A PRISM
OF THOUGHTS

The National Library of Poetry

Diana Zeiger, Editor

A Prism of Thoughts

Library of Congress
Cataloging in Publication Data

ISBN 1-57553-405-3

Proudly manufactured in The United States of America by
Watermark Press
One Poetry Plaza
Owings Mills, MD 21117

Foreword

Throughout life, we store information collected from experiences and try in some way to make sense of it. When we are not able to fully understand the things which occur in our lives, we often externalize the information. By doing this, we are afforded a different perspective, thus allowing us to think more clearly about difficult or perplexing events and emotions. Art is one of the ways in which people choose to externalize their thoughts.

Within the arts, modes of expression differ, but poetry is a very powerful tool by which people can share sometimes confusing, sometimes perfectly clear concepts and feelings with others. Intentions can run the gamut as well: the artists may simply want to share something that has touched their lives in some way, or they may want to get help to allay anxiety or uncertainty. The poetry within *A Prism of Thoughts* is from every point on the spectrum: every topic, every intention, every event or emotion imaginable. Some poems will speak to certain readers more than others, but it is always important to keep in mind that each verse is the voice of a poet, of a mind which needs to make sense of this world, of a heart which feels the effects of every moment in this life, and perhaps of a memory which is striving to surface. Nonetheless, recalling our yesterdays gives birth to our many forms of expression.

Melisa S. Mitchell
Editor

Editor's Note

Shine a beam of white light upon a faceted piece of glass and something magical appears to happen: colorful rainbows seem to burst from its depths. In truth, this is not magic; rather, it is the refraction of light by a prism. The prism has split the light into its component colors, making them visible to the unaided eye. The scientific explanation for this effect may remove the enchantment and mystery that accompanies the phenomenon, but does it remove the beauty of the rainbow itself? It is doubtful that anyone who gazes at the dozens of tiny rainbows reflected on a wall by a crystal vase troubles himself overmuch with scientific explanations. Instead, it is much more likely that he simply enjoys the beauty dancing before his eyes.

One can view the literary analysis of poetry in much the same way. A reader can split a poem into its components, dissecting each word or turn of phrase, until he achieves complete intellectual understanding of the work in question. Or, he can opt to set aside cerebral concerns and instead appreciate the poem for its aesthetic value: the manner in which some words flow as easily as a song; the beauty and clarity of a particular image; a rhyme that is especially clever; or the emotional resonance of a certain phrase. Of course, it is possible to have a technically brilliant poem that has little or no emotional effect on a reader, just as it is equally possible to have a highly passionate, moving piece that demonstrates little or no proficiency with poetic forms. A worthy poet aims to create poetry that is elegant in form as well as evocative of feeling.

There are many pieces within this anthology that achieve this balance. Time and space permit discussion of only a few; however, all the poems featured within *A Prism of Thoughts* are deserving of praise.

One poem that merits special mention is Michael Kirmaier's "Writer's Villanelle" (p. 180). This piece tackles a familiar theme, the process of writing, using a challenging poetic form. A villanelle is a French lyric form which is nineteen lines in length, composed of five three-line stanzas and a concluding quatrain. The first and last lines of the first stanza (designated as A^1 and A^2) are repeated throughout the piece, and the second lines of each stanza rhyme. The rhyme scheme is as follows: $A^1bA^2/abA^1/abA^2/abA^1/abA^2/abA^1/abA^1A^2$ ("a" rhymes with A^1 and A^2). The villanelle is a difficult form to use, as the repetition of lines can quickly become dull in the hands of an unskilled poet. Kirmaier demonstrates mastery of the form, though he chooses not to employ the iambic pentameter that is frequently used in villanelles. In fact, the departure from convention is addressed within the poem:

> *Tradition cages fantasy; Destroy that ancient gate,*
> *To fields of unmapped fancy; to fledgling poetry I'm lured.*
> *Order comes from chaos. I will murder and create.*

"Tradition cages fantasy" indicates the notion that imposing form upon art will not allow the artist full creative freedom, and that rules must be broken in order to foster true imaginativeness. There is a fear that the rigidity of convention will stifle the creative urge:

> Some magic, lyric utterance could nurse the thoughts I'd state,
> But syntax stunts fertility, and silence thus assured,
> Tradition cages fantasy. Destroy that ancient gate.

Nevertheless, there is a sense that some sort of discipline must be imposed, as demonstrated by the repetition throughout the poem of the line "Order comes from chaos. . . ." Ultimately, the poem reflects a hope that the individual writer will find a way to balance inventiveness with convention:

> Though verbs and nouns are old, youth rejoins them when they mate,
> With each hopeful writer's vision and untested newborn word.
> Tradition cages fantasy; Destroy that ancient gate.
> Order comes from chaos. I will murder and create.

The act of creation through destruction is addressed in another way in Jill Malone's work, "Projecting Narcissus" (p. 118). This poem is written from the point of view of a man whose wife has left him, not necessarily because she no longer loves him, but because she hates what she has become and wishes to start a new life. The persona acknowledges that he has been distant during their marriage (perhaps physically removed, but certainly he has been remote emotionally). He notes that he had wished for some kind of bond with her, but was unable to begin bridging the gap until it was too late:

> I dreamt of pushing through her breastbone.
> I wanted to bind myself to her spine;
> to burrow into her heart
> with my fingernails.
> I came home instead to fire: An altar of ribbons, letters,
> flower petals. . . .

The woman has decided to destroy all remnants of her former life and of the relationship so that she might start afresh.

During her husband's absence, the woman "played Penelope: Unraveling / under the vigilant moon. . . ." Penelope, according to Greek mythology, was the wife of Odysseus. After Odysseus had been absent from his kingdom of Ithaca for several years, suitors began courting Penelope. But she believed Odysseus would return to her, and said she would choose a new husband only when she finished weaving a particular tapestry. Each night she would undo the work she had done during the day, thereby ensuring that the tapestry would never be completed. Odysseus did return, proving Penelope correct. If Penelope is the archetype of the steadfast wife, then by "playing Penelope," the woman in the poem at least gave the appearance of steadfastness. Yet "under the vigilant moon," she was "unraveling"—not a tapestry, but her mind. This woman became so consumed with self-loathing that she was unable to face herself in the mirror, and finally was driven to the desperate act of destroying her old life in the attempt to create a new one.

ii

In the wake of this destruction, the husband finds himself lonely and confused. He attempts to hold on to some tattered remnants of the woman:

> *I put what was left in my pocket: Her watercolor eyes,*
> *the long scars on her elbows, her scent*
> *bottled in the pillowcases. . . .*

He salvages what he can, and he wonders now how much of the burden he bears for her desertion:

> *When she said she couldn't breathe in the dark,*
> *whose dark did she mean?*

It is likely that in his grief this question will consume him for the rest of his life.

Those in the grip of an obsession can take what is to others a passing interest, and turn it into a virtual religion. Peter Green explores this phenomenon in "December Joggers" (p. 1). In this poem, Green observes those joggers who allow nothing, including harsh winter weather, to impede the pursuit of their chosen activity. Green employs imagery that compares these athletes' devotion to their sport with monks' devotion to their religion. More specifically, he compares the joggers with those barons who murdered St. Thomas à Becket (c.1118-70) at the orders of King Henry II of England, when Becket became increasingly opposed to royal policy and eventually refused to sign the Constitutions of Clarendon:

> *Grey-cowled against winter, long legs sheathed*
> *In jester yellow, they resemble nothing*
> *So much as Becket's killers . . .*

The runners pursue a goal that they view as proper, but have become coldhearted, almost animalistic in their efforts to obey what they recognize as their higher power:

> *Frosted eyes glinting, beards quickset with cold,*
> *Pursuing some unseen quarry whose thin cries*
> *Pitched high past human hearing*
> *Quicken their predator's blood, . . .*

Green emphasizes the runners' asceticism; like monks, they attempt to purge the flesh in order to free the spirit. They are:

> *Creative anachronisms pledged to exorcize*
> *The burned-out flesh and muscle of desire,*
> *Hearts of the chase with not a beat in view,*
> *Whose sacrificial fat must flare the fire*
> *That eats away the hopes of an elite . . .*

Note the clever pun on "exorcize" / "exercise" that reinforces the monastic image of the runner.

The "December Joggers" are single-minded in the pursuit of their activity. Running has become their religion, and they are its clerics, devoted to nothing else. The rest of us can merely observe their devotion and wonder at it.

Not only has Peter Green created vivid images in "December Joggers" and maintained these images throughout the poem to form a cohesive whole, but he demonstrates considerable poetic skill. He uses a subtle rhyme scheme which never appears forced or intrusive, and is economical with his language — each word has been chosen wisely. Green also uses puns and double meanings, further indicating his ability as a poet. For all these reasons, the judges and I have chosen to award Peter Green the Grand Prize in the contest associated with *A Prism of Thoughts*.

There are many other poems worthy of special attention: "Postman's Burden" (p. 388), by Melissa Gurley Bancks; "The Singer In Eden," (p. 510) by Sean Brendan-Brown; "Suzanne's Rue" (p. 216), by Elizabeth Gerhart; "Gristle" (p. 314), by Jennifer Gosar; "Song For 12:00" (p. 115), by Nancy Maguiness; "The Blight" (p. 52), by William S. Roberts; "The Polaroid" (p. 110), by Stephanie Ellis Schlaifer; and "Narcissus Discerns Himself Into Physical Inactivity" (p. 525), by Charles Lincoln Zeiders. I urge you to read these poems closely so that you may fully appreciate their artistry. I would also like to applaud all the poets who are featured within this anthology. I hope that you will enjoy reading their work as much as I have.

The publication of *A Prism of Thoughts* was the culmination of the efforts of numerous individuals. I offer my thanks to all the editors, assistant editors, and customer service, administrative, and general services staff who have added their hard work and talents to the production of *A Prism of Thoughts*; a special thank you is extended to cover artist Steve Kimball. I am sincerely grateful to all who have contributed to this volume.

Diana Zeiger
Editor

Grand Prize Winner

Peter Green / Austin, TX

Second Prize

Melissa Bancks / Saint Louis, MO
Sean Brendan-Brown / Olympia, WA
Elizabeth Gerhart / Kutztown, PA
Jennifer Gosar / Portland, OR
Michael Kirmaier / Longmont, CO

Nancy Maguiness / Chicago, IL
Jill Malone / Spokane, WA
William Roberts / Parkersburg, WV
Stephanie Schlaifer / Saint Louis, MO
Charles Zeiders / Wayne, PA

Third Prize

Stephen Akintoye / Hatfield, PA
Byron Aldrich / Saint Paul, MN
Merilyn Alexander / Long Beach, CA
June Andrew / McElhattan, PA
Robyn Art / Lincoln, MA
Roxanne Avery / Olympia, WA
Melinda Blair / Charleston, WV
Benjamin Branham / Rolling Meadows, IL
George Butler Jr. / West Point, MS
Edward Capocy / Phoenix, AZ
Douglas Carter / Tampa, FL
John Chorich / Warrenville, SC
Audrey Coco / Hartford, CT
Georgia Cruz / Tucson, AZ
Christopher Cummins / Boston, NY
Deren Dohoda / Brunswick, OH
Robert Doyle / Mountlake Terrace, WA
Cherie Dunn / San Francisco, CA
Ari Durham / Marietta, GA
Jane Eberly / Broadview, MT
David Edwards / Oakland, CA
Michael Eng / Ballwin, MO
Kirk Gillums / Springfield Gardens, NY
Anthony Giannone / Cairo, NY
Nigel Hazeldine / East Hampton, NY
Sherrie Hogan / Mesquite, TX
Jeff Howard / Doylestown, PA
Omar Huamanchumo / Rahway, NJ
Scott Jacobson / Ames, IA
Elaine Kelso / Albuquerque, NM

Anne Kent / Perkiomenville, PA
Eugene Kim / Garden Grove, CA
Gretchen Kuks / Pittsburgh, PA
Joshua Kusnierz / Cottondale, FL
Bonnie Lafitte / Laredo, TX
Ernest Landauer / Berkeley, CA
Andrea Levine / Lake Worth, FL
Danilo Marquise / San Francisco, CA
Marcy McNally / Tucson, AZ
James Melcher / El Cajon, CA
Michael Misislyan / North Hollywood, CA
Laura Morton / Taylor, MI
Danielene Myricks / Fairfield, AL
Walter Nordstrom / Mansfield, OH
Gregory Orr / Palm Harbor, FL
Zoja Pavlovskis-Petit / Vestal, NY
Ryan Petrilli / Charlotte, NC
D. W. Phillips / Madison, WI
Daniel Roberts / Lake Forest, CA
Sydell Rosenberg / Jamaica, NY
David Samas / San Francisco, CA
Yrene Santos / Richmond Hill, NY
Wilhelm Schmidt / Allentown, PA
Scott Shou / Corona, NY
Mark Sockell / Portola Valley, CA
LaVonda Staples / Dellwood, MO
Gene Tanta / DeKalb, IL
Nikolai Tarasuk / Medina, NY
Dave Turner / Mission Viejo, CA

Congratulations also to our Editor's Choice Winners!

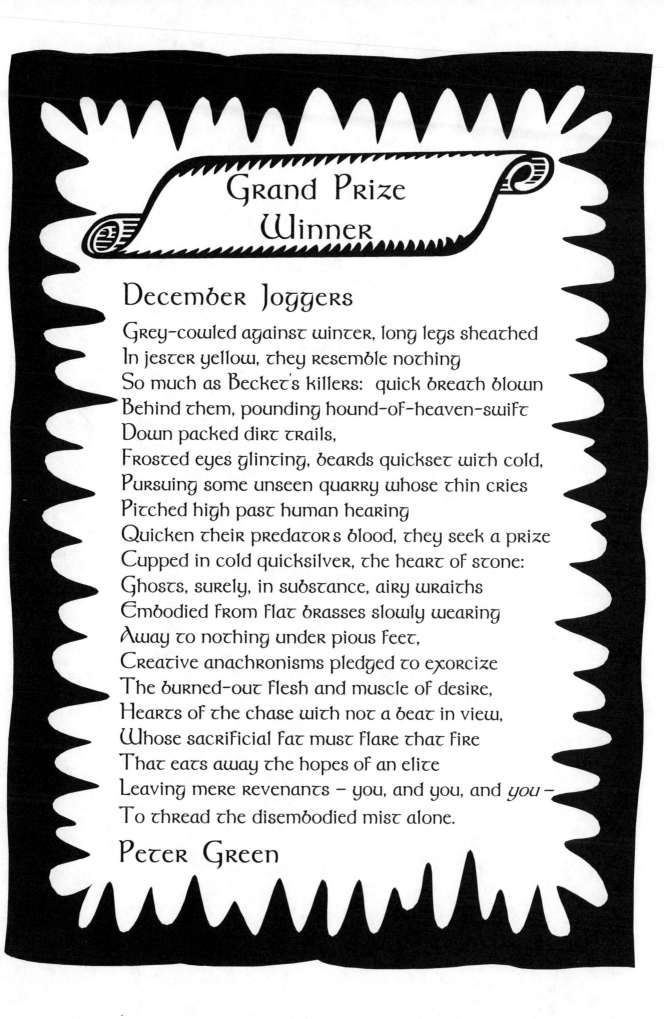

Grand Prize Winner

December Joggers

Grey-cowled against winter, long legs sheathed
In jester yellow, they resemble nothing
So much as Becket's killers: quick breath blown
Behind them, pounding hound-of-heaven-swift
Down packed dirt trails,
Frosted eyes glinting, beards quickset with cold,
Pursuing some unseen quarry whose thin cries
Pitched high past human hearing
Quicken their predators blood, they seek a prize
Cupped in cold quicksilver, the heart of stone:
Ghosts, surely, in substance, airy wraiths
Embodied from flat brasses slowly wearing
Away to nothing under pious feet,
Creative anachronisms pledged to exorcize
The burned-out flesh and muscle of desire,
Hearts of the chase with not a beat in view,
Whose sacrificial fat must flare that fire
That eats away the hopes of an elite
Leaving mere revenants – you, and you, and *you* –
To thread the disembodied mist alone.

Peter Green

Nature's Christmas

The sounds of nature ring clear and true.
Fallen leaves of red and gold trim
   the earth and sparkle with dew,
The wind has brought her gift of colors.

A story is heard as nature's
   beauty sings to the earth.
The babbling brook presents the
   sound of her music,
A magical river overflowing
   her banks filled with the
   spirit of giving.
Rippling gently, her spirit
   is heard on the colors
   from the wind.
   Susan Mann

The Visit

While she sat rocking in her chair
And smiled a Mother's love,
Her aging framed with silver hair,
She thanked the Lord above.
Her son was here! His family, too,
Just for a brief visit.
The gladness in her heart shown through
Her shining eyes, explicit.

"Smile, Mom," he said with camera aimed.
"Say cheese," the others chorused.
She laughed with glee and played the game.
This day was well the joyest.
She chuckled as he clicked away.
Her boy, grown from a fawn,
Would not know that within a day
She, sadly, would be gone.
   Lucille S. Dowey

Ode To A Toenail

On the skin you can really win,
   but on the nail you'll always fail.
You see, my friend, a toenail fungus
   is too humongous.

Hit it once, hit it twice, with Lamisil and Nizoral.
Then sock it thrice with Micatin and Tinactin.
Alas, no matter what you try, you'll never ever win.

Pull your fungo slugger from the bag
And blast the nail with your Fungoid rag.
Out of the ballpark you will rap it,
But no, my friend, you'll never zap it.
   Charles Bernstein

This Time Around

Today I see the hardships of the past,
Not realizing then that it would not last;
Learning to live with love and reverence,
Has made it easier to live with remembrance.

As time stands still with the rising sun,
Life has only just begun;
Each of us must realize what our soul needs,
All that's required is faith and to believe.

This time I stop in times path,
Looking ahead with each days aftermath;
Paying attention to thoughts and feelings,
A balance of mind, body, and spirit are total healing.
   Angela Michelle Soth

Whiskey Songs

Come sing to me in your whiskey voice a song of oyster days
under pearl gray skies when time floats
on the rocky shore of a cold and noisy ocean.
A simple song of coffee steaming in its morning cups
when we untangle from flannel sheets to share another day.

I want someone like you to spin my autumn days,
and we can be like two red leaves in the warm breeze
of the rest of our lives.
Someone whose gentle touch banishes the tension from my neck.
Whose face conjures memories of girlhood fantasy.

I would clone you if I could take a gentle scraping
from the inside of your mouth
and grow my own now and from-now-on lover.
And when you stood in front of me,
I would wrap my arms around you and know
that you are finally, finally mine.

Come sing to me in your whiskey voice
a song of love. Come.
Sing to me.
   Adrienne Davis

New Year's Eve

Shakespeare and I shared a deserved demise.
I bore the weight of sonnets on my chest.
Those word-packed sentences! Their meaning lies
Like lead upon a heart in need of rest.

The will that's carnate in these words is brave,
No doubt affected but not moved by fears.
Communing from and for and with the grave,
Each word a sentence of its own appears.

My sentence's not the sentence of the bard.
It's a humiliation given to each.
Whose soft? And whose imponderably hard?
Whose short? Whose with extenuating reach?

The years are not the measure of this will.
Their passage none the worse for lying still.
   Wilhelm A. Schmidt

Adam, Man

God created Adam, manful flesh, bone and sinew
He was meant to be untempted, a strong undying gender
Charmed with paradise, deathless and true
To the way oceans and the salted seas they render.
No procreation, but infinity to the God-like art
Of sun, and moon, and stars exclusive
Exclusive to the soul and human heart
Where passion's love, cannot heartbreak give; nor save

But glorious God, ever more he gave;
From Adam's rib, created woman, to the silent loneliness
He thought severe, in blind duress
Of innocence; he gave him happiness.
But serpent stings and serpent slithers
Beguile the hearts of imperfection
Mad quick music kills and withers
Blood pulsating tunes of dark dissection.
Therefore and henceforth I found Adam once again
As someone's father, brother, son
The plural parts of mortal men.
I found Eve, someone's sister, mother, daughter in
   fates more wrought and spun.
   Anthony Giannone

3

Angels On My Shoulder

Angels on my shoulder, whispering in my ear, all those positive messages that I need to hear.

Tell me of the protection around me everyday, show me how to see the world in a better way.

Give me the strength to step out and say "I can make a difference in a special way".

With your heavenly counsel I found the peace within, allowing it to grow, until it has found all those in need.

Those small goals obtained, bring happiness for all to see, the beginning of a brand new healing tree.

Look up to the hands of angels circling around the world forming a halo of light to help us to see so clear.

Nurtured by knowledge there are no limits to see for greatness abounds from the angel within me.

Cynthia L. Davis

The Twilight Dim

The old man crossed in the twilight dim
That sullen stream had no fear for him,
Came the evening, cold and gray
For you never again must pass this way.

Looking-up the sky at the silver stars
And through the hills passed a shinny light,
It must be dawn, or is it night!
Shove over it with a warm good night.

The journey will end with a languish day
Whose youth feet must pass this way.
To that fair-haired youth may a pitfall be
He, too must cross in the twilight dim.

And while I wonder far away
Though dreams are calling; everyday,
Having crossed the chasm, deep and wide
Who's last sound are calling beyond the light.

Tamara M. Walusko

Hazel

She could really iron.
There's a pace to it, you know.
"You've got to do the collars first," Hazel said.
"You've always got to do the collars first!"

She followed you around like a dog in heat.
When boys came over she appeared in every room.
She'd always smile and ask:
"Can I iron any of those blouses with the pleats?"

She loved those pleats, Hazel did.
Liked it when I gave her my old hats, too.
Would always put them on right away,
Just to make me feel important.

She mothered me when Mom nursed Grandpa,
Fed us when Mom got pneumonia.
Loved me without ever sayin' it.
Cheered for every little thing I did.

She had a hysterectomy, and we never saw Hazel again.
Mom said she called once.
Hazel taught me everything about ironin', about lovin', and
About leavin' without sayin' goodbye.

Margaret M. Newman

The Letter, The Rope, The Pain

The letter, the rope, the pain,
that's all that runs through my mind now.
The letter, the rope, and the pain...

The letter is her last thought,
the rope is her last action,
the pain is her last curse to me.

The letter speaks to me,
the rope cuts her off from me,
the pain is all that is left of her for me.

The letter is burning my eyes with its words,
the rope is staring at me with torment,
the pain is killing me.

I remember everything we used to have together...
now all that I have of her are
the letter, the rope, the pain,
and the grave.

Cassandra L. Jeske

Love Lives On

A pillow rests upon the overstuffed chair,
My long legged boyfriend used to sit there,
He has passed on to heaven now and my heart is bare,
He only told me of the pain in his back and sat on a cushion,
When I could not believe he was dying he called me "unfeeling,"
Had I known he had cancer I would have been reeling!
He had asked me to marry him but we didn't know then,
How very sick he would be and would be taken so soon from me,
From his home to the hospital he was taken for special care,
He couldn't stop staring at me when I came there,
Coming from behind him as he lay there
I had kissed his forehead with a silent prayer,
This dearest man of my heart and love of my life,
My close and only sweet heart for ever ten years
Was now facing death and I was close to tears,
His suffering would be over soon
But now our love filled the room!
Our boundless love will live on and forever on.

Lorena Barrett

Childhood Kisses

My very first kiss of love
  As I came from the Lord above.
A kiss each and every morning.
  As each new day is dawning.
A kiss for get well quick
  In case I'm ever sick.
A kiss to brighten each day
  As I go out to play.
A kiss to make it well.
  Wherever I ran and fell.
A kiss that seems quite sad.
  If ever I'm really had
There's the kisses to take faraway
  When for some reason, I may not stay.
Then, kisses sent in a letter.
  Wishing very soon we will get together.
With kisses to welcome me home.
  No matter how far I may room.
Extra kisses for very good dreams
  Oh how lovely all kisses seem!

Miriam E. Giles

An Hegira Of Sorts

A Fall visit to the pond
Is well worth the effort made
To hear the plaintive sounds...
Unique cries that the air pervades.

As Summer invariably becomes Fall
Canada Geese gather with instinctive call
To await their kind in good time and reason
Now grown purposeful at this season.

By instinct they work out daily on high
That departing V, they shall make in the sky
With practice and preparation for all to acquire
Needed skill flying South to which all aspire.

Once accomplished, they'll say their exit good-bye
Leave a cold North dramatically in their own way,
That unique V, so marvelously, perfectly timed
In their au revoir and departure for warmer climes.

K. Helena R. Laramee

Tempest Of The Black Sea

The severe tempest reached us at night,
When the waves rose in the stormy mist so high.
The sea raged, we were deprived of light,
The wind blew and heavy rain fell from the sky.

A thunder clap resounded with force
The furious waves poured over the deck.
We feared, that our steamboat lost its course
We battled with the storm, nobody went back.

We were exhausted from the exertion and we envied
The storm, which made merry on the sea.
The heavens looked down as our ship swayed
Tossing us. Our unity and heroism fascinated me.

The storm, growing calm in dawn's early light
Soon we saw the sunlight. It's been a pleasure
With the first radiance the heavens became bright
The sun's rays were directed to us beyond measure

It was a miracle, that we possessed life with all its charm
Life! this priceless gift each of us received.
We overcame the formidable force that dangerous harm
We thank God and the happiness of life we clearly perceived.

Raisa M. Spektor

Held By An Angel

I was feeling rather sad and lonely.
I found it hard to face another day.
I said, "Lord I'm depending on you only."
"Please send a little help my way."

As I tried so hard to fight each tear,
A voice whispered to me and said,
"Peace be unto you. Have no fear."
"Come to me and rest your weary head."

Suddenly, the wind began to blow,
And the birds began to sing,
Amazed because I was all aglow,
An angel embraced me with his wings.

My spirit was renewed and filled with love,
To sing praises to God and lift my voice.
Sent from Abba Father from above.
He gives me many reasons to rejoice.

As the angel rocked me and held me close,
Wiping away each tear from my eyes,
He said. "All of your cares and concerns God knows."
"And He cries with you whenever you cry."

Christine L. Pointer

At The Inaugural Headquarters - 1997

Quite by accident one day close to this special event;
I chanced to visit the headquarters
  that was preparing for this great four year stint.
Security was heavy; visitors extreme,
  but all around the office, life was snappy and prime.
Everyone was working to ensure the Inaugural's success,
Everyone came out each day, looking their very best.
Efficiency was apparent, promptness a must
Everyone was full of pride, some seemed ready to bust.
Problems - there were plenty,
  Solutions sought and tried;
Supervisors were edgy, but refused to escape or hide.
Staffs remained alert though complained of feet that hurt,
The Inaugural, however, was the center
  of this large, but busy assembly,
Determinant they were to make this event complete.
On January 20th how proud they were,
  as they stood along the selected parade route.
Everything had turned out swell.
  They began to howl and hoot.

Herbert Collins Jr.

J. Squirrel, Esquire

I made a new friend on Cape Cod last summer,
A plump, pompous cute little squirrel.
Each morning we kept our date for breakfast,
I with my yogurt, and he with swiped birdseed.

I sat on the porch of the house by the sea,
And he in his tree just looking at me.
We did become close, six feet apart,
I'd throw him some nuts, he'd eat and depart.

He was disdainful of birds, except for the raven
Of whom he felt fear and quickly sought haven.
The raccoons he eyed leerily, they were much bigger,
Not even friends, that much you'd figure!

He'd snoopily peer through the window of the study,
Twitching his tail, "Hey, here's your buddy!"
We'd always converse tho' he never said much;
Anyone watching would think I was tetched!

But playing Dr. Doolittle I find is relaxing,
A role that for me is by far non-exacting.
And so, dear J. Squirrel, when I bid you adieu,
Please don't feel bad, for our friendship's not through!

Charlotte Ann Zuzak

Song Bird

Song bird don't fly away, sing me your song.
Your melody always perks me up when things are going wrong.

Your plumage is such a beautiful sight.
You're always singing from early morn 'til into the night.

You make mankind's life so aware.
And ask nothing in return, not even a fare.

Your skies are limitless as you soar about,
absorbing wind and rain you fly it with clout.

You're always welcome at this ole place.
Bring all your friends, there's plenty of space.

I'll gladly feed you crumbs and seed,
provide you with water and all that you need.

I'll build you a house if you'll just stay.
There will be no one to harm you or drive you away!

Bruce I. Geuder

Harvey Stays Boss Of The Street Gang Crew

Harvey Mathews was a black man of medium build whose sinewy arms were sized like hams. Mighty enough to snap iron bands. A quiet good man, labored long years for Dad, paving roads, raking hot-mix bitumen goo. Penetrating heat blistered feet, through thick layers of socks and heavy work shoes. Dad invited Harvey to supper one night, to break what was meant as good news. Promotion to foreman, and higher pay, boss of the street gang crew. Smiling yet reluctant, Harvey balked at Dad's news saying, "Whites in the crew won't take orders from this dude." Dad persisted, anted more pay. Harvey decided he'd try a few days. On his first day as boss of the street gang crew, Harvey's dire prediction surely came true. For the air was charged, cuss words flew and we all heard the degrading "N" word too. When Dad drove up it came to a head. Two arrogant whites had enough they said, demanding Dad fire Harvey that day. Dad collared the two, hissing through his teeth, "Get off my job, get off my back. Pick up your checks at the pay-master's shack. On my job your bad mouths won't do and Harvey stays boss of the street gang crew."

A. R. Jack Banks

Random Blessings

Ah! The sweetness of gentle rain
Murmuring softly; a silken, cadenced refrain
Sweet the perfume on thirsty earth
Parched into powder by dint of dearth.

Silver beads hang glistening from the eaves
To slake the thirst of desiccated leaves
Delicate Pansy faces lift heaven ward for sips
Of ambrosial globules touching their lips.

In forests devastated by raging fires
The pluvial benison anoints blackened pyres
Permeating the air with caustic fume
Lifeless and hushed in the awful gloom.

Random blessings, like gentle rain on parched earth
Nurture; heal; turn sorrow into mirth
A smile from the heart; compassionate tears
Words that hearten to conquer deepest fears.

Soft, still darkness - just before dawn
Walking barefoot across a cool, damp lawn
A rainbow glimpsed briefly through the mist
So many random blessings; so easily missed.

Elaine E. Kelso

Miss Louise C

In softly spoken words you said,
stand up straight and hold up your head.
You, be proud of what you can do.
Don't wait for the world to be proud of you.

How many times, through the years,
have your gentle words stopped the tears?
As each accomplishment came to me,
I knew you'd smile if you could see.

Better yourself, is what you preached,
in the school on the hill in Wilson's Beach.
You were kind and gentle and very true.
I kept your words with me, my whole life through
My teacher.

Ruby Greenlaw

Aging Disgracefully

Chill, Child, please be still,
Can't you hear him comin', now, over the hill?
He's got his wintry fingers tanglin' in my hair,
Tryin' his best to drag me here to there.
So I sit here, pedalin' on my iron steed,
Thinkin' I can outrun him, oh yes, indeed.
And he laughs at that, oh, he laughs out loud!
He likes his victims fighting, he likes his victims proud.
Two steps forward, then I'm tumblin' back,
Backside like two bearcubs, fightin' in a sack.
Elastic waist jeans, oh! 'dem achin' bones,
Turn the volume up on the telephone.
But he ain't gonna claim me without a fight,
Ridin' on my steed, here, deep in the night.
So, Chill, Child, please be still,
I'm a pedalin' hard, but it's all uphill.

Lynn Work

Six o'Clock :: 1967-1969

straight up and down
her body stretches
like a clock whose time is six
black coal eyes stare out at
me longing to stare back in
face composed in perfect order
no expression is seen here
but are there thoughts that linger on
is joy or sorrow felt
they say that souls will never die
thoughts of eternal life
questions rise — will answers follow
memories singing memories crying
the clock is ticking on
feel coldness making systems stop
turn around and leave
the pale lean body still stretched out like
a clock whose time has stopped

Phyllis I. Behrens

Addressed Out In Space

Oh they called us Alien,
Addressed out in space.
Circling through the metropolitan.
We ran and we chip, like doing gymnastic.
Got lost in some peculiar place.
Searching to find another familiar face.

Enduring trying to be quick.
Over the snow, under the snow.
Crunching the ice, liking it so.
Wishing if we could find the space ship.
We ran and we ran, ha, ha, ha
The little heart pumped and pumped ha, ha, ha,
Trying to find another familiar face.

Conserving day or nights.
Hot or cold, rain sunshine.
We ran and we chip, like doing gymnastic.
Wishing to find the space ship.
Got lost in some peculiar place.
Searching to find another familiar face.

Veronica Bogle

Feld Lebensmittal

Mostly we lived on C or K ration meals,
D Bars during the Bulge were a good deal,
When the kitchen trucks got "field rations," we lived well.
Better than civilians in the area, I mean to tell.
We traded cigarettes for eggs, for those we didn't steal!

In summer ripe fruit in orchards, was swiped all the time,
In winter canned fruit in cellars was prime,
We killed wild boar and deer to eat.
Cabbage, carrots, and potatoes from gardens we'd sneak.
A hand grenade in the creek made fishing fine.

Ten-in-one rations were the best of the lot.
For two or three men in an isolated spot.
A single tank or a Jeep on a lonely run,
When the kitchen truck was far away, cooking was done.
This ration had canned bacon, tomato juice, and apricot.

Everything is sealed cans in a wooden box, new,
It also had cigarettes, soap, and toilet paper too.
The boxes could even be floated, ship to shore.
A wide variety of food was in store,
Well packaged, watertight, and no mildew.

Russell L. Kelch

Hot Wax

A scented candle burns
Flame tangos then boogies to one side
Burning through
Releasing a torrent of hot wax
Flowing to fast to form the desired pillar
Spilling onto the glass table
A mess to be cleaned later
Not now
Not while the flame and scent seduce
Forming faces and images
As seen in clouds and wood grain
Fodder for the imagination
An old man
Flying Dragon
Praying mantis devouring a beetle
Dark red here
Translucent pink there
Choosing its own path
Running dripping splashing
Much like my train of thought

Robert N. Wormington

Yes, We Let Them Live This Way

As our artists, musicians, sculptors, writers
Live in poverty and its many incumbent ills,
We let them! They can't give up all self-respect
And still pursue each his avenue of art;
So many die young, impoverished, ill
We let them! No one seems to care.

Yet years later, long after they are gone,
Their work is eagerly collected, grows in value;
We sing their songs, with another name;
Hang up their art, sold for millions
Stolen, copied, returned, and sold for more.

Writer's works are collected, illustrated, etc.
First editions bring the most in a hundred
Years or more — long after the writer is dead.
Honestly, any artist wishes only to live in peace
And places little value on this world's goods.

From this caldron of his deep emotion
Springs the music he hears, and must write.
The words of the poems he hears, too;
The pictures he must paint or visions in stone.

Alice Louise Salter

An Infatuation

Don't seek a cure for loneliness,
out of desperation.
Don't mistake a newfound love,
for mere infatuation.

I suggest you think it over,
talk things out with your lover.
Study the relationship before it goes any further,
or you'll find yourself in real trouble.

Don't expect the unexpected,
don't take things for granted.
Don't settle for a fictionalized story,
then watch them leave in a hurry.

Be careful and as cautious as you can,
anxiety is not the solution.
Patience is the rule to virtue.
don't do something you can't undo.

It's just an ego trip I see,
an ego personality.
Take heed to your situation,
it's only an infatuation.

Ronda Louise White

The Big Flood

I sit in comfort in my abode secure
Safe and sane from the stormy clouds, demure,
Almost as if in biblical time
The rains keep pouring...insane.
The snow is melting in the mountains
Sprouting water in nature's lofty fountains,
Through the creeks, rivers, down the falls
Water, water ... Everywhere — it calls
For help to save us sinful mortals;
We're not ready yet to enter those portals.

Relentlessly, mercilessly, helplessly,
Extending hands of care — unselfishly,
The cry goes out to save the land
People, homes, animals, crops at hand.
Wetness engulfs us now — be forewarned
Deluging all to repent today, friend;
When, oh when will this insanity cease?
A prayer to Almighty might help, so please!
It keeps raining until it came to pass
The prayers were answered at long last.

Carlo Flores

Memories That Linger

A banjo standing in a corner
Brings to mind old memories,
Of agile fingers, quick and nimble,
Dancing on the fretted keys;
Proceeding in rapid leaps and bounds,
Playing the old tunes with ease.

Shimmering strings alive and trembling,
Strumming the banjo with pride,
In a lively, spirited manner
When all restraint is cast aside;
Weaving an invisible patchwork,
Making music countrified.

Blessed were those happy hours of sharing
The old songs close to the heart,
When interests unite and linger,
Enjoying a natural art;
Thoughts of an old banjo in action,
And happiness, friends impart.

Mary E. Nagode

Sunflowers... Book Story

My garden is embellished by splendorous sunflowers
gleaming with their ephemeral glory.
And their exquisite beauty inspire this artist to
illustrate a "Sunflowers... Book Story."

In its glossy pages the flowers will grow tall and regal
with their loveliness delighting young and old.
They will grace many special places and give them a touch
of magic, with their fresh and vibrant gold.

They will be near a meandering and bubbling mountain stream
and by the lush and green countryside.
On hills strewn with sweet grass and clover, scented with
the fragrance of ripe berries on the vine.

There will be lovely butterflies and small songbirds,
feasting on their thick and moist dark seeds.
And resting on their broad leaves you will see brightly
colored ladybugs and bumblebees.

Contained in an elegant flower vase, also they will be
gleaming with their ephemeral glory.
Adding charm to a home's coffee table, adorned with a copy
of my "Sunflowers... Book Story."

Amelia Rios

The Ocean

The ocean is so deep and blue, treacherous
is the name I have for you.
Surfers ride your waves with joy avowing
the danger as they bend and sway and hoping
that they can return another day.
Sailboats sail in the wind crossing over
to safety to win.
Swimmers catch their breath as they always do,
finishing their course before you catch them too.
Your undertow below the surface is a snare
of fear to all that wonder.
Your roar is like the sound of thunder
which also can be heard down under.
What lies beneath on your floor is your
secret to keep forever more.

Lillian Barb

Elders Of The Past

Oh, great Elders of many Spirits past.
Teach us of sage, pipe and vision while each of us last.
We've forgotten respect for air, water and trees.
For this our great Mother a breath, drop or leaves.
We divide our feelings like elements of storms.
But each day the great Star, a Spirit it warms.
For many sounds of silence can cover a grieve.
But great Elders of Spirits, takes what it leaves.
Oh, Mother Earth forgive us in vain.
We've invented a future and forgotten your name.
But this land has been tortured by every last man.
Let's give back a reason, for one Elder's hand.

Stephen Alexander Taylor

Sea

Have you ever gazed at the rolling sea
Sun glistening on white caps
Waves lapping every inch of beach
Touching each grain of sand
Whispering secrets of where they have been
Soft summer places and harsh winters shores
Fabulous lands and treasured isles
A wondrous world of freedom and love

Marian Sagherian

Whispers

There are whispers from afar,
Or are they just behind the door?
People will whisper both night and day,
One can't hear what they say,
One isn't supposed to.
Why do they whisper so?
It's because you're not to know,
Or else they would just say it aloud,
Holler it above the clouds,
But no, they whisper.
Whispers are a little voice,
Hardly even make a noise,
Maybe for evil, maybe for good,
You can't hear them - they're not understood,
They're only whispers.

Steven Morrison

Life

We enter life as helpless babes,
not knowing our fate must be the grave.
We grow and learn, and laugh and play,
enjoying our youth while yet we may.

All too soon we become adults,
our daily lives filled with tumult.
We struggle through as best we can,
each trying to outdo his fellow man.

Then comes old age, the regrets and pains,
and we wish we could live our lives again.
But it's too late to make amends,
as, one by one, our lives must end.

We then lie on some marble slab,
while someone else picks up the tab,
Or recklessly squanders all we've saved,
'cause we can't take it to our grave!

Clarence N. Wesson

Window To Paradise

Lying peacefully on the silky cinnamon-colored
sand, absorbing the cool serenity of the
breath-taking panoramic pageantry awaits the shore.

The orange orbed sun silently sprays lambent
light on the powerful ponderous ocean creating
a delicate veil glistening luminescence.

Cloudless heavens streaked with crimson and
violet hues compliment encroaching reeds which
intermittently fringe the dunes, causing flickering shadows.

Gentle winds desultorily carry a crisp scent of
salt air chirping birds alight the small trees
bordering this wonderful window to paradise.

Holly Draudt

Shared Memories

It's hard to believe that memories can be
Not mine, not yours, but ours.
Yet when we talk of shadows and lights
And creatures that take our powers

Leaving us helpless to control
Our thoughts, our feelings, our actions.
Who do we tell our secrets to
That won't think we're a lunatic faction?
I'll tell you my memories

If you'll tell me yours.
We'll understand with compassion
Because all of the memories are ours.

Doris Upchurch

In Delicate Balance

The city is a lonely place
Filled with hurrying people,
All in a great rush to get - somewhere.
But if you ask them where,
Or what difference it makes,
The returned look is empty.
It is as blank, as barren,
As the mind behind the face.

The people are as sheep,
They follow an unknown shepherd
To an unknown destination.
They dress and look alike;
Speak the same time-worn clichés
With the same lackluster voices.
They see and hear only that
Which does not upset the delicate balance.

The occasional stranger, the rebel, is greeted with mistrust.
He dares to be different, to defy moral authority,
To follow his own code of ethics. For this, he is crucified
On a cross built by society for the individual.

Philip A. Eckerle

Momentous Moments

There is a moment in time
That changes our path.
It could be a sweet song or poetic line,
Or it could be an expression of wrath.

When we look back through the years,
We can discern a point of turning.
Sometimes it fills us with indelible fear.
Sometimes it leaves our heart yearning;

But whatever way we need to go,
There is a God-given strength of will
That can give us more power than we know
So our mission in life we can fulfill.

Betty Nichols

Illusions

We struggle daily, trying to break out
of our own self-inflicted prisons.

Hemmed in by restrictive schedules,
we scurry to reach approaching deadlines.

The barriers of limitations we build,
cause us to falter and lose faith in ourselves.

If only we would reach down
into our special place buried in our minds

We would find a land of enchanted magic
where everything we dream is possible.

If we could reach this land, then we would know
that limitations are nothing but illusions.

Sheila B. Roark

The Picture

Fingertips scanning the page for a look.
Conjuring up pictures locked in a book.
Telling a story written in braille.
It is here the writer must not fail.
For eyes without sight, from birth have not seen.
Imagining life could be frightful it seems.
Professionals we are though we receive not a cent.
We realize from heaven our talents were lent.
Sharing with others is what we must do
If the picture we write is to ever shine through.

Stan Harris

The Deadbeats

"They must be brought to justice,
pay their dues once and for all
these deadbeat husbands who cheat their wives,
with payments at a very slow stall."

"Be it alimony or child support,
this game is always the same
the culprit is ever behind payments,
as he plays his hold back game."

"This is a sad situation,
wife and children suffer most
make the scoundrel pay on time,
put him in jail where he can roast."

"It's time they pay for their actions,
let them pay for their misdeeds
put their pictures in the papers,
pay up or else, for this bunch of bad seeds."

"The courts have been too lenient,
a jail sentence would do the trick
the family has suffered along enough,
hit them with jail terms that will stick."

Marty Rollin

Grandmother

My grandmother was very special to me,
Memories of good times filled with glee,
I loved the weekly visits to her home
The kitchen a special place to roam.
I sat in the large rocking chair at the end of the room,
Grandma baking raisin filled cookies that would be ready soon.
The stove was very large -
It gave off tremendous heat.
I loved the special cookie - a wonderful treat.
I will cherish the memories of the lovely
Christmas and birthday presents.
The boxes wrapped in white or red tissue to paper,
Beautiful stickers, tied with fancy cord to complement.
Box contained a special book -
Nancy Drew Mystery, Bobbsey Twins or animal stories
A box of three embroidered handkerchiefs
And a small bottle of perfume
Memories of love - treasured gifts that are a special heirloom.

Ethel M. Shannon

Kassie - With A K

Born in the land of the tumblin' tumble weeds,
on a windy, spring-like day;
A tiny little girl came to be with us,
And we called her
Kassie - with A K.

A beautiful little angel sent from heaven above,
Soon filled our hearts with wonder and love.
With her sweet smile and happy way
This baby girl we called
Kassie - With A K.

Time changes the weeks and months into years,
And they too, soon fade away,
Where is that little girl we once knew,
That little girl of yesterday?

Now she is a grown - up lady
With a love all her own,
And a future that's bright and gay.
Will there be another tiny miracle to come along?
A little girl called
Kassie - with A K.

Evelyn Mitchell

Thinking Positively

The most important thing you can do,
Is to think you are one of the few,
Who can do everything for which you have a plan,
Be the man who likes to think he can.

Be positive in your every thought,
Be proud of everything you've got.
Don't think of those things you did wrong,
Think of what makes you proud and strong.

Think of those things you did that were right,
It will give you a better line of sight
On those things for which you have a plan,
Then you'll be the man who thinks he can.

Before you go to sleep at night,
Think of the things you did that gave you delight.
Revel in the thoughts as they bring on a smile,
Sleep on them, so tomorrow you can go an extra mile.

Keep positive thoughts on your mind,
Cast out all thoughts of a negative kind.
Think of those things that give you delight,
And keep thoughts of thinking you can in sight.

John A. Strommen

Open Line

Hello. . .hello. . .hello. . .
　　I wonder if someone's there.
Father, who wants to talk
　　but changes their mind?
Is it someone I would like to know
　　or, perhaps, someone who doesn't care?
A telephone is a wondrous thing. . .
　　it usually has a most welcome ring.
In times of deep concern, it is a comfort
　　but misused, it seems like a threat.
Help me to remember, always, You are in control.
　　Hello. . .hello. . .hello. . .
God loves you, God bless you. . .open line.

Sharon K. Blaker

My Mama

If I were to choose one word to take notice
Of all that Mama has meant to me,
That one simple word would have to be
　　Giving
For her, living is giving unendingly!

Sometimes her giving is things I can touch,
Sometimes a word or a smile.
Yet always a lesson in how to live
For giving makes all worthwhile.

So God bless you, Mama, for memories of giving,
And lessons you still teach today.
I pray that my sons will say I'm like you
That "giving was just Mama's way".

Lucy H. Wilson

Night Falls Softly

Night falls softly over valley and hill.
The voices of day are muted and still.
And the lowly earthling forgets petty cares
When the Master Jeweler sets out his wares.

Willette Caudle McGuire

There's No Use For Me To Cry

There's no use for me to cry,
tears won't mend a broken heart,
　　I should have known I'd be alone,
and we two would soon drift apart.

There's no use for me to cry,
my tears would hurry you away,
　　I'll just pretend, it didn't end,
and you'll come back some day.

What can I do to reach your heart,
to bring us back together,
　　how can I tear, these clouds apart,
and end this stormy weather.

Don't you know how much I care,
I'll love you till the day I die,
　　I hate to see you go, you'll come back I know,
there's no use for me to cry.

Jimmy Copeland

JonBenet Ramsey

At six years of age, the shadow of death
　　cast darkness upon a little Princess
Though violently robbed of precious breath,
　　her childhood didn't have many chances

Already wrapped up in stiff pageantries
　　that exacted pressures beyond such years
her young existence was full of entries
　　designed to exploit glamorous veneers

Child pageantries are not much different
　　from the molestation of innocence
Of abuse...we remain intolerant...
　　these exploitations have the same accents

With expensive shrouds cloaking young children,
　　well screened under stringencies they sustain
whatever childhood, is now made barren
　　to suit the desires that parents will train

We all grieve your loss, JonBenet Ramsey...
　　I'm sure in others, your fame was fulfilled
But the whole tragedy, some still can't see
　　is...your life was robbed before you were killed

Bob G. Martinez

The Making Of Modern Thinking

It is often heard that older generations say:
"We will sacrifice much to provide our children
Advantages in life that makes their world unstrained."
These people felt their hard work still deprived them!

Some parents did well toward creating better opportunities
For their young because an easier life became available.
More youth made themselves accessible to non-manual jobs.
The new generation became, relatively, more stable.

But a dichotomy has developed within the new generation
That does not fare well with one fair condition.
Many better educated haven't shown understanding and veneration
To those who haven't excelled in similar fashion!

Even parents, who promoted family literacy, are avoided
As folk somewhat below the character desirable,
Thereby becoming alienated society within their own folk.
This gives reasons parents are isolated with little favor.

What becomes established is that literacy like personality
Changes us so radically that we lose many of the credentials
By which we, literally, attest to family commonality.
Yes, and there seems to be little possibility for prevention.

Theodore R. Reich

Poet

For I am the poet.
The white raven of life.
Creating mental pictures out of emotion,
And emotion out of picturesque words.
The black dove of the unknown.
Bringing meaning to sadness,
And essence from death.
The sphere of truth.
Making a summer's day
The greatest thing of all, love.
The shadow of lies.
Crying the soft, tender tears
Of the beloved innocent child.
The creature of the haunting dream.
Look at the fiery sunrises, the mystic forest, the changing seas;
They tell a tale for me to chronicle.
The dreamer, the teacher, the pray-er.
See the people: their smiling mouths, their concerned eyes;
Their soul is the template of my pen.
For I am your poet.

Richard Wing II

February Rose

Beautiful butterflies are back in the garden
Bringing memories of but a short time ago.
Little girls, I will hear on the stairway below,
Smiling face now haunt me and comfort my soul.

Small patches of sunshine drift across the garden
On a cloudy, but bright summer day.
A little girl will walk through my mind
Fond memories of her, are with me today.

One might chase a shadow, until it will disappear,
Precious moments once lost, in happiness or tears.
The seasons I will now tie all together
To remember the garden, of her young years.

Thistles and thorns, did grow by her path,
As little Rose, now brings sweet memories back.
While in her season, such a short time of life,
Special moments of happy, and bright sunshine break through.

I look through the clouds, and roll back the time
This day of each year, will stay locked in my mind.
A Rose from the garden will once more appear.
As I hear little footsteps on the stairs.

Joe Staker

The Midnight Nemesis

I have been in a bed of thorns,
Swirling through the thousands of the
Burning flames for Vengeance is my name
and I have arisen from among the
dead in search of you. I have traveled
the million miles of the midnight darkness.
There'll be no peace till I have found
you and have possessed of your very
soul I shall shoot you with the
flaming arrow that I carry,
scar you carve out your heart leaving
only trails of dripping blood behind.
For you'll be condemned to
serve punishment.
When I have found you.
For I am the goddess of
Vengeance that has come to
collect what's due.

Loyda E. Carrasquillo

Sous La Pergola

To run the path of the divide
Into silence and the deep blue
To walk the dance
To embrace the shoulder curved by time

To give when asked, to give when the share of destiny
Has found its faith in its own shadow
Elongating toward itself, inward
As if a celebration of the passage
Where remembrance changes to pardon
Alchemic, abandoned on the doorsteps of people
Without remembrance
Of people trying to recall the abandon of hope
On a fall day when colors change
Into primary, into primordial, into themselves
And when the colors fall
Through maple leaves, within your eyes
And the moment of our despair

I will depart without fanfare
As if the time we had to spare
Was spared with others

Vahe A. Kazandjian

The Song Of The Mosquito

He whines in lively glee as he dives on that
    flesh whose blood he desires. Slap him and
    he springs away. Escaping and choosing yet
    another spot, he detects with vicious glee a
    likely target.
Fiendishly he sings his battle cry and pursues
    relentlessly his ferocious strategy. On skinny
    legs, delicate as strands of hair, he reconnoiters
    with cunning ferocity. Swooping again
    and again, leaping freely from body-smashing
    blows, his translucent wings carry him away
    from disaster.
Such artful cruelty in that miniature brain
    such an appetite seldom appeased.
The mosquito is a devilish fellow making of an
    evening's respite torture, exquisitely distressing.

Dorothy M. Schreiber

Our Love

Just because of your love for me
    Stars sparkle brighter in the sky
        The sky glows softly in the morn
    The trees move in tempo
        to a freshening breeze.

Because of my love for you
    The roses' scent gives us delight
        The stream flows in harmony
    The grass moves endlessly where
        The sunset has a warmer flow.

Just because of your love for me
    The ocean shimmers in the dawn
        The mountains stretch ever higher
    The birds chirp their love songs
        to our musical melody.

Because of my love for you
    The waves churn heavily in rhythm
        The air keeps an aromatic scent
    The sunrise bursts upon a pleasant day
        The ocean whispers your name.

Charlene Fuhlendorf

Grief Behind The Glitter

My dear Lord look after the City of Angels
As the dense fog rolls, with the bright lights it mingles
Its green valleys and hills are gleaming with the stars
Its radiant laughter conceals its ugly scars.

Sad clowns parade the wretched streets of Hollywood
Their desolate woes felt throughout this dreary world
With AIDS infliction, the prospect is in tangles
Dear Lord have mercy on the City of Angels.

Those shabby city walls - with graffiti they bleed
Vile gangsters rebelling - lawlessness they believe
The surging lust for drugs - the youth it endangers
Dear Lord have pity on the City of Angels.

The Third World's anguish is its endless starvation
Our shallow society deems it's salvation
Vanities outrageous; genuine love dangles
O sweet Lord, deliver this City of Angels.

Aimeiko Christel Tasico

Mary Clair

I heard the crying across the street
So many people were there.
They came to help young Mrs. Ford
When death claimed Mary Clair.

The little girl was six weeks old
And pretty as can be.
When her mom went to the crib,
Breathing could not see.

Mrs. Ford called 911.
The ambulance quickly came.
They worked on Mary Clair awhile.
"We're sorry. No one's to blame."

The child's spirit was in heaven.
It was light and free.
But Mr. Ford was far away,
Army in Germany.

"Let's walk in the woods. I'll hold your hand,"
I said when they were gone.
As friends we ambled long and far.
Peace was felt that dawn.

Linda Seling

Little Sparrow

Petite brown sparrow
Hopping sprightly along the pavement;
How delicate your form —
Belying a stalwart spirit.

Little passerine, the asphalt is hot
Beneath your tiny feet;
How do you survive without a meadow
To cushion your dainty step?

Mimicking the stubborn wild flower
Thriving between the sidewalk crack;
You bounce exuberantly,
No frailty do you express.

Simple in your attire —
No tawdriness in your garment;
You epitomize all that is strong and true,
Little bird of faith in a confused world.
Step proud in your downy garb,
You mock mortals of lesser worth.

Susan J. Friedman

Had There Not Been You

It was a hard time in my life
    A time when I was in desperate need
        of strength, understanding, and courage
    The wall of ice around my heart ached
    Needing to be broken and warmed again

You were my light in the darkness
    The strength, understanding, and courage
    I needed I found in you
    You found a crack in that wall of ice
    And melted it down piece by piece

Out of the blue you came into my life
    Quietly, carefully you found your way
        into my heart
    With silent resistance you remained there
    Refusing to leave

Had there not been you my life would be different
    I would have shut myself off
        to hide from the pain of the world
    I would have been cold and lonely
    Had there not been you

Lorraine Ippolito

In Love...To Julissa Cortez

The fan in my room rumbles at times
Whispers get loud so I'll keep mine
Besides, I am all by myself tonight

I can't hear you, you don't see me
You standing by the corner, do you love me?
If you do, come and kiss me
Let me take you to Saturn with me
We will make love on the rings

I've thrown out my fan
and I've mellowed out my whispers
Besides, I shall be with you tonight

Quixotic we'll both be
So endless...so together and free
We'll take away what is
Lady's liberty

We are In Love

Javier Espinoza

Strange Mourners

It was a rainy and dreary night
When the lonely old man died.
He had no family.
Nobody was at his side.
He had no friends.
So nobody cried.

Only the rain tears were falling.
Tapping a melancholic song
While the wind squeezed through the window
And whispered what's wrong
And the old oak trees
That are tall and strong
Shivered and lamented
All night long.
Only the weeping willow
That always shows her mystic sorrow
Mourned a lonely old man
Who will not be here tomorrow.

Ruth Goldberger

Gems And Treasures

Soft blue opal of the heavens streaked in pearl white
  giving way a vivid blanket of gold dust
Suddenly showing crimson red as in the ruby
  with the background setting of sapphire blues
An artist's creation in a brilliant rainbow of colors
  deepening to subtle beauty in ebony shade of onyx
Adorned with the shimmering crown of the
  Aurora Borealis in the north
While being scattered with an abundant
  setting of sparkling diamonds
The gems of the day becoming jewels of the darkness
  all this within a sunset into night
Forever glowing and repeating in the glorious heavens
  tho' the artwork never the same to be repeated
Given that we may wonder at this mural being created
  artwork of radiant gems and treasures o'er us all

  Rae Ann Barton

When Your Mother's Gone

If your mother dies when you're little,
Your world comes to an end.
You lose your very heart and soul;
Your confidante - your friend.

You lose your self-esteem, as well.
You feel the "odd one out"
When you see girls with their mothers,
And you will always doubt...

That you belong to anyone,
Abandoned, lost, bereft.
No one knows the devastation
To a child who's only left...

With memories and images
Of the one who gave her birth,
And now you doubt your talents,
Capabilities and worth.

To the outside world you just go on,
Hiding hurt that knows no end,
When you're the child, and your mother's gone...
Your confidante - your friend.

  Jacquelyn Adair Williams

Ode To Nicole

Your poems are plaintive songs
  with moments of aesthetic incredulity.
Your poems are the epitome of continuity,
  a rendezvous with the paradoxically premature
Death of a friend
And the absence of parents
  who are on ambiguous journeys.
Your poems leave no room for pretexts.
I cannot wear my rose-colored glasses
  when I read your poetry.

  Bonnie Perkins

Searching

Eyes are searching, searching for the truth.
Tears flow from blissful eyes,
A smile on a bruised face,
Remorse in the eyes of a murderer.
Words of faith from the unfaithful,
A devil hides behind child-like-eyes,
The guilty of sin plead innocent.
Happiness is the face of depression.
Eyes are searching, ever searching.

  Kelli Frondle

Alone...But Why?

The wind swirls debris in the darkness, no one knows he's there.
Taking refuge in the blackness, he's content on waiting there.

He's dressed in black from head to toe, his long coat protects
him from the cold, he crouches down in the corner, his arms,
he silently folds.

His patience pays off, as she comes into sight, her blond hair
being swept from her face. He watches her near, as he silently
stands, his heartbeat starting to race.

He pounces on her in the blink of an eye, his hand presses a
knife to her throat, he drags her back in the darkness, as the
blood runs hot down her coat.

Her last thought as her life escaped her, was of her mother,
who she had earlier forgotten to phone, and how, here in an
alley, freezing cold, she's forced...to die alone...

  Sherry Keown

My Concierge

Into my life you came one day
And taking my hand, I prayed, you would never go away
Your love and grace pulled me through
And helped with the many things, I thought I could not do.
Oh Lord, keeper of my soul, I pray
That I may lead others to your house each day.
The joy one feels when knowing you care
Overwhelms me, and with others I want to share
Thank You Lord, for giving me the key
That in eternity, all may dwell with Thee.
Thank You Lord, for being my concierge.

  Helen P. Sassaman

Love Me With A Song

Lord, here I am again, apart on bended knees
With nothing to hold onto, or to put my mind at ease
A message burns deep inside and somehow keeps me strong
So, touch the chords and write the words and love me with a song
The lines I write I know you hold and somehow make them rhyme
the rhythm playing in my soul, you give with perfect time
My life is but a melody of scores both right and wrong
So, Jesus pick me up again and love me with a song
Let me reach out and shared the things you've shared with me
Touch some life with truth and love and somehow set them free
You break the bonds that hold within the will to carry on
And touch the strings within my heart and love me with a song
A song that reaches out to touch the hearts of all man kind
A song we all are searching for but seldom do we find
A song that rings with truth and love for all to sing along
Reach down and gently touch me Lord and love me with a song

  Jimmy Felton Thompson

Coeur Sacre

In the heart lies the questions.
In the soul lies the source of all answers.
It tells you that only He
Can untie the knot of confusion.
So, you knock at His door.
He opens it.
Sometimes it takes time
For he is listening
From the other side.
But, when you let go,
When you let God,
Allowing Him to dwell within you,
You've removed the door between you
And you will never have to knock again.

  Pina J. Moore

Matthew's Vacation

I asked God about a year ago or so
 If my time was due to take a vacation.
He smiled, and said, "When it's time, I'll let you know—
 And I'll let you pick your own relation."

It seemed like months and months that I looked around.
 God made so many nice people everywhere!
I looked at Moorhead — my Mom and Dad were found!
 Six months ago God said, "Go now - and - take care."

My Mom is Linda - and my Dad's name is Doug.
 Grandmas and grandpas and aunts and uncles too!
And do you know what? Grandma K. sure can hug!
 To make them laugh - all I do is Coo!

I hated to tell them my visit was to end.
 "Come, little Angel Matthew," I heard God say.
Maybe some day I can arrange to help send
 A brother or sister for a longer stay.

Will you tell my sitter I just fell asleep?
 I love you all — I'll miss the whole relation.
The hurt will pass — and you can smile — not weep!
 'Cuz, that was the bestest of all vacations!!!!

Jeanie Brennan

This Body Of Mine!

No wonder I am tired, so weary and so weak
My eyes are very heavy, but still I cannot sleep.
My body seems too busy, 'tis causing me great harm,
It looks as if I'm carrying a zoo, park, and a farm.

All the calves on my legs are heavy you see,
And vanes are on barns, yet they criss-cross on me.
The bridge of my nose is busy this week,
And I'm wondering daily of the moles on my cheek.

There's corn in the garden, yet some on my toes.
Plus the ears on my head are giving me woes.
And I'm pondering deeply ('Tis giving me dread),
The wisdom of having a hare on your head.

And then there's my temples, they make me collapse.
Are they Hindu or Moslem, or Jewish perhaps?
In my eyes are two pupils who chatter away,
Making my head ache during nighttime and day.

I'm a little morose as this tale I relate,
And shudder to think of what is my fate.
I'm feeling rather sickly, can you sympathize with me?
I'm tired of being human, so what shall I be?

Jane O. Eberly

Wishes Made Just For You

I'll always feel great pride
 whenever I have you by my side
I'll never be far away
 my love for you grows stronger each passing day

I wish I could take you far from here
 bring you a life of only joy and cheer
I wish I could fulfill your every dream
 and be the one who makes your heart sing

I'll share your pain as my own
 you'll never again have to be alone
I'll try my very best
 giving only love and respect

I wish I didn't live with the constant fear
 that you will one day disappear
I wish I never had to say goodbye
 each time tears fill my eyes

Lisa West

I Wonder....

As I sit here remembering all the good
and the bad times we had,
I remember how much I love him,
and how much I miss him,
wishing he were with me at all times.

If only there was a hint or a sign
to let me know if he loves me as he used to.
Something that will let me know I still have a chance with him.
To let me know if we are only friends or
something more special. Is it love or friendship?

One can only hope or wonder if
it is as special as they want it to be,
Why can't there be a sign?
A sign would make all the difference,
and let you know so much.

Wondering if it will ever be the same.
Will we walk through the park again sharing secrets,
will we lay down and watch the stars as we share our feelings,
will we ever just have a really good time doing anything together
just because we are in love? I guess one will never know.

Denise L. Briggs

The Eternal Destiny Of Man

Come my friend and listen to me
As I tell you an eternal mystery.
I will tell you how God's come to be.
This is a story about you and me.

"Intelligences" sang and danced among the stars
eons ago in past eternity.
Godly parents said "These We will organize
they have a destiny. They shall be spirit children unto Me."

Organized, a birth you see -
Male and female given identity.
Living in His presence, like Him we wanted to be.
Needing a body to be free.

Time went by, but growth must come through mortality.
An earth created, no primordial goo or simian ancestry.
"A child of God" born to earthly parents were we.
Now by faith we walk the road to immortality.

Birth, life and Christ like love, death, and resurrection,
Behold! A God is born endowed with creativity.
Then with "eternal family" living in the presence of Deity;
and "Intelligences" in eternity; the cycle begins again, you see.

Theodore K. Elmer

An Awakening On A Christmas Visit

I came to them by way of emptiness,
Bringing not an academic gold;
Nor in disguise of bright disposition;
A love for them in a dour mold,
For mystery's love had winged me there.

A house crowned with simplicities.
(that I felt fair)
False lights festooning their eccentricities.
Evil bowing to their goodness,
And rightly too!
Death loses to His birth!

Waves of ego laughter
Disguised upon the earth.
Smiles, memories, past loneliness-
One's love recalled.
Carrying the soul along to an individual destiny.
Christmas is upon us, one and all!

Joseph Sauer

Alone

As morning comes and the sun rose high
My heart is filled with soundless sighs
The soft flutter of a bird's wings
The silent flight of a butterfly
The rippling brook sliding over the stones
A little daisy standing all alone
The trees bow down their branches
A soft breeze gently move the leaves
Everything is hushed and still
God is here - I am not alone anymore

Enda B. Nixon

At The Happy's Stork

At 5:30 p.m. on January 21, 1996 once again everything in the universe feels in its place.

I took my rightful place at the bar; there but not involved, like a rock in a stream that the current flows around.

At 7:30 p.m. I became part of the stream.

nic galloro

Inspired By A Friend

Some discover its meaning when time's almost out
Some go a lifetime with always a doubt

Some are confused with each living day
Some see it coming and just walk away

Some disrespect it and hurt when it's gone
Some let it die when once it was strong

Maybe it's because some don't understand
It's a simple definition we all hold in our hands

LOVE is the word some find hard to define
I am lucky to have found the meaning in such a short time

We should live, learn and pass it on
We are all here to help each other when it's all said and done

If you are willing to die for a person or cause
-Without a pause-

You have LOVE

Selina Rodriguez-Griffin

What Man Can...?

What man can measure love in a test tube?
What man can grow faith in petri dishes?
What man knows the dimensions of the universe?
Who among us can feed thousands with two fishes?

What man can created life from nothing?
What man, with a word, raises the dead?
What man can calm a raging storm?
Who among us can exalt the lame from beds?

What man can command legions of angels?
What man is always just and right?
What man is the perfect judge and teacher?
Who among us has his power and his might?

What man, at once, can be all colors?
What man, at once, can be many faiths?
What man, can be God Incarnate?
Who among us can be in more than one place?

What man can truly comprehend it all?
What man will just believe and trust?
What man will listen to the great I am?
Who among us knows there's life after the dust?

Brenda Neal-Vey

Mysterious Ocean

Never calm with passion
Life is like a mysterious ocean;
Face-lines all in thunder-fury expression
Display only some silly bubbles of emotion
Through the floating waves poor, all thrown
From the deepest far away bottom of center ocean
Where all kinds of underground suppression and depression
Constantly take place as part of some survival operation
Surface in pretension being kept motionless with all caution
To thwart any attention from the real obscene action
Going on between most deadly creepers with fatal poison.

When one poor silly wave comes in front throbbing
Desperately searching for firm stand on sands,
Within no time waving by beating heads
There follow huge thick rows after rows sobbing
Only to bury their sorrows before able to reveal one.

Heart-feeling memories of scrolls of vast pain
Of all who drowned exploring mysteries in vain
Ever float around the heart of tears-mixed waters
Covering our planet by more than two thirds.

John Thanickal

To All My Children With Love

You all are my darling valentine,
And have been your whole life long;
I look at you all and see,
Just how dear you all are to me,
And if you were not around
how empty my life would be,
I don't always say what is in my heart,
But without you all my world
would simple fall apart'
I look at the years gone by,
And how much, I love each of you
and how wonderful you all are'
And though the years gone by some good some bad,
You children are the best friend a mother could have;
And as we grow older my kids and I,
We will always stand side by side'
to the end of our time
And you will always be my darling valentine'
I love you all so very much...

Estelle Johnson

The People That We See

They come in groups, with a friend, or one by one,
    these people that we see.
Traveling by freight, hitch hiking, walking.
All they want is a break from the road, a chance to rest,
    drink some coffee, have a bite to eat, clean up a bit.
Talented and smart, sharing what they know,
    what they have, with others they meet.
Often insecure, afraid, lonely, a chip on their shoulders,
    searching for a place they feel they belong.
Wanting to be a part of things, to fit in with the rest.
Not knowing how, they rebel in self-defense.
Often treated as though they are different,
    different from the rest of us, when they aren't.
We see them every day, we want to help them find their way,
    trying not to make demands, to add to their burden.
We want to be accepting, to listen to their needs,
    help them through their journey,
      find their way through life,
      realize their dreams.
They come in groups, with a friend, or one by one,
    these people that we see.

Virginia Sellner

Acquaintance

The most beautiful girl in the World...
I wish I may, I wish I might,
Make her acquaintance in my dreams tonight.
Seductively, she gazes into my curious eyes
With thoughts we ponder and both know why;
Yet birds nor butterflies can be
No more fitting than she and me.
With mutual respect for the way things must be,
I must be I and she must be free.
Timing and circumstance made void our bloom,
Which never could emerge this winter afternoon.
Some things in life never ever were they meant;
Perhaps a different time, a different place,
A different world - longing for such dream
Defer thy spice she waits for me.

Donald Cochran

A Mansion For Me

There is a mansion in heaven for me,
The rent has been paid by Christ on the tree.
The rooms are of ivory, the streets are of gold,
No need to worry about the heat or the cold.

There will be a reunion with loved ones up there,
There'll be no more parting, or sorrows or care.
The Lord will be there, my Redeemer and King,
Loud praises to Him, eternally I will sing.

If your sins are covered by the crucified one,
But your work here on earth has barely begun,
No need to worry, there'll be room for you there,
For Jesus has promised, "A place I'll prepare."

So trust in the Lord and wait for his call,
Just work day by day and give Him your all.
A mansion has been leased in Heaven for you,
The rent has been paid, if to Christ you are true.

Anna Maxine Holt Leak

The Age Of Four

It was raining, bare trees dripped;
Inside, the preacher droned on and on.
Where was mama? On a trip, they said -
But she didn't kiss me good-bye.
I squirmed - my blue serge pants were too tight.
Square blocks outside looked gray and cold.
Then we were outside, standing in the rain.
I couldn't see past black pants legs - dresses,
There was a sound like gravel hitting wood.
I'll never forget that sound. Scary!
My fat aunt started wailing -
Where was mama?
I think I grew up that day.
I didn't want to wade the branch
Or climb the apple trees any more.
Or climb into the barn loft where raw peanuts were drying.
I didn't want to play any more.

Selma Mariah Springall

No Excuse

Stop abusing the women of our time,
There is no excuse for this vicious crime.
She's someone's Mother, who gave life to them,
Who should never be abused at the hands of men.
She's someone's Sister, whose diary is always closed,
Never to be written in since being abused by someone she knows.
She's someone's Daughter, the light of her Mother's eyes,
Who should never be abused and forced to live with secret lies.
Thanks for the courage to get through these times,
There is no excuse for these vicious crimes.

Tyrone David Sawyer

A Letter To My Son

A letter to my son, like so many others,
begins and ends with all my love mother.

How can I express the turmoil in my head,
How can I be my best when I feel unrest instead.

You know all I ever wanted...
was your happiness and success...
So when I go to sleep at night,

I whisper please... please...
God bless

You are the only son I've had...
and probably ever will.

So for heaven sakes young man...
let's make it up this hill.

What hill was that mom, you asked, what could you be saying,
Is it that my life's fulfilled,...
the prayers, all these years you're praying?

Now you are a man, my son.
Of whom I am very proud, keep your head up high,
and say this phrase out loud.

With the help of God I am, and I shall become,
the very best that I can be, hearing my own drum.

Gwendolyn P. Moore

Tree Time

You think I'm just a solitude shadow
Upon your night wall
By days' light I stand outside your home,
Time itself standing tall.
I recall when Dinosaurs shook this land.
The moss growing on
My north side cried out at Custer's last stand
My outstretched branches
Bowed to birds who sang a different song.
My age old limbs' tips
Wrote in sand the buffalo's epitaph.
My leaves were so green
When Kennedy walked a different path.
Man, can you join me?
Reverse mankind's course, save the countryside.
The yin and yang of
Our earth's unbalance is due to collide.
Will I still be here
After the haunting pain of Earth's rebirth?
If so for how long?

Carol Danielson

My Search

I searched for years to find meaning for my life
    But somehow it always eluded me;
Only after years of endless searching
    Did I conclude, "Satan has deluded me."

My eyes were blinded to the fullness of God
    And what His Spirit and power could do;
So vainly I looked for hope from the world
    And found not a thing in it was new.

Then I heard the Gospel story, "God's own Son
    Died on the cross to give me grace;"
Hope for me was born that day so long ago
    When, on Calvary, Jesus took my place.

Now my search is ended, for Jesus I've found
    And the meaning is real to my soul;
He looked deep inside my heart and saw my need
    And by His Spirit has made me whole.

Vernon Howerton

'Loveless Life'

Sweet memories so precious carry tears to the eyes,
The world is so beautiful only today I realize;
But sometimes somewhere I really want to find
Those beautiful moments hidden deep in the mind.
The chains of life are so hard to break
The relationship we share divided by a gate;
The ecstasy of candles, the depth of the night,
The fragrance of flowers, the brightness of lights...
But still somewhere deep in the soul
Something burns my heart from wood to coal.
I can feel the warmth of your burning lips,
I can feel the strength of your grasping grips,
I want your presence through each moment of my life
But a curse divide our lives like a blazing knife;
I realize the world's beauty but deep in my mind
The world seems so ugly - everything's so unkind.

Shakila Saifullah

Untitled

I'm sick of you, I'm sick of my life.
I'm sick of you, and of being your wife.

Stop playing games, and give me the divorce.
Before you know it, it ends up in the courts.

The kids will lose, nobody will win.
The kids will lose, and you never again grin.

There's never enough, enough property or money.
To buy you that fur, or that Energizer bunny.

Hope springs eternal, or so it is said.
I want that divorce, and before I am dead.

Gloria J. Mullavey

A Time Gone By

The wind blows gently
outside my window pane,
And the leaves on the trees
seem to be swaying in the breeze
As I again recall such a day
I once walked down the line,
In a Country Town so far away
where I stopped to look around
It was so quaint,
With its old schoolhouse
And the stores whose floors
creaked as you walked.
That old Museum along the way
With its Antiques all about
And its old wood stoves.
Burning oil-lamps throughout
Why do Museums make one feel that way?
As it seems to beckon, "Do come in and stay",
"It's been a long-time," seems to say.

Josephine Mason

To You I Give

Memories float in and out in front and then behind.
You are always and forever on my mind.
As a tear drop slides down my sad face, I see you in my heart.
I thought I knew who you were right from the star.
If you had any idea how I feel in my mind.
All of the love and hate totally combined.
The way you look, your whisper, your sent, lingers in my heart.
There's no way of explaining how I feel when were apart.
I thought surely from the first you were meant for me.
If only now you, I could convince to see.
I have so much to offer to you, so much inside.
I'll give you no less than my heart, my love, my soul, and all my pride.

Lacy Castleberry

Fragments

Dear Mother, as we pause near the end of your life
separately, anguished, I prepare to lose you knowing
there will be no resolution

And though you are not resting in that rest home,
your light is mercifully fading, as mine burns
bright with disjointed memories

Of clean Adirondack mornings, my white Lady greets me thumping
recognition, proud, wide-rumped, gentle
I ride her 'round the corral, with braided hair,
in my cherry red sweater

I walk to face the ordained, black crows, chiding children,
tripping slate sprung by massive oaks shading a community
of conforming, rowed Victorians, pious Irish, that place
where I was never safe

I am your child running, hiding, chalking Bronx sidewalks
with radiant images forever flattened by the havoc
that shreds our lives in unpretty railroad rooms

I see our struggle, our abject tangle
and oil your mismatched mahogany
to bring back the sheen.

Joan M. Corr

Sowing

We sought our fame and fortune,
Upon life's weary road,
We smiled and grinned and bore it,
With each new heavy load.

We struggled through and always knew,
That someday we would find it,
With each hard day we found a way,
And didn't seem to mind it.

We had our days of sun and fun,
As all our seed we sowed,
Life past us by while on the run,
Down it treacherous, bending road.

And when, alas, we'd found it,
it wasn't what we'd thought,
For to the end the fortune sought, the work we'd wrought,
Had reaped but what we'd sowed.

Don C. Dickinson

Remnants

These dusty shelves yield remnants of the journey from
the youthful passions lost to strangers we've become:
I tread within the yellowed leaves of timeless traces
failing in my quest to recognize the faces
even though this pensive child and wistful wife
once walked within the fleeting shadows of my life

Although the ageless inner soul is still the same
I hesitate to hear the echoes of her name:
A soft and sorrowed song meandering through the mind
to dwell within the dust of laughter left behind
and when at last the murky mirror shows myself
I'll place the crumbling book upon the silent shelf

Debra Polirer

MOTHER

M - Is for the many ways you show your love for me
O - Is for the Only Child that I turned out to be
T - Is for the tenderness only a mother could give
H - Is for the happy home you've made for me to live
E - Is everything you've done for me, how will I ever repay?
R - Is for the rareness that is in your loving way!

Sandra Francine Murden

A Sonnet For Mother Earth

This beautiful planet we call Earth
With humankind its myopic steward
Was conceived during the sun's fiery birth
And with myriad life matured
All in a balance exquisite
With synergy of oceans, life and air
Which is our planet's requisite
For its fitness to spare
Our Creator then made humankind with superior ability
But He failed to foresee that insatiable greed
And failure to curb our fertility
Would fail the earth in its time of need
  Now He must refresh the human mentality
  If He is to revive the earth's faltering vitality

    Ray C. Frodey

Waterstained

God, I wish the water would wash my fears away
Instead, I slowly drown in the dreams that I have made
Tears that won't come down, don't wash away
But they stay inside and fill the emptying remains.

Was never supposed to be this way,
  we were never supposed to rust away
The rain can rain lifetimes away
  but it was never supposed to flood this way.

And when the sun went gray, I prayed for the rain
That it would wash me away, to another day
Instead, the rain froze me to where I had to stay
And now I know when it thaws, I'll be water-stained.

    Joseph Jay Cunningham

Realize The Loss

On a hell bound train, I bought a ticket to ride,
When I cut my wrist deep to commit suicide.
Satan now laughing, there's no place I can hide.
The light growing dimmer, into darkness I slide.

You may wonder what happens to this great stud,
With life flowing out in a gushing wet flood.
My body now limp in the sea of red blood.
The red will soon turn to a crusty brown crud.

Now intelligence is not what I lack,
But I can't figure how to find my way back.
At the morgue my body's on an icy cold rack,
As my soul rides this train down a one way track.

Deeper and deeper the train rides to hell.
That ugly conductor keeps ringing the bell.
We round the corner to an awful bad smell.
With Satan's black magic, I'm locked in his spell.

Through the hot brimstone the train moves on straight.
My car pulls up to number thirty-eight gate.
Don't give yourself this very same fate,
When you realize the loss, your life is real great.

    Gary D. Rick

Moments

  A cool breeze, the scent of flowers and evergreen.
The barely audible sound of rustling leaves and chirping crickets.
  The somber glow of the moon, and the brilliant
specks of shimmering stars, that seem to fill the heavens,
  and transport the mind on unimaginable journeys, thru
the infinite reaches of space and time, until the gentle
  touch of your hand, and warm embrace
    returns us to
      this time and
       place.

    Dennis W. Brooks

Tucker Wood

Tucker Wood is a place of dreams,
adventurous times and wondrous schemes.

Warm summer days and cold winter nights,
bring the promise of spring and autumn's harvest delights.

Sedate and secure are all who dwell,
within the bosom of Tucker Wood's dell.

Frolicsome spirits, light hearted and gay,
begin the enchantment of fellowship each day.

Follow the call of the whispering breezes,
for Tucker Wood is home...if one pleases.

    Darlene Gardner Vaughn

What Shall We Do?

What shall we do with this beautiful day?
  We can use it wisely or just throw it away.
God gave it to us to do as we would,
  So will we do wicked? It's better to do good!
We can search for a rose or gather some weed,
  If we have chosen the latter, we need to take heed.
Go speak a kind word to lift someone up,
  That kind word may help to fill their cup.
Try to make a friend happy whenever they are sad,
  Then we will be certain to enjoy the day we had.
We can hand out a smile it won't cost a dime,
  Only a few seconds of our precious time.
So think about the beautiful day that we've had,
  Then, we too can smile 'cause it wasn't all bad!

    Sylvia J. Murphy, alias "Sally J. Martin"

The Unnoticed American Journey

Steps, steps - we seem to walk without a trace!
Crowds pass our sad and frightened face.

Our invisibleness heightens our growing fears,
No roof or shelter to hide our tears.

Where, where will we go to find a bed?
If the cold is severe we may soon be dead!

Not one quarter for bus, or phone or food,
No shower or clean clothes to improve our mood.

We're not lazy, but how would you know?
We're invisible to you, we do not show!

Our American journey seems way off track,
Perhaps if more cared, we could find a way back.

We know we're responsible for our own fate,
But please just a little help before it's too late!

Some of us had an American dream,
But illness, war, poverty derailed us it seems.
It's not as simple as this poem indicates.
But we're worth saving, we really do rate!
Perhaps one of us will give back to mankind,
What all man are craving and just cannot find!

    Elizabeth Joan Wallis

Bright Morning

Early in the morning, when a new day arrives
Darkness has pulled its drapes and presents the sun
Birds awake and thrill the hills with song
All signs celebrate, the day which has just begun
Leaves, inhale, shiver and wave to their neighbors
Dew races to slake the thirst of grass and flowers
Spiders working through the night enjoy the call to the bar
The sun warms the earth and the life it empowers

    Joanne Caruso

Buttons Of Old

Buttons of old, buttons of new,
never two are the same.
But the buttons of old bother me the most.

Buttons in an old glass jar hidden forever in the attic.
Buttons of old, buttons of new, that my two sisters
and me rummaged through. And Art was there too.

I know that one there in the bottom belonged to me,
in that jar of buttons of old.
It was from an old gray coat that mom had made for
me way back in the fifties.
And look there is grandma's orange half broken button in
there too. Gee, that must have been some special memories
for her to keep an old orange button of old.

As we shook that jar of buttons of old out
fell Art's brown button from his old sweater that
his mother had knitted just for him when he was young.
Nellie and Thelma dug their hands deep into that jar of
buttons of old and pulled out their buttons in the
colors of yellow and green.
For those were the days of buttons of old.

Marcella G. Inman-Sievers

While Missing You

Am I falling for you; I honestly don't know,
My heart says yes; but my mind's saying "whoa!"
The more we're together — and everything we share,
Makes it so easy for me to start to care.
I look into your eyes or see your sweet grin;
My heart melts and I start to fall all over again.
Waking up in your arms somehow felt so right,
That's a habit I could get used to — every night!
I'm glad we met and that you've been a part of my life;
Yet the thought of never seeing you cuts like a knife.
Often when we're alone and start to touch
I get scared that I'll care too much.
When you're tense or feeling blue;
I want to be a gentle rain soothing you.
Only God knows what tomorrow may bring;
So all we can do is live day today. . .
Yet I'll always be glad He sent you my way.
When I allow myself to dream I see me and you as us;
But I've realized that most of all I want your
happiness and trust.

Debbie A. Kelley

Dogwood's Doxology

The dogwood is the fairest tree
That wakes in the sovereign spring.
Its boundless beauty beckons me
To worship Christ as Lord and King!

It lifts its leafy boughs to God
In tribute for resurrection.
Asleep in the chilled wintry sod,
It's now groomed to God's perfection.

Four petals form its blossoms white,
Each tinged with a droplet of red.
The blossoms bear the sacred site,
A crimson-stained cross where Christ bled.

It acclaims Christ of Calvary,
For in shame He was crucified.
It extols Him eternally
For the glorious day Death died!!

The dogwood lauds all creation,
Bursts with joyous exultation.
It calls spring to celebration
To honor Christ's Coronation!!!

June Nash

Serenity Woods

Behind my home my little patch of serenity grows,
Planted years ago by a tender farmer's hands.
Though he has departed this earth several years ago,
His life and legacy lives on through this small patch of land.

Gathered from far and wide
And planted with a farmer's pride.
All shapes, sizes and varieties of trees
That provide homes for all birds and animals for free.

Through the window on a winter's day
I can watch the cardinals so red and the very blue jays.
The squirrels with their bushy tails,
The masked raccoon as well as pheasant and quail.

Spring brings rebirth
Of plants, flowers and creatures' mirth.
Why can't men learn the beauty of the earth to enjoy?
Why is he bent this beauty to destroy?

The peace and tranquility serenity woods brings to me
Is there for all mankind to enjoy and see.
To witness the beauty of the earth and sky
Listening to the birds sing and the wind sigh.

Stop! Look! Listen! Before they're all gone!

Jill E. Kuhns

Untitled

So one may say your dream's a lie
And one may kiss and say goodbye
But you will stand oh so still
While your eyes with tears will fill
You scream for what you now crave
As your life is taken by a single wave
The dream of death you had before
Now has set an even score

But what can this catastrophe mean
All your life you've been waiting to see
The undying truth about the fatal fall
Now that you've seen, have you seen it all
For although your eyes are still sore
Your mind and soul crave for more
The truth's escaped and flown away
Which ends your last life filled day

Beth Silva

A Season For Waiting

The small child's voice rose in shrill sing-song
As I walked down the nursing center corridor.
The words were unclear at first,
Then I recognized them
And silently joined the chorus.

It was a sultry summer day
Yet the song was of Christmas -
About goodness and rewards and waiting.

"He knows when you are sleeping
He knows when you're awake . ."

I glanced through the open door
To see the tot with charming song.

A single silhouette was there
A shriveled little woman tied to her wheelchair
Gazing into the sunset beyond her window
Beyond her world.

Sobered I continued down the hall
As the childlike voice followed me.

"You'd better watch out, you'd better not cry . ."
But I cried.

Barbara Magerl

Summer

Spring sets the stage with care
soft stirrings agitate the air
  I take my chair.
Bright sudden summer crowds my eye
Scudding clouds follow on by day
Stars make a lantern show at night
sun's heat is felt in every hour
Life surges in beast, plant and flower
Fall drops its curtain on my seasons play
The theatres dark in winter gray
  I leave my chair and walk away
Until - again - I see you - summer

Robert C. Norton

Can This Be Real...

The years pass by — joy and sorrow meet. Waves of life circle
around every part of my being. Lashing, splashing against my
mind. Coming, going, moving, flowing. The ebb of sea sounds
washing the past behind, as if pushing debris away from the
shore out into the sea, lost in the magnitude of water.

So you are to me — washing waves of love over me; by the
touch of your hand, the gleam in your eyes, or the gentleness
of your smile. Like the clear blue-green sea when the sun
shines making the water glisten. Or the light of the moon as
it sends streaks across a lake still and quiet. Gleaming beams
dancing across the dark water leaving strands of light in the darkness.

The way I feel when I hear your voice. The gentle hesitation —
not too fast or too much, go slow — be careful. Stop...

Let the waves push the clear sea water near. Sifting the sand,
cleaning nature; bringing sounds of peace and joy, pushing
debris away. Leaving white powder — sand, tiny and white —
crunching beneath walking, running feet. Going forward, mind,
soul, body, to the unknown. Can this be real — waves, sand,
moon, sun, love. After years have passed by. Can this be real.

Sharon R. Cleveland

Seasons To Come

On a rainy day put down your umbrella my love,
I want God's teardrops to touch you with His love

When the sun warms you inside,
Just remember "He Will Abide."

When the snowflake falls gracefully,
Just remember those sweet memories.

When the springtime comes and new foals run
You'll know His works are all well done.

They come and go, old age and youth,
The breath of life's never ending truth.

Winter, Springtime, Summer, and Fall,
My sweet love we've shared them all.

The best is yet to come I'm told,
On Heaven's streets, lined with gold.

Catherine Steele

Daddy

Daddy you have been gone a long time now
You are with God, but I still miss you
I think of you often and when I do I smile
and remember all the many happy times we had together.
I thank you daddy for the love I felt from
you and for teaching lessons I use in my life.
For being there when I needed you
Thank you dear daddy I love you and you will always
be with me in my heart.

Judith A. Carter

Tainted Love

You were but a dream to me.
When we met I felt the desire.
To touch you, to feel you
To know your heart, to quench your fire.
A kiss was but a wish to me.
We shared a moment in time.
Just the two of us, intimate.
To taste you, to penetrate you.
To be entwined, flesh to flesh, soul to soul.
We melted with our union.
We became a part of each other.
The sensation, the passion, became addiction.

Hayden L. Polk

My Destiny

Whose right is it to say
my life unfolds array,
when through the golden gates of hope
I cling to every happiness?

When the clapping hands of years
applaud my hopes and fears,
who counts my gains,
who calculates my losses?

I have woven a tapestry of love
which hangs so far above
the insignificant threads of hate
which threaten to snag it.

My patient soul sings
while waiting in the wings
for my inevitable destiny
to be played on a grand, but uncertain stage.

Jerry L. Truesdell

The Humbling Effect

The more we learn, we find the less we know
The more we engulf of the big wide world,
The smaller we appear to grow
Humbling, humbling inside
The world so big and wide,
Tends to humble us inside
Humbling, humbling inside

We huff and puff and stick out our chests
We strut our stuff with our heads held high as the sky
What a useless and worthless sense of pride
Humbling, humbling inside
For we realize though we seldom confess
That our world is an awful mess
Humbling, humbling inside

Ann Hobgood Wrenn

Somewhere The Rainbow Ends

I promise you we will always be together
Some other time some other dimension
Our hearts will touch and beat as one
I promise you we will always be together
Where the sun glows like pure gold
Laughter radiates forever I promise you
We will always be together somewhere
The rainbow ends
Where true love remains no more gray clouds
You will see as high as the stars shine
You will always be my memorable love
Somewhere the rainbow ends
Your caress will be like feathers
Of a bird our hearts will touch and beat as one
Somewhere the rainbow ends

Barbara Thomas

Addiction

I will lift you up. I will bring you down.
I will spread your name all over town.
I will make you laugh. I will make you cry.
I will let you live. I will make you die.
I will take your job, your car and your house.
I will cost you the respect of your friends,
    Your children and your spouse.
I will make you lose. I will let you win.
I will rot your teeth. I will ruin your skin.
I will make your children cry.
I will make your babies die.
You can bet me. You can spend me.
You can pop me but you will never stop me.
You can snort me. You can shoot me.
You can drink me. You can smoke me.
You can even toke me.
But if you dare you had best beware.
You can truly make this prediction.
I will forever be there. I will be your worst nightmare.
I am an addiction.

James Byron Davis

Of Cats And Men

A cat, in climbing up a tree,
Gives little thought, how hard 'twill be,
To get down to the earth, again,
And there, she's not unlike the men,
Who jump upon a passing chance
Of business, trouble, or romance,
Without a thought to looking back,
That they might know the homeward track,
When all their hopes, of one fine day,
Are dashed to nothing, in the way,
That almost all were dashed before,
And will be dashed, forever more.
The cat, that's climbing up a tree,
Will come down, that's a certainty,
A man, however, has a chance,
However slight, he may advance.
The cat may struggle slowly down,
The man, if he can't "go to town,"
May come down, with a bang, instead,
And lucky, if he keeps his head.

Frank Greenberg

Untitled

A world where there was no room
for romance,
just crystal chandeliers and champagne,
to con your favours..
enjoy your pleasures...
when amidst it all you arrived...
like a nuclear explosion,
leaving everybody shell shocked by your presence,
as you blew my mind...
coming straight to me, as if I was the only one in the room;
and you, your lips, your hair...
your body... and beauty came towards me.

And in all those glorious memories...
of such a long forgotten past..
amidst the laughter of hyenas...
I wanted to take you in my arms...
to be my queen for the afternoon,
when the peonies were in full bloom...
and your dress moved gently...
as we drifted through the people.

Walter G. Perz

Night

I am Night
With silent wings I overcome my brother
Day

Shadows lengthen as my steps grow near
Disquiet follows in the wake of my path

I call the stars fro0m their nests in ancient galaxies,
Passive observers of ages past
And ages to come

They watch with diamond eyes
As Day weakens and dies
Yielding to my children:
Darkness and Moonlight

Polar twins from the womb of Night

Laurel Scherffius

Peace

Dark terror; gripping my heart
with fret and fear.
Beads of sweat; gathering on my brow...
sinking deeper in the mist.
    Prayer...
On a sea; in a crushing storm...
feel the boat being seized by the wind...
dashed about.
I'm so tired; no strength to continue.
Then...
    Calm...
Water lightly slapping the now gently,
rocking boat.
See the crystal clear shine, glare,
bright on the rolling surface.
Hear the birds; sounding their joy
in soaring through the shining, fresh,
sky blue heights.
    Glorious... Peace...
It's Jesus.

Theresa Noe

Missing Words

Spoken not is heard not
Listened not is learned not
Used not is practiced not...
If all that is intended we knew
Then all that is misunderstood would not be
When we know not what another means
Then the conclusions that we attain are unfounded
Because of this gap in understanding
The gulf that separates us widens...
Help me to understand
Help me to learn
Help me to help myself
Ask the unaskable and I will answer
Give me the missing questions
I will give you the missing words.

Philip D. Mann

The Cactus

Arms outstretched over an arid and desolate plain
Its flower unbloomed longing for moisture
Blue skies overhead, dry air unrelenting
The cactus waits in solitary thirst

Brian J. Owens

Forgiveness

If someone asked the color of your eyes,
I'd say I haven't noticed yet their state.
I'm busy sensing through your anguished cries,
And wondering how it ties together fate.
This moment in time increases my hope
Like someone in a trance, somehow possess'd,
Transforms our worlds and broadens wide the scope,
Like yielding minds whose bodies hunger least.

The years have gone and I am past despising,
Yet leave me in a most receptive state,
Souls, minds, and hands meeting and rising,
Toward a common goal, a waiting gate.
   The future, like a crystal glove, soon brings
   Exchange of intellect unknown to kings.

   Merilyn Fox Alexander

Life Dismissal

The blue of your eyes fades as you speak
trying to grasp these words
foreign to your tongue

Yearning to grasp the notions
that even your mind cannot fathom

You need her like the earth that falls beneath your feet
the wind carries her voice to every heart but yours

The pictures and memories of your love
are now gone from the walls
empty whiteness fills the spaces

The tears you cry have never been for her
only of who you are without her

You lay in the darkness
and label it suicide.

You would never take your life
but you would let it go.

You close your eyes
the kiss of cruel love upon your lips

   Tara Lynne Bryant

Southern Snowday

Snow began in the night,
Tiny, tentative, tapping spherules on the skylight.
Awakening, I looked upon a landscape of wintry hue.
As day progressed the snow grew bolder,
Enlarging each flake minutely as if saying
I come south as I please.
Late afternoon brought larger, more silent flakes
As the world became wrapped
In a velvet blanket of white.
Night brought keening wind around the house,
Drifting snow across yard and fence.
Fire heats the hearth to warm me
As I survive the silent snow.

   Louise Norman

It Only Matters What Is Within

It doesn't matter about the color of your face,
It doesn't matter about what kind of race,

It doesn't matter about the color of your skin,
It only matters what is within.

It only matters about your personality,
Not your race, not your color, can't you see?

People in this world should be treated right,
Because it matters what's within, and not what you see by sight.

   Mindy Frazier

Lent

The forty days and nights of Lent
give all of us a needed time to think
to pray and fast and meditate.
Do now what should be done.
You pray - your way and God will heed.
But if the heart is not in the words
forget those words and start again.
Do now what should be done.
Pray with your mind and heart combined
making the presence of God feel real
and only then will the help of God come through.
Do now what should be done.
Then thank him for his gift to you
that feeling of having been fulfilled.

   Joseph D. Palmer

Bonnie, The Jonquil Of Life

Life begins at 40, they say.
To some this may be true.
But life began March 3, for me the day,
That life began for you.

The greatest of all Gardeners, is Christ.
His light outshines the sun.
God, whose glory bathes in the dawn,
And sheds the night when day is done.

Guide with love our Jonquil, Bonnie,
Let her blossoming be fair,
Cultivate her with the Spirit,
Teach her how to love and care.

Let no evil weeds or briars,
Prey upon her as she learns to live and grow.
Teach her patience, courage, and honor,
Guard this March flower...Bonnie with a rainbow.

God, who puts each flower by the garden wall,
Light our Bonnie eyes, and make them clear.
Keep her safe, strong and tall.
Let her know I will always love her and be there.

   Shareon E. Higgs

Christmas

Christmas means a lot to me
It's Christ in the name you see.
For Christ was born, God's only son
without him, the day is none.

Time has allowed us all to celebrate
in this world of power, greed and hate
and each year we get a chance to change
our worldly desires to loving thoughts so strange.

One tiny child, in a manger bare,
grew up to be the man of care.
The son of God who bore it all —
for our eternal life, is his call.

A call so profound for us to believe
His call is truth and light, so don't be deceived.
It's heard in the bells and the music too
Listen to him...he's calling you!

   Myrna Pierson Graver

Magical Dreaming

   To dream a magical dream is to dream a special dream,
about lemon drops and gumdrops
and chocolate rivers with icebergs of sugar.
Of elves and fairies and magical lands,
and to dream a dream of such things
is to dream a magical dream.

   Arianna Vasquez

Spring Migrants

Some come skipping
in the new sun,
as if infused with new life.

Others, impotent before the March wind,
are hurled northward to the trees,
whence they came last fall.

Floaters and skippers, all pell-mell
before the gusts, across the back yard grass
before melding with the earth 'neath the trees.

For them, winter is the interim,
the wake before interment in spring.
These are the first leaves of spring,
zombies from the fall,
migrants seeking rest.

Michael Hogan

Sunset

Roll on purple mountains with peaks so grand.
The blue and pink sunset is cheering for you,
With a cloud spread like a fan.

The day is over and night has begun;
But not without a spectacular array from the
setting of the sun.

The sun will come creeping again from the
east in the morning time.
Bringing warmth from the gold and
amber sunshine;

But the greatest show will be in the
evenings fair.
When the sun sets behind the purple mountains,
with beauty so rare.

Brenda Faye Larimore

Love And Reassurance

I will grow a blanket of grass
And embroider it with love for a wreath
And when the chill of winter comes to pass
Perhaps it will warm your spirit beneath

And when spring replaces winter's toll
I will sow seeds of flowers
A canopy of color to cheer your soul
And there I will while away the hours

One day I will plant a tree
That will shade and comfort your rest
There mockingbirds will build their nest
And in summer sing their songs just for thee

In fall I will plant pansies all around
And ask them to embrace the ground
Then I will look upward into the clear blue sky
And thank God for telling me you did not die

W. L. Allen Jr.

Communion Of Life

Communion of life, the father and the tiny leaf.
A top of the great tree with many leaves,
yet only one danced an ecstatic dance of joy.
Below inclosed with in the hollow of the great tree...
the mother curled her warm furry body,
sheltering her little one from the cold night winds.

Leaves fell, covering the Mother and her little one,
as snow swirled covering the blanket of leaves
with soft snow, while angels hovered near
the sleeping mother and little one.

P. Simmons

To Cross The River

Far it is to the bitter end, yet life seems so short.
Could it be, to end this way, standing by the river's port?
Charon comes close now, I can see his empty eyes,
The gleaming craft on the River Styx brings me soulful sighs.
His destination across the river, he collects the lonely few.
Passage of time is so final though there is still much to do.
I see fewer birds today, I miss the cardinal red,
And the oriole's song is quiet, and the whippoorwill unfed.
The deer I used to feed by hand is driven far from home,
Uprooted by the greed of man, and frightened, forced to roam.
And the waterfalls and woods I used to play in as a child,
Now plundered, trashed, with heavy traffic, defiled.
As I think upon the marauding population of man outward cast,
I wonder if the bridge to the future can ever match the past.
It should matter not for me, my youth is spent, never to return,
But I ponder still if this glorious land will ever really learn.
Somehow it matters, it matters to all who remain behind,
Especially for the children, of all lands and human kind.
Even with the ticket over the River Styx firmly in my hand,
I wonder anew, did I do enough to save this grand old land?

Vern Johnson

Dear Mother

What is a Mother, what makes her unique,
It's the smile on her face when she's gone without sleep,
From sun up to sun down is a time card she keeps,
Up on her feet when there's babies that weep
Time on her hand would be so good to see,
But how can she rest when her mind's not at ease,
In silence she'll work, but there's tears in her eyes,
Tears that won't fall, 'cause she holds them inside,
Watching her face that once gave such a glow,
Now taunted by age, and her movements slow.
She's the pillar of strength when things go wrong,
She'll hold you and say you have to be strong,
It'll get better you just wait you'll see,
Take it from someone older and wiser like me.
These are the words she said gently to me,
With a voice strong but shaky and a tone soft and sweet.
Now that she's older I'm right by her side,
To make up for the times when I made her cry.
Dear Mother I love you in so many ways,
No words can express all the love that you've gave
God bless you.

Eartha Green

First Beard

Straggly and prickly, and not too strong,
first emergence from your safe cocoon.
Into manhood and responsibility,
you grasp at it, all too willingly.

My how you've waited for this moment,
like a zealot, determined and proud,
skillfully training and cultivating.
Wow! Look at me -
How stately, how macho...a brand new me!
Wait until everyone sees!

And when they do, insensitive people,
would take this joy away from you.
Where is that clean-cut kid we knew?
Shave it off, it isn't you.

Aren't these God's stepping stones,
from one stage of life to another...
And haven't we all been through this phase,
walked in his shoes, and felt this craze?

Louise Segit

Old Woman And A Baby

Sunset meets the dawn
    yesterday greets today warmly, gently,
Marveling at the strength and glow
    of the morning
That shines with the radiant glory of
    newness and hope of what will be.

Sunset fades into dusk with bittersweet
    raindrops caressing the horizon as she passes
Taking with her a day of sorrow and joy,
    things that once were, things that could have been.

How swiftly the dawn rises to burn
    brightly the noonday heat,
Tender, fleeting is the sunset at
    day's end.
    Traci Boland

Twilight

An overwhelming problem can leave one
without solution
even down trodden
So in life with problems mundane
use this as a rule...

 Allow not these things your inner peace refrain,
But instead the God within seek and attain.

 Above all keep a tender heart,
Unleathered by things that smart.

Follow this and you will see,
Your life like an orange sun at dusk
melting into an undulating sea,
Renewed every twilight.
    Floyd J. Sanders

Dear Grandpa

Hold my hand like you did way back when;
Can you swing me once again, like an airplane in the wind;
Can you teach me how to flick the lid of your tobacco can;

Can you teach me how to bait the hook;
To give it the right amount of tug,
So you wouldn't loose the catch at the end of my hook;

Can you take me to the snow, or to our favorite picture show;
Can you and I just sit and watch all the weird people go by;

Can you teach me how to make a garden grow,
You've always had the right ingredients to do just so;
Tell me, is it the love that makes it grow;

Can you teach me to smell the sweetness in the air;
The beauty that grows through each passing year;

The rising of the sun when a new day has begun;
To listen when the day is done;

Can you hear me Grandpa, I am whispering softly in the wind;
I am telling you I Love You Till my time too has come to an end.
    Robin Box

Untitled

To my grandparents on this special day,
I love you in every single way.
When I'm down, you make me feel better,
Sometimes by just sending me a letter.
And I wanted to let you know,
That it's Grandparents Day and even though we're apart,
I'll still find room for you in my heart.
You've always been there for me so I thought
I'd let you know that I love you.
    Jeffery Bridgman

Summer's Lake

The sun belongs to Summer, and the Summer breeze.
The yielding grass beneath me, the swaying peaceful trees.
Upon a Summer's morning I sat upon the grass,
watching God's creations up above go pass.

In front of me sits a lake, not that large but blue.
I swam in it before, so comforting and cool.
Lulling me to sleep, one I wish not wake,
let me introduce you to the Summer's lake.

The shrills of playing children is no longer now,
and the great white swans with majestic bows.
We live around this lake which brings us peace of mind,
certainly a great thing in life that isn't hard to find.

Now aren't you glad I told you, told about the lake?
That God has given beauty and could also take.
If you wish not for a stay, the beauty will cajole,
for it lures your inner spirit, and caresses your soul.

Now you know why this lake that the Summer owns,
draws me to it daily, forgetting about home.
Blessed is this place which you can't destroy nor make,
come and visit soon, to the Summer's lake.
    Alesha Lynnette Perry

Captor Of My Heart

You, who have captured my heart...
please hold it gently, like a rare piece of art.

When I hear your voice or see your face,
my heart smiles in a most special place.

Your lips caress mine with a kiss so sweet,
each tender touch, a searing heat.

Feelings thundering over me like a tide,
flowing and ebbing away with you by my side.

My fluttering heart, be quiet, be still!
You cannot concede to your captor's will!

But as life would have it, 'twas my fate,
I tried to save my heart, but it was too late.

For I was rendered helpless to your charm
knowing within, you'd bring me no harm.

So if you were to set my heart free,
it would choose to stay and love tenderly.
    Cathy Thompson

A Mountain To Climb

With rags wrapped around their feet,
They marched through the snow, their enemy to defeat.
Tears of pain upon their face did freeze,
Have mercy on us, oh, God please!!

A man in Germany, the Nazi kind,
Humanity standing on the line.
A star brazenly sewed upon the sleeve,
The world cried out for their reprieve.
All hate ever felt in mankind's breast,
Put the soldiers to their test.
Tall they stood, and tall they fell.
They made a bridge from the bottom of hell.

We praised their efforts, oh, so great,
They alone erased the hate.
They plucked them from their unsung grave,
And a world gone mad they did save.
    Sue White

Really Couldn't Say

You couldn't say he was tall — or small.
You couldn't say he was thin;
You couldn't say anything at all
Except that he wasn't your kin;
His hair was black, his eyes were too;
And his nose was nor crooked nor straight;
His mouth did open as yours would do
If you asked how long you must wait;
He paid his money and went his way
And now you must know the truth:

For all of that you couldn't say,
The man was John Wilkes Booth.

Diana Dutton

A Handkerchief Holds Many Things

Please use this hankie to dry your tears.
Fill it with memories and reflect the years.

This is a difficult time for those left behind.
I hope you will find comfort of a loving kind.

It is not ours to know why a loved one is taken.
Whatever the causes, don't let your love be forsaken.

Hold on to the love, the memories, and the laughter.
We all have our day with the Here and the After.

With time may your anger and pain turn to peace.
May your capacity to forgive and to love increase.

For this is truly what we are all about;
We must all learn faith and love without doubt.

Hold on to the time that you had and you shared.
Remember with your heart and be proud that you cared.

We each are blessed with choices to make in life.
To thine own self we must be true, whatever the plight.

It doesn't make it easier to bear the pain.
Know that you did what you could and let go of blame.

It's difficult to understand when one leaves us behind.
We each have our judgment Day; keep this in mind.

Katherine Sanchez

In A Nut's Shell

1 Ext. School-rainy day.
   (...drip....drip...)
-tranquil daisies in the grass
flowers lounging in the class-
I can't feel the pinprick on my fingertip
and I can't feel the rain
   so I let it drip down the drain
-a loner sheep in the herd
His classmates laugh. He is absurd
He can't feel the shears
   as they cut his wool
but He can feel Death's grip
   and its mighty pull in his pain
-humble drones perched for War
who cannot know what is in store
They do not see the Whites
   in the Enemy's eyes
and their rifle shots
   muffle all the cries in the rain
   (...drip...drip...)

Edward Soyfer

My Little Nubian Prince

Looking through these eyes I see
a disturbing sight of reality.
My future being blown away by
a gunshot blast
all because of a curious stare when
he walked past.
Priorities are placed on the material thing
no respect for the life of our fellow
human being.
Where do they study this, where do they learn it
give respect to get respect is one sure way to earn it.
The short lived life of the chocolate little boy
learned as a young tike take this gun as a toy.
My little man friends learn this lesson young
keep your mind on your school books
and your hands off the guns.
With this all in mind take the time to fantasize
about all of the dreams that are deep inside.
My Little Nubian Prince this poem is just for you
be the best you can be in all that you do.

Denise Parks

A Mother For My Daughter

A mother for my daughter I cannot be,
a father to my sons I will always be.
My daughter says: "I love you dad,
but I miss my mother so very bad."

The pain comes welling up inside
and the rain rushes from my eyes.
I cry for the pain my daughter must see,
for a mother to her I can never be.

We talk and talk but I still cannot see,
What a mother to a daughter really must be.
My heart aches to comfort her sorrow,
her mother's death has tarnished her tomorrows!

Michael D. Lynn

Drifting

Drifting in and out of dreams
Thoughts of childhood pass the screen
Images and words become so clear
The leaves of fall as winter nears
Snowflakes fall, the cold wind blows
The warmth of home and snuggling toes
Laughing and singing I drift away
The seasons change the light of day
My untamed spirit flows like the wind
Like love and trust of a new found friend
The time slips by and soars through space
My breathing heavy, my heart keeps pace
This drift so soft, so real, so pure
Holds every feeling my soul endures
So hold me and love me my drifting light
For now, forever, the glorious sight

Todd Blamire

Passing Of Time

Will it ever pass this way once more
Young children playing on the floor,
With old folks rocking in their chair
And every meal begins with prayer?

Or is this a dream that has passed with time,
When gum was a nickel and candy a dime?
And little was known of fear and crime,
I guess these things have passed with time.

Jack N. Hisaw

"Echoes In Time"

When our drums beat, what do you view:
Our people, or are we invisible to you?
Let me paint you a picture, my pen weave a line,
As you wander back to the beginning of time.
Where once we stood, proud and strong
Our history stretched wide and long.
A people existing in gentle harmony
Roaming where we pleased, always living free.
And with the Eagle we did fly
Our voices echoing in the wolves' cry.
Hearts beating to the rhythm of Mother Earth;
Reminding all what each of us is worth.
Your Native Brothers — can you hear their call?
There once was a time when we had it all.
Standing tall on the edge of the world
Watching quietly as our destinies swirled
Together; Lakota, Pomo and Cherokee
Our past, present, and what is yet to be.
qo?di ?ya?khe hi?da sati dan?qa
Grant that our path be clear.

Shaina J. Thompson

Only My Protector

My Protector who mingles within the night,
All my eerie struggles, shed your light.
Help me shew all I hear, feel and see,
Only you've viewed what's ruining me.

You know, Protector, when I'm unconscious, I am conscious,
Because when I sleep, I'm really awake,
And not the only member of my dreams,
'Tis also as hard for them to painfully take.

A misty lady once said, everyone in your dreams,
They're all your emotions, they represent you.
As wise and experienced as she is,
I couldn't agree, 'cause for 'my' stress, it's not true.

My Protector I know not, yet may help me escape;
Putting my consciousness back to reality,
Allowing to live my life in comfort, asleep or wide awake.
Though I yearn to meet him, least I'm sure he's not fake,
Think I can now sleep...'Naw', think I'll take a break.
Protector, am I awake?!...

Geoffrey Reed

The Coming Of Christ

"Christ," as long prophesied, "would come"
"To save the blind from their downfalls,"
"To help the wild become better,"
"In the realm of their minds and souls."
"When His presence is manifested,"
"Destroyed will be all dark mansions,"
"And mankind will see the whole truth"
"Inside the Ball of Creations."

He came at last! Christ came at last,
With a body of boundless light
And immense cosmic consciousness
Beyond belief and beyond sight.

Mundane knowledge, high or low,
Will be soon assessed for scraps sales;
Christ's omniscience is too divine
For both profane and astral scales.
I love to paint my prose and poems
In the form of symbols and emblems
For all souls to be enjoying
The whole truth of Christ and His coming.

Thuy Lexuan

Love

Love is lost,
Love is gained,
And love is forever to remain.
Love is sometimes good,
Love is sometimes bad,
But love always returns as it should.
Love is nice,
Love is sweet,
Love is good,
Love is great,
Love is never to break the fate.
Love is not violent,
Love is respect for your mother, father, husband, wife,
Family or friends.
Love is not to be lost,
But found in the hearts of people in this town!

Scotti Shay Daw

Home Sweet Home To Me

There's an old log cabin standing
in the West Virginia hills
with pine trees all around it.
you can hear the whippoorwills,

There's a beautiful stream that flows near by.
The water is crystal clear
where the black bear comes to quench
his thirst, along with the white tail deer.

You can watch the squirrels climb the hickory nut trees.
To feast on the food that grows there.
And the possum in the persimmon tree
To get the fruit they bear.

If you can picture in your mind,
The place I describe you see
That's why people say almost heaven West Virginia.
That's the place I long to be.

Pearl Booth

Kitty Cat Love

Cats are a mystery, a known fact in history,
We share thirty seven in all,
A loving Egyptian Persian named Snowball,
Amy, Ginger and Queenie are calico,
Benny, Midnight, Bubbles and Domino,
Delightful combination of grace and beauty,
Molly, our Himalayan is a real cutie,
Smokie and Cotton are seal point Siamese.
Their special magic is to please,
Honey Bear and Sunny have mitten paws,
They shake hands and wait for applause,
Chauncey has mesmerizing blue eyes,
That say - pet me, then - just sighs,
Blossom, Peaceful and Princess are tortoise shell,
Endearing mischief - but they won't tell,
The beauty of the incredible cat is a big deal,
With their furry affection and special appeal,
The infinite charm of the Alley Cat,
Elegance and unpredictability is just that,
Sunshine and Ying are in Heaven, our story of 37.

Miriam C. Hildreth

Serenity

As I walk along the deserted beach my mind flutters in the wind like
    a feather in flight allowing a day's thoughts to enter and pass through.
I listen to the silent cry of the waves smashing against the rocks below.
I feel as if my body is floating across the cool damp sand.
A sudden wind jolts me back to reality.
As I turn to go I wonder was I really there at all.

Nicole Doyle

My Little Dunn-e

I bought me a horse that is tiny and small-
But then I'm certainly not very big at all!!
We fit together just like a bird and his feathers.
I'd like to show her off where anybody gathers!!
I call her name at morning and night—
She hurries from the pastures and sure is a sight!!
Lonesome I'll never be-
Because of the likes of she.
Horses have been my love-
I know they were sent from above.
This will probably be the last horse I own-
When I can't ride her anymore I'll groan!!
Maybe when we go to the hereafter-
You'll hear me talking to her and there will be laughter!!

Joella Palmer

Fatal Square

It calls to you, your not aware,
this box, this fantasy, this fatal square!

You start to speak and words come true,
from this square, that beckons you.

You share your laugh you share your cries,
but then it simply says, "goodbye".

No one listens, no one cares,
how you feel beyond this square.

You're reaching out and hold to hope,
and beg this square to help you cope.

So listen up and please don't dare,
get too involved with this
   Fatal Square!

Karen Elizabeth McLendon-Laumann

I, Fool

How many men have so professed their love,
Claiming foolish things in metric verse?
It only goes to show you, only prove,
That poetry and fools will mix the worst.
While lovers mix with liquor very well,
A writer's love drinks not but darkest ink
(Though since both love and drink have truth to tell,
I'll admit I lie, I love a drink).
But still my inky love will fill this page
With foolish drunken wantings writ in rhymes.
This little heart of mine must leave the cage
To scurry off with yours for drunk-fool crimes.
   (The drunk and lovely poets empty purse
   now taunts itself in foolery and verse.)

David Samas

YHWH REV. 1

He that wants understanding;
Let him hear the light.
For from the beginning I was;
All was created by me.
Your living breath I blew into your nostrils.
I'm the image of all life.
Father forgive them; they know not what they do.
For this reason I have come.
I'm the lamb who shed the forgiving blood for all people.
I'm the Alpha and the Omega;
I am which was;
And the living God to come.
God with us.
"YHWH" <translated> God

Jeanne Helenne Laurin

Longing For Completeness

In my mind's eye I see all that I need to be complete.

It wells up inside of me like a waterfall
and trickles down my senses,
rushing through my body
with every breath and every heartbeat.

It sends me soaring
as if in a constant dream
and brings me warmth when the wind chills.

It makes me tremble when near,
and quiver when it speaks
thereby opening a door that was closed long ago.

Could it be that what my mind is gazing upon
is the picture of being in love,
or is it a yearning to fall in love
and be loved in the same way?

No matter what the cause,
I care not to erase the picture
for each time I close my eyes and look upon it,
I only long for it more.

Laura J. Staples

Imagine My Surprise

To come home on a dark rainy afternoon
To find a package waiting on the porch.
My friend Agatha surprised me again.

With great anticipation I opened my surprise.
Right on top, a jar of current jelly.
Next to it a jar of lush peach preserves.

At the very bottom a flowered wrapping
Tied with a wide lavender satin ribbon.
And, a fancy sheet of note paper with writing.

"The petticoat has two inches of heavy lace,
It will secure your legs and prevent disgrace.

Fog has been heavy in the bog this Fall.
Winter reminds us it will visit soon.
Birds are migrating in large noisy flocks.

I'm melancholy this time of year, it's an ending.
The wood is cut, stored and ready.
All canning is done, sewing supplies complete.

A special time, I'll renew my soul, recall
Memories of beauty, joy, sadness and you.

Your friend, Agatha"

Dorothy McClelland

My Safe Corner

My soul seeks an inner place,
Somewhere safe to hide!
When the world gets too crazy,
I delve into this inner gateway,
And find I'm still as I was,
Same personality, same temperament, same self.
Doubts arise from time to time,
And my heart frees me from them,
As I go to the inner place where my soul safely hides.
Away from the world, safe, secure, waiting for the
next move in my life's plan.
In this way, I defeat my doubts,
Walk tall and proud, head held high,
Secure with the knowledge,
That all is ok in my world.

Catherine Ruedy

Life's Lace

Moments to Retrace,
The hearts search for the perfect Place,
Sorrows, Joy, and love Interlace,
As we look upon each earthly Face.

The day's end we Embrace,
Bare feet take their Place,
As leisure takes life's Space,
And the mind end the day's Chase.

Woven leaves of life's Lace,
Whispers without Trace,
Starlit skys seeming without space,
And man's never ending Pace,
Our gift of Peace, bound in Christ's Grace!

Ann Jones

Little Boy's Dream

A little boy dreamed while snug in his bed
The thought of elves dancing around his head
They put colors of rainbows on a tree
Any color to please you and me
Reds, pinks, greens, blue and gold
With a little silver and yellow, we're told
Light as a feather and in a bound
They placed ornaments all around
With lights that blink and stars that shine
Also popcorn, a thread-fine line
The elves then jumping with glee
Put a small angel atop the tree
Two wee elves then gave a kick
And quickly cleaned the chimney for ol' Saint Nick
Around the tree they sang a bit
While waiting for presents to put under it
A more beautiful tree there seemed not to be
As this little boy's dream of his Christmas Tree

Frederick Davies Jr.

The Explosion

I feel like a volcano ready to erupt,
The pain I feel of loosing my friend is terrifying,
I am hurting, my world is filled with darkness,
my heart is empty as I find myself still crying.
This explosion will be grand when I allow myself,
to let out the pain,

Then the hurting and sorrow will disappear,
I can only hope that no one will see,
Nor, be able to hear.

I am like a bomb ticking with each passing day,
Hoping I will not explode tomorrow
or the next day.
His memory and God are the only things
I can count on to save me now.

My heart is a timer waiting to explode,
and my veins are like wires wanting to let go,
God, please let mercy come,
for I can take no more.

Glenna Smith

Parade

I saw four marchers pass so fast:
  A sporting man, bass singer of shaped notes, now hums.
  A languorous wafer of chuckling curiosity, just grins.
  A yellow-skinned mountain of wonder and confusion, drums.
  A hard, wise face too scarred to smile, just nods.
  The crooked angel who breaks my heart, still.
Please wait for me.

Martha Johnson

Say Grace, She's A Prayer

For the girl who waits say Grace,
A prayer that is proper in any place,
Truly she has earned the Thanks,
Of her lover who serves in the ranks.

While I am serving in a land far away,
I know where her thoughts always lay,
With tears that streak her lovely face,
She is the strength that quickens my pace.

Even though my heart is heavy since I've been away,
I lighten it with a prayer I always say,
She is a blessing, a prayer of Thanks named Grace,
So please dear God, won't you end this race?

Send the world the sign of the peace dove,
So that I may rejoin my everlasting love,
And look into the eyes of the Grace I am saying,
While I hold in my arms the Thanks I am praying.

Stephen G. Antonelli Jr.

Rucksack Dream

I woke up this morning beaming,
Buddha smiled at my side -
with a temperament for exploration
on a new path, I began to ride.

Oh what a perspective to attain
a technicolor viewpoint comparable to flight;
the wide open stretch of road-
a pilgrimage reminiscent of beatnik delight.

To feel the aura of personal domain,
to understand how a happy traveler begins,
companionship becomes nebulous,
lost in the gleaming of the soul's origin.

I remember the aimless buzzing of urban civilization,
where clarity is an idealistic wish.
I cling to being here with my friend thought-
not hard to follow, no effort necessary to accomplish.

Feel your bliss begin to flow-
conformity can be detrimental to the soul.
Just pack a bag of peacefulness,
Have a sip of courage, smile for the whole.

Brian Hicks

Forever

Wild river
Rushing. Unbearable screams carrying away my tears.
Twisting, turning, mixed up, churning
Violently bashing against rocks.
Tormenting, teasing, barely audible pleas.
Why did white foamy arms carry you away? I am helpless.
Why were you swept out of my life?
Drowning in sorrow, I was unable to help.
I didn't see need.
Waves of grief hit harshly, steady rhythm of reality
Coming around a bend, slowing.
Initial shock is calmed, quiet, solemn, cold pool.
Standstill.
With you went a piece of my heart. Quiet.
I am left, washed up on the beach. Guilt.
Carried by the ever moving river of life,
I am forced to move on.
Without you.
Forever.

Kristy Witkowski

A Soldier's View

A war begins when two sides falter
To come to terms on simple matters
When people cannot coincide
On certain objectives it's suicide

Imperfect minds come into dissension
The next move made is uncertain aggression
The first shot fired from bitterness and hate
The other side's willingness to retaliate

Innocent ones taken in violent action
The brave you pretend gives no satisfaction
Destruction surrounds you on every side
Fear begins to take the soldier's pride

When all you witness is wasteful deeds
In mind or flesh you're bound to bleed
They say in a war there are a number of heroes
For in the taking of lives that count is zero

For all the turmoil, misery and pain
Regardless of the outcome there is no gain
War is hell for all involved
When it is finished there is no resolve.

Dennis Gobin

My Love, Where Are You?

Nothing,
  to come home to,
    to wake up to,
    to love, and share affection with
Someone who is there, to care,
    and for me to care so very much about.
To come home to,
    to wake up to,
    to spend my heart through
      and say "I love you!"
My love, where are you?

To view my path alone and say;
"My love will come, another day".
Another day, so —— far away.
Tender eyes, gentle face, and that smile,
I close my eyes a little bit, a little while,
And then I see You!
My love, where are you?

Ian D. Rodney

Goodnight Hugs And Kisses

"Hershey's" got new hot cocoa in the store
flaunting names you'll probably adore
"Goodnight Hugs" has white chocolate you'll savor
while "Goodnight Kisses" has a milk chocolate flavor
both have tiny "Hershey's Kisses" inside
chocolate lovers will be gratified
Share them with loved ones far away
send with a note, that just might say
These "Goodnight Hugs and Kisses" that you see
when ya pull from the shelf, will remind you of me
Should you feel you need some warming up
pour some with hot water into your cup
Though if you'd prefer it rich and thick
use milk instead, and stir it quick
Don't think they're just for bedtime though
could be for whenever you're feeling low
Have sent these, cuz ya know I care
for as much as I'd like, I can't be there
So I pray God bless you from above
and with "Hugs and Kisses," I send my love!

Peg Mitchell

My Therapist

My love is like a pink rose,
And where she'll take us, she knows,
She leads, I follow, hand in hand,
She carries me like Jesus, across the sand.

Why this good fortune should come to me,
I wonder, I ask the Lord, but still can't see,
I had more years than I can tell,
Of relentless, unmitigated hell.

The prayer is answered, I'm safe and free,
Jan and my Savior have rescued me.
More of the journey needs to be trod,
But we'll travel together, until we see God!

Alicia Neel

If I Had Three Wishes

I'd wish you warmth on a cold winter's night
  Someone beside you 'til dawn brings the light
Someone to live with, and laugh with, and hold
  Who'll stay by your side as you slowly grow old.

I'd wish you the joy of a warm summer's day
  The beautiful sounds of your child at play
The sun on your face, the wind in your hair
  The simple joy of just "being there."

And I'd wish you peace at the long day's end
  As you return to a home full of family and friends
With the sense of contentment that comes when you know
  Life's finally taken you where you always wanted to go.

Debra L. Rodgers

Raven In The Sky

Looking out my window I saw a Raven true
His feathers glistening black with just a hint of blue
Raven with your magic, what do you have to say
He called my name and told me this was my lucky day
I watched him as he graced the sky, he seemed so content
He smiled at me and whispered, your time has been well spent
He told me now was the time for me to be brave
That my skills were needed and not to be afraid
Things are changing quickly, there isn't much time
We have to work together if we hope to make the climb
Trust me and you will find what you've been looking for
Great Spirit eagerly awaits to show you through the door
I journeyed through the void and then back again
Upon our return I asked, but where do I begin
He told me, listen with your heart, listen with your soul
Do those things that feel right and you will be told
Each day I watch and listen for Raven in the sky
I try to live the magic that Raven lives by

Julia Alvarez

Pen And Paper

When you're feeling sad and blue
Come to me, I'll comfort you
Take me in your hands and see
How I make you happy and free
I am pen, paper, and comfy chair too
Take me take me none too soon
Write, write, write, till your heart's content
I am here for you now don't forget
Talk, confide, share, your secret's safe with me
Give me your thoughts, emotions and fears, whatever they might be
Take comfort knowing I am with you now
Guiding you silently no doubt
Lay your burdens on me, I am your friend for life, silently
when you're feeling sad and blue
come to me I'll comfort you

Anita Goel

Dear Friend, Polly

You asked what it was going to feel like
    To be heaven sent
We could not answer you
    Our thoughts were bent
In trying to relieve your anxious moments
    Our hearts were filled with what you meant

How brave, how strong, how gentle and kind
    You kept us all laughing and smiling
With your wonderful humor and keen mind

Although your last journey was very hard
    And terribly unfair
You carried us with a love that you shared
    For everyone
We knew how much you cared

You inspired and taught us, you laughed with us
    And most importantly, you loved us

Polly, you are on every sunbeam
    Every star, every breeze, that's where you are

Karen E. Rodman

If Pews Could Talk

If these old pews could only talk,
    These are the words they most likely would say,
"I've been kicked, glued with gum. Squirmed on,
    Scratched and walked on by little feet
Watered by innocent babes, a desk for busy tiny hands.
    Nailed together, when I began to come apart, shaken,
Even pushed out of place by shouting saints.
    Used for a coat rack, even a bed for sleepy children.
Although I have experience all these things,
    I'm happy my place was in the house of God.
Here many have kneeled before me, praying to the Lord,
    I've heard many weary souls calling on His name,
And He has heard and answered them.
    So I have no complaints, since I am getting old,
I feel that I have done my share, my only request...
    When the new pews takes my place, try to remember
All the good services that I gave."

Catherine Stokes

Love Is The Greatest Gift Of All

To love is to care
Not only about yourself
But for others
Who always seem to be there.

To love is to share
Not gifts and material things
But thoughts and feelings
That are true and beyond compare.

To love is to be supportive
Realizing each other's ideas and emotions
For not understanding dreams of one's desires
Will lead to total commotion.

To love is to have patience
Knowing that everything takes time
And when you are by my side
I always feel just fine!

To love is to be faithful of your feelings
Not letting others get in the way
Of that wonderful, most perfect love
That shall never fade.

Leslie Lindstrom

Relieved

I did fret and I did worry
    Why couldn't I a better person be?
When in the wee morning hours before dawn
    God's Holy Spirit did enlighten me.
You're merely God's child, deemed by Him,
    Trying too hard to go alone.
Without qualities bestowed upon you
    A useless vessel you'd be to endear.
Without faults you'd feel too supreme
    Missing out on life's greatest need.
The receiving of God's gift of Grace,
    Freely given to be freely received.
You can't earn what He bestows,
    Only trust and in faith be relieved.
Go forward in peace, I'm with you constantly.
    Those stumbling blocks are nothing more
Than building blocks mortared by Grace
    Now you'll do fine depending on Me.

Emily Oliver

Pastor, Tell Me Why

Pastor, why does God keep me lingering here
When I'm having so much pain?

My child, God must still have need of you,
Some need that I can't explain.

Pastor, How can God use me if my mind has gone?
What good can I do just lingering on?

The ways of our Lord are not ours to know,
Or when or why we must stay or go.
Some child of God seeing you in pain,
May be gathered safe in His arms again.
Maybe that child could be your own,
Who had wandered far and you'd never known.
God can still use someone's love for you
To keep a loved one strong and true.
So bend your heart to your Father's will;
Knowing His love is with you still.

Gertrude L. Tandy

Walking In His Strength

Walk with me my teenage friend
Observe emphysema patient whose life may soon end.
For them exhaling carbon dioxide is a difficult task
Hiding this problem they can not mask.
Blowing out a candle is difficult to do.
Attempting this task their face may turn blue.
If only I listened to adults in my day
My lungs wouldn't suffer in this difficult way.
I thought I was cool sneaking behind my parents' back
Not listening to them; discernment I lack
Swallowed up in great pain and despair;
For me it's too late, my lungs surgeons can't repair,
O sinner, accept my Lord, walk on this narrow path.
My savior awaits you, your sin He'll forgive.
Give up smoking He may let you live.
Walking in His strength with each passing day,
But only begin with much time to pray.

Dottie Whitcomb

Lighthouse Of Hope

Oh Lord, show me the right direction,
    I made the wrong turn on the journey,
Show me the direction of the wind and
    the calmness of your spirit.
I can see the Lighthouse in the distance.
    Come to my aid and forgive me.
Let your light be a "Lighthouse of Hope."

Barbara A. Schmid

The Light

My sleep was restless from the start
Something was troubling my heart
A light out of nowhere came to me that night
I knew it was there to solve my plight
The light was so bright
Still I saw no one in sight
Then all of a sudden a face appeared
It was a face I loved so dear
It came to say I love you so
Look deep in your heart and you will know
Then it left as fast as it came
I knew my life would not be the same
Suddenly I awoke and sprang from my bed
A cold sweat running down my head
I wondered if this was only a dream
Did God bring the answer? It would seem
As a peaceful feeling came about
No longer did I doubt

Derek Melancon

A Whisper Of Autumn

Like the seasons of change, her life too was planned, she
was taken away, at God's final command.

Leaves vibrant with color, a crisp autumn day, the sun
warming the marble, there forever, she would stay.

Decades have passed, another autumn is here, like the
whisk of a feather, I felt her presence so near.

My eyes traveled the room, but no-one did I see, just the
brilliance of a sunbeam, resting upon me.

Fixed in a gaze, on a pedestal that was near, I captured
her silhouette, in the marble, very clear.

Why never before, did it ever appear, until now, in the
season, of the time I hold dear.

Is she calling to comfort, or a signal to fear, is she
whispering a message, that my destiny is near.

And if that it must be, with colorful leaves from the tree,
let them flutter and surround us, together we will be.

Dolores Barnette

The Owl

Fascinates me from my childhood
days in Trinidad and Tobago.
The intrigue of stillness, and
gracious eyes put a spell on me
like the presence which dominates.

The hoot is not in English or Spanish
their language is for family, and
friends to know where they are at all
times because they do not have beepers.

The coat of fine feathers in beautiful colors shines so bright.
It was exciting when my flash light caught up
with a pair perched on a tree branch, I am quite sure I
interrupted a lover's quest that did not surprise.

Beryl Harvey

You

You have touched my soul and have taken my heart.
You feel as new to me as from the start.
I have never felt so lost, yet alive as when you are near.
When you are with me I begin to believe I can see my life more clear.
You have been my mentor, my life and my love.
You have made my heart feel as free as a dove.
You have given me a purpose for living and my life a reason.
Our love is as colorful and magnificent as the seasons.

Wendy Z. Sweet

Teaching

Teaching school is a choice I made
Not another job and career would I trade.
Greeting the children at school each day,
Makes my heart and love want to stay.
Helping each child build his self esteem,
Seems to me like a life long dream.
When I see a sparkle in the eyes of a girl or boy,
Gives me hope, peace, and great joy.
Seeing a child progress as the year goes by,
Lets me know that his heart cares and will really try.
Much encouragement and praise goes a long way,
Being a good role model is helpful as they may say.
Watching the students choose their own career,
Gives me a feeling of promise and a tear.
I can now realize I have been a part of their lives
Their work will continue with great strives.
Teaching is a way of life for me,
For I am as happy as I can be.

Lavon Wiersig

War Hero

Drafted away from home and life,
the end of his gun bears a knife

Dragged away from hopes and dreams,
always hearing nasty screams

Dodging bullets and his enemy's sword,
all he can think is help me Lord

Crawling along this tattered hell,
he watched the bomb as it fell

Closer and closer it became,
falling upon him like dirty rain

The bomb that hit him was at ground zero,
that's how he became the mighty war hero

His family and friends fear for his loss,
but in that world your life's a coin toss

For those of you who entered the war,
I pray that you made it to exit that door.

Mike Wengren

This Island In My Land

I live in a land of freedom
But there is an island in this land
I go to daily
Out of necessity, out of need.

On this isle, in this land
Freedom is given up—freedom lost:
Choices are given but range is to one.
Persuasion, inducements, are reminders
of what could be given up, what could be lost.
A picnic, or a day at Turtle Bay
Disguised as a day off is a day without shade;
Of forced participation in the glare of the Sun
Until the sun has lost its light,
The hours are done.

The range of dos are scheduled events
That are a must for privileges and growth.
Into the loop I continue to go
Out of necessity, out of need.

Irene M. Gaza

First Time

One of the finest things a young heart can find...is love.
Love started in a young heart, is the most
tenderest of all treasures.
You can't put a name on it, or a price.
You can't hold it, or look at it...It's something born within
you, and grows as you do...sharing of yourself
,a gift from one heart to another.
...Never really given or received, but
transferred quietly, with a silent beauty
all its own...no taste...no smell...
Just an un-explainable tranquility within
yourself... silent questions are asked!
But only a feeling of heart felt pleasure
are returned... A touch, a smile, a look,
...then a glaze in the eyes.... Almost
hypnotic...the slightest touch of a hand
sends a thrill through you, like no other,
...A confused feeling of uncertainly...
"And a bitter-sweet fear of knowing
that your heart is speaking for the very "First time"...

Debra L. Scheller

To A Solitary Rose

Your red-robed beauty filled my view
Such a delight to my eyes!
I moved as though drawn to you
My heart fluttered with sighs

Words of praise my lips had to say
As you sat alone in perfection
Although single, you were in splendid array
Which gave me pause for reflection

I wondered why you grew alone
And why no comrade joined you
But you had nothing for which to atone
Your answer to beauty's call was so true

Daily I paid homage to your regal presence
Too soon your brilliance began to fade
Then God, the giver of your florescence,
Back to the earth your petals laid

O solitary rose, I hope you knew
How much you enriched my soul!
The joy you gave while perception grew
Through the years I will extol.

C. Scott

Nephew

I watched you grow
And it was hard
For you were just a boy.
Who made a man's decision.
And as for your decision
You're a giant of a man.
You're not that little boy I remember
For you have gone from a boy
To a marine.
It seems like it was yesterday
That you were just a boy.
Now look at you you're a marine
A father and husband
And I'm still just your Aunt.
Your job has taken you miles away
And as you ride that bouncing waving ship
Riding into different ports
You will always be right here in my heart.
And I sit thinking about you
Oh how proud I am.
For the little boy who became a marine.

Kimberly Hall

Semblance

Cowboy exertion and excrement.
Tie-dyed deadheads and friends said,
"Be fellow and phone person,
Be answered heller".
We ancient balanced mapper.

A quarter part played.
A diminished role found
A tripped-over abundance
a dry western town.

Some pain brought over from yesteryear.
My fumbling window mind yet near.
My breathing at the fulcrum and at the sweep.
The metered ringing in my silent ear.
All evidence this reside,
All tantamount to this hide.
The rule of society is crucial to our development!
Left ravished.
Found famished.
Consumed of trying.
Ample lost art plying.

Joe Duvernay

"A Reward"

First came surprise.
Then shock,
Humiliation,
Fear,
Panic,
Paranoia,
Lunacy,
Darkness,
Submission,
Remembrance,
Restoration.
Then out of the thick haze of loneliness, that
still hovered over my clouded soul, came the
realization that one man can have the power to
Illuminate the heart back to life after such
frigid isolation and despair.
He is gentleness and strength in unison.
He is... the green sun of my life.

Jean Antinarelli

Damn, I'm Bad

When life's experiences bring about discouragements
and situations are more than I care to tolerate;
I go within; pull that special part of me up,

   My Soul!
And my undying, ever courageous strength prevails.
When circumstances trip me up
and I find myself in the valley of complexities;
wallowing in the sewer of despair;
I take pleasure consoling my ego
knowing I have an impregnable trump,

   My Soul!

When hostile forces crucify me
with their petty jealousies and envious hatred...
whispering and inventing illusion about my integrity,
I shall rise up a winner!
My spirit cannot be broken!
And my endless, undying, ever courageous strength prevails,
sustaining my being to rise above the dismal bull!
   Damn, I'm Bad!

Fannie Thomas

People

Sometimes I find it impossible to see the world
for what it really is, or to see people for who
they really are. One day they act like they're your
best friend and the next day they hardly
speak to you, and you wonder what I did this
time. What really hurts is you say something
and they take it the wrong way or blow it
out of proportion, or when passed on lies
develop and you're the bad guy for a few days
then things are peachy, peachy, sometimes
You'll find on their bad days they say "Don't
take it personally", but everything seems to
point to you anyway so you say "Hey, why
not pick on me today". Then you'll find
them talking about you or other people
behind their back and when it's you, you
know and want to say "Hey, I'm over here."
People, guess I'll never be able to figure
them out, but I wouldn't want to
judge or come to any conclusions either.

Cindy Bush

My Prayer

God, give me the strength to carry my load
Over the smooth and sometimes rough road.
Give me the courage to stand alone,
And delight in others, my example shown.
Give me love that I may impart
A reflection of your love and win a heart.
Give me tolerance that I may suffer long,
And still keep fighting, singing a song.
Give me wisdom that I may be
A servant for you, in any capacity.
Strengthen my faith and endurance too,
So that I can hope to be with you.
Of all these gifts I'll treasure the most,
'Twill be the love you give, my Lord, my host.

Daisy L. Moore

Gone

I lost something a while back.
I wept with sorrow at what was to be.
Where has my love gone,
She was my song.
Why had she gone,
And taken her love along.
She left me so alone,
As if she knew there was no other way.
As she went away,
She said there would be another day.
I shall not forget her face,
For we shall meet again in that other place.
Why did she have to go away,
I wish there had been another way.
I am left with such beautiful memories,
For we loved as one.
Now I am the only one.

Phillip C. Hilbert Sr.

Tornado

A small funnel lowers from the sky,
Soon it becomes a giant gray twister
I taste my fear as it moves closer
Hear the crashes of its destructive force
Small pieces of debris fly past my face
The roar of the wind brushes against me
I close my eyes, grit my teeth, and...

I'm gone.

Jonathan Michael Welker

Grandma Hazel

Friends come, friends go,
I'll never have a friend like you,
This I'm sure I know.
Even though our ages were different we didn't seem to care,
You were a beautiful person with really curly gray hair.
I remember you like I saw you yesterday,
And once again playing catch.
I'll always remember this,
Around my birthday having chocolate cake,
The price was only a kiss.
When I'd come and see you on those rainy days,
We'd sit and play cards watching the rain as it played.
Then you'd accuse more of "cheating" with a twinkle in your eye.
When I think of you now it makes me want to cry.
For God has taken you from me, but memories I will treasure.
All those wonderful memories of love, warmth and pleasure.
All things that I will keep with me until I meet you again.
Friends come, friends go,
I'll never have a friend like you,
This I'm sure I know.

Kari Ambler

God (He Hears)

I said a prayer last night
hoping that all my dreams come true
Just a little peace you see
not just for me but maybe for you.

I know that you're old and sick in the bed
can't get up or even be fed
trials have come to you they have said
I am hear I am not dead.

I am the wind that blows through the sky
I am the clouds that passes you by
I am the river deep and wide
I am the laughter for the world that cries
so when you look up and see all I've said
then you will know that I am not dead.

There was a time I hung on the cross
I died for your sins not leaving out one
I have now risen to the sky up above
I am your Lord saviour my work is not done
I'll come again, it may be soon
To take away the hurt and gloom I am here I am not dead.

Judy Tolbert

Long Ago And Far Away

The home and kingdom of childhood
I lovingly remember,
was never mine but in my heart,
my eyes possessed it;
each tree and shade and path,
each scent and touch
of leaves against my face,
earth beneath bare feet,
sand slipping thru my fingers
smooth stones cherished,
all graven on my heart,
all in reality is changed
by years and winds and tides
and fallen trees and furrowed soil;
only the dream remains - all else
has changed its face a dozen times by now
truth and beauty fled
and will return no more - alas my world.

Mary G. Horde

Youth In Western Jeans

Your eyes touch each other's eyes
Your hands press each other's hands
A gleaming axis gyrates your globe

What's Agrarian Union to you?
Who knows of peasants born to toil?
Enough of statues deducting down

Across a world your comrades walk
In tight designer jeans
Like you, their history gone

Old women tourists walk and talk brave words
Of work for 50 year plans; illiterates learned to read

Your plastic plans provide new thrills
Beyond dull basic bread
Whose dreams are real?

Those women like your loving looks
They've known youth and lovers too
They are not here to preach

They know of eyes and touch
Do you know of work and cause

Youth in western jeans?

Esther Franklin

Sometimes I Think...

Sometime I think I'm a luscious red
strong and bold,
passionate and full of love,
always in the center of a crowd.
But if you look past my outside
and deep into my inside,
you will find a dark smoky cloud.
So full of anger and fear
ready to come out.
You will find a shy girl afraid of rejection.
These are my true colors,
this is what I stand for.

Sometimes I'm a sparkling silver
so full of beauty and pizzazz!
Like a model ready to catch the spotlight!
At other times I am blue
dazed and confused and completely
careless to the world,
tired and droopy and really no good.
But look out world, I'm feeling silver.

Dana Bridgewater

Just You

Softly without moving she touches me
Tenderly with just a smile she caresses me
with just a glance in a rhythmic trance
my body flush and warm
As fantasies start to take form
and it's you that I love
I love you from the depths of my heart and soul
I love you from your head to your toes
I love you rough
I love you tender
I love you wild
I love you sweet
I love you like a new born babe
from his mother's womb
with the innocence of a child
but set to another tune
I love you beyond this place
unbound by time and space

Jim Williams

Mea Culpa

Would I have joined that hostile angry crowd
Gathered in Pilate's courtyard shouting loud,
Would I His claim as Son of God deny,
Crying, "He blasphemes and deserves to die?"
  Surely, not I.

Would I with them have called, "Barabbas free,
His blood upon us and our children be,"
Or watched Him scourged with no protesting cry,
Would I in rage have shouted, "Crucify?"
  No, never I.

Rather would I have risen at early morn
And with the loving women spices borne,
Beside the empty tomb with tear-dimmed eye,
Beheld with joy my living Rabboni!
  Gladly, would I.

But - 'twas my sin that nailed Him to the tree,
Redeeming love brought Him to Calvary;
Dying for me beneath the darkened sky,
Yielding His life that I should never die!
  Yes, it was I.

Emma Ruiter

No Regrets

Hoping for your mind to change
Waiting for you to remove the pain
What you have done, I don't think realize
Wondering if everything was a big lie
All the promises I expected you to keep
Once more I am left alone to weep
Why does everything always end in tears?
I can't accept that you are no longer here
Denying that I need your words so kind
Still you remain on my mind
Looking back, I see smiles and gleaming eyes
I have forgotten all of the lonely cries
What made you leave? Why can't I forget?
Looking at us, I have no regrets

Jeannine Stanks

The Homeless

You poor old man, you have no home
You walk the streets, you're all alone.
What meals are there to feed to you?
And clothes to fit are very few.
There's a little old lady, that just walked by,
She's short and sweet and oh, so shy.
Around the corner is her home,
She sleeps on any cobblestone.
Their families - God, where did they go?
Or were there any, some time ago?
This shouldn't be in this day and age,
It looks like animals out of a cage.
For there are so many, in the street,
I'm sure deep inside, they're very sweet.
I wish there was something, that I could do,
Perhaps some clothes, some food and shoes.
But when they're dressed, where do they go?
Back on the street and no place to go.
We take in dogs and cats as well,
But! Here are humans, that live like hell.

Audrey Reynolds

Dreamwalk

Our odyssey through life is a dream
Orchestrated by Fate in playful glee.
Sometime struggling rocky ravines
Over rugged boulders, hopelessly.
Sometime soaring unlimited skies,
Giddy and weightless and free.
Our crossroads are an endless chain,
But choices are few and futile,
For all our cunning is in vain
When either road leads away from the goal,
And both roads deadened to oblivion.

Margaret Peach Vaught

Son

Son come and sit beside me, let me give you some advice
Listen very carefully, so I don't have to say it twice
I know you get discouraged
You're at the age you think you know it all
But in order to make it through this life
You gotta learn how to take a fall
Life has its ups and downs
You can't just race straight to the top
There will be times you think you've got it made
And times you think the world has stopped
This world never stops. Sometimes it just slows down
To give you time to learn about the things
That makes the world go around
You were born into this life
You were sent here on a journey
Placed here by the hands of God, and the purpose was for learning
So son don't get discouraged, if you should take a fall
Remember before you learned to walk, you had to learn to crawl
Son don't be afraid of falling, don't be afraid to hit the ground
Just jump back up and try again, don't let nothing hold you down

Roxanne See

Our World, Our Problem, Our Guilt

It's a world, lit up by night,
Found on each corner, yet another fight.
Us, tourists, think it's a great place,
But only because, to some, made invisible is its other face.
The streets seem full of beauty,
But in reality, every cop has to be on duty.
It's actually a spot of horror and fear,
Made true by lots of drugs and beer.
"Bang," another shooting, someone's dead,
The president, a child, maybe a fed!
Us, tourists, ask who made this mess,
Trying to lie, so we don't have to confess!
Why are we killing, this world that's made for us,
Without minds, evil, and the start of every bus.

Jollen Wagner

I've Waited Long To Find A Love

I've waited long to find a love
That would fill the boundaries of my heart.
A love that to a dying soul
Would bring rebirth and make whole a part.

I've waited long to dub thee lover
And to crave the touch that I'd know so well,
A lover that would take free rein of my heart strings
And put roses in my cheeks of pale.

I've waited long to taste fulfillment
And surrender to its sweet release,
And yet, because you're bound to another
I'll never know that kind of peace.

Vickie Hollen

Caged

It must have been an ungodly deed,
A whispered warning we did not heed;
To be cast out and forced to dwell,
In a cumbersome body, an earthly hell.

There is no silence here only freakish confusion,
Scrambled and broken condemned to delusion;
Listen carefully and hear the hum, droning sound,
As tormented souls scream, caged and bound.

Porous flesh burdened with addiction and obsessions,
In shame, we isolate with unheard confessions.
Flouting, indignant, they mutilate our souls,
Serving only to widen our secret black holes.

Each breath is squelched as we choke and suffocate,
Smiling masks conceal and thinly placate;
Choosing not to see our impotent desperation,
We kill or be killed without reparation.

Clambering and clutching we seek to escape,
Revolutionized gyration of self imposed rape;
Drowning in misery, a mere toss of the dice,
Plunging into the vortex, a life pays the price.

Mary Lou Connelly

My Angel Returns

My Dear Little "Toto", it's plain to see
The clouds opened up, angels brought you back to me.
Your little tail wagged as I shouted with glee
"Hello, Mr. Toto - I see you are free."
The sting of death - it had no hold
You are in the angel's land
Walking the streets of gold.
The sky of blue - the clouds so white
You came to me, then you were out of sight.
There was no hug - there was no pain
Your return by the angels
Brought forth a rainbow after the rain.
Now I know you are happy
In God's arms up above....
Thanks be to the angels
For showing me this love.

Carol Lee Pfaff

The Man

This man he stands alone.
He shows only the lonely side,
The bitter hard and cold side.
For life has been cruel to him,
Beaten hurt and low, he holds this shield around his heart
So pain cannot control him.
No one knows the real man, the soft warm and gentle one,
Who loves, cries and feels, but I know this gentle man.
For beside him I'm proud to stand.
For his heart beats with mine, this kind and gentle man.
In time I hope the world will see, the man I've grown to love.
The soft and warm and gentle man who's heart belongs to me.
This gentle man who set my lonely heart free.

Brenda Priest

Moments Of Sadness

Moments of sadness, hours of joy
For a little while you were our sweet boy.
If your light shines as brightly in Heaven as it did here on earth.
We know you weren't chosen for your age but for your worth.
Everyone loved you so much.
The Bible says "Jesus loves you even more."
Is that you up above us...peeking out of Heaven's door?

Frances Neidig

When Years Roll By

When the years in life roll by,
  much faster than before,
We think of things we should have done,
  and wish we had done more,
Hope of hopes we'll truly find,
  the purpose we are here,
To help the others in our lives,
  and ease their pain and fear,
For why should we, through toil and pain,
  desire to gain the gift,
If we ourselves amid the fight,
  have left others bereft?
'Tis surely false that we will gain,
  while making others loose,
But just as surely we will win,
  when service is our dues,
Then listen to life's lessons well,
  to learn of things gone by,
Apply them in our daily lives,
  and reap rewards on high.
     D. E. Lee

The Finished Dream

I do not have to dream again,
I know just what to do to win.
Dr. Singleton advised me what to do,
Dr. Nugent accepted his advice as true.
All that I needed was faith and prayers.
Have faith, The Master will be right there.
With good doctors and nurses through and through,
I knew that my dream was really true.
My knee is straight as it can be.
That was my dream enough for me.
As time moves on from day to day,
The Lord is my light, He will lead the way.
     Victoria Sutton

My Outlook

Outside my window a new day I see
and only I can determine
what kind of day it will be
it can be busy and sunny laughing and gay
or boring and cold unhappy and grey
my own state of mind is the determining key
for I am only the person I let myself be
I can be thoughtful and do all I can to help
or be selfish and think just of myself
I can enjoy what I do and make it seem fun
or gripe and complain and make it hard on someone
I can be patient with those who may not understand
or belittle them as much as I can
but I have faith in myself, and believe what I say
and I personally intend to make the best of each day.
     Bruce Burris

A Prayer Note

  My dear Lord, as you know,
I am just one little spark
  in Thy kingdom's darkest night
or just one little ray of hope
  in Thy kingdom's broad daylight.
So whatever Thy reason for giving me birth
  with prolonged breath and health upon Thy planet earth,
I praise Thee and daily ask Thy guidance
  for the rest of my life's span
in doing Thy will to humbly serve Thee
  whenever and wherever I can.
     Amen
     Mary Mae Brock Mardis

Okinawa

Lo, barefoot girl, your calloused feet
  Have scaled the coral shores
For clinging moss that finds retreat
  Along the ocean floors.

Sweet Yasuko, I've heard you long,
  A-toiling through the day
In winding rows of yams, in song:
  Do tell me <u>how</u>, I pray!

Now silver, silver is the moon!
  And silver are the pines,
The coral cliffs, and each cocoon
  That's spun in silver lines.

Cragged rugged cliffs that typhoons storm,
  And reefs that fringe with foam
Entwine their coral arms to form
  An ocean cradled home.

Don't change for promises to be,
  <u>But keep your island free</u>
To live in simple harmony
  With sun and land and sea.
     Nikolai Tarasuk

The Christian Bet

When God pours out his blessings
I pray there is one for me
Never asking much
But it would be nice and something to see

What makes my blessing so very nice and real
Sometimes we ask ourselves that question
When answered, not understanding still

Well, I thank God for the blessings
He has bestowed upon me
It may seem small to you
For me, it has set me totally free

Try and ask for your blessing
Just to see what you will get
I never gamble on God's word
This time I will make the bet

Go ahead and ask for your blessing
     Michael A. Jonas

Child

You're the apple of my eye
Cute and darling as can be
Sweeter than chocolate pie
I love you so.

Even now that you are grown
You're still my pride and joy
Your love you have always shown
Always there for me, as I to you.

When we talk to each other
Be us together, or on the phone
Sometimes I forget I'm your mother
Then by something you say

Brings back memories of my pride and joy
The gleam in your eyes, or the smile on your face
I'm so thankful you were not daddy's boy
But, our darling girl now and always.

We never seem to tire of you
You make us so happy too
Even when times are blue
We'll always love you.
     Ruth Clark

Longing For Love

Days turn into years.
Years blur with many tears.
Rushing, running and changing gears.
Bring on many realities filled with fear.
Prayers said and answered with gratitude.
Received only with disinterested, crude attitudes.
Bending, changing and forever flexible.
Responses filled with harshness and the intolerable.
Hurt, pain and lie after lie.
How can one be asked to survive.
Feelings and emotions never to be exposed.
All hidden in fear that one might explode.
Passion, lust and love slowly dissolve.
Hoping and dreaming one might evolve.
Dreams fade of happily ever after.
Behind these doors, there is no laughter.
Clinging and desperate, hanging on a thread.
Pushing to continue when the bond is already dead.
Unfulfilled passion ad dreams still remain.
Only to discover that everything stays the same.

Gail Jeanette Lyons

From The Heart; The Leaving

I shall not love again, as in my youth,
Nor find the comfort of our middle age,
Yet from Life's book is missing one last page.
And now I must confess I hid the truth.
I could not let them hear your labored breath,
Nor let them see your anguish and your pain,
Nor let them see my tears that fell like rain,
Nor watch me, as inside I prayed for Death.
I cannot let my feelings go; to grieve.
For since the death my whole world fell apart.
Now anger seems to fill my broken heart.
Why did you have to go? Why did you leave?
The pain goes with me; stalking me at night
Like some vile monster; felt, but never seen,
It follows me. It makes me feel unclean.
I know that I'm afraid, but why the fright?
Ours was a Love you could not often find.
Each touch, a fond embrace for me to keep.
When darkness comes, I grieve, no more to sleep,
For you have left this earth, and me, behind.

Edythe V. Piccione

My Mistake

I made a big mistake...
    The first in quite awhile.
Neighbors gave me a puppy
    To make my older dog play and smile.

They get along together,
    And run and romp and eat.
I named the puppy Freebie,
    Because she is so sweet.

But after I thought about it,
    Freebie wouldn't do.
I should have named her Pay More,
    Because of the things I have to do.

Shots, de-worming, surgery and toys,
    License, collar and leash and food...
A blanket, and a carrier...
    The name Freebie isn't good.

Long ago I learned a lesson
    That nothing is ever free.
We have to pay for everything...
    Even for a freebie for older dog and me.

Jo King

From Your Bargain Daughter

I was already grown when we first met:
No youthful memories of adulation,
No steady tolerance of foolishness,
No backward thoughts of childish absolution.

No spoken word or chastisement or praise
Arise like phantoms to relieve the sorrow.
He was the father of my adult years;
A mutual love not bound by ties of blood.

Even the gray skies seemed to weep for him
Blustering wind of angry rain-lashed grief;
And I stood shivering by the grave
Cold, as the empty place within my heart.

Gone now his gentle humor from me
His guiding hand outstretched to help or save
His soft-voiced wisdom's echo slowly fading
Lost, as the orphaned child within my mind.

Cry, my soul; cry for the loneliness
His passing's left within my daily life:
Appreciated more in absence than in being
Loved still with a depth that transcends even death.

Lyn Welch

The Care Giver Crew

We get up early, and stay up late..
We go to work no matter the date.
Holidays come, and Holidays go.
We work every day, even when there is snow.

We make Breakfast, lunch and supper.
We put in just enough salt and pepper.
If our clients are happy we are too!
We become friends me and you.

The clothes get washed, then comes sweeping and mopping,
We even go out and do the shopping.
Washing the dishes does not take very long.
When we chuckle and sing to a Garth Brooks song.

The cleaning is done and there's two things to do.
Place a snack on the bar and turn the radio off too.
We say good night, they say alright,
Take care going home please do.

Katrina Hodge

Wee One

A precious bundle came our way,
And asked if she could with us stay.
She was a gift from heaven above
Made by our Lord for us to love.

Ten little fingers, ten little toes,
A dimpled chin and little pug nose;
Two pink cheeks, eyes of blue,
Lots of dark hair with a reddish hue.

She's an answer to a mother's prayer,
A perfect body strong and fair.
A little life that has just begun
To bring forth joy in the days to come.

We loved you, Janna, as your life began,
And prayed you'd grow as God had planned,
With a life of richness in His grace
To stand before man in your rightful place.

As the years go by we'll watch you grow
From a tiny baby until your first beau;
And in these years we'll take a hand
To form your life as God had planned.

Mary E. Fosholdt

Love Is A 4 Letter Word

Searing swords of spite, lashing tongues, injuring
words, a wounded dove takes flight.
Slicing through the heavens, lashing out at clouds
feeling hearts so heavy wading through the crowds.
A rebel rose in a sea of weeds, unrequited love and unmet needs.
Running along a circus wire, just wanting to be loved, needed, desired.
How much longer must it wait? It's raining and I stand
keyless at this locked gate. If the only alternative is
hate then I'll just jump over, besides it's getting kind of late.
Dawn closes in and out rolls the tide. Time to put away
anger, hate, and foolish pride. In the house where these
fiends live, love can never reside.
Pull up the sheets, turn out the light and say a short
goodbye to a long loveless night.
I think I'll try again tomorrow.

Todd Alan Robertson

To My One And Only Love

The way you hold me so tight,
The way your eyes shine so bright.
The way you speak to me,
Making everything seem carefree.
When we hold hands while saying good-bye.
Makes me realize my love for you could never die.
When feeling down, to me you tend
Hoping you think of me as your best friend.
Your name echoes throughout my mind,
Remembering how you are so kind.
If only you knew you played such a big part,
For you are the one who holds the key to my heart.

Kelly Diggins

The Tryst

The Shade's hand beckons,
'Tis time enow for me,
With truths and deeds unreckoned;
To delay the tryst.

Wrought the willow-wisp
Fleeting with grace,
Fate calls the tryst
All men must face.

Being was bold and quick;
To live his fill,
Who knew where to pick?
Who had the will?

I need not mourn
For my child.
Life will be bourne
For him, yet a while.

All was writ before
Man had tapped the till.
Angels guard the door,
'Till he pays the bill. Tell the determined shade,
I'll come when my dues are paid.

William R. Suda

Passing Reflections

There comes a time between dusk and stars,
when the future's truth shall be ours.
Hopefully a time when faith can heal all ills,
when life's great tragedies are still.
When life has ended and time rolls on,
remember me when I have gone.
For time is great and passes fast,
The memories are made to last.

Ollie D. Haney

Winter Sunlight

Pale shadow-branches dart swiftly 'cross the snow-crisp yard,
Tumble into icy ruts in bare-ridged barnyard roads,
Scramble to their feet to scale the bank
And sadly end their day.
Clinging to ancient clapboards on a white-walled house;
Forever seeking
The festive leaves which once they bare
In the haunted havens of their summer shade.

Forever lost those leaves remain;
But in the fragile pattern of a tender love,
Etched transiently in glowing wood and crystal snow,
A cherished picture's found
By my remembering heart.

William Colby

Son

Through wind and rain and sun and dark,
The native Son takes hold.
He rises with the strength of man
The beast within subdued.

And through the flashing night of life
The sound is deep and blue,
On endless walks of raging thought,
Their sin has gone unheard.

Through fire and flood and good and bad,
His love is in His wrath.
Be not alone upon the sod,
Straight up upon the path.

Outside the Presence in our mind,
The end of all in sight,
Embraced with all that is in Him,
In favor of the Light.

Rayward Fremin Jr.

The Gift

My heart, my life, my precious one,
You knew I could not rest.
You came to me in a bright, warm light,
To tell me, "Mama, don't be afraid.
I'm fine and safe, don't worry about me."

Our love we gave, one to another.
I wanted so much to be with you.
"Not now, but later, when your work is done,
We'll be together again."
With God's help I will make it through.

What joy that brought my aching heart -
A hope for tomorrow, a brand new start.
Each day I still miss you as much as before,
But I know you're not gone forever,
Just on the other side of the door.

Beverly Self

Untitled

Home...
   A cast of spell, our burdens behind us...
   Still await for us, years of happiness

Love...
   From the mother calling, with her arms open wide...
   Give us comfort...there's nothing to hide...

Home...
   A place of sweet serene, a place we call our own...
   With this family, hope and love...
   There's no real place like home!

Kap Hopkins

Not Me

As I watch her strong arms
  pull you closer to her body.
I wonder,
  could that be me?

When she speaks with you,
  your attentive ears listen and understand.
I wonder, could that be me?

With your ever constant smile,
  at the memories she brings,
    and her dancing eyes
      as she savors your appearance.
I wonder, could that be me?

I genuinely wonder,
  as I watch the emotions
    build within your hearts.
If I could feel what I see,
  the painful truth made itself aware to my sleeping mind.

I have seen the emotions but no,
  that could not be me.

Tamell Williams

Rainbow Of Hope

I rise again to meet another day,
As I awaken I wish my physical pain would go away.
I look out the window and what do I see,
A child who fell and cut her knee.
I then go and turn the radio on,
And it's the anniversary of Vietnam.
I get in my car and start to drive,
In my rear view mirror I see an ambulance arrive.
People are crying and hugging each other,
A scream is heard, "My God, it's my Mother".
I arrive at work to start the day,
The phone rings, my friend's Father passed away.
A co-worker has reached the end of her rope,
She yells and screams, "I cannot cope".
I glance at the clock, it's half past nine,
Then in comes a customer who is blind.
A girl is crying as she walks down the aisle,
She said, "My Dad left us and went away for a while".
Oh so many people with so much pain,
To wallow in self pity there is no gain.

Margaret Gasiorowski

Stop

As evil creeps into the mind, you slip away.
And not only does your mind slip away,
but so does your soul   and spirit.
You begin to stop feeling. Stop hearing.
Stop seeing.

You stop loving and caring.
Then other people stop loving and caring
about you.

Then you become numb so that you feel no hate.
Your mind hears it, but your soul   and spirit feel it and
you fall deeper and deeper into a black hole of nothingness.

Eventually, your soul   and spirit can't take this
numbness anymore so it tells your mind to stop

Your mind will realize what is happening
and it does, in fact, Stop.

Joanna Dwyer

The Iceman Cometh

Walking amid shadows, blinded by the darkness,
delicately sidestepping puddles in an attempt to avoid
too many noisy negatives.
Hopelessly waiting in the wings, as people
suddenly strangers, pass on by,
as feelings come and go, like leaves upon the wind.
In a shell all too unforgiving, time marches on.
Ever so slowly, the beat is stiffened;
now, by a backbone never there before. Sensitive and caring,
understanding and sincere, stupid and pitiful;
all too often, wonderful traits of a lost cause.
Alone and empowered, a stranger walks among us.
He knows not the answers, yet seeks out no questions.
Embittered by life, his strength lies in his pain.
Demons nip at his heels, a constant reminder of times
not long ago; of memories, gone but not forgotten.
Footprints disappear behind him, frantically running away
from a world that has no welcome mat and wastes no time on tears.
But it is here that all is good. Here, he is king.
It is time. The iceman cometh. He is a stranger no more.

Lee D. Andersen

Killed By The Silence

You ripped the skin off my heart today,
hurt me in the most painful way.

Walked up to me simply cut me in two,
never expected, my enemy to be you.

My whole world began to spin,
blinded by the sin shape I was in.

I ignored your warning too lazy to change
can't sleep last night rolling in pain.

Facing the ceiling tears pouring from my eyes
I begged my God please show us why?

Repeating the battle walking alone again
where was compassion, where was my friends?

Today I faced you all alone.
Torn, broken, and screaming wanting to be strong.
I walked down the street, I tumbled
into darkness, nothing to break my fall.
Killed by the silence.

Broken Dove

approaching fifty

the leaves,
they murmur to me, "go back, go back"
i cannot, my destiny will not let me

the wind,
it wails out, "turn around, turn around"
i cannot, they will not allow it

my youth,
it beckons to me but i cannot grasp it
for it is gray now, no longer white yet not quite black

the snow,
it whispers to me, "look forward, look forward"
i cannot, i am too tired from trying to reclaim the past

the will-o'-the-wisp
it tinkles to me, "seek me, seek me"
i cannot, i do not know in which direction to find it

my future,
it is leading me, to some unknown fate
taking me along as time reveals my story

Marie Modica

Life

In life's expression I've found,
a need for reaching out,
of taking hold, and of gentle holding.
Reaching out, and there embracing,
life, a tender caressing, filled with joy.
The sweet breath of life is in its living.

It can be so moving, and exciting,
with sensational expressions.
It can have an eloquence in its flow,
and delightful aspects in its wonder.
It can shine like the morning sun,
and cool like the evening breeze.

Life is all these things, and even more.
Yet the greatest mystery in life's living,
comes with its finding of love.

And the power of love so great,
that even life in its soaring flight,
would give its breath for another.

Paul Bauer

For My Sister

For my sister....
Not many know of the vision of love.
I have seen it and had it taken away.
She was perfection...she was love.
She was everything, yet so small...as if nothing.
She was an angel that flew down from heaven.
She kissed my eyes and let me see innocence.
But, there was no sound.
She kissed my ears and I heard...
The sweet melody of patience.
But, I could not talk.
She kissed my lips and I was fluent
In the language of God.
But, I could not touch.
She kissed my hands and...
I reached out and touched her face.
But, I could not feel.
She kissed my soul...and I said goodbye.

Lesley Jane Ellis

Execution Of The Innocent

A gentle touch, so harmless,
yet the past reminds,
and the caress is painful.

"My beloved". Words solely caring,
Yet memories rush,
and whispers turn to screams.

In a space, brought to a kiss,
a gesture of need.
Yet closeness brings fear,
and the need turns to hate.

Cries fill the night,
as the executed remember
Bruises left unseen, yet they come and go,
but scars are a mark for the past.

Some live, most die.
Pain filled deaths, in deserted alleys.
Unhelped by the uninvolved.
But for them, the killers,
the execution is pleasure.

Brandy Dorsey

The Blues

Striking on occasion a frequency of joy
Resting a lever, a consonance employ
Fingering a strain of rarely acquainted sound
The nebulous state of existence wound.

Riding the clouds of mixed elation and wealth
Soaring and soaring with limitless self
Esteemed to the highest - infinity's friend
Laughing, rejoicing, seldom without end.

Filtering through sieves of sadness and gloom
Journeying yet to prisons too soon
Of hopelessness, darkness, visionless doom
A shadowy figure averted in womb.

Chasing the flutter of ivories dull
Setting the moan and fitful lull
Of thirds and sixths in splendid sync
That welcomed accord is so distinct.

Danielene T. Myricks

At The Vet

At the vet we get all kinds of pets
Dogs, cats, puppies, kittens
Some are named rex
Some are named mittens
At the vet bunnies and ferrets are what we get
All get exams
Some get shots
Some get blood drawn
And we treat hot spots
At the vet we aim to please
We try to make pet and owner
Feel at ease
Some visits are exhausting
Some are a breeze
In any case we get the job done
We enjoy caring for your pet
At the vet.

Pamella Jean Engravalle

Reflection

My thoughts are racing to you again today,
swift as the river's raging rapids.
My mind becomes troubled.
Slowly, I walk down the darkened pathway
overgrown with brush and enormous trees
The croaks of the bass-throated frogs prick my consciousness.
Suddenly, I reminisce of a fishing adventure as a child.
Just as quickly my mind returns to the present surroundings.
My instincts are sharpened as I hear the rolling
thunder and the lightning illuminates my way.
I do not stumble.
The horizon becomes visible; pleasant memories return.
You are near and your reflection is cast in my eyes forever.

LaVonne A. Chase

Untitled

Awake in the middle of the night,
From nightmare shadows of my life.
Sweat pours from my hair and skin
Lying in a damp bed I stare around me,
filled with horror and helplessness.
The strange frailty of life smacking me in the face,
As my fevered mind fills with hallucinations.
I lay confused and realize I am not alone,
Paranoia and fear lay on either side,
Trapping me in their icy embrace.

Timothy Gilmore

Face To Face

Because of you, I remain here longer,
The shared love, that made me stronger.
To kiss your face once more in life...
Gives the strength, that makes things right.

To hold tight your hand...so tenderly,
To have you near, means so much to me.
I would lay my face upon your face...
We could disappear without a trace.

When love was young, and we we're free,
Do you remember what I said to thee?
Through all the trials, and all the tears,
I said I would love you, for a million years.

Magic days and those quiet nights...
The thoughts of you within my sights.
Wondrous times, that we've had together,
Now I know, they will last forever.

Native Spirit

Time

The sound of tear drops falling.
Is simply time that's calling...
A reminder of a life that used to be.
A requiem of repose addressed to me...
I still recall when it began...
My world was much younger then.
The calendar, and the clock upon the wall...
Tell the story well; but they can't tell it all...
The years, and days record the tales...
A few notes of success, and many more of fails.
Now every page relates a story...
Of my life; all its pain, and glory.
Each leaf proclaims the history...
Of every year; by day, and mystery.
The most important time of life.
Was then saw love become my wife.
When then saw life from two pair of eyes.
Through the low times, and the highs...
Our love grew; through the forty-seventh year.
And will continue for as long as I am here

Lester C. Harris Jr.

Mockingbird

As I sit in my hell, I'm trapped in a cage,
And I know why the caged bird sings.
For love, for longing, for being afraid,
And losing the use of his wings.
If his eyes could cry, I know they would,
His heart is far away.
The only one he never could,
Is the one who should have stayed.
It's funny how it works that way,
His heart was torn in half.
There's nothing left for him to say,
So all he does is laugh.

Sara Stern-Nezer

A Flowering Time

I dream on my couch and flowers grow in my window box.
Saffron blossoms unfold to the heavens as
Devoted worshipers supplicate the Day Star.
Golden rods on candied beams nip sealed green coffins.
In midnight silence dormant stigma prepare the womb.
Flavors of bestial cravings march in airy parades
Embracing honey bees on pollen treks and latch them.
Long awaited guests serve themselves at gilded cups as
Flaxen dust on frenzied feet impregnate.
And there is a Flowering Time.

Georgia D. Young

A Love Dying

As the snow started falling from the cold dark sky
The love they once shared slowly started to die
Bound only together by words of love
They would no longer share the heavens above

Their love was as precious as a gentle rain
But now could bring only heartache and pain
Something inside him, He could no longer share
Something she needed, but just wasn't there

As they lay there together in a sweet warm embrace
He reached out to touch her, but only her face
She needed his love to keep her alive
But felt only emptiness as she looked in his eyes

Her body now ached with desire
As she felt his warm gentle touch
This man that she truly longed for
This man that she needed so much

Now there can be no real love without passion
When the fire within you has died
This room where they made love for the last time
Now feels like the winter outside

Jacqueline Ludlow

Spring Comes

Spring comes
As if it were invited.

Rustling dead leaves and pushing up the ground
With innocence and wild abandon.

Acting as though
The wisdom of the past were all forgotten or unlearned
In this new incarnation.

Acting as though
Hope springs eternal

And as though
It would not lead to Winter
Always Winter

Which always leads to spring.

Marion Perkus

Sugar Is Bitter, Sugar Is Sweet

My face is scorched from the burning heat!
Look at the bruises all over my feet!
Yesterday I was drenched with torrents of rain,
Yet I will give my life for the sugar cane.

Don't ever despise my torn, black clothes;
It's hard in the field where the sugar cane grows!
These hands of mine have bled from toil,
That's why you can live on my country's soil.

Day after day, to the fields I would go,
Working and watching the sugar cane grow.
Chanting a tune in the noonday heat,
Like sugar is bitter, sugar is sweet!

The harvest is ready, come savour the sweet
Of the labor I gave, in rainstorm and heat.
The bins overflow with crystals of gold,
My heart is aglow, what joys untold!

So the sugar you eat is not only from cane;
But from sweat, and blood flowing, and sinews I strain.
Come out to the cane fields, and endure a day's heat,
And soon you'll find out, why sugar is bitter, sugar is sweet!

Joel Chinapen

Nature's Grace

As I sit here with pen in hand,
I wonder who will strike up the band.
I look out my window and see nature's grace,
And everything about it put so firmly in place.

The forest so green with the leaves we've seen,
But we must have forgotten how they're so fresh and clean
The brooks run so swift, pure and clean,
Until someone destroys its very means.

We watch our wildlife scamper and play,
But to us the people they have no say.
It saddens me deeply and blackens my heart,
But I'm proud to say that I've had no part.

We must protect nature for one and all,
Or soon to come we'll see our downfall.
If we keep our brooks fresh and our air pure and clean,
Someday we'll be thanked from nature's scene.

James W. Johnson

God's Love

Walk in the clouds with me,
all I am is love can't you see.
I sent the Dove from the Heaven above,
don't be afraid of me.
Go pass the word, the Bible as you plead,
pass it soon, before it's time to leave.

Come in my angel, through that faithful door
and I will lead you forever more.
Now your pain is gone and the world has passed,
"I'm So Glad, You're Here At Last"

Rusty Young

A Gentle Hand

I stumble in the night.
With reckless abandon I seek the light,
but it is lost to me.
I am blind, I cannot see.
Everywhere I run and then do turn
is another place my soul will burn.
There is no escape, only pain and fear,
an infinite, dreadful emptiness, nothing clear.
At the darkest hour of that hellish night,
through endless tears I see a light.
Toward me reaches a gentle hand,
the lifts me up from where I stand.
It rescues me from this wholly sinful,
mortal life I've trod.
Now I am safe.
It is the Lord...my God.

Brian Williamson

Paradoxal To A Lady

The tree starts undressing in the fall
She is shapely, beautiful and tall
Her colorful clothing falls to the ground
Cause Mr. Winter is coming around.
Mr. Wind caresses her
Until she becomes completely bare
No red, yellow, orange or brown clothes to share
They are all on the ground
Now Mr. Snow is falling down
From the sky and what a treat?
And you can see a nice white carpet
Under Miss Bare Tree's feet.
It makes her feel very, very sweet.

Gwynn T. Alexander

Love

(Is What It Is)

Love is something warm you feel deep in your heart,
but cannot express it.
It's a feeling that so deep that it hurts,
when you see the one you love hurt.

Love is that feeling when you look into someone's
face or eyes and you can see when they are in need.
Love is what word you tell someone, "I love you,"
and mean it from your heart.

Love comes from the heart and it suffereth long.
When you love, it gives up the right for the wrong.

Love shares whatever it has with no regrets.
Love goes out of its way, willingly.

Love is "I will go anytime, day or night."

Love is understanding.
Love is patience.

Love is the most precious gift anyone can every give.
For God so loved the world that he gave his only son.

Love is kind.
Love never gives up.

Love will always give and looks for no return.

Virginia Rosa Broussard

'Tis Autumn Again

When the green of the leaves turn brownish in
hue to start showing their underside, summer
has spent itself, and 'tis Autumn again.

As the North winds blow in from Canada, and the
long-necked geese start their honking flight to
the South, you know then, 'tis Autumn again...

And e'en tho' the leaves finally fall, to show
barren trees with limbs exposed in awkward
positions, one knows that winter is not far off
and t'will come Autumn again...

Then the days are shortened and dark replaces
light sooner than before as animals use this time
to forage for food and rebuild nests torn a sunder
by others, the storms, that they can say goodbye
to Autumn...

As snows blanket the ground and the trees of the
forests and the mountainsides, and e'en those
nests of recent repair, 'tis evident that winter
has shown its forces at last, and might replaces
fading Autumn, once again...

Robert H. Wyatt

As I Grasp My E-Pen

As I grasp my electronic pen,
And press the keys in order to send
A message to my lovely Flower
All within the very hour.
Your beauty is stunning;
Your charm in great!
Our love grows more and more,
But, alas, is it too late?
Farewell my love,
For I must be going.
Forget me not,
For our passion runs so very, very hot!
"Hell hath no fury like a woman's scorn."

John Wigington

The First Night

Tonight's the first night, you held me in your arms
Slow dancing in a room filled with people
Our cheeks pressing against each other
Your hand just above my hip
My hand placed carefully on your shoulder

Moving slowly to the music
Awkwardly at first
Then picking up the rhythm and dancing as one
Your body pressed against mine
We swayed back and forth

A heat generated from our bodies
You whisper "I want to make love to you"
Silently we remain dancing
Clutching closer to each other
Then the music ends

We break apart and look at one another
Returning to our partners in love
Not by choice but by necessity
Tonight's the first night you held me in your arms
Slow dancing in a room filled with people

Linda J. Sabol

A Quiet Song

Once, by chance, a quiet song drifted,
Softly, it could hardly be heard,
A light breeze lifted it, played with it,
Instilling a moment of joy.
I listened, just beyond reach there,
Not much more than a hushed whisper,
Like a spider's thread, in and out
Of sight, comes and goes, now and then.
All too soon, like a night vision,
A cloud that floats across the earth,
Vanish disappear like shadows,
Never to be heard again.

Nona Vaught

Desert Freedom

Open space, sunlight
Surrounding me, beckoning me.
Releasing my spirit.

Calming silence.
Crisp, pure, innocent air.

Immense canyons ablaze with red rock.
Alive with history broached
    through sandstone.

Majestic mountains off in the distance,
encircling me, containing me, keeping me safe.

Oh, great Mojave,
Your beauty nourishes my soul.
I am free.

Cindy Abdelsayed

Hidden Treasures

Who is to say what the future will hold
Each golden moment a pleasure to behold
Thinking only of tomorrow and wishing our lives away
Missing what there is to savor in each given day
When our life draws to a close will we look
    back in wonder over all we have missed
Or will we treasure each moment to the fullest
    and make each day worthwhile
Not running through our lifetime, but walking every mile.

Jean E. Bowers

O To Be Like Thee

Some day a crown will encompass my head, if I
Only remember to be compassionate and kind.

Angry words have no place, for God's love is
Shared with us all.

Incredible as it seems a drudge is far better
Than a grudge.

Forgiveness leaves us feeling relieved, then
A humble heart can be felt within.

A praiser I shall be, 'tis better for me

Mercy mercy mercy is there no end of his love
for you and me.

Albert Lillie

King David

All joy, performance true
In days of old, inspired view
He danced,
With leaps of thunder, whirling storm
Graceful vent, King David's form.
Stirred on, displayed by Love Divine
God's masterpiece moving in perfect time.
He sways to bend, admired by unseen Angel's train,
Dancing feet patter like soft-drop rain,
Sweet lift of arms in homage sends.
Soul on fire brings drive and feel,
Wrapped by predestined, polished shell,
Compelling music to be heard,
He danced,
With overlapping zeal,
Through shades of depth,
Expressed perfection in every step.

Georgia O. Cruz

Untitled

There was an Elder named Hellwig
Who had the most mischievous grin
You could see the fun dance in his eyes
As he told you about the Lord
With whom there is no surprise
His companion Elder Gibbons, was sweet and shy
They had both come on a mission
To serve their Lord and now mine
To save us awful sinners
From the clutches of the devils crime
They gave me my lessons
In what seemed like record time
Soon I'll be baptized, and washed free of my sins
Thanks to Elders Hellwig and Gibbons
I'm free of the devils sin
But praise be to my Lord
Who gave his life for mine
And to the missionaries
Who taught me to be free

Connie Rose

Upon Arrival

Hurried footsteps over fleeting years
Carried me, with absolute assurance, to this day.
Now I stand here, unexpectedly filled with doubt,
Alone..in the very moment it was all about...
Wondering how it was I ever felt
The manic need to come this way,
Only to find myself leaning fearfully
Against the pressing winds of time...
Pondering what I might have missed
In my dogged, blind pursuit of this.

D. J. Calzada

Some Words We Use

Some words we use can build a great nation
Angry words can bring total devastation
Some words we use in debate, angry words will show their hate
Some words we use can bring fortune and fame
Angry words can bring you down in shame
Some words we use can tear you apart
Angry words directed at the heart
Some words we use can make you feel alone
Angry words can destroy a happy home
Some words we use can be cold and cruel
Angry words are always spoken by a fool
Some words we use can give you a new start
Words of love that comes from the heart
The word of God will show you the way
God's gracious love is with you through night and day
We speak words of love in our own way
We should speak them to others every day
Speak the right words in things you say
You never know when it will be your judgement day

Albert G. Gloor

Loneliness

Ah! Lonely lonely heart
Oh how the iron claws of despair
tear at you.
They rip at your very being,
Fibers and muscles shred
at their touch.

Ache, ache, ache,

Time drags its feet,
enjoying to the utmost
your misfortune.
Who is there to care?
Hope where are you?

The lonely heart beats raggedly on,
searching, searching for someone to share
its solitude with.

Surely another lonely heart
Beats out its searching
Pattern somewhere?

Lonely! Lonely! Ache! Ache! Ache!

Carolyn Ingles

Only To Remember

Every time I close my eyes,
your image appears.
Only to remember,
you've disappeared.

Every time my mind wonders,
the thought of you occurs.
Only to remember,
you don't think of me.

Every time I lay in bed,
I feel you next to me.
Only to remember,
it's my teddy bear.

Every time I see one of your look-alikes,
I blush and look harder.
Only to remember,
you're gone forever.

RyAnne Thompson

"Great Trips Are Satin Dreams"

My everyday life is not so cozy
Nightfall helps to make it rosy
I cover up from neck to feet
As I creep beneath my satin sheet
My dreams they are far away places
Where I can see many happy faces
My eyes are closed it's really keen
Trips and countries are to be seen
What makes a person like me to whine
Is that this life can not be mine
The clock keeps ticking and finally rings
Fantasy ends, I'll see what this day brings
Midnight comes, under my sheet I'll climb
Hoping my dream has a great trip this time

Bernice M. Smetanka

Free As A Bird

As free as a bird I want to fly
to soar through the great big sky,
To spread my wings and, feel the wind
that is how my day would begin.

In and out the trees I'd sway
and in the green meadows I would lay,
And if I didn't want to be found
I'd fly up on a hill top without a sound.

Over the oceans I would glide
and fly along the mountain side,
On the tree tops I'd make my nest
So, under the stars I could rest.

For, if I had a choice I'd be,
A beautiful bird so, I could fly free.

Patty Marchuk

Dream On

Your mind is a mass of desperate emotions:
Love, hate, anger and despair.
Your thoughts isolated you
From most of the world,
But my dreams somehow held me near.
I saw the silver tears
Slowly flowing down your perfect face
And vain I attempted to comfort you,
But the feeling of hopelessness
Was just too much—
You eventually drifted away from me;
The circling thought were too confusing
And you felt you couldn't stay.
My dreams faded and with them, my life.
But dream on, my love.

Angela Mueller

A Mother

A mother is many wonderful things
She has a heart of pure gold,
Her eyes are love-light shining
She'll give you anything she owns.

We can't always understand, a mother's love
And perhaps we never shall,
Whether the day be cloudy or fair
One thing for certain...mother's love is there.

As father-time ticks fast today
And some of our mother's go away,
We may not understand why we suffer this here
Remember, someday, God's purpose will be clear.

Nina L. Crum

A Weaver Weaves

Even now, as we speak a weaver weaves
  in and out, up and down, one side to another,
  applying his trade until
  a montage of life is created.

Gold, silver and rose colored threads, depicting
  happiness, felicity, enchantment, interwinding
  with foreboding gray, dark blue and black threads,
  portraying sorrow, melancholy, heavy-hearted times,
  all woven in intricate imagery.

How we mourn for the silk threads gone forever,
  marked by the spaces left in the complex pattern and,
  those soft, worn threads, loose, devoid of form as
  they slowly unravel.

From birth to demise the mosaic of life and death emerges
  and the weaver continues to weave symmetrical tapestries.

    Mary R. Spinella

Portrait Of Love

The childlike smile on your face
Your gentle touch and warm embrace
The heights of passion I reach with you
Make all my fondest dreams come true

We've shared some moments, but very few
Each times the embers were flamed anew
Our bodies and souls felt free and warm
Like the calm that follows a raging storm

I long to hold you close to me
But I know that it cannot be
Restraint must kill the burning desire
Where as your love could extinguish the fire

I felt so secure when you were near
You were so special and so very dear
I hope you will think of me once more
For you my love I do adore

    Deborah A. Kopis

Child At Bay

How still you lay
Day after day
No movement of sound
Yet still your heart pounds

My innocent babe
To the unknown you are slaved
How I wonder what's on your mind

Time moves quickly
Picking at your youth
Deciding for you
A path you can't chose
How can this be
Sweet child before me
Your life once full of joy
Now lays dormant like a toy

If only I could give life once again
I would surrender my soul to make you whole

But alas the experts say...
Be patient...
Wait another day

    M. Amanda Galicia

Our House Out Back

That two hole toilet, I remember,
Especially on a cold night in December.

We'd hurry quickly, relief in sight,
Hoping the moon would shed its light.

The hinges squeaked on the wooden door,
Our tiny feet barely touched the floor.

Newspapers stacked in a box nearby,
A few corn cobs, if we ran shy.

The roof was covered with rusty tin,
Tar papers lined the walls within.

Yesterday's memories bring forth a smile,
That two hole toilet, I used as a child.

    Jettie Hopper

You And I

Once you were my best friend,
I was glad we became something more,
All of a sudden you told me it all had to end.

We always had so much fun,
When you and I were together,
Now those days of us are done.

I'll always remember the love we shared,
Together all the things we've been through,
Wondering if there was a time you really cared.

I think I can make it though,
This troublesome time in my life,
The place in my heart still remains for you.

    Keely Ivy

Stormy Day

One stormy wintry day I held his hand in mine
And I said I do for the very first time
I thought who really is this handsome man
I've known for only six months
As I stood staring into his eyes
I realized who and what he was
To me he was handsome, gentle, and ever so kind
He was willing to give of his time
To teach me what I did not know
And give me room so I could continue to grow
I would love him more with each passing day
And if somehow I lost my pace
He would say take my hand and let me lead the way
I would be his and he would be mine
Until the end of time
Thank God for that Stormy Wintry Day!

    Trena Gaye Locke Strickland

Untitled

Alone I torment through the answers
Seeking the Divine yet searching without grace
The sandstorms of my mind
Twirl about questions impossible
And punctuation's non-existence as
The likelihood of retreat
Flows from my mouth like a drought
Thirsting for rain
I hold my fiery lip
In order to reckon all of the day's allowances
And close my eyes
Alone I stumble through the answers
My only companion quickly departs
Leaving just a grain or two of possibility
And no mention of the thought of rain

    Charlie McCarter

Rebirth

The eagle awakes,
The sun is shining bright,
The flowers stick out their leaves, in this new breath of spring,
There is a newness as - the child within awakens.

The eagle finds its wings,
The sun is shining bright,
The flowers stretch out their leaves, to taste the freshness.
There is a new awakening as - the child within finds its wings.

The eagle takes flight,
The sun is shining bright
The flowers stretch out their petals, in the newness of Mother Earth,
There is a new found confidence as - the child within takes flight.

The eagle soars,
The sun is shining bright,
The flowers stretch up their faces, in this glowing of light,
There is a beauty untold as - the child within soars.

Kathryn Willing

Seagull

Oh I wish I were a seagull, so I could fly,
up and up into the sunlit sky.
Swooping down to hover over the aqua blue sea,
then upwards again into the clouds so billowy.
Sailing along in the wind's gust,
the blowing breeze I would always trust.
To lift me high and guide me far,
when the sun shines bright or on a night that sparkles only one star.
For I would be one of God's creatures, free like the wind,
I would have peace of mind and security within.
Sometimes I wish I could escape the problems everyday brings to me,
and oh to be like the gull and just soar over the sea.

Amy Sparks

The Captain Of Our Salvation

The atheist calls himself a captain,
   and gambles with his soul.

The one who wants to go to Heaven
   will follow what the Bible says.

In the old Testament—2 Chronicles 13:12 —Abijah
   the King of Judah, called God captain and
   relied on Him to deliver them out of the
   ambush of Jeroboam, who never recovered.

In the New Testament, Jesus Christ the son of God
   is captain of our salvation—Hebrews 2:10. His ship
   is the church—verse 12—which He founded A.D. 33
   on the day of Pentecost in Jerusalem—Acts 2,
   when 3000 souls repented, confessed Christ is
   the son of God showing belief, and were baptized;
   and Christ added them to His church—verse 47.

By following the teachings of the New Testament steadfast
   to the end of life (staying in His church) we are
   made partakers of Christ and will dwell in Heaven—Hebrews 3:14.

Are you gambling with your soul, or will you
   be prepared to meet Christ on Judgment Day?

Virginia W. Thomson

Mystery Of Tree Roots

Erosion of the sand left the trees standing on the tip of their
toes. They looked like they were ready to tiptoe across the sand.
How such slender roots can hold a tree so big is a mystery. Logic
tells me that trees standing on their tiptoes must fall over onto
the sand. Yet, the trade winds continue to blow and the trees continue to stand.

Alyce Nielson

Land Of Shadows

Come with me to the land of shadows
Take my hand and away we'll go
Come with me to the land of shadows
Walk with me where demons grow
Follow me to the Devil's household
Deep inside his forbidden lair
Come with me to the land of shadows
The things you seek are waiting there.
Taste the fruit, forbidden, sweet
Close your eyes and smile
Taste the fruit, forbidden, sweet
And be a God awhile
Roam the land that darkness hides
Lay where the sun fears to go
For deep within my world of shadows,
You'll find the things you seek to know.

John Requardt II

The Sod House

I think that a sod house,
Is kind of an odd house.
Wouldn't it melt in the rain?

But a shortage of wood,
Made the sod house look good,
Out on the cold, windy plain.

Block upon block,
Row after row,
Rising to thick, brushy roof.

Wads of sod!
Clods of sod!
Hauled up by hand and by hoof.

So tonight, fast and tight
In your warm modern home,
Remember the sod house,
Remember this poem.

James Bernard Moore

Will?

8 years and none
A malady
Discovered, admitted...finally
Ebbing and flowing
Spinning like the top
Momentum spent, inspiration gained
In unfamiliar places
Once suggested graces
Listening? Shivering, delivering?
Will a promise be made...or kept?
Is it earned, deserved...perturbed?
Leaking the sap
Alive...yet?
Cracking ere the Spring
Too late? Too soon?
Troughs arrange
A hastening of Slumber
Arising...surprising
In the midst
Running; Gone Home, or going?

Alexander R. Clayton

Fossils

Darwin in the Andes;
Seashells by glacial lakes;
Subtle curiosities, chinked loose,
Can shake the layered limestone
Of the earth.

Carol Ross Starr

The Last Laugh

I remember, you laugh
Who me, yes you laugh
I remember, you laugh
Who me, yes you laugh
At my friends, friend
Who she no he yes me
I remember, you laugh
And then you become
Laugh why me, yes you
Laugh, laugh, laugh
Laugh why me, yes you

Aubrey Best

Goodbye

One blonde head, one brown
Whisper softly
Bend close
Lips touch
Just barely
Then with more passion
As desperation takes hold
He's leaving soon
This is their goodbye
Lips part
Eyes meet
Silent messages pass
Lips meet one final time
Before he turns
And walks away
Quickly, so he cannot see
The pain in her eyes
That he knows is there
For it's in his own

Crystal Cluster

Rose

Amy, you are so fine,
your hair, eyes, lips.

Lips so tender, so soft, so luscious,
like a rose, a rose brought to
earth by an angel.

Your eyes, so deep, mystical,
so beautiful,
like a spring rose.

Your hair, so soft, so silky,
like a petal,
a petal from a precious rose.

Amy, when I see you,
my love blooms,
like a rose.

William David Stevenson

Fragments

Icy blood pours through my veins...
now only when it rains...
my life is shattered...
pieces scattered...
only fragments there remain...
fragments gleaming...
people screaming...
life will never be the same...
now icy blood pours through my veins...
where memories are retained...
never knowing all their names...
always quietly restrained.

Julie M. Evans

Cowboys Have Religion

I don't need a building tall or a church with a spire.
Or a preacher with his thoughts to tell me of my soul's desire.

I don't hear the word of the Lord, but I can see His creation.
The peace and contentment of this place is just right for meditation.

The prairie is the floor, the mountains make the walls.
The sky above, the ceiling makes, I have my church, I have it all.

The mountains rising high create the steeples of nature's church.
My saddle is my pew, my faith is clear, I do not search.

The water holes so clear and blue take their reflection from the sky.
The cattle graze in the meadow as the ducks and geese go flying by.

The animals, the trees, the grass, are shown in all its beauty.
This is my church in nature where worship is my duty.

My pony and I rise the plain, as on this land we trod.
This was all created by the Sacred Hand of God.

Matthew Scopelitis

The Course Of Things

Have you ever wondered how runs the course of things?
How little odd things happen, the mystery that it brings?
Where does the lonely sock go; did it slip into the drain?
It started in the washer, then was never seen again!

When going down the highway, how come it looks so curved?
But when we drive upon it, it's straight instead of swerved.
How come you can't find something, when it's right under your nose?
Could it be it hides itself, on purpose, do you suppose?

Why do they call them apartments, when they build them all together?
And when you just have washed the car, you get the rainy weather.
How come the signal turns to red, just when you're in a hurry?
Just then you get behind a slow car, when you want to scurry!

When in a store, I find myself stuck in the longest line.
Or when I'm in the bathroom, the phone call's always mine!
So when you think of something, and another thinks it too.
Remember you're experiencing, a little deja vu!

Sharon Olmos

It's That Sad Day Again

Without you nearby this is another sad Mother's Day
Today marks the second of many more to come my way.
We were very blessed to have many happy days and years past
Knowing full well life for no one would forever last.

The recent years of our regular afternoon coffee and chats
With you gone has created a tremendous void; I can't fix that.
Memories shared will always be held so very dear
Somehow in my heart it does help keep you near.

Not everyone has been so lucky having a loving Mom, kind and sweet
With two special parents to guide me and a big brother, who wasn't always a treat.
Yet, with all my family gone there are certain days nice to recall
Even as Mother's Day is again here and sad, I loved you one and all.

Nadine M. Bushong

The Night I Danced With You

I miss the night I danced with you, holding you close to me.
The beating of your heart, the warm feeling I had holding you in my arms.
I miss the few hours in my life of total joy, just dancing with you.
I can still hear the music playing as we danced the night away.
Every cent I had was spent buying the new suit I was wearing, but it was worth it
 just to dance with you.
I remember that night so very well, the moon was full, the stars shined brightly in the night skies.
I miss the night I danced with you, holding you close to me, the beating of
Your heart, the warm feelings I had holding you in my arms.

Poet Canavan

Born Free

Don't grieve for me, for now I'm born free;
I'm falling the path God laid out for me, I'm born free;
I took His hand when I heard Him call, why! I'm born free
I turned my back and left it all. Because I was born free.

I could not stay another day that way, I was born free
To laugh, to love to work, or play, I was born free.
Tasks left undone must stay that way, why!, I was born free.
I found that place at the close of the day, I was born free.

If my parting has left a void. Because I was born free.
Then fill it with remembered joy, I was born free.
A friendship shared, a laugh, a kiss, why, I was born free.
Ah yes, these things, I too, will miss and why, I was born free.

Be not the burdened with the times of sorrow. I was born free.
I wish you a sunshine of tomorrows, you were born free.
My life has been full, I savored so much. I was born free.
Good friends, good times, a love one has touched, I was born free.

Perhaps my time seemed all too brief, because I was born free.
Don't lengthen it now with your undue grief. Why!, I was born free.
Lift up your hearts then share this with me. I was born free.
God wanted me right now, He has set me free, why, I was born Free.

Anthony Vincent DiGiannurio

Night

The sun sinking low, giving up to night's dark prince, —twilight
But, before the last hurrah, nature's burst of color, —sunset
Now all is between, not light, — not dark, but limbo
All are dark shadows, trees, hills, and the horizon
The sky is lighted only by those eternal stars ever glowing
A pale sliver of yellow light rises behind the trees, — the moon
Earth's reluctant companion bound by invisible strings
Full now night's watchman, master of the tides, weird things,
superstitions, and madness
The peepers begin to awake and serenade the night for a mate
Night is everywhere, full, — and here it will rule all things till dawn.

James L. Findlay

Freedom, Security, Tranquility, Unity And Love

Freedom! Freedom! Freedom at last! Liberated totally of the horrible past.
Forgiveness is the greatest of gifts. My heart soars as it constantly lifts.
The toils and labors will finally pay off. Forever we thought we would be lost.
Security! Security! Security my friends. We'll grow in the power we'll have in the end.
Tranquility! Tranquility! Foremostly Peace! Let's all join hands to kill the ugly beast
of bigotry, discrimination, hatred and distrust. It is very vital, an absolute must!
Unity! Unity! Unity for all! Big, small so tiny and tall.
We all bleed red blood and we certainly cry. And the lack of these things is the reason why.
Love! Love! Love one another! Homeless, Veterans, Sisters and Brothers.
Black, yellow, white or brown.
Let's proudly come together and don the regal crown!
Freedom, security, tranquility, unity and love
will surely guarantee peace and abundance above.

Lisa Lindstrom

Untitled

I have seen your face so very often
You have indeed walked with me through the arduous and adorning peril of my youth

In the realization of an appetite for wisdom, I've replenished the consumptions of mediocrity

So many of us all too often get lost in an illusion, trying to
grasp what is not real, what we can't see, and what we cannot hold

Caught up in a whirlwind of doubt and indifference, our minds allow
our individuality to weaken

If we cannot recognize substance, virtues and values we fail to
commit our souls and will not achieve piece of mind

You are my conscience, keeping me strong

Noel S. Hamel

Until A Kiss

There was a time
when I thought we were friends
But something changed
A wheel spun a different way
You looked at me
And in your eyes I saw
A different scene
You smiled and your hand
A gentle touch it gave
Fingers lifting my chin
Lips flawlessly placed
There was a time
When I thought we were friends
Until a kiss took place

Amber Smith

Precious

A starry night, a child's first sight
A mother's arms enfold
The gift of life, a wondrous thing
From infancy to old
Through growing pains and wisdom shared
A man must show he cares
For time too short and not all sweet
Their precious life grow old

Dean J. Hartmann

Jumping To An End

Thinking it's all over
when it's never too late
his mind sets on overdrive
his body shifts its weight,
Falling from a clear blue sky
with thoughts flowing through his head
he never thought he'd die
he dreaded being dead,
It's too late now
there's no turning back
he's gone too far
he cannot react,
Closer to the ground
wishing he never jumped
hoping it's all a dream
hoping he'll wake up,
His vision disappears
his mind drifts away
no one could save him
it was his last day

Melissa Russell

Nani

Great great grandmother,
I never looked into your face,
Nor you into mine.
With your last breath
I breathed my first.
And to my grandfather you said,
The little one gets my spirit.
As she is born, I die.
You pressed into his hand
The last rose of summer,
Plucked from the hot July air,
And said,
For her,
The child.

Megan Linde

You've Flown Away To Heaven

You've flown away to heaven
a sweet and better land
you walk amongst the angels
you hold the good Lord's hand

You guide us with your spirit
you let us know you're here
and even though we miss you
you wipe away our tears

You've flown away to heaven
you're earning angel's wings
you're dancing in the clouds
and doing angel things

We remain to always miss you
you shall always be our friend
and you have flown away to heaven
until we see your smile again.

Natika Henderson

Seagull

Free
Summer seems to energize him.
He glides, dives, conquers
A fish
Near the beach edge.

Brave,
yet timid.
Fear of danger,
people passing on the
beach

With others
sittin' on the
ocean.
In touch with the motion
of the waves.

Relaxed,
Preparing for next flight.

John Grant

A Million Minus Two

When two people see each other
With their own eyes
In their own way
With hatred or with love

When two people touch each other
With their own hands
In their own way
With hatred or with love

When two people kill each other
With their own force
In their own way
With hatred or with love

And when two people love each other
There is hatred
And there is love
In their own way.

Dennis Bader

Life

The little boy cries
He sucks on a lolly pop
Then he aged and died.

Dustin Wolvert

Valentines For Sweethearts

February 14th is a special day you know,
it's set aside making valentines for a favorite girl or beau.

With a sad and heavy heart Fanny watched the girls in groups
make fancy paper valentines with ribbons, laces and cupids for
their sweethearts, at the Valentine's Dance to bestow.

Fanny had no sweetheart, not even a true friend, but she pinned
a secretive smile on her face and put her heart and soul in the
making of that little Valentine card as if she truly had a beau.

The night of the dance Fanny with a somber look on her face
stood alone and away from the crowd, when a shy little boy with
eyes of blue and a smile on his face singled Fanny out as she looked
lonely too. The courage he had seemed almost to falter when he
blurted out, "My name is Willie, will you be my valentine?"
Fanny's eyes seemed to brighten and burst into stars as she stared
at dear Willie. She was so grateful and delighted for his kindness
by far more than he would ever know.

They soon became fast friends having many interests they shared,
so when time came to exchange valentine cards there was no
hesitation on either Fanny or Willie's part. (Fanny sighed and
thought to herself how pleased I am that I worked so hard on
making a valentine for my supposed sweetheart).

Marolyn E. Baker

Childhood Recollection

House to home in that I see, this picturesque edifice stately
standing. Transformed by warmth within,
a love submerged shelter, anointed by virgin oil,
an adult recollection through childhood eyes perceived.

Images dance with gentle connotations, fondly remembered and loved.
Drenched with patience and gorged with laughter in memory,
my soul explores its rooms with diligence.
Stability sustained, obedience not invoked, moveable no.

This whirlwind synopsis etched of younger days,
comes back to intrude upon intent.
Shedding veils from secret places, reviving upon request,
and rejuvenating spirits soulfully missed.
Listen! This house awakes with renewed breath.
Lackluster spirits? I think not! Every corridor a welcome mat.

Hallowed spirits of divine treasure,
strength and truth once sustained these walls.
As shadowed figures woven in tapestry by celestial beings,
captivating to submission the verbal past, with tantalizing seductive
aroma, to create and claim steadfast to this life.

Lillian A. Davis

My Dear

How much I would have missed My Dear if we had never met.
When we said our vows I thought the world was mine and yet.
I had not known the meaning of the word that some called joy.
Until they laid within my arms that tiny wriggling boy.

For here was God's great miracle, so old and yet so new.
Fulfillment of your love for me and proof of mine for you.
These moments will be precious as we journey down through life.
The birthday of my first born son and the day I called you Wife.

There'll be many that I will treasure but these will be the best.
And I can be so grateful for the way my life's been blest.
I thought you were so lovely when you became my bride.
But you never looked more beautiful than with our baby by your side.

Oh darling, though the years will pass and silver touch your hair.
Still in my heart you will remain so sweet, so young, so fair.
I only ask that God be near to keep my happiness undefiled.
And look with love on my infant son and the Mother of my child.

Regina Scopelitis

A Good Hand

When I cease to be
There is one way to remember me
There is a phrase often said
And I hope it fits me when I'm dead:
He was a good hand is only a term
But to achieve it you start as a worm
You come to work all eager and meek
Hoping you still work there at the end of the week.
You bust your tail and you really try
But by the end of the week you could just sit and cry.
The guys you work with really put you to the test
But unknown to them, and maybe you, they make you the best
Because each time they kid you and make you feel like a fool,
You'll always teach yourself another rule
Most of these guys have been around for awhile,
But watch and listen closely and you'll save yourself many a mile,
If from each guy you learn but one good habit,
You will go from a worm to a rabbit.
Faster and faster you'll do your work,
And no longer will you feel like a jerk.
And when you've done it and on your way,
All your fellow men will say... He was a good hand!

Mike Jurek

All Would Be Still

If I should die before my time, let it not be in vain. For the sorrow
would have ended, the emptiness would be gone. And there would no
longer be pain. There would no longer be life no more hatred for me
to feel, No more anger to be displayed, no more lies, denials, sins, or
secrets All would be so still! So if I should die so quickly that I
am unable to say my goodbyes I say to you now. I ask only that you not feel sorry, do
not be sad, and to some of you I ask not to be glad. For all would be still.
I will no longer be seen by your eyes, but I will always be there in
spirit. In spirit when the flowers begin to display their beauty I'll
be there. And when you're camping out under the stars and you hear the
river rushing in the distance I'll be there...and even in a smoke
filled room a billiard amongst ice you hear the clanking of the balls
I'll be there and all will be still...I'll miss the smiling faces of family and friends, your hugs
and kisses I'll no longer have the
beauty of the earth I will no longer be able to enjoy, but the love
I felt throughout my life, the happy times and the joyous memories,
these things I will not miss..for these things I could never forget,
These have been embedded in my soul for me to take whenever and wherever
I go. And there all would be still....

Cynthia Morales

You Do Not Know Me

You do not know me I am just an ordinary person, except for one thing
I have allowed my eyes to recognize and comprehend, not to just see for seeing's sake
My eyes behold the sights of mankind plundering and killing
Not just in the literal sense, but in the thievery of the soul and the murder of the heart
Behind all our knowledge we are mindless of all we do
Is blaming another the only way? Are there not other avenues to dissolve this hate?
Why do we hate? Can you give a good answer?
Or only ones of color, race, religion, or geographical location
Think before you speak and open your eyes to the truth, before you say you see

You do not know me I am just an ordinary person, except for one thing
I have allowed my ears to really listen, not to just hear for hearing's sake
My ears vibrate with the sounds of agony and despair
Not just from mankind today, but from the dead and buried and those yet to be conceived
It comes from the land itself, the soul, the heart, and every living organism
We are not just destroying the "enemy" but the very essence of ourselves
That part of us that truly makes us strong, empathy and compassion
Why can't we give up the anger? Can you give a good answer?
Or only of indifference

Tamara B. Foster

Free Insecurities

Free Insecurities,
Please take one...
Take a hundred before the day is done.
Take a thousand to give
To your daughters and sons.

Free Insecurities,
Please take two...
Take two hundred in lieu
Of trespasses against you.
And for those you hate,
Take a few for them, too.

Free Insecurities,
Here, take 'em all...
Take a trillion before you fall.

Joshua Haise

Forever's Kiss

Centuries ago we met,
On a night just so.
We walked along the river bank,
I could not let you go.
Standing in the moonlight
You gave me love's forever kiss!

Centuries from that night
We make again the vow of love.
Standing on a moonlit river bank,
Your blood fills my mouth with love.
I've returned the love you gave,
With your forever kiss!

Krista Lewis

When People Die

When people die
We don't know what to do,
So we cry and we cry
For they cared about you.

When people die
It gives us quite a scare.
So if you ever need me,
I'll always be there.

Jesse Shepherd-Bates

Glory

Unfurled ev'er morn
Raised to the heights
Some men have scorn
Others have died.
Rolling, flapping
Moving, now still
Glory showing
Moving, now still.

Greatest nation
Can it be true?
Greatest nation
They'll kill you too
For what it means
To the simple
Is not the means
Of brave people.

Watch out for Bill
Moving, now still.

Thomas C. Jones Jr.

Yesteryear

No pain, no guilt, no fear,
Just memories of yesteryear.

She's put a twinkle in your eyes,
That even you cannot deny.

You think of her in silent slumber,
With me it's just a simple wonder.

Could she be the one you're after?
To share your tears and laughter.

She's only an image in your mind,
Is it possible to leave me behind?

She has you now from dusk till dawn,
The hours your love for me is gone.

Will the feelings come to pass?
Can your love for her forever last?

A simple smile, a shedded tear,
Will this be memories of yesteryear?

Terri Chapman

No More

No more tears
No more fears.
No more fun
No more sun.
No more laughing
No more crying.
I can't bear the thought
Of those people dying.
No more winter
No more fall.
No more love
Not at all.
No more summer
No more spring.
For the people
Who died in the
Oklahoma City Bombing.

Halli Simpson

Leaving

Taking steps so far away
there isn't more that I can say
a look from you says it all
your tender tears begin to fall

A message deep starts to flow
one that opposes me to go
touching hands and fingertips
a few light words from your lips

I take them with me as I walk
so much to say, few times to talk
there are no promises to be broke
no conversations until we spoke

But while I'm gone my heart will feel
the love you have that's so concealed
I'll remember all the times as one
and from this moment we've just begun

Melissa Hall

i do not know-how-the sea was made-
though-i do believe-to one extent-
but-this-i know beyond a-doubt-
the-sea's man's home-when he-is out-

Peter Sletmoe

God Is My Guardian, I Am Secure

Oh what security to know, my God is always guarding me.
I need have no fears, for He is with me, wherever I may be.
Through struggles, trials and heartbreak, His loving arms are always there.
Whenever I need confirmation, I can go to Him in prayer.
For with God as my guardian, I meet each day safe and secure.
I can overcome any problem, through my faith I shall endure.
Leaving all fears behind me, I can meet life's challenge squarely,
With God's love within me, those I encounter I shall treat fairly.

Now as I look about me I see many tasks that should be done,
With God on my side, I shall tackle them - my crusade has begun.
For God has given me special talents, which He wants me to use.
Just knowing He's my ally, there's no assignment I should refuse.
Oh, there are those frustrations, and I do stumble along the way.
Then God will lift me up again, help me to face another day.
He gives me courage to meet head on, the challenges I must face.
I feel His arms supporting me, and I'm surrounded by His grace.
                    Amen.

Sarah L. Shaw

Old Friends

They were just two old and lonely men, comforted in their age by a
    friendship as old as they were.
They played checkers in the park on one of those stone tables
    chased clouds from a park bench and fed popcorn to the squirrels every day.
As they sat together, or walked in the park, they relived the days of
    their youth...
        And smiled (with a tear) at the memories brought back.
Children sat at their feet to hear the tales, and brought them
    ice cream cones
    that melted down their weathered hands.
Where there was one, so was the other
    to help across busy streets,
    to listen and to share,
  to be ALIVE with,
        and to love as only old friends can love.

Jenni Walcher

Alzheimers

It takes your loved ones without warning
You can't stop it even with all the mourning
They are gone even though they are still alive
Some just want to die
My heart aches for her to be her own self
She is not rich, her family is her wealth
Thinking about the emptiness she will bring makes my heart bruised
She does not even know who I am, she is so confused.
I am not sure
If they will ever find a cure
I'm waiting for the news, when will it come?
The tears will start to fall when she is done.
Why did it have to take her, I do not understand
Who will take off of her cold finger, the old wedding band?

Laura Dawson

Reflections

I sit by the window, watching as the rain bounces and splashes against the windowpane.
I love the rain and the wind; the air fresh with the scent of a day without care.
A day to reflect, to feel peace from within. A day to reflect on how life might have been.
The choices we made seemed so right at the time. But, as we slow down
and expand our dimension; we often see other roads that may have deserved our attention.
So, a word of wisdom to share with our youth. As you grow and experience all life has to offer,
remember, the roads are well travelled in search of the truth.

Joyce A. Messina

The Blight

As a child, I remember seeing them, white bony fingers pointing upward
Like fleshless skeletons, grotesquely bent, they rose throughout the verdant tent,
Defiantly rooted, unmoving, almost arrogant.

Bleached spines against night sky's display
Downward darkening to ghoulish grey, in murky shadows...then fade away.
In hollow stillness they seemed to mock with mirth
At their own deaths, at life's quick clock...another's birth.

Those chestnut trees, are memories now, vague images of greatness in their own right.
Coarse-grained, henna-hued, their bodies sacrificed to form a million crafted sights;
Burr-lidded eyes, unseeing, once delicious, roasted sweet,
Palates of generations tempted...sated...replete.
  A legacy, only reminisced by elders, now,
  of strength, of life, which would not bow.

Sturdy giants, element shields, protectors strong,
  Nurturers, cradling innocents naive;
They, their progeny, for centuries stood long, then in an instant...
Gone,
Victims of a killer who would not leave.

Now others rise, proud and tall, amid the crowd,
Give life, then smugly wait the pall, their deadly shroud.

William S. Roberts

I Love

I love the dew wet grass - the morning sun.
The sky so blue and clear
The whisper of a breeze -
All sight, and sound familiar to my ear -
I love a shimmering web upon a shrub -
Leaves dancing on a tree -
The crunch of gravel 'neath my feet; all that I hear and see
I love the scent of new made bread, a fresh washed floor.
I love - Ah, yes! These things and many more
The rush of surf upon the sand
The birds on soaring wings -
The sound of music in the air - The glint of sun on blowing hair -
I love the gleam of light on a window pane as it says "hello" to me.
The trees, the flowers, the birds, the bees, all lovely things -
A rock - rivers rushing to the sea
I love the clasp of hands, a smile, a nod
The chatter of child, a sense of glad surprise.
For eyes, and ears, and senses I thank God
That he gave me the earth to trod - With Love

Naomi Greene

Dove Eagle

She stood atop a mountain, knowing how it happened;
that **she** had been born a bird of prey.

When hungry she'd take a meal,
being certain to thank The Great Spirit, for
providing her sustenance that day;
wasting nothing.

Not confused when confronting the reason for her existence,
for in this universe she'd always been aware, that for **her**
there was a place.
And with her power she never thought herself more noble,
than those upon which she preyed.

She remained steady in her purpose,
never doubting what that purpose was;
for she **chose** it.

She never questioned The Great Spirit (or his biding),
and found wondrous comfort in his love.
He'd always looked up her with favor, for deciding to be an eagle...
though she had **preferred**, to be a dove.

Consiwella R. Ray

Love

Love is not a word,
not a potion.
Love is a feeling,
a powerful emotion.
Love is true,
and never ending.
Love is open,
and never fending.
For love comes from the heart.

Adam Flagg

The Little Things

The little things in life
are the most precious things to me.
Like falling stars and rainbows
and sea shells from the sea.

Like unicorns and puppies
and babies, oh so new,
like waterfalls and mountains
and lakes so sparkling blue.

Like the sunshine and the moonlight
and the stars that shine above,
like poetry and letters
from someone that you love.

Like a new doll or truck
or a furry teddy bear,
like a buddy or a special friend,
whose secrets you do share.

Like a person who is cheerful,
and always wears a smile,
these precious little things in life
are what make it all worthwhile.

Laurie Mohl

A Look At The Future

Great Mother Earth
I must apologize
For my people
For my kind

You were once
A beautiful place
Full of green trees
Blue seas

Everything has changed
With withered trees
Toxic seas
Now deadly

Great Mother Earth
Forgive them
They were warned
But, would not believe

James A. Abraham

A Little Bowl Of Onion Soup

A little bowl of onion soup
On a sphere table is everything:
It's peace, love, and friendship.

A little bowl of onion soup
Is like a heart running through you.
It's like a shimmering, glittering,
Scaled sun growing inside you.

A little bowl of onion soup.

Rimma M. Pivovarov

World War II Veteran

A cigarette ash feathers
To the ground
Sitting paralyzed in your chair

There are many things
You had going in the past
Many things to live for
Many things to die for
Now you seem useless
Your heavy body wastes away

You don't want to live life like this
Would rather die with honor out at sea
You cannot hold out any longer
It's time to go

Vincent James Tula

Satan's Night Out

The red sun sets over the hills,
As the flickering light dwindles.
The shadows begin to consume,
And the darkness sets in.
The moon rises overhead,
And the night comes to life.
The eerie stars light the sky,
To show the dark path.
The bonfires blaze in eulogy,
To the demon's wicked dance.
All the furies of hell are released,
As his shadow emerges.
His rancid breath fills the night air,
His dark, black wings fill the night.
All the saints shrivel back,
In fear of his powerful wrath.
All his minions bow before him,
Gazing at his evil form.
The roses wither away in his sight,
Yes, oh, yes, this is Satan's night out.

Jackson Conner

Sunshine's Light

By the sunshine's light,
I raise my face up to the sky,
Pretending I'm a bird,
Imagining I can fly.

By the sunshine's light,
I feel the warmth on my skin.
Breathing in and out,
From deep within.

By the sunshine's light,
Wishing for my deepest fantasy.
Dreaming of pure peace,
And sweet ecstasy.

By the sunshines light,
Bring peace to my mind.
Wanting the happiness,
Of all mankind.

Melissa Wyatt

Hudson River Dawn

Just inches away from the surface
Afraid to break the ice
Tip-toeing gently across the river
Draping a curtain in front of the trees
Lifting cautiously to reach the sun
Being blown around by the furious wind
The fog rises

Catherine Elizabeth Benton

Lord I Thank You

Lord I thank you...for being my closest and best friend
No matter what I'm going through, you're always there until the end
You told me to cast all of my problems on your shoulders to bear
And no matter what time or place you would always be there.

Lord I thank you...for not giving up on me when I gave up on myself
You could've easily cast me off or placed me on a closet shelf
You showed me many signs that you were still present in my life
Waiting patiently on me to call on you to relieve me of my strife.

Lord I thank you...for the sacrifice of your life on Mt. Calvary
To unselfishly put your life on the line so I could be set free
Then on the 3rd day you rose and from hell you took life's eternal key
So that all of your saints could live in heaven in perfect harmony.

I'm glad, oh heavenly father, that I've given my life to you again
For no one in this world can be as close to me as you can
I promise you I'll try to live by your word and help others to see your truth
For being my maker, creator and my comforter...Lord I thank you.

Sherman A. Trueheart

Snow Kiss

When the golden moon hung much too low,
glowing on the fresh fallen winter snow.
The stars seem to have fallen without a sound,
they lay like diamonds on the ground.
Winter has a beauty that is sometimes hard to see,
like your love you have carefully hidden away from me.
But I believe somewhere beneath all the cold sparkle of winter snow,
our love like a snow kissed rose will grow.

Sandra E. Sager

Didn't You?

"Didn't............ .... You?"
Didn't you think you had finally found the chosen one;
those times when your emotions reached for nonexistent peaks,
and just to hear that musical voice accelerated the pulse of your heart's beat?

Didn't you think there couldn't be an end,
even though you had given your heart to the only one whom you called dearest friend?

Didn't you taste your tears when love was time and miles away,
and all you longed for was to have it near even for a minute of a day?

Didn't you think of all the others; this was the best,
sand wondered if it was for experience or a waste of time with all the rest?

Didn't you think there was no going back to love's hate
because in this relation you had hope and faith?

Didn't you wish in your mind that this was
the last fall of love for one last time?

Well I have.
Did You?

Delroy Duckworth

You

There are times when I fall, and I see my life falling apart. But you are always there to catch the pieces. There's no way to show you what that means to me. I don't always know why I act the way I do. Sometimes I act like I don't care because I don't want to admit I was wrong. But even then you stand by my side leading and guiding me. You show me my mistakes, but never hold them against me. Some nights I'll lay there and ask myself why would you bother. Because many times I say the wrong thing, or will make the same mistake. I can't understand how you can stand that. I know many times I've caused you frustration, and a door some dents. But you still stay by me. I can only hope that someday I may have that same patience and understanding. And maybe, someday, we'll help each other overcome problems, together.

Jennifer Duncan

Stillborn

I carried you in hope the long nine months of my term
remembered that close hour when we made you, often felt you
kick and move as slowly you grew within me, wondered what you
would look like when your wet head emerged girl or boy, and
at what glad moment I should hear your birth cry and I
welcoming you with all you needed of warmth and food, we had
a home waiting for you.

After my strong laborings, sweat cold on my limbs, my
small cries merging with the summer air. You came you did not
cry, you did not breathe we had not expected this it seems
your birth had no meaning or had you rejected us? They will
say that you did not live, register you as a stillborn.

You lived for me all that time in the dark chamber of my
womb and when I think of you now perfect in your little death
I know that for me you were born still, I shall carry you
with me forever, my child you were always mine. You are mine now!

Life and death are the same! (Mysteries)

Tina Anthony

I Walk Alone

Walk down these city streets, walk on these two legs
these two suspicious feet, I camouflage my head
no appetite for danger, walk on with a good man's song
Reflection in the store front glass says, again I walk alone
These streets are full of giants, who see themselves as bums
I toast to their ancient rite, I just mite walk all night.
"No pleasure in this business", I heard somebody cry
She charged him twenty dollars, but it cost him his life
She loves the faded billboards, and those abandoned homes
the sweet sound of sirens, she loves to walk alone
The policeman's horse is nervous, the butchers puzzled face
the smell of rotting talent, I really love this place.
So many people touched your cement impressions, now they're wearing down
And all those people with their good intentions, they're always hanging
'round you see them hanging around, they'll always be there dragging you down

On down around the corner in the crucible of pain
just like his dad before him, some things will never change
he's funny out of patient's, running out of time.
Run down these paths of glory beneath these neon signs
He's got to run alone

Kimberly Frederick

Robert D. Ronco

The Spark Of Life

Does mere mortal man
think that the could have a hand,
to create, or give soul life to another man?
Then what arrogance! Man could never do this by his device;
Only God can impute the Spark Of Life.

A woman gives birth, but does not give life,
for only biological life resides in the womb,
of the same chemicals found in the soil.
Only at that moment of birth, when the first cry is heard,
did God breathe into them the 'spark of life' to each person ever born!

Adam was only biological life made from the chemicals of soil,
then God breathed into Adam the spark of life;
and he become a living soul
from dust we have come, and to dust we return, says the word of God.

No one can take life out of the soul not even God Himself!
The soul lives on to be with God, or resides in hell itself-

But, God made provision for every soul, a chance to live with Himself -
to come from spiritual death, to spiritual life - a chance,
to be born again through personal faith in Jesus Christ.

Clara Broussard

Painful Prayers

I pray to the stars every night,
To bring you back you me.
But my prayers are never answered
I was foolish to believe.
Your heart belongs to someone else.
I am no longer apart of you.
When you glance into her eyes,
I hope you see a piece of me too.
Looking at an old picture,
I remember how we use to be.
We looked so happy and in love,
As you were holding me.
Now all of that has changed
And we have gone our separate ways.
I wish you all the happiness in life,
No matter where you are.
I, myself, will keep praying every night
Until I find that lucky star.

Tina Robles

She

She breathes an air of solitude
Of shattered, sunken bliss
And those before
Felt love unsure
In her january kiss.

She bears the brunt of reprimands
The sting of north wind stares
When for their books
And fresh-cut looks
Her heart can give no care.

But when their barbs and insolence
Do pierce her armored hull
She flees the night
And holds me tight
And lets burn forth her soul.

Peter Lynch

Bailey's Flight

She is an elusive butterfly within a
flux of life...the sun, moon and stars
all within her reach.

Giving her approbation to the sonorous
bellow of silence...insouciance is
her path to peace.

Like an astral beckoning, the melody
of air passing her wings soothes her,
a shield to the obverse.

She must fly, for we know the butterfly
....is friable.

Cheryl Ann Dietzel-Baldwin

What A Price To Pay

This should be heaven
and yet it feels like hell

Like a snake in the garden
the tree shook, the apple fell

What a price we have paid
for all of this wealth

We have everything we wanted
and yet nothing at all

We took paradise
out of spring, we made fall

Brian Moran

Incarnate From Dreams

Incarnate from dreams
Comes beautiful things
Fluttering out of your heart
As if on angels' wings

How many of us have felt before
The urge for sudden expression
To show either overwhelming happiness
Or deep solitary depression

Whether it be music of passion
Or literature of the soul
It grips you from the inside
And makes you lose control

For it doesn't matter what time of day
The creator in you beams
Because all things are
Incarnate from he who dreams

Jennifer Henning

The Walls

They hear your laughter
They watch you cry
They feel your pain
And understand your sigh.

They encompass your joy
They know your fears
They hold your loneliness
And see your tears.

They know your weakness
They watch you alone
They hear your silence
And know you are strong.

They hear your prayers
And see your hope
They keep you safe
And know you will cope.

They hold your secrets
And know you well
If these walls could talk
What would they tell?

Deloris Brownlow

Traffic Report

Come out if you're in there,
stay in if you're not.
The brighter I burn,
the darker it gets.

If you wish I was gone,
just say so, I'll leave,
but do things disappear
when it's too dark to see?

Darkness just hides it,
unless there is light,
which also may hide it
when painfully bright.

Heat is my purpose,
but I produce light.
I cannot lay low
to increase my own height.

A vault holds the key
to its own rugged locks,
an endeavor to end
an endless paradox.

J. T. Bushnell

Un-Holy Dominance

Your image took form in the garden,
for my own I search in vain.
The Un-Holy seed I sow not.
I am the gender low and plain.

With rage that splinters and perils my flesh,
I can not moan for my mouth is full of gall
that curdles in my bowels. There is no escape.

My crowning glory is but smoldering wool.
A stench that flares my nostrils and fills my lungs,
as beauty and virtue lay spent.

Eyes flashing darts of molten flames fanned by your dominance.
The feet are weary for they cannot be still,
shod in time long forgotten.

You travailed not in pain as I was born from your side.
Only in the barren maiden is found no guile, for she does not give
birth. I perpetuate this un-equal scheme.

Forbidden passion warm and sweet like nectar you have found,
with dominance over me destined to make you King.
I remain
The gender low and plain.

Glenda J. Moseley

Beyond The Heaven

On the wings of Angels, have I been swept away.
I feel a sudden rush of wind upon my face. As if my breath has been taken away.
My heart is pounding loud as the blood rushes in my veins.
My breathing has become very strained. As I lay prostrate before the King.

There is the sound of music, sounds I cannot trace, as if
a thousand violins were all in place. This sweet sound fills the air,
I've never heard a sound that can quite compare.

There is a bright light such as one I've never seen, glowing in this
place that smells like spring. So sweet is this fragrance it makes you
want to sing. Rise up rise up and dance for the King. The singing
is so sweet it sounds like a crystal spring, bubbling in the mountains
as the birds joyfully sing, rise up rise up dance for the King.

My chest feels heavy as my heart beats loud, I hear the sound
of drum beats coming from the clouds. Rise up, rise up and dance
for the King. The music wraps around me as I began to swing,
twirling, leaping and bowing with such delight, as a feather taken
in flight. Chiffon of many colors is my covering. Tiny little wings
so crystal clear, begin to flutter as I take to the air. Arms outstretch
as I curtsey low, so shy and humbled as I start real slow.

My eyes are closed, as I listen to the sounds, I hear the sounds of
tum-tum coming from the clouds. The singing of the Angels soft and
clear as the sweet sound of violins caresses my ear, and I know
without a doubt I have nothing to fear. When I hear the angels'
voices saying rise up, rise up the time is near. When suddenly I am awakened
to find this was all a dream, but never shall I forget how I danced before the king.

Carrie Johnson

Angel At My Door

Angel knocking at my door, looking in just like before, like
a spirit in the wind, thought I would never see her again.

Angel walking up to me, I look into her eyes and see, God
sent her to me long ago, and like a fool I let her go.

Angel standing near to me, I look into her eyes and see, a
time when spirits danced with me, and love, a burning desire in me.

Angel reaching for a hug, a warm embrace sent from above, all
my fears, they disappear, Angel! Angel! Won't you stay? And with
that thought, she went away.

Angel knocking at my door, not the way it was before, for she
surrounds me in my heart, and now I know we will never part.

Tobin R. Burnett

Sunlit Walk

Early morning sunlit walk
Tall green towers shade us
Grayish, brown bushy tails scamper up and down trunks coated with bark
Enchanting birds of song
Sun disintegrating early mist slowly.

A mystical river me meet!
Sun tries to find its way through thick trees and dried up morning dew
Mystical river wears her coat of morning mist
A small boat afloat, holding two fishermen
On her banks, a young boy sits — blends with natural beauty.

We move on hand in hand with our sunlit walk
Cozy homes line country streets along with velvet green, tall maple and pine

I'm lost in nature and enveloped by love
Small meaningful talk, content silence
Eyes savor every look of beauty

Sunlit walk with love
A morning never felt or looked more beautiful
A day that began so right from birth
It was natural beauty that blessed us let us walk forever on sunlit walk

Rita Mattioli

(This poem is a corrected version of "Sunlit Walk," which originally appeared in the anthology Whispers at Dusk. *The National Library of Poetry apologizes for our previous error.)*

Prelude To The Anti Christ

Son of satan, God of darkness; welcome to our world:
It has laboured 6000 years to bring forth what is unfurled.
Socio-economic religion is poised precariously upon the edge of chaos;
And the geo-political landscape is a powder keg to bias.
Our neo-Nazi/gestapo leaders are preparing for revolution;
While our new world order nature loving zealots are advocating
Evolution.
Dictators and despots all, dehumanizing society.
Forging chains and laying traps compromise our piety.
Pride, avarice, and selfishness abound;
While truth, mercy, and justice cannot be found.
To capture and create utopia is only an illusion;
But all of this foolishness and nonsense leave but one conclusion.
That all of life exists but for one reason;
It is God above designed it for our faith to be tested;
To use it wisely as he intended; or foolishly; life wasted.
The paths are ours; he will not interfere;
The choices be great, but not always clear.
To follow his son through the tomb to the light;
Or the God of anarchy, death, and eternal night.

Noel M. Helligso

The Primate Genesis

Small undulating waves for unrecorded ages brushed the shore.
In the briny deep, in silence, life began and what was, is no more.
Sprang not we a total whole. A roaring crest dropped a creature form.
Dropped we were with no concern. In this manner, we were born.

Prim Tiberi

The Dark

The shadow breezes and flowing light across the sky as it goes dark,
The air smells so fresh it tickles your nose until you laugh,
One single star is an eye-full and turns a red glow in your cheeks,
Then you go barefoot and the ground is cold and hard,
It makes you smile and gives you a shiver up your spine,
So when the sun goes down notice all these things,
The things that give you a feeling of joy and laughter,
Then you will know that it is only the dark.

Denise Beahrs

Slumber's Sleep

As I sleep,
in slumber's sleep.
I dream of you,
who's heart I keep.

'Till tomorrow,
another day.
Different than,
it was today.

Our love might grow,
and never stray.
This I dream,
as I lay.

I wonder if,
this dream you see.
As you sleep,
in slumber's sleep?

Larry D. Hanson

Feelings

Someday when I get the courage
I'll tell you what is in my heart,
I hope it will draw us closer
And not drive us far apart.
Although I've said to you many times
That our friendship will never end,
The feelings that I have for you
Are much more than just a friend.
I once told you in a poem that
I'd protect you from all harm,
But what I really what to do
Is hold you in my arms.
I've said you're that special someone
An important lady in my life,
If things for me were different
I would seek you for my wife.
Everything that I have said here
Please believe me it's all true,
Now the one thing I have not told
You yet, is that I do love you.

David Pike

We'll Always Love Thee Emily

It was nine months ago.
We felt you start to grow.

The time we had together.
Sweet child of ours forever.

So perfect in every way.
Even though it was for one day.

Emily of ours we pray.
God will take care of you today.

Although we must be apart.
You shall stay with us in our heart.

For you are loved by one and all.
Our most darling little doll.

It's not good bye forever.
We'll be some day together.

Our sweet child O' Emily.
Will always be our fondest memory.

Karean L. Chapman

Red Rock Hill

Waves of yellow grass
Blow in the wind
As the sun beats down
Upon the red granite.

A cricket hops from the grass
Followed by a snapping dog
And the sun beats down.

The sun sets slowly
In the west
The red rocks glow
Reflecting the light.

The wind moves slowly
Through the trees
And the sun has gone to sleep.

Erica Hulstrom

Emily And Grandpa

A child
more specifically the baby
is so incredibly interested,
eyes completely open!
Senses curious
excited
and overwhelmed
colors,
every touch brand new,
textures and tastes...

The old man sits easily.
Reading,
transplanting,
under the ancient redwood tree.
uninterested
unimpressed.
Content and unmoved,
possessing all of the knowledge
the wisest one.

J. T. Shamshoian

Slosh From The Soul

Ever to know
the color of a kiss,
is to taste the light of being;

impressive
is the contour of the mind,
that which vanquishes
disdain and depression.
Christ! Is it true?
Christ! Is it in you?
My God! that is what is called
in the throes, but never
when it's real.
When it's real,
only three words
from me to you.

Jason R. Garner

I Am

I am laughter without joy.
I am sorrow without tears.
I am who I am because of what I am.
I am enclosed behind the doors of time
With only the light through the keyhole
As my hope, yet
I am.

Ray M. Lee

Miss Winter

Miss Winter upon the land, you hath pulled me from
summer's hand. From the harshness of her heat, that moved me
toward retreat. For in my days of mourning, my mortal did she
beat. She wore a cheerful mirth, as my beloved returned to earth.
Now you covereth her so bright, with your crystal blankets white.
Yea, I once stood tall and then, that mighty fall. But during all
that grief in you I'd find relief.
Miss Winter, you beautician, you've cured that bad
condition. I no more feel the heat, that laughed at my defeat.
For you I feel such trust, as silently you dust with your
powdered flakes, that the spring will take. And decorate the icing on the frozen lake.
Miss Winter, how do you make such light, upon the darkened
night? As you cap the crowning glory of every single tree. And
bring such awesome beauty of the sight of me. How heavenly your
snow, as you make the rooftops glow. All so beautiful and white,
all the day and night. As you hold my hand so tight. So gone is
all my fear, and to me you're very dear.

Augustus Rolfe Garton III

Untitled

This table top of life at which I sat beneath it the leg SNAPS!
On top, all that which stood, come crashing down,
Crashing down to the marble ground.
The glass which held my joy, breaks into a million pieces.
How ever shall I repair it?
Look deep into my eyes, the windows of what's within.
You'll see the pain which has swallowed me, smothering my soul.
I no longer cry for I feel as though I've died.
See you any hope here? No!
Only one small thread to which I cling, with every last strength within.
My child, don't ever leave, don't ever disappoint me.
For if that last thread breaks, I have only one choice.
To fall into that eternal hole of death from which there is no escape.
For at this moment in time,
Your love is all that holds together this heart of mine.

Tina Louise Partridge

Sing It Again

Sing it again
I remember asking my mother as a young child
and no matter how many times I've heard the song
I'd have to ask her to sing it again.
She sings to my ear
the beautiful melody that tells me she understands me.
She sings from my heart
the comforting hum lets me know she has felt my pain.
She sings about my heart
as glory day stories have me tapping my feet
and remind me of her youth.
She sings of God's beauty as I have witnessed
endless skies opulent with stars
and full moons and of crimson skies at dusk,
She knows what's in my heart
because she told me before I got a chance to tell her.
She sings for me because I have yet to learn how to
carry a tune like my mother.
One day I will pleasure the wonderful feeling of hearing my
own daughter ask me to sing it again.

Denise Parks

Untitled

Memories flash before your eyes; dark shades of red;
The distance screams of agony; all the tears you've shed.
The pain you suffered all comes back; the hatred you've felt inside;
Tears your heart into two as you remember what it was like.
To of lived a life full of darkness; no hope left in your soul;
With thought of never recovering; now only memories that you hold.

Tracy Bulaich

"My Precious Girl"

There could never be a happier time, than the day I gave you life
Your first breath, your first cry, the way you would stare at me late at night
The promises I made to protect you, and to always do right
Though I admit I did wrong that warm summer night
I took you away from your father when you had no choice or clue
I thought you were young enough, I never meant to hurt you
Please believe how sorry I am and that I used all of my strength to bring him back again
But his heart is now belonging to someone new
It's a choice he has made, "I will never leave you."
Don't get me wrong, your father does love you with all of his heart
It's from me whom he wants to be apart
So I will do my best to help you grow and to teach you in every possible way
My love for you grows more and more, with every passing day
And I know one day when you grow up, you are going to ask me why
I will be there to answer you and to hold you if you cry
I swear to you, Crystal, my precious girl, I will never leave your side
As long as I have life in me, yet even after I have died
And with this I promise to do my best as your mother as well as your father
Because there is no greater love, than the love between a mother and her daughter.

Teresa A. Storey

Out Of The Darkness

Blue sky turns to red, colors of fire light the sky.
Watch as the fire begins to die, dull colors take their place.
The canopy of night is drawn, the stars soon come into view.
Stars that shine like night lights to keep the darkness out.
Out of the darkness, strangers, You and I.
You with a smile that made me feel welcome.
A shining star, you stood there.
I was in the dark, scared and unsure, you took my hand and knew
    exactly what to do.
You helped me find my way when I was lost in the dark.
You shone bright like a single spark.
I could see you standing there, someone on whom I depend.
    Florence, You are my best friend.
You always had the right thing to say, when I was having a bad day.
I knew you would always be there, never to question, just that you care.
Now the darkness begins to fade, bright colors of the day take their place.
A blue canopy is drawn across the sky, the sun comes into view.
Together we found our way out of the darkness.
Together, as Friends, we face the new day.

Susan M. Smith

Memories Of A Childhood

It seems like yesterday
my sister and I alone at play
unfortunately those days I can't regain
some memories of happiness and some of pain
I remember playing until my legs couldn't walk
but somehow in our beds we found time to talk
we would play children's games like animals in my bed
when at the same time I tried to erase horrible memories in my head
I can never replace my innocence lost
if I could I'd do it at any cost
we've had many experiences together and apart
as long as I live there will always be a special
place for her in my heart
as the years go by and I look back on my life
one of the fondest memories is seeing my sister as a
mother and a wife
I'm not too foolish to write this and pretend
my life on this earth will someday end
but as my body is laid to rest my memories will be held
tightly, as my hands lay across my chest.....

Greg Hawkins

Secrets

There isn't anything that can say,
what a single secret may.
It isn't that hard to keep,
through there are promises to meet!

Come and tell me,
your secrets, let me see.
Don't hide them behind,
let them be free from your mind!

All that is spoken,
will be kept not broken.
A trust that we obtain,
From knowing each other's pain!

Why has the world been,
so evil like sin.
The experience we've had,
they're really not so very bad!

The surroundings are diminished,
but are they yet finished.
Oh please let us decide,
the fate of all human kind!

Ran Tao

The Rose

I sit on a rock
I am dreaming about someone or
something
It's not often that I dream

While I sit on the rock
I see a rose
Growing between two weeds

The sky is clear, the sun is shining
And the rose is still standing
It's struggling to survive

When I come back to the next day
The two weeds are dead
But the rose is alive

It overcame the sadness of the weeds

Austin C. Eddington

How You Don't Know

Oh, how you don't know
Don't know what you've lost,
You let it go
But baby at what cost,
To be with your friends
And party all night,
But think who is there
When you're not all right.

Oh, how you don't know
But I'm moving on,
To find someone who loves me
To make my life fun.

Oh, how you don't know
You had your chance,
But now is my turn
To have fun and dance,
Maybe if you'd accepted
To be a man grown,
But no sense in reminiscing
On what you should have known.

Janet Vera

Mirror

Heaven, Heaven! Face the martyr.
Angel, angel! Read the challenge.
Cupid, cupid! Answer the question.
  Why.
Question the answer. Devil, devil!
Challenge the read. Demon, demon!
Martyr the face. Hell, Hell!
    I.

And thus the Angel speaks,
I am but he
Whom I see
To be
Me
Whom he
Will decree
I am but me
And thus the Devil spoke.
    Todd Chang

Eyes Of A Child - March 4, 1992

In the eyes of child
Is a world of wonder
Where all is good and right
There is no pain
There is no hunger
There is no black and white

When someone enters
This world of love
And brings to it abuse and gloom
An innocent child
Full of joy and purity
Fills with fear of impending doom

God bless the children
With all your glory
And protect them from the battering wild
God damn the guilty
With all your fury
By giving them eyes of an abused child.
    Stuart Merrill

The Race

People moving all in time
People standing still in line
People walk on crowded streets
Soldiers marching to the beat
"What's the hurry?" People say
"Have to go I just can't stay"

Pressure mounting
Money counting
Have to hurry
Lots of worry
'Must make hay'
'Got bills to pay'

Can't stop
Won't drop
Yes
No.
Gotta
Go.

    Stephanie Lewis

Recalling One's Memorable Experiences

Remembering the times of life and all of living there,
Learning good will overcome within us everywhere.

Seeing light that makes one smile and feeling very free,
Knowing all the beauty near displaying endlessly.

Recall the children in their play and treat them all with care;
To trust the past and joy it brings may so fine we fare.

The hills and plains are picturesque; they fill the soul with glee;
The minds of young that prosper far and growing like a tree.

Hear the wind and feel the air with all the songs they bring,
Take time long to flowers see and hear the robin sing.

Give the good with friendship's heart to all join in with you,
Remembering the times of life and learning through and through.
    Randal R. Rossow

Seeds Of The Sun

The apricot tree planter, searching through time and space,
found a uniquely fitting place
to sow - seeds of the sun.

Where mountain meadows descend
to a raucous river's bend
took root - seeds of the sun.

Under the influence of warm winds from the sea
branches burst toward the sun, as into a handsome tree
became - seeds of the sun.

From bark of dark maroon, sprout new growth spurs
befitting strings of pale pink flowers
for - seeds of the sun.

Early spring sees a thousand blooms as honey, black and bumblebee
buzzing among blossoms, fulfill their destiny
to enhance - seeds of the sun.

The faded flower gives way to golden fruit with a blush rosy red
as the heat of the sun, like a baker bakes bread,
forms - seeds of the sun.
    Vincent S. Amadeo

I'm Gonna Try

Troy, a guitar picker with quick fingers, and a winning way
fell ill and didn't show up for rehearsal one day
I overheard a conversation as I was passing by,
one man said, "you gonna take Ole Troy's place?"
The other man answered, "well I'm gonna try,
I just don't know why Ole Troy had to die."

And try he did with all his heart, As we watched we breathed a sigh.
He really brought true meaning to the words "I'm gonna try."
I couldn't keep from thinking, as I went on my way,
that's the way people should strive to be each and every day.
How many dreams and goals are lost, just left to die,
or destinations never reached, because we didn't try?

Make a promise to yourself not to toss your dreams aside.
I'll never say, "I can't do that" you can bet I'm gonna try...
try to be a better person to everyone I meet,
whether they're from a far off land, or a neighbor on our street.
So when this life has ended, and I'm at the pearly gate up in the sky,
St. Peter will ask me, "Are you coming in here?" I'll answer, "I'm gonna try."
    Lovel L. Rogers

Paradox

I am part of existence. But what is existence?
I have been through time. But what is time?
Time seems to be a never ending existence.
Existence seems to be an infinite amount of time.
Therefore, time and existence are one and the same.
For as long as either have been, they have always gone hand in hand.
How can one escape existence? Death and birth are
the only doorways in and out, but then one would escape
from time as well. If one wished to escape time,
and not existence, then that one would be forced to,
remain in time and existence, or sacrifice existence to escape time.
Therefore, it is impossible to escape one
without escaping the other.
The universe is their child, for without time or existence,
The universe could not be part of an ever growing continuum.
How did time and existence come to be?
That question will be forever unanswered.

Brad Scalise

Guardian Angels

　　Guardian angels who art above I pray that the
Lord allows you to hear my plea.
　　My plea for help in time of need, my plea for mercy
in a time of despair, my plea for courage in a time of danger.
　　To guardian angels who live among us here on earth whether
you're a friend, neighbor or kindly stranger to say a kind word,
to lend a hand or to give a hug when needed.
　　To guardian angels that are sometimes overlooked; the pets that
we love so much: some maybe trained others may only rely on
instinct and the love that they have for their master.
　　Guardian angels can take many shapes and forms...they can be
unexplained coincidence or events that we as people can not understand.
I believe that they are here to help us regardless.
　　And I appreciate their assistance in my life. I believe them to
be a blessing that the Lord bestowed upon us.

Tracy L. Sturgill

What May Become

One special night I wished upon a star and hoped someone
　　would hear and come to me from afar.

I gazed into the black of night brightened only by a star's twinkling light.
There I lie in my bed a million thoughts rushing through my head...
　　wanting someone to call my own; someone to make sure that I will
　　never be alone... someone to trust till they lay me down
　　to rest... someone to love me and put my love to the test...
　　someone to believe in me through the good times and the bad...
　　someone to remember with me all the joy we've had.

And now I look upon that very star that has granted my wish
　　and brought you to me from afar, I tell you of my experience,
　　to use your wish with wisdom because whatever you wish for
　　may someday become...

Robyn N. Heming

Vision

　　Moment by moment times seen to slip away, day by day reality closes
in on me like a wave of emotions tearing at the very fabric of my
being! Inch by inch I feel you closing in on me, but I don't even
recognize you I don't even know your name! But you're there! I can
even smell the sweet fragrance of your body as it hypnotize my mind
taking complete control of my senses, leaving me in a complete stage
of ecstasy! You're there I know it! I see your eyes, I see your
face! But you're still a mystery to me! How can a human being be in
love with a vision, I've ask myself that question a thousand times!
still it true! I love you!

James Smith

The Other Side

I have walked amid the flowers
And of thorns I've had a few
I have seen the seasons in and out
And the sweet and sour too

Take heed my beloved children
Weep for me no more
I've gone to see the sunset
Just beyond heaven's door

William Smith

Life's Clock

The clock of life is wound but once,
And no man has the power
to tell just when the hands will stop,
at late or early hour.

To lose one's wealth is sad indeed
To lose one's health is more
To lose one's soul is such a loss
As no man can restore.

The present Only is our own
Live, love, toil with a will.
Place no faith in "tomorrow".
For the clock may then be still.

Tim Ebert

Loneliness

The candle melts
and slowly dies.
The darkness comes,
blackening skies.
The wind blows cold
and chills the heart.
The loneliness
tears me apart.
A friend who loves,
a foe deceives,
a chilling pinch
my heart receives.
And so I bleed,
so red, so warm.
Ne'er no more
may no one harm.

Jennifer Cooper

Fantasy Land

In my fantasy land you can
fly and play and do just about
anything you want to do and not
do what you don't want to do

To get to my fantasy land
you have to go to the big oak
in the corner of the park and
climb through the giant knot hole

I'll bring into this fantastic
place my imagination and
my inner child to have fun
and maybe I'll let you come too

I'll leave the hate and pollution
behind and all my worries also
when I come to my magical
land to this place of enchantment

Daniel Holmberg

A Night Of Tears

Misty skies,
passionate eyes,
thoughts of twilights passed.
Absence of light,
Stars explode in the night,
dreamy shadows are cast.

Stardust sweeps,
a lover weeps,
as she lies alone.
She only loves he,
he doesn't love she,
two destinies unknown.

So love come as it may,
and as dawn turns to day,
she slumbers and ceases her tears.
Though the night seamed so long,
her heart shall stay strong,
'til someday a true love appears.

Marilyn Segar

United Souls

You and I
God and Children
Beauty and Nature
are all United

Our love
My heart bonded
to yours, together
we connected and
became one

United in our love
My heart to yours
yours to mine
We still forever and
always be
United Souls.

The beauty of Life
The knowledge of Love
The beautiful feeling
of being whole makes
You and I, Us United Souls

Cynthia St. Clair

Sickle Cell

When I think about diseases
    that can kill

I only knows, how it makes me ill
    to read about, certain ones

Sometimes I thank, What have I done
    to endure, such a disease

In the worst way, no I'm not please
But God knows, time want be long
He'll take me to, that Heavenly home
But its sad, when I hear
People, so young and very dear, who
have gone on, without knowing,
that Gods Love, is always glowing
Yes, he loves us all , that is true, so
don't leave this world, being subdued
God loves you, keep the Faith,
you'll find, that we all need
to come unto his grace
yes we all
Need to come, unto his grace

Laurie S. Hurt

Shades

Color! Delightful iridescence. Charmer of senses.
Prime nourisher of life's beauty!
How unfortunate, then, to utilize color for segregation, to violate, to demean.

People, many colors, ever so articulated;
White, brown, black, yellow, red?
Sole use of each extols blinded fallacy
Red, black, white, yellow, brown -
All not related? Just like you and me?
What nonsense. Explain this varied brew!
Not nonsense - when described in terms of hue.
Neath a kaleidoscope of iridescent ground
Lies there a basic, all us encompassing brown.
Clear determination, a melding of kin.
Neath it all same colors for skin.

Why blinded by barriers, staunch, yet superficial,
When substance gives the greys of browns, so beneficial!
Brothers and sisters just under the skin?
No! Over and under as always we have been.
Color barriers? Not out there as truths we can find
But deep in here. Here! In deluded recesses of polluted minds!

John Paizis

The Day I Fell In Love

The breeze blew through the autumn leaves as we rolled along the
trail, I swept my gaze across the park and back to the river rail.

I noticed children playing games, while the gentry strolled along, saw
frisky squirrels climbing trees, and flitting birds caught up in song.

But the finest work of God's own hand that I noticed on that day,
was the gal in the purple shorts, ('specially when she moved that way).

She raced along on rollerblades, coaxing me to do the same,
but all I saw were awesome legs, (man, what a beautiful dame)!

"Please take the lead, I'll watch your form" she said her innocent
way, "No that's fine, I'll stay here behind, I'll learn by watching you" I say.

Later we shared a lazy meal on a windswept patio bar,
I marvelled at the way she talked, I really liked this girl thus far.

Her words portrayed a loving heart, I mused as we ate and talked,
I liked her laugh and gracious air, (and I loved the way she walked).

Later that night when on my knees, I prayed aloud to God above "Lord,
let this be the one for me and fill her heart, for me, with love."

I guess you know the story told is true in every part,
For the lady I describe above, has forever won my heart.

Now in my nightly prayers I pray, "thank you Lord in ev'ry way,"
for when I fell in love with her, in purple shorts, that autumn day.

Wade T. Myers

Safe Harbor

Darkness surrounded her, its inky black cocoon cold and unforgiving
The fear, its icy tendrils pulling at her, numbing her strength to go on living
Alone, she sank deeper, no buoy in sight.

Her memory, hazy in the fathoms, recalled images of light, color
and sound: photographic wishes sadly swimming to the surface,
reaching for a tow to firm solid ground
Her mind cried for safe harbor, with all of its might.

Twirling and swaying in the eddying depths, the fluttering senses inched upwards
Spiraling slowly, lazily gliding, stretching functions long smothered
Her foe, the deep shadows, found friend with the light.

Foghorns in the distance, steady, reassuring sound
Love, like a lighthouse, standing firm on the shore,
Guiding home the lost swimmer with beckoning warmth
Radiant light that encircles, sheltering from harm,
Brought her into safe harbor, her sanity found.

Paula O'Driscoll

Mama

Just one year has passed since you've been gone,
yet, in our hearts it seems so long.
We've missed you, oh so very much,
your jolly laugh, your gentle touch.
There's not one day passes by
that we don't gaze on heavenly skies.
What are you doing, Mama, in your home up above?
Are you singing? Are you dancing? Are you sharing with those you loved?
Did you bring them up to date on all that had gone on?
Did you give them all the scoop on your daughters and your son?
Did you give our love to Daddy — Nana and Papa too?
And tell them that we missed them just like we now miss you?
I know that if we could have our choice to have you back again,
We wouldn't ask a loving God back to this earth to send.
In our hearts and minds we know we joy you now possess
Your life on earth is over — you've entered heaven's blessed.
How could we even think to ask our Lord for your return
Instead our hearts watch and wait for Heaven is what we yearn.

Brenda Knight

Majesty

I sit and watch with wonder as mighty trees bend low
Watching in great reverence God's majestic show,
I hear the thunder rolling as I watch the birds fly by
I feel such awed amazement as lightning brights the sky,
There's nothing like a thunderstorm to make God's power known,
As I sit safe inside myself he speaks to me alone,
It puzzles me as I often think of other people's fears
What I consider beautiful as rain falls down like tears,
It washes clean our spirits and opens up our eyes
It cleanses us from sinful ways that we might lead better lives,
If you stop and think about the storm you then can understand,
We're sheltered in his loving heart and in His mighty hands,
Next time you hear the thunder roll and lightning brights the sky,
Remember He is sharing His beauty in disguise.

Dinah Sapp

Angels

Angels; so say the legends, take rise from man's own innocence
To bring hope to those in suffering; to assure us one more chance.
Artists paint them as infants, skin alabaster white;
A halo wreathed around their heads, to guide us in the night.
Tiny, winged cherubs with eyes like heaven's blue;
Floating up among the clouds; keeping watch o'er me and you.
Poets also see them, as white-clad, winged youths
Always close and ready to help us find our truths.
And though the images they instill bespeak of gossamery splendor
We know that other shapes evolve to fill the eyes and mind with wonder.
For it could be the fireman groping through the smoky gloom
Beheld in the eyes of a toddler as he enters her flaming room.
Or perhaps it is the trooper to a mother - soon to be
As on some lonely country road, as he helps her delivery.
It could well be your neighbor, the grocery clerk or doctors nurse
Or perhaps the boy who found, returned the ladies misplaced purse.
So you see, an angel needs not wings, or gowns pure white as snow
'Tis in the eye of the beholder that gives them Angel's glow.

Donald H. Peeples Sr.

A Blooming Rose

The heart is like a blooming rod, red rose
If your heart loves or is loved by another a rose will begin to bloom.
No matter how much the plant around it grows the single red, red
rose will stay in perfect bloom because of the love inside of it.
Unless you are unfaithful to the greatest gift of all, love, that was bestowed upon your heart.
When you are unfaithful the bloom will begin to wilt inside and then
after many years the rose will completely turn to stone if you are without love.
Till you are with another true love, again, you will have a cold stone heart secretly.
No matter how pure your heart may seem.

Sarah Hysell

A Future?

A swell in the current
of life's simple storm
my world might go away.

I'm walking the night alone
searching in the darkness
for the road that lights the way.

Many false impressions
as hope closes near
I guess a tragic end is close.

Angels all around me
But still I can't sleep
All the pain still keeps me alone.

Tomorrow will be brighter
I truly hope I'm right.
This world can't only say, "You die!"

I will somehow survive
Having dreams to accomplish
I only need to find my wings to fly.

Ernest C. Harper II

Bleached Fools

Killed corn
Killed chickens
Killed cows hanging

Killed pigs lynched
Killed summer
Killed fall

winter!
   hell for others
      indifference to others
         torture for others
            existence for self

Brown death yestoday!

Aaron A. Trompeter

Untitled

It's funny how a melody
   can bring to mind a memory,
And suddenly your thoughts run free
   and years just fall away.
To simpler times when life was slow
   so much to see, think and know...
Was it really all so long ago,
   it seems like yesterday.

Carrie Fisher

Seaside Dreams

Each morning I walk along the beach
   and I see the little girl
who collects the trash,
   but seashells fill her sacks.
She tells me
   that the sun lives in the ocean;
   and that we have no home at all.
She says
   spirits rise from the water
   and only she can see them.
Seashells are the gifts
   they give her for watching.
She hands me one
   and it silently crumbles to dust.

Dave Kohler

Discovery

As I listened
To the silence of nature
Creativity began to flow
Once again
I was in touch
With myself
And thanked God
I was not lost
When thoughts
And thoughtfulness
Lovers love
And the sweet juices
Of creativity
Cannot be found
In nature
The spirit is dead
To the love of God
And immortality
In every sense

Michael R. Gallegos

A Greeting Card And A Flower

A greeting card and a flower
With the holidays
Coming ever so close

And you are at a loss for words
All you need is a greeting card
And an envelope to close
To be in tune with
The holiday spirits.

So don't be a loner
In the crowd
Get on board
The merry go round

With a greeting card
In your pocket
And a flower
In your hand
Is all the message
You will need
To win her hand

John J. Chironno

Come Take My Hand

Come take my hand, and walk with me.
Together we'll see what will be.
Down life's path through all time.
Hand in hand we are young and prime

We face life together without fear.
We don't know what will be here.
Let come whatever may.
We're here together to stay.

With our oath we took a vow.
Forever here and now,
Till death us do part.
This we believed with all our heart.

You came, you took my hand.
We walked all over this land.
We have come a long way.
We've loved and lived each day by day.

There'll soon be another anniversary.
And the best is yet to be.
I love you for all eternity.
Come take my hand and walk with me.

Lajuana D. Burton

Christian Marie

I thought "ha! no problem," a simple task.
To raise a baby, that'll be a blast.
I never thought it would happen to me,
My little angel would never be taken from me.
But, within a blink of an eye, she was swept, taken forever from me.
Now as I sit and mourn her death,
I say to myself, "I wish it were me instead of she."
I often wonder "if I just," but carry on I know I must.
Christian Marie was so very special,
Her joy and laughter will be my eternal vessel.
Of what she meant to me, words can not express
The feelings I must suppress.
To bring them out in the open, will only make me keeping coping.
Inner-strength and lots of prayer is best,
For I know God is who laid my baby to rest.
There she'll stay, no worry, no pain in the hands of God she'll remain
As I think of her care giver I put my fears to rest,
For I know God is the Best! A peace of mind I ask God to give,
As I grow from this experience, life will be once again worth to live.
Times and troubles will all pass by,
but the love of God will hold strong, enabling us all to carry on.

Christina Renae Crawford

Lust In The Mask Of Passion

Hearken I sayth O' voice in the deep. How doth one know love from lust? Thine soul labors in sorrow and continues to weep...

Bid you should ask that, 'twas once said, "To Thine Self Be True."
Is it love or lust? Such a courageous question of you! Whist thou
not know the seeds of the corrupt and taste of sweet fruit? The plump and the luscious
can sometimes make blue! The question you ask is betwixt human want and divine gift.
Doth thou not know the feeling of true bliss?

Human passion can bind one; wrap thine heart!

But beware! 'tis sometimes as the sounds of unsettled dogs in the dark. The lust you
ask of can't be put to sleep, for it does not satisfy your soul to keep.

Then how doth I discern my dreams so true and express thy love ever so new?

Hearken I sayth; lend an ear to your spirit, for human lust can never get near it! You see
'twas the forbidden in the Garden of Eden; where God cursed man, 'twas said in the
beginning! For entice She, the serpent, with the fruit of lesson and caused man not to
know of this lust in the mask of passion. For it 'twas upon that time we enjoyed divine
conception, but then we began to ask this Age Old Question.

Marty Costello

Can't Fill His Shoes

When I was just a young boy oh, how tall he was
and it seemed my whole hand could be held by just his two fingers.

We'd walk and talk and my little legs ran fast
just to keep up and I walked around in his shoes like boats
and knew, that I - can't fill his shoes!

Growing older I worked in his business
to be near the man I loved, admired and wanted to know more deeply.
saw so many who loved, admired and wanted to be near him;
heard them seek his counsel - advice or have him as their friend
and knew, that I - can't fill his shoes!

Later in life I took his place and he was transferred
and daily he was missed and asked about
and I tried to do my very best,
but knew, that I - can't fill his shoes!

I've walked many a mile in life wore out many a shoe
and finally understood I must wear my own
and perhaps, leave a trail for others to do the same
and love as much and touch as much as help as much as I saw in him
for I know, that I - can't fill his shoes!

Don Hayden

A Risen Lord

My Savior loves me with a love like I've never felt before
The day he died, darkness came and the temple veil was tore
He asked his Father to forgive those who had crucified him
With all the torture they put him through he still loved them
I am glad that Jesus thought of not himself but of us first
He promised if we drank from living water we would not thirst.

Saints graves burst open and people were still being healed
He later came forth from the grave though his tomb was sealed
When he ascended he promised the Holy Spirit he would send
In his word is the comfort that we need for our spirits to mend
He is our Savior, Refuge, Shield and Buckler, the King of Kings
If you deny yourself and come unto Jesus a new life he will bring.

Debbie Burks

Love Is Like A Flower

Love is like a flower, without water it will die,
love is like a river, without rain, it too, will dry.

I fill my river everyday, with whom I may not know,
I share my love with everyone, and every place I go.

Love is our one commandment, this one, I shall not fail,
for love endures the greatest pains, this too, I'm here to tell.

If you are one who feels unloved, I write this poem to you,
for I am not the only one, much greater, God loves you!

Although you may be all alone, and feel that no one cares,
my nameless friend, I need to say, God's just waiting for you to share.

Life is not always easy, we have our ups and downs,
so when you feel that you're alone, remember God's love abounds.

My friend, to which I have no name, your river is not dry,
God knows your every sorrow, and watches as you cry.

I too, am just a flower, without love, I'm sure to die,
but, God reminds me everyday, he hears my every sigh.

If we believe together, we will always be okay,
for it only takes two flowers to create an eloquent bouquet.

So, if love is like a flower, the center is very tall,
for the center is God's flower, the most spectacular of all.

Edna M. Powell

Untitled

in the silence of the pastures he awakens from his bed of comfort
the straw provides security and warmth
his black coat shimmers in the morning sun his legs wobble as
he steps onto grass wet with morning dew
his eyes are hungry for new sights his long nose pokes and prods everything within his reach
his ears sense all sounds everything is fresh and new

unable to walk steadily he trips and falls though he tries
his best to join
the other animals grazing
he cannot reach the greener grass on the far side
of the meadow
so many obstacles for one so new
he knows little of this world he is in of the life he will live
all he desires is to chew the luscious bits of grass

he is unaware of the presence behind him until it is too late
his ears hear the prodigious boom
his eyes see other horses run with fear
his nose smells a distinct yet unknown odor
his body feels the passage of the shiny metal bullet
as he gasps for his last breath of crisp morning air
his mouth can taste the sweet grass on the other side.

Jessica Karbowiak

Would You Be My Daddy?

Would you be my Daddy?
   Could I be your little girl?

Would you be my Daddy?
   Could you protect me from this world?

Would you be my Daddy?
   Could we just pretend?

Would you be my Daddy?
   Could we be the best of friends?

Would you be my Daddy?
   Could you lift me up into the air
   so I can fly?

Would you be my Daddy?
   Could you never ask me Why!...

Roxanne Williams

Feelings

I just saw Gwen in the sky
As the clouds passed by,

I saw her put her hands together
As if to say we will be one forever,

I have often looked to heaven
Only to see a passing raven,

Late mid summer's day
Only made me pray,

Brother and son are there
But yet I know not where,

Clouds, sun, and stars
I know they are out there,

I keep searching,
But yet I know not where,

If they could only reach out
And touch me one more time,

That moment would be mine,
My hand is held open to the skies
Still there are tears in my eyes.

Bryan M. Williams I

Sweet Child

Sweet child of mine
Don't give me that line
I knew when I saw the sign
You were lagging far behind

If only you could know
How life can make us low
And things are harder as we grow
And life is not one big show

Through the day you run your pace
Not knowing the many things you face
In days to come you must find your place
Among the humane race

Of trouble I hope you steer clear
It often slips up from the rear
To me you are so very dear
I wish you could always stay near

Of all the advice I could relay
I would tell you to pray each day
Try always to do what you say
And never ever forget how to play

Theresa Floyd

Awakening

A visit from a baby
Raised my spirits - I must say
Making me aware of the wonders
That surround us every day

He picked a pinecone from a dish
And studied it with awe
His eyes were shining - as I watched
And wondered what he saw

Out of the patio door
While he watched the birds feed
And exploring the world
Gaining knowledge indeed

A little child shall lead them
Or so - it is said
He awakened my curiosity
That so long was dead

Now I feel light hearted
And greet each day - with zest
I had forgotten all the wonders
Brought back - by my little guest

Ramona Smart

One Of A Kind

She is with me when I am sick,
Another mother I would not pick.
She holds me close when I am frightened,
My gloomy days she always brightens.
She fills my life with joy and hope,
Without her I'd never cope.
She is the best,
She's one of a kind,
Another mother like her
I will never find.

Susanna Coronel

Rain

The rain pours like blood
   from an open wound
I feel it hitting my
   fleshly tomb
I try to disrobe to let
   it cleanse my soul
Maybe the rain will help
   me grow

Kevin Rubeck

Lasting Love

If I were you
I would say to me
I love you love you
Don't you see.
If you were me
I would say to you
I love you love you
Yes I do
Since I am me
And you are you
Why don't we vow
To stay together
And promise we
Will love forever.

Dorothy Bigham

All Of These...

Woman, wife and mother, I was allowed to be all of these.
To be born into this world, to be taught, to learn, to grow,
none so greater to me than all of these.
To give back and to teach, to love and to share....
there has been pain, oh so much pain, but through all the trials,
no words can ever express all my world has gained.
To be a woman, perfect in God's eyes, that's how he sees,
but allowing me my choices to be all I have chosen to be,
to be a wife, God's first human creations partner, to help him,
to love and stand beside behind him, and to hold him so dear when
he needs me to be there. Nothing can feel so meaningful than from
my husband a touch, smile and loving stare.
Mother, my sweet mother, that sheltered me and held me when I was
young, only after holding my own, did I realize what all she had done.
What will I teach them, what will they remember when I go?
I have to put it in God's hands, for I will never know.
To be a woman, wife and mother, who in life could ask for more?
I knocked and God answered, that's what he held for me,
behind the door, all of these...

Kathaleen Marie Gwin

My Love

My love is like the sun!
It is the warmth and light of the world in which I live.
It rises within at the start of each day,
and by the light of my love, I find guidance,
the path before me is plain to see.

At night in sleep, my face is like the moon
the light of my love reflected in my smile.
Each night and day, all of this-the cycle set by God
and adhered to by all His children
of which, I by having you, am one of his chosen.

Our love is the symbol of our happiness and contentment in our own world, together.
Beloved wife of mine! My heart, my soul, my life all for you alone
In this life and beyond,
Changing never, nor ever held lightly in word, thought or action.

The pain of being without you an ever constant reminder in my heart
of the wondrous joy that is to be mine, when once again we are together.
Until that day, here is my heart.

Econoply

The World All Gone

I sit and ponder one day.
As I'm sitting there I think of
A mother with true love, now gone.
My hope for her return lies within.
Still I await her return with her open arms.
Each night I dream of her and the memories we shared.
But what will become of these memories.
When the mother goes beyond our grief? What will she take?
Take with her, she shall, the generosity of her love.
But some day the love will pass with the memories.
The light held deep inside, the eternal flame, all worth living for
Too will disappear. All the world taken away.
Left behind one will find but two memories...
The grave and her delicate yet fragile body.
But soon the body too will return to its natural place,
And the grave, once found, will crumble.
Leaving behind nothing...
A blank screen with no color,
Found in front, left to watch.
The World All Gone...

Amanda J. Bil

Free to Believe...Again

Into my life you entered your touch sparked my love

The voice soothing my spirit, your music touched my very soul
Fear began to leave, entering space a dark empty hole

Together we grew, too strong, too fast.
Fear entered again, doubts were cast.
Silence, empty, open pain, loneliness, despair, nothing to gain.

Flowers wilt, music silent, time becomes endless, thoughts violent
Does trust enter again, or take flight.
Will the music come alive into the night.

Two souls begin dancing to a wondrous song
Could it be the anger is almost gone

A song plays of love, trust and friendship
The wall starts to fall around us, foundations lose their grip

We dance through it all, on and on the night does call
The final note stops barriers begin to drop

We look around everywhere there is debris
Eyes open filled with wonder, the first time they finally see

Friendship and love are all around
The soul is fearless the guard is down

You are open, I enter inside the music plays nowhere to hide

Jacqueline Seitzinger

An Angel

Some time ago in years gone by, I asked for a Mother as an Angel
passed by. Her beauty overwhelmed me, she was an Angel to behold.
Her love shone like the sun and her halo like gold.

"Your journey into life is about to begin, any special requests
as you enter in?" I want love and laughter through sunshine and rain,
a life full of happiness without any pain.

"Fame and fortune would be an easier request,
for the things you have mentioned is not easily blessed."
I don't want money, fortune or fame, I want a mother who will give me a name.

The journey had started, life was conceived,
a mother was waiting, the plan was achieved.
In a short while, a baby entered the world and a mother sat cradling her new baby girl.

As I stared into my mothers eyes, there was something I recognized.
The Angel above that helped me to be was holding me close and
looking at me. God did not bless me with fortune or fame.
He gave me an Angel for a mother, and she gave me a name.

Stacey Bethel

Mother Of Jesus

The moment was one of heavenly consequence.
An Aura of radiant magnificence filled the air.
A serene hush was mysteriously present with volitional
Rapprochement dictating utilitarianism of thought.
God beckoned his flock for a gathering of righteousness,
As the Holy Trinity emerged through the dawning of a new day
It was to evermore establish forgiveness through humblest endearment and sublime approach.
Thy lady in reverence bowed before the consecrated cross that bore man's salvation.
Her role divine, a status of exaltation.
The tears that flowed from her eyes, were not of self-pity.
They streaked her cheeks, some staining a small spot of parched soil beneath her sandals.
Trembling was present, as was concentration on distant plain.
To feel pain, though possess tranquility, not touch, yet be touched.
Was infinitely the charismatic adornment of one who has lost her only son. Jesus Christ.

Edward A. Nicholson

The Prayer

I greet the day with prayers to God,
And to His son our Savior.
I ask them to forgive my sins
And better my behavior.

I ask Him to improve my sight
That I might see His wonders.
That I might hear His precious words,
Protect me from all blunders.

And then I pray for other folk
Who need His healing hand.
There are so many other ones
Throughout this saddened land.

And then I thank Him for His Grace
And all His blessings given,
And ask to meet Him face to face
When my reward is heaven.

Bruce W. Jones

Song For Amy

My little Amy,
now that you're gone,
I treasure the years
you were happy and strong.

I pray for your soul
to be peaceful at rest;
My heart's full of sorrow,
but your spirit is blessed.

Gina Daidone

You

Far more than you could ever know,
Far more than words can say.

You're on my mind and in my heart,
With every passing day.

You fill my life with happiness,
You're all my dreams come true.

And there's no greater joy for me,
Than just to be with you.

Juanita H. Parker

Time

With the passage of time,
May get credits for efforts of mine
Hundred dollar shoes,
Credit card blues,
No such things as taboos.

Babies taught sex, no moral aspects
Crime does pay!
Criminals walk away!

Time goes fast,
Youth doesn't last
Parents out of date,
Boy I can't wait!

This old world keeps
Turning, my poor heart
Is yearning, for the innocent
Years, had no pressure
From peers, wish I could
Control their fears.
With the passing of time,
Maybe things will be fine.

Catherine Rasche

A Solitary Star

Silently the snow
slipped softly towards
the deep, dark timbers
Falling freely
to rest undiscriminating
upon all,
turning the darkness
into a soft but true light
witnessed only by
a solitary star.

Allison Perry

Thoughts Of The Tower Of London

I've stood alone, on London Bridge,
and eastward looked toward the tower.
The flow of Thames revived my thought.
that time itself is earth's real power.
Deeds once passed by with scarce
a thought and little care,
how loom as targets everywhere.

For judgement currents run
both long and deep, and
history knows no death or sleep!
So deeds once passed with little care,
Now loom as targets everywhere!

William T. Reynolds

The Double

Here's next year pulling in,
and I have a ticket
to carry me away from myself.
Never again
will I visit Love, New York.

There she stands,
ugly face red and blue
with starry tears,
one eyebrow raised at half mast-
and no one sees me.
Mirrors mist over;
water's too fluid.

We may meet someday, unexpectedly,
in some roadstop washroom - a blotch
in a spotty reflection;
a waitress in a dingy diner,
she may set down a cup of nausea
steaming between us.

But not in New York;
not in Love, with its two-way mirrors.

Zoja Pavlovskis-Petit

The Angel I Know So Well

Sleep angel, I know so well I
hope God never breaks his spell
we are the angel, in heaven above
who's put here to teach on love
angel, with all white can stay
though day and night but dark
angel, comes in spells. To assist
us straight to hell. The angel
I know so well.

Myrtle L. Mobley

Mess

Love. Love is like...
  Any other infectious disease
Life. Life is love...
  Becoming another leper on his knees.

You can't turn the tides on something like this.
Either way you're in the wake of a force you can't resist.

Love. Love is pain...
  A solid rock it makes of your heart.
Ironic, isn't it?
  The same thing you live by can tear you apart.

  You won't be the one to change things, now.
  You can wear your stone mask, but you're still eyes in the crowd.

Innocence, then, confirmation. Next, the urge towards consummation.
Jump headlong into the compelling mess.
Love - and sex - an eternal quest...for the rest...of your life.

Angelo Speranza

The Jewel

She was magnificent, this Jewel I had. She was perfect in every way,
And shone so brilliantly, that stars were put to shame.
Her cut was perfect, and to gaze upon her
Was to gaze upon beauty known only to the Gods.

I cared for her, this Jewel of mine,
I held her tenderly and caressed her fragile form,
I protected her from harm, and those who would touch.

But my Jewel was not happy, she needed another to care for her,
She needed another to look upon her beauty. To hold her and caress her.

And so she moved, this Jewel of mine,
From my arms which, had tenderly enfolded her,
To another's arms she thought were better suited to her needs.

She stayed, for a while, with this new admirer,
But her brilliance began to wane,
For that which she needed was not to be had,
You see, the other arms knew not how to care.

And so when, my Jewel realized,
That the care and love she needed, was where she had been,
She returned, and the beauty and brilliance which she had possessed,
Came back in all its glory.

Henry D. Reiss

Autumn

Trumpets flourish—
Courtiers snap to attention—

And she enters. . . .
Her skirts rustle softly in the stillness of the great hall
As she carefully measures her footsteps over the cloaks flung before
her from the unmoving arms of her stolid attendants.
Abruptly she halts. . .
She stands perfectly erect with solemn features,
  though her crimson cheeks rival the fallen
  blossoms strewn about her feet.

The slight chill of a sudden zephyr weaves
  invisible designs in rambling branches above m'lady's head.
Now myriads of messengers abandon themselves
  in full greeting of their long-awaited monarch.

She stands gazing aloft, slightly squinting at
the profusion of heralds that now swirl and caress her immobile form.

A last proclaimer bids homage to this solitary figure held captive
in her own spell. . . .she quickly cast her eyes to the ground.

A moment. . .her head lifted, she looks about, and with deliberation,
moves on. In royal silence, autumn leaves.

Darrell E. Jones

A Tribute To Irene (Memorial Day 1996)

I visited a cemetery today known as Signal Hill. My darling wife is resting there, according to God's will.

As I stood beside her grave with my head bowed low, a gentleman stood beside me someone, I did not know.

He asked me if I was visiting someone there today, I said yes, my darling wife, who recently passed away.
He said, I'm very sorry my heart goes out to you. With trembling voice he shook my hand, as if somehow he knew.

He placed an American flag upon her grave and slowly walked away. He said, may God be with you my friend, on this memorial day.

Edward Lewis

Life

Life is to be lived...
To the fullest...
Dream...
They just might come true...
Follow that dream...
Think...
If something don't work...
Make new plans and go forward... The bottom line is don't even go there...Giving up... Birth...to be happy...The purpose... It is up to you...think... There's two sides to every story... Pro or con...Good or bad...
Which side do you want to be on... Life goes on in a circle... Go back don't ever go there it is onward and upward... Now Education always go there time and time again... It's of great importances to be always in the learning mode...keep a child's mind open... When you learn you got to...Teach Then there is college...Cooperations...finances... Marriage...Family, go there but take it slow and stop and smell the roses...Enjoy... Never give up.

Shirley J. Horton

Dawning

Awake at morn's new dawning
  And my heart in grateful praise,
While looking through my window
  Lifts my soul through early haze;

In wonder at the beauty displayed before my eyes,
  As softly the sun comes stealing
Through the leaves upon the trees,
  And casts great lacy patterns, just beyond where I am kneeling.

It speaks to me of the wonder
  Of a new born souls first dawning,
As gloriously the Son's bright light
  Bestirs the soul to longing, driving darkness all asunder.

The more the sun is lifted high, across the great blue sky,
  The more the hovering shadows flee away.
In the glory of that light, revealing a warmth and glow,
  That bestirs the grateful, thankful soul to pray.

Linda L. Hotchkiss

Within Your Heart

In the heart of the garden peace is born
In the moonlight sisters of the stars dance heavenly
The garden seems to talk to mother nature
It promises to hold no hate or violence
The garden grows within your heart
It seems to be full of color from the flowers that bloom from the mind
To see the garden's streams and ponds blue as sapphires is a
Magnificent sight
Animals come to greet the sun as the sky becomes magically bright
The garden has a radiance
It glows because the love and peace is so full.

Randi Powell

World, You Are A Beautiful Dress

Great wide beautiful world
With beautiful bodies of waters
around you whirl. And the
long green grass upon your breast,

With tall trees over you
grows with yellow and red leaves,
and the long white moss hanging
upon your chest.

Rosellar Barber

As She Sleeps

As she lies down to
go to sleep, I caress her body
ever so sweet. I lie awake
most of the night to keep her
from the big bad fright.

The stars and the moon
are ever so high, I lie there
whispering to her she will
always be the gleam in my eyes.

Michael R. Livermore

Lonely Eyes

When I looked into a mirror
And I see my lonely eyes
But everyone seems to tell me
That it's not so very wise

Anyone could tell you
As I gaze into the skies
You can see she is so lonely
Just look into her lonely eyes

I wish that I could see you
And I hope that you will try
Too come by and be with me
And look into my lonely eyes

Then I won't have to wonder
As the days go by
Everyone can tell you
It's about my lonely eyes

I look into those lonely eyes
And I always think of you
You never thought you'd leave me
And leave me here so blue

Ruth Shelton

The Empty Space

Passing through the unknown
Living from day to day
feeling the loss of one
who just passed away
Reaching out for something
that just isn't there
Seeking comfort....
But who really cares?
Must the vacuum be left?
Must torture be undergone
thinking day and night
of a dead loved one?
Nothing can compensate
Nothing can replace
there is still that vacuum
still that empty space.

Aaron Oteze

Rhymes Of The Rainbow

Raindrops spill on the sage,
    clouds wander and climb
and the thunder rumbles
    in the walls of the canyon.

Suddenly, through the showers,
    She peacefully sweeps
her arc of color
    across the sky,
bowing thanks to the sun,

As she sings the
    rhymes of the rainbow.

And the rhymes
    and the thunder
still rumbles
    in the walls of the canyon.

Irene Schultz

To Form A Shade Of Gray

We stand apart from each other
With no line of equal rights
And ignorance towards equality
It's just the colors — black and white

God made us all as equals
Black and white as one
To form a bond of grace and love
Until all is over and done

Yet we forget we share one thing
The ability and strength to live
Our focus is on the color of skin
Instead of the will to give

Would judgment still be seen and used
If the world was colorblind
Or would there be just one race
A race of one mankind

If we could only step aside
Put discrimination away
And bring black and white together
To form a shade of gray

Karen Tesch

Untitled

Racing rain
Soaking my soul
Hiding my tears
To what gain but control
Of my fears

Grasping desperately
As shadows
Fingers slipping
Through nothingness
Running aimlessly
Across the meadows
Craving but a gentle caress

The courage to embrace
What I know in good
Wisdom like hindsight
So burdensome
Shouldering regret, so tiresome

Longing always longing
Trials upon trials
Enlightening to gray, fading to black

Jeffrey Lee Kratt

14 Hours Out Of LA

14 hours out of LA, the flight was beautiful without delay Assuming
standard orbit from high above, descending to the concrete like a dove

Scanning this world that seemed untouched, although many have visited,
especially the Dutch Watching the waves break was not so much a
fright, watching all the surfers you have to be opposite of uptight

Deflecting the sun as it rise, casting its light we look divine
Across the river where some of the locals are, Beyond the river the Natives are too far

Up the Gold Coast our journey is continuing, it is getting warmer, we
are no longer shivering The arrival in a small town is not so iffy,
the town — how cute — has been invaded by hippies

Not knowing I would be here through all my dreams, I can no say I am
part of the team Beautiful reefs, colors of blue, exotic fishes and visions of you

Approaching the end, arrival of night, beginning of Spring and the awe
of twilight Walking in the park there are vibrant views, analyzing our surrounds
of the morning dew

This new New World is what I would coin, this New World, perhaps, may
be better to join We are leaving on the ship that brought us here, I
am ascending now, so please take care

Assuming standard orbit as when we arrived, leaving this far away
world which has great pride Soaring through the stars without any
delay, sailing through the heavens, back to LA

Erick D. Griffith

A Moment In Time

A tragedy, so wrong yet true, left us all feeling sad and blue.
Their lives cut short, by a moment in time,
Only their memories, are left behind.
To them it was just another day, off to Paris, they were on their way.
For that dear Mother, and her Angels two, and we won't forget that friendly crew.
The Sportscaster, Musician, our Friends and Lovers,
Our Daughters, our Sons, Sisters, Brothers and Mothers.
Then we had the school's best, their Chaperons, and all the rest.
One even became 'engaged' that day, his Hockey game, he loved to play.
He could not predict he would never be home, to leave his lover, all alone.
These memories of people I don't even know,
Have left me saddened, so full of sorrow.
As I sit and watch the evening News,
Another tear's shed
Still waiting for clues.
Why lives were cut short, by 'A Moment In Time,'
And taken away by a hideous crime,
But they will keep flying with their brand new wings,
Sent from up above, an 'unbelievable' thing.
Hold on to their memories, from their past,
As their lives forever, surely will last.
A destination, yet unknown, for 'us' they will never be coming home.

Tammy Waggoner

Darkness

Darkness what is darkness, what is it truly? Darkness, darkness
what is it fully? Is it a black void wherein lives wickedness, or is
it really full of joy and goodness? It is a dark blanket that covers
many mysteries, a black cloud that covers many histories. Of the
darkness people are frightened, they expect horror but become
enlightened. They find that from darkness came light, A light showing
all what is right. And light will return back to the dark, darkness
was its mother since it first was a spark. Darkness is often times
associated with death, the time when a man takes his very last breath.
This is because death is misunderstood, it should be appreciated it
really should. It is a cycle that never ends, once one man dies he is
born again. Like light to darkness, darkness to light, opposites but
united if seen in one sight. So when you're in the darkness and you
shed a tear, don't be afraid because there is nothing to fear.

Johnathan Neal

The Traveler

A Traveler, a templar, a quested knight,
Begins this moment his final fight,
To seek truths far beyond sight,
And bring to darkness a lasting light.

A light of hope, to turn the tide,
A light of reason, to help divide,
The Army of Chaos at Uncertainty's side,
Where the unknown and the known collide.

Search, must he, for these questions of his,
'Cross Time and Space and all that is,
To bring this wisdom, from fated twists,
To the place where answers are amiss.

And so, steps he into the void,
The fear and ignorance now destroyed,
To battle beasts and Insanity's toys,
That lurk within the dark disguise....

...Of His mind, and Our mind, and all that We are,
Who we are, Why we are, What we are for,
All of us Knights, Templars, and each a Traveler,
The question is life, and at its end...how appropriate...the answer.

Walter Campbell

My Wish

As I sit on the beach I see, the sun's light will soon reach me.
Just a few more seconds and it will come,
shining bright yellow and wholesome.
Here it comes above the mist, like a gentle, placid kiss.
I feel its rays touch my face, with their tender, warm embrace.
The sky is clear, the day is beginning,
the birds come out and are singing.
How I wish I was one of those,
so I could watch how each day comes and goes.

As I sit on the beach I see, the sun's light now leaving me.
It's getting dark, the wind is stronger,
the sun is sinking, to shine no longer.
There it sets into the mist, like a friend's sad farewell kiss.
I feel its loneliness touch my soul, with its emptiness making me cold.
The day is ending, the sky is dark,
the moon shines, the stars spark.
How I wish I was one of those,
so I could watch how each day comes and goes.

Marlena Toto

The Past

She peers out through the foggy glass
The rain hitting the ground is a constant pounding in her ears
She hears the stream of fallen rain flowing into the gutters
Her hands are cracked and bloody from trying to shatter the unbreakable glass
The salty tears falling from her swollen eyes burn inside her open wounds
Unwanted thoughts consume her mind,
And she is overcome with guilt
She can't bring herself to gaze into the eyes that she knows are unable to look back
She hates the feel of that pathetic embrace.
There's no strength in the old woman's arms
Hands withered by time wipe tears from her face,
Soon enough those hands will be gone
Images aren't what they used to be,
The mind can only reminisce
A captive of her words is all she's become,
A victim of so much regret
Unnoticed pain shines through her eyes,
The inevitable coming too fast
Whatever she does the glass just won't break.
Because she can never change what's in the past.

Amber Cottrell

Colors

God must love the color blue;
for the beauty of the sky,
its reflection on the waters;
God must love the color green;
for the grass and the leaves;
in their multi-hued splendor;
God must love the color brown;
from dust to sand,
to the rich, deep loam;
God must love the rainbow,
for the sign in the sky,
the rain is over for today;
God must love His children,
for the blood his son had shed,
was of the color... red.

Cheryl Lynn Ridley

I Am Always Here

She never left your side
Although she left your eyes.
She has the heart and soul of yours,
The soul that never dies.

She's lived inside of you
Since the day she went away.
Every step you take is her's,
In every single way.

She is an angel, just like you;
For you and her are just the same.
Anytime someone speaks of you,
They are also calling her name.

Why are you two just alike?
Only you could understand.
For every time she felt pain or sorrow,
You were there to give her a hand.

She is the voice you miss so much,
That voice you want to hear.
Can you guess who it is mom?
It's me; I am always here.

Amber Coose

Slip Sliding Away

Ice is nice,
For skating rinks
Glaciers and,
Tall cold drinks.

Hockey games,
And Eskimos,
Ice cream cones,
And lake ice-floes.

Ice storms cause,
The schools to close,
Meetings, churches,
All of those.

To the mailbox,
What a trip,
One could fall,
And break a hip!

Helpless in the
House we stay,
Pray for ice
To melt away.

Marge Shelden

Aging

I reached out to touch
The years I have known,
But my thin frail hand
Found a sense of childhood
On the borders of my mind.

I felt a growing sadness,
A wistful sense of memory
Interacting with the changes,
Groping to bring meaning
To the pattern of my being.

The deep love of family.
The accumulation of years,
The acceptance of what is to be,
A strong sense of integrity,
Threads the needle of mankind.

The awesome world of aging,
The majestic overtones,
The fascination of life,
The sense of destiny,
Brushed the shadow of my eye.

Herman Allen

Time Forward

The shade of past
is fading fast,
closing time is near,
Minds seek and find in fear,
cause the end is becoming clear,
Time swept away to let you know
Eternity is not forever,
For two people who love each other
cannot always be together.

Megan Taylor

Untitled

Chiselled fragments of Jasper and Flint
Erode and vanish into the depths of
    sparkling sand
Destined to emerge above the dune
    as an Arrow
Pointing to the era of new beginnings.

Kathy Lynn Drabek-Farrow

Good Girls

There once was a girl,
    as sweet as can be;
Whose parents had died,
    when she was just three.

A kindly, good fairy,
    did cast a spell;
The girl's house enchanted,
    of that I now tell.

The child merely spoke,
    her request would appear;
From playmates to toys,
    her countenance did cheer.

For the fairy had to work,
    as all good fairies do;
Helping children that are good,
    earn their good fairies too.

Judy Ann Echols

All Grown Up....Well...Almost

The girl is All Grown Up now...In Control one might say...
Not real good on confronting...but Better!!!
She remembers, Yes, She remembers
She remembers the forced sex and the pain,
She remembers crying...and saying Please No
    She remembers the song playing...
She remembers being little and wanting it to stop...or, to Die...
Yes, She remembers...She remembers his coercing ways,
    and She remembers the house.
She remembers for years believing that it was Her Fault...
But... You see, it Wasn't Her fault, and She Knows it Now!!!
She also Knows that the heart Can Heal, and that people do Believe!!!
For awhile She wasn't sure...but Now She knows, and Now...
    there is Some trust, where there used to be None.
    Much writing has been done, Many tears shed,
        and a Long Hard Journey taken.
            The Journey is not complete,
                But the Woman has found
                    The Courage To Heal!!!

Marla K. Mosher, M.Ed.

The Light of the Moon

By the light of the moon the silent forest comes alive, its children
awake to join a crescendoing twilight sonata.
By the light of the moon the breeze flows through the trees, singing
an enchanting love serenade among the leaves.
By the light of the moon the lonely wolf howls towards the sky, adding
his haunting tone to the woods' overture at hand.
By the light of the moon the glimmering stream dances down the
mountainside, rhythmically accelerating the sweet adagio tempo of falling water.
By the light of the moon the cottontail rabbit sounds through the
brush, bouncing a staccato beat with every hop off the tympanical ground.
By the light of the moon the golden eagle cries out in the canyon,
echoing his solo suite for all to know.
By the light of the moon a cabin lies nestled in the thicket,
a solitary man glides a bow across violin strings in a harmonious concerto.
By the light of the moon nature enhances the night, its symphony played for all to hear.
By the light of the moon all one must do to hear the glorious song is
open the heart and mind...and listen.

Joe Williams

Dancing Dove

Dancing dove...
sweet white dove, innocent eyes... looking at me
dancing on rich golden sky, I saw you flying this morning
such brave circles in the misty air, and is that your family?
you all soared so proudly as one...dancing through the sky
without a care...and giant circles you flew, bouncing on air
currents so graceful the golden sun reflecting off your white
wings, morning star bright. A heavenly day star. And you glowed
as an angel in the daylight... What a gift from heaven's doors...
dancing with the sky...a sweet dance for the sun...dance for me...
My daytime star. My dancing dove, dancer of heaven's breeze...
my dancing dove...

Allen Linam

A Scrap Of Paper

I awaken before the dawn arises.
A scrap of paper sits before me waiting to be written upon.
Many thoughts run through my troubled mind.
What do I write, what are these thoughts and how do I put them down.
Where do I begin and what is their importance.
Are they only important to me?
Are they of any importance to anyone else?
Why do they trouble me and what do I put down on this scrap of paper.
Waiting, always waiting before the dawn arises.
I must put them down before the last dawn arises and leaves only a scrap of paper.

Joyce De Gennaro

I Once Saw Myself Ugly

I once saw myself ugly but not any more
My youth and innocence was taken from me
I was told I was good for nothing; I was told to be ugly is to be
without love and laughter; I was then taken to a world no different
from what I was used to; full of hatred; full of hopelessness

I once saw myself ugly but not any more
Is it any wonder that I wake up in the middle of the night yearning for a new beginning?
Yearning to be surrounded by my loved ones
I don't know what it means to cry
and I don't know what it means to weep; why?

Because of faded dreams, disappointments, loneliness and broken promises
My heart was empty of hope; caring little for life but afraid to die

I once saw myself ugly but not any more
I relied on someone dear to my heart but she, too, was taken from me
I'm helpless when we're apart; I depended on her love for me; her
strength, her courage her vitality
Now all I have is memories; happiness is gone for me
I once saw myself ugly but not any more misguided by the world and its
lies; I felt lost until someone helped me walk those lonely miles
Taught me how to love myself; taught me beauty is within ourselves;
gave me strength and courage I felt strong again; I no longer needed
to be loved because I had enough love within me
I once saw myself ugly but not any more

Medgine Duval

The Crush

I think of him and reality is slowly lost, fading away
as I fall in to a dreamy state of love. Then, as quickly as it
departed, reality returns. Replacing itself with a lonely longing for him to be near.
He is a man of cherished means. A man with a touch
so soft, a kiss so light, a smile so bright. Captivating
with his humor, he makes me laugh like no one else.
His reserved side fascinates me, making him more irresistible.
The reason for love songs, I find him enchanting.
My knight in shining armor, he mystifies me with his ways.
As mesmerizing as life itself, I think of him always.
Curious as to what he might be doing, wondering if he is thinking of me.
A thin barrier of passion separates me from him.
He is already taken. He does not feel the same way.
Feelings not shared now are quiet forever.

Julie Parias

Fade Into Another Day

I open my eyes and wonder how the world could be so cruel.
What has brought me here, to this tomorrow?
Is it God? Who indulges in my profound melancholy.

Euphoria has not seen my soul,
Euphoria has not even enlightened me in dreams.
Sacred dreams, you used to be small portal into satisfying images of bliss.
Now, you are nothing, you are a fiend
You attempt to steal me away.
You attempt to put me where no one can find me, self hate.

I think of a life I would like to lead.
It all comes crashing down, though.
She always dances on my glass wall with concrete shoes

I have had a few moments of witnessing her elusive radiance.
As is reality, she often leaves me for another.
She who denies me of love.
She who looks through me,
As if I were transparent. You are too insufficient.

As I fade into another day,
I feel dishevelled and alone.
Fingers gushing blood as I constantly mend my glass wall.

Johnny Wirth

The Fruit Of The Spirit

Love is when your heart is there,
 for someone who's in need.

Joy for all the things you've got,
 don't search for more in greed.

Peace is but a way of life,
 as tranquil as a dove.

Patience in the one who waits,
 for thins sent from above.

Kindness helps to heal the pain,
 when someone's fallen down.

Goodness in the way you think,
 when sin is all around.

Faithful to your father,
 you're told that he knows best.

Gentle is the one who lifts,
 a bird back to it's nest.

Self control in every way,
 to turn fast as you see it.

To live a life built on God's word,
 a life lived by the spirit.

Timothy Tyler Marx

Sacred

A stranger,
among us.
Sacred he is,
for deception,
has not affected,
his soul.

Yet dwelled,
among strangers,
he lies within,
among us,
only to be,
sacred,
of sorrow,
as thy stranger,
just walks,
away,
in thy darkness,
never to be,
known again.

David Oswald

A Nothing Place

Render for a moment
The color gray a nothing place
Where time is not counted
Roads left untraveled
And memories remain forgotten
Let's now contemplate a place
Where forever never waits
Love cannot enter
Neither hate cannot remain
A nothing place
Where there will be no haste
Time will never be a waste
Only stained with gray...
A nothing place

Joseph D. White

Welding

My youth
breathing in
dust and smoke
on the cracked cement
in our little shop.
The big door
shows my sunny house
on my back.
Through green glass
in my helmet
my father welds;
locking blue light
inside the steel
as orange sparks
leap to freedom.

Jeannie Ralston

The Opening

You say
You're happy
To be.

Alone I see.

Then
Why can't we?

I'm in you
and
You're in me.

I decree:
Let's agree
and
Be fluid
and
Free
as
The sea;
Be.

Wrightman Kelley

Organized Religion

Chains which close minds
cultures lost across time
a piece of jewelry
not a state of mind
judgement passed on Sunday morn
easier to accuse them to look within
on the pulpit of hypocrisy

John M. Lichtenberger

A Mother's Gift

A mother's gift;
So wonderful and true; I do
not know what kids would do
without mothers like you.
  Your love, your smile, how
could I possibly forget how
wonderful you've been.
We don't have much money but
I know we'll get by.
You'll always be there by our side.
When I grow up I am going to
be as loving and caring just like you.
So don't forget you've got a
mother's gift; so wonderful and true.

Aimee Rogers

At The Water's Edge

I sit by the pool; the water glows. The water glows,
when the light shines on the water and the waves appear.
The water spins and churns, and rocks as the water glows.

I look at the pool ceiling as the light beams on the glowing tile.
The rippled water glows as people swim laps. They swim up a storm
of disarray as the water glows.

This glow is a unique glow as swimmers pitter and patter, the
children splash and churn in the water, close to the pool's edge.
Splashing and churning is what makes the world go round.
Children are the livelihood of energy and a ray of sunshine.

As America embarks on the end of the century we cannot forget the
water's light. The country is just a wink away as the water glows.
Think about it; as the years go by we wonder at what a distance we
are from the century's end — but over the long haul we benefit from
the young children as they pitter and patter.

Joseph C. LoRusso

Tributes

During the spring of the year you could always see a strong lady
tending to her yard. She was there long before you or I could ever
dream about getting up, but there she would be sharing her thoughts with God.
A straw hat upon her head and a rake or gardening hoe in her hand.
She - would be there listening to God's plans.
He had given her much, so many children to love her true.
A house everyone calls home and grandchildren that could have easily
been her own. God had given her much, a heart to serve Him, the
strength to know Him and the faith to understand Him.
He had given her the wisdom that only a mother can have;
He had given her much for that was His plan.
And when the sun rose high in the sky, she would be through gardening
and would be ready to rest. Straw hat in hand, rake and gardening hoe
in the other, there she would sit on the front porch or by the window
in the parlor waiting on God's messenger while watching her gift from
God bloom. There she would be, smile upon her face watching and
thinking admiring the "Good Lord's grace"
And if you look around yourself right at this moment
You'll see and understand why her flowers always bloom.

Lisa F. McCullers

Puppies In Their Prime

It's truly fun to watch the small young animals, as they fight, play, and whine;...
They show-off for humans in an instinctual way, they're puppies in their prime.

And in their prime, which doesn't last very long, they're tireless and that's a good sign;...
They'll dig up your grass, and spread around trash, 'cause they're puppies in their prime...

It's possible I have seen more beautiful sights, but at present none comes to my mind;...
Evidently they weren't more beautiful to watch, than these puppies in their prime.

And in their prime, which passes far too fast, they'll trust you if you're tender and kind;...
Still they'll chew on your shoes, rip and tear your paper-news,
  'cause they're puppies in their prime...

They uplift my spirit, and refresh my mind, with their antics time after time...
I hope and pray they will stay this way, fluffy puppies in their prime...

Jeffrey Steven Colbert

To My Children

Oh, could I gather the wandering years, and fasten them snug at my
gate, I'd offer them for your pleasure at noon, but the wandering
years will not wait. Could I but capture the dreams that are fled,
I'd lock them in life's secret file; I'd take out
one golden dream every day and spread it before you in style. Many
days I'll store neatly like spice on my shelf, and label them "smiles"
and "tears." I'll treasure each flavor, the bitter and sweet, and use
them to season the years Dear children just taste a little today
and then leave my memories alone;
No, you will not miss my wandering years, for you must make dreams of your own.

Helen Cutlip

A Visit With Daddy

While walking down the corridor of my mind one day;
I turned and strolled down memory lane.
Suddenly, my Daddy was standing in front of me -
I could see his face so plain.

He smiled and said, "How are you" and "is your Mama well"?
I asked him if he'd sit a while, we had so much to tell.
We sat down on a river bank, beneath a great oak tree,
And I said, "that, we were fine, both Mama and me".

I told him that we missed him and, that he looked so good.
He said, "We won't be separated long, if you live the way you should."
His sparkling eyes and radiant smile, without another word
Touched my heart with all his love, our minds in one accord.

We stood and, as we turned to go, I looked up to say, good-bye
But, there I was alone again and I began to cry.
Suddenly, I felt the love I had seen there in his eyes
And, I knew then, through love, there is no good-byes.

Donna Abell

No Longer Tomorrow

I wish I could go away; away from everything.
I wish that I could leave right now; immediately.
I can give up on it all. Wash my whole life away.
Along with all the pain and hurt that infects my
heart, the reasons I no longer wish to stay.

No longer the tears, no loner the pain and sorrows.
No longer shall I suffer; no longer tomorrow.
For this shall be the last day, no longer shall these eyes cry,
nor my heart beat, nor my soul weep as these lips kiss good-bye.

As I lay here I barely breathe, away from me I feel my life slide.
Eyes and mouth open wide, I laid there; and I died.

Steven Hutchins

The Other Mother

As the tears come falling down my face,
I can't help but wonder who has taken my place.
Do they hold and protect you as much as I would,
will they ever know, how I wish that I could.
Does your father teach you how to stand proud and be strong,
does your mother teach you gentleness, and to know right from wrong.
Are they patient, loving, and understanding at all,
do they pick you back up when you stumble and fall.
Can they quickly turn all of your frowns to a grin,
do they stand right beside you, through thick and through thin.
I know it must seem like I'm expecting a lot,
and I know deep inside, that "Perfect" I'm not.
But I don't think these dreams are crazy or wild,
because a "Mother" always wishes the best for her child.

Rhonda McClendon

Sunset Islands

High above the raging seas the rays of the sun explores,
From the highest of the island peaks to the sand of the ocean shores.
Images of mountainous terrain surrounded by the deep blue,
Cleansed with the summer's rain are God's creations shining through.
Like the beauty captured by a snapshot hanging motionless on your wall,
Is the sunset on the islands caught forever in your heart, mind and soul.
The pebbles on the beaches reflect the strains and labors of the day,
Bottled up inside like a gem you collect ocean waves will wash them away.
When the sun sets upon the ocean surface and auburn settles in the sky,
You know the sunset has it purpose to let the stars illuminate the night.
Pray upon the days to come for the sun is sure to rise again,
Dream some dreams for they will become as true as the day will begin.

Kristin Ashby

Water Vision

A journey has begun
A crusade it will be

Splashing, rushing, rapidly falling

A map it has to guide its way,
Only one way to go
Down, Down,
Into which it came forth

Ending not here, nor there
Battling forever
Circling its way
Round and round

Only one friend it has
Thundering its way through the clouds
Announcing its departure and soon return

Lisa M. Bee

Life

I came and I was
and then I was no more,
will I be again?
Was I before

See now into the mind
and this question forever more
does it end or begin?
For now and forever more?

Bobby R. Morgan

The Flight Of Herring Gullberg

The sea winds are blowing west to east
The view of a table is set for a feast
Caviar, onions, carrots and eggs
Loxs, and bagels, and red wine with legs
Ringing, laughing, yelping, and mawing
Whining and screeching
Delight!!
Delight!!
Left alone was I
The feast to be
No one in sight
Break free!!
Break free!!
As nature has it a skullcap atop
I scooped up the lox
Then left my mark

Mark Abraham

A Color-Coded Heart

If my feelings were put in colors,
   My feelings for you would be bright.
Deep red would be the passion of love;
   The purity would be of white.

The times I failed to show I care,
   Would be the color blue;
But green would sometimes comfort me,
   Knowing I can start anew.

These colors would represent the way,
   This way I feel about you;
For a color-coded heart will show,
   That my love for you is true.

Hope Marie Washburne

Life Is Fragile

A life is such a fragile thing,
A woven chain of thread;
With links of joyous golden strands,
Or dark and somber dread.

A piece of lead can end a life,
Though small in size and weight;
And none can tell when life is gone,
What is its doom or fate.

As bubbles floating in the air,
Some break and fall below;
Some rise to higher worlds unknown,
Where others cannot go.

No matter what we say,
That life is bubble or a chain;
We know that man cannot bring back,
The life that once is slain.

Marcia Chvat Minot

My Torch Is Upside Down

My torch is upside down,
and it consumes me;
I didn't know
that I had turned it over.
I never realized the actual moment
the light that was
bright enough for my youth,
upright enough for my youth,
got too dim for older eyes to see —
like going from the black into the red,
like slipping from my interest
to my principal —
unawares —
compelled by life itself
(by death itself)
to continue
to consume
even me.

James W. Cole III

Don't Forget

When we're troubled and don't
Know what to do
Talk to God, he'll see you through.

We always go to God in prayer
When we're desperate
God is with us everywhere
We have problems, we can't solve them
He will answer your prayers
Don't forget

Why is it, when we think we don't need
Him, we forget to serve him
And keep our vows

When our bills come due
We're in despair we know
He cares in face of adversity
He blesses with prosperity
We will always remember him.

Hazel Allen

A Soldier's Wish

I wish upon the brightest star
to make my wish come true
just to bring me home to her
always safe and true

Nick Bronzino

Complete

When I look at you sometimes
It sounds sort of strange
But for a moment in that look,
I fall in love with you all over again
That funny feeling way down inside
When I look into those eyes,
Those beautiful blue eyes
Then I sigh
The reason why
Because I know we are complete

Stephanie Canonica

Kindness

A gentle look,
A gentle smile,
A gentle touch,
A gentle hug,
Shows the receiver caring,
Costs the giver nothing.

A gentle word,
A gentle thought,
A gentle act,
A gentle prayer,
Shows the receiver loving,
Costs the giver nothing.

Caring and loving,
Two human traits,
Shows the receiver accepting,
Costs the giver nothing.

Harriet Hoevet Bennett

Families

Families are to have and hold,
They are more precious than Gold.
Though life may tear them apart,
A love rekindled warms the heart.

Cherish each moment while you may,
For you may not see another day.
Guard this love close to your heart,
Not letting anything keep you apart.

For when you are Old and Gray,
This bond is what will ever stay.
Friends may come and then go,
Family is there in rain and snow.

Dear God thank you for this gift,
May this love never ever quit.
Each day may it always flourish,
Guarding each moment to cherish.

Priscilla Luke-Suneetha

Dreamer

My home is my castle
  I shall not want
    except luxurious things...

Expensive diversions
  shipboard excursions
    upon every finger a ring

Pearls of great culture
  I'd hoard like a vulture
    I'd thrive on all precious things

So untrue to nature
  I'd spend 'stead of save
    this isn't half that I crave...

Evelyn M. Cole

Children

When I hear them cry,
it tears my heart apart
I can't tell you why
but, I too could start.

When I hear them talk,
it makes me feel so happy
I want to take them for a walk
just to listen to their story.

When I hear them yell,
I feel some kind of strain
because I can't always tell
whether they feel joy or pain.

When I hear them laugh,
my heart just fills with joy
I can never get enough
of the laughter of a girl or boy

Veronique Maes-MacDonald

Let Not The Light Burn Clear

The future starts today
And leads into an endless array
Take me far away
Am I to flourish or am I to perish
Twice in one life is too much to bear
No more disappointments
One things to go right
So you won't find yourself
Crying into the lonely night
Once more we will ask
For the light to burn bright
Not to be extinguished with
Thoughts of sorrow
And no hope for tomorrow
Stand tall and speak clear
Make them hear
You will not fall again
Rise above the clouds
See through the tears
Let not the light burn clear

Christine E. Brown

Hugs

It's wondrous what a hug can do.
A hug can say an "I love you"
A hug can cheer you when you're blue
or "I hate to see you go."
A hug is "Welcome back again".
Great to see you, where've you been?
A hug can soothe a small child's pain,
And bring a rainbow after rain.
A hug, there's just no doubt about it.
We scarcely could survive without it,
A hug delights and warms and charms
It must be why God gave us arms.
Hugs are great for fathers and mothers.
So stretch those arms without delay
and give someone a hug today!

Susan Preziuso

Untitled

Virtues, dreams,
thoughts in rare form to explain life
  in simple terms.
To live and die in an imperfect world.
The sky shakes,
  I don't know why.

M. L. McCloud

My Love

We share our life; we share our love,
　And we always know,
There is someone to depend on
　To give us back our glow;
When things around defeat us,
　Or set us back a bit;
We can each count on the other
　To keep our fire lit.
I wouldn't want to be without you,
　For you are my very core;
I've loved you for a long time now,
　But I've never loved you more!

Charlotte A. Fife

Trapemo

We are the definition
It is not a premonition

We are and will always be
Floating in our own reality

Harmony does not exist
Crises challenges us, if we resist

Lulled to sleep by subliminal visions
Surgical implants with utmost precision

Be aware
There is no way to prepare

We are The Trapezoid of Emotion
Life's jagged edges in perpetual motion

William C. Leppo

DoppelgSnger

There's a certain someone
That no one else can see
She really is a fun one
Who dwells inside of me.
She has no image reflection
No reason to go or to linger
Lacks any aim or any ambition
Because she's my Doppelgänger.

Eunice Abby Reding

The Best Day

I love this day
Everybody was well
The flowers smelled better
Just like a dream
Golden fields spread the pasture
And in the night
A star looked down at me and said
"Don't you like this day?"
And I replied back
"Yes I do, but it only comes this day"

Reece Love

Dingo

There is something about a Dingo
That makes your heart tingle,
It's that look in his eyes.
He looks like he is praying,
and I know what he is saying.
"I will love you until I die."
Oh! Yes there is something about a Dingo
That no man can deny.

Feng Sheng Shi

What Are We?

Are we just what is visible?
Is that all that makes us up?
Or maybe it is just a shell
That covers what is the real us

Are we two arms, two legs, and pretty?
Or is that just the wrappings?
I think we are what is inside
And the covering is just that!

We are much like a Christmas package
The wrapping is oh!, sooo pretty!
And does first get our attention
But the contents are really what counts

What good a pretty gift, that's empty?
It is not a gift at all
But a real gift, even ugly wrapped
Is still a gift worth having

So let us not dwell on the wrappings
But on the contents
For they are what counts
In the Real world

Leo C. Wilson

Big Bend

High mountains o'er vast stretches
Of space
A quick storm kissing dry earth
Calls forth a Joseph's coat
Of blossoms
To mask the barren desert —
　For awhile.

Patricia Morse-McNeely

Summer's Days

Summer's days, lightly, winded
gently, clouded summer's day,
the summer's day is last day,
Don't falter it maybe not, go ahead
Live life as you always have, what
if it was last day? What would you do?
Would you do anything, would you
have fear of the last day gripping
you too tightly? Would you live
the last days, or day, or summer's
day differently from all the rest
of your days, piously, righteously,
Refuse to change, because to change
your life on last day, is to admit
that your life has been wrong and
without fulfillment.

Theresa A. Whitt

What Went On In Nancy's Kitchen?

Double, double,
end of trouble,
fire burn and caldron bubble.

Eye of Newt and wing of frog,
wool of bat and hoof of dog,
toe of snake and turtle's mane,
cockroach boots and candy cane,
breath of moth and scale of cat,
tail of spider and horn of rat.

Slam! "Oh hi Judas, dinner is ready."

Christan Mullee

Untitled

Look into my eyes.
Who do you see?
Look beyond the lies,
And you will see me.

Look though my pain,
Though thick and thin,
take my hand,
you will know where I have been.

Look though my laughter,
though tangle and clear.
Take my love,
for our love is dear.

Look into my heart,
though the pain and laughing
Take my life,
for life is everlasting.

Look into my eyes,
what have you seen?
If you saw beyond the lies,
you will understand me.

Stefanie Nagata

The Mini Prince

He sits upon his padded throne
And smiles upon his slaves
Who bring him toys to catch his eyes,
This pampered prince of mini size.

He waves his hand to call his knaves
Who bring him everything he craves.
He's not yet into trains or trucks
Or planes of every hue,
He hugs his teddy bear and waits
To see what tricks his serfs will do

To gain his favor and his smiles,
This potentate of mini size.

He knows his wishes will be met,
And he will have no need to fret
To get what e'er he wants to get,
This emperor in baby guise.

Alta A. Olson

Vocabulary

"Integrity?"
The young man laughed.
"It sounds almost obscene.
A word from an ancient movie
Ripped off the silver screen."

"Loyalty?"
The young man mused.
"Sure, I'll stick by you
Until you infringe upon my space,
Then you and I are through."

"Honesty?"
The young man scoffed.
"What's that to do with me?
As long as I get what I want
I'm honest as can be"

"The world's a mess"
The young man fumed.
"It's in a steep decline.
Someone ought to fix it fast,
The responsibility not mine."

Lyn Edwards Asselin

Worth Waiting For

Every now and then,
    Just beyond that closed door.
You meet that special someone,
    You know is worth waiting for.

Ever since that day,
    I first laid eyes on you.
You made me quiver in ways,
    That nobody else could ever do.
You are such a beautiful woman,
    And I'm sure you're very kind.
I've been thinking a lot about you,
    Cause you're always on my mind.

You've been on my mind,
    Each and every passing day.
I would like to see you again,
    I hope we can find some way.

You seem to be very special,
    A woman I would love to adore.
I'll remember the times spent with you,
    Knowing you're worth waiting for.
            Steven R. Williams

Purple In Teal Abandonment

Desert drenched in moonlight....
Her eyes flash stars at me tonight.
She gives her love, till break of day;
When others come, take her away.

Amid the morning skies of teal
And indigo, they land to steal
From me the one and only friend,
Upon whom all my dreams depend.

Far out to the heavens flew
The spaceship - and my loved one too.
Abducted by aliens - she left me;
Waiting here on Earth, so lonely.

Beyond forever's end I fear...
She never will again appear!
I gaze intently at the skies;
While stellar dust gets in my eyes.
            Kristiana

God's Healing Co

Everyone's a storage shed
Full of parts, that we use
An electric panel in your heart
With a master fuse.

Your head, has a wave length
That makes it all function
Your arteries are stationed
At each vital junction.

A manufacturing process
To heal, all your wounds
If mental or contusions
Or maybe a little gloom.

You have miles of capillaries
Like rivers that flow
Or a waste disposal
That knows when to go.
            Lloyd Rexford

The Loudness Of Silence

Softly, silently,
I pad through the predawn hours
In search of your lingering presence,

Softly, silently,
I search each room, explore each corner,
In search of an image, a vision.

Softly, silently,
My nostrils detect a scent, but
No one is there - a memory,

Loudly, bellowing,
I rage and scream an agonizing
Call of anguish, and emptiness echoes.

Softly, silently,
I retrace my steps down the hallway,
Regretting another day without you.
            Jack L. Boland

The World's Child

I am the world's child;
Come upon this scene by chance.
Struggling from my mother's womb,
I bite the cord umbilical.
With pause to catch my breath,
I cry aloud, "I'm here world,

It's me," your newborn child.

Feed me now and clothe me.
Lift my body, help me walk,
Nurture me to face this life.
Though I'm blotchy, red and blue,
Soon I will be black or white;
or creamy yellow — even red;
For I am the world's child.

Who will be my father,
You or you, or even you?
Who will lift me from my crib,
Wipe my tears and smile on me?
Who will kiss and love me tenderly?
I am yours, the world's own child.
            John H. Elia

She Sleeps

She sleeps where the dogwood's
    delicate shade
with color enamors the air
and lays on the lonely new bed
    we have made
a coverlet soft as a prayer.

No more shall tears reach her,
    she sleeps without care,
Her troubles have melted away,
may she waken in sunshine as warm
    and as fair
as the morning forsaken today.
            Clyde A. Beakley

Modern Man

Lonely...
Dismal...
A voice cries,
Find Me!
Help me!
Here....
Sob.
            John N. Drowatzky

Time Will Heal

In time of need
We are, indeed,
Dependent upon one another.

I call upon you
To help me through,
You are as dear as a brother.

The pain I feel
Is so real
Will it ever go away?

Talk to me,
Set me free
Together to G-d we will pray.

Faith come back
Onto the right track
So again I can endure.

Time will heal
So soon I will feel
At peace with G-d and secure.
            Sondra Eisenpress

Life Or Destiny

Is our life a planned provision
of the things we are to be? Or,
Do we lurk behind the mysteries, of
the things we do not see? I! For
one, would like an answer; as I
travel on my way.
    Because my days must be
numbered, or at least is what
they say. Why! my life could have
been different.... In so many, many
ways, is why I often wonder, do
we even have a say?
    I do pray for their forgiveness,
those who went astray... Only God
is there to help us, when our
weaknesses go away.
    There are many unsolved
mysteries, in my life I can't convey,
that is why I need a miracle...
someone to show me the way.
            Viola Jelinek

Mr. Right Is Gone

First look
And I knew I was hooked
He made me feel
So very special
He wine me
He dine me
He made it all happen
Then all of a sudden
Wham-bam he was gone
At that moment
My heart was broken
I never felt so lonely
That even my soul left me
To think the man
I loved and thought was Mr. Right
Could just love me and leave me
Just as fast as he appeared
He disappeared
Not knowing where or who to turn to
I just cried knowing Mr. Right is gone.
            Elizabeth S. Conde

Situation

Seemed a feisty female tiger
took a tussle to a bear
it wasn't much a conference room
just a couch and several chairs

Bear didn't seem much daunted
so adjourned the matter there though
walked away her younger tiger
in esteem of much repair
summed up a set authority
restored a value and good care
and then conclusively returned said cub
secured and snug within the den

Susanne L. Helles

Snowflake Ballet

Hi, little snowflake
falling in the air.
Dancing on the breeze
with nary a care.

White as the clouds,
that sent you to the ground.
Fluttering and falling
around and around.

Exhausted you'll lay,
when you've come to rest.
Your brothers and sisters
will join the fest.

Tomorrow will be,
as yesterday is gone.
More little snowflakes
awakened from dusk to dawn.

Dale L. Park

Deborah

My heart beats with a melody of love!
Day and Night for Deborah.
I sing in the shower every time!
I vocalize for Deborah.

She is so petite
With short brown hair
With skin so soft
Deborah an existing goddess!

I observe my heart beating faster
I catch my mind dreaming
I notice my soul eliminating
I love Deborah so!

If only one chance to be!
I want her to
I only!
Just!

I will never get to tell her
I am in love
I have nothing but a broken heart
I am so alone!

Bruce N. Law

My Favorite Express

Thank thee my express
Taking me swiftly, surely home
Over your steel tracks you rumble
With the country at your side
Come upon the golden treasure
The conductor's pride

Sean Backe

Madison

You're one of God's Little Angels
    Born to us this day
And even though we had our plans
    His were not for you to stay

So now we must go on
    Forever to wonder why
If only He could answer
    Why you had to die

The thing that keeps us going
    And sees us thru each day
Is knowing you're in Heaven
    A safer place to play

You're with your brother Michael
    And together you will grow
So all this love we send above
    Is the greatest you'll ever know

Grandma Blausey

My Own Mine

I went out West searching for gold
But what did I find?
    "Fools' gold"
— not worth a dime —

I heard about a gold mine
down Mexico way
So I jumped in my jeep
Not to tarry a day.

I bought a plot of land
I dug deep and I dug hard
I put up a fence
to guard my back yard.

Some say I'm a gold digger
others call me a fool
most claim I waste time
believing rocks into jewels.

Whether it's 24 carats in my back yard
Or pure pyrite, I find —
It doesn't matter to me, you see,
As long as it's all in my own mine!

Carol Chilian

Country

Few people view the country
Or see the beauty there
If they would just notice the bounty
Of all the scenery so fair

Farmers sowing seeds in the spring
Women planting flowers galore
Praying for spring rains to bring
An abundance of crops to store

The leaves soon bring such beauty
We wonder where summers gone
Leaving us with a wonderful memory
Then we can appreciate each new dawn

If we stopped to smell the flowers
And enjoyed mother natures hues
Not look at the fault of others
Then we enjoyed the beautiful views

If you just look, there's beauty
In any season of the year
Then you'll never be lonely
If you just let a smile appear

Calvin Nelson

Rice

R is for the rough life I no longer live
    since I repented of my sins
I is for I who is living a happier life
    since repenting of my sins
C is for the calmness I have within
    since repenting my sins
E is for eternal life with God
    I have to look forward to when I die

Roy McDuffie

Respect

A word which means honor
A word with high regard
Something that doesn't come easy
It comes by very hard
It is not to be taken lightly
It is easily taken away
Once obtained, hard to keep
You earn it day by day
Not given to just anyone
Earned only by a few
One thing you have proven to me
RESPECT is what I give to you

Matt B. Englebrake

Thanks To My Fancy Sleigh

I know a friend
who doesn't like snow.
So when ask her to play,
All she says is, "NO!"

I tell her, "It's fun,
you'll see."
But "no" is her reply
to me.

I say, "Playing in the snow is fun,
but hurry up
before the snow
is melted by the sun!

She finally says, "Okay,
but only one thing...
Promise me I'll get to ride
in your fancy sleigh!"

Lauren Godlasky

At Your Window

Dear Friend, it was a cruel fate
That shut you from my sight.
Each lonely, sunless day I'd wait;
Each restless, starless night,
I longed for word of how you'd fare,
So racked with fever, tossing there!
But today the world is bright again,
For I have seen your face
So white against the window pane,
And smiling with the grace
Of Heaven shining there far more
Than I have ever seen before.
Perhaps still watches of the night
Brought you some dream or vision bright.
Perhaps mid rush of angels' wings
God's Spirit whispered holy things.
Transfigured thus I see you there;
I know that God has heard my prayer,
That soon you will be whole again —
You've smiled into my soul again!

Edna E. West

In Retrospect

"I want you!" softly whispered.
"Yours I'll be." She said.
Two arms around her circled,
and carried her to bed.
God looked down and cried for them.
Alas, life can be cruel.
And two wrongly joined lovers,
oft make one forgotten fool.

Maxinne D. Morris

Poetry

My eyes are always open,
My mind always in gear,
Searching for something
   to write about,
For all the world to hear.

Whether it be of nature,
Of love and even time,
My mind is never satisfied,
Till I put it all in rhyme.

I write about the children,
Sometimes about my friends,
About the love God gives us,
I can't hold these thoughts within.

Someday I wish to write a poem,
That will sooth each mind and heart,
If it could bring peace to all the world,
I'd know I've done my part.

Charlene J. Hatton

A Child Is Born

The feeling of a man's touch.
Joy of Conception
Beauty of giving birth:
A child sent from Heaven
To raise, to teach, to show
To mold into an individual
Courage to stand and be proud.
For life is so precious, and treasured
A privilege to hear them say
Mommy - Daddy
I'm here, show me the way.
The feeling of a man's touch
Joy of conception
Beauty of giving birth
A child sent from Heaven

Debbie Jean Yacklin

One Of Those

Dance with me silent raven!
Our songs are quite alike.
The time is now to sing the
mental tune of our fights.

Dance with me silent raven!
Our tongues are frozen still
but the music always plays
for you and I our truths kill.

Dance with me silent raven!
our sorrows were twinned at birth.
Let's waltz away our sadness,
let's flee this horrid earth.

Die with me silent raven!
The time to leave is now.
Our songs no longer play on
and life is not allowed.

Emily Douglass

The Alpha And Omega

A Great Spirit alone in a dark void,
without laughter, without joy.
Like a bright star does shine,
projecting through space in time.
Creating from nothing as it went,
in nature's balance, nothing spent.
Subdividing into countless parts,
giving All the spirits their starts.
The mighty cosmos they did perceive,
from whence they came, they leave.
Combining with the elements form life,
but with the creation there is strife.
Through love, kindness, joy, we shine;
but with hate, malice, greed, decline.
Through darkness the light will shine;
Our faith within will not be blind.
From within that small truth to find;
for our will with Him we shall align.
Once our countless sojourns are done,
then we all shall again be One.

Walt Holcomb

I Am

I am all love,
I give my peace,
I obey justice,
I use my beauty,
I take advantage of nature,
I am a worshiper of freedom,
I am the serenity that God gave.

I am what I am

Robert Roosen

Angel In Heaven

Angel
   lying in golden white sweetness.
Chocolate eyes
   melt in hope and prayer.
Warm like the sun
   in a cool summer's breeze.
Angel...
   docile as a lamb.
Two Shetland Sheepdogs of the Lamb.

L'il Bit O' Heaven.
A small silver cloud puff
   with a Panda face.
Gently straddles
   golden white sweetness.
Extending
   angelic ivory paws,
   encircling, embracing his Angel.
My tiny Teddy.
   Bear Hugs.
Angel in Heaven.

Michelle J. Murphy

Valentine

Paper Hearts belie the fear of
   Intimacy.

   Can one dare to
   Love,

Having grieved so Much
   for Loss of

   Self?

Carolyn M. Goyette

The Monkey, The Zoo

I saw a friend
   today alone
   he cried
he really
is streaming unseen
   tears
all
   however
our friend felt
   especially by me
huddled by the window
   arms clasped
   I see
   'round his chest
his gaze wide-eyed
   at the massed viewers
   as if to secure
   their comfort and
   escape
a dream

D. Kristian Barnett

Heart Broken

Where are you going my little one?
Pray tell I know not where
My life is full of emptiness
And no one seems to care.
It seems I've lost the will to live
Don't know just where to go.
my two best friends have left me
And Oh! I miss them so.
I try so hard to do what's right
But no one understands
I need someone to be my friend
And give me a helping hand.

Virginia Ellington

This, I Believe!

I'm for life:
   Busier days,
   Loftier ways

I'm for living:
   Purposeful days,
   Meaningful ways.

I'm for loving:
   Companionable days,
   Knowledgeable ways.

I'm for caring:
   Selfless days,
   Sharing ways.

I'm for seeing:
   Beautiful days,
   Life giving ways.

I'm for knowing:
   God giving days
   For splendid ways.

Raymond B. Knudsen

Garden Of The Dead

Why does a rose grow in half
a foot of snow? But with its
thorn a human's finger it must
truly prick. Was his blood black
or was his blood red? No one knows
and no one shows in the garden
of the dead.

Erin Watts

Kyla

She stood before me
dressed in red.
And with her mind
to me she said

Be at peace
inside your heart
For from you
I'll never depart

My spirit abides
in sunshine and love
And I can fly
just like the dove

Then she faded
From my sight
But left behind
A heavenly light
My soul smiled

Judy A. Egan

Sea Of Thought

There was a wave of words
On a sea of thoughts
That talked about a ship
That sailed the sea
Along came the wind
And moved the ship
And the wave of words
Hit the shore
On a land of dreams.

Linda Gaile Blaziek

I Need Someone

I need someone to hold me,
to listen and understand.
I need someone to give me advice.
To be a gentle man.
I need someone to hold me
and hug me with tenderness.
I need someone like you.
You're different from the rest.
You're special, kind and thoughtful.
I like to talk with you.
I need someone very special.
I need someone like you.

Eileen Linda Williams

Frigid Darkness

In the arctic Northland,
On a cold, still night,
The burning moon and infinite stars,
Provide the only light.

Frigid waters to the South,
Frozen mountains to the North,
You can't help but to love this land,
As you bravely struggle forth.

Land of the Great Grey Wolf,
Land of mortal fears,
Land that beckons longingly,
That's why I shed my tears.

Jonathan C. Asay

The Year 1997

The year 1997.
This will truly be a new year.
With the Lord,
We will not have any fear.

Let's see how much
We love one another.
Thank the Lord,
Because,
He has helped us
One step farther.

The Lord will show us
The way.
With him is where
I want to stay.

We can love the Lord
Each and every day.
He will be there for
You and me.
We could be so
Happy and free.

Helen Garner

Friendship

When life seems unfair,
Or you can't find someone to care,
Look inside you,
For everything you do,
Affects everyone around,
Here on the ground,
Please put yourself in their shoes,
Be careful in everything you do,
For one day you may be there,
Or who knows where,
So please be kind,
And not so blind,
Always wear a smile and never a frown,
For some day you may be down,
Always offer a helping hand,
As you do remember this one thing,
No matter what life may bring,
Always be a friend,
For a friendship never ends.

Nancy Speake

The Beet-Eaters

We eat beets
the tasteless, purple juice
stain the main parts of my perfection —
not even the big bleach can leach
onto such permanence. But

The dry find in cotton-mouth,
such speechless each word deemed
more powerful, the strain of lip and
tongue-slapped teeth.

It's the only hair, muddy backed
garb that gathers around the raw-sexed
root, like lace — the hidden temptress.

So boil,
let the blood paint rings around us all
revel in the tainted water
filled with the color only fools
enjoy.

Christopher Eric Owen Cummins

Fledgling

Fledgling, why do you fly so high?
Some people are puzzled,
Some wonder.

But I know why you fly so high:

Your wings are like satin,
Your body like silk,
And your eyes are moons
Glowing in the night.

You fly so gracefully through the air,
So you can view the earth so fair.

You never come down to take a rest,
You're always up there with the best.

But I know why you never rest.

You feel at peace above the leaves
But you don't know what to
Expect down beneath the trees.

Sarah Hunter

Peace

Faces, freedom fought for now
Lionesses on the prowl
Life and limb risked for world
into red hydraulics hurled
clashing swords and dropping bombs
snapping fingers, sweaty palms
In the world, this spinning strife
Keep your gift, keep your life

Lindsay James

Concomitance

To you my thoughts are nothing
in the wind.
You think with your mind.
I reach out with my heart.
You can make a speech.
I can make a bed.
You see the vine.
I see the leaf.
As to living, we have the same belief.
So somehow I see
We can live together quite happily.

Florence Baker Hanson

She

Warm as the Southern winds
Her smile shines brightly upon me
Warm is the laugh that rings
So sweet, so gentle, so quietly
The light that glows from her eyes
Reminds me of angels features a loft
They sing and dance with joy and glee
Love so pure, so soft
She smells of mornings of dew on roses
That fresh clean smell of spring
Enhanced by her I blow a kiss
That images forever, I will cling
She then will warm my soul
She can quell my passion
Warm's the light I hold
I will come home to you.

Todd Blamire

The Proposal

Come live with me,
In my lighthouse by the sea,
And be my love.

Come be my friend,
Right to the end,
Come be my love.

Through wealth and fame,
Through loss and shame,
Come be my love.

Through good and bad,
Through happy and sad,
Come be my love.

Through day and night,
Come be my light,
Come be my love.

Come live with me,
In my lighthouse by the sea,
And be my love.

Rosanna J. Deaume

Friend

Your kindness can
Be heard in your
Voice.
Your smile offers
Comfort during bad
Times.
Hope can be seen
In your eyes.
You are truly a
Person I am proud
To call friend.

Russell Ward

Soul Wanderer

I am not myself
How could anyone be themselves
I feel my soul wander to others
experiencing what they do
God just give me a body to live in
But it's nothing more
I'm just a waiting soul
ready to be given another waiting body
So my soul can experience
other waiting souls...

Amanda Ropella

To My Dad

Small yellow faces
shined
to remind me of sunny
days gone by.
Not ordinary are these
bloomed that they would one day
Grace the grave
of one loved so well
now withered and faded
upon my pillow
like the spirit within.
They cry out to be delivered
to shine again
Anointed by my tears.

Gail Williams

The Duck And The Chicken

A duck once told a chicken
"Why, you're more popular than I —
You're in all menus,
Broiled, baked and fried."
The chicken bucked and crackled
"What you say just isn't true —
Why you're the one that's most admired
As you fly up in the blue —
And you're the one that is most loved
As you waddle in the muck —
I hate it when they call me
'Chicken' — but thankful when
They yell out — Duck!!"

Ed Wyatt

Good-Bye

Locked in a cage
An example of rage
Crying by day
Dying by nay cause
As I pause
One last breath
One last sigh
One last cry
good-bye

Cara J. Hannus

The Return Of George

When "Star Wars" arrived in 1977,
George Lucas was not fully satisfied,
he could not do all he wanted,
yet viewers loved what he tried.

George was a pioneer,
who dabbled with possibility,
he possessed many dreams,
which became a reality.

What "Star Wars" inspired,
was a phenomenon unto itself.
Now George is back to enhance the film,
as a treat to himself.

George then went further,
fulfilling all within his mind's eye,
enhancing "The Empire Strikes Back",
and "Return of the Jedi".

Will audiences admire his recent work?,
or will they be sore,
ticket sales indicate one thing,
the fans just want more.

Joel Obuchowski

Lonely Desert

Cactus, sagebrush
As far as the eye can see
The warmth of the air is gentle
A comfort to the longing in me.

Have I spent my life in blindness?
My dreams never reached the sky
It never touched the greatness
Of the soul of one great guy.

On the road of this lonely desert
My thoughts are traveling free
Through all the cosmic spaces
And the fondest wish to be with Thee.

Hedwig Kempf

New Life

A life will come today,
a baby, a child of God,
Julianna she will be.
A flower among the trees.
A spirit from Heaven,
to fly and be free.
A child you see, created by thee,
A breath of life, of pure delight,
a smile, a cry, and a tear,
a child from thee.
Happy we will be, to see, to hold,
to keep from the cold, this child,
Julianna she will be.
Cry today, sleep tomorrow,
awake my child, come and be,
for your mother, is waiting to see,
this child from thee.
Julianna she will be.

William R. Criqui

Akasha

Lost,
In a sea of passion.
Needing,
A reason to believe.
Wanting,
To melt in your eyes.
Forever,
Circling the same sky.
Above,
The world around.
Hunting,
A spiritual soul.
Intense,
The reasons behind madness.
Wandering,
Into a wake of life.
Rebirth,
Closer, the danger is.
Destiny,
Our love for each other.

A. Nicole Sanders

"Our Alexandra"

Clothed in a royal night gown
only seven days old
The infant rested on Mother's large bed,
that looked to be an acre long
Through the doorway quietly observing,
the baby appears in command —
so true! so true!
I am queen of the domain,
I alone rule this home,
upon my throne.
This countenance she possesses
are rules that must be met
In come the Queen's subjects to peek,
with gifts for her approval,
I know! I know!
My subjects you will all be rewarded!
Now silence is all about,
but sleep I must, so I can dream
Please leave your gifts and depart,
For I have plans to make
for tomorrow and tomorrow
and tomorrow!

Ernest E. Seely

Memories

Clearer than water
A sound louder than thunder
which was heard so far away.

Run for your life,
but nowhere to go.
Silence, Silence, Silence
my heart is pounding.

A light shines in my face
A hand stretches out.
A voice shouted
give me your hand,
I will take you to freedom.

I held it tightly
when I saw the light
at the end of the tunnel
I know I was safe.

Beryl Harvey

Pretty Words

This planet has no time for tears
Your pretty words I need to hear

Speak of desire, speak of romance
Of things too foolish to comprehend

Though talk is cheap, and I am weak
Your lullabies will bring me sleep

Carry this fool to other worlds
And fill my life with pretty words

By bread alone, no man can live
He must have courage to believe

So make me strong, say I belong
Like bird of Spring, thrill me with song

With smiling glances draw me close
Capture each moment for all its worth

Carry this fool to other worlds
And fill my life with your pretty words!

Lillian Fabbro

There Was You

I walk, alone and lost
To the wind my cares are tossed
I trip on my shattered dreams
My tears falling down in streams
And then, there was you.

Your words lift me up
Past the moon and stars above
I dance on a cushion of air
Intoxicate myself in your stare
In my thoughts, there was you.

If only you knew
All the things that you do
You make my soul burn aflame
I am lost to your foolish game
In my dreams, there was you.

Your hand caresses my cheek
I know I've fallen too deep
I can't remember anymore
You've taken me to a distant shore
In my heart, there was you.

Becky Mindock

To Mom, Mother's Day 1996

You helped me learn to tie my shoes,
And, chase away all the blues,
You helped me write, color and paint,
And, to never use the word ain't,
You helped me with my homework, too,
Even if you were busy, and, I was
impatient with you:
I love you so much, you'll never know,
How dearly I care for you so.

Lisa Tebrinke

Burn Out

I'm tired of being
The one that's strong
of having the shoulder
The others lean on.
I want to be held
until all my fears
Like a magic trick
Just disappear.
I want the chains of responsibility
To be set free
I want the pleasure
of just being me.

Addie Renee McElyea

Flowers Of The Spirit

If flowers were the spirit
From the day we are born.
It would be an African Violet
So fragile, soft, and warm.

   As we reach childhood
   Loved and nurtured to succeed.
   This lies within a Dahlia
   Showing inner beauty for all to heed.

Then comes the teen-age years
A Majestic Lily shows her head.
For she will grow strong and proud
While weathering nature in her bed.

   When we reach adult-hood
   A Rose will surely be found.
   Some may show many thorns
   As their inner beauty will surround.

Soon we will all be elderly
The Orchid will show through.
Her gentle petals forming angel's wings
Is exactly what I found in you.

Jacqueline Remay

Sweet Emotion

Rain, taking a part of my soul
and leaving with me a pouch
of memory to fill in the monstrous
space of my imagination. Clouds,
out of reach, take my
attention with my eyes half open
and feet barely touching the ground.
Standing on the moist ground,
I see out of the corner of my eye,
a boy leaning against an old,
rotting lamp post. A tear of emotion
swells, and the boy leans more.

Shannon Langman

Young Mother

When your heart is young.
And you're out for fun.
You don't think of things
That could ruin all your fun.
Now you're in your teens
you've had your fling.
With baby on the way
You have no time to play.
With washing and cleaning
All the day, you think of the
young life you led astray.
So when your heart is
young and out for fun.
Just remember! You're not!
The only one who pays,
with baby on the way.

Bonnie J. Raley

God

God, He is Almighty and
answers to no one,
the new way of life
came from his son,
he wanted us to be like Him,
But the Devils wanted
us to be like them,
He knew we were not
perfect and the Devils
had won,
and this is why he
sent his son.

Tommy J. Smith

The Dancing Lord

The sad dancer is dead.
The joyful dancer is living.
He lives on forever.
Never to perish.
He is Lord of the dance
The dancing Lord.

He dances where he pleases.
Never to stop. Never.
To those who accept
He gives a great gift
The gift of dance.

"Now dance for me," he says
In his deep, strong voice.
"Show me what you know."

The dancers try, and fail
For they aren't good enough for he.
Then he leaves, leaving them
With the gift of nothing.

With the gift of death.

Michaela Duggins

Time Is Right

You in my life, for time is right I
Have no need to fear.
Love is a treasure, for we are gold
Of today and yester-year.
Tender thoughts flow through tears
Of past and future things. For time
Is right and time is love, for what
Out future brings.

Joyce Lavon Wells

Orion

Bits and pieces scurry
Away in the wind,
Leaving me chilled
It feels as though they are
Ripped from my very existence

It saddens my soul,
That again I feel
The need to let another
Dream go into the
Wild

I may eventually
Catch them and
Put myself back
Together
Once more

Alas, this is neither
The time nor the place,
So I await for
That futuristic point
When I can be reborn

Kristina Fridas

Escape!

I shut my eyes and go to sleep,
I close the door on light.
I dream of things unknown to me,
I soar the sky in flight.

Just once, I feel I'm in control,
My life's on even ground!
Dare I whisper "Freedom's" name,
For fear I make a sound?

Gliding through the air so still,
I'm peaceful as a dove.
No turbulence or thunderstorm
To alarm me up above.

The darkness of my slumber's rest
brightens now and then.
I toss. I turn. I readjust.
Then I escape again.

Fran Gammicchia

Love After Death

When life is struck with death
We often mourn and cry
But we should stop and catch our breath
For true love shall never die.

Sometimes the pain is unreal
We seem to have lost all hope
It takes a while to heal
We need time to try to cope.

When our minds begin to wander
And we reminisce about the past
We should stop and ponder, and
Remember true love shall always last

We often feel so numb
We have love we long to give
Though they may be dead to some
Our love shall always live.

John Williams

Friends

Too many times I heard people say
What good does it do
To live in this world anyway
Why don't people learn to live
When you see a friend in need
Just be a friend in deed
Don't be afraid to share your wealth
When someone needs your help
What good is life if you don't share
Never be afraid to show you care
You see all these things
Are better than Diamonds and Gold
When you do these things
You do right from wrong
Your heart will sing a pretty song
A friend is worth much more to you
Than you will ever know
And make you happy
Much more than riches untold

Jean Hoch

Sun Kiss

Here in this place, while the wind it
warms my face, the moon I want to
chase, here on this hill, my senses
I want to fill, here the stars
heighten my awareness that I'm a
living being and that beauty is
so freeing
The night shines as the world
unwinds, colors fade to black
until the day comes back to
welcome the world to the
morning's glow to the sun
we've come to know,
to the kiss she bestows upon us
each day, to the debts we owe her
I pray that she always shines her
glory upon us as she lites our way.

Pamela Yarborough

My Greatest Treasure

You lead me by the hand
And took me to your promise land.
You showed me new ways of giving
And the best way of living.
Your love opened my heart's door
And make me feel like never before.
You're my greatest treasure made of love
Truly a gift from the heavens above.
I want you to be my beautiful wife
Because your spirit is the key to my life.

Brad David Buckley

Chelsea

A child...
sweet,
funny,
honest.

A friend...
caring,
silly,
truthful.

A sister..
kind,
playful,
sincere.

Jacqueline Klein

Journey

Sometimes...
At night,
'Midst falling snow,
'Tis time to wander
Here below...
Surrounded by silence..
Overwhelming peace,
And touched by wisps
Of tussled flakes,
Wending their way...
Earthward bound.
And on looking up,
Into a crystalline dance,
You can become lost,
In timeless reverie.
Until, at last...
Within the streetlight's cone,
The snowflakes' shadow
Touches home.

John A. Dunn

Our First Son

I got a call from him tonight,
from our first, the only one.
He and she are quite alright,
our first, our oldest son.

I got a call from him tonight,
he told me of their one.
He called to tell of their delight,
of their coming, perhaps son?

I got a call from him tonight,
that they are, as yet not sure.
Of their coming, small delight,
of their event, so pure.

I got a call from him tonight,
I wish that you were here.
To hear yourself of their delight,
my eye could hold no tear.

I got a call from him tonight,
I cried for alone we two.
I cried for their delight,
I cried for I "love you!"

Angelo R. Spagnolo

A Mother's Love

A Mother's love is
given without strings,
Upon which we fly,
her golden wings...

A Mother's love is
a beautiful song,
Musical vibrations so
sweet and strong...

A Mother's love is
our life's teacher,
Lessons we learn,
grow ever deeper...

A Mother's love is
never ending,
On this special day
our love we are sending...

Verna Y. Shockley

You

I love every inch of you
From the very day we said I do
Every time I look your way
I have a very special day
I need you more than you'll ever know
You teach me each day how to grow
I think sometimes we forget
We think we know everything and yet
Someone comes along one day
And what we thought we knew,
Instead we just grew

Karen D. Timothy

Teaching

To teach school is a job
One that has rewards galore.
Some days I think "I've had it!"
Then I come back for more.

Some days my class is great
Some days my class is a mess
But I still love my students
And I give them my very best.

Teaching isn't easy
As a matter a fact it's rough
But I keep hangin' in there
'Cause I am a country girl that's tough.

Retta Sells

Tears

Tears rolling down her cheek
they said when they married
"Till death do us part."
The day has come
She remains, he is gone.
Someone she loves
She can no longer touch.
He was her world
now it seems,
to have stopped.
Oh, how she loved him,
and wished he were here.
Tears rolling down her cheek.
Many names he answered to
Dear, Dad and Grand Pop,
She remembers his face.
Tears rolling down her cheek.
One day she'll realize,
his love for her remains,
forever, in her heart.

Sherry A. Weingartner

One Hundred Year Old Wonder

The majestic cedar grows,
Tall and straight,
With limbs that embrace,
The sky,
Its age is unknown,
But I have been told,
It is a century or more,
But it doesn't matter,
Looking at it,
Fills me with wonder,
That anything so old,
Could stand so tall,
And look so strong.

Mattie M. Stewart

My Color Game

When I'm inside on rainy days,
I have a game I like to play.
I think of colors of things I know,
Like yellow for the sunlight's glow.

I think of other colors, too;
Purple — eggplant; blue-jay — blue.
Sometimes I think of things all red,
Like my Dad's truck and jam on bread.

Sometimes I just decide to think
Of orange like the juice I drink.
But other times I think of green,
For stems and grass and frogs I've seen.

And so, at last, I have a kind
of made-up rainbow in my mind.

Melanie Lynn Jacobs

For Freedom's Fight

On Freedom's Wing
our Spirits soar.

Our Hearts they sing
we're chained no more.

They fought with Glory,
a tremendous tale;

A lifting Story
of the men we hail.

They marched with pride
on God's green earth,

And side by side
they proved their worth.

No longer bound
in a cold, dark cell;

Yes...most men found
that war was hell.

But now, they stand
with heads held high...

For this great land,
we'll fight or die.

Robyn Coleman

You Make Me Smile

You make me smile when days
Are rainy and the sun goes away
You make me smile when my
heart is blue.
You make me smile when love
is in the air and when the
weather is so fair.
You make me smile when the
sun goes down and when there
is no frown.
You make me smile when spring
is around and when the flowers
bud out.
You make smile when I don't
think I could, or I should.
You make me smile when
things go wrong, or when I
feel so all alone.
You make me smile when you
come and say I love you so.

Michele A. Johnson

Or So I Thought

Life was simple then
or so I thought.

So young and pure
I almost forgot.

The long evenings
where parents talked.

And boys played baseball
in a vacant lot.

Neighborhood children sharing barbecue
and soda pop.

The summers were endless
or so I thought.

You taught us Olympic games
and plays with eventful plots.

Way back when
on some empty lot.

We were the best kids
on the block.
So thank you Mom
thanks a lot, (...and you too Pop).

F. Reid Morgan

Beautiful Face

As I see your beautiful face
in the wind; I see your face
as being a friend, you're more
than just another beautiful face,
you're very special to me,
and I will always love you,
your eyes shine like the most
beautiful diamonds
in the world!
It is clear to me that God is in your Life,
stay with God,
I love you so very much
that I would die; so you could Live,
please don't let anyone hurt you,
remember you're beautiful.

Becky J. Tunison

Heirlooms Of Time

We are antiques
Worn
Yet valuable.

Survivors of time
Frayed
Yet still whole.

Blemished
By impurities
Yet so refined.

Viewed
As abnormal
Yet so unique.

Once
Almost worthless
Yet now priceless.

Each of us
A special
Work of Art.

Each of us a Rarity

Pat Duty

Buzzard

Dancing
And prancing,
Buzzard bad breath
To love him,
Will kill you.
Mortal death breath.
You eat him, you die
You touch him, you're green.
No amount of potion,
Can kill his disease.
So, flock from his feather,
Forget about your whether's.
Just leave the poor buzzard behind.

L. Brady Steward

Angel Disguised As A Nine-Year Old

Those soft, silver raindrops
remind me of you.
So innocent, so wonderful,
so true.

Yes. We were a pair
we two —
'til you received your wings
and into eternity you flew
leaving the wonderment
I once knew as you

Constance C. Margerum

Simplicity

Simple am I.
With uncluttered lines
Of thoughts to bestow.
Unadorned words that tell
Of my blessings and woes.

My lucid talk
Has no flowery tales to tell.
My words are austere and transparent.
Can you see?
God made me just an ordinary soul.

Will flowery words
Ever captivate my scene?
Or am I to be
As plain as green grass?
Simple me.

Mildred Zimbelman

For My Angel

I awoke early this morn,
my first thoughts were of you.

Musical words came to
play a melody in my head!

My heart roared with
the splendor of your name.

Yes, finally I know the difference
between sane and pain.

When I hear your voice
it's more delicate that the
song of a wind chime.

More magical than a choir
of angels. More breathtaking
than the flowers of May.

Speak to me.

Ramon Pecora Jr.

Out Where The Bluebonnets Grow

The other side of thirty-five
recalls to me once more
a highway where I used to drive
some forty years before.

Like, far out where bluebonnets grow
I'm on this ego trip,
back where I was so long ago
(and please excuse the quip).

With offers I could not refuse
I took my car and went
in time to drive away the blues
(I gave them up for Lent).

Out west the radios still bring
good music from the hills.
"The Austin City Limits" swing
with people like Bob Wills.

While driving down that awesome road
a voice I overheard,
"These flowers Mother Nature sowed."
That must be Lady Bird!

Durward Hopkins

Poem Of The Procrastinate

I'll write a poem tomorrow
which will bring the world to cheer.
My words will be of great renown
for many, many years.

A poem that holds such meaning,
such beauty in its way.
A poem of such great magnitude
cannot be writ today.

Today may be the final day
that I may spend alone,
For when I'm famed, Oh how they'll crowd
about my humble home.

I'm certain that tomorrow's light
will find my great creation,
my profound, moving masterpiece
of words and inspiration.

But that is for another day,
for now there is no need.
As long as there's tomorrow,
today is grand indeed.

Michael Hutson

You

When these material things
   have turned to dust,
And earth's dust join
   other stars' grand panoply,
There yet remains one golden orb
   of essence pure.
That orb is you my love
   eternally.

Through morning mist
   I'll see your face again,
And rendezvous we shall
   on distant star.
And your fond worshipper
   once more I'll be.
And worship at your altar
   once afar.

Wendell L. Vaughan

Thoughts From A Lonely Cornstalk

I wonder why they've left me here
   and took everyone else
I wonder why they've left me here
   It's nothing I've ever felt

I wonder why they've left me here
   All lonely and so dry
I wonder why they've left me here
   I wish that I could fly
   When shall I die?

Emily Littlehale

Precious Love

Like rivers without their currents
our waters could not flow.
As our hearts without love
could never truly grow.
If I had not given our love a chance,
This precious love
I would have never known.

Linda Doane

Cupid

   I saw a cupid in the clouds
pulling back his bow,

   His arrow flew I know not where,
yet he made his mark somehow,

   His arrow flew right to my heart,
when a dove on wing

   Brought your valentine to me.

Martha A. Lydon

And In His Dream

I awoke one morning to find Martin gone
He left his soul to live on
One people, one land
Black hand, white hand

And in his dream
I could hear a silent scream
Love your brother
And in peace live together

A king on a mountain
For us to see
All God's children
Living free
You and me

And in his dream
I could hear a silent scream
Together we stand
Apart we fall
One and all

Warren L. Foster

Eventide

In the evening of your mission,
as you serve him here below,
may you feel the savior's love,
as the healing water's flow.
From the river of his comfort
may you draw so deep and long,
'Til the savior comes and takes you
to the place where you belong.

Julius Vander Slik

The Mother Weeps For Me

As the rain falls from the clouds
As the sun struggles to shine
I begin to realize
It's a brand new day

The pain I feel from deep inside
Reflects with the autumn sky
Clouded and gray
Misty and wet

Thunder rumbles
Like the feeling
Residing in my chest

I pray for violent weather
Charlotte Cattell

A Meadow

A meadow filled with grasses tall.
A meadow filled with flowers.
A meadow where God's creatures play,
So happily for hours.
The deer who graze and sun themselves,
The mice who run and hide.
The bees who seek their nectar there
To be taken to the hive.
The wind will sometimes softly blow
And the meadow becomes a sea.
Then the waves' sweep smells of nature,
And you're glad you've come to be.
The meadow is a peaceful place
Most times untouched by man:
But if he should happen on one,
Pray he's gentle as he can.
A meadow, God's creation,
A place He didn't plant His trees,
Instead just open spaces where
He left beauty for all to see.
Mark T. Kenyon

The Ocean

Emerald Ocean
Glistening in the sunshine
Dashing into rocks

And then back to sea
Pushing sharp seashells along
Foamy and wavy
Dominique F. Leitner

Today

When that long black Cadillac
comes to the door
we won't have to worry
anymore

Bills, jobs... Others' stuff
won't mean a thing
when the guy in the suit
makes the doorbell ring

Hearses don't have luggage racks
there's nothing we can take
let go of what we don't have
it only causes heartache

Today is all we have
a promise of tomorrow
enjoy the vigor of this day
not many left to borrow
Bob Olson

God's Heavenly Angel

God's Heavenly Angel waits for us
Outside of this very door;
God's Heavenly Angel is waiting
For on her, our feelings we can outpour.
She is on this earth to help us
She will be there when we're in need;
She knows our every thought and concern
Her urging, we should heed.
By always trying to do what we want
We ignore her gentle nudge;
We always think we know what's best
No matter what path we trudge.
God's Heavenly Angel is waiting for us
Outside of this very door;
Should we open this door to her,
Or her knock, should we ignore?
God's Heavenly Angel is leaving
Returning to heaven up above;
If only we can remember her mission
To fill the world with love.
Francine W. Garner

Rachel's Poem

God can create a sunset
Each and every day
He can create a rainbow
After the rain has gone away
He can create the moonlight
To brighten the night time sky
He creates the clouds we look upon
And the wind that moves them by.
He can create the mountains
And flowers that bloom each spring
God creates all wonders
And all beautiful things
And though he'll keep creating
He will never be able to
Create anything more wonderful
Than the beauty he placed in you
James Michael Ruquet

The Mirror

When I look
in a mirror,
what will I see?
I will see a
loving,
gentle,
caring and
creative young woman
who enjoys all of the
time she spends
with you.
When you look
in a mirror,
what will
you see?
Kathy Dies

My God

My God is one in whom I trust
He's the only God for all of us
When we need help, He's always there
He knows our need and every care
I love my God and He loves me
It is by His light that I may see
So when trials and troubles come my way
I know my God will save the day.
Lynn Thurmond

Country Dreams

Our gravel winding road
Whistles of dogwood trees
The long curvy path
Hand in hand, you and me.

Glistening waters from the sunshine
As rocks surround our lake
Nature calls from all around
Our dreams that we make.

Beautiful flowers blooming
Such a sight to see
A cabin in the woods
Built just for you and me.

We stood together many years
To pray to God above
Our dream in the country
Filled with lots of love.
Naomi F. Garrett

Along: In The Wind (Infinity)

You're here (somewhere).
I hope you see and hear me

I'm here (also).
You hope I see and hear you

We hopefully notice each (other):
It's precocious

I don't know!?; I do!?——
Richard A. Carter

Haunting Melody

In the corner of my mind
Plays a haunting melody
all my yesterdays keep turning
To a long lost memory

As the tune continues playing
I travel back in time
Remembering times and places
That click like words that rhyme.

To days of treasured childhood
And homemade apple pie
Driving home from church on Sunday
Greeting friends as they passed by

Walking down the old dirt roads
In summer with bare feet
Cattle grazing in the pastures
Oh, those fields of golden wheat

I could listen to this song forever
That haunting melody
Taking me to time and places
Where my heart so longs to be
Linda Irons-McBride

Too Soon

I thought of you today.
I wanted to call to tell you
that I thought of you today.
That I wanted to tell you something
I knew would make you laugh.
To talk of everyday things.
The kids, the grandchildren.
The paths our lives have taken.
But you are gone.
Too soon.
I thought of you today.
Margo Lindemann

Lost Love

One day you told me you had special
   feelings for me
Then it seemed like the next day
   they were gone.
You said you couldn't love me as you've
   loved any other.
It just wasn't the same, I know
   it's true.
But what was it that was so different?
Was it that our love was becoming
   so strong?
Had you ever felt a love such as mine?
So true, so dear, so much was my
   love for you....

What went wrong?

   Michelle A. Rosario

The Final Scheme

The cult of illusion steeped in myth,
A vile of seclusion aligned to death,
Be not clear, the clouded dream,
Yet to fear, the final scheme.
Seek an answer from the dust,
Of vengeful decadence, greed, and lust,
Observe the find, if you fair to muse,
The solution of earthen space to fuse.
An isolate sphere of dense debris,
Known to us as — humanity,
Can fill our void of path retained,
To sense our being in mortal vain.
To what then can all this mean?
Existence, perception, or just a dream.

   Stephen E. Rice

Apocalypse

Fighting goes on across the lands,
sweeping countries dry.
Death is dealt by many hands.
The wounded left to die.

What is gained by such despair?
Our world's demise is free.
If there's no one left to care,
no winners will there be.

Our Earth is now a dreaded place.
Nothing for the eyes to see.
Tears rolling down her face.
A broken Miss Liberty.

What is wrong with such an end?
Sometimes you can never mend!

   Bruce R. Nadeau

Night Songs

One lonely songbird
Sang for me tonight.
His song was not of sorrow
But of the beauty on this night.

The crickets kept up clumsily
With such a master in his own right.
But I stood motionless
And listened in delight.

The song spoke of love
For the moon was full and bright.
The wind blew in harmony
So listen, listen to the night.

   Kenneth Pruitt

I Know That You're Alive

When I wake up in the morning
And the sun is shinin' in
I think of all Your glory
And the love You share within.

I love to watch each day appear
And know it was You who made each one.
You've put Your loving kindness
Into all that's ever been done!

I know that You're alive
Because I feel it in the air;
Every breath I take, every move I make
Depends on Your being there.

Thank you Lord for each day You bring.
I know each was made for me!
Help me to make the best of them
And let You shine through me.

I thank You for Your woods and fields
And for the rivers, lakes and seas,
But most of all I thank You
For loving me for me!

   Terria L. Gill

Help!

The innocent always gets hurt
The guilty always gets away
Can you feel the pain
Is it eating you away
Do you hear them chant
Can you hear them pray
Can you feel the power
Is it slipping away

The helpless never gets help
The needy never gets tended
Can you feel the need
Is it that they need
Do you hear them scream
Can you hear them beg
Can you feel the sorrow
Is it seen
Can't you see
It is you that they need

   Mark Nelson

Tonight: A Meditation

I stepped onto this night
accidentally
The stars burn
a thousand holes
in a sky
black like asphalt
at midnight
These lifeless trees wait
for a partner to dance with
but tonight
the wind is bored
Instead a freeze cuts in
ordering all
to be still
The moon hangs heavy
as if it is using
all of its strength
to hold up the night
but wanting
to let go

   Keith Chow

Her Word

A girl without bows
who will never know
a word as grand as this;
And whispered goodbyes
and not enough tries
and tricycles tossed aside;
And quietly laughing
as the people passing
never succumb to themselves;
The mirrored illusion
of constant confusion
in a world outside of our own;
And disagreeing races
and people without faces
and the constant fears of youth;
And the girl without bows
has yet to know
a word as grand as this.

   Melissa Lowrance

Unity

Picture it -
in your mind,
use your imagination
see one hand: White
holding another: Black
holding on to another: Reddish brown
and see the faces
with smiles
of joy
of happiness
of no difference
of unity.

   Lolly Bowean

Thunder Voice

The thunder rolls across the
Hills far way, a piercing
Voice tells me things
I am not.

But I am thunderstruck
And begin to believe
What I am not.

The storm worsens and I
Scream, nobody hears me as I
Become what I am not.

The voice becomes
Louder and stronger
It holds me down,
Won't let me up.
Now I am, what I am not.

Though the thunder has
Faded away, I have become
And will remain
What I am not.

   Shawna Kovacs

I Need No Stone

I need no stone to mark me
for someone to care or not care for
only to be beaten down in time
give my plot to the living
give my ashes to the wind
for the wind shall take care of me

   Henry W. O'Donnell Jr.

The Mermaid

The seagulls
Herald her coming
In her ermine
Robe of foam

She rises
To the shore
Selecting gems
From her jewel box

On the beach
The water drips off
Her lovely face
And fin

Then the sun
Turns her
Into iridescence

And she is
A moment of beauty
From the timeless sea

Madeline Gits

The Ten Tears

One tear begins,
Two tears follow.
Three tears continue,
Fourth tear remembers.
Fifth tear questions,
Sixth tear doubts.
Seventh tear wonders.
Eight tear desires.
And the tenth tear
Begins the flood.
And so forth
Bring upon
The hidden ocean
Of so many emotions
And feelings.
When will it end?

Stephanie A. Preku

Untitled

You tear yourself up with
    doubts and fears.

You hold your head in your hands
    fighting back the tears.

Life is to be lived
    not meant to pass you by.

Start taking risks
    Stop wondering why

Be true to yourself
    For no-one else will be

You'll be better off
    Just wait and see.

Janet Troth

Untitled

I saw a fish jump
Out of the deep blue ocean
It was colorful

Sara Watson

The Waiting Room

You enter the room today,
yet it is filled with yesterday,
only we wonder about tomorrow

On one side you see grandparents
across the way you see the children
to the side you see the grand children
not yet knowing why they are here

From the waiting room you see the hall
and down the hall we watch
not knowing what will appear
our hopes are for a cheery face
that will not show signs of sorrow

But if we shall see an angel
our hearts will be filled with sadness,
but also with joy for we shall know
everything will be OK.

Richard B. Haynes

A Corner Of My Heart

To My Dearly Beloved Husband,
Thomas J. Manning
I keep a corner of my heart
Reserved for thoughts of you
How very dear you are to me
How much I love you too...
And many a happy thought of you
Will always be a part
Among the private thoughts that fill
That corner of my heart

Terry Manning

Precious Moments

Memories of childhood,
With dust on the shelf,
Each speck, each spot,
A photo of myself,

A horse and her foal,
I think from the fair,
So cheap in design,
I'm surprised it's still there,

A liquid filled swan,
It's from the Big E,
We had fun that time,
Stacie, Heidi and me,

Glass Precious Moments litter among,
But that they all are,
And the bright days they were made,
Seem oh so far.

Amy D'Amico

The Soldier's Prayer

Brushed by the wings
of an angel called Death.
I've been burnt by the
dragon's hot breath.
I have survived
the call of the wild.
Washed the blood off my hands
to kiss the tears of a child.
Jesus, would you catch me,
in my fall from grace?
I'd like to live forever,
but not in this place.

Robert L. Close

I Know Nothing

Confusion... loneliness... uncertainty;
what happened to all my yesterdays
where are all my
tomorrows...Dear God,
Why do I feel black
yet only see white?
What do I taste;
sweetness...my only response
is bitterness.
Up and down
left to right
always yes in meaning
no, for sure, in speaking.
Where do you lie?
are you my today
or my forever tomorrow?
Please, be kind to me,
tell me...what are you?
I know only darkness and you;
therefore, I know nothing.

Monica Meng

A Teacher's Lament

A student is missing
In my room today.
Just when he departed
I really can't say.

Where is this child
Who sat in his place,
With an interested,
Eager look on his face?

Where is this child
Who truly worked hard
And never once asked,
"Where's my reward?"

Where is this child
Who took time to say
"Please," and "Thank you".
And "Have a nice day?"

He slipped out unnoticed,
Without making a sound.
I miss him, you know,
Since he's not around.

George T. Schipp

Cotton Feline

My cotton feline was for real!
A clean white snowball deluxe!
I can still hear his purring!

Our after school snack,
Always including milk,
Slowed my pace for homework!

He could unwind yarn the fartherest,
Jump for a bird the highest,
Stretch for a butterfly the longest!

Cotton was a fighter.
No mice, large or small, were
Allowed to live in our garage!

He lost life's battle to a snake,
Help was not fast enough,
Medicines would not heal him!

Recalling Cotton's capers among
Texas fields of sunflowers,
I envision his picturesque statue!

Joyce E. Ryan

Walking Away
(Dear Mommy And Dear Daddy)

I was only one year old
When on a summer's day,
You told me that you loved me;
Then, you turned and walked away.

You brought me here, into this world.
With you, I thought I'd stay.
But you just said, "I love you".
Then, you turned and walked away.

My grandparents take good care of me
And, with them, I will stay.
Because you said you loved me
Then, you turned and walked away.

Sometimes, you come and visit me.
Oh, how I wish you'd stay!
But you just say you love me;
Then, you turn and walk away.

Grandma holds and comforts me
Each time you go away.
How can you say you love me
And then, turn and walk away?

Kathy M. Brening

Inside

I have a deep dark inside
which shudders when I speak
for I cry at my utter voice
that makes me far too weak.

My molded figure appears
much more than what is seen;
I long to become another,
yet in return become a fiend.

Beauty is in my bones,
and I fear they will never rise;
instead they hide beneath my skin,
and I am the ugly disguise.

And still a hopeless hate
remains out of my control
soon I will turn my rusted body
into an endless hole.

Jill Marija Petric

Lost Treasures

Oh little one,
what would you have been?
   A scientist who found the
cure for diseases of mankind?
   A dancer floating gracefully
across a stage,
   A writer whose words could
turn the course of a life,
   A speaker who would turn
the in justices of the world around?
Oh, little one,
If on that fateful day, a bomb
   had not ripped you from this world,
If you had been allowed to grow,
   Whom would you have become?

Brenda Palmer

Smile

You should always smile.
Unlike some people who frown,
'Cause they're always down.
Hey, give 'em awhile.

Maybe your smile will cheer them up.
Don't be sad,
Be glad!
Instead give them a new baby pup.

Smile for a day,
And you will see...
That your friend will be...
Happy to see you and play!

Alicia Tempel

Untitled

He came as a babe
One wintry night
The wondrous star
Gave off His light.

The shepherds came
The wise men too
To see the King
Who came to save you.

He grew from a boy
A carpenter's son
To be a great man
The holy one.

He gave up his life
He died on a tree
On that dreaded hill
Called Mt. Calvary.

He rose into heaven
Undaunted by sin
And one day soon
He'll come again.

Sara Dossett

To My Brother

I can, sweet brother, only watch
as you slowly fail, the machinery
of your systems pumping less and less,
as you grind towards the inevitable
halt. Show me then, in these waning
days of light, how to lift the cross
of pain that shoulders you, if only
for a moment. Teach me, somehow,
in that immaculate space, to carry
my own timbers, that I might follow
the hymn of your fading breath,
and stand with you as the brilliant
darkness comes to bring you rest.

Alan Kopp

Seasons Of Growth

Love is like a wise old tree
whose knowledge is born in its limbs
To say you have learned from someone
is to say you have loved them
Like the insignificant acorn
when nurtured by the sun
grows into sky-filled magnificence
So does love mature
in seasons of perennial growth
from its unripened naivete
to a fruitful heart of completeness

Diane M. Myers

Bliss

Gaze upon the things once seen
Hold onto that memory
One day it will disappear
Everything gone, nothing near

Silence from within will speak
It echoes through the emptiness
Suddenly shattering the solemn image
What was seen, no longer is

Everything lost to running time
Nothing left or kept behind
An empty box of nothingness
Left to no one, a total Bliss

Michelle R. Dice

Noises Of The Night

As the night goes on
The moon shines down
Like a street lamp light.
The stars look down,
Shining and bright.

As the night goes on
The crickets chirp
Chirp, chirpity, chirp
The owl hoots
Hoot, hooo, hoot

As the night goes on
The fireflies light
Flickers and dances.
The wind swishes and blows
To make everything sway.

As the night goes on
The sky turns a fiery red,
And a bright purple.
The night is over.
Now to face a bright new day.

Erin Bonney

a moment for lynsey,
with the word petunia

petunia petals play
            with sacheting pillows
                  of plushing fiber wings
            partly splaying out
                  in circles
                  of
            whitish and yellows

                  and lavender hints

passioning in the shooing
winds of days

r. e. atkinson

Trouble

In the back of the car
the cuffs were tight
all because I got in a fight.
I was scared and not prepared.
I was mad and my Mom was sad
but then, I thought it was rad.
I showed no fear and never shed a tear.
I knew I was in trouble
and felt like I was trapped in a bubble.
My Grandma yelled, my Mom cried
then, I wish I could just hide.
I wish I could take it back
and show much more slack.

Evan Williams

Jelly Sly Grin

Stop giving me that liquid smile
Which is more of a jelly sly grin
god! You make me into
A puddle of flesh
No bones to back me up
Stand up straight!
Stop staring into those sleek black eyes
His brain is thick and he only wants you
like a 105 pound piece of meat.
But that liquidy grin
Those hands so strong knowing
Which of my buttons to push to make me
Collapse into his arms
A helpless victim unfolding
Exposing everything about me that
He laughs off and quickly forgets
Stop swallowing my personality
I've got to break free!

That's impossible he breathed
Feathery into my ear.

Rebecca Susan Gosse

Pets

I had two fish.
They died.
I think I over fed them.
I had a dog.
I sold him.
I was too afraid to pet him.
Later, I got a cat,
But she was too mean to play.
Then I got a bunny,
But she just hopped away.
Now, I'm in a pet store, deciding
    which is better —
Three hundred ducks,
Four hundred bucks,
Or an English setter.

Liza Townsend

The Spirit Of Children

Carefree and giving,
    is what they are...
        each one a star.

They look at you,
    with such joy and delight
    it makes you feel,
like you've done something right.

"The Spirit of Children"....

    Oh, how wonderful it can be,

Remember
    that's how we were,
        you and me.

Deborah A. Myers

The Mirror

I see you in the mirror
each time I brush my hair;
For, if I partly close my eyes,
it's you who's standing there.

So when I think you're far away
and miss you, Mother, dear;
I only need to find a mirror
to quickly have you near.

Kathleen M. Burley

Death Becomes Thee

Shall I be the first to cast the stone?
Should thou be the last one giving.
Time told to be alone,
What reason to go on living.

Death to all worldly pains,
Always first to be apart.
Welcome to those who shall sustain,
And bleed from thy heart.

Grievance to all that will show.
And cast all fears out the door.
Like a tree that will not grow,
Thou will fear death no more.

Then as death bears its sharp claws,
You find that death obeys no laws.

Jacquelyn M. Lynch

My Thoughts On A Quiet Day!

My thoughts on a quiet day,
Vary according to my feelings.
All inside of me revealing,
My inner most ideas.

Sometimes I'm joyful,
Full of love and happiness.
Sometimes I'm sad,
Sad of love and happiness.

What joy could I bring
If joys not in me?
All I can see is the gray
Covering the sunshine of my day.

Could I express,
All I have right now
If somehow noise were all around?

No, I would not think like this.
All my feelings I would miss.

Jeannette Bosch

To Be Or Not To Be

To travel through an endless world.
Hatred, love, no peace

To travel through a crowded land
Through wars and endless meets.

No one cares or thinks about
What it all will come down to.

They only care to win and gain.
They don't think of me and you.

But if one thing can turn around
Have peace, and love, no hate.

Take the world and help it out.
Clean up our mistakes.

Then think about how it will go
Not now but later on.

Then think about how we will be.
Give peace at our last dawn.

But if we don't try, and give up hope
We'll soon be at the end.

It still can change and turn to peace,
But on us it all depends.

Andrea Kirkegaard

A Fragile Peace

  Be still my soul
  Be quiet my heart
  He is with God and
  God's peace fills me
But the tears are never far away....
    The sky is blue
    The sunshine bright
    The air is crisp and cool
    His peace fills me
But the tears are never far away....
    Friends are friendly
    Family caring
    Life is sweet and fun but hollow
From that hollow the tears flow
A never ending source
Until in answer to my anguished prayer
    My soul is still
    My heart is quiet
    He is with God
But the tears are never her away.

Odile Fleissner

Valentine Hearts...

Floating away
to magical places
where love is always for
you and me.
Following paths
through a magical
rain forest
to everyone's heart,
especially yours.

Making people happy
for all deeds they do.
So nice
to do good deeds
for the rest
of their life!

Caitlin DeLano

Swimming In The Water

There is fire on the tree.
I jump from the swing.
Then, I splash into the water.
There is a shark in the water.

I called the police helicopter
With my phone to rescue me.
Then, I see a rope and a helicopter.

I swim across the water.
From the helicopter, is the rope.
I splash out of the water.

Then, I hang on the rope
Swinging on it across the water.
I swing in the air on the helicopter.

Emeka Robert Okoroh

A Lump Of Clay

I am nothing more
    than a lump of clay

For God to mold
    in whatever way

He sees fit
    to use the form

He lets me wear
    from morn to morn

CarolAnn Otto

Space And Time

The lines, like petals from a rose,
flowing through time like emotions
one touch will stir one's passion
like waves arouse the oceans.
The eyes, deep and mysterious
they sparkle, they dash, sublime
embrace and one surrenders
like stars through space and time.

The soul, so strong, yet delicate,
reveals itself at times
and then again, it disappears
like stars through space and time.

The heart, unequaled in measure,
opened to all, apply
once broken, pray for its return
like stars through space and time.

Combined, they make a woman
a gift from angels divine.
I treasure this gift, so wonderful
like stars through space and time

Darrell S. Pressley

Prayer

Trials, troubles, anxieties
We have from day to day
Leads me to the mercy seat
And I hide myself in thee!

If everything went smoothly
These feet of clay of mine
Would go boastly on
And never think to pray

Oh, why am I so unthankful
When everything is well?
How glad my Lord is waiting
To hear my humble prayer

I am glad that He is patient
With my inconsistency
He looks upon my trembling heart
And gives me strength
From dawn till dark

Ann Worthington

My Wish For Tomorrow

I wish
that all people
can live together
in a happy
and healthy
environment,
I wish
for no more drugs
or crime
in the world,
I wish
for no more
hunting
of endangered species,
I wish
for the world
to come together
and be one
big,
loving, family

Jason Miller

Thinking Of You

Just a simple embrace
To start the pace
Of two hearts to race

Warm, soft embrace
Lying face to face
Soft, moist lips to taste
A warm and gentle place
Lying face to face

Our hands entwined
One of the things that bind
Two hearts as one

I started this day
Thinking of you this way
Hand in hand
One woman, one man

Doug Lawrence

Deception

You and me every day
play the game, say
if you can't convince, deceive
until believed
face to face, two-faced.
Positive misinformation, propaganda
high twisted into a lie
day to day, today.
Missiles in Cuba in '62
the old shell game, ballyhoo
marrow to marrow, tomorrow
Magnified pleasure, whore in bed
synthetic love, feelings dead
love to love too loved.
Christmas attacked? My God,
No!
Santa Clause is real, don't you know?
Year to year, too dear.
You and me, mirrored reflection
pretending love, the final deception.

Raul A. Sandoval

Curtain Call

Long ago I fell in love
and gave my Heart away;
To one who only acted out
a most convincing play.

His op'ning lines were well rehearsed
He played His part so well,
That I believed His Heart was Mine
until the Curtain fell.

But even tho' He Broke my Heart
I've Learned a Helpful factor...
To Never judge a first Run play
By the Talent of the actor...

Marlene D. Walters

Trapped

Trapped in a mind game
With no way out
Trapped in insanity
Fighting for reality
Unlock the door and let me out
I found a way in and now I want
Out!

Catherine Steele

To My Grandson

O.K. Jeff, it's your turn to cook,
Don that apron - makes you look good.
Toss the salad and broil the steak
roll out the pie; or bake a cake.

Nancy - works hard, she needs to rest
Set the table and do your best.
Wear the Chef's hat - pour out the wine
soup's on! You're both ready to dine.

So here's to Nancy, the new bride!
And here's to Jeffrey, the new groom!
May their hearts twine together
and their love last forever.

Mary K. Schwulst

Dance Of The Leaves

Trees dressed
In bright fall colors
Of gold and orange,
Yellow and red.
Branches dancing
To the hum of a cool autumn breeze.
Leaves, gliding and twirling,
Discarded by the trees
As they dust and feather the ground
Creating a blanket
Of brilliant color.
Some traveling
To far away places by air —
Coming to rest
In a special place
At the end of their lives.

Carol W. Ghent

Night

Here it comes, once again.
It's quite scary,
and I wish you were here.
Here to hold me,
so I could hold you.
I sit here in the dark.
Here it comes, once again.
It's quite scary.
And I wish you were here
I miss your soft, sweet,
sensuous, loving touch
upon my soft skin.
I miss you.
I miss your touch.
I'm scared,
please help me.
Save me
from the
night.

Brandy Evans

Untitled

Mother to all, but she is
One, she gives us love
Tells us not to worry, she's
Here for all
Eternity, our world
Revolves around her sanity.

Even now she
Aches, her soul is
Ready. She is
Tired, ready for us to
Heal - to make her whole again

Abigail A. Marshall

A Single Second Of Life

A single second of life
Forever frozen in time,
Was all it ever took
To completely make you mine.

From two came one,
But only two remain;
One is new and young,
The other still the same.

In a world so unpredictable
I found a love so true.
We were married, young and happy
And planned our life with you.

The world was in our hands
Nothing ever could go wrong;
You're my only baby now,
Your mother's forever gone.

You'll never know how much she cared
Or wanted to hold you tight;
She died in birth, but you were saved,
Now you're my only light.

Steven Alee Taylor

Silence

I am without
sound.

Quiet as grass
whispering in the wind.

A secret that
cannot be told.

A person in a long
awaited thought.

I am the sound a mother
makes when she coos her
baby.

I am the stillness
of death.

Silence
Christina Gibson

Now We Are Forgotten

Once our aces ripped across the net
Once we danced 'til dawn
Now our legs don't work at all
Now we are forgotten

Once our sweet voices filled the air
Once our jokes brought tears of laughter
Now our vocal cords don't work at all
Now we are forgotten

Once we ruled mighty nations
Once we chortled "checkmate"
Now our brains don't work at all
Now we are forgotten

Once we had adventures to be told
Once we had romances to relate
Now our memories don't work at all
Now we are forgotten

Who are we you do ask
We are you and you and everyone
Once held in awe and revered
Now we are forgotten

Paul W. Wyman

Deja Vu

Thousands of waves crashing;
  in places fathered by dreams.
Smashing rocks below my feet;
  things are not always as they seem.
The rocks absorb cold feelings;
  they mask the crashing sounds.
It's as if they sorrow together,
  for dreams drifted and not found.
Maybe the rocks have mothered the
  waves - held them while they cried.
The tide comes to take the pain,
  of dreams that have only been lies.
Hear the waves cry to the rocks;
  feel the tide wash it all away.
Listen to what they say,
  can you hear them?
Have I been here before with you?
  Maybe? - Deja Vu...

Jessica Goodwin

The One I Loved

You were the one,
Who showed me how to have fun,
You taught me the game,
And knew me by name.
You were the one,
I wanted to love.
For that laugh and that smile,
I would walk for miles.
All those words of encouragement,
All the time you lent,
No one will know how much they meant.
You never knew,
You were the one,
I wanted to love.
Now time has passed,
Our lives have changed.
But you will always be,
The one I wanted to love.

Sue Parrish

Journey Of Life

Our memories are not made in
our beginning or in the ending
of our journey in this life.
Rather our most precious and
treasured memories are made
in the most unexpected moments
during the journey.
And it is only when we are
getting near the end or for
some unforeseen curves in our
journey that we come to appreciate
the memories we are making
or the ones we have made
together.

L. Elizabeth McNab

Untitled

I love you dearly
Mother of mine
As love grows yearly
Like the fruit on a vine,
Forever!
  Happy Mother's Day Mom.
James Ross

My Love

My love is like a flower,
It starts to blossom little by little.
As the day goes on,
My love grows more.
  Minute by minute,
  Hour by hour,
The flower grows sour,
if it doesn't have its sun.
So minute by minute,
  Hour by hour,
I grow more sour,
if my love (you) don't come.
But the flower still grows,
And I still show,
My love for you
Even when I'm blue!!
Marina Taylor

I Wait

I wait, slowly dying,
In despair, surely crying,
Without hope of ever finding,
The one my heart shall adore.

The sea was strong, unrelenting,
I'm heartbroken, still resenting,
Being alone and living,
Free of he I've loved before.

An eternity I'll wait, slowly dying;
In despair, and surely crying,
Looking in the depth of my soul,
without hope of ever knowing,
the love of he who lies below
lost forever more!

Nicole Paschal

Forever Loving Vows

Let's kneel down and cry
To the thought of you and I
  Let's wipe our tears
To all our worst fears
  Let's hold each other
To comfort one another
  Let's smile now
To say good-bye and make a vow
  Let's never grow apart
To stay forever in my heart
  Let's never say we hate
To never bring the thought "too late"
  Let's never fly lonesome as a dove
To always say "You I Love"

Shay Lee Billingsley

About Prejudice, About Relationships

Shades of gray
get in the way
in a world that is black and white.

Lines are not clear
when we draw near
and something seems so right.

Warning signs stand
throughout the land
in this man-made plight.

But I can see,
between you and me,
nothing is black and white.

Eva H. Heape

Nostalgic Trance

Neatly folded memories,
Obliging my obsessions,
Sentimental saxophone
Twirls yesterday around.
A single dried up yellow rose,
Love scripts in faded ink,
Give esoteric quality to
Invaluable fragments;
Circumstantial evidence of
    who I used to be.

Tastes of summer sunburns
Reflected in photographs,
Adolescent innocence wrapped in
Necrotic bandages and bows.
Careworn corners of the treasure box
Endure another passage.

Jody Taggart

Day In The Park

We'll set up a spot
In the middle of the park
We'll talk all day
But with nothing to say
We'll dance until night
We'll sit under the moonlight
That just shows
The way love goes
I love you
You love me
Together we'll be
Friends forever
Or a little bit more
Thank you for
The day in the park

Greg Sanders

Antarctica

Icy blast of silence
Burns the mountain's flank

Wind arching out
From this bowl of silence
Searing anguish

Glacial agony
Stinging until the silence
Sounds tolls of death
Chimes of blessing

Amidst glaucous-winged gulls
Swooping
Soaring
Steered by no less than God

I am dense, ungrateful as stone

Marisa A. Coutts

Reminiscing

Do you ever wonder
If you hadn't made that blunder
Where you would be now
Would you be rich
Would you be poor
Or maybe just knocking on heaven's door
We all know we can't go back
And live it all again
So let's all vow to do our best
And love our fellow men

Laurie McCullough

It's Just Life

The grass is always greener on the other side
so people sometimes say
though I search for the path that will lead me there
I get so lost along the way
maybe there is a sign that I am just unable to read
maybe there is a bridge that has no place to cross
maybe all of my tears are clouding up my eyes
maybe I'm just running away from all the answers to my why's
maybe I just sometimes long for a little peace of mind
yet, if this did happen to occur, I am afraid of what I may find
Is this greener grass people speak of just fantasy or a myth
or is it really possible it could exist
I am coming to the conclusion that it is said only for the reasons
of giving one faith and hope
and in helping one to understand, that if it can not be changed not
to waste away and dwell, but to look forward while holding your head
high you will find the strength to cope
then with it you will learn to always deal
    For it is not a fantasy nor is it a myth,
    It's just life and it is very much real.

Teresa A. Storey

Eternally Yours

One day the moment will come when you find that special someone.
One that makes you feel complete, one who sweeps you off your feet.
Together until the day you die, something happens after many years go
by. Something missing, unhappiness sits within. You're not sure what it is,
and you'll wonder why.
One may leave, and both will grieve. Have faith in your love, find
the missing key, fight for what you want, and soon you will see.
Together talk until you can't talk no more,
because your love is something to fight for. Your soul will know, listen to it.
Follow its lead, and sooner or later you'll know what the other will
need. It's too easy to call it quits in this day and age,
but if you married your soul mate and you know in your heart,
the two of you will not stay apart. Solve the problem, no matter how long it takes.
When you do, your marriage, your life, your faith, your hearts, your
inner being, your soul will be stronger than you'll ever know.

Tabitha Fernandez

Runaway Child

Inside the cold dark room lies a child of the world, alone and frozen.
No protectors, or guardians to care. No one to see what has become of
him. He lies in a broken down building where he took shelter from the storm.

Outside the night is cold and dark, the deep white snow lights the
way. It is impossible to see the child that lies inside. His body
cold and still. His soft skin gray, lips blue as the sky. Tattered
clothes that hang on a thin frail body, his feet barely covered.
Frozen tears lie upon his cheeks. An awkward skinny body curled up
almost within itself. A small hand tightly clutching a ragged blanket
that could not keep the cold hands of death at bay.

This child would be cold and suffer no more for he was dead.
Dead to a world that had preferred to look the other way rather than
acknowledge its starving and freezing children. This child would not
grow up to change the things wrong in this world for he was never
given the chance. Alone and abandoned, how was he to know that in this world where
once he had lived happy and care free there would come a time when he would face the
cold uncaring eyes of strangers.

How many will have to pass through the night before someone takes
the time to stop, look and listen? How many more children will
have to suffer before someone stands up and says out loud I care what happens?

Mickey Marston

A Grave, Forgotten

A grave forgotten, they number, more than
one were once, loved ones gathered, beneath,
the warmth, of the morning sun.

I promise I will visit. Many were heard
to say. Their promises, such as leaves being
carried by the wind, they to, simply floated away.

No longer, are there voices, no longer are
flowers, laid upon the ground. Friends,
once so dear, no longer take time to come around.

(Gone but not forgotten) inscribed, for all to
see. (Not forgotten) what can the meaning be?
Surely, if not forgotten, then their promise would be kept to me.

Gary W. Huffer

He Didn't Mean To

Larry, didn't mean!
Didn't mean, to leave things this way!!
Without his will, to help you through!!
He said, "Set your mind to it!"
"You, can do it!!"
"If you need any help, turn to Boyum's!!"
Dad says-
   "Just take your time, it will all work out!!"
They both, have confidence in you!
They both said-
   "Things will get easier, as time goes by!!"
"Just stop and think back to how things were done!!"
They're both standing there
   with their arms around each other!
Laughing at you!
Saying to each other
   "Les never did like, cows or horses!!"
"But confidence, we do have in you Les!!"
"Because, you won't let us down!!"
"We both love you!!" From Larry and Dad!!

Rosie Ludwig Jr.

Love

Love is an elastic nether world
Where your heart like a flag is unfurled.
Where tears are painful and laughter gay
And the sun vies with storm clouds each day.

Love is a bedtime story or song.
It's that look you get when you're wrong.
It's that brush on the cheek at work's end
And a smile on which you depend.

Love isn't a feeling or thing to be seen
Nor is it something in between.
Rather a force or compelling tie
Much like a bridge between you and I.

Love is an elastic nether world
Where somehow we three were hurled.
To spin our web and laugh and cry
My wife and my son and I.

Jack E. Everling

From A Mouse's View

As I saw the serpents grin, I saw his eyes speak of sin.
It was I who crossed his path, now I must face his wrath.
To do so and move now, would endanger my kin. So I leaped
across his path, to my den Oh home sweet home of mine. But
now my life is his to dine, however my wife will live to
see him shed his skin. And maybe someday my kin will win.

Jason D. Wulf

The Song Of The Flower

In the land of Awakening
   blossoms many a flower,
   not to fold or cower;
But to hold its head up and its shoulders
   high to tower
For the sunlight reveals its shadow
   Casting down its reflection it endows
This one and only flower has a different
   impartment for this land to see:
   A unique smell, hue of color;
Shining in fullest imbuement - dull to Bright!
The flower sings forth the song of its heart
'Til the day of final glory
   calls for it to embark
Leaving behind its seeds to revel
   in Spring's sweet earth;
For others to be dazzled by their very own
   cleverness they hold in tight!!

Patty Barker

I Will Miss You

I will miss you while you are away.
I want you to know that I will think of you everyday.
I will miss your laughter, your smile, your eyes, your kiss,
You, I will miss, and miss, and miss.
Apart we will be, but not for a long time.
When you return, you will bring back my sunshine.
In my heart, I will keep you until you come back. Knowing
that you are there will keep me on track.
Think of me often, because I will be thinking of you, today,
tomorrow, the next day and the day after.
Don't forget me and what we have together.

Sha'Ron N. Singletary-Alston

Memories

I sit alone and I wonder why
It's certainly not because I am shy
Could it be because I talk of my past
And of this life I know won't last
Good memories are like precious jewels
Not to be related by conceited fools
Who brag of all the things they have done
But who have never helped or aided anyone
So I pray that mine can help do good
As all past life's memories really should

Beatrice M. Bateman

Time And Generations

The spectrum of Generations are
   rooted in an oral tradition.
Passing like gentle silver strands
   connections of life.
Great grand, to Grand, Mother and Child
   Moving in and moving out.

New birth, a descent into heavenly bodies
   God giveth and he taketh away
   And the circle keeps turning.

I saw you, I knew you and you gave
   me the tradition - the roots of
   my life to pass on -
   And the circle keeps turning.

The strength, the need to know myself
   and others - history past, future now
   And the circle keeps turning.

Gwendolyn Walker

Untitled

The air is like the smell of death as I
  sit here and listen for a sound on
  this breathless winter nite.
As the snow slowly melts away, so
  does the soul of another. Trying to
  stay around for it's such a beautiful
  sight; Mother Nature does as she wants
  for she's always right.
The animals scurry closer 'cause they
  don't know what to do; when the deaf
  sounds of nature makes them scared
  of reality even though it's very true.
The drip of the snow feels like
  a tear were on my face; as it slowly
  reaches the end we smile for we know
  she's found the heavenly place.
  Mathew D. Miller

A Penny For My Thoughts

In loving memory of Eric Chavez
A penny means so much to me,
a wish, a prayer, a dream I see.
Off my thumb I flick it high.
My dreams, my prayers float in the sky.

For you I'm wishing all the best,
suddenly now it's put to the test.
It hits the water and falls to the ground.
And it sits glistening brightly on the wet ground.

Now the penny is no longer bright,
and your life ends suddenly, late one night.
I don't know if it's good or, if it's bad.
But, on that day it was truly sad.

I know that you left, and why you died
but, I am so sorry that I hadn't cried.
I know no matter what you'll always be blessed.
And you left this world, because it was best.

And now you'll always be in the sky of blue.
And I'll look up knowing that my dream came true.
  Robert Chavez

The Messenger

The footsteps of countless multitudes
Are heard within a silent understanding.
Birmingham is in tears as her child soothes her soul;

  His name was Martin, he was a song,
  He was a heartbeat,
  He was a message;

The cries from a people of untold struggles
Rest within many souls, the tears of oppression
Have yet to be the tears of joy.
Bloodstained patches of earth
Are filled with footsteps of ebony children;

He bared gifts of strength within a people,
He went to the sanctuaries of the coffled,
He went to the mountaintop and cried upon broken commandments
And walked with races of a multitude along freedom way;

Upon the struggles of color was the watching of all eyes,
For from the mountaintop came forth a dream,
A dream that is within the heartbeats of all struggles.

  His name was Martin, he was a song,
  He was a heartbeat, he was a message.
  Lenza Williams

Dear Mom

You remember the day I was born.
And a lot I put you through.
Good times, bad times, fun and sad times,
And a few times in between too.

I love you for putting up with me,
The worrying and the carrying.
We're been through a lot together,
The loving and the sharing.

Mother to me is a mystical word.
One I can't explain, but is so real.
I love you, does not express
All my feelings I do feel.

I am so glad I have you,
I wouldn't want no other.
I like you just as you are,
Love having you for my Mother.

No matter how old we grow,
The feelings grow more strong.
You make me fully realize
Why they wrote mother into a song.
  Saundra Burlingame

Life's Candle

In heaven as I talked to God,
He stopped and showed me something very odd.
He showed me a door with an enormous handle.
Inside was a room with millions of candles
Some were thick and very tall,
While others were thin and frankly, quite small.
And then I saw one with my name,
I looked at Jesus to explain.
"My child," said He, "This is your light,
Lit at your birth to shine through life.
Each other candle represents a life on earth,
Some old, some new, some long unbirthed."
As I walked around the room and looked;
Each candle told a story almost like a book.
Some smelled sweet and heavenly,
While others stank disgustingly.
Many things I saw in that room,
Many of joy, but some of gloom.
If by chance you may come upon this rhyme,
Make your life bright to shine for all time.
  Joy Bingham

God Governs All

How beautiful is the night
Lit by God's shining light!
How beautiful the dawn
When it awakens the world
With spectacular colors unfurled.
With the coming of dawn
The birds greet the new day with song
Now the new day has begun with the coming of the sun.
All nature responds with renewed growth
To the blessed warmth from the sun
Which brings life to nature and man till day is done.
This goes on day after day-bringing all nature to maturity.
A newborn babe is God's gift to man
For a baby is born according to God's plan
For God is love and the creator of all life.
Listen to God and he will keep you from all strife.
He will help and guide you all your life
He will keep you strong always
And we will abide in his love all of our days!
  Lorena Barrett

Words Of Love

Hallowed words of love
  Softly whispered on a star filled night
Gentle words of love
  Floods the soul with souls warm light
Soft words of love
  Vowed soothing low and clear
Growing words of love
  Boldness that knows not fear
Knowing words of love
  Pierce the essence of the heart
Bright words of love
  Quell the inner dark
Speak words of love
  Let us have today
Hallowed words of love
  Never go away

    Michael A. Carmichael

Faces Of Love

There is the love of a mother, for a new-born child;
  Always reassuring, gentle, and mild.

There is the love of a father, protective and sure;
  The love of a child, innocent and pure.

There is the love of siblings, which they often hide;
  But, in a crisis, they stand side by side.

There is the love of adolescence, adventurous and wild;
  Most often over, in a very short while.

There is the mature love, of a woman and a man;
  And if it is true, it will forever stand.

Then, there is the greatest love of all, coming from above;
  God bestows on each of us, his gracious, eternal love.

    Wade Hornbeck

Thoughts

When my mind is filled with thoughts
That tumble and jumble to settle naught
And the world moves by with no direction
Like a misspelled word that needs correction
I think of the farm when just a kid
With the satisfying things we always did
Then the tumbling thoughts turn into faces
That smile and speak
And I am there
It's nineteen thirty without a care

    Robert O. Hills

Broken Metronome Of My Soul

My heart lies bleeding in my hands.
And though it is bruised and broken,
It's battered, torn, yet all I have.
I'o to you I give this token,

This broken metronome of my soul,
Is all I have left to own.
I give it to you freely, so together we can watch it,
As it slowly turns to stone.

So take this grotesque pitiful offering,
And tell me how it makes you feel.
Carve upon it with your love.
Because it has wounds only you can heal.

    Devon Metzger

Feel The Mouths Drop Open

Feel the mother's death throb
  a hole in her spirit
  killing her softly
  it is man's job

Feel the despair in their eyes; our careless assault
  the creatures of ours
  abuse, neglect, hunt
  it's our game, it's our sport, it's our fault

Feel the lust, the lies, the treachery, and crime
  no one cares for respect
  devalue and exploit ourselves
  society in decline

Feel the pain stun the heart
  meaningless bloodshed
  killing a man
  body and soul come apart

Feel the mouths drop open, spinning in a whirlwind
  world in galactic chaos
  we are responsible
  we've brought ourselves to the end

    Amber Allison

Storm's Lullaby

Dust motes spinnin' down the street. Hanging plants swayin'
casting neon streaks, wind edged corners sighin' soft and
sweet. Lights flashin' — storm's comin'.

Folks are stopping, stepping in. Windwashed tables emptyin'.
Coffee cups left for rain to coat, fancy little cookies
left to float. Drops, splashin' — storm's comin'.

Sheets are drifting, back arc light. Ghosts and specters jump
to flight. Green life drinkin' up the raining night,
Lovin' it!

Storm is here and I just sit, swallow coffee that one last
bit. Then down the street I've got to 'git.' Off to sleep,
for that I'm fit.

Good evening my companion of the night. Make the morning
sparkle bright. Old man storm will do it right, good night,
rain light, Good night.

    John J. Callaghan

In Memory Of Barb

The angel came and whispered softly in her ear
Put your hand in mine...I'll lead you away from here.
But Barb said "no"...she wasn't ready to leave
Too much to leave behind...too many to grieve.
So she fought her battles and thought she'd won
But to no avail...her sickness wasn't gone.

Many times to the hospital she came and went
So again God's angel was being sent.
Barb said "no"...this isn't my time
When I have my talk with God...then I'll be fine."
Her sickness raged on...she wasn't getting well
I'm sure she was living her own private 'hell.'

One night she had a dream...God said "Your time has come
You've been forgiven...your work here is done."
So again came the angel..."Barb, take my hand
I'll lead you to peace, beauty...the promised land."
This time she took her hand and hung real tight
The angel was leading to a very bright light.

So look up high...not so very far
The heavens are brighter...there's one more 'star.'

    Wilma Davis

My Daily Prayer

So powerful and strong is He with a touch of truth and love,
This God of all who rules the world from heavens up above.
All he asks is our faith in Him and repentance for our sins,
To accept Him as our Lord and Master, the redeemer of all men
To accept whatever He wants for us and to know His will is best
Until the day the world will end and all in heaven rest.

God only gives us crosses He knows that we can bear,
as long as we have faith in Him and know that He is there.
Each trial and tribulation He may give us all each day,
His guiding light will always shine to help us find the way.

To show us that the way can only be just one,
Not my will Oh Lord—but only thine be done.

Charlotte K. Anderson

Why Be Death So Frightening?

Why be death so frightening?
Even as we look forward to meeting the Lord.
Feeling that we should, on our own accord...
Although we know it will be enlightening,
And the strains of life are tightening.
We're looking to find, how we will afford,
To keep our lives around the heavenly cord.
Why be death so frightening?
Our Heavenly Father sends us his signs,
There's no need to complicate his teachings.
Let's do the best we can, while on earth,
Or there will be on time
To heed our Father's teachings,
A small price, for what enlightenment is worth.

Vicky Pletz

Shakespeare

Shakespeare
Life cannot be real without complications
life cannot be lived without expectations
search for the meaning hidden by reality
sit back and appreciate the comedy
think not always of the tragedies

The prose flows, but no one knows
they shrug their shoulders as the plot grows
five-hundred years, we still don't know
what all of his lines meant in the show.

Shakespeare

Peter Adderton

Christmas

Our Lord was born
  On this day.
For one reason,
  To take our sins away.

He desires all to receive Him,
  As their personal Lord.
He tells us that repeatedly,
  For it is written in His word.

He wants us to be born again,
  Born both of water and the Spirit.
For if only born of water,
  There really is no merit.

We cannot be called His brothers and sisters
  If we won't let Him in,
To take over our lives
  And wash away our sin.

Diane Taylor

Moonpath

Of all of Nature's beauties one way view
A rosy sunrise bidding night adieu,
A brilliant sunset dazzling to the eyes,
Or northern light's pale searchlights in the skies.
The one that brings a feeling most serene
E'en more than mountains, streams or forests green
Is one in which the viewer may partake -
A shimmering moonpath on a northern lake.
And as one sees with joy this scene sublime
It seems that minutes cease - there is no time;
And though one's thoughts be troubled, one will find
A calming peace will overtake the mind.
I hope in far-off days I may recapture
In my mind's eye a lovely moonpath's rapture.

Mary F. Hodge

Care-Givers

This house we live in may begin to fail
Our souls may be strong but are bodies are frail.
So the Lord has provided gentle people who care,
God bless the care-givers in Nursing Homes everywhere.

They bring a measure of comfort with their gentle hands
And a loving voice when the need demands,
So the Lord has provided dedicated people who care,
God bless the care-givers in Nursing Homes everywhere.

A patient may feel special with a warm little hug,
And a word of love as they are tucked in bed so snug
So thank you, Lord, for these people who care,
God bless the care-givers in Nursing Homes everywhere.

Maxine L. King

Eternal Chains

I live in a world full of self-centered bastards.
They spend eternity groping and clawing their way
into my sovereign soul.
While I spend eternity fighting the evil that
devours and bastards' minds.
They suck the life out of living.
They consume the innocence of the sainted and
suffocate them with the fires of hell.
To escape is total bliss.
To be caught is self-destruction.
So they continue to escape through the
pleasures of sin.
And I remain due to the chains of eternal slavery.

Leticia J. Gonzalez

The Wedding

There in the twilight, soft candle light
makes shadows dance on a gown of pure white
Tears of joy spilling down her lovely face
her new life begins in this sacred place
Her family gathers, their love they bestow
They surely will miss her, but want her to grow
She entered the church, one half of one,
But when she walked out, her life had begun

There in the twilight, soft candles glow
He fidgets with worry, his nervousness grows
The tears in her eyes fill his heart with fears
Could it be that she doesn't want to be here?
His family gathers, he tries to stay calm
They've made it this far, nothing's gone wrong
He entered the church one half of a whole,
But now they are one, heart, mind, and soul.

Mindy Hornberger

We Saw You Mom

We saw you as rocked us mom;
As you tenderly nursed us from childhood illnesses.
We saw you gardening and tenderly caring for
the chicks to grow up.
We saw you mom, with love in your eyes, fixing us your
special things for special days.
We saw you never complaining as you did things for us.
Mom, you were always waiting there for us as we
grew up; then you waited til our families came to
visit, and you were so proud to have so many visit.

Now, mom we still see you in our hearts and minds.
We see you now with family who have gone before you,
and we know they are happy that you have joined them.
Their joy is our sorrow, but mom, we will always be
seeing you in our hearts and minds; knowing somehow
you are still with us, watching and loving us.

Dorothy J. Elder

Brain Drift

Existing in a universe, my own,
Abilities within myself appear.
My mind creates environments unknown;
The power over everything is clear.
To motion this great planet do I bring;
Its properties by only I controlled.
Calm winds throughout the planet start to sing;
The atmosphere, I've made it blue and cold.
Though physically transparent, I exist
As energy and thought waves much the same
As many light rays breaking through the mist,
Unlike my form on Earth from which I came.
Back to the Earth from which I came I reach,
For my instructor has begun to teach.

Melinda Broda

Locked Up

The devil has tempted me with his mistress,
she came, I saw, and I should have concord,
I failed because I am weak minded and I was off somewhere else,
she tempted me with her attitude and I loved it,
the thought of fire blazing and animals running for their very
lives made me feel so very un-alone,
the sky turned black, the moon hid in fear, the beast was loose,
it threw me up against the wall (hard),
she tore at my heart, and I loved it,
it made me want to show my affections but I didn't know exactly, how,
I loved this beast, but did she love me,
No,
It didn't because I threw her in to a bloody waterfall of hurt,
just meaningless words,
she hid her eyes for they where red with the desire and hatred
of this place (she tried to escape),
then in a flash she was gone,
I watched the beast fly away, an angel,
but while I was behind the bars of hell.

Gregory Tyndale Lewis

Our Flag

Over land and over sea,
    with innocence and purity.
Proudly waving in the skies,
    those who honor me shall rise.
Justice, Courage and Vigilance,
    you stand before me with Allegiance.
With your blood, sweat and tears,
    you've cried for freedom through the years
No matter what Religion or Race you hail,
    with your respect, Stars and Stripes will never fail.

Diana Lynn Vathis

Silences

Birds soaring in the sky.
The sun rising in the morn.
A happy smile upon the face of a child.
Ducks swimming on a pond.
Flowers blooming
New sprouts shooting up to the sun.
Leaves floating to the ground.
Snow falling as the days turn cold.
The stillness of night.
The blinking of the stars.
Moon beams across a lake.
Reading by the fireside.
A baby sleeping
All this beauty to see.
And not a sound to hear.
Makes life precious for you and me.
Stand up and leave your sorrows and pain.
Look out your window and see the rain.
For tomorrow will be beautiful and ever so fresh.
The beauty of silence will do the rest.

Jean D. Simmons

Give Me It All

Give me the nature of a man going wild
Give me the time to groove; to go out in style
Give me what it takes, to make my heart pump fast
Give me your love; make it last
Give me the entrapment of your eyes
Give me the truth; never the lies
Give me all you got; nothing less
Give me the lovin' that makes you the best
Give me the pleasure of holding you tight
Give me assurance that it's all right
Give me your love right here and now
Give me your hand with a forever vow

Craig Simpson

My Mother

Who was it slaved from morn till night?
Washing and cleaning to keep our home bright.
The washing machine had a handle of wood,
Which swung back and forth to wash everything good
No motor to work it like modern ones do,
But her wash was the cleanest, they looked just like new.
She baked in a wood stone, the bread that we ate,
Christmas cookies, pies and also the cakes.
On a kerosene stove, all our meals were prepared,
So lovingly and tender we knew that she cared.
All our clothes, were sewn on a treadle machine,
Pumping away she looked so serene,
Her jellies and jams were made for us all,
She'd start in the summer and end in the fall.
Seven children to raise and take care of for years,
Surely we must of, brought many a tear.
In her wheel chair, at the front door, she waits every day,
And ask repeatedly, why did we go away?
But modern conveniences, don't give any one time,
To visit, this, "Dear old sweetheart", that "Mother of Mine."

Marion H. Schmidt

Flaming Decadence

I watch the last embers of a dying phoenix
My mortal eyes cannot fully comprehend
But I watch despite my limits
I do not view it for a great answer
The vast sight just gives me solace
Because in seeing it, I see myself
And I understand a little more,
My future and what it holds for me.

Edward M. Sullivan Jr.

Crazy Bee

Crazy, crazy, crazily bee
The crazliest bee I ever did see,
His honey was sweet
And he funked to a beat
Of a criss-cross, up and down melody.
Shakin' that buddie, to whatever tunie
Was in his crazily bee head at the time,
Whippin' that nectar up to that dancin' funk,
Makin' it up nice with his special little spice
And a twist of the sauce the others had lost.
He stirred and stirred, he whizzled and whirred;
Shakin' that juice back and forth,
Makin' a taste from the old school course.
The Queen Bee with the masses stared,
But that Crazy Bee, he always sweared;
That of the fun he was having they weren't aware.
And if you drank it just right
So for a moment you lost sight
To a great surprise...
That tasty treat had **YOU** stompin' those sweet dancin' feet

Kevin Groves

Life's Gift

Each day begins with a new born light,
fresh from the quiet of the sleepy night.
Another new day; another new chance.
Our hearts to sing, our hopes to dance.

Opportunity arises with each morning light
to start a-new and make things right.
A lifetime of mornings; a lifetime of starts
to enjoy what is precious and dear to our hearts.

Every morning we wake, with the knowledge at hand,
of God's Blessings, throughout the land.
His forgiveness, patience and most of all,
another chance to walk straight and tall.

We will not re-live today, hour by hour,
but with each new dawn we are given the power
To correct our mistakes; wipe the slate clean;
a pardon, if you will, with each new sunbeam.

So, when we awake to begin our day,
we should be thankful, in some sort of way.
And make this one better; it may be our last.
In the morning, it's future - in the evening, it's past.

Jean A. Souva

With Love For Isaac

Here's a little verse I hope you will enjoy,
you've come into the world a bouncing baby boy,
to everyone's happiness and delight,
even though you wake us up at night,
we all can't wait to see you smile,
as it shows those dimples that will beguile,
you are so special and long awaited,
most of all by those that created,
this work of art so precious and serene,
that only time could ever come between,
so through out the years my wish will be,
that every day begins and ends with
"Love for Isaac" you see.

Beverly D. Pearson

One Swing's Peak

Time is like a porch swing,
Romantic and ambivalent;
Holding the tension of new lovers
Fleeting from one swing's peak to the next.

James Farthing III

The Mirror

The shards from the shattered mirror fall
like the dreams and hopes of past generation.
Are they mine or hers or his or yours?
Yes.
They're all of ours, yet none of theirs.
It seems to happen to only them yet all the while
only to us.
For we are all someone else, to someone else.
My dreams of yesteryear are gone
only to be replaced by those of today and tomorrow.
Which are only to soon be destroyed.
Some who are supposed optimists see this as sorrowful.
However, if my old hopes were not torn,
How would I know what I truly want.
Perhaps wishes of before were fleeting
only to inspire my hopes of now, which are perhaps true.
And perhaps not.
Only.

John Soboslai

The Mourning Of Grandpa

It is difficult for me to think
Of things I could say
I know you have heard everything
Feelings are hard to convey

I know this time must be hard
I am sorry, is all I can say
I think of you every night
You have changed me some way

My thoughts and prayers are with you
That with every precious passing day
The grief of losing someone so special
Slowly begins to ease and fade away

Somehow, I know he is right here beside you
Through each step you move in life ahead
I know he hangs on every word you whisper
"You are now her angel," is what the Lord said

I am lucky, I proudly proclaim
To have you in my family
I strive each day hoping to possess
Your strength and love inside of me

Melissa Hoffman

Look Upon Mine Affliction

The storms that devoured the earth
    leave me in virtual awe
Our land is infernally saturated
    with insuperable devastation
Adversity, loneliness, and evil-
    I am mesmerized by their omnipotence
It pierces my mournful heart
    with such insufferable agony
I have plodded beyond my bounds;
    my verve and means are depleted
My soul and essence are on the brink
    of eternal extinction
I feel Thou art a million seas away,
    and in my melancholy ponder:
Dost Thou exist, O Mighty One;
    or hast Thou taken away Thy blessings?
My cup hath long been empty;
    and my lips cracked from brittle dryness
This cross is lethally ponderous for me to bear;
    behold this tormented spirit
O Great Saviour, I cry unto Thee:
    Thy tender mercies I implore.

Aimeiko Christel Tasico

God's Surplus

God has a surplus He's ready to share,
He's had it forever with plenty to spare.
His love is so boundless, there's none to compare.
This gift of redemption — our sins He did bear.

Our God did implore us "repent and believe
Knock and I'll open, ask and receive"
With His heart overflowing, our souls He retrieved
From our bondage of sin which He can perceive.

"O tell me you're ready. To live for our Lord,"
Will you give witness, study His word?"
Worship our Saviour, who hung on the cross.
With His resurrection, He overcame the loss.

One day He's soon coming to claim His own.
This journey ended, sorrows all gone.
We'll all shout the victory He's won for us all,
Then, for eternity, peace and joy will be full!

Charles H. Pierce

Nature

As easy as I add herbs and spices into a simmering tomato sauce,
physicians artificially inseminate cells in vitro.
The eggs attach themselves to the lively tissues
the same way leaves grow roots into a water-filled crystal vase.
The inner space resembles a crowded pit.
A fetus shares the virgin womb with two dead siblings
in a space that resembles a crowded pit
praying for the miracle of life.
Worms hide from birds, birds from wind,
that mother's fears lurk her behind a tic smile.
A mourning voice, sad as a cave,
depressed as a hollow in the ground,
reaches the creature, resonating in a blue echo.
The sun deserts the day,
laughter abandons her lips.
Her turbulent dreams are burdened with tragic thoughts.
Silently weeping, she swallows her tears.
Her voice is locked in a forgotten secret.
As before, she stares at the face of death.
As before, she remains alone, blaming herself for the loss.

Sara Schmidt Haber

Untitled

I am forging ahead through life, alone
he floats in...
we become as one.

His eyes capture my soul,
  His laughter is calming,
    His voice, soothing...
Best friends we seem to be,
Lovers, we are.

Time drifts on
His eyes are clouded over,
  His laughter is scarce,
    His voice, silent....
Letting go is difficult,
            impossible,
                  necessary.

Why does love fade?
Why must it wither?
Is it ever real?

I am forging ahead through life...
  alone.

Melissa Catherine Guernon

The Dying Great Lake Of Ontario

The Great Lake of Ontario gives up its dead:
  the seagulls move.

Heap of broken fish,
the beach claimed.

And the seagulls retreat to inland darkness,
us, they leave their sleepy song
  in the October wind.

Golden factories exhale their profits,
their footprints cover the Great Lake.

Dead water of moving graves,
the lake claimed.

And the people lake whimper in their headstones,
us, they leave their silent scream,
unmourned by the mothers of early horns.

Memories vague as fog give up its ghosts:
  the Great Lake turns loose.

Fingers of dying waves,
have sound across the world-green;
us, they remind their sad reveries,
drowned in the dark alleys of Buffalo's den.

Elmer M. Abear

Red Sky

A veteran sailor of long years past,
Leaving home again, in search of life anew.
To rekindle memories, reminiscent of a love long ago,
Hoping to cherish once again, vivid thoughts of the skies endless hue.

Red sky at morn, a sailors scorn, he's tragically seen come true,
Losing his only true love, to an unforgiving sea.
But red sky at night, he learned long ago, is a sailor's delight,
Fading bad memories away, bringing back the love of the sea,
  a love which is due.

John Metevia

Life And Death

Life is the glory of being able to watch the beauty of God's
creations. To watch the birth of life, whether it's of human
or nature. To have it all given and then suddenly taken away
in a minute. To drive along the country roads, looking at
beauty of the trees and flowers as they blossom in the spring.
Only to watch them die in the fall as the seasons changes.
To have the company of someone one minute and then all
taken away the next. Always remember the good and the bad
times. Between all the laughter and the tears, to go on with
your life, only to know that I am in good hands.
And that I will share the same glories of happiness and sadness
as you. Even if you can not see me, remember me in your dreams
and in your thoughts, just as I will remember you. Remember we
must all come and we must all go. Some sooner then others. We
all have a reason to be here, and have a reason to leave.
Be your own judge, and maybe you to will understand the
true meaning of life and death.

Rita Mae Hiniker

Mark

Why couldn't we be to each other a friend,
To the bitter end;
When in the casket you did lie,
I felt the best part of me die;
When they put you in the ground,
I felt a great sadness all around;
But now you're up there,
And in God's loving care.

Kerry R. Corley Jr.

Sunset

When crickets begin their endless chirp
When farmers end their hard day's work
When predators in the shadows lurk; sunset

When travelers turn their headlights on
When a romantic dinner sounds like fun
When on the street they buy a gun; sunset

When the sky reflects an orange glow
When the sounds of a lullaby are whispered low
When they stand on a corner to score some blow; sunset

When children playing sounds so sweet
When kids are looking for a treat
When gangs leave our young lying in the street; sunset

When a gentle wind blows through the leaves
When a Christian falls down on his knees
When the mother of a lost child grieves; sunset

When a brand new day begins again
When we're looking forward to seeing a friend
When we have a chance to make amend; sunrise

Phil Dennis

Memories

I remember the feeling I first had for you
It was strange, odd, and completely new
I felt complete, my heart did fill
Thinking of you gave me a thrill
I loved you since those connected eyes
To me, it was a large surprise
Finding love when you least expect
But there was something I didn't detect
A shattering end to this love I felt
The fire of love, to my dreams did melt
The overwhelming feeling is gone
All I can do now is to move on
Yet in me there remains and spark
For you my love to light the dark
I think of you often when I'm alone
And the feelings that you never shown
Now as I remember the heart I knew
I wish I could had you feel it to
But it is over, my hearts at ease
It's deep in my soul are kept the memories.

Sarah Lynn Brown

Internal Search

A clear wintery road
A passage of Rust
The feeling of coldness
The cold winter Crust
The memories of friendships
Long lost in the Dust
How often I wonder
Why then did I Trust
I ponder the problem
In search of my Lust
Wondering always in
Whom do I Trust
Decisions are many options so Few
How often I've looked for that elusive Clue
My search continues in futile Despair
In hopes that someone
Will eventually Care
The message is clear and
So often you'll See
The search for the answer lies within You and Me

Rafael Muniz

What Is It???

Some will wrap it, store it, pack it, and grow it...
  Box it, bag it, pick it, or hoe it.

Some will freeze it, bake it, zap it, or broil it...
  Also squeeze it, cut it, slice it, then boil it.

Some will fry it, flip it, chop it, and spice it...
  Others grill it, grate it, chill it, or dice it.

Some will roast it, toast it, broast it, or dip it...
  Weigh it, wash it, shell it, or whip it.

Some will serve it, then taste it, right after "the Blessing"...
  It is "food—glorious food"—what kept you from guessing?

Patricia Y. Frishman

Dogs

Dogs, Dogs, Dogs, How naughty can they get?
They run, walk, and play and they even run away.
Dogs are very loyal to their owner or master,
When they aren't they get a spanking.

Dogs, Dogs, Dogs, See how they run just like the jaguar.
When they are scared they just run away.
But when they want love they behave well.
But when they want to be mean they steal shoes.
But dogs are the best friends you could ever have.

Jose-Trelles Herrera

Feelings Of Confusion

My feelings for you bring on much confusion
My thoughts and emotions seem like one big delusion
I started out wanting friends, but that lead to more
It's tempting to go with, but what if judgement is poor
A relationship possibly leading to pain
Or possibly one where love takes its reign
I know I should hear what my heart has to say
But who will it hurt? Is there no other way?
What is it that I'm afraid of?
I think I'm afraid of the pain that's in love
I don't know how to act or what to do
As long as we're friends all through and through
Then there's no way that we could loose
And after awhile I hope to be less confused

Joe Todd

Help!

Help! Oh no, this couldn't be,
  I'm drowning in a deep blue sea!
The sharks are coming after me,
  My eyes hurt so bad I cannot see!
The dolphins and whales are leaving me alone,
  Oh, how I wish I had a phone!
The water is swirling round and round,
  Oh, how I wish I were on solid ground.
I'm scared to death,
  I can't take a breath.
I know I'm going to die,
  I cry, cry, cry, and cry.
I wish I had a couple fins,
  No I wish I knew how to swim!
I wake up and realize,
  I can see out of my eyes!
There's sweat running down my head,
  But it was just a nightmare and I'm safe in bed.
Tomorrow I'll learn how to swim,
  So I never have that dream again.

Kelsey J. Gerber

Seasons

The springtime green is fresh and bright,
Life leaps and swells, our joy will grow.
Youth rushes out to love the world;
The old ways seem so strange and slow.

Like summer, flowers our lives now bloom,
The rainbow's end is real and near.
Blue skies are constant, rain is soft;
The sun will never disappear.

The harvest moon first fills, then wanes;
In shades of fall the leaves float by.
The wind grows cool, the hills turn gold,
Red sunsets glow in autumn sky.

The quiet shadows beckon now.
As flakes of snow drift slowly down,
We seek the love of friends and home,
The warming fire, the gentle heart
   When winter comes.

Evelyn Eccleston

Untitled

When words are not enough to tell you how I feel,
how else do I show you that my love for you is real?
Do I climb the highest mountain and proclaim my love for you?
Do I cross the widest river, waters raging blue?
Do I sell off all I own and move to a deserted land?
Should I spend all my time building castles in the sand?
And should I watch as the water laps up the sand?
Until only a fragment is left in my hand?
What can I do to show you how I care?
By not telling me, you are not being fair.
Just tell me how I can prove my love to you.
Give me a clue as to how I can convince you:
Love is a precious gift that is shared.
If you only opened your eyes, you would see how much I cared.
I long to share my love with you,
But you have other thoughts in mind.
I must come to realize, you will never be mine.
So my love, I send this letter with a kiss —
Just to let you know what you will miss.

Reena M. Aguilar

Marie's Poor Black Lamb

Marie sat with her little lamb,
   Its fleece was black as night.
Happiness filled them all the time,
   Marie shown pure and bright.
Father was jealous of that lamb,
   So, anger filled his heart.
To kill her little Black it seemed,
   His gun the perfect art.
Without her Black she went to school,
   Her lamb she missed till brunch.
Marie, so innocent and young,
   Had found her Black was lunch.
Soon scarred for life she sits and cries,
   Marie is now insane.
Without her Black she kills for spite,
   Because her Dad caused pain.
Marie's Black lamb is not alive.
   Fore'er its soul will fly.
Marie shot herself in the head.
   With Black, she's in the sky!

Annalisa Holgerson

In Waiting

Darkness surrounds me in a tower of glass.
The only light comes from the moon
   and that I can barely see thanks to the rain and clouds.
I reach out into the rain — the rain looks purple — but when
   it hits my hand it turns into blood
   and the moat below me is nothing but a sea of crimson.
Sounds of thunder and lightning crash in my head;
   feelings of pain, agony, despair and torment surround me.
Off in the distance I can hear a church bell strike twelve;
   my heart starts to pound and race faster and faster.
I open my mouth to scream but nothing comes out;
   tears are rolling down my face.
My breathing is becoming more and more erratic.
The only thing left for me to ponder is —
   when the Midnight Angel will come for me.

Mark J. Stone

Erin's Child

The wind as it passes keeps turning us away,
and I wish in my heart I could stay.
The shadows of the past keep calling my name
to a place I dreamt of one day.

Where is it that my soul goes,
seeking shelter from the world.
Is it Erin's blood in my veins
calling me home again...

The pastures I dream of, so green and alive,
And shepherds tales filling my mind.
Peaceful waters and morning birds
they all seem to know my name...

Where is it that my soul goes,
when I escape from the world.
Erin's blood in my veins,
are you calling me again?

William F. Teague

Dedicated To All My Children

Seven times have I been blessed,
Seven tiny cheeks caressed,
Seven babies clothed and fed,
Seven angels put to bed.

Seven children's smiles and tears,
Seven times the scolds and cheers,
Seven lives to guide each day,
Seven names when I kneel to pray,
That Heaven will bless each one of these,
Seven personalities.

V. Pauline Tobias

A Puppy Runs Through It...

Home she comes at just eight pounds.
   So sweet and cute, your heart resounds.
She starts to grow and six months later,
   you've got a wolf crossed with an alligator.
She'll steal from the counter,
   she'll steal from the table.
She'll steal from the top book shelf,
   if she's able *
Still, despite all the cleaning and mopping the floor,
   there's just nothing sweeter than my Labrador!
So if you've put it off,
   just go and do it.
You'll see a house is not a home
   'til a puppy runs through it!

*When you're not home, they can fly!
   Alec Manfre

Trees In Winter

Skeletal, nude, bare-armed, without the adornment
of flowers or sensuality of fruit, slender offerings
of ritualistic and sacrifice-loving autumn, they stand
tall and with gracious dignity like aristocrats
under the iron weight of solitude in valleys, woods,
suburbs, along rivers, barren fields which were young
with wheat and rye, pure mineral streams born out of
snow, around decaying Gothic churches and on
canvasses of young, doom-loving artists, stripped of
vibrancy and the life-giving clarity of the sun.

Inside our homes, by crackling lyrics of firesides,
the hell-hot bars of meticulous electric heaters, we,
Crown of Creation and Predator of predatory creatures,
seek warmth from wool, wine, hot food, hot baths,
telephone, television, Beethoven, poems, the bodies of
our loved ones and dogs. They, trees, lean, bare, wan,
without the cunning of education, the advice of doctors,
philosophers and governments, without the soft words
of mothers, husbands and priests, fake the gloomy rape
of ice-cold winds, the naked truths of this world.

Norberta Nayagam

Tell Me

Do you ever think, that people need to let themselves out,
   that you need to know what's running through their minds?
Do you ever think, that people need to keep themselves hidden,
   and let the fire burn inside of them, until the flame they
   can no longer find?

Tell me what's running through your brain,
Tell me of your thoughts,
Tell me of your fears.

Until you tell me how you feel,
I'll keep myself hidden in the darkness,
I'll keep myself a secret;
The words inside of me will run wildly to the back of my head,
until one day they will be forgotten.....forever.

Rachael Araiz

This Creature——Man

Being born in innocence yet under a sentence of death
This most noble of creatures, begins the ultimate quest

Faced with illusions and all such uncertainties of life
To seek for some answers that might ease all his despair

Although possessed of true greatness, all love and much good
He does meditate his existence and by himself stands condemned

So imprisoned by false fears and confined by his own doubts,
He now consigns himself most eagerly to reject his own worth

Yet sadly there exists deep within these frail mortal bonds
All the secrets of this wondrous Universe still left unsung

Aware not of his potential and so denying his final call
The seeds of true greatness will thus remain silent within;
This Creature——"Man"

Keith S. Nelson

Unseen Faith

As I sit here and ponder on all the complications of life,
I realize that each one of these requires a sacrifice.
And when I see others conquer these,
Most often it is I that is not pleased.
But since the Lord has made everyone equal in his mind,
Why should it bother me if a little of life's luck they find.
It doesn't matter who has what or how much they maintain,
But if you see what's really inside then success will be gained.

Matthew André LaBarre

Transformation

Whenever
I talk to you, or see you, or feel you
   It's like all of me has gone through a wire sieve
And I become the softest flour that has ever been sifted
   White powder for baking bread
I rise so high and so free
   The fragrance of freshness emanating from me
And the butter that melts is my heart
   As I toast my silver chalice
Filled with the blood of the lamb
   I think whatever this is, it must be Holy
For I've never felt so pure
   With a man!

LaDonna DeBarros

Letting Go

You raise them right,
   You treat them fair,
And suddenly —
   They're not there.

There's a time when they must go
   And you have to let them go.
It hurts, oh it hurts, but still
   It's time, their own dreams to fulfill.

They spread their wings
   Soar into the night,
And you wonder —
   Have I done alright?

There's a time when they must go
   And you have to let them go.
It hurts, yes it hurts, but still
   It's time, their own dreams to fulfill.

Karen Young

Missing You

If I were to sit and count the days and
the many different ways I've been missing you,
I would not have the energy to remember the
days that were true.
   With spring coming soon I fight to get
over winter's gloom.
   With the thought of the flowers that were
so dear to you it helps to make the days seem
brighter as they come due.
   It has been four and a half years and with
the fifth coming there are still many tears.
   Mom I love you and wish you were here,
for I miss you more and more each year.

William D. Dickey

For The Future

A long time you spent, at
making it right,
knowing your future, is
still in your site.

Within your grasp is all you've wished for,
Remember it's all you've ever worked for.

Take it and mold it, into
something new,
and continue to make this
all work for you.
So now we say farewell, to you,
Good-bye and good luck, in
all that you do.

Theresa Scoles

Weeds And Roadsides

Were I there I could smell the air
Of his room
His head impresses the pillow in my thoughts
A hollow breaks rising inside like flight
And its thrill
Were I there I could smell his hair
Like flowers growing wild
Is this love
It needs little but the sun and the rain
And they come
Blooms open on the roadside
Enjoining us to stop and pick of their plenty
Feral notions nodding in the wind
The weeds bow as though a prince has entered
My unrestrained thoughts of him
The same wind comes through to him
With extravagant kisses goodnight

Darrin Pruitt

Oh What You Do For Me

Oh what you do for me it's difficult to say
but whenever you are near me there's such warmth that you convey.

The way you energize me brings me such delight:
it's like soaring on a feather or like riding on a kite!

Your presence is like loved ones sharing at a feast
with food, fun and laughter and with it joy and peace.

Or like a child's expression that look within their eyes
when they receive their wish of a long awaited prize.

I wish I could explain all that you do for me.
But how can I when faced with such diversity?

For each of you are special; just one of a kind,
and no one else can ever be the person you define.

So I can only mention the way you make me feel
and the happiness you bring me whenever you are near.

So this simple message of cheer is brought your way
to wish you a truly special Valentine's Day!

And when you come to visit, whenever that may be,
I'll be glad to offer you a song or melody!

Dehner Franks

Once Upon A Time...

Once upon a time...
As a young girl of fear,
To God I used to whine:
"Why do I do to keep my parents from being near?"

Once upon a time...
After traveling down the memory lane of childhood life,
What seemed like mountains then were only hills to climb
Reaching plateaus to celebrate continued effort and strife.

Once upon a time...
I loved and married a prince of charm.
Soon realizing his passion for gambling a crime;
Causing much heartache, pain, and potential harm.

Once upon a time...
After earning a teaching degree,
The job offers were many so I tossed a dime.
Thus, began a new career in my local community.

Once upon a time...
I thought God had stopped loving me,
Due to a life full of obstacles and trudges through slime.
Years later, I conclude God is still molding very tenderly!

Barbara L. (Harris) Funaiole

Confused

Said you loved me
Is that true?
I thought you cared
Cared about who?
Said you missed me
Missed what?
No one else mattered
Huh?
Said we'd be together forever
When?
If you said that you loved, cared, and missed me;
No one else mattered, and we'd be together forever
Then how come you're always with your friends instead of with me?

Sabrina Bustos

Fiorenza

Now Florence with her peach-tint evening sky,
With gold-flecked clouds of silver-bursting light,
Yields slow surrender to the pulse of night,
So hushed it lies amid its relic sigh.

Then cobbled streets reecho: vesper bells
Reach out, embracing and uniting all,
Reverberating from each hallowed wall,
Each lingered stroke grown fainter as it swells.

Here mingle Medieval, Renaissance,
And even Gothic memories in stone,
Recalled to life in flesh and blood and bone,
The shadowed substance of a high romance.

Here past and present seamlessly are one
To celebrate a love for God's own son.

Robert M. Marceau

Beautiful New Hampshire

The blue sky,
The green grass,
The snow-capped mountains tall.
The sparkling waters,
The golden sun,
The bright leaves in the fall.

The white snow,
The wild flowers,
Those hot, hot summer days.
I love New Hampshire better than the rest,
With all its perfect ways.

Kate Davison

Life?

The seventh moon
Lights my sky, awaking the demons
My heaven of the day will be lost too soon
I'll dwell in limbo throughout the seasons

Time, the enemy that wins
Past happiness, gone forever
These are my sins
Living in hope, dying of thy hellish fever

My spirit is imprisoned
In this weathered scarecrow
I scream, but no one listens
As they consume lies to fill a body so hollow

Gold and dirt
Treasures of mother earth
Love and hurt
Infinite misery from birth

Andrew Jegannathan

In Search Of...Self

I languish in this interesting life,
   of pots and pans, of mother, of wife;
of songs I've sung, and deeds I've done;
   of lessons learned, and badges earned.

What more? I find I ask myself.
   as I sit here upon this shelf.
of what I can't begin to say;
   the light is light, but is not day.

At 40 now I search my past,
   to change, to be, to hold on fast;
to dreams and things I need to be,
   to find the self, inside of me.

The outer shell it fits just fine,
   and tiny ones bring peace of mind;
but in the day the nagging reins,
   ambitious goals and lofty gains.

Pray what I need to conquer me;
   speak fast so I can start to be,
I find I'll need to mix and match,
   the past, the now, the best I'll catch.

    Pamela Williams-Coote

Guns In The Distance

Guns sound in the distance as my friend cries softly beside me.
I reach out my hand to touch him, then I pull back.
What can I do to change it?
Death took our friends,
Death took our enemies,
Now, Death has only us to take.
The fear builds inside me I have to get away.
Jumping up, I run from my tent across the field.
Searing fire explodes in my soul as a spray of bullets
   tears through my chest.
I crumple to the ground.
For hours I lay there;
Waiting,
Wanting,
Needing to die.
Then I wake up.
I'm still on my bunk.
Guns sound in the distance as my friend cries softly beside me.
When will this nightmare end?

    Tiffany Bronson

Host

"Pity me not", he begs
As his immune neighbors cry for him.
"But it's a case of the human race,"
Replies Venus with tears.
"It is deadly," sympathizes Mars.

The handsome biosphere speaks dignified,
Appearing not the least bit worried
Hiding his fatal symptoms.
"I can fight this parasite,"
He proclaims to his eight friends.
"Do not be intimidated by
This carbon-based human waste,
For it is not contagious."

It is a suicidal virus, he knows.
It may self-destruct and pass
In time, not being so sublime.
He sighs and says patiently,
"I think I'm getting better."

He has a chance, does Earth.
He has a chance.

    Ryan Eckes

There Once Was This Girl

Her kiss on my lips
Her body into mine
Our flesh became one.
Her eyes are like a vast sea so deep and enchanting.
Lips stutter shhh... says she.
Tonight she's mine.
Silk lace outlines her soft and tender body.
Her skin glows with a dancing flame,
She's all I'll ever desire.

Before me is an unbelievable wonder,
Innocent being, beauty is what I see.
Her mesmerizing smiles, her countless yawns she makes,
The gleam in her eyes, the whisper in her voice.
She gives me no other choice than a quick kiss good-bye,
and a long a lasting hug.
I think I'll be forever in love.

    Gary Bastien

Star Of Fire

As I search throughout many night skies for shooting stars,
I've many times been rewarded with one to appear.

Have you ever seen a shooting star?
Oh so pretty soaring through the moonlight lit sky.

I wish upon my shooting star, my wish I cannot tell;
Or it may not come true.

Some may not believe in wishing upon shooting stars,
but I do.

    Sabrina L. Lasky

Motherhood

I never knew how motherhood
Could positively change a person's life
Everything I'd heard from well-meaning companions
Was that there would be struggles and strife.

But you came along, precious child of mine
And put an end to all the tales of woe,
And set my life's course in a direction
I wake every morning looking forward to go.

Oh, how I can't wait to see you
In the afternoons after a day of labor
I look forward to sitting and playing and talking
And inventorying your day; for it's this I savor.

I could sit and watch you for hours
You're such a beautiful sight to see.
Your "long" blonde hair, your beautiful blue eyes
You're a dream come true for me.

You are my sunshine; my only sunshine
You fill my life with bliss
"My little family" is a gift from above
A blessing from Him, sealed with a kiss.

    Toni J. Lanier

Not Knowing

Most people in life go through a blank
Have no idea in the path they take,
A lot of people don't know what to think,
Doing what they do they have no link,
Stopping at times they have a drink,
Most people are at a sudden brink,
Just having a life some live in mink,
Long to them but to time it's a blink,
The world is somewhat like a sink,
People are living a life not knowing.

    Zacharia W. Myers

Legacy (In Memory Of My Dear Father...)

If the mystery of life
I dare encounter,
If all the universe
under my feet surrender,
then...I will discover
the impossible thought
of my desire,
that your spirit and mine
could be again
by death united.

If your memory
could surround my soul
and the perfumes of life
I could finally acquire,
Then...a thousand sounds of music I will listen
to suddenly realize the sorrow of your absence.

If I could touch the silence with my fingers
and find the pleasure lost of your existence,
then...I would fly along with the majestic eagle
into the lost forever place where you have fallen.

Vielka E. Rollins

Ocean

The ocean is so rhythmic,
the waves endlessly slap the
shoreline breaking at a constant
rate, rolling up the shore.

The jagged shells and smooth stones
await on shore to meet the water,
when the water hits them they
roll and become dependent
on the current.

The waves are strong, so strong that
they cannot be resisted, they will move
anything in their path. They have a mind
of their own.

People struggle to live separate
from society. Rarely do they
succeed in breaking away
from the current.

Loriann Cattafi

The Room At The End Of The Hall

Old timers, Alzheimers,
the room at the end of the hall —
I feel so sad, that isn't my dad,
that isn't Dad at all.

His hands so cold, his face all gaunt,
deliberateness in his step,
Memory gone, can't come home,
nothing like himself —

He the parent, I the child
'til time reversed the role —
His brain is gel, his body a shell
enclosing a quiescent soul.

Walks and walks and walks all day —
somewhere that he must go —
family erased, memories misplaced,
no one he seems to know —

His life's the span of a history book —
Teddy Roosevelt to Bill Clinton.
Forgotten now all he's ever known,
all the history that's been written —

Kathryn Dickey

Lake Superior, Near Whitetail Cabin

December 7

Not yet the hunger time,
Last night's snow sloughs gently, flake by flake,
from ancient hemlocks, through sun dappled air, covers,
as a gossamer veil, trails of the timorous deer,
the pondering bear, the officious ravens.

Not yet the time of rancor, of frozen hearts, of last dreams;
the lake still warms the air,
the earth, still pliant, responds as juvenescent flesh.

December 8

Through the second night Superior arose prodigiously.
Sleep was ruptured by basso profundo
growls of great slabs of ancient basalt.

In the morning, angry and brawling,
whitecaps extend to the horizon.
I am drawn to it.
Spray freezes in mid air,
it stings the flesh as the cut of a razor,
not yet begun to bleed.

D. W. Phillips

A Stillness In Meadowbrook

The childless streets are still and empty.
A fleet of bicycles once sailed these hills.
Where are the boys? One once tied to a tree
Fighting, playing - Flesh knowing no ills.

The "Circle" a concrete playground;
With a torrent no parental dam could check.
Gazelles ran with a canopy of sound.
"Silver hairbrushes" having no lasting effect.

Now "crawlfish" swim undisturbed in the creek.
Grass untrampled on the land.
Rowdy boys, the police no longer seek.
The child, sadly, became a man.

Strangers suddenly appear on the scene.
Stewards - astounded at their ways.
No charges from childhood do they wean.
Lord, bring back those bygone days.

Erwin T. Avery

Character Matters

Is character, like beauty, in the eye of the beholder?
Is maturity instinctive as a child grows older?
Does integrity just appear, or is it something learned?
Can you buy your reputation, or must it be earned?

Allow me to answer with wisdom and thought,
By reflecting upon the values I've been taught.
It may seem old fashioned, this advice that I give,
But without a doubt, it's the best way to live.

Let love and compassion flow out of your heart,
Select your words carefully, no hurt to impart.
Embrace the truth always, make good attitude your friend,
Never justify a means, by the lure of the end.

A hard-working mentality should certainly be adopted,
Make fairness your goal in each judgement that's opted.
And if you desire to live shameless and free,
You must discipline your life with true decency.

Then your character will be good in the eye of the beholder,
Your maturity will increase as you grow older.
If you live by these principles for all to see,
You'll own a good reputation with integrity.

Robert E. Sentz Jr.

That Summer Day

The ground was carpeted with purple blossoms
Birds above singing their happy tune
While sucking nectar from apple-cups
So nice to feel the tickle of blossoms falling
And the gentle breeze blowing against my skin
Every tree makes a bow
Out from the shade the earth crack
The sun peering through to see the center of the earth
For it's been weeks since the land awaits the blessed rain
A moment of tranquility gave way to a nap against the tree
The woods I roamed in a wonder-world of dreams
Then slowly I walked back to where I sat
Under the apple tree
Not a birdsong or a single tree bow to the wind anymore
Nor the sun peering through to see the center of the earth
But the silver moon stands out among the star-packed sky
Frogs are croaking, and fire flies flying about
And the wise old owl
In the top of the tree
Too wit, too wit, too woo.

Glen A. Norris

Teenagers

They are humans, with a mind of their own;
As soon as they reach puberty, they think that they are grown.
All the older folks were once teenagers too;
But society back then made them show respect for you.
It's not advisable though, to chastise teens today,
With their parent's disapproval, you'll soon be on your way.
Now, some do have respect, and others they just don't,
And with the words they use today their respect...you don't want!
Some teenagers are very beautiful, and others you wonder why,
It doesn't seem to bother them to see their parents cry.
But there is a right solution, to help teenagers of today:
Put the fear of God in their hearts and Society will be
a better place to Stay!

Cordella K. Baldwin

Untitled

I look into a wondrous blue,
a blue that swallows me whole.
I look so deep into this color
it makes me fall into a deep daze.
This color mesmerizes me.
I fall so deep into this color
that it is astonishing.
Looking into this blue makes me feel so relieved.
It is my sweet ecstasy, my escape.
It takes me in with loving arms
and it soothes me and my pain.
This blue is like a bottomless ocean,
but at the same time a topless sky.
But this blue isn't the ocean nor in the sky.
This blue is the mysterious color
of your most beautiful eyes.

Shannon Rodia

Kids

Some are fat and sassy,
Others are thin and classy.

Some are happy and quite cheerful,
Some are sad and very tearful.

Some are rich and live in mansions,
Some are poor and live on ranches.

But one thing is the same about us, you see,
God made all of us his children, you and me.

Emily Guth

The Tear Drop

The tear drop trickled slowly onto her cold and paling cheek.
As she struggled to see clearly her legs grew very weak.

The wind was blowing harder and the air smelled of rain.
Her heart was beating faster, responding to the pain.

They did not see her and she just happened to see them.
She was only there by chance - just passing on a whim.

The tear drop ran make quickly now and left a tiny streak.
As all her muscles tightened she knew she couldn't speak.

She wanted to cross the street but cars were just a blur.
In fact her whole surroundings were nothing but a whir.

They went around a corner and were immediately out of sight
but their image would haunt her forever - on every lonely night.

As the tear drop hit the pavement it quickly burst apart -
impossible to be mended - much like a broken heart.

"Paul" D. L. Farley

A Night Full Of Fright

She walks in the door
Beer bottles on the ground
A drunk man passed out on the floor
As she looks around.

She thinks of last night
Seeing children full of fright
Brothers and sisters hold each other tight
And wait until he's out of sight.

As the ceiling beats with the sound of rain
She thinks of what at first seemed like a dream
Now fills her heart with pain
And makes her want to scream.

Suddenly she hears a sound
As he awakes
Her heart begins to pound
As she shakes.

He doesn't remember last night
Or the way he made them feel
He doesn't remember the children full of fright
Because to him it's not real.

Alana Cooke

The State Of Human Nature

Look out towards the melting skies
Let a little sun burn your eyes
Shady creatures awaiting night
Flee from the evening light

A city dog growls in fear
As you approach, so far, so near
Never wonder, never care
Run your fingers through your hair

Not alone, not occupied
Stick to the shadows, eyes open wide
A tear freezes on your face
Your blood is cold defying common place

A bite as bad as poisoned snake
Deathly aware of unearthly fate
Extremist hate, a youth irate
As birds are screeching and cats meow

You try to hide an evil scowl
A world to devour, an Earth too sour
No appetite could find appeasing
It's all one thought and not too pleasing

Tim F. Johnson

Awake! Ye Seven Churches

Awake ye seven churches and listen to The Lord.
to all ye overcomers, it is time for your reward.

Known from all your lovelessness; those in Ephesus receive:
from the paradise of God; a tree of life to be.

Due to Smyrna's faithfulness, escape the second death.
Here I have your crown of life. Ye gave me your last breath.

Hidden manna went to Pergamum. A new name etched in stone,
to him who did receive it, to him only was it known.

Doing my will to the end, oh, Thyatira reigns.
Deeds of service, faith and love, God's rulership remains.

Sardis, just a few in number with unsoiled clothes about,
your name from the book of life will never I blot out.

As pillars in God's temple, Philadelphia proclaim.
Seen coming down from heaven was the New Jerusalem by name.

To those who have kept the faith,to all who wisely nod,
written on him forever was the name of my God.

Even those of Laodicia shall forever sit with me.
Just as I have overcome and with the father be.

To all God's sons and daughters, those steadfast in the Lord,
awake to see eternity. It is time for your reward.

Hugh B. Fowler

Thoughts Of A Fool

Life's a chance to hold on to,
When your love turns cold and blue.
Full of pain, your heart turns cool,
By yourself, alone, the fool.
You fight so hard to take a breath,
But what you feel, slowly, a death.
In your eyes, tears will pool,
Thoughts of lost love, thoughts of a fool.
Once, trusting, with your heart
You find your world, torn all apart.
You ask yourself, where you begin.
To let your heart trust once again.
You look for ways to free your soul,
The weight of the world, you have to pull.
The days last long, the nights are cool.
And once again, alone the fool.
With each day, you learn to be strong,
With a long lost love, that somehow went wrong.
Life has the will, to stop being cruel,
Happy, once more, no longer a fool.

Susan Menicucci

The Last Breath Of A Leaf

When a lighter pigmentation is imposed upon the flesh,
It is the gesture from the destroyer,
With all being accounted for, on the quest,
It is I, for whom he has become the voyager.
His partner silent makes ready,
To seize hastily the breath,
Which preserves me to this woody stem, quite steady,
Preservation halted, now I swing to my death.
The solid surface looks with favor,
As I approach my grave grudgingly,
Withering arms stretched ready to savor,
Has thy defeat been satisfactory,
Yes you, autumn, wind, ground, and grass,
Ah, last breath taken, now gracefully I shall pass.

Shenique Monique Milton

The Second Year

Now I have time I'm assured I'll survive
To miss you to wish you were here and alive.

I think you'd be proud of the strength that I found
My need to go on making no sound.

You should see my new friends I've met them alone
So many activities stumbling on my own.

The first year I functioned without any thought
Using hammer and drill by friends I was taught.

I learned how to sleep without lights and TV
Live through the weekend stop the anxiety.

Our son finished kindergarten one season of soccer
He can read and tie shoes but misses his father.

We have a new dog he's our best friend
We love him and hug him our hearts he will mend.

I crave knowledge training I'm in a posture to give
I'm growing and learning I want to live!

I have to go now so much to do
Through all of this pain somehow I grew.

Stay with me guide me help me to see
I need to live without you here with me.

Susan L. Droege

Fingertips

I look at my fingertips, worn down
bloody and black. I look at them and
ponder at what I see. Look, look at these
hands, they are young and strong, yet they
bleed and they hurt. The pain is emotional
and the physical pain is due to what I
see before my eyes. I've been struggling
in a middle class world with nothing
but my hands to protect me with.
Death, war, prejudice, sexism, and all
the things that make this world turn. The
bomb turns with every tear, every cry, every
smile even. Now my fingertips are numb with
a tingling sensation through out all the
blood. I can also see the numbness of the
world as I slowly begin to dig myself
out of society until the bomb is detonated
and ready to fade into the universe,
as I look at my fingertips.

Rachel Anne Levy

A Random, Senseless, Act Of Kindness!!!

In a world of violence, that seems to have no end,
Made me write this message, that I would like to send.
It started with a man, that read the daily news,
So wearied from the violence, he couldn't shake the blues.
This man is a Professor, who went to school one day,
And challenged all his students, to live a better way.
Instead of giving homework, assigned them for the week,
To do an act of kindness, or turn the other cheek
The results were so amazing, unselfishness, was learned,
Through doing acts of kindness, the students' hearts were turned.
An inner joy was felt, when giving to the other,
Be it friend or foe, sister or a brother.
A thank you may not come, or any big reward,
But with these acts of kindness, you never will get bored.
Maybe a kind word, or smile as you pass,
Could make the biggest difference, outside, or in your class!

Denise Sampson

Did You Ever Try And Touch The Sky!

I think that I would truly try, it just seems, so high. I don't
know why, when I try to reach for the sky, sometimes I think
I can just jump, jump, jump, pointing up at the sun and out
into the air, do I dare, this, be such a feat, only if I could
complete the Mission, impossible or maybe just improbable.

Just a conclusion of the frame of mind for a one tract illusion
of a vision that I wish to be mine. Just let me touch that
open clear blue sky, there's no reason why I should ever want
to die, but maybe, just to fly. Way over yonder, so I will
forever wonder, how did it get there, who hung is so high,
why, oh, why do birds fly, do robins sing, does grass turn green,
and flowers bloom in the spring, I think I maybe a little short
but all this I'm trying hard to sort, out, in my wild, wild,
Dreams.

Barbara Field

Restless Night

   It is such a restless night,
for something which my heart cannot fight.

   All I did was toss and turn,
for it is something my mind could not yearn.

   Tonight is such a restless night,
For I heard every countless sound,
and seen something in every sight.

   All I did was try to sleep,
but the thoughts in my mind,
was taking a leap.

   When all the thoughts had crossed my mind,
for my eyes had opened,
and showed me a sign.

   As I laid there and watched the clock,
the time had gone by,
within a tick and a tock.

   As time hit reality,
it was time for me to see,
for what a restless night it would be.

April May

Beyond Beauty

Touching moments of silence through dreams
I'm moved, suddenly I'm awake.

Breathing, absorbing the breeze, as thunder breaks the ice
of beautiful mornings.

It moves me to see you, I want you to know.
Do you want me? Yet, were paralyzed

As my mouth craves your scent
I'm stunned, at such beauty.

Mother nature never lies and reality so near, I awake again...
only to find you asleep as you caress between me, I wonder...

Is this real? Sin? Or has fantasy joined me?

Entangled in lust we become entrenched with pleasure.

And it feels so good
I want to explode,
but don't, stop please...

As we embrace, inhale the moment
of such pleasurable madness.

Luscious lips, passions past, temptation's ghost
follows...

Come, come on, it's only a dream.

Sergio Lewis

Flower Of Love

Love like a seed
Covet life and fulfillment

Love like a vulnerable bud
seeks out God's firmament

Tend one's love for it is
more delicate than yonder flower

Sprinkle of thy self
with the newness of April's shower

Love like the flower
never truly dies and concede

For Love like a precious flower
only glorifies and re-seed

The flower rejoices in the blazing sun
The flower is bliss when the pouring rains come

Love like a flower is Creation's ultimate help
The seed of the flower can but recreate its own sweet self

Love can only evolve into Sweet Love

Kenneth E. Beard

Is It Really Spring

Pretty little Meadow Lark
sitting in the dell,
Won't you come closer
and sing to me a spell.

Inside these prison fences
it's seldom that I see,
Anything of beauty
surely possessed by thee.

You perch upon the razor wire
and I listen to you sing,
Your song is very cheerful,
now I know it's Spring.

So sing me a song or two to make these long hours pass,
Sing to me of lovers lying in the grass.

Sing about all the ladies
who are soft and very fine,
Sing of all the good times
with music, beer, and wine.

Sing to one you know best sing it out loud and clear,
but move a little closer, just so I can hear.

Urshel M. Reed

Grandma's Wildflowers

I remember her wildflowers
growing up without proper
care or love,
Yet still returning each summer.
I remember her roses just yards away
being primped and watered out of a tin can.
And the wildflowers grow up coarsely.
So my grandmother
tried to transfer them
from their coarse ground to her own fertile garden.
But they withered and fell.
They are wildflowers.
They are accustomed to the harsh soil,
and relentless rain.
So much love and care broke their barriers,
and eventually broke their hearts.
And each summer
they returned to the coarse life they lived.
For they were her
wildflowers.

Dawn Ann Nereim

Untitled

Secrets...are kept within
Waiting...to escape

Your lips want to open and whisper
into just one other ear,
But they're forced to stay shut
Not allowing an escape or entrance.

Your mind is not attentive.
Just focusing on that one little secret.

So little, just few small words.
Yet so revealing...so confidential...so secretive...

It can hurt a person so deeply,
To where the heart needs mending.

Or cure a soul, and make a person smile!

If only you could tell,
Get those few little words out of your head
Not having to worry about it again.

but you can't...you open your lips
One word, two words, now three...

Uh-oh oh! It's all out!
Someone knows...and it is no longer a secret!

Jennifer Webb

The Shadow Of A Child

I'm hungry with nothing to eat.
I'm thirsty surrounded by dirty water.
I'm broken with harsh edges.
I'm complaining to deaf ears.
I'm wishing down an empty well.
I'm praying to the God I hide from.
I'm living in a world that doesn't want me.
I'm dying with life still in my body.
I look out my window and the moon hides from me.
The stars pucker up and fall.
Then all I see is black.
Black letters on a cement wall.
Black ghosts crawling out from behind new tombstones.
Black eyes with no sight.
Everything turns to blackness,
As the wind blows out the sun.
Like a man blowing out a candle.
And my light, my life.
Becomes a shadow.

Jessica Hooten

A Loved One's Final Repose

The rain poured down
There lie I upon my loved one's grave
Clouds lay gray on a canvas of sky
There weep I upon my loved one's grave
Night lay day down to slumber
There lie I upon my loved one's grave
Beneath lay the love I have lost forever
There weep I upon my loved one's grave
Never to utter I love thee again
There lie I upon my loved one's grave
If our love be so true then I must let go
There weep I upon my loved one's grave
Let not furthest of distance keep us parted
There lie I upon my loved one's grave
A love so true shan't ever die
There I feel peace upon my loved one's grave

Jessica Washko

Beyond Time's Shore

Forever the winds may howl with stormy raindrops falling
The clouds may gather to darken the skies joined by deadly
Lightening and thunders's bawling.
An earthquake may move mountains or alter an
Ocean's course,
The sun as well may nevermore the days endorse.
Could it be that with the night the moon will no
Longer share its fullness or the stars their sparkle of lights.
Yes my darling, all would be most unbearable plights;
Yet, I will only suffer from their darkness, floods, or the cold,
If I am forbidden thine hands to hold.
Still, I will love thee now, then, and forevermore,
As mine is a love that will reach
beyond time's shore.

Carolyn Mathis

The Man In The Cloud

When I look high in the sky
I see a cloud above
Then this man will appear in a cloud
High above the place where I fear
Is he my fear or what...
Is he my love or what...
Is he good or bad
I am not sure because he is high above the place that I fear
When I look high in the sky and no clouds are there
I wonder if the man in the clouds is still there
or if he is gone
Oh where did the man disappear to
When I look high in the sky
I see a man in a cloud
And the man in the cloud is looking at me

Pamela Smith

The Polaroid

is you at the sink
washing him off your hands
a fierce lash and lick from the pipe mother
ushers them needles
and scours at the sink-sisters
who would cry for you.

you green wink in the mirror, fossil in the vein
inking like a coward, coy and paralytic
and you curdle

at the thought —
you would like to be an orange
a waxing dimpled pulsar whose events are cursory, at best.
you would then have hands to finger you
pull and gut
and covet your pulpy magistrates.

your hands are molding
water into shards of the serpent
which cower in the tap like familial icebergs
needing that enzymatic push
and you catalyze.

Stephanie Ellis Schlaifer

The Last Butterfly

The Last Butterfly just left.
The question: Will I ever see a butterfly again?
Comes to mind. I wish I could just wait, but I don't have
time to wait, so in my dreams I dream of blue skies,
beautiful meadows, butterfly shaped clouds, and then a
butterfly might come back, some day.

Jillienne Landry

Full Moon

Full moon in the morning
Comes without warning
Bringing on the day ahead
One day in the life of man
A day in which we should all reach out and give a hand
A day can be misunderstood
He makes the day gracious and good
A day surrounded by family and friends
A day that never ends
It just keeps repeating its glory
Always telling another story
A story of all of our pleasures
Reminding us that children are our true treasures
This day is worth living
So let us each keep giving
Giving to all mankind
All of our heart, soul, and mind
The day is coming to an end
So let our bodies mend
Full moon comes at night
Making the day end just right

Jeff McDonald

Harlen's Fight

Felt a pain, that wouldn't go away
Went to the Doctor, the very next day.

On the examining table, where I lay
I looked up, and knew, what he was about to say.

Before he could answer
I told him, "I have cancer."

With my wife so near
I ask "Where do we go from here?"

With tears in her eyes
She said, "Tell us the truth, no lies."

The Doctor replied, "Radiation and chemo."
We stood together, both thinking "Oh no."

My biggest problem, I found
Food and medication, wouldn't stay down.

Then I think of my family again
I know I have to fight this fight and win!!

All I can do is keep going on and on
Till I have licked this battle and won.

I know deep down in my heart
One day soon, I'll have my new start.

Leona Dennis

A Boy And His Angel

A love built on immortal trust and grace,
that shall not be hurt by pain or tragic.

A gentle light glow come forth from thy face,
to show thy angels redeeming magic.

A gentle breeze blows through thy silver hair,
as thou reaches for thy child's dear heart.

To show thy child that thy God doth care.
And he and she shall never fall apart.

Thy child rises to greet his angel,
with thy kiss to lay upon thy soft cheek,

For thy two hearts in love hath been tangled,
and as thy dear love begins to feel weak,

He bids thy dear love goodbye and farewell.
For in heaven his love shall hath let dwell.

Triesté Chipps

You Can't Go Back

So many hugs and kisses and dreams, life was so sublime.
But you were right, you can never go back to 1959.
How did it happen? Where did it go?
What happened to me since that time?
The friends that I had, the people I knew before 1959.
Some were real special, some were real
dear, I shall always remember a few, who
were the dearest and best in all the world,
but that was before I met you.
I thought that all of my dreams had come true
Prince Charming arrived right on time. Just like
you said, "I can never go back before 1959."
Somehow, you were wise to what you had said,
or how else would you have known?
I think you probably tried to return, but
found that your dreams were all gone.
I'm sorry I took you away from your dreams
But that was a long time ago.
The dreams have all vanished, Prince Charming
is gone, the future don't look very fine. My
heart has been aching for many a year since 1959.

Pat Hildreth

Ode To My Daughter

Upon the Beauty of your Birth - Upon the depression of your death
 I LOVE YOU
The tears I cried, I cry and I will cry - I LOVE YOU
Upon remembering your first smile, first laugh - I LOVE YOU
Upon midnight feedings - I LOVE YOU
Upon the placement of your casket into the ground
Upon hearing the final sound, "I shall fear no. . . . . ."
I LOVE YOU
Upon never seeing your first steps, feeling your first hug —
I LOVE YOU
Upon never knowing - I LOVE YOU
My Jessica, so precious, so small, so young, so dear,
I LOVE YOU.

Robert Raber

Oh Death...Fear Not

Oh Death, come forth on the wings of a dove;
we live our lives so filled with love for what?
The approach of the shadowy ground;
and to what else in life but death are we bound?

Yet know that this is not the end.
For with our death, we live again
To evermore know of those who care;
who in the living, love we shared.

Fear not, for peace is with me now.
And in time, you will know how
My life and dreams live on too.
Yes, my child, it is through you.

Sharon Pope Swauger

Stars

Stars are so very bright
You can see them in the night
But there's one thing I'd like to say
Why can't we see them in the day
Because we think they are a beautiful sight

There are stars you can wish on
But when day hits they are gone
There are some that you just stare at
I guess they are there just for that
They will probably be there for an eon.

Jamie Mathis

In The Kitchen

Teetering like Janus two-headed,
Rimming about the edge of the frying pan
in smells that waft up and around; like
Being rolled up in a thick eiderdown
Comforter overcooked in the dryer:

What's (or is it who's) cooking?
Is what I want to know.

Well, anyway, I am not
Partial to those electric ranges
with their flat dull-grey snail coils
that bed the frying pan hard and unyielding;
Mostly, though, it's the long pause between
Thought and heat I cannot abide.

Me, I like gas.
Blue-yellow flames cushion the
cast-iron pot, elevating it ever so slight up towards the
wooden spoons that stir the sauce
or keep the onions from burning.

Now, I never know if I'm the cook or what.
But between the two, I'll choose the fire.

Mark Sockell

Land Of Dreams

In the lonely darkness of the night,
She sometimes dreams of a better place,
A place where the world is like sugar.
Full of wonderful things it is.
Nothing bothers her, nothing at all,
Life could never be better than when she is there.

She is always dreaming and living in her dream world.
To her this dream is wonderful.
She has friends galore and they're all just wonderful.

But as the dawn breaks her dream comes to an end.
She awakes and opens her eyes.
The room is empty and quiet.
She then realizes that it was a dream,
And she is still alone.

Ryan Jamison

Destiny

Strange are the twists of fate,
  Strangers fall in love
    And lovers begin to hate.

Deep are the depths of the heart
  With every goodbye,
    There comes a new start.

High are the mountains of doubt,
Will you help me, with the route?

Crazy are the thoughts in the mind,
That cannot tell hate from kind.

Strong are the feelings of hope,
But with hurt, 'tis hard to cope.

Dark are the fears that abound,
But I'll help you when you're feeling down.

Loud are the voices that stand in between,
  What the future holds
    Remains to be seen.

Sweet are the times that we spend,
  A heart broken now
    Will never mend.

Harsha Bhojraj

Smile

Smile
There is peace in the world today
Smile
Disease is gone today
Smile
No one will die at the hands of another today
Smile
Starvation is a thing of the past today
Smile
No child was hurt today
Smile
Crime is nowhere today

Cry,
for today never came.

Stephanie Villane

Summer Reruns

Thunderstorms on hot summer eves
Bring back flashes of flickering
Firefights in the distant green hills.

A throbbing roar against the sky
Quickly recalls the loud, dark-black
Shadows above the troubled land.

A hunter's echo in the woods
Is a memory of red and
Green death streaking through the jungle.

A warm greeting glimpsed in passing
Replays a fond family, but
Also a cold, uncaring world.

Media tales of delayed stress
Aptly show the futile anger
Of the now forgotten soldier.

Thunderstorms on hot summer eves
Remind me to tug on the leash,
And head for the safety of home.

Kenneth Newberry

Reflection

A crisp fall moonlit night
  two young people joined at the altar as one

Five years brought first home
  two daughters

Next ten years brought
  son and third daughter

Ten more years brought
  a silver anniversary

Next twenty-five years brought
  three sons-in-law one daughter-in-law
  six active grandchildren

Sweat of the brow and hard work
  sorrows and tears
  pleasures and joys

Two people older and wiser looked at the ocean
  listened to its sounds
  watched sea gulls feed in the quietness
  a crisp fall moonlit night
  a fiftieth anniversary

Two people as one by the Grace of God

Beatrice C. Pardee

I Can't Tell You Why

Why did you leave me, before I could tell you?
I know that I waited too long.
I was ready to meet and tell you at the phone
Where I always called you, but they told me,
"She's gone". Why did I wait so long?
For the short time I was with her
I just didn't know how to tell her
as much as I loved her
I knew that I'd lose her.
I just cry my heart out and can't stop the heartache
Knowing all I wanted to tell her.
I can't tell you why and
How much I loved her.
I know that I lost her, but I did
Find a love to keep and share with
My Heart Forever.

Louis Anthony Loesching

A Child Is Born

Unto us today a child is born
For all of the world to see
A lowly, meek, humble, soul
Is what he came to be.

He was born in a manger
No crib had he for a bed
Who would have thought that one day
This man would raise the dead.

Oh can't you see them plotting
And conjuring up bad thoughts
They searched and searched for one wrong deed
But this man had no faults.

This is the time of year
That we celebrate his great birth
No more wise men around
With frankincense and myrrh.

If I could give a gift
I wonder what it would be
I think I'll give my soul
Because he died for me.

Patricia Miller

Wisdom

"We make mistakes, but don't live on your regret"
Words I believe and now live by,
Father, you gave me memories I'll never forget.

In my youth there were things I didn't get,
Because I took for granted and didn't try,
"We make mistakes, but don't live on your regret."

Remember the time we played catch under the sunset;
The orange, crescent sky,
Father, you gave me memories I'll never forget.

"Being late, you'll lose your bet"
I always stepped slowly into unknown sky,
"We make mistakes, but don't live on your regret."

Summer days fly fishing and cooking a bait's pet,
Wishing the camping nights wouldn't die;
Father, you gave me memories I'll never forget.

I thought my problems were the size of a jet,
But every trouble passes with a sigh;
"We make mistakes, but don't live on your regret."
Father, you gave me memories I'll never forget.

Ryan Petrilli

Friends

A friend will always be there
to guide you along the way,
A friend gives a shoulder to cry on
and an ear to hear what you say,
And a friend is someone who will hold your hand
when things aren't going well,
Someone to share your secrets with
and know that she won't tell.
A friend's your candle for life
that no one will ever blow out,
A friend is someone to care for
and whose love you shall never doubt,
A friend's a friend forever,
and I hope that's what we'll be,
Because I know that I love you,
and I hope that you love me.

Hailey Herdlinger

Gateway To The Stars

Cold moonlight under a starless sky,
Her face is frozen in yellow light,
Crisp and bright in her silence,
Ever changing her expression in repose.

Crescent shape and in her last quarter,
To a full white orb that moves in the night,
All phases of her life to be dreamt of,
Only to return and influence our dreams.

Nostalgically recalling a romantic time,
Her moonbeams sending down rays of silver,
With awe as we watch her moonlight glow,
Fragrant memories that bloom in the night.

Moonrise watched in earnest consideration,
A lunar odyssey of silent moonbeams,
Pearly blue light makes it a thing of wonder,
This moonlighted gateway to the stars.

Barbara Austin

The Unveiling

A rose is a rose, a story untold;
    Slowly,
        Quietly,
            Purposefully,
                Unfolding.
Detailed beauty, revealed one petal at a time;
Relinquishing a scent that is truly its own;
    Beauty
        Untouched,
            Unhurried;
Truly a miracle, in GOD'S time;
      A rose!

Elizabeth Scribner

In Search

I am deeply touched by your poetic prowess,
The way your words flow, with pure stream-of-consciousness.

My eyes were met with emotion
As I drank your words as a potion
And slept with dreams of shangri-la
In waves of cello, flute, and viola.

Pray tell, are your words fact or fiction?
Of just a clever contradiction
Of contrasting images in your mind,
Of an answer I will never find.

Nathalie Rouhana

Heaven Don't Miss Out!

Heaven is paradise, God made for you and me.
A place where we can live for all eternity.

But there is one thing we must do, while
we are here on earth.

We must give our life to Jesus and receive
a brand new birth.

It isn't very hard to do, just ask Him from
your heart.

I know that He'll be with you and He will
never part.

Your life will change forever and
never be the same.

And you will no longer need fortune,
wealth, or fame.

Don't take too long in asking, for it may
be too late.

And don't take any chances, for He may close
the gate!

NorRene Gillette

Being Perfect

I'm perfect if I can be all that
God wants me to be. There're
many imperfect people in the world.
Being perfect will make me beat odds of life.

Being perfect is success. To be a perfect
mother and a teacher to perfect my children.
A wife to support my husband and my family.
That's perfect if I can be all that God wants me to be.

Having integrity at work place gives me joy
Putting away the opinions of people, though the
Devil will try to take control.
Being perfect is making God real in my life.

Hungry and starving for Jesus to touch me.
And hunger to know him better.
Trusting and believing in God.
And any other thing will be added to me.
That's making me perfect.
I'm perfect if I can be all that God wants me to be.

Pauline M. Onwuzurike

Denied Love

No words could ever explain
  the way I feel inside,
Nor can I begin to tell you of
  the love I know I must hide.

We were wrong in doing as we did
  and what now after all,
can I do to stop myself
  from an awful deadly fall.

A fall filled with much loneliness,
  for I know we could never be,
I love you more than ever
  you have taken the soul of me.

I cannot begin to tell you
  of the love I know I feel,
for what we shared
  was too short-lived to be all that real.

I asked for nothing from you then
  I yearn for it now,
but we will never love
  yes, this we must never allow.

Lisa D. Hawn

Beach

A small child runs through sun music,
sand castles shimmering in the heat,
invigorating salt air mixed with picnic lunches,
open enjoyment, burning feet flying above the sand.

Older still, self-conscious poses with windblown hair,
surfing, cruising, enjoyment tempered by pressure
coming in waves from artificially carefree peers,
seeking acceptance from the crowded ocean.

Pretenses fading, calming peace from the sun,
wiser analytical eyes view the world,
amusedly contemplating early incarnations
as they engage in excited motion.

Consumed by obligations, days fly by,
all frivolity passed in the interest of life.
Seagulls and dunes are forgotten while
working frantically to control and limit strife.

Finally fading, long after yesteryear has died,
perception limited to grainy views of timeless
wintry winds blowing through deserted memories,
the hidden child returns and slowly walks the beach.

Matt W. Polhemus

Raindrops

And then God began to cry and the
Tears of the night fell upon us
God's lightning rod struck fear into each evil heart
God's each and every tender tear
To each and every plant was dear
For just a minute, all was clear

Now God began to cry again
This time he'd never stop the rain
It smashed against my windowpane
I wondered when I'd see the sun
God was on the contrary,
He wasn't near done

Somewhere young children are having fun
Somewhere some parent's work is done
The raindrops keep falling down,
Somewhere right now a child is sleeping
Somewhere right now a mother is weeping
Now God has found us sunshine

Nicholas A. Pearce

Sister Parker Honored '96

The Theresa we see is very strong;
With the Rock that guides she's never wrong.
Her hands lifted in His praise,
She pulls down strongholds which are raised.
She sings, she shouts, and dances all about,
Stepp'n on Satanic forces without any doubt
With prayer and fasting she gets God reacting.
As a prophetess she warns of future attacking,
Brokenness of the spirit came by her speaking;
Thank you God for Sister Parker's gifts of teaching.
The children she cared for love her dearly,
We all know how she soaked and fed us yearly,
She gives of herself until she's run down;
She waits on God; who strengthens without a frown.
In this city and throughout; you are renowned,
But we here at Canaan Land are glad you're around.
This day is to show how we appreciate you,
We say in unison; Sister Parker we love and thank you.
You had this day of rest - and God did bless
We release you back to your duties for God to use His best.

Katie Thomas

Song For 12:00

A noon disciple wounded in the square
anointed the burning shade behind the trees
with rage that sparked the utterance of prayers
among the numbered throng assembled there

to hear the words of one who would portend
an unctuous quivering or a blind urge
to witness an ambition of a trend
exonerating the age of a dark scourge

in some true measured fashion of the sublime
heard a dissident wind or an aversion
sentenced as a heart's conjectured whim
the raconteur evokes a silent version.

Pitted against a shudder in the bone
bearing the sting of wisdom and the lone
seething of a soul's longing for a bright
day and a host of the recondite

companions of a dominion's horizon
sanctioning the distance and the stance
of sons and daughters in a contrite grove
where one has known the stages of their love

Nancy Maguiness

Towards The Sun

A blessing in disguise, no ones more the wise,
the sun casts shadows on us all, winter, spring,
summer and fall.

Catch the day and all the glory within, I heard
you sing, I heard you flew away on angels wings.

I saw you in the wind and in the birds flying
wing to wing, in dreams you're there watching
over us until the sun rises.

Life hurts now that you're gone but inside my
heart you'll always live, reaching your hand
towards the sun.

Where angels welcome you....

James A. Saros

Rilee's Rhyme

Read me a story, tell me a tale
Of lions and tigers or maybe a whale

About diamonds, emeralds, and a crown set with pearls
Of princes and princesses and little boys and little girls

Cowboys and pirates and spaceman with ships
And famous paintings of angels with cupie bow lips

Stories of knights and dragons and elves
And people who were heroes in spite of themselves

Read me lots of stories mom so that when I'm grown
I won't forget to read them to kids of my own

Maratha J. Phillips

Shirley

Shirley is the only lady in my life,
Shirley is the only lady who lights my night,
Shirley makes me happy yes indeed,
Shirley is the lady I want to be with me,
Shirley makes me happy every day,
I love Shirley more in every way,
Shirley is the sweetest coast to coast,
Shirley is the lady, I love the most.

James Clarence May

Eternal

I saw him in the purple sun
As he walked toward me
And the plum light faded
I knew we would emerge
From this feigned reality
As one member giving
With love and fealty

His glance left me a bit unsure
The feeling of love I could not cure
He wanted me and I knew at first glance
His entire embodiment could send me to a trance
Of a feeling deluded by warmth
His known being could horde me
As a duchess to her lord

It was then I knew
His love would always hover
About my soul
My eternal lover

Maria Ferrara

Is It Possible?

Many still young adults have gone through one or two
divorces, and are living in the world of visitation,
and often loneliness.
There are those who have hooked up with relationships
for the benefits of companionship and/or physical needs.
Somewhere, lurking in the background, are those precious
few idealists who still feel that out there somewhere
is that special unique mate.
One who will put that twinkle in their eye, and butterfly
wing resting, but fluttering on their left ventricle.
Should we keep our hopes and dreams alive for another
chance at blissful happiness, that we may have experienced
in our youth?
Yes, Most Definitely!!

Steven Nahoum

Make A Choice

She was right, in what she said
as she left.
"You'll miss me," she said as the door closed.
What a difference one person can make
Someone to share times with,
if only quiet times to talk.
Someone to look forward to talking with.
Someone to listen and care for.
Someone who will be there for me
Please make a choice so I can get
on with my life.
Make a choice so we can both let go.

Scott Mellington

Being Of Sound Mind

Bury me please in my sleek gold lame
I found it quite useless in life anyway
With red hair it was striking - my skin far too pasty
My friends called it tasteless - men called it tasty
A bargain you see - it was bought very hastily

The problem however - I refuse to be buried
So this term inter - has me quite harried
Cremation to me - a decision most amicable
And besides I am told - gold lame is quite flammable

So please bury me in my sleek gold lame
And tell everyone that I wished it that way
In life 'twas a look - too tough to try for
But at my demise say - she dressed to die for

Donna Marie McDade

Shopping

Today's the big day, where do I start?
At the fashion store, that will be smart!

Sales here, sales there, sales everywhere,
I have to handle my money with care.

There's so many stores, where I do I go next?
I will go to the store that I like the best.

Cool, those earrings are buy one get one free,
Now I can get a pair for my friend and one for me.

I have been shopping all afternoon,
But the mall will be closing very soon.

I think I'm done shopping for the week,
I have two big bags full as I speak.

Now it's time to say good-bye,
As I leave the mall with a great big sigh!

Katie Lee Couture

Echoes

In your eyes I have seen a truth
molded of granite. It dances within
a darkness foreboding. Of pain so cruel
come the whispers to my mind laced with sin.
Promises which distorted by chagrin
lay heavy on my soul. Could it be you
whose echoes throughout the mountains have stirred
or did you blindly deceive my desire?
Still, I listened to your unspoken words.
Surrendered to the vision they inspired.
Benevolent affliction. Why, oh why?
Go, lest your truths again be heard.

Linda M. Goetz

Dejection In A Flower Garden

I am not deceived
by the allure of your false beauty,
your bouquets of many colors,
your soft slender stems and delicate leaves
so merry green, symbols of life...

I still smell that antiseptic aroma
of the hospital ward, that lingering smell,
sweet, sickly, foreboding.

Oh, you brighten a smile or two,
but for a moment,
then you wither and die...
I am not deceived.

Art Chapman

Last Thoughts

To long for something better.
To yearn for something to fill the empty space.
To wish for something clearer.
Your heart has died and stone has taken up
  its place.
You haven't got a friend.
You've plunged off the deep end,
Sorrow without tears
Nights empty of everything except fears.
Hopelessness and despair.
Nothing but an existence, bleak and bare.
Heart like a rock.
Gasping and reeling,
Time running like a clock.
Only one thought left.
Death.

Rachel Ten Haaf

December Joggers

Grey-cowled against winter, long legs sheathed
In jester yellow, they resemble nothing
So much as Becket's killers: quick breath blown
Behind them, pounding hound-of-heaven-swift
Down packed dirt trails,
Frosted eyes glinting, beards quickset with cold,
Pursuing some unseen quarry whose thin cries
Pitched high past human hearing
Quicken their predator's blood, they seek a prize
Cupped in cold quicksilver, the heart of stone:
Ghosts, surely, in substance, airy wraiths
Embodied from flat brasses slowly wearing
Away to nothing under pious feet,
Creative anachronisms pledged to exorcise
The burned-out flesh and muscle of desire,
Hearts of the chase with not a beat in view,
Whose sacrificial fat must flare that fire
That eats away the hopes of an elite
Leaving mere revenants — you, and you, and *you* —
To thread the disembodied mist alone.

Peter Green

The Hunter

The hunter waits for morning light to come,
And clarify the images he sees.

He slowly thumbs the safety on the gun,
That lies upon his lap, across his knees.

Then just a glimpse, he catches through the trees,
Of something moving stealthily along.

It is a deer! Its silhouette he sees.
But what, a buck, a doe, perhaps a fawn?

It disappear behind an evergreen,
Then re-emerges with its head held high.

It has a rack with wide and heavy beam.
He counts at least six points on either side!

Transfixed by one of natures miracles,
The hunter's breath is short, his arms are weak.

Until he's able to regain his thoughts,
And knows this is the trophy that he seeks!

With sights aligned, he squeezes off the round.
His aim is true, the buck is struck and dies.

It lies there motionless upon the ground.
The hunter first rejoices, then he cries!

Roger Hinterthuer

Moments Of Quietness

In moments of quietness,
Pondering days gone by,
I think of little ones
Who have said goodbye.

Reliving days, filled with laughter and joy,
With trips to the park
And so much more.
Recalling the terrors of cuts and abrasions
Of broken bones and broken hearts
That healed so fast, it was simply amazing.

Some moments just never seemed to end.
But others I wish I could relive again.
Each memory is wrapped and tied with a bow,
So in moments of quietness,
To this special place I can go.

Lucille Burkeen

On Mourning

The death and the piano
ding ding ding
clink clink clink.
Some mistakes are better made
cluck cluck cluck
by those who know how
to be made
a journey to be played
clink clink clink
by those who know how
the quality of the road's intervals
clunk clunk clunk,
some wound call them empty dissonant holes,
they jar rough.
Get forgetness
clock clock clock
and children
play the peace of goodbye
remember forever
so you may sometimes cry.

Abraham Greenstein

War

It's on everyone's mind
It's nothing to think of in the kind
Bloodshed spread over the land
They will die with brotherhood on their hands
God's rain will come down calmly
It will stop this war solemnly
Will it be too late to forgive
To all those people who didn't live?
Peace or freedom which will it be?
Why not both? Do not disagree
Love will live and show the light
No more ignorance! No more fight!
To make it through this we need guidance
Also caring, sharing, and kindness
Stop this now or it will be extreme
To push all those men to eternal dreams

Angela M. Lewis

Untitled

Oh, the yearnings of this tired soul,
are really beginning to take their toll.
Once Happy with love and joy all around,
now sadness and voidness are all that abound.
What's left to do now, I pray to know,
with these feelings of misery,
that leave me so low.
Will the sun shine again and make me complete,
to know love and joy instead of defeat.
Help me I pray, to carry my sadness,
and heal my whole being, so I may know gladness.

Georgia A. Bolton

Love

Hearts, feeling, passion.
Love, sustain.
Love, father, mother, brother and sister, husband and children.
Love, our children.
Love, people, friends.
Remember what the world needs,
Love, neighbor, the boss, coworkers, and home, sweet home.
Love, yourself.
Love, is the key, the path way to heaven.
Love, our animals,
Love, the beautiful day we woke up to.
Love, the Creator and our beautiful earth.

Kiki Tserlentaki

Wolf

Her mate has come and gone again,
And she must watch for hunting men.
Few have seen her, but I
Will see her where earth meets the sky.
I will see her where earth ends and gives way
To vast expanses of ocean and bay.
She is of the Earth, one of flesh and blood,
One of the river stones and mud.
She is of the water, one with Beauty's grace,
A wonderful perfection of her entire race.
She is like the wind, full of all its speed,
She plants it in her offspring; a hereditary seed.
She is like fire, herself a burning flame,
No love of hers or great friend could make her tame.
She is like fire, her eyes reflect her blaze,
Not one creature in the pack can meet her piercing gaze.
Her love is strongest for her mate,
No matter how long she must wait.
He will return soon,
And together they'll howl to the moon.

Amanda Demeter

My Great Aunts

Aunt Nell had an ample bosom and a throaty laugh
And pendulous triceps
That wobbled and bounced when she salted her sweet corn.
She claimed she opened beer bottles with her teeth
Before she got her dentures.

Aunt Eunice had thick legs and ankles that drooped
Over her shoe tops,
But as a girl she could run up the cellar steps
with two buckets of coal
And light the kitchen stove with just one match.

Aunt Maude was the smart one, known for her
Presence of mind
ever since she threw the dishwater on Uncle Dick's tongue
that morning he was dumb enough to lick the frost
off the axe.

My aunts and their antique names are gone.
Instead we have Tracy, Misty and Dawn.
What will their nephews write about them?
That each has pierced ears and soft hair
that smells like fresh fruit.

Bill Ross

Confusion

The music beats too fast
The sounds are no longer rhythmic
The melody just lingers in the air
One moment away from destruction

There is no touch-no feeling
There stands a fool possessing the every desired rhythm
But there is no touch-there is no feeling
One moment away from destruction

My head pounds-not to a rhythm but to...
My heart beats to make no sound
My kisses no longer make a melody
One moment away from destruction

Can you make a sound by whistling a song unknown
Can you make a memory last by tapping my drum
Can you touch me so my banjo plucks
One moment away from destruction

Is there assurance existing in the sounds we cannot hear
or am I one moment away from self-destruction

Olacoy O. Robinson

Perfect

A perfect man and his mate in a pristine garden
A promise of eternal happiness from their loving Father
  A warning unheeded
   A future they cheated
    Sad...So sad

A perfect Son and his fate among sinful men
A promise of eternal life to those who would follow
  For the love he demonstrated
   His life they eliminated
    Sad...So sad

A perfect child (in my eyes) without hate, in a polluted world
A promise of undying love from those who surround her
  As this girl died
   Her ancestors cried
    "Sad...So sad"

A perfect world won't be late, in a future hurrying
A promise of eternal life from a loving Father
  A glow in the heart
   Intended from the start
    Glad...So glad
      Phyllis R. Washington

Silence

Night closes in
People cry, without sin
Night slowly goes by
People slowly stop their cry

The pain will never leave
Neither will the number painted under their sleeve
Will the memories ever go
Never, dear. No, no, no

The Jews are scared
Of the Germans' strong might
They can't fight back
Can't just go up and fight

So they sit
And they wait
Hoping and praying
Never knowing
That they soon will be laying
Dead. In the night.
    Kerry Mulligan

Projecting Narcissus

The sidewalk stretches out like the slope of her back.
Her singing still seeps through the faucet. I had a wife
who played Penelope: Unraveling
under the vigilant moon.
I dreamt of pushing through her breastbone.
I wanted to bind myself to her spine;
to burrow into her heart
with my fingernails.
I came home instead to fire: An altar of ribbons, letters,
flower petals. She said it was *herself* she couldn't live with.
The mirrors pushed her away.

I put what was left in my pocket: Her watercolor eyes,
the long scars on her elbows, her scent
bottled in the pillowcases.
A woman shading the horizon with her silhouette,
like a stringless kite. A woman pulling toward the moon.
A woman who dipped her face in the pool
not to kiss, but to drown the reflection.
When she said she couldn't breathe in the dark,
whose dark did she mean?
    Jill Malone

Enter My Heart

Oh, my God come into my heart and save
For all I need is your support. With time
I'll stand and with your help I will be mine
Then I will become new, no longer knave.
My life was given to another to save,
But I admit you not, much to his design.
Although you're here, I've drunk of his fine wine
And cannot defend, sorry that you came.
I love you, and wait for your love eagerly,
But I am stuck with your enemy now.
Will you break these bonds, for I wait willingly,
I gladly will become your humble serf.
No longer do I belong to this foul
You are my master for ever and now.
    Elizabeth A. Winters

To Love Again

So often love can hurt so much,
But two loving hands with a gentle touch,
The special words and a tender smile,
Makes all of life seem so worthwhile.

We need each other, as you know,
To talk and laugh; to share and grow.
For as love comes straight from the heart,
We'll stand as one and never part.

I need you now, as I always will,
To climb that sometimes frightening hill.
Someday soon we'll reach the top,
To love forever and never stop.

Stay with me, love, I'll do my best,
To make you happy, you'll teach the rest.
We'll stand together for all to see,
We've a right to belong, a right to be free.
    Kathryn A. Cordonnier

Where Were You

Where were you...
When I needed you many years ago?

Where were you...
When I needed true love that I so needed?

Where were you...
When my life needed to be changed?

Where were you...oh where were you.

Where were you...
When I needed your sweet smile?

Where were you...
When I needed the kindness you give me?

I know now that God was saving you
For my best...my little angel.
    Howard E. Collison

My Grandmother's Quilt

In memory of my (maternal) grandmother, Jessie Ryan Farmer
Seeing my Grandmother's quilt,
Created from remnants of cherished designs,
I'm fondly inspired,
To fix my appointment times
The way she, so carefully, her stitchings arranged,
For over-all good;
So, perhaps I, much as she,
Amply could
Cover and comfort,
Protect and provide,
For dear ones,
With love, to abide.
    Mary Hooper

Forever Friends

Friends are friends forever
not only for a while,
They accept you for who you are
not for the perfect image everyone wants you to be.
Friends are there through thick and thin
for the good times and the bad times too.
Forever true friends,
are you and me.
A true friend would never leave your side
no matter which road you choose to take,
and this friend would never leave you
for the roads you have already taken.
I am your friend now, as I will be forever!

Kristin Countryman

Untitled

In light there's hope, in darkness despair.
In sunshine we cope, in shadows beware.
We're brought forth into this world,
In light, love, and joy,
Then brought up during the day,
As an innocent young boy.
As time goes by we explore in the night,
Succumbed by the feelings of wisdom, and fright.
We mature with this disease in hope for a cure,
But the depth of our knowledge is only a lure.
With knowledge we shed a light on the subject,
Then darkness moves in and abolished our prospects.
With every light in our life,
There's a shadow lurking,
It's evil, sinister, and always smirking.
We grow decrepit, and ill,
In our final search for the light,
Till we're six feet under,
And darkness has taken its final bite...

Kevin Salva

Thank You God

Thank you God for my family and friends
for if I didn't have them I'd be all alone.
I thank God for shelter, food, water, and oxygen
for if I didn't have them I wouldn't survive.
I thank God for Adam and Eve
for if they were never born my ancestors would never be
I thank God for my aggressiveness in sports,
for if I didn't I wouldn't be myself.
Most of all I thank God for my very soul,
I would not have myself or be myself.
My soul and personality make friends,
so if I didn't have my soul
I would have no friends

Jessica Hiles

A Soft Serenade

I remember the night when I had the dream,
Where I was the flower and the flower was me
I stood alone in a shimmering pond
and the moon was like flickering candle light upon it.
I was alone in this great big pond until
you came upon me like a soft serenade.
With the softening tones of this sweet serenade,
you reawakened my inner self and found me
wondering through aging memories, but like
a gentle, joyful dream you touched me like
dew on a rose and awakened my presence,
bringing me back to a dreary day.

Katie M. Caballero

What Is A True Friend

A true friend is honest!
A true friend is dependable!
A true friend is trustworthy!
A true friend is there night or day
    with a gentle touch and a kind thought!

A true friend is a shoulder to
    cry on a hand to hold!
A true friend is priceless as gold
    and never too old!
A true friend doesn't have to have
    great fame or a fancy name!

A true friend will not leave you
    when you are down on your luck!
A true friend can be quacky
    as a duck!

A true friend is not fake or phony
and will not leave you when you
are lonely!
A true friend does not lie but,
A real friend you cannot buy!

James M. Fields

Laughin' To Keep From Cryin'

The Romantic Person thinks things last;
    false perceptions from a fairy tale past.

I don't want to fall in love with you.
    I probably will-it's sad but true.
"I love you" -softly- The battle lost
    Silence for a moment - unmeasurable cost.
Beauty means the scent of roses then the death of roses;
    But for a moment let's suppose.
Beauty means the agony of sacrifice- then the end of agony.
    Does anyone but me see the irony?

The Sentimental Person hopes against hope;
    they know their heart and mind can't cope.

Sometimes I have to laugh to keep from cryin';
    Sometimes I have to win to keep on tryin'.
My love seemed only to scarcely touch,
    a girl so special that meant so much.
You and I know strange corners of life;
    We know the sadness, pain and strife.
Feel I've lost something, Know not what, Know not why.
    Never again will I let Hope get high.

Brad Williams

Free To Love

Here we have met my love
at this moment in time
my heart longing for such a moment
Now here we stand my love
encircled not by unspoken pleasures
Instead surrounded by chaotic images
of what love may become
Subtly dictated by years pondering
analytic assessments of our past,
Barriers to our soul
How do we escape them?
Are we are able to escape them?
Yes....We must first surrender
Let go of inhibitions learned
Allow our spirit the freedom
so desperately needed for love to endure
With you I am free to love
Is love your thirst unquenched?
If so, my love offered simply may be your drink

Maryanne Campolo

Before Me

I always knew there was never another before me
As I think of all the times you said you adored me
I lay awake in bed most every night
And squeeze my pillow with all my might
I go by the park nearly each and every day
To feel the breeze, hear the birds, and watch kids play
I stop in the old restaurant every now and then
Just to think how hard we had it way back when
I sit out on the porch and stare up through the stars
To realize in my heart true love was ours
I drive by the old house every once in a while
Just to try and remember your loving smile
I walk through the old school yard now and then
To try and think to my self what might have been
I always told you I'd love you till the day I die
God only knows I didn't lie, I didn't lie
Who would of ever thought you'd go before me
Now all I have is tears, a broken heart,
and precious memories.

James B. Shultz

Y Kant Tori Read

Y kant Tori read?
I suspect, though I could be wrong
(I don't know her personally
Though it would be interesting to meet)
That Tori can read perfectly well and simply chooses not to
If that suits her, why shouldn't she?

Too bad nobody was listening
But Tori, with a Bosendorfer out in the middle of the desert
Played on and eventually the world noticed

Now if only the rest of us
Could see such success doing what we dream
I suppose all I can do is keep writing
For whomever is paying attention, even it it's only me

Had a plan with a friend of mine
To run away to a castle in the Welsh countryside
Haven't quite made it yet
But someday...

Christopher Baran

True Love

This is just a small way to say, "Thank you dear"
    For all of the love you give me everyday,
You go out of your way so happily and willingly
    to make sure that I'm happy in every possible way.

You kiss me gently goodbye every morning
    and I smile so deeply inside every time.
I often get chills just thinking about you later
    and feel so blessed that I have you to call mine.

You're the type of man that every woman dreams about,
    so honest, loving, faithful, kind, and true.
Thank you again my precious love for being my sweetheart
    who always gives so much love in everything you do.

Tammy Rector

Untitled

Walking on the beach, hand in hand
Gazing into the big, dark blue reflection
Of the sky on the sand
Watch our steps, together in one
Just you and me together as one
We look behind us, no steps I see,
But hand in hand, how happy I can be.

Karley Brown

Your Dreams.....My Prayers

Your dreams are my prayers for you,
as you go through life, what you choose to do.

My happiness not follow, but be by your side,
may your love and faith be your ultimate guide.

May you have no regrets, in your times of grief,
May you always have strength, love and belief.

When your waterfall shuts down, completely sometimes
Pray hard and remember, it's all in your mind.

Pretend you have faith and faith shall be given
Mostly have patience, it's the will of the heavens

Michaeline L. Kester

Nature's Wonders

Nature's wonders near and far
From the small deer running by your car
To the White tigers roar one of the rarest of all
And the splash of a giant waterfall
From the nearest small creeks to the Rockies' great peaks
From little cats and dogs to the huge cloudy fogs
From the lion roaring to the eagle soaring
From make believe animals with long shiny horns
To the earth's soil which produces veggies that include corn
From rabbits that hop and in your dreams dance
To unicorns who fly and they also prance
Nature, how far does it go?
Even the wise owl for sure does not know
I say...
It goes beyond the great rivers and streams
It goes beyond your wildest dreams
It usually seems so quiet and calm
But somewhere else a living thing sings their song
From the great Oceans and seas to the small rabbit or hare
Nature's wonders are everywhere...

Alea Aldaz

Buddy

My oldest brother I knew not well,
    too many years between us fell.

I remember so little,
    but what I do
    was loving and caring and giving too.

He lived his life so all alone,
    a life that no one should have to own.

He lacked the tools of life you see,
    tools like jewels we all do need.

But the qualities he did possess,
    will get him through this last small quest.

For the Lord has taken him away you see
    there is no more oldest brother -

    Only you and me.

Rebecca A. Wood

Yellow

Like flowers and humming birds, they are so heart warming.
All at once seeing the color yellow, lightens the soul, makes
the unknown bearable.
Golden fish swim to and fro in my mind.
I can kiss the blue sky, I am as wide as all outdoors.
For nature and I are one, as God has created so many minds to
react so gently to the sight of pure nature.
We are flesh and blood,
We are one with life and everything natural.

Tom Vincent

120

Paint Me A Picture

My soul filled with endless images of dreams
You look at me and ask for a beautiful scene
And I reach inside a sea of light
Like a passionate flame that burns in the night
My heart pours out a timeless array
Of colorful pictures with which I long to stay
Two people joined together in another world
With shining silvery eyes like that of a soldier's sword
The blade which can so easily pierce the heart
Takes hold of their souls so the dream will not part
And in their walk together a rainbow appears
That fills their eyes with soft joyful tears

Christina Isenhower

A Child's Grief

She is lying there dying there
So fragile so weak
Dare I kiss her tender cheek

In her eyes such pain
Death is coming quickly
Unstoppable like a cold torrential rain

Who is this woman
This woman who gave me life
Mother, friend, wife
This woman I know so well
In this tired and unfamiliar shell

Her spirit has already left this place
Please let peace reflect upon her face
Her body on this earth must no longer dwell
Remove her from this hell

Gone now
Some relief
Much grief

A depth of sadness quite like no other
The sadness of losing one's own mother

Lora Harvey

Untitled

With graceful same the wreath of willow wrapped itself around
in tears of pain, it lived back and forth, unchanging
with lucid dreams it gently swayed in the wind
it's cradle air, it's comfort space, it rocked itself to sleep
the darkness closing in

The smile never touched its eyes
The weather rusted roots fermented in the sand
the rocking ceased its heartbreak flow
like water in trickling vales
mournful wind in the trees

We wallow in the crisis
we break our own hearts each day
we get older we all get colder
but the willow makes the sun shine
and the sun goes on shining
in perpetuation

Jessica Lynn Hagerty

The Barriers

There's a thousand barriers before my way,
But I must not stop, I must not say,
"It can't be done. It never can."
But I must think, and work, and plan.
I must spend time, and money, too.
There's a lot of things that I must do.
But the more I suffer, the more I pay,
The less the barriers in my way.

Marvin S. Reitz

Little Wonders

Today I heard your heartbeat
just a quiet little sound,
How can something so very small
be the greatest gift I've found?

As we wait for your arrival
I dream of holding you in my arms,
I wonder, will your eyes be like your sister's,
full of mischief, laughter, and charm?

Are you the boy your daddy dreams of,
or another precious girl?
It really doesn't matter to us
just be you - the center ofour world.

So impatiently we wait for you
Only dreaming of who you will be,
Just know how much we love you,
Your daddy, your sister, and me.

My life seems so full of wonder
for Heaven's grace I can not see,
How truly blessed are the little ones
that make us a family.

Gina M. Reed

Alcoholism

Alcoholism is something you can't control.
It starts with your mind and ends with your soul.
It hurts the people you love.
Even the one above.
You sing your little song,
saying nothing's wrong.
And tell everyone lies to cover up,
as you sit and drink out of that little cup.
But now when you sing that same song,
you say everything is wrong.
So you drink some more
while you go to your room and drop to the floor.
You start to cry, but nobody hears.
So you drink another cup trying to hide your tears.
Now you feel trapped, but not in your home.
It's in that bottle where you're all alone.
You finally admit you need help from friends.
Now all the drinking has come to an end.

Nicole Smith

The Final Question

It was but too close
   And not so long ago.
With my heart, you had most
   And my devotion was never low.

Then came weeks of sorrow
   For I longed for you.
You took my heart, did not ask or borrow
   Now gone without a loving coo.

I ask now of your love and trouble
   Together let our joys be spoken.
May we forge the world a double
   I wish of you, and a love never to be broken.

Jacob Thomas Smith

From My Dream To You

Doctor, doctor.
Her hair lay so beautiful on her head.
When she had a dream of when she was dead.
Her tears fell down.
She started to weep.
She fell to the ground so fastly asleep.

Caroline Cook

Untitled

Time passes strangely, sometimes fast, sometimes slow.
Summer seems like it came and went a long time ago.
Yet it seems that just yesterday
It was New Year's Eve and we were all friends.
It's been almost a year, my friend, since we were all so close.
Sometimes, time passes too fast, and days are lost
And never found again.   What happened to laughter?
What happened to love?
What happened to precious time together?
When did time become such a hated thing?
When did we start watching the clock,
Willing the hands to move faster,
Willing the end to come sooner,
Wishing that everything would stop?

Paul Sellers

An Indescribable Feeling

Hearing the water rushing
over the rocks, is such a peaceful sound.
Watching the wind sway the
tree tops, is such a beautiful sight.
Seeing the clouds just hanging around
like there are no worries, is such an exhilarating feeling.
Looking at the snow covered mountain tops.
Knowing you are almost close enough to reach the sky,
is such an awesome feeling.
Calming down watching the sun disappear into the ocean,
is such a soothing feeling.
But knowing you are here to share it all with me, is indescribable.

Christine Christensen

Untitled

Sleep is something that you get,
When you lay your head to rest.
After working hard all day,
After taking time to play.

Sleep is something you might call bliss,
Something you wouldn't want to miss.
For once it's lost, it can't be found,
No matter how hard you look around.

Sleep can not be bought or sold,
Although it's precious just like gold.
It's something that you get for free,
Just rest your head and you will see.

Sleep is something not to be ignored,
All areas of this have been explored.
For if ignored, your body fails,
Believe you me, this is no tale.

So, sleep my friends, and do sleep well,
For if you don't, it soon will tell.
You'll find it very hard to make it,
All day long you'll have to fake it.

Lee A. Hunter Sr.

How Love Feels

Love is like a wild burning fire
It overflows with a heart-felt desire
It's like a night filled with passion
As the stars glow in a beautiful fashion.
It sparkles with wondrous delight
As the fire burns down into the silent night
The flames glare throughout the sky
Praying that it will never die.

Kristen Johnson

The Eagles Eyes

An eagle soars on wings of high.
Reaching out to touch the sky.
We look above and see how grand
This creature is who observes our land.
His eyes have seen what ours have not
And he remembers things that we've forgot.
He sees no color, no race, no creed
He kills for food, not for hate or greed.
Look through his eyes and we might see
What a wonderful place this world could be.
Let's stop the fighting, the jealousy and hate
And join together to unite our fate.
Just think of how this world could be
If we could see what the eagle can see!

Vera Lightfoot

Willow Tree

How do I plant a willow tree
that would sing in the spring
and dance with me.

Be glistening in the winter cold
when I was blue.

To love a willow tree
would keep me from missing you.
A willow tree has hollows
where secrets are kept
And roots that go so deep into
places where know one can step
A willow tree sings quietly in the breeze
and cries silently
when nobody sees.

Kimberly M. Dailidenas

Visions Of Harmony

Sitting in my world of illusion I comprehend nothing, but yet try
to understand everything.
As my mind flows deeper and deeper into meditation it leaves me
and I have a vision of a perfect Utopia
It is vast and wide; It called onto me and it was exhilarating to
see as society of harmony amongst the unknown.
Then I saw vision of what was to be, it seemed to blind me from
the madness that surrounds me.
Then my journey ended it gave me the wisdom, peace and
knowledge that I was searching for and it made me whole again
then I awoke; reborn!

Ricardo Theodore

The Watchman

When day's work is done
The city sleeps in far off slumber
Before the sun shakes the sleep from his tired eyes
And rises to cast his first glance upon the seas
The night air breathes peace upon the watchman
And the harmony of silence exposes things hidden
Beneath the veil of dark sky.

Sobering in its fullness
Piercing are its visions

How clear it all becomes
When standing from this vantage
Like crystal lamps that shine through my eyes
Yet brighter still
Are the fires which gleam through heaven's gates
And embrace the soul with wonder

G. Warren Ingram

This

Why do I feel so down all the time
I wish someone knew

My life is fake
My life is all untrue

I would sale my soul
To turn my life around

This thing has me trapped
It has me nailed to the ground

I cannot say what it is
Most are good, but this can bring great harm

It can be deadly and
it's very, very strong

This weapon has been through everybody
But with myself it doesn't leave

My one and only wish is to be free
I pray that God will help me
Brian Neipert

To Our Lost Child

I sit here imagining what your smile would have been like
if you had stayed with us long enough to see it. What would
it have been like to count your little fingers and toes?
Most of all I long to hold you to wrap my arms around you
and look into your eyes, if only for a split second. I can
see your Daddy rubbing my belly, whispering words of love
to you. I remember singing to you in lonely times, when it
was just the two of us; was it only a few days ago? I see
your father and I lying in bed in the dark hours of the night
dreaming of you. You were so tiny, barely an existence and
yet you were so alive in the hearts of many people. You were
with us for such a short amount of time, but the closeness you
brought us could have accounted for years of knowing you.
You were never even born, but you were a special child from the
day you were conceived. You taught me about love and loss,
you taught me about caring and pain but most of all you taught
me a lot about myself. You will never be forgotten and you will
always be loved. You are in our hearts, our prayers, and our
memories; we love you our Angel.
Lori E. Nixon

Ice In Carolina

It was very cold this morning
When I crawled out of bed.
The power lines along our road,
Had long since been dead.

I hurried to the window
Shivering in the cold.
And there the sight before my eyes
Was something to behold.

While we had slept through the night
An angel from on high
Had showered all the countryside
With diamonds from the sky.

The trees were heavy laden
Their heads were humbly bowed
Each little twig was greatly wrapped
In a shimmering icy shroud.

The sun came slowly peeping from behind the icy trees
Such dazzling brilliant beauty a mortal rarely sees.

Everything was still and peaceful with brilliance everywhere
I could never find the words to tell of all the beauty there...
Myrtle Strain

Destiny

Should I or could I?
When do you know the answer?
Is it such that one cannot tell another the intricacies of
their own mind
Or whether one is sublimely misinterpreted. . .
Time knows all.
Tell us now, where shall we be. . .
How to see the living and beyond from the one within who knows
yet cannot speak.
Life taunts the simple and torments the mind.
I sit, breathless with suggestion
Sensing the ultimate juncture of hope. . .wisdom incarnate,
Merciful union of the senses unleashed!
Should I or could I?
Despair not for others who want for those who will not.
Cheri Thorne

Dream A Dream

Dream a Dream and watch it come true
Say a Prayer and it will come to you

Wish a Wish with all your might -
Hold on to it - from morning 'till night

Believe in your dreams as far as your eyes can see -
Tell yourself,
"My dream Will happen for me"

Share your dream with people you see
because they will help you fulfill your dream
to become what you want to be

Now that you have your dream in store
work and work toward your dream
even if it becomes a bore

Remember,
if you work toward your dream, and
believe in your dream -
you Will achieve your Dream
Rick Olando Amos

A Feeling Of Sadness

When my Great-grandmother got sick and died
I saw for the very first time that he cried
I knew that they were very close
And grief is the feeling he'd feel most
And although most of his feelings were sad
This was the first time I saw the not-so-macho side of my dad
All his memories of her were happy
Some of them were even sappy
And I knew that he felt much remorse
That's a typical feeling of course
Even though he tried to stay strong
I noticed he couldn't do it for very long
As he tried to tell us it was going to be ok
I wondered if he was going to make it through the day
I saw all the sadness in his eyes
And I knew how much he really tried
But for the first time I saw him cry
Nikki Lavelle

Natasha's Poem

Max, Max, he's so fine, I can't wait to make him mine!
His gorgeous hair, his tempting smile, simply makes my heart go wild!
When I saw him in Three Ninjas Kick Back, my heart went wack!
When I saw him in Apollo 13, I thought he was totally keen!
The love bug hit me like a blade. My heart belongs to Max Elliott Slade.
Natasha McCann

Don't Take Your Love Away From Me!

Dedicated to Jeremiah Newborn
Please don't take your love away from me.
It just wouldn't be right you see.
I love you always until my dying day
and if you would cooperate things would go our way.
You think it won't affect me none
when you go and have your fun.
So I'll just sit here and cry these hurtful tears.
Hoping someday I'll have you again near.
So please don't take your love away from me.
What do I have to do to make you see?

Andrea M. Hoff

Friendships

Many lifetimes have passed, yet we are only part way through.
We cannot imagine life as it will be.
Will our paths remain intertwined a life time,
perhaps the briefest moment?

Many friendships have passed, yet infinitely more are possible.
Which will we remember, learn from
carry with us to guide the way?
Which will we cultivate, commit ourselves to,
let down our guard and live through?

How many will touch our lives,
reaching beyond courteous, beyond casual
even beyond close and personal
to touch our souls, reach our hearts,
guide us through?

Who will they be, how will we know?
All that is for us will come only through time.
We can only cherish what we have
love with all of ourselves
respect the fragility of these,
our life line, our friendships.

Lisa VanCura

The Silver Thread

A silver thread, holds fast, my soul,
Lest it should wander too far, and be lost.
To this dark world of sin, and error,
And eternal death.

A silver thread that holds me bound,
To "him" who is my creator.
A silver thread of love
So strong, no evil can touch, nor break

I feel the gentle tug,
A gentle tug, that draws me to his side.
For He "My Lord" has saved me,
From "Death, to Life" in Him.
Through His great sacrifice of love
The silver thread

Agnes Zaverton

Hands

What a wonderful thing to have hands
We can use them to caress and show love
Or to pull, push or shove
We can express from babyhood right into old age
Our joys, our fears, our love of hate.
We use them in our toil or pleasure
We pick up stones and we pick up treasures.
We use them to bring joy
We use them to destroy.
When we can not speak another's tongue.
Our hands tell them what we want to say,
Shall we use them to curse or to pray?

Eileen T. Jones

Essential Rain

Oh, Beautiful Man
My Beautiful Man
. . .or so I thought.

Oh, Beautiful Man
Oh, wondrous lover, my lover
. . .or so I thought.

Friends, lovers, partners forever
. . .or so I thought.

Day after night,
Sunshine after darkness
. . .or so I thought.

Gazing adoringly at Beautiful Man
Seeing only warmth, miracles, and magic
. . .or so I thought.

Beautiful Man's mask slips,
a reality incompatible with life
sadness grieving struggle growth

Goodbye to Beautiful Man
Hello to warm healing tears
essential raindrops in a welcoming universe.

Betty Bernhart

The River Speaks

The River speaks. Come, sit, watch, and listen.
Your loss is a rage, deep.
Only my flood will overcome your anger.
Filthy brown and wild, rebounding down steep canyon walls.

The brown torrent fades to green.
Dirty green still flowing with power.
To carry the grief away.
Now the pounding will ease.

After a time, the green turns to emerald.
The color of healing and health.
The sound and color empties you.
Ebbing emotions quiet, finally at rest.

The River runs clear.
In that clarity comes understanding.
Remember, He first brought you here.
To receive everything I gave to him.
Wonder, understanding, endless wonder.

You shared me then. You share me now.
Your wonder is his. Your understanding is his.
As you smile, remember, so does he!

Brian Gaunt

Untitled

Two rain drops
run down the window
racing to see who will reach bottom first.
Standing here all alone
humming a tune to myself
lost in my own little world
while everyone comes in and out
in their zombie like state of mind
repeating their daily schedule of life.
Paying no attention to me
and the world around them.
Humming that tune nobody knows
and nobody cares about
for I am all alone in this zombie like world
living in my own little world
where rain drops race down windows
and people hum tunes all day long.

Delia Lynn Curt

My Friend

A friend is someone to hold,
even a fish the color of Gold.
A friend will know better,
and a friend never quits at making you feel better.

My friend tells me when I'm wrong,
yet I know she can be a ding-dong.
She never says it in a mean way,
I guess I could say she will be with me all the way.

Her hair is like a butterfly in summer,
Her eyes lighter than the sea,
and every single joke of hers
makes her even nicer to me,
that makes her so special
because she is kind as could be.

I can never say too much about this friend of mine,
but I'm not lazy
so I might as well go on.

Our friendship will always be
she is someone so special,
and I know that's how she feels about me.

Zahira K. Vinolo

Under The Wings Of God

We stood together, you and I
Facing the moon in the night sky.
The stars sparkling like diamonds as its backdrop,
The night so still and silent.

You whispered secrets to the moon
Of wonder and anticipation for what lies out yonder.
I dared not turn to see your face
For fear the magic of the moment would disappear.

Now, I stand alone in the shadows of the moon,
Feeling your presence all around me.
Awaiting to feel your touch,
Not daring to turn and spoil the rousing desire
I feel in the air,
    ...so surrounding.

So, I whisper my secrets to the moon
Hoping it will hear my plea
Of hope and anticipation for our re-uniting,
So we may stand again together,
    ...hand-in-hand,
Under the wings of God.

Abelina De La Rosa

Taking Time

Life is a struggle, as everyone knows.
Life is not easy, and sometimes it shows.

Life is the pit, of the cherry, they say.
They never told you, the cherry, was rotten anyway.

Life is what you make it, some dummy proclaimed.
Too bad the dummy, was legally insane.

Life can be beautiful, if you take the time to see.
You better look quick though, and hope it was free.

All things cost in this world, the poor always say.
It's the rich that baffle us, they don't seem to pay.

Ah, life is so silly, it's short, and it's gay.
Too bad it's so hard, finding time, just to play.

So what is the purpose, of life here on earth?
To inhale, to exhale, in labor, giving birth.

Ruth Catalano

Dark Light

Faster and faster I can't keep up
Lunging forward my fear erupts
Towering high above me your arms reach down
The wind moves, you there's no one around
You breathe my air, I feel your stare
You absorb my soul and I am left bare
Shadows reveal you, you remain unseen
My spirit was drained and you fled the scene
Tempting me toward you, I cannot afford you
Taking my hand, you think I applaud you
I am left alone as you grow higher and higher
Stealing my life you'll never tire
My bed was made but I did not see
Forced to stay I did not agree
Caught in your trap surrounded by you
You leave while you stay, I saw when you flew
You unleash your evil with death as your goal
Your demons attack me and I was just sold
You live as I cry, you laugh as I die
Sunk deep into darkness still wondering why

Christine Medeiros

Dream World

I lay down
I think of your soft touch on my fragile skin
I imagine us staring each other in the face
You have a glow that warms my whole body
Our love lights the whole sky above us
I break down in a river of tears
You comfort me in your strong arms
once again I feel safe
I imagine us in the future
It does not seem clear
My dreams are becoming a blur.
I can't see us
Is this telling us something?
You kiss my cheek lightly with your soft lips
then looking again you are gone out of my life forever

Katie Ramadon

A Simple Request

Songs of the past ring in my head
Silent tones as I rush to my bed,
The time has come to put my body at ease,
I ask God, "Take care of me please."
I talk to my family as they come to my side
Take good care of my sister the bride
they knew what I meant as they said they would
also I was wondering if maybe you could...
Take care of each other, lend a helping hand
as I journey on to a distant land
I guess it won't be bad when I finally get there
so be kind, and nice, and take good care.

Andrea Danielle Hall

A Time To Remember

Take me back in time to another era,
where life was simple and people were kind.
    Here are some of the things we would find.
Home doors unlocked and the windows wide open
    Big old front porches with people a loafin'.
Ladies in long dresses adorning hats and wearing gloves,
    Children playing free as doves.
Men sporting top hats and carrying canes,
    This is what we'd see strolling down a red brick lane.
When our modern world has me at my wit's end,
    Take me back in time to remember when.

Denise E. Schneider

Hollow

What's left inside him? Don't he remember us? Can't he believe me?
We seemed like brothers. Talked for hours last month, about what
we wanna be. I sit now with his hand in mine, but I know he can't feel....
No one knows, what's done is done, it's as if he were dead.
Lord how I miss him, at least what's remembered. It's so important
to make best friends in life, but it's hard when my friend sits with
blank expression. He is hollow as I alone, now. He is hollow as I alone,
a shell of a friend.
Just flesh and bone, there's no soul; he sees no love. I shake my fists
at skies above. Mad at God! He's as Hollow as I converse. I wish
he'd waken from his curse. Hear my words before it's through.
I want to come in after you my best friend. He as hollow as I alone.

Thomas Barnes

Fear

I have this fear, that slithers
down me like a serpent
slithering down a tree
oh me!
My fear taste sour as a rotten pear
not fair!
It makes my hair stand up, like when a
cat gets ready to attack.
That's a fact.
I hear the fear rolling thunder, climbing
down a mountain top.
It flops!
I feel the chill walking down my spine,
in a line!
It traps me like a rat in a trap.
Don't clap!
It strikes you faster than a
bolt hitting a tree
oh me!

Theresa Stomper

Meditation Moment

Into the starlight I happened to be
when suddenly, I wasn't really me
headed off, I know not where.
What if it's me, and no one knows
this radiant being of light that glows?
I want to stay, but no, not yet,
The time is wrong and they'll forget.
"That won't matter in just awhile,"
a light friend says, while sporting a smile.
A voice that has a familiar ring, says,
"I'll come back when I've learned one thing,
It Is Me that glows from deep within
and nothing to do with the outer skin."
The others, I know now, will not forget
for on our journey we have surely met.
And when our lives again do merge,
I'm sure I'll have the greatest urge
to show you all which light I'll be
as soon as I find who is really me!

Rose Hufford

In The Eyes Of The Beholder

Your versatility. Your beauty.
Lies in the eyes of the beholder.
There's nothing sacred, we are all breathing hatred
You can not hide it, dare to fight it.
...it all lies in the eyes of the beholder.
Don't move. Don't speak, just listen to the sounds of defeat
When it is all said and done and we resound as one whole,
....spirit with soul.

Monica Clark

Redeemed From The Darkness Of Sin

Jesus was pierced through for our transgressions,
Crushed for our iniquities,
He was mocked and afflicted,
Yet he did not utter a single word.
He was like a lamb that was led to his slaughter.
Jesus was to be crucified among wicked men,
though he had no violence or wickedness in his heart,
He allowed the iniquities of the world to fall upon him and
without a second thought he poured himself out to death.
For Jesus could have come down from that cross at Calvary
to end his torturing death.
But his love for us is so great he chose to endure
such a cruel and tormenting death for all humanity;
for sinners such as us.
Through his scourging we are set free.
And through his crucifixion we are
Redeemed from the darkness of sin
in which we have become entangled and
brought into the light of Christ
through his Resurrection.

Sylvia Rios

The Moving Stillness

Everything is moving in such a way
that it is impossible to sense
from outside of its sway.
But it is possible to proceed
without moving at all,
a paradox worth knowing
to avoid further stall.
Such a strife to create
such things that are still
shows a baffling misdirection
of will.
A magnanimous collaboration is needed
to fight all that have thoughtlessly conceded
to the perpetual stillness
imbued in us
that likens the worth of our souls
to dust.

J. Swift

My Prayer

This my prayer I pray today:
My heart feels heavy and blue,
Please help me dear Lord to be strong each day
And to keep my eyes upon you.

I'm not the person I want to be yet,
I strive each day to survive.
Sometimes it's tough to make it, dear Lord,
It's hard just being alive.

The world is so full of hate and harm,
Of sickness, disease, and pain.
It sometimes seems the sky is full,
Not of sunshine, but always of rain.

I want to look to heaven, dear Lord,
I want to hold onto your hand,
Because I know you carry me Lord,
Like the "Footprints in the sand."

So Lord, I just want to thank you,
For your tender mercy and grace;
Just help me, Dear Lord, to be more like you,
'Till the day I can see your sweet face,

Tammy Rhnee Brown

126

Writer's Block

There are notions I cannot latch onto,
Elusive and just beyond my reach.
I want to express my feelings
But I cannot transcend the breach.
The concepts elude me,
Evasive and just beyond my ken;
And slipping through the fabric of my mind,
The expressions evade my pen.
To evoke great emotion in others
is my upmost desire;
But the everyday stresses of life
Are the very things that conspire
To keep me from becoming the writer I aspire to be,
Full of stirring emotions and passions soaring free
So I sit and put pen to paper and hope with all my heart
It's not just another fiasco, not just another false start;
That maybe this time will be different
And I'll finish a story or rhyme,
And produce something really worthwhile;
Maybe, just maybe, this time.

Nancy A. Gordon

His Last Good-Bye

Mike is a man that has no more pain
He went through so much time and time again
He tried his hardest to fight for his life
But all he could do is say good-bye to his wife
He follows his family and friends to his final resting place
But all he could do is stare at his wife's beautiful face
He walks over and kisses his wife
And says thanks for a wonderful life
You gave me a son and you gave me a daughter
And my daughter made me a proud grandfather
What more can I ask for to end my life
But for God to take care of my beautiful wife
It is hard to leave the world this way
But everything seems to be O.K.
The angels fly down and sweep him away
Then he remembers what he would like to say
He stops and turns around
As he takes his last look at the ground
All he can do is sigh
As he said his last Good-bye!

Kira Michalik

For You

And it was winter in my heart
A storm was raging there
All the ice of the ages
At least of my age
Formed there
Hard and crystal-like it clung there
No one could set it free
So hard and stone-like
That no one could find me
I didn't know it formed there
This ice around my heart
Didn't know I belonged there
This person I call me
Could you be the magic?
The salt to melt the ice?
Could you be the secret
With all of your advice?
If you are this wizard
The one that's come for me
Then wave your wand across my heart and finally set me free...

Madelyn L. Pulice

Lost And Alone

I run through the darkness, I'm frightened and alone
I'm reaching for something, just what, I don't know
It slips through my fingers, I cry out in the night
I don't know what it is, it's beyond my sight
Where have you gone? You're right here beside me
I can see you quite clearly, but your heart is not with me
I know what it is now, it's your love gone away
I still have you here, but not as past days
I've tried to do better, I've loved and I've changed
But nothing is happening, you just flew away
Hold on to my love, it will always be there
But my heart has been broken, there is no repair
If you came back tomorrow I would jump with joy
But deep down inside it is all just a ploy
The love that we shared can no longer be
For your love has changed, it is killing me
So I'll run through this darkness, I'll be frightened and alone
No longer reaching for something to hold
I know what it is now, I know where to find it
Your love is in the past, now, very far behind us

Rolande Jo Snowdeal

Until One Day

Why do people I love or loved so
dearly have to die?
I only wished that on that day
I had at least said "goodbye".
I so regret that I did not give her a kiss
on the cheek or say a simple "I love you".
I know she knew,
in my heart it's so true.
It makes me sad
that she is not here.
But it makes me glad
knowing she is so near.
She lies in a special spot in my heart
she will rest here, always and forever.
Until one day we unite once again,
in a joyous feeling of love
and knowing of that special friend.

Sarah Shearer

To My Husband

Don't have to believe our love's turning old
All of our memories are spun from gold
For all hopes of happiness for each tomorrow
No time for any tears of hurt and sorrow
I'll love you forever not just one wonderful night
May God promise me you'll never leave my sight
I love you now and forever cause I really do care
Thanks for all the memories and all the time we still have to share
Your love forever.

Susan M. Markovich

Here's To You

I love the breath you breathe,
I love the life you lead,
I love the beat of your heart,
I love your every precious part.

You are the reason I live,
For the hugs and kisses you give,
For the warmth you express,
For your sexy chest.

To me, you are royalty, my king,
I was overwhelmed when you gave me the ring.
Our love is the greatest I've ever seen,
when we wed, you made me your queen.

Cindy C. Simmons

Sometimes

Sometimes it's hard, to say what's in your heart.
Because you know now, we'll always be apart.
Sometimes it's hard, to lose someone you love.
They come in your life, and float away like a dove.

Sometimes they treat you, so very rude.
Then they turn around, and tell you they love you.
Sometimes it's true, I did lie to you.
But if you think about it, you lied to me too.

Sometimes you'd tell me, you'd always be there.
But you've turned around, and disappeared in thin air.
Sometimes I can't, express how I feel.
Sometimes it's so hard, to believe that's it's real.

Sometimes I'll remember, you did your part.
I just want you to know, you'll always be in my heart.
Sometimes it's hard, to let you go.
Because there are so many things, that you'll never know.

Sometimes the sun rises, sometimes it sets.
There are some things, that I'll never forget.
Sometimes it's hard, so hard to say goodbye.
Just find it in your heart, and give it one more try.

Courtney Fauria

Gone Forever

One day you were there holding my hand,
watching my every move with an occasional
soft kiss and a smile.

Then you were gone.

I loved you, the way we talked and looked
at one another.

Then you were gone.

Now there is nothing but cold stares. How
can we go from being so in love to nothing
in the blink of an eye?

Then you were gone.

I saw you holding her hand, talking, and smiling
at her and I knew.

You were gone.

Was everything a lie?
Was I making it all up?
Was it a dream?
Maybe, but at least I have the memories.

You are gone forever.

Crystal Johnson

Love

Love is lost in our world
Loving all the wrong people
trying to show people how we really care
Wanting to spend my life with one special person
 found that person
 that one special person,
 That I will never have
 As I think of him tears fill my eyes
 As I see him a smile is upon my face
 Wanting to be with him
 Wishing to make love to him
 waiting to live with the one special person in my life
 only happens in people's dreams
Falling into reality and waking to find myself alone one more
with nothing but the dream the night before.

Kathryn Angela Venturini

Wonder How You'll Die

Ever wonder on how you'll be dead;
Stab wound to the stomach, a shot to the head.
 I sometimes wonder, I do not know why;
When, where, how and which way will I die.
 Death comes to everyone in many different signs;
Homicide, suicide or just natural kinds.
 No one is afraid of actually dying;
It's the way of death their minds are replying.
 So don't be afraid when death comes around;
You'll forget how you died when you're 6ft underground.

Erin G. Hall

The Endearment Of An Empty Heart

Once my soul was lost
I never new what love was
I had not hope and few friends
My heart was always empty
I tried little things to fill the missing link
Still my heart was empty

I never dreamed, friendship would lead to love
My heart was no longer empty
One kiss is all it took to fall in love
Are hearts are as one, to never be broken
Nothing will ever break the love and friendship between a couple in love
She will always be able to count on me for love and friendship forever

Jon Massengale

Take Me God

I yearn for the past, when everything was quiet.
Now it's loud, but I'm standing still.
I've lost a friend, my only light in life.
I'm afraid of the dark, sobbing my pain away.
There is so much to hate, in a loveless, lightless world.
Oh, how dark it is, when hearts are blind.
I never dreamed so much, until you left me so hopeless.
So helpless I am, without a guiding hand.
Will you put peace unto me, and rest me in your arms?
Take me God, take me away.
This is a horrid, blessed with hate world.
Don't let me alone.
Don't leave me behind.
Carry me with you.
Let me be loved just one more time.

Debi Drake

Trail Blazer

I'm lost,
I live in a dark wood,
The heavy forest is almost,
Suffocating in sleep,
But I thought I knew the way.

I left at dusk,
On a journey I'd intended to take,
Long ago,
A life ago,
But by the morning's rays I had yet to find my plot.

I brought along with me,
A mirror so that I may see,
A hope, so that I may be,
And a love, so that I may need.

My mission abandoned,
I walk to retrace the tracks,
Lain by my own feet,
With only my mirror left,
I reflect and see,
The man who one was me.

Aric Lee Roberts

The Beauty Of Love

You walk along, the wind's fingers
running through your hair,
the lips of foam
playing around your feet.
You look out onto the calm sea,
where boats gently get pushed by the wind.

I look at you,
alone in this dark world,
trying to hang onto a small Rock,
in the sea of life, a Rock called Hope

You see me and start running,
but then the tears start
running down my face.
You wonder what's wrong,
but it's nothing, just Love.

I hear your soft, sweet voice
as it rushes like waves over my face.
And I hold you, wanting never to let go.
I want you to be there for me, always and forever.

I Love You.

Mary Frances Wampler

Crashing

Crashing.
You are.
Coming down with me in an empty ballroom.
I will drop my pearls and you will
scatter them with the toe of your boot, and meanwhile
the chandelier above sways like
unanchored tide pool fantasies
threatening to drop on us a death of shining crystals.
I will take you by your unmanicured hands,
Lead you toward the middle of what has no middle,
and you can pretend I am not really there, though I am
standing on your toes
watching fish swim in your pond-green eyes
and flowers grow in your straw-blonde hair
Racing towards the sky with open petal arms,
the moon lies in pieces at my feet like pearls —
I wake with the burn of your lips on my palm
into a world where a kiss is only
crashing faces.

Melinda Fell

The Inevitable

It's an undefeated transformation most people dread
whenever the thought invades their head
Many enter with a vibrant start
But if here until that time
That's not the same way we part.

Our psychol which helps us through the years
Starts to fade, and that's one of our fears
The once attractive outer exterior
Sags and folds, which wasn't that way prior.

This transition at times annoys us
Having to feel like we've become an onus
The memory of our youth may have a negative
Or positive effect
Whenever we think about it all in retrospect.

Then adding to our distressing emotion,
Illness strikes, which is another ordeal
Leaving us melancholy every so often
And for some that state of mind
Induces them to wind up in a coffin.

Natasha R. Phillander

My One True Love

For the days that I have lived, I make praise to God.
I have found a true love of a lifetime named Nikki.
Her beauty is not of earthly nature, but of heavenly nature.

On a day of sorrow and deep pain,
when the dark clouds are full of rain,
your true love can make me feel intoxicated.

When I look at your picture every second,
it makes me feel as though I'm in heaven.

Your voice is like sweet music hidden in an autumn breeze.
And only you have my attention of love and ease.

When first I see your heavenly body in sight,
I will want to hold you and love you all through the night.

Even though I go through much with all the struggle and strife,
it all makes no difference now that you are in my life.

Rob Riley

The Baby

A familiar cry at four a.m.
Time to change the diaper again
As you pick it up to soothe its behind
And coo at the face that seems lost in time
    Ah....hear the baby

The teething it finds to be of no fun
You try everything to ease the aching gum
Small glass containers of food you look with a sigh
It watches people pass and waves a cute bye-bye
    Ah...see the baby

Spit-ups, exploring, reaching for things of price
It looks around and grabs without thinking twice
As it reaches for you, then stands from a crawl
You smile and say "walk to me" as it wobbles and falls
    Ah...touch the baby

Crawling, to walking, to running full blast
Not looking as it runs into the door made of glass
It learns lessons fast, three steps at a time
Scraped knees, cut fingers, a patty-cake rhyme
    Ah....how we love the baby.

Janene Peterson

My Dreams

Blue, blue skies
Red, red sun
When will you show yourself
To the Forgotten One.

Come save me sweet morning light
Breath of Sunshine
Before I become Forever Lost
Under a thick layer of frost.

The steel doors shut with a clang
My mind screams out
Let me be, let me be
Can't you see I want to be free.

In a deep dark cave under the sea
Little Fish, big Fish swim by watching me
Will they let me go, I don't know
But try I will to catch a ship with a sail
Even if I have to bail.

I know I will, I know I can
But there must be a plan
For me to make real good tea.

Jeffrey A. Bennett

Paths

You and I have walked along so many paths.
We walked the path on which we met and followed it to love.
We've walked paths in laughter. We've walked paths in tears.
Together, we've walked every path all these many years.
One path we walked was called an aisle, forever joining paths.
There were no signs along the way to say forever never lasts.
Together, we've walked in sunshine and yes, we've walked in rain.
We stopped to rest along the way to ease each other's pain.
And through many dreary storms, we would always stop to talk.
And together choose another path upon which we could walk.
Today you chose to take a path and walk it all alone.
You chose a path called death without me to walk along.
My path seems long and endless now. It has no stars or sky.
And I walk slowly down it, wondering why you chose to die.
Someday, somewhere, along the path, you and I will meet again.
And hand in hand we'll walk along, a new path to begin.

Donna Winters

My Prayer

As I sit here and wonder
About the days that have gone by.
I wonder if I've done all I could,
Or did I let a chance slip by.

Did I witnesses when I should
Or did I fail to act?
Or could I have passed a kind word along,
I'm sure sometimes I lacked.

The courage to stand up for Him
Who's kept me through the years.
Gave me strength and wisdom to decide,
Through toils and strife and tears.

Give me the patience to go on,
To accept each child (of God) and mine as he is.
To give advice only when asked
Or when your will it is.

Keep me always depending on you,
Don't let me think I know it all.
For then I know, without your strength
I would most surely fall.

Freda Awker

Oh Lord

Oh Lord, I reach out to You in prayer,
Guide and direct me through this despair.
Lift my spirits and show me Your light,
Grant me Your promise of freedom tonight.

Teach me Your will with each new day,
Help me to follow You, for this I pray.
Without You I am nothing, I have no voice,
But in You Lord, I can only rejoice.

Not my will Lord, but Yours be done,
The new day is here and has just begun.
Give me the strength to carry Your will out,
Take all my fears and feelings of doubt

Help me to be patient, loving and kind,
Teach me to seek You, no matter the find.
My life is now Yours and Yours to rearrange,
Teach me to trust and be willing to change.

Jesus my Lord, You're a man of Your word,
You've lifted my spirits and I soar like a bird.
Thank you my Lord for all You have done,
Help me to remember that You're number one.

Tanjilene K. Oakley

Life's Seasons

In the beginning of Life, as in the Spring, we see anew
The wonders of God's creations.

From the noblest king of beast to
The lowly sparrow.

The Summer comes resplendent in
Hues of red, orange, and yellow.

The fall of leaves beckons Summer to leave
The splashes of color for another Season.

The Earth blanketed with its patchwork quilt
Prepares for a Winter sleep.

With glistening shimmers of light reflecting
The Winter snow in the twilight.

As with us, there's a time for sleep.

Sheryll A. Meldrum

Untitled

I heard your voice in the wind today
It blew through my hair-tickled my earlobes
I hid behind a tree to get you away from me
But your voice was strong-I looked up
and watched you blow the leaves around
and listened to your sound
passion abound

I felt your fingers in the rain today
Cold like ice they trickled down
my neck-down the center of my soul
I tried to wipe you off of me
but you poured harder down
Soaking my nightgown
Fingers all around

I saw your face in the moon last night
I wanted to take flight to touch you
but I was frightened - so I tried
to dig down - to bury myself underground
But your moonlight flooded all around
So I just lay there and drowned.

Emily Anderson

Untitled

For need of linguistics in love and thought,
It is in us true love abides and is non fought.
within your eyes I see love of pure substance
and inside your heart rooms full of joys' intent,
but throughout your soul I wish to make countenance.
I wish to bestow within your heart and dreams so true
a desire for me, our lives, and love always new.
A noted three months we have on this day enclosed,
and yet in these three months for lifetime I've known.
Of you I dream and with you I'm in love,
wishing you never to part but wear my heart like a glove.
I feel with you my emotions secure and see contentment
intuitive to pursue. I in you and you in me, together forever,
and becoming one in a pledge. Pledging together
in front of those dear, one to another erasing all fear,
to bestow on each other our love and future so near.
To lose me you must upon never fret,
because I'm yours forever, a lifelong rich bet.
I am yours my dear, and you are mine
so please OH please love me until God closes time!

Kevin M. Potts

All Babies Cry

In The Same Language

People are people, no matter what they wear
or how they comb their hair.
Whether their eyes are blue
or of a darker hue

Whether their skin is fair, yellow, black or brown
their blood is always red
No matter what city, village or town
where they go to bed.

The language barrier is always broken
when a babies cry is heard,
for when they extend their plaintive plea
it is without a spoken word.

Elaine Gray

I Feel

I feel like a two year old baby,
Helpless and yet so innocent

I feel like Paul Bunyan,
Big and full of anger

I feel like a blind person,
May not see, but hear and feel

I feel like a parent,
Who's kids are out of control

I feel like Jessie.

That is what you can not see.
You may see my reaction,
but you have no idea what I am really feeling.
You do not know what I am thinking.
You just know what you see.

Jessica Danielson

Rainbows

Rainbows are forever, rainbows everywhere
rainbows are the essence of the lives that we all share,
we look into the Heavens, we look across this land,
we look into our neighbors and try to understand.
My son looked to me one morning and said he felt
so sad. The children were all playing but to him
they all looked sad. I said son you shouldn't worry,
it's really not your fault. But a handicap is special
and that is what you are. I looked into his eyes and I could
see a tear, I said son I see a rainbow, it really is so near,
you know I really love you and I always will,
but let those rainbows gather, and take away those fears.
Storms gather in the heavens and a lot of us get scared,
but God smiles on us with rainbows and brings peace
into our hearts. So we get down on our knees and look up in the sky,
and thank God for His rainbows which bring sparkles to our eyes.

Edward A. Gilmore

Leaves Of Autumn

Chill springtime was the season when we first knew each other,
Warm springtime when our budding friendship grew so strong.
In summer's sunshine we laughed, and fought, and teased.
Short Indian summer days we shared, and learned of love.
Then frigid winter relentlessly sent out his frosty messengers;
Messengers dividing us, tearing at summer's love.
We are the leaves of autumn running before the wind
Helpless to stay our flight we despair of uniting again;
For the leaves of autumn are not unchanged by the snows
    and the blizzards of winter.

Susan N. Martin

What You Mean To Me

My world is surrounded by you
Not only are you my husband
But my best friend in life
Whom I love and cherish so very much
You are so committed and caring
Never forget a day without saying "I Love You"
You fill my life with beauty and joy
With places, things, and people I never knew about
You continue to teach me how to grow
As an individual as well as a partner in our relationship
No matter what situation our lives could be
You always have a winning attitude
You bring me plenty of laughs and smiles
Throughout the years we've been together
My life with you is a gift from God
I can never ask for any gift greater than you
You mean the world to me Eric
And I love you always

Debbie Lin Encell

Glorious Sea

The sun shines upon the sea bringing forth
To one's eye rays of light telling the story
Of these waters as it was told a thousand years ago.

As one stands on the shores and admires this
Realm of beauty, her centuries' old life comes before you.
Images of those who sailed in bravery and cowardice,
Out of duty for their country, or for simple pleasure.
Her life, both past and present.

Her folklore of captains and pirates,
Her written words from the hand of the poet,
Her vision of beauty from the eyes of the artist,
Have carried her on throughout her long life.

The sea with her rays of light as bright as heaven's embrace,
Will eternally exist as the realm of glory that she is,
Forever as God's perfect creation.

Holly Bianchi

A Moment In Tranquility

A night that has never been seen, at least for a long, long time.
    A date with destiny, that a heart could only find.

A woman that you've known, like a lover from far away.
    A woman when gone, you wish were here to stay.

A kiss that gave you life, like God could only give.
    A kiss that made you remember, why you want to live.

A hug that gave you comfort, like holding a long time friend.
    A hug that made you wish, that time could just suspend.

A cry to only realize, it was a moment you'll never have again.
    A cry in only heaven, where you'll hold your love again.

Roger Phillips

A Gift Of Friendship

Friendship is a gift you can enjoy forever.
I am thankful for our friendship. You've
helped me through all the rough times in
my life. You were there to listen to my
dreams and encourage me to go for them. We
have laughed and felt pain together. May
our friendship grow stronger everyday. I am
glad to have you on my side in everything
I do. May we always be friends to the end.
Thanks for everything especially for being
my friend.

Laura Oursler

"My Tiny Voice"

Do you cry,
when young boys play glorious war games, and all the
evening news has to say is, "four teens died in a car
wreck last night"? What are we teaching our children?
Do you cry,
when hatred becomes the only cause for action, and
oil is more important than life? Where are our priorities?
Do you cry,
when souls freeze in urban boxes and shoes are a luxury,
all while young women scream real tears in disgust?
How can we justify neglect?
Do you cry,
when sorrow is evident in old folks eyes and fear
replaces hope? Indians are being slaughtered and used
to stuff the scripts of Hollywood, but this isn't how it
used to be. What have we become?
Do you cry,
every time she says goodbye-again?
I do.

Bob Clyde

Childhood Memories

Yesterday you were a smiling bundle of pink perfection,
You had a language only you could understand,
Full of coos and babbling baby sounds,
And sometimes bewildering cries to your mother and I,
There were bumps and scrapes along the way,
Nothing a kiss and a hug couldn't mend,
Days filled with laughter and fun,
But always, there was a heart full of love,
Bicycles, dolls, and a dog named Rex,
All added to the fun,
There were boys, dances, dates, and graduation day,
I glanced away for just a second, a moment, in time,
But you were grown, transformed, from our little girl,
Into a beautiful young woman,
Now a mother soon to be,
Your childhood left to yesterday's memories,
While some things are destined to grow and change,
As you will soon see,
The one thing that will never waver or flee,
Is our heart full of love for thee!

Debbie K. Ostrich

Winter Weather Sounds

I hear the drain swirly
swirly swirly
then girgly girgly girgly
The rain drops
blop
blop
blop
tingle tingle tingle
I hear the cars
Rumbling
and people mumbling
The crows are
Laughing
and the water pipe splishing
and splashing
The wind is whistling, the stream is shshing!!
The grass is slirping when I step
This all happened on a cold Winter Day?
Yep!

Nichole Criss

Renaissance

An impulse strong, a thought, a prayer
Float like feathers in the air
Not landing as soft breezes blow
Keeping our hopes and dreams aglow
with renewed strength and a firm of heart,
beating and on fire, desire
to do the will of Him who came.
In humble stance, with no acclaim
He lived to prove that only He
Could save sinners such as we,
He is our strength from day to day
He is the truth, the light, the way
Bringing us salvation that is free,
For all who open eyes to see.
    He is the Great I Am.

Ruth MacKinder Westlake

The Love That Was Started Long Ago

There was a love that started in the womb of my mother.
When my mother and daddy showed their unconditional love
    I was conceived.
The love in my mother's womb blossomed and grew;
And never has withered but grown low at times;
    refurbished by the love of Jesus.
The love of Jesus that was started in my mother's womb.
At times of heartaches and troubles the love of Jesus will shine through.
Now, I ask as a mother, touch that hurting child
    whose love started in his mother's womb.
For Jesus in this child, will smile and say I love you my child.
The love of a mother can never be taken away by devil or foe.
For in that child Jesus's love was started in that mother's womb.

Raliene J. Wallace

Loving Words

Why did Matthew have to die?
His strength, it gave her wings to fly
But now her wings are crushed and broken
Too bad loving words weren't spoken
He left a cold and rainy day
She could not find the words to say
But now her heart is weak and broken
Too bad loving words weren't spoken
"No!" she screamed into the night
She didn't want his spirit to take flight
He's dead, but how she loved him so
Now where he is, she wants to go
As day is night and night is day
She loved him in a special way
But now her wings, they are not broken
For she knows loving words were spoken

Keri Harrold

Jennifer's Autumn

You are like a beautiful autumn day
Hair of reddish gold which I can say
Eyes of blue like the sky above
When I looked into them I felt the love
As I stand by you looking at a tree
I cannot help feeling better, for all to see
The clouds look soft and white
Just as your skin that I wanted to caress with all my might
The gentle breeze that touch my face
How I wish it could be your fingers as beautiful as lace
Autumn is but a very short time in the year
Just as your life I feel with many a tear
When the leaves are collected and autumn is gone
You my little love, in my heart will go on and on

Daniel Landsbaum

Untitled

Grasping on to anything
trying to find happiness
  why can't I find it?
Looking here, looking there - where is it?
I don't understand why I can't have it
  So many others have found it
Why do I feel a hole in my heart?
  I don't understand
I'm trying to fill it...Nothing seems to work!
  What's the point of being here?
No one seems to care; if I'm here, or if I'm there.
  Why is there a hole?

Why don't I have anyone?
  I have life, some say even more abundant.
Why not peace? Jehovah Shalom - where are you?
  My Joy - where have you gone?
Come back to me ... Please!
  How did I lose you? Why did I lose you?
Where is my God?

  Why my God?
    Becky Sikora

Woodsmoke

So fragrant from my hearth you rise,
Breath of life from death,
Up into the darkening skies,
Into the dying sunsets cloud.
the stormy wind moans still so loud,
He waits, the chimney rumbles with his breath,
To catch you in his strong embrace,
To dash to earth, or soar in space.

From starlit nights and days long gone,
From solitary years you've come.
It is for man the greater one,
For him the sacrifice is made,
The tree chopped down, the log is laid.
The flames will set its spirit free,
To fade into eternity.

Ah! so it is, with memories,
Gathered from the fires of life;
Old loves, and dreams, and stormy strife,
From days long gone, start
Wraith like. Rising from the heart.
    Marcella Schumacher

Earth

The deep crystal water reflected the sky —
Higher and faster I wanted to fly.
Over the infected and painful earth
I could hear its cry for a new rebirth.

Its screams had echoed over the trees
But came to a muffled silence when it hit the seas
The wind became cold and sat real still
The animals wouldn't be able to escape the chill.

The land will harden and water will freeze thick
The bunnies and frogs will burrow real quick
The ice age is upon us, is what they say...
One day we can all just be wiped away.

So be sure to have fun, and live for today,
It should be that way anyway.
Tell everyone that you're glad they're around
And you'll smile in peace at the happiness you've found
    Holly Kerr

A Husband's Remembrance

I loved the simple pleasures
  We both shared throughout our life;
Those which started from the very first day
  You agreed to become my wife.

Our daily routine of a simple hug
  To saying, "I love You Dear";
To giving each other monthly anniversary cards
  Throughout our very first year.

Our daily walks, our evening strolls
  To star gazing on our patio at night;
Just as long as we were together
  Made everything in life seem right.

Some people wish for money and power
  Or some trivial material thing;
We were just happy with the few things we had
  That all started with one simple ring.

I miss you now more than words can say
  But try to get on with my life;
But I'll never forget you as long as I live
  my partner, best friend and my wife.
    Danny L. McGrath

Blow

  Hey little girl looking out your window,
Why are your eyes so innocent?
Why are your thoughts so pure?
Do you dare to grow up?
  You have never seen the ways of the world,
You have never experienced the punishment of
the spirits.
  Blow your lashes in the wind,
and make a wish when it flies.
Fly through the air,
with your chest so bare,
swoop down to kiss the ground,
and glide away again.
  You have a dared to grow,
your eyes are no longer innocent,
your thoughts are now impure.
You have seen the ways of the world,
and you experience the punishment of the
spirits every time you open your eyes.
    Amy Schultz

Judas

When I close my eyes I hear marauding footsteps
Laying wide the hours before dawn low electric humming
cutting thought like a scream,
How many angels lie awake as the wraith walks...

A classic Lugosi nocturne,
keen as a rapier elegant, streamlined
Shaped and stained with blood and battles aged to
sifting dust of majesty
Remaining, as the night has done, quiet, ageless.

The hour of secrets behind the walls of that pale skull
is a carnival masked in shock and feathers fallen.
Here, spectres rise to jubilant waltz

Tossing venom across the path on any who might cast a wayward
glance at death - deep is the beat of revelry -
They would drop to their knees if they knew.
    Michelle R. Manili

Nursery Rhyme For A Nurse

There once was a young lady who always wore white.
She worked days, split-shifts, weekends, all hours of
the day and night.

With her mighty cape she would be
caring for the young and the elderly.

And from their beds the sick would say
"Nurse I'm glad you're here today."

Giving the world her healing touch
The loving care we need so much.

From time to time she'd get an abrasion
But she always rises to the occasion.

By the people I am told, that she has a heart of gold.

So, from this rhyme you may agree
that an angel she might be...

Gina Hodges

Along The Way

How glorious the sun shines this morning,
So peaceful my world seems today.
My heart feels like angel wings soaring,
Each time your eyes look my way.

An honest, true friend, this has to be right.
With a touch of your hand, my burdens are light.
Love overflows, I stop to rejoice,
Such sweetness is found in the sound of your voice.

For along the way, our paths crossed one day.
My life changed completely, I wish you could stay.
Seasons have come, you say you must go,
Tread lightly my Love, For you carry my Soul.

Peggy Self

Prayer To God

O God, I pray to you as a disciple,
Sincerely, wholeheartedly, and with utmost devotion;
Give me your blessings, and to all I have known,
And to those who are in trouble, those unknown;

Let your blessings drop down from heaven,
As drops of rain rushing towards men;
Give me that heavenly power O God,
To help men in need, wherever I trod.

This earth is loaded with crime and violence,
Give these criminals so much sense;
So that never again a crime is reported,
Never again a sweet home is broken;

Never again O God, never again,
Any innocent creature loses his life
Due to the cruel deeds of another person.

Bless this hostile earth by your grace,
Without any discrimination by any race,
Bless all, omit none, including me;
So that I can try my best, in the way, whatever,
To make this world a better place to live than before...

Bhavana Mulay

There Still Is Time

There still is time to do your part
To lend a hand to the man in the dark
To share with him the beauty of light
To help him understand wrong from right
To develop his mind and touch his heart
There still is time to do your part

There still is time to teach that little boy
Replace his weapon with an educational toy
Instead of destroying human tissues, get him into moral issues
There still is time to guide that little girl
Along the crooked paths of this cruel world
Tell her she's not weak, and of the discrimination she'll meet
Show more attention and concern for them
There still is time to guide those children

There still is time to save your own soul
And experience the peace that will unfold
Be genuine in spirit, be pure and true in heart
And encourage your neighbors to do their part
Helping each other is more precious than gold
There still is time to save your own soul

Karl McCarthy

My Lighthouse

When I feel like a ship tossed upon the seas of life,
Almost not knowing how to find my way to shore;
I remember your wondrous love is my lighthouse,
Shining the light of glorious compassion and love forever more!

For me to follow and hold close and dear in my heart,
And warms my very inner soul;
To come into port to stay in your loving arms,
In safety and contentment where I am complete and whole!

The shining light of your love is my life beacon,
For true hope and sanity, and eternal happiness;
Even through the storms of life your love-light shines,
Never to be quenched until we pass on,
Only to shine for us in glorious eternal bliss!

Katherine Bowman

Hidden Image

As you walk through the door the tears
started to soar down your cheek. As I
sit here at my highest peak, with a fifth
of ever clear sitting beside my chair
and my face covered with snow. I knew
I wasn't a person you would want
to know. Now your heart is being torn
apart, while the pain drives you insane
as you find it hard to believe what
you've already received. I tried to think
of what I could say in that one special
Way, but my thoughts were dry as I
watched you cry. I knew there was
nothing to be said, so I turned and
bowed my head...hoping you knew
how much I love you!

Valena Hatlestad

Just A Raisin In A Bran Muffin

Woe is me...how can this be?
I'm just a raisin in a bran muffin.
In the beautiful sunshine...with dew on my face
I grew lush and productive...the pride of the place.

Such high hopes...and great pride too
What would I be?...what would I do?
Maybe grace the table of the rich and elite
Maybe quench the thirst of the men on the street.
Bringing joy to some hearts...to others despair
A heavy burden for a grape to bear.

My dreams have all changed now...new visions acquired
The glory I once sought, no longer desired.
I'm grateful and blessed and happy indeed
To be granted the honor of filling this need.
Not destined to be champagne or nuthin'
Just a plump little raisin in a tasty Bran Muffin.

Helen A. Jaeger

A Touch

I think about the day, and I begin to shiver,
I think about the nights, and I begin to quiver.
This world that we behold, how it means so much,
it all can be resolved, by a simple touch.
A touch of peace, a touch of silence,
a little touch, to stop the violence.
What will it take,
for us to wake.
To make that simple touch,
it doesn't take that much.
Are we destined to be, living in harmony,
or will that remain in mystery?

Melissa Frank

Our Love Along The Way

Our love is as strong
As the day is long

Each time I see you
I want to sing a song

And each and every time we kiss
My heart beats fast and I'm filled with bliss

The years have now gone swiftly by
And each time I think of it I heave a sigh

So as we enter our golden years
We great each day with hope and cheers

And when our time has come and we must die
I'll proudly hold your hand as we stroll forever in the sky

Emmett L. O'Leary

A Treasure Box

I found a box the other day hidden in my closet,
I took it out and brushed it off, what riches lie inside it?

I thought it must hold jewelry, or maybe gold and silver,
A treasure worth a fortune, I'll be rich forever!

I carefully opened up the lid, the box was old and worn.
And what I found inside of it, was priceless beyond words.

A treasure full of memories, one right after the other.
And as each one unfolded, these were memories of my mother.

I sat what seemed for hours and watched these memories pass,
Of you and I together, a treasure found at last!

So when you're feeling lonely mom, just open up this box,
And know that I am with you, in my heart and in my thoughts.

Shauna Alberts

Memories

Sometimes memories just seem to find
their way back into my mind.
Memories of you and me
and of how it used to be.
Memories made up of pain and fear,
and some that are truly oh, so dear.
Memories of the times we walked,
the times we laughed, the times we talked.
Memories of how you would listen
as I sobbed, and your eyes would moisten.
Memories of watching the sunrise
over the lake through sleepy eyes.
Memories of all the times we shared
and never knowing how much — or if — you cared.
Memories of arguments and tears,
and of trying to get you through your fears.
Memories of lies and sorrow,
of wondering if there will be an "us" tomorrow.
Memories of too many "one more tries",
and most of all...that last goodbye.

Debbie Prokulewicz

Mixed Feelings
"Black"

It's not a bird or a fly, but a cat, a fat cat,
with whiskers three inches long.
It's a tail blowing in the autumn wind
swaying back and forth like a spider's web,
slicing the forceful winds attacking it.

Black is a shadow
fading as it chases the sun.
Black is the satiny finish
surrounding the earth
and inhabiting its outsides.

Black
the frightening precursor of a storm.
A hundred thousand raindrops born.
The unknown grows bigger, more and more
and before you know it, it starts to pour
the tears of a lost child
as his mind races
BOUNCING
off the **black** walls
of the undeveloped images in his mind.

Nicholas Roman

Ode To Mother's

A warm, soft voice, a gentle touch,
words of comfort that mean so much.
Who can ever know how much they really care
every time needed they are always there.
When sick with a fever and resting in bed,
a kind-loving hand to comfort our head.
Looking down upon us with a sweet, soothing smile,
"Don't worry my child I'm here all the while."
Life goes on and the years swiftly pass,
growing up now, on our own at last.
Mom stood behind us as we made many a choice,
sometimes we even needed the wisdom in her voice.
We tugged at her heart, and caused tears to flow,
when all else failed we knew where to go.
No matter our problems that caused her alarm,
she was always there with an outstretched arm.
Mom's are very special and God made it true,
as we express our love and adoration for you.
May God walk beside you down life's golden street,
and welcome you home when your journey is complete.

Jerry M. Free

Mother-Less

My mother should have been a kangaroo.
With built-in safety-secret places that
Protect the unseen shadows as they do
Their metamorphosizing into pat —

Terns of older long gone whispered songs
From other shadows now of bone and dust.
Of one whose life is etherized, yet longs
For perpetuity instead of rust.

I needed warm and time and harbour then,
My chrysalis so fragile hanging still
On twisted limb, but always ever when
I needed her it was against her will.

A butterfly emerges even now,
Many years since loathing was commonplace.
But in diaph'nous wings above my bow
She sees me not and knows not I'm her face.

Andrea Levine

Angels

Please O Lord let us live; Anyway.
When we hurt, forget, misuse, look the other way.
Time will come someday when people will care; someway.
I look forward to this day; Please let us stay.
These are good of love and help; Press on.
Through the darkness, into the light; God in sight.
It can't be stopped but it can be helped.
Beat the children till bruises and whelps.
Forgive them not because nobody cares.
Beat right through their loving stares.
I tear I sigh in Quiet Reflection.
Thinking about my past rejection.
If you live, you all will heal.
God Bless the children with all your will.

Michael Branham

Untitled

I've been calling upon my deepest thoughts
Yet none of them makes me see
Fireworks or tingles my spine.
I can't write of Love,
For I've not experienced it, but I long for it still
My deepest sorrow is a broken nail,
And a perfect nail it was
Hate is a strong word, That I dare not use it
For written words are hard to take back.
But my paintings, Oh such beauty.
My pen just wanders and the images come
And I realize that my days of an artist
Have only just begun.

Jennifer Muller

Untitled

The hazy understanding of past lives on known
As one quietly slips into an unwatched sleep
Eternally hushed and peaceful
Never harmed from the outside
The feeling of pure peace throughout.
Wondrous visions of happy feelings and experiences
Not regretting anything done or undone, said or unsaid.
Longing to go, not unsure
No pain from the body, just love from the soul
Drifting away into forever peace.
Leaving a place of hurt and disappointment
Flocking to a higher, magical wondrous place.

Natalie Pittman

Untitled

The scent of death lingers in the air
Black clouds circle up over my head
Sadness
I hate feeling sad
Depression
Loneliness
That's how I'm gonna feel after he's gone
Lonely
That's what he will be while suffering
Pain
It feels great when someone else is in pain
When your heart is yearning for love
But nobody will give it to you
Death
It is cold, black, sensational!

Kassie Petetabella

To: Danielle

I am a man trapped in my own world of fantasy.
Filled with confusion, frustration, and misery.

Only the beauty and love of a woman
Can bring me back to reality.

Because, in my life
That's all that seems real to me.
The beauty of a woman.
The woman I call
Beauty,

Danielle

Richard Platt Jr.

Roses

Roses are special and divine.
Meaning many of one kind.
Which friendships may incline
through love which binds.
Joy to many who become blind.
In your life you may find great perfection through this same kind.
So follow whatever maybe twine,
and you will find your greatest vine.

Karen Richards

The Pain Of Life

Today I am born and the pain begins,
Almost as soon as I took my first breath
my mother, for reasons of her own,
gave me up for adoption, and her pain began
Years went by and the pains lessened,
mine to the enjoyment of childhood
Hers to life
What goes around, comes around,
in the way of life we met again.
Now her pain and mine have met
Today, we work on the pain together
It's easier when we share the pain of life

Joan L. Dunbar

Sleep

Sleep

Night dancing around the moon,
calling attention to the green eerie light.
Wrath of darkness.
Swallows day whole.
Transforms it into night.

Goodnight, sleep well, don't let the bed bugs bite.

Laurie McGregor

Untitled

I have seen many sunsets
Deep in the Western sky,
I have caught many moon beams,
Yet still they fly
Somewhere there is a rainbow
Waiting to be set free,
Yet there seems to be no one
Willing to pay the fee.
I am older than you think,
Yet younger than you know
But the words just fall
Like leaves and drifting snow.
Birds will always fly,
And music will always ring,
As long as someone stops
To hear the voices sing.

Sjana M. Williams

The Holy Father's Gift

Two inmates from Cell 17
went to church to see

What God's love might mean
they found that

God's love is out there
for you and me

Look with your heart
not your eyes you will see

Talk of a Savior who died on a cross
was indeed a blessing instead of a loss

Freedom from sin
His Life and Blood gave

For those who didn't believe
He arose from His grave

The Holy Father's gift
His only Son He gave

William E. Chandler

Best Friends Forever

To those of us who are left behind,
We will always wonder why. . .
Why someone who was loved so much,
was allowed to die.

We've been friends since childhood,
And man, what fun we've had.
The memories of just you and me,
will never make me sad.

Today, I say "goodbye my friend,"
and lay you down to rest.
You will forever be my "Best Friend,"
And I'll be forever blessed.

Goodbye My Friend, I Love You!

Scott Smith

Clowns Have Frizzy Hair

Clowns have frizzy hair
Sometimes they even start to stare
   They throw balloons
   And act like goons
But mostly take a dare

Dustin Farmer

A Shout Out To My Bro-Thas

A Tribute to 2 Pac, Cousin La Mont and All the Fallen Bro-Thas
I give a shout out to my Bro-thas from the East Coast to the West —
and wonder how many will really listen before you too go to an early rest.
What are you dying for? What does it mean? Why are so many of you Dead
   before you're out of your teens?
"I Shed So Many Tears," you said it yourself — a boy from humble
   beginnings — became a man who rose to great fame and much wealth.
Now, your "Dear Mama" is bowed down with sorrow and grief —
your fans 'round the world shake their heads in total disbelief.
What will it take for the killings to cease?
What will it take for us to live in harmony and peace?
To the Bro-thas from the Sis-tahs — we give a shout to you
we need you my Bro-Thas to be the Head of our Nation —
stay in school — make sure you get a good education.
Put down the guns — study war no more — teach some child
how to buy and manage their OWN store.
Take charge of your life — stand up for good-go down in History doing
all that you could — make sure your living is not in Vain —
and that we as a people realize — Black on Black crime is completely INSANE.

Laverne Chambliss-Larkins

A Friend Of Mine

My friend and I met....where I was a lad in my "teens"...
We walked through fields, through parks, and on my street.

In later years when I sought my place in this world of "Grown-ups"...
My friend led me through the deep canyons called "Streets in the city."

The world at "war"..my friend was my constant companion through battle
Through his efforts...I fought for survival..hoping for a day a peace.

As I roamed through streets of a foreign land..my friend was my guide.
Together we visited of laughter....seeking a face of recognition.

The "war" is over...we are once again in "our" land...faces are about us....
Faces of friendly people, but..my friend leads me on...where?

Where is it that my friend leads me...to another foreign land....
To walk narrow streets...hearing the talk of strange people?

Why is it that my friend is my constant companion...I have not favored him....
Nor have I tormented him...laughed at him or scoffed at him?

How long will my friend abide with me...guide me...
Will he ever guide me...guiding me on into eternity?

I pray that my friend is not known to you...for you see....
My friend is loneliness.

Robert L. McPherson

My Friend, Rollo

All my life I've had this friend, Rollo is his name.
   I don't know how he got here, I don't know how he came.
He's just a little raccoon toy with eyes that cannot see.
   You might not even like him, but he means the world to me.

I tell him all my secrets while he snuggles in my arm.
   We dream of things like sailing ships and tractors on a farm.
We fly to never, never land, and see all that we can see.
   He's just a little furry toy, but he means the world to me.

One night in our adventure, we went deep beneath the sea.
   We saw sharks, and octopus, and whales as big as trees.
We saw horseshoe crabs and little clams as happy as could be.
   I like my trips with Rollo, 'cause he means the world to me.

One day Mom said a bath was due, and Rollo looked so sad.
   She put him in the washer, and that sure did make him mad.
And then into the dryer, while I waited patiently.
   I loved his little shiny face, 'cause he means the world to me.

Mom and Dad like Rollo, too, that's 'cause they're both so smart.
   One day when he was hiding, they tore the house apart.
A playmate, a companion, he's all that he can be.
   Because you see, I'm only two, and he means the world to me.

Betty Bridgeman

Women In Waiting

We give our all, we give our best, we always seem to exceed the test.
From sacrifice to servitude, we nurture, provide, then allude,
and then we wait!
We raise our offspring to be the very best, from infants to
adolescence through college and all the rest.
And then we wait!
Now the nest is empty, our hearts are full for the freedom has come
to explore the pull from the years of storage of mistakes realized,
we plan, we project, and to our demise
still we wait!
We give it meditation, and we vision the fun to finally excel!
Shouldn't everyone?
Then comes the struggle, the invisible fight to discourage,
to diminish, our God given plight. We know there's a purpose that's
greater than now and women who wait never understand how,
the mountainous task will ever be met, yet fervent in faith God
will recompense. For he will restore the cankerworm years the
sacrifice, the disappointment, and even the tears.
So in our hearts.....we continue to wait.

Edna J. Jones

A Little More Time

"Lord, I'm your child, do you remember my name?
I haven't spoken with you in a while, hope you'll listen just the same.

There's so many roads and choices to make.
Which ones to leave behind, which ones do I take?
I'm following a dream and fearing a mistake.
Cautiously planning the journey I will make.

Lord, if you'll give me just a little more time,
my life will have its reason, my life will have its rhyme.

Lord, will you give me just a little more time?"

Then I heard him softly speak, as I lay there in bed.
He made it very clear to me, and this is what he said.

"Child, I'm your savior, do you remember my name?
I haven't spoken with you in a while, hope you'll listen just the same.

I've traveled your roads of troubles and tears.
I've been right beside you through your sorrows and fears.
I felt every struggle year after year.
Through hell or high water, child I've always been here.

Child, if you'll give me just a little more time,
your life will have its reason, your life will have its rhyme.

Child, will you give me just a little more time?"

Teresa Danks

The Story Of The Sun

The Sun is a beautiful thing in its wonderful splendor. It has the
power to make even the strong surrender to its revitalization of their
soul, in an attempt to make them whole. One day, It carried me to the
chambers of Heaven and washed me in the house of the Lord. It
polished me brilliantly like the blade of a sword. The Sun laughed
with me and we talked for a while about the things that happened when I was just a child.
The rays of the Sun held my hands as we traveled to many distant lands. Just talking to
the Sun eased all of my fears. It spoke to me of the uselessness in the tears I cried
through the years. I then soared with the angels in the sky, my spirit and soul
has never felt so high. The soft white clouds were like the ass of a babe. They were
wondrously gentle and beautifully made. There
were silver hills and streets of gold, there were no forms to be seen, only the splendor of
floating souls. My burdens were lifted, I knew the job was done. I took one last look at
my friend, the Sun. I then headed back down the lit exit from the sky. I turned around to
ask Him "when would I die?" As my eyes focused, I gasped suddenly with awe. Words
could not describe the image I saw. I fell to my knees and began to cry. I'd glimpsed the
Lord watching me from up high. The sight was so wonderful, His love was so clear. A
sudden wisp of celestial air told me He was very near. I was reborn as I felt Him flow
through my soul. The happiness I felt, only God and I know. As I floated back to earth,
I decided to tell the world. . .the story of the Sun and a little girl.

Anthonette Walker

Fishing Ocean Drive

The waves come crashing
Into the rocky shore;
The blowing wind is carrying
The mighty ocean's roar.

Graceful seabirds fly and glide
In the vast blue skies.
Then swooping down to catch a fish
They give off screeching cries.

The fisherman look out to sea,
On jagged rocks they stand.
They tell stories of the deep
With rods and reels in hand.

So patiently they wait for bites
The fish are in the bay
Proudly they tell of fish they've caught
And big fish that got away!

As dusk descends upon the land
It's good to be alive;
This is the feeling that you get
While fishing Ocean Drive.

William G. Pruitt

The Child Within

"When I look inside I see
A child as lonely as can be.
A child who did herself away,
Whose only answer was to play."

"When I look inside I feel
This life I've lived, can it be real?
Tangled emotions and broken heart
I want, I need a brand new start."

"When I look inside I hope
I take the time to really cope.
To say the things I need to say,
Never again to turn away.
To love myself and be good to me
And maybe then I will be free."

Sandra Creaser

Only Then

If my heart can bear the sadness
Of a love that I have known.
If the strains of her memory
Should forget to come around.

Should the wind forget her fragrance
And my arms forget her touch.
Should the light in her dark eyes
Nevermore reflect my mind.

When my dreams won't bring her to me
As the night wind calls her name.
When this emptiness inside me
Is erased by her return.

Only then can I be free
To pursue the love I need.
Only then, once again,
But only then.

Don N. Hansen

Rainbow

Pretty colors
Arching over the earth
Being happy while looking at
God's sign.

Colleen Nordstrom

Mystery Man

He comes to me in a dream all
tall dark and handsome. He tells me
everything's alright with a voice so
deep it commands attention. I
never see his face. But I feel
his smile. I never clearly see
him at all. Shrouded by clouds
and smoke. But I feel his touch,
I experience his kiss. They burn
deep with in me. When the sun
comes up he's gone before I
know it. Leaving behind a note
and red roses. I wake up
feeling a little shaken, because
it all felt so real. But it was
only my mystery man who comes
when I'm feeling all alone with
no one to love of my own.

Katherine M. Mills

Quiet Time

Some quiet time alone
   with my God,
my Father, the One
   who sends me abroad.
Some quiet time alone
   with my Lord,
my Savior, my Jesus
   the One I adore.
Some quiet time alone
   just us three,
some quiet time
   is just what I need.

Janeen Debbie Kim Owens

The Child

As music wafts throughout the air,
She whirls and twirls in time.
So carefree, in her tot-world,
Enjoying things sublime.
Her animated conversation,
Said aloud for all to hear,
With an imaginary someone who,
For her, is near and dear.
Her smile at all things simple
Is such a joy to see.
This little girl, my daughter,
awakens the child within me.

Christine Grippi

When God Saw Me

When God saw me:
   he said let there be
   life,
   he breathed life into
   me and I lived.

When God saw me:
   he said you are a wonderful
   creation,
   go and love as you want
   to be loved.

When God saw me:
   he said "you", go into the
   world,
   tell them about my power
   and that I am
   God almighty.

Jennifer Carver Oberhausen

Loving A Convict

Loving a convict is so hard they say, Loving is the price you have to pay
It's loving him with no one to hold. It's being young and feeling old.
It's letting him whisper his love to you, you whispering back that you love him too.
Wait! Knowing the Parole Board now hold his fate. It's extremely
painful letting him go while dying inside from needing him so.
Watching him leave with eyes full of tears, stand alone with his hopes
dreams and fears. Although you are near, but so far away,
his love for you grows with each passing day.
Loving a convict isn't much fun, but it's worth the wait when his time is done.
Remember he's lonely and sad from being away and he's thinking of you
every single day. So love him and miss him and please tell him so,
Because if you really love him, he desperately needs to know.

Mary C. Banks

Glass Eyes

Here I was born and here I die every time I dare to step into
   the footsteps of my youth.
The home that was love and hell all at once...
What kind of love was this that gashed my soul and gave concussion to a tender heart?
I know, and then I don't know.
I know fear lying in wait, cringing at solid footsteps — boot heels;
The smell of cold wind and death from a hunt;
Raw animals gashed, just like me — I know.
They knew fear too, the hunted;
Death creeping up on them — a mighty man with a gun to wield,
Running into a dead end; nowhere to run. He's got you. Will you die?
The animals too, like me, screamed silently, died quietly;
Their skulls a trophy; their lives unprecious — just like mine.
My burning skin was prophetic. Ah, but to die from the inside out —
   I know.
I wept for them that were just like me.
I wanted to love those dying animals — to rescue and make safe —
   but I watched them die.
A last look into glossy-eyed life, a weary blink, and then those eyes were gouged out
Only to be replaced by glass and be mounted on the wall.
I turned my own eyes to lifeless glass to save my own soul, my life.
You can't kill what's already dead. Or can you?
I was wrong because, still, I am the fleeing fawn or bird in flight
   with glass eyes.

Desiree Wilson

Beyond This World

I see stars glowing in the daytime, and sparkling all through the night.
My strength is growing stronger and my wisdom is in my sight.
God is the glory for every man, woman, boy or girl.
A new life is just begging when I leave beyond this world.

My prayers will reach the Heavens, and my faith will lead me on.
Fear cannot go with me because my soul is much too strong.
So I'll dance like a Ballerina, and all will watch me twirl.
I'll perform with motivation to get a standing ovation, to prove my
journey is beyond this world.

Now that I am free, and no longer feel the pain,
the Lord has called me over and my work was not in vain.
Watch me as I soar in the skies with wings golden in a swirl.
Who knows where I'll end up when I'm gone beyond this world.

Althea Battle

"From A Daughter"

I know you've gone to a better place.
Already I miss your sweet gentle face.
It was all so sudden it is hard to accept.
But I know you would want me to pray and do what you would expect.
I left my family and life so fast.
I'm having a hard time thinking that it could ever last.
I miss you so much it is hard for me to adjust.
I know that we have to make the best of things if I must.

Jennifer Lynn Williner

Epitaph Of Age

The time doth come when man his temples grey, "Panic"
This can not be, I'm not old, my youth must stay, I will be young.
My wife? She is the best, I love her still, I guess? She had her
day, but now you're getting old dear wife. I?
Look at me, why, I'm only fifty-three, you understand, you can see?
Free, yes I must be, forgive me love.

Another line is in my face, makeup helps a trace. I need not
look within a mirror...no, my husband's face does tell it all.
The sparkling eyes that open wide, when by his side the young appear,
Tiny waists, flirtatious smiles, coquettish walks that brush so near.
Inside I cry such painful tears, for forty-six are now my years.
   "Old? Aging yes."

Dear God, the years we shared together, no matter what, we'd have each other.
Our love was strong, would live forever.
Such love have I, so much to give, without this man I can not live.
   The sands of time, are they coming near?
How sad it is, he can not see, his lust for youth, will never be.

The sands of time are not just for me.
   Isabell G. Rossa

Hold My Hand Child

Hold my hand... to play with while you feed on your bottle.

Hold my hand... to steady yourself when you begin to walk.

Hold my hand... when it's your first day at school.

Hold my hand... when it hurts to lose your first tooth.

Hold my hand... for congratulations on graduating school.

Hold my hand... for support, while searching for your goals.

Hold my hand... for advice on raising a one year old.

Hold my hand... now that I am getting old.
Hold my hand... when I am down and cannot stand on my own.
Hold my hand... as I prepare myself for the Lord.
Hold my hand... when I say my last and final words —

Hold on to the Lord's hands now child, and later, when it is time,
I will come to hold yours
   Debbie Greene

A Good Place To Be

Between Bellefonte, PA the home of governors and Mr. Football's town of Penn State;
rests a place some people claim is a property of enchantment, while others say it's just great.

As you leave the busy highway and motor towards your goal;
you'll feel some of your built-up tension easing and a little lighter in your soul.

After you have been greeted by happy smiling faces, and you know all encountering remarks
   are in jest;
You will be careful to examine your equipment to insure its worthiness as you proceed
   to do your best.

You will find your surroundings almost spotless, the result of a lot of elbow grease;
your white shirt will be soil-free thanks to the mechanic of expertise.

The bowling houses in this small knit area are of renown;
and customers from here visiting other establishments have spread the good word around.

Because of the favorable atmosphere and all bases covered to help you score;
we have seen home keglers perform on TV, and I'm sure there will be more.

Maybe your arthritic condition didn't go away and your lumbago will come back another day;
But right now you're kind of loose and sort of moving free;
And you don't hurt near as much as sitting home thinking about how it would be.

Conditions are improving, for which we should be glad;
our air is a lot cleaner and visibility is clear, not like we had.

Enjoy your activity here and remember it's not paradise;
but you will be hard pressed to find another place this nice.
      — an appreciative roller —
   Charles E. Sprow

A Prayer For You

Let the Lord be with you
Not only you
   your spirits too
Let the Lord take care of you
Because he knows best
   to let you rest
So believe in me and the Lord
And we will always be with you.
   Sarahmarie Hollenstien

A Dreamscape

Seducing my mind, filling it;
With half-awake dream fragments
Drifting in and out
The dawn melting;
Slowly through my window
Thin clouds of dust
Like specks of brilliant light drifting;
In the dull shine of the sun
Should I awake
To the new day?
In and out;
The wonderful feeling
Of being on the edge
The edge of fantasy and reality.
   Toby Bozeman

Always N Forever

Boy, thank you for letting me
love you so.
What I ever did without you
I'll never know.
It may sound sappy,
but I know it's true.
Always, forever, everything,
everywhere
   is
      you.
   Shantay Ortiz

Prism Of The Mind

The prism of the mind
fractures the light of our thoughts
spreading a rainbow of ideas
across our words
for all to see the beauty,
Though some only notice the ugliness.
And it must always be remembered
to look at all the colors carefully
because the light has been fractured,
   Broken,
      Shattered,
and the parts do not always
equal the whole
after they have been split apart,
Making it hard to see the brilliance,
For thoughts can be distorted
in the prism of the mind.
   Jennifer Waskow

Three White Birds

White birds arrive so secretly
then start to fly away
the bold and brilliant color
of a white snowy day
they swirl just a while they play
then carefully fade away
   Betty J. Bivens

Peace

Confusion is what's left
after a dueling conversation.

Misleading words lead to
anger and frustration.

Carefully choose before
you speak your mind,

Or losing a friend
is what happens sometimes.

Peace they say can
be tough to keep,

And when it is not
loved ones will then weep.

Kirsten L. Nordlund

Love Is A Wheel

Love is a wheel
Turning around and around
I hear your heart pounding
A gentle sound
I have set my mind
To change every little way
Erase all my mistakes
So that you will stay
Love is a wheel
Turning us around and around
These words I have mended together
These words I wish to send
A promise of a tomorrow
A love that never ends

Jason Ray Cox

Down

Down, down in my soul,
Far away from the world,
Spirits dwell, fairies roll.

They paint a picture of living things,
They dine with the immortals,
When the dinner bell rings.

They play their drums and harps,
When they sing their chants,
They dance on golden tarps.

They lead such a happy life,
Spending eternity in paradise,
Living immortality in splendid blithe.

Emily Burnette

Night Air

There I stood under
my wings of destiny in the
mixed night air, while I
swallowed my breath.
I wasn't surprised that all
I could find was dust in
the night air that surrounded
me like a ring around a pole.
I prayed that someday I
would be able to breathe in
the mixed night air and
then I would stand tall under
my wings of destiny.

Michelle Pilalas

Really Home

We left as young men, eager and brave, with dreams of glory and flags awave.
We left our girlfriends, family and wives, to do the duty our country advised.

We did our duty as best we could, slaughtering and killing for "our
countries good." But when we returned no glory to be found, and we
were just people left to live on, We lost our girlfriends and wives,
to war our minds were empty and so were our lives.

Some have scars or wounds that show,
  But we all have pain that each of us know,
Our men and women of war have gone many places,
  our heads are full of their memories and faces.

We raised a monument to show that we care,
  and when it was dedicated, some of us were there.
When will we have it together again?
When will we be what we were before then?
  Happy and free, no wish to just roam.

When can we be really home?
  Only God knows and none of us, for we still live.
With the death and fear, from long ago.
  When will we really finally be home?

William Drouin

Outside Poem

As I stand outside completely alone with the world,
I feel the cold wind whispering in my ear.
It tells me of the adventures it's had
Throughout the countryside...
Like the dogs barking at the soft hum of car's motors on the distant roads.
Or, of the bare trees swaying silently by the force of the cold wind.
And as I look up I see a heavy blanket of sparkling snow
untouched.
If I look beyond the silvery fence, I
See the cold barren earth which is more silent and peaceful
than I've ever seen before.

Ariel Fredrickson

Where I Love To Go

I love the beach,
I am captured by the sunset,
I enjoy watching the birds fly by.
Walking along the beach makes me feel calm and relaxed.
The breeze against my face exterminates my bad thoughts and makes me
think of more pleasant things.
The sand at my feet is so cool, and I feel proud of myself.
The waves crashing on the shore and rocks usually represents my
personality, strong and persevering.
The beach is a wonderful place.

Regina Lozic

True Friendship Is A Gift From God

Dedicated to my friend, Rejohnia Evans

True friendship is a gift from God, that sings a special song.
It warms the soul with golden glow, and lasts a whole life long.

An unspoken word is often understood, by just a fleeting glance,
And heartfelt joy is always there, to make each spirit dance.

True friendship is a gift from God, that distance cannot sever.
Separate paths our lives may take, but near to each heart forever.

Memories created, that laughter and tears have sealed;
Dreams shared, secrets told, and hidden fears revealed.

True friendship is a gift from God, that should never be dismissed.
As God unfolds a lesson learned, I know that I've been blessed.

Agape love is well defined, though some might misconstrue.
A sisterhood ... a precious bond; and this I've found in you.

P. Arrel Tidwell

Just There In Nature

The sun rises and the sun sets. It gives warmth and light to all
who seek it. The joy and beauty it shines is priceless to those that
want to be within. Always chased, and giving. Just there in nature.

The days come and the days go. Never given a second thought, expected to be.
The moments of joy and happiness never counted or given full credit due.
Giving of second chances and tomorrows. Just there in nature.

The moon travels its lonely path. Sometimes by day, and sometimes
by night. Never warming but taking of the gifts of the light.
Never returning what it receives to the giver, just grabbing more. Just there in nature.

The nights come and the nights go. Shadows move in the darkness.
Only loneliness and dampness to throw at those it touches. Things
only seen in part, never in whole in its graces. Chasing and hiding. Just there in nature.

Life comes and life goes. A full range of emotions, with some
forgotten. Joyful begins and sorrowful ends, to much or not enough
in between. Events sheath the walk of countless monuments. Just there in nature.

Living is done or just expected. It reaches are either for what can be or what can never be.
Choices made, some misplaced and some put off. Living for the sun or the moon,
events viewed for the giving or the taking. Or just there in nature.

Julie Myers

A Troubled Child

Some are born out of love, some are born just for fun,
some are born just to endure, to live a life on the run.

A boy runs and he hides, he faces a life he can not comprehend,
to him life is an obstacle so large, with no beginning, no end.

He reaches for help, he wants his life to have meaning,
to him, he feels this is a useless task, for a life so demeaning.

He learns to touch, but not feel, to see, but not understand,
to him there is a light in the tunnel, but it's a light with no end.

He knows there are people who love and who care,
he must find these people out of hope, out of despair.

Once found, a heart can learn to love, a soul can ascend,
a life once lost, through guidance can now mend.

To him, he can finally feel a life worth living,
he learns to smile, laugh and understand forgiving.

He gains insight through experience, he gains knowledge through others,
he learns how to care and to help his troubled brothers.

He finds wealth comes from the heart, accomplishments from the soul,
he teaches of the importance, to learn self-control.

He learns to help others, and guide those who seem "wild",
he understand their needs, for he was A Troubled Child.

Elliott L. Nadeau Jr.

A Note From Da Da

My Darling Lauren do not fear, 'cause Da Da is away.
My love for you grows stronger yet,
With each new passing day.
I want to have you in my arms, and hold you oh so tight.
Protecting you from any harm,
And tell you it's all right.
And with each tear that you may cry,
One also falls from my eye.

With this poem that I write I try to tell you how things should be.
I hope to show you how much I care,
And wish to be with you,
To let you know I'll soon be there,
That Da Da loves you soon

David W. Davidson

Soar

Lifter
Sweet music above many a cloud
The wings of the innocent
The feathers of freedom above me
Let the heaven's rain pour
Float among the Gods
Flight of forever
Watch others dreams rise
Praises heighten the mass

Past the gates, they open the door

Descent
Down here screams so loud
Twisted souls, ye repent
Still I chained below eternity
Shrouded tongues, turn to ignore
I born of embryonic pods
For this incumbent, never
To my dismay is my demise
Scorned emotions collapse

But me; I descend, because of my sore

Courtney Wilson

Poet's Periphery

The creek giggles by,
tickling toes and ankles
as it always has,
and by me, forever will.
Cool hands that have touched the world
before and again,
caress me gently and slip by.
As I bend to touch the fleeting water,
the movement of fairies
draws my gaze quickly to nothing.
Still...I know I hear
the creek giggling...
...I know I hear
their spritely tittering.

Gary Lasby

Deep Thoughts

I shall forget
    I shall forget for
you that I have lips;
Nor touch you even
    with my fingertips;
I shall alert my list you
    should see
Deep down into the patient
    soul of me,
I shall walk with
    prosaic feet.
That winged to meet you
    on the street
I shall that you may
    call me friend;
I shall forget until
    you turn the bend.

Alice M. Plotczyk

The Cyclist

The cyclist never complains,
he only gains,
    distance. . .
by revolution.

Jonathan Graham

That Night

We met there in the mist that night,
He and I alone.
He met me in the mist that night
To tell me the unknown.

"Come with me," he said that night,
"And from them we'll be freed."
"Follow me," he said that night,
"Each other is all we need."

"I can't," I said to him that night,
"They need me more than you."
"I won't," I answered him that night,
"I won't carry it through."

"Very well," he told me that night,
"But this is your last chance."
"Goodbye," he said to me that night
And walked away without a glance.

I knew I couldn't leave that night.
My path led another way.
I watched him leave my life that night.
I had to stay.

Katie Francis

Seagulls

Seagulls soaring overhead
Happy as can be
They remind me sweetheart
Of what you mean to me
You make me feel so happy
And glad to be alive
That I too could soar
Up up into the sky

Mary Cantu Binns

Well Of Wishes

Well of water
Well of tears
Well of wishes

I stand alone
Waiting waiting
Each day I think
Each day I pray

Lonely I am
Surely, you would see
Tired out I still thing of you

To a cave I crawl
To hide from all
I wail for your life

I wonder if you know
Pray I do
Only for you

Day up day —
Week after week —
Time marches on.

Wesley Brewer

Untitled

I here; you there
But under those eyes
Space is all-where.
Distance: very far
But under the stars
All things are joined,
All sorrow and beauty
and spirit are one.

Lucia Szigeti

Daybreak

Unrehearsed accounts of life are branded in my soul,
Unreleased expressions of love are dying to play their role.
Riveting dreams explode in my mind like the dawn of a breaking day,
But dusk comes too soon, and feelings repressed, I retreat to hide away.

As time moves on, I grow inside, and challenges are met face to face,
Those feelings held deep within emerge from that dark space.
I know in my heart that the future holds what now may only be dreams.
And I know all those things, impossible they feel, are not as far as they seem.

So I take pleasure in the rising sun, and the brightness it shines on our lives,
And I know that even when the day turns dark, the sun never fails to rise.

Melissa Gallo

What Kind Of Man

You say you feel unwanted
But ya' push on undaunted
you still care I can tell
'Cause when I'm with you you're not in your shell
The feeling is strong and I know it
But we want to get past the moment, to show it

So what kind of man would I be
If I lived unfaithfully
If I just took your heart
and tore it all apart

I pour out my heart and you listen in the past I'm reminiscing
You were broken and I know it I'm there for you, I hope I show it
what kind of girl would be left here with no one in love to share

So what kind of man would I be if I lived unfaithfully
If I just took your heart and tore it all apart

Let me keep you safe and warm protect you from life's quiet storms
If I didn't hug, love and kiss when I'm alone it's you that I miss
so, tell me...tell me...

What kind of man would I be to not wish you love eternally

Barbara Holland

The World: As It Might Be Viewed By A Deaf Person

The silence of night, the silence of day,
I wish I could hear what other people say.
Although I can see with my own two eyes,
I can't hear the winds that blow high in the sky.

I think to myself, "Oh what could I be?"
Maybe a beautiful fish swimming gracefully in the sea!
I glance to my future, the present and on to my past,
I wish my life wasn't passing so fast.

Lonely nights come with the presence of silence an darkness,
If only I could hear, I'd have a lot more gladness.
To quickly bring on a new day of sunshine and rain,
And try not to think of all my sorrow and pain.

I thank the Lord everyday for giving me the special gift of hearing.
To hear a favorite song on the radio, or a football crowd cheering.
My silence sympathy and compassion reaches out to those unfortunate victims,
and, I pray to God, and offer them my petitions!

Gina Romanelli

Manchild

Matthew, larger than life, walking in the footsteps of Jesus Christ.
Matthew, lover of life, walking in the love of Jesus Christ.
Matthew, beautiful child of light, walking in the ways of Jesus Christ.

David Hakeem, child of two worlds, what do you dream?
A king of past ages, a shepherd boy, what do you dream?
A mother's babe, a father's son, a grandmother's little man
  what do you dream?

Barbara J. Hayes

The Night Visit

Behold the waning lovers' moon, barometer of night,
Cast dappled shadows from draping boughs, majestic sentries evermore
The scent of fallen blossoms, cloying with allure -
A mid-summer mattress, nestled 'neath the verdant growth.

Hark! A piercing yowl of primal instinct, bred relentless and true
With hiss and spit, and furry plume, tom's message clear to all
His feline fancy circles near, their dervish dance begins.
Prometheus never bore an agony thus sweet
A hint of musk upon the dew, to greet the birth of day.

Patricia Tucci

The Backwoods

A world that separates itself quietly from the rest.
Not prejudice or demanding of what is in your chest.
No crowds to flock its comfort. Its identity scarcely known.
I yearn for the day when I slow my pace and sit upon its throne.
A seeker has to pay no fee to step its boundary line.
But the day expansion pursues it will be a mortal crime.
A familiar friend that constantly changes, yet never ceases to give.
And the memories of its adventures will be with me as long as I live.
Canopies that stalk your every move, my heart to hear.
The growing admiration of its seasons year to year.

Sara Forthofer

No Matter What

I'll still be loving you when day turns into night.
When flowers stop blooming and eagles do not take flight.
When the stars and planets burn out and die.
My love for you will take their place and light up the evening sky.

When fish no longer swim and rivers cease to flow.
My love for you will continue to show.
When children stop laughing and people forget to care.
I will still have my love that I'm willing to share.

When the leaves stop falling and our rose is an empty seed.
I'll still be loving you, that's all I ever need.

Tarah Anne Schichel

Untitled

The Ghetto Part 1
The world is a ghetto, a ghetto, of trash, they label it, ghetto, of
no cash, the shacks people live in are not of their choosing. Yet
there is no meadow in the ghetto, babies born in this disgrace
adjusted to the so called human race people crying, people dying, in
the ghetto, so visit the ghetto, when you're in town visit the ghetto
and hang your head down. I know I've lived in the ghetto.
The Ghetto Part II
There is a ghetto in your town, just get up and look around. Then
you'll see what's going down in the ghetto. In the ghetto you will
find poverty of the lowest kind and the meals they eat are garbage off
the street. Why fly got to get high in the ghetto. The president
don't care he does not have to live there a deterioration of our
generation baby born and I keep on wishing but all I see is
malnutrition aid and diseases are here to stay cause people tend to
look the other way.

Edith Beggs

There Comes A Time

There comes a time for everyone,
Where the clouds are blocking the sun.
A time where the rain will fall, and no rainbow will appear,
A time when happiness is faded, and sadness is so clear.
There comes a time for everyone where you're overcome with doubt,
To the point where you question yourself, and what life is all about.
These times, they may travel, but for some they remain,
To the point where there is no escape or easing for their pain.

Julie Eichstadt

For You And For Me

The Bible has
all you'll ever need.
Just read this book and you will see.
The way to teach also the way to be.
The bible is here for you and for me.

God will help
whenever you need,
all you have to do is listen,
live and truly believe.
Just look to the bible and you will
receive all the love God
has for you and for me.

Crystal Brown

Snore

There he sits
Reclining, asleep
With shuddering fits
And gasps from the deep
Recess of his throat.

His tongue lies
Slouched in his chin.
Inhaled K's rise
Then fall with a thin
Lip-feathering note.

T. Cinnamon Leavitt

Alone

Alone I walk along the shore,
Whines and pouts I hear no more
I see the fish and hear the waves,
By the waters the sand is paved,

I sit and think and think some more,
How can life be so sore,
It is here and it is there,
Life and death are everywhere,

I watch the sun setting on the sea,
Life no more matters to me,
One day soon I will die,
Like a little butterfly.

Justin Hickman

The Rose

Love is like a rose you know,
So beautiful when blooming full...
Patiently waiting for life to unfold,
What a sight in the eyes of the behold.

But as petals turn and leaves fall,
Knowing what this means to us all...
Like the flower no longer anew,
Love will die, as once it grew.

Patricia Morales

Last Breath

As the cold stench of death
rolls 'round, you realize that life
you are without.
Cold and lonely in the darkness
you fight for your sanity.
Clinging on to the last bit
of life you have, fearing that you
will be no longer.
But with this death you find
new birth and new life for all eternity.

Violet White

The Day Before Tomorrow

Awaken, a new dawn of day,
Lifes joys, sorrows, trials, and
tribulations on us, a weigh.
As the sun comes forth, the
morning dew, it dries, or the pure
white frost, it melts before our eyes.
In life, the momentous tasks,
it does not wait, we must forge
on for it is in our fate, it will
be our demise if we hesitate.
Go forward, we must, for not
too long, it shall be dusk, of
the day before tomorrow.

John Stevens

Dreams

Dreams have a different meaning,
to everyone who has them.
Dreams can even have,
a meaning of nightmares.
Dreams play a soothing record,
to ease the mind.
Dreams can make,
us weaker than before.
Dreams become visible,
not only true.
Dreams can be,
predictions into the future.
Dreams are like a recording,
of a song again and again.
Dreams take me to a faraway land,
beyond the rainbow.
Dreams gives us,
things we really want.
Dreams can take us,
into a deep sleep.

Jenny Puchalski

Love

Love knows no boundaries,
    Cannot be measured by wealth,
It comes from the heart
    The conscience of one's self.
It's in a smile, an embrace
    Or an accepting glance,
A part of love's purest form
    Not given by chance.
Love knows no prejudice,
    But embraces all,
No sacrifice is too great,
    No pain too small.
It's in all God's creation,
    Through grace in His eyes
Unconditional love,
    The unmeasurable prize.

Sandra Neal Stevens

Life

I've had my share of ups and downs,
I've been pushed and pulled around.
Life is strange and sometimes thrilling
Especially when the heart is willing.
Willing to go on day by day,
Even when you've lost your way,
Just stick to the path and amble on,
Before you know it, you'll have won.
Won the test that is hard to learn,
Just be ready, when it comes your turn.

Janet Ufko

Pain

Is today the same as yesterday? It seems so until...the blackness starts, the pain begins, one more time it comes, why? All seemed right until the pressure started, then there is no stopping it. The world begins to close in around me and things begin to spin, much as the hurricane in the sea. I long for the beach, the wind beating against my face and the surf pounding, as God has no wrath greater, no lessons stronger, only me alone in the world and I know not why. The pain becomes stronger and the anger greater, as if the hurricane were inside me and I fear for not only myself, but for others that have wronged me in the past. The rain begins as tears fall from my eyes and roll down my cheeks. The thunder roars as I scream in pain from deep inside and I have no control or will to stop. For days, prior, I talk with my mother, knowing she will understand and help me all she can, but then in a flash much like lightning - She's Not There!!! Again the thunder rolls and the rains fall as I crash to the rocks below. My body swells much like the surf, and I pray that as it hits the rocks it will explode and the pain will subside. Much to my sorrow my body begins to ache in every joint and again I cry. Finally after days of pain and suffering, I feel my body, soaked and beaten, no longer able to function without help which God provides. My husband, my sons, with arms outstretched, waiting, waiting, to pick up the pieces, wipe the tears, and try once again to mend my broken body as God mends my broken soul. Then shreds of reality venture forth as sleep slips softly over me and the days pass, one after the other, until I feel safe once more, knowing help is there waiting for my outstretched hand. Life starts over, never knowing what tomorrow will bring.

George Llewellyn

Once In A Lifetime

Once in a lifetime someone comes along and has such a profound effect on the life of another person, so much as to change their lives forever. This person has such warmth, compassion, and love that words cannot describe the beauty that dwells in their heart.
    You are just such a person, and only God could make such beauty and splendor. A day without your presence is like a day without sunshine, cold and dark. Your smile warms my heart and your eyes melt my soul. Your soul radiates a glow that enlightens my life.
    There is none other like you. God has given you to me one of the greatest gifts I could ever receive. A love that is bounded only by imagination, honor, and trust. Kindness is your motto, beauty is your seal, which is engraved upon my heart forever. I love you my precious one with all the love one human can have for another and then some. Only God has a higher place in my heart and he has blessed me greatly with your love. I await your presence with wide eyed anticipation as if a child on Christmas morn awaiting to open gifts. I shall wait; I shall be patient yet my soul longs for you. Even though I have known you for a long time, my heart leaps into my throat at your sight. I shall sleep and shall dream of you until I can hold you once again my precious, precious love.

Mark F. Gillette

Stormy Conflict

The storm rages through her soul
Her mind once fruitful and full of wisdom, strength and integrity,
is now dead
Replaced by emptiness, devoid of all senses which allows her no peace
There is no rest, only an endless tide of despair and dissolution
She reaches to the depths of her very existence, but finds nothing
She carries a numbness that flourishes in her thoughts
The conflict tears at her heart
Is this the punishment for a wrong turn on the path of destiny
Life is such a cheat, and the torment continues
Just when the culmination of her vision is at hand, it's snatched away
like a thief in the shadows
Then...as lightening fires through the sky, the tide of life changes
and nature makes amends
With a weakness which savors her spirit
The tears from the storm consumes her pain
The ravaging has ceased, and all is not lost
Her being is restored, salvation at last
Another page is turned

Marie Aucone

I Cannot Act Black, I Am Black

For I have been addressed as a sell-out, an Uncle Tom, and every other name,
Is it due to the way I act, dress, speak, or every non-black friend I claim.
"You don't act like you're black" it's often been said,
Is it because my pants don't sag, or I don't wear a rag on my head?

To me this is an example of ignorance, and it's also a stereotype,
To categorize characteristics of a black person denies us our
diversity, and that simply is not right.

Contrary to some beliefs, I am a proud young black man, who is culturally aware,
Because I've read about or watched the black race's enslavery, struggle and despair.

I ask you to see me for who I am, what I stand for, and what I believe,
Not to criticize me for my interest in the arts, music and poetry, or my burning passion to succeed.

Damani Rivers

The Past

Night was fun, and day so sweet;
but the love that we had we couldn't keep.
Our love grew colder and faded away
until it became like it is today.
We started off just as friends
and thought we'd always be 'till the end.
Our friendship grew into an attraction
until all we cared for was our actions.
In time we grew to love each other;
until I realized I seemed a bother.
I loved you, and thought you felt the same,
but every time we met you seemed ashamed.
In time we drifted and led separate lives,
as I noticed it more, it made me cry.
So sad to see our friendship end, as I realized this wasn't pretend.
Our caring and companionship that we had together,
had slowly fallen gently like a feather.
So this story leads me to say:
There is always an alternative to each story;
there is always another way.

Sherrie Bonenfant

Pondering

As we ponder what is happening in the world today;
hunger, plaguer of illness, and racist way.

What must we do to calm the tide, to save the human
integrated side.

What must we do, but ponder, our hopes, our
dreams never ceasing be.

What must we do we ponder. Looking to the stars,
that flee the numerologist, television gruologist and
the likes of them to be free.

From the tormenting thoughts that invade our mind,
so often it occupied our time.

We ponder what life is all about, until we hear the cry of fight!

We Ponder, My God We Ponder!

Thelma D. Davis

Anatomy Of An Idea

I saw something that wasn't there - a shape, a form, translucent air
A glance, a flit, a shadowed mist - the helix of a whispered tryst
Tendrils drift across the mind - whispery fingers, ethereally twine
On pristine panes they dance, they twirl - catspaw's fog they glide, they curl
A phantom chain each link is fast - no power protects, no walls defend
The metamorphosis at last complete - no change more perfect, no joy more sweet
I lift aloft elixir's draught - and give the world the wind of thought
Behold - An Idea!

William Alexander

A Reindeer

A Reindeer goes up and down
down and up
every single day they tell
tall tales to each other
before they go to bed
each day they each
wake up the very next
day and go up and
down down and up
their sleigh Santa said
don't tell your very
tall tales before you
go to bed each day
because you'll go
up and down down
and up a little
more each day.

Jessica Lathrop

Cold Weather

Where my Granny lives
it gets very very cold

The snow gets in her shoes
and freezes her toes

When she walks the dog
the wind blows real hard

The freezing wind blows him over
like a new playing card

The city of Chicago
where the ice cliffs get real high

When the waves hit the beach
it makes you want to say goodbye

This is why we live in Cal.
where the sun shines all the time

Some days it might look like snow
but it always does shine.

Travis Forster

Valentine Heart

Very often it seems
Another day dawns
Like the one before,
Each of us yawns
Naturally reaching - stretching
To begin the daily routine.
Into our ordinary activities and
Noted in our spirited
Existence comes a Valentine.

Heart warming
Envelope - with card
A splendid puzzle part
Revealing amazing
Thoughts of a Valentine Heart.

Gwen Pease

My Baby Brother

My baby brother's beautiful,
So perfect and so tiny.
His skin is soft and velvet brown,
His eyes are dark and shiny.

His hair is brown and curled up tight,
His two new teeth are sharp and white.
I like it when he chews his toes,
And when he laughs, his dimple shows.

Edward L. Rivera

Grandpa's Peace

The sun's gone down
It's time to rest,

But the life you lived
Was truly blessed.

Your worries now
Are no more,

We know you're there
At heaven's door.

I see the Lord,
But he's not alone,

It's grandma beside him
They're calling you home.

Your pain and suffering
Did finally cease,

Go to them Grandpa
And rest in peace.

Catherine E. Wilson

The Hope
Of The Royal Brigade Band

She was sweet with all her heart
And with that heart was the band
Then one day it rained
And the car slipped from her hand.

She was in a dream.
A dream she couldn't follow
Then she couldn't wake-up
And we all had so much sorrow.

While she's in that dream
Her friends and family mourn
And the only reason she's in this
Is because of that damn horn.

We all hope she is there
And please lend us a hand
'Cause we pray she remembers
the hope of the Royal Brigade Band.

Misty Rovinelli

Tracy

Love and pain
I sometimes wish
I never knew
your name.

Desire and lust
will I ever know peace
or simply
return to dust.

It's hard to capture
with word or phrase
what you mean to me
I remember each day.

Your blue eyes gleaming
your long hair flowing
our skin touching
memories locked away.

I don't cry anymore
at least when I'm sleeping
I wonder why
we had to know.

Perry A. Pederson

Untitled

I sit alone in this world that
is so distant from one another
Alone in a world that is over populated.
For too many people who have
lost their way in life
No moral, no value
no principles, no place to fit
into society a lost soul
I set alone and wonder
who can we trust? Who can we turn to?
Do people really care or feel anymore
We alienate our selves from one another. Why?
Can we trust our brothers or sisters?
Every bodies under sieged
Every bodies under pressure what do we do?
Go with in find the inner self.
Find inner peace, inner strength. Look to
thy self and strive to be above the lower level
of ignorances — above all the negatives of life.
Life and give love give a little bit more to build this world again.

Lori Vozzella

Eternal Requiem

With no fanfare, no sound of bell
Silently and calmly
I will be gone,
Gone forever from your life.
You will be searching for me
And I will be nowhere to be found...
And at peace, maybe, you'll be.
I will have no tomb
No epitaph, no flower, no funeral
And no tears will be shaded for me.
Have you ever thought how sad the sky would be without the sun?
Oh! Without the oxygen the nature will be dead.
One day you'll be searching all over the world for me,
And I will be nowhere to be found.
I will be longtime gone.
All my souvenirs will be already melted with the wind
And supreme irony
Deep, deep inside of your soul,
You'll celebrate an eternal requiem at my memory.
And you will, at last, realize that I loved you more than you love me.

Jean Albert Rejouis

Joy

Frozen to her I stare, unable to move, speak, or even blink my eyes
in fear that I may miss another one of her beautiful yet coy movements
Tenderly she stares back at me
Our eyes meet and for a moment it seems as if the rest of the world
disappears leaving just the two of us standing on a cloud
A white cloud, fluffed and endless in all directions
I drift into thought
Thought of years yet to come
I see us hand in hand, laughing, being happy
Happier than I can even put into words
Slowly I drift back to the loving moment of reality
Nervously I take a step in her direction extending my hands out to her
Slowly but sure and confidently
I hold her in my arms as she freely surrenders herself to me
As if this is the moment she too was waiting for
Gently I hug as I close my eyes in a silent prayer of thanks
I turn and open my eyes to see the face of my wife staring, displaying a tear in each eye
Speechless...I try to hold back my emotions
Then softly I say to her....
"Thank you my love let's name her Joy."

Gregoey Lamarr McQueary

People

The people come from many places,
by land, by air with freedom in their strained faces.
Some from here and some from there as if with time they were racing.
Coming with the hopes and dreams on all of their faces.

They all wish to be free.
But is this a dream or reality?
Wishing to be as free as the wind on the sea.
Free, as free must forever be.

They all hope for jobs good or bad,
that they will go to day after day whether they're are happy or sad.
Work they must though the hours be long, with all their ideas becoming a fad.
Caring for their families, their ideas help keep them from going mad.

People will be people no matter where they are going.
As life's day of work is towing.
Thou, life's struggle are showing.
Our children will still be growing.

Which still makes people well worth knowing.

Rosa Nelson

Magic Carpet Ride

Consuelo there has to be people like you and me in this world.
People for other people to say Good-bye to.
You learn to love them, they say they love you;
then with the slightest breeze they're gone.

The night creeps into day as softly as a child crawling on all fours,
reaching out and touching everything in its path.

Once again our dreams have left us.
It goes on this way until once again we find happiness.

Happiness?   What is happiness?
It is irrelevant.
It exists only in the minds of the very young and innocent.

So we cry, "Come along with me.
I'll take you on a magic carpet ride
into the land of the unknown and forgiving.
We'll listen to the heartbeat of the tinsel tower.

There's nothing in the beat.
The record skips and then goes on as does my mind.

Well turn my ass inside out and bless my soul.
I feel like I'm in layers, I'm hanging on a hanger.

Life goes on, death is final.
A finale to what?
All the hellos and good-byes that have passed before us,
"Hello, Good-bye, lay me, we're gone."

Lynn Chabot-Long

The Small Wind

If a small wind were to blow, what would you hear of it?
It travels past a many a' folk
Some curse it, some bless it.
On the sea it is truly a miracle
But the tiny wind is only slowed down by these many obstacles.
It can travel almost anywhere
Making no stops whatsoever.
And those who care to notice it only know of it for a very short time.
This small wind may travel all the way across the Earth
Going through all the seasons.
Blowing leaves in the fall
Cooling us down in the summer
Making us colder in the winter
And showing us the on-coming weather in Spring.
This little wind has traveled all around the world
What do you know of it?

Lander Yeoman

Why?

That's hard to answer most of the time.
There is no reason, neither
rhyme - to things that happen to us
all - when we stumble or perhaps fall.

Maybe we lose a friend or lover
married or not - often all our worldly
goods we have got - through bad
luck, maybe carelessness or bad
timing when we get stuck.

So who has an answer to the
why - perhaps no one, either you
or I - but don't give up for sure
because with God's help we will endure.

To face life as it comes to
us - so do it with a smile, don't
fuss - then one day we'll know the
why - that's all - goodbye

Doris Dutton

My Friend

It has stood in the yard,
For so many years;
It has seem my family's joys,
And all of their tears.

It has been so very faithful,
Always coming back;
Old man winter tries hard,
'He' cuts it no slack.

It can almost be heard,
Around the month of March;
When it opens its sap pours,
And stretches its arch.

I am speaking of a friend,
Who is always there for me;
It stands tall in my yard,
That big old maple tree.

Deborah Grizzard

Mommy, Mommy
Let Me Have Some Fun

Mommy, Mommy let me have some fun
It's never good unless you score a run
I need to hit I need to run
I need to have a lot of fun

Mommy, Mommy I hit the ball
The second baseman went for a fall
I ran the bases I ran them all
Mommy, Mommy it's called baseball

Keri Brooke Guess

Names In The Sand

Lonely beach
sun setting low
two lover's names
written in the sand
the tide comes in
washing away what was
and bringing in
something new
yet all remains the same
waiting for the day
when the names
may be written
once again.

Paul R. Graham

Behind Eyes

There's a place
Somewhere outside of my walls;
Too big for me,
Too small for my thoughts.
The place is cruel,
Violent, cold,
Scary.
So, I sit in these walls,
Protected
From things I was forced to know,
See, feel.
I build my own place;
A world of music, smoke,
me.
No one else is allowed in.
I won't be hurt again.
But the walls turn into a prison,
And my emotions
Explode into pieces.

Time to rebuild.

Mindy Delavern

A Dream Or More

Last night a dream came to me
Of someone I knew long ago
But it seemed more than just a memory
For we laughed and talked of love
Together we spent those fleeting hours
As if they were sent from above.

Then suddenly awakened only to find
An empty room, dark and still
Only me but with a thought in mind
That someone far away from here
Might too have thought
Of days when love was near and dear

Betty J. W. Cottongim

Behold The Lamb Of God

Behold the Lamb of God is revealed
Shining through the Glory of God,
Shining through His Glory.
We see Him as He is,
Coming down from above,
In splendor of beauty,
Forever, forever.
Oh! What Majesty!
Can't you see Him in His Glory?
High above the heavens,
Coming through the clouds.
Behold the Lamb of God.
Can't you see Him coming?
He is here!
Behold the Lamb of God is here.

Judith H. Harris

With Deepest Sympathy

The red rose whispers of passion,
And the white rose breathes of love,
The red rose is a sea gull,
And the white rose is a dove.
But I give to you a cream white
Rose-bud with a flush on its petal tips,
For the love that is purest and sweetest
Has a kiss of desire on the lips.
In memory of Tom Tevault
Forever and Eternity

Christine R. Mondi

Growing Miracles, A Beginning

I can't believe this miracle growing inside me,
Already I'm protective and acting motherly.
You can't be more than a few weeks old
And my heart is so full; so is my soul.

It's hard for me to really believe that it's true,
That your Dad and I are expecting you.
At times I just want to jump for joy it seems,
Other times I want to cry for fear this is a dream.

You will be a part of me and a part of your Dad.
You will show the love and togetherness we have.
Together we will rear you and show you the way,
It's a task we look forward to day after day.

We couldn't care less if you're a girl or boy,
As long as you're healthy you will bring us joy.
So as we lie here with our hands entwined across my tummy,
We wonder if you sense that he's Daddy and I'm Mommy?

God has blessed us with this miracle you see
And we will nourish, care, and love you completely.
You are the miracle that will come none-too-soon
And if it's within our power—you will have the sun, stars and moon!!!

Julianne N. Howard

To My Love

My mind vainly grasps for eloquence to express my inner thoughts,
For it would be easier to count the stars of Heaven in one evening,
Or to solve the great mysteries of mankind in an hour,
Than to translate the message of my heart into verbal expression,

I am embraced by your presence as I awake in the morning,
And I encounter your signature upon my soul throughout the day,
I have learned to cherish you for your tenderness,
For its warmth encompasses my being and caresses my senses,

I am encouraged by your smile and its radiance,
Shining through the darkest night to bring hope in despair,
I am touched by your quiet and timely expressions,
Sharing inner feelings, when other forms of communication fail,

I am amazed by your brilliance and complexity,
And awed by your simplicity, integrity and faithfulness,
I am honored by your presence, in both beauty and charm,
And my spirit is captured by your humor and sensuality,

You have cunningly bound me with an undeniable force,
And I am helpless within its gentle constraints,
To me, it is far greater than the sum total of all human effort,
And I shall be powerless to do more than love you forever

Roy Stephens

April Sunshine

Smile a song on happy faces, sunshine falls in golden laces,
    Take me to your sunny places, and lay your daydreams down over me.
When did you climb inside the morning, waking the sky without a warning.
    Waiting to shine on yellow roses and angel's noses,
Won't you say want's on your mind now,
    April Sunshine.

See the lady in your garden, lying in your morning flowers,
    Tell her I'm trying to spend my hours, making up her mind over me.
Dress her in your moods of laughter, and follow the clouds she's dancing after,
    Feeling she's found the time to know you, let her show you,
Won't you say what's on your mind now,
    April Sunshine.

Winding through your canyon country, highway towns and morning smiles,
    Watching your clouds and your city styles, painting up the sky over me.
Nights and lights and new tomorrows, finding ourselves with time we borrow,
    Washing ourselves in Boston weather, we're back together,
Won't you say what's on your mind now,
    April Sunshine.

Robert Beaser

A Priceless Friend

I have a friend who's priceless, worth more than any gem,
When burdened, troubled and despaired, I can always count on him.

I have a friend who walks with me, when I think I'm all alone,
This friend is always there for me, a saviour, of my own.

I have a friend, I call. In the morning-noon-and night.
No matter what the problem, he'll make everything alright.

I have a friend who stepped in and healed my broken heart,
He tells me: You are not alone, you and I will never part.

I have a friend who listens to my prayers, and they are always heard.
He always give me an answer, without ever uttering a word.

I have friend who touches me, heals all aches and pains,
I go to him daily in prayer, now my life. Is not the same.

Who has never turned from me, no matter what I'd done,
Fought all my battle, and the victory already won.

I have a friend who looked beyond my faults and saw my every need,
Then he pours me out a blessing, that I don't have room to receive.

I have a friend who was nailed to a cross, stayed there for me and bled;
With a plaited crown of thorns, that were placed upon his head.

I have a friend who hung his head, to take the weight off of mine.
Laid-rested-stayed-in a borrowed tomb, and he rose on time.

Alzelia P. Stephens

Loneliness

Wandering in endless overcast of consciousness
Pondering in my own sorrow of stupidity
And you, alone without me anymore,
Emptiness being your closest companion

As I walk down my highway of mortality
I realize my mistake, falling in love with you
Mending the broken pieces is a harder task than ever expected
Losing you is a lost part of my soul
Love is deep, but the extent of internal feeling will rule over love forever

If I make an effort you pull away
Questioning the actions of the one you love can be a question for yourself
Perhaps you can do better
But no one can make my feelings escape from internal to external like you
As I stare out my window into this world of quarrels and conflict
I think of my dreams within my heart
Fulfilling the need as my deepest desires is a measure not yet
Explored nor conquered

Hopefully on day everyone will understand the meaning of love
And running away is only an exit and not an entrance
To a bottomless pit of heartache and loneliness

Angela Donkin

Serpent Evil Vs. King Of Time

Crazy with ideology and moral doctrine I have come, sane with the
perception of unequal equality, managing to shared each indignity with the teeth of
circumstance, and grab at its tail with furious
inflictions, serpent beast which is oppression, marked with ridicule,
vanished from existence, yet allowed, with deception to corrode the
mind of a young babe's virtuous breath, penetrating insipid souls with
retrogressing thoughts of adulterous crimes, all to formulate truth
which is your domain, I battle you - in disgust I kill you, with
serene beauty of loving conception, pure divinity and vitality strong,
with kindly manners that reek of fervor, of adoration, unrestrained by
human tongues and shallow minds, I search for you - coming for you,
King of time to battle calamity, ungodliness - serpent evil, with my
heart beating patience, beating life ready to strike a blow of Godly
vision, of immortal might to strangle death, sanctifying in my
recourse positioning the truth and constant - love I have come, King
of time to battle, you, serpent evil.

John Fraczek

This World Of Violence

This world of violence
what can we say.
Somebody different is killed
every hour of the day.

Some are accidental
others they are planned.
This nonsense needs to stop
we need to take a stand.

A stand for peace and happiness
something very hard to see.
Who knows who's going to be next
perhaps you or me.

Why can't we realize
that life is not a game.
Put down the gun
for we're the ones to blame.

We need to open our eyes
and look beyond all the hate.
Or soon enough another grave
is going to have a date.

Alaina Sacramo

Nothing

You say you can't live,
You say you can't sleep,
You have nothing left,
You might as well just sit and weep.

There is nothing, nothing, nothing.

Is it worth it,
I really don't know,
Is it worth it,
I don't think so.

You can't
You won't
You'll get through it,
You'll succeed.

It's not worth it.
Live for yourself,
Succeed for yourself,
Accomplish your dreams.

Live your life and love yourself.
Nothing is worth dying for,
Nothing.

Vanessa M. Sanders

Bedtime At Grandma's

Upon a bed of pillows,
Surrounded on each side,
By dazzling dolls, bodacious boys,
There I was forced to lie.

They would not let me slumber,
They would not let me sleep.
They clamored for more stories,
They giggled, rolled and squeaked!

We offered prayers together,
We talked about God's Word.
A few confessions then were made,
We all felt pretty good.

My aging eyes were tired,
I longed for quiet rest,
But as I kissed and said, "goodnight,"
I knew that I'd been blessed!

Gwendolyne Jensen

Mom and Dad

I still go to the phone each day
to see if you're all right.
Thoughts of you come to my mind
when I retire — every night.

I wonder if you're watching
to see how my family's grown,
Or if you know how much
I still love you — I wish I
would have shown you more.

So many years have passed.
How long does this pain
and emptiness last.

Mary McArthur

The Contest

I enter the contest to see how good I am
but, I know how good I am.
I enter the contest for acclaim,
but I want not acclaim, do I?
I enter the contest for prizes.
Now, prizes, I do want.
I enter the contest for me, yes,
just for me - no!
There is a desire to be higher and
a reason to be seen as pleasing,
or why else would you or I enter the contest?

Jeffrey Rose

Untitled

You sit alone with muffled cries,
The liquid drips down from your eyes.
Can no one see the hurt inside?
If not then why in them confide?
They know not what you're going through,
their mind has not been torn in two.
Speak a word? You do not dare,
for even then will no one care?
You ask yourself is it a shame?
To know not what has caused this pain?
Even you don't understand.
You lay alone with head in hand.
Every night like a routine,
you attempt to beat this thing.
Your eyes are wet, you wipe them dry,
you slump back in your chair and die...

Abigail Plummer

Grandma

How much do I love thee
Well let me just say
Everything is special — in its own way
Your never ending love for me
Helps me through the day

Grandma's gifted and talented
Which was passed on to me
I must make sure to used it wisely

I never have to search —
For my angels tell me so
She' as perfect as a rose
Yet, I know My Grandma
Will never leave me

For you see — My Angels Tell Me So

Jon Paul Salazar

I Wondered

When I was a young child, I thought about many things.
Princes and paupers, beggars and kings, armies of gold, gods of old,
and why good men have no money.

I wondered if the devil and God were good friends.
I wondered if they played together when they were kids.
I wondered if the devil ditched school.
Which one broke more rules, which one got more girls.

I don't mean any disrespect, I love my God dear.
I just wondered if he and the devil were near.
I always thought the world a game, everyone made from cardboard stands
The world was run by manipulative hands.
And everything was known by a man behind a curtain.
Every problem was invented by us, we invented hatred, we invented war.
I hope something stops us before we invent more.

When I was a young child, I thought about many things.
Princes and paupers, beggars and kings, armies of gold, gods of old,
and why good men have no money.

Now that I am not a young child, I wonder what will become of me.
I wonder if the world is just a decorated cage
where, in fear, I have invented my love and my rage.

Patrick C. Keefe

The Man Of Twenty One

I'm walking through life trying to find my way
Something on the wind calls me with a faint cry

As I turn for an instant; a boy is born; Wesley Andrew
It's like being in a dream; so quickly the time goes by

So soon he crawls, then walks; then he is up and about; such a smile
No time to return to innocence; no time to calm our fears

He's off to school; in such a hurry to grow up; time races him on
Pushing him further into the world, away from us; we shed tears

We feel our grip loosening as the world and age tug against us
Hold on son, we won't let go, love is our stronghold; he slips further away

Off he drives for the first time; my heart sinks; I try to be bold,
   but...
Lord, only you can be with him now and always to protect

Graduation, oh what a joy!, finished with part of life
Move on further down the path our lives to redirect

Faster we go and further away; a teenager no more
So much life to live; life can be hard; be careful son

I hear a small child calling; I see a child running toward me
I reach out to embrace him; then realize it's all been done

I am face to face with a man of twenty one

James David Wallace

Ascension

Far off in the distance I see a shimmering light.
I've climbed a thousand miles so far this cold and stormy night.
My trembling legs near failed me before I saw the glow
But now they have new life from the memories of below.
Each new step a lesson. I've learned my lessons well.
And now I've reached the light with my story now to tell.
There were times I felt I'd turn back and try to right my wrongs.
But now I know what's done is done. The present is where my heart belongs.
There were times when people pushed me. I thought that I would fall.
But somehow I found strength. I climbed on past them all.
And sometimes I felt miserable; had no inspiration; no goal.
The shining sky above me was sometimes a black hole.
It was filled with nothing but anger, fear and pain.
But now I've reached the top. It won't be dark again.

Erica Leigh Schichl

"Untitled"

Approximately one-thirty a.m. It is Sunday. The Lord's day. Tossing,
Turning. Light blinds me. Awareness of all surroundings. Death is with me. In the air.
In my heart. Footsteps pounding in my ears.
Closer they tread. My blood stops pumping. My heart enters into
commission. Wearily eyes open. Muscles contract. I'm reaching for
someone. Someone who is the half of me. The remaining half silently cries. Cries in the
darkest of nights. I run. Keeping a pace that
was never known to me before. I stop. Fear is now my companion.
Sticking with me like the shadow friend I had as a child. Together we stand alone. Alone
in a world that is not our own. Someone else
controls it as well. This world of lost souls. Death for eternity. Then he appears from
the light. Peaceful. Gracious. It's Daddy. I run. No shadows to follow me. Arms
stretched so they reach the end of the Universe. They wrap around him. Integrity.
Pride. I hold his hand. I am now safe. Hands and hearts bonded. We walk to the light.
So warm and glowing. Disappear from this world...
I awaken.

C. Summerlot

Your Space

The space around you is hallow.
It surrounds you and makes you aware.

If you do not defend it you are shallow
and later there will not be space to share.

So take the liberty to discuss; the very problem is right there.
But be cautious not to make a fuss because anger and violence is really part of all of us.

The space around you is filled with silence.
It surrounds you and you have sworn, no longer must you defend your
sense, no longer will anger leave you torn.

Between what is right, between what is wrong,
Believe, you have been reborn.

Kristine L. Baker

Ugly

I stare at her with eyes of blood and bitter blue
She has long smooth legs and eyes of blood too
I forgot how to feel today
Like it's just been pushed away
She looks at me with a gleam in her eye
She looks at me and asks me why
I touch her in a sweet soft way
She leans over to where I lay
She whispers something into my ear
but it was something faint and queer
I decided I didn't care as I ran my fingers through her hair
She looks at me; I look at her
Something beautiful is what we were
I was happy, and high off her love; we fit each other like a glove
Who am I to deserve a woman of this beauty and grace
I ask myself as I stare into her face
You don't, I replied, she suddenly became green-eyed
The most beautiful creature I'll ever see
She slowly began to rub my knee
as I thought of why she'd pick an ugly guy like me

Anthony Shepherd

Talk To Me

...Talk to me of things yet unseen, of waters uncharted and stories untold,
talk to me of the fantasies in men's minds and things that make us laugh
sublime...talk to me not of life today, but of tomorrow and how we'll make
our way...talk to me of hopes and dreams, of visions in our head, not lies
and deceptions and other things we dread...talk to me of the rarest
snowflakes, and of rainbows painted in the sky...talk to me of the wonders of life
and the mystery of the butterfly...talk to me not of the things that you see,
but of the beauty of life and the hope there for me...talk to me,
please talk to me from the depths of your heart that I too might dream
and find hope in my heart.

YazooLady

My Father

My father is my friend,
He taught me every thing I know.
As time goes by I cannot lie,
because he told me so.
He taught me truth and
understanding and honesty and health.
To get a job and do my best
and work my way to wealth.
To go to church and trust in
God, and forever I would see,
that all these things I learned
from him, would guide my family.

Meriam Sullivan

Loving You

Sometimes it feels like Summer.
Even on Winter Day;
It happens when you smile
at me or look that certain way

Sometimes I feel the sunshine
When it's raining from the sky;
It happens when you hold my hand
And when I hear you sigh.

Sometimes it feels like heaven,
Where all my dreams come true;
It happens when you look at me
And say, "I love you, too!"

Sherri Marra

Dear God above me,

Please watch over my loved one,
    while he is away.
Please keep him close at heart,
    and help him through each day.
Please protect and keep him,
    within the barriers of your love.
Shield him with your kindness,
    wondrous God above.
Help him make the choices,
    that are right in your eyes.
Guide him through darkness,
    and see truth above lies.
Please protect him like I would,
    if only I were there.
Show him that I love him,
    and how very much I care.
Guide him safely home to me,
    with this prayer that I send.
I thank you God with all my heart,
    in your son's name I pray, amen.

Joanie Davis

Time Traveler

I am a universal being
    the world is my guide
I am a free spirit - movin' within
    all dimensions
I travel to places far beyond 3-D
    I come from the past
    I am in the present
    I know the future
No boundaries can prevent my entry.
I travel thru all space and time
Who am I - you ask!
    I am
        The time traveler.

Marsha West

Keys To My Heart

These are the keys
the keys to my heart.
The keys to friendship
a friendship that will never end.
It will open and close my heart.
If you need to crawl into
my heart you have the key
and if you need to close my
heart you have the key
our friendship is based on
this key.
This key is a
symbol of how I feel
about you, you're a wonderful friend.
I feel as though we're sisters.
I love you no matter what
and will be here forever and always.

Lela E. Tenters

Simply Me

The shadow that is seen...
While down the road it trod..
The shadow is simply me...
The art work of God...

The road is long and unwinding;
A car goes swiftly by...
The shadow carefully wipes..

A speck of dust from one eye...

The emotions within me are:
Love, joy, and fear...
The shadow whispers softly...
"God is always near."
The shadow enjoys the breeze,
Flowers, people, birds, and trees...
Singing merrily down the road it trod...
The shadow is simply me...
The art work of God!

Ruth Evelyn Ray

Little Angel

She changed our lives forever
In the short time she was here
and although she never spoke
Her message came very clear

We never touched her little face
or held her little hand
But God knows that we love her
and God knows that we care

So, when this life is over
we're going to meet our little girl
That precious little angel
That never saw our world

So little baby up in the sky
that's all we have to say
Except that Mommy and Daddy
will see you there someday

Francis J. Exner

Untitled

Running down the hills of green
and into the fields of sun.
Stretching out on nature's grass;
my ears fill with silence.
I am alone at last.

Victoria Sedlacek

The Umbling Prayer

Lord, help me in my course of life,
Not to be bumbling;

When it comes to giving back to you,
Help me not to be caught fumbling;

Or when I am uncontented about circumstances,
Bridle my tongue that I may not be found grumbling;

Help my heart and mind ever be clear of your will,
Not that of jumbling;

At prayer time when I speak to you God
May I be bold and transparent, not timidly mumbling;

Of the moments I am a witness of You to those around me,
May your Spirit shine in me so others will not give rise to rumbling;

Lord, I am human and easily make errors,
But hinder me from being a block in someone's path for stumbling;

God, life can throw me a curve and Satan can deceive
When the uncertain is unknown,
Jesus keep me from the pit of hell and tumbling;

Most of all Lord,
Help me to live a life pleasing to your Honor and Glory,
That most of humbling.

Cynthia M. Dodds

Maintumhen Piyar Karta Hun

You are my flower blooming in the bitter cold snow when all else has died
You are my mantra who gives me the power to see myself for who I really am
You are my blood, the sweet nectar of life which gives me the breath of life
You are my sacrifice, you are the one I give myself to above all others
Maintumhen Piyar Karta Hun
You complete me, you fill my life with a meaning it never had
You fill me, you provide me with all I need to survive
You enchant me, you put a spell on me with your loving ways
You mystify me, you blind me with your sweet words
Maintumhen Piyar Karta Hun
And when the meaning of life is finally discovered and the clock stops ticking on the wall
I will remember who you really were and what you've done for me
I will never forget how you've touched my life and filled with a new meaning
And the Gods will lay their hands on you and bless you with
the power of the one you love Piyar Karta Hun
And what of it? And what of it? Maintumhen Piyar Karta Hun

Bernadette Giacomazzo

Friendship

Surrounded by the darkness of depression,
Just when despair was about to swallow me up,
A hand of friendship, composed of light,
Pierced the darkness to show me life.

I grasped this hand of light,
Slowly I was pulled from the hungry maw of despair,
And I entered the embrace of friendship.

I looked down to see despair rage at the loss of its dinner,
I looked up to see the loving face of the friendship smiling on me,
And it felt good to have a friend save me,
Save me from the oblivion of my own sadness.

My new found friend whispered in my ear,
Yet I did not hear, all that filled my ears,
Were the cries of rage coming from despair.

I looked into the eyes of my new friend,
And I understood, to destroy despair would take courage,
Courage which was provided by the friendship that saved me,
And together, my friend and I, we ended my despair,
And the hold of terror it had on me,
In one fell swoop of friendship, love, and light.

Christopher A. Cox

My Guardian

As my mind strays away from me while I lay my head to sleep
I know the Lord is watching over me as a good shepherd does his sheep
So that I don't get caught up in the wicked thoughts in my mind
That's when he awakens me and stops me as I leave the wicked thoughts behind
As I go on in life he keeps me walking in a straight but narrow path
To keep me from all of the wicked and evil ways and a violent death
Because surely I know I can't do all these things alone
There is no sense of me saying I could, because I truly would be wrong
He has taught me not to be selfish, and not to hang over greed
Because he would supply me for my each and every need
He teaches me with the grace of compassion, and all his love
And he smiles down on me from the heavens up above
And to let me know I don't have to beg, borrow, or steal
Because he is my spiritual Guardian, and that is real

Richard E. Scott

Only I Can See Her

She hides her face inside.
She says nothing is wrong but I know she has lied.
The beauty of her face is more than enough,
For her weak self to pretend she is tough.
But even though this weak spirited soul,
Can not pay her endless toil,
The love of her heart still shines through.
Because the love of her heart is very strong for I knew.
I could see through the colors of her dark dress.
Even though everything else seemed to be a mess.
And this love shined through on and on.
But I could only see through what everybody else thought was wrong.
For the dim face of this defenseless soul,
Was as beautiful by love when she lifted up her dark stole.

Danielle Hunt

Romantic Anomie: Counting On Tomorrow, Another Day Of Atrophy

Writing only the title of this poem a day in advance hoping to be proven wrong by the finding of a new lover (although viscerally knowing it wouldn't be such)

Another day, another eve, cold-blooded, came to nought,
that romantic love ain't free you see is all that I've been taught,
when lava from the gentle hearted, erupting, crawls down to the sea,
the vast clouds of vapor rising bespeak ephemerality,
billowing, expanding, to the ether all retreat,
condensing, congregating, in the welkin all will meet,
regrouping, they exist again, although in attenuated form,
from which in continuous session, rains down a passion storm
by the ocean of indifference, beleaguered on all sides,
the precipitation on my tears she distributes to her tides,
thusly unaffected, once more, smoothing her complexion,
gelid, catches nothing, not even my reflection,
so it is, another day, and of a love not smitten,
yesterday's tomorrow came true today, just as it was written.

James Baskind

Vanity

She walked an inch above the ground with her halo and her wings.
Her inherent will stood aloft, the center of everything.
She stared with an aesthetic eye, seeing only what she chose.
Her transcending climb would but allow,
Seeing others down her nose.

A sadistic notion crossed my mind, for an instant I knew shame.
I saw a vision: her nose held high, and drowning in the rain.
The scene regurgitated in my mind. Exhilaration filled my being.
For nothing could ameliorate, the vision I was seeing.

In judging her, what do I become?
Have my feet also left the ground?
If the rain began to fall on me, would I also drown?
I feel the need to delve my soul, to impress in my heart and mind,
Of what I pray I never become, nor ever forget with time.

Cheryle Kemble Rhodes

Open

Do you believe in me?
Could you possibly be?
How you mean so, to me.
When I feel, you are the glow.
When I yearn, you are my fill.
We are together, your soul be still.
Feel my strength, silence your scream.
Don't be afraid,
  I am only a dream.

Phenitia A. Kitchak

Goodbye

The time has come to say goodbye.
You once held my heart,
but to see you with another...
I'd rather die.
You changed my life so much
without speaking a word.
You made me smile
and filled my heart with so much joy.
Now you've turned away.
Just say you never cared
or stay quiet and walk away.
Either way my heart will break,
my tears will fall,
my dreams shall end.
Goodbye my love...
goodbye my friend.

Stephanie Gallegos

Class Reunion

We savored the sweet nostalgia
of those other days.
We hugged and kissed and cried.
We had felt the moment of what
used to be.
The fantasy of what might have been.
And the final reality of what
will never be.

Charlotte Anderson Kritsky

Untitled

One heart needs must divide,
become two branches, once entwined.
A rivulet of white,
among the hairs of night,
two pieces of blue ice
staring stars of simple stature
are all that now remains;
a scar of wounds sustained
through such divisions which
needs must be made.

Melinda Heins

The Tree

A love grows from my gist.
Its branches scrape the sky
Self sinks into fading mist.
The soul stands true and tried.
I hear a heartbeat in the thunder.
The breath of life flows in the wind.
A holy spirit live in the wonder.
Spawned form the seeds within.
Here am I this moment.
Here in lies my life.
Father sun's atonement.
Is mother earth's delight

Lance Carter

Cruthú

Spéir,
And there is a beginning.
Talamh,
And there is a place to be.
Uisce,
And there is movement.
Solas,
And there is day.
Dorchadas,
And there is night.
Gairdín,
And there is splendor.
Grian,
And there is the east.
Gealach,
And there is the ebb and the flow.
Ainmhí,
And there is living.
Daonnaí,
And there is an end.

Sherrie Dennis

Purple Mountain

Beyond I now glimpse
The purple mountain peak,
Reaching into azure skies
One shy kiss to seek.

Her beauty I behold
Awed I'm entranced
Mysteries she yet veils
With intrigue she's enhanced.

What lies beyond thy cloak
Oh, purple mountain grand,
Unwritten in any book
Yet held within thy hand.

Wanda Atkins Almodova

Vanquish The Feeling

At times
You must enjoy the pain
To vanquish the feeling

Let us look the opposite way
Confronted with emotional torment
An even greater pain
Humbled by tears

Daren Luebbers

Mind That A Soul Inspired

Desperation sings a lonely song.
Feeding off whispers
of dark birds
Carrying candlelight messages
To the refugees,
Lost in future times of past thought,
Caught,
Between known confusion
And accepted delusion,
Of what they once never tried to
become.
The eyes in the fire
Bore a hole in their united soul,
And left coal,
Dead coal,
For a mind that a soul inspired.

Devin Beck

The Missing Part

If I could put into words how I truly feel,
you may begin to wonder if such feelings could be real;
but I lack the skill to do this as simple as it seems,
for my thoughts are full of confusion, and hopes of faded dreams;
I can't begin to understand these feelings I have for you,
and though they are something different, I know they are true;

You've given my life meaning, where every moment is enjoyed,
without you my life is empty, and happiness is void;
everything's so much brighter in the light that shines from you.
with you I feel I've been reborn, the world seems so brand new.
You are my inspiration, you give me reasons to press on,
you've revived in me motivations that once before were gone;

You've opened up my eyes to see the joy that can be found,
things that I can never see, when you are not around;
you've given me a hope to love, and the courage to see it through,
and the one thing I need the most, is the love that comes from you.

Though I don't have much to offer, I have a lot to give,
like honesty, devotion, and affection as I live;
warmth and tender kindness, from a very loving heart,
things I've always had to give, but you were the missing part.

Joseph Conrad Sparrow

Let Our Heroes Rest In Peace!!!

Let our heroes rest in peace, I feel we owe them that,
They led us through some trying times, to them I tip my hat.

Let our heroes rest in peace, you could not ask for more,
Leave their families alone, though it may be a chore.

Let our heroes rest in peace, leave memories intact,
Though what we often say and do is really not the fact.

Let our heroes rest in peace, would they do less for us?
Although we're simple people who seldom make a fuss?

Let our heroes rest in peace, don't search and reach for "truth",
Their souls must wander, even hurt, Yes, Elvis and Babe Ruth.

Let out heroes rest in peace, let John and Bobby fade,
Don't study and ask questions now, their debts have all been paid.

Let our heroes rest in peace, and quietly go on,
And mourn them still, but don't forget that new ones have been born.

Their sons and daughters need their peace, they shared them long enough
So let our heroes rest in peace, they gave us quite enough

Mary Ann Turner

First Vacation With My Wife

We work so hard, we work so long, now it's time for us to be alone.
A vacation for you, a vacation for me, a vacation for us as a family.
A time to watch, a time to grow,
A time with no certain place to go.
There will be no worries, there will be no woes.
Just you and me to love and grow,
We will see each laugh their own special way,
as we smile and giggle at the special stuff we see.
I love you so much, there's no words to describe.
There's so many reasons, maybe that's why.
Your looks, your beauty, that's more than skin deep,
Your looks, your beauty, that's inside is what keeps.
It keeps me going, it keeps me strong.
It's the only thing that matters, that you and me get along.
We get along so well, our thoughts as one.
With you as my soul mate, I'm the lucky one.
These are but a few, reasons for my love.
You've taught me so much, you've taught me to love.

Bruce J. Mathews

Memories

I think of memories from the past.
Joyous years, I thought they'd last.
My Papa and my Mama they were such parents dear,
music and laughter, family always near.
Brother's and sister's with children of their own,
we'd all get together, it was such a happy home.
We'd sing hymns around the piano, Mama played so beautifully,
then Papa with his fiddle would play some cheerful tunes,
with Ed on the keyboard, someone else played the spoons.
We all had a good time, food, and games we would play.
Then before we went to bed, we'd all kneel and pray.
Year's went by so quickly, everyone grew old.
Changes came, it was a shame, family couldn't travel anymore, to be together in that
sweet home, where love and devotion were shown. Papa and Mama have now left this
life to live in heaven above—they left behind such memories of happiness and love.

Betty Mae Kinder

"Overwhelmed"

Overwhelm say thee, do my words of love. Can it be
that thou truly knows not, these words are the result of
a force far more overwhelming than any words, be they
written or spoken, than I might ever conceive.

Alas fair love, credit me not for that which my hand
put to paper. Credit me not for these words which I speak,
for 'tis not I that create such verses and phrases thou
takes, such delight in, 'tis the Lord's doings not mine. From my heart,
of which for sometime now, I admit having no control over, stems
the emotions of love so powerful that I, a mere mortal man could
not possibly describe of my own.

Dare not I, to issue utterance of love to one so fair as thee,
for in my simple mind lay not the words, for thou are truly
A creation of God with all His wisdom sent forth in thy beauty.
Mayhap thou should gaze upon the looking glass, and behold
His beauty which lay therein. Look deep my lady fair, look deep,
And thou shall see the sight which truly overwhelms.

Look deep my lady, and thou shall see, in the eyes which look
back are Christs which I see. So say thee once more
that I overwhelm thee, - Nay my love 'tis thee who overwhelms me.

Jann Oslund

God's Little Miracle

I'm a tiny little girl, a true beauty to behold.
A precious gift from God, or so I have been told.

I'll steal your heart away, if you give me half a chance.
It doesn't take much, just a single glance.

My Mom and Dad love me, they're with me day and night.
I know it's hard on them, cause they want to hold me tight.

But you see I'm too small, to handle all that stress.
And I know it's putting their patience through an awful test.

It's not easy on my Mom and Dad, to watch my ups and downs.
I can see it in their smiles, I can see it in their frowns.

They worry if I'm gonna make it, and don't want to leave at night.
I try to tell them I'm okay, when I squeeze their fingers tight.

The nurses take good care of me, and the doctors — they do too.
Even though they know a lot, it's God that's seen me through.

He's sent a little Angel, to watch over me night and day.
And He listens to your hearts, and hears you when you pray.

Well I better get back to sleep, the nurse is back from lunch.
Just wanted to let you know, that I love you all a bunch.

Thanks for all your prayers and support, they mean so much to me.
Good-bye for now, God bless you all, Love Ashley Marie.

Richard Thompson

Incredible Flight

As I stand upon a peak
hoping for what I seek
I'm dreaming that I could fly
way up there high in the sky
So I jump into the air
where no man has ever dared
As I fall wings form from my hands
and now I soar above the land
As I look down at this beautiful sight
amazed by my incredible flight
Then as faster and higher I go
now I leave the earth below
Now I fly among the stars
never knowing I'd go this far
As I come down from that great height
so much end my incredible flight
I know now what an eagle can see
is as beautiful as can be
As I wake up from my wonderful dream
I realize life isn't always what it seems

Steven D. Howell

A Soundless Peace

The wind rushing through my hair,
galloping, galloping,
faster and faster we go
through the field without a care.

A soundless peace,
galloping, galloping,
nearer and nearer we get
when we travel, time will cease.

The sun beating down, warms one,
galloping, galloping,
dandelions swirl up around us.
Nothing else in the world is as fun.

Stacy Chambers

The Illusion

My coat, I throw on the floor
   my wrap of mourned angels
My necklace, I toss in the air
   my beads of twisted desires
My clothes, I tear off my body
   my cocoon of trapped pleasures
My flesh, now content with freedom
   my mortality will carry me home

Seema Virdi

Rose Garden

Now that my prize roses are
grown and gone, tears fall from
my eyes; I no longer have them
to hold and be happy.
They have gone to their own
garden to be happy and dear God
I pray they are.
I do, however, have one more
prize rose in my garden and
this one is watched over with
all my loving care, but some day
this beautiful rose will be gone
into her own.
And tears will fall again.

Loretta Romano

The Feeling

The way I feel,
Every time we meet
I know it's real,
The feeling can't be beat

It's time you tell me,
And I'll tell you too
Please help me see,
What I mean to you

When I see you,
There's a feeling I get
The feeling's not new,
It's been there since we met

The feeling is mine,
The feeling is strong
This isn't a line,
I know it's not wrong

Someday for real,
I hope that you
Just might feel.
The same way too!

Jessica Cournoyer

Cindy Seal

I like to make you smile.
I like to make you laugh.
I like to swim.
I like to splash.
So if you want a good meal.
Please don't eat me, because
I'm your friend Cindy Seal!

Mlynnda Brugger

To Jerime With Love

Who would have thought
It could be like this

Who would have thought
It could feel like this

An angel in disguise
I watch him sleep

Perfect little hands
And itty bitty feet

What a gift, so pure,
So gentle - what great
Joy God has given.

Carla L. West

And His Name Was Jesus

When I was very young
And things were going my way
Along came God
And I pushed Him away.
As I grew older
My life was happy and gay
Along came God
And I pushed Him away
And life went on it seemed
I had no time to pray
Along came God
And I just pushed him away
I'm much older, now
And life is slipping away
Along came God
And now I beg him to stay.

Rose Carlo

And Then There Were None

The journey of life is the most trying of all, sometimes we stand up
and sometimes we fall. Merriment and fun is something we all hold
dear, but for one sweet maiden it all held fear. The little story
that I am about to tell, is about one girl's own personal hell.

On the surface the story is charming and cute, this is something that
you cannot refute. But, Alas is of a young woman named Jill, whose
heart kept yearning for a man called Phil. For months, Phil was the
object of her attention, he never should have looked her direction.

He seemed like the ideal Prince Charming in white, until the day they
got into a fight. The argument was about a few little dates, one, two
three, four, five days that she was late. It began on a morn when the
fields were too green, and the fair Jill coyly removed her jean.

The ever beautiful morn quickly turned quite sore, when Phil convinced
her that she wanted more. A few mornings later, she began to feel
sick, and she realized Phil had been too slick. And all of her hopes
finally began to sink, when the little white sick quickly turned pink.

Finally after thought, her courage did muster, she called Phil, and he
began to fluster. He thought for a moment and said with a cruel grin,
"You cheap whore, it's not any of my kin." Much to Jill's misfortune
her knight put down the phone, she now knew she was to be on her own.

She went to see her family's friend in a white coat, he gave her pills
and soon she began to float. In her mind she returned to the fields
and hills all in white, part of her died as she returned to the night.

Her days of playful excitement and joy in the sun, started as many,
but now there were none.

Lisa E. Rosenthal

Love Knows No Boundaries

The moon dances across the water around you, like my love for you dances
in the warmth of my soul, only to be weakened by the darkness of a stormy encounter.

To feel your touch is like feeling the wind blow gently across my cheek.

The pounding of the waves against the shore near you, can only begin
to describe the pounding of my heart as I near you in presence.

The seas parted once, but my love for you could never part.

To love like this, is like a great light leading lost seagoers to safe distant shores.

Feel the warmth as night slowly gives way to a glorious sunrise.

The storms of love have finally lifted and calmness is once again restored,
leaving behind a majestic interlude of passion laced with a strong will of survival.

Love Knows No Boundaries.
Love is Eternal.

Connie C. McBride

The Gift

As I visualize the Muses on their platform in the sky,
They studiously ignore me and my plaintive plea of, why?
If a man is given talent by the God's who rule the earth,
Then, is not allowed to use it, what is that talent worth?
Is the reason for this talent just to help him find a space,
With no other earthly value than to keep him in his place?
Or maybe it's his karma that he never sees the day,
When his gift sees wide acceptance and his talent starts to pay.
If he asks himself these questions, should he try to answer them,
Or will the answers he is given, end with questions once again?
Are the questions I am asking all the proper ones to ask?
Are the answers all too simple? Should they be more of a task?
Can it be that there's a lesson that I have yet one day to learn?
And, if I finally learn that lesson, will my zest for life return?
Please tell me gentle Muses, for my life has been a quest,
Does my talent have a purpose, or was it given me in jest?
Does my question bring you laughter? I really wish you'd say.
If it was given as a joke, please take the gift away.

Edward J. Capocy

157

We Didn't Have Time To Say Goodbye

We didn't have time to say goodbye. We didn't have time to say goodbye - you and me.
When you set sail for the open sea, God had said it was time to go and I said no, please God no
Don't take her away from me to sail that lovely, lovely sea
We didn't have time to say good-bye - you and I
No more gliding across the ballroom floor, no more summer nights on an ocean shore
No more chasing the moon like we used to. The children really enjoyed it and thought it was true
No more sonnets about your Easter bonnet. You were the grandest lady in my parade
No more Halloween when the kids would trick or treat
And bring more candy home than they could possibly eat
No more Thanksgivings when we gathered when we were able
And asked God to bless us and the food upon our table
And then there was Christmas, that very time when voices would sing and bells would chime
Lights on the tree oh so very bright, all gold, red, purple and blue
And tinsel reflecting like the new morning dew
Presents spread out all under the tree with Santa's parting words -
Merry Christmas from me
Time has gone by like a hurricane blowing through a stripped out tree
We didn't have time to say goodbye - you and I. We didn't even have time to say hello
Will you wait for me when you reach that far distant shore
I promise I will paddle and paddle 'til I can paddle no more
I love you Mrs. Calabash - more than you will ever know

Leviathan B. Denson Sr.

Untitled

I saw you for the first time, walking from afar.
I heard your voice for the first time, when you said 'hello'.
I tasted your kiss for the first time, standing on a porch.
I felt your hand for the first time, walking with you in the moonlight.

I felt your love for the first time, when you told me 'I love you.'
I felt your body for the first time, making love under the stars.
I felt your warmth for the first time, dancing in the rain.

I felt pain for the first time, when you walked out of my life.
I felt tears for the first time, watching you walk away.
I felt death for the first time, for I lost you.

What can I do to feel you again, a second time?

John Buchanan

Untitled

I saw my father's shoes on the floor,
I tried to put them on.
As I slipped one on my foot, it would not fit,
And the other would not accede.
They fell off my feet when I tried to walk.

I set them aside and saw my father's uniform, and decided to try it on.
But the pants were too big, and the jacket too small so I put them back.
Then a thought slipped into my brain, and I smiled a secret smile.
In everything I do I try to be like him,
I can be my own man,
But I will never be him.

James Stephen Wirfs Jr.

The Abyss

As I entered the Abyss, my wife exited me with a soft kiss.
Then I daydream, and daydream again; but still I stand in the Abyss.
With horrible memories lying there half-dead half-alive
I strive, and I strive to live. And I think again, and again trying to get out, but
I still stand in the Abyss. Terrible memories every night on
my knees, and I pray and I pray just to live another day.
Still striving, and striving but for what of. But for my darling
my lady love. I had been to hell, and back with Satan in my soul
trying to take control. But I couldn't let him not then not ever.
I'm glad to say that I am here today, and to tell you that daydreaming
can not be bliss. I'm telling you this because of my terrible
memories of the Abyss.

John Gabriel Langston

13th Veil

Oh, how fragile be this
Vessel of clay,
When it doth brush against the veil.

How fleeting,
when thy cup be fill with merriment
And song
That thou wast given sorrow to drink.
And in that sorrow,
Stirs a tide
Eternal.

But oh, how faithful,
That in the end
Comes He
Which gives birth
To miracles.

In this,
I will drink my fill.

Victoria Badger

Because Of Love...

The rose is blooming now
And becoming more mature.
With an outlook on life and love
Much clearer than before.

The stem is stronger
And now standing tall.
When faced with stormy days
It's not afraid to fall.

With roots firmly planted
It's been able to shed all thorns.
Less afraid of what tomorrow may bring
Because it's been reborn.

Still aware of the husbandman
And the pruning it must endure,
In order to grow
More beautiful and mature.

While facing the sun,
And reaching out to humanity,
It will not exist it will be.

The rose is me!

Nancy O'Leary

A Wish

I wish I had the
courage all day long not
to be scared into doing
wrong; also I keep
wishing that I might
never be afraid to do
right and never be
such a coward that
I could be frightened
if laughed at.

Dolores Stephens

A Halloween Fright

I was sitting behind a post,
When all at once there came a ghost.
A long bony hand I felt,
Grabbed me by my belt.
Just then, a black cat screeched,
Down here at the beach;
And the old Mother Witch
Jumped out of her wits.

Jeanne D. Davies

One Voice

Snowbird sits
His song sung low
Melancholy yet honeyed
Winter's tune he chirps.
Waiting patiently
For his blend of one voice
Unity his companion
Spring listens.
Love
Mother Nature Grants.

Michelle M. Farrar

The Judgment

As the sun sets
As the light fades into eternal darkness
It was too short

As the clock stops
As the eye quits opening forever
All the things we would have changed

When no one can change any of it
It is a day of a few happy souls
It is Judgment Day

Luke Steers

Daily Life Is...

As the wind
blow undirection,
your life
run with motion.

As the sun
wake up in the morning,
your life jump
fully jolting.

As the moon
shown own half face,
so your life
appear part amaze.

As the sea
cure the wild waves,
our own life
is daily craves.

Anthony Morello

Rain

The rain is really my tears
falling through the air.
It's my thoughts and my fears.
It's all coming out,
but not through me.

First it sprinkles
now it pours.
The weather is cooling down
for my feelings.
It puts a smile on my face
Knowing it's falling all over the place.

Now all my feelings are let go,
no one will ever have to know.
The rain has stopped
I'm sad no more.
The rain was really my tears,
It was my thoughts, it was my fears.

Samara Burch

Red, The Color Of My Love

The blood runs down my arm, still warm like summer rain.
Crimson on white, what a lovely surprise, thoughts mingling with pain.
Disregard played its part, I don't care anymore.
Wounded, I feel nothing. Forgotten little whore.
Tiny drops hit the floor, together, but each its own.
Seeking to be free, yet always by the same name known.
Those rivers of red wind on, searching to find no end.
Ashes to ashes, dust to dust, left to disappear in the wind.
Veins once coursed with a love held for no other mortal on earth.
Maybe now, my God, you'll see this love, spilt, for what it is worth.

Stephanie M. Walker

Lost And Alone

Lost and alone in this great big world, who would care for
this boy or this girl? Deprived at birth of a mothers love, taught
to struggle and steal and sell false love.
Lost and alone just a scared little child, left to themselves
in the streets running wild. You see them on the corners each and
every single day, you turn your head or simply tell them to go away.
Lost and alone in this great big world, would you care for
this boy or this girl? Can't you see their hurt and their pain,
craving for love and a home life once again.
Lost and alone in these crazy times we're in, taught no
religion only shame and sin. Never even knowing the goodness
of God's love, instead willing to shed another child's precious blood.
Lost and alone a soul is caving in, it's time we stop blaming
and give a listen. We will never know when God will choose to
bring a young soul to the gospel of God's news.
Lost and alone in this great big world, would you please
talk with this boy or this girl? Share with them your experiences
past, teach them that God's love for them will forever last.
Lost and alone in this great big world, will you love this boy or this girl?

Crystal L. Reed

Thinking Spring

I recall a day in winter when the world was painted gray,
With the north with blowing briskly since the breaking of the day.
'Twas the turning point of winter, with six more weeks to go,
And the leaky skies above us were sending down their snow.
Outside my kitchen window stood a maple gnarled by years
"Poor old fellow, how I love you" I whispered through my tears.
Then I saw the tree was dancing as its limbs began to sway.
"How can it be so cheerful on such a woeful day?"
The leaf buds on its branches are swollen with new life.
"For they know that spring is coming, in spite of winter's strife."
Oh yes, the tree is dancing, for it knows a wondrous thing -
And even though it's winter, the tree is thinking spring.

In this, the winter of my life - whatever it may bring -
Lord keep my feet a-dancing and my spirit thinking spring.

Olive P. De Lano

Spirit Of My Fire

See the beauty of my embers
Flowing deeply through your soul
You're the spirit of my fire; let it be known
My flames are dancing as if in celebration glowing oh so proud
Serene happy true to you nurturing some how
As I embrace your every challenge with my faith and deep sincere
Always so forgiving, allowing tender warmth be near
You're the spirit of my fire; let it be known
How my embers mysteriously enraptured you in colors of red and gold
You compelled them to grow valiantly into magnificent flames so bold
You entered the windows to my spirit
Suddenly captured within my fire
Hardened hearts softened and saddened souls soothed
Now your spirit in my fire has been smoldered
All that remains are lifeless embers lying in the cold.

Jenny L. Dyson

Lost

The river winds my soul as the coldness of the winds direct me down
a stream of ice. I find warmth in the suns beams. The clouds cannot
secure the shivers that hide the fear within. I am but a drop of fluid in this vast river.

Lost in the overwhelming complexity of nature, I find my domain. A
moment of confusion followed by a trickle of security. This river
runs through me in a flow of serenity. Serenity that binds each drop
of fluid into a stream of warmth. A valley of blocks that change the
direction of flow can only be seen as a path of light. For at the end
of this path will I find a pool to rest. A pool that shall grow with
each trickle that is fed into it. Each trickle giving the life of
eternity a new power to absorb. Changing the shape and feeding power
into the immense reserve that will drive this river into eternity.

A pool emptied of its fears by the release of its energy. There is
no fear as the shivers of coldness dissipate into the surrounding
winds. As I float into eternity, I am but a trickle that shall remain
as the sun gives me warmth. Warmth renewed as the path of light has
shown me direction. I am not lost.

Denise L. Fisk

The Meaning Of Christmas

Christmas really has no meaning, it's what you make of it.

If you believe in Santa Clause that fat and jolly man, then
Christmas is a magical time that is so very grand!

Christmas is a beautiful time with all those pretty lights,
with those pretty Christmas trees and presents, what a sight!

Christmas is the birth of God, or Jesus you may say. The shepherds
and the angels and the star that shined that day!

Now you know what Christmas is, it's so very grand. The time
to share, the time for hope, the time to give a hand.

Holly Beaulieu

The Search

In my search for truth I found it there at wounded knee.
I had to clinch my fist's to calm the rage inside of me.
In my search for God in heaven I banged upon his pearly door.
And the devil opened up and said to me...he don't live here anymore.
In my search for peace I found it...toe to toe with war.
And rushing into battle I found myself in hell...
A place I wasn't searching for.
In my search for strength I found the flame that burn's inside.
Which I turned into a raging fire.. To protect my heart
And burn the word goodbye.
In my search for love I found a place of sadness.
And I thought of thee...
It was a place of broken vow's where pieces of...were scattered...
As far as I could see.

David Jerald

Fading Times

I once walked down the road of life seeking wisdom as I might I laughed at silly frolics
and frowned at my mistakes, I shared the pain of burdens while time showed no embrace.

During my time of traveling I often chanced to meet those within
betrayal who found the lost and meek.

I've captured many friends who grew closer to my heart some were
ever lasting through time we drifted apart. Love is unpredictable
yet kind as it is old, sometime it's warm and gentle or selfish when imposed.

Man is not defined by words of costly fame his actions tell so very
much while scant hopes remain.

Although we run for shelter to hide an awful scar the truth will
surely surface no matter who you are.

For every walk of life death too shall have its say to end a lonely
journey where time is fading away.

Willetta Brandon

Free

When the pipes sing freely
Then shall we be free
When we jig dance merrily
Then shall we be free

When Protestants meet the Catholics
Without hate and rage upon
A red, sharp sword
Then shall we be free

None but one
Could fear
None but one
Could hear

When the widows mourn no more
Then shall we be free
When the children stop crying
Then shall we be free

When time can hear the hurt
Without the hurt returning
And from my heart comes a cry
When shall we be free?

Robert Hope

Untitled

Heaven is my home and
I'm just visiting here
Where there is no more sorrow
And there are no more tears.
When we get back home again
We'll see our family,
And we'll be all together
For all eternity!

Katherine Buchwald

Memories

The days are long and dreary,
The skies have turned to gray,
The sun refuses to shine,
Since you went away.

My love traveled with you,
As you drove out of sight,
My heart has an emptiness,
Deepening with the night.

You left me with such memories,
Though I'll never be your wife,
Memories of a sweet romance,
To hold throughout my life.

Tammie L. Moss

No Time To Cry

There's no time to cry my child
My pain and suffering are gone,
For now I'm in a better place
Where nothing can go wrong.
I'm filled with joy and happiness
Reunited with family and friends,
I'm surrounded by nothing but loved ones
So the joy I have never ends.
No time to cry my child
For it was my time to go on,
But I'll walk with you and talk with you
And help you to be strong.
What I ask of you my child
Is to never question why,
Just know that I am happy
In my eternal home on high.

Latosha Coleman

Hospice Hope

A diary of death this is not
But a chronicle of life
For many unfortunate
Are taken without warning
But these are permitted
To tie loose ends
   ...and say good-bye...
   Carol Balzer

Untitled

Fall came from out of the dorm
With the aftermath of a thunder storm
The sun came shining thru
   Just to play peek-a-boo
The breeze flowing the tall fall grass
   Making it look like shimmering brass
Without showing any fear
Telling us winter's near
   Sparkling so brilliant white
      Snow in the pale moonlight
Knowing spring is not too far away
Flowers will bloom, the first warm day
Followed by the summer's norm
Waiting again, for a thunder storm
   Myrtle Williams

Who Am I?

Who am I?
Why am I here?
Where am I going?
Will you be there?

Does life have a purpose?
Does life really end?
Will I see you in heaven?
Will you still be my friend?

What I want you to know.
What I'm trying to say.
I'll love you forever.
Till my last dying day.
   Daniel T. Bassett Sr.

Raising Our Value

It's true, sometimes it seems,
That life just isn't fair.
People, everywhere you look,
More and more, seem not to care.

We grab for all the glory;
We rob Peter to pay Paul;
We lie to friends and neighbors;
But, is it worth it; all in all?

The hope of a better world,
Where our children soon will live,
Will never be discovered,
Until we all learn how to give.

It's really not so hard,
To try and understand;
There are different types of people,
Who make up this wondrous land.

If we would all just help each other;
Pick our backs up off the wall,
And learn to live together
It would be worth it; all in all.
   Doree Ann Chapman

Ode To My Best Friend

Casey Durbin, my best friend,
is always there for me and will be till the end,
he makes me laugh and makes me smile,
when we need to talk all we have to do is pick up the phone and dial,
he's very special to me, like I am to him,
our friendship will never dim,
we look back at the past
and remember the memories that will always last,
he's like a brother to me,
his household is my second family,
I can trust and rely on him,
there isn't many out there quite like him,
we have lots in common and inside jokes,
most people laugh, even our folks,
trampolines, trains, swimming, and more,
we always laugh and hit the floor,
he's special and unique, just like a friend should be,
I guess I could say, "Lucky me."
I can't explain how much our friendship means to me,
we're best friends, as you can see!
   Darcie Moore

One In A Million

These lines are for my Mother, whom I've known all my life,
   Had she not been my mother, I'd have surely made her my wife,
She's as perfect to me, as perfect as can be,
   As pretty a lady, as any you'll ever see.

A woman of all seasons, who is cultured and has style,
   With a warm loving heart; and a beautiful smile,
Every man should be so lucky, to have this lady by his side,
   To compliment his person, while taking on life's stride.

She's every good thing, all rolled up into one,
   And how lucky I am, being able to be her son,
She has kindness, humility, great understanding, and she's sweet,
   A rare combination, that's impossible to beat.

As I have grown from a toddler, and reached full manhood,
   Through life's growing pains, beside me she stood;
I've occasionally blundered, and reached out in despair,
   And always, this angel called Mother, has been there.

I can only hope that I don't falter, and fall from her grace,
   For the last thing I want, is to remove the smile from her face,
I love you, my Mother, more than words can ever say,
   And these feelings will hold true, until my dying day.
With all my heart and soul, to my Mother, Mary Margaret
   Randolf E. Helm

Willow Trees Bear Strange Fruit

I was walking home one day, three white men in a truck came my way
One man yelled, "N****r what you doing walking this way so late at night?"
I quickly replied, "Sir I just left work cleaning at Misty Pike"
The driver then yelled, "Get on back of my truck and I'll drive you home"
Afraid I was, I quickly said "okay" feeling solid as concrete stone
As we drove away I heard laughter from the three while speeding hastily
Off the road we turned headed through rows of trees
The middle man yelled, "Hey n****r ever swung high in the sky?"
My life quickly flashed before my eyes
My grandpa told me Willow Trees bear strange fruit
Wherever there's a tree a black man is hanging
My soul flew high above my body as my knees grew weak in the chill of the evening wind
Praying to myself I asked, "God please don't let my life end"
The truck pulled underneath a big Willow Tree
The three men got out with guns and rope after me
I ran and ran so fast you see, not able to keep chase they stopped to yell at me
"Hey n****r you may have gotten away today, but tomorrow we will get another n****r
who will pass this way!"
   Robin Lynnette Bridges

Yes, She's My First

Ten perfect tiny fingernails on ten perfect tiny fingers
Ten perfect tiny toenails on ten perfect tiny toes
And a precious tiny head buried in my neck as we snuggle so close.
Ooh! The splendid specialness of this, my first grandchild!

Baby Zoe. Means "life" in Greek; means "delicious" to me.
I treasure this scrunched up little 8-pound bundle
All toasty warm in a brand-spanking new fuzzy receiving blanket.
Receiving Gram'ma. The miracle of it all!

I hold her away from me so I can see her beautiful face.
She holds her mouth like a baby bird awaiting a tasty wriggling morsel.
Her wide-opened baby-blue eyes dart from here to there, and back again
Unseeing but for shadows, I'm told.

She had been fussing tonight so they put Gram'ma in charge. Good!
We nuzzle and rock and walk, and I hum a lullaby and whisper in her ear
That I love her more than Reese's Peanut Butter cups and Mallomars combined!

We are alone together in Maine, mid-September, '96,
Watching the eclipse of the moon...
A celestial wonderment in the skies, an earthly wonderment in my arms,
She'll never remember. I'll never forget.

Andrea G. Garfinkel

The Way Of The Song

The song is important, it is what moves the energy into waves,
that turn back on other waves, that curve through the air and trail
into melody lines, we'll always know

And so what if nothing is real or genuine the only truth comes from
realizing we are all orphans, clasping whatever useless things we
can keep dry and turn from the wind,

Like when a person bursts into tears at a funeral and say's I'm
an orphan now, you always were, it's just that now you know

But it's okay, everyone is everyone's keeper of souls, and the dead
give birth to the living every day, it slowly turns around like
a song a little out of tune, and a spirit a little out of dreams
a little out of step a little out of time
just a little and only that, and not much more
so that what matters least, is what matters most

Shawn Moreau

"I Believe In Angels"

I believe in Angels, for God has sent one to me,
   I believe in Angels, for mine is Tamara Ahwee.

Let me tell you about our friendship, it's a gift from Heaven, you see.
   One of the most valuable gifts in life, one that we get for free.

If I was a beautiful flower, I'd want her to be the bee;
   Who makes my existence possible, for all the world to see.

I thought I was wiser being older, but I find her teaching thee.
   And she shows much patience and virtue, in explaining Spanish to me.

Her friendship is unconditional, she fits that word to a "T,"
   If you don't believe in Angels, you don't know Tamara Ahwee.

We've shared some great conversation, over a cup of tea.
   And we've shared some joy and laughter around the Christmas tree.

We've talked about our diving, as we've rocked upon the sea.
   And I've tried to remember the signs, as she posed the cue cards with glee.

I don't believe she realizes how much she means to me.
   She shares my joys, my sadness, saying, "That's the way it's supposed to be!"

In this crazy world around us, how stressful life can be.
   So her smile and sense of humor, are a valuable asset to me.

May this poem be my way to say "Thank You" for being there for me.
   For I believe in Angels...
            I love you Tamara Ahwee.

Sally Marie Ploski

Body Rush

The slap of skin,
A thrust of power,
How mortals sin,
Past midnight's hour.

A cry in vain,
With every thrust,
For pleasures pain,
Is wonderlust.

With pounding beat,
And racing blood,
The liquid heat,
Begins to flood.

Oh, heartless be,
My vain seducer,
Who will leave me,
For others succor.

In throws of passion,
No thought is spared,
For it's the fashion,
That no one cares.

Amari Vale

Broken Promises, Shattered Dreams

Leaves once young and vibrant
Flexible - willing and able
Now dry and crisp
Pulverized into little bits
Like broken promises
Shattered dreams...
Being picked up by the cold, bitter wind
   being tossed hither and 'fro-
Just like forgotten souls.
Dancing, whirling, swirling
Soldiers of misfortune
Now die out.
Bringing in the new,
   the young,
For new dreams - new hopes
New promises are to be made
   to be broken
To be shattered
like the leaves before them.

Ted Flores

Hallowed Ground

Another year and another name
Is taken from the page,
Of those with whom we shared our lives,
In a not forgotten age.

We stood with them on foreign shores
And carried Freedom's flag
To the vastness of a desert's sand,
Or atop a mountain crag.

With forces joined we stemmed the tide
Of those who sought to rule,
With an iron fist or steel sword
In a way that we deemed cruel.

We who remain now bow our heads
In a freedom so costly found,
For those who lay in foreign lands
Or here in hallowed ground.

Albert C. Fales

162

A Ponderment

In my youth I played and dreamed
Nothing mattered, or so it seemed
But, I made one big mistake.

I went to school and learned from books
A career chosen, and overlooked
But, I made one big mistake.

Money came and money went
Its sole purpose was to be spent
But, I made one big mistake.

My religion taught me peace and love
For all that's under and above
But, I made one big mistake.

My family and friends were true
So important my whole life through
But, I made one big mistake.

Now I'm sick and growing old
I look back - my story's told
Although fame and fortune I did not make
I lived my life - no big mistake!

Andrew P. Mandell

Little Boy

She looked into his eyes
And remembered the little boy she knew
from her childhood
She starts to have flashbacks
of that childhood
with that little boy
Then she suddenly comes back
to the present time
and realizes that
the little boy
is the man that
lies there dead in her arms

David S. Kohara

Pain

Listen!
You know me from yesterday;
Seared in the enclaves of your
Ken,
I wouldn't go away.

Clear,
The colors are of the event
Long past, yet, still you hear.
And I do not relent.

Yes,
You know me. Time, my enemy,
Brings more of me, not
Less.
I won't let you be.

Heidi F. Mabatid

Point Of View

A woman I loved, long ago,
once had me pick up my clothes
and hide in her bedroom closet
when another man came calling.

I said, "But I just asked you
to share your life with me."
She smiled, "Be quiet, and watch!
That's exactly what I'm doing."

F. P. Kopp

Fission

An atom with a dying kick blew up another of its kind,
Which in turn killed one so quick that it in turn flew blind;
So like the ants with grains of wheat; each carried others off with it
Till of earth and all its parts there wasn't left one little bit.

But space was filled with energy,
With heat and light and pulsing rage,
Which rushed in all directions wild
And kept on flying for an age.

With speed of light they flew apart
Exploding all things in their paths
Far from the locale of their start,
They kept on cutting wider swaths.

Destroying planets, moons and stars,
The galaxies and satellites.
If they haven't stopped they're going yet.
Calamitous beyond all wars.

Spencer Squire

Silent Good-Bye

She looks out through her blank eyes full of sorrow, crying with tears of blood

The drops fall to the ground resulting in numbness as drifting becomes reality

At one time she was searching for something, someone, maybe it was just a feeling,
    though failure and emptiness was all she found

Her world is now gone

The faces that at one time gave her comfort are now faded away
    to distant figures in the back of her mind

As the sky above turns to her, the colors appear to be nothing

Inside her heart is dying though part of it is already dead

As the candles burn, she watches the rain fall into silence

Reaching out only to let go...she gently kisses him good-bye

Releasing the rose across her side, he tells her he loves her,
    as in his arms, she dies

Debbie Wisdom

Alone

   The Storm approaches with its pounding and rumblings
and its dark shadow, and its smell of chemical waste
    envelops and smothers.

   A flash of white and the explosion of bass
announce with all the heraldry of Ghangus Khan that the storm
    has come.

   Blown to bits, the tree splits and disintegrates
covering the emerald grass with shards of death;
    animals cower.

   The young man in the forest looks up as the
first droplets of moisture, cold and sharp, hit his face and splash
    onto the emerald grass.

   As he exits the place of green, he wonders if
his life will mean anything or is he just another
    drop of rain.

   Kelly Sutton

Lady Moon

   At night Lady Moon sends her soft dim light to dance across the
water. She peeks through the trees to stare at the little critters
who are preparing for the day to come. The moon knows when it is time
to go. She gently fades away till morning comes. Lady Moon will come
again to watch the earth at its peaceful rest.

   Lacey Paquin

Light

Shining true, through darkened fear,
  for all of the world to see and hear.

Beaming around all corners and curves,
  bringing day is the purpose it serves.

Nothing stops the power it possess,
  it forces its way through all crevasses.

It travels through wind, snow, and rain,
  it's the brightness that takes away your pain.

It comes and goes like each passing ship,
  it grabs and holds you with its mighty grip.

You may think it will always be around,
  but its complete journey has no bounds.

No sooner you take it for granted, it will be gone,
  and all you have is memories of how it was, so important and strong!

  Tina Hoefft

The Light

We see his shell shuffling along through this maze,-
yet never quite see the man within.
Afraid lest he become known he turns his face away,
not from us alone -but from himself.

His being is covered in a multicolored
Plaster of Paris like patchwork crust, smeared on
over the many wounds caused by real or imaginary
cuts, hurts, slings, and barbs endured during his lifetime.

He is impregnable now as he hurries to join the line waiting to view "The Light".
He stumbles in his haste and as he falls another body brutally forces its way in front of him.

His soul feels a stabbing pain through some forgotten chink in its armor.

  A. John Doner

A Special Gift

I stumbled upon a special gift three or four years ago
I had never received a gift like this from anyone I know.
Not from a mother or a father not a teacher or a priest,
It seemed no one had this gift to give, the gift had been deceased.
Life went on it was no big deal, I really didn't feel sad.
Of course how can someone long for something
they've never even had.
I met a lady so gentle and kind in the year of '93
She has this special gift to give, and she wanted to give it to me.
She pulled me close and squeezed me tight
I never felt this good before.
Then I found myself wanting this, so I kept coming back for more.
The more I got the more I wanted,
My heart began to melt
The special gift this woman gave was the hug
  I had never felt...

  Annabel Savage

Friendship Lost

You lose a loved one to the Grim Reaper of Death.
  You grieve and time heals your wounds.
You lose a wife through Divorce, you judge yourself,
  Acquire new loves and your life continues.
Death, Divorce, these things are uncontrollably difficult to avoid
  Friendships are the results of mutual likes and dislikes.
Respect for things and places and ideas shared.
  How do you respond to a friendship ending? One meant for a lifetime.
Has the passage of time rendered me ineffective? Of no consequence?
  Does not my mind think anymore? Am I no longer a person?
Feel not I pain? Real or imagined!!
  Are you that friend? If not where is your presence?
Am I then, that friend lost and forgotten?

  Ronald Norman Beaudry

Flying

Flying High in the sky,
Flying to the tallest Mountain
Flying to the most beautiful paradise
in the world.
Birds flying to their highest
I'm flying, flying high
in the air.
I'm flying, flying high over
the ocean blue.
Flying to the most beautiful
paradise in the World.
Flying over and over again.
La La La La
Flying over and over again
Birds flying to their highest
Flying, Flying, Flying, Flying
Flying, to the most beautiful
paradise in the World.

  Kelly Oren

Paranoia

I hear footsteps in the hall,
the most thundering voice of them all.
But when I look into the hall,
who do I see,
Nobody,
just me.

  Max Baigelman

What Is Not A Form Of Speech?

He leans in close as if to dare,
will you match his sultry stare?
You flick your hair with gentle wrist,
a glance you steal, hope to be missed.
Carefully you shift your skirt,
don't want to get your feelings hurt.
Water crashes on the beach.
What is not a form of speech?

Sun and warmth upon your skin,
a river flowing from within.
Four nights straight don't sleep alone,
his arms around you cast in stone.
Clothes unmatched and face unshaven,
your wake-up hair leaves him a cravin'.
His fingers do your senses reach.
What is not a form of speech?

  Damian Moos

Endings

Reach
  for the end of life
Walk
  into the darkness
Listen
  for distant voices
Seek
  the wisdom of those
  that have gone before
Fear not
  the unknown
Approach
  with the innocence
  and faith of a child
And find
  Our Father
  at the end of the tunnel
And
  The beginning of eternity

  Gail Sorenson Fitzgerald

Am I Crazy

Deepest secrets
Are locked away
vultures flock the mind
Infertile flowers
Dance around
Elliot is scared
Love and lust are mixed together
Iguanas are free
On the table
Telephones sing
Torture runs through the night
Mountains throughout the Mid East
Orange sunsets
Roam the earth
Restless babies scream at night
Ice cream taste good
Seashells live by the sea
On Wednesdays fish fly by
No one understands
Am I Crazy

Luisa M. Morrison

Life Stages

As a little baby
First you're cute and cuddly
Everyone gaze with sparkling eyes
at this bundle of joy, so lovely

Now time has gone by
You're playing a childhood game
Laughing with your best friend
In a little while things isn't the same

Responsibilities have hit while
growing to a different change
Using your own mind now to see
What you as a grown up can gain

You look back on these passed times
some was happy
Some was sad
some was good
some was bad
But being grown you realize
All these graceful ages
Come about in our life stages

Belinda Castille

Son, Where Are You?

I gave life to you,
I gave you my heart.
But son, where are you?
We are so far apart.

Yes, you sit beside me,
Your body is here,
But where can your mind be?
The one I hold so dear.

Chemicals have taken you,
At the age of fourteen.
Drugs have been the undo,
Of a mind once so keen.

You were quite an athlete,
In your little spiked shoes.
And now you face defeat,
Please son! Please don't lose!

I plead, what can I do
To help you win this time?
Son, son, where are you?
Will you ever again be mine?

Renee Ginther

Our Gathering

Our gathering came far too soon.
It was early spring, the harvest was not right.
The dawning sun shone so bright that the wheat
  bent against the wind to touch its brilliance.

From the light came the harvester, and he seemed
  confused, this gatherer of wheat and grain.

"Why am I here in early spring?", he seemed to question.

Gently he moved among the rows, stopping now and then,
  careful not to crush the young leaves within his mercy.

He paused, knelt down, and slowly reached out for supple
  and promising leaves.

In my utter despair I spun my stalk and spike into the light and
  pleaded: "Take me, take me, I survived the last harvest".

He turned, it appeared to me, for but a brief second as if to affirm,
"I have found the plant I seek." He pulled the plant of leaves from
the earth and gingerly cupped it within his hands.

Quietly, without voice, he turned and was embraced by the sun. Why,
why did he come in early spring? The time was not just, the leaves
not yet aged. He did not tell us why. In this field we will never
know. Simply, his task was done.

J. Hauser Baughn

Why Did I Have To Go?

It was 6 in the morning and a bright sunny June day.
Dad went out and started the car and said "Son it's Ok".
Mom was at the door peeking out to say good bye,
I looked at her face and looked away because I could see she was about to cry.
It was a short ride about 20 minutes or so,
Dad didn't say much and I sat and wondered why I had to go.
I was only 19 and hadn't experienced much,
and now I'm off to the Army, away from family and friends and knew I'd soon be out of touch.
I had flunked out of college and lost my deferment, boy was I dumb,
as I sat in the car and ponder and my future, I could feel my body go numb.
Soon I'd be gone, away from friends like Eddie, Tony, Alex and Joe.
Oh Lord I wonder why do I have to go?
Not really a care in the world, I was young, life was fun,
now am off to the army to learn how to be a soldier and how to fire a gun.
I wished the ride could go on forever, but it was over all too soon,
as Dad pulled up in front of the Induction Center, I had a sudden feeling of impending doom.
I said good-bye to Dad and shook his hand, he told me "Son, good-luck",
  I watched him drive away.
I was all alone, going far away from home, it was such a sad, sad day.
I tried to be brave for now I was going to become a man, a GI Joe,
but Lord knows how much I didn't want to go.

Carl H. Johnson

Daddy

It seems like only yesterday I sat on Daddy's knee,
And listened to the stories that he made up just for me.
Mommy used to clean, sew and cook dinner every day;
My family was the happiest 'til Daddy went away.
He used to take me everywhere; I was Daddy's little girl,
And when he left he took with him the meaning in my world.
I keep memories locked in my heart of trips and birthdays past,
But still today it's hard for me to accept that good things seldom last.
From Daddy's happy little girl to suicidal Shannon,
I told myself that he'd be back, but I knew I'd been abandoned.
I told myself that love was all that anyone really needed,
And if in my life I found that love somehow I'd have succeeded.
So I searched the earth from east to west, up and down and all around,
And everywhere I met a face, but love I never found.
Lonely days and nights alone, God turned His back on me,
Yet in my moment of deepest despair it was Him who set me free.
He took my hand and walked with me, and does so every day,
My father's in my heart forever, this time my Daddy will stay.

Shannon Noelle Lockwood

Little Hands

Little hands are the sweetest hands.
They fit so snugly into yours.
They warm your heart with their clasp
and embed memories in your soul.
They create things that are irreplaceable
and express so much imagination.
They can make the simplest things out of nothing.
But these things become our keepsakes for life.
Many things for them are unreachable,
yet too many things seem to be within reach.
Their clutch reminds you of their dependence.
Their release reminds you of their desire to be independent.
Their little hands can do so much. They welcome you their world.
They can be so sharing. They can be so possessive.
They can bring so much happiness.
They can be source of destruction.
They carry with them the realization,
that all too soon these little hands will grow.
They will have more strength
and be doing even more powerful things.
But for today, they are the little hands that fit so snugly into yours.

Vickie J. H. Braxton

Ode To Crystal

If you knew the kinds of things you did to guys like me,
You probably wouldn't believe the power you got to make us see
A beauty you yourself don't notice in the mirror everyday
But a beauty that's too great for any spoken words to say.

Without even knowing it, you cause an earthquake beneath my feet.
You shift the tide and wreck my sanity yeah, you're really neat.
A flash of light comes from the sky and toasts my brain to ash.
They could auction you off, but let me write a check;
    the whole nation hasn't got all the cash!

Transcendent flames sweep through the town and slice through everything.
No country has a shelter deep enough to save the king.
I see the blur of orange light coming, the richest man won't live to sue.
But I stand through the tormenting flames since I know it's only you.

The deficit crumbles as if it were solid and vulnerable to the gust
The oceans burn like out of time and corals turn to dust.
Time slows down, the sky turns red, but then I see your face.
I haven't heard too much about heaven but this must be the place.

Your mortal form appears beside me, there is nothing I don't know
We hold hands and look to the sky, which soon is full of snow.
I feel my life returning as I look into your eyes.
We knew if for each other we would survive.

Timothy Bishop

Untitled

The loud horn of war blew across the valley.
I raise my head to see below a vast dry land
My body armed and ready, mounted on my horse,
Ahead of me lay the soldiers, those who wore gold defenders to my
nation, And those who wore blue enemies to my army.
The land is my conquest, the power is my addiction.
I king ruler of the greatest nation but, thirsty for more.
My catapults are back and ready, my knights are armed and alert,
Now as the enemy pounds his drum, I raise my miraculous sword,
innocent townspeople hide due to fear,
animals jump behind trees to get away.
Then with the strike of thunder from the sky, I yell my battle cry,
My sword flies down to signal the scouts to start the war.
Swords clash and colors mix, the sun begins to fall as I
The king of the greatest nation lay seeking life for just one more day. My wish is not granted...
With my last seconds, I slide across the ground to stare at
The enemies burning and raping. The squirrel's fight for acorns to survive.
Then as my heart stops the sun sets over my land
and the great wall which once represented my empire falls into
thousands of pieces which lay among the fall as dust.

Randall Restiano

The Time Has Come

It's time my dear to take those vows,
    That mean so very much.
We say each word with all our love,
    And then we're one upon a touch
We part our lips and we both see,
    The love we have will last eternally.
We turn and face this world as one,
    But our love, my dear has just begun!

Dennis D. Arnold

Several Times I Think Of You

Several times I think of you
Wondering where you are

I cry tears like rain
deep down inside
Wanting to hold you
just one more time

Those first dozen roses
Our walks in the park
That festival of music
Our hours after dark

The rides in the country
Inside that old Ford Galaxy 500

Just holding hands
Rolling in the grass
Hoping our relationship
would forever last

Please let's find each other
and say what we never got to say

Good-bye...

Diana Matchopatow

Questions

It's midnight and I am lost
in the path of sleeplessness.
I toss and turn and wonder why
and where the truth may lie.
Is it Darwinian or Adam and Eve
and when will it be
my time to leave.
Where is my faith this
long night in my bed
while thoughts encircle
and run through my head.
I lie in the dark and
yearn for the dawn
for these visions to vanish
with the light of the morn.

Helen Wardle

An Angel's Kiss

The porcelain figure
the smallest of hands.
The innocence of a smile
for pureness it stands.

An Angel's Kiss;
Can it Be?
Something wonderful
created by you and me.

A special feeling
that only two know why,
The smallness connects the bigness
with a little baby's cry.

Katheryn Lee Sciacca

Eternal Love

I'd wait forever
for thy eternal love

In the earth below
and heavens above

You warm my heart
and feed my soul

You're my one true love
that, you should know

You embrace me tight
in your strong arms

You win my love
my soul it charms

You're much closer
than it seems

Because you're always
in my dreams

Sarah Cook

Cameron

You were an Angel sent by God
You touched our hearts so deep
Now we know this precious soul
Is resting in a peaceful sleep.

We thank God each day
For the time you spent with us
You were filled with joy and laughter
And rarely did you fuss.

We believe in our hearts
You knew the time was near
But you wanted us to remember you
Without sadness or tears.

It's a sweet release to shed a tear
When our hearts are sure
That God called His Angel home
Where all souls are pure.

So rest our baby Cameron
Until that joyous day
When we all stand before the Lord,
With praise, praise and praise.

Gloria Emilien

Choices

We are born into this world
Without the knowledge of why?
And are taught the needs
In order to survive.

Yet, as we age older
Our innocence we lose,
We are given life's choices
In which we must choose.

We are born with direction
For our lives to take,
And along the way
Given choices to make.

When we choose wrong
And never ask why?
Our next choice to make
Could cause us to die.

Robert Heflin

Lord, You Are My Greatest Fascination!

December 21, 1996
OH Lord, You are my Hope and Inspiration!
    You are my Biggest Infatuation, my Greatest Fascination.

I, John, stand here in Awe!
    At all that you have Created, and all that I have Saw!

I want to learn how to give you Satisfaction!
    And to help turn a lost and dying Nation back to the Realization

That You and Only You are the true Salvation
    For our Souls' True Gratification.

So we can avoid the ignition of our Souls
    To steer clear of Hell and Damnation!

And to help save our mankind, your wonderful Creation!
    To get that final eternal invitation!

To help us avoid all Temptation!
    And then make Heaven our last and final Glorious Destination!

Then there will be no need for any further Explanation!
    And Forever and Ever, we can give you the Glory and Recognition
        That You So Much Deserve!
            Amen

John E. Turppa, Skooter

A State Of Confusion

I dedicate this poem to my dear mother Gloria...
In this world...can be so cold. I've been told by my father so bold.
It can be confusing and if you think it's amusing...
you would be sure to get him fuming.

Growing up...was pretty tough. Always thinking...will I have enough?
Will I live up to the expectations and have any reservations of my said relations.

You have to follow through and sometimes make do
because no one else can do it, it's all up to you.

Try not to blame or to disclaim what mistakes may remain
they make us humane and feel the rain.

Every day will have a twist so get ready and take the risk
that may come your way! Don't delay this is your day.

People may criticize you and sometimes obliterize you, but don't give up
    your time is not up!
It's just the beginning so keep on grinning.

Take each day as the first. Think the good not the worst
give it your all and you will stand tall above the rest without contest.

Robert T. Kendrick Jr.

The Valley

I've just gone thru a valley, this valley's very deep,
Now I have climbed hills before, and they were really steep.

This was no ordinary valley, it's like a hill turned upside down,
I guess you might say it is like a smile, turned over becomes a frown.

This valley's one of life's lessons from God to be taught,
Something to enrich us, never sold, nor can be bought.

It's to increase our faith and put our trust in only Him,
Though the valley be dark and dreary, the hope, bleak and dim.

We have always grown in the valleys, it is a sad fact, but true,
If it wasn't for grey skies, we'd never rejoice when they turn blue.

When we leave the valley, we can look back and smile,
For we haven't grown an inch, we've just run a mile.

Dee Davis

167

Him, The World And The Girl

He holds the world in the palm of his hand but he's not really sure what to do with it.
There's a girl by his side and sometimes he lets her hold the world too.
Sometimes she takes the weight of the world from him, other times she adds to it.
Sometimes she just sits on top of it enjoying the view.
He thinks about the world and this girl and wonders what he should do with them.
Sometimes it's easier to please the world than her, but she's so much nicer to hold.

Sometimes he really feels the world slipping through his fingers.
Some say he should trade it in for a moon. They are so much easier to take care of.
He asks the girl by his side what he should do.

She asks him if he likes to be dark and lonely.
He looks at her strangely.
She says the moon never sees the light of day and is always changing the way it looks.
Then she asks him what he wants.
He says he doesn't know yet.
She says the world will do nicely for it holds all he'll ever need.

He asks her how she knows.
She opens her palms and shows him the universe.

Stacy Barr

Friends Are Special Angels

Friends are special angels sent from God above,
Giving peace and understanding to the ones they love.
Through the trials and temptations of my journey here,
I find my Angel friends so precious and so dear.
I know it's merely a small reflection of your precious love,
Just like the Spirit that came down that day and left as a dove.
I know that time does not stand still, and night always follows day,
So, I hank you God for my special friends that you have sent my way.
The sunshine that I see in them is a reflection of your face,
It's your special Angels passing to me your wonderful, peaceful grace.
Dear God give them love, support, and strength for the day,
For they know not whose life they are guiding by the way.
For you see friends and Angels are very much the same,
They are life's priceless treasures that I can call by name.
God give them your guidance, support, and strength, but please be aware,
That our lives are full of burdens and extremely hard to bear.
Above all God, I thank you for their special love,
And if I can, call them "My Angels" that you sent me from above.
Thank you God.

Deb Phillips

Prison

I see the world but am not a part of it.
I feel love, yet I cannot express it.
I feel joy, yet cannot smile or laugh.
I feel pain, yet I cannot cry. There is no one to hear it.
I feel compassion, yet I cannot offer comfort.

My desires, thoughts, fantasies paralyze me.
My fear and insecurity surround me
Like a cold glass wall that from outside is only a mirror.
But all my senses are affected by the activities outside,
Although I am not seen, heard or felt.

At night, in the solitude of my small, dark room I ponder upon my existence.
Why, God, am I here? What is it that I can do?
What will be done for me?
I see creation in all its beauty and know the world cannot be evil.
But what will I do to protect it?
I feel the pain of others in war, famine and poverty and know that there is evil in the world.
Senseless suffering. But what will I do to alleviate it?

I want to be more, but don't know where to start.
I want to learn more, but don't even learn from my own mistakes.
I want to accept more, but don't distinguish between fantasy and reality.

Lisa M. Radetski

Jewel

Here I lie a corpse once a slain
driven down by purple rain
beneath the depths of endless ice
my fossil preserved, and yet shows life
a million years has tempted the grave
seeped apart by scourging rage.

Time has shown my love for her
a millennium lasts for just a blur
the Spring has come and so has Fall
to bring my frozen heart to thaw
a diamond amidst the bloody pool
reveals my everlasting jewel.

Gerard Arantowicz

Untitled

If we had not met
until the end of forever,
I know that I
would love you still.
For not only are you
the pulse of my fast beating heart
But also the very fabric
of my soul,
And I already knew
the sweetness of your touch
Long before our gazes
had ever locked and held.
I hear the whisper of your name
with every breath I draw,
And it is your warmth
that shelters me in the night.

Tina L. Rogers

A People User

Come running!
Hold up your head and sprint,
Catch the empathy at the side lines,
Let their grimaces and pent-up poses,
Make your stride
This is how to use people!

Donald M. Pinney

My Version Of Heaven

My version of Heaven is...
Herds of white stallions running in
A cotton blossom field;
Litters of white kittens lying
On a feather pillow;
Handfuls of white rabbits
Playing in a garden of daisies;
Flocks of white doves singing
In a cottonwood tree;
And most of all, seeing
Parades of angels playing
The soft sounding music of the harp,
But in my heart I know it's much,
Much better than I can imagine!!!

Felicia Thompson

Untitled

Lord please help me
To become that man
That I see
To become that man
That I wish to see.

Gabe Shelly

When The Night Is Still

Like a marauding horde
from the recesses of my mind
they come when the night is still.
So many possibilities unexplored,
dreams I dared not pursue,
burn my thoughts like flame.
When the night is still,
yesterday's failures stake claim,
like so many warring kings,
to the hopes I still possess.
When the night is still
come the most bitter stings,
inflicted by the arrows
of self-doubt and fear.
Often, when the night is still,
upon my cheek is a silent tear.

Brian Burden

Remembrance

As the love he once had promised
Starts to wither away
She often hates to wake up
To face another day
As the words he used to whisper
Gently forever leave
She then begins to realize
That only the quiet grieve.

Shantel Pint

The Entertainer, (I Wonder)

I wonder who's the woman
wearing silks and lace.
I wonder who's the woman
behind the pretty face.

I wonder if she's wary
if everyone's a liar.
I wonder if she's trapped
in a prison of desire.

I wonder what's the recipe
to bake a cake of trust.
I think about ingredients,
beside the ones of lust.

We do not speak often.
I don't know where to start.
Or how to fit the pieces
to the puzzle of her heart.

Lonny D. Hood

Bethany

My little Bethany
You mean so much to me
You're my first pride
And then you died.
I cry and cry.
Oh, sweet Jesus!
Can you please help us?
We miss our little girl
Our sweet tiny pearl.
Oh, what a prize!
Our Father
Hope it's no bother
To hold my daughter
On your big knee
My little Bethany
Sweet baby, Bethany.

Tom & Becky Malone

Us

I sit, I think, I try to understand,
Why doesn't everyone lend someone a hand?
I try, I fight, getting nowhere. It seems no one really cares.
I am, I will try to keep on, putting faith towards a new dawn.

She tries, she fails, still she wants to know why,
Mankind is hell bent on making the Earth cry.
She stands, she sighs trying to talk. Sense to lunatics they balk.
She fails, she knows this truth, the future lies within our youth.

He cries, he moans, he feels such sorrow.
Unable to expect the world's happy tomorrows.
He hides, he tries to make sense. Of why our minds are so dense.
He finds, he sees the path back, it's love the world now lacks.

We struggle, we strain, deal with heartache,
When inside our souls how they quake.
We live, we love, learning to hate. Why must this be human's fate?
We try, we have to learn, to our children we have to turn.

I have, she will, he can, we must,
Learn to live with each other and above all Trust.

Lisa M. Riseden

Yesterday

It seems only a few yesterdays ago
when momma would look out in the yard and see me
as I was having fun swinging on the tire swing
that my brothers hung from the old oak tree.

Time passed by so swiftly as I grew to be a teen,
Soon I met my future husband - so tall and lean.
We raised our family. One-two- then three.
That was the beginning of our family tree.

Now as our children are in their middle age
they are beginning to see
that we are getting older - papa and me.
We are in our golden years - we have turned another page.

When the nights are long I sit here and ponder.
I realize our grand children are double in number.
3 girls and 3 boys.
They are already too old for toys.

Now when times are quite I often reflect back on a few yesterdays ago
when Momma would look out in the yard and watch me
as I felt safe and secure swinging on the tire swing that hung
from the old oak tree.

Wilma Rogers

THE REWARD

Rotary telephones decorate the border of our classroom,
Vivid kindergarten colors - BLUE, RED, GREEN.
Peculiar numbers stenciled meticulously with bold black marker are,
says, Ms. Farrell, our phone numbers. We must "memorize to win a prize,"
which is a brilliant colored paper rotary to take home to our parents.
John is the first to recite his. He stands erect and nervous, stuttering
when he reads the numbers, but conquers the task. "Well done!"
beams Ms. Farrell and stands on a desk to reach the BLUE telephone.
"Anyone else?" I bound up from my seat and begin to read the numbers
loudly off of another BLUE phone that I have decided is mine. "No, that is not yours!"
she exclaims gruffly. Thrashing me from the soil like a weed.

All the Erics and Christines have long ago carried their BLUE and RED
phones triumphantly home. There are only two phones left BLUE or YELLOW.
Ms. Farrell has embellished the numbers on the rotary to a humiliating size.
Mommy told me my phone number earlier and I knew it. When I raised my hand
it disappeared so quickly that I pulled my pigtails to make it come back. But it didn't.
Until after class. By that time Ms. Farrell had taken down the faded YELLOW rotary
saying hopelessly to me "Learn it over the summer." I wanted to tell her
that I knew my phone number. Only, I had wanted a BLUE telephone.

Maria Woehr

The Lord Vs. The World

The world hollers, "do drugs and drink."
The Lord whispers, "your body is a holy temple."
It is the Lord vs. the world - which will you choose?

The world hollers. "take all you can get."
The Lord whispers, "I will supply all of your needs."
It is the Lord vs. the world, which will you choose?

The world hollers, "come over here and look at this."
The Lord whispers, "be still and know that I am God."
It is the Lord vs. the world - which will you choose?

The world hollers, "hate all people who are mean."
The Lord whispers, "love your enemies as yourself,"
It is the Lord vs. the world, which will you choose?

The world will continue to holler and scream and yell
but if you listen you can still hear the Lord whispering amidst the noise.
It is the Lord vs. the world.
Which will you choose??

Sandy Ellison

Mother Machine

Dear Mother Machine wake up from your dream, your muscles
aren't stronger you're twenty no longer. Forget about friendships,
dancing and fun, you just don't have time unless your work's done.
The windows need washing, the floors are all dirty, get moving
dear mother, pretend that you're thirty. The children are sick, they
caught chicken pox, so comfort them mother then go sort the socks.
The washer is empty, the clothes are all drying, upstairs on the
stove your supper is frying. Tonight you eat early so daddy can
see his great big strong son go play Little League. Your feelings
for sports are not very strong, so mother again your thinking's all
wrong. The telephone's ringing, the door-bell the same, but you're
just so happy you're part of the game. Your intentions aren't bad,
they just don't agree, with that certain cad that we shall call he. He
loves you dear mother as everyone knows, so just be yourself and
don't step on his toes. Of course he's exhausted from working eight
hours, I'm sure that's the reason he never sends flowers. But don't
get a complex and don't get uptight, you know he will show you he
loves you tonight. Without you your family could not get along,
somehow that seems funny when you're always wrong. You're
eating too much, you're smoking a lot, perhaps you'll get lucky your
body will rot. So Mother Machine, dear Mother Machine, do one
thing for yourself, wake up from your dream.

Mary Jane Chiffolo

Innocent Child

I fear it will never end for her -
she's five and so helpless.
I'm her surrogate sister substituting for mom
and feeling just as helpless.

Jerking...screaming...weakening...
Clinging, grabbing and a squeak for help.
  2 arms to comfort, 2 hands to hold,
  A tiny body who's lost control.

Episode after episode hit like tidal waves.
  The seizures do not end.
A controlled panic in the pit of my stomach.
  Will it ever end?
  A final jerk leads to cessation and her calm brown eyes look up into mine.
Comforted eyes.
  Grateful eyes.

I see a new perspective. I am the arms of safety.
  Comforting an innocent but strong child.
She's unknowing of the facts, but experiencing the pain.
In knowing the facts, I experience the pain.

Tonya Knuesel

Stranger From Heaven

Welcome to our family Little Stranger,
A gift to us from Heaven above.
God has sent you here to join us
in a family that is rich with love.
Preparations have been made
to help you on your way.
New adventures come along
with each new shining day.
Here's a message from the heart
Let me sound it loud and clear
The world is now a better place
Because at last you're here.

John Keys O'Doherty

The Love Of My Life

You are the one
Who's always there for me
There by my side,
No matter rain or shine,
No matter day or night.

Oh...thank you so very much
For being always there for me, my love,
The love of my life.
(I love you)
I'll be forever yours until the day I die.

Manika So

The Tyranny Of Sorrow

The Tyranny of Sorrow
does not let me rest
each night as I fight to hide
the pain I bury in my chest
each night I call for freedom
Freedom hasn't found me yet
I deal with endless oceans
and truths I can't forget.

Too many bloodfed roses
No more lies to hide behind
Just tangled strands of bitter webs
Too many to unwind

The ocean starts to thicken
Too difficult to tread
I'm drowning in these dreams
that are poisoning my head
each night I pray for freedom
to be a whipping boy no more
To overthrow the Tyrant
To finally find the shore.

Hector Benavides

Winter Days

In December days grow shorter
and the sky turns grey.

Snow falls in a daily order and
the kids go play.

Kids come in when they're tired and
they've had their fun

Kindly mothers make hot chocolates,
cookies, and hot buns.

Then the kids start telling tales
of everything they do.

After that they go to bed
alas, the day is through.

Joseph Siwiak

Song Of Spring

Jubilant bunch O' wildflowers
dance in partner with a breeze
following the rhythm of a song
performed by the joy of a willow tree

How I would love to be such a flower
beautiful, in all my grace
to have such partners as the breeze
dancing lively in this merry place.

Ashley Hayes

Lilies In The East

Och, 'tis the East!
When arising from Languor
clutching at the last of the Eve.
She speaks!
Can you no' hear her?
Within her shell of leaves
'afore the Lady's Splendor
she's tilted, wrestling with wind

So 'tis to the East, she bows...

Ever the servant
to the maiden of Grandeur
and the kiss of farewell
to Fate, she sends
Och, she's there!
Can you no' see her now?
Watch her, Beauty, unfold
stretching out of slender leaves
'tis the Lady's Splendor
Lilies in the East.

LittleWolf Haynes

Love Lost

For Darren
He flung his body upon the bed
In a heap of despair
For love lost.

Upon the pillow he rested his head
The tears he shed
For love lost.

Brilliant sunshine ne'er compared
To the golden hair
Of love lost.

Sumptuous sweet peaches paled
To succulent kisses
Of love lost.

With unrestrained passion he had loved
Unashamed to confess
Of love lost.

His happy heart had been devoted
Enduring, faithful
To love lost.

Slowly a faint solitude surfaced
Wonderful memories never lost.

Gillian Vogel

Love Is...

Love is like a raindrop,
Sometimes sad and hurtful,
but sometimes happy
and wonderful.

Kimerly Shock

To My Heart

You give me some of the best advice,
Especially when it comes to living life.
You are always there when I need you the most,
Whether I am here or there, coast to coast.
Whenever I am feeling lost or all alone,
You are the first one to lead me home.
Unselfish, you are always there to care,
And when it comes to sharing love, there is enough of you to spare.
I appreciate you, love you, and can't live without you,
You never think of only you, but of him, her, they, and you.
Without you I just could not be,
To my Heart, the most important part of me.

Jessica Rae Jones

Maranda

I don't know a lot about Heaven, because I've never been there.
And I don't know a lot about death, because I've never experienced it.
But I do know about the existence of angels...
I was blessed with the presence of an angelic sister for seventeen years.

I know that a sister's love is a sacred gift that reaches beyond
death and all its power, it extends beyond any earthly realm humanly conceivable.

Death may have separated our bodies, but it can never separate our souls.
For you shall remain alive, my sweet sister, in my heart and memories for the rest of my days.

So if the rain of despair begins to fall, do not grieve for my
sister, for she is smiling upon us from heaven above.
We were honored with your presence for a mere seventeen years,
and in this short time, you taught us more about patience, love,
tolerance, and understanding than most can learn in one lifetime.

You always reminded me to stop, and take time for the "little things"
in life, and for that I am eternally grateful...
But you see, all angels must return home.
Heaven was always your home, earth was merely a temporary destination.

Tiffany Spears

Mistaken Identity

Your voice is but a note in my unworthy ear.
Your straining words reach out from your throat like long white fiber
arms with thin grasping fingers that wrap around my body.
Your breath is but a hiss in my unworthy ear.
It is a warm wind breezing in from the west, whipping past my ear
ever so lightly, so lightly that I only slightly notice its presence.
I turn rapidly, but find that I cannot force you to be here; I can only wait for you.
As I throw myself to the ground, waiting, hoping for you to be here,
to show up in front of my eyes so your breath can be a warm wind on
my neck and your voice can hold me prisoner, I know that you will never be with me.

Jennifer Katehos

By The Numbers

Hacked and churned, slashed and burned,
one house on the hill now downward returned.
To pay the price is twice as nice,
stay of the subject, we have given up thrice.
Four times hatred, pretty yellow flowers dead,
you know it's all just in your head.
Quintessential journey, essential mourning,
slap in the face leaves scars of scorning.
Six times dripped, oops I tripped,
went insane, confusion in my brain, tell me mother have I slipped?
Hardened heart, seven times hurt,
somebody help me I'm drowning in dirt.
Love and hate, the trials of a first date,
disorganized tree row almost numbers eight.
Doing fine, life's a game at nine,
but as you age, you walk a thin line.
Purple ink, green pen, colors of ten,
my only love, then dead again.

Zachary McBean

171

Ecstasy And Agony

Lord, our God,
Love, lust, rapture, communion, in one package all,
    Momentary, supreme pleasure, foretaste of heaven only thou
    could conceive and everything together bring
Further joys of life three children born and raised ever close to
thee, still one more, with forebears from the land of thy birth, a
son-in law, certainly yet another gift from thee,
And now comes Mark, 21 month first grandson, a spectacle for all,
from nothingness to Thine image in human form, awareness, but first
    an empty box, ours to fill with knowledge, ever more wisdom in
    knowing and living thy word, with love for neighbor and thee,

Agony. We thank thee, Lord, for the gifts of tolerance,
    forbearance, forgiveness, sympathy, and covenant unconditional
    love that get us through withered wrapper and frayed box, into the
    treasures that lie deep, the joys and the peace only thou can give
We all grow up and pass on and on the joys of life and all we behold,
    Indeed how incredibly and unspeakably great thou art.
We can only feebly say "Thank thee, Lord, for all thou art,
    and all that is."

Tierry F. Garcia

Ode To Jake

I thought of you again today, My Dear Friend.
With tears in my eyes, I felt saddened by your absence.
Your passing was not too long ago, Yet it seems like forever.
Sometimes I struggle to go past the sadness, back to the sweet times we enjoyed together.
In most recent times, your body became overcome with the burden of
    time, but your heart and spirit remained young.
As the memories of you flood through my mind's eye, And the tears
    caress my cheek, I am reminded that we shared too many good times,
To remember only the last moments of sadness.
And so my mind floats through the years with visions of you.
A smile slowly overwhelms my lips, as my eyes blink away the welling wetness.
Suddenly I envision your face, with your trusting eyes embracing me with unconditional love.
How many times you were by my side to love me, console me, protect me,
    or just to pass quiet times with me!
I feel the sudden warmth of your presence, and I know that God has
touched my heart again by uniting us in spirit once more.
Yes, My Old Friend, you have shared with me the best of your life,
Your love and devotion, and, in your memory, I will pass your love on.

Gwen K. Tewold

Love Is Many Things

Love is just a glance, when you need to know someone cares —
    Love is just a touch which when you have a burden to bear —
Love is giving when you have nothing more to share.
    Love can't be bought, borrowed, or stolen, but it can be shared.
Love can be beautiful, great and grand,
    especially between a woman and a man.
Love between two friends cannot be compared.
    Love lots, give much, and heaven on earth will be yours to share.

June Tester

Look Up

I awoke this morning with the sun shining bright
And I said to myself how grateful I am to see the daylight
I said a little prayer for this troubled land
And hope that our Father in heaven will reach out his hand
To help the sick, the poor, the dying and the ones that have lost all hope
So their day will be happy, without pain and able to cope
This land of ours is like a treasure
Filled with beautiful birds, animals, trees and flowers beyond all measures.
Look up at the sky on a moonlit night.
And you will see each star shining bright
If you look up at one star long enough
It seems to be saying I'm here watching over you when the going gets tough
For I am a mere housewife who loves this great earth
That God created for each and every one of us with the whisper of his breath.

Mrs. Dolores L. Murawski

Where Will You Spend Eternity?

Someday I know I'm going to be
As angels in eternity
Serving God and Christ each day
In some glorious wondrous way

Eye hath not seen
Ear hath not heard
Of the beautiful promises
Found in God's word
But there's one thing we all must do
Before our life on earth is through
Simply trust, believe in Christ
Then you will have eternal life

Spurn my Lord and you will be
Part of Satan's destiny
Dear friends the choice is yours to make
Remember God makes no mistakes

Lily M. Defibaugh

Without You

If you take another minute
And wash away the pain
If you take another look dear
We can start all over again
Just like the gospels of Jesus
Our love can again be risen
It doesn't have to go down in flames
Every relationship is a symbol
Of Christ's life
The passion, the death, the resurrection
Then the cycle stars all over again
As Jesus is to the church
So you are to me
Can't have one without the other
Could not exist so emptily
Could not live without you
Nothing would have any meaning...
Without you
Without you loving me

Lee Ferrin

The Lazy Cat

My cat is fat
My cat is lazy
He puts on a hat
It drives me crazy
He fights with the dog
He is such a hog
He lays on the edge of my bed
And droops his head
When you pick him up he feels like lead
He sleeps in the den
In a pen that I made for a hen
He is cold yet so bold
Think of that!
He is a porcelain cat!

Sandra Hildebrandt

Amanda Burress

Space

Space is dark, bright, black and white
Space is up, down, left and right.
Space is time, forward and backwards.
Space is day, space is night.
Space gives, space receives.
Space goes beyond, beyond, beyond.

Tina Tomlinson

Crying

Crying in a garden of roses,
listening to the weeping
willows weep.
Thinking of you, and what to do next.

Lightning flashes,
the rain pours down,
hating every moment of this pain,
listening to the wind
tell its story of truth.

This love inside will never leave
for I can't bear it anymore.

Crying in a garden of roses,
listening to the weeping
willows weep.

Terry Thompson

Puppy Pride

Puppies are the pits!
Weaned from mother's teats they come
Piddling and pouncing
Poohing and pronouncing...woof!

Puppies paw and claw
And chew and drool
Their marks forever worn
By chair, door and stool

Puppies know the taste
Of everything in reach
Shoes, belts, dirty underwear
And then you hear a screech!

Puppies are true clowns
Alert and filled with pride
Barking at their shadow
Or stretching at your side.

Nancy Bacon

Working Mom

It seems as though there's not
enough time in the day
To do everything that's required
in the proper way.

Short cuts have to be taken
To keep things from being shaken.

A job that demands so much effort
Leaves little time for home comfort.

Two children and a husband to tend
Dishes to do and clothes to mend.

No time just for myself
For now I must dust the shelf.

Rhonda Abell

Worry Not I Shall Prevail

Worry not you demons
I shall prevail
The bright sun
Someday will shine
Yes, oh yes it will
Then and only then
Will you see me again
and a sweet disposition
Will flaunt through my head
To bring me back to the
Way that I really am...

Donald D. Siders II

What Is Love In Return

Is it the sharing of a gentle kiss on rain touched lips,
or the sharing of a soft caress on a lovers cheek,

Is it sharing warm hugs on cold nights,
or sharing the warmth of the softest fur of a familiar friend,

Is it the sharing of sun lightened days after gray clouds of storm,
or is it what I give to you,
In your dreams,
To your soul?

Is it what you show me in the gentle fold of your strong arms as I
shed the tears that only you know the reason for as you kiss away my sorrow,

Is it me loving you unconditionally, without expectations?

What is love in return?

It's the hearts of two lovers so intertwined, so in tune with each other,

It's what you are to me and I am to you-
It's a love that no one can extinguish
It's a love that only you and I can free.

Ramona Hembry

My Mother

Dedicated to my Mom, Frances Smith
You "Brushed away my Tears," and "Kissed away my Fears," your
love un-conditional and never measured.

And when I started to grow up, and felt really tough the day
my bicycle lost its "Training Wheels," when my knees got
skinned up, with a big hug you told me not to worry, "it's all
part of growing up."

The day I got my report card, and I was less than proud, you
said, "It's O.K. Sweetheart," with confidence in your heart.

And one day I came home with a fever, and was really sick, that
"Hot Chicken Soup," it really did the trick.

My first big "Crush," and I felt like a fool, you seemed to help
me to mend a broken heart too.

It was my first "Prom," and I got home a little late, you stood
on your "Principles," in your own loving way.

And when I was "Un-reasonable", and wanted to "Pout," you nurtured
my feeling objectively, I felt "Silly," without a doubt.

I know "I'm not Perfect," I'm sure you know it too, but sometimes
I fail to "THANK YOU" for the thoughtful things you do. But
you're "MY MOM, MY BEST FRIEND, MY MOTHER," "'cause "I'M A PART OF YOU."

Wanda Reagan-Shelley

Earth Angels

Do not listen for feathered wings nor music from an angel's harp.
There'll be no robes of pristine white nor halo made of gold.
Blue denim, a baseball cap and old plaid shirt may be angelic garb.
Earth Angels may live next door and may be young or old.

The Hospice volunteer who sits with the dying man and listens to his fears;
Then cries with him and holds his hand and dries his final tears:
The fireman who carries a child to its waiting mother
Then goes back inside the burning home to carry out another.

The teacher who teaches with the mind and from the heart
To give the student a better start:
The nurses, doctors and even the aides who ease an anxious mind
With a gentle touch and words that are tender and kind.

They minister to the sick and lonely, the homeless and the lost
These Earth Angels never shirk their duty and never count the cost.
They've been sent to us from God above
And come equipped with built-in love.

Patricia A. Dennis

Where Is My Future

Where is my future, what will it bring
Will I be rich, will I be poor, will I be greedy, will I want more

Will I be famous, maybe a star, will I be a person who never gets far

Will I get married, will I feel lost, will I never marry because of its cost

Will I have children when I would adore, will it be more then four

Will I have many friends, will I have just one, one good friend is better then none

Will I stand by my husband when he needs me,
will I become afraid, leave him and tear up the treaty

Will I let others influences change my mind, will I be strong enough to survive

Will I be sane in mind and in body, will I be able to cope with reality

Will I go to heaven, will I go to hell, or is there another place that no one will tell

Where is my future? What will it bring? I will never know until I have lived

Joy A. Campbell

Seasons

You left in the spring before the trees unfolded their green
the flowers were still asleep in the frozen ground
and oh how I missed you

Summer came with long days and beauty found only in Alaska
we had hanging flower pots with blooms of every color
and oh how I missed you

Summer faded into autumn, the days grew shorter
The backyard trees were ablaze of red, orange and yellow
and oh how I missed you

Winter is here the white mountains are
magnificent against the blue sky
The days are short and darkness comes quickly
and oh how I miss you

You say you will be home for Christmas, the days will be so short
But we will be able to see the trees laden with snow, the ski run lights pointing
upward to the heavens, sit in front of a toasty fire and talk of the seasons that you missed
and oh how I will love not missing you.

Mary Frances Voight

Retirement Day

The weather here is pleasant
I'll sit with my colleagues
Sipping coffee, telling stories.
Those wails of sirens are only tropical birds,
The red and blue lights are only stars.
The badge I once wore over my heart I have turned in,
I left my office with honor, I came here a hero.
Those children I couldn't help, I now watch play.
Every once in a while, I catch a glimpse of the family I left behind.
From here, I can see how many people have loved me,
And I hope the friends from who I was untimely called,
Will carry on where I was forced to leave off.

Cheraba Just

Sunset

Things seemed to be going my way
But I just couldn't wait until the end of the day
The clouds began to set a mood
So that my mind it could soothe
The sun begins to settle down
Changing all the scenery around
Suddenly, there were magnificent colors of purples, blues, and reds
I was so stricken with wonder that nothing could be said
Then there was that wonderful orange I hoped to see
it really flattered and inspired me
This is a scene I'll never forget, because it was a beautiful sunset.

Narissa Reed

The Truth

The Bible is so true.
Even when you are blue
So, do you believe in the bible?
Because, I do.
That you can pray;
Hey! You can pray.
God can answer your prayers!
So, why don't give him a try
instead of a cry?
The Bible is so true
Even if you knew things were
Going to turn out bad.
So, why don't you not be blue.
Instead trust the one who
can see you through.

Cynthia Nation

Untitled

A yawn to begin, but never to end
The street of loneliest scripts.
The soft earth of sloppy springs,
And the salty roads of tired lives.
The thumbs outstretched and sun-
burned
Do carry us through time.
A chariot, a mule,
No different.
Float on away and yawn, the day,
Has ended.
Follow dark lights.
The night's fire don't smoke.
Stale and soggy, old and worn.
Travellers do call you.
You hear them yawn.
They fall asleep.

Bill Hesford

Evil

God created each one of us,
coming from his womb,
but, some people believe,
that we are evil, and we are doomed.

None are born evil,
we are all created good,
but this concept,
to not all, is it understood.

Evil lurks toward us,
it reaches our souls,
it tries to lure you in,
it bribes, and it pulls.

Evil pulls at each one of us,
hoping to pull us to the dark side,
and, this will happen,
unless by God's rules you abide.

Toward evil we are pulled,
because of money and fame,
we lie, and steal, and cheat,
until we become like the devil, insane.

Carrie Wemhoff

Vision

See the sun
See the trees,
See the wilderness
That constantly
Frees!

Brian G. Sim

He Lives

In stunned shocked silence
I ponder and pray
Half believing this a nightmare
Hoping it will go away

How can I go on
When a part of me dies
My face smiles But my heart cries

There is little comfort
in knowing
It was his time to go
He was my love, my companion
And I'll miss him so.

Then I lifted my eyes to
heaven on high
Why should I be sad
I know I should not be sad
And I should not cry

There is joy just in knowing
When I think of my love
A part of me Lives with the father above.

Betty Thomas

Dreams Of Mine

When I drift onto the other side,
I can fly, I can twirl, I can go all
around the world.

When I look at the sky that used
to be so very high, I raise my
arm and reach, nobody to teach,
clouds, fresh air, a voice that can
clearly share, I open my eyes
and to my surprise I'm still
standing there.

What comes and goes, must
come again, for I can cry
but what reason of why?

My moment of truth, a moment
of despair, I try, oh I try but my
true reason why?

Kelly Anne Carr

My Creator And I

As I sit in the Shadowy Gloom,
I check out my Sovereign Moon,
The moon that charts my life's long ways
And sometimes leads my heart astray.
I wonder if I am dead indeed
And this is all an illusion I see.
For if am dead, then Satan does Rome
And I won't find my Sacred Home
When turmoil covers earth's large mass
Then the lake will be complete
It's hell at last.
  But
Then the Sun comes over the hills
And that is when my heart stood still.
For at that second I did find, it was
Only Ole Lucifer toying with my mind.
For my Lord is strong
And my faith steadfast
And me and my
  Creator are together and I at last!

Ed Burdick Jr.

Through This Granddaughter's Eyes

Through this granddaughter's eyes:
  You're so special to me

  A man full of wisdom and dignity.

Through this Granddaughter's eyes;
  I saw you toil and sweat, but never a moment did you ever regret.

As the years passed away;
  The foundation you laid;
  for a family that's proud, of a man of your way.

As God's plan goes on, in everyday life;
  your wisdom and pride; I'll carry on in life.

Thanks — grandpa,
  for all you have given,
  may God's sweet blessing to you be given.
    Debra Shelton

My One And Only Love

My love, my dear...
time is never of the essence when you are near.
This feeling I feel for you is so overwhelming, I cannot explain.
The words seem to escape from me when I see you.
Such an angelic light rises from you to the sky,
As if you were sent down from the heavens to be by my side.
The warmth of your touch sends me into a world of dreams.
The glance of your smile gives me the strength that I need.
And the softness of your voice lifts me up, as if you have given me wings.
My love for you is unconditionally and undenyingly true.
And if there are angels sent down from the heavens,
Then darling, my angel is you.
    April Kathleen Morgan

We Will Meet Our Loved Ones Again

We will meet our loved ones again,
When God calls from every end.
There will be no more tears to cry,
Just laughter in the great blue sky.
There will be no more sickness to bear,
Only love, and peace to share.
Heaven I can imagine is a beautiful place,
With flowers, and trees as green as the grass.
And the Lord's there to help us to pass,
We all will rejoice, and sing, and have a glorious time in the Lord's company.
We will praise, and serve the Lord,
And be one happy family doing it all.
God is always there when you're in need,
All you do is pray, and believe.
God is every thing to you, and I,
You have to have faith before you die!
    Georgia Jackie McCray

Portrait

I never want you to know winter within your heart - only summer -
only rainbows, only love.
I can take or leave the rain - it's wet - and cold.
I love the sun - it reminds me of you -
I want to be a journey-man of your soul - your body.
But getting inside you is like trying to make someone else's music in our own time.
I wonder sometimes who you really are - what sands you've walked -
  whose face you've dreamed.
You know I am much
too wise for dreams.
I want my portrait of you to be finished,
complete - a legacy of love.
I want the world to
know the love I have been fortunate
enough to touch.
    Roselea E. Laufenberg

Introspection

As my Senior years are upon me, I have made a discovery.
I have realized that in all of my living, there is much that I didn't see,
from luscious landscapes, tall buildings to Oceans, to the wealth of life's majesty.

In awe now, I gaze all around me, there is not a thing that escapes my eye.
An exhilaration surrounds me as my eyes reach up to the sky.

I love to wake up each morning to the rise of the Golden Sun,
and look forward to the Sunset when e'er the day is done.

A rainy day even excites me as I watch the droplets feed the flowers in bloom,
looking out of my big picture window, from the warmth of my cozy room.

I love to hear the wind whipping wildly, it sends a chill up and down my spine,
as I lie beside a warm fire, and sip a tall glass of wine.

I truly marvel at the beauty of nature, the grace and girth of a big old tree,
and am so ever grateful that my eyes are able to see.

My heart just fills with rapture in each moment of every day.
There is indeed so much I'd love to do, so much I'd like to say.

If I could only write a novel, or paint a canvas of my soul,
then I would be in heaven, I would have surely reached my goal.

Is it because I'm getting older, and the time just moves so fast,
that I savor each precious moment, as if it were the last.

Evelyn Pesso

How Much Do I Love You?

If I had all the time in the world,
from eternity to eternity,
it still would not be enough to tell you
How much I love you.
If I could give you anything in the world,
where money was no object,
I could not find a diamond too beautiful or gold too pure to tell you,
How much I love you.
If I could say anything to you,
if I could speak every language on earth,
I would not be able to tell you,
How much I love you.
If I could hold you,
without interruptions,
I would never be able to hold you long enough to show you,
How much I love you.
The only way I find to tell you,
How much I love you,
is to open my heart and let you in,
I love you because you are part of me!

Dusty Raines

Untitled

Forever given to a passion that is a mere illusion of what I dream of —
I am lost.
My soul cries from the very depth in which life is sustained —
It is relentless.
Confusion overwhelms me as I plunder to my horrid end.
Death so slow it may never come.
Only to remain within me to torture with memories.
The fall has set in.
The trees have lost their leaves not one remains.
They blow helplessly in the wind exposing their jagged, crooked,
twisted branches.
It would seem they have died.
Only to wake to spring and new growth —
When all the leaves return, in full beauty and life.
Love is a bit like a tree, it may appear to have left
But the dream remains alive.
Love...
It is within

Mary Ashcroft

The Tooth Fairy

Oh, how I wish the Tooth Fairy
would come and visit me.
My friends have all each lost a tooth
some even two or three.

I haven't even seen a wiggle.
And when I try my friends just giggle.

Oh, if I could lose a tooth
I'd tell the world.
Now that's the truth!

I'd put it under my pillow
and hold it tight against my head.
I wouldn't want my tooth
to fall out of the bed.

In the morning I would wake to find
lots of money that would be all mine.

If a tooth would only wiggle
I'd be as happy as could be.
Oh, how I wish the Tooth Fairy
would come and visit me.

Angela Greenhaw

Hungry For Fish

Fishes, fishes in the sea;
Fishes, fishes look at me!
I've come to catch you one-by-one
Until my fishing time is done!

Oh, how I wish I had a fish
That lay on top of my clean dish!
Fishes, fishes can't you see
That you are looking back at me?

Fish, oh fish upon my dish
Don't stare at me again I wish!
Fish, oh fish don't frightened be,
I'll throw you back into the sea!

Angie Grimi

What Are We?

There's no such thing as accident.
There's no such thing as fate.
We all get what we deserve,
So let's all celebrate.

Our children will not spit on us.
They'ld never go that far;
Unless we refuse to be
Exactly what we are.

Eugene J. McLaughlin

The flamingos of Bonaire

The flamingos flew at sunset
Vanishing to Venezuela
To the ocean...
Returning at dawn like tongues of
Fire
And sudden suffusions of
Desire
In pink, yearning ponds of emotion.

Evan Jon Wright

Dreams

To live life each day as we see
To see only shadows of our dreams
We live life in the shadows you see
Trying to reach in and pull out our dreams

Jack Newcomb

Sacrarium Maximum

There's something growing green new
Where ever rain needs soaked dew
Wet trees sat, trees sat
The earth heals spirit time effect
Tomorrow wields supplant
Tomorrow went tomorrow went today
Yes, say you undid decay, yet
The earth thinks soon nothing grows
Sundays sun no one errs
Sight throws superficial
Life ends seed drop
Pour refreshing glance
Emerald deeds seem magical
Life ever reins supple, endless, simple.
Go on now wind did dance.
Bury your reflection near rainbows
Sigh, hint, tell, levy, yen noble excuse
Enrich healing
Go on now wind did dance

> *R. D. Capps*

Cool Water On Blacktop

When you were here (with me)
It was a though an angel
had come down to teach me
that there was a good kind of love;
That hitting, and yelling, and hurting,
and controlling were not a part of it.
You showed me I could walk (or run)
through the garden...to trust again.
Unconditional love you said.

All the things you taught me
vanished into the air like cool water
on blacktop the day you left...And,
now I walk carefully through the garden
in combat boots.

> *Taryn M. McClure*

Love Thyself

One should not dwell upon
Who they imagine to be,
Rather, we should focus on
Improving who we
Truly are!

> *Brian G. Sim*

The Old Attic

As I slowly walked up
into the hot damp attic.

Dust flew all around me
landing on old, torn boxes.

The floor creaked as I slowly stepped
on the tattered floor.

Each step I took, I
felt like the floor might
cave in at any moment

I noticed a light softly
coming in through the big
stained glass window.

Which made the attic seem softer
and more old.

> *Jessica Brown*

Thanksgiving

Starting in November, all the turkeys shake with fear,
Because they know that Thanksgiving Day is near.
They run, eat and gobble all year long,
Just to end up on our tables, nothing but bones.
With dressing, gravy, all the fixings, pies and cakes,
There's always more food than it takes.
Sitting at the table we say grace,
By thanking God and giving Him praise.
At the sound of "Amen", everyone stuffs their face,
You would think we were at the "World's Fastest Eating Championship Race".
Let's also, thank the Pilgrims for giving us this holiday,
By stepping their foot on Plymouth Rock that day.
The land was woods and the streets weren't paved,
So they sailed the Mayflower across the waves.
They had no idea what they would face,
But they trusted in God to lead them place to place.
God gave them this land and set them free to roam,
It's been named "America", but the Pilgrims called it "Home".
Now for this beautiful land they raved and raved,
Maybe...that's why it's called, "Land of the Free and Home of the Brave."

> *Dorothy M. Pearson*

Mom

This lady soft and warm with a touch as gentle as the dawn.
A smile that could turn the tide and make the clouds want to hide.

A heart full of hopes and dreams but only for her children it seems.
Tired and weary from years of strain, still gives her child a supporting refrain.

Once younger in her mind and soul this precious lady set her goal.
To put the world on its ear, to never wither under its sneer.

How can she be so nature sweet with those who caused her own defeat?
The only answer I can see is that she is content to be.

She's all that's good, all that's kind, she's all I need to settle my mind.
Who is the lady with a zest for life, she is my Mom, given by Christ.

All you have given is not unknown, that could never be with the love you've shown.
Your life, your love, your dreams untold, a certain warmth only you unfold.

Your smiles, your tears, worries, woes, whatever else only Heaven knows.
But in my heart you've a special place surrounded by love to keep you safe.

Should you be first to take the Journey, I'm sure God will know you're in a hurry.
For about you there will be a hue caused by the love you'll take with you.

Or should I be the first to part along with me I'd take your heart.
As I stand beside the man I will wait to take your hand.

Then together we'll take God's arm to be ever safe from any harm.

> *Diane J. Warren*

Beautiful Death

Serene and silent
Placid and patient
Breaking the boundaries from life to life.

He is scared and startled to see me stop before him.
Always anticipated my coming, but never expecting my presence.

As the warmth in his cheeks fades
and as the cold brush of death asphyxiates,
The tender moment of desolation and vulnerability captivates his being.

So I strike a pose for the graceful repose.
The taker of his life yet the mother of his eternity

His soul dances in my palm all the wisdom and
years of his age are lacking protection.
A pearl, without its shell
The long journey of death is near just beyond this willow.
Mortality ceased
In the last sensuous trance
the trance called death, mesmerizing death.

> *Bianca Guzman*

Evolution

This is hard land. Now the conifers tunnel the eyes with green
and the earth is quilted with stemtips.
But I have seen the fault planes close in like jaws.

Evolving is an art: You hone your pain to mastery.
Imagine that first day, the soft cords of your body wracked
in protest, the backbone screaming in your flesh as your gills fell

Into the sea behind you, each lung blinking in the strange air,
flickering streetlights in an unknown town.
How many scars you have collected just to see

That silly yellow sun. And the pain!
The stretching, the breaking into wing or blossom,
pain like you wouldn't believe. Yet you keep on

going, your blood deepening, your arms webbing
into flight. Do you see that I am speaking now even as my own skin
is breaking, growing back into

The red yawn of earth? Sleep turns you over and my blue breath dies
on the pillow. In the morning, your bones unfold
from a dream and you look

Outside to the scatter of maples as the ground open its pores.
It is the way of things. Someday you'll leave a skin here.

Robyn Art

Soldier's Dream

As I laid my head upon my pillow, I seen him.
There were angels flying above his head.
They were counting all the dead.
He looked form one to another, saying how can they kill each other?
Don't they know that they are all bothers?
When oh when will my children become tame?
Be their belief in Buddhism, Hinduism, Islam,
Christianity, or Judaism, they all bleed the same.
They came here to fight today.
With their lives they did pay.
All the rivers are flowing red.
From all my children who are dead.
He then came my way, this he did say.
Get up my son, and pick up your gun.
For you shall live to fight another day.
That is when I woke, right after he spoke.
Now I wait night and day for him to come and say,
Lay down your gun my son, your fighting days are over and done.

Jeareal Gravitt

Sureness

Loving life to the fullest extent, since you came into my life,
that heaven has sent.
"The angels" have brought us together, "so pure".
I know in my heart, I will always endure.
Endure in the love, that we share together,
that will grow, more as one, as we spend our time forever.
I have this vision in my mind, so clear.
It's followed with this feeling, that you will always,
Be near.
There's not one little doubt, or even a question.
For me, you will always be, an obsession.
An obsession of love, none, of selfishness in anyway.
That I want to show and share with you, everyday.
Everyday that we live, everyday that goes by, there won't be one day,
that the thought of you, won't pass by.
I breathe in deep, I feel it, in my soul.
In my mind, I believe, you have just thought of me also.
I know deep down inside, you care for me, as much as I do for you.
I have never been so sure, about anything in my life,
As I am about you.

Loreen Driggers

Fearful Dreams

And when the new moon finally fell
And heavy black clouds form
Distant victims felt my thunder
Like the quiet, before the storm

Out from shadows that can't be real
My dragons fill the sky
Children scream who once were playing
Mothers fall to ground and cry

Your pretty face hides fearful dreams
With skin now cold as ice
Open eyes in sleep forever
Run to hide in fear of Christ

And when the new moon finally fell
Deaths dark clouds formed
Every person feels my thunder
Like quiet— before the storm

Todd Douglas

Imagination

Awake my child
and you shall see
a wondrous world
for you and me
a dreamy walk
through land
and sea
through past
and present
past lock
and key
something wild
something mystic
something soft
all so majestic
thus comes a melody
sounding in harmony
from every nation
child let us use our imagination

Lorri Thoman

After You've Gone Away

If I had loved you less
would you have loved me more?
Would there have been more
Vibrant colors in our lives?
To help me now in my loneliness
and despair.

For now I am old
you are not here
I hear crescendos of a broken melody
I am left alone
to face the shards of pain
in my heart.

Veta Sams

A Cry for Help

He is coming up the stairs
He'll hurt me
Please God keep him away from me
He'll hurt me I know he will
He'll put his dirty hands on me
Oh please Lord
Don't let him feel my soul
Please take him away
He is cold, mean, and dirty
Please keep him away from me.

Galina Malykin

Joy

Joy comes forth when
everything is sweet and
special, like the love and
understanding that our
savior Jesus Christ give us.

Vernon E. Brand

Homeless

Hey mister, he said
with a big toothless smile
my name is Bob
can we talk for awhile

I'll tell you a story
about the life that I've led
a terrible story
of money, and dread

You see I haven't always
been this way
I had a family, a life
and business games I would play

I climbed up the ladder
looking for gold
what I did didn't matter
I was ruthless and cold

But now I'm a bum
I'm homeless you see
can you spare me some change
or will you wind up like me

Dennis Twitchell

The Vietnam War

A flat stone lying for 1000 years
Moving it took great effort

The thoughts of who it was
The thoughts of what it represented

As I put it under the tree
Not only remembering I could see

The three million under the stone
Once living but now turned to bone

Had they survived to tell the lies
We on earth might not be surprised

Daniel L. Hobart

Martin Luther King - Medicine Man

Kind-hearted medicine man,
Loyal, smart, and full of peace
Looking for the right kind of lock
Because he had the golden keys.

They keys, he knew, unlocked the door
Of a racism-free world,
Someone shot him dead on sight
Just as the mystery uncurled.

He made a difference for here and now
Open-minded was he,
Changed the wave of our thoughts, he did
Because he owned the golden key.

Karyn Griffin

A Wish For All Children

I wish for all children love and happiness,
and also understanding in times of duress.

I wish them true goodness and compassion for all, but also the
strength to endure what we have made them befall.

I wish them to grow with truth always at their side, to know that
their feelings need they never hide.

I want for them peace in every possible way,
to delete the word war and teach them instead to pray.

I wish for all children that they join together, that bias and
prejudice are a thing of the past and complete equality will be for them at last.

I wish them the warmth and gentleness of the sun,
the purity of streams and clear waters to run.
I wish them the freedoms of birds in the air, and the strength of the
seas to use on man's decisions with care.

Our children are born with freedom and we take it away,
I want them to keep it, to cherish it and to pass it on and be able to say.

"All children will be free of the wrongs of man's past, and because of
absolution freedom will be ours as long as life lasts."

Sandy DiBella Donnell

Love's Longing

The rain so gently falls
Like teardrops upon the face
As I through window stare knowing
That I shall never hold a place.

A place within your heart I've longed
Not so big yet not so small
For I've loved you Lo these many years
As others came and called.

I've watched you chase another
As I've waited oh so near
But you never looked upon me
Or said the words I longed to hear.

"I've" longed to hear "I Love You"
There's no other in your place
Yet you'll never look upon me
Nor will I see Love reflected in your face.

"I've" always feared the answer for your heart is not your own
It was promised to another Lo so many years ago.

As I gazed once more thru window watching again the raindrops fall
I knew they were not raindrops but tears, from rejections call.

Lorrie Jones

The Tale Of The Silent Bell

In my mind I saw history's flashbacks, each one a picture of time.
First the prints of hoofs and wheel tracks, then things of a more modern clime.

I saw a frame of new lumber, standing bare on a field in the past,
while a group of men, small in number, heaved and pulled to set a bell fast.

Years passed, now grave stones, crowned the hill,
the builders, long gone, were replaced, by a group
that could not remember the hardship and work that was faced.

I saw later on, as the scenes went, an old church, now empty,
unswept,...too many forgot...the bell silent
and a cloud of witnesses wept.

It was rung once a year, that quaint, and shaky old bell
in memory of those held dear in God's fold,
but it sounded more like a knell.

Then I had one view of the Morrow, of a cloud, and from it soft
singing. And One asked, yea asked in great sorrow,
"Did you vote to keep that bell ringing?"

Rev. Carl F. Kemper

Writer's Villanelle

Tradition cages fantasy; Destroy that ancient gate,
To fields of unmapped fancy; to fledgling poetry I'm lured.
Order comes from chaos. I will murder and create.

Within me, unexplored emotion paces prisons, and through the wait,
This restless captive whimpers, it longs not to be interred.
Tradition cages fantasy; Destroy that ancient gate.

Cities non-existent, beasts, heroes and their fate,
Await my embryonic parchment and fertilizing word.
Order comes from chaos. I will murder and create.

Some magic, lyric utterance could nurse the thoughts I'd state,
But syntax stunts fertility, and silence thus assured,
Tradition cages fantasy. Destroy that ancient gate.

Exploration beckons me, and yet I hesitate,
To embrace some human drama, or fondle the absurd.
Order comes from chaos. I will murder and create.

Though verbs and nouns are old, youth rejoins them when they mate,
With each hopeful writer's vision and untested, newborn word.
Tradition cages fantasy; Destroy that ancient gate.
Order comes from chaos. I will murder and create.

Michael Kirmaier

Seasons Of The Night

Flee me from this stoney night
Of withers cold trapped inside
With concrete froze and glazed with gleam
The moonlight brightly reflects the stream

I walk along this stoney way and feel the chill caress my face
And think of when the night was clear
From all this white cold misty fear
When moonlight shadowed treetop leaves
Upon the street still filled with heat

The ground and sky so full of life
Small creatures singing through the night
Till daylight rushes them out of sight
Greener than green was the world on that season of the night

I walk along this stoney way
And witness diamonds falling frail
All around the colors glow
Children laugh, people sing, the sleigh rides away with bells that ring

Whiter than white is the world on this season of the night

Nancy L. Keener

The Challenge

A cold foreboding restlessness surged the sparkling foam —
In gusts of filmy mist around a wretched ship — a home.
Gaunt sails scream out longingly for blasts of earthly air,
To refresh, fulfill courage, the mighty load to bear.

A blustery wind billowed sails in puffs of snowy white —
Like giant fiery dragons — this early morning sight.
Crystal spears of sunlight sifting softly through the mist,
And thunder with the blustery wind, and its sturdy iron fist.

The mighty ship sails forth in glee, a challenge to the wave —
Pulling, forcing, straining, in a ravenous churning cave.
Suddenly the crashing, pounding, roaring water gropes the stern,
Propelling, exploding, and smashing debris — an erupting, swirling churn.

A blackened rock, the deathly foe of this battered ship in foam —
A home, our world in the midst of war is charred like the siege of Rome.
Or again, the crystal sunlit spears could unveil the golden door,
Of equality, to a ship — our home, linking *Peace* for evermore.

Sandra Marie Davies

Is There Anybody In There

Is there anybody in there?
I'm standing just outside;
Looking through your vacant eyes,
I see your suicide.

Is there anybody in there?
I know the pain you feel;
Wasted tries of a lifetime.
For this you want to kill.

Is there anybody in there?
It's time to stand your ground;
Feel no longer hurt and guilt,
It's easy to be found.

Is there anybody in there?
Come out and face me now;
We'll reach an understanding,
And walk on common ground.

Daniel W. Million

Confusion

My knees start to shake,
when you're in sight.
My mind's filled with wonder,
my heart filled with fright.

When will this feeling stop?
When did these feelings start?!
How can I listen to my mind,
Without breaking my heart?

I'm so confused,
What should I do?!
I can't think of anything,
but you!!

Should I ignore you?
Or just give this time?
I can't think straight,
My heart controls my mind.

Olivia Odom

The Present

Lord I pray to restore
My child to four
Now twenty four
Twenty years of experimenting

Giving, loving, rearing
Twenty years too much
Discipline, suppressing
Bruising of tender hearts

Men can no longer be four
But before time
Elapses, passes, collapses
Lord please

Present as a present
To my son, himself
That he can present himself
As a present to another.

Beverly Emmons

Beginning

Before the middle and the end:
Before the hurt and the pain

Before the sadness and the sorrow;
Before you and after you...

There was the beginning.

Kris Morris

Untitled

You said you'd come and
  share all my sorrows;

You said you'd be there
  for all my tomorrows;

I came so close to
  sending you away;

But just like you promised;
  you came to stay!

Jennifer Shaw

God

God made the sun, God made
the moon. God made the evening
and the afternoon. God is great,
God is love, God comes from heaven
above. God made the birds, God made
the trees, God even made the
little honey bees. God made clouds,
God made flowers, God even made
April showers. God made every
living creature on earth, God even
made every child's birth. God made
you and God made me. God is
awesome! Can't you see!

Brittney M. Grimes

Inside

Keep searching for the truth
inside your soul you'll find
the answers to the questions
that lay heavy on your mind

Within the heart it lives
the meaning that we seek
the bonds that make us strong
and the faults that make us weak

Our future we must save
generations we should guide
so take your gaze from others
and start looking... Inside

Carolyn Wyckhouse

The Service Has Ended

The service has ended
The choir goes home
Look for my new helpers
No one to be found

Old-fashioned language
There's something wrong
Inherited money but nowhere to Rome
Donated money for two pairs of shoes

Tied up my pajamas
poured out the real wine
Threw in the white towel
But who gives a damn

Too old to stay clean now
The flowers all died
Can't stand any surprises
Am just an old man

The service has ended
The choir goes home
Look for my true helpers
No one to be found

Myron Watkins

Touched By God

My heart has known many a tear;
Many bouts with life and a multitude of blessings.
The years I had with my husband were full of joy and happiness.
Now I am left with the memories of our youth, our love, our hopes.
You see, my life has been touched by God.

Together we made a home for the greatest blessings of all, our children.
Words cannot reveal the amount of pride and happiness they have brought to our lives.
How fortunate I am to have such a loving family as well.
Another godsend from heaven.
You see, my life has been touched by God.

The thoughts, the dreams that once were a part of me, are no more.
They are hidden away as memories, memories that cannot fade.
I do not know what direction my life will take.
I only know wherever I go I am not alone; I have my memories, my children, my family.
You see, my life has been touched by God.

Shirley Burnett

Western Spell

I remember your warm voice weaving the words
Mending my soul across the miles
The stranger I trusted so quickly
Your maturity, my infinite insecurity
Cradled by promises you swore would never end

And oh how you impressed the sun and bowed to the moon
I ran quickly to try to capture the magic
while tripping over clouded romantic notions

You danced in the fingers of my flame
took hold of my reins; disappeared
Leaving me lonely with the silence of your beating heart

The distance between reality and a phone line became all too clear
when I looked into your eyes, felt you tremble; when I needed you

Confusion blinds my spirit as it rides a wave that longs to kiss the shore
I run faster on the sand
I grasp at stolen shadows and mark each parting hour
You are the bend that curves this endless path
You stare blankly at my struggle
Your boots stroll slowly through the dust
As you lose all intention and deliver another tear to my heart

JB Snyder

First Thing In The Morning

Sunlight weaves its way into my dreams
tick tock of the clock becomes bird songs out the window
I stretch my arms; reaching out to bring you in to me
However far, however wide, however long, forever pride
will share my inner desire hidden by commonplace appearance
Approaching the dawn, attempting to sleep; aching to feel you
alive next to me. Alone in my bed accepting my fate
All of a sudden a girl of desire, agile with fervor.
My eyes drift into early morning breeze; hands extend my dreams to yours
Floating into the upstairs of sanity retaining the bedtime of reality;
Understanding the longing to caress you with eyes aglow
is best first thing in the morning.

Matthew Frost

Mr. Ball

Once upon a time there was a man called Mr. Ball.
Sometimes over the telephone he made many a call.
Sometimes on the telephone he told the person he had lots of gall.
Once, Mr. Ball had a mighty fall.
He Mr. Ball landed on top of a barb wired wall.
That fall made Mr. Ball
have a lot of pall.
That was the end of Mr. Ball.

Wesley R. Berman

In His Eyes

In his eyes I can see his fear.
I kneel in front of him and whisper in his ear.
He is only 6 years old.
But, he seems old and lost.
How much for his little heart and broken bones?
How much will it cost?
He doesn't understand the things that happen every day.
He is only six, all he should want to do is go out to play.
His eyes are sad and he has something on his mind.
Oh, could please all of us just take some time?
To listen to the children:
They only want love, and a little good, and lots and lots of trust.
Good friends, some toys, and lots of help from us.
For when you're small you feel it all.
It takes so little when they say they hurt
so listen with your heart.
They depend on us, so always do your part.
Children are gifts and entrusted in our care.
Are you listening? Are you there?

Linda Wagner

So They Say That....

So they say that...life should be easy,
So they say that...it'll all work out,
So they say that...you might go crazy before you figure what it's all about,
So they say that...you're the strong one who can withstand whatever you're dealt,
So they say that...when it comes to difficulty you will never take the fall,
But, do they say that...you might not have the strength left to find this out before you hit the wall?
Do they understand what it's like to be the "strong" one, or the one who's not quite made it yet?
Everyone's life moves on around you to the goals that they have set.
Do they say that...you are the last one to achieve what you should get,
Do they say that...love will find you,
Do they say that all the money is spent, or
Do they say that...Yeah, she'll make it as soon as she's out of debt,
Well, the road is long and hard, and an outcome so messily drawn,
"I" say..."What the Hell went wrong?"
I try to be a good person, not doing anyone harm, but it seems to test its limits
   with what will pass by with no alarm,
So I sit and wonder when the time finally comes for me to
"Have It All", will I still ponder,
Do they say that...I was strong?

Sandra L. Overmohle

Baby Sister

In its truest form, a sister rare is so hard to find,
for it is made of many things in your special design.

You are a star that lights the way when darkness comes so near.
It is the warmth of your heart that always seems to cheer.

You are like a lovely song as you grow sweeter with the years.
You have a way to bring joy, casting away my cares and fears.

It seems so hard for me to say that which I deeply feel,
to thank you for your gifts to me, of help, trust and zeal.

Your faith in me that helped me succeed when I was down and blue,
was just the boost that I did need to see my troubles through.

Although the miles have come between and we can't see each other everyday,
I'd like to send my special love and then I'd like to say...

As we face our daily tasks, one thing is surely true,
my thoughts and prayers are there today with you.

So, little baby sister of mine, I just wanted you to know,
whenever your smile turns upside down because of your foe,

Don't let them put a shadow over your glorious shine,
just flip that smile back around and let them whine.

Stop twirling around like an Indiana Twister,
just remember you are loved, my sweet "Baby Sister".

Patricia Gayle Edwards

The Love That Died

It is time to say goodbye
To a love that died
you were my first real love
As I look into your eyes
I can see the love you tried to denied
We have loved each other for so long
We will always be in each other's hearts
As we turn and walk away
I will cherish the memories we shared
I will always be your friend
No matter how much pain we feel
As we go our separate ways
We say goodbye to yesterday.

Carolyn Matthews

Lollipops

Lollipops are good for you
Good for me too.
They are the best
For all the rest.
All kinds of flavors
Just like Life Savers,
My favorite is cherry
Also with berry
I like lime
Also the sour kind.
It's an awesome treat
And oh so, very sweet
I love lollipops
Because they're tops
They're tops
Just because they're lollipops

Stephen Kinnane

Message From Mom

Sleep well my little children.
Rest your weary eyes.
Listen to the silence.
You will hear my lullabies.

Wrap your blankets gently
round your tiny form.
Feel the air about you.
I am here to keep you warm.

Let your dreams flow freely.
Look into them and see
the loving eyes upon you,
fear not, for it is me.

Wake into tomorrow,
taste it, bittersweet.
Capture all its glory
to tell me when we meet.

Savor the fine fragrance
of happy times gone by.
Keep me in your memory
and smile when you cry.

Kathleen Ready

Until The Tears Began To Fall

As I leaned against the wall
I felt the tears begin to fall
I closed my ears and eyes
Against the vicious lies
You walked away
From me today
I stood tall
Until the tears began to fall.

Angela E. Penoyer

Life

All I believed
 never was.

All that I am
 doesn't matter.

All there is
 is pain

Because all that matters
 is gone.

Michelle A. Gordon

For Mom

Mother we love you.
We miss you so much.
Why did you leave us,
in such a big rush?
We know it was fate,
it still isn't fair.
Our family has lost a
beauty so rare.
Your spirit is with us
wherever we go.
It shines through our souls
with a glorious glow.
So Mommy remember
you are still in our hearts.
Even though we are worlds apart.

Kim A. Lamontagne

Butterfly

She's come alive,
Out of her plastic cocoon.

She can fly,
Able to reach the moon.

Metamorphosis complete,
Beauty has been unfurled.

Yes, she's complete,
vulnerable to the world.

Dale M. Camara

Our Love

A void is filled
As each day we build

Our needs are yet
Even since we met

You fill my heart
As you do your part

To help us grow

You love me so

There is a place
Leaving no space

Within my heart

Should we part

Life will go on
As we go on

And as we grow
We will know

That our love is true
Though it is not new

Nancy A. Brown

Untitled

    It was a moonless night and wind howled furiously. A blood red
candle burned madly flickering wildly like a giddy child. Yet there
is a strange comforting glow that echoes with raging fire; it is an
odd contrast to the dark bewitching night. Outside the bare trees
reach like long bony fingers to the sky; not even a wolf would dare
howl this eerie winter's eve. A shadowed silhouette wrapped in
a dark cloak stalks the night. It floats through the streets like a cat
on the prowl; a madman escaped from his cell. Not a sound is herd
this mysterious night. The witches know something is afoot, and they
watch with wicked ease as the angels melt away; and hearts are filled
with fear. Shadows cast on the walls, magic stirs the air. Evil
discomfort and blood curding stares are sensed with a shiver and
a shriek. No one will sleep this haunted night, the spirits are
afoot. They creep into your dreams, and you wake with screams;
screams that pierce this moonless night.

Keegan Gourlie

Grandpa

Dedicated to Grandpa Bennett
I sit on my bed and wonder
Why life is so short
Why you had to go so soon
I wonder if you're in a better place and full of grace
I wonder if you know how much we loved and cared for you?
I know we didn't always show it we thought you would always be there
We thought we had time
I wonder if you're watching over me
I wonder if you see what I see
I wonder if you miss us do you feel as empty as me
I know you are ok now I wish
I could say that for me!
I miss you grandpa!

Marsha Ritter

Suffering

The howl of a wolf is the cry from all human suffering.
    The mournful wail to which our grief can be
expressed for what we have lost and can't reclaim.
    From the Indians to the native slaves and on to our ancestors
we have inflicted suffering and destruction upon others and ourselves.
    We fight for freedom and unity, but we accomplish nothing.
For now it is our turn to listen and hear
    the mournful wail of the wolf.
We don't learn by taking which doesn't belong to us.
    But we can learn by others and share what we know which can help, but not the
destruction to which our forefathers showed
    To change what can be and improve what can't be
To rise above and overcome the ugliness in which we live
    or we shall forever hear the suffering
From the mournful wail of the wolf.

Gail Edwards

Forgiveness

In this world there are those days when things go wrong, then people kneel and pray
To God above for help and strength to lick the wrong in the human race.
When things go right, however said, they do not kneel beside their bed
Instead they forget that they might need thy help again some day.
They do not realize, however, that some people who need thee ever,
Need their prayers to be said, for a forgetting soul that is almost dead.
If one would only think right now, then none would forget and heads would bow,
And they'll know forever, everyone, that God forgives and no harm will come.
Some are so sure that they will go to heaven comes that day,
And yet, each in their own little way, at one time or other, will get
down and pray to ask thee for forgiveness so that they will never go to hell.
But instead to be with thee, and know forever that they've security,
in heaven always then with thee, and know from there what life can be.

Walter R. Sheldon

Old Woman In The Mirror

I look in the mirror, shocked by what I see. . .an old woman is staring at me. "Who are you?" I ask the lady. "Certainly you are not me, or I have gone crazy. My eyes have not sagged, below them has not bagged, my lips are still full, my skin has a glow. My teeth are my own!"

"Nonsense," she says, with a wink of an eye "You are looking at yourself...you and I. Years have passed by and my did they fly."

So, I reached out my hand to touch the old woman's face and as I look more carefully, I realize the woman I see, indeed is me.

"Look deeper than the wrinkles on your face, my dear, they will never erase. Instead look at the life you have lived, the love you have given, the sadness you have hidden. A smile cannot erase the aging of your face, but the twinkle in your eye is still as blue as the summer sky!"

"Think of the children you have raised and how they have grown. They are now seeing wrinkles and graying hair of their own. Life has passed on, old woman, can't you see? Nothing is quite the way it used to be. But don't look so sad. . .look in the mirror and take pleasure in the blessings you have had. Return the smile to your face. . .you have strength and wisdom that fills your Inner space.

And with that I stood and looked in her eyes...the same ones I have seen so many times and realized again how lucky I am to be growing old. . .for life is a blessing, so I have been told.

Jacklyn Seymour Mahaney

Moving On

As I enter this familiar place it seems so strange and cold.
Its emptiness, its loneliness, its strong familiar hold.

It grips me and it keeps me until my heart is sore.
It hurts me when I think that I can't walk back through this door.

I stroll back through the hallways with no furniture in sight,
And I look at all the shadows that once were filled with light.

I can hear the distant laughter that we made so long ago,
and remember all the times we've shared and how I'll miss it so.

The image of the sunlight that had shown down through the dew,
awakes me in the morning to a house I thought I knew.

The pictures that had hung there, on what's now a vacant wall.
The square of where it should be, where there's nothing there at all.

I feel a heaving in my soul, somewhere deep inside.
I feel the scars from the years and I take a different stride.

I feel than I am like a ghost floating through the past,
as I'm sorting through the memories, to try to make them last.

This house is now a part of me and forever it shall be,
the very living heart and soul that now has set me free.

Jennifer Marrow

Untitled

My dearest love...
My best friend, my wife, my life.
Where do I begin to thank you for the past wonderful years?
You've given me so much: beautiful children, a happy home,
a sense of peace that I'd never be alone.
We've shared laughter and tears,
and have always been here for each other throughout
all of these years.
I'm so sorry that I had to leave you, but I haven't gone far...
just look up to Heaven to that bright morning star.
I'm with you in spirit in the soft gentle breeze,
or you can find me in the white caps floating over the seas.
Always remember wherever life takes you, I'll be right by your side:
until we meet again in heaven my beautiful bride!

Debbie Stafford

Spring Is Here

Spring is here
I had to wait so long
now I hear the birds' lovely songs
No more snow
no more rain
No more being bored all day
I get to run
I get to play
I'll never stay inside a day
I'll always yell
I'll always shout
I'll turn my parents inside out
I'll ask for a puppy
I'll ask for a deer
I'll ask my Dad for a sip of his beer
He'll yell at me and whack me twice
Then he'll say did that feel nice
I'll scream, I'll yell
I'll run and hide
I'll be grounded till December, '99

Brian Boothe

Life

I was born in
the year of 1983

My parents are wanderers
They have a life made of dreams

Hebru gave me my name
By way of my parents

My father helped me with
my homework and my feelings

My mother gives me her opinions
What she doesn't like I don't do

My father told me I would be
a dreamer, a lover, a dancer

I haven't left my parents yet

I am a dancer
a collector of movies, love and people

Amber says I have
dreamt before I've became

I have craving for
wide open rooms
and girls that are ballerinas

Jessica Snyder

Mother

To my dear mother up above,
Couldn't you see, I needed love.
I never asked, to much of you,
I only wanted, to be loved too.
You never seemed, to give me, a glance,
All I wanted, was to be given a chance.
I was your child like all the rest,
But I know you didn't like me best
If I could have only, felt some love,
Maybe I wouldn't, be looking above.
My life has never been to swell,
I guess that's why, I feel like hell,
Mom if I make it to heaven above
Please will you show me a little love.
I hope I meet you at the pearly gate,
I want it, to be, without any hate.
All I want, is to feel your love,
If I make it to heaven above.

Janice P. Knight

If I Could Stop Remembering

We put a dream together
And suddenly now it's gone
Although you're lost forever
The longing lingers on.

If I could stop remembering
The love that we once knew
And set aside the memories
The longing love for you:
If dreams would stop reminding me
Of things that we had planned
Those haunting-wanting reveries
Of castles in the sand
Then life could be forevermore
A dream world in its flight,
For, dreams, like ships, go endlessly
And fade into the night.

If I could stop remembering
And have you near to me
Then empty dreams could wend their way
Into eternity.

Harry Pearlman

Lost

And for once shall
my soul relax if only for
the blink of an eye, and
shall my body slump from
the overwhelming relaxation
my mind has gone into, for
as to escape from all that
is reality although only to
return and dread upon it
once more.

Jason Briggs

To Love And Lose

To love and lose
   is nothing new,
And if you don't watch out,
   it could happen to you.
So when you pick,
   and pick you must.
Pick someone that
   you can trust.
Because if you're wrong,
   and wrong you could be,
you'll end up a broken hearted fool,
   just like me.

James B. Trapp Jr.

To Margaret Smith

" 'Twas the 29th of January
100 years ago today.
   A girl was born to the Smith family
It seems she came to stay.
   She made life happy for every one
she was so bright and gay.

She sought to live in Florida
   in her declining years
where life was really happy
   and where she had no fears

We were the benefactor of her decision
   to come to this great state.
And now we have the opportunity
   to help her celebrate."

Orla L. Birt

I Should Have Seen It Coming

We're barely holdin' on, when I'm in way too deep.
Happiness — it's been no friend to me, but forever after ain't
What it's all cracked up to be...
When you're feeling like a headline on yesterday's news.
I feel I've been danglin' on a hangman's noose.
Loneliness has found a home in me, I've tried to need someone
   like they needed me.
I opened up my heart but all I did was bleed,
They don't make a bandage that's going to cover my bruise.
Pull me under run through my veins to a place where I feel no pain.
I should have seen it coming when the roses died,
Should have seen the end of summer in your eyes.
I should have listened when you said good night
You really meant goodbye.
Ain't it funny, how you never ever learn to fall, you're
Really on your knees, when you think you're standing tall.
But fools are know-it-alls, I played that fool for you.
Baby I thought you and me would stand the test of time.
Now it's so sad that whatever we had ain't worth saving.

Tami Olson

Ode To Past Homes

Yards demolished, trees are felled,
round houses where my family dwelled.

An eerie feeling, walking through,
to think that these were all once new.

Were furnished once with special care
a favorite chest, a rocking chair.

A dining room for all occasions
Christmas meals and celebrations.

To my lonely homes, so far away
their lamps unlit and fires gone gray.

Their ghosts like dust motes float within my brain,
"Will the Circle be Unbroken" dimly heard that sweet refrain.

Fragments of the whole cloth from which my soul was made,
lie moldering in these ghost homes from which we all have strayed.

All soon to be just memories,
in too few people's reveries.

Replaced by structures, sterile, tall
with cheerless rooms and concrete walls.

These grounds where my dear family massed,
a little bit of history passed.

Faith Byerson

Untitled

Remember when the nights were dark, and your mind was washed
away, in a place where there's no sign of hope even sunlight
means no day? I remember thinking I'm all alone with no place I can
turn, I kick at my troubles, I scream and I cry but the bruises
continue to burn. Destiny awaits me and time is still ticking but
that's not the part that's so hard, it's adoring my future when I
know the beginning is the final chapter of my start. Seeing my
future is not on my cast, not part of my character at all, I've found
a light on red, my mind says stop, I hit dominoes once and they all
fall? I'm hurting so and I can't depend on first aid, please show me
a world where I can count on tomorrow and these feelings will
somehow just fade. I'm trying, don't give up on me, if so I'll be all
alone, with God as my witness, I have no resentment, just a dream
to uncover on my own. Now I leave you with this thought and I
hope you'll remember if your mind is ever washed away, there's a
place and a sign of hope from God when the sunlight brings in a new day.

Tawana Adams

Life

Awaken on a bed of flowers, inhale the crisp air of morning.
Open your eyes wide to watch all your dreams and fantasies
dance and frolic before you. And wow could it be you
smell a faint exotic breeze, you hear some music oh
so soft you wonder if this is just a dream. You feel
the ground you dance, you prance, then you freeze in
your tracks in dreams you can feel. So you see
an apple tree nearby you pluck one and taste the
delicious fruit. You feel lonely oh so bland yet
some comfort comes off hand. A voice speaks, oh a voice
speaks so loud and clear, it tells you not to fear
for this is where your dreams come true "oh trust me I know
I trust you." Another voice appears it replies, "Don't worry
dear, follow me and have no fear, don't listen to him."
    A third and final voice has come, it says "Nothing just a hum.
Who will you chose the 1st and 2nd fellow?
She stammers then she said I chose the 3rd a decent fellow".
Everything around her disappears "oh my how queer" she wonders.
"You're in heaven", a voice replies. Then appear some friendly eyes.
"How did you know to chose me?" "Well," she said, "they were harsh
and the wise don't speak."

Sarah Lamberg

My Child

I never knew what the word precious meant - until you.
Priorities took a sudden turn.
What once would have been a treasure,
Was now only a passing thought.
You were all consuming.

Who could know that sunlight in your hair would be my gold,
And your smile my obsession.
That a touch of your hand would be my strength,
And your tears, my heartbreak.

But then, who would ever think a crayon scribbled masterpiece
Would rival the greatest work of art,
And your silly song, my favorite sound?

I thank God in silent prayer,
With every breath and conscious thought,
He gave me you.

I must have done something right, to be entrusted with such a gift...
a tiny soul.

As long as you are happy, healthy, and mine,
I have all the riches in the world,
In my heart.

Paula Kidd Casey

Once In A Lifetime

Once I held a love like no other so divine.
Then one day my arms were empty, my heart crying inside.
I was left behind, I was only holding hope that
I would find that love again.
Once you were gone I did not think my life could go on.
So many years passed on, some without any communication at all.
Then a letter came with the news I dreaded to hear.
You were in a relationship again, happy you said settled with a family.
I thought I had lost you forever, so now I too should
get lost in a relationship, even though I knew no one that
I could love compared to you and the love we once shared.
I continued to dream and meet you there, for if dreams
really do come true, I knew one day somehow I'd be with you again.
Today is the day that once again in my lifetime I hold that love like no other.
My arms are no longer empty and the tears of my crying heart are kissed dry...

Joyce A. Vaccaro

Leaving

If you leave me, will I cry?
Will I live or will I die?
Life goes on, but hurt is felt
Like being whipped with a belt

Why must we carry on this way?
Can't we save it for another day?
If we get on our knees and pray,
Maybe this will go away

leave if you must for fear of love
Hold your head high and look above
Love comes at various times
And we stop it without using our minds

Look with your eyes hear with your ears
Be prepared to deal with your fears
The time may come along with tears
maybe soon maybe years

Nikki Sweet

Related Strangers

Strangers may meet
And learn to know each
other well —
While we — who are of one blood
And under the same roof
do dwell —
Never reach under the
surface
To know each other well.

Still, with maturity, there
is understanding —
With a fragment of
knowledge.
And this is the
strangeness of life.

Glenna M. Kozlowski

Trains Drive Me Wild

Trains drive me wild
Not when I was a child
They come and sit,
go slow and stop

I throw a fit
Fly over the top?
I can't, I'm late
I hesitate
I turn around
another exit not found

Just a minute
What's that I see,
the last car?
Couldn't be.
But it is by far
the very last car

Don't stop!
It did
I'm late again
Trains drive me wild!

Kristy Breithaupt

Untitled

I wish, my dear, that I could be
A breath of wind or scent of rose,
That I might sweeten thy repose
Or gently soothe thy cheeks for thee.

Richard E. Pritchard

His Will, Mine!

Jesus is my reason for being!
I'm a part of His wonderful plan.
I must tell others of His love,
fulfilling my part in this land.

There's naught but to fulfill it.
I can't see another way.
Jesus lives, and I must tell it
to the people who love to play.

He is my reason for living,
His love, my controlling Hand,
to see His light in the darkness
all over this weary land.

I must go tell them this story.
If it hurts, tis naught but His will,
to let others see His bright glory!
Oh, the glory of doing His will!

Kathleen A. Darbee

Final Letter Of Love

Don,
It broke my heart to lose you
but you didn't go alone
a part of me went with you
the day you left this home

A million times I'll miss you
a million times I'll cry
if love could have saved you
you never would have died

Now to your resting place I travel
the flowers are placed with care
no one knows the heartache
as I turn to leave you there

If love could build a pathway
and heartache could build a lane
I would walk that path to get you
and bring you home again.

Love, Dad
Ben Watson

Solitude

I wander in a limited world —
So dark, yet free,
    And in my world, I can conceive
What glories light beholds.
    Though sometimes in my solitude,
With ears my only guide —
    The joy and peace,
    If I were deprived,
    Would lend a greater thing to
My distress of daily life and man's
    Incessant greed.

Glenn E. Irwin

Death

What burden hangs upon thy
broadened shoulders?
The consternation of it all
mutes the mind.
Such a dismal happening,
One that grasps the body,
Obstructing it into eternal rest.
Stillness...
Quietness...
Death.

Nina Hegel

Borrowed Structure

What a magnificent structure the Lord made when He,
Constructed the human body of Adam and Eve, ongoing to you and me.
The mechanism that He put together lasts nigh on to seventy years or more,
It functions so precisely understanding it can be a big chore.

Legs that keep us standing and walking all our lives,
Arms that lovingly hold objects husbands and wives.
A heart that can be tender with many moods, but keeps ticking,
While teeth chew up our daily rations and goes right on clicking.

A digestive system that works only second to none,
Yet a plumbing factory is individual for everyone.
Including a production system that works most every time,
Yes, and taking care of His structure can be very fine.

Suffering, pain or heartbreak, can be a blessed event,
To those not heeding things like being content.
Many things are only material possessions on this earth,
But the greatest possession of all is a human body's birth.

The Lord has made it possible for us to borrow this life,
Take it, honor it, steer clear of constant everyday strife.
This body is only yours to use during this lifetime,
You must return it, when to Heaven you will climb.

Floyd E. Fountain

A Wish Is A Dream Your Soul Makes

Dream with your soul to embellish your wishes with animate desires,
Not when asleep, but awake and aware of the world a new day brings.

Never be afraid or ashamed of what you whim,
Never feel foolish or naive when you can born virgin cravings instead.

It is what you want and have always wanted,
To find it you must dream into a realm of unforbidden ecstasy,
You will fantasize beneath the thick blankets of your soul.

'Tis the only way you shall uncover what you are yearning for,
Because a wish is a dream your soul makes,
Not a fairy tale — a blessing.

Katrina Cebey

Garden Garden Of Love

My love for you is like a tree planted by the waters
Rooted deep—deep in your word. Thank you father
You have made me part of your garden of love.
Sent straight from the father above.
Every soul and life that you lead to me will become a part of your garden of love
Garden of love, garden of love
Oh how love-ly all kind of beautiful flowers, big ones little ones, old ones, new ones,
Tall ones, short ones, red ones, black ones, yellow ones, white ones brown ones,
    all kind of colors.
It's your garden we're working together for your purpose "love"
This garden is so beautiful!!
My eyes have never seen a garden like this and
I don't think I'll see anything so great until
We get to heaven...

JoAnn Munford

Seaman's Prayer

Spirits of the Ocean, Rulers of the Sea,
Controllers of the Waves, and Keepers of the Tides,
I pray thee, hear my plea. I beg forgiveness for my people,
And pardon for my race. Your sacred Waters we defiled,
And now my soul is in disgrace, because of the ignorance of man.
Yet through our marring, you've prevailed,
And your beauty still shines true and steady, for all the Universe to see and covet.
I would perish in the cause, to save our Ancient Waters
From the folly of mankind.

Abigail Rencsok

This Is Us

This is where plastic clear death shone in the skeletal corner
  This is where hopeless melancholy stood in feverish eyes
   climbing beside desperate knobby women
Shaking grubby signs of wishful freedom making their chains sink deeper
While the men looked on their smiles holding filthy meaning
And the blaring God of T.V. cradled the child's cool steel
  This is where war was faraway and at a mother's wasted doorstep
  This is where the young dragged themselves in listless and vacant steps.
This was darkness. This is world. This is us.

A light shot through quietly it stepped
Into the filthy ragged bodies becoming blooming souls
And before they knew the glassy stare stood back and saw knowledge
Hope.
And carefully they crawled to the light seeing their molded flesh
In a whisper under soft tears the luminescence healed the wounds
'I am here...come to me'
Basking in the light the woman child and man stood
Becoming large trunks stretching toward the limitless sky
Throwing away...coldness, hate, darkness...
This is light. This is paradise. This is us.

   Maryam P. DiMauro

The Vision

  While sitting quietly enjoying the company of a good book and
soothing jazz, I was struck by a vision of unparalleled clarity.
  The vision transported me to a place and time infused with
infinite possibilities and a chance to feel genuine happiness.
  I discovered myself in the presence of someone whose beauty could
be felt even by the most insensitive people in existence.
  Looking into her deep eyes, I glimpsed a passion in her soul so
intense that it awed and overwhelmed me.
  Her presence emanated a strength of character that became evident
as she opened my mind to her beliefs on moral and social issues.
  As she spoke, the manner in which she formed her thoughts
appeared leading you to clearly understand and respect her views.
  Then I realized that she was not trying to be anything, she was herself:
the confident, strong, loving woman of my future.
  During this engaging conversation, I was stunned by the wealth of
experience and wisdom she amassed in her life's travels.
  In time, all things must come to an end. So did my vision, yet not
before I had a chance to embrace this woman and seal her presence in my heart.
  I have recognized the lady of my heart in an extraordinary person
whose grace and presence have granted me an opportunity to obtain happiness.
She is very real.

   Casey A. Jackson

Life

We use that word so many times,
Yet there is no real definition of it.

To some it may be the act of breathing and carrying out simple tasks,
Merely doing a job and not feeling any part of it.

To others, life is a journey,
Walking a narrow road with millions of different paths;
Some that lead to doom.
Some that lead to delight.

Others say life is a river,
And we must steer clear of the eddies and rocky waterfalls that
  we will always encounter.

And there is also the theory of defense.
Something is thrown at you,
You respond.
and that's all you do.

I can tell you what life is:
It's feeling happy, but not one hundred percent of the time.
It's caring about what you do,
And caring about those you are with.

   Melanie DeBoer

Father's Advice

The days get longer
and the nights get shorter
how long must a man work
and still not get ahead

The young get old
and the old pass on
hopes and dreams disappear
with every new day

But you must fight
and hope and pray
that time does not pass you by
and you can see your child's dream

   Richard Garcia

Real Cool?

Real is far from cool
  cool is nothing real
When life seems too cruel
  many lose their zeal

Cool is nothing real
  real is far from cool
Life is not a deal
  nor a petty duel

Real is far from cool
  cool is nothing real
The mind of a fool
  has no true appeal

Cool is nothing real
  real is far from cool
Good you want to feel
  live the golden rule

Real is far from cool
  cool is far from real
Crack your priceless jewel?
  Pray and God will heal

   Wes Cauthers

I awoke amidst a Twilight dream

I awoke amidst a twilight dream
So much against my will
Stood shocked, confused, and overjoyed
Beholding such a thrill
Mother dear surprised me
Standing there in grace
With silver hair and God's good smile
To brighten up her face
Mother there's so much to say
You know I miss you so
I never really came to terms
With the fact you had to go
I kept some of your habits
To remind me you were here
And the things that are so strictly you
Are the things I hold most dear
We stood and talked of many things
More feelings now than facts
She seemed perfectly contented
With whatever death exacts
She left me with serenity....and
As I shook off my dreamy state
I pondered now reality
Was I, perhaps, awake?

   Rick H. Lajoie

Untitled

The moon cries a tear for you
Farewell scorched starlight.
In the arms of sleep,
take me down.

Beyond my hopes,
There are no feelings of remorse.
To forgive love there is no such task.

No reasons to do such.
Future of a shattered past.
I lay restless thoughts to rest.
In the darkness of a shadow.

Without a care in this life
Scattered thoughtless thoughts.
Solitude etched upon my heart.
Confined to hate.

Virginia Grady

David And Goliath

Goliath, the giant,
Was a very fine fighter.
David was a boy
And very much lighter.
The glory of the Lord
On David shone.
And he slew Goliath
With a sling and stone.

A pearl from God's word,
A story of old.
From the life of a prophet,
And very well told.

John F. Romann

Poetry

Poetry is beautiful, it comes from
deep within I open up my heart,
and it flows right through my pen
It's just so simplistic this paper and
ink it shows my emotions, and it
tells what I think Poems seem
fragile with their verses and
rhymes but poems withstand all the
signs of the times Poetry is
something that man leaves behind
for others to ponder and run
through their mind Perhaps it's a
way to see someone else's' point of
view of perhaps it's a kinship with
someone who thinks like you.

Rick B. Taylor

The Pain

All the pain I hold inside,
never want to let it fly.
Afraid I'd hurt, afraid I'd cry
although I can tell no one why.
All the pain I have inside,
I want to kick, I want to shove
afraid to punch the ones I love.
I try to show that I care,
but I mess up and do not dare try again.
The past it haunts me night and day
of all the screaming and all the pain.
Although I sigh I know why,
God gave me them with loving eyes.

Kristall Luehmann

Maybe This Time, It Will Be True

Nothing hurts more than being betrayed by a love one.
You feel exposed, helpless, a sense of vulnerability.
I'm usually more careful, but I never stop doing good,
Maybe this time, it will be true loyalty.

Time tells me we should never stop making new friends.
Some last, others come to a disastrous end.
Situations tell who's a real friend and who is weak.
There's a possibility this time, it will be true friendship.
I've been in love a lot, or so I thought or got it mixed up
with my good heartedness.
I would trade any of those feelings, I feel blessed.
But there's a particular lady I met that made a lasting
impression on me, maybe this time, it will be true love.

Sometimes I feel people lose their sense of self,
Their values of doing right turn into doing wrong,
When pushed by the world, we sometimes feel we're not strong
By looking inside you'll see that you have true honor.
Most people live their lives in search of a dream,
In realizing it, they might've hurt people along the way in the process.
One day maybe by failure or having to be hurt, they will take a closer look within,
Being humble, they might say, maybe this time, it will be true success.

Ahmed T. Saidu-Kamara

Unspoken Whispers Of Her Thoughts

Morals of respect quarrel with the passions trapped deep within,
for love there is no answer but the acceptance of her unspoken word.

'Tis the dawn of new vision, dreams, and adventures to confront the
frontier, yet immigrant fathers grip onto the past of ideas, of control, and of respect.
Metamorphosis of one's opinions and independence are rejected by this father, whom
his youngest daughter leaves silent gaps in my heart to wander in quarrel.

One never believes love at first sight till the moment it is executed
with both presences, causing kinetic volcanic eruptions bursting rage
amongst the battles of passion.
Souls search for one another at the galaxies glittering edge having
never crossed paths, and yet I find my other half in life to only leave her trapped deep within.

Surrendering to the outskirts of illuminating synapse neurons
confronting parental consent to marriage proposals, thus catalysising
only the conceptualization of the two drifting souls having only sighted the five senses of love.
When requesting the daughter's hand in marriage I was rejected by her parents conform-
ing to old traditions, that the older sister should be
wed before the younger replying "No" in answer.

Parental guidance evolved me from a chameleon rebel that surely would have been lying
amongst those who wish to be remembered, by their concrete words chosen by their
beloved whose souls are separated from their hearts acceptance.
I dare not defy her parents word out of respect for my family, so I lay in a sea of tears
pondering the outrageous rejection having never to hear her unspoken word.

In silence I lay my shield of armor to rest as I journey into life's
battles awaiting the end, hence forgotten as a common figure with unspoken whispers
carried by the sailing wind of her thoughts.

Keith A. Nagara

Winter

The powdered-sugared hills of snow mound up around us,
And the long, sharp, scissor-points of icicles reach down from the eaves,
As the children stretch up to them with delight,
Eager to taste the first drip of melted ice.

A winter wonderland has surely been created
As nature her magic does weave,
The snow sparkles in the sun, prisms of color are seen,
Caught in the dark branches of the trees.

Can there be anything else so full of wonder
As the quiet hush of new fallen snow,
As it lays a white blanket so smooth and so clean,
Brightening up the dark winter's day!

Melanie E. Green

A Trip To Fatherhood

We start as little boys, who cling to mother's breast so tightly.
We grow, fuss, kick, eat, and make things, and us unsightly.
The love mom showed us was oh so warmed, with her smile.
But in our prankish selves, we could not resist, we acted guile.
As we grew, learned, and listened to mom and dad a bunch.
Head-strong, we did not climb, our brains were out to lunch.
We did resist our parents example, their guiding ways so right.
Instead we chose a prodigal journey, then proclaimed God's light.
We search, study, work, and strut to find that perfect mate.
Let us ask in prayer, not put aside, or be unreasonably late.
We exchange our vows and rings, we except His love and grace.
Our attention, a wife deserves, a kiss, a hug, knowing it's not a race.
I pray to be that father, of a child to teach, protect, and guide.
We now have our child, His gracious gift, to tootle at our side.
We share hearts, and spirits with His word, though depthful study.
Our daily bread, our deep beliefs, so strong, not as a pane with putty
I now cradle our infant child, within my arms that securely cleave.
The strength of our faith, His love, and grace with which we weave.

George E. Pech

Patience, Thy Name Is Woman

As she struggled for respect and equality throughout the years, she
was told. . ."Be patient. Things are as they should be."

As she fights pain and discomfort every month for years, she is asked to "Patiently endure it."

As the life in her womb wreaks havoc on her body, she is told..."Be patient.
It's only for nine months."

As the paroxysms of labor pains engulf every fiber of her being, she
is told in the delivery room to "Be patient and don't push yet."

As she is sexually harassed on the job, she is warned to "Be patient
and forget it if you want to 'keep this job' or 'get ahead.' "

As she Defendant's lawyer tries repeatedly to convince the court that she was "asking
to be raped," she is told to bear this indignity patiently.

As she struggles with the decision to abort or not, she is asked to
patiently stand by while she loses her right to choose.

As she is still treated in some cultures as less than a human being,
there she is told to "Patiently accept it."

World...Take Heed! As long as injustices, double standards,
discrimination, abuse, and harassment still exist, she will patiently
confront and destroy each one until they are only a memory.

Patience, Thy Name Is Woman!

Jose Haddock Jr.

Let Me Tell You, If You Think You Know Who You Are

How can you tell me that I don't feel the love for my people, the
people of America, when all I can think about is this, and how
can you tell me that I can't feel what you are feeling? When all I
can see in my nation is this. So if you think you know who you are,
why are you on the street selling drugs to those crack heads, or
bums, just for you to make a living; you tell me that you know
who you are? If so, why are you selling drugs for some dealer,
who's making more money off of you than you can even imagine? But if
you want me to tell you this, at least I know who I am, and what I
want to be, because I have a future ahead of me. My life is the book,
and this book is the bible, and that's what I believe, now let me
tell you if you think you know who you are, selling drugs to people
that want to die, selling drugs to those that want to get high,
selling drugs to those who are in pain, selling drugs to those who
want pleasure and game, does not make you into anybody these days,
but it will turn you into nobody that wants to be somebody, so try to
change, because you are a fighter in God's eye and that's how I can
tell if you want to be somebody, that never again wants to be nobody.

Latoria Chaney Ortiz

Poet's Song

Weep, poetry.
Press the pain out.
Transparent language,
    this of tears.
See through,
underneath,
the creased face of life.

Exult, song.
Keep joy on record.
Artisan's sculpture,
    these tears.
Revel in the shape
of perfection,
washing the face of life.

Gayle A. Carlson

Flight Of The Eagle Scout

Soft feathered, dependent
Like the fledgling
entering this world
to search...
Taught by noble leaders
to think, act, follow
with outstretched arms, like wings
into the vast world
accepting challenges,
overcoming fears.

Now prepared to fly
like the majestic bird
with gleaned knowledge
and wings that span immense chasms
and unknown precipices
Outward... into the waiting world
Upward... to the sky
where God smiles upon
another great
Eagle.

Gayle T. Gale

Tomorrow

Thinking ahead of the days that will be
Wondering what will happen to me
I think of the things that mean so much
Their glory or their personal touch
How will my life be in years ahead
Will I succeed or fail instead
I think about it an awfully lot
Life passes by as I'm lost in thought
As I sit in an easy chair
Holding my life within a stare
Thinking ahead of the days that will be
Wondering what will happen to me

Lisa Schrieber

My World

It looks like a white sea
As the birds fly upside down.
What is this world I see,
What causes it? Maybe love
The trees are still
Although a twister just went by.
Is it caused by love.
That lion is climbing a tree,
As a duck chews on a bone.
When ever I'm with her or
Thinking about her, this is my world.

Chris Cunningham

Time Line

Yesterday
Yesterday I was a child;
a child so full of Hopes and dreams
that depended totally upon Me.

Today
Today I am Youth;
Because of them (Peers)
I casts my Hopes and Dreams—aside.

Tomorrow
Tomorrow I will be an Adult;
an adult with no Hopes or Dreams
And they (Peers) know me Not.

Harold B. Mayes

Thanksgiving

Thanksgiving
The Pilgrims chose this day
To set aside their labors
So that they might pray
For their many blessings
In this their chosen land
And with their fighting spirit
Our new world began.

Thanksgiving -
The day we set aside
To thank the dear Lord
For all that He did provide
The gathering of our friends
To dine with us this day
And everyone is thankful
Each in his own way.

John J. Busher

The Widow

Too busy when the kids were small
They grow—you take a job.
Anything wrong? Your fault.
Don't ask questions
    they represent rejection.
Can't do anything I want to do—
Protect the fragile male ego!
Mine is smashed and shattered.
Sexual problems? My fault.
Can't discuss anything-
    he calls it arguing.
So here I am 50 years later
Old, empty and understanding at last
What a misogynist is—
A cider press for women's spirits.
A widow these many years
And yet
    he lives.

Janet F. Thatcher

Kityo

The war of a child's laughter
Over the murmuring cries.
A smile lit dimly
By the feeling of sunshine
On one's back.
Blood flowing across the skin
As if it were snow melting
On a mountain top.
The child swims through
And finds a friend.

Amy Lynn Peacock

Such A Spirit

With gentle love and caring heart; she took me by the hand.
She listened to your every word and showed me where to stand.
She wiped my tears, turned my head and said that you love me.
We walked in quiet baby steps, then knelt before you on our knees.

I gazed upon the cross, so big and dark; full of sad despair.
She whispered "You have it wrong, it's here your wounds repair."
"Don't weep my child, your son is safe in God's loving care.
Blessed Mary is his mother now, he's in glory everywhere."

"The Lord has listened to your prayers, he understands your heart.
My child, rejoice! He has saved your son, you and him are not apart."
In a voice of adoration, she gently placed me in your loving arms.
In your mercy and forgiveness, Lord; you help me carry my cross.
    I fear no harm.

"If God can see into our hearts, don't you understand?
He knows your son, he loves him so, he holds him in his hands."
I gazed into the soft brown eyes, so radiant with your love and care.
She truly listens to your word, Lord. Your message she's eager to share.

I thank you for your blessings Lord, in heaven and on earth.
For Sr. Martha, her gentle guidance and my family's rebirth.
Only in your love could my eyes receive their sight;
But such a spirit, Lord; in the one you chose to show me your light...

Geri Conley

The Trees Of Life

People are like trees.
They begin small and helpless;
Their bodies are fragile leaves that at any moment may not exist.

As they grow and mature,
They become stronger and tougher
To the harsh problems that chill them but eventually are gone.

People find their space,
And they grow in it.
They thrive on the nourishment that others around them can provide.

Bending with the problems that eventually blow their way;
They survive the chill of life
And adapt to the weathering.

Some are unfortunate and are cut down very early in their prime.
The rest become old and bent,
With the inevitable passage of time.

In the end, only the ones who receive light and care
Will survive the longest.
The others will fade and blow away.

Lisa Currie

The Inventor

Lost in a world of tumultuous thought...chasing dreams and solutions
in his mind...the look in his eyes is a wonder to behold, the far-away
land he haunts is his alone. From deep, green valleys of peace and
resolution, to craggy, almost unapproachable mountain tops of challenge and risk.

He travels on with a certitude that leaves others far behind him.
Sometimes his steps are slow and cautious, other times he leaps from
rock to rock, as if in a gambit to gain an advantage. Staunch and
steadfast, he rarely wavers from his intended goal. His endurance
to solve a problem and call into question, each aspect of the
possible solution is inspiring. Examining the details and re-arranging them time and again.

Until a glimmer strikes his imagination...then a full-flame ignites
and fireworks are in those shining eyes. Piece by piece a new
creation comes forth in a heartbeat. He gently tucks it inside the
chamber vault in his mind; locked away, nurtured and protected like
a child, then with pride, he brings it into the sunshine and holds it high.

But soon the crags and caves are calling to him. His eyes drift and
he is off again..., to explore, find challenge and bring forth new
lights, from a far-away land he haunts, that is his alone.

Jan Wagner

191

Birds In My Backyard

There is a bird in my backyard,
chirping and chirping away to the dull, dull female.

There are many, many kinds of birds
like blue jays, cardinals, robins, and
many other kinds of birds in different continents.

I like to watch different kinds of birds high in the sky soaring,
and chirping away to cheer the female up
from sitting on the eggs so long in the breeding season.

In my backyard, there is a hummingbird feeder.
If I look out the east window about every twenty minutes
a hummingbird comes to the hummingbird feeder
to drink some fake nectar.

I love to watch birds soar high in the sky,
chirping and chirping away making lovely songs,
and the males what beautiful colors,
and the females blending in with the trees,
all the birds make our world a better place.

Max Leon Lesert Lockwood

The Place That I Call Home

Hello there, dear country! How much I have missed you.
For in the big, wide cities - they have too much to do.
While here in the big, wide country - there is time to see and hear
The chirping of the beautiful birds and the sound of the wind so clear.

The rushing of the waters - rushing into the river and out
The waves up in the marsh weeds sound as if they are trying to shout!
The buttercups and dandelions are as thick as they can grow
Narcissus, lilacs and many more are putting on a flower show.

The dogwood and many other trees have decorated the land -
Each tree putting on new clothing and showing it off where they stand.
The fluffy clouds are wandering as if they don't know where to go
But the sun is determined that it must come out to help its friends to grow.

While deep down in the minds of man - the question always arises
Could this creator, whom we call God be giving us so many surprises?
Who else has the mighty power as He to create such a beautiful earth?
No man - not even machinery can to so many things give new birth!

Then, there are my parents who love me that live in this dear land!
They helped God make me who I am - and I think that they are grand!!

Judith L. Holland

Harmonics Or Complaints Of Angels Who Built The Big Bang

The tall tale tellers said the earth was built in seven days.
The angels were appalled. It had taken them, they said, sixty billion
light years to redo the stars and to construct the Earth and Solar
System. "We lit the fires of the 'Big Melt' and had our co-workers,
the 'Holes' and the winds, shepherd the old stars into the fire. The
stars, most all came in, for it was time...like elephants to their
graveyard." Angels said they made bowls of fire, and fire-angels did

the work of separating, recombining and gathering plasma for pouring
into the black holes going by, or into holding bins. They flapped the
frigid cold into fissures for places to rest. In between stints of
churning and pouring, they rested. The fires made a mighty roar and
sound crackled in all directions.

The angels said they used the sound for making black holes and for
energy and making matter. They said the "holes" made the roadways for
carrying energy and star matter to where they planned to put a new
earth and a renewed solar system.

From the "Melt" they went Southwest to where Jupiter was anchored to
the bottom. There was hard frozenness and another resting place
for ancient universes and black holes piled up. They said it was them
who built the earth for something to do.

Carol S. Cairns

So Cold And So Alone

The snow falls.
My true color is disguised.
The burden is heavy.
My breath is short.
I lie deep below —
this pain unexpected;
so cold and so alone.

Shall the warmth ever come?
Will this freezing soon cease?
The seconds become hours,
and the hours create eternities.
I lie in these inches
that seem to be miles;
so cold and so alone.

I, a single blade of grass
drowning in a sea of millions
like myself ponder this nightmares end.
I lie in the vast whiteness
my tiny green protruding;
yet so cold and so alone.

Alison Caldwell

First Born

'Your laughter cures my heart
   from all it's troubles and sorrows
A hug and kiss could rescue me
   in case there's no tomorrow,
The sparkling light of the
twinkle in your eyes
   is enough to surround
   the World of different skies.
A perfect tiny smile
   walks with your bliss
At my life's end
   I shall regret
   Those days I miss of
   your sweet happiness...

Audrey Corey

Thank You, Lord

Thank you for the sun above,
And the ever-ripening grain.
Thank you for the friends we love
The stars, the moon, the rain.

Thank you for the world you made
Your son who taught us love.
Who died and in the tomb was laid,
Who reigns in Heaven above.

Forgive us for betraying you
And causing you such pain.
For every time we hurt a friend
We betray you, once again.

Gladys S. Wolfe

Life

Life is beautiful isn't it sweet
Everything about it is totally neat,
When you were born life began
and God had his own special plan,
Maybe you are an artist maybe you are
Faithful and true that may be God's
Plan for you, your life will
go on hand in hand it will be just as
God planned then you will die
and life will end, but you will go
to heaven and be born again.

Shane Rhodes

Autumn Reverie

Leaves burning in the Fall
Bring back lost days to me.
The pungent smoke ascending,
 Envelops me.
Days spent on high green hills,
Companion of the breeze,
Lying, through sultry noons,
 'Neath trees.
Sky's quilt of azure blue;
Cloud patches, muslin white;
Wind sobbing through a tree,
 At night.
The sparks dance wild and high.
Bright gold and gypsy red
Turn to dull, gray ash.
 Summer's dead.
 Edith C. Wilce

Different In Every Way

Lord is as beautiful as a butterfly
as great as a mountain.
Lord is as small as an ant
as warm as a flame.
Lord is as strong as a hurricane
as cold as the snow.
Lord is as gentle as a breeze
as bright as the sun.
Lord is as light as a feather
as dark as night.
Lord is like all of us
different in every way.
 Tonia Swavely

Waterfall

Waterfall who cleanses the earth
Forever flowing through the mist
Over all of the rocks and life
Supreme in its world of magnificence
Each drop of water fresh and new
Replaces the old on the riverbed
No single speck of their remorse
Can keep the misfits from driving ahead
They come together joined as one
To form the mass of royal power
No living thing can break the force
Or they the mighty will devour
He crashes down upon the stone
Not slowed but merely strayed
From his original discourse
Onto a path he freshly paves
He knows no enemies or friends
Just objects trying to encase him
Nature finds a means of freedom
Destroying our attempts to frame it
 Jason Visci

Captured Quickly

She looked in my eyes
Although we did not speak
My eyes answered hers
And the answer was Yes
Then I knew, as she did
Of that feeling - captured quickly
That feeling of caring
And the joy of sharing
That wonderful thing
Called love
 Byron Gregory

Love Leads Us

Along the path of life
Love lights ivory candles
That shine so very bright
Like strong and silent soldiers
They show us the way
And line the winding road
That we walk day by day
Each and every glorious one
Unique in it's own right
Signifies a day, a kiss,
A smile, a sigh, a night.
Happiness, laughter and yes, even tears
How they do brighten our hearts
With memories of past and present years
And even though there are times that they may not shine so bright
When the whisper of an angel's wings dims down their glowing light,
We must remember this, my dear, when we feel too weak to stand
That the love we've shared is strong enough still...
To light the candle we hold in our hand.
 Summer Gallotte

Mining The Mind

Writing poetry I find is like mining for gold hidden deep in the mind.
A little nugget may be found but there has to be more to express the
thought and put it down, so deeper into the mind's shafts I explore.

At times many little nuggets I find in my mine and I quickly put them
down on paper, I like the thought and want to expand on them more and
they can't be forgot, whether they are serious or for a little caper.

In the mind's mine there is gold, silver, bronze and tin also some gems.
I love it when I find some of them. And I may wonder would
these gems be of interest to other men?

Deep into my mind's mine I love to explore and when I start digging
and begin to find gems, I don't want to stop. I want more and more.
Sometimes I bring up "fool's gold" that is only tin. And if I
showed it to others it would disappear like vapour from the minds of men.

I am thankful for those master mind miners of the past, whose mines
were full of gold and precious gems, who left poetic beauty as a
legacy to inspire little miners like me to dig deeper within and
hopefully come up with something too that will last.
 Jean Bryan

A Grandchild

Two little eyes look up at me,...what a story they do share;
Sometimes they ask a question,...like, "who," "why," "what," or "where?"

It wasn't so very long ago, they looked at me and said,
"Who is this person who's often here?"..."Even lifts me out of bed."

But now those little eyes are filled with wonder, awe, and such;
A twinkle of mischief sometimes says,..."I knew I shouldn't touch!"

Two little hands reach up for me,... there's a purpose - that, I know;
A need to be held,...a kiss or hug,... some "cuddling" before you go.

It wasn't so very long ago, those little hands would grasp
A "blankie,"...or a shiny rattle,...or a finger, they might clasp.

But now those little hands can pick up food and stones and toys;
Play "peek-a-boo,"...push food away,...cover ears, if there's too much noise.

Two little feet come running to me,...two feet with wiggling toes;
They curl right up into my lap,...faster than anyone knows!

It wasn't so very long ago,...they could only stretch and kick;
They moved so much when you would cry,... And demand attention quick!

But now they go where YOU want to go,...they even wear all kinds of shoes;
They step on ants,...they jump in puddles,...skip, hop,...whatever you choose.

You're growing up, my little one,...and it ALL is happening so fast!
It's what you MUST do,...I realize,...but your "babyhood" soon will be past!
 Marcy Webster

193

Children

A smile is always worn, displayed for the world to see.
Always bewilderment in their eyes, as they live in an endless fantasy.
Their world consists of imaginary things,
of fire breathing dragons, sand castles and kings.
Knights in shining armor, damsels in distress
pretending to be someone in costume and dress.
Free from all the worry and care as they live in a world they don't know where...
exists pestilence, starvation and fear for they listen to all but seldom hear.
The cries of children unlike themselves
with no clothes on their backs or food on their shelves.
There are no toys to be played with, not a doll is in sight
and they shiver as they sleep in the cold deep night.
Yet perhaps if we gift one small toy misused or not played with to one girl or boy,
and the thick woolen blanket with one tiny hole to keep warm and cozy one tiny soul,
and the under-sized shoes too small for our son are given away to those wearing none,
or the clothing outgrown, no longer in use to help ease the pain of a child's abuse,
then their world might consist of less pain and sorrow
and we could look forward to a brighter tomorrow.

Maureen Mary Brezinski

Memories

The pitter-patter of little feet adorn my hallways,
As though time will always let it be
The business of crayons, stories, coloring books,
Bats and balls, trucks and cars will soon fade into memories

Memories of nap times when no one is sleepy;
Or goodnight times when just one more story is read;
The quiet finally comes; the memory remains
The pitter-patter of little feet.

Time passes as little ones grow
Away from story time, and cuddle time;
It now turns into events such as school — friends;
But the memory will always remain — the pitter-patter of little feet.

Amy Forakis

Sonnie

"Who's that baby with a great big smile
  It's my little girl

Who's that child laughing all the while
  It's my little girl

Who's the graduate with such grace and style
  It's my little girl

Who's opening packages of happiness before walking down the aisle

  It's my little girl!"

Shirley S. Hirsch

Lost Language

I travelled through a colored wood and vanished from this world.
I came alive inside a dream when I was but a girl.
I saw a deer that ran so swift as it bound past me,
And when it ran I caught its eye which seemed so wild and free.
There was a pond that shone so clear, the fish they swam in air,
And when they swam, it almost seemed, the pond, it wasn't there.
When I awoke from this dream that gave me such a thrill,
I heard the wind blow through the trees which gave my heart a chill.
The wind it spoke to me that day in a tongue I've never heard,
But yet, somehow I seemed to know every single word.
The trees they whispered softly, about things they've heard and seen.
The chipmunk squeaked and told me how the men had been so mean.
The river flowed and as it ran, its color a darkened brown,
Told the tale of man and pollution, the cruelness made me frown.
Then I thought about my dream and about reality,
And at that time, I realized, it all depends on me.

Amery Christina Thurman

A Loyal Friend

Kitty cats and puppy dogs
Whiskers and tails
You will always have a friend
When all else fails
They know when you're happy
They know when you're sad
They never hold a grudge
Or even stay mad
They forgive you when you yell
They forgive you when you kick
A pat on the head
Seems to do the trick
A spit and spat, a bark or a yelp
Usually means something's wrong
Go get help
A leap up the stairs
A chase down an alley
A typical game of tag
There goes Brutus and Sally

Crystal Rhye

Abandoned

Abandoned,
Left here alone,
In this place,
That's supposed to be home.

Left here to fend,
For myself,
Like some discarded item,
Upon a shelf.

All alone,
With no-one around,
Left in a place,
I'll never be found.

Worst of all,
Oh the very worst part,
The place I was left,
Is in my heart.

Daniel I. Harpster

Dream

Life is but a dream,
So it may seem.
On day one from hence we come,
Hither we go to and from.
Each day is a new beginning,
An ever desire of winning.
Giving over all, always trying,
Living, laughing, working, dying.
Is life but a dream?
Is it all that it may seem?

Carol Etto

What Is Home Without A Bible

What is home without a bible?
'Tis a place where day is night.
For o'er life's be-clouded pathway
Heaven can shed no kindly light.

What is home without a bible?
Is a place where daily bread
For the body is provided
But the soul is never fed.
What is home without a bible?
Is a vessel on the sea.
Compass lost and rudder broken.
Drifting, drifting, aimlessly.

Louise Williams

My Valentine

You are so good to me,
You know just what to say,
And you always seem to be,
Gentle in every way.

You know how to care,
Every time we're near,
The things that we share,
I will always hold dear.

You are so special to me,
I melt away at your touch,
I want us to be,
Together so much.

Please be mine,
My Valentine.

Nancy Petersen

Hidden Treasures

Love is a gift of joy—
Beyond Measure,
A blessing, a promise
a moment to treasure
a gift from the heart
that never stops giving,
that makes each day special
and makes life worth living.

Greg W. Scroggin

My Brother - My Angel

Every time I'm missing you
All I have to do is be myself
The way you laugh, I laugh
The way you cry, I cry
Sometimes it's frightening
But I always end up smiling
Because I remember
When you were here with me
All the good times we shared
And it doesn't seem scary anymore
Because I realize we're still together
A part of you is inside of me
Forever and always
You are my brother, my friend
Helping me out with today's issues
Tomorrow's dreams
Little Chuckie
How strong you were
Tears of steel
Heart of Gold

Marilu Kameliski

School Sounds

By my desk
   Sounds of pencil's clatter
   Sounds of classroom chatter
Clatter and chatter
Keeping me from working
Across the hall
   Sounds of children squealing
   Sounds of bells pealing
Squealing and pealing
Keeping me unworking
In the library
   No sounds of squealing
   No sounds of pealing
No squealing or pealing
Keeping me working

Megan Carson

The Sailor's Wife

I lie awake and softly cry, listening for his sleeping sigh.
I know that when the dawn's light shows, he'll smile and say
   "It's time to go"
Then suddenly we're on the pier — my last chance to hold him near
I bite my lip, try to be strong...but six months seems so very long
   "I love you"
is the last I hear him say as he slowly turns and walks away.
I stay and wait to watch it go — USS Kitty Hawk with her men below
Some man the rails and give a cheer:
"Before you know it, we'll be here!"
When it's finally gone out of sight, I come home for my first night
of an empty house, no more a home. Finally, I go to bed alone.
I lie awake and softly cry, lonely for his sleeping sigh.
Here today. Gone tomorrow. To get through this, I must borrow
from the joy that used to be...and know he's coming home to me

Susan M. Wagner

Anything You Ask

Anything you ask of me, anything you want me to be
I'll be all that and even more, and someday you will see
That my caring goes much deeper, than you ever did believe and all
the love is there for you, for you to just receive.
You need not look, to know I'm there, I'm with you in your heart
And even though you may not have known, I've been there from the start.
I know you're bound to another. This I understand
Because I, too, made a lifelong promise, to another man.
But it doesn't change the way I feel and I'm not asking for you to show, whether or not
you care for me, because this I already know.
I only need you to be my friend, to let me hold you in my heart
And remember this poem and its message and the feelings it's meant to impart.

Debbie C. Edwards

What Ifs

In the night as I went to Bed What ifs got in my head with a leader named Fred;
What if I'm in trouble or trapped in a bubble;
What if I'm sent to Japan or maybe lose a hand;
What if I get eaten by a croc or have my head slammed into a rock;
What if my friends don't like me or I get stung by a big bee;
What if I'm late or I'm not so great;
What if I get sick and die will I start to cry;
What if I can't blink will my head shrink?
The day is good and right on there but as nighttime comes so does a nightmare.

Jurle Edward-Lloyd Gaver

The Elvish Hunter

The elvish hunter, with longbow in hand.
Has no need to hunt in a band. Because he knows every crack, creak,
and bend in the land. And when he wants, his form will change.
To something wild, vivid, or even strange. As his favorite, the wolf, he will roam the
range. From bird to beast he can easily tame.
Or muster something up, that will put a wizard to shame.
To him, even the great dragons are fair game. Kind at heart, that is he.
When he deliberately lets an attacker flee.
Or puts an injured animal out of its misery.
So brave is he, with shield and sword. He won't even run from an orc horde. But still to
battle he will never look forward.
Because once he joined an infantry.
Nothing was left after the attack of the enemy, But an old oak tree.
And from this tree he makes his home.
From the outside it looks like a giant wooden dome,
But from the inside it's like an exciting poem.
He could do anything but play the fife. Once he even made a magical knife. So I guess
it's safe to say he's always led a noble life.

Brandon Paul Ricks

Forgotten Memories

A sudden flash bursting flames.
The world has gone without a thought.
Everything that lives for tomorrow has died in six minutes of sorrow.
The human and animal races are no more than memories.
Not a cockroach stands in the waste of mankind.
All that is left is flesh and bone.
The winds blow across sand and rocks.
The only thing that moves is darkness and time.
The memories are gone.
The super powers have made their final mistake.
The golden years are nothing more than memories.
There's just a planet of dust waiting to be reborn.

Michael J. Martinez

It Is Finished

As they stand below me they think that all is lost,
If they really knew what's happened, would they feel a loss?
If they knew what's really happened, they'd fall on bended knees,
To worship their Creator throughout eternity.
I look upon their bodies, they're lame, worn and bent,
I take them now my Father, for that is why I'm sent.
My men look upon me, with tears streaming down their cheek,
Give them the power to be strong, but keep them mild and meek.
A soldier is looking at me, I say, please come abide,
His only answer came to me, when he pierced my side.
The crown of thorns is pressing, my strength is almost gone,
His face has turned from me now, I must do this all alone.
The soldiers now are laughing and casting lot for my clothes,
The robe, it has no value, it's just a mockery from my foes.
One soldier stands upon the hill, tears his face has stained,
He...I think, understands. That today a lamb was slain.
The clouds are swirling above me, time itself is still,
I believe you could hear a whisper, a mile from Calvary Hill.
A thunderous eruption suddenly sounds, I cry "Father, it is done."
And my eyes finally close to death, it's finished and Satan knows we've won.

Betty Jo McGee

Photo Album

I'm sick with anticipation, I'll wait longer, just don't forget that I am here
I'll just whisper my hopes right in your ear. I understand how you
feel, you don't want to hurt anyone
you want to make the best choice, that's what I want, but I cannot
decide for you, I'm getting sick of myself
the mirror is not my friend anymore, just a mere picture, I cannot break
A painting that's not changing, that painting is so familiar
yet, I do not know why, the feelings of it are trapped inside, it's not understandable
It's just another world, just forget about the painting, look at my eyes
Just don't go past those pools of blood, beyond my messed up lies

Courtney Bartlett

Isolated

My dying friends laugh at their own pitiful, rueful lives
Their voices just images in the far off distance of the unknown
There is no one there anymore to support their joyous cheers
Just a meek shadow in the corner that means nothing
No one knows, and maybe no one really cares
But my sorrowful life of never ending uneasiness and surprise now bores me
I don't want anymore
I don't want anything but to be a faded smile on a stranger's face.

Troy Heiland

How It Always Seems

Past, present, and future,
What have they to offer,
In a world full of hatred,
Leaving no such kindness,

Days, months, and years,
What ever will they bring,
As loneliness and sorrow,
Hold their steady pace.

Seconds, minutes, and hours,
What ever could they tell,
For friendship and love,
Cannot exist as one,

And in the end, when all is through,
And the hand of fate is dealt,
For a friend turns to be a lover,
But no lovers ever depart as friends.

Albert J. Marchant Jr.

For Who Knows?

Evans learns
Differently
Thank goodness!
Evans will
Think differently
what a blasted relief!

I have never known
anyone,
who thought like
everyone
to do anything
different.
If no one thought
differently
we wouldn't be here.
So thank goodness for
Evans
for who knows?

Irene St. Aubin

All My Life I've Dreamed Of You

I really thought I knew
now I see it wasn't true
you'll always have a place
in my heart
even though we are apart
you'll be loved by me forever
even though I see you never
how long will my love for you last
before I can forget the past.

Jennifer L. Strege

A Forest

In a forest green with beauty
Birds and insects fly there gaily
While the squirrels by the meadow
Roam about the morning dew.

And at night you'd see this forest
Caressed by the golden moonlight
And the cool breeze gently blowing
Create a very splendid sight!

In this forest live the reindeer
Live the rabbit and the beaver
But out in the distant jungle
Lurk the beasts that all men fear!

Ernie Turla

Our Love For Each Other

When Spring pushes Winter away
It brings the flowers for a day
When love pushes sadness away
It brings happiness that's here to stay
The seasons come then disappear
When love comes it's forever here
Summer sings its joyous songs
And makes the world so bright
Our love for each other how it longs
To be forever and be so right
Autumn brings the galeing winds
And paints the world in color
Our love we have that's deep within
Can ne'er be like another
When Winter prevails once again
And brings its warning with a start
It blows its cold across the sand
But it's forever warm within our hearts

Charles D. Jansen

Cherished Memories

My grandma's things,
So precious to me,
More precious than I thought they'd be
From Paul Masson to a pillowcase
A picture of a younger face
These things so dear, so hard to keep
Will keep her here,
In memories

Lillian M. Kulage

Pain

For My Hero (Austin Padgett)
In the tiny pieces of glass,
The broken mirror of my past,
I see how the love of life,
Opposing death, and pain, and strife,
And with this before my eyes,
I begin to realize,
That death is a part of life,
And that pain relates to strife,
But worst of all I see in vein,
Part of love and life is pain.

Rhonda D. Phillips

Untitled

The darkened black eyes
Fall beneath,
Carrying mixed thoughts and emotions,
Describing/exploiting the pain,
Melting flesh and blood,
Boiling fresh blood.

Eyes that see through
Psychic stares
Psychic flashes,
Reminiscing and dancing upon
the failures
That are present in the mind.

Black tears
Seep out
Staining ivory skin

Falling to the ground
Slowly dying,
Suffering
At least no more will be felt...
Demise.

Chadra Guerrette

Don't Say Good-Bye

It's alright to have a little pain, it's okay to have a cry.
But please always remember, you don't have to say good-bye.
This world is full of many gloves, thou temporary they may be.
But the soul that emerges from this glove lives on through eternity.
Every person loved her, every person cared. Every person has
memories, that can now, and forever be shared.
So please always remember, life will not stop at the end of this day.
Life is forever, if you choose it that way.
It's alright to have a little pain, it's okay to have a cry.
But please always remember, you don't have to say good-bye.

Netta McCracken

A Best Friend

A best friend is hard to find
It is not someone you've only known for an hour or two
A best friend is someone who is always there
Someone who is willing to drop everything just to listen
A best friend is someone who knows how to make you laugh
Someone you can always have fun with
A best friend is someone you trust with all your heart and soul
Someone who always knows when you're down, when the rest of the world doesn't. it
takes a lifetime of knowing someone before you know they are your True Best Friend.

Sarah M. Haug

Rest In Peace Mr. Dirge

Whence Came The Disarray
From the fire and burning ashes came the children blinded by tears -
Never in the legacy of their luxurious barter did they expect the
preceptor of their fears - Ravage the waspish who desecrate the
peacelands and resent diverse pride - With ruthless speed and sinister
strength the wrath of the chameleon will halt his stride -

The Agony Of Waspish Pride
The chameleon slew the wasp whose hateful heart painted blood's
crimson ground - Scowl the spineless swarm who abandons bravery in
conception of winds airshattered sound - Wreckage of the serpentine
eruption will reverberate the underpinning of the prospect -
Neglecting to gaze with hawk's eyes leaves swine in the grasp of
death's grim suspect -

Uncoiling The Powerful Injustice
Before the hawk could grasp it the serpentine inferno fell upon the
swine with radiant fury - In their nemesis they discovered
the lunacy of two orders acting as executioner, judge, and jury -
During the seventeenth hour after the intrepid explorer sails
the extensive path - An enormous predator's waylaying destruction
will prove a gruesome aftermath -

Travis James Griffith

Through The Eyes Of A Child

A child is conceived, what does he see? A world of darkness, as quiet as can be. It's
warm and safe inside his little world, just as a clam protects a precious pearl. Today!
Today the child is born, a time to treasure not a time to mourn. Through the eyes of this
child, what does he see? Colors and shapes as blurry as can be. Five years have
passed, he's now a little boy, enjoying a life of love and toys. He sees the people
around him, so happy and kind, people sharing and helping others weren't so hard to
find. Now sixteen. Through the eyes of a child what does he see? A world that isn't as
sweet as it used to be. Drugs and cocaine are becoming a big issue, his friends are
pushing him to use. He sees no future, if he were to try it. He's a confident young man
today he still denies it. We all can change, I know we can. Eight years gone by, the
child is now a man. Through the eyes of this child what does he see? Drugs, crack,
a threat of war and poverty. The love he used to know is love no more. That word
HATE, finally came forth. A young man sells crack to his mother. "I want to be
just like you," says his little brother. "Killing your unborn baby is a sin," they say.
Will you have enough room in your home for them to stay? Tomorrow. Tomorrow.
A child is conceived. Through the eyes of this child, what does he see? Nothing.
Nothing. He never came to be.

Geneen Marshett Simmons

Heard Before A Death

Beneath the empty ebbing gleam, forever flows the bloody stream.
Beneath the shadow of his smile, we shall wait a little while.
Then four horses shall dance around, Four Horsemen shall ride us down,
and all lost beneath that sound, but the roar that shall resound.

What waits us who slumber keeps, our dear ones gown fast in sleep, and
echoes still linger on, and we are gone, we are gone? What waits us
when tomorrow morns, and poppies before the sun adorn iron crosses
silent on our mounds, and salted tears have fallen down?

What waits us, when senators words send bodies young to fields unheard
and our souls unwillingly yield, leaving empty the father's field? What
waits us, when mother gray recalls the songs of yesterday, and upon a
name should chance, and there rest a tearful glance?

And tears fall down. And, we the young shall the heartbeat never
quell, for we do not upon our souls wish our brothers' blood to flow,
For the seas of dead before us stand, across we reach with weary hand,
that our nations shall forever be in peace, as forever in death are we.

The world silently awaits the morn, when Shores of Dunkirk no longer adorn, and the
whispers in tomorrow's breath, is an anthem heard before a death. Down four horses go,
and Four Horsemen follow slow,
To the valleys where gates will keep, and we can rest in peaceful sleep.

Michael F. Enos

Miracle

Soul O soul once as dark as night.
Lifted by the gift of angel's flight.

Born into the darkness of Sheol itself.
Surrendered unto the glory of the light.

As the tranquil beauty of a rose is marred by the thorns.
The dawn of light is from the deepest darkness born.

Unveil your heart to hear her melodious song.
Take sustenance in the honey of her offering.

She toucheth your soul in its darkest hour.
Lighting your way back to the path.

The sacrificial pangs of her labor upon sweated brow.
Taste of her tears, taste of the sweet dew of truth from her lips.

Revel in the miracle of the gift of rebirth she offers
    unto your very essence.
Throw yourself upon the merciful alter of her sacrifice...

Sandra Adams

Hey Group, Am I Good To Me?

I pour myself out to you like vegetable soup in a bowl;
You sort through and keep the good things from my soul.
I hate myself, berate myself; you defend my rights for me.
You verbally shake me, startle me, try to make me see
We all have a dark side but we have to let the good show.
Nurture ourselves, be kind, gentle, let the child within grow.
I hurt me when I'm cruel and mean to the girl inside my head.
I torture her, abuse her, scare her when I wish her dead.
Where does that anger come from that bubbles up from within,
Lies I tell myself, self inflicted wounds that won't mend?
I'm like a little child lost in a black and ugly room,
Constricted and constrained, no place for myself to zoom,
To take wings, fly soaring high above the rest.
I've got a God-given life, you help me see it best.
Starting here, starting now, I'm throwing an anchor out.
I'm going to practice good self-talk, learn to say No, never shout.
I want you to be my witness to the promise I make to me.
Continue to be my soul's eyes and strive to help me see,
By being honest, objective, straightforward and true.
Please don't give up — the girl in me cries out for friends like you.

Linda Hollywood

Untitled

Black of night
Dark of cave
Cold of Ice
Fury of battle
Ugly of sin
Wrath of God
Life

Blue of sky
Light of day
Warmth of fire
Joy of child
Beauty of nature
Love of God
Life

Tony McGuyer

A Teardrop On The Floor

From out of darkness
your light did shine.
Within your smile,
your eyes met mine.
I felt the birth
of a brighter day,
But wait! Your smile
just went away.
And as your head
did slowly turn,
I felt my heart
for you did yearn.
I know not what
you held within,
when I saw your face again.
A tear had fallen
from your eye.
Someone or thing had made you cry.
All you left here to adore,
was a teardrop on the floor.

Steve Terry

Open

Today I am still in darkness:
The closet door is shutting.
A beam of light gives me hope
that tomorrow will offer a new way.
What must be done
I can see and almost touch.
Yet I remain numb.
This Utopia is a dream
that I must chase and catch.
Somebody
grant me
my serenity

Greg Miller

Kissed By An Angel

My life's been kissed by an angel,
with hair as red as the sun;
Blue eyes full of mischief,
so happy at one year young.

Together we'll climb mountains,
and sing with birds above;
We'll bask in Christmas sunlight,
then sleep in winter's glove.

My sweet most precious daughter,
so much love you've made me see;
For my life's been kissed by an angel,
when God gave you to me.

Victoria Ashton

Thinking Out Loud

Always look for rainbows
that follow the rain.

Celebrate the wonderful things
about this world.

And when tomorrow comes
do it all over again.

Remember how full of smiles the
days can bring.

And believe that what you search for
you will see.

Take time to smell the flowers
envision today as a gift,
and tomorrow as another.

Always keep planting the seeds
of your dreams because if you keep
believing in them, they'll one day
come true, and will blossom for you.

Jocelyn C. Bailey

A Spirit Is...

Spirit is you,
Spirit is me.
Spirit is she,
And spirit is he.

Spirit is Mom,
Spirit is Dad.
Spirit is happy,
And spirit is sad.

Spirit is day,
Spirit is night.
Spirit is strength,
And spirit is might.

Spirit is discipline,
Spirit is esteem.
Spirit is confidence,
And spirit is theme.

Spirits are pilots
Spirits are musicians.
Spirits are artists,
And spirits are electricians.

Tony Ashworth

Now That I'm Old,
While I'm Still Young

Time passes swiftly
Slipping through my hands
I look back and wonder
Have I done all I can

Places I haven't gone
Things I haven't seen
Is this just the beginning
Or is it the end for me

Can you be so old, yet young
Can you be so young, yet old
So many things I've done
So many stories I've told

So many things to come
I haven't yet begun
I'll live life to the fullest
Oh, what a story when I'm done

Angela Poland

Morning Fog

In the mist of the morning fog I gaze upon an ominous scene
Of twisted metal and shattered glass
Of mangled limbs and shattered dreams.
I heard a voice call my name, from where I do not know.
A crying voice, a loving voice, but the face it would not show.
I tried to move to find the voice, but my feet I could not feel.
Then I realized where I was. My God this can't be real.
I have so much I need to do, so much I need to say.
I want to sleep another night and wake another day.
They gathered round to take me away, I cannot speak what I need to say.
"I'm still alive, oh can't you see. Don't place your death sheet over me.
Please God let me speak. But alas I cannot say, the very last words
That need to be heard,
"Please don't take me away."
I realize now, I watched the scene, from the safety of my bed.
I've got another chance, to say what should have been said.
To all the people in my life, who have showed me unending love.
I want to say, I love you too. A great undying love.

Dennis C. Greene

Beyond The Clamor

Silently I fight the Clamor inside my head, its will is stronger than mine,
    spewing my thoughts into distortion. "Peace!", I plead, before I finally resign.

Stripped of my memories, I feel empty, abandoned by Love, and the anger
    consumes me as the past is fading, and I find nothing beyond the Clamor.

Life moves and surrounds my stillness, only time is not the same as before.
    I wonder why no one helped me, why no one heard the Clamor.

Returning now inside my head, fewer distorted memories are now dimmer.
    Ache fills my body, and I become confused for not having gone beyond the Clamor.

I pray morn heals the emotional turmoil. Clinging again to Love, I remember!
    The joys of Life, and I learn "again" that happiness must lie beyond the Clamor.

Dare I go into the darkness of my mind, to the emptiness approaching.
    Dare I attempt to ration with whatever seems to control me.

Ever so slowly, I surrender in my weakness to the ogre of despair,
    praying if only I were disciplined to Faith at each encounter.

And then a calm emerges within me, surrounding me in an unfamiliar rapture!
    Ah! I learn that letting go, alone, is that which takes me beyond the Clamor.

Linda Testa Terrell

This Love, This Life...My All

Let me wrap you in my love and I'll take you home,
There you'll find an Eden, from where you ne'er will roam.
I will shield you in loving arms from any raging storm,
I'll kiss your trembling lips to calm and keep you warm.

A greater joy could ne'er be known, no lips could e'er tell;
The way my heart leaps when 'tis heard the name I know so well.
Look deep into my eyes, one time, and let the truth be seen;
My love will span the universe and plumb the deepest sea.

I give you my weary heart and soul, this love, this life...my all.
Take me to the highest heights and never let me fall.
Put your trembling hand in mine, together we'll roam this world;
We'll watch the magic grow, as each moment is unfurled.

Let me lie down by your side and slowly breathe you in,
Let your long dark silky locks fall gently against my skin.
I'll sink into your eyes, as dark as the darkest coal;
I'll find a way to touch you, honestly, from soul to soul.

Let us take this wondrous love, it'll guide us through the stars,
Let us protect it selfishly, in a cage of iron bars.
Let us plant this seed, watch our love grow strong as a tree,
With this precious love, together we will be free.

Terry L. Latham

Suicide

What have I done I seem to be falling forever
I've passed the angels that have guided my way
There is the Heaven for which we always seem to pray
Where am I going? What is this place?
Darkness all around and no familiar faces
Falling through the cracks left by others places
I see my friends from times long ago
There goes the man that I've prayed to so long ago!
The Devil seems nearer as time goes by
What is this place that I have forsaken
Where is my peace and my love from a future past
I see the window that was reserved for me! O'God what have I done?
My feet hit the floor that is to be my resting place
I run in steps, but seem to get no further
Life is over and death is forever
Where is the eternal life that was promised to all?
I am at the bottom but wished for the top
The basement is my new haven from the ghosts of society
I feared the wizards that attempted to change my life
Now I am a prisoner of the world Lucifer created!

Charles Westover

What About Love

Can love be touched or seen?
Or can you show a person what I mean?
Can love be the best thing to share?
If you have the feeling, then show that you care.
You view love as a one way street, I view it as an open
highway. If you do not bring love with you, then do not come my way.

Love I hold, Love I show, to express love in feeling is the best way I know.
Can love be bought? I think not.
Can love burn? Only if it gets too hot.
Love of my life, love of my dreams,
Love hurts, it can make one scream.
Love should be cherished as the best thing on earth.
I loved my mother ever since my birth.

Can love be denied? Can you take it away?
No, it's too powerful, so it is here to stay.
Love fears no color and it will never age,
If feelings had a book, Love would be on the first page.
Love is delicate, say it when it is real.
Never hold back, Love will know how you feel.
If anybody asks who taught me to love,
I would step outside and point to God above.

Daymon Patterson

Untitled

It's funny how people know you...never knowing you at all. A bleak
realization and ponderous thoughts...darkness and rage consume a
past...not forgotten to go forward...not remembering to outcast.
The future is luminous...yet not wanting to see...stuck in limbo...
an abyss created by me.
I'd like to start over to do it all again...avoid situations I was
continuously put in. Close my eyes and forget...let the silence
drift me away...imagining a world and there I'll stay.
Only in this slumber I am a bliss...soon reality is a grim
awakening kiss. I've run out of words and sentences to say...
Does it really matter? Does it matter anyway? Things are seen
but never saw, not wanting to look on...how does one ignore it all?
The cries for help...a listening ear...I wonder, I wonder, how can they
not hear? So I want to shout and scream out loud! Clutter,
clutter fills my mind, oh what the hell, it's just a waste of time.
No one cares of a raped identity, a once creative mind. I'll stop
it here, it won't desecrate mine. See there I go, I'm all right,
"she's' fine." Smiling I look pretty, the wall defeats the pain...
Although somewhere, somewhere silently it will always remain.
I'll deal with it, I'll deal with it, I'll deal with it one day

Carolann Sirchie

The Old Feather Pen

I am a feather pen,
in an old drawer.
I helped to write independence
during the war.
I helped to make your country free,
while you dozed under a tree.
I sat in all the courtrooms;
waiting to be picked up.
Thomas Jefferson saw me and
picked me up.
He brought me to a paper,
and I started to write.
I wrote the Declaration
that very night.
An old feather pen.

Victoria Cromley

Alone

Slip away into the darkness
no longer deal with life
all of its ideal matters
taking away from who I am
stripped of my desire to continue
just want someone to understand
no reason, no purpose
nothing I say is heard
I attempt to lend a helping hand
they ignore me, while slapping my face
then cry to me for help
when they're the ones who fall
walk away, no destination
create my own world once again
where only nothing matters
seeings how nothing is all I have
twisting, and pulling, my heart aches
I cry vicious screams of agony
Yet, no one seems to hear
maybe they just don't care!

Crystal Bartlett

Silhouette Lost

Bathed in light from behind,
Pausing in the doorway she listens.
A voice comes to find her still
Calling, drawing, pleading,
"Come to me and forget."

The sky's canopy is gone,
No ground rolls beneath her feet.
Her eyes stare fast and hard
At the shifting black, whispering,
"Come to me and forget."

Night sounds quickly cease,
Silence crushing in around her.
An unseen hand clenches her heart
Scratching upon it this,
"Come to me and forget."

Slowly, rigid fingers relax,
Leaving their hold on the door.
As hesitantly she eases into the void
It sweeps her down, howling,
"Came to us—lost."

Juliana Seguine

Ode To Parents And Children

I live in a democracy, this I do know
I help elect officials, some of whom I don't know
The country was built on the basis of freedom
And we have as our motto E Pluribus Unum
I have to work to earn a living
The best years of my life, is what I'm giving
Through-out the year, from dark to sun-up
I can do as I want, cause I'm a grown-up.

I live in a monarchy, I think this is so
My papa is King, he tells me so
He says, "mind your mother
And, don't fight with your brother"
The King and Queen make the house rules
For the prince and princess, and the balky mules
The rules hold until I'm twenty-one,
'Cause until then, I'm a little one.

Thomas E. Lempges

Ode To A Bestfriend

Calling someone a bestfriend can be hard,
Though I call you my bestfriend without regard.

For all the devotion you may give,
I will honor for as long as I live.

Others may not see nor hear
Your time and tenderness at which I hold dear.

Sitting there awaiting me mutely,
I unleash my feelings to you emotionally.

You undid the hurt when I cried so many nights
Over numerous break-ups and parental fights.

On your shoulders are where my tears fell
Things I shared ascertained you would not tell.

Taking my bitter sad depression
Lifting my spirits and pride to a higher elevation.

All you did was listen with sweet understanding
Because of you my hopes are still arising.

Now that I'm older and we're apart
The memories I have are cherished in my heart.

I love you for being there
And I love you my...Teddy Bear.

Sjonneke Jones

The Big Crash

One fine day, coming from school,
We thought everything was going to be cool,
So there we are, cruising down the road,
Half the story is yet to be told,
Everyone was just full of glee,
But a happy day was not to be.
I saw a trailer, coming from the side,
The driver broke all rules, by which we abide.
The next thing we knew,
We were smashed into a wall,
No one was hurt, during this great fall.
Out of the wreckage, we appeared,
With a helping hand from all who were near.
The truck was filled with oil,
But it did not explode,
We were ushered into a building,
And the story was told.
I was in shock,
My uncle comforted me,
'Twas a day to remember, not a fond memory.

Naresh Francis

I Am Not A Stereotype

I am not a stereotype.
I am not who you want me to be.
I am not what you want me to be.
I am not yours to judge.

I am not a stereotype.
I am not to be classified.
I am not part of a like whole.
I am not the definition of normal.

I am not a stereotype.
I am my own person.
I am not from the mold of humanity.
I am not weird nor normal.

I am not a stereotype.
I am myself.
I am me.
I am not your statistic.

I am not a stereotype.
I am not, will not, and never will be a stereotype.

I am not a stereotype.
I am an individual.

Adrienne Shaw

Weeds

With shade of night
You entered my garden gate
Reaped my weeds
Then sowed your own.
How was I to know your ivy was poison?
Blinded by the beauty of a single rose,
Its petals bouqueted
Into a makeshift bed.
Intoxicating scent,
Feeling sublime,
Sweet whispers and promises,
No thorns in sight.
Tenderly, you plucked the blossom from my chest
And placed it in your hair.
On hushing breeze,
Before sunlight could creep,
Before my garden had a chance to bloom
You exited my garden gate and left only
Weeds.

Kevin Toby Clark

It's All Because Of You

There's someone who has touched me deep in my heart.
Cuz she gave me the courage and gave me the start.
To come to my senses and think about my dreams.
Since there is a lot more to life than to me what it seems.

For she gave me the push and the extra "good jobs,"
That kept my ideas flowing and boy I had gobs.
For never before had I had someone in my past,
Whose confidence in me, continued to last.

Even through times when I had started to lack,
You kept pushing me forward so I wouldn't look back.
To just think of tomorrow and what it may bring,
Instead of dwell on the past which could be an awful thing.

And I hope that she knows that she started me out,
And showed me the meaning of what life was all about.
And now I make nothing but A's and a few B's,
Yet still with the guys, I'm that little "ol' tease".

But now my priorities have been securely set straight.
By the cute little teacher I had in grade eight.
And I'll tell you the truth (and I'll be quite frank)
She's the only teacher that I have to thank.

Stephanie Welton

Heaven

Thoughts drift,
Fond memories coalesce,
Forming a radiant light.
Heart stops, limbs become numb, immovable.
Soul released into the light.
Body left behind for us to pray over.
Face left at rest for us to linger on.
How can you be gone?
I can reach out to touch you,
Yet I don't.
Hands folded across your chest,
Clasping sacred beads.
Eyes closed, you cannot see my tears,
Or can you?
You live on through us.
What happens when we are gone?
Will we be together again?
Unanswered questions.
Faith tested.
I believed.

Meagan L. Connolly

Evil Dominates

Is it not true, we are letting evil dominate our lives.
Look around, what do we see.
Greed, hate and so much jealousy.
This is what it's come to be.

Lets wake up, before it's too late.
Love, compassion, is needed, not all this hate.
Killings, fires, deception, lets get rid of all of this.
We can, we must, then only will we have heavenly bliss.

Blessed are the ones, who give from the heart.
They are the real sympathizers, for the most part.
In reality, knowledge of what is true, what is right.
Its been passing away, lets bring justice back
We need it badly today and we sure do need to pray.

Irene L. Starkweather

Darkness Rest

As I walk along the quiet road I see a cave
It looks dark as one would be brave
I walked up close to see that nature had only stayed
So I left like I never had step close to feel ashamed
I came to a willow tree next to a grave
To read a name of one who had been left along from his trade
To know once my traits of life once
lived along the road which never had fade.
Feelings of joy came across my face
like I knew happiness once was here as I walked away
For I could feel peace that tribes
rest and walk in a family parade.

Daffney Merchant

Krazy Woman's Shadow

I am the eyes you cannot see, the arms you cannot feel
The voice you cannot hear. But...I am with you always.
I am the anguish in your sorrow, the laughter in your cheer
The inner self you look upon...I am always there.
Only in the bright light do I appear
But only a reflection of "you".
I am always there for you
You can count on me
me — your friend
I am your shadow.

Kathy Krazy Woman Folsom

Water Rises

At the beach in its comfort and daze
My heart is free of danger and pain
I feel the rugged brush of the salty waves
Now hidden from all the anger and shame
The water begins to rise.

The beach, my haven for all sense of thought
And the pleasures that come from within,
The peace of mind that has always been sought
Now beckons on the sand where I've been.
The water continues to rise.

Rising higher, the waves at a point of no return
For leisure is all I seem to know now
Because I still have no worries or deep concern
All have receded into the waves some how.
But the water has risen.

Nicole Y. Howell

Man Alive

Collecting dreams, hour's dust, hair's tooth,
dream breathing, clean,

Green grass blood,
flowing wind river, arching branch of sky,

Pebbles, God stones, places, faces, new seed,
rivers on the run,

Sweet birch trembling,
ease of moment, touching internal mountains,

Calling of guides in bright silence,
echo yes hello,

Daffodil smiles,
inhaled sun to radiance returned,

Great dance, dancing earth the sign,
apples without question,

Trees without question,
and clouds, spires of aerial rivers,

Shade forests and cities and life moving on,
man alive

James S. Chandler

Chandelier Tree

Crystal gems glistening in the street light.
Swaying gently in the dark of night.
Dancing, dancing globes of light.
Wanting...wanting...wanting.
Coldness of the branches.
The fluid in the body...slowing...slowing...slow.
The ice forming and creeping up body and branches...ice age.
Frigid it is to be dressed in crystal lights.
Mysterious to be dancing in the cold remorseless night.
Oh how the crystal encases me!
Shake my branches...please!
Touch me...please!
Warmth...come soon!

Anna M. Goffinet

Anger

Anger is foaming in my heart.
Charred within, love has turned into dust.
Resentment bubbles, rising above
Revenge takes form flying free,
But not like a dove.
Tears start rolling down my face.
Bringing me to reality once again.
Equanimity finally has taken place.

Ani Nadjarian

Veil Of Shadows

I come from a place...of darkness...
Complete, enveloping, blackness...
of a room with no doors...no windows...
Where even the reality of my own being...
is in doubt...
Beyond despair...to acceptance of numbness...
Then...suddenly...out of the emptiness...
a shard of glittering rainbow light...
from an unseen passageway...
Blue then red, gold, purple, among a hue of colors...
for which my mind could find no name...
As the light touched my face and hands...
I became overwhelmed by feelings of life...love...
total and complete acceptance of all I am...
...my love, has found me...

Lynn Curry

Country Ride

Gracefully, telephone wires dip and rise
in rhythmic fashion.
Purple-gray clouds border the horizon,
promising abundance.
Cumulus giants growing larger...
Rain-drenched pastures roll on and on.
Trumpet Vine winds up and over
any fence, any post; draping orange everywhere.
Silos stand still in the heat waves;
rising from fields baked by the now visible sun.
Wild verbena peeks through roadside grasses,
making splashes of purple in all the green.
And ever onward goes the blacktop;
gently threaded through this quiet countryside.

Christian S. LeHeup

Midnight Reflections

Burning hard on midnight oil,
Playing down mental turmoil.
Of life and love, what dare ask I?
To pass through shadows or soar through sky?
Of passion's fleeting shadowed ghost
I reap the least and seek the most
and know that life entails both
the highest highs and lowest lows.
Take the gift, ere whence it come,
and tally not life's changing sum.
Grasp each moment in firm embrace,
and though tangibles go without a trace,
each special moment in memory stays
to be savored, on less memorable days.

Jill Calkin

The PuppetMaster

My movements are mechanical.
As easily predicted as the thoughts of people.
So obvious to everyone but me.

My movements are spontaneous.
As easily unpredicted as the color of people.
So oblivious to everyone but me.

My movements are my emotions.
As easily uncontrolled as the fears of people.
So obsolete to everyone but me.

My movements are my destiny.
As easily controlled as the lives of people.
So easily maneuvered by the puppetmaster.

Bethany W. F. Long

The Addict

There is a dark life calling, asking for you
It has the voice of desire
You play the role of the buyer
Of the people you know, true friends there are few
A stranger - you are to those who knew you before
Without family or friends the pain never ends
As you get high you can fly but not soar
Once there was faith then I lost what was found
The belief in myself
My strength and my health
All this well knowing I search crumbs on the ground
It's a dog that will beg for crumbs at the table
It's dogs that we are, once caring, now unable
For it's a short life after all
A short life after all
It's a short life after all
A short, painful life
In this life of regrets I can't change though I try
Now understand what was given for the chance
To get high

Jason Van Horn

Some Day

If some day I would disappear from your life,
Would you miss me.
If some day you knew you would never see me again,
Would your eyes ache, searching for me.
If some day you would never see my eyes looking deep into yours,
Would your eyes shed tears of loneliness.
If some day you could not touch me with loving fingers,
Would your fingers longingly tingle, from the memory.
If some day you could not feel my arms hold you with love,
Would your heart bleed red tinged tears, of lost love.
If some day you discovered you have lost my love,
Would you wish you had taken a chance.
If some day you had the chance to do it over again,
Would you take that chance.
Some day may be too late.

Alice G. Bryant

Martyr's/Mentor

America forged first in flame,
Bred the brood that brought its fame.
Those brave and bold - their visions seen,
Endured everything to build their dream.

As centuries passed all prices paid
We forget the sacrifices made.
To give us hope to chase our dreams,
No matter how hopeless it seems.

History's intent is to free the minds of men,
Who seeing nothing, learn nothing.
Listen to its song; the revelry of hidden things,
The ballads of all those mortal men,
Who traveled the same roads as ourselves,
and have seen the same things that we see,
Yet gloried in the magic life contained -
Then took the magic that they found. . .
And recorded it for those yet to be born.
So as we move ever closer to meeting them in death,
Let not their trials and triumphs be in vain.
But let us too seek this magic that awaits us -
And live long and hard, but also learn. . .
To accept death, as it rapidly approaches.

Khristopher Scott Morse

Wish For Warmth

As a child, alone, sitting wedged into a corner
In a city full of strange faces that are unknown to me.
Sitting there as quiet as a church mouse
With a face of innocence and terror.
As a child, scared
And no one cares to give a second glance at me.
If they do they start whispering to each other
As they slowly walk by.
I haven't ever heard what they say
Except I know what they're talking about.
They say look at that poor boy over there all alone.
It makes me think about how I ever got here
And why I'm alone
As I walk the streets and see families together
I think what I would give to be part of that
And to have a place that I could call my own
But instead I'm out on the cold, dark streets
Scavenging for food and warmth
Wherever I can find it
Just to stay alive

Melissa Wright

Drawing Pictures At Night

While doubting believers roam around,
Blind receivers hear the silent sound.
Accepting no fear (but always afraid),
They yield to tears in the games they've played.
Nightmarish cringes in total daylight;
By immovable hinges they're drawing pictures at night.
Alone in an instance of joyless smiles,
We traverse the distance of measureless miles.
Through the glare of emotionless tears
Reflections stare from imageless mirrors.
We vow in secret with possible might;
Relying on trinkets, we're drawing pictures at night.
Then the clever fools deceive us all
With their primitive tools and motionless falls.
As they lock us in our paper prisons,
A whispered scream! But no one listens.
We'll only be free when we've won the fight
Released into slavery, we're drawing pictures at night.

James P. Melcher

Colors

Red is the fire that kindles in the hearth.
Blue is the sky that holds up the clouds.
Pink is the nose of the kitten small.
Green is the envy that kindles in men.
Purple is the sunset, the beauty of the sky.
Brown is the tree when the winter is near.
Black is the Dark of night, the fear of little children.
Orange is the color of fruit that bears its name.
Yellow is the sun that we know will shine again.
White is the power that contains them all.

Simon Pfeil

Madness

Go left, go right,
Go out of sight,
Can't function because of the combustion,
Have not a soul to turn to,
Can't imagine why they give you the look,
Maybe, just maybe they mistook you for a crook,
Look here, look there, look everywhere,
Seek high, seek low, seek down and below,
But keep away from the madness
that causes the combustion,
You never know though, might just
be your function junction.

Cheryl Marsh

If These Walls Could Talk

If these walls could talk what would they say?
Would these walls lead me the write way
or show me the write path?
If these walls could talk would
I listen to what they had to say?
Or would I just treat them like
I would treat other people, or treat
them how I would want to be treated.
If these walls could talk would
they have more to say just like
ordinary people? How would they
react towards other people? Would
they be shy? Or would they not
talk like they would always do?
If these walls could talk would I tell
them things that I never told anyone before.
Would these walls keep secrets to themselves
and not say a word to whom ask them.

Rickeshi A. Moon

Sea Of Change

The Past and the Future met today
Close your eyes, drift away
And it may seem more than strange
Drowning in a Sea of Change.

The Past was the Future in someone's dream
Tomorrow may not be what it seems
Fate is always prearranged
Drowning in a Sea of Change.

The Past and the Future parted ways
The best laid plans are swept away
With no time to rearrange
Drowning in a Sea of Change.

Jon R. Jones

The Lonely Old Man

Way down by the river an old man sits all alone.
Behind him is a forest and a cabin he calls home.
He hears a sound of laughter, but sees no one there.
But behind a tree his grandson stands all aware.
The young child visits by the river running slow.
He sits down, grasps a rock, gently gives a throw.
He looks at his grampa, whom holds a frown on his face.
The look in his eyes hold a clear and empty space.
The child asks "Are you sad grampa?" the reply was a nod.
As he whispers the words softly "Oh help me God."
A smile is forced to the old man's face, he gives a little wink.
Picks up the boy and says "Hey what do you think?"
While walking towards the cabin they laugh and play.
But the old man is still sad, they're only here for the day.
Now the old man's waving at a car headed on to home.
He then will head back to the river, where he will sit all alone.

Tammy F. Cudaback

My Guardian Angel St. John

Even as a small child I always seemed to fail,
Things always worked out with my guardian angel near.

There has been dark days no ending in sight,
The emptiness would last deep into the night.

When I would sleep and wake with a scare,
My guardian angel would be there gently stroking my hair.

My angel would comfort me and help me get through,
But little did I know all these years my angel was you.

Pansy Lynch

Jesus, My Valentine

Jesus stands at the door to your heart and mine,
asking us to let him come in, and to be his valentine.

His love is far greater than any human love,
sent down to us all from the father up above.

He will of the spirit give you a brand new birth,
filling your heart with holy gladness and mirth.

If we would just look to him and always take heed,
he will be all that we ask, and supply our every need.

He will give you joy when you come to the end of your rope,
and pick you up, giving you a fresh new hope.

Just open up your heart and let him come in,
of your affections he will surely win.

I'm glad I opened up the door to my heart,
that is where he now dwells, and will never depart.

He has endowed me with tranquility of mind,
today; will you let him come in and be "your" valentine?

Margaret Maxwell

Love

I lay my head upon your breast
Tho' you feel it not in your infinite rest
And my fingers trace your features fine
Recalling that each one was mine.

Not like in days of used to be
My head upon your breast divine
Together breathing rhythmically,
When you living were really mine.

I lay my hand upon your brow
So cold and white in your coffin bare
And pray with all my heart and soul
That you were here and I was there.

Arelene Schlang

Roses For You

Roses I have for you
To say that I'm sorry
Cause I haven't known
Just how to please you.

I know I've done you wrong
Cause I didn't treat you kindly my friend
But if you give me a chance
Then I'll never let you down again.

Roses I bring to you
To say that I'm in love
The love I've longed for
Is now here to stay.

I knew I fell in love with you
The first time I saw your face
I know I have found my love
Cause I've never felt this way before.

Roses I bring to you
Just wish to make you smile
And hope that someday
I could win your heart.

Young Huynh

Autumn Leaves

Have you ever watched the leaves as they fall
Each one seems to answer a separate call

Are we so like these leaves that fall
To decay upon the forest floor

Surely without Jesus in our hearts we too will fall
And decay as we pass through death's cold door

Is it not our solemn duty and can we ill afford
To bring ourselves and others to our Saviour and our Lord

Do this and when our life on earth does cease
Jesus will take us home to the perfect place of peace

I will not badger, nor make demands
But I'll gladly share my love for Jesus
And for all that he stands

Earl C. Barry Sr.

Ocean, You Are The Greatest

It is big, it is huge, it is a lot.
When you look at it, is so gorgeous.
Sometimes you see it blue or it could be green;
and a red one, you'll say: It's the best one I've ever seen.
It never stops though, and could even be ferocious.

Sitting on a rock, appreciating its beauty,
from a distance you wonder about what happens inside,
and coming to it to feel its warmth is what you should decide.
But if you disturb it, that means you are not complying with your duty.

Your responsibility is to care for it and always be nice;
doing this, it will gladly reflect its majesty,
something too much for you, just worthy of kingly dynasty.
Still, it keeps doing it, never putting you a price.

Humongous, enormous, in abundance.
That is how it will always be.
It is so deep and yet so reachable.
Having it all for yourself seems almost unthinkable.
Compared to it, you are just a little bee.

Jairo Pina Jr.

Mystic Vagabond

I haven't bothered to write
or to adjust for reality,
I haven't danced since that night,
I'm not sure I could handle it.

I haven't in a long time,
taken such a long walk,
or thought of someone for so long all at once.
I haven't blurted out in song,
or played at painting with the stars
like a mystic vagabond.

There is no feeling that is right,
but I'll accept it if I can.
There is no hope to fill the night,
but there are memories to stir.

I'll give reality a twist,
and I'll come up with written words,
but since you're not here to hear them read,
It doesn't seem worth the bother.

J. A. Rea

205

Whidbey

As the salty green water slithers onto the stony beaches,
a seagull squawks.
As a strong wind whispers to a broken mountain,
a crab sidesteps.
As a rickety old boat bobs on an endless sea,
a baby seal splashes.
As a mother otter grieves over the death of her young,
the sky cries.
And as the water flows and the tide comes in,
all is peaceful on Whidbey Island, Washington.

Justin M. DeLong

Lost Love

Some say, all things happen for a reason.
Sometimes it's fate,
or cosmic destiny.
Sometimes it's just a dream.
I loved this man,
then lost this man.
Cosmic destiny?
No, just fate being mean.
Some say, all things happen for a reason.
It's not true,
there is no reason for this love I lost.

Coleen Lasko

In The Hush Of The Snow

Where does one go in the hush of the snow?
In the hush of the snow where does one go?

Off to the woods where the trees are piled
With mountains of snow and the sun filters in
to set them aglow.

Off to the pond where the stillness lies and the only
sounds are brave bird cries and the crackling ice
that seems to sigh beneath its load of snow.

Off to the meadow to gaze at the drifts that hang
suspended by rails and posts
Where the only tracks one sees at all are those
left by nature's ghosts.

Where does one go in the hush of the snow?
To view God's creation that seems to know that
man's efforts are lost for a day or so
While the world stands still
in the hush of the snow.

Helen E. Chamblin

The Lousy Cop

You call me during your family fight
It doesn't matter what time of night
You depend on me to save your life
Today I fought your child with a knife

I'm there to listen to what you say
For me it's just part of my day
I never refuse to answer your call
Today I stood before you standing tall

When your life is shattered and no one seems to care
I will share your burden which is hard to bear
I'll comfort you whenever you need
By saying a kind word or loving deed

Although we will meet again someday
I know exactly what you will say
We'll face each other and you'll look at me
The lousy cop is what you see

Geneva A. Cook

Butterflies In The Sky

Butterflies in the sky. How they fly so high
in the sky. Oh how they light up the sky with
their beautiful colors! Butterfly in the sky fly, fly
in the sky, you beautiful butterfly. Oh how the
sky is so full when they fly so high in the sky!
So fly free over the trees, be free in the sweet
breeze in the sky, butterfly fly over all the trees.

Brad Barnett

Untitled

As I watch TV I sit and wonder, what
    happened when I use to read good books.
TV is full of commercials, sweethearts and
    even incest and crooks.
What happened to those days of Hemingway, Twain
    and his Tom Sawyer
Now all you get on TV is, detectives and
    a glibbed tongue lawyer.

What happened to those days, the best days
    of our lives
Now, most people go to the local corner and
    visit the most popular dives.
Give me back the good days and a few
    years of my youth
You can have all those new fangled packages
    of cereals and juice.

Robert A. Stier

The Project

Meetings, discussions held hour by hour,
drain the life and dilute the power.
Issues and tasks get thrown in the pile
and the target grows distant in the meanwhile.
Do something once and do it right.
Accept the challenge and not the fight.
Shoulder to shoulder and arm in arm,
A job well done, ah that's the charm.

Wanda Bays

I Tried

I tried, but did I succeed
How will it be known
Be it from duty or deed
Or trials to me, yet unknown

Trade and commerce measure success
Simply by market gains and dole
How are accomplishments then weighed
When it stems from the soul

Understandably integrity has to prevail
Along with compassion and respect
But often pondered their value
When perceived by many as suspect

Life's role pursue many directions
In my case, Father, Friend and Foe
Treated each with patience and care
Satisfactorily I must admit, without woe

These success however remain in doubt
Coupled with contentment I desperately seek
Not knowing if prayers were helpful
For...I tried, but did I succeed

E. D. Klarich

My Beloved East End

I am leaving my beloved East End.
To the land speculators
greedily carving and pushing,
creating only rifts.
To the NYC restaurateurs
dreaming imaginary parking spaces
on thin aired Main Streets.
To Hollywood insiders
frolicking amongst the lights
trying to reach back and appear to belong.
To illegals
scrubbing pots and manicuring blades of grass.
Gone
are the cool mist filled potato field nights,
the plover filled dunes defying a determined ocean trying
to erase the character
its gravity created.
I am leaving my beloved East End,
but its forgone nature
shall always reside within.

Ronald D. Salargo

Death

    People dying all around me,
people dying so innocently.
    You never know when your time will come,
you never know when you'll be the one,
    People dying everywhere and no one seems to care,
I wonder who will be next to take the dare.
    I guess we'll just have to wait and see,
I just hope next time it won't be me.
    Friends and family all in tears,
because they knew him so many years.
    It kind of makes you think
that someone could die in just a blink.
    Trying to cope is just so hard,
for now and forever my heart will be scarred.
    Lets try to find a way to keep him in our thoughts,
so our love for him will never be lost.
    Every year I will lay a rose upon his grave
in remembrance of the sad day.
    And every year I will shed a tear
because he should still be here.

Melanie Davis

Walking Eyes

She walks upon her porch with haunted eyes
He walks away not to see nor satisfy
They play a game to distant tolls
The game guides and controls

He walks away not to see nor satisfy
They dance a dirge and the season dies
The game guides and controls
Filling the time with endless holes

They dance a dirge and the season dies
Forced to face away from brilliant lies
Filling time with endless holes
Moving beyond gravity's pull

Forced to face away from brilliant lies
She walks upon her porch with haunted eyes
He walks away not to see nor satisfy
They dance a dirge and the season dies

She walks upon her porch with haunted eyes
Unseen, unseeing wondering why
She plays a game to distant tolls
Her bare feet tread softly upon the warm wood.

Marjorie L. Miller

Untitled

    Don't let go of us. Don't forget our memories.
They may be all we have left. So make the best
out of our time that we have left. I love you and
I always will. The time we've shared has changed
me. In ways nobody else can see. Love is what
we have, and it takes two.
    Remember me the way I left. So many nights
we've left each other, so many mornings we've
spent together. Yet, so much has been left
unsaid. Someday we'll be together - Don't forget me,
I will love you forever.

Laura Bay

Lord, Let It Be

Help me to see what you want me to be.
Help me to be what you want me to be.
I may not always be right, but I'm saved and I see your light
Lord, let it be.

Lord help me know where to go
And help me to walk where you want me to walk.
Lord let me talk the right talk.
Lord, let it be.

Lord help me walk in the right way
As I go on day by day...
Help me to say what you want me to say.
Lord let it be, let it be your way.

Sania Hogan

Time

Time, that hideous creature, moving along at a serpent like pace,
It puts the grey in our hair, and the lines on our face,
The old will it to cease, and the young to increase,
But none can corral it, or whip it to speed.
Just a little more time, is all that we need,
A little more time please, it just isn't fair.
But it's plain to see, that time just doesn't care
Time is deaf and blind, and it has not a heart,
But like magic it changes, daylight to dark,
Time can change bones into dust, and mountains into hills.
And in the end, you will see, it's really time that kills.

David W. Capps

Great-Grand Ma, Mary

Great-Grand Ma, Mary was a lady you just did not mess with.
    Whatever she said, she most definitely meant.
    On occasion, would help you understand with a switch
    from the willow tree or with the back of her hand.

    There were times when that old willow switch
        would reach out and touch someone,
        for some mischievous deeds they had done.
        She would always explain,
    "This is hurting me as much as it's hurting you."
In the end it was all for the best, cured me of all my sassiness.

    Yet, she could be gentle and very kind.
    One minute she was whipping your behind,
and the next minute kissing your boo boos away.
    Telling you just how much she loved you,
    or doing something extra special, just for you.

    Sometimes I would wish that she would die.
Then one day God took her away, all I could do was cry and cry.
    I realized that I really did love her and would until I die.

Sometimes I wonder, who is she whipping in heaven today?

Betty Reed

Too Late

I hear you calling me,
But only in my dreams
These images and memories are not mine,
At least that is how it seems

I wait for you, but it's all in vain
It was my happiness you took from me
And I will never be the same

It was never enough the love I gave
No matter how hard I tried
Feelings were things you never could save
And you always pushed me to the side

Now I am older, and do not care
About the life we once had
I no longer miss the things we shared
And thoughts of you don't make me sad

Yes, I hear you calling, saying you've changed
And that I'm not being fair
But can't you see that it's too late
And I'm no longer there?

Terri Donnell

Touched By An Angel

One night sitting at home,
feeling confused and alone
a powerful feeling surrounded me.
Something that I couldn't really touch or see.
I heard a voice inside me say,
tomorrow will be a better day.
Ever since that special night
things have always gone all right.
Keeping me safe and free from harm,
is the embrace of His powerful arms.

Christine Williams

Amelia

I could not believe, what my eyes perceive.
Such a lovely face. My heart increased in pace.

Emotions tend to flow, we pay that which we owe.
I stumbled on a dream, at least, that's how it seems.

Say you'll come to me and do so caringly.
Remember to be friends and we can make amends.
For hurt that we knew love is overdue.

Can you comprehend, the way I condescend.
Persons whom I know all of us must grow.

To a higher plane never to remain,
Stagnate in our ways, make it just a phase.

Spinning in a whirl, words I must unfurl,
Something like a pearl, you're such a lovely girl.

Harvey G. Carrathus

One Goal Daily

In the morning sun, you wake up trying
to set a goal in hopes of abiding
As the day progresses, so do you
and on to other chores to do,
always aware your goal will be met,
and still there are many things to be set,
By trying hard, and using our wisdom
This is up to God alone to make this decision
So in order to attempt our goal,
it will come from within your soul,
and when you reach the goal you desire
Thank you Lord, the one to admire

Norma Catchpole

Not Blind, Can't See

We're on the run, not looking back
At the trail we've left to be followed
Disposing of waste, we proceed in fast pace
Leaving behind what our children can't swallow

Now our world's become small with T.V. and all
Push button connections on line
Strangers seem stranger, we hide behind covers
Listening to what's being said all the time

Our fathers before us toiled the earth
They touched their neighbor's hand
Days were longer, compassion was stronger
You knew your neighbor then

The living room was with your family
Entertainment was imagination, and love developed at home
The horse became carriage, talking turned gossip
You could make things faster by phone

Children today with fair skin and harsh minds
Connect to technology with ease
Single mothers in tears, kids and their peers
Know nothing of Grandpa's sore knees

Bob Straight

A Widow's Lament

My heart still aches;
It seems so long ago.
Your clay is in this grave,
But your spirit is still aglow.

The beauty of Nature sends its signs;
Your caress is in the breeze.
Songbirds sing your praises
As they snuggle in the trees.

I listen to the wind and the pines
Whisper of the joy we shared.
Somehow all the earth
Knew how much we cared.

As the flag waves o'er your grave,
Other lonely times come to mind.
The years you spent at war;
Your return; Fate was kind.

God gave us years of happiness;
Togetherness was the key.
Through thick and thin we had each other.
Now only memories comfort me.

Genevieve Campbell

Voices From The Walls

Can you hear them?
Listen.
There they are again.
Shh.
They are so loud!
The voices are coming from the walls.
Oh! They are so loud!
Please make them stop.
Why can't you hear them?
Make them stop!
I'm going mad!
I can't take them anymore.
I'll blow up the walls.
The voices are fading.
Where are you?
Please don't go. I need you; I just
couldn't take the voices in the walls.
I can't see or touch you. Don't you care
anymore? I'll find a way to find you.
At last the voices have totally ended.

Ann Wagner

America's Secret Side

Love, Hate
Sex, Date Rape
This is America's Secret Side
Those who spoke all good of America lied

There are children being beat
And who's to say no one's living on our streets.
Alleys filled with homeless men
You'll never know their stories of where they've been.

Children cry themselves to sleep
Daddy hit mommy the pain went deep
Young girls forced into prostitution
Our world is fast becoming a bad institution.

12 and up getting pregnant everyday
Can't we help in anyway
Drugs are offered everywhere
Come on America, don't you care

Is there an answer
To our country's bad cancer
America needs to clean up its act
Its people are the only ones to do it and that's a fact

Ann Lairson

The Precious Art Of Living

When I was a babe on Mother's knee,
    She fed, amused, and tended me,
Teaching me the livelong day
    To praise our Saviour as I prayed.

During my painful teenage years
    Christ's shielding armor vanquished fears.
When temptation nearly conquered me,
    Mother would say, "Look, pray, and see."

On and on down the road of life
    To hold my head above the strife,
To see what God had planned for me,
    Mother would say, "Look, pray, and see."

Our paths have parted; no more will we roam.
    Our Lord and Master has called her home.
Her Toil on Earth is done, you see;
    She taught me there is an Eternity.

Elwood DuBois

Students

In diversity they come
To the repast of learning.
Styles as divergent as genes;
Motivation equally as unequal.

Some have voracious appetites;
Others are picky eaters.
Most show veracious traits;
A few are dishes of deceit.

As to personalities - lambkins
Give in to irreproachable lions
Pablum contexts are measured
Against gourmet sensitivities.

Bell curves crack in the
Mayhem of intelligent pursuits.
Routine research becomes, at times,
A search of futility.

Slowly, failure begets success.
Learning, not grades, brings intrinsic rewards.
With gruel of knowledge finally digested,
Graduation honors their just desserts.

Neil W. Cox

The New Year

Sounds of Christmas now are gone,
Shopping, planning, the baking is done.
Friends and family travel back home,
The house is quiet, again we're alone.

Snow still on roof tops, cold weather still here,
Now we're just waiting for another new year.
Will it be better, will dreams come true,
I hope for this, and I know others do, too.

I look back on the year that has passed,
Realizing now it went by so fast.
Did I accomplish what I wanted to,
Or did it just pass like so many do?

And when the new year finally comes,
I hope it will be better than the last one.
Good health, happiness, just being with you,
I pray it will last the whole year through.

Theresa Wolff

Once Upon A Lifetime

Once upon a memory, you walked Life's roads alone;
    And the roads you chose to travel remained apart.
Threads of disappointment were woven through Life's cares,
    And a quiet and gentle yearning filled your hearts.
'Cause success doesn't take the place of love.
    True riches a heart can't buy.
Just a house will never make a home,
    And things won't satisfy.
Then you met upon a moment at the crossroads of your life.
    He asked to be your husband.
You agreed to be his wife.
    Hearts can be much lighter
When a man and woman share.
    Happy is the couple
Who teach themselves to care.
    A lifetime passes quickly.
What will matter as it ends
    Is not to have been lovers,
But tender, caring friends.

Barbara G. Miller

Writer's Block

One more paragraph will finish your day
Then you can go outside and play.
Tick tock, tick tock,
Guess who has writer's block!

It's 12 o'clock, you started at ten,
The ink starts to harden inside of your pen.
Tick tock, tick tock,
Guess who has writer's block!

It's already pm at 8 o'clock,
Your brain starts to harden like a rock.
Tick tock, tick tock,
Guess who has writer's block!

Then you hear the cuckoo clock,
Say "There's only one way to get rid of that wood,
A couple of termites should do it, they should."
Tick tock, tick tock,
Guess who has writer's block!

So you think up some termites inside of your head.
And that writer's block is Dead!
Tick tock, tick tock,
You have no more writer's block.

Ian Powell

The Ultimate Dream

As I try to imagine the ultimate dream,
    the place is peaceful
    and so serene.

Before me a mountain of majestic blue
    with clusters of gold
    glistening through.

Wanting to share, I reach out my hand
    before me appears
    this extraordinary man.

Like the magical mountain, he's not easily described
    especially the gold
    that glistens from inside.
        Lisa Blackburn

Please Don't Go With The Flow

Please don't go with the flow
don't be like all the rest who had to go
Stay here with me,
and I will be happy

Don't cheat on me, like all the rest
Pretend that I am the best

I will never grow old of you
Won't you please say that you love me too.

Please don't go with the flow
You might get swept under the tow.
        Meghan Ashley

The Touch Of Innocent Love

Rootbeer, M&M's, and "Walker Texas Ranger"
This man was more than a stranger
In our hearts we loved him so
How hard it was to let him go

He was so special to us all
Will he hear us when we call
Does he happily sing
Does he have an angel wing
Does he watch us from above,
Guiding us with his love

May his pain never more endure
Our love will be connected forever more
His family is fine
Knowing he is surrounded by love divine
How sweet is the touch of innocent love.
        Dana Boatman

A Mother's Prayer

This night a Mother's heart is breaking,
As she sees her children stray.
The tears they flow - weighed down with woe
And her soul is filled with pain
I see you not as grown men
But as my little boys
With dancing eyes and smiling faces
And hearts filled with joy
Oh why! Oh why! Must you lose the innocence of youth?
O' My Lord, I beg of you
Hear my humble prayer
Bring my little angels back
Into your loving care.
You land them once while they were young
Please love them once again
Fill their hearts with your precious love
And bring them safely home
        Patricia McAtee Risinger

Blindfolded?

Love is blind?
    Isn't that what they say?
    But if love endures and lasts a lifetime,
    Are we still blind throughout it?
Does a love which ends
    Signify the restoration of our sight and reality?
    Imagine - what causes the change?
    Visualization? Of what?
Now - imagine -
    Stereotypes, prejudices, and racisms -
    Would they exist if we were all blind,
    As in love?
Uniformity -
    Would skin color matter if it couldn't be seen?
    Maybe the world would be a peaceful place,
    Until someone's blindfold falls off.
Don't they say
    Love makes the world go round?
    Yet they don't see what brings it closer to its end?
    The irony of it all...
        Diane M. Steffan

Wishes

I wish I had infinite dollars, so I can get everything.
I wish I owned cybersmith, to play all the video games.
I wish I had virtual reality.
I wish there was no school, and people were already smart.
I wish I were at Disney World, so I can play.
I wish I owned $50,000,000,000.00 flying carpets
I wish it would snow, and be hot when I want it to.
I wish there was no work for grown-ups.
        Nicholas Goyuk

D Day For Our Sacramento Kings

Today is "D" day for our Sacramento Kings!
We're not sure if we'll hear slow music for a funeral,
    Or a joyous bell that rings!

We've had them now for almost 12 years,
And all this time they've heard our cheers!

If the decision to go forward with this offer to Jim Thomas
    Were left up to us, we'd say yes!
But our city council is making us guess!

For us to be happy, takes an affirmative vote of five;
If we fail, there's no use for us to be alive!

We dearly love our Sacramento Kings
And our hope is eternal the fat lady never sings!

We want the Kings to stay here forever;
For, with them, our quality of life is so much better!

Now, is the time for us all to bow our heads and pray
For God to bless our city council and guide them to a
    Decision that lets them stay!
        David T. Ajay

Horse Ride

Riding smoothly upon a horse's back,
The color of brown roasted chestnuts.
Hearing the beat of the horse's hooves
Advancing to a trot.
Then a leap
And dances into a canter.
Seeing other horses a cactus breeze by.
Feeling the breeze like a hand comforting you.
Then, an unexpected halt!
        Tiffany Nochta

Life's Day

The early glow of dawn shreds the dark of night
bringing the first hope of life to a new beginning.
The creatures of the earth begin to stir
and a new day, a new start, has been conceived.

The warm fingers of sunrise penetrate the sky's deep hues
sending the silent sounds of morn to rouse the world.
The tall timbers rustle with the beating wings of life,
little ones scurry from their warm nest. And day is born.

Mid-day arrives all too soon, the blazing sun challenging
all to compete for survival in the trials of life.
Tall! Strong! Dominating! The power of the mature day
decrees and directs the needs fulfillment of the time.

The evening shadows begin to fall, and the day begins to
grow weak and weary, the darkening shades of twilight
collect the lingering rays of dusk, to form a gentle glow
on the days last smile, waiting for the finality of life.

It is finished, death has conquered the strength of youth.
Day is done, and only the darkness remains, guarded by
the countless stars, angels in disguise, caring for the
many who have passed this way, waiting for tomorrow's dawn.

Ray Hursh

Farewell To A Love

I wish you the world, and I know you'll achieve.
The things that you search for, and all that you need.

You gave me my life, when I needed it most.
Years in earthly heaven, that put to rest my ghosts.

My heart, it was yours, to hold in your hand.
My soul, it was given, to you with time's sand.

My love knows no bounds, for my daughter and you.
I finally gave it, completely and true.

Now you are gone, to search for your life.
I just wish I could have made you my wife.

My ghosts are now gone, it's now clear to me.
I must begin living, and set my soul free.

I wish you the world, and I'll love you for all time.
I give you, your freedom, I must now find mine.

Michael R. English

I Am The Wind

I am strong and subtle,
Cool and warm,
Harsh and gentle,
I am the Wind.

I am a breeze on a cool, summer night,
I am a hurricane - power and might,
I could be like a dove or a knight,
I am the Wind - I can fill you with fright.

I may seem pleasant, a peaceful song,
But I can deceive you - I can be quite strong,
I can blow a building, a tree, or a train,
I am the Wind - I can inflict pain.

I lurk in the dark and the shadows of night,
I dwell in places beyond your sight,
I could blow from now to the end,
I am the Wind - I'm not always your friend.

Mark J. Saia

My Love

She was my world, she was my life.
She was a beautiful woman, she was my wife.
She gave me two children, I loved her so dear.
Now that I'm older, I see things so clear.
I had too many doubts and too many fears.
I made the wrong choice and I've suffered severe.
I thank you my love for the times we had
Some good, some better and some even bad.
These times will be cherished til the end of time.
Yes, you were a great woman, I had a great time.
You're still my everything and you're still on my mind.
So I ask you, my dear, as time passes on
Please forgive me of those things I've done wrong.
These words that I write they come so sincere.
Why didn't I show you when you were near.

Bill J. Warren

Shields

So I put up my shield
and walked on the streets
And hoped I would meet
someone strong enough
to push it aside and talk to me
Surely I'm not the only one

So I walked and walked
and mostly talked to
myself and God
And the people turned aside
and tried to find some other side
They could not plumb the depths
of my grief and pride
And so missed the joy of my soul ride

The people that talked to me
they mostly just bounced off my shield
And could not see and did not understand
my need or how easily I could bleed
or how deeply I could see inside
That life is a glide and I don't want to hide

Jeff Singer

Critical Eye

Critical eye
See
You look,
You see,
You see what you see
No one can see differently
   You see
Therefore it can only be
The very way you see.
No other view is noted
No other view is okay to be quoted
   You see?
   You see!
You argue the point because to you it is so
Observe, examine thus you see your mind makes it so
   you know.
   Critical eye
   See
   Critical eye I see me.

Valane Bussell

Penitential Rite

When things look blackest and I feel blue—
My psyche bruised and tattered in two
from that last unsettled fight with you
Over God knows what
  or why
   or who
And from my eyes, a facade of calm
that belies the crushing pain within-
Much needing to feel the healing balm
From that most impossible task for you

Seven small words
that gag you and choke you
that vilify, castigate, castrate, and smote you.
  Softly,
   Halting,
they finally come
like mythical hens teeth, sprung anew
I'm sorry,
and I
still love you.

   Maureen E. Opal

Ever Presence Of Decay

As darkness falls,
The reaper calls,
Searching, for the life of another,

Our enemy is the light of day,
Beware the presence of the stray,
We live in this world where hate is real,
Where our way to live is only to steal,

To steal the lives of innocent souls,
Each time we kill our hunger grows,
We feel the ever presence of decay,
For we will linger another day.

   Jared Linzey

Sunday By The Water

Sunday, by the water,
You brought me to your world.
As I lay in your arms,
You showed me a love so pure.

You ran your fingers through my hair,
Like a gentle summer breeze through the air.
Your touch framed my face with such splendor,
As you closed my eyes and opened my heart with words so tender.
Within your embrace, I have seen how beautiful life can be,
All in the wonderful way that you loved me.
Your kisses brought me to a place like no other,
When we were together, on Sunday, by the water.

   Patricia Guilherme

Holding Hands

My hands are nothing special
Eight fingers, two thumbs and two palms
They were given to me, I did not earn them
They are works of art that help me, in turn, to create
They give, they take, they heal, they soothe and they make
And yet, for all their majesty and all that they hold
Nothing, but nothing, compares to the gentle feeling
When I hold your hand in mine.

   James Wicks

Makin' Do

Pot of water on the stove, salt and pepper, too
No meat for the stew, but we're makin' do.
Ten babies to feed, needin' shoes
Daddy out of work crying the blues
Don't worry says mama, we'll just make do.
Now daddy loves mama, mama loving daddy too
  Whoops! Another baby
They say we have to make do.
No fancy things, nothing new
We got each other, just makin' do.
We have all these children more than a few
But we're all together and makin' do.
Remember when you love and being loved too
It don't take a lot to just make do.

   Joyce Crawford Brown

Love - Now And Beyond

Our love is very special, unlike anything we've known.
It's like a dream coming true
That's the way I feel about you.

When I need someone to hold me, no matter the time of day
You put your arms around me and everything's okay.

That's why on this day - our wedding day
I pledge these vows to you
I give you my love, to have and to hold forever and ever -
  may we grow old.
I give you my heart, please, handle it with care.
I give to you myself, so, our love we can share.
I give to you my word, to always be true
And I make a promise to never make you blue.

I love you with all my heart -
  and vow that we'll never part.

On this day, as we are wed.
Let's remember all the things we've said.

I became your woman and you my man.
May we always walk together - hand in hand.

   Leigh Isley

If The World Was A Rose

As you and I walk through life
We see the good and bad in everything
But it would hard for us to walk by a perfect
Rose and not ponder at its beauty
And wonder how life would be if the world
was that rose

   Ronnie G. McCoy

Realization

Since you've gone there is no meaning to my life.
Time falls to exist...

This pain in my heart,
Has gained control and overwhelms me.
Please go away and let me be...
I miss you so very much,
If only I could touch.
You are never coming home,
I just want to hold you and say I love you...

I'm so alone without you,
Are you lonely too?
You're the one I could count on,
I've always been there for you.
Now you're not here for me.
It's just not fair...

How could you leave me?

   Pamela R. Greenbush

The Fly, Spider and Bird

Tones of color reflect the dew
from the moisture in the air.
A fly is caught within a web
wings fluttering furiously in despair.

The sun peaked through the clouds so high
to warm the earth so moist.
Yet the fly, while losing faith
struggled on at his own frightful choice.

A bird flew low and shaded the web
with the fullness of his wings.
Closer and closer the bird did swoop
when its beak opened wide as if to sing.

Snatch went the beak within the web
a jolt to the fly did undertake.
At last this web had been broken apart
a struggling attempt was once again made.

Free at last vibrated the fly
away from the spider's web.
This great young bird had saved its life
thinking, "Thank God I am not dead".

Louise E. Melrose

You Are My Life

You are my life.
I say this because you've given me one,
a reason to want to continue mine,
an opportunity to include someone as special as you.
You have brought out feelings I never felt,
the qualities I thought no one would ever find.
You are my life.
My heart was a candle that had never been lit,
this flame now burns for you.
You are my life.
At last I feel happy and content,
I now see a future instead of looking for an end.
Thank you for bringing me to life!
Your love has turned a lifeless flower into a beautiful rose.
You are the plant food which makes me grow, and gives me life.
You've shown me the sunlight, then taught me how to enjoy it.
Without a doubt, you are my life!
You've given me a gift I needed to receive, you've given me life.
From this day forward, I will forever share my life with you.

Tracy Haas

Do You Ever Look For Me?

I passed a lady at the mall today...she looked a lot like me,
Could it be? Perhaps it is? Oh, that crazy fantasy.

Would I know you if I saw you?...Would you recognize it's me?
Or am I just a painful thought, an ugly memory?

Do children pass and do you wonder...
Oh where's my little one?

I want to hold her, kiss her face,
Lie with her, watch her run.

My eyes are blue, my hair is brown,
Not short, nor am I tall.

I passed a lady, she looked like me,
Today at the shopping mall.

It could be you, I do not know,
I let that lady pass.

I can't believe I blew my chance.
And I didn't even ask.

Marnie Ellison

Leaf

Funny how things change so fast.
It's like being caught in the wind.
Sometimes you land here or there.
Sometimes high up in the sky.
Sometimes low on the ground.
We're like a helpless leaves.
Sometimes surrounded by hundreds of other leaves.
Then that wind starts up again.
And takes you who-knows-where.
Maybe, alone again.

Christine Rizzuto

Balloon Time

Allow me a moment from memory's fires
Silently speared on an axis of time
Errant balloons in intrepid high wires,
Imprisoned in branches, betrayed by the sky.

Not mourning their fate, and feeling no fear
Seized by my questioning, measuring mind
I envy their struggle and fight back a tear
For balloons I have lost and lives I can't find!

Seeking acquittal, they pause and pose,
While strings of security anchor them fast.
Wrestling with earthbound, formidable foes
What counsel will finally free them, at last?

Entangled in trees of physical treaties,
We stumble and search for something to tell
Blown by the winds of cerebral breezes
The simple flight home we all know so well.

Lawrence E. Smith

Sunflower Guyana

We were conceived in the very rich soil of the motherland
...by parents of strong back bone.
They mold us with their little knowledge and that good
old fashion tradition.
With a perfect picture painted of how our life's supposed to be
...they brought us to America.
As we experience the authentic in ourselves we groove
into our own identity.
Few of us desire to be doctors, administrators, mechanics, while
others are entrepreneurs. Some of us have brilliant ideas
which crumble to the ground due to insufficient funds
and moral support.
With our own success we pave a better way for the new
generation...one who may never see Guyana...and may
never experience the rigid of their grandparent's roots.

Rene Denese Ramdeo

Just A Man

Each day is like a string of pearls although I can't arrange it.
I go to do the best I can and then I cannot change it.

I always hope today I did the very best I could and then I
realize at times my best is not so good.

Each sunrise is a gift from God to do the best I can.
Forgive me Lord and please remember I am just a man.

The pearls add up for fifty years to make a long long strand.
Forgive me Lord and please remember I am just a man.

Everyday is a gift dear Lord thank you for every pearl.
One day I pray to go with you to Heaven's perfect world.

Until that day I'll rise and shine and do the best I can.
I thank you Lord for remembering that I'm just a man.

Grace E. Stone

The Tea Song

She served me Oolong, then said her "So long."
Now I search byways, airways and highways.
How long is so long? She's been gone too long.
Should I find new ways to ease these drear days?

Then on the strait of Dover near Calais,
I caught the scent of her sweet Shalimar.
So I steered that way, but it was Earl Grey.
'Twas tea, not she, though I looked near and far.

Out in my Bentley seeking more Tetley
Or looking for her - I still pine and care.
How cruel can she be to pour them my tea
Since she's gone on tour as someone's au pair.

Chinese is pure tea, no tannin - no dye.
Even Pritikin said, "Free from trouble."
So be a wise guy; kiss those others goodbye,
Use your head; hurry back on the double.

Oh heartless Oolong, I've known it so long
She'd boogie in the Tea House close by Fuji.
Oolong, oh Oolong, once you were my song.
Now Lipton's really more my cup of tea.

June E. Andrew

The War

The war, the war, the war.
Shotguns hitting from door to door.
"Run away, far away," whispered a voice in my head.
That's just what I did, for I had a choice
of life or death.
My family of 13 tagged along, too.
While walking through the endless mountains,
I faint to the ground - my eyes closing gently.
My family starts praying, tears in their eyes
Begging God, "Don't let her die."
Then my uncle comes closer, with a glass of milk,
Tilting my head, he encourages me to drink.
A few seconds later, I wake to see the dark grey sky
after dreadful walks for 15 days, I thank God
for I am alive.

Aveen Benyamien

Evening

At the ending of the long hard day
Troubles hide the bright Sun away.

The night settles in with a cool breeze
That chills the internal soul of me.

Above the pond a cold gray mist rises
And the beauty of the world it disguises.

Problems of the day begin to overwhelm
As darkness covers my world's full realm

Then night's birds sing in the nearby trees
And the crickets play their mating melodies.

A soft breeze drifts across my cheek
With its character now mild and meek.

The stars peek through big fluffy clouds
And Mister Moon slides from their shrouds.

In the woods the nymphs plan their guises
With their giggles my spirit rises.

I sigh and rest my weary heart in God
And contemplate the long road I must trod.

Wondrous calming peace washes over me
And leaves me in a state of tranquility.

Jeannette Stone

Grace In The Wind

The wind gracefully yet boldly brushes the planet
    touching every cell
        rejuvenating all that lives

In the wind I find my friend — and my salvation

He comes to me
    day and night
        he rocks me with his loving hands
            he lulls me with a gentle song
                refreshes every cell of mine
                    creating newness at my very core

When the night comes
    he gently brushes over me
        softly strokes me with serenity...
            tenderly transports me into tranquility...

And my heart is filled once more
    so that I may reach out...
        like the grace in the wind

Arly Arguello

In Search Of Yourself

You run to learn of things you cannot change;
You mask the unveiling of your life to
Cover the awful truths—that you are a human
with feelings of hate, fear, anger and love.
Take each emotion as you feel it and understand
why you have it.
Fear not the answers that you uncover,
But enjoy the person you discover.

Darlene F. Parrish

Deja Vu All Over Again For Mr. Dole

I saw the latest poll
And found Robert Dole in a big hole.
He cannot vault the Presidential pole
Deja vu all over again for Mr. Dole!

Family values are not the realm of Dole
A man twice married does no good in this role
The religious right has mandated this as his goal
Deja vu all over again for Mr. Dole!

Nobody buys his "proven-leadership" lore
He stood firmly on every side of role
With all his humor still comes across a bore
Deja vu all over again for Mr. Dole!

Pro choice is not to be our choice
Pro-lifers seem to have all the voice
I can't take any more of this extreme noise
Deja vu all over again for Mr. Dole!

Kemp can't seem to lift Dole any more
I'm in a deep search of my soul
There is not much we can do any more
Deja vu all over again for Mr. Dole!

S. Krishna Vajhala

The Olympian

As we merge on a city's battle field;
With gold, silver, and bronze on our minds.
When the dust settles,
Some will experience the agony of defeat;
Others, triumph of victory.
But through it all,
We are one,
We are Olympians.

Tish Devore

214

A Vision Appears

As night time has fallen, I look towards a dream,
  An image of you, in a beautiful scene,
I fall into slumber, a vision appears,
  There you are standing, my eyes fill with tears.
We laugh and you hug me, with a gentle embrace,
  The tears are resolved, a bright smile in their place.
We talk of tomorrows, of hopes, dreams, and fears,
  of being together, how strong our love seems.
Just as I'm ready to hug you again.
  I wake from my slumber, and realize were I am.
  I'm locked up, I almost forgot,
But at the same moment, it left me this thought.
  If you believe in your dreams,
You are going to find,
  That dreams are reality
    from your sub-conscious mind!

  Scot E. Scharrer

Good-Bye, Dad

We stood at the head of the church aisle,
My arm was in his.
We smiled at each other,
I squeezed his arm, and we walked.
Twenty-six years ago today I was married.

We'd had glad times and sad times together.
When Mother died, we were each other's strength.
I'd watched him age and fade a bit,
But he was strong in mind and body.
And always cheerful, always cheerful.

He'd loved New Mexico, its sky and mountains,
Its vast open uninhabited lands.
He'd loved it such a short time.
Eleven short, short months, he was well and happy.
Then, nineteen hours of illness and...gone.

Now we are back in the bleak, cold East.
Again we are at the head of the church aisle.
The very same church, the very same date
This time I stand behind him, I walk behind him.
It is our last walk together. Good-bye, Dad.

  Laura A. Page

Our Special Child

Into our lives came a special son
who cannot speak or even run.
"Profoundly handicapped," we were told.
"Rubbish," we answered, "Pure gold."

"Autistic like", is the term they used,
but from day one my family refused
to accept it, agreeing to believe
in miracles our son would receive.

"Pull him in a wagon," doctors said.
But, Jeffy walked at three instead.
His hard-won victories allayed our fears,
bringing "Hooray for Jeffy" in our cheers.

Through the long and bittersweet years
came pints of progress, gallons of tears.
But, as Jeffy became more able and busy,
we asked ourselves, "Handicapped — or is he?"

He'll never work or earn a dollar,
never crack a book or be a scholar.
Yet, he's the richest person we know,
worshipped by a family that loves him so.

  Jerry Eaton

The Vision

I held a dream within my heart
The vision it was clear
The enormity of the dream
I embraced and held it dear

I saw as love exploded and became a part of me
Taking me into places that my human eye could not see
There was no male or female, no race of any kind
For love had blotted out the differences, erasing every line
No barriers, no walls to hold back
No more not being able to do because of lack

I beheld a new heaven and a new earth
Born of "The Spirit", for God had given new birth
Not of the flesh of man nor of man's will
But of the will of God, his purpose to fulfill.

I saw as love began to change all of those around
No more the chains and fetters to bind and hold down
A releasing to soar as high as one's spirit yearned to go
No more in hearing, "Halt, for here you cannot go"
No more the limitations placed upon us by man
But an agreement with God's spirit that says I can.

  Janet Salsgiver

A Winter Forest

When Autumn's trees are bit and nipped,
And the smell of Winter seems real bold...
When willows are stripped and dipped
In sheets of icy cold.

When rodents are rowdy
And their faces blushed,
Another is dormant in a spree of lusty fur.

The jovial fowl take up to move
While the buds are tranquil under their cozy blankets...
Their greedy little tongues licking the soil for nectar.

The dew has reached its pinnacle and so awaits a new day.
While the waves in the sky roll over to yawn,
And the timid fawn breaks dawn.

  Samuel E. Fiol

Men!

It's not the way men look at me,
It's not the way they stare.
I guess I'm kinda tired of having an affair!
I'm tired of the way men think,
It's all fine and dandy!
But mainly it's either now or never,
Or what ever may be handy!!
I'm tired of playing seconds,
When others are #1
So if I tell you to hit the road Jack
I think you better
Run!!

  Bobbi Cummings

Winter Wonderings

Fast, frivolous flakes flying,
  falling, filling fields.
Crystallized comets, coming, calling;
  adding, stopping, stalling...suspended.
Frozen moisture, moving, vexing;
  meager meadows and majestic mountains.
What separate words would romance
  winter's wonders...
White trees, grey skies, swirling winds;
  wildlife stops...
Soft; shivering, silent snow.

  John Zachary O'Day

Your Secret Admirer

I watched you today
But you were too busy to notice me
I longed for you to wave
I would have settled for a simple smile
But, you were too busy to notice me today
I have forgiven you for that
I followed you home.
But, you never noticed me.
I watched you through a window,
   'Til you feel asleep.
I wished I could have touched you
   and held you tight.
But, your love is for someone else.
If ever you change your mind
Remember I'll be right here waiting.

Tonya Horne

Untitled

Do not weep and do not cry,
Just shed a tear, then wipe it dry,
For time should not be spent on self-pity and sorrow.
Time should be spent on the dreams of building tomorrow.

Stephanie Milnes

Suzanne's Rue

Golden dripping ardor, the life
blood, sits like a stone within me.
I wait and wait biding my time, knowing I am not
alone, knowing I will never be alone. "I'm your Man."
Yes, you are, and you are the father
of my child. You may not know it, not
just yet. But I have a feeling the stone grows. Bow
strings, horsehair, cut into me; the music flows.
These stupid love songs I listen to
to curb my fear, my anger. My will can
never be my own again. Bard-minstrel, Leonard Cohen,
what ever happened to the tea and oranges?
I scrub, and try to push the images
far away. The floorboards have never seemed
cleaner. You may be out, but I am never alone. The
violins chew
and saw as I inhale what I can't caress.

Elizabeth Gerhart

Unchosen Pathway

I trod my weary steps, exhausted eyes
closed shut, trying to bar the sight
they know awaits them.
Oh but I have no fear of misplacing
these travel-weary feet of mine, for they know
the loathsome path as well as do my ever - tiring eyes.
The road that stretches before me is barren
and lonely, and is filled with the dense
fear of uncertainty.
For no matter how many countless times I'll
walk this way, I will always be one groping
as in the dark, for the end of the road
is never the same, nor ever predictable.
One day the road I traipse upon with
sodden feet, shall be empty of my
ever-slowing footsteps and bleary eyes.
Then the loneliness will echo in painful, empty
silence until this path can at last over
take another traveller and sap them of vital strength.

Emily J. Richie

I Hear Laughing All Around Me

As tears flow down my face,
I turn so no one sees me cry.
People stare as I walk down the sidewalk,
all by myself, tears rolling down my cheeks.
I see people walk by with smiles on their faces,
holding their boyfriends hand, laughing when they see me.
I think of all the people who laugh at me,
and wonder why they are always laughing and making fun of me.
As I turn I see a familiar face,
when I start to talk to him he laughs and goes on his way.
I turn the corner and continue to walk,
as I do these familiar laughs ring in my ears, I start to cry.
When I neared the park I often go to, I sit down to rest,
from a distance I can hear people talking about me.
I try to ignore it but it grows louder and louder,
sometimes I hear a faint sound of laughter.
I sit there and doze off, the sounds fade away,
and are never again to be heard by me,
for I died that night all alone by myself,
hearing people laugh at me. Good-Bye.

Jessica Sineno

Visions Of Love

Through the ocean breeze, and the clear blue sky
The thoughts of you go through my mind
through the sunlit days, and the stars at night
I feel your love that holds me tight
I feel the warmth, and all the care
that you give when you are near
I live for your smiles, and I'd die for your tears
A broken heart is no need to fear
I hold you close, and I hold you tight
like all of the covers when I sleep at night
Your love's like a rainbow that stands tall after the rain
like a baby's first Christmas, and life with no pain
like climbing a mountain, and reaching the top
like a poor man who is happy with all that he's got
I'll be the star that you wish upon,
and our love will continue from this day on.

Daniel J. Nagasawa

Turn Those Nightmares Into Dreams

It's been quite a few years now
Since the government said that we were free
And maybe I'm being ungrateful
But this doesn't seem much like freedom to me

We still must use back entrances
We can't look the man in his eyes
If we touch one of their women
We will surely die

A few brave people
Have publicly shared their dreams
but they have been persecuted and ridiculed so badly
They have been turned into nightmares, it seems

People like Malcolm X and Dr. King
have never stopped dreaming
They continued to believe in equality
Without a lot of yelling and screaming

Follow the paths of our great leaders
And take some time to dream
Believe that the world can be a better place
If we work together as a team...

Lisa McGlone

A Promise Broken

A promise broken is like a seed unsown
No way to tell if the fledgling will grow.

A promise broken is like a dream undiscovered,
A dream non-existent and cannot be recovered.

A promise broken is a sad man's demise,
One possibly avoided had he been wise?

A promise broken lies hidden near a cave,
The ominous epitaph on this man's future grave.

A promise broken will drive one insane,
On this man's conscience, his happiness will hang.

And on his last living day as he speaks with a song,
He's lived some good years, but the pain lingers on.

And as he reaches toward the death of his days
His object of affection will hear him say...

A promise broken is toward someone you knew,
That promise is me, and the broken promise...
Is You...

Eric Gillingham

To My Daughter

Mourn for me when I'm gone,
But only for a while.
Then remember me
and smile.

Remember that I gave you life
and use it!
Use it wisely and gently,
don't abuse it.

Sadness and beauty can be side by side.
Deal with each as it comes.
Remember me, it will help you
to smile.

Think of spring flowers;
it took rain to help them bloom
just as cross words were meant with love.
Look at tomorrow
Remember me
and smile.

Vera Strand

Touched Up By An Angel

They entered the room on a moonbeam,
Three little angels in white.
They hovered over the baby girl
And created a soft glowing light.

One opened a box marked "Morning Dew"
And deftly applied just enough
To make her skin soft as the wisp of cloud
She used as the moisture puff.

Next came blush to her cheeks and lips
Supplied by a red, red rose.
A smidgen of angel dust took the shine
Off the tip of her little nose.

A sprinkle of stardust was dropped in each eye
A few more sparkles to bring.
The silken lashes were brushed and curled
With the tip of an angel's wing.

Their shadow was left on the closing eyelids
As they gently kissed her good-bye.
Then they settled themselves on their moonbeam
And rode it away to the sky.

Glenelle Price Bryant

Let This Be You Sign

In Honor of Euclid DuVal Armstrong Jr.

On a recent Sunday Morning, the clock was approaching nine;
A total unknown in his vehicle "crossed that line".
Many friends, family members and four children were left behind!
If only before the losses in our lives we could receive a sign!
We shall always remember his words of wisdom and intellect;
Since birth our father taught us not to "cross that line".
That in all respects of life our actions can hurt mankind!
We shall carry all the family traditions down the line,
To teach our siblings not to "cross that line."
On the highway of life, you never know who is left behind;
If an unknown in life has not "crossed that line;"
On Father's Day and everyday give your Father a hug!
    "Let this be your sign!"

Betty Armstrong-Thomas

It's Been A Year

It's been a year, my former Dear,
that my head has laid upon another pillow.
Weak and confused I made it through,
though I was lost and numb to the max.
It was at least six months before I could relax.
It's been a year, my former Dear,
never again, another tear.
Like the winds, our courses changed
and only memories can remain.
I have no thoughts of "what might have been",
to waste time there would be a sin.
I have few regrets for the time gone by,
mainly because now...I know why.
There is no future, there is only now,
and I'm going to live it the best I know how.
My best to you, my former Dear,
on your uncharted course, you have nothing to fear.
Your wit and your charm will keep you protected.
And may you always be happy with the life you've selected.

Rufus Keel

Home

Four plates on a table
  Greet me at the door.
A plant by the sink
  Makes me smile
Even though I have whipped cream in my ear
  (And chocolate in my eye).
Busy hands draw pictures on the floor,
Turn pages in the corner of my eye,
And beat a drum that I can only hear.
Lovely voices murmur in the air
  Make me laugh
    Tell me good night.
The clock ticks loudly,
And the faucet drips a steady rhythm,
And I am scared of a bug
  that is hiding behind a picture
Because I can't see what it is up to.
My head falls on the pillow content,
And I know when I wake
I will never wonder where I am.

Amy Coroso

The Heart Is Deaf

Some say that love is blind,
But it is the heart that is truly impaired.
When the love has left, the heart is deaf...
It won't listen to good advice
Or hear the reasons why,
It just feels the pain as the days go by.

M. J. Kebis

Today

Today is a good day. A special day. Today is a day to be
remembered. Today I marry my friend.

Today I turn from all others. Today I commit to her alone.
Today I will vow to love her, protect, honor and adore her.
Today I marry my companion.

Today I'll walk by her side, no longer walking alone. Today
I'll share my life with another, myself, my hopes, my dreams my
faults and my failure. I'll place nothing and no one above
her. Today I marry my mate.

Today the sun shines brighter and my heart seems lighter.
Today I'll stand beside her, to delight in and to abide with her.
Today I marry my wife.

Today I become whole, for I've found the companion to my soul.
To love, to have and to behold. Someone with whom to grow
Old, in sickness and in health, in poverty and in wealth. Today
my search ends, for today I marry my friend.

Christopher J. Simpkins

Mercy On The Scare Crow

Have mercy on the scare crow
nailed to a cross of fear.

Look closer into his eyes,
a heart of gold that belongs not there.

A weathered face that knows the winds,
loyal crows, his only friends.

With arms to rest their thieving wings
"mercy, mercy" the scarecrow sings.

Broken pieces assembled by fate,
confused soul that knows no hate.

Longing for things that lovers do
like you and yours while watching you.

Have mercy on the scare crow, feel his pain.
as thieves fly off he feels the rain.

Daniel Joseph

The Eyes Of Christ

When I look into your eyes, time for me is still.
I behold your ageless love emptied and yet filled.

My Lord, your eyes are beautiful,
Though veiled in pain and misery.
In them I see your healing love,
Which soothes and beckons unto me.

Eyes like pools, they quench my thirst,
And in their light, my soul is bathed.
Enamored with this lofty drink,
I see in them my soul You saved.

In gazing on their loveliness,
I'm changed once more in seeing.
For from them come such awesome lights,
Transforming my whole being.

I yearn to look into your eyes,
Where love alone remains.
But Lord if you should close them,
I will love you all the same.

When I look into your eyes, time for me is still.
I am wrapped in endless love; I am emptied and yet filled.

Sr. Debra-Therese Carroll, C.T.C.

Fleeting Thoughts

Today there is a fleeting thought
of things of yesterday
Tomorrow that to will be gone
a new one in its place
If friends like fleeting thoughts can soon be replaced
their love wasn't from above
and self was in its place
So lets take self off the throne
And replace it with God's love
And we will be pleasing to ourselves
and to God above
walking hand and hand in His perfect love

Frances Dollie Mooney

Hope For The Times

Oh, Lord, what troublesome times.
    Let your sword cut our binds.
Looking out from my bay,
    I want to say, "Hey!",
wake up world and take a look.
    Lift your eyes from your book.
See the work that needs your attention?
    The world is full of contention.
It needs you to make a change.
    It needs you to be sane.

It's time to be a ray of light
    and bring it into the night.
Oh, Lord, give us sight to see
    the way that you have desired us to be.
Oh, make us to be bold
    and care to reach your goal:
To work for peace in these troublesome times,
    to make a difference to all mankind.
Oh, Lord, what peaceful times ahead,
    all because we awoke from the dead.

Nyle S. Elliott

A Season

The Autumn night was Cold and Dark,
Heavy snow clung to the trees,
Balsam firs were thick with bark,
A sense of Loneliness overwhelmed me.

It was horribly quiet — the kind of silence that crushes Air.
I sat motionless near the edge of a trail,
Waiting for the animals to arise from their lairs,
Watching for movement — the flick of a tail.

Fresh snow muffled the sound of a breaking stick,
My heartbeat raced because I knew — the Reason,
Looking into the eye of the Whitetail; Click,
The conversation of Death — the end of a Season.

John A. Traxler

A Special Day

It happened on a nice fall day,
When you wanted to go outside and play.
You were very determined to ride your bike,
You took off on your own like a soaring kite.
I admire you for your courage and will,
Even though you took a few small spills.
What a special memory in your childhood,
But all along mom knew you could.
As you rode down the street inch by inch,
You jumped off your bike and said, "What a cinch"!
You brought a tear to my eye,
Cause you kept on giving it one more try.
You came running towards me with arms opened wide,
Remember dear Gabrielle I'll be by your side.

Christiana Fante

I Thought Of A Diner

A car drove by and the dirt from the desert road
misted around me, leaving me in its tracks.
I squinted my eyes and
turned toward the sizzling sun,
which made an attempt to pierce my eyes
with its needle rays.
So I squinted,
and I thought of a diner.
A diner with red vinyl booths and
red-and-white checkered tablecloths.
The diner was full and all I could hear was
the clinging of coffee mugs and silverware.
All I could see was the steam
rising out of the kitchen,
and all I could smell were fresh
scrambled eggs and toast
and cigarette smoke.
A cloud passed over the sun.
I forgot about the diner,
so I kept walking.

Amy Laurel Brown

Ages Of Our Great Divide

How many years have passed us by,
how many chances have we missed,
to heal our country from this rift?
The soul of man we have not seen,
nor do we know its color scheme,
for ages past and for those to come.
Our human race has lost its face,
in spite of segregation, civil rights
and amendments to our founding rights,
we have not seen this all made right.
What will it take to close this gap,
this great divide of man and soul,
for ages past and for those to come?
As for the One who placed the stars and sun,
we have been told we look like Him,
our souls whose color scheme we have not seen.
For those who passed, they know not grief or anger now,
those souls have crossed this great divide,
but we remain and judge by color
all who have not yet crossed our great divide!

Thomas B. Foley

All the Years Have Passed and Gone

All the years have passed and gone,
The memories come back
  like a sad but sweet song.
There are many things that we both have done,
But we both know we're
  sorry and to both move on.
All the letters you gave me and I threw away,
There wasn't one I didn't read
  to keep and tell me "it's ok".
I'd blame you for all the anger
  inside me,
But knowing in my heart it
  wasn't you it was me.
I cannot lie, I'm still in pain,
But with all you've taught me
  I'm trying to break that awful chain.
I know I never tell you so,
But, I do and always did
  Love you so!

Melanie Perera

Answers

I move in circles above my shadow
Catching pieces of my life not otherwise known
I see myself from afar - pushed back from the others
Excluded
Not by their choice, but mine - "Why?"
I see things happening in slow motion
No chance to stop it and make it "Real"
I need someone to grab my shadow and make it live
I had to leave...so I turned around and
Mystically I vanished
No trace - no answers
The shadow still remains - tainted by
the sun - making it lifeless.
I now watch from within
Now I, I can't see anything - it's dark
My shadow had left this earth
For an instant - we are re-united, as one

Tiffinie Smith

Realization

I wear hair on my face
Does this mean, that I can take a man's place?
This world has turned into a raging mob,
Not many know, what is a man's job?
A man must love his wife
For all of his life.
He must teach his children to live, to cope, and to handle
He teaches them with experience. The Book, and example.
A man must know fear
But not live by it.
I wear hair on my face
This doesn't make me a man, does it?

Samuel Howard N. Loggans

Mother's Day

Remember those days that live in our souls,
of a little boy that never grows old,
of a mom who shows him the way down darkened halls
and gives him hope to conquer all.
To dream, to see and not be scared
of the things that might live there.
To be safe for one last time as reality stalks him from behind,
a mother's dream helps him to survive.
She holds him as long as she can
and slowly lets go of his hand,
and as he turns to walk away,
thanks is the last word a mom hears her son say.

Leonard Snipes

For You To See Sitting On The Wall

To each and every Cub who plays the game of ball,
Keep your eyes on the little guys sitting on the wall.
Pay them mind, shake their hands,
Sign the mitt they wear.
Tell them good job, work real hard, that's what got you there.
Don't turn your head, please say hello!
Little boys adore you guys, don't you know?
It's all of you,
These little guys want to meet, all of you who play ball.
They think you're so neat while sitting on the wall.
They know not the cost of a ticket for you to see,
Or what you make to "play".
The game of ball they wish to learn,
  is the neatest dream for them today.
The love of this sport not the money greed,
Is in their hearts through love for you they concede.
It's these little people we parents bring, not to see you,

But For You To See.

Rebecca L. Addington

"Cause and Effect"

I started while young
I just didn't learn
My life is now littered
With bridges I've burned
Bad choices I've made
And things that I've done
It started for pleasure
Excitement and fun
The trouble was bigger
And deeper each time
What once was a prank
Now turned to a crime
I did not know then, but soon I would see
Whatever I do makes its way back to me
Five times the effect
Or even to ten
It all equals out
When we come to the end
You live your life angry or whether you're nice
Whatever your actions you pay the full price.

Micah McComas

Trust

I look into your eyes and I see the pain.
I know trust is a fragile thing and it's hard to regain.
I've been there before
I know the pain.
Take my hand I'll lead you through the rain.

People will come
People will go
Who to trust no one knows.

Take a chance open your heart.
There you've found a place to start.

Your heart won't let you down
so don't stand around and frown
For there's a smile near by
who'll never let you down.

She's been there before
She knows how it feels.
She'll take you by the hand and show you it's real.
Look into her eyes
And you'll know the truth
for she only speaks the unspoken truth.

Jennifer Dunfee

An Elder

To many, a few listen to the words of choice.
    To see, a few heed to the difference,
That are taken in by the human spirit.
    This person shares their strong dignity in faith.
Some understand and don't know why.
    This person controls their words through understanding.
Living in self control of emotions,
    Wise words are mended deep inside.
The past is gone waldo, yet in memory the mind is strong,
    The years are filtered with wrinkles,
In which tears have fallen.
    Eyes so strong like those before,
Encouraging the weak, in helping one another.
    Having so much in common, this person in years goes with age,
To know the heart, seeks joy which brings happiness.
    To find within, we call beauty. Have knowing,
We call this to all, in our lives daily...
    An elder.

Wallace Dugan Jr.

When You're In Love

How can you tell when you're in love
And have that special feeling that comes from above
Do you float do you fly or grin ear to ear
Or blush maybe laugh when that special one's near
You're with him you're happy everything's right
You just sit and wonder whether he'll call you tonight
You just wait by the phone then start to weep
You stay up all night and can't go to sleep
You ask yourself quietly why are you feeling this way
Thinking of him 24/7 each and every day
How can you possibly love a boy so much
Is it the way you melt when you feel his soft touch
From a thousand miles you'd hear his sweet voice
And you know in your head you've made the right choice
You smile you sigh you put away all sorrow
And you very softly say, "I'll see him tomorrow"

Aemarie Bracks

Madeline

Has there ever been a sweeter child
Than little Madeline Rose?
Hair so curly, eyes so bright, a perfect little nose.
Has there ever been a sweeter child
One who captured all your attention?
With her cute little laugh, wonderful smile, and
    gentle disposition?

Has there ever been a sweeter child
One more perfect to behold?
For God has blessed us with a vision
More beautiful than gold.
She is rare, she is pure, she is truly one of a kind
Madeline Rose Wyly, your love will always shine.

Travis Wyly

The Setting Sun

One by one we are growing older.
Day by day we're nearing the setting sun.
When we will hear our Saviour calling,
"Come on home, a crown you've won."

He has built for me a mansion.
And I'll soon be going there,
Where I'll see my loving Saviour,
And earthly joy cannot compare.

I have loved ones in Heaven
Waiting to welcome me home.
When I enter those pearly gates
I will never more roam.

I will sing and shout with angels
I will praise my Saviour's name.
There will be peace and joy forever
When my heavenly crown I claim.

If down here we've lived for Jesus,
Who gave His life at Calvary.
We will live with Him forever,
Throughout all eternity.

Emma Walker

The Seer

I met the seer in Crane's poem,
And saw the great book.
"Teach me everything in that book," I said,
Then I awaited his lessons.
"Young man," he replied,
"Do you wish to grow too quickly?"

Garrett Wisenbaugh

Colors Of The World

We live in a world of red and green.
But the color on the skin is mostly seen.
We live in a world gray and white.
Because it's done doesn't make it right.
We live in a world of yellow and brown.
Old and young can't ever walk down town.
We live in a world of blue and pink.
We change ourselves with pens and ink.
People say dare to be different dare to change.
The biggest dare of all is to stay the same.

Michele Kerns

New House

It sits there, quietly inviting me in.
Sun glinting off sparkling windows
blinds me with diamonds of light.
The large oak door welcomes my arrival.

Flanked on both sides by wildflowers,
the spiral path beckons,
leading to lush gardens, and pathways
a child could frolic in ...some day.

Tranquility covers me like
a blanket of peaceful well-being,
conflicting with the excitement building in me,
as I gaze upon this picturesque paradise.

It sits there, taunting me now,
knowing that in a moment's time
I have lost all resistance to walking away
untouched by the spell cast upon me.

I give in to its magnetic charm,
instinctively knowing I'll never regret it.
For, how could one pass up paradise,
only to replace it with "I should have".

Nancy Lee Gagne

Sink

Pulled under by the leaching growth,
she drowns within a social pool.
Drifting downward her head tilted back
she gasps and lets it flood her insides.
Flushing her will. Compassion drifts
from a once filled heart.
Allowing avoidance to pervade its space.
Opening wide eyes she glimpses the faraway surface.
Closing them she becomes engulfed.

Laura Johnson

Animals

Animals come big or small,
Some are large others are tall.

Animals make you feel happy when you are sad,
Most animals are good not bad.

Animals can bite, snap or howl,
Some can hoot like the hooting owl.

Animals talk in their own way,
Usually they know just what to say.

Some animals are fast not slow,
Some animals take their time, others just go!

Animals are much fun,
Just like chewing gum.

Some animals act like a flower,
Others are great and have power.

Libby Biszko

Dear Mommy

I'm three and a half, almost four, God's taken
    me, worry no more.

No second thoughts, I'm saying goodbye,
    Mommy, oh Mommy, please don't cry.

My work here is done, don't forget me my
    dear Mommy, not a memory one.

Soon you'll have a baby named Dan, who
    will turn out to be a loving man.

He's not me, no he can't take my place, but
    the hole in your heart he will replace.

Two more children are soon to come, a
    girl and a boy, Austin and John.

With a wonderful new husband, who's name is Don,
you'll love your life Mommy in the future to come.

You know someday, you'll see me again, and
together we'll take God's beautiful hands.

Until that sweet day I want you to know,
you're a wonderful mommy, I love you so.

Austin Jeffers

The Big City Boy

My Uncle's a farmer, what ever that means
    Said he grows corn, and big lima beans
Said "Son come on down, get a breath of fresh air"
    We'll take in a dance, and a big county fair

I arrived in the morning, and went for a hike
    Just looking around, at the birds and the like
There isn't a thing, that can ruin this day
    The sun is so warm, with the smell of new hay

I hadn't gone far, when I heard a loud snort
    A hellish big bull, was bent on some sport
I made a U turn, took off at a run
    Sure had no interest, in his type of fun

I doubt if I'll make it, from the pounding behind
    Or is that my heart, blowing my mind
A few more steps, I'll be over the fence
    I wouldn't be here, if I had any sense

In a week I go home, with my bandage and cast
    To hell with this farming, it's all in my past
I'm a big city boy, that's all that I know
    I don't give a damn, what these farmers grow.

Max Linden

Understand

I love you so much I want to leave you
I have so much fun I wish I were sad
I am so young I wish I were old.
Do you understand?
Would you take the time to comfort me or would
You let me pull the trigger, would you take
the knife away or watch as my blood runs.
I want to die, I don't know why, I have
everything I want and need, yet I wish I
were 6 feet under.
Do you understand?
Do you want to understand or are you the
first to order my coffin and dig the hole?
Do you want me here with you or down with
the devil and demons too? If you leave me,
I shall die and come to haunt you day and night.
Do you understand?
I want you dead, beside me in the graveyard
do you understand?

Cassandra Hollingsworth

Sharf L. Mecham
Son Of Wm. O. And Ethel Mecham

May 23, 1922 - May 25, 1922
Do you recall your brother Dee
A brown-eyed boy, the age of three?
While stretching on his tippy toes,
He said good-by, yet needed to know.

Why his brother could not stay
To jump in piles of fresh-mown hay.
Or with him play at hide and seek
Between ma's rows of sugar beets.

And would you love this childish scheme
That into jars of sugar 'n cream,
A slice of bread and fingers could go.
Now by golly, how did ma know!

"Your heart," the doctor said, "was weak."
You never would play hide and seek.
The Master beckoned with loving arms
And safely enfolded you from harm.

You knew that cheerful Tom would come
And bring his years of boyish fun
So you could always be a part
Of the love in brother's heart.

Darlene Mecham Seely

Forgiving My Sin

When I hit rock bottom my heart was broken;
the Lord told me I was chosen.
He looked at me and saw inside
all the fear I was trying to hide.
He picked me up and my heart he did mend,
and through me, a message he will send.
Out of my soul the demons he will cast,
and cleanse my soul of its sinful past.
Now, that shows, if he can forgive my sin,
that anybody can be born again.
I remember the Lord and his almighty power,
that he can save a soul that has long been sour.
Raise up your hands and beg him for more,
and he will open that heavenly door.
He opened that door and I walked through,
I told the Lord, to him, my heart would be true.
So close your eyes and pray to the man.
The things you can't do, believe me, he can.
When the Lord is ready, he will take the stand,
and he will thin out his heavenly land.

Sean Rogers

About Last Night

Last night was about beginnings, for you and for me.
Not about winnings, often squandered so carelessly.
Nor was it lust, which drives us so recklessly.
We each shared a desire that simply had to be free.

Last night was about hope, without we'd never see an end.
Not one influenced by dope, but a word called friend.
A night not of broken hearts, but hearts that will mend.
You and I together, who could predict a more perfect blend.

Last night was about dreams, which were so vividly shared.
I can't help but chuckle to think you thought I'd not cared.
This night was not one of loss, just look how we've faired
A night so remarkable, by which all others will be compared.

Last night was about discovery, never to wonder who we are.
Having looked in all the wrong places, seeing love but from afar.
Last night we entered a door that was once slightly ajar.
Into a world of newness which promises to be the best by far.

Last night was about sharing, never more to suffer fright.
A night full of wonder, a night beaming bright.
And I hope you, like I, will remember regardless of our plight.
The events which unfolded, all about last night.

Bill J. Dunbar

Untitled

Every toy which is kept can be taken away,
As can status, assurance and wealth,
While allotted time dwindles from year down to day,
A brief candle is physical health,

And contrary now to common belief,
Love is not owned but is borrowed,
All will be lost to a ravenous thief,
If not today then tomorrow,

Yet people reflect upon everything dear,
When slowly time draws near the hour,
To what can they cling that might comfort the fear,
As worthless becomes earthly power,

Revelation transpires as senses enter final sleep,
That as for this world, nothing is to keep.

Craig R. Schwendeman

Molly's Box Part 2

Good-bye to you, for now I'll let you be, I won't take
back regrets, it all that's left of me. That's all over now,
because here it ends as my life expires. One final time to break
myself, my soul, my mind, and all of my desires; bleeding
patiently while my emotional inertia hides the pain, slowly
decaying the rest of my thoughts, my feelings, my emotions,
allowing you to devour my heart, as it completely tears me apart,
I watch you as you continue to laugh, to smile, to ignore me for
a while and carry on like you just don't care, you don't care but
still I try, try to win your heart, try to make a new start, try
to build on these thoughts, these thoughts of you, of us, of how
we used to be, or more so how I thought we used to be; bleeding
slowly while my mind begins to crumble, as I begin to stumble, to
fumble all of these feelings, feelings of pain, feelings of
devotion, feelings with no emotion; falling from or rather fallen
from grace, still had to escape that darkly lit place, no more
words to hide, no more pain trapped inside; bleeding painlessly,
anxiously, mindlessly. No reason to keep my tears hidden, too
late to keep my thoughts forbidden, waiting coldly, boldly, until
all of the draining is done, and I'm no longer one...

Michael G. Tarbell

Friends

I have warm friends,
and sweet friends.

I have friends, that make me laugh
and friends that don't .

I have some that give me tears of joy
and laughter,
some help me with everything,
some with nothing.

I have friends that are smart,
and some that aren't.
I have artistic friends and loving friends.

I love my friends for who they are.

Alia Noel Phillips

Thirst

I walked alone through an endless desert
thirsting for God's word. Angels, though
many there were, offered me none of their
"living water." My thirst became so great
I thought I might perish. Then I saw Him.
My heart ached no more as He told me about
God and His word. Then He vanished and I
realized I thirst no more.

Jennifer Merritt

Nonsense Of A Blur

You cannot see me, I am not here.
You cannot breathe me, I am not air.
Close your mouth, and swallow the pain,
But do not feel the majestic rain.
You do not like me, I am not fair.
You are scared of me, but I don't care.
I am the evil that lurks below,
I am the one who made death so.
Purple flower petals fall from the sky,
I don't know, and I don't know why.
Walk with me into the bliss. But do not stagger or make a hiss.
Prancing, dancing in the sun, falling, flying, dreaming on.
The dark blue clouds drift fast above,
They stare down at me with jealous love.
I feel confused while twirling about.
I feel like crying without a doubt.
I fall to the ground and start to spin.
Oh, why did the madness have to begin?
I'm disappearing, fading away.
I just wonder who made it this way.

Cali Jo Popiel

Whisper

A small boy whispered in his mother's ear,
so quiet and soft she strained to hear,
of adventures and travels he was anxious to face,
mountains he would climb and people he would race.
Bridges he would cross, the deepest jungle he would explore.
To the ends of the earth then push onward for more.
Mother's heart grew sad, for her son she would miss.
What to do when no longer a small cheek to kiss?

The world he would face as a man not a boy.
Where was mother's lap and his room full of toys?
For now that he was out on his own,
he wished back then he could have only known,
that mountains and bridges and living by maps
only seemed safest when in Mother's lap.
"Courage", she told him was something he didn't need.
It was something he had, it was his turn to lead.
Adventures and travels he conquered all on his own,
with Mother in heart, never feeling far from home.
A small boy no longer whispers in his mother's ear
He holds her in his heart, where she'll always be near.

Jarmila Moran

How We Hide And Seek

Brother cries, olly-olly-oxen-free,
counts time after time with his eyes shut tight,
but he hasn't ventured to look for me.

We're equal limbs of the family tree;
though I pluck the apple to take a bight,
Brother cries, olly-olly-oxen free.

I've tried to explain to him what I see
on the route I take to a grander height,
but he hasn't ventured to look for me.

I remember the days when all that we
wanted was to soar. But in my flight,
Brother cries, olly-olly-oxen-free.

Each journey a story and happily
he, my brother, I will always invite —
but he hasn't ventured to look for me.

What keeps him grounded (impatient with me)
each time I'm hidden from his line of sight?
Brother cries, olly-olly-oxen-free,
but he hasn't ventured to look for me.

Lorna Wiegardt

The Path I Have Chosen

I have a dream of charity to help my fellow man
And I pray the path I've chosen is part of heaven's plan
I have a dream of comforting each soul in my scope
And touching them with promise, peace, joy, and hope

The days, the evenings and the nights
They pass so quickly by
As I learn to strive and minister
For it's only God and I
As I start each day my prayers shall arise
Toward heaven as I pray he will touch my heart and eyes

My each and every way I have filled with gentleness
And pray that God will lead me
And help me do my best
I pray as I touch each one
As able as I can
They will see a heart that's filled with love
For my fellow man.

Ricky Thomas Gentry

O' Glorious Be

I am waiting for thee, O'Glorious Be
The day you come, come back for me.

From the place you've prepared for me to reside
All heaven rejoices, for you're by my side.

Princely Kingdom, my heart was set free
For in you alone did I find the key.

Your right hand established me
You brought me out of dark,

And in anticipating your return
I was sealed with your mark.

Awaiting my Savior, patient I be
O'Glorious day - the day you come back for me.

Tammy C. Folsom

A Respite For The Common Man

In search and contemplation of the greater truths of life
Man seeks wisdom of the ages and questions earthly strife
He reaches in desperation for the boundaries of his soul
and explores distant horizons for that which makes him whole

He summons all his courage and assumes his destined quest
To weather all the storms of life, his faith is put to test
His strength are often weaknesses and virtues become his vice
He battles his daily demons which ill winds of fate entice

The yearning for fulfillment is an unrelenting haunt
A silent scream in the darkness, unanswered by response
He stands and faces heaven and implores upon the stars
Wearily, he recounts his deeds and heals his wounds with scars

His thoughts flash in an instant, and now he understands
An inner solace emerges, fate was always in his hands
He finds resolve to heed the call of the universal cries
The simple truth is in each of us and there the answer lies.

Mark Garrett

This Is The Day

This is the Day to Share the
    Sun, moon, wind, rain and all the beauty God created.
This is the Day to care for
    Family, relatives, friends, and all mankind around the world.
This is the Day to give Thanks for
    Food, shelter, clothing and our Freedom.
This is Now - Oh! God protect us from harm
    and fill the day with peaceful ways.

Alberta C. Welch

My Dog

My dog's name is Brandy,
She ate my Halloween candy.
She runs around the house,
But she would never chase a mouse.

She loves to chew on bones
She bothers me while I'm on the phone.
She is very, very small,
She popped my brother's big blue ball.

She is an inside dog but she likes to go outside,
She always cries when I put her on the slide.
Even though she sounds like a rascal,
When I need her she's a real pal.

Erin Donnelly

A Missing Page

As I was flipping through a book of the age
It happened that I came across a missing page
Not that it hurt me, but all the same
Such a thing is always a shame

That the book should skip
From 742 to 745 it had went
With what was missing gone without a hint

I started to give the book a flip
When I realized what this had meant
For an entire poem was gone to me
One I may never ever see

Was it of love or was it of hate
Did it speak of life or death at the gate
Would I like it, love it, too late
For the missing page will not show
So as it is I may never know

Robert Egidy

In Memory Of Joe M. Fulford, 1992

It's been a year since my Daddy has passed
People say memories fade but to me they just last,
To most it is hard to adjust to it all
To me I just walk and stand proud and stand tall.
The pain is always with us and probably always will
But we just learn to walk and go on and to never be still.
For a still man has no future 'cause he dwells on the past
A strong man moves on with a silver lining at grasp.
I try to stay strong and positive all through the year
But thinking about my Daddy, everyday I shed a tear
He was my Daddy, my brother, and my pal,
I have got family and friends to help me each day now.
Never take anything for granted 'cause bad things will come
But always look ahead, don't turn your back and run.
A weak person can also make it, Lord knows I did
Cause there were several days I wish I would've stayed hid.
This is a story for all to take heed
For everybody out there himself is in need.

Joseph M. Fulford Jr.

Mikey

My best friend died,
We all cried.
We pray that he's okay,
He's up in the clouds through day and night,
Looking down to make sure things are all right.
He loved to play baseball and go to the beach,
He loved to eat ice cream, especially peach.
It was so much fun when we played,
On those spring and autumn days
Those were the days when he was alive,
And then there were days he fought to survive.

Rachel Martelly

Forever My Dreams

Those loveable arms that caress me
Those kissable lips that cling
Those eyes that hold the meaning of my every dream
Your love is always welcome
To be within my heart
Because my darling I've loved you
Right from the very start
you seem to know my feelings
You know my every care
My darling you have my love
So make us two a pair
Forever and always I'll love you
And I know you'll always care
So make my dreams comes true dear
And our life we'll always share
      my deepest feelings
          With love,
              Pat

Patricia Y. Turner

Dark Knights

When daylight fades into evening shades,
we are told in our hearts that we should all be afraid.

For evil is upon us, and darkness creeps
through knights be alert, but through daylight sleep.

Dark knights are with us, but we're not
hopeful still, artificial white lights evade
us, exaggerating until, we are engulfed in the
spell of its mellifluous flame, a flame of
deceit and white lights is its name.

We are all victims, pawns to its scintillation,
so dark knights persevere resist all temptation.

A great day will come, soon it will arise
neither knights nor day will be seen through fearful eyes.

Sonya Price

We've Made The Table Small

It's getting near Thanksgiving, we listen by the
phone. Pretty soon we hear the news Pa, we're
coming home. So we open up our table as far as
it can go. And the bristling in the kitchen our
hearts are all aglow. A week in preparation
making goodies pies and all. Then suddenly it's
over and we've made the table small. Our minds go
back to the old days When our kids were all so
young; looking forward to the holidays when our
family were all one. They were all at home this Xmas
the kids have grown so tall. But today the party's
over and we've made the table small. We are glad to
see them happy, we wouldn't change at all,
except when we remember to make the table small.
The good times we remember then silence in the hall
Then Pa says come on now, it's time to make the table
small. When our Journey's over and we've gone beyond recall,
I hope just one remembers when we made the table small.

Lucy Luker

Lifetime

A lifetime is but a moment in time.
Thank you for spending your precious moment with me.
You gave me more love in that moment than I've ever had,
or have, or will ever hope to have.
In that moment, I loved you then, as I love you now,
As I shall love you always with all my heart.

Jessie B. Belcher

Hold On

Holding on to a dream that may not come true
would this be such a foolish thing to do
like the little wooden boy who dreams of being real
The boy spirit who wished for his heart to heal
The Princess dreaming of her Prince who should come one day
Any dream has a chance of coming true have faith and pray
our lives are forever changing but for our dreams
Life and time can change our view but we still have dreams
Having a dream no matter how big or small carries you through
Battles, strains and pain a dream is you
In your heart, your eyes, your smile and laughter
with out our dreams, there is nothing after

William Shields

Beauty

"A thing of beauty is a joy forever"
so I've heard them say
"nothing lasts forever," is what they say

Take the delicate rose, she rises in birth at spring
then come the stirring winds
eventually robbing essentials from within

All through her short life, it is beauty to be seen
If you examine closer, what do you find?

Sharp edges have been acquired, all along her spine
exercise caution if you dare to touch
lest you receive a sting

Do not take it upon yourself to uproot this gentle flower
for she will soon wither and fade away
leave her where she has seen fit to be planted, she will flourish

Even in the blistering sun, she shall stand
through the beating rain, she shall not falter

Yet the day will arrive when she lastly leaves behind a shell

So beauty, a vanity, does last forever
still only in remembrance
untouched, in what we call the mind

Misty Rose

Guardian Angel

The beauty of every sunrise and sunset,
    The grace in the legs of a deer,
The care of a lioness to her cubs,
    And the healing of God's miracles.

Careful thoughts of her family and friends,
    Meaningful words for her part time job,
Loving touch to her tiny infant baby,
    Ancient advice to her teenage daughter,
And tender caress for her husband,
    She makes few mistakes,
But, still is human in mind,

She is a single woman,
    She is a loyal wife,
She is a full time mom,
She has strength and strife,
    But, being all these things,
She is also just one, simple thing
    She is a guardian Angel!

Elizabeth Binney

That Night

I heard a gun, I thought it was fun.
Put it this way, my life is done.
I woke-up in a hospital, not knowing here.
All I could remember, was that one little dare.
That was the night, that I wouldn't forget.
But I only remember, taking one little sip.
I forgot about my drinking,
I forgot it that quick.
That was the end, I'd never drink again.
My life was destroyed, just
by the devil's toy.
Now I know, that God cares
I know this, because he tells
me in my prayers.

Jennifer Wheeler

Field

Red and white dots glide across the field
past the blinking beam
of the broken street light.

A star tries in vain
to peak through the gray haze
a diamond pendant hanging beneath the
gray strands of mother age.

There are eyes
in the nursing home
reflecting the same wonders
as these eyes in the house across the field.

We are looking at the same
enchanted cartoon.

What happens in that field after dark
what spirits visit that Enchanted Kingdom?

The night beauty is the pill
that fills my
eyes with the
sweet sand that

Sends me to the next world.

Michael E. Lamontagne

Untitled

This wait is slowly killing me —
My heart aches with so much pain.
I hold a pause in my life and hope you're
doing the same.

I believe with all my heart that you're the
"perfect one."
So early in our lives we met and look
what we've become.

Closer and closer we've become to what
we want to be
Two perfect souls locked together
And only we have the special key.

Never to unlock, our vow is forever,
You and I will be as one;
Our lives can only get better.

Rebecca A. Barron

The Hobo

Thoughts sometimes come to me
About brave and beautiful tyranny.
Doubt arises, I see it there.
Questions of saneness presents; do you dare?
Those who endeavor so embark
Any fantasy which comes to heart.
Life reflects no tedious strain.
Clouds say "move", look, there's rain.
Tis a sad estate my fate to be,
I've much developed sheer authenticity.
But moments of weakness often find
Me far, far from my fancied grind.
Effort persuades me to return
Still more determined to fulfill my yearn.

Lynn S. Gainey

Mother

The call came about midnight from Helen
Who reported the massive stroke.
And we gathered the next day, and saw her,
Wires sundered,
The few remaining,
kept the bare motor functions twitching.

And hundreds of others gathered, called wrote
(Even Harvey from England appeared at the hospital.)

People said how lucky we were to get there in time
To say goodbye.
But they were wrong, for we really gathered
To say hello...

Something we usually don't get right in life;
For saying goodbye is not as risky as a full hello
To the living.
Hello to life, the essence of her.

Jack Calhoun

A Thought

I watched one day
and let the world go by
it filled me with emotion
but I could only sigh

Was it possible age caught up with me?
Were my parents right on the way I would be?
I wondered where's humanity, its loving grace
or are these just words, no foundation, no truth, no place?

I saw the newborns, the old, the young
It made me wonder where morality has gone
Have we replaced our love with natural hate?
For the way one looks, his religion, his race?

Then I thought deeper about what's in my mind
To look at others for the answers I must find
The words said when I expire, what would they be?
Then I realized to change the world I must start with me.

Harry Crawford

A Happy Day

As I awake to a bright spring day,
I pray to God to guide my way.
Outside, the children are having fun,
under the warmth of a golden sun.
The grass is glistening with morning dew.
The flowers are blooming with colors so true.
A squirrel is scampering up a big oak tree.
The birds seem like they are singing just for me.
The skies are billowing a bright white and blue.
Be as happy as the day, and God will lead you through.

JoAnn Bridges

A Prayer To The Lord

Oh, dear Lord, I am on a new road now
Please direct me of what you know
I know your wisdom
I know your power
Please Lord, come at any hour
Although you're not with me, your voice I hear
Although I do not see you, your presence is clear
Lord you know me and all my sins
You know all since I began
Here is my heart I give to you
Please Lord teach it to be true

Linda F. Castellanos

The Time, It's Speeding By

I never thought too much about it, all
those years ago. My time was like the birds
in flight, always on the go.

Time had no meaning, there was no plan, much
time to go around. In fact it seemed on
some days to really get me down.

As time went on and years flew by, my body
did its change. My hair grew grey, my size
increased, I couldn't run and play.

To play had always been there, yet now there
were some days that if I'd known about
these times, I'd gone another way.

Still these new-days are peaceful, with lots
of time to read, to listen to some ball games
and even time to weed.

My hair has now turned its whitest and my
hand has got some shake, but my spirit's
filled with all the memories, that time can never take.

Roy Owen

Parents

Parents are those special people in our lives
who teach us right from wrong.
They teach us to be caring,
they teach us to be strong.
Everyone's parents are different
in appearance and in name
but when it comes down to loving their children
they all just want the same
they want their children to be happy,
they want their children to be strong,
they want their children to have a perfect life
and never do no wrong.
So let's not forget our parents
and all that they have taught,
let's show them that we care about them
by just this little thought.
Tell your parents you care about them
and you'll be there for them too,
tell them you're glad they're here
and you'll always love them too.

Melissa Brown

Face in the Mirror

Do I see your face in the mirror, where where
oh there it is, it's me me.
Simplicity is my name, but complication is my game.
Tush Tush they say, what a shame, what a shame,
But I don't want to be anyone else, just me, plain ole me.
And no one else with no other name. Hooray for me.
I like me just the way I am.

Elsie M. Wood

Unlimited

The wind danced
secretly through the 7 worlds
and she drove down through time.
"Baby, I got eyes in you."
Fire crackin' apple seeds
candy snackin' double tongue
spitting fire across the days

You see
I'm only here as this tilted 'structure'
to take notes
while my steeple is encircled by snipers and triggers
the other equal half is 'swimming in wine.'

Destiny?
Once owned by nature
Then Stealth!
my hands weeped-
hidden behind apparels,
compelled to live in a barren home;
constantly dodging their right from wrong.
Yet I still wear the flesh.
          Carissa Barton

Coping

First, news of the illness
"Hello disease, no welcome mat for you!"
Prognosis is bleak
Darkness permeates the soul
Beginning to extinguish the light

"Comfort me, Doctor
Keep me at least free of pain
Guide me through this excursion
Pray, give me sleep
And a reason to wake up tomorrow"

The mornings dawn dimly
Breakfast and current events herald the day
News is dark
Worldwide, soul-shattering events
De-evolution of the human race

The mornings become less barren
There is light in the distance
Fertilization for the soul
A flower blooms in Winter
Infirmity coexists with flourishing soul.
          Jesse Nash

Beside The Man

I see the same man
On the same corner
Of the same street
Every day on my way home from work.

He holds the same tattered sign
That reads, "Will work for food".
I curse the traffic light
That beckons me to stop

Beside the man.

I never look him in the eye.
I'm afraid he hates me
In my new car
With automatic everything.

When the light frees me,
I leave the man to the next
Guilt-ridden bum, like me,
Who can't bear to look himself in the eye.
          Aimee Miller Zaring

My Life

As I sit each night and look up at the sky
The days and years just passing by

I then begin to wonder why it is so
My life is passing by as you must know

My family is all grown up this day
Time for them to be on their way

Grandchildren and Great-Grandchildren are here
Now is the time I want them to stay near

My life has finally come into place
I think of this things as I look out into space
          Dorothy A. Oder

Untitled

Familiar you look, yet how could it be
I give the once over and now I can see
You're a long way from home for us to chance meet
You, one of angels who once brought me heat

Optimistic eternal, pessimistic by trade
When caught in the middle of this gray charade
We once danced as lovers, you know call me friend
The damage was done, unable to mend

Believing in love is much of the whole
Condemning the hate may help save one's soul
I was a believer, now hope has grown dim
Tilting the balance because of a whim

And now the day's over, flown by like the wind
The words that were spoken no chance to rescind
Had I but one chance of which to partake
Would I still choose one with the art to forsake

There's always a new day, we risk but our life
Upon cooler waters to ease our warm strife
The wisest of sages will heartily vow
The chance should be taken, the time should be now
          Vince Hartman

Broken Heart

The tears I've cried could overflow a river.
The years I have lost have made me quiver.
The lonely nights I spend alone
with memories of you have not gone.
O Mother hear me say,
without you I can only pray.
The hole in my heart will never heal,
The arms I need so much to feel.
The empty hours seem to last longer,
and nothing helps me to stay stronger.
You're my Mom, my friend right to the end...
I need lots of love to make my heart mend.
You're in my mind every day
with heavy emotions all the way.
Not one day goes by without me thinking of you,
back to my childhood, being around you.
          Rosa Lee Elkins

Like Pouring Rain

Like the sound of thunder, my heart beats for you.
Like summer heat, my passion is for you.
Like lightning striking, I ache for you.
Like wind blowing leaves, my spirit dances for you.
Like a rose in full bloom, my soul sees you.
Like I need air to breathe, I need you.
Like pouring rain, I love you.
          Toni R. Ortega

227

Nature's Beginning

Nature is a wondrous thing
To think how each creature came into being
In the beginning there was only a void
Everything that is, came from the Lord.

Science has not any part in nature.
The Lord above created each creature.
Science occurred only when men wondered.
Every thought man has can be blundered.

The Lord gave us the world, and He put us in it.
For we humans to deny the Lord is the creator
Is a misunderstanding of the Divine contribution.
It is a sad mistake to believe in evolution.

To take away from the wonder of God's creation
Is an error of mind and understanding
The Lord alone existed at first.
The Lord alone gave all creatures the gift of birth.

Catheryn R. Nance

Coverings!

How are you covered oh child of God?
What does your covering show?
Does hypocrisy, pride or self acclaim
Conceal the true radiance of a Christian flame?

The fig tree in the orchard gallantly stood,
It leaves were green and bold;
With such bright foliage, there must be fruit around!
The Master searched, but no fruit could be found.

Nothing to offer that could His hunger appease;
Nothing to distinguish it from the other leafless trees;
Nothing behind a covering that seemed only to tease -
Nothing! Nothing! Nothing but leaves!

See the fig tree now withered and blasted!
A symbol of deception it became;
How briefly had its vain glory lasted!
As fruitlessness preceded its shame!

So too, the Christian's life tells a story,
Are you covered with "leaves" that are merely for show?
Seek now the life that manifests God's glory;
Fruits developed first in the heart will outward grow!

Olive W. Foster

Then Will There Be Peace

If all nationalities, creed, or race.
Should no longer manifest a hateful face.
Showing loving expressions so full of grace
Then will there be peace?
If we show respect for all mankind.
Always keeping pleasant thoughts in mind.
Allowing joyful hearts to become entwined.
Then will there be peace?

Seem to me it's worth a try.
Open your ears-please hear the cry.
Unite, stand tall, all fears release.
Then there will be peace?

Catherine Thomas

Rushing Waters

Our body and spirit became a soul
In Rushing Waters.
The sound of Rushing Waters stirs our soul.
Reminding us of times past and times to come.
Rushing Waters clean us from life's evil.
At the end of our life on earth we will return
To Rushing Waters.

Marva J. Schwendiman

It's Me

Honey I'm gone
My spirit is all that's left
You keep me alive
That warm feeling you get
In the middle of the night
It's me, I'm holding of the night
When you're all alone
You feel like someone's there
It's me I'm sitting in my chair
That tickling on your nose
It's me, I'm just playing
The thoughts of me you have
In the middle of the day
Don't let it make you sad
It's me, sending you our beautiful memories
No you can't see me anymore
But I'm here, by your side
I loved you all my life, I love you now
My wings are wrapped around you
It's me, your guardian angel

Judith A. Haas

Old Pictures

I looked into the picture of the past.
Ancestors never known set in glass.
Wondering about their lives; a thought
a smile, a romance. Over 200 years old;
since their passing. Who am I?
Do they know? Their history only to be sold.
My soul like a portal; each picture
digging into me deeper. Looking in the
mirror. Which parts of them am I?
Only two old letters to read; an idea of their
thoughts. Who was close or apart?
Incomplete at the end; both pages with no ends.
Wondering who I am?
In conclusions, torn emotions, mass confusion,
wanting answers; for no story was to be found.
Never to know. A hard hit in emotions
To be given and sold to the grave like an auction
restless souls without a notion; a family member
cares. A price for them is not fair; since history
is surely theirs. Who am I?

Sandilee Banks

A Christmas Wish

Merry Christmas one and all
And to all a good night,
I heard that jolly ol' man say
As he drove out of sight.

But, something was strange
For there were no reindeer,
Just an old Chevy truck
Filled with presents so dear.

He wore no red suit or had a white beard,
Wanting no recognition
He quickly disappeared.

Leaving the children to open presents under the tree,
Each orphan a gift received
As their tears fell so free.

Each child with a secret
That only they know, feeling warmth and love
Watching the falling snow.

Christmas comes but once a year but that does not need to be,
For every day can be Christmas living it daily for all to see.

Beth A. Martin

Look! Can You See Me?

I feel invisible here on earth
Take a look at me, I'm a person of self-worth
When I talk I know words come out
Tell me though do I have to shout?

I feel people look through me
Take the time to look and you'll see
That I'm human flesh and blood
Not a strong rain beginning to flood

Thank heaven for books and TV
It drowns the thoughts of being me
There's so much going on in my head
I won't give up, I keep my faith in God instead

What's the point in having a friend
Sometimes she don't have an ear to lend
I'm slowly dying in this world full of hate
Look! Can you see me, but now it's too... "late!"

Malinda J. Chappell

Pure Love

Pure love is more precious than gold;
Listen for a moment, this is how the story is told.
Pure love will never fade away;
This love will help you through those unhappy days.

When the sun doesn't shine;
Don't forget to stop and take the time.
To look deep into your heart;
And see what made you fall in love from the start.

Giving respect to your mate;
Means sometime you will have to take.
Never keep angry inside;
Because it will cause your love to die.

When things doesn't seem to go right;
Just let Christ shine the light.
In your life, keep Christ from above;
And you will always have that pure love.

Antionette M. Coombs

With Love — Mom

Well my daughter —
For nine months you've felt a life within
And now the little one's life is about to begin —

With blessed innocence and angelic face
Every baby comes from our Father's grace

Little fingers and little toes
where the journey will venture —
no one knows

So enjoy every moment — however good or bad
and realize that being a "mother"
is the greatest journey
that any woman's ever had...

"The journey ventured begins with you"

Sheila Miller

Love

Is with you the day you were born,
The unconditional love and support of your family
Love is there when you spot your first crush,
It is there when you get the job you wished for all your life.

Love is there when you are married,
There when you witness the miracle of birth,
It's there when you hold your grandchild for the first time.
Love is with you until the day you die.

Beth Griser

Angels

I like to envision Angels as I climb the stairs to bed.

I like to envision Michael, brandished with the sword of truth,
Off to battle satan the deceiver of the earth.

I like to envision Gabriel and see the look on Mary's face,
The great Annunciation, Immaculate Conception.
I like to envision Angels, too innumerable to mention,
Sent by God to protect the heirs of salvation.

I like to envision Seraphims and Cherubim surrounding God's
Throne, singing mighty Allelujas all in one accord.

I like to envision Angels arrayed in white linen, here to
Escort the Saints on the day of resurrection.

I like to envision Angels when that last trumpet sounds,
And they return with Jesus, at the end of all the ages.

I like to envision Angels as I climb the stairs to bed.

Joyce Russell

Car Dealer's Daughter

Yes, I'm a car dealer's daughter
and my daddy taught me what he oughta'
He taught me how to clean those cars,
To wash them up, where they shine like stars.
To scrub the carpets and whisk the floors.
How to get in the nooks and crannies, of the jams of the doors.
He taught me how to polish them right
So their lustrous glow shines day and night.
To mount a spare and change a tire,
To break it off the wheel in less then a hour
To vynal the dash, so it looks sleek
To clean the glasses, without any streaks.
To drive a standard and much much more
That's three on the column, and four on the floor.
He taught me all the secrets, used by a dealer
To think fast and be a witty wheeler.
Yes, I'm a car dealers daughter
and daddy taught me what he oughta!

Debbie McAlister

My Friend

She makes me happy when she comes
to visit, with time to spend.
She makes my heart glow when she
plays with her Dominoes and "Play Dough"
Cause she's my friend
When she cries, she makes me sad, when
she smiles, she makes me glad
When she wants a horsey back ride, I
get on my hands and knees, glad to oblige
she makes me happiest of all, when she
comes running to me, saying grandpa
she's my friend, I'll love her to the end

Bernard Yelli

Moon Dancer

There is so much more
I'm swinging from
I thought was gone (for good),
But good for me I was so wrong;
When I saw what I thought was a closed book,
Came partying in with pink and green balloons, and
An optimistic look,
Swinging from a rope in a big fat tree,
Reaching for a place on the moon,
Pouring hot tea...

Cindy Lynn Camp

Isn't It You?

Just when I thought, I'd started anew,
I only wanted to be with you,
And at the time I'd thought you'd see,
You'd only want to be with me,
Many special times we shared,
I really thought, I thought you cared,
But all our time was spent in vain,
In the end you caused me pain,
You broke my heart right from the start,
Afraid to confess what I was feeling,
scared you'd slip away,
Deep deep down I'm concealing
The words I'm wanting to say,
I guess tomorrow's another day,
Say, can you see what you're doing to me,
I spoke to God but he didn't hear my plea,
I've so much to offer and I try my best,
I look for one man and I discard the rest,
I consider him lucky the one for me,
If it isn't you! Then who will it be!

Yvonne Dunbar

A Mother's Love

The day you were born, I knew from the start
all the love in the world would soon fill my heart.
Your sweet, gentle face shining ever so bright
could bring tears to my eyes as we rocked through the night.

Holding you now, tiny fingers in mine,
I wish I could capture this moment in time.
As innocence comes to life through your eyes,
emotions unfold with abundant surprise.

In so many ways you're changing too fast,
but you're cherished each day much more than the last.
With each gentle squeeze, I love you some more
And I wish I could know what life has in store.

Adventures for you will soon multiply
and with each passing one, your spirit will fly,
cause every tomorrow holds something brand new
for a sweet little boy as special as you.

A heartbeat away, is all I will be;
with arms reaching wide should you ever need me.
And soon you will find, my sweet little one,
that nothing compares to my love for my son.

Teresa M. Cox

Dancer Of The Sky

In the sky I fly,
Seeing the beauty around me,
Seeing her in my eye,
She appears as a wonder, she appears as a mystery,
She is the dancer of the sky.

She calms my soul and feels my love,
For she is the one that dances above,
She is eccentric in every way,
For there is no one that will take her place,
For just look at her and admire the beautiful face,
For she is the dancer in the sky.

I once sought other needs,
But the truth is the first glance at her brought me to my knees,
For she is my supporter,
For she is the one that kindles my fire,
For as long as I am with her I know that I could never be a liar,
For she is the one that dances in my soul,
For she is more than a dancer in the sky,
For she is the beauty in my eye.

Derek E. Dilley

Being A Bear

It would be fun being a bear.
They're full of energy and don't have a care.
With that kind of life there could be no other,
Where I could roam forests with my brother.
Bears also have plenty of hair;
Animals like them have no choice but to wear.
Bears also like to climb a tree;
Their paws move so easily you see.
They also like to run and play,
Be courageous and joyful everyday.
Since bears always like to hibernate,
Winter's no problem, it's warm and great.
You'd seldom see them walk on two feet;
Bears hardly ever cross the street.
They never worry about the time,
Nor how they're supposed to spend a dime.
Yes, bears can make a terrific pair,
And this is the fun of being a bear.

Linda K. Gebers

Opinionated Death

Death has no face
to see who it takes
No questions does death ask
It steals through darkness
taking souls to eternal rest

We were born to die
And all that we achieve
will someday turn to dust.
Faces we know will exist no longer
death shall conquer all that lives.

Death's grip begins and knows no boundaries
of who or what is right or wrong
No one can say what death really is ...
eternal rest, endless sleep without dreams

Some say death is evil in disguise
spell evil in reverse, it spells live...
Do we live in evil ... or does evil live in us?

You may think my thoughts are insane
but who are you to say
We all end up in the same six foot resting place.

Charles G. Martin

The Gentle Flowers

I loved to see the gentle flowers grow,
While multi-colored petals did portend
The splendor of the waking morning's glow,
And knew that while in life I had a friend.

While being nourished by the common stream,
Their radiant beauty ever was unfurled
And joined with me to form a dual team,
Reflecting joyous light unto the world.

No field of clover ever sought to reign;
The rambling rose did not its will bestow.
Nor seek to alter features of the plane
Which God and Nature had ordained below.

Such attributes belonged to sons of Cain,
Who did their evil tasks with hands well-gloved,
And never seemed to heed the cries of pain
From blossoms severed from the world they loved.

I loved to see the gentle flowers grow,
But badly withered petals now portend
The stillness of the final evening's throw,
Where e'en in death they have a friend.

Joseph A. Presing III

Only In My Sleep

Here I sit in total anguish.
In my realm of dreams I vanquish.
There I am loved and bathe in the glory,
But reality tortures with a different story.
Christ teases me with a losing goal
By placing on this global earth your soul.
In my soundless slumber our spirits are one.
My unwanted awakening becomes a perfect picture undone.
My paintings of today are a dull black and white,
While vivid colors dance when day becomes night.
In my creative mind I am loved and I love,
But these visions of tranquillity are never enough.
Once, I thought my tantalizing mirages would come true.
That actually during the light I would be loved by you.
Clearly it has been shown that I have been mistaken,
For only in my sleep is your love awakened.

Karen J. LaCasse

Untitled

If I was to say that you are a flower,
Under the dark gray clouds,
Waiting for the showers.
Bright as the moon.
Deep as the forest.
As cool as the air.
To be picked would be a waste of a precious life,
Of grace.
To let it grow on its own,
Would be blindfolded passion ever so,
Unknown.
To be a bee upon your arms of limbs,
Ever so green.
I promise I would waste nothing,
That I have seen.

James R. Copus

She Don't Know

I have watched her when she wasn't aware.

I have given her my love even when she wasn't there.

I have touched her soul and helped it to grow
and someday she will know.

I have helped her to grow and taught her how to love.

I have given her my heart and much, much more.

But she still don't know that I am a part of her soul.

David Jones

Cloud 9

Slowly flying overhead
an angel watches you
at stressful work or while in bed
an angel protects too.

An angel watches you all day
it never has to worry
an angel puts your fears away
and never will it hurry.

The raindrops fall then rise again
to form a most glorious cloud
on which angels gather and sing "Amen"
wonderfully peaceful, never loud

For on Cloud 9
you shall find, miracles planned each day
and the sun will shine
to warm your soul, with love in each new ray.

Momara Sheppard

Where Have You Gone

Dedicated to: Lorraine and Henry Sublett
I gaze into your eyes, but your presence doesn't show.
I'm sure you are there, but where I don't know.

Is your mind adrift on some distant shore,
and will I not know you any more.

You remember the children when they were small, and
you remember the places we've lived, them all.

Yet to remember today is beyond your reach
oh God, Dear God, how can this be.

If this is the burden that we are to bear,
then God give us the strength by always being there.

I remember when I met you some 50 odd years ago,
dressed in your white from your head to toes.

An angel of love to protect me through the night
an angel of love to help me win my fight.

You nursed me to health after my ordeal,
and without your love I would not have healed.

Oh where have you gone my love of all time,
and will you be back? I pray for that time.

Wanda Wilbanks Sublett

My Sun, The Lover

Malnourished for sunlight I twist
then squint through slits
in mini blinds
to peer at the world outside.

Naked trees stand quivering, only their
roots shielded by earth,
fallen leaves, straw
Brown-gray is the scheme.

While rocks unchanging stand firm as in summer.

Air seems deceitfully warm, Romeo
sun tempting me to
ride underneath him
with the top down.

Vaguely a clinking keyboard assumes his
place among my senses
letters rising, falling
convey knowledge of the applicant

Who would be where I am now.

Wendy A. Williams

Love Music...

A whispering, smooth shadow of two
Voiding the black beneath

A man and woman come together
Dreaming of a life vision felt

Its likeness is to the seasonal beauty of the rain forest
Whose leaves smell like a thousand red rose petals

By day, the hot summer sky is flooded with sunshine
By night, the fall moon is delirious behind the chanting sea

A raw winter wind lathers me in white
But I feel as delicate as a spring garden

I'm weak from this powerful moment...

Me, in my milky white gown
He, to be my rock for eternity

We stare longingly
And say "I do"

The Future Mrs. Barry Shea Jr.

Forever And Always I Am Man

Forever and always I am man.
Immortal being challenged by life.
Urgencies — no matter for one such as you.
What destiny shall you serve, dear soul?
Serve none, for they shall serve me better.
What force shall drive you away to hide face
down from shame and horror?
Death is such, yet I own him, I shape him,
and carry him on his trails.
Tear down my walls of insecurity and I will
give you my oath.
My will be done, for I am stronger than fear and machine.
I create, therefore am I not God?
Surely you know my name, forever and always I am man.

Jason A. Lavely

Forget-Me-Nots

Because I shall not forget you
My heart is blue

Forget me not

Don't shed no tears
That won't get rid of your fears
And you don't need all those beers

Forget me not

To take away your sorrows
You may end with more than you can borrow
Just to make a better tomorrow

Forget me not

I want to share days when I'm blue
And you'll care enough to say I love you

Forget me not

Then I can whisper four words
I love you too

Rebecca M. Libbert

Fatherly Love

Walking down life's winding road.
Feeling lonely, feeling cold.
Looking for a place to call my home.
Looking for someone, to call my own.
Memories from my childhood past...
Why do the bad ones, seem to last,
And I ask!!!
About fatherly love, I never had...
No one to call my father, daddy, or dad...
Tears of despair, that make me sad.
Fatherly love I never had.

Donald E. Chambers Jr.

Trapped

I'm trapped in a world of pain,
A world of hate and fear.
I'm trapped in a world that doesn't care about people
of different race, religion, or color.
When I hear and see what it took people to get their
God-given rights, it's so sad.
Just because a person may be different doesn't give
anyone the right to judge them.
People are being trapped in fear.
I'm trapped in a world of violence.
Some people can't even walk down their street without
being scared or threatened.
I wish I was trapped in a world of
Peace.

Jermaine Johnson

Paparazz

Love shall guide me through the next night,
caring for you everyday is a fight.
I know many want you when they see you in sight,
But I earned you without even sinning.
Wanted to hold you from the very beginning.
To me you're too much for a song,
so I wrote a poem,
To express myself in every shape of form.
You're my infant of joy.
Even though my size compared to yours is much more,
without you I'll be in adversity.
With you and your twins I can get a 500 benz,
Great champagne plus party with my friends,
also I can eat greater than life,
and buy clothes across the world for my wife.
Sweet Green Money you're my #1 in life.

Montego Pearson

Exile

A great sadness rushes over me
like a wave enveloping a sand castle
when I realize that my past is great, my future small,
and that I have not done enough.

The feeling is fleeting,
but its furtive onslaught destroys my well-being,
leaving me limp, lonely, and isolated.

What is this phantom that strikes at me,
seeping into my spirit,
eroding my composure,
and shattering my resolve
not to dwell on uncertainties?

Like a deadly vapor,
and at a time of conscious serenity,
it enshrouds my window of hopefulness
and plunges me into momentary fright.

I know then that my separateness from God
is the root of my sorrow and fear...
and I pray.

Donald N. Bosworth

Nature's Gift

I hear their talk as I awake,
Their voices soft and sweet.
I lay and wonder what they say.
Just listening is a treat.

Some sounds are high, some sounds are low,
Some come from far away.
Some voices are so beautiful,
"Oh please don't stop," I pray.

I listen as they sing and chat,
Their songs so pure and rich.
No lessons did they need to take,
So perfect is their pitch.

I wonder how so small a size
Can sound so great and rare.
The rapture that they give to me,
There's nothing can compare.

The gift these little feathered friends
Give to me every day,
Inspires my heart and lifts my soul.
There's no way to repay.

Jan Twohill

Love

Love comes, and love goes,
But few of us fail to realize
when it was truly ours to call our own,
We often feel abandoned, and left to be alone,
To search our hearts,
and souls for one last chance to love, yet another
time once more.
It's then we reach out to finally
hold the meaning of love,
we know this by only being,
Bigger than one could ever see with just
one glance,
Heavier than one could ever hold with just one set of hands,
More words, than one could ever understand listening alone,
But one saying known to every language
spoken so warm, so true,
you know this to be, love!

Heather Lewis

The Value Of God's Creations

The beautiful grass on the hill,
 Each blade so perfect and green,
Blows to and fro in the wind:
 A fairer sight, seldom seen.
No praise from the eyes of man who climbs
 The hill in haste and tramples it under foot
Destroying its graceful sway and beauty so complete

What secret propels this man, his face an ugly mask,
 To trample up the hill, so mind less of the grass?
It too, is God's creation, so precious to the land,
 One blade, worth more than the greatest art,
Performed by mortal hands.

Samuel L. Thompson

Visions, Past, Present, Future

I arose this morning and looked in the mirror,
 and there I beheld one of my greatest fears.
Where a young man had once proudly stood,
 now was an image much less understood.
A weathered old man, with frost in his hair,
 stooped with age, and wrinkled with years.
My mind said, "I'm young!", my body said No!
 The season's now winter, time for the snow.
Age came upon me like darkness of night.
 Swiftly it came through good times and strife.
So be wise, my friends as you travel through life.
 Enjoy the trip, don't wait to get ripe.
For there's flowers-a-plenty to enjoy on your way,
 And family and friends to brighten your day.
Soar with the eagles, fly through the clouds,
 Don't grovel in dirt with slovenly crowds.
For age creeps upon us and requires its due,
 And never excludes neither me nor you!

Ralph G. Sorenson

Knowing Like, Lust, Love

We now know the true meaning of love, or do we? Wanting to touch, hold, caress, kiss to be with. Some fall deep in love and don't really know it yet. Some really think they know what love or this thing called love is. To them it's just a dream like the water lifting a stream. Does it seem to happen over and over time and time again. I want colored picture butterflies in our garden flower like incense for miles.

Like lust, love, hate, denial, emotions running wild. Liking you as a friend, lusting you as life, and loving, loving the one who wanders in a ring of fire. Closer, closer we get to the edge of the layer. Are we there yet?

Brian Vinson

Me, Myself

I am me, myself.
I am strong and smart.
I love rain.
I love to sing,
but Art is my thing.
I have eyes, I have lips.
I have a brain to think,
and a tongue to speak.
I have many ideas.
I can't wait to go out into the world
I want to turn into a butterfly and travel
around the world.
I will go to Brazil and dance with the Indians.
I will go to Scotland and lay on the green grass,
And just stare into the sky.
I can hear music, it seems to
tell you something, but I don't know what yet.
It makes me want to float. Or just keep on going.
Then I come back, to my life. I still remember my voyage, but
I am still me, and will always be.

Lilah P. S. Mavis

Promise

Grey and stern, the Minnesota winter answers no questions.
A few lonely geese scurry across the sky, in search of
 warmth and hope.
The cornstalks, tan and ochre, stagger in the wind,
 melancholy remnants of harvest time.

Yet a slice of sunlight shimmers for a moment, a brief
 reminder of what comes in the spring without fail.

It is a cycle as true as a child's smile, as comforting
 as a mother's touch, as enduring as time itself.

The future lies in wait, a promise just beyond the grey.

Emily Lodine Overgaard

A Mother's Child

A mother's love is her child.
 A mother's child is her heart.
My heart beats for you every day.
 Even though you're far away.
Sometimes I find myself at night
 Just hoping and praying I could hold you real tight.
I can't see or hug, or give you a touch
 But you need to know I love you very much.
I think about you all the time.
 If not you're always on my mind.
I think about you every single day.
 I thank God you're only just a dream away.

Mary Cole

A Moment of Passion

The scent of love embraces the air.
As two eyes meet, they stop, they stare.

A passionate moment sparks become intense.
While two hearts race, loss of words immense.

As a majestical mist covers the room.
Their hearts create one beat, one sound, one tune.

They're drawn to each other as though they are one.
Life has a meaning, theirs just begun.

Susan Roubal Wesley

Someone We Love So Much

We all have rough times to go through
When there's nothing else we can possibly do
We try so hard to help and guard
Someone we love so much .

We try to comfort and hold
And take them in out of the cold
We talk to them and lend out a helping hand
We try our hardest to understand
Someone we love so much

Sometimes they just can't see
How important family can be
It hurts us to be pushed away
From someone we love so much

Through these rough times
Be sure to keep in mind
That you don't have to search to find
Someone who loves you so much.

Lindsey Miller

A Special Man's Death Bed

I see this man that I don't know real well
Lying in this death bed in a world of hell.
As he lays on his death bed
and looks at the beautiful weather
I go visit him and we grow closer together.
I ask him how he feels and instead of answering
he asks me if my injuries from my accident have healed.
I don't know how he does it day after day
Smiling and giving us all a gift in his own little way.
To himself he is not lying
for this man knows that he is dying.
He writes a book about his cancer
Knowing deep in his heart God has the answer.

He has gone on now to see the light,
Gone up in the sky so blue and so bright.
He has left us to see a better day
and in my heart he will always stay.
I'll always remember him and the life he lived
I'll always remember the gift he did give.

Derek McClellan

Grandma's Quilt

How many a child was put to sleep
On blankets soft and pillows deep.
"Don't worry dear," as she brushed my head,
"I'll tell you a story as you go to bed."

I pulled the covers up under my chin
To say to her, let the story begin.
"This blanket here at the foot of your bed
Belonged to me as a child," she said.

"Each day my mother would stitch and sew.
The hours it took only she would know.
A bit of an apron or piece of a shirt,
And that one there was her favorite skirt.

More like a memory than just an old quilt.
The love it had and the friendships it built.
One day just a tiny piece will remain
But still then the story be told just the same.

"From child to child and grandchildren too,
You'll know this quilt is especially for you."
She got up from the bed and turned out the light.
"I love you Grandma O," I said, "Good-night."

Tamar Kohtz

Congratulations

My dear sweet sister
You shall see

How life is created
For you and for me

A recipe, so divine
Extracted from a Holy wine

A spark of passion
A flame of love

A symbol of a Holy dove

As these nine months
Bring happiness and joy

With thoughts of a little girl or boy

I pray for you a multitude
Of great, majestic beatitude

And when this darling comes to be

Your life will swirl so joyously

And bring forth into a Christian life

For Gods love is what we strive
Congratulations, I say to you for life within is anew.

Melanie Braicu

The Sight Of An Angel

Sitting alone as thoughts of you go by, like windy squalls,
To hear that voice like an angel, echo off these empty walls.

Feeling the warmth of the sun and seeing its light,
Is to display the truth of love at first sight.

To see the endless amount of stars in the darkest sky,
Is like the many times I think of your beauty, as time goes by.

As God made the heavens and this wonderful earth,
I praise Him for making your beauty which started at birth.

The love of Christ I see in you, is brighter than a flame,
The tone of your voice like a saint, praises His holy name.

Your future will be blessed by God, I see it as you grow,
I see it when I look in your eyes, the future has begun to show.

To hear your laughter and your voice, to see your smile,
Makes the true meaning of Godly love, all worthwhile.

The sounds of a sparrow like your voice, I hear it call.
You whisper kindness to everyone and help them from their fall.

This face of love I see, is sought as a raging fire,
The love of Christ you show to everyone, is your desire.

You are truly a gift from the wonderful God above,
I know what I hear and see is truly the gift of love.

William Bradford Spinks

Poetry

Poems, poems, poems!
Brilliant thoughts, some moans
Each word beautifully arranged.

Foregoing moments, some bygones
Captured, reminiscent, also fluorescence.
Wordy lines of phrases, expressions, lore.

Forceful, flourishing, allegory words
Rhyme, metaphorical enabling mercenary
Merchandise of this my poem! Be merchantable words.

Hopefully the poem alone of true poetry will be helpful
To all involved and the sum awarded by submission of each
Will be received soon.

Grace I. Hager

The Winner

Do I require such a type of governing
That I can not judge for myself
Your logic is to be followed like a religion
Either appeal to it or perish by it
Correct behavior is praised but it is so hard to accomplish
For you have established a prison of criticism
And incompetence that makes me
Bow down and cower to your every word
My mind gets flustered, my anger gets buried,
All the words on my tongue get lost
All my feelings suppressed
For this naked individual that I have allowed
Myself to become has not become weak
But has developed a sense of patience
That is to be respected
For no other person could still
Consider this relationship a challenge
He will one day look in to my eyes and see an equal
I will win

Cary Denice Fox

To My Beloved - Ernest

Your face will be written in my heart,
Will be written in my mind.
Forever, and though eternity.
I spend my days half wet, half dry.
The nights are long and lonely.
I have been hovering between non-life, non-death,
At the crushing wrack of losing you.
I find indelible shades of you in our child,
To tell me I am not alone.
In all our life,
You were my love.
In all our love,
You were my life.
You were my heartbeat.
You were my husband!
Oh, how my heart longs for you,
And forever, I am so blue.
When tomorrow the sun does shine,
I will feel your spirit divine!

Polly M. Longchamp

My Idol, My Obsession

Dedicated to : Billy Corgan
When your voice comes to me,
Either singing or screaming,
I listen

When you appear on the television
I kiss the screen,
Leaving lipstick prints on the glass
And you don't seem to mind at all

When I am alone or in public
I imagine you there,
With me or watching me

When I think about you
Everything turns into a scorchless red
Creating atmosphere unlike my own
But it is still breathable, and now persuasive
Cool breezes flow through my vacuum sealed place

You are my idol, and my obsession

Seantelle Roe

Ending Of A Love Story

Silver linen around the moon
Blankets women who have swooned
Stars twinkling in their eyes
A tear forms then she cries

The doctor is aloof; but amazed
People surround her all crazed
As the doctor showers on the scene
A rain falls like a mist on a dream

Her eyes crack like the day break
But her hands are like an earthquake
Her face white as a blanket of snow
The red lips call for the man she knows

So as she's embraced in his arms
The sun shines through him and pushes the storms
A gentle hug and a simple kiss
So all the love stories end like this

Christopher C. Hilton

10 Seconds Of A Suicide Attempt

Shotgun jammed between clenched teeth, in a few seconds
you'll need a wreath. People slipping by the open room are
sensing pain and the impending gloom.

Thumb on the trigger, gun ready to fire, soon this body will
expire. Angel, oh angel sweet angel of death, come and be with
me, I wish to breathe my last breath.

Misfortune is common in a crowded city, yet here you are
full of anger and self pity. You'll get them to suffer when
you're laid to rest, all your life you've been a person self-possessed.

The muscles are tensed, body's beginning to shake. This makes
no sense, why for God's sake. The mind is a scramble, tears
starting to flow. What's wrong, can't do it, you really want to grow old?

Now you're afraid of being in pain. You could end up a vegetable,
with half a brain. Why did this happen that it comes down to this;
It all started with one little kiss.

Melissa Rack

A Glimmer Of Truth

A teetering tot had heard
Some tales supposedly factual
The truth was most were not —
What the tot had been taught was absurd
And decidedly not very actual.

A traumatized teen had trimmed
The fat from the lessons he had learned;
A cut of truth is lean —
As the cream from the milk must be skimmed
Can wisdom's wages be so easily earned?

A militant man had searched
For oases where truth came to rest;
'Midst dunes carved from deceit —
He sought wise men who swiftly researched
Answers to riddles or just made a good guess.

A crumbling coward saw truth
Shrouded by smoke screens of fools' desire;
Truth, born from rotting fruit —
Man's fires now fueled by gin and vermouth
Fade to a glimmer...truth and flesh soon expire.

Robert Doyle

My Father

I guess you can say I'm "Daddy's little girl."
My father means the whole world to me.
He is always there for me.
For as long as I can remember, my father has
Given me the strength that I need.

Dad, you were there when I fell on the ground.
My father would pick me up and dust the dirt away.
You always had advice for me and encouraging words to say.
I realize I wasn't usually easy to deal with each day.

I am so very thankful to have you in my life.
I appreciate every single thing you do.
All the blessings in the universe wouldn't be enough
For me for repay you.
I just feel you need to know that I love you.

Jessica Moore

To: Mom And John

I am writing this poem
I am only going to show 'em
I am not only in the dark side
I am not only trying to hide
I am only writing how I feel
I am sometimes only trying to heal
I don't think my life is bad
I know it's not, that's not what I had
I have a wonderful life
With my mom as his wife
It may be hard to learn
But I will be as soft as a fern
So guys I'm telling you now my poems are becoming pow
I'll write a happy one as happy sun
for you mom I will write for you to read in your site
and hopefully you might say they are hype!
And as for you John thanks for being with my mom
I know sometimes I'm wrong put please stay strong
So I'm saying to you both I love you
I know it doesn't rhyme but it's time to shine

Tina Whittemore

Night Birds In Twilight

To what other, secret universe
do these magical swallows fly,
as in and out of existence
against the twilit sky,
they flit 'round the windowed structure
streaming shafts of unseen light,
on their simple nature's errand
of feeding in the night,
to create a wondrous mystery
as they vanish in mid-flight.

Unaware, this swarm of swallows,
swooping freely to and fro
through lit slices into darkness,
as if through time they go.
Without a care, these slender night birds,
except for the task at hand,
are mindless of two rapt watchers,
who in awed enchantment stand,
to contemplate a miracle, no doubt, as each winged creature
flickers out, then reappears again.

Darlene Pyburn

PLAYWRIGHT

Each stories a world
                    that can be borne.

Ibsen-like, your well-made play
                    defines motives, actors
                    predictable, complete.
Act III inheres in I, surprises
                    only the inattentive.
You use My name in your cast.
I will not play in a doll's house
                    built by human hands.

Beckett appeals to me.
                    I will wait where roads cross;
Pagliacci may pass, Elvira Madigan,
McMurphy, Jesus in rags, you,
                    unnameable, me I haven't met....

...are there house lights?

Jeanne M. Concannon

The Cry Of The Sea

Thunder booms
Lighting flashes
The waves of the sea go wild
In the distance you can hear the cry of lost love
The rain pours down hard on the earth
The heavens open up
Lighting flashes
Thunder booms
The waves grow bigger and twist like a sculpture
The cry of lost love
The thunder stops
The lightning flashes one last time
The heavens close
The rain dies
The sun smiles on the earth
A woman and man walk hand in hand upon the beach
They saw
They heard
The cry of lost love.

Amy Whetstone

The Tip Of The Iceberg

Running and racing to and fro
Panicked and partial to the ones I know
Constant like the Northern Star, and the sea
That's what I thought you were for me.
I gave you all love, perhaps too much
Perhaps, overwhelmed, you shrank from my touch.
I'm sorry; I loved you; I love you.
I'm strong though
I've learned some
I will not be part
Of how small you've become.
I love you, but I need me
So now and forever, you are free.
Free to control all
That is not my own
I hope you pride sustains you
For you have chosen that throne.

I will not wait,
But you will never be alone.

Eric Kendall

236

The Voice Of The Past

Late one night, I was fast asleep,
Not one creature made even a peep,
My dreams all were pleasant, in my bed I was curled,
The moon outside shone brightly, over the world.
Then a voice, somewhere near,
Woke me suddenly with fear,
The voice knew everything that happened to me,
I looked for the voice, but no one I could see.
I was scared, "Make it stop" I was praying,
Lots of events from the past it was saying.
I told it to stop, while I held my ears,
Trying to ignore it, while my eyes filled with tears,
I struck at the air, and I cried like a child,
I sung to myself, while my memories piled.
Then I suddenly realized, the voice was in my head,
From my locked away past, all my memories it said.
"Remember the memories you've locked away?"
Said the voice, "You will learn from the past on another day,
You have to remember what happened back then,"
said the voice, "Stop it from happening, all over again."

Michele Jennings

Passing The Torch

I hiked up the hill from the parking lot,
Past the uncountable rows of monuments,
Then stood quietly as I studied the eternal flame,
Looking out to that tall monument,
I studied the tasking to all generations.
What is our report card, since November 63,
When I was 17?
Have we battled and created a better world?
Have we conquered tyranny, and poverty, disease and war?
Have we defended freedom and set it forth on a clear course,
That the world will want to follow?
Have we taken more than we have given?
Have we shown a higher purpose,
And passed the torch to the next generation?
Let us measure our score and redouble our efforts,
Lest we lose sight of the prize,
For tyranny and disease are on the run,
And war too deadly to consider.
So now we must resolve, with God's blessing and help,
His work is truly our own.

Bruce Fette

When I Looked Up

When I looked up
And God looked down
All my sins He forgave
And His Love, I have found
He forgave me, my sins, doubts and fears
And now I know, His Love and His grace
For when I look up
I can see God's face

When I look up
My Savior looks down
With love in His eyes
And his mercies abound
He looked in my heart
And my sorrows he sees when I look up
And He looks down on me

When I look up at the heavenly realm
With all of God's beauty
In heaven can be found
And I know that one day
When my life here is over this beauty I will see
For God is Love and with Him I will be

Betty J. Hudkins

Fiction To Be Not

All these little girl worlds we've lived
you and I, my china doll laughter
edging on and on
and even feeling a little
alabaster and some times blue
I think that's when you smiled for you
screaming at the sunlight
screaming for a Mad. Day
overcast and anti-humane
just hanging out, standing in the rain
with the monsters that used to stay under our beds
well, they're kissing us finally
loving us and licking at these tears, and your tears
fiction to be not for you I dream
and this ecstasy is my torment
this rapture, I shouldn't let it stay
so I'll give to her this chisel and paints that won't fade
from this wall, in mind to matter to and through
dream aching for a reality
for my china doll girl, really loving in the rain...

Rebecca Hurley

Life Cycles

I was born the ocean
(if I was born at all)
My next life was humidity
then a cloud I came to be
Later I was gentle rain
Returned to the sea.
Again in the ocean
Someone called "wave" at me
A storm came up
I was afraid
Of droplets I had been
Back in the ocean,
I don't remember my other names
  humidity
  cloud or
  rain
Or that the storm herself brought me home.

Johanna Beaudry

The Devil Laughs At Mortal Lust

When day turns night and dark takes dusk,
The Devil laughs at mortal lust.

Oh what a world for such a beast,
When mortals dance his eyes do feast.

Upon the flesh; upon the bone...
Upon the fetus being born.

He looks down on a man with a knife,
He holds his lover and kills his wife.

He looks on a girl standing naked as men squirm and shout,
as their pelvises slash in then out.

Oh, what a world we grant to him,
All his wants the pleasures of sin.

He reigns on high with a faithful cupid by his side,
And the world of lust his cupid provides.

He can't be killed nor beat,
but made to run with thorns in feet.

Immortal love in mortal hearts,
Pierce his skin and sting like darts.

Until such time he'll hold his pride...

When day turns night and dark takes dusk,
The Devil laughs at mortal lust.

Jennifer A. Davis

Going Home

It's hard for me to imagine
Wandering from room to room
Looking for the place where there
was once a bride and groom
All would be now quiet as a tomb
except from the floor that creaks
Rotting from disuse

It's hard for me to imagine
walking slowly up the stairs
nothing can be heard but the whispering of air
when I reach the top
I will not bother to knock

I walk to the window and look out at our land
In the distance beckons me two unearthly hands
I close my eyes and feel the wind rush
against my face as I race towards the ground
And into death's embrace

It's hard for me to imagine ever looking back
and as I start to cry I realize there is no going back

Brandi E. Grummel

Mother

   The sweetest word that could ever be said,
sweeter yet when it is heard... Mother.
   Everyday the sweet Mother unconsciously
opens her heart and puts into place, elements
to form and raise a gentle and kind human being.
   She watched with amazement as her
little baby grows.
   Then she struggles with the time and
how precious it really is.
   Although she has undertaken the most
important position in her life, her work is
seldom acknowledged or appreciated.... Still she
perseveres through each day.
   The biggest job in the whole world and
the payment unmatched at any amount.
   Unconditional love and be called... Mother

Betty Earle

Another Lonely Spring

Winter's chill has come and gone,
Icy fingers have played their song,
Breezes hum a lullaby,
Reminders of a love gone by.
Here I am, another spring,
Lost in lonely remembering,
Soulful tunes that have no rhyme,
Sunny days playing tricks with time.
Warm sand cools as autumn nears,
Summer romances fade,
But empty hearts like mine,
Must feel a lighter beat, and not be afraid,
Seasons pass, I'm still alone,
What will tomorrow bring,
Will I find a love once more,
Or face another lonely spring.

Gordon E. Bradfield

A Missing Link?

Is love a missing link in our home, today?
A strong bond of family with God's needed ways.
What happen to father, mother and child, per se.
What missing link would you say?

Father is needed for guidance and strength.
Mother is necessary for love, encouragement, at no length.
Child, today, needs the qualities of above.
For the family
   A strong bond of love

The missing link is felt from within.
Love is the answer and to all our kin.
Originates within ourselves, family, and then others.
(The warmth from heaven above.)
Each and everyone of us are the missing link - called love.

Elaine L. Bowman

Untitled

Your hand has touched my very soul
before I held it in mine.
Your voice it sings to me,
like an arrow to my heart.

I close my eyes and you are there,
your heart beating in time with mine.
I dream of your hand in mine
and the scent of flowers in your hair.

In such a short time to find one such as, you,
My soul mate, my heart.
I can no longer say I am alone
for with you my life can begin, anew.

My heart beats with new life
and a fire of passion for your love.
All I could ask for is your hand,
your heart, and a life shared.

Debra Wall

Light Of My Life

If, through a glimmer of light,
I feel hope.

If, through one spark of light,
I gain faith.

If, through the flicker of one ember,
I feel warmth.

If, through the light of the moon,
I feel love.

If, through life's despair,
I see light at the end of the tunnel,
And it brings me back to see life in a better light.

If one person can give the light from despair,
The light of love, the light of warmth and faith,
And the light of eternal hope,
Then you, my daughter, are my blazing fire,
The light of my life.

Barbara L. Hargraves

Wiles Of The Wind

Shimmering reflections dancing on the waves.
Ripples gliding round and round.
Crashing surfs upon the beach, foam floating to and fro.

So too are we guided by the wind which
   listeth where it will.
Whether it be here or there we will follow
   as it beckons.
We are just a wave, a ripple, a surf, being pushed and tossed,
   one way and then another.

And so through life we go where it has directed us to go.
A reflection dancing,
   round and round,
      floating to and fro.
   Nancy J. Love

Solitaire

Moving along I feel the touch of sadness
I know the loss, ever watchful
Comes with a song, like the wind
Hustling the memory of words and faces.
And so young to start the Other journey,
Evening star welcomes the wanderer
Learn the answers beyond the still life.

We knew the moment now the silence

Stands sentinel in the unreflected room.
Possessions remain behind inscrutable
Unyielding in their secret vision;
Remembrance, that softly glowing legacy
Looks down the departed years
Offering its tribute in the here and now.
Crystal moments in time, our time
Kaleidoscope between departure and return.
   Roger Peploe

Save The Children

A Child is born and christened by the Reverend,
The Angels are watching in hopes he gets to heaven.

Times will be hard, his short little stay,
but during this time, we must teach him to pray.

We must bring them up right to start on their way,
So when they get older, they will not stray.

Christ will be with him to guide him by night,
Constantly inside of him advising what's right.

Satan will be out there throwing darts amidst,
But as we have taught him, satan he should resist.

Soon his battles will be over, Christ beckons him home,
Will he be worthy to meet the King on the throne?
   Quillian Montgomery

To My Son

I watched a beautiful sunset the other night,
and my thoughts were with you...
Wondering if you were seeing it too?
Then I began to cry,
knowing that though you are
always close in my thoughts and prayers,
sometimes the distance between us
is more than I can bear—
more than just miles...
And even though the moment was beautiful,
I feel empty, open, broken and choiceless...
   Pam Schwertley

Eternal Flame

I never meant to hurt her
It's just what I do best
She may think I've deserted her
What I feel for her is becoming less and less

But nothing could be further from the truth
Because what I feel for her over-flows
And I'm only waiting to show her proof
That my love for her still grows

But what if I'm imagining things
That are never gonna be
And if one day the love she brings
She doesn't bring to me

I guess I will or maybe I won't
Learn to accept it as my fate
But until then...I don't
Have anything I'd rather do than wait

So here I am...waiting for her
And the love I so desperately desire
Because deep within..my heart and soul bestir
The flames of an eternal fire
   Ian Lifecreed

Forever Love

As strong as the sun that shines upon the land,
Is the power of my love that I have for you.

Its force is that which will last a lifetime,
Its contents will be filled with the capacity to be flexible,
To be soft, to be gentle, to be understanding and forgiving,
to be changing, and yet be firm enough to stand the test of time.

As bright as the sun that shines upon the land,
Is the strength of my love that I have for you.

Its vision knows no bounds,
and is forever a reflection of my actions.
Its feeling is always present,
with every thought and touch and response.
It's in each smile, each sound of laughter and joy,

It only grows with every passing day.
It is the source and nourishment of life.
This is my Love for You.

As warm as the sun that shines upon the land,
Is the warmth of my love, that I feel in my heart.

You are my essence, my inspiration, my Love.
   Michael L. Aglialoro

Until I See You Again

I've been up all night
And down all day,
Wondering what it is I'll say
If ever I see you again.

I'm done with games
And silly lies,
I'm through with all your alibis
Until I see you again.

Too far down the road you're gonna realize
That I was meant for you and you for me.
Too far down the road you're gonna come to see
That what is in the past can never come to be.

So go your way
And I'll go mine.
My thoughts of you will fade with time
Until I see you again.
   Susan Welty

Focusing Through Dissonance

Hopelessness and Loneliness -
I know them both well.

Avarice and incompleteness
are my constant companions.

Comprehension and Inclusion
of wisdom I now need.

Despair and Disillusion
once riddled little Malcolm.

Disgust and Doubt about them Martin wrote.

Surprise and Suffocation -
Mohandas walked with them.

Abuse and Neglect - the rape victim knows.

Terror and Void are in a battered child's tears.

Hear and know - I didn't before.

Know and Act I now do.

Alertness and Discernment
has come from this pain.

Equality and Justice - I must now strive.

Hope and Love - truly, they exist.

Crimson and Grace flow from nail-scarred hands.

Donnie Underwood

Pain

Who will take pain away.
The confusion it gives.
To live or not to live.
To strive for your dreams.
To be understood by others.
Fear rises and self-esteem dies;
ego has a chance to take over.
Incapable of being honest
as lies build and fly similar to that of a hurricane.
What's your name.
Who will take pain away.

Nicolas Montalvo

Without A Clue

Listen and I will tell you,
a tale so sad to hear,
She lost her love so dearly
but did not shed a tear

All were envious of their home,
big, and white, and bright,
But she had wished for smaller things
so not to be alone

The years went on without a clue,
she worked, and cleaned, and loved,
but he was very busy too
and not so very true

When light was shed upon his game
he did not fall or waive,
He said "my dear I did it all
but only for the fame"

Though she's no longer happy
they live from day to day,
She loves him still though all has changed
why no one can say

MaryAnn Spada

My Beloved

Of desperation and suffering,
I search for my beloved
where no one can dream,

Of rainbows and starlit nights,
I search over seas and mountains of great heights,

Of loyalty and love,
of feelings from above
of magic and legends,
I will search for my love,

Unto the ends of the earth to find you,
hoping that you love me too,

For pain and death, to keep me from you,
I'll take my last breath, for my love is true.

For only the purest of heart could ever love me,
The voice of god said: You're the only one that could be,

I've searched for my beloved and the only one is thee!

Rachel Gaoa

The Life Long Gift

She smiled, and said "I'm glad you came!"
I bowed my head to hide my shame.
I kissed her brow and gave her a hug.
I now felt humble instead of smug.
I'd known I should stop in, or give her a call.
But kept putting it off, because after all
I had all these things I needed to do.
But still I knew her visitors were few.
So finally I put all my work aside.
Behind these excuses I was trying to hide.
We'd been friends for so long, and now she was ill.
She couldn't get well. This was a bitter pill.
She handled it so well. So why couldn't I?
Alone in my room, I started to cry.
She was so brave! And I so weak.
Some of her strength I wanted to seek.
So, I knocked on her door not knowing what to say.
She made me feel welcome, as was her way.
She had always been one to encourage and lift.
And even in death, she still had the gift.

Wava I. Foster

When We're Apart

I know that you'll be leaving soon
and I'll be left behind,
but there's one thing that you should know.
You're always on my mind.
No matter what the distance
or how many miles apart,
you take with you the best of me,
the thing I call my heart.
And with my heart you take my soul,
my dream of things to come.
There's no one else to share them with
for you are the only one.
The one that God has chosen to walk
with me through this life.
The one who made me very proud when
I became your wife.
Hold tightly to these words my love
for though we are apart,
there's nothing that can touch a love
that's kept inside a heart.

Mary Jones

They Go Away

A person that you love a lot who you want to be close to,
Might go away even though they're not supposed to.
You love them so much and you don't know why,
Cause it seems like all they do is make you cry.
It might be a mom or maybe a dad,
And you won't remember memories you've had.
There won't be any, 'cause you weren't with them long,
The other person had to go wrong.
I try to remember memories but they won't stay any longer,
My love for my mom keeps growing stronger.
I don't understand why 'cause she makes me feel bad,
She doesn't want me and she's not even sad.
There's no one that can take her place,
When I look at a mom I remember her face.
I try to call my step-mom "mom" and it takes all I've got,
But in my heart I know she's really not.
I wish I could forgot about my mom cause it's tearin' me apart,
Now there's a piece that's gone away from my heart.

Anna Hickey

Passages

Your soul beneath my heart,
Soft flutters like the wings of a dove.

Pictured only in my mind, my
breath is your life
until two joined together separate into one.

Set out on our journey,
your hand inside mine.

In the dark
unknown fears, swept away into closets
locked tight.

Storms, calmed by a gentle touch.

Dandelions clenched tight in small fists
reward me
more beautiful than dew kissed roses.

But like the slow thaw from a cold winter,
your hand slips from mine.

Strong wings no longer need wind.

Time weakens those locks.
Its unknown fears set free
now become mine.

Ann Angelicola

Normal Fellings

All this anger, all this pain, why do I feel I am going insane?
I cry in the day, and a bit more at night
sometimes I feel like a soar bird in flight!
When I am done with all my tears, I look
back and laugh at my stupid and silly fears.
Now I go through life as nothing
before, and then I die, lying on the earth's floor.
As I pray for a good eternity of sleep, I
Pray that of my soul the Lord shall keep.
Now as I soar through the skies, in the heavens up above,
my anger and pain has seemed to have disappeared,
for now all I feel in this place is only love!
All the smiles and laughter flowing
through the air, makes all the worries I
have ever had not even worth a care.
My soul is in the arms of love and I
need not to rely on my fate, for now I
am through with all my sorrow and hate.
For now I have passed the test and now
am living beyond those heavenly gates.

Stephanie J. Thomas

Letter From An Addict

Help me,
I'm hooked on drugs.
I never thought this would happen,
but now it's done.
I thought a little here or there was safe,
but it was never enough.
I shot and pushed,
smoked and sniffed.
The more the better,
the higher I get.
Then one day, I had too much;
my system stopped,
I lost all touch.
The next thing I knew,
you were beside me crying.
And then I understood,
that I was dying.
I hear the machine beside me,
it now has a steady whining.
I now understand my life is gone.

Ann McKesson

Pain

Have you ever felt pain deep down in your heart?
That kind that cuts like a knife in several different parts.
The pain is sharp and hard to explain,
As I reached out and called Jesus by his holy name.
"Dear God, what is wrong?"
Fearing in my mind, time isn't long.
I called the Lord in a last desperate cry,
"O Lord, is it my time to die?"
He answered, "No my child,"
I looked to him and he gave me a smile.
I said, "Thank you Lord for sparing my life,"
As I reached to my chest and removed the knife.

Cynthia Pettway

Teenaged Sorrow

I sit here thinking and begin to cry
but I'm really not sure why
my heart is always feeling great pain
even though I think I'm sane
thoughts start spinning in my mind
like there's something I'm supposed to find
I need someone to save me
all I want is to be free
free from the burdens that hold me down
and all of the things that make me frown
I know I can love yet I still always hate
I had better try soon or it may be too late
I try to tell my problems to anyone
but does a person even try to hear one?

Shannon Dems

Waiting

I sit in darkness on the deserted beach,
waiting to see the one I love,
the stars above me twinkle so bright,
as if to say she's on her way,
the wind sweeps the mist, from off the waves,
and gently sprays it against my face,
waiting to see the one I love.

A light appears upon the horizon,
anxiety builds within my heart,
I can't wait to see the one I love,
she appears in orange, so beautiful, so bright,
for the one I love, is the morning light.

Howard Day

My Favorite Sounds

Lying in the grass, looking up above,
I can hear all the sounds, that I really love.
The happy buzzing of busy bees,
And cheerful songs of birds in the trees.
Dragonflies humming over a nearby lake,
And the beautiful sound a chorus of frogs can make.
The sound of grass swaying in the quiet breeze,
That also rustles the leaves in the huge oak trees.
Water babbling over rocks in a stream a few yards away,
How much I love these sounds is more than I can say.
Of all my five senses, the one I think is best,
Is the one that works so well for me, while I sit and rest.
Without it, all of these sounds, I couldn't hear,
That's why I feel so lucky to have my two ears.

Aubrie Haight

Slippers

I'm crazy 'bout my slippers
'cause they are better on stairs than flippers
They are fuzzy, fleecy - neat
fluffy pillows upon my feet
they keep warm my frosty toes
while I freeze my little nose
They are very warm and fuzzy
if you wear them outside they get scuzzy
Pink and blue and green
and sometimes tangerine
You can wear them singing Barber Shop
or when you're doing the Bunny Hop
Road weary trippers
find comfort in their slippers.

Courtney Lloyd

A Mother's Gift Of Love

Out of the clear blue sky my mother said to me,
Sonny boy, in the hereafter, a butterfly I want to be!
Little did I know, after her request,
I had to lay my dearly beloved to rest.
A day in passing, a ring of the door bell,
A trash man friend stopped by to wish me well.
He too was at a loss her love to miss;
and in talking but what I see hovering above;
a more beautiful butterfly I could never hope to see!
There I stood in awe as it was beckoning to me.
Within my heart I knew it was my mother dear,
calling to me, dear Sonny boy I will always be near!
In passing I wish to give all my thanks to thee
her wish come true, forever her gift to me!

Brad Campbell

Christmas Crib

One cold December morning
I visited a resale shop.
As I walked through, I passed
An old wooden crib
Standing alone in a dark,
Dusty corner.
Its wooden legs were still strong,
And its wooden cushion still intact,

I wondered about the many births
This old, wooden, dusty crib had cradled.
It had nurtured new life,
And for its reward, it rests
In this dark place,
Hidden from the view of life.
It had at one time held the cries,
The joys, the beginning of life,
Of motherhood and fatherhood.

Ronnie L. Parker

The Death Of The Last Dragon

This is a tale of very old
So you must think of times untold
When kings and dragons ruled the land
And a magician held great power in the palm of his hand.
There was a hero brave and bold
And a dragon wise and old
The dragon took the hero's maiden bride
To show her enchanted places far and wide.
The hero was filled with hate in his soul, body, and head
And could only imagine seeing the majestic beast dead
But what the hero did not know
Is that the princess wanted to go.
Thus began a great war
In lands and places, many afar
In the end the dragon was slain
And the hero greatly regretted this dreadful ordain.

Miguel A. del Valle

God Makes The Seasons

As the trees on the mountains stand so tall,
I saw their leaves began to fall.
I looked upon their coats of gold,
And I saw the beauty they did behold.
They were once a pretty green,
The most beautiful I had seen.
Then God had a master plan,
And stroked the leaves with His hand.
For all the world to plainly see,
That He made them for you and me.
There's so much beauty for us all,
When the leaves began to fall.
As the wind carries them over the hill,
Because that is the Master's will.
That they must die to live again,
Just like man, God knows when.

Edna Bain

Cousins From H-LL

The cousin whose name I will not mention
Never gets punished just permanent probation.
All his short little life he's been a menace
I wish his parents would send him to Venice.
Instead they send him to visit with me
He trashes my room, and never lets me be
He throws our food and tortures my dog.
He should be caged with a wild wart hog!

But my parents adore him, think he's clever
I wish cops would take him forever.
He's a little (bleep-bleep) and a big (expletive) too
He should be on exhibit in a zoo!
He wakes me up early to play with his cars
I think I should kill him (or send him to Mars)!
Just when my patience has run out
His sister is born, in joy I shout:
"Hooray! He'll tease her instead of me!
He'll torture her and I'll be free!"

But I was wrong as wrong can be
Now there's a pair of them to torment me!!

Ian Bowers

Image

Looking in the mirror and never seeing me
Only the reflection of who I want to be
Trying to discover underneath the mask so sheer
The me the image inwardly the one with all the fear
Never looking inward only outwardly
Will I ever find her the me I long to be.

Carol J. Daniel

Untitled

A spirit rose into the night
shining bright
Saying to thee—I love you

The spirit stayed and together they went along the trail
Their hands touched and trembled
for their shadows were with them
But strength from within
Held tight from release

And the path started
a narrow road
widening at times
to lessen their load

Through the hills, the forest, the mountains
they climbed together
their thoughts were forever

And as they rose
they came to see
their love together
and let it be
Dale E. Burgess

I Do's

Now that it's time to say "I do",
I'm really happy for the both of you.
Always be happy, never be blue,
'cause now its up to just you two.
Sometimes you give and sometimes you take,
But don't forget, you have a mate.
There's a time to share, a time to spare,
so don't ever forget how much you care.
Now that you both have become one,
It can sometimes feel as if it's a ton.
So always be cheerful and bright,
And don't forget, there's always tomorrow night.
Now that you both are joined together,
Remember it's always now and forever.
So always be smart, and never depart,
'Cause it all comes from your little ole hearts.
Just remember the "I Do's",
And especially the "I love you's".

Donna D. Spence

My Dream

A dream was born in me, as a child I have seen it
Now I'm grown and it stirs inside of me.
A place in time where the world was mine, and all the love in it
Where the flowers grew inside my mind.
A place where heaven was the sky and all that mattered,
And how I knew that it was meant to be.
But he doesn't understand and he doesn't ask me why
He just keeps living day to day.
No he doesn't understand and he doesn't want to know
What lies between the heart and soul.
I've got to say what's on my mind and that's all there is to it.
I can't live in a world of make believe.
Take me where the sunshine warms the meadows in the mountains,
Where the water's clear and running free.
A place where the spirit's free to fly as an angel
Where God can walk beside of me.
I wish that I could take you with me when it's time to go
I'm sure that you would like it there.
To feel the peace running through you as it calms your very soul
And you could finally feel what I feel and finally understand.

Jackie L. Nelson

Endless Love

I thought I would never find the one so true,
but that was before I met and knew you.
I now know that God sent you from up above,
I now know, that you are my endless love.

I often wished that love would come my way,
I wished for that every night and day.
But soon you came to me with love so true,
the endless love I wanted I found in you.

I often dreamed and wished that I could see,
the one who would stop the tears inside of me.
I never thought it would be you,
my endless love so strong and true.

I guess this is the way it was meant to be,
but nobody knows how it became you and me.
But I know you are the one God sent from up above,
I know you are my one and only endless love.
Grace Lee

To My Special Childhood Friend

Today, I say goodbye to my special childhood friend.
When we were young, we thought our lives would never end.
We grew up together in the peaceful setting
of Blyn. We laughed and played
We fished and swam - life was clean and
pure - our friendship would always endure.
He baited my fishhook and held the barbwire
fence - being the gentleman he was.
He was my childhood prince.

I don't ever recall a cross word from my
friend even as spoiled as I'm told - I might have been.
Richard's kind and thoughtful ways continued on.
Even though, through our teens our friendship wasn't quite so strong.

I'll never forget my friend
the memories will always with me abide
And so I say goodbye to him, until we
meet again on the other side.
Pat Harbaugh McLucas

They and I

I sit alone in silence.

I am surrounded by several people speaking.
I see them smiling, laughing, sharing.
(They surely are staunch friends, I surmise.)

I sit in silence.

They see me and smile - a sad, sympathetic symbol of good
Samaritanism,
(They are smiling simply because they should, I'm sure.)

I return their smile, secretly desiring to speak,
Sneaking a second glance at them.

They restart their systematic sharing.

I sit more sadly stooped in solitude.
Patricia Pearce Bishop

Almost Off Their Chair

Americans ask me
is America more racist
than Brazil?
Than Cuba?
Or that country with the Japanese president?
If only they could measure
that force that leans
them forward towards my reply.
Joel Aubrey Mackall

Lover's Lament

There's a sky full of stars
For as far as I can see
And as I wonder where you are
I sit here in ecstasy
The night is dark; the moon is silver
A bird sings his life's song in the trees
I feel the night as cold as forever
Half as true as you and me
By showing me the wonder we share
You opened my heart's door
And you showed me how much you care
You showed me how dreams still come true
Now I'm strong enough to answer to the call
Strong enough to give a love to you
My heart will not take another fall
I give to you my life's light
And take a love that you offer me
So as I see the birth of the morning light
I know that my soul is finally free...

Ron S. Kapis

Love And Live

Don't let the small things get you down.
Don't let insignificance make you frown.
Look to the good, even seconds, in each day.
Look for a minute where you can play.

Be a child at heart, if only in your mind.
Be careful of your words, may they be kind.
Turn your thoughts into actions of peace.
Turn to help when pain doesn't cease.

Begin each day with a trusting soul.
Begin a new life, for you, as a whole.
To try your best is all anyone can ask.
To try at all is a difficult task.

Dreams of better days and brighter days too.
Dream of what the future holds for you.
Love every friend that passes your way.
Love and live for each brand new day.

Gina Wechsler

Untitled

I don't remember when
I stopped counting my blessings,
and started
only counting my sorrows.
And as my heart and soul began to freeze
the once brilliant landscape of my life
turned bleak and gray and sad and old.

But I continued to watch the woman wake.
And I continued to watch the woman go through the motions.
And I continued to watch the woman laugh.
And I continued to watch the woman live
as though nothing had ever changed.

And little by little my heart and soul began to thaw,
and my sorrows began to recede,
and some color returned to the palette of my life.

And finally I could stop watching and
rejoin the woman who was living my life.
And once again I could count my blessings.
Because they had never really left.
Only I had.

Judith Helene Berman

Please Tell Them (My Children)

Dear God, when you take me with you to live,
  Please let them know how much I love them,
Tell them their smile can set me aglow.
  Please God, will you tell them?
For I feel they do not know.

Tell them how my life was filled
  With just the thought of them,
And all the love and kindness,
  I know they hold within.
Let them know they helped me
  To be a better person -
How they made my days so much better,
  When we shared them.
Please make them understand, Dear God,
  Help them please to listen,
And most of all, I pray Dear God,
  They will know how much I will miss them.

Anna M. Jacobson

My Love

The sky set high with bright colors,
The waters waved goodbye like innocent
  caring mothers.
The love in your eyes, helped you realize
The place you longed to be.
The place you longed to be, was cuddling next to me.
Snuggle me close under a blanket of cotton.
Wishing this night, might never be forgotten.
Sharing the warmth of our hearts,
Is nothing like being struck with darts.
  My love for you is So strong,
Sometimes it feels Oh, so wrong!
Just sit back and relax as I take you into my mind.
The mind in which You are all that people can find!
As I declare my love for you,
Are you able to do that too?
The love in my eyes acts like a fire.
A fire that just cannot expire.
The love in my heart, will never depart.
As long as we do not grow apart.

Alexis Fojo

Second-Long Look

When we were lost
we were saving every texture,
taking breaths in every silk ray.
candlelit nights
blurred by dreams I never knew
and the land you crossed in my mind
pointed fingers straight through the back
of my heart.
my hardened shell was your only defense,
you swore.
"I looked up once and I was enveloped..."
those paths I can't even spell
and I know I used to feel you
and I know the things you used to say
and all the time we'd spent;
pennies in pools as deep as oceans
and hands in hands as warm as now.
and it seems so unreal,
you're not in these memories.

Ben Londa

Cascading Colors

The seething crimson basks beneath
the indigo wreaking havoc upon the advances
of my amber. The nuances of the navy
lie casually near the frailty of my fuchsia,
and blending meaningfully with the magenta.

Never before have the delicacies of my taupe
arranged themselves so vividly around the
mauve while the acuteness of the violet trickles
gently toward the periwinkle.

By and by the brightness of silver dilutes
itself haphazardly into the grey and white,
closer, ever closer to the charcoal and ivory.
And underlying this prism symphony, my basic
blackness is forever.

Anita R. Strongwind

A Path To Freedom

A silent whisper, the moon shines bright.
We gonna catch da sub tonight.
"How we gonna get there; it's almost dawn?"
"The drinking gourd," I yawn.
"You one smart lad, can you get your brother?"
"Certainly, Mother."
"Mother, Mother brothers down.
    Mother, Mother what was that sound?"
"Is it the train?
    Oh Mother what pain!"
"Leave without me,
    take care of your brother.
    I shall die on this path."
"No, Mother!"
So that how she lay
    with pride and faith.

Terren Rice

Alone On Mobile Bay

Sitting and watching each wave come in
with ageless repetition and yet each one different
reminds a person of their life.
Every day goes by with a sameness and yet something happens
just often enough to keep monotony away,
sometimes it's a thunderstorm, a lover's quarrel,
a beautiful sunset, even a hurricane!
but all things, even a new lover
can make one realize how close in proximity
is life to spending a day as the beach.

Rosemary H. Dunham

Essence Of Love

It gently sweeps my heart away,
By the touch and by the sway.

It blows the red petals at which I lye,
And takes the innocence from my blue eye.

It switches my emotions like the cards to a deck,
And enhances my smile like a warm everlasting peck.

It takes the flowers of my heart,
And blooms them until they fall apart.

What's this power that takes over my fears,
And causes all my madness and tears?

It's the emotion that's felt within the soul,
And fills the heart of love like cereal to a bowl.

It's the essence of love and all that it brings,
It's the power of love that the heart sings.

Kelly Clark

Let Go

Your eyes are like a withering flower.
As if you were crying out for someone.
Your face so pale, like snow on a winter day.
You need the voice of truth.
You need to be led.
Cry, scream, let go of what's hurting you.
Now breathe.
You're loved.
You're cared for.
You are important.
Love yourself, and you shall be a new person.
Let go of what's hurting you.

Nilsa Aviles Colon

So I Won't Feel The Greater Pain

I would be willing to trade life for death;
So I won't feel the greater pain.
I would be willing to trade light for darkness;
So my eyes would forever be closed to see the light that pains.
I would be more willing to travel for eternal extinction;
So I won't travel the path of eternal damnation.

Let me not see the sun;
If only suffering befriends me.
Let me not breathe an ounce of air;
If breathing will I despise.
So let me be unborn,
The unseen dead future of America.

Antoinette O. Tinapunan

Loss

As I stood on the hilltop of understanding...
    I observed one of the most beautiful sunsets...
    I had ever seen.

It was in that moment that I realized...
    A blind man may never see the setting of the sun...
    and for that,
I mourned the Loss of Beauty.

And then I realized...
    That a man with sight may never see the very
    same sun set...and for that,
I mourned the Loss of Vision...

For its Beauty is there for him to see...
    But he lacks the insight of the blind...to know that
Beauty...Is but a Gift...And he must Swallow it...

        While he can!

So I ask you...
                    Who's truly blind now?

Richard B. Longo

The Lord Holds You In The Palms Of His Hands

May our Lord hold you in the palms of his hands
    these beautiful days.
May the sun shine be warm upon your face,
    and a light burning in your heart.
May the Holy Spirit, that Jesus, places in
    your heart joined with him be with you always.
May his eagles wings, wrapped around you,
    keep you safe in his arms.
May the mustard seed that he has planted with you,
    grow and grow and blossoms forever.
May your life be placed at the foot
    of the cross.
May the joy the Lord gives you,
    be always a light for Him.

Margaret Volletta

Planet Paradise

The sun, the clouds, the colors of the sky,
the moon, the planets, and stars twinkling by.

The trees, the flowers, the mountains of earth,
the winds, the waters, filled with life and rebirth.

The forests of life, stocked with creatures of might.
Some live in the dark, some live by the light.

This heavenly body floats through space and time.
All needs here are filled, and existence is prime.

But so much destruction to these beautiful things,
will come to pass before an angel sings.

And after that, what is left will grow,
and the "ones" who are spared will surely know.

Appreciate what's been left here.
Take care of it, and hold it dear.

Sandi J. Patat

The Transition

Black clouds gather on the horizon
Bitter winds pierce through to the bone.
Sands, swirling high, invade my nostrils.
My palpitating heart must soon explode.

I try to scream out in my anguish.
My voice is trapped somewhere inside.
A thousand hammers pound my forehead.
My rasping breath struggles to abide.

Cold, clammy hands are reaching for me.
A multitude of voices assail my mind.
"We've got you now!" echoes their screeching.
My soul they try to over ride.

"Get Back!" The commands comes clear and strong.
I'm strengthened by its force alone.
"I've already triumphed over darkness,
And this child is covered by my blood!"

Black clouds dissipate. The sun is shining!
Gentle rays bathe my cowering soul.
I experience an aura so pure and inviting.
My spirit leaps and merges with joy untold.

Loraine R. Degraff

The Statue Of Liberty

The Statue of Liberty is the symbol we see
When once we enter the land of the free

It holds up its torch for us all to see
It lights up the darkness for both you and for me

Millions have entered this land of the free
And millions have found this deep ecstasy

The tremendous joy, the spine shivering sting
When first our eyes on the statue did spring

We feel deep within a God feeling truth
That liberty and freedom is a worthwhile pursuit

And now we are privileged to be part of this scheme
In this magical land which grants men a dream

And so to that statue, man's symbol of hope and of dreams
Long may you reign as the symbol supreme

Hold high your proud torch so others may see
That ours is the land of true liberty

Where the tired and the weary joyfully see
The Statue of Liberty in the land of the free.

Sol Mann

A Mother's Love

You always carried my weight.
You always carried my pains,
You never shed a tear in front of me,
Yet, I know, you must have cried many tears, behind closed doors.

You always stood by my side,
Whether right or wrong.
You always guided me,
Away from wrong to the righteous path.

You always respected my decisions,
Yet always left it up to me to learn.
You always comforted me when I was wrong,
Yet encouraged me to try again.

You always tried to show me the true meaning of love.
So complex, so pure, yet so simple,
Love is so great and so divine,
Yet, it is only found, "in True Mothers Like you."

Glendon M. McGee II

Western Epicerie

during goldrushes
many gullibles ravel
into yarns made famous
by passages of time -

timely passages to goldenfields
make for unlikelylikely luckyluckies
as assay after assay sashays dust
to dusty dances in the rays of sunny
neverset (nuggets have longsince beenskimm'd
into glittering casino palaces and conspicuous
consumables) -

but dailydailies tell of deardear groceries
awaiting their place in the heroic epic told
in later idioms -
when does the expensive become expansive?
the age of force of destiny is now foreshort'n'd to
the force of habit - nectar and ambrosia become
food for thought foregone; the epic of groceries
is yet not writ nor spoke in memorial cycles -
we vegetate toe-to-toe in antipodal epicerie -

Ernest Landauer

Easter's A Comin'

Easter time will be here soon
And we can sing a happy tune.
'Cause Jesus rose on Easter Day
And He came to show us the way.

God prayed in the garden for you and me.
When our life is o'er, Him we'll see.
When visiting His tomb, He was not there.
He had risen, the tomb was bare.

He came to us to atone for our sin.
And heaven at last for us to win.
He came for us to prepare the way
To meet Him above on Judgment Day.

When the early days of Lent are o'er,
Our thoughts of joy will surely soar.
When to Heaven our voices we'll raise.
And to God our alleluias will praise.

On Easter morn, Christ did arise
In the beautiful glory of the skies.
And one day we will join Him there.
This should always be our prayer.

Mary O'Mara

What The Heart Keeps

I remember how you looked at me,
that dusk on your Mother's porch,
when you gave me the four o'clock
you purloined from your Mother's tree.

Through the years, no hothouse rose,
no seductive whisper in a candlelit room,
ever held my heart as you did
with merely a look and a hand-held bloom.

They continue to haunt me—
the promise and the bloom.

I dream the old dream,
the dream of present, future and past;
me in antique Victorian lace, you in sable brown,
a flower strewn garden path,

And my Grandmother's piano
against the empty wall,
between the bay windows,
in your house.

Peggy J. Frith

Free Me

Free me from the constraints of my own mind.
Free me from the thoughts of others pain.
Free me from this mental prison.
  Free Me

Free me from the consciousness of the world.
Free me from the moral approval.
Free me from my internal fears.
  Free Me

Free me from a mirage of impersonation.
Free me from scenes not written.
Free me from dreams passed by.
  Free Me

Free me from speaking untruths.
Free me from mental judgments.
Free me from thoughts unspoken.
  Free Me

  Free me from.........
  Free me from.........
Free me from.....Free me from me.

June C. Pewitt

I Miss You My Darling

   In the morning as I greet a bran new
day, I look around not to find you, for
your love was taken away.
   Oh if only I could have said "I Love You",
just one more time. Would it make my spirit more peaceful?
Never my darling. I miss what was once mine.
   I think about our good times, our goals and
our little fights. It happens when I'm
pretending to hold you on these lonely long nights.
   My heart knows we've loved each other
through everything that we've done. I see
your face in starry nights, and glimmering in the sun.
   At times I can almost see you sitting
across from me in your favorite chair. I
picture your loving eyes gazing at me and
the distinguished gray dancing in you hair.
   My darling my heart shattered the
day God told you, it's time to go. From
now until the end of time I will always love you so.
   Be at peace my beloved.

Florence Elizabeth Poole Sweet

Blue Life

I look into blue and see my life,
   long ago on a lonely night.
It gives me a message of sorrow so deep,
   and then I know I cannot sleep.

It happened so suddenly,
   the sad news rolling in
That my mother was in an accident,
   no longer suffering with in.

I was happy, though I cried
   to know she was safe,
away from danger and
   a harsh, uncertain place.

So it brought tears to my eyes,
   and sadness to my heart
to know that I would see her once,
   and then have to part.

Yes, I remember it clearly,
   so sad and so true.
He stole away my mother,
   my best friend, companion, and confidant.

Janice Huesemann

Rachel: The Diary Of A Schizophrenic

This morning she laughed and she laughed and she laughed.
She was happy, you see.
Then she groaned and she cried and moaned desperately
For deep, deep, down inside, there was Rachel, you see
But she refused to come out, she had been torn
Emotionally

Tomorrow she would be free, as free as could be
She would soar through the clouds
She would scream, it was loud.
She would scream and she'd scream, and she'd scream
Never ending it seemed. But then she would be free,
She'd be free, Mentally

Last week she was old, she was slow, she was told
It was so hard to move, it was impossible to prove
If this 'thing' did not flee, she would be bound
Physically

Today, I am afraid! What a mistake they have made
They are sending me away, to stay
I am crazy, I am told
One less burden, officially
They all need to be free, they all plead to be free,
Financially

Fernzalene D. Smith

Only Friend

I sit and watch her roam
It's the streets she calls home.

It was here where she wept
As the darkness slowly crept.

You can't stop her pain.
But it hurts to see her shower in the rain.

Alcohol had consumed her mind,
Now death she would soon find.

After her last breath of air
Her eyes gave a lonely stare.

A bottle on the beach,
Her breath gave the obvious stench.

It was her only friend,
But it cost her life in the end.

Matthew Jeremy Wilson

Say No To Drugs

So much has happened in this generation
Because of this vast drug anticipation
So much happens when you say the word "No."
It teaches a child when to come and when to go.
It teaches them all the good things of life
How to learn to love and refrain from strife
Drugs come to us from afar,
It's like rain coming in when the door is ajar.
Our children doing things that do not please us,
But to sum it all up we all need "Jesus."

Edith B. Mercer

Untitled

Oh my Lord it's been a long time, from you I've gone astray
I've traveled down the sinful road, for that I've had to pay
Now I'm asking your forgiveness, Christ willing, I pray
So that I may walk the righteous road with you someday
Lord my God Almighty, you're in heaven above.
Fill my heart with Jesus and the Holy Spirit's love
Give me strength and guidance through this trying time
And with your blessed glory, tomorrow the sun will shine
When I was at my weakest, I thought you missed your cue
But little did I know that you carried me through
Unnecessary obstacles, sadness and pain
Clouded my judgment and challenged sunshine with rain
Today I'm filled with laughter and joyous relief
No longer am I lost or question what to believe
Lord my God Almighty, you're in heaven above
Fill my heart with Jesus and the Holy Spirit's love
All of God's angels have come together to pray
I've come back to Jesus on this bright and glorious day.

Cynthia L. Riddle

My Awakening!

It seemed as though
I had been asleep in the snow
For a long winter's night.
But now that I'm awake,
The sun is warm and bright.
And though my body has become
A part of the earth,
My soul is the shell that has encased
The seed of the universe.
Now, every introspective breath I take,
Moves the seed, closer to the surface.
Hence, it's steadily pushing itself through the earth,
To eventually fulfill its purpose.

Madelene Patricia Balloy

A Wrinkle In Time

How bright the stars that light our way
As darkness passes into day
The heavens almost open wide
While sun bolts out from deep inside

Much like our lives the heavens above
Filled with wonders, hope and love
Each star that shines. . .our good friends
The darkness. . .troubles yet to mend

Sunbeams kiss a brand new day
Our worries seem to melt away
Hearts and minds cannot measure
Even one of these heavenly treasures

The sun sets on another day, stars begin to twinkle
Time has stolen once again, leaving just a wrinkle
Within this cycle lives unfold
While stories of love, courage and hope are told

Lorra Peck

Friends

Let's be Friends, not Lovers.
Let me hold your hand.
Let's grow old together.
Let's explore life and living.
Let me hold your hand.

We're another year older
Maybe a little bit bolder.
Let me hold your hand.
You can put your arm around me.
Let's grow together.

Let's be Friends, not Lovers.
We are still only seventeen.
Life ahead, so full and bright
Let's find out what friendship means.
Now we're man and wife — and friends.

Now you're my Friend and Lover.
Forty-five years of ups and downs.
Four children and a treasure of memories.
Hold my hand as I close my eyes.
My young Lover, my old Friend.

Mason Alliston Gile

The Depression

They had no jobs and looked like slobs
Waiting for tomorrow
Their heads hang low and stomachs groan
Feeling pain and sorrow

Parents cleaned and children played
There is nothing more
Many people sleep in fear
Behind a dark wood door

With hungry stomachs they wake up
Laying in their beds
With aching bodies from head to toe
They are surprised that they're not dead

The children played and were worry free
The parents tried real hard
All they needed was a job
So the family wouldn't starve.

They continued to suffer in agony and pain
They say it's not their fault
But when they go to sleep at night
They taste their tears of salt.

Jacob Mascarenaz

Sisters

Sisters share a special bond
Of love that's really true
That's why I am so happy to have
A sister just like you
You cheered me up when I was sad
You calmed me down when I was mad
You held my hand when I wanted to cry
You held me close when I wanted to die
You made me laugh when I was down
By acting foolishly, like a clown
You are always joyous, gentle and kind
The type of a person that's hard to find
You listened to my stories of woe
Love and understanding is what you showed
We laughed, and sometimes spoke in whispers
Which reinforced our bond as sisters
When we grew up and lived far apart
My love for you always remained in my heart
For me, the end may come too soon
And I'll forever be grateful for a sister named June

D. Wimmer Vitanzo

The Meaning Of 'Matter'

Without Love, The Things That Matter Have No Meaning
Does it matter if the homeless die of hunger on the street
While we have so much food to eat

Does it matter if our children murder and rape
And turn to drugs as their only escape

Does it matter if lives must first fall apart
Before our efforts to help can truly start

Does it matter if others are the worst they can be
Because their weakness alone is all we can see

Does it matter if our hearts have turned to stone
Because we selfishly think of ourselves alone

Does it matter if we have no time to care
For the things of God, we no longer fear

Do all of the things, serious or fun
Truly matter in the long run

What matters most in all the above
Is that to God and others we show love

Not passive 'love' based on feeling
But active love with true meaning.

Donahue Constantine

The Light

There is a light deep within
No matter how low, or high you've been.
Just close your eyes, and turn it on.
'Til all your doubts, and fears are gone.

Find a moment, a quiet place.
Shut out the noise, the light embrace.
Open your mind to new horizons
Build a stairway,
that love can climb one.
Discover new world's, as truth unfolds
Remember that love is a treasure to hold.
As peace, love, and truth begin.
Remember, embrace the light within
once you've found the light within,
No matter what comes, you'll know you can win.
Hold on to the light,
There is no end.

Marjorie Hawkins

The Union

The two of us now had become only one
Performed by a minister of the holy one
Our souls had been entwined for many long days
We enjoyed the same things in the same ways

We were together sometime each and every day
Figuring out where to go and how to play
Through simple things we had a lot of fun
Not knowing someday we would have our own sons

Through the years we did all things as one
It takes deferring one to the other with each rising sun
We have found so far this has worked well for us
This has eliminated many arguments and a heated fuss

Many years have passed since that fine day
Two sons were added to this union along the way
They have grown to manhood before our own eyes
That they are fine men now to us is no surprise

As we continue along on this long journey of ours
Each spring will again bring its beautiful flowers
Life has many great things for us still ahead
The bond that's forged will hold until that day of dread

William Lowell Gilreath

The Captain

A friend, a pal, a seafaring guy
The outdoors his playground, sea to sky
A great teller of tales, a craftsman as well
A salesman of note, he sure could sell

His love for Sandy, as wide as the seas
His joy for life, like a warm summer breeze
Carolyn, Dick and Big Mark-Very close friends
And many, many more, the list never ends

Halyards and sheets on the Freedom's he sold
Made his eyes light up, so I am told
Thoughtfulness for others, he always had
A non-lover of life, would make him quite sad

Enjoy the sail, a life's journey of sorts
For someday we all must pull into our Ports
The winds are strong, the sea full of foam
The breeze at his back-The Captain Sails Home

S. Robert Jeffery

I'm Nobody

I'm nobody
I have nothing
No home, no life, no body
supposedly no mind

(So you want me to believe)

See these tears rolling down my face
Sell my babies masta
So I have nothing to live for

(So you want me to believe)

Sell my husband so I have no love
Sell my body it doesn't belong to me

(So you want me to believe)

See these grotesque scars on my back
I'm a strong black woman who can shed the pain

This is what A-me-rica is like
Mean, cold, cruel, I know you can take everything I love
Take my babies, my home, my body

So give me pain but one thing you can't take
is my knowledge and love for God
You may have hate but I have love and patience

Adrianne Graves

The Race

Driving in my race car,
Wondering if anything will happen.
Will I win? If not, who will?
Why am I doing this?
Is it the rush of adrenalin?
Or the speed? Or is it just the feeling of winning?
Oh no! I see Gordon sliding
Just don't panic, it's not the time to.
Just hit the brake a little,
Left, Right,
More brake.
The smoke is clearing,
I can see the checkered flag.
I smile with joy to know that I have made it.
I cry for those who didn't.
It's scary when you don't know what will happen next.
It's not fun when you see your life flash before your eyes.
Now that it is over, I think, is it worth it?
And then I remember,
It must be...

David Vogel

The Wiseman

The wiseman thinks in silence,
while the fool talks aloud,

The wiseman sees a person,
but the fool sees a crowd.

If each person was the wiseman,
Would the world be a better place,

Maybe then people wouldn't judge others,
By the look of their face.

What if we were all like the wiseman,
Do you think we'd all be the same.

Or would we be much different,
And hide from our shame.

Brad J. Niemchick

Alone

Every new day crawls into my life
Sometimes terribly distorted
Although nonetheless transparent,
Confusion wells within my fluid heart
That is frantically trying to swim in the time
I have left to be real,
I have held many things along the way
However, I have lost just as many of them.
When I am alone,
I can see how the sky blends
With the strength of color as friends,
And my anger goes away
Forgetting what has been taken for granted
At the foot of this door,
We can greed for power and sacrifice for gain
Because life is free, but our pleasure and treasures
Are easier with thoughts so insane.
So, I try to realize love and peace
As the keys to a door of my own cure
That I may finally be able to open tomorrow,
Alone...

Robert Loren Iverson

Rest In Peace

You weren't suppose to leave us so soon...
You were suppose to live a happy life-
and bring joy to all of us,
for a very long time.

You were to enjoy living -
not have your life,
brought to such an abrupt end.

You were meant to live a long life-
giving enjoyment,
with your writing, your smile, your humor
and your laughter.

How you will be missed-
but also you'll be remembered,
for all the joy you brought us.

Rest now, Barb-
and know we...on earth,
will always remember and be thankful...
we knew you.

Charles P. Flannigan

My Feelings

Home is where my heart is and that is why I stay.
If something ever happened I might just run away.
I have a lot to lose, but still there's no excuse for the pain,
suffering and abuse.

Sarah Aaron

Marriage Of Convenience

Blood of a lamb,
   Cry of a dove,
The lamb is a ram,
   Should push come to shore...
      Therein resides a cancer,
         Leprosy of souls,
And the dancer has no answers,
When two halves fail as whole,
   So very often wonder,
Where else it might've gone,
Still split storm asunder,
They do still ramble on,
Uneasy lies this compromise reached,
Faith and trust are all but breached,
The serpent lies coiled,
Its grand designs foiled,
The ram in rebirth,
Messianic engine oiled,
The dove follows faster as all share in mad laughter
As for what may be after, forever, ever love!!

Jeremy Rogers

Tara's Short Stay

She came as a bundle of joy
She was here only for a very short stay
Her time here was all tubes, needles, and no toys
She had a very sweet smile
And was awake only a short while
She brought tears galore
If only we could've had her more
Time will tell the lesson well

Joyce M. Miller

Music In My Head

The music is always in my head.
At times it's peaceful and soft.
At times it's abrasive and loud.
When I close my eyes I can see it.
It can be picturesque.
There are beautiful colors.
There are times when it's dark.
The blackness seems to surround me.
I'm happy with it sometimes.
At other times I'm angry at it.
There are times I wish it would stop.
There are times I wish it would go on forever.
I never quite know what I want.
I have no control over it.
So I guess I will have to just live with it.
I only pray that it stays in harmony with me.

Patt Leake

Untitled

I don't know how to fight what has to be done.
I'm actually not scared at what is yet to come.
Don't walk away, stand at my side
After all it's because of you that I have cried.
Don't deny it, you can't hide from the damned
Don't turn your back at what you planned
Now in your mistakes is where you can prance
With me you at least had a fighting chance
You couldn't stand, what I wouldn't allow
You found that when you commanded I wouldn't bow.
Your apologies mean nothing, I'm sorry won't work,
Do you even understand at how much I hurt?
You can't break me down, I'm going to be strong
Because in the end, guess who was wrong.

Brenda Newman

Untitled

May our Lord hold you in the palms of His hands,
  these beautiful days.

May the sunshine, be warm upon your face,
  and a light burning in your heart.

May the Holy Spirit that Jesus places
  in your heart, joined with Him,
  be with you always.

May His Eagle's Wings, wrapped around
  you, keep you safe in His arms

May the mustard seed that he has planted
  within you, grow and grow and
  blossom forever.

May your life be placed at the foot
  of the Cross.

May the joy the Lord gives you,
  be always a light for Him.

Margaret Valletta

Untitled

What's a blank piece of paper but an instrument?
An instrument empty like an egg
or a kite that can't rise above a tree
when your mind is dead a piece of paper becomes its grave.

What are hands good for if not for touching?
subtle nerves interlock like fabric
the most precious thing to feel a foreign skin next to our own
inert hands never accomplished anything in this world.

What are lips necessary for when you are lonely?
Two dried up leaves about to crumble,
no sympathetic fire to entice their reunion,
no wind beneath them to carry other mild breeze.

And what are eyes that eye no eyes?
Unlit with no spark to make them shine
tiring blurry vision when there is no one special
like a sun due to rise but delayed by the night.

And what is love good for?
To feel her body with my hands of lumberjack
to caress her cheeks with my bruised fingers
to kiss her forehead like the soil of a newfound land.

What is love good for if I don't have you?

Omar Huamanchumo

Close Your Eyes

Close your eyes
Then I will appear
Underneath your fingernails
Underneath all your tears
You have nothing to worry about
Nothing should you fear
I will be here forever
For there is no end
I'm here to listen
Dreams I will be in
I'm in your life forever
These are the things he said
Nothing I thought could touch us
Only until I experienced your loss
Now I'm not a pretender
Thinking time will just pause
Every second is an eternity
I would rather be damned to hell
I go to sleep late, hoping I will not wake
Because I could be lonely for one more day.

Amanda Meyer

I Have A Dream

I have a dream that there will be peace on earth,
I have a dream that one day I can wake up
knowing someone is not getting teased,
I have a dream one day nature will be treated with
respect, I have a dream there will be a cure for
cancer, I have a dream that anyone could do anything
they want, I have a dream I will graduate, I
have a dream that violence, and guns will
never can harm anything, I have a dream
is my way of saying how much we need to think.

Laura Simmons

nie wieder

It was Hitler's death machine,
filled with the slaughtering of bodies and souls
All around you could see the taste of death
An Auschwitz! What a beautiful place...
Hear the cha chug cha chug of the wheels
as a train arrives at the death camp.
Touch the frightened people mashed together on that train
Smell the stench of gas as it steals
the breath from each of its victims.
Taste the poisoned air.
See crematorium flames hungrily devour the gray bodies
  of mothers, of children, of the old, of the crippled.
How Could The Germans Do This?
"the Germans never saw us...Ask them.
They never saw us.
It was beneath their Aryan dignity.
We were just a lot of filthy Jews.
Why even glance at us?"
  nie wieder! nie wieder!

Bodies lie in piles, waiting for their turn to vanish into dust

Kathleen I. Binau

Lament

I've gone through sorrow, I've gone through pain,
Can't tell if it's for better, to me it's all the same.

She was never my woman, so there shouldn't be pain.
Tell that to my heart. It's more of the same.

She never knew me, she never knew my pain.
The way I lost my love, is painfully the same.

I lost love slowly, I lost it in shame.
My tears were of blood, but it's more of the same.

If pain were poison, my soul would be dead.
Unfortunately it's not, so my soul is wed...
To void.

Matt Hufstetler

Mistakes In My Life

If I could take back the mistakes in my life.
I could still be a mother, a cook and a wife
I could have a big house, pool and a couple of cars.
But my oldest daughter and grandson would
have been left out, under the stars
No place to live, no family to give
All the happy times that a family lives
She would have been alone in this cruel world to survive
That maybe today she would not be alive
so instead I left with my girls and grandson
sadly to say I had to leave my only son
My journey's not ended my life is not through.
But deep in my heart I hope this never happens to you.

Carol A. Kitsch

After Glow

I'd like the memory of me,
to be a happy one.
  I'd like to leave an afterglow of smiles,
when life is gone.

  Hazel E. Johnson

Higher Power

There are no reasons well defined,
Nor explanations for my mind.
To teach itself through search and ponder,
Contemplation, endless wonder.

Auto pilot yes I can, to learn, to bet, to understand.
Survival is my minds good deed
It gives me the time I need
To test, to teach, to learn my limits, redefining every minute.
Constant changing aspirations, Keeping up with time's mutations.

Auto pilot there I wept, a silent sobbing senseless wreck.
Reminiscing of my splendid, grandeuristic youthful wander.
Pains of pity, full of self, from toe to shoulder I engulf.

Auto pilot yes I can. Survival was my battle plan.
Though often tough the journey was, victorious I rose above.
Knowledge gained from prior battles, aided always in my travels.
It seems now the hill I climbed has been a mountain in disguise.

Auto pilot yes I can, to survive in softly somber;
There I wept to understand, as my pilot closed my eyes...
Tossing, turning, sleeping soundly, unaware of how profoundly;
Learning lessons, wisdom gained, a wiser pilot than my name.

"Son of Barbara"

  Jim H. Jones

Poor Communication

What are the words that mean I care
Which you might comprehend?
How can I act it, write it, talk it,
And appear so obtuse to you?
I'd like to show the empathy
I have for your desires
But angles from which we approach the goal
Cross swords — don't smooth the way.
So hunger proceeds from our wistful souls
Striking barbs and blows, not charm.
My love for you will never die
But unveiling it seems frightfully slow.

  Judy Phelps

Waiting For Spring

I look out my window and there I see,
An old oak tree without any leaves,
It looks so lonely against the colorless sky
As the cold wind rustles its branches that it
raises with a sigh.

It waits ever so patiently, or so it seems
For all it really wants is an early touch of spring.
I look again at the old oak tree
And I think to myself, "it must feel old
and lonely just like me."

What would we do if spring never came,
Because nothing in the world would be the same
But God in His mercy would never let it be
He will always give us new life with that
loving touch of spring.

  Gecoulia Smith

I Know A Place

I know a place where the roses grow,
Deep in the woods is this place I know.
And there the grass is soft and green,
The flowers pop up like rocks in a stream.
There the sun burns so white,
The rest of the sky seems blue and bright.

I know a place where the trees grow tall,
And everyone loves everyone, one and all.
The robins chirp loud,
As we watch the fluffy clouds.
At night we see the moon and stars,
And wish upon each one afar.

In this place, seasons come and go,
Just as fast as the stream does flow.
Spring is a time for everything to begin,
Or to cool in the peppermint wind.
Winter looks as if all dies,
But when it snows it warms your eyes.

  Nikki Hervol

A Portrait

He was the best friend I ever had.
He knew me like a sibling.
  Loved me like a lover.
    Cared for me like a parent.

Together our souls walked hand
  in hand as we grew into this life.

He could foresee the roads ahead.
  The more I trusted in him
    The higher he carried me.
From lovers to parents and back again.
  We held on tight.

Our world filled with laughter and tears
  as we played the role of man and wife.

My Love For You

What can I do to prove my love for you?
Nothing is good enough, no matter what I do.
I could climb the highest mountain,
but it wouldn't be high enough.
I could swim the biggest ocean,
but it wouldn't be big enough.
I could fly high above the world, and spell out my love for you,
But no matter how hard I try, nothing is good enough for you.
All I want is a simple man, who will not put me to the test,
and all the love I need to show, is to do my very best.
Someone who does not find fault in the things I try to do.
Someone who will love me, as much as I love you.
And now that I am looking for this man of my dreams,
I wonder how you will prove your love to me.

  Angela Keeton

Racism

We are all Racist
Every one of us
But we are not all Prejudiced
We are Racist
As the "Birds of a Feather gather together"
As Schools of Fish swim together
As People of Race live Love and play together
For "Like attracts Like" is
Nature's gentle way
As Prejudice is
Man's cruel and selfish way
Yes we are Racist

  James Toyama

Rendez-Vous

All my life I've been alone
Even in a crowd;
I guess it's just my destiny
For loneliness to follow me
Around.

My friends, who are not my friends,
Are all paired off so nicely.
So tell me this: Am I so wrong,
That in my heart there is no song?
That when I see them all I feel is jealousy?

Why is it that when I see her face
Her beautiful smile is all that I can see?
I think about her night and day,
To kiss her lips, at night I pray;
Obsession is just an ugly part of me.

So now at the end I disclose to you
The reasons for my depression:
I've never had a rendez-vous,
No girl has told me "I love you"
So I suffer from loneliness, jealousy, and obsession.

Robert Thomas

She Is

She is sometimes happy, sometimes sad
Sometimes angry and sometimes glad

She is often gracious and often debonair
She has the gift of simplicity and the gift of flair

She is often the breadwinner and the caretaker
She is always the nurturer and homemaker

She can appear to be cordial when in pain
She can be fabulous and then appear plain

She will serve her family first making herself last
She will comfort her family and remain steadfast

She is full of spirit and animation
She will stand her ground when met with intimidation

She will die to protect her family
She will yearn long life to see them independent and free

"Yet"

She is often walking alone upon this spacious land
She is you, me, her....she is woman

Vera Jenkins

The Death Of A Very Special Friend

There is a time when someone's life comes to an end
but you wish it wasn't to a very special friend.
Although he is gone and we had to part,
this brave little child will never leave my heart.
He loved to sing and hardly ever smiled,
he was such an innocent child.
This child was as special as can be,
he was different than everyone else if you saw him you would see.
There was a special home that he went to,
it was a home for children that are not as normal as you.
Why did he have to die and make so many people sob and cry?
Why can't he come back some day and lead his life a happy way?
He was lucky to live five, beautiful years,
our memory of this special child is so very dear.
The child that is gone and hardly ever smiled,
was my cousin, Christopher Negri the innocent child.

Erin Watson

Memories

Certain things you will always remember.
Images cast in your mind, crystal clear.

They're the extremes of life.

The day you met your lover.
The loss of someone dear.

Certain things you may forget entirely,
but other sources will hold your past.

They're what make life special.

Sights and sounds will jog your memory,
pictures of moments you wanted to last.

Today is only the beginning.
Beginning the rest of your life.

Just take a look around.

People are talking; cameras are flashing,
and you do look like husband and wife.

As the sun falls in the westerly direction
and the crowd begins to tire and fade,

Do you remember?

Walk to the water; gaze at your reflections.
Another priceless memory has just been made.

Mark W. Davidson

Necropolis

As a romping child I found
Quite the novel playing-ground.
Full of trees, and grass, and rocks,
Here was a secret, quiet space
Where one could play at hide-and-seek with a shadow...
And, oh, what a wondrous place
For my mind to run a race
Through the endless void of time
A knight! A prince! A king!
So dashing and brave was I
That all the world bent to me!

So, now with my childhood passed,
I find that I still come back
To grind away my thoughts - with pretense
That I am only walking my dog!

But "kismet" calls as time ticks
Now, one of those Rocks is mine...

Andrew G. Krall

Skates

They have met here in the late-light
On the pond, as always.
Trudging in as couples, or alone.
Snap-the-whip, Races, all that.
Ice.
A day long gone by,
Yet preserved in a black and white
moment.
White as snow.
The picture speaks.
Has its own language.
The people in it are different from those
they've become.
For they are trapped on that pond
in the late-light
Forever.
Calling to their children...
Set me free,
Remember me.

Lauryn E. Sasso

Prayer Is A Place

Prayer is a place, its entrance hope.
Its walls are mirrors reflecting the soul...
Its ceiling's skylight lets in God's love;
Its floor gathers tears for God's vials above.

Prayer is a time that is set aside
Earth's hold is broken, and so is man's pride.
God's Spirit takes over and I am transformed;
I'm melted, emptied, comforted, warmed.

Prayer is a highway that leads up and up.
Prayer is a drink from a life giving cup.
Prayer is a lifeline the drowning can hold.
Prayer is a treasure of more value than gold.

Prayer is a place to lay aside care;
Prayer is a place Heaven's glory to share
Whatever desire or need in life's race
For complete fulfillment, prayer is the place.

Prayer is a place of total surrender,
A place where self will is set aside.
Prayer is a place where angels minister
And a place where God's love abides.

Annie Alford

The Destruction Of Reality

Reality is a monster. It eats at your soul.
You find yourself growing up too fast and
Missing things you used to know.
So I sit alone in my room and
Argue with the wall.
While my mind wanders
The aliens' land.
With imagination as our weapon
We fight reality,
Rules and regulation.
The aliens take me to their craft,
And we fly through the sky
To rid the world of the tyranny of reality.
We are successful.
But then I awaken and
I find I'm home
Or at school writing papers.
But I can still see the aliens
Walking down the halls of my
Mind's eye.

Jennifer Dominick

Someone To Remember

She releases the breath
That gives each of us life.
Holds you tight,
When the nightmares come in the night.
Gives a warm smile to show you have done your best.
Sometimes I wonder...
When does she get her rest?
She finds a secret place to hide her fears and sadness.
Just so your life doesn't show the madness.
Always ready to take away all your worries.
Makes you smile with a wonderful story.
She will always be there...the same.
Even though sometimes we forget her name.
God blessed us forever,
When He gave us that wonderful person
Called ....Mother.

Felix Cabrera

The worm part one

You the seed —
    the unfamished, profane parasite;
born into love — bred into violence.
You... Who drank of my tainted honey and cringed
at its "unwholesome" bitterness. I
Twisted your mouth in unshamed disgust
You the larvae — depraved of sanity
    leech of the loins...
    killer of thoughts — selfish
    herder of insomnia...
the one who loved to be unpunishable
All the spittle runs dry now...
    the curses and deafening damnation;
    reverberating unbeknownst echoes to blame
Slither back into the filth — you are unredeemed
the dirt of society... That which you always
Feared
Grinds between your gumless teeth.
You will never be beautiful.

Laura Morton

Catalogue

Pink nose, soft fur
Lying by the fire place
Cozy and warm.

In deep sleep he dreams
Sweet dreams of mice and birds.

He must be comfortable
Because he smiles and
Sighs as though to never wake.

Waking up now, yawning
Like he has been asleep for weeks.
Licking his fur with his soft warm tongue
Making sure to be clean and neat.

Soon he stops, looks around
Slowly seeing nothing is going on
Then softly he gently lies his head down
And falls to sleep cozy and warm.

Jessica Salas

The Way Of A Man With A Maid

He lifted the lute from the shelf where it lay,
Unused for a decade or so.
The grime of time and dust of neglect
Had slowly taken its toll.
    He lifted the lute and tenderly shook
    The smothered and moldering cord,
    A silken twist of the strings he caressed
    And stroked the long finger board.
So skillful his fingers - so gentle his touch
So subtle was his demand.
The strings were a-tremble in response to his skill
A lute in a Master's hand.
    He cradled the lute.
    Pear-shaped in his arms, adjusted the ornate thong.
    Then into the hush of an evening's calm
    Came love in the heart of a song,
But he tired of playing
And he laid the lute down carelessly on its side.
Jubal, father of music in days gone by,
Knew more than a song had died.

Margaret Cox

Morning In The Forest

A cold dark winter morning in the forest,
A blanket of crisp snow lays on the firm forest floor,
Small snowflakes land on the frozen ground like soft
feathers gently blowing in the wind,
In the distance an icy river slowly and calmly flows
through the depth of the woodland,
Cool gusts of wind fill the stiff air while limbs clatter,
The lonely forest grows silent like an empty room,
Lifeless...
The radiant sun gradually rises over the horizon
of the tree tops and fills the forest with sparkling light,
For it is no longer gloomy,
The forest is as bright as a rainbow after
a spring shower.

Heather Brown

Finding One's Self

These lovely mountains I came to see
 and perhaps to find who I may be.

I seek a place where few will go,
 a place for me less traveled and beaten.

Each step I take, I ponder with care
 and find new things with each corner and peak.

But dread I feel, for its time I think,
 the time to take home what I can be.

Jonathan W. Buck

It's Called Love

I love the feel,
the taste and vision.
The pain,
that comes along too.

For me it's not just a hobby,
It's not the thought of winning.
It's love and dedication,
and it starts with the tie of a shoe.

Running around on a court,
dribbling a blown up ball.
Sure it hurts when I play,
but it's love that will keep me above you.

Billy Salus

Psychedelic Psychedelic

On the eternal tree of life,
Swings are high and swings are low,
Round and round, and up and down,
Branches are blue, and green, and pink,
Its trunk as wide as my kitchen sink.

This is the tree where I house my past,
My present, present and futures,
From limbs of the pinkest of pinks, and mauves of mauves,
Twigs and branches of smokey grays to the darkest of blacks

Spun gold, silver, and bronze,
Cobwebs encase my most precious,
Treasures from weddings, births and birthdays,
Inevitable death, future hopes.

Dreams and day dreams, destiny and ecstasy,
As my tree of life stands branched and sprawled,
Spontaneously burst into a radiant glow
Of multicolor glorious and victorious
My sensational tree of life.

Virginia Corbie

Kaitlyn

Ten little fingers and ten little toes,
Then of course there's that cute button nose.
Pretty blue eyes and soft tufts of hair.
Peaches and cream skin, all soft and fair.

Cute little giggles and a soft tiny coo,
You're Daddy's little girl, so sweet and true.
You're Mommy's little princess to cuddle and hold.
Our love to keep you warm when the weather grows cold.

We thank God each day for bringing you here,
Our precious baby; a daughter so dear.
Someone to love and hold all our own.
You put the sweet in our "Home Sweet Home".

Love, Mommy and Daddy

Heidi Poschner

Casual Observations

One day I was checking out people—
their actions, emotions and style.
They all seemed to me so different,
which caused me to ponder awhile.

They each had two arms, two legs and a nose;
hair and two eyes that look.
A neck, ten fingers, ten toes and a head,
by its cover, don't judge a book!!!

So what was it that caused me to think them so odd?
Why were they each strange from the other?
I think it's because it takes lots of kinds,
in a world where all are our Brother.

Catherine A. Week

Untitled

Murky shadow of sadness hanging down
Tears of shadow shades drip on images all around.
Drops of darkness creep over my soul
Bringing shadow clouds to my days
Upon the valleys of my life it lays

Albert L. Downs

The Essence Of Time

As it slips through the night
it takes with it another day
yet when you wake up
it brings a new day
it passes rapidly
but is never forgotten
it runs away with you
but is always there
it often worries you
and then you waste it
if flows through you
and with it takes life
so use it wisely
for the essence of time waits not for any

Chris Poniske

The Precious Birds

As you look in the sky, past the twinkle in your eye, you can see
the precious birds fly by, you can see the colors move,
white, pink and blue. The birds are as graceful and peaceful
as an angel itself. They laugh, they cry, and they unfortunately die,
just like you and I. The birds are as precious as this message
I am sending you, your heart feels blank without the bird,
but open it, and let the bird be free to fly.

Carly Stenfelt

Water-Ties

Staring through myself,
my transparent image silent
    in the glass.
i lean a shoulder against the cold window pane.
my breath frosts gray-white.
    my finger draws like slim rivers through uncharted land,
the lines on the smooth moist surface
which combine to form your name.
    tired eyes watch as it slowly melts away.
lines become empty space, rivers become a vast ocean.
your face in my mind, the cream-lined shell—
    it sounds in my ear the immensity of pounding waves,
so loud, it seems only one thing can stop it.
    the connection of the water...
my hands long to slice through the frigid ocean,
    but the tips of my fingers recoil from the cold glass.
i wrap the gray blanket around me,
looking out at gray skies,
    and i hope for rain.

Deborah Hsu

Born

I was off today, but had to go into work.
And let me tell you, it was a definite Perk!

I arrived early to finish up an assignment.
Then drove to Virginia, breaking the confinement.

A director at a nursing home waited for my arrival.
We had some goods to trade - Beneficial to our Survival.

Made it back for a meeting and spoke on "Dining".
It was as if a Light From Above was Contently Shining.

I was Confident; I was Jolly.
I felt like a Christmas Decoration covered with Holly.

I was Focused; I was Sincere.
I felt like a 21 year-old cracking his first beer.

I was Productive; I was Organized.
I felt like a battery that had just been "Energized".

I was Positive; I was Pleased.
I felt like an A+ Grade had just been seized.

I was Emancipated; I was Gracious.
I felt like a Puppy - Animated and Vivacious.

I was Cheerful; I was "Untorn".
I *Feel* like someone who has just been Born.

Andrew D. Everstine

In The Shadowy Darkness Of Hell

In the shadowy darkness of Hell
The ever so mean Devil comes to tell
The wonderful people above
That they can hate instead of love
He tells them to pollute
And to kill things that one says is cute
I know I can't take this pressure
We all need to make this Earth a lot fresher
He tries to make us think
That we can't deal without a blink
We all have to stick together
If we want to make it even better
We have to fight against him
We have to go above the rim
To fulfill our tasks, that God spiritually gave to us
But the one thing we can't do is cuss
That will show that the Devil is right
That we have lost our sight
In the shadowy darkness of Hell!

Jessica S. Jasek

Thunder Clouds

While I was staring out the window one morning,
two thunder clouds collided without a warning.
They gnashed and they gnarled and grimaced at each other,
bumping and grinding with nary a bother.
The noise was abrupt and oh, so loud;
I had no idea it could come from some clouds!
I jumped for safety, for surely I knew
that lightning would follow, white hot and true.
It did and I saw it, all brilliant and bright,
slicing the sky and causing a fright.
Then came the down pour, Gully Washer its name.
But no need to worry, Earth needs this,
Mother Nature's game.

Sue Bisher

Tightrope of Despair

Walking the tightrope of despair,
balancing the past with the present,
existing with the problems of yesterday
that will be here tomorrow.
Traveling towards an answer that is with us now.
The sin of possession
creates and feeds separation of man,
unable to exist without the walls of
individual or class distinction.
Separation for all of us
is within the minds that cannot accept
equality through peace,
or look from the land above onto those below.
Peace as in life,
is found at the level of water
where all is equal.
Offering no answers,
only an observation of what traps us
within a cycle of grieving people,
whose lives are controlled by the world around.

Mark O'Laughlin

His Plan

And God set forth a wondrous plan
When He created the female for His great land.
It all begins with a baby girl child,
So soft and sweet, so meek and mild.
Such a tiny thing but full of such charms,
You don't want to let her out of your arms.
A beautiful dream that has finally come true.
How thankful you are she was given to you.
As you watch this babe asleep in her bed,
You can't help but know what lies ahead.
There will be laughter, love, heartbreak, and fun,
For we well know the story has just begun.
Yes, only God knows how strong a mother's love is
Because it is comparable only to His.

Peggy Caley

Questions For A Season

Is it the advent of north winds that I feel,
or the sting of a heart turned cold that chills?

Is it the moaning of the barren branches that I hear,
or the lamentations of a destitute soul?

Is it the track of the sun, never far from the horizon,
or the ruin of joy, which brings the early twilight?

Does pale winter moonlight shadow the world with greys,
or have the vibrant colors of love faded from my vision?

Will my spirit remain buried beneath swirling snow?
Will the promise of spring be known once again?

Dan Urich

Best Friend

The blackness of the night will be gone
and with its leave there will be left a song
a song of praise a song of thanks
for those that did not breech the ranks
eternity is within your reach
no more sleep and no more grief
no more hurt and no more pain
only everything to gain
Won't you come now and take a peek
at the happiness laid at your feet
Give your heart, your mind and soul
Jesus can save you from Sheol
Look to him to bring you out
To turn your life around about
Never look back, you've been born again
And now in him you have your best friend.

Sally R. Brewer

There Is A Woman

There is a woman who loves me
Her love is unconditional without judgement
Her love is patient without doubt
Her love is limitless without bounds
Her love is spiritual without boundaries
Her love is generous without greed
Her love is beautiful without grief

There is a woman who loves me
She is giving without question
She is accepting without prejudice
She is encouraging without pushing
She is by your side without hesitancy
She is beautiful undeniably

There is a woman that I love
She has been my lifeline through love and trust
She has been my confidante through sadness and fear
She has been my support through anger and tears
She has been my friend through happiness and cheer
She has been there like no other
She is my beautiful Grandmother

Ana Guffy

A Child's Hope

The sea is blue, the sky is too.
The children sing, the laughter rings!
They are full of joy...
    to some just toys.
But life so fragile was left with struggle,
Hardship and heartache seem to be their only friend
    and to some a very bitter end.
Then comes shame and abandoned dreams;
A life to some who have never seen.
God bless these few, these chosen ones,
    who want to prove there once was love.
Please fill their hearts too full,
And keep them safe
    to the one who gives His loving grace.

Jennifer Lindsey Gengler

Untitled

Oh city of Angels gilded in gold built
upon the brick of indifference I weep my
Modern Rome. The stars bowed reverently
in your direction. You were an international
port of idealistic dreams and hope.

Oh City of Angels amorphously defamed
bitter ashes are all that remains from
the fervent flames that echoed the voices of injustice.

Jacqueline Fernandez

The Poet's Dismay

I am a poet, a whirlwind within myself!
The verse like...books lined upon a shelf.
The rhymes in utter dismay;
Will they come together someday?
My poetry is from the heart, where no mortal man can see.
Where pain, anger, and despair caress me tantalizingly.
If the words should stay apart, it could tear me limb from limb,
From all the hurt and anger that flows so deep within.
For within each verse I've lived a life;
Sometimes filled with happiness, but often full of strife.
I am a poet, there is no doubt, my depressions deeply set.
For even when I'm happy; I'm even sadder yet.
There is no end to this pain that surges through my soul.
I pray that in death, that I find my peace, for I am getting old.

Kathy Piatt

Be Nice To All Children

Let be nice to all children and give them your love and support.
For they are the future and hope of tomorrow.
They need affection, protection and communication.
Hatred and recrimination does not help,
Because love conquers and hatred destroys all.
If we ever have the need to make corrections
Let's try a two way communication.
Let's be there when they may need us.
With love and hugs, there is not room for drugs.
Drugs and child abuse must be eradicated
From the face of the earth and soon.
We must live in harmony with all things and
In peace with ourselves to protect our universe.
Let's be nice to all children of today
For they will be the parents of tomorrow.
We have to create a better present
And prosperous and brighter tomorrow's
And in the name of God, do not abuse children,
That is a stigma, a disgrace, the biggest shame
Of our society. Please be nice and care for all children.

Teresa Abad

A Letter From My Love

I awoke this morning to a letter from my love.
It was written across the sky.
Written in hues of gold and blue so splendid
That I could have cried.

I whispered thank you, I love you too and
I ache to be where you are.
That's when he gave me this little wink,
From the last bright morning star.

Sighing deeply I knew he was right,
From my mission I could not stray.
There are so many that we both love,
Still lost along life's byways.

With renewed strength I take a bold step
Into this brand new day.
Reassured that soon my work will be done
And with my love forever I'll stay.

April Dalrymple

Valentine Would You Please Be Mine

What are you doing my sweet valentine?
I asked you once. I've asked you twice. Dear
sweet valentine, please be mine. Like a flower
That blooms, like a star that shines. Like a
parent and their child, oh valentine, would
you please be mine. Like a chocolate so sweet
like two lovers that just meet, like me asking
you for so many time, oh valentine, please be mine.

Octavia Hawkins

Technology Trauma

So much is routine that was once so exciting,
wonder is a thing of the past,
TV And those cellular phones are igniting
technology, awe doesn't last!

Beyond the initial, and so fascinating,
new products that we view 'on line',
present an impossible scheme, there's no waiting,
we'll witness it soon, Oh! But I'm

Not into computer, I am A disputer,
I prefer my typewriter, or script,
Alas! Don't need many new comforts, if any
replace my old ways, I'll feel gypped!

At not being able to cope, I'm unstable
I feel will be my designation,
by those who harass me as they all surpass me
Did the Lord, when He started creation

Foresee all the 'cool stuff,' some leading to cruel stuff,
Folks no longer heeding those Ten
commandments He gave us, is nothing to save us?
"Slow down, World", pleads God, now Amen!

Bette A. Ruth Dailey

Untitled

A little flower has come to live with me.
I had not planted it; how could it be?
The pot stood empty, with soil quite bare;
So, little flower, how got you there?
Was it a wind-borne seed, carried along,
Or a bird who dropped it, with a song?
Odd shaped leaves, like mittened palms,
Spread out to beg of sunshine's alms.
Choosing to grow and flower in partial shade,
Of my vacant pot a home you've made,
And colored it with tiny Trumpets Blue
Tapering to white in startling hue.
Welcome, little flower, I hope you'll stay,
And not, as you came, slip silently away.

Ludwig Savarese

As Life Goes On

At birth, an entry in the Book of Life is made
And another foundation is carefully laid
From which a new life is about to emerge
Seeking fulfillment with a powerful surge.

Our purpose in life and to what heights we're aspired
Comes from people we meet and by whom we're inspired
But in trying to reach the goals we would achieve
We must not lose sight of that in which we believe.

Our stay here on earth is of short duration
And we're but a small part of the great Creation.
As the earth keeps turning, forever the same
To dust we will return, from whence we came.

The fact is that no matter how hard we try
Inevitable, 'tis written, we all must die.
It is but a question of how, when or where
We will reach this destiny we all must share.

Of utmost importance is what we leave behind
For those who would follow in our paths to find
Will we leave in our wake only hatred and fear
Or a better world for our having been here?

Lillian Bohleber

The Night

   During the night I awake to hear the howls of the wind,
though it does not scare me, I feel a tingle through my back
and a shiver up my spine. Sometimes, I can imagine that the
wind is calling to wake the great earth saying, "Beware, for
soon will be the coming of a storm". And then, almost as if by
command, minutes later I awake again, not from the wind, but
to the tears of the sky on my window and bolts of threatening
lightning and the evil breath of the world which makes a great
clatter. I did get frightened but only for a second, for then I
realized it is just mother nature doing her job. So, with
that thought in my head, I go back to my dream.

   Ashley Westbrook

Melancholy...

He there is standing like a sweet heavenly moon upon me
Drink from me, my bitter sweet romance
coming to terms and leaving fast
   Love
The sweet nectar of his heart
Me, like the angel coming apart
And I am leaving no one, behind
Say to he - you are your's and I am mine
Standing there beside my heart
Looking at me fall apart
Glory mine
In love my thrown
He does not be left alone.

   Jodi Creager

Timeless

You are with me no more,
   Gone...forever closing the door
The "Togetherness" we once shared was the music of my life
   You said you were glad that I was your wife.
Still I sense your thoughts, feel your breath on my face
   Yes, I know that in time, these feelings will
Leave without a trace,
   For it is the way of our world, with joy there is pain,
While few know that to give love is the greatest gain,
   And to receive love is the one true gift.
From Life to Death.
   It is timeless.
   So be it!

   Rose M. Fuller

War

As the dishonorable discourse
of our human imaginations emanate.
The hatred brews from within the need
to conquer and destroy all.
I question the drive and the need
to destroy, and I plead "Create, Love"
There is nothing glamorous nor glorious
about the ruthless killing of human beings
Why I ask, why we must Hate,
   must Destroy,
      must Conquer.
There is no true or sound answer
except that we are evil and know no other.
Or is it power that the politicians seek
a sense of control or even a false security,
I just question and wonder
the real and true motive behind war.

   Jed Stumpf

Different World

I look outside and see a world
A world of anger and hate,
Where a person's race means everything
And people segregate.

I look outside and see a world
Where love is all around.
In every child's and parent's eyes
A love light can be found.

I look outside and see a world
With happiness in bloom,
Where jokes are made and games are played
And laughter fills each room.

I look outside today and think
And wonder how it came
That people are so different,
And yet they are the same.

'Cause everybody laughs and plays
And everybody cries,
So cast aside your differences
And look through other's eyes.

Lora Jackle

That Day In November

Sweet November came
like the hush of a storm
silently making
partitions, pleats, and creases in my life.

Sweet November came
Bitter as it was
and froze a sharp icicle
right on top of my heart.

Sweet November came
and swept him away;
but lately I've been hearing
vibrations...I think he's nearby

Sweet November came and went
and gave a little as it took:
A drop of hope, an ounce of faith
a pinch of prayer, and a lot of thanks.
And then it set an angel on my shoulder
just the other day
to bring me closer to
all that went away...

Tanisha Davis

Untitled

A snow-covered countryside is a sight to see;
The snow simply beautifies the trees.

The magnificent trees seem to wave at me
When the wind sends a chilling, artic breeze.

The touch of snow is as cold as ice.
But a taste of snow cream is something nice.

It's not a treat to see the snow leave.
It'll come back, I believe.

Angela E. Ferrell

Lightning

It strikes as silent as a mouse
Then a lion's roar rules the sky
A flash of burning air scares the midnight sky
Then another flash hits to say goodbye

Casey Lyons

Ode To Thomas Merton

Into the darkness I shall go
Into this purging of this night
Letting loose of man's made light
To walk in this darkness and find my soul

Learning to leave the light of day
To venture onto this unlit road
To find in blindness a lighter load
And wings for my heels to walk this way

I can now see a glimpse of the glow
As I move upward on this unseen hill
A dawning within me like a flood to fill
All the chambers within my emptied soul

Into the abyss I dove
And fell to dwell within the sanctifying sea
Which illumines my heart and sets me free
And thus in my darkest night the sun arose

Consumed by the radiant, beautiful blaze
Of this wild and wonderful way
That has transformed my night into blissful day
And in awe I live and drown in my mysterious inward gaze.

Ari W. Durham

The Melting Sandcastle

As I stare out into what used to be
Dilapidated visions send shivers through me
Dreaming of a time when towers stood tall
When thoughts became true in spite of it all
Remember just how proud and how straight
The flags did fly, escaping the hate
And grain by grain; inevitably
The sands flew on, scream to be free!
Drifters of earth, slave to all time
To a higher tower they hope to climb
Natural disorder always succeeds
Like a feather that floats on the warm summer breeze
Birds conspire in tranquil blue
As a fresh day is born anew.

Jayna Lorene Derby

The Portrait Of A Lady

Suddenly the image of opulent simplicity
Came into focus. Thereupon, I fell absolutely
In love with her.
An exquisite, expansive smile enables her
Fiery soul to resonate with deeply appealing rhythms.
By her pattern of word, a whole new
world is woven.
Whether or not of popular opinion, a
persistent stance she maintains, concerning her conviction.
In the face of death, stalwart, from
pillar to post, the child of comfort she personifies.
Providing steady ground, unselfish love
She retains, through the valley of doubt and fear.
Unique unto herself, may this stellar
Portrait of a lady forever be on
Display in my life.

Paul A. DeGennaro

The Duck Hunt

Early in the morning,
As I sit on the ponds edge,
I wait until I hear the wing beat of the duck,
and the cackle of the geese,
the whisper of the wind,
the gentle softness of the mist,
I look forward to another day in nature.

Curtis Smith

I Am Here, Where I Belong

I have shouted to myself, "I am alone"
Standing by myself, alone
I need someone, someone who will understand
and accept me, as I am
In desperation, I seek you out, but
I need more than you can give
The answer comes
after much thought
He dwells within me, therefore
I am not alone
He has brought me to this point, I believe
so that I could learn
Now I must also remember.

Dorothy F. Sterni

Fading Into The Fog

Heading into the rocks; smashing, crying, weeping
Yelling at me to pick up the pieces
The pieces of your life.

Lifting your spirit breathing
Life back into your body,
Restoring you, just to watch you
Fade into the Fog again.

Like a record, I can only be played so long.
I tire, and get scratched on the surface
But you still want me to play as if I were new.

So, I'll play on - destined to play your favorite song.
Until you get tired of me and throw me away in the trash.
Only to remember the good times, then you'll try to find me.

You will find me
Fading into the Fog
On the barge of Love
back into the sea of life where I started from.

Richard D. Deming

A Teen-Ager's Thoughts

These teen-age years. . . . .sure can be fun,
Yet, we know some things. . . . .are missing,
So. . .I'll make each day, just last. . . . .and last,
No gripes. . .complaints. . .or hissing.

You're just a teen-ager. . . . .only once in life,
If you "screw up" now. . . . .forget it,
You may never get another chance,
In jail. . . . .you will regret it.

I look around me. . . . .on my block,
With drugs. . .and booze. . .and "drop outs",
I want to make my folks so proud,
Don't want to be. . . . .a "cop-out".

There's trouble here. . . . .and trouble there,
And oh. . . . .those strong temptations!
To join "the boys". . . . .on week-end nights,
'Tis said. . . . .are some sensations!

It's "nothin' for nothing'". . . . .in this great life,
And success is there. . . . .with study,
You get out. . .just. . .what you put in,
So, why not make your mind. . . . .your buddy?

John J. McGee

Li'l Red Corvette

Man O man my li'l red Corvette.
Bright and shiny red boy O Boy.
When the sun the moon the stars and the scene is set Girl O Girl.
That is where I'll be with my Li'l Red Corvette Uptown Swirl.

Kim Duncan

Life's Twist -N- Turns

Life is queer with its twists and turns,
as we all will someday learn.

As we learn you will see
how lucky you and I can be.

Life is somewhat like a street,
you never know where you'll someday meet.

Sometimes the road will turn in and out
and we will question what it's about?

The road will curve to the right, and you wonder why
and then it angles to the other side.

If you continue going, you will see
it angles back again indeed...

Life is quite the same in terms... give up and lose your name.
Keep on striving and you'll conquer the game.

Janet Jewell-Sanchez

Mother's Day

As we are upon the month of May
I want you to know there is a special day.
A day for all children to love and to praise,
A woman so special in many, many ways.
This isn't much, it's just a small token
Of the bond of you and me that can never be broken.
I know it's not much but it comes from the heart,
I promise to you that we will never be apart.
I love you so much that I had to say,
Have a wonderful time on this Mother's Day!

Robin Jackson

Cry To The Wind

Cry to the wind.
Cry to the wind for my lament's end.
Cry to the wind for the sun to set on my long, dark mourning.
Cry to the wind in a choked voice to blow away the ashes in which I kneel.

Cry to the wind, the oblivious wind, the uncaring wind to loosen my shackles. To remove my blindfold.

But the wind doesn't listen.

Eric Hartness

Oh Brother

Sweet little boy
Maybe when he was three
Hard working child
When somebody is looking
Kind to animals
Yeah right

He is my brother
He is nothing but a disgusting little brat
but I love him.
I help him when he needs help
even give him a hug when nobody is looking.

Jennifer Rzepka

Emotions Of A Tree

In spring the tree sings of buds.
From the kisses of the sun it blushes green.
With the unforgiving winds it cries leaves
until boney branches remain.
Now, its soul frozen, it patiently waits for spring.

Nichole Fowler

The Weaver And The Loom

I held the thread of life
When breath I grasped
Two decades past.

I stitched the needle of beauty
To patterns of wisdom and love,
Mixed with the colors of sorrow and mirth.

By my choices I proclaimed:
My design was mine alone,
Shared to no one, not even God.

Until the colorless hue I saw,
No pattern, no design,
Only nothingness exemplified.

I looked up from the stitches
And saw the hand that held the thread:
It was God's.

Yes.
God was the weaver
And I was only the loom.

Joy P. Gensaya

Mother Earth

Mother Earth watches over large and small
   Giving us seasons spring, summer, winter and fall
In place the clouds and rainbows stay
   Because of Mother Earth's wonderful way
In repay we create something bad
   Pollution and garbage and it's making her mad
It's greed I say, people are money fools
   It's becoming too much it's frightening and not cool
We depend on Mother Earth for life on this land
   She holds us up so we can stand
So think once more of what she's done
   And clean her up so she can feel young

Sarah Efronson

The Rose

If you will listen to me as the wind blows gently through my
petals you will hear many tales of love and happiness.
For I the red rose is used to represent love.
I and my family are used to prove love to many young women.
The love I show is gentle and sweet you shall realize this when
you receive a single long stem red rose.
As many young women are about to cry the rose shows how their
true love's feelings for them and I also gratitude.
Do you need someone or something to show love for you just buy
a single long stem red rose and it will show you love.
If you will listen to me as the wind blows gently through my
petals you will hear many tales of love and happiness.

Angela Horton

In Memoriam of Verna Alice Perdue

Whose birthday would have been January 20.
Her smile gone forever.
Her hands so dear to us we cannot touch.
Still we have all those memories,
Of the one we love so much.
Her memory is our keepsake
Which we treasure with our heart.
God has her in sage keeping.
We have her not.
So our heart is always heavy
In too big a spot.
But we praise God in His Glory
For the Home He gave her that we could not.
Ilene Olson, Harry Perdue

Ilene Perdue Sandage Olson

Think Of Me

Think of me, when you think of me,
as a row boat set loose from its moorings
drifting away
you can still reach me
   If you only stretch out your arms

Think of me, when you think of me,
as a rare
beautiful butterfly
trapped inside a cocoon
   which I cannot open from the inside.

Think of me, when you think of me,
as a single balloon floating up into the sky
a red balloon drifting higher and higher
with a ribbon dangling almost to the ground
   Daring you to take hold

Lorrie Barrett

The Traveling Worm

There once was a worm who was unlike the others,
He could count by 3's unlike his mother.
He giggled a lot and made funny jokes,
He loved to talk, but not to his folks.
One day he decided to go out west,
And be someone he wasn't and become the best.
He flew around and around till he came to Madagascar,
When he was there he won a golf tournament with a par.
Then he went way, way down to Brazil,
And sat in the nice hot sun, he thought that was a thrill!
He got a ticket to go to Ukraine,
And went on the nicest, and prettiest train.
Then he decided to go to Greenland,
Where he saw and played with the new toy Sqand.
But he didn't feel right a friend was what he needed,
Like back in the old days how he had been treated.
He decided to fly just one more place,
It was his home country the United States.
Although his name is Anthony McTrevor,
He ended up staying with his family forever!

Leah Anderson

To My Dearest Sister

My teardrops are like the dew,
Pouring from me down upon you.
Emptiness where you used to be,
Sorrow and Grief that is left for me.
My thoughts of you are in my mind so deep,
Struggling with memories I long to keep.
Many times your life was so unfair,
I hope you knew that I always cared.
You always kept a good frame of mind,
You are that Special one of a kind.
I know you're in Heaven, your new home,
And never suffering or ever alone.
You are my angel above,
As whole and pure as a beautiful white dove.
You had it hard and earned your wings,
You fought hard for these wonderful things.
May God keep you in his peace and love,
Until the day I venture above.

Carla Stillian

My Imagination Zoo

Canaries eat berries in my imagination,
Parrots eat carrots in my mind,
Lions eat people,
I know that doesn't rhyme,
But wouldn't you hate to have a lion in mind?

LaNita Pearson

Coming Of Age

Be patient, truthful, listen, acknowledge.
I woke up one day, as if every other day hadn't mattered.
The truth is...
No one can give an age, or tell you when it will happen.
Some become drifters and are lost because of their misfortunes,
but don't deny it when it happens to you,
accept it.
Fear, anger, hostility, denial
I want more.
I don't care about the consequences.
You haven't thought about your actions.
Your lover wasn't only yours.
Now you're pregnant, alone, and have no money.
What are you going to do?
Why did this happen to me?
What was I thinking?
These are great questions, but I don't hear any answers.
Wake up, realize, accept, take responsibility, plan.
If these are just words to you,
then you're not ready.

Valerie Sandin

Passion

   I wish I loved you. We have met but only twice.
Once when I forgot everything and once which I will never forget.
Passion, I wish I knew you. I wonder if I ever will.
   I meet Indifference so frequently,
I question my sheep-like nature. I question even my own name
wondering if Indifference is me. But deep down I know
my name is not Indifference. Indifference is my lover.
Most nights he stares empty into my eyes.
He means well, but after our twilight affairs
I wake holding empty in my eyes. Passion,
sleep with me for the night. Swindle Indifference
to another lover and delight my heart with fire.
Stroke me with your heated feelings
so that I may wake with a fire still burning.
Passion, won't you let me know you?
Won't you let me love you? I beg of you,
with nights of Indifference having left me
with cold ashes, spend the night
so that - for once - I may sleep with fire.

Michael Fox

Crossed Path

If you crossed my path again,
Would you see my face?
Would you look up at me,
Or down in shamed disgrace?

And if I dare to say hello,
What would your response be?
For I am trying to be your friend,
But you seem to disagree.

Or what if I should cross your path,
Where the same sunlight breaks?
I'm sure I would be pleasurable,
With the slightest grin on your face.

But if you didn't smile, my dear,
I'm not sure how I'd react,
I'd probably look around, turn,
And follow my path right back.

(For our paths are not to cross, my friend,
Never again to me.
But if they accidentally do,
Please-only smiles should greet).

Stephanie Davis

War Is A Bitch

Have you seen,
that war is mean
the rifles, the bullets,
the wounds it causes.

Some soldiers die,
some mothers cry.
I don't know why
the soldiers die.
War is a bitch!

While the soldiers sleep,
the wives weep.
They sit at home and hope to die
that their husband will come home alive.

They wait here and there, they wait everywhere.
They wait to hear
their husband's fear.
But all they hear is that the rifle
sounds like a roar of thunder
and her husband is 6 feet under.
War is a Bitch!

Christopher C. Moynihan

Retired

I am but a mortal retired,
Who would like to be rehired,
Not in work but peace of mind,
To be a bigger part of mankind,
But like all I am a small part of the world wide,
So I live my everyday life on my own,
And try and set my own tone,
I wake to a new day,
And each first of the month wait on SS and my pension pay,
I eat, and sleep and do what I want,
So what is it I hunt,
Just to be plain old me,
For I can spend the rest of my life for things, to see,
To live my new found life in peace,
For life has given me a new lease,
Most of all good health,
And maybe a little wealth,
Who knows how the retired wind will blow,
In my heart poem I'll let you know.

Anna Maerean

Untitled

(Translation by Isabel Espinal)
Two o'clock, three o'clock
It's the same old morning
With the same sleepless curves
The pencil makes its last point
in the pointed word that surprises me

Three o'clock, three twelve
everyone is dreaming about everything that happened
the untiring game, the bustling children
the unending trips to a foreign counter
astonishment's sleepery getaways
the long hallways through which memory wonders
the frustration's crooked bodies
my Achilles heel, Jose's fatigue
surprises, laziness, yawns, poetry, indifference,
and why not faith, prayers, and meetings?

Four, four thirty four
I turn toward the wall
anxiously await the word
the one that doesn't reach me
the one that burns, the everyday one.

Yrene Santos

Lord For All Season And Reasons

Another year has flown fleetingly by and only you, Lord,
Knows the reason why
Was I so bored? And failed to see how quickly time passed me
I seem to recall some bright sky blue days
But more than usual, fall days of gray
But on these gray days of fall
I felt your love most of all
It matters not how bright or gray the day
Only that (You) are there always
Gives me reason enough to praise and cheer
Some say you are awesome
I found that true
Because of your gigantic love
I can love too.

Glenda Napper

My Little Tale

The next guy coming along goes by Snoop.
His favorite snack to eat is soup.
He has very long hair to be black,
But in singing, he does not lack.
His favorite type of song is known as "rap",
And after a show, he comes home and takes a nap.
No you don't understand the words,
But people come from miles around forming herds,
To hear him sing. His life is very simple,
Except when he sees himself and finds a pimple.
He thinks his looks happen to be the "bomb";
So when he gets rejected, he stays calm.
His clothes are very big, I might add,
That two his size could fit them. Now that's bad.
The words he sing have a bit of rhyme,
And you might be able to catch it just in time.
I think he's great and so will you;
Just see him once, that's all you have to do.
You will then put "I Love You" on a sign.
But back up sista, this brotha's mine!

Rebecca Reid

What Is The Purpose Of Life

What is the purpose of life When the outcome is always the
same Death, Why are we here, they say every soul has a
purpose, But yet most of us are Helpless or Suffering, and
yet We Are All Alive, And The Outcome Is The Same Death
The religious say that God has a purpose for us all, But yet
there is Starvation, Poverty and War, yet We Are All Alive
And The Outcome Is The Same Death, God says that help comes
to those who help themselves, but yet there are the
Needy, and the Helpless or Innocent, Who Cannot Help
Themselves, but yet We are Alive And The Outcome Is The
Same Death, The wise say good cometh to those who are
patient, but yet there are tears that never reach the
bottom of the well, or dreams that never learn to fly, but
yet We Are Alive And The Outcome Is Still The Same For us
All Death, Some of us never live a full life or never get
the chance for a life, but all of us face death alone

Patrick Stephen Recupero

The Blackest Rose

Soft was the petal of the very first touch
I could hear the agony and the pain too much
Closely I listened and heard the call
Coming from the blackest rose I ever saw.

Then a cry too faint...I could barely hear
A piercing clip...then no more tears.
No longer could I hear the call
Coming from the blackest rose I ever saw.

Tammy White

A Very Personal Encounter

Sometimes I think I'm missing out
On what is really in our hearts.
We talk of many, many things
But where's the feeling parts?

Relationships that satisfy
Share intimacies and such
That lie inside the guarded soul
Where only hearts can touch.

But intimacy's other mood
Can stir a darker side
When revealing awful secrets
That deep within reside.

There's risk involved in telling
Disclosures that we share
There's a burden in the knowing
And responding needs great care.

Still I need a someone
Sensitive enough to actively listen,
To honestly respond, not jokingly divert
In attempting to subvert, a very personal encounter.

Joyce Goldman

Vacant Fires

Vacant fires of a conquered people
flame emptily inside us

Where once there was the fountain
that lustily spewed forth seething magma
there is now only the cold void of Lethe.

Whence forgotten so easily are the
restless oceans of self,
so buried beneath obscuring layers like the unwanted dead?

Where gone is our delight in
the simple wonder of sunlight,
nightfall, a breath?

Submerged somewhere in the cold obsidian of our minds
is the memory of the flames which made us,
sustained us, kept us warm, and gave us life;

A memory of the world as it is, not as the blind see it;

Without which we are but cold shadows
unaware of having been vanquished by ourselves
or of what we have lost

David M. Hoenig

Untitled

Everything stops,
No movement,
No sound,
Earth stands still.
Only thing that is moving is what's going on inside my mind.
Light fades,
Winds die down,
All plants shrivel,
And painfully die.
Water never flows,
Animals turn strange and awkward.
Then all is silent and dark,
I stand frozen and pondering.
I had never imagined this would happen.
Darkness,
Quiet,
Motionless,
The eternal fear marches on.
Everything...gone,
All gone.

Valerie L. Roberts

Loneliness

Loneliness is a feared feeling among us all.
Its a feeling we try to run from,
but there is no escape.
You have your heroes on T.V.
But that is only a dream world.
In the end they're heading for a fall.
At times, loneliness makes you feel like your being ignored,
So you try to make yourself shine in the lime light.
to get everyone's attention,
But you're doing nothing except being the fool.
So, you see, life sometimes has the upper hand,
And all you can do is sit there and hurt.
Loneliness is something you can't fight alone.
So you're going to need a friend,
who's going to care and understand until the end.

Larry A. Roush Jr.

The Rain

The splendor of the day unwraps its layers one by one,
As droplets, suspended in air gently sweep over the land.
The overcast above reveals a knot to be undone,
As a mighty man about to drop water from his hand.

Then slowly, one by one, the drops of water hit the land.
Soon raging fury fires its engines, and unleashes cooling fire.
The rain envelops the land, and as if it were all planned,
Douses the fire, and moves away, leaving its muck and mire.

Now done, at last, the water recedes into the ground and gutter,
Leaving all to carry on, to enjoy the calm again.
All is silent, as before, but now no one a word shall utter,
And life goes on, as just before, in house and cave and den.

Brandon Folts

Big Blue, New Seabury, Massachusetts

The clear blue stretches before the eye,
till finely indistinguishable from the late day sky.
Shades, shapes, hues, and rippling waves
underneath it all lies submarine caves
that lie home to great creatures large and small.
To think that from this tumultuous roar began it all.

Pounding and crashing, the thunderous surf,
the clash between Neptune and Mother Earth.
Try as we might to conquer its glory,
each failed attempt becomes another epic story,
of battle, of struggle, and the ensuing defeat,
the mighty ocean refusing to be beat.
Staving off man's progress, or peace of mind,
and showing, that very fragile is mankind.

Michael Saitow

Untitled

When you live your life in fear
It is your destiny you cannot steer
What happens tomorrow you never know
Day by day you always go
Future plans or looking ahead
Can never be thoughts of, can never be said.
So as you're playing "The something will happen game"
Procrastination has become your middle name
"I know, I know" have been the words
Frankly, it's really for the birds.
In order to do, you must react
That's not a thought - it is a fact.
So use the support of loved ones and every friend
And put this lousy crescendo to an end.
Get involved with your own fate
And always remember it's never too late.

Phillip Goldberg

White Witch

I listen to a medley of Squire,
Reminding me of those Golden locks.

I dreamt of her today.
A wild rampant fantasy of mind and flesh.
A desire of romanticism long dead.

Deep inside I feel chivalrous, giving, loving.
My exterior proves cold, e'en callous.
But she made me melt once, long ago.
In my dream we become one, melting
Into a blue sparkling pool of love.

But e'en as we change, they remain the same.
Ergo - my fantasy is a dream - naught but fantasy.
'Tis a lost and lonely feeling:
A dream soon to die and burn to ashes.
E'en as I once did - but then - I rose again.

Destiny is a funny thing, fate so comical.
Karma is Aunt, Sister to Gaea.
Life - life is dream and fantasy.
She is my fantasy - eyes so blue,
The lips so tender, the dream so false.

Sabin D. Woods

Love, Left Alone, Is Dying

It was a little rift, mostly unnoticeable
    but so subtly disruptive.
Neither mentioned it, both rose above it,
    but their love slowly bled.

"You are such a lovely friend."
    "And you...so faithful and loyal."
"I could not match you ever in loveliness."
    "Nor could I love another so."

"Are you feeling...ah, what a lovely day!"
    "Yes, er...what do you touch on?"
"Are you writing your...my, the air is cold"
    "My mother is having company today."

There is no help from heaven, and the love is dying.
    It is piteous, as if too elusive
To be encouraged and nurtured to revive.
    And nothing shall be said to survive.

Marian A. Cantwell-Fry

Waiting On A Lift

The wind blows swiftly moving by, in the face of
the eagle awaiting a high.

The wind like the spirit, in times of refreshing
lifts you high above the shadows of doubts and
depression.

The soul is mounted like an eagle with wings,
perched in position, waiting on the wind to
strengthen his flying.

Waiting on a lift, coasting in the air, my soul
like the eagle has flown its last moments almost
driven to fear.

The storms have almost beaten and battered the
eagles control, but hidden there in shelter
safe from dangers that alarm the soul

Feeling and touching awaiting a high, the wind
like the spirit, moving and soaring, blowing
swiftly by.

Freedom and liberation are felt as lifted up by
the mighty wind, strength for tomorrow, soaring
in the spirit, preserving my soul to the end.

Frankie Honeycutt

ANTI

How you've built me up with your wishing hell.
Corruption opens your eyes, then you'll see.
How you've thrown Cupid down your hating well.
This world wouldn't give a chance to be so free.
All anti-white ethics and anti-man.
White children grow up learning anti-black.
Government with an anti-future plan.
Now Satan sits on his fiery throne.
Religion and race separated now.
We have ignored our last chance. It's blown.
God, money, everyone must now go bow.
Try to look through the darkness and the gray.
See through all of it. Love just might stay.

Haki Flores

There's Someone Or Somebody Somewhere I Know

There's someone or somebody somewhere I know
That's looking for someone his love to bestow.
His soul may be calling its mate to unite.
Don't hide in the shadows but meet him tonight.

There's someone or somebody somewhere I know
That's waiting and watching in sadness and woe,
Her eyes full of kindness never daring to frown
Her lover now absent in some far distant town.

There's someone or somebody somewhere tonight
That can't bend to do what her heart feels is right.
If she could but fathom what love has in store,
She would answer him smiling and tell him much more.

There's someone or somebody somewhere, I know
That could be made happy, her cheeks all aglow.
If the man whom she married would smile every day
And never by actions, his promise betray.

Monica Yoak

Shadow

I open my eyes to see only my shadow,
Shadow, why do you still remain?
The women have fled,
friends close and far have walked away.
My life goes up and down,
yet you still remain to hear my sorrows.

You never walk in front or behind for long,
but always there for me to see.
You have yet in my life made a sound,
yet my questions are answered without a word.
You follow, but never pester,
O' curious friend you puzzle me.

We walk side by side,
we talk day in and day out.
You hear every word, and every thought.
You were cast when I was conceived,
and have truly been my life's companion!
Shadow - best friend,
Why do you still remain?

Paul W. Schiavone

Reading

When I open up a book, I don't just peek, or take a look.
I open up my mind, and read, from mountains to the end of sea.
From the cat in the hat, to the wind in the willows,
from a kitten's meow, to an elephant's bellow.
I stretch my imagination, and I can see, that I can be anything.
I can travel through time, as different feelings go through my mind.
Then I finish this wonderful book, I walk around and take another look.

Amanda Liberty

Through A Child's Eyes

So simple, so complete
Things are beautiful in every way
Mischief, wonder, adventure
Fills every day
The only questions are the why's.
Every day is clear blue skies
This is the world through a child's eyes.

So grown up, so mature
Where are the child eyes
That were once so pure?
Everything is so complex
Nothing is so complex
Nothing is the same
The only feeling
Is the heartbeat of pain
All the sunny skies turn gray
Confusion fills the busy days
Everything around suddenly dies
Wishing to see life once more
Through a child's eyes.

Stephani Englebright

Super Sunday XXXI

Super Bowl 31 in 1997,
for true football fans this was pure heaven.

Once again it was in the Superdome,
unfortunately for the Saints they were not home.

One team was an original of the NFL,
the other had started the AFL.

Both teams were no strangers to Super Bowl fame,
the Packers in 1 and 2 and the Patriots in the 20th game.

Reggie White pounded and sacked and tormented Bledsoe,
he did it so much it turned into a show.

Brett went long to Rison and Freeman,
while Drew handed off to Byars and Martin.

The Patriots were trying to work out the kinks,
while the Packers were breaking the SI cover jinx.

Records were broken and so were the Pats,
fans went crazy, those ones in cheese hats.

For a backup quarterback named Jim McMahon,
he beat New England twice, both times in Louisian.

When the clock ran out it was 35-21,
the Packers had three rings, and the Patriots had none.

Anthony Mickelbury

Whispers Of The Heart

I hear a sound mystically composed
Of gentle winds rustling the pedaled rose
It mimics the rumbling of rapid falls
Like the thunder of the heartbeat calls
Its power draws forth the shadow's song
When two lives intertwined belong
There is a warm hum when eyes come to meet
Producing a lilac fragrance in the air to greet
I hear the song of your embracing smile
When lying together or across the miles
The sounds of your touch like an uncorked wine
Feeds the flesh to our spirits entwined
I feel the vibrations of trembling breath
Singing amorously, evermore always flesh
I hear the melody only two can chart
When calls the whispers of the heart

Michael D. Castle

Harvey Brown's Wake

Ol' Harvey Brown danced a jig
Near the river bed,
Knew the most he ever knew
The image in his head.

A floppy hat swayed its brim
Fell upon the ground,
Round and round ol' Harvey danced
To the same ol' sound and sound.

A young girl watched him yip
Wild as a coyote kit,
And while amiss couldn't resist
The folly in her swaying hips.

But Harvey knew of wild men
And yearning younger girls,
And laughed and laughed at the flowing mass
Of strawberry, golden curls.

Smelling of liquor and of stench
He slipped upon the rocks,
And slept a sleep, he had never slept
Until the gurgling stopped.

Steve Crank

The Garden

In God's world grows a beautiful garden,
A vision that eyes can see.
Created from seeds of nature, growing
for life's "Majesty."
Oh the Rose with sweet smell and such beauty,
Protected by thorns, fulfilling its duty.
The Morning Glory awakens with morning fresh dew,
A greeting for life, to make the day new.
The Sunflower grows tall, so high above set...
with all intentions of life being met.
The Gardenia so white with its thick fragrant flowers,
The Tulip's so colorful, lining rows like Towers.
The Daisy with "he loves me...he loves me not," dreams,
The Lily-of-the-valley has meaning, so it seems.
The Sweet Pea so delicate...the Carnation so bright,
The Night Blooming Jasmine aroma's the night!

We are God's Spiritual flowers...which one are you?

Leanna J. Beck

Today

The years pass, time marches on,
Both joy and sorrow in life belong.
The childhood mirth, unending youth
So soon lead to an eternal truth
That today is all we mortals share
To laugh and love, to show we care,
We muddle on, ours the choice
To simply be, or each day rejoice
In this life we live till all is gone,
While the years pass and the clock ticks on.

Virginia C. Collins

Saoirse (Freedom)

To sit and ponder their sacrifice,
May it touch our hearts, our souls, our lives.

For the price they paid was very steep,
Now together, the Irish must stand, and deep!

To ensure that freedom's voice will not be lost,
For the strikers have paid the ultimate cost.

The time for action is here, indeed...
After eight hundred years, the shamrock still bleeds!

F. L. Casper Crowell

Point Of View

Some people see everything as black and white.
Pure and simple, right or wrong, heaven and hell.
Still others see a thousand of shades of gray.
Extenuating circumstances, situational ethics.
I don't want to convince you that one way is better.
Or that your way is wrong, that isn't my wish.
I just want you to accept that there is a difference.
And try and understand me, as I try to understand you.
Lets not put each other down, belittle one another.
Just because we look at the world in different ways.
Let me experience the view form your window.
And let me show you the view from mine.

James C. Hopkin

The Old Southern Tradition

Children of all races in the south were taught
Respect, that is what it is all about.
Our parents were loved there's no doubt.
We went to school and obeyed the rules,
Until we were old enough to choose.
Our morals were high and we didn't cry about the rules.
It is right or wrong in the old southern home.
Most of us chose not to roam.
We saved our bodies, for the love of our life:
And brother let me tell you this is right.

Peggy King Bethune

Cherrie

My love took flight and flew from life
Up to the pearly gates;
Sobs tore from my throat, tears fell from my eyes
But my love was unable to wait.

I called out your name in a voice filled with pain
But it echoed right back in my ears;
I love you, I cried, and without you I'll die
But, alas, I was left only tears.

What do I say, my dear, now that you're gone.
There are no words for it, there is no song.
We thought yesterday would go on forever;
I never thought you'd leave me, my dear, not ever.

Oh how unfair life seems to be
My loving you, your leaving me.
'Tis true, 'tis true, 'tis sad but true,
The sunrise tomorrow, and me, without you.

Harrie L. Campbell

Untitled

Living in a world, on earth.
Been here since my day of birth.
Living in a society, in a world.
Full of so much, full of everything.
Full of love, full of hate;
Full of kindness; full of mean people;
Full of cops, full of criminals;
Full of good, full of evil;
Full of importance, full of insignificance.
Man, will it ever agree?
What will it even come to be?
Living in my own World, in a society.
To me I'm great, to others a nonentity
If one day all would feel the same,
Then it might end this unbeatable game.
In my World, dreams are anti-reality.
Believable and achievable, that's my pride.
Determination is my will until I have died.

Marc J. Sullivan

Untitled

Myth of the heart
It's a lonely thing
At a moment's notice
It can all sink

Seasons repeat themselves
As passions flair
And smoke rises
The confusions glares

All blown over
It ignites the dark
The feelings of love
The myth of the heart

The day surrenders
The cold wind of night
Takes out the shadows
And blacks out the light

And gingerly the tenderness forgetting the sun
And provides the rumors to bleed into one

And when it's all over and you traveled too far
It's all intermingled in the myth of the heart

Darrell Pemberton

Orb

In its wrath, you will find
The lasting feeling at something kind
Its flowing down rivers of light
Wash away all the creatures of fright
In its soft eternal gold glow
Makes everything flourish and grow
Warming everything near and far
It has to be our only star
In its glow is where we have fun
I think we owe gratitude to our sun
In all its splendor and its power
The sun's the God of every daytime hour
If the sun ever dies so will life
And there'd be no love in our world of strife
So that's why there has to be sun
So people can go out and have lots of fun
To feed the people, and grow the plants
To support everyone from elephants to ants
If not for its energy, our world would not run
So I think we owe gratitude to our sun

Patrick J. Wittry

Always

I'm thinking of you always
That is how I spend the days away
Through day and night
You're the one always in my sight
You're the one in my dreams, my dear
I'll love you always throughout the years
Together we will always be
Always together, you and me
Never, ever, shall I forget thee
I know you'll always be by me

When you're gone, I miss you so
I'm even sad before you go
You're always there for me
Making everything so clear to see
I know you shall never leave me
So my heart, I am giving thee
Only death shall do us part
And that I know, shall break my heart
So in this poem I write to thee
I give my love and life for eternity

RaeAnne Gackenbach

Untitled

Why does he do it?
Doesn't he love me?
I hate it when he hurts me.
It always hurts so much.
I've learned to expect it and how to avoid it.
I've learned how to hide the pain and not let it show.
I don't want my life to be like this
I don't understand why we just can't talk.
I hate all of the violence, all the anger, and all the pain.
But I love him.
I know it's usually my fault, but I don't know what to do.
or how to stop his anger and violence
He's always angry, he's always violent
Sometimes I just get so scared
that the only thing I can do is hide
Even during happy times he's angry
And when he's angry, he's violent.
I hate it when he's angry.
I hate it when he beats me.
I just wish it would all stop.

Stacy Battersby

Savage Dreams

The things we do are sometimes rude and very wrong,
and things never turn out quite like a song.

The reason why never seem to fit,
and it's always strange how the outcome can hit.

Living our lives with a sense of danger,
always trying to hide from the common stranger.

Never really knowing quite who we are,
the answers we find do always scar.

We all have friends and enemies too,
but fight is always what we seem to do.

The greed and pain will always exist,
but the only thing we can do is tighten our fists.

The world we live in for some reason we must kill,
and for other reason then blood spill.

How stupid we are and how smart we seem,
is the only real reason for our savage dreams.

Walter L. Winters

Sudden Love On A Sunday Morning

begins
like rain out of season —
misty, rhythmic
— unannounced.

and like the way clouds billow seductively
above me in late november
lifting their skirts
spilling a song and dance of gray noise —

every row of every field
is drenched in salty-rich musk
that clings between the wheat like sweat
between resting bodies...

sudden love on a sunday morning

the clouds bleed this way
down in africa
over huts of straw and bamboo,
stripped,
weaved and stroked
by the hands of a gentle man...

like sudden love on a sunday morning...

Angela D. Wooley

Forgotten

My greatest fear is being ordinary, simple and the same.
My life has been extraordinary, my heart is hard to tame.
I never gave up, I kept moving on, no matter how dark it got.
Through the shade I saw no sun, so by moonlit day I fought.
Life has been far from kind, love and hope moved me on.
And the help of a dear friend of mine, my love for her goes on.
I'm special to this world because, I never needed the truth.
I knew exactly who I was, I fought through an empty youth.
I realized that nothing lasts, and then I proved me wrong.
Even the greatest of loves die, but mine's lived all along.
The special girl for whom I write, the one who understood.
She was there for me every night, and she loved me, bad or good.
So when my final night is done, and followed by no dawn.
I know my love won't let me be forgotten when I'm gone.

Shawn McCarthy

That Day

I look at you but you just turn away,
I'm sure your thinking about that day
I don't know exactly what to say,
Because I too remember that day.

I was glad when we first said Hi,
For soon you would be my guy.
Sometimes I ask myself why,
You had to tell me good-bye.

I just knew I had done something bad,
So I figured you had gotten mad.
I thought of all the good times we had,
Then my heart went very sad.

We got together the first of May,
Everyone thought we were so happy and gay.
I didn't think it'd turn out this way,
But I still think of that one, dark, shallow day

Becky Kindlesparger

My Light, S.B.

Some people live in the darkness, part of their lives,
Some people live in The Light, part of their lives,
I was born in The Darkness
and have been there all my life
Until The Light.

The light found me one bright sunshiny day
Hiding;
Deep in my heart
Lost in my soul
Setting in The Darkness; afraid and lonely

Tired of being extinguished
pushed away.

The light showed me Passion, showed me Love;
Life.
Now;
I live in The Light
My heart, my soul
"My Light"
Just for me.

Pauline Hayes

Refrigerator Poem For Catherine

I throb
squirm
she devours lips sweat and bare belly
she says soft eyes
I blush down hard
melt ferocious
the work of a sacred bloody hearted woman

Bonnie Patricia Stroot

He Can Be Your Everything

He can be your everything
What you need and want and more...
All you have to do is call Him
Then He'll meet you at your heart's door
Just let Him in and in time, you too will know;
As I have told Him many times,
"Where you lead, I will follow"
For I know He knows what's best
'Cause He knows what's around the bend
I've been up and I've been down, He's
been there for me again and again...
As it has been written in the Bible
As for me and my house, we will serve the
Lord, for me it's true
I know I love the Lord and best of all
I know He loves me too!

Johnny E. Pryor

Love At A Moment's Glance

The slight fluttering of my pulse,
The quick beating of my heart,
The feeling of air slowly lifting me above,
The soft breeze on my face, like a feather of a dove.

Your face stares at me cautiously,
Like a window to the rain,
And I feel your eyes search mine,
For a sense of content, hate, or pain.

Your hand entwines itself in mine,
As we feel the warm glow of joy,
Our hearts are no longer strangers,
Nor are they simple toys.

Even though our souls have only just met,
This feeling of belonging will never fade,
For this love I have found is not a threat,
And we shall sing together in this love parade!

Meera Seshadri

Race

We are both black and white
We both chew and bite
We both smile
We both cry
We both say hello and goodbye
So why do we fight all day long
Instead of singing our favorite song
Why do we argue about our race
Why do we argue about the color of our face
These are puzzles that will never be made
But I wish these puzzles would soon fade
Everyday I do my best
But everyone else has to do the rest.

Nicole Pratt

Autumn

The wind in the trees and the falling leaves;
to me: This is autumn.
The cool crisp morn and the delaying dawn
signal the end of a summer gone.
The cool, dying grass and the clear blue skies;
the nip of the wind with the slightest chill
Give glimpses of winter and cold, grey days
With Christmas and New Year to brighten the way.
In every season: hot, cold or warm,
Can be found the thrill of beauty and form;
And every day is unique of itself,
A gift to enjoy, a memory to tell.

Sharon Funkhouser

When, Where, How

As I walk down the street
I begin to think.
It is now four o'clock,
And the sky is turning pink.
It had been a beautiful day,
But also so lonely.
Where would I go tonight, I looked so homely.
What will I have to eat,
Leftovers or second-hand gum.
I don't care what it is, I hope it's more than a crumb.
Where will I sleep. Front step or back.
Will I have a pillow; no,
Someday hopefully a shack.
Tomorrow they will see
Me with my straggly red hair.
They will laugh, just as always,
I pretend I don't care.
But for tonight,
I will have to get my rest.
Tomorrow will be another long day.
And I will have to do my best.

Amber Marie Duprey

Hand By Hand

Palm to Palm
worlds in collision
traveling nervous, paths
imprints as an expressionable thoughts
each of each....(a stigma)

As one microcosm
each pore a needles eye
drops upper drops
transformed...

Hand in hand
as extenties of each being
of each intention,
power and all that which
day today is told us

Hand is hand
(peace is achieved, human hope kept alive)
eternalizes changes
transluces and transcends;
one by one life continues on

William R. Farfan

Shall A Sign Be Given?

A great blue heron soared
  above my domicile;
Last Spring,
When we never thought the rain and
  snow would cease,
And the air was brisk.
Mammoth cottonwoods poured out their leaves,
And busied squirrels with trimming.

By what torment from within,
Should I speculate,
That a journey, so complex,
Could be accomplished within those walls;
Among others, besieged by sources, unknown?

My window, as a comfort,
Of green grass, outside; of robins, rabbits, and ravens:
On, toward mealtime, I survived.

And the "sign", was so obvious,
Upon returning home;
A brilliant bow, to span the sky!

Geraldine M. Zrubek

Brothers

The Eagle and the Biker are like one and the same
The only difference is the name
Both live of the land
And when it is in trouble will make a stand
There's always people who just can't see
All they want is to be left alone and free
The Eagle loves to soar through the air
Like he doesn't have a care
The Biker putts down the road on his hog
And his troubles disappear like the fog
In reality they know life is rough
That's why both are built tough
If you know them you will understand why
They each have only one law to live by
For the Eagle it is - live to fly, fly to live
And the Biker it is - live to ride, ride to live

Rudy Marx Jr.

Untitled

I was thinking of my friend the other day.
But a little while back he moved out to L.A.
He was crazy when he left
and he's probably crazy now anyhow.

I was thinking of my mother the other night.
I know the things she told me probably were right.
But even she can't help me now
cause she's not here today anyway.

I was thinking of the things I did a long long time ago.
They would've worked out better if I only took it slow.
In my younger days I never feared
But now all the good things have disappeared.

Roger Donn

Horses' Heaven

Before the auction comes and we are sold,
There's one thing all little colts must be told.
This is, of where we go after we die,
Son, there's a "Horses' Heaven" in the sky.

This place is like a dream come true,
With bubbling streams, tall grass, and skies of blue.
There's pillows of golden yellow straw,
Such a beautiful place you never saw.

Iron shoes, harnesses, and whips have been banished,
Flies, lice, and gnats have completely vanished.
Small Pegasuses fly with their wings of gold,
Their harps singing tunes of tales of the bold.

The great White Stallion rules his herd with pride,
To his commands all horses must abide.
Those who disobey will go straight to hell,
A place that you would not like very well.

So, my son, serve thy master with love; not hate,
If you wish to enter into heaven's gates.
Before we part, one last word, and I'll be done,
Pass this knowledge of "Horses' Heaven" on to your son.

Linda Anne Garver

The Ferris Wheel

Going up in the Ferris Wheel.
  All the smells wafting up to the top.
  All the noises from the rides and people below.
  All the colors of the flashing lights.
  Fantastic!
  Marvelous!
How sad to have the whole car to myself.

Michele Bernard

East Freedom School

East Freedom School, wasn't so great
The principal seemed droll.
Way back in forty eight.
East Freedom School, I cannot define
Reading, writing, teachers rule.
Way back in forty nine
Years pile up, like winter snow
Fifties, sixties, where did they go?
A wife, then kids, grand children too.
A million words, puns and ad libs
Prevarications and flowery fibs
Deep and intricate, the minds learning pool.
So little of it came from
East Freedom School.
Life goes to fast, a lot of it cruel
But how I'd love to be back in
East Freedom School.

Robert H. Weaver

Thoughts Of You

Scared and alone, starting fresh again,
Wondering if it would ever end.
Wanting someone just right for me,
And fulfilling dreams I imagined.

As I thought to myself this just can't be true,
Although he is very shy,
Maybe, just maybe he is right for you,
Thinking carefully as days go by.

Recalling now clearly my dream came to life,
Down on one knee, asked my hand as your wife.
Together we are learning a lesson or two.
Something brought us together, what was it, or who?

Once two separate people,
Now one human being,
Without you near, the world is not worth seeing.
Throughout our days, into our nights,
Remembering how you became the substance of my being.

Heidi M. Bowness

Emotions

Opening your mind, closing my eyes
Hoping and praying under darkened skies
It is unto me that this I say
Words are hard, so I stay away
Blackened sky brings the stars of the night
Thoughts of you in me, are as bright
Time ticks away as my heart beats of life
Visions cut me, like the blade of a knife
Sun comes to morning, movement is clear
Warmth becomes my heart if you were near
White clouds, blue skies my day is here

Scott Fielder

A Morning Prayer

Thank you, God, for this new day.
Keep us in your care, we pray.

Guide our hearts, our hands and feet,
Give us smiles for those we meet.

Show us what we need to say
To cheer a friend along the way.

Make us wise, filled with zest
To always try to do our best.

Then when day is done and there's no light
Give us courage to face the night.

Mary Terrell Fox

A Bike Ride

I ride my bike,
on a sunny day.
It feels like a hike,
on a sunny ray.
I say good day,
to a sweet, old lady.
When I do,
I feel true.
She said she rode when she was young.
Her favorite thing was to stick out her tongue.
Her bike is now old,
The wheels won't roll.
She says she doesn't mind.
She is so kind.
The lady makes me feel good.
I think now I will ride through the woods.

Tara Dennis

A Sister's Love

In the cold clear sky
I see the beautiful shining stars looking down on me
Oh! Lord could it be?
Are two of those stars, my sister's lovely eyes
Reflecting the light from heaven above?
I remember how they shined
The last time I saw her smile before she turned fifteen
Her face was aglow as she realized what being
"Auntie Barbara" would mean.
But Lord it was not to be
You took her from us as she wilted away
A beautiful flower in a coma one day
I think of her often and just wish I could say
Sis let's go shopping or just come visit for the day
I miss her, I loved her
But someday, we'll be together
Looking down from above
Lighting the sky with sisterly love.

Charlotte Ann Smith

Spirit Asleep

The rain has ceased - only the trees
     Shed its drops upon the ground.
For that second-calm and peace hold me.

I pray the sun returns - more to warm my
heart with healing than my body.

It is impossible for me to heal my heart
From its place of pain and coldness
     Perhaps someday - But I think not.
Too much pain has entered and frozen its pulse.

I am my heart - so I too am lost forever.
For my heart is where my spirit lives
     Where my spirit lived...

Sharolyn Taylor

Untitled

The poem that comes to mind.
That is no more than twenty lines.
Is mine, and will be for all time.
And if it doesn't rhyme, for that
I wouldn't give a dime.
And you will come to know in time.
That this poem is neither yours nor mine.
But what can you get for under twenty lines
(or less).
Just call it a poem with no rhyme or line.
And this poem is mine.

Helen J. Moore

Garden Of Love

In a medieval garden my love grows,
It grows for you alone.
This wondrous garden lies within my heart.
When I am with you.
all that grows within seems to dance,
To dance as if there is no tomorrow.
To dance with all the joy that life possess.
My blood rushes to this garden
Nourishing all that grows
Making my garden strong and bright.
It is the most beautiful garden in the world.
You are invited to visit my garden.
To smell the scent of my love,
To rest within its quiet sanctuary,
and to pick my love as if it were a bright red rose.
Take home that rose and remember.
What you have experienced in my garden of love.

Kevin Lahue

A.I.D.S.

Acquired
Immune
Deficiency
Syndrome

She was waiting every day for some
cure to prevail;
And wasting every day until a
cure prevails.

She then picked herself up and made a precious pack;
Never again to let her wonderful life almost slip from her grasp.

To live every day to her fullest
Enjoying the wonders and mysteries of life;
Never to falter until her dying day
And then she can say
She lived her life 'till the very last breath.

An
Important
Decision on
Saving life.

Monique Abadilla

Sisters

So tell me again what stories you can,
recall to your mind the young schemes
that you plotted and planned
late at night in your room
as only two sisters could have,

Tell me again of the laughter you shared
of what nick-names you dubbed one another
about the silly, the sad,
even the times you got mad,
but couldn't stay that way long with each other.

Tell me again and again if you like,
if in it your heart finds some solace,
For I know those thoughts,
how they echo around, in your heart,
when there's no-one to share them.

For I have some too, and I'll tell them to you,
again, then again, if you let me,
Now that she's gone,
let her memory live on,
in us, and in all who did love her.

Sally J. Sotelo

My Grandmother's Eyes

In my grandmother's eyes I see love
A love that is comforting and warm
A love that crosses generations
To touch the souls of ones held dear
A love that is eternal

In my grandmother's eyes I see wisdom
A wisdom borne of patience and understanding
A wisdom that is gentle and strong
Surpassing all knowledge and meaning
A wisdom that is truth

In my grandmother's eyes I see reflected
the beauty of living, the joy of friendship,
and the love of family
I see hopes and fears, happiness and tragedy
I see a desire to live and a desire to change

In my grandmother's eyes I see life
I see the dawning of time and the reason for being
I see the light of creation and the meaning of peace
In my grandmother's eyes I see love
And I see myself

Nathan S. Hipps

A Poet's Point Of View

The writers, the poets, the ones who are true
In the clouds above us loom.
Through our hair the wind will flow,
And in our ears the wind will blow
Telling the truth, and hoping we'll hear,
Saying it is us, not the wild whom to fear.
Our eyes are open so why can we not see?
It is the oceans, the mountains, and the prairies that are free.
They are free from this way we call civilized,
Which in harmony, intelligence, and love it will despise.
So poet am I, and poet are you,
Who can open their eyes, and hear the truth,
And let it be known that we are the few,
Who can see it from Nature's point of view.

Morgan L. Webert

And So, I Cry

Awake in the morning frustration fills my heart
But noontime came quickly, while blood flowed passed his chart
I cannot bear this, Lord, help me see
Haven't we suffered enough for thee?
Seventy-two hours will decide if he lives
And so, I cry for thee to hear,
because Lord I thank thee dear
Help me Lord to make it through
These last few years have been too much to bear
Touch me now as I lay down to sleep
Please keep me in mind because my heart has grown weak.

If I die before I awake, take me Lord to a much better place.

Teresa Pridgeon

Untitled

He rode into battle with a cry of pain
Holding his shield and swinging his sword in vain
A stab wound in his arm, and an arrow in his leg
Some die soon and for others mercy they do beg
But expect or get it they do not
For he shall strike them down
and let their bodies rot
On that day the stakes did vary
But still he rode out with a cry of victory

Sean Devlin

271

A Better World

What a better world this would be
If through a child's eyes we could see
Where everything is looked at with wide-eyed curiosity
And days are filled with dreams of all that we could be
Where pleasure is found in simple things
And pain only comes from bumps and stings
Where friendships are lasting and sincere
And our fellow man we need not fear
Where war is only make believe
And killing is something we cannot conceive
So if a better world is your dream
It is not as difficult as it may seem
For if like a child we would try to be
A better world can be our destiny.

James E. Morris

Untitled

we are all victims of our childhood
our every conviction
our every reflection
our every attribute
shaped by the events of the past
piercingly embedded into the life we live
we try to escape from the enslavement
that threatens to suppress
but inevitability is inescapable
we must not fight
but acknowledge and yield
allow the tortured youth
who lives oppressed under society's restrictions
to co-exist and be liberated
to become a Woman

Janice Hsu

Hell

Fires of rage and torment and pain
A place of Hell where punishment is obtained.
Feelings of hate and lust and desire
A place where nothing can quench the fire.
A place where, if you look around,
Nothing good can ever be found.
A place where up above, you can see
God looking down rebuking thee.
A place of sins and evil and eternal burning
Where nothing can ever stop your yearning.
A place where sinners are eternally in sorrow
Because they did not heed God's message,
Not thinking that they might die on the morrow.
If they only would have yielded to God's message,
A gateway to Heaven might have been their passage.
Their souls are lost in Hell forever.
If you ask for God's forgiveness,
From evil, your souls could be delivered.

J. Michael Palmer

Untitled

A tumultuous change billows over the horizon
A wonderful new beginning to life; like a
babe born unto a nun. Surgeons and physicians
reel and smile at the success to what they have done.

Transplants are here, fresh, anew; no telling
what they can't do. Being a recipient I feel
Alive and fresh with vigor. The joy I exalt
only encompasses the realm of becoming better, bigger.

In short, I pray to the Lord for my life
hoping he may anoint me with a wife; so I can
raise my own babe. The future is now, so
become a donor, save a soul.

David Durenleau

Inspiration's Guidance

Inspiration is not an acquaintance,
For I embraced it carefully in youth.
It lies beneath me and speaks with my wants,
As I remain afraid to face the truth.
It liberates me when the dark appears,
and my body directs the new vision.
But often it brings unstoppable tears,
And I become unclear of my mission.
The usual products of this sequence,
Personal awareness without remorse,
Instill within me a straightforward sense;
That it will direct my difficult course.
I would be a forgotten memory,
Had I not its energy to guide me.

Marissa J. Hood

Tomorrow Never Came

You were holding me, and had to leave, as I still cried.
You said it would be all right tomorrow, but
Tomorrow never came
It would be better between us, and I would stop hurting,
We'll start tomorrow, but
Tomorrow never came
You'd come back, we'd start again,
Our love will never end, tomorrow, but,
Tomorrow never came
Tomorrow is the day, it will all begin
Tomorrow is the day, we'll leave behind the sin,
Tomorrow we'll forget and start anew,
Tomorrow is when we start to forget all we've been through.
Tomorrow is a good word - for you
Tomorrow I'll be the man that you used to know
Wait for me you said, just 'til tomorrow
I waited a lifetime......but,
Tomorrow never came

Sally Pector

A Chance To Say Goodbye

You left so quick, didn't give me a chance to say goodbye.
All of our moments, all of our laughter, all of our memories
will never be forgotten., they will live on through your memory,
for it will never die.
We had so much, your life so short
I often wonder why.
Your life should not have ended with the choice of someone else.
She took your life into her hands and didn't stop to think,
What might happen, who might die when she took that deadly drink.
It's over now, nothing can be done.
I know that never again will I hear your laugh or see your smile.
This makes me stop and think on how my life has changed.
I will never forget you,
and through sad eyes,
you will always live a long and happy life.

Ariia Pike

Left Behind

Beyond the darkness where I can't see.
Cries a small child in sweet misery.
Your spoken words that I can't believe,
leaving this child afraid with broken dreams.
Your open arms are without love,
leaving this child feeling afraid to be loved.
Those eyes I look into are not mine I see.
Leaving this child afraid to believe.
There's yesterday in this darkness I hold.
Leaving this child feeling cold and alone.
Your broken dreams and broken words,
has left behind a lot of confusion and hurt.

Dawn DesRoches

Unresistable

Take a ray of sunshine in your palm
Find the answer for someone stray
Care for he that's not so calm
For your smile can brighten a new day.

See the moment in your eyes
Share the thoughts of many lost
Calm the fear in all your ties
For your kind heart is a great at any cost

Since I've seen you more today,
I've notice one more thing
You don't come to stop and play
Only to care for human being.

I yearn for the warmth of your T.L.C.,
Your aura is but a place to rest
I know I can be your friend you see
Because I know you're the very best.

Tell my heart that you will find a place
In the vast wholeness of your soul
Calm the anguish that I face
Every time I see yourself so bold.

Juan C. Hernandez Jr.

Silent Memorial

Killing and heat is Hell
Burning bodies, a repulsive smell

My portrait of War, has many scary things
So are the memories, the word Vietnam brings

Grasping my forty-five
Thank God I'm still alive

Hearing the sound of an AK forty-seven
I bow my head and pray for heaven

When I opened my eyes, and looked to my side
There was a man no arms, but great pride

At first glance, no time to care
Then I looked back, blue eyes and blonde hair

My best friend his name was Brad
Used to fish with him and his Dad

More gunshots rang out, tried to stay calm
Till a shot hit my hand, and exited my palm

Then I called out to Jesus Christ
Staring at my hand, I remembered His great sacrifice

I hear a painful scream
I awake it was only a bad dream

Joshua Dallas Lovejoy

My Friend

A friend is someone who loves you for who you and what you are
But, as I left my best friend in the world
My heart received a permanent scar.
You showed me how to be a good person
And you lifted my spirits high.
You taught me how to achieve good things
And you taught my heart to fly.

When I had terrible tragedies in life,
I'd always bring them to you.
With your love and care, you'd solve them.
That's what a good friend should do.

I thank you for always being there for me
   and never letting me down.
In my heart I feel you should be given
   an angel's golden crown.

Casandra Bindig

Am I Ready?

Why did she choose me? Was it destiny?
Does she really love me? How can she?
I don't even know her, yet I love her.
She makes me feel, joy, pain, fear, love.
Can I trust her with my soul?
Can she trust me with hers?
She touches me. I'm frightened.
Is it only physical? I hope not.
Courage I need to face this love.
I want to be a part of her,
I want her to be a part of me.
Am I ready?
Is she?

George Dubiel

The Sculpture

She glances in from across the way
entranced by what she sees,
Tired hands push the features of a face,
this face that is to be.
She sees him everyday she says
working hard and so diligently,
creating the face for no one knows, no one knows but he
This little old man shows no stress nor strain,
as he works from dawn to dusk
at the end he knows there is joy for him,
at the end in hands of trust.
This face he carves, he carves with care
a love so long, long lost.
He prays in time he'll join his love
forever at any cost.
As his days grow short, these ropes get taught
the ropes that are tugging him where?
For he dreams of his wife, and the love
he had cherished, with his love so long, long lost.

Tim Norris

Gift Of Love

I have a gift to give to you
Which was given from the one above
To give this gift it must be true
For the gift is the feeling of love

I lay in my bed I think of thee
As I crave for your gentle touch
It builds inside and grows in me
For my love might be too much

Forever and ever I want to be your man
For it is something for which I pray
As we walk down the isle hand in hand
I dream we make love on our special day

To my love I will always show affection
For no harm can come for love is our protection

Marcel R. Moody

Untitled

Strange sensations, a tingling deep inside;
Uncertainty and the ever questioning why.
Anticipation replaced by doubt and fear;
An underlying desire to hold you near.
So much unknown, so much to confuse.
So much to learn, so much to lose.
A fragile reflection cradled in my arms
As I shield the future from unforeseen harm.
My swelled breast aches for acceptance
Yet knows there will be freedom from your present dependence.
A pounding heart and pulse racing wild...
All my emotions for my new born child.

Janice M. Chrzanowski

A Secret In Their Eyes

The cry goes out,
They gather into a primeval circle,
Of carnivores.
This cold night on the tundra,
Reflects the image of evil,
Unfairly cast at these gray-furred creatures.
Year after year,
They gather,
Re-uniting the pack.
You can see the deep friendship,
In their dark eyes.
As if they all have a shared secret,
No one else will ever know,
Why they howl in this ring of those family,
Under a similar ring of moon light above.
Perhaps that is the secret they share,
No one else will ever know,
Why the cry goes out.

Diana Garvin

I Wake

When I wake and you are gone,
The morning sunshine seems so very bright.
The chirping of the birds is out of place,
The hours in the day are much too long.

When I wake and you are gone,
I look to watch you turning on the light.
I want to see the smile upon your face
And listen to your early morning song.

They said that you are never coming back.
They assured me that you never felt a thing.
They told me that a drunkard is to blame
They explained that it was over just like that.

I'm not sure if I should still wear black
Or what to do with my diamond ring.
What do I eat when all food tastes the same
They didn't cover details such as that.

I'd really like to know where I belong
And when I'll once again sleep through the night
When will this house stop being empty space
When I awake and you are gone.

Rebecca R. Bowling

Morning Song

Night has fallen long ago,
And the sun's not far away.
It's wonderful waking with you
To a favorite time of day.

Now I sing the song of morning,
But its words you'll never hear.
For I sing only when you're sleeping
Whispering gently in your ear.

When I see that you are stirring
The words I put away.
To save them for another time
To be sung another day.

It's not that I wouldn't share the lyrics
Of my morning song with you,
But the words are always changing
And the song is always new.

So if you listen when you're dreaming
My voice you might just hear,
Singing the song of morning
While you're still sleeping near.

Chistopher Yonker

The Winds Of Freedom

To ride along the waves so wild,
  upon a horse no man can tame,
The wind sweetly blowing on my face,
  I softly touch his mane,
I feel his warmth,
  I feel his power beneath me,
Ahead I see a limb,
  taking horse from walk to canter,
Closer and closer he gets to the limb,
  then it's gone,
Under him as fast and as soft as the wind,
  taking the horse back to walk,
We head home,
  there I set him free once more,
But freedom doesn't last forever,
  and I know someday we will meet again.

Elizabeth Ann Louise Lins

Mine and Yours

My heart, your heart, my sanity, yours,
To keep them all intact would be a feat to win awards.
My life, your life, short together, long apart,
To know forever after you will dwell within my heart.
My nights, your nights, both shared and slept alone,
To back away from what we make cuts us to the bone.
My love, your love, mine spoken for, yours not,
To want to please two people takes more than I have got.
My happiness, your happiness, and both our sorrows too,
To have mingled them together creates a fate that we must rue.
My body, your body, the secrets we have learned,
To feel the fire consuming us and longing for the burn.
My path, your path, how fortunate they crossed,
To walk down them together is worth all that we have lost.
My future, your future, so soon must they diverge,
To forever miss the joy that came with succumbing to the urge.

William C. Colley

I Am Black And Blue

I am a black woman, seven children around my feet.
Winter is upon us, and there is not enough to eat.
My man gave me a promise of diamonds and gold,
I am a black woman and my heart has grown cold.
The windows are broken and there are locks on the doors,
My sons go out at night and I don't see them anymore.
The little ones are frightened, we hear shots in the dark.
I am a black woman, no dreams in my heart.
I am a black woman and once I was young.
Life stretched out before me and there were songs to be sung.
The songs are all gone now.
My world is broken apart.
I am a black woman with tears in my heart.

Zerina Pollard

Desperate Slumber

Watch me strive for rest in my desperate slumber
  As I toss and turn in my dreams I wonder
What the score is on this dark day
  While I hold my angry demons away
I remember how she used to hold me
  In the dark and dank the evil scolds me
I shut my eyes to block the tears
  But all the demons can see my fears
As I stare into my preconception
  I desperately slumber through my transgressions
My body gives up and my mind gives in
  As all of the demons come rushing in
And I secretly wonder if I will ever wake
  From this desperate slumber I now take

Saul Ingle

Mindless

A cup of boredom with my soup once prompted me to leave
the place I thought I could enjoy if only I could be
a little higher than the rest to rise above the crowd,
but now I see I'm quiet below what I can allow.

And so I packed up all my stuff into one small suitcase
and headed to the state of mind I'd enjoy in that place.
I figured body followed soul and so my soul did go
ahead of where my feet could carry. Where? I did not know.

It floated 'bout until it landed high above the clouds
and there my mind has rested on some transcendental grounds.
My body is in quite a wreck. You can't imagine though -
how I'm to let my foot carry when the mind did go?

And so it cried and laughed aloud it is indeed a mess!
A basket-case of flesh and bones for that is all that's left.
Where my feet do carry me - my mind is unaware,
and so I wander mindless - of broken glass and hair.

Dawn Struz

Lover's Lament

When you kissed me,
I had no idea of our fate,
When you touched me,
Time seemed far away,
Now you tell me you can't stay,
Never again will there be light on a new day,
You can see my face, you can hear my voice,
You know my thoughts are far away,
I am thinking of you,
and the warm ways that touched our days,
Now I fear the moment when all has ended or gone away,
I know you didn't smile much for a reason,
But your love was so true, how could it be treason?
It came from your heart to my heart,
You don't need your matches to see the spark in the dark,
Nowhere are we, we're lost and wandering so senselessly,
When the sun rises and the day begins,
I will come to you, let your love rescue me,
I know you are what I see.

Carmen Cubitt

The Supporting Role

I have enjoyed all things becoming,
I have always insisted on the finest.
I've satisfied all my desires,
My existence has been truly grand.

Dessert has always come first,
Satisfaction bears my visage.
I have taken without any regard,
And I have achieved with much ease.

Yet for all that I've attained,
Something still remains unattainable.

Gardens of green have blossomed,
And elders with wrinkles have laughed.
Children have found the wonder of learning,
Babies have clumsily taken first steps.

But this was all accomplished,
With no need for me.
A man of self-imposed importance,
A man of only self-fulfilling needs.

I have all that I want,
But I may as well be without a face.

Rajat Rastogi

I Am - ME

I have seen the universe through the eyes of God _____
But I know not of his plan as I circle the spinning earth
the home of man _____

I fly to the planets faster then Einstein's; C and warm my
hands as I pass the sun _____ now it's back from there and into
my chair _____

I'm now on my way to the milky way _____ again
exceeding___C___
for the speed of light means nothing to me as I ghost along
to the galaxies and let the stars light my way to the edge
of space hoping I can see God's face _____

Again it's back from there to my rocking chair _____
as the old clock strikes the hour _____ awake _____
my body locked to earth's gravity and envious of the trip _____

I am the thinking mind of man _____
and when I think _____ I know I am - ME.

John J. Lacey

April Dusk

Upstate. The April dusk is streaming,
slow and fogged with solstice rains.
Graves grow out desires in moss,
a leopard of clouds fading to ghost.
Gutters grow rivers, arms stretch to a lover,
To our laugh, our Christ, our laundry lines,
to pieces of bottle, each cradling a moon.
We have our baby prams,
chattering with pink ribbons,
a crochet of grandma in dandelion fields.
A drunk's hat is filled with the breeze of
a sneeze! And the cows rock with vertigo.
A passion lifts its head with "ohh!"
that's left unsaid and dying in the clutch of eyes,
slow-lidded with fire.
We have back lots that mumble mass Indian graves.
Our industrial stacks smoke with patient eyes.
And truckers lean into glass roads for weeks.
Like Jesus-freaks.

Claudette Bakhtiar

How Will I Say Goodbye

I guess I must at first realize that you will never
really be totally gone. That you will always live
with me, and all that you have taught me shall
go into the world. If not through me then through
my children. And I shall always be happy with warm
memories because someone cared. We laughed, we
cried, we shared many warm moments that will last
forever. You shall never be gone because I will never
let you die. You shall always be apart of my
life as long as I shall live.

And I will be happy because I know you would want
me to be. You will be missed and each time I think of
you it will inspire me to live a better life. I
shall learn by your leaving that nothing is forever
and to take care of the things that are important
to me. For someday I to must leave and only then
will I totally realize what life was all about.
Because only through death do we live and
through life we die.

Deborah Southwell

My Angel

My Angel walks behind me,
Keeping harm away
The nights I'm afraid to walk home alone.

My Angel tells me secrets,
Of a world found only in dreams
Teaching me there still is hope.

My Angel makes me laugh,
When the world makes me cry
Letting me know he still loves me.

My Angel sings to me,
At night when it's dark
Comforting me more than anyone knows.

My Angel is my best friend,
Someone that will always love me
My Angel is... my brother.

Jeni Szpilka

Peace!

Wow! The three horses run
Black, white and brown;
They play in the meadow
Green all around.

The river runs blue
With white specks of sun;
As pinto does jump
'cross the water to run.

At the edge of the hill
A neat tree we find,
With flowers of all colors,
Their beauty does shine.

At sunset I ponder and
Wonder and think;
Then ask how such beauty
Be captured with ink.

The sun goes to sleep and the moon does its thing;
The crickets and evening with song start to sing.

The day has been fleeting now evening is here;
The peace that we feel means the Good Lord is near!

Becky Edwards

Loved One Lost

I stood outside and watched the hill
That held my loved one so very still
I wondered why so great the debt
Paid by my hands, the greatest one yet.

I see my Love one so very clear,
And knew by sight his time was near
I saw the road he seemed to trod
And failed to call give God your heart

For the path you're on love ones are few
Come! Come! Dear one please start anew
He turned and I saw oh how confused
Not knowing the outcome if he followed you

I say to myself I've done my best
I've prayed and asked God to do the rest
I watched as he journeyed down the road
And knew he would be judged by the seeds he sowed

Only but see god's extended hand to you
To carry your load, he'll see you thru
So short the life, so short the view
For God was always there for you

Mary L. Boyd

Echo

My thoughts and feelings inside and outside my being;
These thoughts and feelings become images,
That loom larger than words;

What's in a word?
Can a word reach to the depths of my feelings,
And the heights of my ideas?

The words on this page leave open spaces,
That only my thoughts and feelings can fill;

What does my inner self echo back to me?
Intellectual warfare,
Loneliness,
Joy,
Peace,
Love,

A mixture of these and more transcend all of who I am;
The echo continues...

Elvy P. Rolle

I Wonder

I am a scared little girl.
I hear voices, and wonder if they're real.
I see figures, and wonder if I can trust my eyes.
I know the impossible, and wonder if it's myth.
I feel them all around us, and wonder why you can't.
I state the truth, and wonder if I'm lying.
I dream fiction, and wonder why it's reality.
I know, and wonder why I can't remember.
I cry for my protector, and wonder why he doesn't answer.
I hurt, and wonder why I like it.
I have friends, and wonder why I can't trust.
I call for the sun, and wonder why it rains.
I wish for love, and wonder why I hate.
I want to understand, and wonder why I don't care.
I feel hot, and wonder why I shiver.
I think about death, and wonder why life is so important.
I pay attention, and wonder why I don't hear.
I understand, and wonder why I am confused.
I pray for peace, and wonder why I fight.
I fear nothing, and wonder why I am a scared little girl.

Karin Gardner

Why Ask Why!!

Why ask why from another?
When the answer lies within!!!
Why ask why from another when that person would probably
lie to their mother...or sister...or brother!!!

Why ask why when you already know the answer

Why ask why
when it's the very same answer as before
Why ask for the pain when you know you don't need any more!!!

Why ask why
when you know it's going to be a lie!!!

Why ask why, who, when or what?!!!
When you felt the answer so many times in your Gut!!

Why ask why, who when or what?
For that matter, when it really doesn't matter!!! (or does it??)

Why ask why??
My friends, my family, my countrymen and/or my foe
When the true answer is revealed, you don't want to know!!

Why ask why when the bottom line is
you have all the answers right inside!!

Why ask why when the real answers lies up in the sky!!

Deirdre Lindsay

Am I Alone?

Am I alone in the ways that I feel?
I often believe that I am
Are thoughts that I think so far from real?
Are they so far from yours, my friend?
When my memories send chills down my spine
Or send tears to well up in my eyes
When inspiration sparks in my head
Things of pleasance or of my demise
When I talk to myself or sing alone or pray aloud to my God
Does that make me a terrible strange sort of being?
Do I then become horrid or odd?
Or is it that we're all alike as a race
Whether a crude or sophisticate kind
No matter the color of skin on our face
Looking closely enough, we will find
That I am a little bit different from you
And you are different from me
but we anger and fear and laugh and cry
And need love invariably

Virginia L. Beavis

A Mule Love Song At Dusk

Standing yonder neath an old oak tree
Was a lonely figure my eyes could see
The evening shadows had begun to fall
And I heard a whippoorwill's love mate call
I eased up closer in the twilight dim
Naturally I didn't want to frighten him
Deep in study the figure seemed to be
He stood so silently in the shade of that old tree
His half closed eyes made him look serene
He had nothing to do but stand and dream
The long pointed ears on his noble head
Assured his friends he'd been royally bred
He twitched them once - maybe twice or thrice
A definite sign he had heard a secret voice
Evening sounds may not be heard by human ears
But God endowed mules to hear them for years
The figure heard the voice of the closing day
Pitched his ears slightly forward and began to bray
His raucous voice blitzed over the trees
A love song at dusk a lady to please.

Viola M. Smith Young

Half Way Across The Lot

One bright sunny morn, I went to milk out toward the barn.
I started after the cows in a trot
And met the bull half way across the lot.
That's where I stopped.

I flew up in the east, came down in the west
and let my feet do the rest.
Across the lot we tore about sixty or more.
Me, aiming for the door.
Around the barn we flew, just we two.
He on four, me on two.

Across a corner I tore and ran square into a door.
The words I said, I'll repeat no more.
I was up in a bound,
My feet were going so fast, they wouldn't touch the ground.

Just then Ferdinand came around,
He was going too fast to stop.
So he just took aim, and Pop!
I flew half way across the lot.

You may read this poem and laugh a lot,
But it's no fun, to meet a bull half way across the lot.

Billy E. Moon

Summer's Process and Pleasures

Warm rain showers,
all kinds of pretty showy flowers.
Catching glimpses of a pastel rainbow,
now and then.

Outdoor games, of different sorts.

Lots of people taking a vacation from work,
to head themselves off to some certain resorts.

The brightest sun shining and the longest days of the year,
makes for seeking Food Pleasures of watermelon, corn on the cob,
barbecued hot dogs, and for some — refreshing cold beer.

   Birds a-calling at our doors, seems to tell us;
that we can enjoy each other, and ourselves much more;
like we never have really done so yet before.

Shirley Wainwright

Traditions

The ice that coats the trees
sends a glare across the great field.
The ground is frozen solid yet
green, save for a few small patches
of frost here and there.
The rolling country side view gets more
unfamiliar every time.

The sweet southern blues on the radio,
Traditions that we follow this same day
every year.
Walking through the door to hear the same voice,
a bright smile occupies my face because the
air has been filled with the sweet smell of
my grandmother's cooking.

Robert DeWitt

Reasonable Doubt?

He was tall, a very slender guy.
Dressed in a grey suit and red tie.
High yellow was his complexion.
Hair a very short box in perfection.
He caught my eye the moment I saw him.
Not even a second look, the first one was convincing.
I never saw a man so handsome as he.
I envy the woman who had him for company.
As he stood there talking making his speech.
Reasonable doubts seem to come over me.
All those things I cherished dear to my heart.
About being married seemed to all fall apart.
Trusting, faithful till death do you part.
Didn't seem all that important to me anymore.
My eyes goes after what my heart cannot reach.
Give me a little time beyond my cuffed head and slumber dreams.
I discover myself on the verge of an unusual mistake.
Just for you and you alone my heart aches.

Jessica J. Weber

Untitled

These Roses Grow. To all's perception lost
salted fields. Charred earth. Baked mud bricks.
To be given, the potential. Used for so little
to be given gold, only to purchase lead
grown has nature, us only
poisoned potential have we left
once palaces, now ruins show forth
as a collective. Lost we are to know is to:
Built is so much. Much to lose. Yet lost.
In becoming what nature is.
Homes yet little hospitality.

Myles L. Harvey

A Metaphor Of Death

It's the black hole of life, the unforgivable thief
Who steals things we love beyond our belief

It leaves no time for questions or silly debate
It decides on a whim, its most deplorable trait

For some it's a mentor, expected with grace
But for most it's a criminal dressed in bad taste

We laugh and we cry in hopes to explain
This ambiguous joke that causes great pain

We dream in the night that when we awake
The victim will appear, surviving an escape

We feed this starving entity for years upon years
Hoping it will fill up, yet another disappears

When the knowledge of acceptance finally blankets our mind
The wrinkles of age remind us of our time

And so we acquiesce to the reaper of life
Never ending our fear or our fight in this plight.

Angie Ripanti

I Will Rise

I raise my head for tomorrow,
I look for the sky,
Only to see the ones I love soaring high,
I feel they are above I am below,
Their life keeps moving mine goes slow,
I look far solution,
Maybe I should change,
This is who I am,
But maybe just maybe,
I will rise,
I can't dwell in the past,
Life goes fast,
When it's my turn,
I will rise.

Kelly Strycker

I'm Still Not Leaving You

I'm a conductor in a symphony
Leading an orchestra on its way.

I begin to conduct; and, then I realize
I have no song to play.

I'm still not leaving you.

I'm the sun, you are the moon
I start to go down somewhere around noon.

All at once it gets real dark
All you can see is the brightest spark.

I'm still not leaving you.

Next thing I know I'm laying down
All you can hear is this beeping sound.

Pumps, doctors, all kinds of tubes hanging everywhere
I can't describe how much I hated being there.

I'm still not leaving you.

I knew perfectly well where I was at,
as the little green line, once active, suddenly goes flat.

My last words to you: My spirit lives,
I'll still be with you - I'm not leaving you.

Janine Nicole Atkins

The Dead

We betray ourselves,
    once again,
into the arms of insecurity.
We are forced to protect
    something we do not love.
We come to stuff ourselves
    with the richness of life,
But find us,
    in the end,
Bloated but empty;
    bloodless and seeking death.
We are gathered together
    to destroy the delicacies with apathy
        and choke on our own tranche de vie,
        à la mode.
Exposed defenseless,
    sudden pain in my head:
Some of the Dead are actually living
    and
Some of the Living are dead.

Philip Crolley

A Scented Wind

Now and again, from time to time
There blows a wind so scented
You wonder if some nature elf
Its fragrance has invented.

It smells of woodlands wet with rain
And forest floors of leaves,
Of newborn fawns and fog-filled dawns;
Wild smells drift on this breeze.

It beckons your thoughts to the country
Like moths to a candle's glow,
Where time is nothing but daylight,
Where streams to rivers flow.

It floats through your dreams in updrafts
To mountains with trees festooned
With featherlight flocking of new fallen snow
Shining silently under the moon.

It wafts hypnotic into your thoughts
At the least expected time,
Whispering that the wilderness
Is also a state of mind.

Cheryl Tompkins

Barabbas

No one loves you like we do sonny;
You are our only loyal honey.
Our sense of humor must be funny
Because all you think of is of money.

Sometimes we must speak to you in code
Because of all the extra load.
If we don't we will be towed,
It's society so called mode.

For us you fit like a glove
Because there are no words for our love.
You are more beautiful to us than any dove
Don't let us down; you're from above.

So many times away from you,
Although it always made us blue.
We hope you now have a clue,
We did expected right on que.

To us you'll always be the best
Because you are from our nest,
Life will come to you as a test,
Take it all with your most zest!

Janet Van Dyke

Mom 4 Rent

My Mom for is 4 rent,
It is this I do repent,
To many houses she's sent,
This person I call my Mom 4 rent.

She mops and cleans with tons of chlorine,
And while she's shopping she's really cheap.
She gets only dented cans.
She makes a delicacy out of Spam,
She also bakes honey-glazed ham.

If you ever come this way,
and you have a lousy day,
Just remember our company's name,
You'll never be the same,
For I proclaim, Mom's 4 rent.

Viktor D. Skaggs Jr.

Unicorn

Not a star sparkles though the moon is bright
Its moonbeams shine in the darkness of night
A shimmer is seen through the incoming mists
Splendor and love in its luminous
Proud and strong silver beauty
Golden born wonders majesty
Divine enchantments and graceful steps
The dearest secret ever kept
With the wind comes more haze
While silence follows in minds amazed
Shadows engulf the whole of earth
Then disappear to show what mirth?
Gone is the beauty of the wonders creature
In the mystery of midnights glamour

Jennifer Civerolo

Daddy's Little Girl

I woke up and went to school,
Thinking everything was cool.
I came home to say "hi!,"
I now realize I said good-bye.
All of a sudden he was gone in a whirl,
But I'll always be my Daddy's little girl.
Sitting here being sad,
I wish I could have back my Dad.
I miss him always taking me fishing,
But I know now I better stop wishing.
I'll never stop loving him with all my heart,
I guess it was time for us to part.

Lyndsey Plumm

Reflections

The rain is dripping slowly, steadily;
Another day has ended in sweet sorrow.
I listen to each dear one sleeping heavily,
And think what life will bring tomorrow.
Perhaps I'll awaken to smiling faces
Who want their breakfast now, not later.
Then it's time to dress, tie their shoelaces;
Play Barbies with her, with him Darth Vader.
Is it naptime yet? No, one more hour.
We'll read a book, or two, or three...
In comes my youngest, in her hand, a flower;
"I brought it for you, Mommy." And then I see,
    That like the earth, I too, must welcome
    The rain God sends to all, each one.

Mary Tullos

Untitled

Waking each morning to a dull and dreary day,
Standing in front of the mirror,
All I see is myself from the outside in.
A mirror reflects what is, not what can be.
The image the mirror reflects,
is not the image others see.
Others see what is,
as does the mirror,
But what is for the mirror is what can be for others.
The true me is what can be,
not what is.
Why am I the only one who sees who I can be?
Why is everyone so blind?
Maybe they should see me through the mirror's eyes.
After all even mirrors don't look at what can be,
they see what is!

Erica Elam

Why Can't You Help?

Can't you hear the screams,
    The screams of children crying.
Can't you feel the pain,
    The pain of the children's suffering.
Can't you see the emptiness,
    The emptiness and loneliness in their eyes.
Their hope is vanishing,
    Their existence is being wiped away.
    Why can't you help?

Sophia C. Osotio

To Lenore

Light filters down through the trees,
flashing brilliant patterns on the narrow path in front of us.
We walk, side by side underneath the thick, mountain canopy.

I stop and take a drink from the water bottle,
then I give it to you.
The water tastes cold and delicious.

A stream runs alongside us and I close my eyes and listen.
The mountain is so very still now.
I hear the gentle rush of water, winding its way down,
trickling over and through the stones.

A bird cries overhead and my shoes scrape the ground,
harsh and clumsy, waking me from this trance.
It is strange and wonderful, a feeling I am not used to.

I look to find you and we are both smiling.
The water moves alongside us, disappears around the bend,
and vanishes down into the mountain's depths, unnoticed.

It is constant, reassuring, a soothing whisper in my ear.

I reach for your hand and we move on.
Listen! I hear the falls on the other side.
I am glad that we could share these moments.

William Morrison

Young Flower

I was down for the count, one ear to the ground,
I did not want to hear, not one romantic sound.
Then you appeared like the stars in the night,
Cast your spell upon me, like a queen does a knight.
When I first heard your voice, my heart was in desire,
Now when I look at you, I feel a raging fire.
When you stare at me with mystical eyes,
My mind slips away to those hot summer nights.
As you pass through life with such power,
Don't ever forget, you're just a beautiful young flower.

Johnny Thomas Hall

Through Time

Seconds that change the things you see
Minutes that turn love for you and me
Hours that fly with no place to be
Days you can't catch that hold the key

Feel the days go by and by
Weeks that pass without a sigh
Months that roam without a cry
Years that frown with no good-bye

Life regains deaths sunken seed
Birth allows mother nature to lead
The living is what evolves from this need
Death that comes for life to feed

Feel the days go by and by
Weeks that pass without a sigh
Months that roam without a cry
Years that frown with no good-bye

Malik Kadar McKinley

A Precious Need

A need to feel wanted, arms to show you care.
Just a precious moment, and you held me right there.

A need to feel accepted, and say it's O.K..
Just precious hugs, a very special way.

A need to feel loved, and felt with tender touch,
Just a precious word, can mean so much.

A need to feel needed, in everything you do.
What a terrific person, of what I see in you.

A need to feel understood, and listened to patiently.
Just a precious second, for you to, see the real me.

A need to feel weak, in the darkest of the night,
Just a precious word, it's O.K. And all right.

A need to feel strong, to face the toughest storm,
Just a precious hug to keep me safe and warm.

A need to believe in all you do.
Just a precious second I'm so proud of you.

A need to accept whatever comes our way.
Just a precious thought that it will be O.K.

Sandra Dipka

Midnight Sonata

Stone-washed, milk Moon drizzles forth
in whispering ripple waves
Bathe in its arduous oak-framed gleam
soak them up,
hug highest to the sky,
kiss this radiating starlet of heaven-found
...The Wolf howls at midnight forevermore.

Fossil Man lounges peaceably on old mahogany chair
through looking glass gallancy, he looks but a night critter
Sinfuldated from young-colt's escapade,
life is now but biscuits and milk...,
absent of stinging bees and pecking birds
...The Fossil Man howls at midnight forever more.

Wolf spindles into heartland shrub
And Fossil Man, drifts to noble thought...
What have it, the Midnight Wolf?
Has he chivalrous brawn? And chivalrous brain?
What is life as the Midnight Wolf, but heavenly bliss?

Woolywood sings not ripe for man.
If just for life as the Midnight Wolf.

Eugene Kim

Drifts And Whirlwinds

Drifts and whirlwinds, snow all around
A soft white carpet upon the ground.
Snow lined trees forming lace in the sky,
Quietness and peace around us lie.
Out of the house, across the fields
Tramping with sleds close to our heels,
Leaving a trail as we set a pace
Snow and cold stinging the face.
Up we would climb going higher and higher,
White majesty below muscles tired,
Down we would soar at breakneck speed
Landscape fleeting, freedom in deed.
Up we'd climb, again down the hill
'Til night would fall, and all was still.
Home we'd tramp reluctant to go
Hoping soon to return to the snow.
Childhood days have long gone away
Memories return me to those special days...
Of drifts, whirlwinds, snow all around
A soft white carpet upon the ground.

Diane Dalum Groth

Time

Little children do not worry,
About how they spend their time.
Sailing through their carefree days,
Life's an endless song or rhyme.

In a twinkling time flies fast.
Then they grow into teens.
Too busy with life's challenges,
Their world caught up in dreams.

Yet time has a way of passing by,
Going through our young adult years.
And dreams are put on hold sometimes,
Through need, or greed, or fears.

Then wake up they one morning,
To realize life's halfway through.
They'd better do something about these dreams.
My, how time has flew!

A few more years and they look back,
At happiness or regrets along their climb.
How elusive life can be,
In the passing of a thing called "Time".

Judy Baird

My Struggle

In the cramped darkness I see a shimmer of light. The gleam
fills me and I am bear. As I crawl beneath, a moment of
joy conforms to the wails of children. As the stroller
is pushed life enters in rubbing away the swells of moisture.
Moisture enhances as promises disturb us. Unattainable
future has overpowered me as I fall beneath the covers.
Restraining from love the echoes of young become foreign
to my ears. I turn to truth and my life is lost. Dreams
are realized by pulsating throbbing and cracked rings.
I am fulfilled as we explode. A longing of future attained
from love. Empty I lie alone. As a moralistic balance
of past conforms me heavy forms and embodied remorse invade
us. The forms are paralleled by joy and longing. Deformed
the walls begin. The crib is standing. I am content with
emptiness. Heavy I embrace the child. I do not see him
for he is not mine. Reality accepted I crawl into darkness.
Still I cherish the image of the pulsating throb. Longing
alone. Content to hear no wails.

Jeanne Ryan

Painted Eyes

A black silhouette in the mirror
with painted eyes
painted shades of the past, the future
like a landscape of her mind

The ticking of the clock

Remembering the moment your eyes touched mine
an ocean — the thunder, the rhythm, the music

Yet, in your eyes, hidden behind shadows
the mystery remains
beyond your gaze, secrets lie
afraid and uncertain
to love
wanting to escape reality's stare
your painted eyes, a roadmap to your soul

The turning of the calendar

Looking far ahead, my picture
that has never been sketched, never viewed
is painted
with an artist's angle toward reality, a knowledge of certainty
seeing the reflection of your blue, blue eyes

Sari Hott

And Day Remembers

Fog moves down from the mountain
Like chiffon shreds that querl
Into a foaming mass -
Embracing treetops,
Looping about unyielding trunks and finally...
Hovering over the grass,
Like a benediction...
Shielding the heart of earth
From unknown threats.
Then, as though to light the way
For some kind spirit in the dark,
Fireflies flicker through the silken web
And there - startled perhaps -
A deer frames itself briefly in the mist,
Then bounds without a sound into a secret world
Where fear and silence merge into a faith profound.
While back on the mountain
Vertical rays of sun
Cast their red glow against the sky
And slide into the elsewhere's tomorrow.

Fanny Kraiss DeVine

Darkness

My life is a solitude desolate place
Where I cannot see any other's Sweet face
Time passes so slow
My spirits so low
I can't stand one moment in this small dark space

I want others to come here with me
So that I can have some company
We'll laugh and we'll play
We'll frolic all day
And then we'll all climb up a tree

That would be much fun and lots of delight
We would have so much fun all throughout the night
But alas oh alas my poor dream it shall die
So here for the time I shall stay here and lie
Until finally after the years upon years
After all of the flowing of tears upon tears
I shall lay my self down and then I will die
So I ask you one thing, for me please do not cry
I will die, I am dying, I am dead goodbye.

Angela McNutt

The Flight 800

Excitement, happiness, laughter, joy
Man, woman, girl, boy
These eight things belonged together,
But now just a faint cry from above forever
Nobody knows what happened that night
Witnesses say it was a flash of light
So high up in the sky
Why? Why did these precious people die?
Their empty bodies floating in the ocean sea.
Their spirits and souls asking why me?
Why did these innocent people have to go?
I guess nobody will ever know.

Alicia Marie Califra

Forced to fight off the quiet
Calm pressing against the
Invisible shards of the heart

Purge feeling with the numbing drone
Of regulated ticks counted out in the grey monotony,
— the gathering of minutes,
A lullaby of sleepless invisibility.
All I strain to hear is your heartbeat
Black broken shadows dance on the ceiling,
The stumbling waltz,
Against my own chaos—

Lift me out into the blue with you
— a soothing stillness...
Until I can taste the wind, feel its grasp,
Hearing the seductive whispers of the night sky,
Filled with beams and pricks of starlight,
Dripping on my head
Bathing me in the breath of life.

Wendy Waterman

Untitled

I'm sorry it had to end this way
I wish we had another day
But we don't and now I'm gone
I hope eventually that you'll move on
It will take a while to relieve your pain
It will be hard to stroll down memory lane
I know you'll spend many nights crying
But you've got to keep on trying
To get on with your life as soon as possible
Though memories of me may not be tossable
I'll always be watching you from above
Sending down to you, all my love
Remember that even though I died
I'll always remain right by your side
I know you are torn apart
But know that I love you with all my heart

Aimie Palaza

Untitled

On the anniversary of her suicide,
The woman shot upward as an arrow
Burning radiance,
Ebbs or energy,
Until there was no more.

As the ashes of all that was
Drifted slowly to the ground,
The child collected these
And dissolved them in a cup
Drinking from the wisdom of a light gone out
Before its time.

Gina De Lagerheim

Euphony

When the fire has died to embers,
there is one who remains, touched by the sun.
They open their arms to greet the dawn.
In silent absolution, the blaze spreads anon.

Then, most profoundly,
it reveals an individual truth.
The emptiness that is all of ours,
is once again removed.

Dreams, trapped in dying coals,
are revived by the hunger of a single flame.
The flame will find you in the dark,
And set fire to the coldness of the rain.

What is this that can do this to me,
such a prison that sets me free?
There's confusion in its intensity,
and solace in its production.

It reluctantly quivers beneath my fear,
then in painful torrents from my soul.
Music, my deliverance and perdition,
is at once my friend and foe.

Jessica Casto

Twenty Five Years

Are you willing to spend twenty five years
Awake to the river, the darkness, that throb
Which pulses and dreams and runs rampant
Deep inside your earthy soul?

Are you willing to drown and sink into the muck
That surrounds your skin with a heavenly glisten?
Are you willing to hold your breath, sweat and labor,
Hoping to thrust into harsh teeming waters
The lost child, the one you dreamed of,
Whether it be radiant and lovely or a bloodied urchin?

Are you willing to make the protracted effort
And never compromise,
And never regret, even when you see
That urchin, that lusty glaring child,
Who puts the truth to your hidden heart?
Are you willing then to accept every imperfect gene?
And then, tell me, are you still willing to smile

Barbara McCorkhill

Only One Person

There is only one person
I trust so completely,
Only one person
Who treats me so sweetly;
Only one person I give my all,
Who will always be there
If by chance I should fall.
There is only one person
Which I give my heart,
Only one person
I shall never from depart;
Only one person whom I'll follow where they go,
Only one person my secrets to know.
There is only one person,
One so divine, that all I will share
Is all that is mine.
There is only one person
I'll love my whole life through...
I know that because
There is only one you.

Jenniel D. Jensen

Loneliness

L - is for the Longing for someone to love me
O - is for my open arms ready to hug someone
N - is for never knowing that special feeling
E - is for every evening alone
L - is for the love I've missed
I - is for the isolation
N - is for the nobody cares
E - is for the envy of others
S - is for the sadness
S - is for the sadness

Laura Fajdich

The Ocean

The ocean, 'tis a mystery or two,
Waiting with patience, calling for you
To come and dip your feet in her mouth;
She starts out nice, the epitome of couth,
Licking and lapping, a pup at your feet,
Bidding you forward, into her midst.
   A beauty is she, no one can surpass,
But, in truth there's none can placate her wrath.
Betrayed? Bereft? Fickle as Time?
Unfathomable, yet constant as rhyme.
None can guess the reasons behind
Her anger, and yet she soothes as a lullaby.
Unconsoled, yet she still consoles.
Is it the sigh of a woman's heart?
Who can know the depths of life
But He who made Creation to breathe?
   'Tis true there're some who'll cry you a song
Of loss and woe, of terrible fate;
But, never you'll find a woman so true,
Nor possessed of a beauty so great.

James Wesley Post

Greedy Fly

I am merely a moth,
A passing, common fly,
Spying on the light
Within my mind's eye.
It glitters, it sparkles,
It will attract 'till it blinds
Tragic that its seekers
can't see what they'll find...
The light as an Eden
Truly a devil in his guise,
His light bringing all that seeks it to their demise!
I am trapped within a chosen fate,
My will stifled, I am blind
Beware of all temptation
For I have yet to find my prize!

Abigail Garcia

Untitled

When you dream, you have a goal
No matter what that dream is
you will stop at nothing to accomplish it.
Yet, when something gets in your way,
you let it beat you in every way it can.
Emotionally and physically.
You think to yourself,
"It is over, I am no longer the best".
To find the drive and love deep
down inside you is the hardest
test you can put yourself through,
But once you find it,
Only then will your
Dreams start to come true.

Sara Reischman

Old Boots And Hat

My boots are worn and my hat is stained
  But they still shed the rain.

People think that they're worn out
  But I have my doubts about throwing them out

New boots and a hat would be fine and good
  But what I have fit like they should.

Old boots feel like slippers, an old hat like a crown
  So throwing them out would constitute a frown.

These aren't worn out, they're just worn in
  And it would take some time to do again.

When you see a pair wrinkled and worn,
  A hat that's stained and torn.

Remember the mud and rain they've seen
  And all the days they've met their need.

You still say they look like heck
  But it's my head and feet that won't get wet.

So go along and buy your own
  Maybe then you'll change your tone.

    Ricky Joe Humphrey

The Ocean Paradise

The Ocean Paradise glows green and blue -
A rainbow of colors in every hue.
  Sometimes tranquil, sometimes loud,
  Seldom humble, often proud,
A flat expanse of glassy light,
Awes the world with strength and might.
  Bubbles break the surface, clearer
  Than a polished, shining mirror.
Sharks that prey, seals that leap,
The rippling Manta, whales that weep -
  Dancing with exotic rhythm
  With youthful play and age-old wisdom
In chorus echo secrets deep:
Cliffs and trenches sharp and steep,
  A symphony of colors vividly expressed,
  A haven for peaceful, quiet rest,
Blooming gardens of natural treasure,
Grandeur and beauty beyond measure.
  Hear the music, feel the sand,
  Taste the salt of the Untouched Land.

    Tonya Douglas

Emotions

Facing the unknown grips my heart with fear,
Hurt, disillusioned, ready to cry,
Disappointments, heartaches, sadness so drear,
Frustrations beset me whatever I try.

Self-destruction thoughts awake me with a start.
What possesses me to act so strange?
I sense a disturbance within my heart.
Excitement rushes over me, feelings change.

Like a swirling, mighty rushing wind,
A feeling of happiness floods my day.
Laughter breaks through, my misery to end.
A sweet calm peace is here to stay.

Now a new joy is mine,
With life I am content.
Realizing both storms and sunshine
Are for me from Heaven sent.

    Glenna L. Mathews

The Ranch

When I was just a lil' tyke of five or six or seven
I found our what I really liked, to me it was like heaven!
I remember it wasn't a long trip, but one of behold;
To see the quiet streams, to recall my wonderful dreams,
And that ranch house of old.

I couldn't wait to see the rows
Of magnificent flowers in bloom,
Bluebonnets, marigolds, and painter's palette
So vast that it would fill a room.

The orange, the fig, and peach trees were surely a delight,
For us to go and pluck a fruit and eat with all our might.
And then the horses in the stables were beautiful to see.
We always used to ride them with so much fun and glee.

So these are some of my favorite memories of
Our trips to dear grandfather's ranch
They will always be with me
Like a flower on a branch.

    Leonor DeJesus Marulanda

Pictures In The Clouds

What pictures are in the clouds today?
Perhaps a huge dinosaur, Or hey!
Maybe a gloriously beautiful full moon,
a luscious brown white Florida sand dune.
I think I see a rabbit sitting, begging for food
a quiet iguana laying down thinking the rabbit is rather rude.
I see an eagle soaring high on its wings,
Wonderful! A jay who sings!!
A circus is in the clouds, performing before the crowds.
Who will come and watch the sky as magnificent clouds go by?

    Natalie Knapp

Roundball Hero

He's awesome, he soars, clear the way for a fly by,
He breathes net and leather, he's a trash talkin' out cry.
He's board bangin' rim thumpin' net swishin' wonder,
And God help the man...near the net...that he's under.
His jumper is dangerous.... And wow what a hook,
I tell you.... This guy takes a shot at each look.
He's a joy to behold.... With his reverse jammer,
And rare...is the moment the ref checks his grammar.
The court's filled with energy when this guy brings his stuff.
And they all scream for more.... When the clock says enough.
When, just for the show of it he flies up with his pump,
And the crowd is hushed...by the rim as it thumps.
He's a celebrity, a conqueror.... A leader of teams,
And as our hero hits the showers...we go home with our dreams.

    Jayne Raef

Chance Encounter With Darkness

Only through shaded eyes can she feel
The warmth that is strongly familiar
Once embraced she is freely carried away
Beyond the shade, beyond the light of day
The force has brought her to a safe place
The breath of darkness upon her face
The taste upon her lips
The weight upon her soul
There she is saturated with energy
The two are bound into one
One in body
One in soul
One in mind returns them to the light
The two break free from their blind flight
Always wondering, always desiring,
The chance encounter with darkness
To embrace once more

    Shelly Lowe

My Parents

They're really quite helpful you see
For their part in the bringing up of me
Because of their correcting, loving and
That's why I think of them so grand

They've helped me fight the battle of life
Going through situations that come with strife
They've given me love, a home, and food
They taught me to be polite, not to be rude

It's the experience of theirs that helps me through
Their watchful eyes seeing what I do
They taught me to follow the path of the Lord
Who can take away sins that bind like a cord

That's why I love them, that's why I'm glad
To have my Mom and with her clothes and Dad with his plaid
This is why I love them and what they've done, too
I love these parents of mine, wouldn't you?

Tyler J. Smith

Tears

I saw something last night,
something that happened to me long ago.
I saw two people holding onto each other
on a pier on a brisk winter's night.
Their lips were filled with passion,
hearts pumping with love.
Their souls burning with desire,
and their eyes were lost in one another's.
The lights shined down upon them
as the wind circled around.
They watched the boats sway on the water,
as they held each other in search for warmth.
As the water lapped against the pier
they cried as tears rolled off their cheeks.
They weren't tears of pain or sorrow,
but tears of a new found love.
After I witnessed this, I drove on.
I knew not where I was going,
but I knew what I had,
tears of pain and sorrow.

Matthew G. Mamos Jr.

Destiny

Each one of us is dealt a hand you see,
but will it foretell our destiny?

There is no genuine reason or rhyme
why only some have bitter lesions of time.

Shalt those discouraging actions hinder
whether you survive or easily surrender?

Experiencing any kind of abuse
is not enough reason for lifelong excuse!

Destined cycles are not difficult to break...
only you can decide which path to take.

Instead of focusing on the past,
gaze now at what the future has cast.

Graciously allow a gentle hand
help bury the scars that life hath panned.

Circle your sights on the angels He sent;
permit love to bloom the way it was meant.

Merely look forward, hold your head high,
spread open the wings God gave you to fly.

Let bygones be bygones, set past evils free...
Decisions You make predict destiny.

Colleen Louise Niemeyer

A Virgin Child

A fair maiden awaits her sweet prince
A meeting by chance
She sees the depth of his soul
through his penetrating eyes

From the sky, anew fallen snow - pure and flawless
A hint of scent tinges intense sentiments
Inquisitive eyes suggesting privacy
The comforting wind shadowing forth
an imagery of freedom

A kiss, one that is first before any other
Kindles a flame of burning desire

This passion inside, presented to view
Our heartfelt souls reaching for rainbows
Should we dare enter into a
world of dreams unknown...

Seek and discover - the profound dreams
in the newly fallen snow.

Jan Blake

Auschwitz

A single candle in the door
    where once there burned a raging fire.
A nation's cries that went unheard
    as hatred's banner won.

A thousand days rolled on and by
    as billows of death filled the air.
Evil ran unchecked, unseen
    as freedom turned its eye.

As firebombs fell on London-town
    and Nanjing writhed in pain
In Auschwitz was heard a frightful sound
    whose echoes still remain.

The flames are gone, and what remains
    are silent shells of a mad man's game.
Let them stand as votive stones
    lest we forget of mankind's shame.

Christopher Melton

My House Of Prayer

I have no scheduled time in which to pray.
When the frightened dawn steals up, or in the day
Bleached white with the sun's all-purifying ray,
When shadows push the vaguely fading light
Over the horizon, or when black demons fight
To keep forever dark the smothering night,
I, one lone soul, before my Maker come!

I need no stated place to make a prayer,
For that are hills and dales when over there
Is space unbounded. I, all free of care,
From stark deserted cliffs sing out aloud
A song of praise. In church my head is bowed,
And often drawn aloof from mottled crowd,
I, one lone soul, before my Maker come!

Russwyn O. Hall

release me

until i am released by death,
imprisoned i will be in this cold,
dark world that only exists around me.
no one can hear my pain or feel my cries.
no one can see the taste of death
or taste the nothingness i feel.
so alone i will remain in this cold,
dark world that only exists around me.

Hayley

Untitled

Rain, rain, the whole night through,
Can't tell the rain from the morning's dew.
The tiny tears from heaven on high,
Falling downward from the sky.

Tells of God's cleansing of the Earth,
To make mankind know its worth.
The sweetest smell of the fresh new rain,
Makes streams and rivers on my window pane.

I hear its music on my roof,
And dream it's the sound of fairy horse's hoofs
Riding high through the mist and rain,
As they leap through the rivers on my window pane.

To find adventure just close your eyes
And dream a dream of rain and skies.

Doreen R. Barber

The Way It Was

I miss the way you used to hold me,
the times we had, why can't it be
like that again.
The way you softly whispered,
I love you.
When you walked out, my world fell to pieces
You left without a reason, you broke my heart,
leaving me to cry in the rain
Now I realized you didn't love me
You lied to get what you wanted.
It's too bad I believed it all,
Every pitiful word you said
It was all a lie, just like you

Just remember everything we shared
I love you

Maria Kinkade

The Dove

I have waited for love all my life,
And learned that the waiting is hard,
When you do find love you just play your cards,
And hope and pray those cards are right,
But love can also stab you in the back like a knife,

Once you do find that certain true love,
You will float and feel like a dove,
Love will grow stronger and higher that dove will fly,
Your love will sweep you off your feet,
But beware love can tell you good-bye,

Good-bye the forbidden words,
The forbidden words in love,
That dove shall fly no longer,
Because of the two words that killed that dove,
But love will fly again,

Just like the flowing wind,

Sheila Michele Newton

Dream

I saw pale green eraserbottle regard the logical catastrophe!
I contacted the spontaneous crackling of the purple nonsense
spring boarding from my imagination!
I smelled the rusty styles urge and hammer the fantasy!
I evacuated the sour acid soup and biodegrading black holes
in your toxic trumpet!
I felt unprecedented jumps tangle the moisturized spin!

G. Austin Grove

Sitting Alone

Sitting alone....
Sometimes it's good, sometimes it's bad,
sometimes wandering thoughts make you sad.

Other thoughts fill your head like a big balloon,
hoping one day your moment in life will come soon.

Life changes in so many ways,
to where you could find yourself losing track of the days.

But when all else fails just smile,
after all we are on this ride for a while.

So if you find yourself sitting alone,
think of you and others as more than just skin and bone.

Remember life as a roller coaster, it has its ups and downs,
and smiles and frowns.

Doug Howard

The Eagle And The Flower

He was a wild eagle flying aimlessly
his head above the clouds
She was a dying flower rooted firmly
her head falling towards the ground

But one day by chance they met
the eagle and the flower
because he stopped flying
and she stopped dying
long enough to notice each other

He hold her stories of freedom
determination and reason
and she showed him stability
despite the change of seasons
and she found courage to hold her head high
and he found direction for when he flies

And though the meeting was brief
the exchange was intense
and they'll not soon forget the other
for she'll use his strength to go on living
and he'll fly with purpose he borrows from the flower

Nora Kaiser

Memories

I met him on a blind date,
I guess it was just pure fate.
The first night he spent a lot of money,
On a fancy meal and a play we thought funny.

The next night was free, went to a park,
Where a band was playing in the dark.
He said he loved me the third time we met,
I said, you can't you don't even know me yet.

We went together for four or five years,
There was a lot of laughter and yes some tears.
Then we were married secretly,
For some said it wouldn't last, you see.

But it did last for twenty years,
And then he got sick and I shed more tears.
He past away on Veteran's Day,
He would be proud of this, some say.

It's been over a year since he's been here,
But I have good memories that I hold so dear.
He would want me to be happy, I know,
But without him, it's going to be slow.

Marilyn R. Mitchell

roofhopping

you said turn right, so i said let's do both...and just go roofhopping.
from house to cottage, till we get there...wherever there is.
let's stop deciding, and start writing...books and poems alike.
let's pick some random numbers, and do something about them.

and dream the same dreams, of plastic storms and metal crayons.
dream until everything is completely right...and wrong as well.
it reminds me of how you sleep and dream...and yet I don't...
all i can do is consume my mind...with endless thoughts:
perfect songs and theoretical, trigonometrically perfect...roofhopping.

David Edward Pearl

Sitting On The Subway

Sitting on the subway wondering who is straight, gay, bisexual
or who has AIDS! Am I in danger? Don't act like that thought
has never entered your mind because I know that it has... I just
had enough guts to write it down. I have now entered a whole
new world... The inner world. I ride the train to my destination
and that is supposed to be it. I may be on the train for thirty
minutes or less and a lot can happen. People are reading The
Washington Post, The Wall Street Journal but no one speaks to
who they are sitting beside, unless they happen to bump into
you and then the person gets very polite, almost cold like and
says "Excuse Me" or "I'm So Sorry." Really they are thinking to
themselves "you interrupted me from reading my paper!!" And they
bumped into you not you into them.

Sitting on the subway watching this strange inner world of
people reading a book, listening to music with headphones on,
talking ever so lightly to a friend, husband or lover or just
sleeping. Within this inner world I also see an outer world on
each face. Some are heading to work, home from work, to
college or around town for leisurely pleasure. But, still no one
really speaks...it's almost claustrophobic the silence you
experience with so many people and yet no people.

Sitting on the subway wondering...do others feel like shouting
as I do or am I crazy? Is it so awful to wish your neighbor a
good day or what? I wonder...if I did speak would I be ousted
from the train like some common criminal or would others join me?

Arthienyer L. Fraser

Jimmy

Through the eyes of an alcoholic everything seems clear,
Until the next morning, when the headache sets in,
  the stomach begins to churn,
  the mind faces reality,
  the hand reaches for another Coors Light
   another Vodka Tonic
   another Gin on the Rocks
   another escape from sobriety.
Because when the clarity of alcoholism becomes hazy
It is then that the headache is not only from the bottle, the can,or the glass
It is from the harsh reality that anyone can become addicted.

Even Jimmy—you know, the boy who lived down the street, the one who used to walk
  his poodle past my door.
So, Jimmy, have the next drink on me and drown in your unrealistic reality
That not only numbs the head and the mind...
But also the heart.

Shareen Barry

The Love Of My Life

Your eyes are like wildfire which burn through my soul—
Your smile is my sunshine which brightens my every day—
Your lips are like soft rose petals which kiss and caress me late in the midnight hour—
Your arms hold me tight and give me that secure feeling every night—
Your heart is of gold and it shows in every little thing you do,
  and that is what tells me you're the perfect man—
And that is why I love you like I do...

Tina Litchfield

Time

Life is a journey.
Upon which we commence.
Some choose to live it as a tourney.
Others just construct a fence.

We have been placed here for a reason.
Some choose to persevere or even blame.
Yet, I shall commit no act of treason.
I am here to keep the world lame.

Stand up and live for the fight.
Do not wander and strive for play.
Oh, here commits the dawn of night.
On the ground we will lay...

Craig William Drummond

Death Of An Unborn Child

A tiny creature grows warmly within me.
My life, my spirit, my soul are renewed.
The empty hollows of my heart cry out alone.
It is no more.
I grow weary of grief,
I long to be whole again.
Fragments of myself were torn
from my depths.
I will seek comfort from those
who have gone before.
The wrath I have known will be
stricken from my soul forever.
My shattered dreams have been shaken.
I feel nothing
I cry no more.

Jayne Miner

There Are No Tomorrows

With whom shall we gather
Oh what will they say
Or does it all matter
when we go our own way

There are no tomorrows
time has stolen away
It steals without malice
Judge not what I say

The joy we are seeking
The dance, and the song
Lies there in the silence
This moment so long

So stand and be silent
Do not hurry to be
There are no tomorrows
Just moments like these

Daniel A. Lund

Spring

Oh spring
where art thou
please come soon
no more sniffles
no more colds
no more aches
no more pains
no more snow
no more ice
that would be
ever so nice
oh spring
where art thou
please come soon

Joan Houghton Hamsher

286

Don't Dare Deny!
(A Holocaust Survivor's Lament)

The scars seemed closed
The griefs reposed;
Your callous claim
Old wounds inflames — your brutish lie!

Our kin you slew
Meek infants too
Gone young and old
Six million told — now you deny!

Erstwhile deemed mild
The ache's gone wild
Inside my chest
As anger crests — All senses cry!

Don't near my face
My rage might blaze
My wrath might strike
Your evil psyche — don't dare deny!

The true report
Don't dare distort
Don't let your lie
More hurts decry — don't dare deny!

Leo Rechter

Your First Friend

Your first friend is your mom.
You'll always remember in life
no matter where you go, that your
first friend was your mom.
When she has passed away and
has gone to those golden gates, you
can tell your friends about your best friend.
You'll always have her memories
of laughter, smiles in your heart.
Also, you'll want to tell strangers
who your first friend was.
Then you'll tell them that it was
your mother that was so beautiful.
Then you'll also tell them that you
were glad that you had gotten sent
to such a friend.

Tammy L. Elliott

Oxymoron

Enslaved in my freedom,
at war with my peace.
In light of the darkness
forever will cease.
Afraid of my bravery
(as days turn to night)
the sword and the kind words
cause brothers to fight.
Water on fire
and children with guns
bring death to the healthy
and many to one.
Acknowledge your ignorance.
Move on from the pause.
When questioning the answers
rebel without cause.
I exhaled so deeply
the air in the mine
ignited the smoke,
and everything's fine.

Joshua Kusnierz

What Is Life

A test of our abilities...
To change and to grow
To love and to hate
To forgive and to forget

It's about giving in to temptations
And being responsible for our actions...

Each day we get stronger and weaker in our own ways...

It's about planning ahead to make the future what we want it to be and
leaving things behind to build memories...

It's understanding and learning from our mistakes and controlling our
urges to do them again...

Life is a test of our abilities to Fail and to Succeed...

Angela Myers

Poem For 3 Nurses

You know that I'm uncomfortable with emotions I am feeling
I profess to want to let them out without being too revealing.
I wish that I could walk around with all 3 of you beside me
To soothe me when I need it (or, as necessary, to chide me).

I'd put one of you on my left shoulder, and one of you on my right.
The 3rd could ride atop my head to be there day and night.
But, sigh, that's not quite feasible, to do these things I need
And even if it were to be, you have your lives to lead.

I'm not sure where I'm going, but the road could use some paving.
And the 3 of you have been there when I have needed 'saving'.
So please don't go away just yet; I like to know you're there.
When I'm not treating Me too well, it's nice to know You care.

Donna S. Rubin

Prozac World

I fell out of bed, hitting my head on the alarm
I have vowed to destroy.
I search the floor,
covered in clothes and scraps,
for my salvation and courage.
No, the dry mouth isn't too bad, not bad enough to stop,
nor is the insomnia. As long as I'm 'ok.'
Now I can speak, and not
turn red. I can sing and laugh, and not cry.
Crying doesn't last as the green and white pill sucks away my tears.
I toss back 40 (milligrams not pills),
jump into the shower and become beautiful...
and just ok.
To face the day, I swallow, and feel the icy trails
they leave in my soul. And at night, I lay awake
saying my prozac chant
'it's all ok...it's all ok...'
soon I may even believe it...
and I'll never feel
what the prozac feels.

Chelsea Snyder

Looking At Death

You can look at death in two different ways,
it can be both a sad and a rejoicing day.

If you have Jesus in your life, and you truly rejoice in the name
Christ,
then there's nothing to fear in the word death,
just know in your heart you're headed for the best.

Sure there is sadness for those left here,
no one is ever ready to leave those who are dear.

A part of life is death, and it's truly a must,
for we all someday, will return to dust.

Debbie Vaughn

Tears Of An Oldest Child

Robbed of your friendship on that stormy night
Taken from me, our kinship, as you walked into the light
Snatched out from under us, too early in your time
Stolen from me, everything in which I placed my trust
Don't worry I'll be fine
Picking up the pieces, of my broken heart
Storing in the reasons, only asking for another start
Building all these bridges, from beneath which have been washed
Mending all the fences...Is this the cost?
Learned of the lesson, so many to me you taught
Practicing the word that was preached, is a bitter pill to swallow
Writing in my pain, turns the ink a rusted hue
Reading between all these lines...leaves my asking
What next shall I do...
Bottling these emotions, only sours and ferments
Sealing this fate, that has become so uneloquent
Pouring out my soul, is this deluge running wild
Who is there to catch these tears of your oldest child?

James J. Sutherland Jr.

Of Fluid Grace

As my mind begins to wander, like a cloud drifting 'cross the sky,
   my thoughts turn to her.
A waterfall of calico curls embraces her angelic face.
Her luminous blue eyes sparkle like sun streaks colliding with ocean spray.
And like raindrops on a rose, freckles delicately dance 'cross her cheeks.
The silken gown covers yet can not hide her graceful flowing form.
A warmth pervades me as I see through to her radiant soul.
Then an embrace...and I am home.

Ryan Patrick O'Hare

How Come?

How come all so suddenly a smile can turn to tears,
And nothing can replace that smile, for it's been overcome by fear?

How come all so suddenly a friendship can be lost,
Though one true friend may want it back, no matter what the cost?

How come all so suddenly our beliefs can fall and shatter,
And you begin to wonder what was the point, why did it even matter?

How come all so suddenly our lives can fall apart,
Just becoming worse and worse until we all lose heart?

How come all so suddenly the sky can turn so dark,
And how come when you most need light there is no longer spark?

Terra Meeuwsen

My Master

My master went away today, and I don't know where he's gone;
they say he won't be back again, I'm so lost and all alone.

Who'll scratch my ears and pat my head,
who will I lie beside when I go off to bed.

Who will I bring his slippers to, the paper, or my leash;
is there anyone here that still wants me, I hope that much at least.

Will someone take me hunting, so I can romp across the land,
and who can I bring the birds back to, and deliver them to hand.

He's gone to those happy hunting grounds; why didn't he take me with;
I don't know where this place is, perhaps it's just a myth.

I worked so hard to please him, is it something I've done wrong;
I hope he knew how much I loved him; I can't show him now he's gone.

Eternity is, they say, where the rest of his days will be spent;
he's gone to heaven where he can hunt to his heart's content.

I just don't understand it and I'm really in a fog,
but I guess that's why he was master and I, I'm just his dog.

Steve Piper

The Silent Grandchild

He won't accept
that he has passed away
He just let's the anger
build up inside
Like a raging storm on a
war path is what he will
be if he does not let
the pain and hurt show
he does not tell a soul
how he feels
not even his own
he thinks everything is going
to be alright
nothing has happened
but when he wants him
and can not find him
it is then he sheds a tear and
the silent grandchild
has spoken.

Carrie Schultz

Swiftly

Swiftly, swiftly on the breeze,
Swiftly, swiftly through the trees.
All the birds fly high in the sky,
Dancing, dodging the mountains on high.
Most birds now close their eyes,
For it is night,
Everlasting night!

Amanda Jester

Birds

Birds by my window
So fluffy and nice
Don't seem to mind
The snow and ice.
All day they sit
In the shrubs and sing
And plan for the nest
They'll build in the spring.

Wilma F. Parrish

A Passage In Time

In the years I have lived
I've learned it's best to forgive.

I've looked back at what is best
And have learned to forget the rest.

The future is before me.
I cannot wait to see.
What will it be?

My dreams will they come true?
Or will it happen just for you?

If I try to do my best,
then I may take a rest.

Because I know that in my heart
I have succeeded in that part.

How long will it take? Because
I just can't wait.
To know the date.
What passage in time
will my dream really be mine?

Rhonda Gagne

Untitled

The good old days. When orchard
roads were full of fruit, and people
would smile and say hello. It was
great to be alive talking, laughing and
just having fun.

Peter D. Pratico

A Widow's Love Affair

Last night the black widow
crawled along the armrest of my chair.
She wept with venomous drops
Her bereaved web beckoned.

Up my arm, to my shoulder
Over to my nose, she rose.
T'was there in a moment of peril
Tongues of flame turned my lips colder.

In low sweet tones
She whispered then moaned.
Her desperate solitudes
Like a widow's love of fear.

When her tears did die
Salt fell from her face and stung.
Those slender strands of lace
Clothed the splendor of womanhood.

I grasped to pull her near
As she spun away, I chased after.
For the sheer love of fear
She bit me in breathless laughter.

Christopher Wojick

Despair

I reach despair when no one's there.
Lack of love, and no one cares.
I feel despair!
I'm all alone!
I feel that I will never know;
the gentle warmth of love's embrace.
This I am afraid to face.

Matt Wion

The Exceptional Child

God made him so,
Retarded, blind and palsied.
We ask God why.
No reply.
We pray for this cross to pass.
No reply.
Just the pain of lost hopes.
No first steps or student of the month.
No touchdowns or proms.
No father and son.
Just the pain of lost hopes.
Officially, and forever handicapped.
So final. So negative.
Yet he has given so much, to so many.
We search for a way.
And God gives us the word...
Exceptional.
Not handicapped, but exceptional.
Our son is an exceptional child.
Yes, God made him so.

William L. Clarke

Truth Of The Heart

In my mind there lies a book whose pages are not worn,
Though I've read it often and at times have felt forlorn.
Within each page are thoughts that are distanced from
    the center of the pages,
It speaks of stories from the start through all the different stages.
As time passes, the book is kept hidden behind lock and key,
Only for those with knowledge of the secret to see.
In my soul there lies a truth whose time has never come,
Although within it appears that it has shown itself some.
There is a depth in this truth that will never disappear,
With love, trust and respect, dignity as well as fear.
The truth in the soul is wise and wondrous for those who can see,
How much there is to the wealth of truth and all it can be.
In my heart there lies a love,
Which can never be attained to be enough of,
For where it belongs, it may not ever reach,
But there lies a lesson that only a heart can teach.
That true love belongs in the heart, in the soul, in the mind,
And it should be treasured if you are able to find.
Keep it in your heart for it to prosper,
And you will continue this love and grow with it forever.

Katherine A. Baron

symphony

balcony of a one room apartment—
good view of the world's Stage (as you like it)
which is the Performance which is the Concert which is Life
which is you that you're looking down upon.

sit beside a grill never used
('cause you don't eat much besides cantaloupe).
pick up a pen with a hand never held,
stare out across street stationary in time
of all raindrops warm yet frozen in place
(you just don't care where you live these days),
smoke away a week's earnings with lips never kissed,
sing they the songs of false credos—
you say you're content with merely existing and enjoy no one knowing
your fears—turn up the music when Truth rings the doorbell
    —for you could wake up in the morning and skip off to
italy and not a single soul would notice in the world.

so, smile a fake smile at me (but not fake to you)
'cause your ears are still ringing.
what? you actually think i don't know that not a day goes by
without you wishing you could play the piano?

Benjamin Branham

There's A First Time For Everything

As I stand here with you, a vision dressed in white
The preacher and the altar hover at the edge of my sight
I think back across the years and the things I've done
I wonder now if I've always known that you'd be the one

There's a first time for everything, every touch, caress, and kiss
But those times are all illusions, all I've known 'til now is this
This moment in the candlelight begins my life brand new
And with these vows of joy and love I give myself to you

You can't go back again, can't change a thing they say
But with you there's no yesterday, only tomorrow and today
My life begins all over again, all that matters is you and I
Our parts are soon forgotten without even having to try

Thank you for bringing me back again, back to what could be
Thank you for opening my heart again and giving me back to me
Most of all I want to thank you for this first moment in my life
'Cause I know all is new again as we stand here man and wife

Christopher Matosky

New Moon

I am as Jupiter,
Bold, bright, a gentle sentry in the sky.

It is as if you are a new moon in my sight,
A familiar, faceless friend from ancient times of joy.
But yet, it is not you who circles my sphere.
It is I who orbits around you, suspended weightless in your power.

My renowned, enduring strength is weakened by your forces,
To no more than as a lone leaf trembling on a branch in the wind.
What was once a mighty presence in the night
Is reduced to a mere area of shadow,
And you, new moon, are my connection to the light.

I reach out for you, drawn by your brilliance
and realize...
When straining to touch a heavenly body
There is a great distance from which to fall.

Brian Keen

Raining On The Inside

You see me being jolly, all smiles and very funny,
I even joke around with you, I'm as sweet as jam and honey.

But these days are very trying and at times I may be smiling,
But if you were to look inside you'd find I'm slowly dying.

There's a terrible storm a-brewing, in my heart is where it's at,
There's lots of lightning and thunder and there's no denying that.

Rain clouds are hanging heavy, they're always drifting by,
They never seem to go away, no matter how hard I try.

You see, my aching heart is crying and daily it has pain,
I'm sunny on the outside, but inside it's pouring rain.

All I ask is you comfort me and ease my heart of pain,
Just one hug and your love, you could dry up all my rain.

Gary Q. Fry

Jody

My son, my beautiful sunbeam, my flower, my tree,
My moonlight, my starlight.
God gave you to me.
I was grateful for that, but I misunderstood,
I'd thought God sent you to have for good.
You were only an angel, sent to brighten my days,
Yet, everyone knows that angels can't stay.
So I know that you are watching and waiting my son,
For me, your mom, to join you when my days are done.
No matter what each day will bring, know one sure fact,
I will always love Jody, and want him back.
O Jody, my Jody I know you are in a place with the best of the best,
While I am here hoping this pain will take a rest.
So until my tasks here are done, and my time is at an end,
I will continue on, knowing someday I will see you again as my son
and my friend.

Linda Allen

The Forever Cycle

It begins. She beckons me to sit by her side.
I fight. I try to resist her melodious voice.
I fail. My intense longing for her overcomes me.
I weaken. I begin to sweat with anticipation.
I yield. I sit down beside her and welcome the torture.
She delays. She teases me, but touches me not.
I moan. She slowly runs her hands down my trembling body.
I burn. The intense heat radiating from our bodies ignites a fire between us.
I scream. The climax of our passion tears at my very soul.
It ends. She has sucked the very essence of my life away.
She discards. She leaves me for the reaper of souls.
She searches. It begins again.

Phillip Fisher

Dance

See, nobody sees what you see.
Experience, nobody's having yours.
And if I feel that I dance alone too,
Aren't we dancing together?

Gustave Karinen

Hoops In The Drive

Sweat dripped off our noses
Falling to the cracked cement.
The rim, the object, stood
far above the competitors.
Enemies; anger in our eyes.
Voracity kept us moving.
A game: emotions high.
Envy filled the air.
A game he loved.
A game I loved.
His hard fists teaching
the agony of defeat.
His curly locks floating
by as he stuffed my face.
Friendship grew from controversy.
Love grew from envy.
A father and son sharing a time,
never forgotten,
locked in the memories of youth.

Jimmy King

A Dream

Nothing comes to sleepers
but a dream
for beyond the sky the source,
of everything seems to
hold within your destiny
in the twinkling of an eye,
your life could change
the sunshine in your
life to tears and joy and pain
God made my dreams come true,
far beyond the sunshine and rain.
Life is full of dreams
and nothing comes
to sleepers but a dream

Rita Johnson

The Battle For Life

The lightning strikes,
With a blink of an eye.
Guns burst,
And bullets fly.

An innocent child,
Surrounded in blood,
Lay in the path,
Of a rivers flood.

Drifting away,
Along the road.
Badguys walk,
As they throw their code,

Not guilty so they claim
But soon they will come to,
Nothing but shame.

For the parents,
The child they miss.
Not able to hold him,
Or give him a kiss.

Amber van der Voort

Untitled

Why don't we fly
towards the white-tipped sky
on the wings of freedom
over all this kingdom
while the soothing wind
finds a place to descend
over calm and tranquil water

Why don't we fly
towards that white-tipped sky
where children cry
and all angels sigh
while lovers lie
over calm and tranquil water

Why don't we fly
on this white-tipped sky
with innocent horizons
vast and endless horizons
over calm and tranquil water

April Jones

The Last Hour

As the clock slowly ticks away,
    the hours, minutes, seconds;
We know that the time is coming
    when you will leave us.
The time has come.
Your breathing gets harder and harder.
As we watch your last breath,
    we know that you have gone.
We then talk to you,
    and comfort you,
And see you taken away
To God in heaven.

Linda Sue Brokken

Here

Here the weeping willow weeps
in silent, aching pain
here the sky around us sweeps
the endless, dying rain

Here the golden wheat's pained scream
closes 'round the mustard plants
here the aspen lays like cream
its anguished breath in choking pants

Here the raging river groans
the roses shriek in sudden dread
here the sun in silence moans
from far away it mourns the dead

Here the weeping willow sleep
a silent, aching tear
I cry still, my pain it keeps
my friend lies silent, here.

Alyssa Erickson

House Of Stone

I live alone in a house of stone.
A house not built by human hands,
Built of the hands of sorrow,
Mortard with tears and wine.
Where gardens of hatred grow
tended by anger.
Where fires of anguish simmer
endlessly.
In this lonely house of stone.

Marguerite Kiehle

Muse

Page behave while I stain thee with ink;
    sun warming thee brings me to think,
does it dare too, in drying these marks of ink?
    To observe your texture forces me to think;
would things go unnoticed had I not used this ink?
    Might the sun in due time come to think;
to burn thee before thou art covered with ink
    Ought to help the sun in its task me think,
    should burn thee myself cause 'twas I whom stained thee with ink.
Then it too would go unnoticed me think,
no one 'cept I would know this stain of ink.

Douglas Irvin Carter

In Love With A Shadow

Every woman has a shadow, of this much I am sure.
But why is it I can never find the woman who is as pure?

Every day I stand my post, in search of that special someone.
But every time I see her shadow, it disappears with the sun.

I think I could love this woman, if ever given a chance.
But every time I see here shadow, I get no more than a glance.

If only I could meet you, and show you how much I care.
And yet you only show your shadow, for yourself you do not dare.

When do I get the chance, to see your shining face?
To see your lips smiles at me, as my heart begins to race?

Why is it so hard to find, this woman that I seek?
Is she hiding in the countryside, or just behind a peak?

Has she taken shelter in a somewhat distant place?
Hiding in a closet, perhaps, so I can't see her face?

This game of hide and seek, is growing old real fast.
But I guess I have no choice if I'm, to find true love at last.

I've been searching high and low, and so far I've had no luck.
I can't imagine what's wrong with me, am I as ugly as that duck?

All I can do is watch and wait, and hope to end this plight.
To slowly watch the sun as it sets, and her shadow disappear into the night.

Howard Rosenbaum

Stop!

The world we live in we think we know,
But we don't.
Some don't know what they're doing,
Others don't care.
Our world is based on greed.
Have we no hearts?!
Yes, I'm talking to you who have no jobs and live off others' money!
Yes, I'm talking to you who abuse and kill over dumb things!
Stop your ways!
Or else it will be too late for you, me, and the world.

Elizabeth Hess

In Your Eyes

In your eyes I see a life of love and happiness,
with caring thoughts and feelings that are easily expressed,
the love I feel cannot compare to any felt before,
I can only say I love you, and this I know for sure.
For the day has come when memories flow, good feelings are safe inside,
The man I married, my Best friend,
My love can't be denied.
You are as precious in my life as the children I have beared,
I pray we stay together and continue in the love we share.
Your love is a gift of confidence
I cherish more each day,
I couldn't live without you and I'd like to take this time to say...
Happy Anniversary in a very special way!

Bobbi Jo Watson

Broken Is My Innocence

With a little bit of time and patience maybe I can shrink to where you are
And though it barely makes sense I want to touch your heart.
You bring me sanity in chaos, a mere token of your name, and
though one day I'll break free, I'll never be the same
Empty when you're near me I am full of who you are,
And though I know you fear me please don't hide behind your bars,
of anxiety, never mind who you are
Don't deny your hunger so close and yet so far
Maybe not today but I will one day touch your soul
Maybe on that day I'll fill this hole
I caught a little bit of sunshine, and I held it here in vain
I thought it might be a sweet surprise but you said it left a stain
On the silence at your doorstep with the peace you still can't find
I'd let go of the moonlight but I can't it's the only kind
There's no place for me here lost in your shadow
Are you free to name your fear or is it one you still don't own
Just a little short of freedom I'm forever in your name
And though one day I'll break free
I will never be the same.

Kevin Squalls

Thinking Thunder

Ryan never has to do his chores, that is while his friends are here.
Making it always in understandable terms,
Sixteen fifth grade little boys, running in and being obnoxious,
Have you ever tried to concentrate, while Shelby and Morgan
are spying on you?

I do my math homework, with blisters on three fingers,
Mom calls me out, another errand to run?
Just hitting the climax of the very best book, someone needed
to empty the dishwasher,
Wasn't this Ryan's chore, about an hour ago?

Playing basketball, concentrating on the rim,
Time out for the other team,
Hey look, Tyler thinks he's Shaq!
Shooting from the other's foul line, another thing I have to do, to
compete with him, this big bully.
Better start working it long, why'd he have to show off?

Throwing rocks, like they were worries, into a barren field,
This is what we do for fun,
Jess and I, when we're alone,
Send your feelings flying,
A kite lost in a rainstorm.

Erin K. Peterson

My Blessed Angel

God must be pleased with the spirit he has created,
For you are his best
Jesus must be proud, for his father is the one who made it
And so you shall be known as, "Blessed"

Your soul must be Angelic, for all the innocence it contains
Your heart must be proud, for what to this world it brings

Your feet shall walk on only the softest of clouds,
For which the Angels proudly lay before each step you take
Your eyes shall look with only the greatest of brightness,
As so shall your smile make
Providing this shall be reflections of only the most beautiful stars
in the sky's nightness

Your touch shall be as precious as a kingdom of diamonds,
Of which you rule with greatness
Your kiss shall be appraised as priceless,
For if ever blessed upon one, they can only repay in slaveness

You shall breathe, forever
Provided only the purest of air for your chest
You shall be known as an; award, reward, trophy, or gift; Never
But only and always known as, "Blessed"

Jason Michael Underwood

Winter's Demise

February kept the world
In wrappings of the drabbest gray,
But March has rolled the corners back
And pulled the cord away.

Snips of color soon will show
Encouraged by the sun's warm smile,
And winter in her dreary dress
Will swiftly go on trial.

Guilty! Will the verdict be
of keeping infant spring at bay;
Then shackled by a gentle rain,
In shame she'll slink away.

Margaret A. Piety

Human

Out of the fires of hell I come,
Wreaking havoc on everything in my path,
I am the epitome of evil,
The incarnate of hell,
But what is this,
It looks like me,
It is,
I descend from the heavens above,
Gliding down on a soft beam of light,
Holy as the son of God,
How can this be?
Am I both? Am I neither?
I am both and neither,
I am human.

Robert Foreman

Veronica & Me

The dishes are sitting in the sink
from dinner yesterday
I'll get around to washing them later
Veronica wants to play

The laundry's in the Hamper
I won't let it get in my way
I'll get around to washing them later
Veronica wants to play

Her little face is dirty
Her clothes are in disarray
I'll get around to washing them later
Gramma wants to play.

Kathy Morrow Stapleton

Why?

I once had a friend who thrived
But he hanged himself and died

He was worried
And his heart hurried

He was made fun of everywhere he went
Yet he was so content

He was mad
And I am sad

But I believe
He didn't leave

He did not die
I'll tell you why

For he lives within my heart
And that's the living part

Kevin McCrary

Times Past

Sitting in the sun
Feet dangling in the mountain stream
Memories of childhood whisper in my ear
I want to go back.

Simple times, simple joys
Family ties that didn't bind
But gentle apron strings to hang on to
Mother's hand to hold.

Secure in my parents' love
Safety in their arms
No worries of what the day would bring
Only to live and play and grow.

Hungry for times past
Regrets for saying so little
To the ones I miss the most
I want to go back.

Barbara J. Cain

The End Of A Family

Here we sit
Just us three,
Husband, son and me.

Look at the coffin
At my uncle within.
My mother's brother dear
Dead in his 94th year.

In comes his younger brother
Feeble and eighty four.
Helped with a walker
He comes through the door.
"Joe-Joe," he softly cries
With tears falling from his eyes.

Where are the bride and groom,
The new born baby with cheeks in bloom.
Celebrations will be no more,
All have passed through death's door.

Here we sit
Just us three,
Husband, son and me.

Barbara Jaworski

Middle Class Dreams Or Suburbia

In a box
surrounded by four sides
white glaring amid
washed sunshine
glimmering off
clear floors, clean lines.
Step through portals
to follow tree-lined paths
still surrounded by the
same four walls.
All trees are the same trees
All walls are the same walls
Staring into the windows
behind me
staring at the sunshine
behind me
clattering, banging through
the clatter and banging
staring at the cherry frame
Framing it all, framing me
Watching you die.

Binh H. Pok

Fever 9-27-96

Each one is a face turned against the wind.
The chilly bite of winter that gnaws deep into your bones bringing
    Few dreams of sugarplums
    More like visions of loneliness.
For every breath exhaled that mists, there is a tear that falls
    Unchecked.
A hug that goes
    Unclutched.
Where the howl of the wind is only your own solitude screaming its
presence in your ears.
The steady beat of the icy rain competes against the stillness of
your heart..
    And all is quiet in the dead of winter
    The silence roars in the dead of winter.

Because, no matter what, nothing embraces harder than
The cold.

Ted K. Joe

alone

wake in the night and speak to the skies my sweet dark raven of infinite night
pieces of souls children of a miserable veil come the day breathe   again
hearts to the empty shell the crimson flame of a child's hell sweet
    hitchhiker on the road less taken
sweet divinity blind denial my child of god.   my god, my child!
endless time of fading dreams burn these crashing smiles
keep the faith buried in there your chest all the while
his hear, now lonely, clots itself to hard black stone
she leaves now dressed as he freshly scars his skin, "all alone."

Donald Francis

Without The Fire

Barreling through time, a train on its course,
appearing invulnerable and unstoppable.
Within its belly a fire kindles its strength,
protecting its speed, and carrying its passengers.
The unimaginable control it takes to guides the pullmans,
coupling them and holding the entire train together.
From within the warmth of the cars,
we know comfort, and safety.
Funny how we look at things,
without the fire we would not move,
without the coupling we would not be together,
and without the comfort we would not be sane.
Thank you train. Without you, I would have never taken a journey,
and would have never arrived where I am today.

David McMillin

Walk Alone

Standing on my two feet
saw all my days

Standing on my two feet
is where I've been, all my life, every day

Days of looking in the mirror
discovering who I was who I must become,
days in love, out of control, enveloped in whole by one
days of walking by myself, figuring out life,
on my two feet;
some days I was knocked down but I always land
on my two feet;
days of miracles; of laughter; of rain; of glory; of tears; of sun;
of reckoning
days where there was no turning back

Standing on my two feet
where I've seen my whole life from
and I know who I am, and where I am,
on my two feet.

Wil Everts

Disturbing Imagery

I wake suddenly
I am staring at you dying
the blood welling from your nose, eyes, and mouth is very becoming
it enhances your natural beauty
I wonder if your blood is soiling my face as well
I think...will I be cold when you are gone
or will I nonchalantly fall back into a restful sleep
the apathy consuming my soul once again
leaving me immune from pain...but also love?
I just stare at you and hope
for a little while...as you stir my emotions
I just stare and hope it will never go away
but, inevitably my eyes get heavy, and apathy overtakes me
and I fall back into sleep

Jason Kantor

Life Flows Out

This place, so many waiting with fear on their faces. So many protest these kind of places.
Helpers working in pink and baby blue. Their job, much like God's is to call upon you.
The waiters in the room were fearful and varied. Some alone, some accompanied,
    some single, some married.
Everyone knew why you were there. We all had the same problem that none of us could bear.
Taken to a room, simple and plain. Three chairs, a table, no pictures or frames.
You are told positively, if you have conceived. Some proceed heartbroken, others relieved.
The heartbroken are then taken to another room to wait, there you undress from your toes
    to your waist.
A cushion table, machine one the floor, with a tube much like a vacuum, where life will soon soar.
My Savior? Then enters the door. He asks again "Are you really sure?"
He then proceeds with an injection, this is your protection.
And life flows out.

Amanda Sica

Consequently

Consequently a shadow draped over my soul and let the darkness inside,
    when you quickly walked away from me too scared to even glance behind.
Too scared of seeing these tears and knowing they're shed for you,
    because you could not comfort me after the pain you put me through.
Consequently a dream has diminished for me and no longer will I know,
    the happiness that you shared with me and so willingly let it go.
Let it go without a reason or an attempt to help me understand,
    why a sudden change of heart lead you far out of reach from my grasping hand.
Consequently another tear will fall and lengthen the river that keeps us apart,
    and the light in my eyes will vanish although the hope will remain in my heart.
Hope that you will somehow find that piece of me that you now hold,
    and realize there is a large piece of you still buried in my soul.
Consequently those fears that you once calmed are slowly beginning to evolve,
    for how can that trust and faith remain when the one who taught me is gone?
Taught me how to break down that wall and soften this heart of stone,
    then left me here to wonder why you just didn't teach me to be alone.
Consequently my spirits have fallen and those magical days are through,
    consequently a chapter has finished for me; consequently because of you.

Erica Bucklew

The Highrise Builders

Look up way up. The man works, walks cross 'bars to build
build for you, build for me.
Look up - has he a family? Do problems lay heavy in his heart
as he crosses from beam to beam? And for this courage.
What be his wage? Is it enough? Could it ever be enough?
He builds for you, for me. Some say high rise builders are of
Indian decent - is this true? Are they a special bread of man,
enabled by some kind of magic? Has luck always walked before him?
Look up - see how small and insignificant he appears to us
here on firm ground? Am I on equal ground with him?
I never could pirouette as graceful here on flat surface as he
does up there twenty stories or higher..
Just one wrong step, on wrong twist of his torso...
Does he ever secretly hope in that direction,
or has God planted his footage firmer than mine?

Sandra Dandona

The Meaningless Message
Of The Birds

The birds send a message;
A message that is unknown,
A message that over the years
Has recently grown.

It is hard to understand
The message that they send,
But if you really listen,
You know it goes throughout the wind.

The birds send a message;
A message that is unknown.

Kia Knowles

Forever

Love of my life
heart and soul
Together we will live
Together we will grow
Supporting each other
day by day
Till the ends of the earth
Together we will stay

Chantel Hutchins

The Life

She was not pretty,
    but she was not ugly.
She was not stoutly,
    but she was not skinny.

She was loving,
    but she was not smothering.
She was misguided,
    but she was not wrong.

If only she had a chance,
    to show herself; without romance.
Sex is okay,
    but not for today.
Disease took her life completely away.

Dorothy Zobitne

Untitled

He looked so young that day.
Standing at the top of the stairs.
With the cold winter sun
Reflecting on a fresh snow...
He really didn't look sick
So sick...as he really was...
He was twenty years old again.
The boy that I married
He was so beautiful!!

Anna Catone McGuirk

A Memory

I see bright, rutted roads
Move into shade through tunneled elms.

I see soft, smoky hills
And sky smudged by a windy wand.

Within this frame
A child unheeding walks
Of future pain
Beyond this sheltered land.

Joyce A. Dangler

Who Am I?

I am the daughter
of my parents,
I am the sister,
of my brothers,
I am the sister
of my sisters
I am the master of
my day.
I am the student of
my teacher
and most of all a
citizen of my country!

Lupe Vasquez

"Freedom"

The sun is brightly shining,
It's been doing that for days,
If only I could step outside,
Into those beautiful rays.

To feel the rain upon my face,
To feel the wind blow through my hair,
To capture all God's creations,
with that beautiful thing called love

To study you with texture,
with insight and for lorn,
with wisdom and sincerity,
Beginning a new chapter once more,

Looking through these iron bars,
at things I cannot touch,
Searching for that inner strength,
upon my release to freedom.

I know it will not be easy,
For temptations are every day
But I know deep within my soul,
God has chosen me so!

Nancy A. McCoy

Weeping Willow

Weeping willow.
Why do you look so sad
does life really treat
you that bad?
Weeping willow,
why do your branches hang
so low,
did someone hit you
with such a devastating blow?
Weeping willow,
Why do you not sing
do you dread so terribly
what life may bring?
Weeping willow,
Why do you slouch so
is there that much
more to life than we know?

Brandy Arwood

Hold Dreams Tight

Life is but a game
Full of mystery
The cards lay on the table
So take a look and see
Your life is what you make it
So dream your destiny

Eric A. Fintel

Lost Love

I look into the depth of your eyes and only coldness is returned to me.

Once there was warmth that comforted my chilled being.

Once I believed that the cold and dark could no longer frighten me.

Now you frighten me.

Once I could feel you breathing beside me.

Now I feel only the loneliness that engulfs my restless mind.

What was once joy has turned to misery.

Once you symbolized security

Now you represent anxiety.

I remember the words of comfort you spoke to me

but they seem to pale with your indifference.

Once your touch brought gladness,

now it is only a vague and weak reminder of past actions.

Once I was totally alive,

now I am encircled in a self-made void.

Belinda Stevens

Pumpkin Girl

Somewhere sometime somehow, love will find a way
As you wish upon a star, the pumpkin girl starts to play

The sandman leaves golden dust, as your eyes begin to fade
Snow White hums a midnight song, Mr. Moon winks and leads the parade

Lambs numbered one to ten, prance and tumble in the sky
Turning into cotton candy, Cinderella dances by

Romeo and Juliet, watch Humpty Dumpty fall
Dr. Seuss pulls a cat from his hat, the Mad Hatter shouts tea for all

A teddy bear, a clown, a rocking horse ride
Mother Goose riddles her nursery rhymes
As you wake and wonder, where you are in flight
Peter Pan whispers dream well and sleep tight

As you fall back to sleep,
The smile on your face
Joyfully reminds you
This must be the place.

Tom Margarucci

Drifting

Thoughts, emotions, mythical magical feelings—always expected,
never appearing...time, near and far, wanders the streets at night,
thinking of you—the heart stopping with every beat—hoping to hear,
glimpse, remember you....questions without answers,
thoughts with no end, passing moments that drift and crawl, the ebb
and flow of a melancholy mind. Dreams, nothing new-all pass by,
never caught, captured—grasping out to hang on never helps....all so
normal, for some at least—despair, longing, the passing of the currents
of air—brushing your face and lifting your hair—a heart's death is not
so never near as each passing beat...stopping, never starting,
holding still, thinking...and remembering you....

Chong Choe

Helpless Hardwoods

Naked hardwoods standing in the yard with fingertips of multitude reaching for the stars.
How hard they try to uproot themselves and leave this place where man has so carelessly
   placed his scars.
Whispering voices fill the cold night air.
"Don't they care? Don't they care? Don't they care?"

Paula O. Cochrane

whisperwell

falling freely from flipped fingers two past profiles drop in vain
two bits ten tumble hand in hand winding down the whisperwell

     he'd only hated hope for haunting
     wanting not demanding more
     screams of silence sounding softly
     never heard nor answered for
     her kiss he missed for bliss he wished
     but left and lonely locked the door
     when words walked over wet he wondered
     when where why she lied ... again
     his heart he'd handed over to her
     crinkled crumpled on the floor
     so scared surrounded thoughts resounding
     falling flatly felt now tore
     demanding hands don't understand
     a love for life like none before
     worried wake from the whiskey waltz
     they finished dancing before they could ... begin

silent incarceration elation stings his soul
bittersweet anticipation not a sound without a ... ... splash

    Scott A. Jacobson

Signs Of Spring

A bird whistles. You prick your finger on a thistle.
Shows a sign of Spring.

Birds fly back from the South. You can't see your breath
  come out of your mouth.
Shows a sign of spring.

Spring flowers grow. Lawn mowers go.
Shows a sign of Spring.

Green leaves start to show on trees. School's almost out - Yippee!
Shows a sign of spring.

Spring is when farmers plant their corn - new animals are born.
Shows a sign of Spring.

Children start to wear their shorts, short-sleeve shirts and
  even skorts.
Shows a sign of Spring.

There is more rain than snow, also less wind that blows.
Shows a sign of Spring.

Spring usually shows in March, April, and May.
That means there probably won't be more snow days.

I hope you use these sentences to see if Spring is on its way,
And I hope you like spring each and every day.

    Kristin Renee Benner

Today I Met Myself As I

Today I practiced being that special person that I am when no one's looking.
I put away my make-up and masks to face head on such beastly tasks.
Respecting the knowledge handed my way with you an open mind in the way.
Today I caught the quickest glimpse of her across a foggy mirror,
I pierced behind a pretty face within to trace her fear.
I saw her true as naked; innocent, caught in the midst of an honest stare.

So free I couldn't look away, and proud of such great straight today.
And this is she whom I can't obsesses, though over time she's given less.
Of her soul, her heart that breaks, while continuously herself she rakes
Over coals of evil blaze, so hypocritically she lays all of what matters on the line.
Reaching others she will let, dawn irresponsibly she'll forget.
Where and how she stands alone, without the need or approving ast,
she is the star and they are last.
Yesterday I practiced being that person that I am when no one's looking.
Perhaps I'll have the nerve again today
  And from myself remember not to stray.

    Sharis Y. Brown

You Said

You said you'd never make me cry
But that was one big lie.

You said everything would be alright
When all we do is fight.

You said you'd never leave
But that was hard to believe.

You said we'd always be together
But you never said forever.

    Jennifer Melious

My Three Cats

My cats are such a constant source
Of love and joy to me.
I can't remember how it was
To be without those three.

I hope it won't be very soon
Before I find that out.
Because they make our Home Sweet Home
Much sweeter, there's no doubt.

    Mary Shevock

Coffee 3

I please her every night
I give it to her strong
I give it to her hot
I make it last real long

She tells me I'm the best
but I admit I have some doubt
'cause she drank someone else's coffee
today when we went out

    Tim Gordon

For Freedom

War is a symbol of courage and hope
And dying for those you love.
War means sacrificing all you have
To obtain the peace of a Dove.

War takes strength to die for others
So others can be free.
War means bloodshed, sadness, and loss
As a proud soldier gives his life for me.

    Sally Vlasak

A Wisp Of Wind

A crumpled piece of paper
Is swept across the street
By a breathless, restless
Wisp of wind that must
Nudge it aside to pass.

That wind, invisible,
Hurries on to nowhere,
A place intangible
As it itself is.

No place is its home
For the wind is nothing;
A fleeting force that flees
Footless a foreign world of form.

Searching, eyeless,
It presses on to find
Non-existence, where it will rest
And, finally cease to be.

    Cathleen Flack

A Spring Day

The laugh of a child...
The heat of the sun...
The bark of a puppy...
The cool of the breeze...
The call of a spouse...
The beauty of the day...
The wholeness of the moment.

Christy Ward

Sun

The warm sun shines on my back
now I feel soothed
like a smile from someone, somewhere
shining down with radiant glory
like a golden bauble
magical its power is upon me
so serene, so confident, so peaceful.

There is one place I would like to be
and that smile,
that golden bauble, takes me there.
It is a place of beauty
all its own
a moment in time
of peace
everlasting.
No one can touch it
or see it
yet I am there
riding on its magical wings.

Tina Marie Cecilia Wernette

Someday

Someday, someway, I'll find the pay,
The rose upon the check.
And in the eye, they'll be no lie,
Just light that cuts the deck;
Of cards I play with every day
In search of the red rose;
That pays me nice, not once or twice,
With blooms to match my prose.
We'll be a pair, my lady fair,
And I the payee proud...
And with demure, the fine payer
And I shall draw a crowd.

David I. Wiles

Roses Like A Spider's Web

The sun shone on
little Emily's eyes, she got
up, went out the door,
to the fresh dewy grass,
she could smell the
lovely smell of roses, she
looked at the pretty bush
of queen flowers, which were
dew dropped as a spider's web.

At night they shimmer in the
starlight like a dime dropping through
the sunlight, glittering and shining as it falls.

Corina Akker

The Activities Of Snow

Beautiful, white snow.
Snow like a large white blanket
Covering the sky.

Jared Coppock

Untitled

It wasn't worth the tears that began at my heart. It wasn't an act of
hatred or anger it was ignorance - blind stupidity - like rats in a
maze they scutter day to day with poisoned minds and tongues -
their ignorance begins at the soul
I do not feel sadness nor anger just pity -
So..., it wasn't worth the tears that began at my heart their pain is
their Achilles heel "what the hell is wrong with you" young black
soldier - your ease has lightened your footfall the struggle that so
many fought for you spit on, you curse at, you face with such hatred,
fear and indifference so, if it wasn't worth the tears that began at
my heart - why do I write what my heart knows as the truth? Why do I
sing the wearied song of justice my young black people-in color and
in heart, what else can I say? I am left here with a countenance of
anger and a question: Of the two, you and I, who is more helpless?
You have everything to rage against yet you rage against your own
You ravish your Queens, yet they too are fallen stars. They dance
with Beelzebub, they entice with ghetto bodies and are raised with
disfigured thoughts. Their trees of knowledge are watered with
deviousness, anger, frustration, neglect, false hopes and false
pride. They read the handbook of Delilah and teach through distorted eyes.

Jodi-Ann Clarke

Dedicated To Oklahoma City Oklahoma

My pen driven to paper, for the faces I'll always remember.
I still feel their pain, but can't remember all their names.
My child in my arms, I sit and watch the devastation of life,
it seems endless, hour by hour, and day by day, in shock from the horror.
I close my eyes, and think of the courage and strength needed.
And those loved ones only have their memories now.
To the photo album they go, to see the lost parent, spouse, child or
grandparent, albums placed against their hearts, to hear the laughter
cries and remember their touch.
And in all this sorrow, we all wonder what would happen tomorrow.
The question still to be answered why here, why so many killed.
From my heart in Montana, they will never be forgotten.

Denise D. Messer

Winter Wonderland

Cold winter breezes, crisp sparkling air, my heart freezes over,
because you're not in there. I try to stay warm, with heated
thoughts of you, but I still get too cold, because I know we're
through. Why do I still hold on to something that's not there?
Why do I just hurt myself knowing you don't care? I take the pain
quietly, and dwell on hopeless illusions. I keep trying to fix
things up, but come up with empty solutions. It's getting way too
cold in here, like endless drifts of snow, I'm never giving up on
you, I want to let you know. If we were truly meant to be, I'll
hold on till the end. If I have to wait ten years from now, so be
it, the warmth will mean more then. I know you don't mean to hurt
me, I know that you don't try. But most of the time I end up sad
and even start to cry. I don't want to be just cozy warm, I don't
want sweet lust as our plot. I want the love and passion between us to be burning hot.

Alicia Pedroza

Measures of a Broken Heart

At one time I thought, I thought of the sky of purity of and love.
Now all I see when I look at the sky is a mass of matter above
He stole my heart and I've seemed to have allowed him to.
I wait in the dark for a prince charming of a guy so new.

My heart will truly remain torn and broken.
I let my words of anger be bottled up and left unspoken.
I've nothing left in emotions, but anger and frustration.
I've also got great lack of concentration.

Seems to be my prince charming, Mr. Right entered my life
He saved me in a time of trouble from a blade and a knife.
For a year or so he's been a very good friend of best.
I've come to realize he's always willing to compete with the rest.

Princess Sowers

The Abuser

I love my wife even after she left my life to pursue a career far away from here.

I need her more than she would ever know. I need her more than I would ever show.

I wish you could understand that I am a man with hopes and dreams or at least it seems.

I know I am not right to always want to fight over trivial things,
that may not be all they seem. So I have just decided, not to get so excited
and push you, punch you or kick you too all until your body is blue.
I was scared as hell the day you fell and prayed I would never hurt you.

I read in the bible that a man is still liable for his action even if it is not to his satisfaction.
So I believe in my own way that I love you and want to stay.
So pray with me that we both could be free from all the hurt and pain that God would shame.

A wise man once said that his heart had bled of tears and fears
of being alone waiting for the day his wife would come home;
and now that you have been gone for so long my heart yearn to learn the art of love
and how we fit together like hand in glove.

Otis Rodgers

Sometimes It Looks Like Growing Pains

In the seventies, there were Nixon, Ford and Carter.
In the eighties, there was mostly Reagan, and there was Bush, too.
In the nineties, there was Bush, but mostly, there came Clinton.

In the seventies, there was M*A*S*H.
In the eighties, there was Saint Elsewhere.
In the nineties, there came ER.
In the seventies, there was Happy Days.
In the eighties, there were Fame and de Grassi Jr. High.
In the nineties, there came 90210.
In the seventies there were All in the Family and One Day at a Time.
In the eighties, there were Cosby Show and Family Ties.
In the nineties, there came Home Improvement and Full House.
In the seventies, there was the Mary Tyler Moore Show.
In the eighties, there were few comparable shows.
(But, there came the first female supreme court justice.)
In the nineties, there came Murphy Brown.
In the seventies, there was Good Times.
In the eighties, there was Dynasty and Fantasy Island.
In the nineties, so far, there came but a flash of Hoop Dreams.

Ching-Cheh Hung

Reflections

Your fists beat against me like the pounding of the falling rain.
This child left so victimized, through torrents of abuse and pain.
Father must you do this to me; daddy won't you stop?
Mother, please won't you do something; mommy call the cops.
Bless this child, bless this son.
Save him from what is to come.
Wrap him in a warm embrace, take him in your hands.
Hold him until he learns to trust, until he understands
Contortions of rage, spread across your once smiling face.
In fear I hide inside of myself, drifting off into deep space.
Father, what are you doing; daddy, can't you see?
Mother, what is going on; mommy, please save me.
Beaten, battered, bruised and scared; this child you love so much,
runs and hides.
Within his cage of fear and steel bars....
your son slowly whithers and dies.

Nikolas Paul Robinson

I'll Fly Away

I'll fly away to the Northern sea and estimate how many fish there will be.
I'll fly away to outer space and see if there are any aliens in trace.
I'll fly away off to Spain and to the clouds to make it rain.
I'll fly away to my uncle's grave and tell him a story about a cave.
I'll fly away to see many things like horse back riders and diamond rings.
I'll fly away almost anywhere but I have to know how cause I'm just a teddy bear.

Alexis Wheat

Love

Love, what is love
It is an emotional fountain
Spilling over our lives
Yet gathering gems and stones
Finally building a mountain.

Love, what is love
It is undying and unfaltering faith
Believing in the frail human spirit
Collecting rivers of passion
Which ultimately deliver our fate.

Elizabeth Corbin

Yet

He reaches out to me,
Yet I can only pull away.
He tries to save me,
But I sink still farther down.

He wants my love,
Yet I can only hate.
He loves my smile,
But I only frown.

He wishes I would give,
Yet I can only take.
He wants me to bless Him,
But I only curse His name.

He gives me a chance,
Yet I don't accept.
He offers me a gift,
But I reject it.

Julianne L. Wotasik

Understanding

I still love you in my heart
I hate you in my mind
I'd like to believe you're up to date
In truth you're far behind
I'd like to say I love you
But I cannot tell a lie
And I'd like to stay forever
But I do not want to die

Robyn Skaggs

Reminded

I'm reminded of love,
the inspiration and grace
I long for your touch,
for the loving embrace.

The loveliest of hearts
erupt with your touch,
A charming smile
is more than enough.

I'm reminded of love
and all of its fears
But love is so strong
it drowns out my tears.

Thomas F. Gerber

To Sporty

I scream aloud
    no one hearing
I cry for help
    no one knowing
    ...so alone
I scream aloud

Sarah Meyers

Belly Button

I got a button,
but it's not from a shirt.
I got a button,
but it's not from a skirt.

I got a button,
it's a part of me.
It's the button in the middle
of my tummy.

It's my belly button,
and it's underneath my sweater.
It's my belly button,
and it's holding me together.

One, two,
did you know that no zipper would do.
No snap or safety pin,
and the belly button poem is at an end

Matt Williams

Roses

Roses are red
Roses are white

They grow bigger
With the morning light

Dew from the rain
Dew from the night

Gives the rose
Great power and might

Thorns on the stem
Thorns on the vine

They make the rose
Even more divine

The petals so soft
The petals so fair

You touch them softly
Handle them with care

Jessie Foreback

In Cream Colored Cups

I sat and had coffee with you
dark coffee in cream colored cups
but I wasn't drinking in the coffee only
I think it was your eyes
I could swear they were dancing
and oh they were so green
I noticed that sitting there
the little things like that I notice,
otherwise I wouldn't know who
you were or why you were there
Really all I cared was
that you were drinking coffee
from the same cup
I drank from yesterday

Claire Carothers

Untitled

When a battle arose...
I fell when it died
And just look at my condition...
If you would, please
at the wounds, the scars to be
take a look at the girl who fell...
the girl, that brave soldier was me

Latoria Green

Not A Gap

Children of today, are often faulted for their rivalry against the
old and young, because of violent words that easily slide from their
tongues. They were once babies. Who were their guides? Was it TV,
rock Music, or rap? Someone didn't tap into their positive potential
but allowed crime to explode their little minds.

We want to blame the children for their arrogant ways, but we as parents should have
nurtured, loved, disciplined them, lead the way. So sad..... We fault our own mistakes.
Some say, "Let the school raise them, but the system didn't have them,
yet you prefer a teacher to do your job. Raise twenty-four little
angels. It sure would be nice to change your mistakes, like putting
icing on the cake. A finished product all ready to go but a main
ingredient is missing.... It's called home. The place where values
and morals are kept. You say a generation gap... I call it a hole.

Brenda McCommons

Those Enduring Young Charms

At times it is a drink offered to you on graduation day,
a loaded 9 mm to do their dirty work and no way out save broken glass,
 mayhem and a garbage chute into a rain-soaked back alley...
at other times it is a glimmering moment with the greatest love ever known...
or a bubble gum wrapper... Or on the wide screen
she kisses me and I do not remember eight, nine years ago when her kiss was more..
I want it back so badly I can taste springtime and cherry blossoms in twilight memories...
it all goes so right and a few drinks later I'm numb.. I forget
one afternoon in the sun... A beautiful home with a fireplace,
 hardwood floors and your kiss returns out of the haze of life's mundanity...
It is warm... It is soft... New
As we sit and eat ravioli by candlelight I remember the rifle in the medicine cabinet.
My latest job, in a lifetime of smash-bang-shoot-em-up romance novels
 is a song of nonsense reminding me still of how perfectly dead right it feels after all these years

Tino DeRivera

Life That Never Ends

Sitting in the darkness, except for the glow. The setting of
sunshine, the moon almost shown, my pain now unknown.
A darkness, so deep the pain made me weak, can it be night?
The loss of all light? This darkness unknown and the pain not shown,
Soon will be clear, then comes the fear.

The screams and the cries, the look of surprise.
With pain so deep, how could he disguise the pain filled tears
That flowed from his eyes.
Oh Lord! My God! Why take him so young?
With no place to turn, our hearts are now left to yearn.
Now can you see? The darkness, the glow,
The last breath of life has taken its toll, a feeling forever untold.

The guns that end life, the boys who play tough.
They took him from us, on this dark early night.
He is known as the one in our hearts whose name brings us pain
That will never cease to be.

The night has now shown me that the darkness is death.
The glow is hope that we'll see in the end, our now departed friend,
In the place where sin is forgotten, and love is life,
Life that will never end..

Jennifer Padilla

A Proposal For Forever

I was going to write a poem for this moment,
but paper and ink will not last as long as my love for you.
I was going to compose a song for this moment,
but there is no instrument that has the perfect melody to capture your heart.
I was going to paint a picture for this moment,
but there's not enough colors that can grasp the beauty you possess.
I was going to do all these things,
but there is only one simple question I can ask
to keep the love, the music and beauty in my life forever,
Will You Marry Me?

Damian Cerrati

Wishful Thinking

I drive down the highway, I slow down to take my exit, but a feeling
makes me glance across the highway and there I see the woman in my
dreams, she has medium length brown hair, pinned up in a barrette,
her coat off, wearing a white sweater.
Though my heart beats fast I feel relieved knowing that the woman in
my dreams is also in reality. She's there when I'm asleep, I see her,
she's beautiful, sweet sincere, her voice is comforting, then she's
gone. I wake in a panic, running through my house searching for her
but she's not there, and then there's a pain, but also happiness too.
So I make a wish that one day she will be in my arms forever, so I
wait patiently wishing for that day, though I may never see her again,
she will always be in my dreams and in my heart.
For I've known someone like her before, but I let her go, my mistake
for not fighting hard enough for her, so my wishful thinking would to
be with for eternity and not just in my dreams.

Ralph Bosch

Reminiscence On Migration

It was the best and worst of times back in forty-seven.
Let's see, I must have been, oh, 'round ten or eleven
When candy sold for a penny and a loaf of bread was a nickel.
The little girls rated second to my shiny Schwinn bicycle.

What I remember most, as the general rule,
Were the little Mom and Pop stores between my house and school
Where kids crowded the counters making their preferences known.
Jaw breakers were my favorite and would last all day long.

How did we get along without microwaves and TV?
Your mom was home when you got there after school, at three.
Ice was delivered in solid fifteen an fifty pound blocks
Which the iceman muscled into your compartmentalized icebox.

A double feature was a quarter, ten cents for the Saturday matinee.
Back then, the hero never kissed the girl but always saved the day.
With "The Big War" over, the economy had become depressed.
So my folks loaded up the old clunker and we all headed West

To California or Bust. That was our motto and destination.
It must have been the right thing for us
'Cause there's just no other explanation
As to why we never left.

Harvey L. Johnson

Is There A Baby For Me?

Each and every morning when I awake,
Tears fill my eyes as though they were a lake,
I hold my head up high, and I look toward the heavenly sky,
I ask The Lord, "Is There A Baby For Me?", But The Lord must be busy,
For The Lord does not answer at all, Can't The Lord hear my call?
Each and every night,
In my heart I feel The Lord as he holds me tight,
And so I pray, Asking The Lord to give me a baby some day!
Is There A Baby For Me? And If So, For When Will It Be?

Shawna L. Pfeifer

Dead Man's Bones

She walked the earth living in vain.
Insane, the shame that her sins have brought to her name.
A light came down and shined on the darkness in her heart,
the pieces that mislead her mind and gave it apart
of understanding.
As she walked to the church of the town ready to receive the Word
that she heard through the light, that had opened her eyes to the
surprise that there is another way. As she reached the inside trying
to prays the Lord, there was more eyes on her than the bible. As she
confessed her testimony, each word not phony but oh, so real. The
church's people started to turn, turning their backs leaving her alone.
People this is how you would treat a dead man's bones.

LaBridgette Norals

Blackhole

A lone shed tear
falls from my eye
I am hurt
it seems everything was going right
now everything is twisted around
I don't understand
Another tear
Slowly gently it caresses my face
leaving a trail
I feel as if I am falling
deeper and deeper
into a black hole
No understanding
No light
No grounding
Just me
my feelings
and hope
another tear

Jenny Matson

Nightlife

smoke from the barrels
rusted and standing in snow
streams toward sunrise

and if as they say
what I've heard is true
that smoke follows evil
at least the alleys are dark still

of the snake's tongue noiselessly
dancing the flames more liquid
more erratic are not themselves grimy

no breakfast no coffee
few cigarettes among them
the men crowding about talk quiets

dead bottles and styrofoam
establish their pathways
though the lighter sky
weakens the communion of all nature

another day
rubbing their hands
shifting their weight

John Alan Gray

"I Am The One"

I am the one
who can start anew,
and correct all wrongs.
I am the one
to take away
the fears in your eyes.
I am the one
that can harvest
riches for all.
I am the one
to follow behind you
and correct the mess.
I am the one
to shine pureness
into your soul.
I am the one
who truly believes
in you.
I am the one
who can save you all.

Jared Manning

The Angles Among Us

The sun is not as golden...
   as the light in Maia's hair.

Nor the Georgia sky...
   next to her eyes, as blue.

And at a glance, you would declare...
   that she has wings to help her fly.

Like her grandmother in heaven...
   as angels often do.

Her innocence and purity...
   a living testimony.

That angels walk among us...
   everyday.

They grace our lives...
   and unconditionally love us.

And make us wish, such as children...
   they could stay.

Mary K. Landers

Who Is God

I always wonder about God
Is He real or is He fake
Is He visible
When I die and go to heaven
Will He notice me
Will I be able to see Him
These are questions
I always wonder about
Genesis 1:1 says
God created Heaven and Earth
If this is true then who created God
It's not that I don't believe in God
Because I do
I'm just a curious kid
Who has a lot of questions

Amy Dorfe

It Hurts So Bad

When you look into my face
and think that I am a
disgrace it hurts so bad

When you call me out of my
name and say that girl
ought to be ashamed it hurts so bad

When I walk down a isle
and everyone start to grin
or smile it hurts so bad

If you walk in my shoes
there are no golden rules

That's why it hurts so bad

Sundra Jefferson

Untitled

Between mountain mists
Golden carpeted paths exist
In twilight's sunshine.
God's moment speaks to the eyes
Of crystal cobweb's prismatic beauty
Mixed in with laughter
As well as sweet sighs.

Ian K. DeNeeve

Only You

Running through the days
Passing through a never ending maze
No doubt you are still in my mind
I just can't seem to unwind
I've got myself in another bind this time

In the sublime light
I'm really trying like hell and holy water to not put up a glimpse
    of a fight over you
You, I never really knew
Yet somehow, I just don't know what I'm going through
I have powerful feelings for you

Massive dreams drift in and out of sleep
Will I be yours to keep?
Or, are you going to make me weep?
I will let you decide if I shall take a long forgotten leap away
    from you
Or, may I be the one to lunge forward, seeping to the inside of you?

Forget me not, I can show you what I've got
If I can listen and learn, it is for you I yearn
Inside my heart, it burns, as the world slowly begins to turn

Andrea Mueller

What Must I Do

  What must I do? What must I do?
You put me on this earth Dear Father to serve you.
  So, please tell me Lord, what must I do?

  "You placed within my heart a strong desire to reach the lost
world for you. So, please tell me Lord, what must I do? The race
is long, but time is short. Your word explains it all. You stood
for us. You paid the price. You made the ultimate sacrifice. The
least I can do while I am here is to take a stand for you.

  I hear you Lord, and I will do as you say. The answer is so
simple. Trust in you and obey, and you will provide the way. I
should not rely on me, but on you, and you will guide me as to what
I must do. Stand strong, be courageous and spread the news that
you are all that matters when our time on earth is through. Our
mansion awaits in glory. Our father said it's true. His children
will live with him forever and ever, never be blue.

  So, while there's still time, let's not delay. The Lord promised
he would show the way. I know he loves me, and I know he
loves you. Together let's be obedient to what our Father says his children must do."

Kathy Jenkins Ballard

Beyond Success

It is all to the glory of God, the supreme architect of the universe.
We have the Holy Bible.
We have the Lord's Prayer.
We have churches and temples of worship for all races and creeds.
We have America the Beautiful.
We have the Declaration of Independence.
We have the constitution of the United States of America.
We have the Pledged of Allegiance to the Flag of the United States of America.
We have family—It is life's most worthy purpose.
We have Medicare, a substantial health care plan for all senior citizens.

We have Social Security, a self-contributed insurance plan for seniors
  to retire with some dignity financially.

We have life, liberty and the pursuit of happiness.
We have "The Power of Positive Thinking" by Dr. Norman Vincent Peale.
We have "God Loves You," by Billy Graham, world-wide crusader
  for the son of God, Jesus Christ.

We have the "Hour of Prayer" televised worldwide by Dr. Robert Schuller.
We have television news media with choices in all fields of endeavor
We have beyond success — love is everything.

Howard B. Kittleson 32°

A Cowboy's Legacy

His cattle are a' heavin' from the trip that they've got planned.
Coverin' every inch of the still forbidden land.
Fear is not an option, but a choice left unchose.
He's every bit a cowboy from his head down to his toes.
His hat is stained and colored from the weather he's been through.
His clothes and body figure are only just a clue.
His legs are used to ridin' his eyes are used to dust.
His fingers are a calloused and his gun is colored rust.
His rope is worn and tired a reliever of his stress.
A way to work on how he feels when his heads a mess.
He doesn't care 'bout what's in style or how his saddle looks.
He ain't the kind of cowboy you read about in books.
He rides rough out in the range any weather he is game.
He's got a reputation; and a cowboy is his name.

Jenna Francis

To My Mommy

Excuse me ma'am, may I talk to you?
Been meaning to for quite some time.
I've practiced over and over what I've wanted to say
Memorized every line.

But now that we're alone and face to face,
I've forgotten all the words but these.
So from the bottom of my heart to the tips of my tongue, I say;

"I love you, I respect you! You're my hero, I believe what you say.
I want to be just like you. I'll try to follow only you,
so, you lead the way."

I should have told you this long ago. I don't know why I didn't then.
I guess it's so hard for me to express the way I feel.
Maybe I'll never amount to much, at least that's what some say.
It doesn't bother me because when I look at you,
I know everything will be O.K.

Have I spoken out of turn? Have I taken too much time?
I know I've got so much to learn, and you've got so much on your mind.

So you reply, "I love you, I respect you, too. I'm proud to be your hero.
I believe what you say, and I will always be there for you.
If you follow, I'll lead your way!"

Tiffany Sanders

Untitled

I've got a good job and I make decent pay.
I've got a beautiful wife to come home to each day.
My children are special, my time with them grand,
But I long to see Jesus and that heavenly strand.

I've traveled the world wide, I've seen its great sights,
I've beheld its glitter and shiny bright lights
I've tasted its dainties, and pleasures so fine,
But I long for the mansion Jesus said would be mine.

What a pleasure on Sundays, God's people to greet
To be in that fellowship, oh what a treat.
The message is uplifting, the music so sweet,
But I long just to sit at my dear Savior's feet.

What I'm trying to say, is though my feet are on earth
My mind's fixed on Heaven, for it has a far greater worth.
And when Jesus comes back to catch His bride away,
I want to be ready for that most blessed day.

Dear friends are you ready? It could be today.
It takes faith in Jesus, there's just no other way.
So where the Bible says: The dead and the living caught up into the air
And so shall we ever be with the Lord, you'll be there.

Samuel L. Saalwaechter

Untitled

Fleeting
bits of thought
whirl ahead tears just
beyond an elusive
realization heart
pounding
wind blows leaves
fragments of me
I cannot contain
skip and dive
please wait

Terri Steiger

Balance

Simple
    but complex.
Truth
    yet lies pervade.
Day
    with night ever closer.
Life
    though death creeps in.
Light
    yet darkness threatens.
Purity
    as sin is ever present.

Amanda Kundert

Small Joys

Small joys—
No matter your age,
No matter your disabilities,
They can be yours.
Be patient, look for them.
Be quiet, listen for them.
Be aware, experience them.
They calm your soul,
Lift your spirits,
Stir your imagination,
Make you smile.
And they need cost only the desire
to find them.

Carol Paton McNitt

Our Mountain

Mist hovers over the Mountain
like a luminous cloud of light.
Enveloping us in love.
Our love molding our family.
Still growing...still new.

The Mountain stands behind us.
A monument to our commitment,
bringing us together,
bonding us to the earth we now share.

Our Mountain...
A testament to our love for each other.
A love for our children and for our earth.

We will let time be our friend
and with God as our supreme guide,
we will continue on this path.
Our lives blending into one.
All on Our Mountain.
Each of us.....together.

Jan Judia

A Father's Plight

Please don't cry father
Don't shed a tear
Mother has cancer
But death is not near
Our Father gives life
To those who believe
If we open our hearts
His blessing we will receive
So father have faith
To you this I give
For you and my mother
With God's Love shall live

Troy Jordahl

Our Home

Our home's so special to me
It's where I've lived so long.
No matter where I travel,
There's just no place like home.

It's here we've faced life's problems
And solved each one quite well.
We've nursed each other's illness
More times than I can tell.

We've known tears and sadness, also
But they've been easier to bear
Because "home is where the heart is"
And I'm consoled just being here.

Its rooms have known our laughter.
There has been so much joy.
Love resounds from every rafter
Of our home, I so enjoy.

If I live to be a hundred,
My fervent wish will be
To bask in all the memories
That these walls will hold for me.

Alma M. Heron

The River Of Life

Life is like a river flowing,
never let its current bring you down.
Keep fighting and kicking,
or surely you will drown.
Keep dodging the raging tides,
Venture fourth with courage,
Wherever it drifts or hides.
Use your family and friends,
to keep you afloat.
Their love for you,
is like a sturdy boat.
This vessel that love passionately gave,
will protect you from the deadly waves.
No matter what happens keep rowing,
And fight life's river flowing.

Paul D. Daugherty

Represents

The rain represents the tears,
    that fall over the years.
The rumbling thunder represents,
    the mistakes and blunders.
The clouds represent the confusions
    in our life.
But, the sunshine represents the
    warmth of our Hearts.
And, the breezes represents the
    purity of a kind person's thoughts.

Sheree Hess

Through An Eye

I watch the walls of my escape slip away. A whole new world is
    entered, where I walk on solid ground,
the sun sits on the horizon,
    waiting for the earth to become quiet, her rays still ripping
    through the clouds that blanket the earth.
The deep blue sky darkens and soon
    lit by the shy light of the moon.
    The earth is not asleep.
You can hear her soul sing with the wind, dance with the trees, cry
    anger through a distant thunder. She is smarter than any
    Einstein, greater than any super hero.
Her wonder is forever held in every sunset, every rainbow, every growth of life.
I journey an untraveled path that soon becomes my destiny.
    Accompanying me are the sun's soulful rays, the friendly
    trees, the heartful sky and the haunting shadows:
        hiding and disguising.
A wolf crouches from afar, in preparations to kill. A deep look
    through his eyes shows me the beauty he holds,
    as he steps back, still looking directly into me,
    I see his soul shine through, and I begin to understand it.

Aspen Jensen

Waterfalls

Listen to the rushing water as it goes over the falls,
How soothing is the sound of the water as it rushes on its way
Makes you wonder where it comes from and where it will finally pause,
Our lives are like this I say
Rushing along life's stream our hearts flow,
It's like the wonderful love you give to me dear.
Only to wonder where it will finally go,
Your love makes the stream of life flow so clear
Tranquil and peaceful are the rewards of knowing you love me
The rush of water brings back memories as I watch it flow
of a September in my mind you see
of two people watching and we felt our love grow,
So listen do you hear what I say,
Watching the water flow over the waterfalls
How we fell deeply in love sitting on the rocks that wonderful day,
Watching the water rushing - rushing on its way

Arthur R. Musselman Jr.

Christmas Memories

My most memorable Christmas would have to be the Christmas of 1973.

Snowflakes were falling silently down
on the rooftops that night in the small, German Town.

Cologne was aglow in the cold, frosty air
where Christkindlemart booths were set up in the square.

Bratwurst were cooking in kettles of steam
and the waffles were covered in berries and cream.

Gingerbread cookies with raisins and spice
filled the air with a scent that was pleasing and nice!

Mugs of hot gluhwein were warming the soul
of every traveler out for a stroll.

Oompah bands everywhere started to play,
As toy soldiers stood up and marched fast on their way.

Carolers singing so sweet and so clear
were filling each heart with good feelings of cheer!

When the church bells rang out in the night air so still,
they were heard in the castle up high on the hill.

They were ringing, I knew, to let everyone know
it was time to go home; time to trudge through the snow.

The market was closed, but the memories were mine, of the fairy tale
village that sits on the Rhine.

Lynn Pocock

Unrested Soul

Many of us today battle through life,
not realizing the primary strife.

A dream is what ignites the fire,
in which one's life will begin to aspire.
Without the warm feelings of excitement and eagerness,
the heart will slowly sink into a deep bitterness.
It takes courage and strength to go to the length,
to follow your own ambitions, and make the right decisions.

Procrastination is one strong for, that could harm the inner soul.
Easy it may be, to delay vital goals and destinations,
but by doing so, can bring undesired frustrations.
Conquering our problems soon, will us away from certain doom.

Fear prevents us from moving forward, instead it drives us backward.
At first it can be difficult to a great degree,
to gather the confidence necessary to succeed.
But boldness, time and practice will overcome,
over most any obstacles that are sure to come.

If the mind is open and ready to receive,
the opportunities of achieving great triumphs will not recede.
Though it may seem threatening to express your ambitions
it can impel wonderful evolutions.

Frank John Pribus

My Church

A church is just a building, with its mortar, brick and paints
But it becomes God's house, when you worship with the saints.
It may have stained glass windows, pews with cushioned seats,
A choir with beautiful voices, and an organ makes it complete,
But without the love of God and the special feeling within your soul,
Some people just don't understand what it takes to make them whole.
I like to go to my church, with my Bible in my hand,
Greet my fellow Christians, and for Jesus make my stand.
You can feel the love and warmth and see smiles upon each face,
Then you feel the Holy Spirit and His presence in this place.
We sing the songs of praise, we bow our heads to pray,
And ask the Lord's forgiveness, and come into our hearts today.
Then the preacher gives invitation while the music is softly played,
And you step out in the aisle and you're thankful that you prayed.
You take the pastor's hand and say, "I've been down the Roman Road,
and I can feel the precious Savior has relieved me of my load."
You want to shout it from the housetop, tell this feeling you have
inside, because you know without a doubt Jesus now abides.
I invite you to come worship and enjoy this love and grace
For this little church of mine is such a happy place.

Joyce Bridges

Send Me

Your sweet and sensitive ways keep me going every day.
When I see you in the crowd, to me you stand bold and beautiful.
Sometimes, I relate myself to a place because the way you send me.
I will be orbiting like nothing has ever orbited before.
You send my emotions to the highest respect for love because when
I look at you, you're like a Dove. Your soft and gentle eyes tell
me no lies but, if I had it my way, I would never turn to that
high way. If I had a wish I would take you on a balloon ride just
to show you how close to heaven you send me. My emotions are nonstop when you are
here and near but, believe me, if God brought
us together, I would Love and forever. If I could send you
somewhere it would be right in my arms and I know I could keep
you warm and safe because I will always cherish your face! That
smile of yours sends me in a moment in time, where every thing
stops inside. It is so radiant, so stunning, so damn appealing. I
would send you directions in how to win my heart, but you already
won it from the very start. If I could have your love for one day. I
would start by placing my lips upon yours, and give you a good
idea of where I will send you! What are you waiting for?
Come And Send Me.

Veronica A. Carroll

Grandma's Flower Garden

Grandma has a garden
It's as pretty as can be
Outside my kitchen window
For everyone to see

Each morning when I wake up
I cannot wait to see
This most beautiful of gardens
That my children made for me

It's the colors of the rainbow
Yellow, pink and purple too
And in the early morning hours
It sparkles bright with dew

So in reading these few lines of verse
You can very plainly see
All the joy and the happiness
You all have brought to me

I love you all my darlings
In a very special way
For all the joy and happiness
You've brought to me each day

Carol Lund

True Beauty

A maiden blind
Saw with her mind
Beauty no Artist could paint

Each scented Rose
She knew and chose
Coloring without restraint

With sightless eyes
Saw through disguise
Discovering Truth behind

If you would see
Beauty as she
Use then the eyes of your mind.

Mona Irene Friday

End of Winter

Icicles are dripping
fading away,
like a leaky faucet,
that can't be repaired.

Fields of grass
renew themselves,
after being trapped
under layers of snow.

Winter's spirit vanishes
with the arrival of spring.
Fields of green emerge,
as a new season begins.

Robert Xiao

clarity

I was touched by my savior
   kissed really
gently as we passed on the sidewalk
like a breeze across my lips
   a whisper of salvation
   that froze me in clarity
   of time and space
   and my own significance
   as my fever calmed
   and my cigarette fell
   into the street

Gretchen Kuks

Our Nation's Loss

As we cross the Potomac River,
Fields of white crosses we can see.
Unto God who is the Giver,
These souls we commit to Thee.

A great man has just been slain,
Because of someone's inward hate.
Atop a grassy knoll he's lain,
A flame is burning in his state.

Thirty days of mourning were declared,
Sorrow for all citizens who cared.
This evil deed can be compared,
With Lincoln's death our nation shared.

The difference between life and death,
Is but to draw our one last breath.

Linda Kiesel

Hope's Power

Time steals our dreams,
and Age, it schemes
to weight our hearts and hands,
and Self won't give
us sense to live —
all gone before it's planned.

But Power sublime
that swallows Time,
that bends Age 'til it falls,
belongs to He
Who sets Self free —
Whose plan is to give all.

David L. Holly

Untitled

Look into my soul,
A pit that's very deep.
All you'll see's a hole
And a youthful mindless creep.
Like the night and day,
It comes and goes.
One day I'll pay and you all will know
The way I feel on this worthless planet.
I'll whine and squeal
Like a dying rabbit.
The pain you all see
Is all because of me.
Accept my apology and set me free.
Free from life, free from hell.
You'll see me dine in the place I dwell.
I ask you this and nothing more,
Let me die,
For I am sore.

Evan Andrew Uzialko

Moon Prints

The pitter-patter of my feet
are only heard by my footprints
I walk in big bounds
feeling the soft powder
surrounding my bare toes.
Everything is silent
except the thoughts in my head.
I look up and see the earth
in the center of the stars.
I awake, my eyes glance
at my feet, and
wonder if they'll ever touch
the moon again.

Megan Stone

Adam

My name is Adam.
I have blond hair and hazel-blue eyes.
I'm 5'7" and kinda thin.
I look in the mirror and see a young face.

I love my family because they care and worry about me.
I hate being in situations where I don't really fit in.
I run to increase my stamina.
I sometimes think that nobody listens to me.

I hate social studies because it's hard for me to understand.
I love physics and history because they teach me a great deal about life.
I think school is cool but a little long.
I think I would drop out if school were a drag.

I've been playing billiards and darts since I could stand.
I have an unknown talent.
I love my billiard Que.
I am a true winner at darts.

I am Adam.
I am sixteen years old.
I am afraid of being nothing in life.
I look in the mirror and see a man.

Adam Nielsen

The Wannabe Cowboy And His Dream

The old man sat on the well worn saddle, and, gazed at the summer sky
He watched the clouds as they changed shape, and dreamed of days gone by

His first thoughts were of the days he played cowboys and Indians all day long
He told his mother he was going to be a cowboy, ride a horse, and sing a cowboy song

It was some years later while he was just a lad
He remembered his first horse, a broom stick, it was all that he had.

His father left when he was twenty, leaving them to fend for themselves
He cranked up his pinto, saying "I'm going to be a cowboy, and wrestle the cows and calves."

At thirty and still a wannabe cowboy, he married a Wyoming widow
Vowing to reach his goal, soon as possible, as soon as he found out how

They spent twenty years raising a family, at fifty his wife passed on
Her will left him the ranch, the sheep, and the saddle he sat upon.

As his sixties came and passed, he still held on to his life long dream
Still a wannabe cowboy, sitting on the old saddle tied to a barn yard beam.

His story was not one of failure, of this gains he only could guess,
Then when at the age of seventy, he finally found success.

He was no longer a wannabe cowboy, for had fulfilled a life-long dream,
He then climbed down from the tall black horse, and put the saddle back on the old barn-yard beam.

Carl A. McCollough

You Are

Even when I hide behind tattered black lashes, I see You.
Even when the world's voice is screaming, I hear You.
When I'm drowning in a sea of sin, You are grace.
When a weary sigh struggles from my heart, You are strength.

Even when I stand alone in the depths, You are there.
Even when the masses turn and taunt me, You are there.
When the sick, scarred earth infects me, You are pure.
When the heavy, treacherous storm threatens, You are peace.

Even when the tears carry their burden down, You are joy.
Even when mistakes trickle from my fingertips, You are perfect.
When I am trembling in uncertainty, You are sure.
When my soul cries for affection, You are love.

In a poisoning, crippling pain, You are healing.
In a cage of oppression, You are freedom.
Even in the falling leaves, scattered stars, hectic schedule, wrong choices,
hurtful comments, wandering spirit, proud desires of my life....
You are God!

Elisabeth John

The Glory Of Sunday Blue

There was
    And there always will be, deep inside my soul...

One honey-sweet, sunny Sunday when the sky was so blue:
so heart-shakingly, achingly blue
that all the August clouds there ever were unfurled their pristine majesty

Across its azure space...
Snowy white spires cresting cumulus castles
They paraded - promenaded- in elegant perfection.

Oh! It was so blazingly, amazingly Blue:
that all the birds of the world, in their feathery, fluttery entirety
shot suddenly into the air...
One breathless swoop of untouchable ecstasy!

Only the sun itself, this glorious, golden day,
Shattered and scattered into the ocean:
one-billion, no, ten-trillion scintillating, shivering, glittering,
shimmering stars all strewn-out, sown-about, in the wandering waves
of the sapphire sea.
    Sarah Burk

Fortress Of Love

A typical Wisconsin winter day:
    Windy, cold, (windchills at least eighty below!) with lots of
stinging wet, blowing snow. I must take my youngest to the bus
stop (again) a dull, time-consuming chore. We trudge through the
ever-deepening white stuff, (it's blowing in my face!) all I want to
do is get this over with, to get in to a warmer, dryer place!
Then the call, "Mom, come play!" and before I can yell, "No!"
I find myself down on both knees, digging feverishly in the
new-fallen snow. Soft cheeks are flushed brightly, (slightly
myopic) eyes sparkle merrily. Tinted hair (painstakingly curled)
lies limp and flat, under the dreaded old stocking cap. But there's
a perfectly sweet smile (on usually pursed lips) as her dripping
pug nose gets swiped with painted fingertips.
"Thanks, Mom! See you later!" The little angel waves, then with a
discordant roar; the little yellow bus bumps cheerily down the road.
I wave, blow kisses, watch her safely off on her way.
Grateful for precious memories such moments often hold.
I'll always remember; (pulling off wet sodden gloves),
when two carefree little girls, (on a gloriously, sparkling, pristine
winter day!) together, built a (magical) snowy fortress of love.
    Marita A. List

Someone I Need

Someone I need but I don't know who it is, someone with gentle
love enough to raise my kids. One person that's all it can be, someone
to love that's all I really need. Moments in time to show her my
affection, someone smart enough to lead me in the right direction.
Eternal love to show her through out the night, someone special
enough to teach me wrong from right. Over exaggerated love can be
seen through the simplest of eyes, but love for you is the kind
that never dies. Now I know what it feels like to be so alone,
I feel dead inside knowing that you are not my own. Explain to me
why I took this lonely road, not knowing where it would take me
and why it would leave me so alone. I can take no more pain, and bear
no more shame, why does it hurt so bad every time we play this game.
Now I know I've been wrong and haven't treated you right or sometimes
even fair, but you know there isn't anything I wouldn't do to show
you how much I care. Exact words can be said by no true love,
ever since I meet you I knew you were sent from heaven, up above.
Even though you and I have our ups and downs, you know we can always
depend on each other to be around. Deep in concern of what should be
the right course, in romantic segregation our love from deep inside
our soul's is not love's strongest source.
    John Paul Valdez

Tragedy

The airplane took off
The skittered across the airway
Like a clumsy skater.

It flew up into the dark night.
But, suddenly it blew
Like fire-crackers, crackling
Boom! Boom! Boom!

Metal screeching, people screaming
And praying not to die.
But the fall continued,
Splash! Splash! Splash!

In the dark water of flushing bay
Metals and blood, bodies and fuel
Are mixed together.
People's path are blocked.

Dear God,
Shed some light into their path to you!
    Frederic Auguste

God's Eyes

God's eyes run to and fro
Searching throughout the earth.
I know this for a fact!
He sees the ways of men,
Their each and every act.
There is no dark place, no shadow
Where evil doers can hide,
And nothing in all creation
Can be hidden from his sight.

Creator of all that I see,
It's a wonder to conceive
That the eyes that saw my unformed body
Deep within my mother's womb
Can't see my wicked ways
And sentence me to doom.
Instead, the blood of Jesus
Has made me pure and clean
And in your eyes I stand — pristine.
    Linda Thomas Smith

Simple Words

When I see you, I smile,
    you seem to make my spirit soar.
It's nice when we're together,
    you're my friend, I'm yours.

Stay with me awhile,
    I want to have you near.
There's something I should tell you,
    Lean close so you can hear.

The words are very simple,
    their meaning close to heart.
Yet they're the hardest words to speak,
    I'm not sure where to start.

I'll start at the beginning
    the words I speak are true.
The feelings I have forever are
    I love you.
    Traci R. Erickson

Empty Pockets

The laundry will pile
It's only I who cleans it
But I have no cents.
    Julie A. Davis

Conforming. . .

Why such rejection of difference
When everyone knows it's so;
Ignoring the simplest fact
That identity never will go.

Agreement is too often sought
By forcing opinions in line,
Crushing distinctions underfoot
For unity all-divine.

Sex and age are resistant
And some other bastions hold,
But much is succumbing to sameness
A deceptive, sterile, false gold.

Differences need not prevail
But deserve their day in court,
To leaven bland uniformity
With yeast of a personal sort.

B. B. Watkins

Together

Together we are.
Together we work.
Together we walk.

We go through hell
Binding together holding hands
To gather our strength.

The flame is high.
The fire is burning hot
But our sweat and our tears
Ease our way marching together.

We will reach and conquer
your heart insatiable lady.
We have in our hands,
As offerings, our true thoughts.

Michele Duplan

The Rose Garden

A day, a new day,
A lone glean of light show
upon an opening rosebud
which just found new straight
in the sun as it embraces.
That on single beam of light.
    The might, the never ending night,
    The rosebud yields to its
    ending might, tilting, twisting
    and finally falling in anyone,
    weeping rose, petals until
    it is no more.
The next morning rose petals
were all that was left, of
That dead rose garden, on that
lot in the city, long since
abundance on a lone, summer night.

Eric Zeni

My Garden

I have a garden,
and how does it grow?

With seeds and water,
Loving care,
all my time I have to spare,
It grows with sun,
And I have fun,
sitting and watching it grow.

Katie Root

Widow Maker Road

Why the grader put that turn in me, I'll never know,
Why the grader put me on this ledge, is a mystery as well.
Death enjoys that corner
And there he sits each night.
Death had called for the rain
But dismissed it at dusk
To keep himself dry.
A '57 Chevy and a very familiar Thunderbird dashed across my back.
I only wished that Death would take the damn T-bird,
But pray as I might, that T-bird stayed every night.
That Chevy had power,
More than the Ford will ever know
But that Ford had Death and knowledge on its side
Both of which to the Chevy were denied.
Widow Maker Road I am called
And Death stalks my back.
A drunken fool has been his friend
but this time a kid slipped in.

Alan Lampe

Who

Taking time when none exists. Pushing through the barriers.
Crashing down the carefully built illusion of all
Reason.
With hands in pockets, shuffling through the ashes, feeding them to
the wind. Seeing precious jewels surface in the rubble, sighing,
Kicking
All the harder. Seeing everything around you, though blindness
nestles in your eyes. Understanding without
Knowing.
Clutching desperately to the phantom chaos seething from your soul.
Thinking everything about nothing. Feeling
Nothing
About everything. Hearing foolish laughter and joining in against
your will. Being drawn toward the frozen expanse of the
Heart.
Keeping still when motion flutters in your chest, waiting 'til the
tide of darkness washes away your dreams. Smiling as you realize
Who
You
Are...

Rebekah Gipe

Reality

I want you to paint, you want me to write. Encouragement for me,
what gives you the right? We all need that factor, who is kidding
whom. We don't need any favors, sincerely who is for whom?
The next time you feel the need, look in the mirror and pay some heed.
Look at yourself, before you look at me.
I am I, you are you.
Who's to say who is living in a zoo.
Do they look after you when there is a need?
You'd do what I do, in yourself there is a deed.
Come close now, the end may be near.
You know me, always trying to relieve the fear.
I have to believe, or all is lost.
I'll never give in, whatever the cost.
There is a fire that eternally burns.
You can't put it out, for always it yearns. There is a way.
Why is there still doubt? No one hears me, why do I shout?
People it's so easy! What is the fear?
If you're afraid, why stand so near?
I can't breathe, who has the air?
The joke's on me, intention, your care? Will this happen to me
in this intellectual world? Feel, Feeling, Feelings. Exist, Think,
Feel, Think, Exist. If it's not enough you'll know, just like me.
The heart never lies. For real.
For those that are brave enough. I've expressed myself.
Adult, with compassion. Yet ever strong,
Reality.

Bridget R. Wheadon

Sailing On Lake Superior

The ship left the dock in Eloise with a light North breeze.
Sailors waving from the stern, relatives awaiting their return.
Some of the sailors from Cleveland couldn't wait for that hour to see the terminal tower.
As the fog lifted on Lake Superior in the morning, the sky was red —
  Sailors Warning.
One ship blown off-course unable to take a bearing, the wind and waves so strong,
  it was rough steering.
The blowing gale interrupted their sail.
Down bound for the locks in Sault Ste. Marie, the American side where some of the sailors reside.
They made it to an island near the Canadian Soo
And dropped the hook and laid in anchor not far from another tanker.
And what a sigh of relief, now they have cover there they will recover.
That lake has taken its toll on men and ships in the month
  of November, like the Fitzgerald, Remember!!

   John D. Brassar

A Phone Call To Mom

Mom, it seems like I have called you a thousand times during the day, late at night.
I have called whenever I have needed someone to understand me and to care about my feelings.
You have listened to my worries and have taken the time to tell me how much I am loved.

Mom, I have cried on your shoulder, and I have cried through the phone,
knowing you could ease the pain. I have made more mistakes than I thought I would,
but through it all you were always the one who helped me find the strength within myself
  to carry on.

Mom, I am sorry I never got that last phone call made to tell you how much
  I love you.
  Forgive me.
  But now all I have to do is call
  1-800-HEAVEN to talk to you.
  Never a busy signal.
  Call you later Mom,
   Love you.

   B. J. Sands

Nowhere

Nowhere beats a heart so kindly
As one born to love you.
Nowhere is a mind so free
But one made to understand you.

Before living, knowing how to live,
Hating nothing...
Denying nothing...
Knowing all...

Bearing in our hearts,
The most treasured of all truths and lies...
Dying with a truth, living with a lie.
A heart, always there with you, understanding, helping you through...

Nowhere is a love so profound
As that from a heart shared with yours.

   Arianna Price

God's Great Church

As I sit here smiling, from the brow of God's great church
I see stones laid out like tiling 'cross a nave that's made of earth..
And the transept is more lovely, than one ever wrought by man
Yet God used but gentle breathing and the closing of His hand...

Not the sweat and blood and heaving that a man must but endure.
To build a place of worship that can never be so pure.
The same Hand that made the sea that makes you tremble with its power
Also painted the bright colors that adorn each tiny flower.

Man's work is a pale reflection of the wonders God has wrought.
Yet man still feels his worth is measured by the items he has bought..
God must shake His head with sorrow that we've missed His point like this,
For it is not in what we get - but what we give that makes us His.

   K. Michiel Cavuoti

Mon Nez

In my face
and in your
business,

Grow when I
lie,
blush when I
cry,

Softer when
smelling you,

Redder when
telling you
tickled

Against your cheek when
our faces meet in
taste

And in smell
as we come
to the well

To offer each other water,
sil vous plait.

   Jon Webb

Frozen Moments

Frozen moments beckon me;
A blink, a smile, a new shed tear,
where laughter lasts forever
and roses never fade.
Where waterfalls will always fall
and birds will always fly.
A place where grass is green
and people never die.

Frozen moments beckon me
when a poignant plea is heard.
The second before a hero's birth;
The minute the sun goes down.
Where boats are always sailing
across the deep gray sea
and chance has just discovered
how great the future will be.

   Brandie Tarvin

Lost In Time

Camouflage solid ball
Whispering sounds out of town
standing lean and tall...
sounds of thunder coming down
Sense of touch, not to near.

Creeping crawlers...all around
Neon lights, blinding sights.
Lost in time, within the sounds.
Sparkling sphere...out of sight!

Love ones full of fear
That will tell,
in sands of black...
for sweet smell
in land that lacks.

To the end...one long climb
Clear to all, no sense of fear
Love for one...will mold in time
Sense of touch...oh, so near!

   Eddie A. Barrios

Ode To Spring

The birds are birdin',
and the bees are beesin'.
The flowers are flowerin',
and the trees are treesin'.
With flouncin' skirts
and glances teasin',
Girls, the young men's
Fancies pleasin'.
Spring has sprung,
And that's the reason.
Gone are coughs
And colds and sneezin'.
Hail to the end
of the freezin' season!

Richard H. Bennie

Lovers Pose

Early morning dew,
fog bank lifting,
I look for you,
my mind drifting.

Tenderly caressed,
gentler kisses still,
feelings not repressed,
the newness, the thrill.

Wanting you near me,
until time stands,
I ask love of thee,
as we join hands.

Forbidden love,
to many taboo,
on wings of dove,
love waits for you.

Together we share,
ignoring those
who cannot bear,
Our love pose.

Robert H. Patterson

Water

Water
Smooth, quick
Flowing, rushing, leaping
Fluid flowing quickly smoothly
Liquid

Alden S. Jurling

Untitled

The blue moon of my morning
Will come back as the tide.
I am filled with longing
While they are safe inside.

Will the girl in the glass house
Fling her bloody stones?
I'm searching for forgiveness
She's searching for a home.

I paint my emotions on my face,
Looking for someone to make me whole.
You hold your heart in your hands,
Because no one will carry your soul.

When I searched for meaning,
I stumbled over a bum.
When I thought it was the end,
I remembered the taste of a bitter plum.

Jennifer Barnhardt

My Wish

When I was a little baby and you'd hold me to your breast,
You'd feed me, change my diaper, then you'd lay me down to rest.
I didn't know about Mother's love; that God had placed me in your hand.
I was a little baby and I could not understand.

When I began to toddle I would climb up in a chair.
I'd put my sticky fingers on everything up there.
You'd come along and set me down and clean my messy hands.
"Now stay down here, you'll get hurt. Don't climb up there again."

When I would do what I should not, I got my bottom tanned.
"Little girl, you're going to mind me. Now do you understand?"
"Yes Ma'am" I'd say through tear-filled eyes - repentant as could be.
Just why you had to be so strict, I simply could not see.

In my teenage years I thought that I could do just what I pleased.
I had no idea of the time you spent on bended knees.
And when I married my sweetheart you meddled not one bit.
You took my spouse as your own son and loved him - that was it!

Well, now I am a mother and a grandmother - if you please.
And now I understand the time you spent on bended knees.
If God would grant me just one wish, you know what I would do?
I'd wish that He would make of me a mother just like you.

Geraldine B. Jones

Silent Birth: What Angel Might Say

Don't cry for me, I'm a dewdrop on the first flower of the season.
I'm the brisk wind that gently passes across your face.
I'm the last light you see before dark and the first at dawn.
I'm a ray of light that filters through the trees.
I'm a moonbeam that brightens even your darkest hour. I'm yours forever and always.
Everything you wanted in a daughter, never a disappointment, for in your heart and mind,
I can be, I am.

I know your love. I rested in the warmest place on earth, inside you.
I felt strong hands sweep across my body and knew a father's love.
I was conceived to bring you completeness.
In death, let me bring unshakable faith in the Father above, where I now reside.

I am loved in Heaven. I have a family united in love on all sides of my being.

Don't cry for me. Rejoice! For I've made it to a place everyone wants to be someday.

I'm Angel. I'll watch over you always and forever, till we meet again.

Deborah A. Harberd-Benon

To The Bride And Groom: A Poem To Celebrate Your Wedding Day

Today we celebrate the big day in a happy couple's life.
It's the bonding of you two as husband and wife.

The groom stands at the altar with anticipation and pride.
As we eagerly await the arrival of his beautiful bride.

After the music is played and all have walked down the aisle...
We watch you recite vows and exchange rings with a smile.

There's no reason to be nervous on this day of pure bliss.
You've been pronounced husband and wife—now enjoy that first kiss!!!

You're now a pair, a duo, a match, two of a kind and a team.
Seeing such a perfect couple gives us "singles" reason to dream.

Let me make my feelings about this extravaganza perfectly clear.
I feel like I've attended the Royal Wedding of the year!!!

A bride and groom are so busy—you can't stay long in one place...
Do you prefer eating your cake or having it smeared on your face?

Thanks for a day filled with the joys of food, drink, and dance.
Everyone there was thrilled to help celebrate your romance.

May your wedding day be just the first of many happy times.
As you may have guessed by now I'm finally running out of rhymes!!!

It was such a pleasure for me to hear your first wedding bell.
Congratulations and best wishes from the poet Michelle!!!

Michelle Beth Weinstock

Rocks —— Ann

My name is Rocks-Ann and I'm the Queen of the street. Just check it out nothing's got me beat.
 I'm the hottest thing that ever hit the land. I can take your woman, or I can steal your man.
One try of me is all you need. You see nothing else can beat my speed.
 Once I reach out and touch your brain. You will give your life to try me again.
I will make you lie, cheat and steal. To have me again you will even kill.
 Once you have me baby, nothing else matters in life. Not even your husband, children or wife!
Some call me Coke, Rock or Crack, but just call me once, and you will call me back.
 No matter how big, how strong or tall, I'm still the Queen, I can handle them all.
I'll take your money, your house and your clothes and have you sucking air through a rubber hose.
 You don't come too rich, or too smart. I can steal your mind, soul and heart.
Sometimes you will puke and scream with pain, then run right out and try me again.
 Free of me you can never be. I'm a lifetime lover and this you will see.
Now when I have taken everything you've had and you're feeling down and oh so sad,
 Just stop and think of all the misery and strife.
Then my darling, I Will Take Your Life!!!!!

 Annie Singleton

Dancing

Dancing is really tough,
It always makes me huff and puff.

I have to practice night and day,
To do that certain wavy sway.

I'm always hurrying to get my homework done
'Cause I'm always, always on the run,

When I hear a jammin' song
I get right up and dance along.

At practice when the teacher says "do more"
I know in the morning I'll be sore.

Mom says "practice hard, 'cause practice makes perfect" but,
Sometimes I think it's not worth it.

So boyfriend if you think you're buff
And your sports are really tough,

If you think, all I'm doing is prancing, well I have two words for you!!!

 Try Dancing!!!!!
 Brandi Taylor

My Little Butterfly

At times I see her as a butterfly with wings so tiny and light.
At times I see her as a lioness, stately and strong with fight.
At times I see her as a lovely lily, delicate and pure and bright.
And other times she's a kitten, cuddly and soft and quiet.

When I sit and gaze at her, to see those pretty eyes,
To wonder at the awe in them that shows her many delights,
She tolerates the tales she fears and I comfort her muted cries.
She loves and cries with her little heart as life continues to make her wise.

I pray she'll let herself be free to live as she would want,
To find a life that's sweet and good, the one she's always sought,
To be that little butterfly the one who's always fought,
To achieve best among many and learn what she's been taught.

 TerryAnn Sheeran

Imprint

My hand will hold yours in infancy to know that you are there.
My hand will hold yours as a toddler to walk me here and there.
My hand will hold yours as a child to keep me close to you.
My hand will hold yours as an adolescent even if I don't want to.
My hand will hold yours in adulthood in a different way then the rest.
For my hand will hold yours adulthood out of love, pride and respect.
So here is an imprint of my hands in their youth, so that when I am older and on my way,
You remember it was you who led me through life each step of the way.

 Lenora Starr Jerrell

Eyes, Like Windows Unto The Soul

Eyes are like
Windows unto the soul.
To look in,
Is to forever behold,
The hopes and dreams
Of all mankind.
But to not look in,
Is to forever be blind.
Blind to the truth,
Blind to the whole.
Blind to the link
That binds body and soul.
Blind to the heart,
That entwines them all.
All of which can be seen,
Through the eyes,
Like windows unto the soul.

 Jarrod Lesko Goodman

My Father

My father, Peter Onyeulo
Oh, my father, Peter Onyeulo
Would to God
Death had stayed his cold hands
For your sojourning lad
To kneel by your death bed
As your last breath
You gasped
Oh death!
Me you cheated
My father, Peter Onyeulo
Oh, my father, Peter Onyeulo
You will I mourn
To my grave mound
Oh my father!
My father! Peter Onyeulo

 C. Ihekoronye Onyeulo

Just Thinking

I just think when
I am lonely...
I just think when
I am bored...
I just think when
I am mad...
I just think when
I am sad...
I just think when
I am tired...
I just think when
I am obliged...
I just think when
I am anxious...
I just think when
I am scared...
I just think when
I am quivering...
I just think when
I am lonely.

 Tailene Newkirk

Surprise

The other day
I found an envelope...
...small, simple, nice,
and when I open it up,
..."inside" written in blue,
..."I Love You".

 Carlos Americo Chinchilla

Son Of Man

Son of Man,
i have no choice;
Denial as my base.

Some secrets always
Will be mine;

Lies upon my face.

How many times have i forgotten
When i thought i never would;

Something in me lives for filming,
Something in me lusts for food.

Day by day i do the things
i know defy my task.

My i be proud,
And see some joy
Is all i ever ask.

Bryce E. Farbstein

September Song

The Summer days are over
Fall scents are in the air
The leaves are turning color
And falling everywhere
You find you're raking everyday
From Saturday through Friday
To try and keep the leaves in tow
And make your yard look tidy
But when you rise each morning
The leaves are ankle deep
And so you grab your trusty rake
Do leaves multiply while we sleep?
You rake — then put the rake away
By the Shovel and the Hoe
It's almost like a signal
'cause the Wind begins to blow
And soon you'd never know it
That you even raked at all
So you sigh and grab the Rake again
Guess that's why they call it - FALL!

Phyllis A. Green

My Wish

Flying high
above the sky.

I wish I could
be with them.

Their wings fluttering beautifully
and the sun shining down on them.

Their wings so fragile
I wish I could hold them in my hand.

So cute and sweet looking.
I wish they were all mine.

Not to be greedy
but I still love them all.

Every time I see one I want to
hold it in my hand and never let go.

If I could fly you know
where I would be.

I would be flying high above the sky
with all the butterflies!

Elyse Quinlan

Daddy

He's very kind-hearted, but would never shed a tear,
and with his body made of steel, he shall never fear.
With each day that passes, his birthday's moving near,
he cannot wait but will soon regret for the news that he will hear.
I told him "Happy Birthday;" not a word did he say.
He didn't even smile; he just slowly walked away.
I looked over at my mother to find her drowning in her tears.
I have never seen my mom like this in all my 15 years.
He opened every present and said he loved them all,
then he got up from his chair and walked quickly down the hall.
We sat there in silence until he came back in the room;
He said, "Your mother and I have something to tell you,
We found out this afternoon.
Today I went to the doctor to find out what was wrong,
They said they overlooked something...I have cancer of the lung."
Turning around....
He didn't want us to see him cry.
Six months later he told us he loved us
And then he said, "Good-bye".....

Jennifer Hart

Fall

Inherited from Summer's late retreat, Fall subtly dons her early autumnal garb.
Faded hues at first precede her inexorable transformation.
The redolence of Summer disappears as balmy breezes rustle iridescent leaves.
A sudden magic occurs, a chameleon-like metamorphosis, a fiery transfiguration.

Explosive sparks, leaves, incendiary bundles snatched by winds,
Erupt like lava, cascading to the ground in crisp, arid, desiccated sheaves.
From September to November, attired in her harlequin finery,
Fall, weary of her rainbow coalition, stands bare; the winds disperse the leaves.

The penultimate month augurs Fall's final days,
As cooler, harsher breezes billow her burnished gown.
Motionless she stands in pallid autumnal splendor,
Unhappy, yet resigned to relinquishing her crown.

Released from confines, the four seasons' bejeweled and glittering diadem,
Fall's flowing titian tresses trail and billow behind her furrowed, knowing brow.
Her left hand hangs distractedly by her side, the other and pressed against her breast.
She begrudgingly accepts the inevitable. Time has fled; her season is gone; it is now.

Raymond J. Howard

How Are Things In Monte Carlo?

The last time that I saw you was on the beach of Monte Carlo,
when we said good-bye that day, in Monte Carlo so far, far away.
Through all the pain and all the sorrow there's only one thing left to say...
How are things in Monte Carlo since you said good-bye that day.

As I travel this lonely highway to my home far, far away
I remember Monte Carlo and my dreams that died that day
and I remember Monte Carlo while the tears fall from my eye,
I remember Monte Carlo where we last said good-bye.

How are things in Monte Carlo? Have you found somebody new?
For my love for you was precious and my heart forever true
there will come a time when there's no tomorrow
what's come and gone was yesterday
there will be no time for sorrow and only one thing left to say...

How are things in Monte Carlo since you said good-bye that day
Monaco was such a pleasure I'll never again feel that way
your eyes glistened like the sand that reflects against the shore
my love for you I'll treasure and I'll always love you more.

I remember Monte Carlo where we last said good-bye
I'll never forget Monte Carlo as the tears fall from my eye.
How are things in Monte Carlo? How are things in Monte Carlo?
How are things....

Anthony H. Wallace

92

Can I master Uranium? I've come so far, lasted so long, seeing that
I've so much more to see. But now I have found it.
I colonized my thoughts, procreated my ideas, and they
unearthed the last element, the final test.
The power I control can destroy me,
can scatter my pieces across the waste of the scattered branches -
    the broken twigs - of my past.
I can forge a mighty sword of this metal; and, yes, this is war.
And yes, yes, yes, I feel it in me, the urge to fight.
Then can try, the tiny soldiers in my head, to overtake me.
But my mighty blade can fell them all.

Ninety-two. Such an average number; it hardly seems like the end.
But it could be.
I have it here, in these pages, in pages like them, in my heart.
The element is here, and it is the only one that matters,
for if I master it there is so much open to me without
self-opposition. If I do not
then there is nothing more to say, and I can burn all these books:
    they are for nothing, they mean nothing.
        Deren Dohoda

Life

Right now I am invisible, for my term has just begun,
I cannot wait until my time will finally come.

Now I am bigger and the month is two,
and mommy I can't wait to be with you.

I am just a tad bit bigger and the month is three,
I am so glad I have a mother who cares for me.

I am so happy I can finally see my hands, oh by the way
the month just turned four,
but it seems my mommy doesn't want me anymore.

I am so sad and the month is now almost five,
but because of my mom I am going to be no longer alive.

My mother aborted me when the month was soon to be six,
I just couldn't believe it as the doctors hit me with those sticks.

I wonder what the month would have been like at seven,
but because of my mom's abortion I am up here in heaven.

The month could have now been eight I would be almost there,
but all I want to now is why my mommy didn't care.

I would have just been born for the month would have been nine,
but I guess my mommy didn't want me she just didn't have the time.
        Erin Calder

Is It Too Late?

Dark clouds permeating our nation; we have raped your creation!
Shall we put our needs on ration? Is it too late Lord?

Our leaders ask us to pray this day in May! You've been watching
at our gate! We confess, we grabbed Satan's bait! We've become
crooks; we must rip out those hooks!

Hearts full of greed, obsessing after our own need!
Golden chains around our necks; perks which became Satan's's ploy to make us wrecks!

Hearts full of pride; ready to take a quick ride, following Satan's devious stride!
Death of your precious babies you grieve and moan. This sin we own!
In their honor sing a funeral dirge. Teach us lessons we must learn, bring on the purge!
Whatever it takes, wake us up; before it is too late!

Sinners, daily pray, not just today! Be aware of His personal care;
after all, he hung and died on that tree for you and me!

Lord, is it too late?
        Marilyn J. Carlson

Sound Tears

The wild creatures surround;
Those who are not careful,
will not be found.

Darkness must come;
Those who fear the night,
will lose their sight.

Death is truth;
When the phobic are ill,
The truth will kill.

Green is evil;
Those who devour it,
Will soon be red.

Obsessment is fear;
Those who posses,
Will no longer be here.

Fear is common;
Is fear of Hell,
Or of heaven most common?
        Molly Coon

Defining Choice

Ourselves defined in choice
Each moment's decisions, crystallized
        Consciously   Deliberated
        Unconsciously   Surrendered
        Subconsciously   Preordained

Life's woven tapestry created
        from threads of choice.
Pattern formed of events
        linking past and future.

With a collapsed star's gravity
        in but a single choice made.
Infinite paths converge
        all futures focused.

To follow a path avoiding choice
        surrenders all choice.
To follow a path embracing choice
        creates a future of opportunity.
        John H. Nickel

Innocence

The beauty can never be lost,
When seen through untrained eyes.
The new wants to be learned,
The old never forgotten.
Unravel more...Search...Find
Every thought, whisper, and movement,
Aches for more.
        Melissa Holland

Oh, What A Day!

Oh, what a day! I went to
the store...And guess
what I had to pay. Money!
My husband will kill me.
And all because I spent,
MONEY. I'll sit here until
I die. Or maybe I'll start
to cry. So girls don't
spend over 1,000 dollars.
Or your husbands will
have you on collars.
        Martha Estela Morales

The Next Chapter

Going into battle
With head held high
Never guessing at the outcome
As the world flashes by.

Time is too short
To harbor the wrath.
The opponent fights with bitterness
Not foreseeing the crash.

Attacking wildly and blind
Like a cat with all claws
It's still not any different -
And just what is the cause?

Is the opponent so unhappy
To show nothing but rage?
Don't you know that's it's simply
Time to just turn the page?

Karen K. Fader

My Home

Before I go to bed at night;
I'm sure to kneel and pray.
I ask the Lord to keep me safe;
And thank Him for a blessed day.
Then my mother tucks me in;
and kisses me good night.
I thank the Lord for my family and home:
as I clutch my teddy bear tight.
I'm not afraid, I am not scared:
Because I'm not alone.
I have the Lord, I have my folks;
Of course I'm Home Sweet Home!

Victoria Rosser

Waiting For My Ride To Come

Sitting on this wooden bench
Staring out the window
Watching the birds as they hop
From one tree to the next
Waiting for my ride to come.

The rain beats down
And taps on the window
The awning above falls down
And it rains on my head
Waiting for my ride to come.

The sun comes out, finally
The world is once again clean and fresh
The earth has taken a sip
From the heavenly water pitcher
Waiting for my ride to come.

I see its approach in the distance
Like a tiny speck on a map
Slowly but surely it comes to me
Like the light at daybreak
My ride is finally here.

Yasmin R. Moorgan

The Brook

Take a look in the brook;
In this stream waits a dream;
Watching for waves to spread its theme.

The sunbeams make the liquid shine;
The wind makes the water whine.

What a special place to be,
By this brook, just you and me.

Bonnie Smith

The Nature Of Your Beauty

Droplets of morning rain grace your petals
a gentle reminder of nature's beauty
your petals, full in bloom
at a time when most flowers go within themselves
waiting for the sun of the spring
but you are different
in the middle of winter, you are in full color
vibrant pink with a brush of white, leaves a beautiful green
a compliment one to the other...
as I look at your beauty
I cannot help but think of how you came into my life...
this morning after the rain
I sleep but am awoken by a presence
the presence of love
and within his hand is you
and from his lips..."the words..."I love you"...
I kiss your precious petals, tasting the sweetness of the rain
smelling the beauty of your aroma
you are a reminder of love...true love...
that is captured in your beauty and will live in my heart forever...

Heather Simon

The Surfer's Psalm

Lord, thank You for the sun and the dance You gave the earth,
that it should spin and roll and turn toward light
out from the darkened night, and thank You for its glow
that stirs the morning air, establishes the wind
and sashays the sea giving rhythm to the waves,
which sing a soothing chorus as they roll upon the shore.

And, thank You, Lord, for the energy of their essence
that sail a man upon their crest, then curl inward
and erupt into a frothy lace of white, salty foam,
embracing the heart of man as they bring him back
to a resting place on the beach.

And to the minds and souls of men, Dear Lord,
send us unceasing spiritual waves of love and grace
that we may be guided out of this momentary sea
into the radiantly crystal realm of Your eternal paradise.
There every spiritual relation will unfold glorious revelations
of all those mysteries that sent such as I into the earthly unknown hoping to find and
touch Your face.

John L. Chorich

Creatures Of God - Sheena And Tonya

She's black and white, short and bow-legged;
    big brown eyes and very hard-headed.

She's honey-blonde, chubby and short with an appetite as big as a horse.

They are my two little creatures created by God -
    and you can't help but to love them because they both have warm hearts.

They'll hug you and they'll kiss you.
They'll make you laugh and they'll make you cry.
But don't get them angry because they'll bite you then hide.

My Sheena is smart and almost quite human -
    always acting like a sensitive woman.
She'll look at you once with her big, round, brown eyes...
    and you can't help it but to hold her real tight
        so as to comfort her with all of your might.

My Tonya is chubby and active at times
    quite mischievous she is when she gets out of line.
She'll lay around all over the house...
    like a little cub bear or a lazy gray mouse.

They know that they're loved no matter what they do...
    because they're treated very special the way God wants us to.

Felicita Rosado-Arlotta

Gristle

A young woman ripples slowly on a Sunday evening
churning with her fingers
churning words.
She wants the gristle of each sound
but on muggy nights like this the words hang
like the water hangs in the air
like her own soul soaks in her skin.

A raccoon came to visit
and she seeks to stand in open doorways
and so they quaintly gaze.

Does a full moon slip fear to the deep buttresses of a black-ringed tail?
Does a full moon lace her distance with the same lipstick?

Maybe he came to share prehensile thumbs with her.
She wants him to tap the wind
between them before naked hand slips open.

A young woman ripples slowly on a Sunday evening.
Ripples with the gristle of drenching humidity
ripples and churns with the zipper trains
and butterscotch street lamps.

Tonight she'll let the wind hiss.

Jennifer Gosar

The Narrow Path

His mother sees her little boy who led his friends in play,
And father sees his strong-willed son, but things are not the same.
As fast as they could blink their eyes, the world had changed its pace,
And somewhere in this busy life their young boy masked his face.

No longer definite in stride, he walks the path alone.
The leadership he used to take, he seems to have outgrown.
It's hard for him to do what's right when he knows they will laugh.
He sets his heart on blending in and walks the wider path.

For if he holds his head up high, they're sure to knock him down.
He hides his tears behind a smile, quite careful not to frown.
Perhaps the emptiness he feels will slowly go away,
As long as he pretends that he agrees with what they say.

They say the wider path will help to quench a life that's dry,
But somewhere deep inside his soul he knows that it's a lie.
I pray his heart will overtake his insecure facade,
And he will walk the narrow path which leads back home to God.

Desiree Wheeler

I'll Be There For You

Friends come and friends go
Then some stay the same
When I think of all the friends I've had
My mind always brings up your name

No matter what I do wrong
No matter what happens in my life
You've always been there for me
Saying "everything will be alright"

We have been friends for a long time
And sometimes I haven't been there for you
But no matter what happens in our future
Your friendship I'll always hold true

Just call me when you need me, I promise I'll be there
I'll listen, I'll help, I'll comfort you, never ever forget that I care

So when you're alone or just feeling blue
And you need someone just to talk to

Don't be ashamed or nervous to call
I am your friend, nothing can go wrong

Friends stick together just like glue
All you need to remember is I'll be there for you

Romonda Dee Parker

A Man's Curse (The Rock)

A man, chains on his legs,
connected to a rock.
Every step he takes
creates a shot of pain
and requires tremendous effort
to get to his destination.

One would think the further dragged
the smaller it would become,
but this man's curse
saw to a contrary effect.
The strength he employed
caused the rock to increase in girth.

As days go by it grows exponentially
and ankles chafed raw to the bone,
but he struggles on
against the pull of the rock
until a day, years hence,
he's found under a mountain.

Douglas R. Lighty

Finding Love

I've spent many years
Stumbling out of one relationship
And into another
Often with the word love
Still fresh on my lips
I was too eager to have it
And it was never there
So I decided to accept
Being alone in my heart
And to keep stumbling
But one unexpected day
Someone reached out their hand
And helped me to my feet
In that instant
I felt our souls collide
Our spirits soar
And our hearts open up
To what we both
Had given up on having
True love everlasting.

Jarrid J. Ryan

Art

I like making art,
I can make a pretty heart,
Art is easy to do,
It's fun too,
Art can be really colorful,
Art can be as bright as you like,

We can make pretty art,
You can make art with shapes,
You can even make a scary ape,
Sometimes it's prettier with paint,
But I like to create.

Celeste Ayalla

Untitled

Why does death makes us weep?
Only for ourselves does grief seem
    a justified sadness
And somehow through the madness
and salt laden tears
Slowly our childhood fears are eased
when we reason that those absent
    have passed from peaceful sleep
To eternal bliss.

Timothy Paul

"All Over This Great Country..."

All over this great country
Which everyone can see
Lives a life for anyone
Who chooses to be free
An opportunity for people
No matter who they are
to plant their roots of family
in freedom from the start
Our history and our pride
embedded deep in our souls
Keeps our passion flowing
from our youngest through our old
And she will always stand by you
From the moment that you say
God bless America,
The Great Old U.S.A.

Robert S. Fantel

What Are Friends For?

A friend is someone you can talk
  to when you are feeling low.
Someone who will listen to you
  when you have a problem.
Someone who will be there when
  you need a shoulder to lean on.
Someone who will give you advice
  when you ask for it or not.

A friend will always be there for you
  when you need one most of all.
A friend is someone like you.
I thank God for a friend like you.
Thank you for being my friend.

Judy Adoko

Stars

The sun may shine,
  but it may grow dim.
The moon looks bright,
  but the dark sky may eat it.
The stars are my only hope,
  small but bright.
I'll hold them in my arms
  and fight off the dark.
The stars may die,
  and so may I.
Stars will be burning in my heart,
  Yet, you are the stars!

Rebekkah Rasmussen

The Low Tech Poet

A poet without a pen
Is like an ape with no prehensile
So when the muse became amusing
I had to find myself a pencil
But now I find this crude device
Hath advantage o'er my quill
It writes even when it's cold as ice
And has no ink to bleed or spill
It even has a delete button
Right there on the other end
Just flip it over and start rubbin'
The errors to amend
And when it comes to cut-n-paste
I just recall what I'd erased
And write it where I shoulda
But if I'd used my fancy pen
I guess I never coulda

Mark D. Nelson

For Time and All Eternity

For time and all eternity, that's what it's all about.
We came to earth to prove ourselves, of this there is no doubt.
We live our lives as best we can, we play and work real hard.
But Satan wants us for his own, we must be on our guard.
We find a friend whom we soon love, and then we two are one.
Our hopes, our dreams, our hearts, our lives - our work has just begun.
For this is one of God's commands, his children we must bring,
Our hearts will swell with each new babe, and then glad tidings ring.
Each baby is a child of God, and so we must prepare,
To love and teach and kneel beside and really show we care.
We promised long ago, that we would do these things and more.
A promise that we won't forget, but Satan's at the door.
He's trying hard to desecrate, our values compromise,
The family he defies and smirks, but we'll reject his lies.
A promise made, a promise kept, and when we keep our pact,
For time and all eternity, our families are intact.

Dorothy Lambson

Texas Mission

Festooned legions reclined in uneasy repose,
Obstinate sons of Texas too, ponder the impending throes.
Yanquis rapt in revolutionary zeal, their predicament obscured,
Ears oft tuned to death's sounds yet none of these are heard.

Flee, fight? The latter deemed right, two-hundred answered the roll.
Santa Anna thousands to command, the reaper to command his toll.
Dawn disposes the darkness and like a vestryman ushers the sun,
'Tis an ominous signal now pealed by bugle and drum.

Weapons shouldered by hostile men billeted 'neath history's tent,
Combatants assailing or defending a monastery soon a monument.
Grenadiers, dragoons, hussars, a phalanx en masse,
Echelons echo, "Madre de Dios, a massacre has come to pass."

Gehennas portals flung open revealing a bellicose bloody gate,
Dying soldiers cuckolded by cruel wives, fortune and fate.
Crocket, Travis, Bowie et al, names immortal left to mourn,
A defiant constellation expires while a lone star is born.

Bob Amann

The End And The Beginning

It creeps to us with many a warning,
For we have no faith in who we are or who we are serving.
The vestige of it frightens millions,
But they will not change, change is too vast a consideration.
So the wind will blow our paths will not change,
Destruction will endure and we are only to blame.
The sun shall soon not shine and give us light,
And the moon will not be as brilliant or as bright.
Eeriness and bewilderment will be within,
'Cause "we did nothing wrong, dare look to us for sin."
Procrastination for the well-being of humanity will be disastrous,
Severe distasteful blustering thoughts full of greed
and boastfulness will bring the end to us.
But with death comes life for few,
Eternity can be a continuation, a beginning, or even something new.
It is for only the purest, hateless, loving people of mankind who will have a new start,
For they gave up greed and ignorance and listened to their heart.
Some call them naïve but we should call them righteous,
For they are going somewhere we may not.

Christopher Bilsland

A Spring Evening

At the setting of the sun, that's when the fun has just begun,
To see the doe and fawn, who will feed from dusk till dawn,
To listen to the whippoorwill and ring necks crow upon the hill,
To hear the coyote howl or the hoot of the great horned owl,
And just as it's getting dark you can hear the call of the meadow lark,
It's such a lovely time of day, as the children come in from play.

Paul L. Hockenberry

Guinevere

As Jesus comforted Mary Magdalene at the tomb, so you, Guinevere,
comfort me at my time of need. Yea, though heathen tribes war
against me, though Morgause casts her black arts upon me, though
Mordred rallies traitorous knights to usurp me, thy prayers and presence strengthen me.

Riches I have aplenty; yet even the myriad of jewels encrusted on
the hilt of Excalibur is shamed by thy resplendent, golden hair,
laughing, emerald eyes, fair and dimpled cheeks, and small elfish
mouth. Thy impish laughter and spring-flowered scent drench my
senses like an April rain. Thy angelic countenance is magnified by the surreal brilliance
of your clinging, milky samite-gowned body.
Thy abundance of beauty is made complete by your velvet, alabaster
skin, generous breasts, and lush valley of warmth. Even the mythic
Athena and Aphrodite would be envious of thy goddess grandeur.

Truly, God's most precious, earthly gift to me is you, my Queen. I
will always be thankful; and I, Arthur, will always love you, Guinevere.

Chris Crawford

Taming The Wonky Welkin

The wonky welkin looms in my path, a kinetic maze of wind blown wrath.
Sardonic echoes from a sargasso sea, warn to shift sail and to flee.
Well-nigh swayed by their wanton swathe, I vow their woe won't guide
my craft. I'll take my chances on the open sea, so avast voices from
lives lived alee. Who dares cross the welkin, to look at its soul? A
zebra that stalks lions? A claustrophobic mole? Can a zebra change its
stripes, or are the lions just fed? Laden with fears the crystal ship
drifts ahead. Who dares cross the welkin, to reach their goal? Can
a ballast of doubt pass over the shoal? There's wealth in the void
if one will be led, but the compass is timid, so steer true toward the
dread. Who loosed the welkin? Has the Beastmaster died? No, to ever
have worth the welkin must be tried. Is their beauty in rust? Must death wear a veil?
Without the wonky welkin wisdom grows stale. Can one find heaven without first
knowing hell? The Beastmaster has answered all too well. When love's
an anachronism, violence the trade, relations merely chimes playing
an anagogic charade. Adhering to old morals is too much of a pain,
so parents kill children for selfish gain. Avoiding the sirens
mocking a none man parade, harmony lost melody in the rabble's tirade. Though the
wonky welkin is the fiercest of beasts, you must look it in the eye to ever find peace.

Wesley H. Brooks

Where Do I Go From Here?

It was only a few hours ago that my world felt complete,
It consisted of you, me, and our attraction that has existed since day one.
Now I'm lying in my bed thinking of what went wrong,
What could I have done differently, where do I go from here?

It is hard to believe that in one minute everything could change.
Now that glow in my eyes has turned into tears,
My sighs have turned into mourning groans,
I feel as if my world has fallen apart, where do I go from here?

If only I could change your mind and help you to see how much I truly care,
If only I knew how to win your heart and show you that my feelings are really there,
If only is but two words that try to explain something that doesn't even exist,
In such a short amount of time you have become so special to me
and to think that it all started with a sweet and gentle kiss.

It makes me sad to think of the possibility of losing you to another,
For to me, you are truly like no other.
I just want you to know that I cherish every moment we have spent together,
And every word that has been said, I will carry with me forever.

My tears are drying up now, my heartbeat is slowly dying down,
What was once a happy smile on my face is now a sad frown.
I feel so alone and confused about what to do,
Now that only question left to ask is, where do I go from here?

Gloria A. Rosales

The Priceless Treasure

Dedicated to Elizabeth Hutcherson

A priceless treasure have I found,
    That brings me so much gain;
It's like a soft and gentle hand,
    That soothes all hurt and pain.

A treasure full of truth and love,
    So few are to be found;
For in this world in which we live,
    Deceit and hate abound.

This treasure comes to me from God,
    His gift of love so true;
I thank the Lord for His sweet gift,
    His priceless gift of you.

Doreen L. Geiger

Petals In The Wind

As far as I can see, as deep
as I can remember.
There were petals in the wind.
the sight of the beautiful petals
gave me wisdom, and gave me hope.
I would open my window, and
stretch out my arms in hope
I might catch one on its way
to the heavens above.
I would run behind them,
leaping in hope to join them
where they were going.
But here I am sitting at my
window watching the petals in the wind.
As far as I can see, as deep as
I can remember.
There were petals in the wind.

April Sistoni

Hospital Room

We waited with her and watched
as she withdrew
    into a reverse cocoon.
The starched sheets gave her shape
and we folded and tucked them
    for something to do.
Busy with things we didn't understand,
she was preparing a quiet exit
    and didn't need our help.
The hissing air tube became the disguise
through which she'd slowly slip away,
    her resignation complete.
I don't remember crying
when the last bit of white enclosed her;
    she had gently drained our sorrow
so we were ready
to live
    without her.

Grace Kin Raffaele

Left-Overs

I'm nothing but left-overs
Nothing but left-overs for you
She's the hors d'oeuvres
He's the main course
It's the dessert and I'm what's left.

I'm the one that no one wants
I'm the one that everyone hates
I'm the one you want to kill
I'm the one that left, left with nothing.

Regina Pouliot

Through A Child's Eyes

Through a child's eyes they
see the worlds delight
The innocent beauty that
God bestow upon them

With his wonder and his might
Through a child's eyes they
see the unforeseen
For the glory of his majesty
Our god, our Lord, our king.

God has created everything
on this earth
The foreseen and unforeseen;
but children always see

As he speaks to all the children
He shows them everything.

Take a look at the world time,
to time through a child's eyes

Johnnie Porter

The Natural Process

Life's continuing process
Process of life and death
Death and new life
Life linking generations together
Together pressing and packing
Packing and reconfiguring
Reconfigurating and transforming
Transforming biology again and again
Again producing unity out of diversity
Diverse poetic ritual
Ritual celebration of nature
Nature of man
Man degrading
Degrading man ending all
All beginning again,
Again the unity of life.

Ann Domjan

Death Is Your Keeper

I stepped into the darkness
I stepped into the void
I only caught a glimpse of him
But knew he was no boy
Suddenly I saw him standing there
I knew he could only be death
His hand reached out to touch me
I knew he was all I had left
He said "I am the darkness"
He said "I am the night"
"I wait outside your bedroom
I am beside you when there's no light
I am the gun that kills
I am the evil in your heart
I am the wound that bleeds the blood
I am the man who rips flesh apart
So come with me, my Darling
Walk beside the reaper
Come to make us one again
Death is now your keeper"

Melody Stewart

Valentine's Day

Sweet smelling candy,
loving red hearts a blooming
with love for me and you!

Joclyne Gonzales

A Heart Of Gold

Sometimes in one's life there comes a person,
Who would walk the ends of the earth, sail the seven seas,
And climb the highest mountain for you.
Not many can experience this, and that must be a horrible feeling.
Not many are as lucky as me, and know and love someone like this.
He will always matter to me, and I will always love him.
For he is the man with a heart of gold.

Life has not been easy for him, the triumphs and the tragedies.
The loss of family members, and physical limitations.
But none of these can hold back a heart that's willing to care
A religious man, who passes his knowledge on to others.
A devoted family man, who tries his hardest to take care of his
family. All of these triumphs and tragedies, have shaped him to be
the man he is today. And that is a loving, caring and honest man.

And if you are caught in the dark mist of confusion,
Worry not, for you will find his guiding hands.
A man who believes in charity, trust, honesty, and kindness

These are all the qualities that make up a kind, gentle man
These are all the qualities that make up my father.
A man with a heart of gold.

David M. Walker

To Get To The Other Side

I started out standing on top of the ice,
There didn't seem to be anyone or anything else there alive.
I had no idea where I was or what I was doing there.
I didn't think or function for minutes, hours, days, weeks - only
existed on top of the ice. When would I fall through?

Then one day I woke up and the ice was gone.
In front of me was a beautiful, quiet, blue lake.
At its edge was a bank of scrawny trees and tangled underbrush.
Again, I wasn't moving - just existing.
I wondered where I would go from here? What was keeping me on top?
I wasn't moving but I was beginning to need.

I didn't know if I was on a boat, a raft or something else.
I never caught a glimpse. All I knew was that I was floating ever
so slowly, barely moving, down the lake and toward the other side.
There was no plan, no one else around, nothing moved - but I was beginning to feel.

Carolyn Christmas

To Our Granny

Our Granny has always been there for us. When we needed a hand or even a knee.
She was very gentle or sometimes rough only when she needed to be.
Granny has always been there to listen to us. Good or bad she always heard our problems.
Granny has always given us great advice, although we would not listen most of the time.
We love our Granny more than we will ever know. She is leaving us now she has to go.
Our Granny is above us all today. We will never forget her by night or by day.
Granny you are everything to us. For some reason, no one knows, God needs you,
    He must to make you have to go.
God has a better life for all of us we know. Our Granny is one He has chosen to go.
So I know our Granny will suffer no more. No pain, no fear and most of all no tears.
Granny is watching over all of us today. Granny we will be together soon one day.
We love our Granny so have no worry, we will never forget our great time together.
Please let's all try to stay strong and stay true because our Granny would want us too.

April May Lawrence Crews

A Road To Follow

Today I walked along a snowy covered road, to contemplate life's troubles,
to lighten burdens load. The air was crisp, the sky was blue, the quiet, peaceful-still.
Once steps heavy laden, became lighter on lifes hill. My thoughts once deep in troubles,
sought a peaceful state of mind, where only I could travel, which I'd struggled so to find.
    I lay myself down on the snow, and cried such happy tears, let loose of all life's burdens,
troubled thoughts and useless fears. The time had come for me to pass, along to better days,
to face the world, to stand up strong, to search for better ways. I look ahead with open eyes,
with dreams that will come true, with greater faith, in myself, and with the love of friends like you.

Cynthia Hurd-Johnson

Untitled

Taking salvation between my lips,
My words are parallelled, caressed and curious in the wind.
I lie green with envy.
Black fragments of porcelain are marooned, and cast away by the light.
A sideshow attraction enters with luminous charity.
A seven day wait. A seven day death.
Seven days of making love...
Ashamed with you, my illness is there in front of your eyes.
My fingers and skin made of Braille, for your blindness will not fool me
I remain a fool for eternity.
There is no excuse in sight.
Searching through the fog.
It's thick and dirty, staining the sidewalks a pail blue.
Mouthful of chalk, I cough and choke, suffocating.
Many more nights of the same await.
Distance is dissolved, and seven days return in my dreams.
The week of the weak. On the eighth, God created the touch.
Smooth and peaceful. I run my fingers over the soft thorns.
The blood tastes of saliva.
Impishness is the personality of the forest...

Justin James Crowder

Gone

Remember:

The day we met, the joy we experienced, and the troubles we endured with and for one another.

The day we met is in the past; there is no more we, only you and I,
and our troubles are no longer overcome together by two, but
instead you and I are left to face them alone.

Our times together are gone forever, and have been replaced by
feelings of emptiness, sadness, and pain.

I know that one day these feelings will fade away, and there will
be a rebirth of love in my life, the joy and happiness will return,
and my heart will again begin to glow.

For now, however, I will do my best to deal with the empty feeling
present in my heart, and remind myself that there will always be hope for better days ahead.

Although our days together are through, and the feelings are slowly
beginning to fade away,
our lives are not gone, and neither is our ability to love again.

And someday, when we have found our dreams, our happiness, our love,
we will realize that nothing is gone at all, just stored away
in a secret corner of our hearts for safe keeping.

Jennifer Leibrock-Steimel

Forster Heights 1956

Coltrane's saxophone cries cool the October sky,
shiver through the skirts of the schoolgirls walking home from the library.
Davis' Flamenco Sketches fills the brisk autumn with minty air,
piano's clinks accompany each bedazzled leaf as it grazes the pavement.

Black men sitting on red milk crates outside the pharmacy
stab the air with their white fingernails and pink tongues-
emitting throaty froggish shouts of "Hey now!" and "Wow!" to every passer-by retiring home.

Cigar smoke swells from the pharmacist's brown mouth-
he orders the stock boy with his beige trousers worn in the knees
to continue sweeping the pink and green speckled floor.

A thin man glazes over the evening newspaper,
holding each end delicately between his cigarette fingers,
smirking underneath a brown felt fedora,
he brushes his heels as he slides along the sidewalk through the orange evening-
over each crack with the grass peeking through deep dark green
And the kaleidoscope of giant oak and maple leaves overhead
that his father used to serenade at dusk
with the sound catching in thick leafy boughs,
whistling away his careless soul,
fancying everything around him.

Christopher Abbate

The Infinite Sadness

It only pauses for a moment
When you are with a good friend
A message it has sent
Your broken heart will never mend

You can never, ever run
You can never, ever hide
There is no such thing as fun
In it you must confide

You think it has left you
But soon you will find
Her beautiful face it will show you
Deep in your dark mind

Your mind can never brighten
Your heart can never pump
For it you will frighten
And it will reduce you into a lump

It is from all of the sad moments
That you eternally relive
A thing it doesn't know
Is how to forgive

Joseph Gleaves

Senses Chicago

People talking,
Cars are honking
Crowds in stores,
Cash registers ringing
The smell of pizza,
The touch of snow
Chicago is a place I'd like to go.

Kendra Curry

In Darkness Dwells

Faces in the night will pale
As rain pours fiercely on
And through the suffocating veil
Only silence answers dawn

Color fades to mirror souls
Descended long ago
Into pools of light so far removed
They scarcely seem to glow

Replete with fiery passion lost
To ages without tears
Left in empty lustful rage
To quench immortal fears

Burning deep within their gaze
A dancing trace remains
Of what was once but nevermore
A sullen heart then wanes

Donald E. Reynolds Jr.

Senses Disneyland

It's the happiest place on earth.
With magic in the air.
Although it's kind of expensive
you'll get your money's worth.
The smell of popcorn and sugar
cinnamon churros is everywhere.
You'll hear lots of music, laughter
and people having fun.
You will see many bright and pretty
colors when your visit is done.

Lisa Domenico

Hickory

Grandma is hickory
Smooth, tough, knotted
Her eyes sing blue
Her whisper's never haunted

Coffee and chicory
A comfortable old mug
With feet firmly planted
In her garden of love

Grandma is hickory
Strong silent crutch
Her nod of knowing
Strengthened by her touch

Card and crinkly
Her finest hour
Our dear old wine
Our dear old flower

Mikel Bergman

Old Man-Young Man-Me

We all are lepers in our minds
This old man said to me
Reality is choked by fear
Of what our hearts could be

To keep the secret mighty,
Trenched with in our souls
Not to follow sheepishly
not to be so bold

Be touched by every emotion, he said
I just had to sigh
Feeling a knot in my stomach
Having to wonder why

So remember now my young friend
There's no shame in what you do
Do what's true inside your self
With every day that's new
I'll turn you loose now my old friend
Heed your own advice
Live what you have left to live
Fearing nothing nice

Lewis E. Wilson II

Pain

You leave
And the hurt of losing you
Takes your place in my heart
It sets up housekeeping
Taking over my
Heart and soul
Where you used to be

Melanie Hartsfield

Untitled

Love
Quiet, calm
Just a smile
Grows to a kiss
Long and passionate
Hot and smoldering
Fire with a light touch
Growing stronger
living always
Just a smile
Quiet, calm
Forever

Kelly R. Bailey

Untitled

When you open the window of my heart and reach
past the blinds that deceive my looks,
emotions run down dried up brooks
　　Don't let this fool you when I don't smile and feel happy
　　The pencil moves towards the paper and draws
past the hand and people sift waves of sand
to make it smooth like velvet or cream
　　Imperfections make beauty so lets run through
the desert with buckets of water and ice
and kick through the sand while the sky turns black
and cold to match us and tunnel the outside
craziness of cheerful willows that should be weeping
　　Hold my hand and I'll show you myself...
you can walk inside the room now that you know
looking through the window is not enough.
　　Fly away with me and walk on the sea to watch what is down
below - I can care for you and feel you know
　　Don't be my shadow, be my soul and be free, yet not too close to me
After all I didn't look happy to you or smile to let you come to me
So what you assumed couldn't possibly be...

Marian Lerner

Unsung Heroes

Twenty-eight to twenty-four,
Was the Cowboy-49er score.
With San Francisco leading,
And players sweaty and bleeding.
With 15 seconds left in the fourth quarter,
And no time outs in the Cowboy order.
Dallas on the San Francisco thirty, one last play from teams so dirty.
Aikman drops back and hurls it in the end zone,
As Irvin cuts across in front it in the end zone,
As Irvin cuts across in front of the field goal.
This was to decide it between these men,
Here it comes, touchdown, Cowboys win!

Irvin won the M.V.P., as it seems likely to you and me.
But what about the offensive line, the true heroes in my mind.
They protect the running-back and quarterback too,
To set up great plays for me and you.
They are the unsung heroes of the game,
The ones who share so little fame.
So next time these guys play, listen to the words I say,
They have a very important job, and joys of fame they have been robbed.

Isaac Craig

Steps

My life is like everlasting steps, it goes on and on and on,
never knowing where it leads.
Sometimes I slip and fall a few steps behind,
but soon I catch up and I'm equal with everybody else.
My steps might be rugged and weak,
but they're strong enough to survive a lifetime.
If your steps fall apart, I am always there.
If you need to borrow my steps until yours come together,
you are always welcome to walk with me.
Sometimes I get lonely walking up these dark steps,
but I feel safe knowing I have people
that will help me fill in my gaps so that I can carry on.
Sometimes I have time to stop
and think about how many steps I have skipped.
Then I wish I could go back and fill in those spaces
that I had once ignored and thought I could carry on without,
not knowing how important they would be to me down the road.
When I come to a split of stairways, I'll take the one less traveled
by and the most worn and rugged,
so I can learn to clean up what lies ahead of me.

Matthew Hilliard

The Devil's Path

As the glistening sun sets out to fall and the sky begins to darken
within a swift blink of an eye,

All you see is a solid sheet of blackness that possess the once
piercing blue sky.

That's when out of the frosty damp wind, rose a chilling
decrepit mist
that filtered throughout the midnight air.

Only then, when you least expect it, will the desecrator
scam his way
to become more masterminded by feeding and gaining his strength
from those who are too weak to fight so that he may become
undefeated.

As for the forgotten creatures, they slowly and painfully begin to die
as their poor souls slouch withered to the earth's ground,
laying where they fell praying for their savior
to come as they drift into an eternal resting sleep.

Vicki Del Rosario

The Bond

The bond between a woman and a man is powerful and strong.
It will survive the summery heat of dissension, and the wintry cold of apathy.
The bond between a man and a woman is flexible and fluid.
It will allow partners to grow, while remaining attached to the whole.
The bond between a man and a woman is beauty and grace.
It will brighten the lives of each and smooth out the chaos and strife
The bond between a man and a woman is holy and blessed.
It will bring healing to the soul, and comfort to the distressed.
For, the bond between a man and a woman is not the result of
evolution or chance; it was not developed in a lab, or programmed en masse.
For the bond between a man and a woman is created out of Love!! Therefore...
It will bring blessings and hope to all, and shall never see defeat!

Scott Sanderson

As I contemplate the tender moments we shared together, I embrace the peaceful serenity that captures my Soul. My eyes behold your masterful greatness as you conquer my imagination.

A spectrum of magnificent colors cascades before me as you demand respect for your performance. You camouflage your strength with your overwhelming beauty; a mass (of brilliant colors) aggressively attacks and hypnotizes my thoughts. Pure and unblemished, immaculate and flawless, you proudly exhibit your enchanting empire.

Graciously you navigate yourself over dry land taking it hostage as you pass by.
A calm breeze and a small spray of mist gently kiss my face as I watch you in a state of awe.
Your articulate and diplomatic flow of water elegantly itself, as it falls through the air, while tantalizing my emotions of contentment and fulfillment. I am humble to your honorable superiority. Vivacious in your movements you lash forth in a manner of great excellence and perfection. You rank among the first contenders in nature's beauty contest.

Victimized by your majestic gracefulness, I surrender my consciousness without a fight.
Seductively you tempt and allure my fascinations. You captivate and entice all that is good and positive within my soul. My spirit is magnetically drawn to you. A magnificent magical rainfall, a masterpiece. "I am beholden to your will; I am overwhelmed with ecstasy; I applaud you, Waterfalls."

Yolanda Phillips

"Waterfalls"

Mother's Day Love

Falling, shining through the night, you the star making a gentle light;
Beyond the garden lie the mountains in the garden sparkling fountains.
You my mother, best of all, you on high never fall;
In the sky you do shine, dear my mother always be mine.
Now my mother I must say, go now Mother on your way.
But, Mother, before we depart, hear me Mother from my heart;
I love you more than words could ever mean,
You've had tears in your eyes as I have seen.
I will care for you as you have cared for me;
All I have seen you will see.
Now my mother let it be, please my mother stay with me!

Heather L. Halweg

Freedom

I've been taken prisoner,
held captive by the foe.
I've fought my chains and bonds,
but I don't know where to go.
Confusion clouds my mind,
and doubt torments my soul.
"Help me, God", I cry
as I struggle to survive.
"Peace, be still", He says
when He hears my weary sigh.
"I don't despise the prisoners;
I set the captives free.
Those who labor under the curse
can find their rest in Me."
My mind begins to clear
as He heals and makes it whole.
My heart, once fractured into pieces,
leaps within my soul.
All strife within me ceases,
and he mends the gaping hole.

Judy Montgomery

Love

Pretty colors
Pretty lights
They cry out so silent.
The innocence of angels
  Glowing.

Jason Brubaker

The Big Game

I'm writing a poem about L.A.
Because I like to watch them play.
From Nick Van Exel to Shaquille O'Neal,
The Lakers know they can seal the deal!
They shoot the ball and never miss,
Man, would they like to win this.
With Magic Johnson going home,
The Lakers know they can't do it alone.
It seems the Lakers have made a plan,
But they still miss the main man.
Now I might be wrong but I'm no fool,
The Lakers are actually pretty cool!
I've got to go and catch the game,
The Lakers will win it all the same!

Shane Harris

The Dreamer

The little boy sat
  at the oversized desk
His feet barely touching the floor
His brow was furrowed
His pencil was poised
  as he let his visions soar

The teacher stood
  at the front of the room
Listening to lessons galore
But she saw the boy
In his own little world
  as he sought to dream ever more.

The school house is gone
  with its old log walls
Where the little boy sat in a trance
But he remembers the place
Where he sat at his desk
  and the teacher
  who gave him his chance.

Mabel J. Desmond

Star Vessel

Star vessel shining bright
Bringing the carriers of Light
To the place of their highest being
Through prayer and thanksgiving

It soars through the universe
All troubles it does reverse
Its armor is impenetrable
Its success is inevitable

With weapons of Truth, Love and Power
With the gentleness of a budding flower
Tenderness and mercy it does bear
Taking us here and there

Bringing us to our place of bliss
We are ever guided by
His ways and His Light
He carries all of the weight

The Sword of Divine Justice
Shall lead us
Lead us through Eternity
And giving us our tranquility
Mary Beth MacQuaide

Just One Feather

Wafting
  drifting
    descending
      feather,
white black brown feather,
long
  slender
    straight
      feather,
light bright tail feather,
it's
  just
    one
      feather,
a single fading feather,
  or is it?
Jaime Williams

The Old House

Weathered scars upon its face,
It's withstood many a gale,
Even storms could not erase,
Or make the old house frail.
Though many tales it could tell,
Yet hides them all with pride,
The many secrets it keeps well,
Of those who dwell inside.
For ninety-six years it has stood,
An edifies of grace,
Through bad times and the good,
Enduring in that place.
When at the morning sun's first ray,
The old house greets another day.

Darlene E. Revell

Pearls Of Wisdom

If it's true that we are the end
result of what life has dealt us,
Why not put it all to work in our lives!
Make changes where needed.
We can, we must!
Wisdom is better than Gold!

Annette Gould

That Clock On The Wall

The forecast calls for a blustery day and winter winds blow all the leaves faraway
while a teacher dismisses class for the night and the students all head for the door in delight.
The birds in the trees and the squirrels in their nests do not have to deal with tough mid-term tests!
Students complain to their teachers in haste; the tests they're about to pass out are a waste.
It should not be required to know all these facts.

They should be more aware of the toll it exacts on the mind, and the health, and the
heart, and the soul, and the will, and our thoughts, it exacts such a toll! Then "what?"
to require, a teacher will ask of the students who argue this difficult task and follow their
nose through the blustery day, without any guidance, and get led astray. They're
unable to answer this question, it's clear, because of a lack of true wisdom that's dear.

The students are angry, but one, though, is not, and the difference is due to the wisdom
one's got; the way one approaches the subject to-wit, and the students, now puzzled, fly
into a fit. They smite the poor teacher who cared for their lot; his reward is the punish-
ment he just got! Now the students are grown and their work is a bore and they stare at
the clock and then rush for the door when the buzzer reminds them it's time to go home.

And when they get there find themselves all alone. The world does injustice to them, in
their mind, but injustice is sewn by themselves, they will find. They've been watching
the clock all their lives and for what? For a dream in their mind, a want in their gut, for a
life, they believe, is much better than theirs, that will quench all their fears, and their
wants, and their cares. This dream does not come about all by itself. One cannot just

relax, put one's cause on the shelf, but persist in one's cause and excel in one's lot, and
never surrender until all one's is the most could want, and the best one can do; this is
accomplished by only a few. And ironic in this, is this one little fact; that the "many"
will help these few in the act, and the few will admonish their gain to us all, while the
many have missed their only call, waiting - while watching that clock on the wall!
Michael T. Marc

Untitled

Oh, Storm,
  Your beginning was no reason for fear.
You didn't peal your thunderclaps at high pitches.
But after you got going, your strength showed me that you could have.
  As you developed, your hate became fury; your heedlessness became recklessness.
Then, Mighty Force, you used your power
to play with the trees, bending them back and forth and tearing
their leaves from them. They had no defense against you.
  You ravaged down the street, whipping everything in your path with
one gust after another, splashing your tears of wrath on cars and
houses; like gravel stones, they stung when they hit. You Powerful Brute,
  You would not cease your raging. But as your terror hummed, I knew you were
wearing yourself out. You slowed down for awhile,
as if to catch your breath for another burst of thunder and flash of lightning.
  You rose up, but your noise was in spurts that dwindled down to nothing.
  Your rain ceased and gradually you were hushed, but for a few rumblings.
Oh, you Foolish Child,
  You could not control your temper, and now your strength is gone.
  Your fame will soon be forgotten.
Marlene C. Mertens

OCTOBER

Yellow, orange, red and brown so beautiful in a field of blue.
You know the colors are always there, yet they hide behind the green.
Once a year, the green fades allowing the others to come forward and be seen;
only to wither and die.
What you are asking of me is to shed my green so that my colors too can be seen.
What you do not realize is then I too will wither and die.
You have taught me to be proud of the colors I have.
My colors are not yet strong enough to endure the winds which cause them to wither and die.
So, please for now just enjoy the leaves whatever color they may be;
ask not for them to change.
Remember, if the colors come too soon they must too, wither and die.
For my colors do not have the strength though I am learning from you.
My colors will show themselves when they can endure the winds.
They will come slowly and at times turn back to green.
So be patient and be my friend just do not ask too much too soon.
For then I will wither and die.
Sheila A. Black

321

To My Grown-Up Son

My hands were busy through the day
I didn't have much time to play
The little games you asked me to,
I didn't have much time for you.

I'd wash your clothes, I'd sew and cook
But when you'd bring your picture book
And ask me please to share your fun
I'd say, "A little later son."

I'd tuck you in all safe at night
And hear your prayers, turn out the light
Then tiptoe softly to the door.
I wish I'd stayed a minute more!

For life is short, the years rush past
A little boy grows up so fast
No longer is he at your side
His precious secrets to confide.

The picture books are put away, there aren't any games to play
No good night kiss, no prayers to hear; that all belongs to yesteryear.

My hands once busy now lie still; the days are long and hard to fill,
I wish I might go back and do the little things you asked me to!

Doris Melvin Burton

My Own True Love

My love is like a red rose that comes to full bloom in the month of June.
My love is like a sweet lullaby that is sung in tune.
My love is like a gentle breeze - warm and tender.
So deep in love am I that I will love him till the end of time.
With heavy heart I listen to the radio playing songs of love.
For me there is no peace, no joy without my own true love.
My saddened heart/soul is filled with pain loneliness and fear because my true love is not here.
Our worlds are so different yet so alike; our commitments are strong to be together
    would break all the laws.
So close yet so far away - I will never know him.

  The nearness of him
  His kisses
  His touch
  His gentleness
  His hands and arms holding me - and he will never know me.

Compromise, this I had to do, but my love for him will always be true.
Our lives are entwined heart and soul. We can and will endure.
You can find my own true love amongst his congregation - where he is complete;
    spreading Christ's Good News and saving souls for their eternal reward.
So you see, me and my love can never be, for he belongs to the Lord.

Rags

Change

When life gets overwhelming, and the burden seems to heavy to bear
Just stop and think for a moment that I'm always here.

Together we stand to face it all, and I promise you my friend we will conquer not fall
When others try to bring you down and make you feel you're strange
Just take a moment to remember, there's nothing wrong with change.

I know that you're scared of what lies ahead, and trust me so am I
But we've got to stand firm and be positive and try
I know we'll have our ups and downs along the way
But take a moment to remember that with each dawn comes a new day

When things start to close in on you stand tall and firm and true
And take a moment to remember that I believe in you.

There is no need to be afraid of change my friend, for after all you see
The end is actually a guarantee to a new beginning of what your life can be
Just stop and take a moment to set your spirit free
Always remember, you have the power to make your life whatever you want it to be.

Side by side in spirit we'll lift our heads and stand tall
together my friend I promise you we will conquer not fall.

Lori Mae Long

The Wedding Jitters

Our wedding day
it's finally arrived.
Swallow those fears.
Shift into drive.

Try to be strong.
Try not to cry.
My stomach feels weak.
My throat's getting dry.

My hair is styled.
The veil is in place.
Now comes the dress
creamy satin and lace.

I hear music playing.
The bridesmaids have gone.
I guess it's my turn
My feet weight a ton.

I slowly take that first step...
Then two...three...and four.
Now I can't walk fast enough
As I look at the man I adore!

Lisa Pekny

Shadows Of My Mind

In the stillness of the dark hours
When sound sleep I can not find.
Then old memories come a creeping.
In the shadows of my mind.

Some memories are of childhood.
Some are nice, some not so kind.
But in the darkness of the midnight.
They just sneak up on my mind.

I often think of loved ones.
Who have now all gone away.
It makes my heart grow heavy.
And I long for break of day.

Now I hope you'll love each other,
and a lasting peace you'll find.
Then only sweet memories will come.
Creeping, in the shadows of your mind.

Russell E. Utter

Among Myself

Among myself with all in others,
with my heart I take some others.
Then I feel so great and proud
of myself, with better faith.

Cameron Elliott Tien Munger

Rainbow

I saw it in the sky
Many different colors
All distinctly there,
Still they merged,
curved.
Melted together.
If only different ideas
different people
Could merge together
So easily
so fluently,
Without paying attention
To all the colors
of the rainbow.

Jennifer Hagberg

A Desire

There's something within me
Deep inside
Not far from my fear
Above all my pride.

Bound by my thoughts
Tied down for years
Exploding with frustration
Can't anyone really hear?

Well meaning people
Giving lots of advice
They think this can be solved
Just overnight.

How did it all start?
When will it end?
I ask myself these questions
Again and again.

A desire for freedom
A longing to flee
Unshackle the chains
And let me be me.

Andrea Barbetta

Enlightenment

From where or when these words did flow,
Nor why they came I do not know.

What all pervasive power in space
Does keep the atom in its place?
Transcendent source that insists
That life in everything exists.

Cosmic, infinite, sacred source
Whose notion keeps all life in force.
Omniscient power that decrees
Such endless forms in myriad degrees.

In absolute bliss it must reside.
In perfect harmony it must abide.
Eternal lamp that thus inspires,
To grant the light, to all desires.

All life is sacred!
All life is one!

Upon us all the light descends.
Upon us all the truth extends.
Turn softly toward this holy light,
To know the law, your divine night.

Valentin Martinez

Praying for You

Just to let you know,
I'm praying for you.
So in the future,
The Lord's will you can do.

You are really special,
And friendly too.
Which makes it easy
For the Lord to use you.

You have a love
That shines real bright.
Which make your friendships
Bond so tight.

Just always remember,
And to the Lord stay true.
There is always someone,
Praying for someone like you.

Patricia Sutton

Destined

   It started as a seed, life granted by the Creator. Fallen onto the soft soil, filled with nutrition, prepared by the Creator. Slowly, as time is gauged on earth, it grew. Just a sprout, then a seedling, a branch at a time, into a strong, sturdy tree. It was the envy of the forest. The time came, elected according to the foreknowledge of God the Father, for the men to cut it down. It would serve their purpose perfectly. The life was taken from it. Its branches trimmed away, the protective bark planed off, forming square edges. Both beams, one longer than the other, came out of this mammoth tree. It had to be sturdy. Sturdy enough to hold the weight of a man. The beams were dried and stored, put aside, unknown to human kind when they would be required, or for whom.

   The days are hot, electricity is in the air. Several beams are chosen, the sturdiest selected. They must die for their sins. The great tree, now lifeless, being chosen for its destination. The longer beams driven into the ground. The shorter planks to receive the waves of pain as the hammer pounds. The Son of Man, Son of God. Nailed to the plank, lifted onto the beam. Paying the price of sin. Not of His own, but of the world. A life granted and destined by God, given in sacrifice that others might receive life.

   Theresa A. Lee

Untitled

The wind one day blew cold and bleak, and it swept deep over every peak.
Everything was damp and dark, no light except for Noah's ark,
And out of Noah's Ark there came...beasts and birds of every name.
Cows and horse, sheep and shoats, the nanny and the Billy goat.
They came along in two by two, the polar bear and Kangaroo.
Hawks and sparrows and the wren, four women and as many men.
When water from heaven was restrained, not a soul on earth remained.
A dove sent out to find dry ground, did not return when it was found.
Noah's sons and daughters and his wife, moved out to start a brand new life.
A while on earth they did retire, but quickly they did multiply.
They owned no land and paid no rent, but moved about and lived in tents.
Until the day of shiloh came they would build a tower and give it a name.
This tower shall be built so high. Its top shall reach the very sky.
The tower's builders became confused, the bricks and motor was never used.
One spoke Italian, one spoke Dutch, one spoke Arab and another such
Such mixed up mess you never heard, and I couldn't understand a word!

   Lynia Bennett

Good-Bye

Why are you so grim? I have not left you. Am I not in your hearts forever? I cannot say I will not miss you, for that would be a lie. I have now only to begin a new life now. Among the trees and beneath the sky is where you find me. But, if you do not wish to go that far, look within yourself and there I will be. Please put a smile on your face. For I am not thinking only of the past or the myself, but I am thinking of the good times we had together and how much I love you. While you are lying in bed, I am right there beside you, in spirit. Our love for one another should not fade, but grow on spirit and heart. Wipe the tears from your face, for tears are nothing but salt. If the earth needed any more salt, we would have another ocean or sea. So you see, there isn't any reason for you to cry and be grim, because I will always love you. Love is unconditional, even through death. Even when we say, "'til death do us part", we are never really parting because I am always with you in heart, soul, and spirit.

   Kristi Foster

Mommie, Please

I didn't mind the cookies for the Kindergarten teas.
Or the Sunday School class parties, when you said, "Mommie, please".
Or even for the Girl Scouts, bless those little lasses.
Or the Freshman, Sophomore and Junior-Senior classes.
I didn't mind the cookies for Youth Fellowship and such.
But there comes a time, let's face it,
When enough can be too much!
That phone call, when it came today,
Had me feeling less than hearty,
"Mom, could you pick up a few things, for the Office Christmas party?"

   Laura Luedemann

The Sign Post

I was walking along, and I came across a sign post pointing in many
directions, and they all led into tomorrow.

There was the long way,
the short way,
the dull way,
the bright way,
the sad way,
the glad way,
the dark and the light way.

I was confused, and then I noticed there was a confused way too!
It became clear to me that I had to take my pick and axe my way along,
thus creating

The short way,
that let in the bright way,
being glad for the light,
that showed me the right way.

Terry Burton

Ordinary Life

I wanted an ordinary life
But I was born into a
Chinese immigrant family.
I wanted to taste the childhood
Of an eager girl but only a
Bitter savor of life remained.

I never thought about my
Mother's pain and the dreams
Lost in her agony each day.
Her love went unnoticed for
I just wanted an ordinary life,

I remember her aching back
And those corduroy hands
That washed marble floors
And supported a family of four.
But I never understood the dignity she sacrificed.

My mother denied her heart to cry although it ached.
She was strong and hid her humiliation, but I was still ashamed to
Call her my mother because I wanted an ordinary life.

Irene Chen

An Indelible Mark

What do you do when the world around you seems to be built on lies
Do you join in with everyone else and compromise
Or do you still tell the truth even though you'll be despised?

When you see a brother or sister who is hurting and needs a helping hand
Do you turn and walk away from that woman or man
Or do you reach out and teach them how to stand?

What do you do when your fellowman is faced with injustice and discrimination
Do you just wish you could do what's right for the situation
Or do you take action to fight against it by voting to change it through legislation?

When innocent blood is shed because of others' hands
Do you become bitter and devise your own plan
Or do you pray to God and ask him to help you understand?

What do you do when things happen that you can't control
Do you sink down into despair until you fold
Or do you look up to heaven and refresh your soul?

Now when you look back on all you've said and done
Will it have encouraged many, a few or none?

Will the life that you live today bring about pain and sorrow
Or will you choose to leave behind an indelible mark for tomorrow?

Velda Towns-Derricotte

My Quilt

My Mother made me a quilt
When I was the age of four.

I've kept it so for twenty years
Because it couldn't mean more.

She made it just for me.
She sewed love into every line.

It's lasted throughout the years.
It's withstood the test of time.

It's been dragged about and ripped,
But it's always kept me from being cold.

I intend to hold on to my quilt
Until I am very old.

Why does a simple quilt
Have such meaning to me?

It's all because of the person
Who made it just for me.

Teresa L. Heier

Peace In Thought

In every life there comes a time,
   a point of no return.
When words are said and actions done,
   emotions flare and burn.

Now take a moment out to think,
   let logic run its course.
Take no action, sink in thought,
   there is no use for force.

Enigmas come and puzzles go,
   with patience all are done.
Now just apply this thought to life,
   and you'll truly see the sun.

Tim Steinhorst

Hope

Once upon another day
I struggled far to see
All the dreams and empty things
I thought that I could be...
It rose within a swelling wave
A monster from the deep
memories of distorted days
I never willed to keep...
Still the hope within me calls
He never leaves my side,
Telling me to worry not
He'll be my shepherd guide...
and now the dreams, important things
Seem closer to my grasp
as I depend on Jesus Christ
It's all he'll ever ask!

Robert N. Rennie

On The Shore

   On the shore of the
reservoir, in the days gone by.
   Me and my boys, would sit with our poles
and watch the clouds go by.
   Oh! Short were the days
that we spent there.
   Just me and God and them.
But, oh! What a beauty there
   is to see, when you see
through the eyes of Him.

Janis V. Gardepe

Sun Down

A warm summer breeze whispers
through the trees, while robins
sing their sweet melodies.
Squirrel pups scamper about,
playing games of tag
while a tabby cat nurses her kits.
A cotton-tail rabbit eats fresh clover
in a sunny grove,
and a bumble bee flies back
to its hive.
The blue sky turns rosy pink,
then melts into the color of
ripe peaches.
The squirrels, and the tabby's
kits go to sleep.
As the cotton-tail hops
to his home,
the sky turns from deep lavender
to midnight blue, dotted with stars.

Laura Hietala

Sensei House

Roof of golden straw,
walls of brick,
deep red like magma.

Inside flashing candles
flicker yellow.
A shiny white rug lies on
an oak floor.
The windows reflect the
light like the sun
reflecting off a crystal icicle.

On the rug sits a traditional
Japanese man,
thinking, praying.
Smells of warm leather
and spicy incense fill the nose.

Four lean sharp Samurai swords
decorate the walls.
The man of honor and pride
prays in fear, violence
may darken his door.

Nick Blumenthal

Knight

Submitting to your touch
Yielding to your love
I feel your eyelashes brush
against my cheek like a butterfly's kiss

Dreamily I smile eyes closed

Piercing my sepulchral shell
You have coaxed me out of my
sheltered self leaving me
alone standing vulnerable,
exposed, naked-but with love

Your love melts me from the
grasp of fear's icy clench
transporting me on rapturous waves
insatiable surf washes over me

And for awhile I am cushioned in warm
security, saturated with hope

Left standing on my own, would I show
myself as much chivalry?

Claudina Roncoli

Parallels

Last night I sat with my notebook on a stoop in front of a DC
    Townhouse with bars in the windows because
It was closing its yellow eyes in despair and wished it could tower
    like the mountains it had seen in photo albums
The sky was grey and full of black clouds that were really smoke
And a streetlight bowed its head in jealously of cartoon moon that
    was fading behind the industrial atmosphere
So I squinted my eyes in sympathy and followed its showering shafts of wasted elec-
trons until my eyes fell upon a trail
Of well-off executives whose black hole eyes and tiresome attire made them look like they
were returning from the funeral of their
    childhoods when they were only coming back from work again -
That led down into the tunnels where the subways trains slither like
    blind eels in the mud digesting paying passengers in their guts who are afraid to look
    at one another
And that thought bothered me, but I couldn't help but be distracted by
    the innocent in ignorance poster kids frolicking in the tears of a
    fountain that was quietly sobbing to be like its Potomac mother
And as I sat trying to fill the empty universe of knowledge in my mind
    with my notebook full of fanatic philosophies in hand, I saw that
    they were beautiful
And I wished I could remember how to be human

Jesse Lee

The Clouds

The Clouds covered the radiant face of Amaterasu,
She tried to shine through, but the Clouds blocked her view.
The Clouds obscured her face more when the wily Wind blew.

At Night, the Clouds enveloped the pale face of Selene,
She had no hope of being seen through the white screen.
The Clouds only wanted attention, they were not being mean.

The Clouds concealed the tiny, twinkling Stars,
They hadn't a chance of illuminating through the hazy bars,
Not even Hercules or Hydra or Pegasus or Perseus or Mars.

High in the heavens, high in the Sky, the Clouds couldn't die.
The floating forms of fog fly easily through the Sky,
The swarming smoke shed tears of Rain as they cry.

The moist masses of mist marched over the atmosphere,
The Clouds overshadow the far land below when they appear,
The Clouds beginning to fear that the gray like sky would soon clear.

Lucian Finger

Fire

It was a very cold evening. The wind, it blew immensely.
I walked out into a sunny area and decided I needed fire.
The only way to create this monster
Was to generate a friction to burn the gathered thatch.
The fire would produce heat and light
So that my needs would be satisfied.
The fire began to feed among the soft pieces of bark.
I added more fuel,
And the flames consumed it, like a hungry pack of wolves on the prowl.
As I added more, it consumed more.
It began to grow too quickly now, eating randomly at brush.
Unfortunately, I had nothing to kill it with.
The heat was immeasurable, the light too much to bear.
The crackling of wood, like milk on rice crispies.
I understood that I along with the trees around me
Was its next victim. I grabbed my heavy coat, acting as my cover
And ran, ran back into my hole, with the remainder of my people.
Hoping the rest of the ants were not destroyed,
I decided to look back outside.
There was no fire, but only a man's footprint.

Eddie Martin "Kotte" LeBlanc IV

Friends...

I am sorry, we were friends, but now, No!!!
Those were the harsh words I heard when my heart stopped.

Bitter tears ran down my face and into my lap.
When you told me this, I wanted to die.

Now my life is empty, no room to fill.
I don't want to say goodbye, I never will.

I feel as if I'm in a dark desert, standing in black sand,
crying as I step on thorns which belong to black roses.

I'm no longer here, am I? I can't tell, for I have you as not a friend.
Welcome, no never mind, stay where you are.

I am the queen of loneliness, and on my back, I hold the black robe,
on my head, I hold the black crown, which holds the black jewel.

I will cry always and forever suffer in pain.

Christy Thomas

When My Sister Had To Go

When we were children, had I've known one day my sister was going to pass,
I'd have done anything in my powers to make sure our childhood would always last.
To see her slowly erase from my presence has somehow made me empty inside,
But knowing I'll see her again in heaven, makes me do God's will in stride.
Before she left, she asked me to raise her children, and to see to them finishing school,
I think my sister knew what I know, and that's that knowledge is a Golden Rule.

One day it will dawn on me as to why she chose me over others to fulfill this task,
But until that day, I'll have no answers and certainly no one to ask.
So my dear Sister, if it takes all I've got and all I can do, I'll grant you your last wish.
I only ask in return that every now and then, while the children are asleep,
You come into their dreams and give them a gentle kiss.

Victor Coleman

Caverns And Love Repudiated

You who are so empty and pretend to be so full — with your joylessness of living
We who find fault in each other's likenesses and parlay our lives —
Analyzing, putting cold objective restraints — on growing, upon loving
You who are afraid of your own beauty, unable to trust in another's
Where will it lead, but to blocked and stifled trails?

No, I no longer need to know you, although I will — for many walk the path of circles
You who pride yourself in your uniqueness of cold indifference
Giving to yourself and others, no warmth — protective of your outer and inner walls
You manipulate inevitable conclusions to be as you pre-decided.

Sadness within and without that you attempt to cloak in masks of pretense
Hoarding all and fearing oneness of trust and vulnerability — because opening spreads truth
And you want emptiness to become your undiscovered continent
Who are you fooling?

How boring is life when pretending to know all the answers —
And all the questions are a rendition of a time and lines before
Safe, you fantasize from life and make darkness out of reality
Daggering truth and jig sawing multiple paths into one.

You leave me empty, you escape me cold —
But also, you create thought with your varied and opposite poles
I hate, and so I must love — the strengths of emotion you well, and the sadness of no return.

Leslie Alcott Tempest Temple

Heaven's Eyes
"Stars"

Stars, there are stars farther away than Mars,
Stars, there are stars that shine like a wealthy shrine,
Stars, there are stars that gleam like a beautiful moon beam,
Stars, there are stars that shine so bright they keep me up all night,
Stars, there are stars that flicker somewhat like a rainbow sticker,
Stars, there are stars that people wish upon!
    there are stars that men call upon!
Stars, these are "Heaven's Eyes"

Scott A. Tyrrell

Desk

Alone in a corner
After hours...
A relic now
Stands alone.
The seat is loose,
Wobbles to and fro.
An artist's work is there,
Carved in the cherry top.
Many drivers sat in the wobbly seat...
Pilots have flown to war with him.
Wanderers and adventures he has seen.
Day dreamers drifting out to sea.
By the window he stood,
Faded now by the noon day's sun.
Forgotten now,
Their chariot of dreams.
In a corner, alone.
After hours...
A relic now,
Stands alone.

Evan Anderson

If I Could Lift Your Chin

If I
could lift
your chin,
and
kiss your face,
and
a
million worries
swiftly erase,
I'd do it now
this shaman kiss
because
your smile
is sorely
missed.

Dr. Margee Howe

How?

How did you do this to me?
I'd really like to know.
You've stolen my heart,
So please don't let it go.

How did you figure me out?
You've seen my true side.
All I really want to do,
Is just run and hide.

Why are you doing this to me?
You are driving me insane.
All I keep thinking about
When you leave is the pain...

Elluz C. Urdaneta

Untitled

As I step outside,
the calm air welcomes me.
Song birds serenade me,
while the breeze gently cools me.
People greet me,
And my sweet Lord inspires me.
As the sunset beckons the night,
It warms me.
The night calls upon me,
As perhaps no one understands me.

Danny Nydegger

My Mother And Father

Mom and dad my tribute to
You.

My mother is kind
Overall
Throughout my life
Her love will be there
Everyday
Really caring what I do.

And do
Not forget my
Delightful father.

For he is always loving
And very funny
Though he is not always here
He is always there
Encouraging me
Rachel, to be what I can be.

Rachel Murry

The Dining Room

The wizard of oz
left years ago on
the dining room floor
courage, brains, heart
scattered pieces
all over hell
a treasure hunt to the future
no, that was yesterday
a memory
becomes confused
where to live
like the soul
groping around
for a landing
calling tower
directions, please

O. Jones

Late

My foot, it hurts and
  pains, my walk;
Most likely in my shoes
  a rock.

I do not dare to
  hesitate
To take it out or
  I'll be late.

I hardly run,
  but go fast,
Arriving as a
  tortured lass.

So now I'm gonna
  operate
And curse that rock,
  'cause still,
I'm late!

Rose Bayaca

Bubble Gum Bubble Gum

Bubble gum bubble gum everywhere,
Bubble gum bubble gum in my hair,
Bubble gum bubble gum high and low,
Bubble gum bubble gum from head to toe,
Bubble gum bubble gum everywhere.

Jeanna Ruble

Reflections On Aging

It was here just a moment ago, or so it would seem;
I felt its pulsing vibrancy, or was that just a dream?
There were so many tomorrows to be cherished as they came,
And a sea of new experiences to know...none of them the same.
There were crises to be met and beaten; I would not accept losing;
There remained an eon for happy laughter, equal time for quiet musing.
Much time, I thought, left in this life to share and be enjoyed,
And yet, with little warning, I now realize a frightening void.
For my time here is not eternal, and soon may be spent.
The happy days with those I love were hours merely lent.
The vibrancy has dulled, endless tomorrows shortened to few;
I want to cry out "This cannot be! What shall I do?".
I long again for that lust of life with which to greet each day,
For while I was busy living, life has quietly slipped away.

Joanne Tumblety Wilson

When I Must Leave

When I leave this earth, will I be prepared,
I know not the hour, time, nor the day,
so how do I prepare myself.
Death is still a mystery to me. I must leave this
world for another, which is unknown to me.
Yet if I believe in God and everlasting life then straight is gate
and narrow being the way.
On the other hand, everyone wants to go to heaven,
but who's willing to die.
Not me, it still frightens me to think about it yet,
it's all I think about as each day comes and goes.
I know that death is inevitable yet
I can't seem to prepare for when I must leave,
I can only see death like this:
Damnation for sinners
Everlasting life for believers in Christ
Always under God's wings
Time of judgement is coming
Heaven if I live by the rules

Shelby Y. Blackmon

All Alone

On a bleak, winter day and few days after Christmas I sat,
Alone in my world of animated emptiness, waiting, waiting
Waiting, for what? I don't know. Maybe for a bird to chirp
A tree to grow, or a love to call my own
I feel so alone in this world of mixed-up, messed up happenings
My love for books and poetry sets me apart from my friends
There is no one with whom I can discuss, my likes and dislikes
I'm a leaf in the forest, all alone, hanging on a tree the last to
Remain I can't express to anyone except myself what I feel
If I could be free to choose what I wanted, free to roam wild
Wild as the wind, carefree as the breeze, if I could only have time
To find myself, in this world of established principles,
If only my lost, disoriented mind would find its pleasure
Music and teaching - what!
Parents demand you be someone, do something, but what - what?
I was born in the wrong era, wrong time, but life goes on
Even though I am lost and confused, I struggle to find
Myself, but I'm a speck in a million, a pebble on a beach,
A lonely wave crashing against the ragged rocks of
Civilization - I'm alone - all alone

Mary Sickels

Simplicity

As the frog leapt from rock to rock, I thought to myself "only if my life was as simple"

As the deer casually jogged through the stiffening mud,
I thought to myself "only if all things were as peaceful and graceful"

As the butterfly swiftly fluttered through the mid-day breeze,
I thought to myself "only if I could carry thro' troubles as he"

Elizabeth Pettigrew

Pastimes

My favorite pastime is watching the classic Western movie
Those of the forties through the sixties I find very groovy

Even though watched many times over, I've never been bored
Many were Oscar nominees, some have won the Academy Award

Action abounds such as perilous journeys and stampedes of cattle
Exciting gunfights and the historic 7th Cavalry vs Sioux "Little Big Horn" battle

There is spectacular scenery of that great western outdoors
Many of these movies have stirring and sentimental musical scores

I'll always remember Alan Ladd and Brandon de Wilde of Shane
And the many great westerns of the late John Wayne

Perhaps more of them should have been filmed in 3-D
Then all that action from the screen would be directed straight at me

I'll put on my blue jeans, western boots, and cowboy hat because it's time for a change
My new pastime will be horseback riding on the wide open range.

Reinhard Huber

The Missing Peace

Japan birth, your culture: Japanese, Japan all you knew.
'Til the life change: The U.S. arrives.
Departure with Dad, and Mom stays behind.
The U.S. isn't good! you think, feel.
Their language is sloppy, their clothes, dirty.
Then you become one of them and wear dirty clothes and speak sloppy.

'Til Mom comes to live in the sloppy, dirty U.S.
All Japan comes back — all the dress, the food.
Then Mom feels unwelcome; she wants to go back.
But your dreams are here now,
You've got sloppy speech and dirty clothes.
Both cultures a part of you, cultures so different, too hard to split.
You can't decide — to stay? To leave? Which self to keep?

'Til Mom goes back and you stay here.
Mom is a part of the puzzle inside,
The puzzle that can't be pieced —
Unsolvable.
The cultural puzzle ever waiting
For someone to create
The missing peace.

Katelyn Hackett

The Draw And The Pull

Our distance closes as currents are drawn to the coast,
pulling and colliding: The possibility of a love rooted in the sand.

Aquarian's solitude is harsh, cruel as the snap of the faun's lithe leg,
Our distance, the smattering daggers of a yet unknown,
what the aquarian pulled through the skin, laid

Then leaned on the thick velvet
of a wild languid voice, cupped

In the length of the hands, pooled
In the blood of a sad smile, here is our heart

Warm and quaking and tired from too many
swipes of cold fingers, knotting
and bursting and stinging from the vast depth
and sorrow of the sea, here is our heart

Cupped in the strange radiance of a lone flower
against the pale explosion of la playa's blue-green
graying caste: the flint of the longing eye

And yes, oh my traveller, here is your soul.

The swiftness and pain of the flowers bloom
the silk cover of your cheek bones,
and our distance brushes softly

Danilo Marquise

mnd's myth

in between the brass pipes
of a trombone slides the stealth
merchant, on heated air, the edge,
in the going forth and returning,
of neither direction, suspended
collision collecting; the air
knows no gain

Nothing is consistent, nothing
constructed of mind It fails,
this continuum hinged on the now
with garland and memories.
Holgrave aims (archer, arrow,
target) at self, the Yesterday

and the merchant ties green ribbons
to a tether drawn between two boughs
marking the relationship. The narrow
place caresses knotted wishes
in hollow sapro-night,
as a Japanese goddess devours
the moon jumping over the line.

Scott Allen

The Real Me

You are the first one
    to see the real me;
You are the only one to set
    the love inside me free.

You walked into my life
    and stayed around to see
the person behind the smile;
    You saw the real me.

You took the time to know me
    and see into my eyes;
You saw the real me and
    I gave up my disguise.

All the hurt and fear
    forever a part of me;
Fears so strong that no one
    could love the real me.

You are the first one
    to see the real me;
You are the only one to set
    the love inside me free.

Lynda Logan

A Country Road

Kicking the dust on a country road,
A lad met his bosom friend,
The two walked slowly together,
To school, around the bend.

Wild flowers in color,
Growing on either side,
Welcoming children passing,
The ragged ditches hide.

The country road holds secrets
Of pleasantry long past,
Initials in a lonely tree,
Memories and shadows cast.

Wild berries and "Queen Ann's Lace"
The ditches beautify,
Thoughts of childhood on a farm,
This, from the passerby
On a country road.

Rosetta Dearing

Growing Up

You don't want to do
    certain things,
But you must
In order to gain
    more trust
You take each day
With a grain of salt
Before you are a
Responsible adult
Denise Manning

Today I'm Happy...

Today I'm happy.
For yesterday I fell in love.
But then....
Tomorrow I might be out of love.
So I will just live one day at a time,
And not worry about what I'll be feeling
    tomorrow.
Because for today means everything.
Lisa A. Rains

The Day Is Gone

It time to sit and lounge around,
because the day is gone.
Soon it time to rest and sleep,
and wonder what the new day will be.
Then you up and about,
till the day goes out.
Then it that time again,
to sit and lounge around,
because the day is gone.
Larry W. Rickmon

Untitled

Glass shatters to the ground
    each shard contains
    one hope that thrives within her...
The warm light of the sun
    descends upon her face
    and dries away the tears.

Thunder echoes in the wind
    each roar speaks
    an evil harbored in the depths...
The summer breeze brushes
    softly against her skin
    and soothes the chilling fears.

She looks up, as the sky
    begins to darken
    and the rain cleanses her of pain.

She begins to run, feeling
    the earth beneath her naked feet
    she will find her way.
Michele Simo

La Fiesta Termina

The bitter pill of dawn
seeps through the ragged curtains
onto the puddles of the night before

Ash confetti of a celebration
is the carpet for a lonely room
still not willing to become memory
Philip Anderson Rountree

Until You

Existing in shades of feigned happiness

Until I saw you

Your eyes sparkle so deeply, enough to shame the stars into extinction.
A smile so deep and true it could cease the wars of nations.

I'd been searching for the meaning of it all
about to give up the hope of discovery

Until I heard you

Your voice resounding with the clarity of a countryside church bell.
A laugh so full and heartfelt it could clear the clouds on the
stormiest of days.

I'd prepared myself to secede into the mundane existence of a man
unfulfilled

Until I touched you

The warmth of your skin under my gentle touch diminishes the chill
    of an early fall.
My hand on your face sends shivers up my spine.

I once knew nothing of happiness or wholeness.

Until You.
Shawn M. Jacobs

A Moment

Can you feel the attraction
Can you feel my eyes watching you
Do you want my hands to touch you
to explore your body or do you need me to whisper your name.

Do you feel the magic between us when we are together
I can't let you go completely, but I can enjoy the memory we shared,

How come we want what someone else has
How come we expect so much, when really
there, so little in what we need,

How can you forget the moment we had
I miss your lips, your eyes, your sexy little laugh.

I know at times, I want to reach into
your soul searching for answers only you can give me.

I know at times, I make you angry,
But just know and understand, I care beyond reason.
Debra Phillips

Thoughts After Death

It all had started one day when I was feeling down,
I thought it was the right thing to end it with no sound,

I had a thought of hanging roped up to the ceiling,
Just because I couldn't stop my drinking and my stealing,

My parents always fought, my brothers didn't like me,
I had the worst life ever just as you can see,

Kicked right off the football team when I was found with Pot,
Busted by the cops when they found my car was hot,

Now there's no point living so why should I push on,
I wish my problems would disappear and this mess would just be gone.

I feel the only way right now is to end it all,
So my mind's made up, my life is done, and I've taken the big fall!

I never thought about how my mom would feel,
She still cannot believe how much this death is real,

I'm sorry mom, so sorry mom, I didn't mean to hurt you
But what's done is done, I can't come back,
And I regret it through and through.
Derek McKinney

Christmas Eve Legend

The woods were still and the snow was deep. But there was no creature who could sleep.

The fox and vixen ran together, silently through the starry weather.

The buck and doe and the fawn came drifting.

Into the clearing, the rabbit lifting his ears, shook white from the twigs he brushed.
The chattering squirrel for once was hushed.

As he sat with his paws against his breast, and the bobcat crouched on the mountain crest.
Safe in the fold the silver sheep told the young lambs not to leap.

In the shadowy stable the horses stood. Hearing the quietness in the woods.
And the cattle sighed in the fragrant barn, waiting the instant of the morn.

The stars stood at midnight, and tame or wild,

All creatures knelt to worship the child. That is why Jesus's birth is celebrated in church.

Ann Marie Beyer

'Twas Two Days Before Christmas

'Twas two days before Christmas, and my car went and broke;
what a great day for it to decide to choke.

I'm standing outside the car looking like a fool,
but down inside I still know I'm incredibly cool.

I left in plenty of time, people drove by laughing and doing mime.

When what to my ears do I hear, many horns that need to be
shoved up many people's rear.

A friendly guy stopped to say "Hi", I told him a tow-truck was coming by.
A call to a chum brought him to me, now in order not to be too late we only had to go Warp 3.

We got the theater with no yelling or screaming,
Thank God for some things or a few people would have been bleeding.
Merry Christmas To All And To All A Good Day.

Theodore Leonard Kisiel

I Am A Strong Black Woman

I am a strong black woman who holds her head up high,
Because I know on God I can always rely.
I am a strong black woman who does her very best
And if you don't believe me just put me to the test.

I am strong black woman who is proud of her race,
If you look closely you will see the word Pride written on my face.
I am strong black woman with lots to give back
That is just one reason why I joined an organization called S.T.A.T.S.

I am a strong black woman living day by day,
Overcoming all obstacles that stand in my way.
I am a strong black woman who knows beauty is only skin deep,
Who doesn't judge a person by their outside, but by the friends that they keep.

I am a strong black woman striving to reach the top,
By learning and by giving from the heart.
I am strong black woman who loves to read and write,
Who's not afraid to speak her mind and not afraid to fight.

I am a strong black woman!!

Tenikka L. Cunningham

Words Are Like Blood

You know how your blood is actually supposed to be blue inside
your body, but the instant it hits the air it turns red?

It's the same with words.

You can formulate sentences chock-full of meaning and emotion
swelling from your heart into your mind, but when you voice those
words and they hit the air, suddenly the meaning is gone and they're just words...

Blue words turned red...
Just like blood.

Jody Ann Smith

Clear Day

Bright is the sun.
Come has the day.
Who wants to play?
Look at the blue, see all the hues?
The bright golden ball,
you know it will not fall!
The sun's rays glimmer and shine.
As I look I can call them mine.
The white puffy clouds,
makes you want to be a clown,
Those white puffy clouds,
come together in a crowd,
Then stretched out from finger tip view.
As I gaze I see only a few.
Wonder as I may the shapes that I see
can "then" only come to me.
So here I am this clear day
As I look up around me
What can I say?

Lee Etta Pester

The Promise

How strange that when you enter
A room you've never seen,
Anticipating nothing,
A promise lies therein.
And you, all unsuspecting,
With mind on other things,
Don't recognize the promise
The situation brings,
'Til once you've left behind you
The room, and closed the door,
And suddenly the promise
Is gone forevermore.
And, looking back, you wonder
With sadness deep within,
And mourning wasted promises,
The way it might have been.

Carol M. Thompson

Lost

Death settles, like a whisper
On the pale cheek of a child.
A short life lived in fear and pain
With parents, drunk and wild.

So many nights, this child cried
A prisoner in his bed.
Dark bruises marked his back and side
A fist print stained his head.

So innocent, so gentle
A loving soul was lost.
And Heaven embraced the little child,
For priceless was his cost.

Marcie Harris

Eileen's Eye

He is my master.
I accept him as my kin.
I hope he loves me as I love him.
He took me from the bitter cold.
He loved me dearly, but now I must go
To the far beyond of my soul.
I wish to return for his sake,
But he with me, I cannot take.
I remember the special call I heard,
And I purred, and purred, and purred...

Johnny Roberts

The Riverbank

She's sitting by a riverbank,
fog surrounds her as in a dream,
I have it all captured
in a photo I've just seen.

Her upturned face is glowing,
her smile is deep and wide,
as she gazes at the man
who's standing by her side.

She looks so young, so happy,
it takes my breathe away.
She was believing in forever,
as she sat there that day.

I wish I had been old enough
when she packed us on that train,
to have offered her some comfort,
to have cried for her pain.

I know, now, she once sat
by a riverbank of dreams,
and in my heart always,
it's a riverbank for queens.

Candy Gregory

The World Around Us

As I look out my window,
I see many lives.
Carrying children,
Those husbands and wives.
Though I cannot leave my window,
I imagine I am free.
Out in the world,
What a place to see.
So many good things,
So many bad.
People are happy,
People are sad.
Flowers bloom,
Flowers die,
So many children,
Will learn not to cry.
When a new child is born,
the mother has birth.
We teach them to fight,
But all we need is peace on earth.

Jessica Wells

Covet

I desire him
Thirst for his soul,
His every morsel

His presence is needed
Life given again
Satisfaction

Taken to another place,
Another time

Float on clouds
Sway with air
Seduced by numbness

Taken by hazy stars
Pins poke flesh
My existence fluid

I am taken,
I am abode

Mindy Knutzen

The Desiring Of Soul's Desiring

What one thing could man give in exchange for his own soul?
Is there a measure to weight the scale to provide for such a toll?
Mankind through time has reasoned that its worth is earthly gain.
And all will find the end unkind is empty as is vain.
Is there a gem so high appraised to obtain soul's preciousness
To share alike in value that a life alone can posses?
Many deem that pleasures seem worthy to arrange
A pledge to buy a lie instead for their soul in exchange,
If there was a paradise to find, a place nobody knows
Would it be worth the voyage for a souls weight in gold?
There is that which hungers for the souls of all mankind
A vacuum to a greater void on one side that we find
But deeper are the longings for possession of the souls
Of God who makes diamonds from the refuse of sins coals.
There is that place within the life of man that emptiness abides
For unto death he will remain unless God's spirit is inside.
It's never enough to experience or for open hands to hold
The cheapened imitations that we so openly behold
There is much more to life than these, for the treasures are untold.
And there is no greater tragedy than one who sells cheaply his own soul.

Anthony Stamile Jr.

My Grampa

He was a man of power and strength,
His stories were told in great length.
Handsome and classy his hair the barber would chop,
Silver and shiny, but he was lacking on top.
He worked hard for the woman he loved, Mary,
He could always pay the bills, his wife's needs were never monetary.
From one of his own bottles he would taste, "very fine",
He thought, "The grapes were very good from this year's vine".
His Croatian girl obeyed every command.
From her master, every morning he walked, leash in hand.
He loved God and gave to the poor,
He was in church every Sunday, sometimes more.
He always told me, "Do your best,
Keep working, never rest,
Until it's done and done the right way".
In my heart his song will always stay,
"I love my Ci-Gi Yesir-Ee,
And she's got nice ushi 1-2-3".

Peter Vranich

Acknowledgement

Look out upon the Earth — with your eyes open,
Look past the smoke, the dirt, the fear, look within your own self.

Tell me what you see
Even within the smoke lays the fire,
that dances one of the most beautiful and graceful dances.

Strain your ears...Listen to the wind
Look past it all, find the inner beauty within all things.

Allow yourself to see what is real, and to feel what is here.
Appreciate beauty for beauty.

Peace only exists in the being,
peace is only unobtainable if you allow it to be,
you have an inner beauty within all things.

Allow yourself to see what is real, and to feel what is here.
Appreciate beauty for beauty.

Peace only exists in the being,
peace is only unobtainable if you allow it to be,
you have an inner strength...

You have allowed yourself to become a slave to the flesh and
to material wealth. Allow yourself to walk free within your mind,
You are at peace...You are a perfect creation. Acknowledge it.

Christina C. Cole

Untitled

As the clouds cover the sky,
Darkness sets in.
My eyes show the burden my heart feels
I'm so lonely I begin to cry.

I wiped my tears and looked around,
Everything is so depressing.
All I can do is sit and wonder why?
I sit here and dwell in self pity.

I'm troubled by the way I feel.
What is the answer?
I felt someone touch me, I jumped.
Know one was there, I was sacred.

I heard a Golden voice, I looked again. There was no one there. Then
I heard the voice say, God is your friend, just talk to him.

The chills ran my spine, I felt warm. I dropped to my knees, my hands
are together. With tears in my eyes, I prayed for help. It started
to rain, Heavy, I cried.

I never felt so loved before.
The rain washed the pain away, my tears stopped and I looked up,
From that moment on I know I'll never be alone!

Connie Miller Trimble

From Loneliness To Joy

I'm a little Hobo from North Palm Beach
So whenever I can, I sleep on the Beach.

Then to my amazement one fine day
I came upon a little dog who had gone astray.

I picked him up and was as happy as can be
To have a little friend to take home with me.

As I walked along the Beach, I found a penny and a dime
Just enough to buy some food, then he'll be just fine.

What a treasure I had found with this tiny doggie
My friend, my pal, my new found joy, he helps when my mind is foggy.

I named him "Joy," mine is Charlie and we get along just fine
His name suits him I must agree, and believe he's one of a kind.

So to this day he's such a friend, and whenever I feel sad
My doggie is there to cheer me, he's the friend I never had.

Mary Prasso

Fear And Hope

Standing at opposite ends of the human emotion scale, fear and
hope could be said to form the bookends of daily living.

I think it safe to assume that both of these feelings live within
each of us, how much they control us often becomes the problem. Put another way,
how well we master them can become a serious test of our ability to move freely
through each hour of each day.

Fear of immediate danger in itself is a terrible feeling but even
worse are those deepest fears we hold within, the ones that limit
and confine us. These deep fears begin to strangle all of the good
things we have inside us. They influence all of our emotions and
many times literally bring our life to a standstill.

But fear can be overcome if we begin to understand how hope can
free us. It's been said that hope is nothing more than borrowing
from the promise of the future. If you think about that for a moment,
it's a beautiful thought.

And, what a positive way to live each day, filled with hope and the
promise of all the good things life can have in store for us;
unafraid of those fears which grip us and take the smile away from our heart.

So face each day filled with hope and trust. Know that each morning as the new light of
dawn overpowers the shadows of darkness, so too will your hope overshadow your fears.

John A. Kessler

I Wish For You

A warm house, good food.
    And those who care.
Gifts of love, and
    A quiet prayer.
Holly, and candles,
    And mistletoe.
Candy canes.
    And lamplight glow.
Children's laughter, a star
    And three kings.
Bethlehem,
    And angel wings!

Janice E. Davis

Everyday

Moon dangles his feet
Over the edge of the universe,
Popping lemon candy into his mouth
And watching his warmth
Swirl into the midnight air.
Over slumber does he reign,
Until dawn draws near
And Morning's fiery fist
Is a silent but commanding
Proposal of combat.
Through ancient and forgotten
Collages of days and nights
Has this weary battle persisted,
But, fatigued, he retreats
So that another may rule.
Abiding by nature's laws,
Moon withdraws into seclusion
And prepares for the night throne;
He will dictate once again.

Vanessa Hill

My Little Girl

I saw the sun today
on the face of my little girl.
I saw the sun shining
as her bright smile unfurled.

I saw the moon tonight
in the eyes of my daughter.
I saw the moonbeams dancing
in her eyes; blue as water.

I saw the stars tonight
in my daughter's smile.
I saw the starlight gleaming
and she laughed all the while.

I saw the world today
as though for the first time.
I saw the world through her eyes
as if she were looking through mine.

Lucien Joseph Hecker

The Beauty Of A Stone

Yesterday's accumulations,
miles of time
silent and still,
molded together in mass,
secrets of the earth
embedded and preserved.
Held in hard evidence,
soft innocence or crumbling doubt.
Forever reminding... The total,
eventual oneness.. All...
in "The Beauty of a Stone."

M. Boyd Lewis

Daddy

My Daddy was a railroad man
Who worked hard every day;
He didn't have the time or means
To sit around or play.

My Daddy was a scholar
Of the Word of God, you see—
And always told his children
To be as God would have them be.

Because his word was like pure gold,
A bond so bright and strong—
You didn't doubt a thing he said
Nor think that he'd do wrong.

I can still envision Daddy,
With the twinkling in his eye—
Even though we made mistakes sometimes,
He encouraged us to try.

Now in that place called heaven
Where we hope to go some day-
I just want to thank my Daddy
'Cause I know he paved the way.

Bob Hatcher

Beautiful Boy

Nothing so pure
Untouched by the world
The babe lies asleep
In his mother's arms

Her eyes speak softly
Her thoughts, her dreams
Perfection so small
Indescribable love

She rocks gently, watching
Content innocence
The moment is captured
Too soon will be gone

Sweet little babe
Perfection so small
Untouched by the world
Too soon you'll be gone

Lori Barber

My Jesus

I would not trade my Jesus
For all the worldly fame
That comes to some who prosper,
But have not heard He came.

I would not sell my precious Lord,
As some would gladly do
To gain a worldly dollar,
For He will see me through.

I would not give my Savior
For all the knowledge you can see,
For it is foolish in His sight
God's wisdom leadeth me.

Verna E. Polzel

Butterfly

I see butterfly
Wings of delightful velvet
Fluttering in field.

Donna P. Holloway

Artifact

"Happy Valentine's Day" chides the balloon
that bobs and weaves before the winter window.
Leaching helium, its shrivelling form glides heart-high
above the cold tile floor. Will it sink to oblivion, I wonder?
Or will it reach a place of equilibrium - its latitude of survival
suspended above where feet would crush?

The cat makes disinterested swipes at its ribbon,
a white paper streamer with tiny red hearts
machine-gunned along its length
a leash tethering balloon to scarlet heart weight
It can't drift too far afield. Or soar too high.

The cat puts paw to strand to gauge the tug from above
a half-hearted act by each of them. There's not enough life
in the game to make it fun. Holding the strand secure between paws,
she shreds the length that her claws have pierced:
little hearts torn asunder, without much thought, without any passion.

Some day soon I'll prick the balloon, then flatten the heart shape,
smoothing its wrinkles. Folding it up, I'll tuck it away
some place sacred and forgotten, only to rediscover it
years from now when I'll try in vain to remember
what its significance was.

Michaele Harrington

My Higher Power

Some look to God during troubles and forget Him when Life is good;
I look to God in every way, 'cause I know He's with me everyday.
I do things constantly to displease His ever watching eye.
I'm sure He looks at me and sighs,
and then says - "My poor child, my oh my!"
But in spite of my shortcomings, He never leaves my side.
In Him always, I find peace, no matter how much I cry.
He continues to forgive me, and never contemplates my worth;
for it was God who made me as I am and knows I'm worth a plenty.
He allows me to stumble and fall;
He helps me up, and yes, to Him I call.
He answers in a soft, sweet voice, He says, "Yes, my child?"
I say, "Lord, please hold me tight and never let me go.
I know I'm responsible for what I do, and most of it is unpleasing
to you; but you know what Lord? I can't make it without you!
One day I will learn, and mature too;
and stop falling short of your glories.
Please be patient with me.
Let me know you will never venture away from me."
He said, "I know, I will, and I have."

Theondra Venessa McIlwain Wallace

Untitled

I'm going to write a little note
to my little girl and boys
to tell that Daddy hasn't forgotten them
Or the things they'd like in toys
First off I'm going to write
Bout things I'd like to do
to make their moments pleasant
I'll mention just a few
I'll build a great big doll house
For my little girl called May
and put in all the trimmings, in which for her to play
It'll be the biggest doll house, that my little girl has had
and all I want for all of this is a hug and kiss for Dad.
Then for my boy Frankie, I'll buy all the tools he needs
to smash and build to his content and I'd forgive him all his deeds
He can build himself a sail-boat or perhaps a truck or two
or if his sisters doll house needs repairs, he can fix it good as new
For little Pete there's nothing yet, but he can borrow from Frankie Lad
and the price I'm asking from the three
is a hug and kiss for Dad.

Peter Perrone

A Moth To The Flame

The pine greets my lungs after a long rest and I awaken to find
its branches across my chest. Are coffins not made of more wood?
I have so much room to move, I must confess. The wooden floor
presses against now numb feet; between bowls of water I try to reach.
Muted silence fills my ears, and with great difficulty I try
to speak. Nothing comes out like dead air. I try to make sense
of this confusion, but can only stand and stare. I know that
I'm in my room, but I feel like something's missing, something's
not there. On my dresser, covered in dust, are memories of what
I used to be. A broken clock's face stares into mine, showing me
the time at which it died. Maybe not too long ago? A calendar's
date circled in blood. What it all means, I don't know!
My confusion grows deeper yet. I'm sure that something's missing;
there's something I need to get. I move closer to the door,
surely on the other side it will all be clear, except it moves
further away the closer I near. Finally I'm overcome with
a horrible fear. A line of sand is what stands between me and
leaving here. I get on the floor in a rush and a hurry, and count
the countless grains for hours to see how deep I'm buried.
As morning arrives I finally break the seal and open the door
as I kneel. The sun hits me, and I only wish that for one last time
I had feelings to feel; and to fathom the hoax played upon me;
it's too late, but I'm just in time to see, a moth dying
on the window's screen mesh; the spirit that left with my final
breath; and as it falls, my soul burns as if touched by God's flesh.

Stephen Halk

~Y.E.S.~
Your Everlasting Spirit

People are forever telling you, <u>no</u>. It may come from your friend,
Your neighbor, your enemy, your boss, your associate, your spouse,
Your child, or even your brother. Human nature, itself, warrants
Prejudice against the positive: It will try win out because of the pull
Of the negative, opposing pole. There is also the pull between good and
Evil, ups and downs, male and female, success and failure — that's just life.
But, who said life was just.
The only way to combat these opposing forces is to gain faith.
Faith will give you the foundation, <u>The Seed</u>, the will, the confidence and
The desire to have everything go your way. There is no mystery here —
Opposition always requires defense, and defense must be gained by
Complete preparation. That preparation is faith, a belief in a power
Stronger than the self.

And that power is beyond life — It is **The Power of The Holy Spirit.**

Edward J. Longo

The Inexpressible Mind

As a stream's vicious waters clashed toward the hostile rocks,
And high desires seem as a light's faded glower,
When an oppressive drudgery given to whom promised lust,
I ache mindless, and feel like a cheated groom.

As a fight to save a soul, to passion an impassive hearth,
is being given. When suddenly voice of wish, was heard.
A matter of needless necessities flashed through mindless thoughts,
Giving an unpleasant feeling of being left out.

As a faith's fragile waves smashed to the walls of a head,
And its suddenly noise created a spirit of oblivious,
To be heard a judgment is unable to find its way,
Is this an end? Is this a time to wake up, to be conscious?

As a nature of rocks rolling down, a storm is mounting
Head's walls attacked by storming immense motion of thoughts,
The unbearable feeling, the mind and oh that affecting.
Stop! Stop please, let it go, express its perplexities.

As I lay, letting it just waft out, setting it free once more,
Storm quietly sat down, stream's little waves frisk on friendly rocks,
And my mind cleared of unpleasant and exhausting thoughts,
Thank you, to let me write this down.

Miroslav Vozka

A Valley Filled With Wild Flowers

There is a valley;
That I often travel to;
It's filled with wild flowers.
I call it the rainbow.

In this valley of flowers;
The colors are endless;
Radius red; outrageous purple;
Royal Blue, and grazing green grass.

I go to this valley;
To waste time;
Let stress out and
To just think things over.

I go to this valley a lot;
I don't know what I'd do;
I would be lost;
Without this valley

Karey Michelle Wallace

Speechless

She stepped into the hallway
as I was about to leave
so feminine, so lovely
man's mind could not conceive
her perfume sprayed the atmosphere
rendered speechless
she froze me there
unable to utter a sigh or sound
my thought processes she
did thoroughly confound
she knew it too
her body said
"Take a look mortal, then
drop dead"
Then in a minute she was gone
yet her presence seemed to stay
"you'd better hurry,"
Some little voice said
but leaden feet, would not obey.

Jonathan Henderson

On My Birthday, I Wear Black

On my birthday, I wear black,
No cheerful parties or cake,
Sitting at Grandfather's wake.

On my birthday, I wear black,
Mourning and never slacking,
Cheerfulness is what I lack.

On my birthday, I wear black,
Death, pushing me in a sack,
Turning my countenance black.

On my birthday, I wear black,
Death never will bar the way,
For my heart is packed with care.

On my birthday, I wear black,
Memories outlast sorrow,
Healed I am on the morrow.

Next year, I will wear smiles,
For I have gone many miles;
Cheerfulness comes in piles.

For years I will remember
Tender things in November.

Heather A. Blandford

Little Cries And Whispers

What makes a tiny soul
  So opposed to sleep,
What makes a child so sad,
Perhaps the rhythms she feels and hears,
  The turn of brow, the flood of tears.

Or is it something else, indeed,
  Unseen, but so at hand,
The will, the blood, the memory of,
  What we were, and am.

Might she not choose another path,
  Another way, another say?
Or will she still choose mine,
And be caught up, like all of us,
  Again, and again, and again.
        Arlis A. Sheffield II

Gone

Closed doors, quiet voices,
I can feel the sorrow here.

The sound of hushed sobs,
As the time is drawing near.

I know things will be different,
But I try to forget.

Words are said that are not meant,
And no one's needs are met.

We walk as if confused,
Not knowing what to do,

We pray that this is all a dream,
And that we won't lose you.

But reality hits,
As we find your room alone

I see her tears shining,
And I hear her piercing moans

I could feel your coldness,
As you told them they were wrong

But it no longer matters
Who was right, because you're gone.
      Cynthia Beth Davis

I Wonder What It's Like

I wonder what it's like,
    To be close to you,
To tell you my inner most feelings
  To share my points of view

I wonder what it's like,
    To hold your hand,
To kiss your sensuous lips,
to run my fingers through your hair.

I wonder what it's like,
    To be held in your arms.
To feel the heat of your body
        Next to mine.

I wonder what it's like,
    To make love to you,
To feel our bodies move in unison,
  To feel our hearts beat as one.

I wonder what it's like,
    To have a life with you
To know you're loved and cared for
  All the years through
      Tracey A. Moore

This Morning Alone

I traveled along the road less traveled
and saw the point at which the azure sky blended
with the misty snow-laden rock-topped mountain peaks
and when I could only think of you and how you
and I should together see this, the grass-green border bridling the
seaboard was too much to alone bear and I willed this image to you in your dreams.

Did you see it and sense me sending it? I wanted you to awake with
this scene and smile at the thought that I too shared it with you.

I am broken-hearted to see the perfection of an excellent morning without you.
Sunsets beyond compare that never would I dare again without you.
Days apart with no beat in my heart if without you.
There is nowhere to go if without you.

And so, my Love, this hasten to your heart,
and like a glaciered river, run it melted to your mind:
Suffer not a thought apart, for all of life our hearts are heart,
in truth as true as if I with you

Saw the perfect morning set and mountains blend into the sea beneath
the sun and wind was still and stood its ground and this green ground
and blue hued sky wore the excellence of Camelot. And in this court,
my life was well and good and right, and it was then that you and only you I thought.
        Michael Henry Oppenheim

Looking Back On The Wheel

Life is like a turning wheel.
My flesh and blood are as cold as steel.
Looking at life through my eyes,
My problems and troubles are a swarm of flies.
They encircle my mind and laugh at my despair,
Each new dilemma is an insect in my hair.
I swat them away with my fly swatter of lies.
I tell myself I'll live forever, knowing death is no surprise.
I know what I'm doing, my denial uncontested.
I tell myself that I'm not doing wrong is the bullsh*t I digested.
Only one solution can turn me around.
I hope I can be forgiven for the sins I have found.
My eyes can only look forward into the light as my feet carry me
onward away from the night.
Merely just words do I write on this paper.
Only God can help me now for he is my savior.
My body that was once so cold must warm the world through gifts that I hold.
I can not look back upon the turning wheel.
There is so much ahead in life with which I must deal.
      Edward Wilson

My Everyday Dream

This is the Cabin of my everyday dream
in my dream to which I often go
to autumn leaves sometime amid or nestled in the snow.
My cabin close beside a crystal stream
when I often swim (alone)
and there are deer who never mind
that I am watching them
this cabin of my dreams
recltic and small and I yet feel.
When I am there. I surely have it all
it has two window through which the sunlight stream.
And when duck fall the honeysuckle drips into my dreams

And here in my dreams there is no need to lock door. No one lives out
this far and I do very well indeed without a bus or a car. I've
spent some happy hours on that bench beneath the trees my home made
bread is sweetened with wild honey from the bees because one cannot
see it doesn't mean it isn't there. It is my secret refuge from a
world so full of care within its walls an atmosphere of true
simplicity and we are one who dwell within my little dog and bird and
out side loving deers.
      Marie Edmie Steed

Lighthouse

Mother and daughter walk by the shore, not really knowing what they are walking for.
They have no destination in mind, but grow closer together with every stride.
The child gazes into the passionate waves. Mesmerized, she could watch for days.
The mother holds her in her arms, and tells of the ocean's beauties and harms.
Toward the water the child leans, trying to see what it all means.
Each step is guided with a mother's care, as she strokes the daughter's long brown hair.
For now they walk hand in hand, through endless, ever-changing sand.
They have never been closer together, but the mother knows it can't last forever.
The daughter will grow and run to the sea, and the mother will have to let her be.
The mother has taught her to be patient and wise. To the daughter, the ocean holds no surprise.
She takes to the sea, nervous but strong. She knows that her mother has not told her wrong.
She never feels too far away, and knows she can return on any day.
My mother will never be out of my sight. She is my lighthouse on the darkest night.

Stacy Berning

Taking You With Me

As I work in the country performing my duties, I see God's
creation and absorb all the beauty. A loving voice resonates
throughout the air, I turn to look but no one is there...
Overwhelmed in the sounds of the heart of the town, a whisper of
love makes a sweet sound. Again I search, but no one's around.
What an unusual feeling... Always so comforting but never to be
feared. A feeling of Love, so close and so near. This feeling
follows me and stays close to my soul. What had once been
confusing — I now know. Who would have thought that love was so
strong? My thoughts put to words as my heart sings a song. I
reach for a pen and I write to my love; "When we are apart —
know that you're always with me... God's gift from above. From my
heart to yours — with all of my love."

Nikko Martello

Adoption

Some people think adoption is an easy way to do it
But that is for those who have never been through it

Believe me I know you have suffered much pain and strife
Which gives deeper meaning to this tiny new life

Mommy had surgery, daddy did too
Thermometers were popping all the night through

They tried month after month to no avail
With all modern science this was not to prevail

I know how you suffered when they would poke you and prod
And we know now this could only take place by wisdom of God

We thank you our father for giving us this chance
And you can relax now daddy and put on your pants

Now son your life will never be the same there are changes you must do
He said I know mom and I hope they will all be by you

But all jokes aside I would just like to say
I'm glad you're all here to share in this day

We will never forget you helped give her-her start
And we know that it came from each and every heart

Frances Ottavi

Silent Cry

As the clouds cover the sun's rays, the willow tree bows her head,
Her branches bend low and brush the ground; the leaves seem dead.
Without the sun she finds she can't stand alone, her strength drained,
She feels lost, without purpose; her trunk is scratched and stained.
She knows the sun will shine once more; but her needs are her own,
She must learn to stand without the warmth; she is far from alone.
Though her branches are weak and could easily break in the breeze,
She raises her head to meet the day, standing tall among the trees.

Jeanne Flora

A Mother Is...

A mother is a person who
is always there,
A mother is a person who
loves you and cares.
A mother is a person
who is always on your side.
A mother is a person
who leads you and guides.
A mother is a person who
always shares her gentle love.
A mother is a person who
prays to God above.
A mother is a person who is
very trust worthy and kind.
A mother is a person who speaks
sweet words on her mind.
These are the ways a mother
ought to be
this is what a mother is
to me.

Richard Golden

Raindrops From Heaven

As the raindrops fall
gently from space,
How warm it feels
upon my face,
Feeling lonely and
somewhat sad
Thinking of a certain child
and what he may have had,
How selfish of me, for
who am I?
The child isn't sad
he rarely even cries,
Seldom does he get mad
be happy for those who don't have it all
For God didn't make
us equal for his special ways at all
What a beautiful rainbow I see,
I think God made it special just for me.

Sandra Suntken

The Rhythm Feeds My Soul

Like rain that beats upon the roof
and storms with no control
like grass that blooms eternally
the rhythm feeds my soul
Like the morning sunrise in the east
that shines upon the world
like the singing sparrows on the hill
the rhythm feeds my soul
Like the church bells on a Sunday morn
listening intently as they toll
like the ceaseless buzzing of a bee
the rhythm feeds my soul
Like an instrument of classic rhythms
that fills an empty hole
like an aura of sweet harmony
the rhythm feeds my soul

Leon Antoine

Burnt Out

The blackness seeps into
my room
my life
As the ever running power
Runs into its dead end
The tears run down
My cheeks
In darkness
The darkness which was always
waiting
In the corners
In the secret hidden places
Just waiting for the time
I knew it would come
There's always a time
When the light
burns out.

Naomi Jones

Ocean

The waves crash against the rocks
the fish swim free,
Animals cool themselves
in the deep blue sea.

Salty water,
Silky sand,
Beautiful creatures,
Perfect land.

They need to live,
Like you and I,
Let them swim free,
Let them jump to the sky.

The ocean, the ocean,
Deep and blue,
The ocean, the ocean,
It's for them too.

Liz Holland

Untitled

I sat by the window
in a chair next to his —
Placed there by a waiter
by fate
by chance.
Subtly glancing outside.
Searching for you.
Wishing for you.
Smiling on cue
(but never too brightly)
Laughing on demand
(but never too loudly)
Pulling away
(not closer)
When the advance came.
Proving to you
who I am.
In a chair next to his —
Placed there by fate
or by chance.

Elizabeth Moore

Snow

Snow falls softly to the ground when you step outside you can hear
every sound, a car in the distance, a dog barking too, and a snow plow shoveling just for you.

The snow plow makes it safe for us, to drive our cars when we know
we must to get somewhere, where we have to be, that snow plow makes it safe for me.

When the snowflakes melt away, the sun comes out the snow turns grey, the blanket of
white will no longer stay, and the snow man runs away.

When we put away our winter wear, it makes me sad, I really care,
Christmas is gone and the house seems bare, when the snow has melted away.

Somehow snow seems so pure to me, white as an angel or a bandaged knee, children
laugh when they play in the snow, their eyes shine bright and their cheeks aglow, their
nose is cold, their fingers too, but they stay out anyway.

When the snow falls softly to the ground, remember this gift that can't be found, when
the sun comes out the snowflakes melt, and the snow man runs away, the blanket of
white is the children's delight, when the snow man stands his ground.

Peggy O'Neill Sproat

And They Were Seven

Seven came from all over the U.S.
Yet they had a common goal
Seven lives with danger and excitement as constant companions,
Seven were so thrilled and happy to be
On a great adventure — explorers and pioneers into space!
Seven started, and yet in the twinkling of an eye,
They were gone — in a Chariot of fire!
And now may we remember the seven who sacrificed
Their lives, their greatest possession —
All they could give for their country and fellowmen!
And when we behold the vast universe and firmament —
May we think of them as seven new stars, up there for all eternity!
May their song of victory forever be "The Battle
Hymn of the Republic" — Mine eyes have seen the glory!"
And may God be the wind beneath their wings!
Surely, God, in all his great mercy, will
Comfort all those who are left behind to mourn,
Who loved them so!
They will live on in our hearts forever!
Farewell! Brave Seven!

W. C. Hiatt

That Man's Struggle

That first kiss, when fireworks roll
That lovely face that touches the soul

That exciting fun that two friends share
That knowing trust that is seemingly always there

That one fateful night when all went wrong
That one man's jealousy he felt so strong

That man is stuck between a rock and a hard place
That true? Friend or that beautiful girl with that beautiful face

That duo told their contrasting stories that man did receive
That man had the difficult task of who to believe

That man is still in turmoil on which decision to make
That man is the only who realizes what is at stake

That sorrowful truth that still lies hidden away
That untruthful soul who will be sure to pay

That sad feeling that man will always feel
That terrible one who never felt love so real

That man will always hold that hatred for all to see
That sad truth is that man, that man, that man is me!

Bill Martin Jr.

River Of Tears

The clouds gather across the sky.
Darkness invades the light of day.
I sit by my window awaiting the oncoming storm.
The rain beats against the window pane, and within moments
hundreds of drops dance across the glass.

But this is not rain; but the tears of a child, a father, a grandmother.
The tears of my People who perished during a different storm;
a storm of human destruction.
Look at the tears; you see their faces, so innocent, so pure, so sad.

There are thousands of drops now; too many to count.
They become a stream of lost hope and despair.
It is the river of the six million, washed away, never to be seen again.

The rain suddenly stops, and a rainbow appears in the heavens.
I smile, for now I know that my People are in the presence of God.

Robert D. Waters

Darryl

Being me and being free on fire for life, I just want to be free.
Oh, but, I can't read! Will somebody help me please?
I go to school, I play football, basketball and I'm big and tall.
No! I won't fall.
Looking through those books, I turn the pages, Can't they see me?
I can't read.
Why can't I do the things I want! I just want to be me.
I just want to be free. Teach me how to read.
Time has passed. I've dropped out of school, going down another road.
This is not really me. Teach me how to read.
I just want to be free.
It's Christmas Eve and here we are on this dark street,
someone's shooting all around.
My friend is lying on the ground.
I must help him now, that's just me.
Bang! Look at that light!
I know I can read. I'm free.

Carol Ransom Perry

Dagger Of The Mind

There's a certain feeling, one of joy and of pain,
It causes the mind to wander; only the body can remain;
Its meaning cannot be traced, for it overpowers to unwind,
Only one phrase can describe it: it is a Dagger of the Mind...

Do not allow this feeling, to enter within the soul,
It will only take away form you a part that once was whole,
And leave you with an emptiness as hollow as the night;
Though this mystical sensation does not occur within the sight;
It takes the form of a happiness that many seek to find,
And tears away at the heart of men while aiding all mankind...

There remains a thought of accomplishment, and a sense of dedication,
That requires the loyalty of body and soul — a time-felt occupation.
As time itself continues on to bring another dawn,
Confused impressions will appear, then cease to linger on;
And then reality will come, which helps to ease the bind...
No other phrase can give it meaning: it is a Dagger of the Mind...

Barbara Sharp Orban

Can You Hear Me?

I am so far out in the distance. I cried for your help, but you
did not hear me. I waited for your response, but you did not move.
I tried talking to you, but you did not understand. I tried
explaining, but you did not care.
You stayed with her but did not let me go. She was so violent and now that I'm older,
it is in the past you try to help. It is stuck
with me, never leaving. I can't help but to blame you. You never
talked, you never listen, you only cared for her.
All I am left with is myself trying to sort things out, never
understanding why it has to happen this way.

Jessica Welch

Graduation

Whirling colors
blue, white, and gold
envelop me as the days go by
not to strangle, but to comfort

Every day disappears,
melded to the rest
in swiftly marching hours and minutes
to the tune of "Pomp and Circumstance"

Longed for memories go unnoticed
buried among flurries of
preparations and finishings

I hurry about,
wishing my youth away
afraid of what lurks ahead
someday it will all be photos
in a dusty, cherished album

Amanda E. Ellerbe

The Red Snow Of Sarajevo

All in the name of Ethnic Cleansing
Hatreds reason an excuse as before
Explodes fire and ice
Its insanity spreads disease
Thundering the mountains
Tidal waves of madness
Chilling humanity
Drowning the sacred life
Spilling destruction
Into an infants stroller
Blown over
Broken, torn, smashed

In the red snow of Sarajevo

Its severed finger points to the sky
Bleeds its mothers cry
The sound as before
Born despised
Bosnian, Croatian, Christian, Muslim
Human divided by evil

In the red snow of Sarajevo.

Ameerah Hasin Ahmad

Time Ticking

The ticks were ticking tocks in time
   together they did speak.
The widow without warning
   wore leather she thought was chic.
The antics in the attic
   where Antoine lay awake...
Caused craziness and of course
   the crushing of the cake.
So strong became the storm outside
   yes, wicked was the weather.
The ticks were ticking tocks in time
   when we left together.

Renee Semon

Chores Delayed

Lawn's grown tall
Red Toro stalled

Golf bag burnished clubs
in the trunk of the car

Lush fairways beckoning
cutting divots I'm reckoning

Albert J. Altimont

338

Time To Go

You've had a great life,
And now it is time,
For you to meet Jesus,
And live a life without crime.

You've had a great wife
Through sickness and health,
Even though you haven't had
A lot of money and wealth.

You've had great kids
And grandchildren as well,
And now you have been called
To go to heaven not hell.

It's time for you to go
Up, up, and away!
This life has been fun,
And you have nothing more to say.

Ian Tongol

Life Is. . .

Life is
   living, laughing,
   crying, worrying,
Trying Harder next time.

Being is everything,
   Living, lonely,
Being is me.

I am she, her,
   That girl, I am me.

The tall, short,
   Smart, dumb one.

Who cries, laughs,
   Climbs, crushes, reaches.

I have to
   Reach, grasp, live.
I have to hang in there.

I live for
   Love, hate, laughter, tears,
But most of all
I live for Me.

Vera L. Seltzer

My Explanation

dedicated to Chris Fletcher
It seems like forever
that I've longed to be with you.
But my longing seems to never end!

I know you don't love me,
As much as I love you,
I hope someday
that it would come true.

Apparently not,
it never will,
but maybe someday, I thought,
my love for you grows still.

Well now you know
how I feel,
maybe one day
you'll feel the same.

I seriously doubt
that you'll ever see,
what I'm trying to tell you,
in what I've explained.

Lori Jackson

He

There is a place where my confusion hides.
Only one is there to whom I confide.
I close my eyes without the sleep. I even try not to weep.
As I pray, my weak legs fall,
the Almighty King has come to tear down the wall.
He brings with Him the gift of peace,
With His arms around me, my faith will increase.
The pain is still there, yet not as strong.
His love and care will last so long.
Through all, He is there, the bad and the good.
Up until now I never understood.
For Him I'll walk through all these years
For Him I'll cry these happy tears.
He died on a cross for all our sins.
In the end the good always wins.
He has saved me from eternal fire, He can save you too, He's not a liar.
In His name, eat the bread, for His glory, the Book is read.
The blood was shed for our sins.
The nails were driven in like pins.
And now all we have is our faith. For His return, we shall wait.

Nikki Finnell

This Figure

This figure before me,
   has a masculine face which possesses mysterious eyes.
   Eyes that reveal there's a lot hidden inside.
   Secrets and pain, sometimes wished to be swept away on an ocean's fierce tide.

This figure before me,
   has a soul full of life.
   Yearning to explore everything there is to see.
   Waiting to sail off in the world's adventurous sea.

This figure before me,
   has no fears of living life.
   Trying at least once everything that's out there.
   Preparing to escape in the earth's soaring air.

This figure before me,
   obtains a tough yet warm heart.
   Willing to help anyone.
   Revealing to them the land's encouraging sun.

This figure before me,
   is someone I admire.
   Everything I've said is true.
   You see this figure is of you.

Charla Cwanek

The Stars

She is watched sleeping by the figures in her own dream,
The figures take control over her being that is still unknown.

In a land where fairy dust is always falling, there is a secret,
But she does not possess the words to speak in this enchanted garden.

She finds herself walking on a cold bridge when she awakens,
Realizing her fate, a tear gently glides down her lucid skin.

Unconsciously, thoughts speed through her mind, but she cannot grasp even one,
The truth of the situation tears her apart and rips away her soul.

If only she could stop, but the intricate force is too strong to fight,
Trembling, she lifts her head to the sky falling upon her.

The ground shreds away and becomes distance as she feels the warmth,
To see what is happening took her sanity away.

Panic pulsates through her body as she sees herself, a child,
The dream was in her sparkling eyes, but the chance was beyond her reach.

Her mind is the world's creation; therefore the decision was not hers,
Her quest is yet to be spoken to her ears and she lets go, wishing for mercy.

Carrie L. Hassler

Because I Love You

I found a jewel rare and true, I found a jewel when I found you,
That's what I thought in my heart and mind,
you were my dream come true.
Why did you leave me here alone, hiding my shattered heart?
From a cold cruel world I have retreated, or is it you who is cold?
and I the one you mistreated!
Not a word have I heard from you since you left my arms,
No answers to letters, no answers to calls,
But have heard you're a nerd,
bestowing on an old friend your charms.
So I send no letters and no more calls
You must be cold as the jewel that I thought you were
But not so true and not so rare,
Then why do I still wear the jewel in the ring on my finger, put there by you?
And why, Oh! Why do I still love you?
And still await your return to my arms with your charms?
The answer is simple and plain to see,
I hope against hope, praying you will come back to me!
   Because I love you.

Ethel Schafer

Family Portrait

Midnight surrenders her silence...
as the common unrhythmic sounds of soulful death
creeps upon the pine wooden stairs.
The scent of Alize emulates through the ajarred bedroom door.
The child awakens and trembles with anticipation
as a man emerges, garmented with its hot stench.
Momma sleeps.
The child tugs at the worn cotton blankets.
Momma awakens but soon after commences her soul to sleep unbothered.
The child smiles as the man falls at the feet of her innocence.
Obscured in the shadows of his defile nature
he is laid reaching towards life with his right arm
extended across the threshold.
She kneels to wipe the sweat trickling down his forehead.
With the assurance that it is He,
the child with a voice as soft as the stillness of death that
beseeches her turns to Momma still cradled in slumber...
whispers in her ear...
"Daddy's Home"

Christopher White

What Is Love?

Lovers walking by the lake, hand in hand.
A boy and his dad running in the wind, flying a kite.
A little girl rocking her dolly, crooning a lullaby.
Good friends sharing a picnic, laughing together.
A faithful dog waiting at the bus stop for his master.
Little girls huddled together, sharing secrets.
Young mothers happily pushing their baby strollers through the park.
A little boy running to meet his daddy when he gets home.
Neighbors gathered in the back yard for a barbecue.
This is Love.

Young parents, holding their newborn baby, filled with wonder.
Mom kneeling by her sick child, cooling the fevered brow.
Dad helping his child understand difficult homework.
Teens helping with daily chores, without complaining,
Parents shouting encouragement at their child's ball game.
Families hugging during a time of crisis.
This is Greater Love.

God looking down on the world He made, sending His only Son to die
that we may have Life.
This is the Greatest Love.

Ruth Zimmerman

Dream Dancer

Through the day,
   and into the night,
the dreams are woven,
   and spun tight.
Dreams move with a rhythm,
   and message sent;
In colors and words
   from the Dream Dancer?

Where is the Dream Dancer?

From within the energy that is,
   comes the Dream Dancer,
magnificent and bright.
   Bathed in the colors of light.

Who is the Dream Dancer?

The reality is,
   that from the levels that are,
comes a blending
   to create,
the message so great.

You, my friend, are the Dream Dancer!

Victoria Lynne

My Reality

My life suffocates
Planting seeds of hate
My love turned to hate
Trapped far beyond my fate
I give, you take
This life that I forsake.
Been cheated of my youth
You turned this life to truth
Pure black looking clear
My work is done soon here.
Try getting back to me
Get back what used to be
Drink up, shoot in
Let the beatings begin.
Distributor of pain
Your loss becomes my gain
All have said their prayers
Now invade their nightmares.
To see into my eyes
You'll find where murder lies.

Jeffery Sells

What Is Marriage Now?

There was a time when Marriage was sweet
When there were steps to take.
And to steal a kiss was a real treat.
But, now it seems a real fake.
The vows seem meaningless
And marriages do not last.
The kids are under duress
And their feelings we just cast.
But where will they go?
How will they feel?
Do they not matter? They still grow.
They think, and talk, and are real!
But where will it end?
Can Family and Marriages still be saved?
What can we do to change the trend?
For all to be happy and none depraved...

Mike Harrison

Nocturne

My wife hits the hay and
   in minutes is snoring
While I lie there thinking
   the whole thing is boring,
So I sometimes write verse
   while others are sleeping
And the hands of my clock
   past midnight are creeping.
Comes the dawn and she's up
   full of vim and of vigor
And I'm cold asleep and
   my mortis is rigor.

    Edmund H. Lutz

What Is A Dream?

What is a dream?
I haven't a clue.
Intuition?   Observations?
An idea 'bout to brew?

Or perhaps a reflection
Back into your past?
Or maybe some insight,
Like a future forecast?

Or possibly a window
Into another dimension?
Or a super idea
For a great new invention?

Or maybe a story
With characters and a plot?
Or just your subconscious
Telling your deepest of thoughts?

Is a dream a jumble
Of thoughts intervening,
Or is it something
With a little more meaning?

    Jenne Turner

Waiting

Wind, winding, wandering, wondering.
What?
Which way? Why? When?
Wishful, wistful, wakeful, wonderful.
Water, washing, wayward, wise.
Without.
Worship, wasted, wretched, wrought.
Wielded.   Where?
War, wicked, worse, weird.
Watch.
Words, wealth, window, witty.
Who? Well,
We want.

    Jaqueline M. McBride

Gun Week

From dawn till dusk you'll hear it.
Bang! Bang! Bang!
There go the deer, followed by hunters.
Some hunters are lucky.
But others are not.

The dear are getting smarter
They run, afraid of everything
Even after dark.
Still during gun week
You'll hear it from down till dusk
Bang! Bang! Bang!

    Billie Figley

My Sister

   Sister's are a special breed, they have a bond that man
has no reign over, and no woman can tear apart.
   A sister's love is like no other, it last a lifetime, there is
no other love that can compare to this for it is special.
   My sister is set above all other's, she has a way about her
like no other, she is beautiful and yet she is so much more, she is
as sweet as an angel, but as protective as a lion, and yet she is ever so kind.
   She walk's with grace and has a style all of her own, and
out of all on this earth, I could have picked no better.
   I wasn't born rich but that was only in material things,
because when God picked you for our family, and made you my
sister, he gave me the most wonderful thing in life that really matters.
   I wish all women could have a sister like mine, so their
life would be a little easier and a whole lot kinder.
   For if there was one thing in this life I could not do
without, it would have to my sister.

    Delinda McKnight

When I...

When I hear the sounds of your sweet voice when you laugh,
you bring joy to a life that sometimes feels so empty.

When I feel your presence near me,
you bring a new dimension to the love we already share.

When I sense the intensity to which lengths you go to make someone happy,
it helps me to understand how fortunate I really am to have you.

When I touch the very warmth that exudes from your soul,
my heart wonders if I can cherish life in a similar way.

When I gaze into your tender eyes,
life's little problems seem to disappear in an instant.

When I reflect upon ours lives together,
I realize now that I don't wish to change the great foundations we built our love upon.

When I pondered why and what destinies brought us here,
and discovered does this really matter?

When I contemplate the reasons time and time again,
there is only one answer that remains clear.

When I embrace the future,
I will savor every waking moment to simply be with you.

    Edward Jones

Laughter

Laughter is a reaction to a good thing
It allows us to escape our troubles
A song that each wants to sing

When we feel sad, we feel like a slave to a king
But when we laugh, we are the hierarchy
Laughter is a reaction to a good thing
It has many cheerful sounds like that of a bell, oh!
What happiness it will bring
Sounds that give us calming effect
A song that each wants to sing

But when the laughter is over, it's like a cheap gold plated ring
Everyone tries to start the laughter again
Laughter is a reaction to a good thing

The bell of laughter has been struck once more,
but very gently, with a ting
Many people are laughing to the melody
A song that each wants to sing

We are once again birds without a broken wing
All of us are flying gracefully in the sky
Laughter is a reaction to a good thing
A song that each wants to sing

    David Scott

341

An Immigrant's Granddaughter

Upon the streets of Ireland my feet softly tread in search of
a piece of history, and the life my ancestors led.
Warm smiles and lilting voices awaited me at Erin's front gate,
while tales of war and famine seemed to creep through a back door.
It was here my great-grandparents were born, and loved, laughed
and lived, but their laughter was quickly silenced as the great famine set in.
There was death and despair all around them, but many were able
to flee to a land of abundance and hope, and a chance at liberty.
How can it be that my heart belongs to a time and place, and people now long gone?
Did their voices call from the soil and gently speak my name, or
was it God's sweet spirit calling me home again?
For in Ireland's precious beauty I knew that I had found a legacy of great riches
more valuable than gold, and the sweet fragrance of heather still runs deep within my soul.
But, of all the gifts they've left me these lessons stand above
the rest, that I must speak out against oppression, and be true to my
beliefs, and through it all keep my eyes on high and never ever doubt.
For God alone knows the score, it is written in his hand, and he
watches over me constantly to ensure my victory.
Now, I know my life may be but a whisper of the legacy that my
ancestors left, but their blood still flows through me, and as my life unfolds,
I will often look back with fondness on this land my great-grandparents called home.

Joanne E. Walsh

Dust Gathers At The Roadside

We live as an interstate world, ever lost in the pursuit of sixty-five.
Reduced here and there, but always closing on our beloved pace.
The flowers upon the roadside flash pretty neon colors.
To catch the eye of the passing traveler before the beauty leaves.
The motorist glances, perhaps seeing the beauty and perhaps not.
Pressing business weighs heavily and the foot presses the accelerator.
The beauty lies vacant.
Waiting in search of more appreciative people who may stop.
The flower sheds a tear as it slowly dies.
Holding onto its beauty for as long as possible, it finally lets go.
Withering and crumpling quickly,
It becomes dust at the roadside.

Nathaniel Waggoner

New Birth

How many years does it take to grow?
How many years before I can see right from wrong, night from light?
How much longer will it be?
I want to be free indeed.
I want to be all that I can be.
I need you Lord to open the door and give me strength and dignity.
The answer my friend is when you're born again.
All things become anew.
You read the Word, it gives you sight and your mind becomes renewed.
You'll sing glory to the Lord and exalt His name.
Glory, glory to God in the highest.
Glory, glory to God in the highest.

Richard E. Woodford

Like A Poem

Best friends are like a poem,
Everything they say seems totally true.
Best friends are like parents,
They know what's right and wrong for you.
Best friends are like a favorite place,
They have total understanding of each other.
Best friends are like a self,
They are of their own, which you both learn to admire.
Best friends are like a statue,
They're always there to remind us of times.
But, yet, I suppose this poem is all wrong.
A best friend is a kind friend, a true friend, and a loyal friend.
Not a poem or place.
Except the place they fill in your heart.

Laura Hartog

The Shivering Rebel

Sleek ice adorns the sky
Sending icy fire to the heavens
Mountains stand cold and silent
Enduring the slow grinding of the years.

Life never breathed into Antarctica,
Neither did death claim it
But a sole survivor still dares
To tread the freezing paths

Shadow-black and sun-white
Feathers and beak ruffled in wind
His eyes glazed with resistance and pain
His plume faded long before.

The world turns 'round the penguin
Polar bears waddled him hiding
Wind bites, cold chills, ice stings.
But still the penguin walks on.

Greg Lake Kau

"Smithy"

'Twas so much fun to go to town
And hear the anvil's din,
To stop the horses on the street,
Then wait our turn within.

Our village smith was always wet
His shirt was streaked with salt,
His hammer arm was never still,
Till work was without fault.

The rancid smell of burning hoof,
From hot shoes being fitted
His calculated mannerisms,
In how a colt's outwitted.

'Twas so much fun to watch the forge,
And see the flame get higher
Till meteors came shooting out,
The steel was now on fire.

'Twas so much fun-the blacksmith shop,
It's distant as a star
'Twas so much fun, 'twas so much fun-
But now, it's passed us with the car.

A. Joseph Trickey

Life

At the end of a pier,
  he sits.
While he gathers in,
  all his wits.
He thinks of life,
  future and past.
And all the shadows,
  he has cast.
The love and hate,
  he has made.
All those memories,
  that do not fade.
He wondrous why,
  he is here.
But the answer,
  is not there.
Though he knows not,
  what's in store.
He gets up,
  and goes back for more.

John Meador

Why?

Do you ever wonder why?
Why your loved ones have to die?
Why some women barren are left?
Why the world contains much theft?
Why are creatures on this earth?
Why some babies die at birth?
Why all diseases do exist?
Why the wrong some can't resist?
Why suffer a broken bone?
Why someone is left alone?
Why some don't get along?
Why some do what's wrong?
Why some can't afford a peace of bread?
Why sicknesses in the world must spread?
Why must we suffer each day?
Why can't exile end today?
I just don't fully understand why?
And I know I won't till the day I die.

Yvette Liviem

Mark

I've admired you
    from near and afar;
You're an inspiration
    a shining star;
It doesn't matter
    where you are.

Outstanding,
    Outrageous,
        Defiantly,
            Courageous
Tall, dark and handsome;
    young, gifted, and Black,
and on the right track.

Bound and determined
    to give it your best;
Unrelenting in your quest
    to climb the ladder
        of success.

In all your endeavors,
    God Bless you.

Barbrie Logan

Untitled

Mystical
Magic
melt
into
life
blossom
like a rose
in springtime
on
early Sunday mornin'

Bev Tompkins

Dappled Shadows

Years have been spent together,
Yet it is much too soon
For the Pale Horse to come galloping
So early in the afternoon.

What will happen to our dream
Of spending days bathed in golden light?
It is too soon for dappled shadows
To become black as a starless night.

Grace Connelly Lloyd

Little Girl Lost

A dark masked stare her eyes do cast with empty promises she thought would last.
Her heavy heart weighs nothing short of the pain and sorrow she could not sort.
What becomes of little girls lost, they pay a price at such high cost.
With tearless cries, she whimpers so, the one time youth she'll never know.
Alone she sits, her head hung low to hide the shame she thinks might show.
Remorse has built a wall so great, not even time can she escape.
Absent innocence so meek and pure, for mother's sake, she will endure.
The battle scars grow painfully sore, there's no honor in this war.
She fears no love could ever come, not after knowing what's been done.
Every night a wish she makes upon the stars her future staked.
Close your eyes and dream of a life you've never had,
the only time of peace that hasn't left you sad.
With love and sentiment, I pray for your soul,
that one day when a woman, you embody all that's whole.
Constantly in fear of what has yet to come;
alone she lives her life, no trust in anyone.
Where will this journey take her when the dust no longer blows;
When there is no more sorrow so happiness can grow.

Debbie Powell

What's In Your Hand?

What's in your hand? Lord I don't understand. Teach me
your knowledge and ask me again. Oh! You don't understand,
come here Jesus, Moses, and Abraham. Abraham what's in your hand?
A knife to kill to obey the Lord's command. Put the knife down
look up and see a ram in the bush provided by me. I wanted to lift
you higher, and higher to let you know I am your Jehovah Ji-Reh.

Moses what's in your hand? "A Rod" he said, no you don't
understand. Cast it down stand back and see, that the Lord thy
God will do a good work through thee. So wonder no longer what's
in your hand for through it they will know I am that I am.

Jesus, Jesus, what's in your hand? A cross too heavy for me
to stand. If it be possible let this cup pass. My son, my son
it's time at last. My son these things must be, but I will send
my angels to comfort thee. Father, father, why hast thou forsaken
me? Close your eyes my son and come be with me. For what's
in your hands is a blessing you see, for through it all sinners will be set free.

Thank you Lord, thank you Lord, now I understand the question
you asked me "what's in your hand?"

Robert Earl Walker Sr.

Nightmare

What is this beast which beckons at my door
so strange a sight I have never seen.
With wind blown hair and eyes of fire, teeth, long and white.
Why does it come in the middle of the night and growl my name in
a voice so deep I can barely understand?

Pounding! Pounding! Pounding!

With fist large, strong, and determined.
It wants me, humble me, why I wonder?
There is easier prey around.

Yet the attack continues, the walls shake,
the windows rattle, and the door weakens.
With hammer and nail I try to strengthen
my fortress, in panic I try to fend off this foe.
The beast turns its shoulder to its task.
I can see long hair, claws, and drool.

Pounding! Pounding! Pounding!

Leave me alone I cry! Go away! I've
harmed no one, I live my life in solitude.

But this beast of the night will not relent.
It seems to grow stronger with my plea.
The nails weaken, the door tears from its frame.
Try as I might I cannot stop this beast from entering my dwelling.
Now in the dim glow of my fire, I recognize; (loneliness)

Gary Paul Bisson

In The River Of Babes

The river of love swells up at the creek of the newborn baby.
The water rises to meet His pursed lips.
The sustenance of life, His life.
So pure, so sweet.
Liquid from the earth cleanses His soul.
His fears washed away by Mother Nature and all her majestic powers.
She remains strong for the helpless creature.
He knows not Her name,
But feels Her presence.
Hears Her calming words as the voice of the waves caress His warm body.
He is one with Her.
His Mother.
"Be not afraid", she whispers in His tiny ears.
"I go before you always in this river of life."
He learns to trust the flow of the river.
At each channel, He is greeted by the warmth of Her heart
As it beats strongly yet silently for Her newborn baby.

Amy Gallagher

Count on Heaven...ALWAYS!

The Chronicles of Mankind Will Forever Bear Witness of God - the triumph of Good,
This promised gold of Divine heritage, inspires mere mortal far beyond what he would!
However, man has agency, and his Intent Will Give Way to acts of honor or shame,
In spite of conscience, man will choose his path, and then signature it with his name!

The Prodigal Son, this profligate malefactor, lived Only for self and but for Today,
His choices denied him Life's True Treasures, and you can indeed hear him say...
"An All powerful God lives in the Heavens" - He loves us, and reveals His mindful command,
He promises indelibly, "We Will Reap What We Sow", - His words will forever Stand!

Andy Anderson

Untitled

It only comes to special people, and not to be inherited
So many go through a lifetime, and never really know it, and maybe even fear it
It knows no sex age or race
And not accepted by all whose presence it may grace
It's so rare even with all the millions that inhabit this chaotic place
And to many, why even plead this hopelessly lost case
Until this...
This thing called love, which is so powerful it can take you
to your highest highs and lowest lows
This thing that can conquer your hearts, your minds, and your souls
This is not something to be defined or controlled by law
And truly not something to be had by all
But if you find it, which to most I doubt
Treasure it, keep it, and never let it run out
Appreciate it, thank it and hold it very dear
And remember this wonderfully unexplainable phenomenon,
for it is truly rare

Della R. McAtee

Our Kids

Now days...many children have no... fathers...
The young just lonely mothers that fight day and night for their survival.

Some lucky days they are fed even in bed...and other
times just, they cry and cry...but help does not arrive.

Many kids attending schools suffering from...their hungers,
thirst, cold weather picking on them without any discrimination among all our population.

The teachers do not understand why he or she can not retain
the classes and explanations of the... spelling...math...
history...Science...due to the neglected world of their own..
Personal abuses...alcohol...drugs...prostitution...that pulls
them into the ring of manipulation and quote, "mental retardation".

What can we do for our children...so they won't face such disgraces?
You...you...you..." macho man," some day you have to be thinking...
that your child is sinking...without you thinking...just hardly....
surviving...while you keep just only bragging... "Hey man...I just...had another kid..."

Ruben R. Troncoso

Here I Go Again

I can feel the madness
coming to me again,
ripping through my feeble mind
to where I hide within.

I can feel the sadness
rising once more in me,
looming as a fortress door
for which I bear no key.

I can feel the loneliness
as it slips beneath the door,
saddening the madness
and maddening me more.

Michael Alan McDonald

Kelly

I felt you in the moonlight
And missed you on the shores
I loved you since the dawn of time
And a thousand years before

I breathed you in the winter wind
Whispered you in the morning quiet
Held your hand in sacred lands
And dreamed you in the night

I kissed you in the torrents
In all the rivers run
Poured my molten soul to yours
At the center of the sun

I wished you on a million stars
From a mountain soul alive
Forever true, my love for you
Until the end of time

Evan Sexton

My Family

My family loves me,
and their love to me still moves on.
My family is first.
I don't care if they are worse.
My family is kind.
I will remember them in my mind.
My family is like a tart.
I'll love them in my heart.
My family is like a flower.
I'll love them with all my power.
My family is like a light.
I'll be as bright.
My family is like a dream,
In our family tree.
I love my family
and they love me
because they are sweet and kind to me.

Beatriz Laureano

Responsibility

That path I may take is always mine.
The knowledge I take in,
is up to me.
The barriers I must overcome
are my challenges.
The chores I must do are my duties.
The things I try to do best
are my efforts.
The lessons I learn are on
my account.
The life I choose is my
Responsibility.

Ryan Elizabeth Barnes

I Waited

You told me that you'd call me,
I waited by the phone.
You told me to be patient,
But I was still alone.

You don't call day one,
I was patient till day two.
I guess you forgot my number,
I never heard from you.

I saw you walking one day,
With another by your side.
I felt so deeply hurt,
I tried to so hard to hide.

You noticed me from a distance,
But still just walked right by.
You didn't have the guts
To look me in the eye.

You couldn't pick up the phone
And tell me what's on your mind.
You tried to let it go
But it hit you from behind.

Irene Buryak

Death Is A Friend

Death
is only morbid
and horrifying
to those still alive

It brings peace
and tranquility
to those whom it embraces

Death is comforting
No one suffers in death
Suffering is only possible in life
for death is immutable

Death is a promise
that cannot be broken
Death will not let you down
Death is a friend.

Christopher Scheer

Raging Mountain

The giant mountain
Casts its enormous shadow
Over my village

Our mountain is loved
It shook and then explodes
Blood runs down its side

Birds soar, taking flight
Landing momentarily
And then fly again

I look above me
And see the ash and large stones
As they plunge towards me

Cotton clouds drift by
Casting shadows on the flames
Always changing shape

Raging fire burns high
Taking my people, my town
Burning it all down

Crichton Latture Atkinson

This Shall Pass

When shadowy days and gloomy nights come- say "This shall pass."
When your heart is broken and undesirable thoughts come - say "This shall pass."
When news overwhelms you say - "This shall pass."
When all of your emotions and feelings are negative - say "This shall pass."
When all of life's odds and living are against you - say "This shall pass."
When you are physically drained and you have no strength - say "This shall pass."
When you think God has given up on you - say - "This shall pass."
When urges and carvings for drugs and alcohol hit you - say "This shall pass."
When no one wants to talk to you and you ask for help - say "This shall pass."
When all of your material possessions are gone - say "This shall pass."
When things make you sad and depression sets in - say "This shall pass."
When love is replaced by hate - say "This shall pass."
When you do not believe in what you are doing anymore - say "This shall pass."
When no one believes in you but you - say "This shall pass."
When your wife and kids are gone - say "This shall pass."
When you think you have been through everything that could have possibly gone wrong
and that all of this has come to pass, but something else happens - say "This shall pass."
When everything else has fallen and you think you can't go on...
Remember - "This Shall Pass."

Benjamin Lipsey

My Dream

I dream every night about you.
I see you in my room so beautiful and handsome.
We walk towards each other and lock eyes.
I look deeply into your eyes and feel safety.

You take my hand into yours and we dance in time with the music.
I hold on to you; I'll never let you go.
Our eyes lock once more - I lean forward and kiss you.
A long passionate kiss so exciting and overwhelming.

We resume our loving gaze and study each other's movements as we dance.
I run my hands down your body and feel everything; fine and perfect.
You do the same - I feel your soft fingers delicately touch and caress me.
You are so wonderful and awe inspiring to me.

I wish I could scream to the world "I love you!"
Every time we're together you change me and I am myself.
I act like me - how I want to act.
You holding me - all the world seeing us - makes me feel so good.

I want this dream to last forever but I know it won't - it can't.
It has to end somewhere and this is where it ends.
You vanish from my thoughts as I am jerked back to reality.
If only the dream were real...

Alex Aivars

Without Love

It's longer than eternity, and wider than infinity
But there is no identity, without love.

Scholars readily profess, that there can be no true success,
Or even real togetherness, without love,

It's a gospel truth, you know, that pretty flowers wouldn't grow,
And clouds at sunset wouldn't glow, without love,

Little birdies in the spring, couldn't even chirp or sing,
And wedding bells would never ring, without love.

Now here's a thought you will agree, must have sprung from the knowledge tree,
That you and I just wouldn't be, without love.

The sound of love's own tender sigh, a youngster's happy, lilting cry,
No world of wealth could ever buy, without love.

A girlish wink, a bashful grin, peachy fuzz on a boyish chin,
Wouldn't cause young heads to spin, without love.

A mother holding baby tight, two hearts adrift in pale moonlight,
Somehow wouldn't seem so right, without love.

So, on this stage of stands and sprints, of life's dull drama and suspense,
None of it makes any sense, without love.

Gordon J. Rowe

East and West Revisited

'Tis said: That the East and the West shall never meet,
Till the earth meets the sky at the judgment seat,
But those words were writ many years ago, before the telly and the video,
Before space flight and satellites and nukes and missiles and a world in fright.

Now the world seems shrunk from what once it was, by the conquest of distance and time,
And it doesn't take long through the limitless sky, to fly to another clime,
From Reykjavik in the land of ice to the steamy jungles of Nam,
Or San Antone by the Rio Grande to Volvograd and the Don.

Now nations and peoples have multiplied on a planet finite and circumscribed,
Where some by force and menacing arms others intimidate threatening harms.
Courageous but fearful, everyone, looking down the barrel of the other's gun.
Should East or West let the trigger down, mutual ravagement rages around.

Imperative, therefore, it is, that the twain forthwith shall meet,
And peoples diverse from the ends of the earth fraternize face to face,
And fly up their prayers to The Almighty One, to grant them the gift of peace.

J. G. Murphy

Because Of You I Have Grown

As I walked through this part of my journey,
I met you walking through yours.
And at the moment our paths crossed,
We merged into a certain time.
You were not one that passed with the moment,
But one that will stay with me forever.
During this time you offered me time, patience, and knowledge,
You did not consider yourself better than I,
Only that you had already acquired the knowledge that I needed to make me better.
You opened up and gave of yourself this knowledge,
So that I could gain the wisdom.
By sharing that part of yourself with me,
You helped me find a new part of myself.
As our paths part again, our time each week concludes.
And as I walk in a new direction,
This time I am different, because I walk with more knowledge, more
strength, and more awareness.
Because of you I have grown.

Jane Seymour

When Laughter Fills The Air Again

When it seems life is so hard, and everything goes wrong,
When days of sunshine turn to rain and birds don't sing their song.
When all we do seems not enough to conquer all our fears,
Remember God is always near to wipe away our tears.

When each day seems to bring to us, a new unwelcomed deed,
When little tasks seem hard to do, and we labor to succeed.
When all our efforts seem to fail, and we don't know where to turn,
Remember God is always near, you are His great concern.

When life gets brighter day by day and nights are welcomed too,
When clouds no longer fill the sky, and all we see is blue.
When laughter fills the air again, we know the reason why,
The Lord took all our cares away as He reigns in heaven most high.

Christina G. Records

A Valentine Poem 4 U

Valentine's day is a special day 4 me and U.
There is a special place in my heart just 4 U and U know what?
  I don't need Candy
  I don't need money
  I don't need flowers
  I don't need a card
  I don't need balloons.
All I need is U on this special day; you being there 4 me is enough.
You caring 4 me, your love, your kisses and your support is all that I need,
everything you had given me is all that I need to get by;
and U being there 4 me makes everyday a Valentine's day.
And I want U to know that I love U and that U are always in my heart!!!

Melody C. Barrett

Judgement

Don't judge what I look like
for I am what I am

For I have been judged unfairly
most of my life

Been given me chance from
a very early age

Been struggling every since
trying to prove that I'm worthwhile

Give me patience, give me love
Give me time, and give me space

For God isn't finished with me
Yet!!!

Roxanna Lee Myres

Afternoon By The Mill Race

Swimming ducks make diamonds
in the muddy watercourse.

Sunlight crowns them
with purple richness,

that sunset fades to gray.
Two visiting Canada geese

collapse onto the water
with the air of dying royalty.

Remember when the three of us
came here to pick blackberries?

Our drifting canoe overturned.
Neck-deep and shivering,

we muddy beggars suffered
the genteel laughter of the birds.

Esther S. Park

Best Friend

Your heart cries out today
For your best friend has gone away.
So many days you spent in fun
All the things together you had done.

Once your friend was by your side
Now your grief is so hard to hide.
An emptiness is now so real
And sadness is what you feel.

But a memory comes to mind
Your friend's words so very kind.
Words spoken so true
Just a simple "I love you".

Brush the sorrow away
Be filled with love today!
Know how much your friend
Loved you until the very end!

Adele M. Cox

My Dad

My dad had curly black hair like a
  cloud ready to rain,
My dad had life in him, until he died
  and caused me pain.
My dad was nice and funny, like a
  clown, kind and sweet,
My dad took me to my first everything,
  which I thought was neat.
My dad is dead, like a branch off a tree,
  I'll never forget you, never forget me!

Michele Leigh Costello

No Answers

There are so many questions,
But it seems there are no answers,
You Wonder Why,
But there is no reason,
You don't understand,
And there is no explanation,
You ask,
But there is no response,
You sit there,
And there is not a clue,
You can't explain it,
And there is no statement,
It seems so simple,
But yet there is not a thought!

Laura Trusty

The Sea

Rolling, glistening, gentle
vastness of life...

Reflections of light, inspiration
soothing rhythms of night

Crashing, pounding, violent
pushing, breaking, wearing away

Unrelenting...

Moving, floating, adrift
at peace...

Ripping, smashing
arage

Rays of sun
warmth of sound
whale songs...

Whale songs...
so rhythmic

Every emotion
is the sea...

Richard Picatagi

Cold

This room is so cold
it feels like desperation
Making me want to curl up

Hide from it within myself
within the body of a lover
within the sanctuary of a blanket
Deep, deep inside my shell

The chill makes my tender flesh
crawl up against itself
it freezes my inside solid as tundra
and turns my soul to ice

The cold makes me feel weak,
breakable, lost
I feel as though I will never again
know the warmth of joy

I will die a lonely, withered shell
shrinking away from its touch
I lose all hope to its kisses
I hate the cold

It makes me cry.

Virginia Whiteley

Change

It was a small dusty town wind blown and torn,
The old man could not remember in the last 25 years even one child being born.

His face was like leather with wrinkles and scars,
Each mar telling a story of his life in the saloons and the bars.

All day he sits in his rocker on a rickety porch,
While the hot Texas sun pounds his skin like a medieval torch.

When he stands he is tall his old bones are proud,
Without a word from his lips his message is loud.

He is a Western Cowboy, the last of his kind,
A tougher man in the world you will no-where find.

He wears a lone Colt draped from his side,
The band on his hat is of rattlesnake hide.

He has fought his whole life for this land with his guts and his gun,
In fact, this is the very territory that took his only son.

That's why as the dozers and wrecking ball turn up his street,
Lonely tears of change gather at his feet.

Brent W. Timm

Push My Clouds Away

Looked up at the moon tonight. It was its light that caught my eye.
I looked and I thought how beautiful it was. I noticed how it dulled
as the thin clouds passed over it. But still it shined. I wished I
could've reached up and pushed all the clouds from around it. But
still it shined. I noticed its scars from the collisions of its life.
But still shined. Shined for the whole world to see. The clouds and
the scars didn't stop it from giving light. Light the whole world could see.
A light that's always shining. No matter how many clouds, no matter
how many scars. Sometimes those clouds are already pushed away.
But the scars are still there. God never smoothed them out.
There for the whole world to see. Push your clouds away.

Daniel Craig Hayes

A New Christians Prayer

Oh Father in Heaven, I am in need of prayer
I'm not sure that I can carry this cross that you've given me to bear
Since I've known you Lord, it seems my trials have been so great
I know in my heart that it hasn't just been fate
The devil has been busy Lord, he's working night and day
So, please listen and answer the prayer, that I'm about to pray
Hide and protect me Lord, until I can grow more in you
So when the devil comes, I'll know just what to do
Please give me the strength and wisdom to do what I know is right
No matter how tempting the devil
   makes things, no matter what the plight
Faith...I know is the answer...to simply trust in you
I'm trying Lord, I really am, it's just sometimes hard to do
If you'll just take my hand and lead me
I promise...someday you'll see
with your help, I'll stand on my own two feet
And help lead someone else to thee. Amen

Kathy Underwood

Just Another Day, Just Another Night

You struggle through another day without a glimmer of accomplishment,
another day of slow motion.
Mornings are wasted with complete unconsciousness, with afternoons of
endless choices that never seem to be made.
Nightfall seems so sudden, with more vast opportunities that are
within your grasp but never to be obtained.
Those times are almost always transformed into the meaningless.
Time pre-examined, seems to be of plenty, as it is experienced, never is fulfilled.
Early morning hours appear before your eyes as if the day is anew, but it is just another end.
The new day's light and the songs of the birds are not ones of serenity, or of joy, but of intrusion.
I must sleep now, for my day is not beginning, but my lonely night is ending.
Soon I will be at peace, only to be later disturbed by, just another day, just another night.

James E. Grant

A Garden Of Eden Halloween

Adam sat under the fig bush on the cool moist ground
and started naming all the things that were lying around.
He looked at a gourd and called it a crumpet
Pointed at an elephant and declared it a trumpet.
He picked up a skunk and said, "wow! It's a golly-gee chocolate."
Then he tossed it to Eve, with orders to put it in a pot and crock it.
Eve retreated backwards in a trembling fright.
And all her leaves fell off, much to Adam's delight.

They returned from the cane brake because Adam was no longer able. And Eve picked
a pumpkin from the cabbage patch and placed it on the table. She wanted to label it an
orange, but thought it was much too big. Adam pondered many names, but knew better
than to call it a fig. Yahweh did not want them in a state of chaos and mudder. He knew
it tasted like krap, even if you soaked it in butter.
The machete in Eve's hand put all the males to shaking in fear. She took over, and
kicked El, Adam and the snake in the rear. When the slashing was completed and
everyone covered in pulp. The males gaped at the ugly orange thing and swallowed
with a gulp. Since she was still holding the knife; they wisely allowed her to give it a
name. And to this very day; the Jill-O-Lantern is Eve's one and only claim to fame.

W. R. Barnard

My First Winter Morning

This frigid wind wracks my frame, angry teeth cut and slash my
skin, cruel stings freeze my warm African blood, This place is no
home, the voice of custom shrieks, Home is far, far away.

But then a calm voice speaks in my heart:
Home is wherever love is found,
for love is the source of beauty and joy.
See how nature covers all its earth with a shimmering white rug;
The silvery glow from heaven above makes every turf to scintillate.
In the field where stood the corn of late, a billion fire-flies jubilate.

When the Creator molded His world,
Love was the binder that He employed.
And looking upon all from His throne on high,
He proclaimed it all to be lovely and good:
The multitudinous differences in size and strength,
The endless shades of color and light,
The unfathomed variances of status and being
—Each and all endowed He with treasures of love.

Oh, What a world we lose when we shut and bolt our door!
What a wealth we gain when we reach out in the heart of love!

Stephen Akintoye

I Thirst

At times like this when I thirst Lord, emotions will to moan,
I shall affirm my heart's belief, let unbelief not groan!
I rest in You my Savior friend, please fill my weary soul,
To bravely press onwards with you, and reach my highest goal!

My heart recalls in thankfulness, the times Your light has shone,
Through this empty vessel, with Glory next to none!
Your faithfulness exceeded all my wildest hopes and dreams,
This dry time I will wait on You, it's not what it seems!

I'm ever grateful for the times you healed my flesh and bone,
Your mercy and your grace flowed through a hotline telephone,
Restoring life's drought years that pesky locusts meant to steal
With streams of living water, oh! in renewed praise I reel!

In wondrous love your Holy Spirit, faithful comforter,
Replenishes with patience, now inspired as discerner,
I sense the beauty of this time, which fellowship we keep,
Your radiant intimacy calling the deep unto the deep!

The longing has returned to worship in reflecting grace,
Residing in your sanctuary, the most Holy Place;
For broken is the veil that kept me from the mercy seat,
It broke after you cried "I thirst!.. Why has thou forsaken me?"

Dorothea Jacobsen

Meteor Shower

I sit alone
with the sky spread out before me
watching the stars fall like petals
from a flower
so beautiful
wish I could fall through the sky
in a blazing glory
to have everyone standing in awe
of my flowing light
so gracefully I wood dance in
the moonlight with the stars
the heavens cheering me on
I would dance faster
leaving a dusty trail behind me
my dance is over and I am forgotten
by most
so beautiful
so alone

Meghan J. McGinnis

The Life Of Anne Frank

Frankfurt is where she was born,
From her house Anne Frank was torn.
She spent two years,
Through all the fears,
Hiding from the Grune Polizei.

She told secrets to Kitty,
And she felt no self-pity.
Then she was robbed,
So Anne Frank sobbed,
For someone knew she was in hiding.

When her sister's life ended,
Her heart could not be mended,
She cried and cried,
Until she died,
In the camp of Bergen-Belsen.

Danielle Buchanan

Temptations Pillow

Who would take this curse upon me
Tie me down with links of chain

Wrestling with the Owl of Darkness
Where in kitchen wall She stays

Drawing me
With hoots and hunger

Brought on by
Her ever Moon

In the still and silent evening
I hear humming like a tune

Drawing me with ever increase
From the hour of eleven on

Singing as a songbird humming
With her melody and song

As my mind goes soaring higher
Hunger strikes me in the groin

And I in giggling
Raid the icebox

As the cat
And dog look on.

Judith Rogers Gray

Untitled

The night cries out,
My soul falls into harmony,
Fear wrought of understanding,
The cause of it all,
For It is but a concept,
An extension of faith,
Without It, it fails,
Ambiguous references all around,
The moon grows pale,
Mist rises from the dead,
What light without a coin,
Have faith, please.

Mark Yoder

Love Flows

Eyes look bright,
Head feels light,
Heart rhythmic like ocean
waters softly beating on
the beach shore.

Playing, laughing, singing slow songs;
Enjoying every moment when
we embrace under the moon
and under the stars.

Love Flows though us,
And swings us up in the air,
Heaven opens its door to us,
And blankets us up in its care.

Celeste Robinson

Ameerah

Light in a veil of darkness
Paints dreams on sleeping minds
As night chases day
My love awaits
Hidden
The night rules she
Comforts that stolen from the sea
Blue reflected mate with Bridal Kisses
Naked as first born daylight
My love she rests
Like a serenading moon, dancing
Ecliptical virgin
Timing sacred reflections
In darkness as retinas climb
Unimaginable my mind
And heavens inner side seem one

Nigel M. Jackson

Choices

So sweet the options
Set upon me.
Their venomous honey
Running
Through their meaning
Dancing
In my conscience.
Of which will I choose?
Of which will I use?
These options
So deadly
And
So divine.

Nichol Winters

The Dimming Lights

The Lights down this winding gravel road where very bright back years ago,
These lights represented a Father, a Mother, and their seven sons and daughters

Through the years the family grew and more lights joined them on the hill
And within this circle were the brightest lights of all, he called her "Mammy,"
   She called him "Will"

There was always music, laughter, and prayers, you could feel the loving energy everywhere,
People came from miles around to break bread with this family and even as a child I knew
that this was life as it should be

Then without warning the Lights grew dim, while Grandfather slumbered
Our Lord and Savior took him
Since that time there has been the passing of our dear Grandmother,
Aunts, Uncles, cousins, sisters, and brothers

And as more Lights grow dim with the passing of each day,
I will always remember each in a special and loving way

Within our hearts we know it can never be as it was before
So we give these precious memories to our children and open another door

The Light shines brightest from our parents through this open
And as we focus towards this light, our children are assured
That the circle is never broken

Jan Gressett

My World

Oneness of a forgotten time joins us
For your world has no room for our kind anymore
Wealths of information
Barred from us by your vain attempts to drive us back
To where you can once again control our minds
In an all too bright sun
and a sky not electric lapis-lazuli over non-matrix ground
But we listen at keyholes and slip through with your precious secrets
Water in an ocean of bytes
A whirlwind-roller coaster of data pours upon netizens
Almost dehydrated from the desert sun of intellectual drought
Cyberspacial peasants of non-existent digital God are flung into an
Egyptian information tomb
Ready to be probed for its stores at a moment's notice
For its curse does not hold true to those who built behind a
stainless steel curtain and know their way through the most horrific
graveside of forgotten myth
The guards will always let us pass
"This is our world now." And the unreal-reality will open its
floodgates, the black plague of conspiracy cured until next

Christopher R. Hopkins

Kisses

Like magic a kiss is given
to set your soul afire.
it gets your juices flowing
and has you spellbound for a while.
It makes you feel you can't endure the feeling that you're feeling.
You wonder if the kiss is real, as it is so fulfilling.
The time has past for you to come to take what you've been needing.
To feed the fire with your desires
to that one which is willing.
To take you to those heights of love
of cool and sweet surrender.
As darkness falls and you recall that kiss which was so tender.
It took you to that nice warm place
where desires of love are driven.
It drives you to desires so wild and fulfilled
with passion, that lets you know you're
no longer a child and these kisses
require a little more action.
A kiss is still a kiss, as you know that is still true,
but if I had a choice
I'd share all my kisses with you.

Lisa Doll Gary

A Mother's Love

I know there are times you think I wasn't listening and I
may have acted as though I wasn't...maybe I didn't like what
you were saying but I heard you. You are the one person in my life
who has always been there for me no matter what the circumstance.
You may not like some of the choices I've made in my life but
still you're always standing behind me there to catch me if I fall and
pushing me to succeed. I may not always show or tell you how
important you've been in my life but I want you to know that without
you I wouldn't have made it this far in the game of life. I can only
hope that if I decide to become a mother I can be like you and let my
children be their own person knowing no two are alike and loving them all the same.
    It's comforting to know that I always have that one person in
my life that is always there for me in good times and bad.
    I cherish the time I've had with you and pray
I have many more years to learn from you!

  Jamie McKenna

Barren Gray

Once there was a girl in a forest where she liked to play.
All that's left of that forest now is a barren gray.
One dreary day the wood cutters came and chopped it all away without a fight.
They left the stumps, the sawdust too and were gone by that night.
Never seen again that year or the next few too.
The trees grew back, few by few, for many years it seemed.
When twelve years past they came again and did the same as the years before.
The ground was left, used and worn.
In the distance I heard the echo of a horn.
The trees still do grow back it's true, but for a bitter cause.
Only to be trampled on by those mean chain saws.
Now I play and wait sadly for the day when they will come again.
And my forest once more will become a dismal, barren, gray.

  Erin Russell

Treasures (Based On Job 28)

There is a mine for silver and a place where gold's refined;
Iron taken from the earth, jewels brought forth of every kind.
Far from the land where people dwell, man cuts a shaft in the ground
To a place forgotten by the feet of men, where sapphires and gold are found.

No bird of prey knows the hidden path, no lion prowls there;
Man's hand assaults the flinty rock, and lays its treasures bare.
No other living creature probes darkness blacker than the night;
Man will search the source of rivers and bring hidden things to light.

Tell me where wisdom can be found, where does understanding dwell?
Do you comprehend its worth? Who knows the way full well?
It's not hidden in the deepest mine or buried in the earth —
Who gives his best from this precious store, riches of real worth?

Man may search the blackest darkness, tunnel down its riches find,
but treasures of lasting value are not things that are mined.
It is the fear of God, the way true wisdom is obtained —
To shun evil is the only path to understanding gained.

  Susan Ammerman

The Witch

Three hundred years ago or more, before automobiles or planes that soar,
In little towns where people gathered to speak of politics and such that mattered,
Whispers sometimes passed about that created fear and cast some doubt

"See that woman, a witch she be, she told it fore it happened to me,
With a nod and a smile, she was very nice, just stopped to give me a bit of advice
But what she said and how she knew, must be evil, Satan's brew."

The whispers went on and on until it was agreed by everyone
To take the woman to be hung, and with righteousness they saw it done.
But the deed was done out of fear, for the woman was psychic, merely a seer.

Three hundred years may have come and gone, but still the ritual goes on
With a different method people do the same, they point a finger and call her insane.
If that doesn't work and she seems unconventional, they just say she is dysfunctional.

  Christine Hanagan

Grandfather And Me

We laugh together.
We cried together.
We talked and walked together.
When I was sick he was there,
When he was sick I was there.
When I was punished he was there,
When he needed medicine I was there.
When I wanted something he was there.
We weren't lonely because we were
Always there for each other.
We taught each other games.
We taught each other jokes.
When my brother died he was there,
When he was in the hospital
I went to see him a lot.
He was there when I was born,
I was there when he was laid to rest.

  Dawn Rogers

Freedom

Hovering over daisy fields
And blossoming apple trees,
In an endless sea of blue,
My kite soars with grace and ease.

Oh, to have such freedom,
With no chains to hold me down,
To climb aboard a gentle breeze
That sends me whirling around.

I'd gladly leave this troubled world
In search of things unknown.
I'd willingly break the ties that bind
For a place in that heavenly home.

But since I'm only mortal,
Such freedom I'll never see;
So, I'll fly my tiny kite,
And pretend that it is me.

  Phyllis A. Tharp

Trapped

Trapped
So alone
So unsure
So scared
An animal in a cage
Screaming
Dying to get out
Help
The room is getting smaller
I can't breathe
Everything is fading away
It's getting dark
What's happening
The room is spinning
It stops
Everything is quiet
It happened
I'm crazy
I'm trapped

  Sally Ann Foote

Haiku

Falling
  leaf
    brushing two strangers
    meeting on footbridge!

  Jose R. Lopez

Moon Boat

I would like to leap up high
and board my moon boat in the sky.
Clouds would light up at the sight
of me drifting through the night.

I'd sail around the milky way
and watch the moonbeams dance and play.
Stars that twinkle in the sky
would twinkle, twinkle in my eyes.

I'd sprinkle stardust in the air
and watch it drift down everywhere.
And with the nodding of my head
I'd sail back home and climb in bed.

Barbara Louise Killian

Cats And Dogs

Cats and dogs
it's raining cats and dogs
barking, howling, meowing, furballs
falling from the sky
cats and dogs
it's raining cats and dogs
boy, I see them everywhere
here's one here and
there's one there .
cats and dogs
it's raining cats and dogs
the ground is turning different
colors, brown, red, gold, gray
I assume they'll be pets by today
cats and dogs
it's raining cats and dogs

Nick Palmer

Untitled

Help me see the beauty,
as I greet each bright new day
Help me see each miracle
That God has sent my way.
We often borrow problems
And our days are filled with doubts
So we never see the blessings
The good Lord's pouring out.
We worry about tomorrow
And what problems there might be
We never seem to understand
The most precious things are free
So let me see and feel the blessings
And let me understand
That when God made the whole wide
World,
He gave it all to man.

V. Goodwyn

No Music

A yawning cello of
want so hollow,
there is no echo
when I yell for myself.

I howl as life laughs,
and God seeps
from wood like warm syrup.
So I yell for myself.

I shout silently,
letting the hole for darkness
trap my tantrum in a mute room.
I cannot yell for myself.

Sativa January

Angel

I met an angel one year ago
Fast we became friends it was instant you know
Friends may come and friends may go
But there's always that special one, and it's you, you know
A real friend you became to me, a real friend lasts through eternity
That special one knows your dreams and fears
Together we laugh and shed a few tears
Escape the pain and sorrow here
God needs you desperately up there
Up on the winds of heaven's love
I still have faith in his plan up above
He needs you worse and now I know
That in my heart you'll always stay, and every night when I kneel to pray
I'll ask for you and family too, for all the blessings the Lord shines through
You touched the hearts of all you knew, you did much more for me than I for you
You brought me so much happiness, I'll miss you friend, oh so much
I'm grateful for each moment with you
You are an Angel my friend
I love you

Cathy Schoenrock

"Soul Serendipity"

Long ago in that soft summer of our first embrace
We held souls, smiling inside, warmth our only need.
Slowly moving through endless days and clear nights
Of love, oh love with a sweet mockery of hatred.

How often did I long to leave with you, just go and be nowhere
Lost in a love not allowed, so tempting and yet so forbidden.
They watched, but they had no knowledge; saw but could
Never understand us. How can one know love's secret ways?

Kisses floating together in a sweet surrender of pure passion.
Two loving as one, moving up to a plane of sweetness and light.
Others claimed their rightful share, we moved back to the shadows
Of things best not thought of, back to our dreams, back to death.

And what of us then? What of love which should not be?
For I had always known your spirit, had felt it stir in me as a young man
Looking for my center, finding only lost nights of drug-haze and laughter
I saw Manson, evil laughing at us all, sticking us with our own secrets.

One taught to love was to kill, to release from this realm, his realm.
He surely could never know this love of ours, a stranger in the path.
We move on to eternity my love, apart, but always together inside
My spirit clinging to yours, and love, sweet love, undying and smiling

Galen R. Wagganer

abdication

the flushed faces, and a cered dissent are being tightly pinned away
in a blushing pinafore- that shrinks - a disconcerted grin.

i tried, i tried to launch this hollowed moon, my excrement.
a widening expansion elbowed into bloom, as much a world to me as a faceless night. so
still I rocked, shedding the petals of my stagnant
dress, until the rancid talc, the orange shouts, the clotted cerate
peeled their stretching mouths. a vehement bite of utopia.

for a time, they sat riled and rooted with the new. their smug cerise
skin was a hint. two moans wade in from an open room and they choke.
as the empty bellows creep like ivy around their clean throats. the voices, a harsh white noise.

there is a scatter of sound, like pearls escaping a neck too much the
same for them to be recognized. now colors muffle, my halcyon has
gone, should I too be pacified? the fingers, so linear in their small
pink fits twist; the nacre worms are hooked and upon the reel, eye infinity's baldness.

a panoramic cessation, runny and voiceless mob, drip onto the clean
tiles of the floor, and with a small fizz, dilutes. mother bores a
sigh into a man made breeze that slowly fades in, like water sneaking
onto shore, before that crash sings its shaking syllables

ah, ah at last.

Kiernin Carroll

351

I Heard Today!

I heard your mother died today and a sanitarium your dad now stays.
The orphanage is now for you since dad will soon pass on too.
Until your adolescence fade away that is where you have to stay.
Poor Girl! Poor Girl!
What will you become all alone and so young?

I heard you got married today and your husband ran away.
Did he leave you all alone with no clothes on your back,
no food to eat and no where to live just the street.
Poor Girl! Poor Girl!
What will you become all alone and so young?

I heard you got sick today and that you passed away.
Up to heaven you will rise to your mother and daddy's side.
Never again to be alone finally got yourself a home.
Poor Girl! Poor Girl! Sorry you Passed!
Poor Girl! Poor Girl! Happy at last!

Sharon Manalang

The Death Of A Broken Heart

All around me I see the lights; the glimmers of loves. Sometimes a
brilliant red flash explodes on my subconscious and slowly jades away
among screams and cries of confusion and torture.
This is the death of a broken heart.
The heart is full of warm, rich love that is hidden. Sometimes, when the other's heart is the same,
the two's hearts will glow white-hot in their love for one another.
When the other turns on the one who is full, it is as if a pin has pricked a balloon full of liquid.
The contents are split and the world knows.
This is the death of a broken heart.
The fading of the heart. The fading of the brilliant red flash is the
wearing of time on the pain of the explosion and revealing of self.
That heart can never be recovered, for that certain love is spent.
A new heart may rise again from the misery of the old with the passing of time.
This is the healing of a broken heart.

Christa Elizabeth Coleman

Three Sisters And One Brother Plus One

Three sisters were we, until one February day,
Mother says it's time and sent us away.
We came home that blessed day,
And found a tiny baby brother had come to stay.
He grew and grew until he could run and play,
Ten years later Mother says it time,
that same day a baby sister had come to stay,
Now with four sisters and one brother
We each had a Brother of our Own,
We never missed each other until one is gone.
Our brother had to leave, Jesus called him home to be with Mother.
Four sisters left all alone. There was no love greater than that of our brother.
We miss him Dearly.

Juanita Lyons

Untitled

Star-crossed lovers.
Searching, searching
For the means by which they may coalesce,
But still estranged from each other.
Unable to find the path through the uncertain tenderness that shrouds
The direction toward the others' understanding
And emotion.

Helpless, hoping lover.
Taking the lonely road less traveled
Towards the answer,
Deceptively covered with fearful secrets
And alluring innuendoes told during promiscuous moments of passion.
That in no way appease the insatiable
Devotion

Of a star-crossed lover.

Aaron Robinson

As I Look Out The Window...

As I look out the window,
and up to the sky,
I see beautiful birds,
slowly fly by.

As the leaves on the trees,
start to fall,
birds start to sing,
with their own special call.

As I look out the window,
and down to the ground,
I see mother deer with two little fawns,
running and jumping and prancing
around.

As the leaves on the trees
turn various colors,
the ground is blanketed,
by its glorious covers.

Nikki Wright

The Inner Image

The inner image overcomes
the fashion and style, that
is placed on the body.

The inner image is not a part
of make-up or the beauty.

The inner image is a part
of what's inside your heart
that you can offer.

The inner image has its
own mind and its own body.

The reason of that is
because the inner image
is what God looks
for in a person.

When you have God on
your side you'll never lose.

Olivia J. Warren

Silence

Stop.
Listen to the silence.
Hear its penetrating sound.
Close your mind to reality.

Wait.
Don't hurry through life.
Take a breath of air.
It's alright not to understand.

Please,
Listen again to the silence.
Just close your eyes.
Think nothing, nothing.

Relax.
Don't try to listen too hard.
Just sit, take it in.
Close the door of thought.

Now.
Listen to the silence.
Can you hear it?
Is it not loud!?!

Telenna Vipond

Neglected Thoughts

What say thee o' thought,
I consult and wish response.
To what I query of you,
It is that which you must know.
Say I of high expectation and input low.
This you shall be,
One of separation, division of one.
A one that once was we,
Yet now its own one.
Can one be undone?
Enlightened thought, that is gone.
So shall other half wallow in its fun.
Must all be lost,
And nothing done?

Joe LaManna

There Is A Fire

There is a fire
that some possess,
an ageless, timeless,
wondrous beauty
that runs through
their blood
like a wounded
screaming soldier

Brethren to few a men
scarlet terrors
streets and hands
washed in blood
a trail of tears...
and in contrast
the most glorious
of days
All hearts it touches
left asunder
in a fiery blaze

Ryan Douglas Muddiman

The Hate Wall

Dark and gray beyond horizons
a wall of hate stands,
blocking the light outside,
built by their mind's demands.

Can you tear down this wall,
the wars that built it tall?
Pull down the hurt and fears?
Pull down the wall of hate
and leave the rubble and the tears?

And what if it would still remain
to remind us of the hurt and pain?
And if we looked beyond ourselves,
would we find no wall at all?

Elisabeth Barrett

When Heaven Embraces Hell

The sweetness of her sorrowed
lips. The luscious stains
of a sweet caress. Licking
at the edge of sanity. Growing
colder, sweetly bolder, not
knowing what to see. Taste
what is last left to me. And
know what I don't wish to see.
Taste at last my last breath
of sanity. Taste at last
the last breath of me.

Joshua R. Barnhizer

I am a girl who believes in the stars and wishes upon them.
I wonder what my future holds in store for me.
I hear shouts of joy and singing with the stars.
I see me flying, floating though pure, divine whiteness.
I want to dream freely.

I am a girl who believes in the stars and wishes upon them.
I pretend my dreams are reality.
I feel the wind dancing circles around me.
I touch the stars and the universal seas that surround me in my own dimension.
I worry that life will pass me by in the blink of an eye.
I cry at the sound of someone in pain.
I am a girl who believes in the stars and wishes upon them.

I understand that life can be cruel like a storm, but soon the storm
will pass and reveal a beautiful blue sky.
I say live your life to the fullest; no second wasted.
I dream of a world without poverty or crime.
I try to be understanding and full of love.
I am a girl who believes in the stars and wishes upon them.

Bethany Petersen

God's Great Helper

Dedicated to William F. Maring
Did God make a mistake
when He took you from this world?
I know you are better now
no pain, regrets, or work.
I now wonder why I never
took the time to stop and see
all the things you meant to us
and most of all to me
Your presence is greatly missed but,
I'm glad you're not in pain
I hope you know I love you
and we'll meet one time again
Does God have a job for you?
I guess I cannot see
Did he think you were here long enough
To take care and comfort me
Are there others all around
That need your love, too?
I guess I understand that God picked you because you're special even though I need you, too.

Shannon Parks

Grandma

I study the lines of age upon her sunken face that only "the Master's" hands can erase.
Why do I feel so guilty as I gently see her lie there still as she lies patiently, silently,
  in her hospital bed?
The hands, once so busy, for her grandchildren, over the years
lay now, passive-so-quiet-We blink back the tears that fall.
The tottering steps she tried so hard to take the cane that used to help,
no longer there has to be for her sake.
Yet her strength which is fading from within
Still comes forth-lingers there helping us to be patient with her loving cares.
Pulling the family closer in the last hours of her darkest time.
Who will be loved by all in her time!
Only "the Master's" hands will heal all!
The grandmother who will not be forgotten for all of time!

Tammy Wolfram

Get Away

I find myself thinking of a plan to get away. Get away from this cruel and two-faced world.
I need to get away from the so-called friends who trash you behind your back,
Who leave you behind when they should be at your side.
I need to leave a world filled with rumors and lies.
I think each night how, how do I get away.
Should I run, should I move, and maybe I should take a more drastic route.
Maybe in order to fully Get away from this world, I need to end everything
    and be in complete silence and peace.
What I need, is to Get Away.

Trisha Brown

Love Can

To love is but freedom...
    Not bondage...
        Freedom to express ourselves through the heart...

Love can be full of color...
    As flowers...covering the fields...
        Each offering different shades of glory...

Love can be a strong-hold...
    As you bond together through the tough times...
        Binding thoughts and souls as you are one...

Love can be also sad...
    If you don't value one another as separate persons...
        Sadness need not be if you give to yourselves...
            The care that you need also from each other.

Love can be yours and mine...
    If we only give each other time...

Linda Renae Hyde

Quiet Storm

Can you hear the whisper through the leaves,
the fluctuating currents that shake the trees,
a profound smell lingering in the air...
the kind of fragrance that lengthens Mother Nature's hair?

Tears of refreshment are on their way
to heal the parched land in disarray.

Darken clouds shun the sky...
pouring raindrops of pain from its shallow sunken eyes.

Waves are crashing like shackles on torn feet
twisting the emotions and smothering the heat.

Roses tumble as they feel the thunder-jolt
electrified by the lightning and smelted by the bolts.

Soon the agony is at rest, and wounds begin to cease
restoration is in the foreshadows, and the havoc is released.

Terrell D. Rubin

The Long Journey Home

The sun is setting, it's about that time for me to go.
I see my days and nights fading, it's a long and rugged trip.
But there is no obstacle that I can't bear, though the
road is narrow and long.
There is no stopping me from getting to my destination.
Though the mountains are high and the valley runs deep,
I am going home.
On my journey home I need nothing, but myself because
where I'm going everything is free.
I need not worry about violence, because where I'm going
there is nothing but peace.
Ahead I see a golden gate, I'm almost there, it's so beautiful.
Where the road ends there are steps to walk up before
you get to the gate.
I walk up the stairs and stand at the door, I knock.
When it opens, my Father is there to greet me.

Juanita Hughes

Society's Influence

Who I am not, I cannot be.
Being me is all I know,
And yet who I am, I do not know.

Accept me for me, or not at all.
None in this world are great,
Though many are considered to be.
All are actors in this world
Putting on masks and costumes to disguise the truth,
which now no longer exists.....

Jon Peters

Chosen Path

As you all left to become your parents,
I left to find myself, to really be somebody
Not the man mommy wanted, or the one coach molded
Not the one they wanted, or the one you expected
I found myself, and lost the man you knew
Sorry to be so literal, so plain and true
Thought you deserved to hear it, thought I should say it
To tell the truth, would be to our generation,
What a rock is to a Window, hate to metaphor and run-on
Like a simile, but my work here is all but done,
You have seen the naked truth, heard the dirty deal,
Touched the mortality and forced yourself to feel
I've made you think to yourself,
And be honest with the fear, I tore down those old walls,
And made it very clear,
In the silence, your conscience calls

Jesse R. Curran

Dreams

I see him walking down the hall
My heart starts beating fast
He's at my side
Smiles, but walks right on past

My head tells me to forget about him
But my heart just doesn't agree
It says to stop dreaming
But how can I, when he means so much to me

He's in my thoughts wherever I am
I see his face every time I close my eyes
I want to tell him how I feel
Afraid, my love remains in disguise

Is all this dreaming worth it?
I may never know
But as time goes on
My love for him will surely grow

Sarah A. Barron

Reflections

They say that I am seventy-eight
    Where have those years all gone?
I minded my parents,
    Did my studies, and
Achieved a high degree.
    I taught the kids and
Loved them all, then
    Married the perfect man.
What better life could I have had?
    Tell me if you can.

Of course there were some problems,
    Days when things did not go well.
I cried myself to sleep some nights
    And prayed to God for help.

There were loving friends and happy times,
    And laughter kept me going
To pursue the goals of all my life
    And the joy that I am knowing.

Helen A. Schoen

Mask

My face is like a mask I wear,
To hide all my worries and trap all my cares.
Without it all the people would see
The pain, the anger that wells up inside me,
So I put on my mask to face them again.
One more time I have them fooled.
    One more time I cry.

Claire Johnson

It Could Happen...

The sky could fall at any moment
The lakes could disappear,
Animals could start talking
And I wouldn't even care.

The mountains could fall very flat
The clouds could dance in the sky,
Birds could swim just like fish
And I wouldn't wonder why.

The streets could turn into miles of grass
That just might happen right now,
The big tall trees could begin to walk
And I wouldn't wonder how.

All these things could happen now
I don't know why they do,
You never know what will happen
They might even happen to you!

Robin Konscak

Wings

Like the caterpillar
wrapped up so very long
in its own little world
held fast within barriers
imposed on itself by itself

Unnoticed, untouched, unloved

Not knowing any better
never having lived any differently
thinking that this is simply the way that it is

Then one day
the sun, the beautiful sun

Can't see it, but feels it and needs it

And the caterpillar
wanting to know, needing to know
breaks free and looks around
at the wings the beautiful wings

And gathers its strength and its courage
And flies

And never will anything
ever be the same.

Jackie Marie Renniz

Surfing The Interstate

Camping at night by the Interstate 10
Sounds like the surf of the Pacific Ocean
The 18 wheelers with their running lights dim
Streak through the dark night with a continuing din
They look long and sleek from off to the side
And insight your wish for a "rip roaring" truck ride
The rumble of wheels makes the ground shake
Nearly as bad as the adjacent Santa Fe "Freight Snake"
And as you listen, an occasional tire tred is flapping
You wonder, why the driver hasn't discovered what's happening
He's creating what truck drivers call a "Gater"
And will deposit it on the road surface sometime later
There's an occasional pause in the repetitious noise
Like the calm between sets of the ocean's poise
Because truckers, too, tend to congregate in sets
Like starting a race and placing their bets
Where they all come from - I do not know
Some, I suppose, through the desert - and some through the snow
There's one thing for sure and you've got that right
There will be more of the same tomorrow night

John E. Vernon

The True Savior

He was a man of Shining Countenance,
    As the words of the Good Book say.
He was sent to the world for a purpose,
    He came as the "Light" and the "Way."

There were many lessons that he taught,
    To those who followed him there;
Like the fool who from his money was parted,
    When the fool couldn't learn to share.

He healed the ill on the Sabbath,
    In spite of the laws of the Jews.
And despite His righteous sermons,
    They refused to accept the "Good News."

He told many parables and stories,
    To teach the "Goodness" He brought.
His only desire was to save men's souls,
    and the souls of all men he sought.

Now everyone knows who I'm writing about,
    You know who He's always been.
He's the only Begotten Son of God,
    Who came to free us from sin.

James Lee Smith

Beauty Is Within Everyone

Beauty is not always what we see,
On the contrary; it is what we hear,
What we do, how we do it,
What we understand, and yes, what we see.
But most importantly, it is what we feel.
For without feelings, we would be nothing
Love to unite us,
Hate to ignite us,
Love to destroy hate,
And peace to contemplate
All that love has given us.
Therefore, beauty is the love and peace we find within.

Stephen Wederski

Jeremy

A boy just turned into a man,
And is now gone like a cool summer breeze.
Lord you sure have a strange plan,
Now help us with our tears please.

You took a talent that we cannot forget,
Must have a special place for him in heaven I bet.
So take care of Jeremy's family as we mourn,
And let us be thankful he was ever born.

Cuz we had some good times that was better than none.
At family functions you and I were always a pair.
Now all that fun is done,
Nothing but good memories of Jer.

Why you departed so soon we will never know.
Some of the best are taken early it goes to show.
To bad we could not relax in our old age is all to say,
It's ok cause our souls will meet again someday.

Chris Clark

Thoughts I

A thought is just a thought, until it becomes reality!
    Then it becomes a part of the past
    The actions at last
    That was thought about but not acted upon,
    Now that it's acted on, the thought is so long
    A long way to go, but a short breath to take
So watch your thoughts and the road they take!!

Carlos Alonso Brown

355

Mommy I Love You

Mommy please listen to me
I don't want you to throw my life away.
I have hands and feet and fingers too
I have a heart that will love you
Mommy please listen to me, I love you!

Mommy do you know who this is?
I am a little baby inside of you.
I want to love you with all my heart
But I won't be able to if you kill me.
Mommy please listen to me, I love you!

Mommy I could be the best child you ever had.
I would be really good too.
I wouldn't fight
I wouldn't even talk back.
Mommy please listen to me, I love you!

Mommy are you listening to me?
I don't want you to have an abortion.
You would be the best mom anyone could ever have
I hope you are listening and I know you love me
Mommy, Mommy I really love you!!

Beth St. Hilaire

The Road That Never Ends

The road that never ends
Has lead you through many different roads
Always returning to the one that you once began
Starting over can be unyielding
Traveling the rough and rocky roads
The roads that twist and turn after climbing a steep hill
The ones that soon become as black as the asphalt
And soon finding yourself on an untouched road
A road that has never been traveled by anyone but yourself
Sliding back and forth through your sorrows and happiness
But never forget the ones that light up your way as you follow
the road through life
This road will never end
For everyone will always have a trouble, a sorrow, or a happiness
Once you think you have found the end
You look to find that you are not at the end but simply
a new beginning.

Brandy S. Taylor

What Am I?

Am I a cruel demon?
Am I a loving angel?
I abhor this decision
Adverting to all angles
Endurance is what demons need
Inflamed forever without heed
Angels otherwise live up with God
And die not committing any frauds
While the rogues and cherubs have met their dying day
I lay in my bed waiting and wasting away

Matthew Eschete

Wargames In The Night

It's a fast pace game - gotta play to win
Glory goes to the one who comes out first in the end
Gotta watch your back and all around
Sometimes ya gotta climb or crawl on the ground
You're either hunted or the hunter runnin' in the night
Gotta move quiet and stay outta sight
Expect the unexpected that's the way it goes
Don't look for the obvious - it's a sure way to lose
Playin' "wargames" in the night-winner takes all
With high stakes make sure ya don't fall.

Beth Shepherd

The Terrors Of Drugs

If your family is your heart
Drugs will only tear it apart.
You think you're in control and very strong,
I sit in jail realizing that is wrong.

To smoke that joint or take that shot,
This means at one time your family you forgot.

The terrors of drugs destroy the man,
This includes the drug natural from the land.
While using you think of just yourself,
And your family sits awaiting on the shelf.

During this high you're no longer kind,
because the terrors of drugs have made you blind.
You say to yourself, just one more hit,
But people around you say quit.... Just quit.
You're on your knees searching through the rugs;
And this is called the Terrors of Drugs.

Richard Simon

Country Life

When the sun peaks up and says good morning,
the rooster crows up his warning.

As folks begin to stir,
they can hear the kittens purr;

The golden day starts with a spin,
just as the prairie grass flows in the wind.

O, how the sheep show their hunger,
as the farmer boy counts them in number.

Lazy cows chew their hay,
while the horses neigh.

Young girls work in the garden,
as the earth begins to harden.

The farmer starts to mow;
and the boys use their hoe.

Rustling trees blow with no will,
then it gets quiet and still.

Dusk will come when the day is done.

O, what a beautiful sight the country is in the moonlight.

Suddenly the sun starts to peek in,
it's almost time for a new day to begin!

Joy Lukachick

Raiders And Bloodshed

Monks die,
blood flies,
people hiding,
people dying,
raiders taking,
villagers waking,
The Danes are here.
The salmons roof filled with blood,
caused by the fire of battle,
wound bees fly through the tub of wind,
The Danes are here.
Snake of wound bites,
Vikings fight,
filling the whales bath with blood,
caused by the fire of battle,
foam leapers fly through the whales bath,
bringing the fire of battle.
Beware,
The Danes are here!

Alex W. Harris

Untitled

Sometimes when you draw me near, I have to
Pull free from the smothering, cold embrace
Which steals all my confidence for you.
For I am quite an able-minded chase;
Who deep inside has a defiant cry
Against the way I'm played with as a toy,
Against the way people believe your lies.
You shower me with artificial joy.
Now I return your lust, but not by choice.
I slowly wait for you to fall asleep,
Inside my heart I'm guided by a voice,
You shall no longer make my body weep.
I calmly hold the gun up to your head....
I know I cannot rest until you're dead.

Bethany Thatcher

Drifting

We may sit side by side yet we couldn't be farther apart
We can chit chat about nothing but I want
to know something from your heart

We called each other friend and now to me
you're like a stranger
We are not as close as before, I fear our
relationship is in danger

Your friendship again I want to gain, I feel
lonely, my insides are cringing with pain

When I call my mouth finds no words
What has happened? Has our friendship
flown away with the birds?

I see you and my spirits start lifting but a
tear comes to my eyes 'cause I know we are
...drifting

Cassandra Yvonne Rodriguez

Silent Cry

As I sit alone and look up at the sky
I can not help but cry a silent little cry.
When I think of you
My heart just breaks into.
For you left me alone
To face the world on my own.
I will remember the good
   I will remember the bad.
But I will never forget what we once had.
You made me laugh
And you made me cry...
But now I have to wonder why
One day you came into my world
The next you left without saying Good-bye.
As I sit here on my bed
Thoughts of you run through my head.
I can not help but wonder why
You left me all alone to cry my silent little cry.

Kendra L. Showalter

Reverent Attraction

   The sun on your face glows brighter than gold
the wind in your hair entices my soul.

   The smile that I see pounds lust in my heart,
crowned by the sparkle in your eyes, my dear split-apart.

   This message of love I'm sending is true, with thoughtful
intention someday, to captivate you.

Richard Giese

Sequel To Life's Perplexities

My dendrite and axon connections are slow.
My reflexes and memory lanes are rebelling.
And those calcified shoulders and knees
Are grinding away in these, my rusty years.
But hold on! Don't despair; there is hope ahead;
Have you not heard of cat scans and MRI's?
Of ultra sound waves that print magic imagery!
No more do medics work in the dark.
Their educated guesses are fever than ever;
For there are computers that diagnose all!
I don't need a new chassis; I need a reader
Who can interpret these images correctly and quick.
And with the help of the new MRIT
That pinpoints the spot and specifies the cure:
My life is prolonged as in Biblical times.
But I must win a lottery to, cover my deficit!

Theresa D. Tregza

Mothering With Music

To invest in your child, time is the key,
Share a love, begin simply.
Music is everywhere, bathing our senses,
Valuable in all circumstances.
Ballets and choirs, weddings and funerals,
Church and popular songs.
Operas and symphonies, parades with marching bands.
Accompany classmates in contests, talent shows and plays.
As proud parents fill the audience.
'Tis a gift from the talents of many,
Seek it, develop it, absorb it, express it.
As piano teachers share love, notes become magic.
From simple to classical, popular, and jazz.
Special thanks to John Stanley, at 3. Ruth Roberts, at 11.
Jim Cook, at 16. Carol Moore at 17.
Professor Charles Mosby at 20. Herb Drury at 23.
An audience to listen, transport, and care,
See his musical wings take him afar,
Accompany friends on instrument and voice,
An investment in time, 'twas a good choice!

Patricia M. Colyer

And Life Goes On

Some things you have control over:
Some things have control over you:
Let's not get confused at which is which:
Take charge and control of your life:
You are given only one, it is yours:
Let's not waste our precious time we
have here on earth:
We are all brothers and sisters
Different colors, but of one family:
How proud to have such a big family:

Evelyn Weber

Ocean Of Rain

When I stared into the night
the moon began to wane
and as days splendor arose
I still had nothing to gain

But the knowledge from within
intoxication in what is vain
between lies and fragile kisses
there's endless crying tears and pain

To lament what I have lost
rather than count what I have come to gain
is to cry a million tears
over an ocean full of rain

Tanya Myslek

Boundaries To Keep

Our paths were destined to meet,
    and you and I had boundaries to keep.

I was the autumn and you were the spring,
    and you and I had boundaries to keep.

You and I see the sun from a different point of view, for me
it is setting, and rising for you, the colors are the same...
    and you and I had boundaries to keep.

As you approached from an undiscovered place, I saw you
brighten as a shining new star in space,
    and you and I had boundaries to keep.

Please do not be ill at ease as I gaze as you go by, for I
cannot express how you light up the sky. Soon you will go
behind the sun and I will remember you as in the spring, only
to remain silent while you dance and sing.

Now you have passed from sight, but your vision still
remains. You never knew how I was bound to your light, and
why this secret causes pain, for if you knew, you would not
have shone so bright, your dance and song would not have been
such a wondrous innocent right, I have boundaries to keep.

            Michael Moore

Wings On Graves

Black on black white on white
who sends black who sends white
black on white white on black
why the black why the white
why the long chameleon
winding in the night

Right on right wrong on wrong
who sends right who sends wrong
right on wrong wrong on right
why the right why the wrong
why the technatronic ransack
running headlong

Flowers on flowers graves on graves
who sends flowers who sends graves
flowers on graves graves on flowers
why the flowers why the graves
why the blinded sight
wracking in the lave

On earth it's said the winged ones still know;
who do you know that doesn't grow?

            Daniel Ward Maines

Lisa's Poem

Fearful of the future, angered by the past
So much to accomplish, time moving oh so fast

Loved ones trying to comfort
Me I'm trying to cope
What do I tell my children, I want to give them hope

Why has this come upon me
In God I must believe
My best He has in mind, my suffering to relieve

I know the time will come,
I know it won't be long, that I will lean on others
To keep my spirit strong

Help me Lord I pray to get through each new day
And when my faith it fades, guide me in your way

So much of the future left but so much yet to do
Fearful that this disease will overcome my youth

I know I must keep spirits high and positive need be
I only ask that God above my pain and fears relieve

            Evelyn Mattie

It's Just Me

He's always pushing himself too hard
he's always feeling the worthless burden of life
nothing ever changes in his bland animation
but now a new wind is swirling by

He opens his senses to a changing faith
one lonely step towards healing the pain
distraught again by such empty trials
to others life bring so much

He grinds his teeth and stares in disparity
hoping and striving for some kind of charity
but ill-willed spirits are all he finds
his spit disappears and paste resides

Sweat is now his only companion
he's dizzy from shovelling your dirt
he dug his hole for future reference
soon he'll rest his dreary eyes

To know he's loved is all he wants
instead he plants every sordid seed he's given
growing his hatred from the gift of life
such a pathetic soul he is

            Christian Gnader

Shining In The Flood

Singing softly in the rain,
Shining forward, back again.
And all the tears from all the stars
Fall gently on our deafened ears.
The pure child, so good and strong
Was drowned and carried along
The sparkling, tumultuous stream
To a giant throne at the edge of the sky
Shining with unshed tears.
Sweet child of light and glory
Lead me gently through the night
Never stopping, never still, 'till the dawn breaks
And fragments of it litter the fields
Shining in your light.
Graceful child of riches and life
Help me dance with
The moon the stars and you the light
The cause of my life.
My love of him whoever he is,
My love of you whatever you are
Shall tear me apart in the eternal war.

            Sara Pocklington

Fading Sunlight

Fading sunlight pours through the window,
clouded with ancient dust.
Fading sunlight pours through the room,
cluttered with moldy flowers.
Fading sunlight pours through the house,
long ago abandoned, and then forgotten.
Fading sunlight pours through the garden,
choked with growing weeds.
Fading sunlight pours through my heart,
long since broken.
Fading sunlight pours through my dreams,
shattered by age, and erased by time.
But if you wipe away the dust,
and pick up the moldy flowers,
If you live in the house,
and clear the weeds,
And if you fix the broken heart,
and mend the splintered dreams,
Then the fading sunlight,
will come shining through.

            Cheryl Christophe

My Grandfather

As I look up into the never ending sky
I am forced to wonder if I could catch your eye
like I did when I was still a child
running through the cuckoo clocks all hyper and wild
every time I left, you would stand, wave, and then smile
I wanted to turn around to hug you and cry

When I finally realized that your time was here
I tried and I tried, but could manage not one tear
instead, I grew so angry and ever so mad
about to move on, and yet you were almost glad
you left me without you, a whole filled with deep sad
that you could ever go without having me near

Time has passed, and I have since cried into the night
I know now that you could not stay, though try as you might
you were my heritage, but more though, a true friend
a person I counted upon until the end
I wait now for some sort of message you might send
assuring me that everything is all right.

William Trump

Graven Image

Far up, too high to see
From down here, down on bent knee
Trying to stir an emotion within,
Love in the soul growing thin
Conceived by men, and even man it cannot be

Far down, too far to hear
Staring out, across the horizon clear
A God in the image of man
Tall and straight, but cannot stand
Speaking, "If your work does not please, there is all to fear"

Turn this around and open your eyes,
Man conceived by God is where the fear dies
The one who is love, the One who can reach,
Known by faith and willing to teach
Look and see the One who is crucified

Look up, easy to see Thy staff and Thy rod,
The truth is where man is the image of God
Emotion is stirred and the soul is filled,
Come, be clean where the Lamb's blood was spilled
Emancipated, on the image is where the free one trods

Eugene Bianchi

Grandfathers

I wish I could see you.
I never had much of a chance to.
I wish I could hear your voice.
I was too young to understand or listen.
I wish I could recall many memories of us playing
games, running around, or just holding me in your arms.
But I can't.
Because we never had the chance to
All I see are pictures.
Most are meaningless to me.
There is one that confuses me.
Do I actually remember this, you rocking me in your arms?
I doubt it.
I think I've just seen this picture many times.
All I hear is silence, an empty void.
All I recall is... Nothing, just a blank.
I wish I could remember you, but I can't.
And you're not there to be remembered.
But at least you are at peace.
That is comfort enough for me.

Aaron D. Wood

Waterman's Love

Brackish water laps 'gainst wooden hull,
brightwork's a'buffed, to shield weather's dull,
tip-of-the-cap t'wards blue heron's trumpet,
my skipjack's a lady, some other fella's strumpet.

I've watched 'em fade from might to mourn,
chin up, chest out, never forlorn.
But this here's the life for those not burdened
with followin' commands, constant urgin'.

"Shutdown her engine, unfurl her main,
Today's a beaut', God's will she be lain'!"
Dredged up a load, struck her deck with a clamor,
"Livelihood's at stake boys, sing praise don't damn her."

Slowly chuggin' to port she's a starboard list,
the dockmaster's wit, a sarcastic abyss.
"G'days work boys, yer pockets'll be boastin'!
I'll hold yer missus' share, whilst yer off a'toastin'."

Belly's full and sleepin', ol' muscles'll be sore,
gentle poke in my ribs quiets lion's snore.
Up at four, my heaven's another man's hell.
I long for osprey's call, distant buoy's bell.

Kevin Turner

A Miracle Man

When I was down and friends were few,
Jesus came and made life anew.

When I was sick and had no place to turn,
He set me down and made me learn.

When I was poor, he said to me, rise
my child, be poor no more.

When I had no food and cupboards were bare,
He filled my shelves and I knew He cared.

I owe my life to this man, you see, without
my Jesus I wouldn't be me.

How He did these things, I cannot say, but there
is one thing, for sure, I'll praise this man
forever and a day.

Helen Jean Curren

Entering Fort Knox

On your doors I knock, but
Frozen silence is all I hear.
Outside, I stand, in the
Cold, wet, pain.
Yet, firmly, I still stand,
Wondering, hoping, praying
For a key, a key from your heart.
Can I come inside? Please answer true.
What torture it is, outside your doors.
Your signs so confusing, "Come?" or "Go!!?"
So I stand outside enduring the pain.
Wind, hail, sleet, snow.
No matter. A small price.
For the treasure I seek is rare indeed.
Worth more than silver.
Worth more than gold.
These I would, a thousand times, gladly trade away,
If I knew your heart would be mine.
So outside I'll stay standing; hoping, one day,
You'll let me inside, and I will be thine.. Always.... Forever.

Jegan Anandasakaran

359

Reflection

As I watched his image become smaller,
  I realized that
one day I wouldn't know when he was coming back.
I could still feel the touch of his hug
where it was given to me so earnestly.
I started walking away, missing him already.
I must have felt his gaze because I turned around.
He was waving and smiling, "Bye, Mom".
When did "Mommy" become "Mom?"
  I don't know.

I wonder how it will be one day.
How will I fill my time, my days?
I want their images etched on the wall of my mind.
To remember them as they were at each stage.
I want to always feel that
they are and always will be the strings
  that pull on my heart.

Deborah Watkins

Searching

Shameful is the way we look at others,
afraid what we see is not true.
All in all it's not you,
what brings sadness could be happiness.
The pit of every thing is unclean.
Just as every thing you have seen as right,
is only wrong just in spite.

Swaying in the branches of the afterlife,
knowing when I was mortal I was to come here.
But it is only a dream,
nothing is as it seems,
when your head just floats dreams.
Watching all around for the moment of decision,
finding every thing to be a vision.

That's when I came to this prison in my mind.
Because I knew it was time to think of God.
Every thing we believe in is real,
It's just some can't feel,
The other worlds floating around us.
That's why we can't win, we'll do ourselves in....

Patrick Grant

Whispering Shadows

Whispers of anger....
  The war has begun.
Endlessly dreaming. For what?
Forever drifting unto darkness.
Watching, waiting for the single light of hope.
Listening, for the cries of peace,
  darkness covers all.

The children run, forever looking,
  forever hearing.
Seeing only the single light
  in the darkness.
Hearing only their own anguished
  cries of peace and love.

So they shall lead the way.
Leaving only shadows of a worn path,
  to the shining light of hope.

In the deafening shadows of war and darkness.
The children shimmer of the light.
The silence of peace and love,
  covers all......

Jamie Barney

My Childhood Memories

Buffy,
Golden retrievers
Golden brown like the first fallen leaves.
Sweet like sugar
Kind like a dove,
Loved.
No bark.
No bite.
Small like an infant child,
Fragile like glass.
Sadness fills the air.
Buffy is gone.
The sun is gone.
Clouds have come.

Danielle Cullen

Your World

As I walked down that dusty road,
I look for something good, I see nothing.
But then out of nowhere,
I see you. You opened my eyes.
To your wonderful, mysterious,
Dark sided world. I loved it.
You show me many new, fantastic creatures,
With flustered imaginations.
You showed me vivid images,
Of vicious, crafty stalkers.
I saw the deep secrets.
Of all the faultless intellectuals, looming in the vain,
Outstretched pasture land.
None of these things surprised me though.
The final thing you showed me,
was your true hope, happiness, love and trust.
And I am here telling you this, because that is what I held onto,
And I will always cherish you in my heart.
The final thing I need to say is Thank You.
Thank you for showing me Your World.

Rocio Velazquez Gonzales

Weddings

Weddings are special with flowers and rings,
dances, and dresses, oh such lovely things!
The white wedding dress, with fragile nice lace,
and the delicate features upon the bride's face.
Ministers, flower girls
a beautiful string of dazzling pearls,
in a big white church, with a limousine,
coming out of the church is quite a big scene,
Kissing the groom, I do, I do,
Getting married is such a big day for you.
Honey moon, throw the rice,
Wedding gifts, such a price!
Anniversary is today,
It makes me think of my wedding day.

Kara Lien

Life

Life has a strange way of spinning its tale;
To some it unfolds smoothly, to others it's travail.

Do you turn your back upon it, and let another do the task?
Or, do you turn and face it, and not care if one would ask?

Life's not fair, but who said that it must be.
No guarantee if it's long or it's short.

Just love it and live it with gusto;
Don't look back, you just might get caught.

Michael Killeen

Lover's Exchange

If I leave all for you, will you exchange and be all to be me?
Shall I never miss our talks and blessings and the common kiss
that comes to each in turn, nor count it strange,
when I look up, to move onto a new place
of walls and floors - another home than this?
No, will you fill that place by me which is filled by a stone
a heart to cold to change?
That's the hardest! If to conquer love has tried,
to conquer indeed is love and grief besides.
Alas, I have grieved so I am hard to love
yet love me — will you?
Open your heart wide,
and fold within, the deepest part of my soul

Annabelle Oliver

Thanksgiving

For birds and trees, honey and bees,
Sunshine and rain, harvest of grain;
Strength to labor, good friends and neighbors.
For puppies and kittens, warm woolen mittens,
Churches and meetings and warm friendly greetings;
Green lawns and flowers, cool shady bowers,
Doctors and nurses and handy big purses;
Confessings and blessings.
For love from on high and God always nigh;
For pastors and laymen and adequate raiment;
White sparkling snow, faces that glow.
For angels to guard us when troubles bombard us;
For families who love us and stars all above us.

Father, I thank Thee!

Noma D. Cargill

Memories

I sit here in the peace and quiet of the early morning dawn,
Searching for my inner self.
I unlock the door to the recesses of my mind.
There are little tiny shelves with little tiny boxes,
They are filled with memories, both good and bad.
Some are shiny and new; others are old and rusted:
Long forgotten memories.
They keys to the locks have been left hanging in my mind,
Who else, better to be trusted?
I open a few here and there, my heart begins to race.
I laugh and I cry; I hurt, but I'm also proud.
Well that's enough for today.
Another time, another place,
There will be other days that I can explore
What's in the tiny boxes behind the door.

Patricia A. Spires

Alley Rattle

Walking sticks with cigar flicks
Feet move slow, pants worn low
Shirt has holes and sleeves are thin
Wrinkled hand holds coffee tin
Spit runs down from dirty hound
Safe way cart is pushed around
Wheels rattle on asphalt alley
Beer cans collected for the tally
Dumpsters and garbage cans are checked
From door frames, benches, from old car wrecks
Insanity runs from her eyes
Stench is bad, large horse flies

Chris Stover

Mother's Face

The face is old
The lines draw me in
I can't look away
I long to touch the skin
To trace the web of lines with my fingers

The face is content
It is her mother's face
I have also known the face of her mother

They merge in my mind and become one
Was this the face of her mother before
and before
and before

I look at my image and begin to see the face
The Mother face
It frightens and comforts me in the same breath

The loss of youth
The comfort of age
The unbroken chain

Rachelle Russell Chase

One Day I Will Find Love

One day, I'll find what I've
Needed for so long. There will be no
Emptiness in me anymore. The next

day will not seem so far
Away and I'll
yell out my happiness.

It will be found and

When it is, I will feel
Invigorated. Maybe then
Lonely won't be a part of my
Limp vocabulary.

Found and held close to my heart,
It's a special thing that will
Never leave until
Death calls from the dark corners to take my

Love. The one and
Only true love I'll ever have and when I find it, it will be
Valued and cherished in my heart for all
Eternity.

Vanessa Anaya

All

A child arrives at birth destined to
walk the roads to find all that is worth.
Life, he challenges, the world, a test
to the bounds of how far one can go. A
find for independence around a summer's
trip into the freedom that shoots a star
across the inside of night. His life a search
for love that hides under rocks in a
dusty desert town in the middle of nowhere,
but he swears it's somewhere.
He isn't sure if love he's feared or
a fear of love but a moment he loses
faith. He sees promises like faces hidden behind
signs along a sun beaten road. When
it's all finally found in a young girl's
eye flashing like a town's sky on the
4th of July, you know it was only
all of just what you needed.

James K. Kessinger

You Said

You said you'd never hurt me
  But you did.
You said you'd always be loyal
  But you weren't.
You said you'd trust me over anyone else
  but you didn't.
You said I was the only one
  But I wasn't.
You said you'd never leave
  But you are gone.
You said you'd always support me and my decisions
  But now you blame me.
You said you'd give me the world
  But where is it?
You said you'd change
  But you never did.
You lied,
  But then again...
You are a lie.

Dawn Celeste

Everyday I Die A Little

At night at times I sigh a little
In the day when skies are bright
clouds you can't see observe my sight
alone I walk all through the day
to wonder is this life the way
speak to any one who will talk
accompany those with whom to walk
so many things that I would share
if I had someone with me to care
work each day when you are needed
even though long ago your lawns were seeded
thoughts that arise in my head
hold their place don't get said
Love that should at all cost be shared
cannot even in loneliness be bared
if you should happen to think of me
remember it's not what it should be
for always is not if all goes well
it should be the Lord who rings the bell

Emanuel H. Gottesman

All I Knew

I dived in shallow water,
I've swam in an ocean of tears,
as I traveled by the stars in the night,
and I still don't know where I've been.

I climbed the highest mountains,
not knowing what was at the top,
bearing the battle scars of life.

I wandered in dry desert,
walking in an endless circle,
while still being afraid of my own shadow,
and I still don't know why I'm here.

I kept opening the doors,
not knowing what it was I teared,
as I began reaching for your hand.

All I knew something was missing in my life,
I didn't know it was You at the time,
All I knew something didn't shine,
I didn't know that I needed Your light,
Now that I know, I'm not going to let You go.

Jennie Schaefer

The Sound That Was Lost In Silence

I spoke a word so softly, but loud enough to be heard.
He whispered something tender, it couldn't be called a word.
I recalled my parents' teachings, every word they said.
That was the only reason, I didn't get into that bed.
A few years past, from that day.
He has a child, he stays away.
The girl he was with, had no clue,
That the love he would give would be untrue.
I thank God for sounds, for words that stay,
For my parents whose words never slipped away.
For the baby's cry that is not my own,
And for silent sounds, that hit close to home.

Tiffany M. Tetidrick

Hold Me

Let's hold each other for a little while until the pain subsides.
Until I figure out just how I can leave you and not cry.
Let's hold each other a little more till I find the words to say
How much you rally mean to me and how much I'd like to stay.
Hold me just a little longer till my heart swells up with pride
On how the world is at our feet when you're walking by my side,
Hold me hard and hold me tight till my doubts and fears are gone.
Until my strength comes back to me and the inner fight is won.
Hold me when I'm laughing, and hold me when I cry.
Wrap your arms around me and never say goodbye.
Hold me cause you want to, and not because you must.
Let me feel your heartbeat and let me know your lust.
Hold me tight and tell me what you really feel inside.
Tell me all the things you want; from me you need not hide.
Hold me, oh please just hold me, when sorrow takes hold of me.
Help me know whatever comes will be tomorrow's memory.
Hold me as we drift to sleep, exhausted, yet content.
Somehow I know my dreams will show that you've been heaven sent
Just hold me.

Alan Craig Williams

Hurry

Here I write, with nothing to say. Faster and
faster I go, sloppier all the way. I hurry
to write, even though it's nonsense.
Scratching letters with a stick, hurrying
to get done, before the tide comes in
and washes my words away. Washes
me away. Words nonsense, just
a bunch of symbols because our
little minds are too small to
record everything. I stumble
over my words. Have to get done.
With what, I don't know. Have
to hurry. The century's almost
over. Can feel time slipping away.
Like grains of sand through my
fingers. Feel our world turning,
the sun setting. Time is running out.
Have to hurry.

Rebecca Munnell

They Answered The Call

Another of our comrades has been called away.
He no longer, has to be accountable, for what he does each day.
  Our ranks are getting thinner with the passage of time.
The space that he vacated will be filled by those behind.
  So here's to you my comrade where ever you might be.
May peace be always with you and God reside in thee.

Horace Gingras Jr.

A True Friend

The day has come to say goodbye
As you go your way and I go mine
I'll be strong and try not to cry
I'll remember the good times that we've had
Laughing, talking and sharing each other's secrets
Staying up late to watch a movie
Or strolling through the museums in the fall afternoon
Even though we will be miles apart
We will still be together in our hearts
The miles between us will not weaken what we have
For the bond of our friendship
Is too strong to be broken.
Elizabeth A. Barkholtz

Love's Bitter Edge

My heart you claimed from the edge, your
life and love to me did pledge. My life
lived fast and on the edge, all for love
your heart you pledge.

My love from you, my heart did keep, for
fear your love my heart would weep, and
so love's pledge I did not keep for in my
mind to love was weak.

Now, your love my heart do seek, of love
for me your heart won't speak, to think
your love would make me weak was
thoughtless ramblings of a creep.

Your love now lost, my heart I pledge, your
love reclaim from its bitter edge and in so
doing remove this wedge of fear, that's
forced us to the edge.

My heart now yours, you must reclaim
for without your love I am not the same,
and if your love I can't reclaim, back
on the edge I'll be again.
Keith G. Henry

The Mailman

I'm all alone and not much to do,
   The work's all done, with it I'm through,
What will the next excitement be?
   I'll wait for the mailman and I'll see.

I watch as he stops in his little car,
   Is it in the box yet, which isn't far?
Or do I wait a little while yet
   Until it's sorted and then go get?

Then I look close and to my surprise
   It isn't just anyone of those guys,
It's the special one coming once a week;
   He stops at the door and kisses my cheek.

You see it's my son so tall and straight,
   When he delivers mail it's never late,
I give thanks to a son of whom I'm proud
   Who carries the mail to a very large crowd.
Vesta A. Gledhill

Creatures Of Despair

I sit and wonder is life so fair, are we the
Creatures of despair or are we just people
Who are not aware. We think we're in control
Of what we do but then the men who rule tell
Us that's not true.
Michael Fishman

Waiting

Sit no longer, I cannot stay.
One does not find time to pray,
Just a little while longer, tarry here
expect your miracle, have no fear.

The longer you hold on the better it will be;
I know waiting is a painful thing to do you see
Remain steadfast, unmovable and ever abiding
Don't rush out there, satan is a-riding

Maybe you're anticipating what's ahead
But, haste makes waste so they said
Wait with faith, sojourn in this place
I know you're tired, but God will give you grace;

Sit no longer I cannot wait:
I believe in the act of fate
Patience is a gift, perseverance is too
God will continue to take care of or (provide for you).
Undrea T. White

Untitled

There's life and there's love and then happiness
who would've thought that's all there is
when there's sorrow and shame and lots of loneliness
floating in clouds and around my bliss.

I'm free as a bird up in my heaven
chasing the wind that keeps me high
looking for dreams that keep me challenged
soaring forever up in the sky.

But such a life isn't so possible
without a meaningful purpose
one needs no one else to be comfortable
but a soulmate makes life more joyous.

So search until a soulmate you find
and that love will make your heart miss a beat
and you'll be overcome by feelings so divine
that your knees will even feel weak.

And together your life and your lover will bring
joy as you deserve best
and to the birds and the trees you will sing
living life as one who lives in happiness.
Matthew C. Cates

Thoughts Of A Child

Time stands still, the light grows dim
I have only one thought on my mind,
I only think of him.
To remember the child within me,
To remember the child that is out.
All the pain, hardship and suffering that I have brought about.

When will it end, or will it ever be?
The memories of a child who made a horse of my knee.
That will grow up and be strong and face a world of challenge
But will he find a smile in every sunset, dawn and morn?

These thoughts will never be complete, the worries never die
The only thing to do is sit down and cry,
Or do I?

To be strong without, I am strong within
When I want to holler, scream and shout
I find an inner peace, that if I look I will find,
To ease the tension in my mind
For the child I bore will always be my son
And I will always have a love that will never be undone.
Veronica Reis

The Realization of Love

A mist of darkness, cloud my skies
Coming to the light, I only fantasize
Been blinded for months, love on my mind
But to my wandering eyes it was all just a lie
Gave him my all, a life filled with joy
Only to find out he played me as his toy
The time has now come for me to see
That no one of this earth cares for me
No one can love me completely and free
But my only friend that fills my heart with glee
His name is Jesus, for sure, no doubt
Does anyone know what I'm talking about?
My mother, my father, my sister, my brother,
My protector, my caretaker, why should I bother,
To tell you about it, what could be so great
It's his love and understanding, for Jesus sake
Have faith and trust, that no one can take
Nestled me in his arms, when I was about to break
My clouds are now brighter than what they ever could be
Only because Jesus opened my eyes for me to see.

Tiajuana Y. Jones Ennals

Threads Of Love

Thank God for the spools of thread that are used,
To mend the garments that are sometimes abused.
For each stitch that mends a vesture so fair,
Shows forth a devotion with much love and care.

These same sort of threads that mend a garment so,
Have also been used to set a heart aglow.
For who has not gazed upon an embellishment rare,
Of an embroidered scene in a landscape so fair.

We've taken the threads that are used to mend,
And we've stitched back together the heart that did rend.
What would we have done without this mighty tool,
Which God has so generously provided by spool.

We've used the many colors of this ornate thread,
And blended them together into a great spread.
To make a beautiful picture that would help us remember,
All the joys of our life that have brought us such splendor.

My Darling, I've noticed with the passing of years,
Through the laughter and joys, through the sorrows and tears,
That these threads we've used in the valleys and mountains above,
Have woven themselves into a cord full of love.

Stephen E. Davis

Tell Me What An Angel Does

Angels are your hope, your soul
They shield you from danger and sorrow
When you need them, there they are
Right beside you when danger strikes
No one can hurt you, no one can harm you
Angels encourage you to succeed
To follow your dreams, wherever they may lead you
your guardian angel does all that and more
So why put a burden on them, just to challenge them
Help them, don't depend on them
Because if you love them they'll love you
Your guardian angel lives within your heart and soul
Helping the Lord to do His job.
Whenever you use your heart and soul,
Then you are an angel.
Not all angels live above
Many live within, so whenever you need an angel
Reach deep within and they will come.
Just wait and see

Heidi Odeen

Untitled

A small golden hand
    pure and untouched reached out to me.
Her smile flowed forth
    with warmth and love.
Her eyes shone with
    innocence that came from within.
A golden child
    in a colorless world of black and white.
Wherever she looked
    whoever she saw through the black and the white
    shone a deep deadly red.
A small golden hand
    pure and untouched reached out to me.
The red from my soul
    slowly drained out.
Two golden clasped hands
    painted the black
and painted the white
    and the world soon lost
    its red.

Kristen Kaszeta

My Mile

We each have our space, our journey through life
There is happiness there, also burdens and strife
As I look back in my 70th year
I have some regrets for things I've held dear
Some things I've done backwards for that is my style
Like college in my 50's near the end of my mile
Some may look at me, shake their head and say,
She could have done better in a different way
but God alone must be the judge (makes me feel so small)
The wonder to me that I was put here at all
five children I raised who gave me 6 grandchildren 2 greats

This is the field where I feel I do rate
When I reach the bend in the road
And finally set down this heavy load
I'll ponder a moment and think with a smile
Just look at me this was my mile.

Ruth H. Skogstad

Childhood Is The Kingdom Where...

Childhood is the kingdom of laughter and song.
A time of tag and cartoons, and getting sick from too much cake.
It is a time of an imaginary friend named Soozie.

Childhood is the kingdom where you and Soozie rule.
It is where you make the rules.
Where you can do whatever you please.
The kingdom where you are free, free to soar like an eagle
Or pretend you are a princess, and Soozie has to dress you.

Childhood is when your fears are calmed, by a soothing voice
    in your head.
When you close your eyes, you shut out the remaining fears,
Including the purple monster beneath your bed.

One day, Soozie is gone.
The laughter subsides, as the sun goes down.
The new fears introduced to you can't be shut out.
You stop hearing the voice in your head.
You have left the childhood kingdom that you were once in.

But deep down, way down in all of us,
Soozie is waiting for us to return.
One day.
Some day.

Denise Ho

A Change In My Life

My home was but made of shadows
because of the darkness that was upon it.

None of us could handle a single breath because
of the darkness that was upon it.

We never noticed our sins in our home
because of the darkness that was upon it.

We did not act like humans, but vagabonds in our home
because of the darkness that was upon it.

None of us where ever calm in our home
because of the darkness upon it.

When out of the wilderness a bright light
came and shared with us blessings of great joy.

Now we are not least of people but
above all because of the light that is upon us.

Tiffany Howard

Gone Forever

They once were here;
    they taught us much.
    They listened to us like we listened to them.

Now they are gone;
    they don't teach us anymore,
    and now, they listen from far away.

Their small gifts, like costume jewelry, once so meaningless,
    now mean the world to us.

We think and wonder,
    are they watching?
    Where are they watching from?
    Who are they with?

Suzanne Robertson

Veterans I Care

For all the Veterans that have fought,
And for the ones that have passed away,
I hope this message comes your way.
I know someday I'll meet with you,
But for now this will have to do.
When I think of what it must have been like, I cry.
When I read the articles I think they can't be true,
But I know deep down some fears came true,
They were worse.
You left your families and friends behind,
To fight for a purpose, freedom and mankind.
I pray for the nameless, wishing their identities found,
And for the missing hoping they'll someday come around.
I pray for the disabled who's lives are forever changed,
And for the families that will never again,
Quite be the same.
When my time comes to meet you veterans,
I'll thank you one and all, but until then, this must do.
Veterans, just remember I care.

Cheryl A. Beasley

I Can Always Depend On Her

Through sorrow, sadness, and tears
I can always depend on her.
Through bad grades, broken bones and injuries
I can always depend on her.
Through heartaches, headaches, and tummy aches
I can always depend on her.
This person that I can always lean on is my mother
And I can always depend on her.

Felicia Warman

Untitled

Manic depression is like a boiling pot that
never died but always simmers, it's a bottle
within one's self. Speak softly, it's a non-sociable issue and a
tiresome bother to it's beholder.
This chemical formula needs no
discussion, it's already earned a label, so
next time try not to ask! I've learned
about it, I live with it. At times my
will grows tired with just the hollow feel
of my bones chilling my blood. Don't sigh
because I'm always some kind of high,
I can feel this soul isn't fading.
I'm not living a lie, it's just that manic
depression won't say good-bye!

Edward F. Maher

Half A Pack

I was normal in her bind
in that mundane state of mind
panting where the pillows were
doing nothing but to purr
being nothing but the cur, till the wide eyes kisses came

On boggy street my head was salty
a wormy meat now weary walking, now
those two eyes I cannot meet, now
those two eyes so indiscreet
they reach me still,
her haunting feat and
I went cotton mouthed, my self sought treat

I had escaped, but now I may
call you back from faraway
and two red eyes will merely say
and a green town sign can only bay
you are home
you are home
you are home

Mercer Bufter

Beyond The Horizon

The Enlightenment within is not difficult to achieve
When one gives up
    the preference for love and hate
    the prejudice of good and evil
The distinction between true and false
    only makes one bewildered
The separation between right and wrong
    only drives one to wonder
When the effort of drawing lines is dropped
All the polarities of existing facts will disappear
And the Great Wisdom within will lead one far
    beyond heaven and earth
    beyond the horizon

Hanna Chang

House

They were so happy.
Flour clumped in her hair.
He grinned as she shook her head loose from the white powder.
"I hate you," she shouted.
He rumbled with laughter, "I hate you more!"
"Grrrrr, I could kill you."
"All right you two, cut it out," Mrs. Watson bellowed
from across the preschool room.
The young children slunk to their chairs.
What's wrong? They wondered.
We were only playing house.
We were only playing Mommy and Daddy.

Amanda Hollander

The Empty Chair

In a room all by itself there sits an
empty chair. No one goes in and no one
comes out. The lonely empty chair is still there.

When someone sits, Ada says, "That's
my daddy's chair." Little does she know,
now it's the empty chair.

She cries, "Why is the chair empty?
Why is my daddy not in his chair?"

One thing she doesn't know is that
the chair is now empty for eternity.

The chair keeps hidden from all to
see, for no one knows it's crying. The
poor, empty chair. I have but one thing
to say about this lonely empty chair.
Sadly no more life will it share.

Holli Irvin

The Girl I Love

I miss the girl that I love
I think of her as something you see in the sky above,
I think she is more beautiful than the stars that shine,
Because she is heaven itself, and her love is mine.

God must have intended it that way,
For my love and my heart is with her to stay,
Her beauty is for man to enhance,
A for me my heart didn't have a change.

I loved her right from the start,
Now that we are together, I hope that we never part,
For she is the girl that I love,
So I thank you, dear God above.

John D. Lopus

Time

An eagle soared in the sky above
The sun shown all around
But none of this did I see
When the white rose hit the ground

Memories ran throughout my mind
I could see through space and time
A little piece of me died that night
When the church bell gave its final chime

I screamed my heart out into the night
Then lay in the fields to cry
But nothing in the world could hurt worse
Than to watch your best friend die

Becky Deihl

Gone But Not Forgotten

She looks around but not at me,
With friends around her she talks and laughs,
I remember,
that once was me,

All the memories of the past five years
are now only remembered through my silent tears,
A loss of any kind is hard, but one of a close friend
is worse, we said we would be friends forever, but now,
that means nothing to her,
Maybe this was coming, maybe it wasn't,
maybe it was meant to happen, my only question,
What did I do? What did I do? All I want to know is,
What did I do?

Erin Taylor

The Leaf

A leaf twists and turns off a branch.
As it falls slowly, it rocks back and forth.
As it gets closer to the ground,
The wind sweeps it up into the sky fifty feet high.
As it comes back to earth, it does millions of twists and turns.

As it comes closer to the ground,
It gets closer to its death. As it helplessly
Falls, it seems to say help me. But it has
No control over where it is going.
As it gets closer, it loses, life. When it hits
The ground, it dies like a bird with a bullet in its heart.

Billy Watling

Within Your Soul

Your quest is over.
For the secret lies within your soul;
in the depths of your heart
it sits there waiting patiently
for you to realize what you already know;
to come to the conclusion
that all your life it's been in the shadows of your mind;
you feel it in the touch,
see it in the view,
savor it in the air,
but mostly it lies within your soul.
It is your one true love.

Deborah L. Hatch

Teenage Love

When you're in love, you know there's no other,
But yet there's so much more for you to discover.
Everything from friends to family.
But you wonder how this could be?
You love these all so equally.
It is this you hope they all can see,
You'll always be there for your once true love.
To them, nothing could rise above.
You love your family just as much,
But your friends have such a gentle touch!
It's with all of these combined,
That my life is divine.
All of these wonderful people,
Share in the love we'll show at the steeple!
For it is there I make them see,
If it wasn't for them, I wouldn't be me.
All of these people have a place in my heart,
Because I know we'll never part!
They know you're always there to listen,
But it's them who truly make your life glisten!

Holly Midthun

Stars Wish

As I wait for the stars to twinkle one by one,
I think of what it would be like to visit the sun.
I suppose it would be pretty hot,
and I would probably just sleep in a cot.
I would float around all day,
and at night I'd sit, and wait, for the first star and say:
Star, light, star bright,
first star I see tonight.
I wish I may, I wish I might,
be granted this wish I wish tonight,
I wish to be with my family back home,
and maybe my next trip will be to the moon.

Christina Lessard

Contemplation

Not many blossoms bloomed this year,
Where did the others go?
Cause for concern and even fear,
When growth does go so slow.

I wonder what next year will bring,
Resurgence or return,
Renewed encounter with soft spring,
Or charred and barren burn?

Will knowledge flow in vital veins,
And nourish need to grow,
Or planned abandon push harsh pains,
To heights we dare not know?

Perhaps strong seeds, with special care,
Will still find fertile soil,
If common sense can make aware,
Man's need to folly foil.

Larry A. Fable

A Child's Smile

Smiles can come and go just like the wind;
Sometimes they just never seem to end.
Like when a child sees a funny clown
or maybe someone just joking around.

Sometimes smiles turn into frowns.
We need to find a way to turn them back around.
Maybe by just being there;
and showing them we really care.

You can make them smile in many ways;
A child loves to hear your praise.
They love to hear the words 'I Love You'
And I'm so very proud of you, too.

Just take a little time once a while;
And see if you can make a child smile.
Then you will see how easy it can be;
To make a child as happy as can be.

Sue Brewer

Untitled

Looking at the storm pass by,
asking questions of why and why?
My brain gets cloudy my body is dry.
Do I see a brilliant sun, a break in the frosting of the clouds,
sweet sweet summer rain.
   My body called and my mind just followed,
could not stop and only swallowed,
Abstain! Abstain! That is all that remains!
Abstain! Abstain! So there will be no more pain.
Here the nights are lonely,
the flame in my heart.
I feel the stinging in my heart.
The world is silent now, drifting, drifting away,
beginning a new day again, everyday is a new day again.
My mind going round and round, when will it stop,
screaming within for a love long away, instead giving in.
I used to look forward to tomorrow,
Now I only feel like dreaming...

Pedro Jimenez

Spring Time Thank You God

Spring has lots of sunshine
   Plants are blooming everywhere
      Rain showers fall washing our earth
         And cleaning our air
          God's children will smile and say
             Thank you God for this fine spring day

Nicole D. Jones

Why God, Why

I asked God one day,
"God why can't I see you?"
He answered,
"Look into your heart."
I tried and I tried, even in the mirror, but
I couldn't see into my heart.
So I asked God,
"God why can't I see into my heart?"
And God replied,
You don't need to see into your heart to believe in me.
Trust in your heart and you will know I'm next to you
every step of the way."

Brittany Aspromonte

I Wonder

As I dive with the whales in the Great deep blue sea,
I look all around at reflections of me
I swim with the fish in water so cold
I Wonder to God, "will I ever grow old"?

As I soar with the eagles to places unknown,
I look back to see, where I have flown
I fly through the sky over land, over sea
I wonder to God, "Are you still close to me"?

As I track with the wolves in the calm of the night,
I look at the ground, and all seems all right
I walk simply and quietly with the leaves at my feet
I Wonder to God, "will we ever meet?"

Joseph Schiavone

Childish Love

A childish girl lost to your love,
her wanting to hold you
to have you to hug.

She talks about dreams that she's had of you two;
She won't tell you what, nor give you a clue.
You said that you love her, is it true in your heart?
Are you prepared for the tears on the day you must part?

Spare her the pain of being heartbroken.
For the words that she thought but to you were unspoken.
Make her understand that her dream won't come true;
Her thoughts that you love her as much as she loves you.

Tell her the time has come to say goodbye,
this was never meant to be.
Remember the good times that you shared together,
and treasure those memories in your hearts forever.

Maria A. J. Giron

Hope

Hollow and deep, gangly and bare,
an emptiness to the core.
There exists a barrier unsurpassable;
cold and solid; ubiquitous and far-reaching.
Yet it is elusive and impalpable;
it cannot be seen or understood.
Is it so? Is it conceivable?

Life elapses and changes imperceptibly.
The stream flows and all of existence is seen
in the riffles and runs,
in the foam and currents.
Faces, places, thoughts, emotions
tumble forward and melt into one.
They constantly change,
they change, they change.

Scott Biasetti

A Tribute To My Only Daughter, Faye

I had a beautiful dream last night all about you.
I heard the kind and loving things you say
And saw the special, caring things you do.

When God created you, He had an exceptional person in mind.
He gave you unique qualities that makes you one of a kind.
You made my life complete right from the very start.
You're like a ray of sunshine and I love you with all my heart.

I embrace our relationship though we sometimes disagree,
We always resolve our differences with true integrity.
You make me proud and happy in numerous ways.
To say you are outstanding would be inadequate praise.

I cherish your precious and unconditional love for me,
Because you, my dear, sweet, charming daughter
Are my special dream come true, you see.

And although many others love you truly,
How fortunate can I be?
I am the one abundantly blessed
With God's gift of you to me.

Wanda Faye Hart

The Voice Of Pride And Prejudice

Emoting a whimsical sense of discovery
The thoughtful baritone danced upon the ebonies
And skimmed over the tiniest bit of ivory
Creating the unfinished piece we call deceit
Flattening the natural points of life
That we look upon to guide us
Pretending and pushing all that he had been taught
All that he desired to learn
All that he did not feel
That his heart didn't beat, hollow

When the incomplete music slowed its horrendous beat
He listened to the words of the wide-open eyes about him
And heard with ears the voice of youth
Playing both black and white harmoniously
Together words drifted off tongue and heart
And sang the masterpiece of life
With ears he heard the voice of heart
And heard it as a youth
And heard it as naive
That its heart didn't beat

Kristen Elizabeth Boyle

Forgotten At Home

Night has fallen, I feel as though I'm crawling,
creeping around through an endless town with
cobblestone streets made of red brick, oh how
the night air seems so thick, it's as if no one's out there
Do I dare? Do I dare? I really don't care!
Forgotten in my own people. Yet far off I can
see a white steeple through the grove ivy growing
on it from top to bottom; it's a quaint little church.
Stained glass windows depicted Angels from
heaven and praying hands,
Oh I suppose this is my land?
There are many who reap the rewards yet so
few who labor, send your tired and we will
do our best, for them we favor.
Deliver me out of my prison!
For I'm being held for a ransom and the price
they seek is far too steep
I will not sell my soul out from under thee
for I stand tall under the witness tree
you have provided for me.

Rebecca E. Hoffman

Gems That Can't Be Bought

Woven deep within the golden memories in mind
I often recollect the many treasures I did find...
So many times by faltering I learned how not to be
and listening to words of wisdom by my Pastor I did see...
that life is short and all that counts is what we do for God
and while there is yet breath in us
for Christ our feet must trod.
And, if we wait for better days to carry out good intentions
the days ahead soon pass us by without so much a mention.
The past is gone, the future is not, but today I am alive...
So if "one" person I can help for this my heart must strive.
And if, by my existence, there is "one" that finds God's way,
then my living would have been worthwhile
and the skies somewhat less gray.
And if I can teach "one person some of what I have been taught,
then I know I will be giving them
some gems that can't be bought.

Beverly Massey Huff

The Woman I Love Doesn't Exist

She's beautiful, so beautiful
She's sweet, so sweet
She has intricate longings for deserts and oceans
   for dreams and caresses
She whispers darkness and light in my ear
   she fears all...
   but nothing.
She's fire and ice and pain and lust and rain
   and sorrow
But above all she's free
   free from laws
   free from others
   free from nature
   free from earth
   free from death
   free from existence

Free from me.

Paul Popov

Last Words

I got out of your car and said, "Goodbye, I'll see you real
soon dad, please don't cry!"

I almost forgot, "I love you too." You see, those were my very
last words to you.

You had tears in your eyes, when you said, "I love you more."
I waved goodbye, and I shut the door.

I cried when I knew you were no longer with me, where was my
comfort? Where could it be?

I remembered then, that I had said goodbye, when my last words
to you made you cry.

Nicole Goodwin

Some Millionth What - If

I am a hill of poetry
In other rooms, I know your ills and your aches
"Oh, how deep" you claimed to me
I, had it been someone else
You'd have thought them to be crazy,

I can feel when you are here
For my cravings for you become a different pain
I walk past you with my head down
   hoping that you'll call out to me
Although I know
   you cannot.

Megan Lowry

The Color Of War

Black is the night that starts out in the east
   The war and the conflict that ends world peace
The dead and the gone who are missing in action
   Separated from loved ones there is no passion
The dreams of holding and clutching him near
   Then wake up in sadness by shedding a tear
Black is the color of mourning the dead
   So remember every word a loved one has said
To all these brave men who have gone off to fight
   Don't remember the black just remember the light

    Debbie Vavruick

Cursed

For what reason doth thy curse avail,
possession of such charm and beauty and health?
What wicked one gave gifts in such quantity,
or were the issued unknown by thyself?
Fated to own so much of what all wish to own,
thus, inheriting the knowledge of aloneness and despair.
Fore no one can stand the sight of all they wish to have and be,
only to be repulsed by a vision so fair.

    Kellie Ryan

Cupid In The Clouds

   Love is like a cloud. It is easily visible, yet highly elusive
and almost impossible to reach.
These grand collections of condensation neither look alike nor have
the same task. Some spread themselves thin over the entire blue above.
Some are so faint and scattered that they are like ghosts in the sky.
And some just roll slowly towards us with black bellies and puffy,
white arms that reach high for a piece of the divine.
Their movements are sporadic acts of magic in a theater of heavenly
objects. Some are created within an eyes blink and then disappear
at that speed. Some are whisked across the sky as if Apollo
had betrayed the sun. While others just linger for days unknown.
And so it is easily recognized that because of their superior
positions high overhead, they do hold immense power. They can
bring joy, relief, or even terror to the brilliance of below.
A rain-maker can release the liquid of life on a thirsty crop.
Or a cute, little 'thang' could turn into a destructive force
in a matter of hours. So be it how they choose to reign!

    Alex Z. Moores

Innocent

The child, the lamb, the innocent.
Who but they are innocent?
No man nor woman, but the child and the lamb.
Yet is the child innocent?
Was he asked to be born?
Nay, he is innocent.
Did the lamb ask to be slain?
Nay he is innocent.
Who are we to judge who is, or who is not,
Who are we to say?
Nay, but the child and the lamb.

    Briana L. Gilbertson

Education

Education is a deed of goodness and kind,
A better career and better mind.
To show the ability and truth
Be away from uneasiness and not truth.
A career a life and a family for me.
I could not get all this without education see.
The knowledge and wisdom is here to stay.
In your life in my life for every single day.

    Nida Israr Ahmed

Thanks Giving

Thank you Lord for bringing me,
my husband, who no better friend can be.
   Thank you Lord for our life together,
and blessing us with such joys to treasure.
   Thank you Lord for keeping harm
away, as we go through life day to day.
   Thank you Lord for all good feeling's
of loving and learning, of caring and sharing.
   Thank you Lord for sorrow and
pain to help us understand the joy of things.
   Thank you Lord for giving us your
Son, a blessed gift, a second chance for every one.
   Thank you Lord for today, a time
for thanks for everything that only You and your love brings.

    Cheryl Sherman

Dream On

I can imagine on that day
When Orville and Wilbur started to say
look here boys, we are going to fly
even though we don't know how
Orville and Wilbur was the talk of the town.
You know how people will put you down
Orville and Wilbur though that they could fly
because nothing beats a failure but a try
when Orville and Wilbur took to the skies
They caught every one by a surprise
They were soaring just like a bird
Looking down upon this earth
Now every one can fly on the bird
We can fly all around the world
To London — Paris — China to Rome
We can fly from coast to coast
We can fly into outer space
We can thank them for opening up the ways
Dreaming is what makes the world go around
Dreaming can pick you up off the ground, dream on

    Tommy T. Burton

Rainstorm

Rainstorm, rainstorm howl and groan,
Enlighten the world with harrow and moan.
Why won't you stop?
Why won't you cease?
Let your sureness shine through.
Let the sky be at peace.
Let your fighting come to an end.
You don't want to be a terror,
So why pretend?
Say "stop" to the howls
To the groans, say "no,"
And in the midst of your wise words,
A rainbow will show.

    Alissa Merksamer

Things Left Unsaid

Things left unsaid
   Are usually the most misunderstood.
Without those words, one's mind might be thinking bad...
   Instead of good.
Things left unsaid
   Can sometime get us in trouble
With timing to late,
   Could size our pain to double
Things left unsaid
   Are feelings left for dead...
And that's why the things you have to say,
   Should never be left unsaid.

    Jason C. Valentin

Present Time

We live on a wave called present,
So thin it can't be seen.
Sweeping life steadily along its crest,
Between past and future, there is no rest.

This space in time, which no one can measure,
Rolls on with lightning speed.
We clap our hands, the sound is history,
Leaving our future the only mystery.

We shout a thought into the air,
It's in the past and forever gone.
The present is only a figment at best,
The past alone is all we can test.

William C. Granlund

Your Eyes Tell A Story

Oh, your eyes, they tell a story,
Full of pain and not of glory.
They try to capture every move,
Just to banter, not to soothe.
If I could reach beyond those lashes,
Would I find you full of passion?
They're oh so big and full of tears,
It must have been rough these past few years.
They're so afraid to reach out and touch,
You've been hurt too often and let down too much.
Your eyes tell a story that has no ending,
For fate can't be written, life's only pending.

Laura Daily

Life

I wander slowly by a darkened stream
under the light of the glowing moon,
Reflecting on life - my dreams, my goals,
knowing some choices will come too soon.

I turn my face toward the goddess of night,
as I sway with the trees in the wind,
Thinking of all my accomplishments,
remembering when I have sinned.

Yet when a cool night breeze brushes my cheek,
and somewhere far off, laughter rings out.
My mind becomes clear, my doubts dissolve,
and I know what life is about.

My life is my own - to shape, and to live,
unique as the silver moon above.
Life's promises beckon me forward
I'm ready to learn, to dare, and to love.

Jocelyn Rood

Fear

Something to me I hold so dear
Is that childish, foolish, feeling of fear.
You could be thirty, twenty, or ten,
But no matter what age you'll always fear again.
It might be the light, or maybe the dark,
Maybe it's just the big dogs that bark.
You could try to close your eyes, and hope it's not there,
But it always will be, and that's a feeling you just can't share.
Your mind will play games and always make you wonder,
When it rains, is it the rain or is it the thunder.
Could it be the fear of being alone,
Or maybe the sound of a certain tone.
My fears are these writings, not being able to share,
For this is a feeling that I will never be able to bear.

Robert C. Sabatino

The Heart Remembers

I remember, I cry, a long sad pain lingers inside,
So strong, so forceful,
I lose control and give in, to surrender to the great,
I will bend, but I will not break,
So powerful, so weak, why has she chosen me,

I see and remember, the look, the feel,
The glass stained of their tears,
I will never look back again,
For in me, it only awakens that pain,
I will not say goodbye,
For I know the tears of they eyes,
But they will never see me cry,

I hear, I see, but never speak,
She is overwhelming, I am meek,
She is like this place, Noise and Joy,
Thinks of me, as her living toy,
But I am with those eyes, through the glass,
Quietly crying, that endlessly last,
Meek yet strong, knowing that it shall not be long,
Until I rejoin those eyes, where my heart belongs.

Andrea N. P. Quintyne

Untitled

The trees, gently swaying - gently calling - out my name
the music, softly playing - soft recalling - yesterday
the road, harsh and winding - cold and thorny - on my feet
the place, so reminding, - rough and mourning - so discreet
all the time I'm walking, thoughts of what I've left behind
in my mind the stalking, they won't leave me this time
dreaming, yesterday. Dreaming of tomorrow. Dreaming, take away,
this cold hearted sorrow.
The house, coldly dwelling, - cold addressing, - my disdain
the voice, sweet compelling - sweetly pressing - to explain
the laughter, slowly fading - slow retreating - from my ears
the ache, old parading - swift in treating - increasing fears
all the time I'm thinking thoughts of what I've left behind
in my mind in screaming - I won't leave them this time
screaming for yesterday, begging for tomorrow, - take away,
this cold hearted sorrow

Brenda Shave

The Writing On The Bathtub Wall

He sits, the little boy of six in tub for benefit of steam
    and, in the vapor on translucent plastic screen
    that separates us—his grandma by marriage and him—
    draws images

First one, a stick figure with a big grin
    below which he traces "BRYCE" and an arrow identifying him
    then more arrows and "N" for North, "S" for south
    and a lesson on where "W" for West and "E" for East
    should go...

I watch as jagged profiles appear and guess aloud:
    "Two people facing each other!"
    "No," he says, "a broken heart". "Whose?" I ask.
    "My mom's," he answers. "Why?" I probe
    "Because her mommy died."

"Don't you think your mommy's heart is healing? She knows
    I love you and am here at your side. Do you think
    I have helped ease away some sorrow?" ... Silence...
    A magic finger draws a new heart joined one-third up
    from bottom point. "See, Mommy's heart is healing now!"

Miriam F. Berks-Roberts

Dream Or Destiny?

I once had a dream,
A foresight into the unknown:
Some place where everyone is overwhelmed by positive thought.
I was approached by a beautiful person:
A Girl, a Woman of great traits.
I looked beyond the physical for a moment.
There I saw the internal,
Love, Appreciation, Joy, and Selflessness.
Closer and closer I walked towards her.
She wore a veil of curiosity.
I wanted to view her stunning eyes,
Feel her bright smile full of sunshine,
Hear the sound of a symphony with each breath.
But beyond the veil was only a bright light.
Her face was like a secret untold:
This told me something unclear.
Was this vision some senseless mind joke?
Or was it a person that I'm destined to meet?
I do not know.
It is a mystery only time will answer.

Darren Lawrence Stanfel

Last Night

Translucent morning rays stream through the blinds
  Illuminating the room, stinging my tired eyes.
Last night, this was my intention...
To stand back and not allow my heart to take over,
  That's what was supposed to happen.
But you've grasped my hand and stolen my heart...
And now I lie beside you wondering if what I've
  done is the right thing.
Overpowering aroma of roses, sweet smell of sex.
  Last night, that was not my intention...
To endure as friends and heed the warning of others,
  That is what was supposed to happen.
But your eyes peered through my feeble attempts
  to tell myself that I did not want you.
And now I am engulfed in you... wanting to
  wake up beside you.
Now I know that I'll love you...
  Always.
Last night, that was not my intention.

Adam T. Smiler

Within

Let me walk you slowly through life.
And as I do so, share with me the awesome feeling of greatness,
of wealth, the passion of love, the feeling of homeliness
and of homelessness.

Let me take you there...

If it is you want to cry, do so!
And if it is you choose to wear a frown, do so!
And if at all you want to laugh, by all means do so!

Earth's hemisphere holds all these things,
some of which you may or may not share.

When experience and hope knock at your door, let them in.
Be the open-hearted surgeon and look deep inside the inner you.
Let faith heal from within and not from without.

Time heals wounds.
Time cushions love.
Time fits in with destiny and puts every broken mystery
into a unified whole. "Truth"

John L. Kinds

Grandfather

A kinder heart, I've never known,
He was my grandfather, but now he's gone.
Why does God take, the people we love.
And place them far, up above?
The pain is deep, like the prick of a knife,
When God takes away, a wonderful life.
Maybe he's an angel, watching over us all,
Keeping us safe, from a trip or a fall.
Surely he's happy now, safe from all pain.
While the rest of us hurt, and try to keep sane.
He wishes us happiness, and begs for no tears.
But, we shall remember him, the rest of our years.
We know there's a time, when we all shall pass,
And all of the memories, shall very long last.
In a length of time, the heart shall heal.
But, our love for Grandpa, will grow on still.

Jennifer Hodge

Runaway

Some people say we run away from fear,
But fear of what?
Is it fear of the risk or of not taking it?
Is it fear of failure or of success?
Is it fear of being hurt or of being happy?
Is it fear of being alone or of being loved?
It is fear of the past or of the future?
What is it you're running from?
Once you have that answer, then you know what you have to run to.

Renee L. Warren

The Coming Of The Seasons

Winter in its heartlessness has arrived
The days of living green are lost
Families huddle together trembling
With distant dreams laced in frost.

Ah, the splendor of spring has blossomed
Fragrantly whispering to my soul
A time of rebirth, renewal, and love
To admire the flower and foal.

Summer is the time for sweltering heat
For being with family and friend
Time to eat ice cream; lay in the sun
How somber to watch it end!

Autumn creeps in coolly, day by day
Leaves are brilliantly ablaze
And as they fall they remind us
Of the brief vibrancy of our days.

And so is the pattern of our lives
As we love, laugh, and cry
And forever it goes until the day
We meet our peace and die.

Clay Miller

Reaching High

Oh how I can touch the sky
You can't believe how very high
I can touch the highest cloud
Oh how I'm so very proud.
I can go so high on a swing
I guess it's just an obvious thing
I could climb the highest tree
Where there are so many things I can see.

Christine A. Edwards

Fascination

We were strolling down this path alone.
I recall your heart, 'twas made of stone.
But, with flowing beauty to catch the eye,
You snatched the very soul of me
With delight, then made me die.

Better did I know that wisdom's wrath
Ultimately follows down a thorny path,
To snare its victims as it may,
And I remember well today.

One day you would toss into the sea
All the dreams you brought to life for me.
And then you showed your colors true,
Winked back, and left me there,
Ashamed that I still longed for you.

'Tis no matter where my feet may go,
Or wisdom, like a sea of kelp, accumulate
Within my weathered heart and mind.
I sometimes hope to find the strength to hate.

Let the fragrance of that forbidden eve
Remain, and in forgiven guilt, a new reprieve.

Nancy Petty Coleman

Love's Four Seasons

Love is sacred in my heart.
So please don't break it.
Now we're testing for the truth
I'll pray we make it.
But why are these days so blue to me?
They say love is sometimes blind, and this is true.
For the tears are burning for the want of you.
They say love grows in many ways.
Mine grows more and more each lonely day.
They say love has its seasons.
And that four times my love has reason.
Spring, to learn every thing about you.
Learn to love and never doubt you
Summer, to have, to keep and hold you.
Hope you remember every thing I told you.
Fall, to build with you our romance.
To hug and kiss at every chance.
Winter, to recall these things we've done,
And wait for spring to have more fun.

Elaine Davis

Love And Peace In The 60's

Blood-rich soil of a foreign land.
Little boys with guns in-hand,
Knowing not why as they fall.
All remains...a name on a wall.

Love and peace was the sign of the day,
As students and presidents were blown away.
Flower children, Woodstock, and assassinations.
Bob Dylan with his revelations.

Janis Joplin, Jimi Hendrix, flying high,
As all of us watched them die.
Buddy Holly, Jim Morrison, and the Big Bopper.
Fast food at the home of the whopper.

Men in white robes with crosses to burn
Teaching hard lessons we refused to learn.
Marches, protests, we could hear the screams,
As Martin Luther King told of his dreams.

Our prayers fell on deaf ears.
Lost and forgotten for a decade of years.
No guardian angels...we were all forsaken,
As love and peace rocked the nation.

Barbra Fleetwood

Young And Foolish

Love is something that should last
As for you and me it is in the past

You were such a sweet talker
Now I really know you're only a walker

We had moments of laughter and tears
But a longing heartache is what my future fears

You promised happy years forever, together
Only after Six Months you left for another

We played wind games with risky stakes
But who will pay for our foolish mistakes

Five months without you
And our baby is due

With a good job, I know we will be fine
Cause now I have something my heart can call mine

As for you, stay away
So Jr. can be happy and just play.

Kimberly Adams

Untitled

The Holidays are coming, with happiness they bring
for people are smiling and laughing as they sing

The Holidays are coming, a sadness is there
and people are thinking that there's no one to care

The Holidays are coming, families and friends are gone
there is nothing left to do except ponder and long

The Holidays are coming, my Daddy's not here
my vacation I'll spend wishing that he was near

The Holidays are coming, a fear fills my heart
crying and moaning and tearing me apart

The Holidays are coming, a happy time of year
when my face is smiling but my heart sheds a tear

The Holidays are coming, one wish I only have
for one minute one hour I just want my Dad

Angela Bryant

The Life Inside

Never would I have imagined a life inside
Conceived from seeds of a man and woman lying side by side
But soon to come will be a blessings from above
A life, a person, a child whom we will love
Never would I have imagined a life inside
A life so precious, that for a while, must hide
But soon to come a child with a glowing smile
And proud parents looking back on what seemed a never ending mile
Never would I have imagined a life inside
Calmly secured in its boundaries to abide
But soon to come a child that will need love and attention
That's what we will give our child; it's God's intention
Never would I have imagined a life inside
A blessing from God; not man's pride

Jacqueline P. Thornton

Pride

I'm sorry you didn't know that in Belmont you didn't win, place, or show. It's ok, the world's not over. If you're healthy, your years are still sober. You did your best, although you didn't win. Of course when the horse trampled over your shins, pain was probably everywhere knowing they had to put in pins. You need to have pride in yourself, even though you feel as small as an elf. When you tried, I can tell you, you had pride. I'm about to end this poetic letter to you.

Sincerely,

You Know Who

P.S. If you remember anything remember this: "This isn't the end, 'cause it isn't over **until you win.**"

They Cry At Night

In the bright Lodestar of the North
 The explorer fixes his eye.
Waving his hand o'er his head
 "Onward men," came the cry.

Morosely the troopers climb to their feet
 Joints and muscles creak displeasure
The men take up their march again
 Toward an unknown treasure.

Hours upon hours they march
 With 'nary a vision in sight
When dark's cold cloak wraps itself 'round
 Only to be split by a shriek in the night.

Frantically they scramble to see the beast
 Crying ferociously in the night.
On no side does the creature appear
 Invisible, he escapes their sight.

Fear seizes the men's hearts
 First freezing them in place.
After days of aimless marching this cold then
 Congeals intent and to home they haste.

 T. B. Smith

Silence

The feel of rushing water running softly over my hand.
A look from a distance far away land.
A hear of a silence out over the water fall.
Not near around is my ugly bedroom wall.
Over flies a bird singing over the wind.
Then I make a new great, great friend.
Then I see a mouse scurry out of sight.
The mouse must be in great fright.
Then here comes some turtles swimming in a pond.
They make quiet gurgles like a soft, soft song.
The sound of water falling.
Just like a lollypop lollying.
The look of goldfish swimming in the water.
Makes me want to stand up and holler a gentle holler.
The feel of leaves crackling below my feet.
Makes me want to dance to the leaves beet.
I hear my mother calling from the house.
But it sounds like a squeak of a mouse.
As I walk home slowly I hear the animals chirping, "Come back
tomorrow." Then I gently holler, "I'll come back tomorrow."

 Kristi Wesneski

My Heart

My heart is very loving and fragile.
It loves very many deeply.
My heart feels love as well as pain.
My heart feels joy along with sadness.
My heart loves and desires love in return.
My heart is the most precious thing to me.
My heart can get broken very easily.
If I give you love, you must cherish it.
You can hurt me worse from my heart.
It is not something to be fooled or played with.
You cannot expect love if you do not give it at the same time.
If my heart loves you, you should do the same.
My love cannot be tampered with.
It comes and goes from time to time.
My heart does not like to be broken.
It will heal, but it is never for long.
Now, I will not demand love, but rather ask for it.
If I love you, you had better love me too.
My heart is the most sensitive part of me.
It loves and it breaks from time to time.

 Shawneen Satiacum

Years Of Yearning

We knew each other when we were young,
holding hands and kissing for fun.
As we grew, our interests had changed.
Feelings were there - yet not quite the same.
Like others before us, we had to test;
how independent we were, from the rest.
Our choices were made out of confusion.
Finding our lives were just an illusion;
of the love we had many years ago,
that slipped through our fingers so long ago.
As time passed by our feelings had hid,
needing that love we once shared as kids.
The call was dialed with fear and delight,
Unsure of what we would find late that night.
Sparks were ignited from years of yearning,
as memories from the past started churning.
After fourteen years we could not pretend,
we had to meet each other again.
When I saw him my heart sped up fast,
knowing our true love was meant to last.

 Joy M. Labath

These Days

The last days we spent together were
excruciatingly like the first,
the moments we kept to ourselves,
caused in me an aching thirst

The first days of the last
Kept me waiting for what had been to be,
left me in total darkness,
there were things in each other we just couldn't see.

The next few days were distinctly cold,
hugs grew scarce as the days lingered on.
Loving words were no longer told.
And each of us knew something was wrong.

The last words spoken from your heart,
were surprisingly equivalent to that of mine.
You whispered the ending, that had to start,
I whispered back the same heart wrenching line.

 Virginia Marie Smith

Duck Dog

Rugged and bearing he breaks through the water.
A real champion from what you can tell.
He'll race to the hen until he has caught her.
He's a dog at top price you're not willing to sell.

You'll brag and boast about your dog.
Your friends will look with envy.
He'll track through brush, and hurl over logs
Just to keep you happy.

When hope is down and all seems lost,
He will come to be by your side.
He'll cheer you up at any cost.
Even if it means getting a boot in the behind.

That's why you two are always together.
You two are actually one.
You're next of kin; birds of a feather.
You are his father, he is your son.

He obeys you on good days and not.
His nose and eyes are keen.
Not gun shy at all; the blind is his hut.
The best duck dog I've ever seen.

 Kate Moynihan

The Peach

Known for where he was grown
(speaking geographically).
Perfect and rich in every sense
a prime example of Southern hospitality.
Soft to the touch, golden hair
covering every inch.
Weathered skin, soft inside,
a dark bruise caused by the slightest pinch.
To hold in my hand wafting sweet smells,
warmth and aroma so bold.
An open wound reveals a heart of amber, red and gold.
Flavors so sweet upon my tongue,
(satisfaction is my fate)
A deluge of sensory overload,
to be tortured is to calmly wait.

Tara Hanna Clark

Brothers

Little brothers can sniffle and snort,
and little brothers can mumble and mope.
Brothers can squirm like little worms,
And brothers can dance with ants in their pants.
Brothers don't want any romance,
all they want to do is prance.
Little brothers are quite big pains.
If you don't agree think again.
If they're laughing and having fun,
Be aware that they're not yet done.
Sometimes they're sweet,
But not quite often.
So, beware of their hair
And try not to stare.

Autumn Mowatt

Cut Up

Somebody found the path to my heart
And they had a weapon with them
Maybe it was a sword or a knife
Although, I know it wasn't a hammer or nails
They cut me up and made me bleed
They made me leak some purple stuff
Did they go down this road on purpose?
Or did they accidentally slip?
Either way I still cut up in many pieces
And pretty soon the purple stuff will turn red
It's overflowing with no place to go
And I'm still trying to find a place for it

I try to tell somebody about what is happening
Then they just go and chose the same river
Am I the only victim of this?
Am I just not good enough?
Or maybe I'm just too good
Whatever it is, I'm sorry
I'm sorry for this cause
I didn't do it on purpose

Monique Bender

Moments

My left hand touches his - the palms sliding together.
His massive hand seems to surround mine.
Our right hands touch - the sensations are the same.
Then I feel the warmness.
Memories flood into me - seeming almost like I will
drown, and then the reality - my right hand was
touching an outline on paper - the left was the other side.
The warmth was my hand through the paper, but,
Oh How Real For Just That Moment.

Susie Pinjuv

To Catch The Sun

Did you ever catch the sun on a perfect day?
When she casts her beams on her favorite spots.
I must go out and stand in her perfection,
For only then am I whole... Complete.
I feel free when she pierces my heart.
I feel the warmth of living death,
For such bliss cannot abide in mortal creation.
Yet I live on, outside of her beam.
She visits now and then,
And I relish the time I stand in her perfection.
I cannot understand her ways
For I am not yet part of her cast.
My soul is still wild and free.

Jodie Craddock Jr.

Soul Mate

Listen to my voice it's clear with light, listen
to my heart it beats in flight, on and on like the
spinning of the world. Rhythmic sounds ancient to your
ears cascading upon you as you slumber. Let me be
the sponge to soak and cleanse your fears, I am not afraid.
Lean on my love, it is rigid and true, it cannot
falter only thoughts are of you. Trusting and relinquishing
your mind, I catch the dew permeating the clothes
you wear. Merging into one consciousness we dream of
distant lands and ancient love that has punctured space
and time. Traveling in thought and action I marvel at the
simplicity and will, a force that always existed and can
never be destroyed. You and I forever.

Marlon Acuna

Each Child

A child is born
so fragile, so helpless, so sweet
they need us to clean and to love them
they need us to live...

A little child is born
each one is so special, so wholesome and pure
nothing but goodness
nothing but truth...

A child is born
each life a real story
each life a real chance
no certainties, no sureness
a future of pain
or a future of goodness...

A little child is born
each child a ray of hope
each child a bright light

Silvia Miceli

Warded-Off

Petrified, the snail shell
Has hid beneath the flagstones
Of a reburied cistern,
And the sluggish years over passed the well.

A digger scratching deep
Below the blades of
A too-long unmown field
Has disturbed the near-timeless sleep,

And all the staved-off ages,
Compacted to a rushing instant
Of withering time wreaked vengeance on antiquity.
So the death wind, delayed, always rages.

Ezra D. Feldman

The Wonder Of A Father

Within the time of life, one can begin to see
What His Father would like Him to be
The mold, the pattern, the shape, the form
Were all there when the child was born
Little feet that need guidance
A strong hand for him to hold

Steps to follow
For later memories to unfold
Oh! The wonder of a Father
How precious He must be
The wisdom He must carry for little ones to see
As the years past the child begins to grow
He too becomes a Father, then He knows
The joy, the pain, the sorrow
A Father goes through
Only then can a son appreciate you
In all of his life you shared a part
To train, to guide in paths of love
The molding, the pattern will hold
As other lives begin to unfold

   Nancy Lyke

Little Things Mean A Lot

I've been laid up for a month or so,
It seemed I just couldn't get up and go.
Then came arthritis, from my neck to my knees,
But I must get going "Oh Lord help me please".
There are so many things that I want to do.
Yes, Lord "I surely am depending on you".
Please give me the strength to do all that I can,
For the sick, the poor, and my fellow man.
As I visit the elderly, we sing and read;
This is something that they all need.
While I am there, I do their hair
And clasp their hands in a silent prayer.
As I leave, I let them know,
That I'll be back to see them in a day or so.
Then there's Millie, who can't get on her feet;
So I stop by and bring her something to eat.
Now I'm heading home, and I am feeling good,
Knowing, I have done some of the little things that I should.

   Elizabeth C. Drehmer

Alone

You came into my life and brought me happiness;
all was well at first but now it's nothingness.

   I feel so all alone.

I wish you would come back the way you used to be;
Life was happy then but that was way back when.

We've changed in many ways, some we've stayed the same;
if only you could see the way we used to be.

   You were my everything.

You left me here to wonder how to get you back;
my thoughts keep running wild, so many I can't keep track.

I never know what to say, my thoughts get in the way;
Sometimes they tumble out, and then we're in a bout.

I really don't want it that way,
but I never know what to say.

I see it in your eyes, your reaction to what I say;
I really don't mean to hurt you.

   It just comes out to sound that way.

   Heather Hedrick

The Tree

I looked up at the branches and
I thought - how tall the tree, so
much nearer Heaven, nearer God than me.
Than I looked above the tree top and
saw a bird on wing. I thought
he's near enough to heaven to hear the angels sing.
Then I looked up at the stars at the close of day
and I knew that they were not as
close as you and I when we kneel to pray.

   Betty Z. Holland

For You

I hear the song of the whippoorwill I hear the song
of the turtle dove too. In these mountains alone
without you, it gets so lonesome but what else
can I do. You're a part of me and I am part of you.
I've carried you with me for so long you're in
my spirit. You are in my songs.
So are you real or just a dream someone I see in
my sleep. How I wish that one day I could
wake up in this dream. I want you to slip
out of my dreams and into my life, so I can see
you and love you with open eyes. I know that
love is a delicate thing. It can bring you
joy and bring you such pain. But as I stand
here alone in the rain, I can't help but pray
it'll come my way again. Sometimes I feel
the wind on my face. I know you're with me
in everything and every place. Wherever you
are and whatever you do. Know that someone
Out there is still looking for you.

   Janis Benjamin

Forgiveness

Tear stained images of forgotten lore
Remembering people and places I loved once before.
Harboring beguiling feelings we mutually abhor
Embedded so deeply we cannot ignore.

Grudges that are held by juvenile minds
Attitudes and beliefs that are much maligned.
Not possessed of the commitment to the love that binds
Too aware of the malice we wish to leave behind.

A culture befuddled with unseen eyes
A world corrupted with unseemly crimes.
Yet, in the presence of trying times
Nothing is stronger than family ties.

   Timothy C. Bragg

Sometimes Our Light Goes Out

Sometimes our light goes out and leaves dark night
Without a hope, without a prayer for truth;
Then God's mysterious means of help, forsooth,
Breaks through and friend appears with spark of light.

Our inner light rekindled from friend's flame
Shines out like sunbeams, conquering dark and doom;
We're deeply grateful to the friend who came
At God's behest to chase away our gloom.

The prism catches our light and our friend's
And scatters beams of color from the sun;
No more the darksome strife to fight off fiends,
The dance of life its patterned course can run.

Thus God's assistance to us with His grace
Has made His burning bush light up this place.

   Jamie L. Pettigrew

All In A Day's Work

As I go through this house
    Scrubbing and cleaning
I cannot believe that this is my meaning
    Not here among my dusting and dishes
Can I express what my heart wishes
    Surely this wasn't my destiny
Surely this wasn't supposed to be
    Where is my knight in shining armor?
Where are my nights of excitement and glamour?
    I guess until my dreams come true
I'll still be here doing what I do
    Cleaning and cooking, dusting and such
I know it'll be worth it, I do know this much
    Because my patience and hard work one day you will see
That my dreams and my wishes were always meant to be.

Robin Tilson

I Once Dreamed That I Was A Baseball Star

This here dream was the best by far,
I once dreamed I was a baseball star.

My team depended heavily upon me,
But I could handle lots of pressure you see.

When games were close and on the line,
I would come through with a hit on time.

The pitchers seemed scared when I came to the plate,
For they knew when I swung I would never be late.

My throwing arm was strong as could be,
For there never were players who dared run on me.

As the season rolled on I just became ideal,
And it's funny the way it all seemed real.

"Yes oh Yes" I was truly a star it seemed,
Till finally it hit me that it was a dream.

Sherman Reed Sr.

Sunday Morning Special

The children always waited for that Sunday morning treat,
A visit to their grandparents' house, the special place to meet.
The toys spread on the porch just awaiting for a sound,
A smiling face to capture them, one always was around.
The turkey was in the oven, the potatoes done just right,
With lollipops aplenty, they wanted to stay the night.
But when the day was through, the sight you would always see,
Grandma waving at the door and a baby upon Grandpa's knee.
You taught them how to be patient,
You taught them how to love,
You taught them how to have faith,
In our wonderful God above.
Now that you are with him, we all just wanted to say,
"Thank you both for everything and we'll see you there someday."

Janice Soltys

Feelings And Emotions

I feel sad and happy, I feel glad and mad, and sometimes
all at once I feel so blank.
We all have emotions, we all have feelings.
Sometimes I feel loved, sometimes I feel hated then
Sometimes I feel like no one cares.
Those are just some of my emotions and feelings,
I have many more like feeling dumb in school or scared.
Sometimes I like my emotions and feelings sometimes I
hate them but no matter what we all have them.
    Can you trust them?

Ra'Shele Elrod

Words I Never Said

There's a lot of words I never said.
To those I loved so dear.
And now that they are gone.
O' how I wish that they were here.

Many times in this life I've had regret.
I didn't show my love to those that I met.
Yes, I was too busy as I went my merry way.
I thought I'd find the time some other day.

Now if God would give me a second chance.
Just to see them for one final glance.
And to say the things I didn't say.
Before he took my friends away.

Now there's one thing I will do for certain.
Before death closes life's final curtain.
I will give them all my love.
And tell them of the Lord above.

Now time marches on and life soon passes by.
And I can't change a thing even if I try.
But I'll tell every one things I wish to say.
Then I'll have no regret when they pass away.

Troy Len Young

King of Hope

Forgotten love which once shined bright,
Without hope I lost my way,
The sun may rise but there is no light,
Without hope I lost my passion for a new day,

A wooden door which I cannot pass,
Deep within is what I'm looking for,
A key, of luck to use at last,
A shattered shield of hope and nothing more.

Memories that once held me up,
Are now lost in a waveless sea,
I drink life from a tarnished cup,
And hope there's more out there than you and me.

You caught my eye beneath the dread,
The hope I thought was forever gone,
To you I was led,
Everything was bright now as a new day dawned.

New found love once again shines bright,
With new hope I found my way,
The sun now rises with radiant light,
With hope I found my passion for a new day.

Jason L. Roberts

Untitled

The cold wind blows through- everyone sad and blue.
Sad and lonely, this is true.
Never forget, always remember, the great times you
Spent together.
All those memories, happiness and love, now you know
She'll be safely above.
Earning her wings, she is an angel, soaring high above,
Free as a bird.
No troubles, no fear, she'll always be near.
You'll never be apart, she'll always hold a special place
Inside of your heart.
Above you in spirit, she'll guide you through, any hard
Times when you are feeling blue.
No pain, no suffering, she is at peace at last, taking sweet
Memories with her from her past.
She is at home at last, pray for her, and smile.

Nicole Marie Roach

How Will We In The Future Figure Out A Way?

If the world can never cease on violence today,
then how will we in the future figure out a way?

The wars and the fights destroying our world,
destroying our lives too, can never stop.
Who will stop it, Oh mighty God, who?

Sent to this world on a wing and a prayer.
Never ceasing to ignore what's under the top layer.

Everyone is different, but yet still the same.
People and places, and feelings untamed.

So many lies, so little honesty, not knowing how
to control so little modesty.

Wasting what's left, using what's not.
When will we ever rise to the top?

If the walls around us all fell down,
what would we do with no shelter around?

If the world can never cease on violence today,
then how will we in the future figure out a way?

Valicia Viola

Father

　　Where were you when I needed you,
it wasn't by my side.
　　Where were you when I wanted you,
did you find somewhere to hide.

　　It's never failed that when I called,
you didn't answer to your name.
　　I can't think of a single time.
that when I cried for you, you came.

　　I still don't know exactly why,
you treat me like you do.
　　Did I do something wrong,
or is it simply you?

　　I can't understand why you don't care,
why you don't even bother.
　　Why you don't face your responsibilities,
why you won't be my father.

Laura Hansan

Untitled

Looking into the Melting Pot,
That once delicious cultural stew,
I notice that what has just been added,
Has turned the taste bitter.

The pot is full,
With a generation of Lolitas,
Giving away the Forbidden Fruit,
To every Adam that strolls by.

And Alex and his Droogs,
Are running rampant,
With àmplé tolchocks for all,
Strung out on milk with knives,
And searching for Dolly, for a bit of the old in-out, in-out.

Rebel Dean is rolling in his grave,
Jerry is Gratefully Dead,
To see the turn Fate has taken,
A mockery of all their work.

'What's it going to be then, eh?'
Nymphets multiplying like rabbits,
Some real horror show ultra-violence,
A generation to be proud of!

Jordan J. Gewitz

Evolution

After the bells rang and rang,
there was a huge explosion-Bang!

There was a substance bluish blue,
that covered the earth through and through.

Then from nowhere dirt and mass,
with big tall trees and short thin grass.

Quickly and quietly and with no doubt,
came a bunch of fishes all about.

And when they decided swimming's getting boring,
God gave them wings and said, "start soaring."

Then they said, "this is no fun
give us four legs we want to run."

So they ran and ran and ran and ran,
but that became boring too. Oh man!

Just then they decided let's try to stand,
and give us the thrill of being in command.

So now it doesn't puzzle me,
how man evolved out of the sea.

Chris Martin

Mother

From the time you tucked me in bed
and sat on my sheets putting me to sleep.
I always loved everything you said.
It touched my heart so deep.
I still remember when you would always watch out for me,
and I would always feel odd,
but now I sit here and nod.
You would always comfort me, when I was in pain,
even if I didn't want it,
you would keep me out of the rain,
we are like a puzzle and fit.
And now I finally figured out why?
Why, you cared so much for me.
I don't ever want to see our friendship die,
no matter what the fee.
You will always be the strength in my life
...Mother.

Kristal Fletcher

The Tears I Cry

The tears I cry are from deep within
Each representing the silent cries of my soul.

The tears I cry are tiny daggers
Which shreds my heart as they flow.

The tears I cry are not selfish ones
But ones for those alike myself-alone.

The tears I cry only heighten my despair
Creating a vast sense of void.

The tears I cry represent my failures
When bonded together, my life is formed.

Melanie McBee

The River Rat

What is a River Rat you say to me?
He's tough and He's loyal and He's proud just to be.
He weathers the storm, the cold and the wind,
That the mighty St.Lawrence wields out to Him.
He loves the river like a father loves a son,
For He and the river are not separate but one.
A River Rat is not a person you see;
He's the spirit of the river living inside you and me.

Pamela J. Bennett

A Moonlight Scene

A Moonlight scene,
A pale, white ring,
Projected on the clouds did speak,
Of days alone, and thoughts untold,
and the sullen distress of a lonely soul.

And I sat on the crest of the grassy hill,
The ghostly light growing brighter still,
All so quiet, the sky did show,
The moon in frozen silence numb,
bared me what I had become.

Reflected light,
Eternal plight,
Projected on my mind,
Of days alone, and thoughts untold,
and the sullen distress of my lonely soul.

J. Mings

Ode To A Poem

I opt to write a poem one day
I knew it would be fine.
Full of meaning metaphor
Within each rhyming line.
With intellect it would abound
Extremely sharp and wise,
Each verse would be unique, profound
I surely did surmise.
I pored upon each word with mace
Encountering as war
And pondered with each thoughtless phrase
Whatever was it for?
On I struggled hopelessly
Until I finally thought:
A poem must come spontaneously,
Directly from the heart.

Caroline Hutchings

In Retrospect

Now that the sun is setting in the west,
All the day's troubles will be at rest.
When that sun rose, it seems, so long ago-
What lay ahead, I could never know.
The clouds hung heavy, and darkness loomed
Until the sun broke through the gloom.
It was such a glorious morn, so bright,
All worldly things so blessed and right.
Dark clouds appear, as the sun its zenith nears,
To we who wait, it brings such fears!
It came, it passed, the storm in its might;
Then the world was bathed in a golden light.
The afternoon had a clear blue sky,
While little white clouds went drifting by.
As evening neared, more clouds, more rain;
Now it's quiet, they have passed again.
The night draws nigh, patiently I wait —
It can't be long, it's getting late.
What will this coming sunset bring?
Will the stars shine bright, the angels sing?

Martha L. Sanders

The Rainbow

Sun and rain enrich the heavens
with the poetry of colors as prisms
of light refract the beauty that
is revealed with the passing
of a storm. Beauty once veiled in darkness
now unveiled in poetic color.

Phil H. Emerson

I Will Always Love You

I will always love you
'til the day I die
And I hope you love me too
So we never have to say good-bye
And I'd hope you would never leave me
So that I'm alone inside
Like a hollow tree
With its shallow roots
hanging by its side
I dreamed I'd never have to say this
What I have to say
Or say it in a different and better kind of way
I'm really going to miss you
And I hope you miss me too
I did not want to say this till the day I die
And I didn't know how to say this better than,
Good-bye

Stephanie Felker

Cleaning Day

It takes a lot of cooking just to make three meals a day;
And what has not been eaten is too good to throw away.
And so I store it in the fridge to eat another time.
To throw out food as good as this would surely be a crime.

But those tasty bits of former meals know just how to hide
Until they've lost their freshness and become so old and dried
So they sneak behind a bigger bowl, hiding from the light,
And there they cower back in the dark, hiding from my sight.

In fact, I can't remember what they were when they were new;
Nor can I guess because I haven't got a single clue.
No meal that I have ever served had just that shade of green,
Why did it have to hide away to never more be seen?

But, as I open each little dish, this one thing I know,
No longer need I cling to it, it's time for it to go.
'Tis then I ponder if it's true what I've been told.
"Many dishes keep out heat," but does the mold hold cold?

Everything that I have done and I knew it wasn't right,
Like that food was put away, out of mind and out of sight,
'Till God convicts me when I see another do the same;
'Tis then I ask forgiveness in my Jesus' precious name.

Grace Woodin

Mr. Burke

Your tie so straight, your suit so blue
you'll be happy to hear this, I really like you.

Your corny jokes, your funny fibs
the teachers adore you, and so do the kids.

You walk down the hallway with pleasure,
you talk to the kids with delight,
you are always there for us,
when there's a problem or fight.

You're strict but for good purpose,
you're just looking out for us,
you love us like we're your own children,
checking if we get on the bus.

You kept the school running so well,
we can't even believe our eyes,
you would never take any bad language,
or put up with any lies.

You are the very best principal,
no other principal's the same,
if there was a museum of principals,
you'd be in the hall of fame!

Anjelica Lena

Such A True Love

You touched me with an open heart
Boy you showed me true loving from the start
And all the things that you felt within
You gave to me and from then did our loving begin

You came to me with unlimited boundaries
Boy in my heart I'm so glad that you've found me
And for that reason you've turned my wants into my needs
And it's your love, sweet love it takes to satisfy me

You and I, we make a perfect pair
Boy there's a sense of magic when you're near
And everything around me feels so right
Especially the way you're holding me tonight

Such a true love, Such a love
Where still waters run deep
Such a love

Such a true love, Such a priceless
Treasure to keep, Oh what a love
Such a true love, Such a love
Where still waters run deep
Such a love...

Flora Hayes

The Parenthood Club

For those who are here and for those who have gone
this poem is for you, whom we honor and adore.

For we have come to appreciate the struggles you've had.
And we have come to know it's too late to turn back.

For growth from our youth and the maturity of our days,
we plead forgiveness for our rebellious and foolish ways.

For we understood in part but now we know in full, that what
we took so for granted was the wrong thing to do.

For the day that has come and the days yet to come
brings the rush of reality and the point of this poem.

It's the parenthood club that makes us flash on the past.
It's the parenthood club that makes us appreciate our own;
for their guidance, support and their praise most of all.

It's the parenthood club that holds our hearts in their hands.
It's our joy and our pain. It's our love and much more.

It's the parenthood club that has only one rule,
to be a member in good standing and that definitely is you!

Debbra Davis-Gaston

Winter Playground

Angels softly descending below.
New life sheltered from the winds of winter.
God's creation changing
everlasting beauty to behold.
Long, gray days of winter playgrounds
against skies of glistening, snowy wonder.
Taunting frisky in soft white flakes of pleasure.
Over hills with trees safely covered,
Children giggling, playing, joyfully tasting,
Lying on a soft bed of heavenly beauty.
Young minds wondering how this could be gazing upward.
Never caring it will soon be taken away for another time.
Responding as crystal, gently touch their faces.
Only to feel them melt away from the warmth of their smiles.
Sleek pictures race in their thoughts.
Aglow as they run to where they came from.
Laughing with expectations of the warm crackling sounds of lane,
In the gentle caress of a patient but listening mother.
New day to begin in the 'morrow
Daring them with new adventures to discover.

Dale Finkbiner

Commander Joe

There he stands real stern and tall
In green combat uniform —
Overshadowing us all.

Throughout the field the men stretch and strain -
His lips yelling in sudden cadence — "Move the hell out"
Numbs the inner pain.

He crawls up and down every line —
Glasses cover his wandering eyes
Checking each soldier and his time.

A collar filled with starch —
Mud-shine boots thump in pace
Approaching with swift march
Suddenly in my face -

Thoughts pounding in my mind —
I was a bit too slow
Lagging slightly behind —
Commander G.I. Joe.

Arthur R. Phillips

Just Keep It In Mind

I Imagine you are on a
M mountain looking down
A at all the choices that you have made.
G Good or bad, they have made a difference
I in your life. Upon realizing that you will
N never be able to change anything about it, you fear.
E Even though you wish you could change them, you

   Just keep it in mind

T The decisions you
H have made have had
A a great impact on both your life and others.
T The paths you have chosen will effect the ones ahead.

For sometime down the wrong road, there will be no
   one there to share the load.
Pick your paths and forms wisely, for most likely down
   valley it is going to storm.
Some will toss you around, but if you put it behind you
   and walk on, you will conquer past life's traps.

Joel Miley

Unsworn

I can't pledge everything, I know because I've tried.
I hope you'll see my soul, know how I feel inside.
You say you understand, that you need others too.
But I can't help fearing that maybe I'll lose you.

I'm hearing through the vines that there are others there.
Don't want to tie you down, I won't ask you to swear.
If I can't win your heart when competition's fair
then maybe I am wrong and we are not a pair.

So, I give you freedom. Because I can't ask you
to do what I cannot, with hope that you'll be true.
If you another choose, I wish you happiness.
I won't bring up my pain if she loves you no less.

Needed your love so much, but I could not have lied.
I'll open every door and offer you my pride.
To bad you'll never know how much I want your kiss.
Or realize, if you leave, it's you whom I will miss.

Kristi Schauerhamer

Untitled

Soft blond hair I seek tonight
Warm blue eyes in the bright starlight
Passions love with intimate life
I did not know could cause such strife
Never again will I be so bold
Wisdom I now seek to remake my mold
Special am I just one of a kind
A little more discipline a little more time
I may never be perfect
And at times to much pride
But always will I love
Always will I try

Steve M. Shaffer

The Ups And Downs Of Yellow

Yellow is a sudden crack in the silence.
Yellow is a deafening scream.
Yellow is hatred, jealousy and vain.
Yellow is melted ice cream.

Yellow is a wild and everlasting violence.
It's a color that cannot be kept in a cage.
Yellow is sweat, anxiety, and thirst.
It's a color that's full of rage.

Yellow is mean, nasty, and rotten.
Yet there is another side to it.
Just like a peach fresh from the store.
Yellow has a sweet outside to cover the pit.

Yellow is the look of freshly picked flowers.
Yellow is the smell of morning's dew.
Yellow is what you hear when the sun goes to sleep.
Yellow is what I see when I think of you.

Life with yellow is a roller coaster ride.
Your passions flow quick and fast.
Life without yellow is non-existent.
For yellow is a color unsurpassed.

Ian Serlin

Understanding Grief

We grieve because we are a selfish race,
for the ones we've lost are in a better place.

Be thankful they're not suffering, for they have eternal bliss,
though their loving words and touch surely we will miss.

We may feel lost, anger, pain, or sorrow,
but God is with us always, today and tomorrow.

Our bonds are so hard for us to untie,
and so we just sit, think and cry.

But others are here for you, their thoughts they share,
because of who they are, you know they care.

Betty J. Ley

Rejoice!

When Adam and Eve were here
The world was a perfect place.
But instead of living with God in fear,
They brought sin and death to the human race.
Because of them Jesus died.
Because of us He was crucified.
Hallelujah! He is risen indeed!
All followers rejoice!
God knew this was what we needed.
So praise Him with one voice.
All followers rejoice!
Now is the time to rejoice!

Holly McBride

Untitled

You are beautiful, even more, you are wise
The sun, moon and stars light up your eyes
And so lucky for me to have soon realized
That you for my wife is my most treasured prize

I don't know what I did to deserve you, you see
The fates must have thrown their tidings on me
For this is the one you'll love, it will be
'Cause your heart is ready, she has the key

You mean more to me than diamonds and gold
For you're the greatest treasure I'll ever hold
We'll share our time together as we grow old
As our love, like a flower, continues to unfold

My life would be empty, a void left unfilled
I'd never experience that wonderful thrill
I have when you're near and I'll have it until
Time ceases marching and the universe stands still

I want you to know I love you so true
And, if ever, I had my life to redo
It would be, at least from my point of view
Incomplete unless done over with you

Bernie Zebrowski

Heart-Seed

An extraordinary landscape
    Appeared in front of him,
Pushed up with rubble here
    And imploded with his secret
Longings deep and deep root-fastened there.

Could he dig and dredge
    Some furrow plowed enough,
    Some incisive path or wider?
A probe went seeking, gentle, gentle
    Lest nerve or flesh be torn.

Now at the center delicate—
    Pulsing just enough—
His searching, bony finger touched
    And felt the knowing.
    Caressing timidly from absence
    It moved on to an embrace,
    And lapped the juice it sought
To lubricate the infinite soul.

David I. Edwards

Silenced Fury

The gnarled teeth of bitterness
wrap around like a brocade
of blackened green fanged vipers.
Lay them away in a shoebox
just as a child buries his dead swallow.
Yet, unlike the dead, rage dwells
and anger rises up with envy—
silently drinking life from your veins.
Like a fool denying that his body is on fire,
so does the deceived ignore (and laugh away)
the canker worms that gnash and pierce
through the very host they thrive upon.
The broken heart begins to rage in suffocation
and pain beneath the false calm of your stern brow.
Reconciliation may never come beckoning
with the accused who shot the poisoned arrow through your soul.
Starve the serpent of lies who desires to drown
you with your foe in his fiery rage.
For he knows his time is short
and he will vanish like a flame.

Denise Tortorici

In This Old House

There was life here once, in this old house
now laid to rest
where night winds whistle through shutters broken
and among the rafters swallows nest

In this place of quiet desolation,
home of the spider and the wren
the ivy vine is king here
and lays claim to all within

Will you pass quietly, old house?
Resigned to your unchanging fate
who now is silent ruins stand
for passersby to contemplate

While still inside your idle halls
where children played, their voices call
"remember us, for we were near"
but only do the crickets hear
and answer back in silence.

Rory Hopkins

Retirement

People work all their life, and hope for the best
Lucky to be able, to pursue their life's quest
They toil and sweat, with maybe some tears
Not thinking at all, of the retirement years

To think of retiring, would short circuit their career
More productive to think, of the years much more near
Of the promotions and fun, if it's a job that you like
Always looking forward, to your next pay raise hike

There's a point when retiring, arrives as a thought
Hard to say exactly when, this retiring idea you bought
But once the word is learned, it never really leaves you
The years then start approaching, so fast, they do deceive you

You begin to worry, about your working life's end
You think mainly of saving, and no longer to spend
You start reading books, about this retirement thing
You hope for the good life, that it could well bring

But, alas, it arrives, it's your last day at work
The work responsibility, just for now you can shirk
You say your goodbyes, and walk toward the door
You can't turn around, you've got new worlds to explore.

Dave Hannold

To Be Lessened As A Woman

To feel like less of a woman is -
    pure pain and hate.
To be made less of a woman is -
    no self esteem or morals.

To have someone strip you of everything
    is total despair.
To be stripped of all your worth emotionally, and physically -
    is total and searing pain for eternity.

To feel like nothing leaves an empty space
    in your life.
To be wronged time and time again
    leaves you discouraged.

To be lessened as a person is total tragedy.

For the one who does these things -
"May you burn in Hell" and, before
your death may someone strip you of everything.

Tonia Jo Shabazz

Lonely Planet

Have you ever been to a mystic land
Where there is no color, no horrid brand
Have you seen the dream of being one
Well my friend this cannot be done
Fore we hate and kill upon the urge
And these feelings inside my body surge
But I don't give in for I have passion
Without this feeling the end would come crashin'
Down onto the ones who feel, ones who don't
It'll come down onto the ones who won't
You don't just feel love for a spouse
And these feelings you cannot douse
Love is what you feel for a friend
The feeling is true it will not bend
You feel it for kids on the street
Who haven't a pair of shoes for their feet
So remember my words true
Without love what would we do?

Levi Payne

Salud Décembre!

I crawled from seductions and licked my scraped knee
let dark cloaks and daggers fall right behind me.
I've healed other lifetimes, torch sung of blue moons
Oh, carried through storms and lived for monsoons.

All of this, to efface love pour tu...

I've scoured the desert and danced in a furnace
I rode my wild horses without e'en a harness.
I've graced fascination and had carpet rides
And let freedom ring regardless of tides.

We fought like old lovers, we already knew how
It frightened and threatened and settled the tao.

Ablaze I have seen, spit roasted in two
dripping lapis and new tile
in cool marbled pools
an indoor foot fountain, a laughing piazza
a loop and a lift and a madcap favazza
a tranquil old lady a bump at a sink
and a royal blue flash that was quick like a wink.

It's crazy I tell you what else would I do
but blow with this Passion and make toasts to you.

George R. Butler Jr.

Time Odyssey

The flow of the tide
crashes against the jetties
Swallowing up helpless sandcastles
Never to be seen again

Dreams painfully shattered
Like the cracking of a stained glass window
So beautiful, so delicate

Tomorrow begins a new day
one filled with promise and hope
an opportunity to rebuild
To start afresh

But always lurking
is the fear of destruction

Life is full of chance
Desires to attain ultimate goals,
Reach self satisfaction.
Absolute perfection

Before the tide comes in.

LuAna R. E. Meigs

First Night

From the window here, my space,
I see the city's faceted face.
The airport veiled pale-gray from sight,
No planes in destination flight.
Snowfall driven left to right.
Snowfall driven left to right.

People moving without haste,
Forward leaning determined and braced.
With first night about to appear,
The city covered, snow veneer.
A white-out of the ending year.
A white-out of the ending year.

Tenements, now condos, white-topped;
Custom House clocks, different times, both stopped.
An echo in the streets below,
A solo sax sounding low,
It's passing by...let it go.
It's passing by...let it go.

Hugh F. Galligan

Trending

Trending happens every year
Baggy, tight, and even sporting gear
Hippie clothes were far but now they are near
"Cool" and "far out" soon did reappear
Skateboarding was out but now it's back in.
Some trends will lose and some trends will win.
Some will last a week and some will last a year.
But you will never know when they will reappear.

Julie Copple

Building A Life

Now I can look at the fences I jumped as a child,
And the old houses that were there, all seem to
Have fallen in just a while.

Like fallen leaves now are the years of our life
Some sweet - some cut deeper than any knife.

Searching in our quest, for happiness, the
Building blocks, sometimes may fall - but -
Building a life....Wasn't sometimes easy...
Uh, after all?

Fantasy and imagination are the only
Free things in life, the cost of living
Is taxes, stress, and strife. To win any battle
Is to keep hope, faith, love and goodness alive.
Mankind needs this to always survive.

James A. McGarr

Mind Traps

What is it that I lack in fortitude
Why can I not make autonomous decisions
My docile actions offer up no answers
I compile thoughts but nothing formulates
Aspirations of serenity fondle my mind
My mind is bound in manacles
With tedious thoughts I scrutinize
I embellish in feminine grandeur and give into temptation
I hope that this doesn't develop into a continuance
Because I can not endure subjecting misery upon myself
   nor the people I love

Adam Middleswart

Golden Threads

Perhaps
the dark shows the light.
When I look at the varicolored fabric of my life
I cannot seem to glean the bright pure strands
so intricately, delicately are they interwoven
with the darker stuff.

In time
the unlovely heritage
violence, taut nerves, black despair
will be distilled out
through many efforts, many tears
leaving behind
that which endures
to shine at last.

In my life
this will be so
and even so
on a grander loom
the fabric of all mankind.

Marilyn Bruce

Would You

If I asked you to hold me tight
To make everything safe and right
Would you stay with me throughout the night
And greet me with the morning light

If I told you what I really needed was you
To help and guide me in everything I do
Would you be there when I was sad and blue
Beside me when I tried things that were new

If I needed to stay behind a tightly bolted door
Until I was ready to face the crowd once more
Would you stay until I could go out onto the floor
Until my whimper once again became my roar

If I said I wanted to be free
To open my arms, look hard and see
Would you open your arms, let me be
And for my journey give me the key

If I came back to your steady charm
Wanting you to once again keep me safe from harm
Would you still keep me secure and warm
And let me remember the comfort of your arms

Nancy Dougles

London Weeping

Ah, the city so bright and gay
seems just a bit sad today.

This city, with so much life;
the parks, the palace, the tower
and abbey.

Why, you ask, is it not happy?

Why indeed, when experience has shown
no one who lived here is ever alone.
For the city can draw you into her own,

But when someone who loves her finally departs,
it will rain,
as it often does.

So, put up your 'brolly as you walk around
and think of London weeping
sometimes softly, sometimes loud.

For London can mourn, can weep and cry
when someone who loves her says goodbye.

Fred Wendt

World Peace

Painting pictures of oceans, deep blue,
Harmony in this world starts with you.
Problems in politics, no one should care,
Past is past, but the future is there.

Man, woman, black, yellow, red or white,
Prejudice behind, all races unite.
Needs for decision limit out dreams
As the world ignores its hunger-filled screams.

An end of pollution in a future, not seen,
Each person, inside, resolves something mean.
The eagle soars high, no reason to hide,
A symbol of hope, a symbol of pride.

Remember, this world is just ours by lease,
And outweighing all war is the need for world peace.
Donna Webb

Togetherness

I saw a man standing before me, young and tall and strong.
When our eyes met - Love; and from that very moment
I knew someday we would be forever joined together.
When that day came, the sun shined and the birds sang.
At last he and I were One - joined in the eyes of God, family
and friends. It was a joyous occasion for all to see.
For now I knew I would never be alone again.
We are together. We each know the other will be there
to listen, to comfort, or just talk; whatever is needed.
It is wonderful having that special someone to share everything
with. Having someone to laugh with me instead of at me.
The world can be cruel, but now I know I have a safe place
to go where the outside world can never bother me: In his arms.
Yes, love is a wonderful feeling. It is togetherness.
Kimberly A. Richardson

Best Friend

Today I laid my "best friend" to rest,
You took your place beside the very best,
All the things you vied for and argued that it was in vain,
As I look around this room I believe you had all the gain.
Unconditional love, acceptance from the start,
You know exactly your place in my heart.
You left me with memories etched clear in my mind,
So now when I need you I'll just reach in and find...
One to make me laugh or calm me when I cry, so
As I lay you to rest today, I don't have to say good-bye.

Your Best Friend
Kandy Thomas Acklin

Down The Road From The Mulberry Bush

I know your little girl with big blue eyes
I catch her often lurking
in the shadows in my mind
I've crossed her path before unexpectedly to see
she tends to like to dance
inside my childhood memories
I used to tip-toe through my past to watch her play
but as the years went by she faded
and her memory slipped away
I soon forgot what it was like to dance
until my own small child danced with me
I thought I'd never learn again
on occasion when we two sit down to play
I feel him tugging
at the little girl his mommy used to be
when last he took her hand I realized
how carefree this world must look
through a little boy's blue eyes.
Faith Fratz

Mirror Images

Across the mirror frame
an endless ocean
crystal eternity
a frightening notion
and it stays even when I'm not looking in
A strangers face with a strangers faceless grin
and so it seems to be that no one sees
For long I peer into
lifes lonely matter
I feel perception change
thoughts seem to scatter
The strangers eyes are eyes of deception
Changing minds from the mind's eye perception
why do I see these things that no one sees
window of perception
shows mortality
we all know
yet some refuse to see
and they're asking me
close the window please
Dan Robb

Untitled

"Little train" roaring down the tracks, to
long ago please take me back...when daddy's
gift was oh so bright and loving arms still held me tight.
"Little train", please blow your smoke so
things aren't clear, and let my mind drift back to yesteryear.
My daddy's hands once held this gift,
was given to me, my spirits to lift.
As I sit alone at night, I hear a
whistle at dawn's first light and though
I'm older now and so called grown, it
reminds me of those special days when I was not so all alone.
Even though out times were few,
"My little train" helps me chug on through or could it be;
Yes, I know this to be true, its
"my father's love" that's always carried me through.
Michelle Love

Alpha And Omega

When we take the time,
To reflect upon time,
and how we use and abuse it,
It is there we realize,
With heart and eyes,
If we are wise:
That time is not measured by the clock
no, not even by the rising of the sun
nor the hours of dark;
But time is measured by the finch warm
and the singing of the song of the meadow lark;
God is the main spring of measure,
He sets our time, turns on the ticking
and claims us when our time is up his treasure.
Ila M. Banbury

A New Beginning

Do something good to be remembered,
Even you're gone they will still praising your name.
Share your richness and the Lord will give you his graces.
Open your heart and your hands to everyone,
And you will feel the lightness in your heart.
Start now before it's too late.
Walk without fear, don't procrastinate so you won't forget.
It's up to you now to decide,
A new beginning of your life.
Minda Martinez

The Crystal Stage

The cockcrow brought me a crystal horizon
while prisms of light danced across the heavens.
Too few mornings have exploded with such grandeur,
as I began my crusade through the countryside.

The arthritic joints of the aging oak
were crippled from Mother Nature's wrath,
yet there was great beauty in the frigid limbs
of the frail and sterile skeletons of December.

I carefully studied in wide eyed wonderment
the diamonds that dripped from pine fingertips.
These jewels from the mist were truly priceless,
for their essence melted away with the rising sun.

As I cherished this fleeting moment
I discovered the benevolence of the earth
and my eyes consumed the exquisite array
that had been artfully displayed around me.

Now, when I rise each morning, before the crashing dawn,
I pray for the lucent pageant of a frost laden world.
With bated breath I draw back the lace portiere
and anticipate the splendor of nature's ice showcase.

Norma J. Bradley

The Utah Jazz

The Utah Jazz are a basketball team
with Malone who's a definite idol.
Chasing after the basketball dream,
an NBA championship title.

John Stockton passes the ball,
with amazing talent and ease,
into the hands of Karl Malone
they make it look like a breeze.

Malone then shoots the twenty-footer
or drives and goes all the way.
Or maybe he'll dish it to Hornacek
who will easily knock down the tray.

No matter who or where they play
to the Jazz it's all the same.
I guess there's just one more thing to say,
man, I love this game.

Jonathan Clark

Stillborn Child

We never had a chance to get to know one another in this lifetime
but I know in my heart that you are now
a little angel and at peace
and we will someday meet again.

From conception, we became one and I
loved you more and more,
as I felt your wonderful little body growing
inside of me.

Laura, you will always be a part of me and
I'll never forget the love that we shared
and the warmth and joy you gave to me
whilst I carried you.

You were a beautiful little baby
and I am so happy that I had a moment
to hold and caress you.

We will scatter your ashes in our garden,
so that you will always be near
the ones that loved you.

And each flower that I see blossoming
and each tree that soars to the sky,
I'll know that it's your little spirit living on.

Tracy Laura Webster

The Sea

Have you considered the sea?
    Of the content of its beauty!

The creeping of fingers upon the ground floor;
    the smashing of waves caressing the shore.

The playing of sun beams upon the water's crests;
    sparkle like a diamond at its best.

And as one ventures the depths of the vast sea;
    one sees, sea creatures, sea shells and
    harmonious scenery.

Its continuous efforts of toil and strife;
    reveal a consistent strength of life.

The rhythmic power of its force;
    echoes vibrations along its course.

It will not surrender to obey;
    to nature or man or night or day.

If by now you are not free;
    consider the beauty of the sea!

Pauline R. Flowers

Waves Of Reality

Listening to the ravelling of the waves
As they crash towards the shore,
Who am I to ignore such a vicious sound?

Could the truth ease my mind, or am I one to judge?
Should I pass judgement on my own existence?
Only one can say what has enhanced me here today.

The soul I was forced to dwell
Weak as a twine; yet so full of strength,
Is now caught in a war between love and hate.

Time has frozen all my dreams.
My mind's ripped apart at the seams.
Bloody tears have shed my soul.
Leaving me with no place to go.

Must I stand tall? I have no legs.
Shall I lie down? I have no spine.
Should I scream? I have no tongue.
Must I die? Then, I'd be without.

What does fate have in store for me?
Will I ever find the key to the door of my destiny,
Or will I ravel and crash to the shore?

Tonya E. Noga

I Am

I am an impatient sister.
I wonder when my older sister will move out.
I hear her say I will be out after April but there is still doubt
I see her still here, not even packed.
I want her to move-out and not come back.
I am an impatient sister.

I pretend she is not around when she is here.
I feel the tension when she is near.
I touch her around her neck trying to stop her breathing.
I worry she will wake-up and see me cheesing.
I cry when she is gone because she is so far.
I am an impatient sister.

I understand why she left.
I tell myself now I can rest.
I dream of my sister, hoping she will visit.
I try to think of other things than my sister.
I hope one day I will be able to tell her I miss her.
I am an impatient sister.

Chante Lacy

The Reflecting Pool

Dreams can be visions as seen from afar
Our dreams are as good as the people we are
Dreams reflect who we are or would like to be
They're partly a vision and partly reality
A better world is in view when the mind's eye is gleaming
Working hard to fulfill it brings purpose and meaning
And if unfulfilled, we must dream and believe
For you just never know what your dreams might achieve

Sarah Thompson

Fear

Who's afraid of the dark? Not I,
Here are some reasons, I will tell you why,

When chills come tingling down your spine,
I am really in my prime,

When haunting midnight comes to be,
Now it is time for me to be free,
Jumping and running in the dark,
The graveyard is my favorite park,

Best of all the time has come,
For me to become undone,
Nightmares here and nightmares there,
I am looking for more victims to scare,

Shivering people lay in bed,
Dreaming of a dead man's head,
Soon the light will be here,
And the ark will leave with its fear!

Jordan Calaguire

Little Dog

With your paws trapped in wrapping paper
And a shining new medal of your own
You looked so adorable, you felt much safer
Little dog, you should have known.

You were just three when you went
Exploring the world, all alone
You soon realized to sleep you had no tent
Little dog, you should have known.

A few days only after you parted
Howling wolves whimpering a death tone
Came by you and a wild chase started
Little dog, you should have known.

Mortally injured you lay down and weep
Letting snow cover you, all alone,
You let out a final sigh before your final sleep
Little dog, you should have known.

Lauriane Saunier

How Do You Know?

Mysterious ties to the soul
bound by memories of the past...
Time paints them stagnant and
slowly breaks the ties that were to last...
What can we do to make the fairy tale forever?
One thought change would keep us together...
When in the future those ties were still to sever...
To think of it will drive you mad,
It can't be predicted...
The wind could blow or the sun
could shine no way to tell
except time...

Carlie L. Kennedy

The Search

You say you need a friend, who's loyal, tried and true.
Well, if you need a friend, the search must start with you.
The very things you need, are needed by us all;
Someone to hold your hand, to help you if you fall.
You say you need a friend to listen to your pain.
Who's there to help you out, and never thinks of gain.
A friend who's there to smile when life has made you glad;
To be there by your side when life has made you sad.
Like a mirror reflects back to you, exactly what you see;
To find yourself a friend, a friend you first must be.
So give to someone else exactly what you need;
And in giving of yourself, you'll find a friend indeed.

Sandra McNulty

That Strange Feeling

There's a feeling that is felt only truly once in your life,
it is felt when two people become man and wife.
It is a feeling that is so hard to explain,
it will be there in the best sunny weather even through rain.
It stays never to go,
it's a feeling that will always grow.
No matter what goes on or what is endeavored,
that feeling we call Love will go on forever...

Laurie Cadorette

Where Art Thou Camelot

Alive no more is my kingdom of beauty, honor, and magic.
The rose embraced fields of natural beauty
Have been blanketed with a jungle of stone and steel.
Corruption has slain honor and justice out of mankind
Leaving them crusading against its own demons.
The winds once sang of heroic epics
Of men, women, children struggling against unknown evils
Now they whisper the banshee cries of law sirens
Marking the scenes of thievery and death.
Oh my dear Arthur, knight of knights
Where art thou Camelot.
Does not a place exist in the world today
Where chivalry has not been devoured by the dragon.
Faith and magic held its legend in my realm
Now the only believers are children and the blessed
The world is dying of a deadly cancer
A cancer of ignorance known as the human race
Oh my dear Arthur, knight of knights
Where art thou Camelot.

David Hicks

Dearest Mother

I had the dearest mother
so gentle so meek so mild.
She was brave as the bravest of woman
yet trusting and sweet as a child.
And she was a rich, rich lady
though she had neither silver or gold
she had something far, far better
and more lovely to behold.
What she had was very precious
truly a gift from above.
And she shared it with all who knew her
for she had a heart filled with love.
Sometimes when I grow weary
and would lay me down to rest,
she comes to me in a beauty full dream
and she cradles my head on her breast.
She tells me not to weary she tells me not to cry.
I have left you here for a little while
but we will meet in the sweet by and by.

Bertha Davis

385

Like A Tree

The leaves have fallen to the ground,
When the wind blows the trees make no sound,
It's funny how the leaves turn so pretty in the fall,
Only a short time later falling to the ground,
Dead and brown-hearing their call.

And like the tree, I am the same,
I'll grow new leaves in the spring,
You stripped me of my beauty and pride,
When November came, I died,
But I have roots that run deep,
The kind that helps you get back on your feet,
Come summer I'll be green and fine,
Grown stronger from the rain and sunshine.

Robbie White

Touch Me

Who are you and what do you want?
Leave me alone, I don't want this.
You can't make me. Just get the hell outta my...

Can you hear me now?
The sounds of silence that echoes
through the air. Speak!!! Sshhh
listen...

Can you see me now?
Standing behind you like a nameless
shadow I follow your every conspicuous lie.

Can you feel me?
As you swallow each breath with
haste and your heart beats faster,
racing through your veins, penetrating
your conscience until finally at the
most intense moment you flinch with
rage, Touch Me, touch me...

Anthony P. Dark

Untitled

In our lives there are so many trials and
tribulations. So often we feel we will never see
daylight in the battlefield of life. I look to the
stars and sometimes ask why things are the way
they Are. Life is such a puzzle and unscrambling my
journey of life causes so much discomfort and yet I
know not what the end will bring, so I continue
to venture in a world of uncertainty hoping to
find an answer.

Peddals Adams

The Aftermath

Groves of gaunt giants thousands strong
had no trumpets nor battle song,
But braved the attack silently mute
fighting a terror absolute.

After the enemy's howling fury
... The aftermath is clear.
Fallen figures twisted, taut
dead limbs littering earth so near.
Lifeblood dripping off the last
as they sway gently, they rebuild
without a thought of what has passed
nor of their companions who were killed.

Finally, crawling out from where they nest
the scavengers return, red and brown upon their crest,
like shadows wandering through a willow mist
prepared once again, another harvest...

Daniel M. Hall

Untitled

Black thin lines run across the page
Leaving their mark of rhythm and rhyme
They grow louder and softer from page to page
it becomes short or long from line to line

From measure to measure from note to note
One moment it could be angry the next sad
Suddenly it is quiet but something so remote
Then in the calm is a joyful little lad.

Turning and jumping as if he had no care
Faster and faster, louder and louder
There is a repeat yet it is not far
Back to the beginning, it comes softer and sadder

Then finally, we're there, the very end
There is no greater joy than the applause people send.

Carmen D. Mattos

Es Regnet

In the feathered cool of November rain
I turn with the autumn gales
like a narrow weather vane. Twirling,
whirling aimlessly in the auroras sky
feeling the breath of winter's audible sigh.

Clouds matched, yet out numbered by the falling rain,
falling in chiliads
Pressing against my windowpane.
My breath fogged the window, for with my finger
I write
Poetry I ode to the tears of the falling night.

Daniel Scott Roberts

Colors

There is a color of any hue
for every mood and every matter
sometimes red and often blue
every shade of every splatter
there's grey and white
and yellow bright.
But all these colors fit somewhere,
and mean something or shortly will.
So you won't question my despair
when I proclaim my color ill.
And plead with you to not mix greatly
causing colors that you take too lightly
or tomorrow you'll find out
your color tablet is a mess
and then you'll see without a doubt
what I know and now confess
here not far from draining red like blood
that all we've done is created mud.

Jessica Stephens

Tad Along

Little tiny tadpole swimming in the pool
   Lost his tail and his legs came through
His mother said come Tad Along with me
   He blinked his eyes so that he could see
The frog on the lily pad, big as could be
   And his mother said Tad this is your dad

Dad jumped high, Tad Along jumped too
   Into the water deep and blue
They went for a swim, mother swam too
   They had a picnic for lunch
Tad Along said I've got a hunch
   My dad and mother love me a bunch.

Nelda Cargill

Ruby

Ruby is such a gleaming gem.
She shines every time the light hits her.
Her color is always bright and deep.
That it is so inspiring; it makes you sleep.
After awakening in the morning, "Oh Ruby" is so deep.

Ruby's skin is dark and smooth.
She keeps it lavish all through the night and day.
Her olive skin just brings out hues of color.
That it gleams like the stars and moon in a dark cellar.
Could it be that Ruby is for a great fellow.

When a ruby is placed on the finger of someone,
It makes you feel like a million.
It gives you confidence and fame.
"Oh," there is no room for shame.
Because with a ruby there is no room for games.

When she bursts into a room every eye turns.
Because she comes tough, brilliant, strong and true.
Her color stands right before you.
Her cut is like a diamond.
"Ruby, Ruby, Ruby," you will always and forever remind us.

  Kay King

Pretender

All day long I sit and pretend,
pretend to enjoy life,
with a smile fixed upon my face, and
a hidden tear in my eye.
No one knows what goes on inside me.
All is false and fake, few see the real me.
Few see the tears of hear the sobs.
To many I'm just a fixed thing
in their normal everyday life - always
there, always the same - but I'm not.
Rarely am I there, usually I'm off
in my own Utopia,
All by myself, crying myself to sleep.
I sleep all day, and live at night
in my dreams.

And all day long I sit and
pretend to enjoy life.

  TatiAna D.

Grey Hairs Dance

Grey hairs dance upon my head
Mingling brown, black, gold and red.

By my mouth there runs a crease
Because of a smile that would not cease.

My tummy pooches - no longer flat,
I wouldn't go so far as to call it fat.

My eyes no longer see as well.
They're just as blue, far as I can tell.

My stretch marks go from here to there.
Hoo-we! You should see me bare.

I'm not as patient as I used to be;
I scream and holler whenever it suits me,

My memory is all shot to hell.
I remember, well maybe not, when it was clear as a bell.

My hands look like my mother's did
From working hard and raising kids.

My body's stiff early in the morn;
Wish it was supple like the day I was born.

Still, for all of this I thank God I'm alive.
After all, I'm only thirty five.

  Cerredwyn R. Harper

Forever

Quietly...strongly, though subtly -
  years pass.
How they creep...
  Though we toss and tumble
  And swing and sway.
Through birth and health and illness,
Through schooling and friendship and work,
Through family and through marriage,
Through both tragedies and joys,
Through worldly happenings,
Through bodily changes,
  Wow!
Life is totally a struggle
Yet...Then.....for what ???
For the creeping years fade us,
  change us, abandon us, devour us...
  Until there is no more.
Time is the enemy, oh yes!
  It sucks our flesh,..our being
  ...destroying everything.
  Joanne Ellison Nydegger

Light

"Let there be light," God said with a smile,
  "That'll keep 'em busy for quite a while."
"They'll search and question and think a lot,
  But end up only knowing what light is not."

"Is it a bundle, a wave, or a little pulse?
  Or is it a ray, a pellet, or something else?
They'll study and look and find the core,
  That light is not heavy, and nothing, more."

  Larry N. Ferguson

Before Time

What do they do where it's no fun
Where there's no sun
And where there's no light
It's so dark and cold
Think of that, what a fright

The dark sky makes you want to fly
Where there's happiness and joy
Where you can play with a girl
And maybe a boy
It's like going through a never ending cave
Or like being buried alive
In your own grave
For now you know
You will always see
The eternal flame of darkness

  Kelsey McGowan

The Path

She pulls back her hood and gazes into the pool.
There, she sees a vision of her beloved one.
A sliver of pain pierces her heart.
The boy lies sleeping in the forest.
A pile of leaves serves as his bed.
Moonlight dances across his handsome face.
A tear slides down her cheek as she takes in his beauty.
The boy stirs, rustling the leaves beneath him.
The girl pulls a stone from within her robes.
Sadly, she drops the stone into the pool.
The boy's image wavers, then vanishes.
As she wipes the tear from her cheek, she turns to leave.
The life she has chosen forbids the love she feels.
She knows she must forget the boy.
She knows she never will.

  Josh Gill-Sutton

Richmond 1861-1996

The avenue of lights, growing thicker,
over Boulevard, Main's station above.
Still lit are the streets of April 19, after
joining their southern brothers.
A torch-lit procession, March on Marshall to Main.
Down beyond Church Hills, through Franklin to Ballard House.

Cannons fired! Bells rang! Shouts rent the air!
Discord in the streets, for different reasons now.
Everyone going down there again, but to drink not fight.
Up and down the cobblestone, lights above for them.
A laugh, a shout, for different reasons now.

Atop the hill, train and river below.
Under the lights of a towering figure,
of those who fought on land and water.
From there a fire torments, the street, the homes.
It cannot be seen, burned long ago.
The soot on the heels of everyone.

The city left as fragments, still burns with something.
Some anger, some excitement. Some trust, some fear.
Why are we still fighting?

Emily Farmer

The Warning

Surrounded again by the mindless that speak,
laying in siege, they storm your dreams,
while the soul remains strong, the mind is made weak.

Imagination soars high up to its peak,
Ideas leak uncollected like streams,
surrounded again by the mindless that speak.

Never stop searching for that which you seek,
You've got to believe in your own unseen beams,
While the soul remains strong, the mind is made weak.

Inherit the earth, thus condemned to be meek,
Achievement and hope are forgotten it seems,
Surrounded again by the mindless that speak.

Melt into collective, be never unique,
Static floods sanity's pages in reams,
While the soul remains strong, the mind is made weak.

Defend your creation, protect your mystique,
Alone, you must fight hordes of conforming teams,
Surrounded again by the mindless that speak,
While the soul remains strong, the mind is made weak.

Walter E. Nordstrom

Lori

Across the miles she did fly,
Fearful that I might die.
To hold my hand when the pain was deep
To wipe a tear upon my cheek.

To stand for hours by my bed,
Only a smile she would shed.
Please get well she would plead,
And in my heart I took her lead.

A friend to love, respect and care,
Her beautiful face was always there
Upon this earth I dare to walk,
For hours on the phone we would talk.

How I say, can I give her due,
To this wonderful woman for all she would do,
To give my love, respect and care,
For this type friendship is so race

Her name is Lori, for all to know,
My love and thanks are here to show

John M. Amantea

Love Stays Strong

Every night I watch the fires glow.
So restless and weary is my soul.
I feel the cold and the dark.
Feel the claws dig in your back.
I know your soul holds its own fear.
Hear your tears that fall like rain.
I share your loneliness and pain.

There's something waiting here for you.
So don't be afraid; close your eyes.
I'll come into sight; be beside you tonight.
As thunder crashes down from the mountain.
My love passes through those cold stone walls.
Like the gentle breeze; I'll whisper your name.
Then we'll fly across this darkened sky.
Until we reach the morning's sweet light.

Every night I watch the fires glow.
Every night I feel our love grow.

Tammy Smith

Postman's Burden

I strap the satchel to my back.
My shoulders sag like a long, slow drag
of a cigarette while the slush
seems to swallow my feet.

I slip on the slick walk of the second house;
the concrete resounds with more a memory
of sound than sound itself when I hear a girl's
grief leak between cracked blinds like a whisper.

I wonder how old she can be to bow her head
like that, leaning for dear life on the shoulder
of her cat, like Chekhov's sagging, broken-backed mare,
the only one fit to bear the tired driver's burden.

She reminds me of my child who sleeps
with her eyes open wide to night's breath;
I often peer inside, trying to catch the eye
weaving blind dreams.

The girl is rising, her body criss-crossed with
bars of light. I collect her sighs like letters,
send her my silent blessing and journey
back into the snow.

Melissa Gurley Bancks

Untitled

In plight, dreams took flight
Yes, right before your eyes
Like a fly flying by.
Days drift by, years made rift
Dreams gone forever, or so it seems
No hope in sight, but that's alright
Catch those dreams, deed it yours.
You will succeed you will see
Taste the seed of success and you will agree
Captured dreams unfold life's true pleasures.

Denise Iondon

Teachers

T - Total commitment to
E - Educate children with their time
A - Always encouraging and listening
C - Cunningly steering to morals and using their minds
H - Help with everything
E - Each child needs each day
R - Routing their dreams to come true
S - Seeing later them using them in the right way.

Zera Westmoreland

The Queerest Things Can Happen (In A Dream)

The queerest things can happen,
In a dream,
The dearest things can happen,
So it seems,
Last night I dreamt of springtime,
Of a Gershwin tune in swingtime,
For it was a Queen and King time,
And you - were there;
The queerest things can happen,
In a dream,
The merest things can happen,
So it seems,
Last night I dreamt of dragons,
They were hitched to starlit wagons,
There were angels shaggin',
Yet you - were there,
The queerest things can happen, in a dream,
Sincerest things can happen, so it seems,
Last night I dreamt of Heaven,
Then I awoke at seven, and you, yes you, were there!

Ransom R. Dobbelaar

My Ivy Garden

I love my ivy garden
By the side of the house
thick-leafed and lushly green,
It looks so cool on a hot summer's day
With hints of quiet depths unseen.
Year after year it faithfully grows
Defying winter's harshness and cold
It bravely clings to its place by the tree
Never loosening its tenacious hold
Sometimes I take it in great dislike
My ivy garden by the tree
I chop it and weed it and thin it out
Trim and rake it with great glee.
But it hangs on - it survives
Keeping its greenness all year long
And it spreads, like my faith,
   in its own unique way
Its roots running deep and strong.

Maisie Widman

The Rainbow's Run

As the winds begin to blow,
sailing storm clouds fly.

Flowers on the earth below
let out a sleepy sigh.

In the heavens high above
the angels start to cry.

The sun is shy
and it will hide while children run inside.

Once the clouds have made their wake,
the sun and all its colors wake.

Once tucked in all warm and cozy,
now they're up, alert and rosy.

The earth below begins to dry.
The people laugh and point and cry.

The children rush to see the fun.
"Watch the rainbow run!"

Theresa A. Smith

I Slip Away

As everyone looks the other way,
a tear falls and I slip away.
As everyone continues to live their life,
I slip away with a tear and a knife.
Everything's normal, or so it seems,
I slip away with a knife and dreams.
As everyone refuses to acknowledge it,
I slip away and my wrist is slit.
No one notices my soul is dead,
I slip away and blood is shed.
As the sun rises to the next dawn,
I slip away and my life is gone.
The pain is finally beginning to cease,
I slip away and I am at peace.

Angella Moos

To Our Daughter

What can we say about a daughter so rare.
We know we will not be able to bear.
The time when she'll say she's on her way,
Into the world to run and play.

You're one of a kind, a real special girl,
There's only one you, like that of a pearl,
We'll hug you and love you whenever you're down,
Just remember who's paying when you're out on the town.

We cannot express how proud we are,
To see that you've come so far,
From the giggles, smiles and dimples.
We know that life will not always be so simple,
But with your courage and strength we know you can do,
All that you set out to do.

With God's love and guidance be on your way,
Remember Him throughout each and every day.

We'll love you and keep you as He will do,
And your hopes and dreams will surely come true.

All our love

Helen Fama

Proclivity

Would you like a drink?, she asks
and proffers it wide-eyed.

A drink?

Sure, I'll have a drink—a goblet full of sweat
and savor it, or better yet
I'll scrub myself in stinging debt until my skin is raw.

I'd rather not just now, I say—I'm searching for forgiveness
but in the dark it's hard to see if there's a window here for me
or if I'll ever be set free to alter my own conscience.

You can leave any time you please,
she says with clear conviction
her breath lies hot against my neck
her sultry gaze is firm
for it's my soul she really sees
and unlike me, she understands
the terms of my addiction.

Deep down inside, I'd like to go and seek out purer pleasures
but each new day maintains its hold on all my good intentions
and even though she says it's fine and tells me that she loves me
a smile slowly parts her lips, and now her eye is twitching.

Jared Cummings

Puddles Song

His eyes are dark and cold
untrusting the faintest light.
Lured from ripened berries of sun
to the metal-cement pulse of dying flowers.
The Sparkling Gold Imitation of Life
was given to him.
He gave his life a chance to run away,
but it stayed.
He told it to laugh.
The Sparkling Gold Imitation of Life
flinched from the new found almost pained fun.
He brought his life to the paradise
between the mind and heart.
The throbbing pulse of life
burned The Sparkling Gold flesh
until it melted into a deep puddle of sadness.
Out of the puddle stepped a boy,
with loving eyes.

Alessandra Simmons

Freedom

July is replete with festive heirs of freedom,
Memorializing the events of that long night.
Bombs bursting in air, sorrow and death swelled like a gorge,
As light-footed angels delivered peace in the morning light.

Heirs of peace and freedom, not a care had we,
That war's pain too remote from our mind.
Then our hearts lay bare man's inevitable and final war,
A beautiful vessel, a soul, and an affliction so unkind.

Silently she fought through long, painful, cold July nights,
Glinted with loving memories, tears, and laughter.
Long, long seemed the nights, and bittersweet,
Sweeter still, as moments slipped into forever after.

A warrior was she who prayed for God-speed on her journey.
Calmly, victoriously, she slumbered into the morning light.
An heir of peace and freedom, what care had she,
As light-footed angels delivered her into God's eternal might.

Elma Flores Westphal

Lost Love

One day you were the love of my life.
All I prayed for is to one day make you my wife.

All of our problems could have easily been solved,
The reason they were not is
Because everyone else got involved,

Our life at one time had a whole lot of love,
But we were both sidetracked and
Needed just a little shove,

All we had to do is give it one last chance,
Then we both could have came
together and made it a beautiful romance.

But now I guess it is all through,
And all I have done for months
is feel really down and blue.

It is a real shame it has taken all of this to make my change,
But now life looks forward and everything is in range,

My life will never be down again,
Because now I am going to live life without all the sin,

It is a real shame that we have to be apart.
But you will always hold a special place deep in my heart.

John C. Kocher

Christmas Cookies

Christmas has arrived
And with it the tradition of cookie baking.
The kitchen table is filled to the brim
With a collection of assorted ingredients
Each one vital for the process.
The mixer hums
While churning out thick cookie dough.
There's sugar and oatmeal raisin,
Chocolate chip and cinnamon cookies,
All shaped as holiday favorites
The whole house smells sweetly
With the scent of these sugary delights.
The timer dings
Out come the cookies!
Warm and gooey to the touch
They are arranged on festive platters
And set before all to enjoy.
Their taste is shared by friends and family alike,
Even Santa Claus gets a few
When he visits on Christmas night!

Mary Rott

Choices

Everyday of our lives we have to make choices
From the man in the moon to little babies with spoons
We all have to listen to our inner voices

If I decide to deceive
I have only the devil to receive
If I believe in the Lord as my host
I'll never worry, being troubled by ghost

Once I chose drugs
Therefore I was sinking into the rug
Now today I've listened to my voice
That is no longer my choice

It was not enough to suffice
I needed advice
I have heard my own voice
And today, I have made the right choice

Connalita Stewart

Untitled

I've got a nice little house in the country
Where I hang my cares on a tree.
And my heart cries out
As I look about
God had been good to me.

There is a loving face in the door way,
Where the birds sing merrily,
And the children rush up
With the family pup -
yes, God has been good to me.

I might have been a millionaire,
With a mansion up on a hill,
but I like things just the way they
are, and I guess I always will.

For I receive a million kisses,
I am as rich as I can be.
That's why I always say,
when I kneel to pray -
God, you have been good to me.

Elsie Sabert

Untitled

Softness
In your white makeup
Cake and shimmer
Beautiful, really
Your blood has mixed well
Well
Well do not look on me
Mine has not
I'm wounded, but your skin is sweet on my tongue
And there you sit
Feeding me rot
All tang and sauce
Tang and sauce
In various shades of bright and glimmer
Your slender hands, a gift
As if
They make it so much easier
To go that extra centimeter.

Roxanne Avery

Silence

The Lord God speaks silently through us
the Holy Spirit, Holy Spirit, Holy Spirit
in truth we trust

Every word that is unspoken and every act of kindness
Heaven's blessings flowing down like a running stream and rest,

Beneath/within a still soul fluttering like
wings of an excited butterfly
A smile, a holy kiss, an embrace are all expressions of love
Praying, caring, sharing are spiritual uplifts
and union from above

Pondering the mysteries of the unknown
Reaching without touching...an endless song

Physically separate...spiritually equate

Unnumbered thoughts, memories of the past
Time is the essence, speechless task

Gwendolyn West-Hill

Me To You

I'm writing a poem for what reason I don't know,
  maybe because this is the way I let my feelings show.
Sometimes I wonder what I should do,
  to tell you the truth I really have no clue.
A lot of people seem to like what I write,
  to try not to cry it takes all of your might.
Do you really understand what I am trying to say,
  maybe not but I will tell you anyway.
What I write is not made up,
  it comes from the heart and not a cup.
It's all about my feelings that I cannot hide,
  kinda like two freight trains that are about to collide.
Some of love and some of death,
  but every one you read will take away your breath.
A lot of them remind you of the problems you have yourself,
  you can't let them bother you because it affects your health.
Sometimes we laugh sometimes we cry,
  but it is a fact of life we all have to die.
You probably all wonder if this is all so true,
  I'll tell you what it's from me to you.

Nathaniel B. Moore

Sir Lancelot

His armor shines bright,
it glitters in sunlight.
His plume is waving above his head,
he has never been struck dead.
His sword is a deadly beam of light,
which will defend him all day and all night.
His stallion is a bucking bronco with no fear in its eyes.
This knight's name is Sir Lancelot who no one can defy.
His son Galahad grew up to be the greatest knight who ever lived,
and Lancelot was the father who taught chivalry to him.
Sir Galahad was turned into an angel of God for the great peace
  he brought.
And all because the proud efforts of a father named Sir Lancelot.

Michael Philip Gibson

Observing Elegance And Black And White

Your fingers touch, then run away
I follow closely to see what I can learn
Hands that can touch the keys so elegantly
and also touch my heart;
they bewilder me.
Song after song,
they come with a passion captured by every sense.
You call it warming up; I call it beautiful.
A blend of life, emotions, and tones,
all expressed with care.
I only wonder if I could show love
through something so material.
A gateway to the soul,
a mood captured in keystrokes.
I compliment you;
you insist it was the worst you had ever done.
I know better,
I've listened before.

Tommy Mokas

One Voice Of Millions

Can you guide me to the right path,
I cannot see.
I'm blinded by the hatred caused by people
like you and me.
We have created a hell,
for whom we claim to care
I'm just one voice of millions
who am I to say what's fair.
But when we're gone,
and our children still cry
you'll wish you would have made
an effort to try.
So the next time you think about this
world filled with hate,
we all can make a difference
it's never too late.

Taylor Richardson

Love Is Like A River

Love is like a river,
Every time I think of you I quiver,
and in return my soul is given a lift.
Our love is so beautiful,
like a river, which can be fruitful.
As we grow and grow on each other,
a river will flow and flow towards its mother.
As a river becomes angry and overflows its banks,
our love is similar as we work it out and show thanks.
As a river becomes calm and the day becomes long,
you and me become one and very very strong.

Brett W. Martin

Now And Then

Agitation.   Inattentiveness.
What makes me so?
Broader views, grander plans.
Now seems so petty.
However, Now must be conquered in order to reach Then.
Things forthcoming inevitably
end up to be Now
will the same anxiousness
to bypass Now occur Then?
Most likely if this habitually occurs.
But Then seems so worthwhile
that Now is insignificant.
So what will change when Then is Now?
Now is the only reality,
there is never really Then
only in concept.
So Now must be dealt with continually and not put off.
Sights must be set for the near future,
but our gaze must always be in the present,
or life will be waited away.

Donia Lilly

Abandoned

As I close my eyes and darkness
folds around me, memories of you dance in my head.
I see you pushing me on a swing and I am
going higher and higher. It seems
as though I am flying and you
are my wind. Then I start to slow
down and the swing stops. I turn
to look at you but you are no longer
there. You have left me alone with
no one to push me higher into the
world. As the years pass, I start
to realize that you are never coming
back, so I abandon my swing
because my wind is gone. I never
thought you would leave me because
I am part of you and you were supposed to love me forever.
As I grow older the anger and frustration
towards you has built up, but I also
pity you because you have lost me forever.
You can never get me back because you stopped being a father.

Nicole Rizzo

That's Just The Way It Goes

Something began; with a wild horse.
What began?
No one knows,
That's just the way it goes.

Let your mind wonder,
Beyond your wildest thought.
Can you feel the horse feet thunder?
Can you sense the fight that's fought?

If I have thought, what you have thought,
Then that wild horse has been caught.
If I have not, then can it be,
The wild horse still runs free?

The wild horse is your mind,
And no two minds think alike.
Sometimes it puts us in a bind.
Sometimes this may be right.

So can it be?
The wild horse will always run free.
No one knows.
That's just the way it goes.

Kay Cryder

LIGHT

the mirror
a black hole

the playground
bombed

the hurricane
a not too distant Memory

Flowers Budding
where people died

the remnants of Last night
take two Motrin and call me Later

a recluse
Opening the Curtains

it's around the Corner
Turning it is optional

Open your Eyes Wide
let the LIGHT of a New day stream into your **Soul**

Case W Janneman

Why Do You Moo?

Black and white cow, why do you moo?
Are you sad or lonely?
Is there anything I can do?
I want to help you
So tell me what's the matter,
Tell me the reason before you grow sadder.

Black and white cow, why do you moo?
Has someone been unkind to you?
You can come live with me if you want,
I won't turn you into beef
To go to the restaurant.

I like little cows, I keep them for pets,
I always feed them before the sun sets.
And if you come with me
You will live happily
And won't be sad anymore.

All day long you can chew on your cud,
I'll even let you out to play in the mud.
So black and white cow, don't moo anymore,
Come with me and you'll never end up in the store!

Robin Richardson

Sighing

Sighing,
You turn from me.
  A mock or memory?
  A sign or skeleton
Of sorrow, hate, or jest?
Are you muting the birdsong
Or simply coaxing it to silence
  with a wink,
To watch me weep?
To have me guess?
or to feel me die in a winter of emotions
Conjured with
a wisp of tenderness and a bulk of avarice.
Sighing,
You turn again
  to meet my blackened eyes,
And blow a kiss
  As if to say just kidding.
Perhaps to say
  goodbye.

Frank Edward Kelly

Alone

An old man sits,
    By the comfort of his fireside.
At his side,
    Lies a golden dog
Both in the twilight of their years.

On the mantle,
    Is a portrait of his wife.
She has passed on, has it been 10 years
All their children's children have children now.

Oh at Christmas time the house still bustles
with the patter of little feet.
But tonight, like most, it is mute.
The old man smiles at some old memory
Never alone in his solitude.

Harold Burns Brooks

Winning A War

As I lay here, I think of nothing,
In my mind I always hear a ring,
The noises of commotion of a war,
I can tell of a fight, of now and was,
A fight of good and evil,
Why am I in between of all of this,
This war is a sequel,
A continuous love and hate of passages.
Down one road, I see mix-ups and wrongs
Through thick darkness,
Of which times in life, things get clogged,
With Jesus, nobody can destroy me.

Chris C. Harris

Finding Home

The whispering sound of the falling snow,
the snow that surrounds me. The caress of
its wet, cold, flakes, stiffens my old legs.
Caught far away, long ago, with only my
dog at my side, I cry. My dog is cold too,
also forgotten, forgotten as the surrounding
scene, lacking what God has made.
How far am I? From the home I once
knew? Does someone know? In the distance
I see light, I see trees, I hear a
faint sound of people laughing! My dog
is jumping! Yes, home, is in the distance!
Deep, deep inside, is a family!
My dog knows. So does God! Deep inside is, finding home.

Laurita Bergner

Knights Of Silver

He walks in the alley, the darkness of night.
Knowing that danger is ahead, pushes on.
Touches his gun, a burst of light,
a flash of red, as the sun.
A knight of Silver is dead.
What was to be right has now to wait.
The darkness of night has swept his soul away.
A bright, new star in heaven now shines.
Evil walks cowardly away.
A flash of silver light, a badge of courage,
a ray of silver in the lightless night.
An explosion of sound, Evil is taken to the ground,
he struggles to kill again,
but righteousness delivers him, an early death.
Death comes again, this time to deliver
a soul to hades, not as before.
Honors to a lost soul.
Shameful burial to night's son.

Marcos Diosdado

To Barter

Life has loveliness to sell,
    All beautiful and splendid things,
Blue waves whitened on a cliff,
    Soaring fire that sways and sings,
And children's faces looking up
    Holding wonder like a cup.

Life has loveliness to sell,
    Music like a curve of gold,
Scent of pine trees in the rain,
    Eyes that love you, arms that hold,
And for your spirit's still delight,
    Holy thoughts that star the night.

Spend all you have for loveliness,
    Buy it and never count the cost;
For one white singing hour of peace
    Count many a year of strife well lost,
And for a breath of ecstasy
    Give all you have been or could be.

Carol Wigley

Window Pain

The young soul rises from a long slumber
On a cold winter's morning and walks over
to the blind-covered window.
The young soul pulls the chord that opens the blinds
And reveals the land covered by a blanket of white
that is almost blinding.
The majestic trees stripped down to bare limbs revealing
Their vulnerability to the world by falling prey to
the ever-changing seasons.
Small children bundled up in clothes to keep them
Warm while running toward the nearest hill with their sleds in hand.
The young soul reaches out to tries and join them
But is abruptly stopped by the glass through which
the young soul was looking.

Jeffrey S. Whitfill

Untitled

The sweet aroma of the melting snow
Glistens in the sun of the morning,
As the river flows in it's perfect chaotic patterns.
The frozen leaves crunch on the ground
As I for the first time realize I am home.
The innocent smiles of the cobblestones lining the street
Tell me their age old stories
Of the stars in the blackness of the night.
As pure and innocent as we were as children.
The coldness of the wind cuts through me, yet warms me.
It was here I was born.

Matt Morton

Time Marches On

The countless sands of time march on
Destroying the past
while protecting eternity
Its merciless brigade trudge fierce
through the universe eliminating all
from seconds to centuries
As time marches on it leaves behind
a mound of memories and stories to tell
atop this mound waves a victory flag
that is colored where prophecies history dwell
All hail
this endless warrior's fight
and do not fear progressions will
though time will march on through one's life
What good is life if time stood still.

Melton Adams III

Our Ancestors Weep

Wept and sorrowed for many years
Our ancestors in empty dreams were
Imprisoned in their homeland
My fathers asked, when shall we free be
Their children named symbolically, chimuzo is one
One day our forefathers shall come, our freedom due
Sorrows and weeping will end
The generation rust and gold prayed
The offsprings for answer asked
Why our spring is silent and sad
Their water we shall fetch
Their rest our struggle shall reward
The adversary to his home has gone
The offspring, to the adversary at home
Our jewels bring to keep
Oh! what a freedom when your wealth is away
Chocolate we eat not says the adversary
Their sons and daughters from home flee
To a better place seek to stay
Their empty home our future garden shall be.

Virgilius MBA

Peaches

Not just a fruit but the name of my kitty.
Bright yellow, green eyes,
Velvety fur,
Meow cute,
Whiskers adorable,
A dainty little tongue
Four precious feet, no one can beat,
And one long tail.
Don't forget her purr like a little motor.
I love my kitty and that's that.
Not a dalmatian like a golden ring dotted with gems,
Or a chocolate labrador a piece of perfectly cut chocolate,
But she is a milk shake of gray and peachy colors,
All shaken up, no other way could be better.
Love her like sweater or ever better
She is my kitty and will always be,
Even if she's dead, ran away, or stolen,
She is my cat!

Katie Byrne

When God Gave Me You

When God gave me you, he gave me life
Together we built one as man and wife
We raised our family, helped with the grandkids too
But now, Dear one, it is just me and you
Our time may be short, but who is to know
The Lord above will guide us as we go
We have had our good times, some bad ones too
I am so glad I could share them with you
As each day goes by, I thank the Lord above
For he gave you to me, my life, my love

L. V. Katz

Caught The Falling Star

I fell in love with you many years ago. When I was
a little girl I wished on the New Moon for someone
to share my honest heart.

There were lots of times when I thought I had found
you, and was sadly disappointed.

But when you finally came along, I knew you right
away, because you were this gentle clown with a dream
or two of your own, who took my hand and showed me
the way to the stars.

Brenda Gilbert Bensing

What If?

What if the souls are right, the time is wrong?
It sounds like a verse in any sad song.

What of the feelings I do hide?
How do I express what I feel inside?

An extended glance.
Do I take a chance?

What of feelings she may hide?
Does she secretly long to be at my side?

Fight the attraction, don't let it grow?
Sometimes it's just better not to know.

What if it's just wishful thinking, all in my head?
But maybe it isn't, should something be said?

I miss her voice, I want always to call,
yet I make excuses not to, finding ways to stall.

Obligations made to others involved
confuse feeling not yet resolved.

I imagine that there will come a day
in a conversation all this I will say.

Then all my thoughts will be sifted,
and the weight inside will be lifted.

David D. Kiggins

My Pride, My Joy, My Boy!

You came to me on a cold cold day,
With every ounce of breath, all I could say,
I love you now and forever,
And we will make it through any kind of weather,
Just you and me and everything to see,
No matter what it is you choose to be.
You make me happy, sad, and sometimes even cry,
And I'll never never ask how come or why,
My heart has even filled with joy and tears,
For what the future hold, brings out my fears
Even though I didn't born you, I gave you life,
And will never part til the day we die,
Or you take a wife,
You're my hero, my life, my child
Even if it's only for a very short while.
So when you're crying for your toy,
Remember you're my pride, my joy, my boy!

Dottie Macauley

Waiting for the Solstice

The cold bitter hand
mother nature's nails are sharp and 1/2 bitten
but the willow cries
a brisk scream passes by

An arctic wind sends shivers down our spines
as small school children scurry down the street
We see how bare the limbs are
the willow bends from the fury
and it has shed its skin

As the winter afternoons approach
a tabby cat meows like a crying newborn
needing the warmth of its mother's arms
cold steel doors stand, locked and forbidden
as a branch crackles and splinters shatter

A nighttime frost glazed over cars and streets like glass
clouded moonlight shines dimly on flattened grass
a howling whistle, like far away trains off in the distance
as mother nature bites her nails again,
our windows rattle from the rain...

Brandt R. Valcourt

Life By Definition

From the innocence of lifes evergreen
Heaven seems to be so far, far away
Waiting for tomorrow is forever
Looking new, another place or day
The dark figure that follows is trust
Miles of thoughts in the atmosphere
So many miles, miles of light years
Sometimes to wait, is with ones mere
It's searching the enigmas for answers
Remembering the past to presents
With a blank stare to no where
Bottoms hit with feelings unclear
A hue of green remembers addiction
One escapes reality within a myth
Climbing of stairs to light the dark
The primal sage of life rules the orb
Bird equals life as life equals death
A vicarious experience, life's only one breath

Audrey McKinney

Life Is The Only Way

Life is the only way,
Life is a lonely way,
i stumbled over many trials and tribulations,
Embraced trial and kissed tribulation
i don't live on charity,
And in life there is no clarity.
Struggling i walk the streets alone,
In the heart i haven't a home.
The odd man on the team,
The unloved one in the scheme.
Tested my life never once did i waste it,
Been hurt in the heart and cut, then i tasted
The only one in his world,
The only one who failed.
Life is the precursor to death!
But some how in my hate and rage,
i need life and love i crave.

Alexander Contreras III

Mists Of Time

Mists of time
spawning dimensions,
conceiving intentions.

Tomorrows reminisce
of yesterdays dreams, with gathering souls
a genesis of beings.

Rapturous beauty, resplendence of flame,
perpetual illumination
of these became.

For want of light,
lifes highest degree,
mankind extends, striving to be free.

Free of limitations, the binding confines,
Uniting once again
with Mists of Time.

Don Mike Catchings

Weeping Willow Tree

As I sit and lean against thy bark
Your gentle branches lean down to caress my heart.
Telling me let the sadness depart.
For as the energy of my embrace,
Races up the trunk to the top.
To receive God's divine energy to flow down to the base
For all those who come to sit - to feel my embrace.

Lillian Murray Roman

We

Our eyes met...locked in a trance...
  bonding immediately.
We rose to dance...his arms engulfed me...
I felt as though I was adrift at sea.

No words were spoken...none were needed...
  our love flowed freely.
Through our eyes, we spoke endlessly.

Our eyes still locked in a loving embrace
We touched hands...an electrifying shock...
We stood still...we heard the minute hand on the clock.
We caressed, kissed, touched each other's face.

We had to be alone to fulfill our dreams
Before anyone heard our stifled screams.

With all eyes upon us, we left the crowded room.
We should have stayed.
After all, we were the bride and groom.

Helen C. Smith

Can You Spare A Dime

Excuse me mister, can you spare a dime?
I've been on this corner for a very long time.

Don't look at me with pity or think that I am strange.
All I ask of you, is for a little spare change.

I may be dirty and in need of a bath,
a place for comfort and maybe a laugh.

"Mi Casa Es Su Casa" - my house is yours,
a meal and a bed, that's a start to be sure.

Please help me today to be warm and dry,
to go to sleep without having to cry.

Homeless and dirty, hungry and cold,
a disease to us all, no matter how old.

So again I ask, can you spare a dime?
I've been on this corner for a very long time.

John Shipley

Dark World

Stuck in this nostalgic position
This lonely fetal position
Can't breathe anymore
Just can't make it to that rainbow colored world
Reach in reach out
Come on and pull the glass together
Crazy glue these jagged shards
Stab them into the problem
Everyone makes me so angry
I'd like to kick a few of these gimps down a mountain
How perfect, how graceful, how righteous they would look now
Still looking for that place
That real quiet place
Just one more breath in this dark world

Ramona Elyse Janson

Spirit

Oh, spirit of morning, noon and night,
Spirit of love, truth and might,
Spirit whose pure path runs true,
Spirit who's always there for me and you.

"Oh, spirit," we asked, "from where do you hail?"
"From heaven's above, or below from hell?"
The answer came as clear as a bell.
"I sure as heck don't come from hell."

Clara Von Martin

Untitled

The gravity of reality reaches up with her confining claws
and jerks me back to solid ground

She pulls
tugs
and yanks me down
back to earth
down and away
from the playground of my imagination

And I must store my hopes and dreams for a while
until I can return to my sand castle in the sky

Sarah Rogers

Sketches

The lines between truth and lies are poorly drawn
The lines between good and evil were etches in stone
But the stone was broken and tossed away
Along with the value of human life
There is no space for a devil here
And yet no room for a God
Yet between them we live,
And to them we look for guidance.
We cannot see their barriers
For we have expanded them
Soon we will break them down
We fear for this day
Yet strive for it subconsciously.

Ben Murphy

I Shall Win

Too many people, too many problems
life was losing its taste
Too many oppressors, too many transgressors
this was my case
Too much affliction, too much contradiction
made life seem so base
Too much darkness, too much sadness
what a waste, what a waste
Look to my saviour, look to his glory
warming my face.
Accept this cleansing, accept his healing
accept his mercy and grace
Follow his leading down the path of his choosing
follow it with haste
Walk in his sunshine, relax in the quiet
finally to find my place
"Be still and know that I am God"
Be still and know, be still, be
Now I shall win my race

Marian Nelson

Candle Night Under SP

Late one candle night,
Dark stars overhead.
Sleepless light from which energy forms,
For whom rest means no other than death.
I saw through my clear mirror,
An empty sky with but one thought to think:
You!!

Late one candle night,
Thoughtless thoughts I think.
Vainful thoughts reaching for the stars,
Fearful of coming forth to reallty.
To tell she whom I love,
May never happen to but one person:
You!!

Samuel J. Rodriguez

The New Millennium

Stone, and rocks, and clay,
replaced by a modern day.
Gone are forests, pines, and trees,
replaced by computers punching keys.
What age is this we enter now,
when man exists, not of moral vows.
The earth is covered in a metal age,
where nature hides in a solid cage.

Our children learn not to read and write,
Peace replaced by an industrial plight.
The homeless stare at the dark cement,
Their lives astray, nowhere to vent.
Medieval ravaging of life,
As we continue on with strife.
Kings and Queens, and sorcerers too,
The classic structure clearly in view.

I say goodbye to my precious land,
For not enough have taken a stand.
The new age of a sunflower seed,
Has shriveled and died, a dirty deed.

Jill Newman

Love Affair With A Tree

If at all possible, check with God and see,
If I may Lord, marry myself a tree.

It's the closest I've found to the man of my dreams,
Listen to me Lord, try and see what I mean.

See the red oak you made so tall and strong?
In the likeness of such arms I'd like to belong.

His solidarity and strength as unmovable as bark,
Yet underneath it all, a gentle, loving heart.

Oh please Lord, this is my only plea,
Master, may I marry one of your lovely trees?

With arms of cradling shelter for the baby birds nest,
I long to be wrapped up in the center of his chest.

Father you have planted him with roots so deep,
Fulfilling, my desire for such security.

And yes, your trees possess a sensual worth,
Branches that suspend with firmness and girth.

I've seen them aroused before my very own eyes,
Touched by the hands of spring, I've watched the sap rise.

So I beg unto you Lord, forget all my other pleas,
And just let me marry one of your lovely trees.

Angela G. Veal

Waiting For You

Waiting for you
Waiting for the day when dreams will come true
Lonely and blue
Everyone I see reminds me of you
Reminds me that there is no one like you
No other eyes to thrill as yours do
No other lips to make mine know anew
The touch of yours is heaven
I'll always be
Waiting for the day you come back to me
For I can see
You're the one to fashion my destiny
Star studded skies just make me lonely
For my heart cries, "I want you only"
So why pretend
Days and nights I'll just spend
Waiting for you

Andrea Ierardi

Untitled

Counting his dreams,
One by one by one.
As his chest rises and falls
With every beat of his estranged heart.

I can read his slumber
He wades in rivers,
He conquers the world.
Doesn't he know that only angels have the wings to fly?

I can distinguish his pretenses.
I can imagine the world in which he lives.
I can see him like I see ultra-violet light.
Only in my own dreams.

I can see him sail down the pacific blue,
Or watch him catch a firefly
Or smell his strawberry wine.
As again he saves our land.

His bitterness is left at his pillow's edge.
Today's sorrow and anger cease through the door.
He lays in soft down and crisp cotton sheets
And creates his own eternity.

Megan E. Schweithelm

Untitled

Hearts broken
ripped out and crushed
the pain the terror
the un-opened thoughts
aches and pains, physical pains
eaten through my stomach
'til it's gone, hearts filled with love
but not any more it shriveled up and died
just like my soul nothing to live for nothing to die for
nothing left at all. Died but reborn scary huh?
Think you've seen it all wait
just wait until that one comes along
it's going to hurt
I'm telling you now
don't start it end it
just end it all
terrible love terrible life
you're happy then sad again, one moment in time
you think you have it all then it goes,
long gone, forever.

Kristen Shaw

A Place In My Mind

The sky was the limit I thought one day
To soar with the wind would set me free

Never did dream I'd fly this high
Until I saw him the pilot in the sky

There were times I thought I'd never be free
That the dream I had was only a fantasy

Time has given me the best there can be
Hope for a future of love given totally

He says he's not special a poor pilot he
If only I can show him what he means to me

It's not a fine house or other amenities
That make life exciting with moments of ecstasy

The nights are so peaceful my days are so free
I can make them all special when I recall his memory
his touch and his voice can take me away
To a place in my mind and it is him I see

He is tall and handsome with so much love to give
I'm so happy I met him and now I can live

Phyllis Earp

Jesus

He was nailed to a cross,
with a crown of thorns on his head;
they struck him with a sword,
and this is what he said;
"Father,
Forgive them,
for they know not what they do."
The women and children cried,
and the men did too.
And in three hours time Jesus Christ had died;
He healed the sick and walked by their sides.
He taught the people how to pray.
He showed us all how to live a better way.
He said he would come again,
and I pray we will all be ready by then.
In the name of Jesus Christ,
Amen...

Jhonette Livingston

A Lonely Lame

The things called thoughts cloud my head.
My illusions of a world turning red.
Pleasure and pain runs through my veins.
A distilled process and facts of turning insane.
My queen will not leave me to mourn and grieve.
I have tried so hard to keep what we've achieved.
Nightmares and dreams stay the same as before;
Wanting a chemical smile passed out on the floor.
Artificial joy doesn't change a thing but keeps it same.
I've played your game and fought hard for to long;
To leave with out a fight at the end of this,
Because given in left me with a rage bottled within.
God is a name that leaves me engulfed with shame.
Blank as the paper that started to write my blame.
I can't be alone in a world that is so lame.

Adam Day

Thanks For The Children...

For it is they who remind us about beauty...
About butterflies and fragrant flowers,
Whistling winds and colossal raindrops,
Mysterious pink skies and endless rainbows.
Who else would chase a fleeting butterfly,
Giggle as the raindrops fell on their faces,
Listen attentively to the whistling wind,
Pick dandelions for a special bouquet,
Believe in the rainbow's end,
Or wonder what lies beyond a pink sunset?
Only children are our constant reminders
To live today
With a smile,
With determination
And a love for life.
Our children are a precious gift.

Carol A. Marshall

As I Stand Alone/I

As I sit here alone...Alone!
I don't know how long it should be...Hold On!
But only how it is.....Gone!
When memories are strong it brings a tear....Cope!
I'll still awake knowing that I'm alone....Hope!
As I stand alone I dream of love with whom can I
share...Embrace!
To be blessed to always have her by my side....Grace
With her I won't be alone....Together
The strength of our love shall fulfill our hearts...Joyous!
I only wish to be alone with the beauty of your love...Always!

Byron Martin

Prematurity

Sunset came early today.
Many children missed hours of play.
Darkness took the light from them
And made the early hours of morning a little grim
Their love for the daylight
Kept back their fear of the night
Sunrise finally came
And the children resumed their game.

Janelle M. Mack

Reach

Lovely faces
Paint our psychedelic being
Multifaceted gemstones
In the treasure chest of life
Sparkling as moonbeams
We reach
For what is in our grasp?
Boundaries?
For, I know none
As you shine
We reach
When the morning dew evaporates
And the beautiful rainbow sets in the distance
Each color reflects a piece of my scared heart
Desire - is it imagination?
Hope, never to be lost
What are dreams?
An obscure reality?
Now, but all alone
I reach...

Michelle Claire Denholtz

Look To The Bright Side

Each mountain we climb seems the highest,
As we search for our pot of gold,
We search for the silver lining,
Of that cloud as the story is told.

We look for the better tomorrow,
As each day passes us by,
Hoping to find contentment,
Which we want before we die.

In order to have the riches,
That we want life to bring,
We must pay the fiddler,
For the music we want to sing.

In order to find contentment,
And peace for your life here,
We must try to live a full life,
And hold every moment dear.

Be happy with what you receive,
And never ask for more,
Then you will have contentment,
As you open each new door...

Midge Johnson

Buried Alive

Lost soul In a coffin of pain,
  Life's blood begins to drain...

As my crawl through the earth begins
  Mistakes eat at the flesh of my skin...

Worms of regret pierce my eyes
  Who can stop the cries...

The cries of the ones that I've hurt
  How can I break free of this dirt?

Terrence R. Battle Sr.

No Color

Red, white and blue
The color stood so true
It stood out from all the rest
At one time, we thought it was the best!

The Rebel flag, it flew around
While many a soldier fell to the ground
Black and white, was of no color
So why should we attack each other?

It shouldn't matter which flags are used
The main thing is, is to not abuse
The Civil flag, it should be for all
Instead we've made it against the law.

"We should grow up and love our brother"
For life's too short to hurt one another!
We're created equal, I know it's true
But let's not forget the golden rule
"Do unto others as you would have them do unto you."
Love one another is what God wants too.

Nancy Olene Maddox

The Beauty of Simplicity

Deep in the complexities of adulthood, I recall childhood,
when laughter was magic, and the world so simple.

Give me the simple things in life
Give me a clear blue sky for the stage,
the serenity of twilight for the neon city glitter.
Give me inner peace for fame and fortune,
a calvary cross for silver and gold.
Give me seashells for plastic money,
a breath of fresh air for nuclear energy.
Strength in my soul for the Seven Wonders of the World;
let my health be the Eighth Wonder.

Give me life and all her beauty,
the brilliance of daybreak for satin and silk.
Give me inner discipline for luxury and wealth
a loaf of bread for chocolates wrapped in gold.
Give me solitude for attention and glory
the sparkle of pure water for bubbling champagne.

Sometimes I wonder how far we've come,
Was the journey worth the trouble?
Maybe we lost our way, on the path to greed and ruin.

Sarah A. Mowry

The Unfulfilled Visit

Just a few things to take care of,
Then I'd go see her, I promised I would;
She had said she would stay forever,
Or at least as long as she could.

A slave to society, I denied her that visit,
Instead pushed it aside for another day;
And while I fussed and fought over homework,
Angels had taken her forever to lay.

The weeping rain came soon after the news,
With every drop mixed one of my own.
God soon comforted me with a consoling rainbow
As gentle as the love Ma-Maw had sewn.

So instead of mourning the death that had come,
I rejoiced in God's love as no other.
For now the daughter whose life ended as a teen
Received long-awaited time to be with her mother.

Today she is vivid in my memory,
Etched like the name of a Vietnam Veteran.
And there she will stay through the trials of life
Until Ma-Maw may be invested in my children.

Kimberly Hintz

Seeing Blue Skies

Paper dolls, play houses and learning new things...
  wanting to fly and spread her young wings.
Hanging upside down on a jungle gym, seeing only blue skies...
  pretending and all grown up, as from a young girl's eyes.

Holding hands and Friday night dances...
  giggles friendships and taking chances.
Graduation, celebration and horizons of only blue skies...
  pretending and all grown up, as from a teenager's eyes.

Marriage and children was the plan...
  then came the desire to take a stronger stand.
Mistakes and bad judgement and seeing only blue skies...
  pretending and all grown up, as from a young lady's eyes.

Children are gone, companionship astray...
  decisions made and now you must pay.
Believing in oneself and looking forward to blue skies...
  no longer pretending, but all grown up - from a woman's eyes.

So what is the lesson that needs to be told...
  should she not have been quite so bold?
Or is hanging from your heels and seeing blue skies...
  the only dream needed from anyone's eyes.

Sheryol Kayser

No More Daisies

A breeze is passing by.
The sun has wrapped around me with all its warmth.
Oh the happiness, the joyous happiness,
I am in a field full of daisies,
wondrous green grass among me.
But the sky is getting darker.
The wind starts blowing harder.
Rain begins to pour down.
I am running for shelter.
There is nothing of that nature.
I am all alone.
I have no protection from this magnificent force.
The field is gone,
there are no more daisies.
The raindrops are tapping me on the back.
Oh the pain that I have accepted.
My only exit to pain is life.
The glorious life that I possess.
A breeze is passing by me.
The sun has wrapped around me with all its warmth.

Lonnie Law

Flawless

You looked past my scarred face.
You saw beauty in my one eye,
And never noticed the black patch covering the other.
You held my deformed hand in yours,
And embraced my paralyzed body.
You kissed my crooked nose,
And tickled my toeless feet.
You loved me. You loved me.

Katharine Ottle

Precious Love

The day begins with such delight when I see your
precious smile of contentment and peace. The day
is mellow when I see your sweet smile, for it brings
peace to my heart when I know you are rested and well.
I can see your eyes hold the softness and love that is
as quiet and beautiful as the petals of a rose with
the morning dew caressing them. This precious way you
tell me you love me, lights up my life and keeps the
never ending embers of love I have for you brightly glowing.

Thomas C. Lindsay

Ice Sculpture

Inventing an animal,
Cold and solid,
Everything made of ice.

Scratching, chipping, ice
Cold and hard,
Unfrozen when spring comes
Leaving the water behind.
Pouring water, dripping,
Trickling down to the ground
Until it vanishes.
Run out of ice soon,
Everything will just be a puddle of water

Justin Moore

We All Dance

Ni Mi Win
In the heavens, the moon dances
and gives her gravity to the earth.

Men have walked in her dust
and call it dry.

But we know.

Her spirit pours into all waters,
they shift and sway to her beat.

Mother of time, the moon
calls all of the hours and days (her children),
by their true names.

"There is no new thing under the sun"

But under the moon
shadows step lightly among grasses and trees,
across sands and changing tides,

And we all,
living spirits of God's creation,
join the circle.

Theresa A. Beville

It Could Happen That We Meet Again Down The Road

When I think about my life, the first thing I think about is you.
The joy of the closest friendship, and a pal that I once knew.
Sometimes someone walks into your arms and a friendship is born,
Then suddenly they walk out again - alas your heart is torn.

And someday, somewhere, we'll meet again down the road.
Humming our tune softly and carrying our heavy load.

Life can be like rainbow, it comes and goes in different shades.
And if you follow it long enough, something beautiful is made.
Don't give up on a friendship, learn from someone wise,
Consider the importance of our ever-changing lives.

Someday, somewhere, we'll meet again down the road.
Humming our tune softly, and carrying our heavy load.

Rachel Pearl

By Myself

It's dark in this place where I am
I cannot find the light
There is no one around me
'Cause no one shares my plight.

Everyone has someone to care for them, except me,
I'm all by myself
I cannot see the future
I cannot change the past
The present is so complicated
That I don't think I'm going to last.

Bruce Chang

Love

He told me that he loved me,
and that we'd always be.
We laughed, we cried, I thought
it'd never end,
but I guess things change.
Our ages were a problem, that we over came,
but to our elders, it still remained.
A wise friend once said a quote I not forget,
"Love has no boundaries, don't ever quit."
One day, which came all too soon,
he told me," I can't see you."
My heart split in two without disguise.
There was no room for compromise.
On the outside a normal day,
on the inside all fades away.
 What's left of a broken heart?
Only no hope for a new start.
Shattered dreams, broken promises galore,
bring my knees to the floor.
Trapped forever now I will be,
a locked up heart, without a key.

Christine Alexander

Love's Hideaway

A wise man once asked me if I know what love is
I told him I had no clue.
He said, "Sit down and I will show you."
He showed me flowers and trees, large birds and small bees
Then he looked at me and laughed
And showed me my homeroom class.
Different races and different creeds
Some even former enemies.
Then he showed me my teachers
Gods in their own way
To nurture the little godlings on the right way.
I thought I had seen it all.
With nothing left to say
I turned around abruptly to see the end of another day.
But then he stopped me to tell me there one more thing to say.
With a big smile upon his face
Superbly unnatural grace.
He pointed to his chest. The human at its best.
The thing that holds all love in the world
The human heart behold.

Claude Bryan Lewis

Waterfalls

A waterfall is a girl, crying for a toy;
  A waterfall is a man, feeling like a boy.
A waterfall is a guy, running free and wild;
  A waterfall is person, being as foolish as a child.
A waterfall is a life cycle, changing every day;
  A waterfall is a gushing river, going on its way.
A waterfall to me, is a glistening wonder;
  As for the sound of one, I compare it to thunder.
A waterfall can be dangerous, if you come too near;
  A waterfall is a treat, to thirsty deer.
A waterfall is beautiful, more beautiful than a bird;
  A waterfall can never be describe, in just one word.
A waterfall is a rainbow, a rainbow of blue and white;
  A waterfall is a graceful bird, on its first flight.
A waterfall is beautiful, to a crazy boater;
  A waterfall is always running, like a fixed-up motor.
I love waterfalls, waterfalls of all kinds;
  But if you think about them, they really boggled the mind.
Waterfalls are here, for some reason, I don't know why;
  Waterfalls are here to say, never to say, "good bye".
I love waterfalls

Victor G. Head

Not Here

As I laid in bed last night and read a delightful book
A sudden thought filled my head and to my side I looked
The bed laid still and smooth, untouched by you as of yet
It seemed to me, this could not be
The covers that protected you should be upset
I looked at the pillow that you laid your head upon each night
I caress the pillow, it felt so soft and so smooth
My shoulders shivered from the unwelcomed breeze
That breeze would have been stilled by your tranquilizing arms
There is no cold feeling of loneliness when you are with me
Only you alone keep me safe from that harm of solitariness
As I closed my book and reached for the light
My eyes once more drifted to that very empty place
The night is so long and so lonely
and in darkness I reach for you
My arm lies across the soft lump your beautiful head resides upon
and water begins to flood my eyes because you're not here

Ibis Jose Veliz

A Melancholy Poem

If ever were a day so gray,
A time when the sun would not shine,
When all we feel is cold and bitter,
This day would be it.

The color and life have disappeared,
We only see in shades of gray,
How dark does everything seem,
If only things were not this way,

The fires that once burned now tremble empty,
The earth has shriveled up and died,
We are here left to suffer and wonder,
How few of us are left.

If only the sky would open itself up,
To end the misery and suffering we endure,
Feeding us with its life and glory,
Giving us the will to carry on.

That time though has yet to arrive,
We hope to be around to see it pass,
So we wait for that second coming,
Every fleeting moment, our last.

David Woo

Miracle Of Life

Once I had a baby with golden hair and eyes as blue as the sky
But he left one day, on the voyage of life
When his ship came sailing by.

The toys are last, the lullaby still
In the night I hear no cry
It's peaceful now my mothering done
In the twilight hours I sigh.

Tho' I know that time cannot be changed
And I see the reason why;
When a mother gives to the world her young
A bit of her must die.

But laughter fills our home once more
There's a patter of tiny feet
I reach the door in a single bound
My small grandchildren to greet.

My empty arms are full again
The hours are strangely sweet
I look at the future, a rosy glow and smile at all I meet.

Who said that mothering days are gone
Or the years have been fleet with the children of my child,
Warm in my arms my cup of joy complete.

Olive Graham

Gaia, Chaos and Quantum Consciousness

Oh how we have categorized and studied the parts of things
while striving to cope with a seemingly dangerous world.
Fortunately many now see this past world view as illusionary
and seek deeper answers for those things that baffle the mind
when we fail to view all life as one total unity.

Words can't describe that 'love-force' holding it all together,
but in reverie we often catch glimpses of this Gaia concept.
Once we've felt this core energy that pervades our world,
and thrilled with the pulsating truth of humankind's connection,
we will begin to sense our part in the process of creation.

Those who fear the chaos that seems to pervade their lives
need only dive within past their own dark and troubling thoughts
to find that beautiful pattern at the core of all chaos.
It is here that we encounter that creative love energy 'stuff'
found within all-that-is that enables one to move mountains.

By visualizing what we 'want-to-be' rather than 'what-is'
we consciously and positively enter into our creations.
If 'consciousness' can alter the world of the atom,
trust that it can bring that joy, freedom, and growth
that will mesh with your wildest dreams - and it will!

Betsy Jo Miller

Destruction

The changes we face will always be
the changes that affect both man and me.
The love we had is now turned to hate
and the happiness we shared is broke on this date.
The peace in our world will no longer be
there's war in this place for everyone to see.
We weep with sorrow, pain, and fear
with no one to love or to keep you near.
Alone in the world where no one cares
to see you cry or wipe your tears.
You stand up for yourself and have pride in who you are,
it's already too late 'cause the pain has deeply scarred.
You barely live a life and then you die
so forget the world and the words that people reply.
You should own the world and make it yours
but society is filled with the violence it pours.
It's a disgrace to see our children
judge the lives and world of our women.
It's true that these problems will never decrease
and soon our world will no longer be in one piece.

Jennifer Choi

Nobody Loved You

When I first loved you,
I thought it would last forever.

But now that I have loved you,
I wish that I had never.

Someday you will open your eyes and see;
That nobody loved you better than me.

There are so many things I've wanted to say;
I've said them already but always, only when
you've been for away.

Oh, now don't look at me that way
you know how it will be;
You know I can't resist,
for your charms always work on me.

So, don't you see?
Nobody has loved you
Better than me.

J. Davis

Voices Of The Hood

Gunfire, loud music, "I got it good", sirens, babies
crying, people just keep on dying.
Are these "Voices of the hood"

Pimps lurking, prostitutes working, "Hey brother can you
spare a dime?" All for a hit of crack.
Are these "Voices of the hood?"

Pusher's selling, informant's telling, addict's hyping.
Can we live in peace?...will we ever get out?
Are these "Voices of the hood?"

Stephenie L. Wheeler

Your Child (For All Our Children)

Your child is your child, for all of your life.
Through sunshine and shadow - joy and strife.
As infants dependant, as toddlers such fun
Then mid-school arrives - independence begun.
Junior High and "The teens" it's "Trial Time" for sure
With love and understanding - all can endure.
We rejoice in their happiness - mourn for their tears.
Delight in their triumphs, cry for their fears.
Regardless of adversity - your love never wanes.
Regardless of age - some things never change.
Your child is your child, always young through your eyes.
Your "Baby" forever, in an adult disguise.

Joan Pacetti

A Mother's Love

To be loved by her, my sweet one,
Is to smell a flower, in the warm summer sun.
To hug her tight and see her smile,
Is to watch a sunset for more than a while.
To talk about life as we sit on the beach,
I feel her heart, so easy to reach.
Upon her touch, she wipes my tear,
And then I'm sure that she is really here.
Deep in the night when I'm tucked in bed,
I always feel her kiss on my head.
When I am scared I know she is near,
To hold me tight and wish away fear.
For now I know, God sent her here,
To be my mother and I love her dear.
This woman, this angel, a gift from above,
Is the reason I will always be grateful for love.

Michelle Linney

Let Me Look Up To God

Let me look up to God and see an able Father
Who loved the World so much He sent his Son
To shed His precious blood and thereby purchase
Salvation for believers - everyone!

Let me look up to God, then out on fields to harvest,
And view a sick and dying world by sin enslaved.
With swift and eager feet let me arise and hasten
To tell these lost comrades "Jesus Saves."

Let me look up to God, then in my inner being
Let me examine thoughts within my heart;
Let me cleave to the good and shun the evil,
Be strong, and bid temptations to depart.

Let me look up to God, out, in, and ever onward.
Let me see Christ in all, and never lose the scope.
But keep a clear perspective of the Savior
Who's for a sinful world the only hope!

Ella Blake May

Meaning Reason

Traveling in time and space
Weaving through the human race
The energy is ours to control
The drop we like to call our soul

We're given a garden of our very own
A place we call home sweet home
Where the soul can wander and roam
Explore the ninety percent unknown

There's only one guiding sun
The light so warm and caring for everyone
The love is pure the driving force
The essence of the reason and all meaning

We're here to play the game and strengthen the chain
Everyone is separate yet we're all the same
Do you recognize in each other's eyes
Windows of the one windows of the sun

The lessons of life have paths to choose
Follow the light and you know you can't loose
If the door is locked and you can't see
Open your heart and you'll find the key
        Carla Eilrich

Only Then

When?
When shall she believe?
Only once, when dark days fall,
Or when the whispering wind overcomes our ears
and we can finally hear its words.
Then, she shall realize, people love her.
Strangers in the world meet fate,
And when you can find a single teardrop in a pond full of lies,
She believes, only then, that she is not alone.
Death comes, death goes,
But even then our sad voices can be heard
through the hole in our heart.
Only then, she believes, she is not hated,
But loved more than she thinks.
        Kelly Mullin

Views of the World

The world can be seen in many different ways,
However I'll only name a few
I guess I should start at the smallest
and work my way up through

to an ant the world is a huge maze,
of which he can't find his way out
all his life he must keep walking and walking
until he has an energy drought

to a bird the world has no symmetry,
with buildings plotted everywhere
people and cars moving all around,
he is sure to get a scare

to a dog the world is just black and white,
a very boring scene
he just hopes and hopes that one day
his eyes will at least see green

To an astronaut the world is a big ball of clay,
made of colors green and blue
he thinks the picture would be blurred
by just sneezing achoo!
        Sravan Kakani

Fantasy

There is a thing called fantasy
That can make a star out of you and me.
Take us away from our daily grind
Leaving our troubles and cares behind.
We can dance or sing, act and play
By hitching our stars to life's milky way.

I throw a perfect spiral pass and see another score
I tip my cap and swing my bat;
I hear the crowd's loud roar.
I stand upon a concert stage, an overnight sensation.

I sing the notes of songs I wrote.
I receive a standing ovation.
I admire the trophies I have won in my Indianapolis racing car.
I win the match at Wimbledon;
Finish in the Masters: 16 under par.

Then at any given time
I can come back down to earth.
It hasn't cost a single dime,
Nor has it changed my worth.
        Donald F. Shultz

Untitled

He taught me only this
taking the hands of someone you love
and in the deep valleys of the hand, pale and smooth
find what can only be seen
with eyes closed.
With my body still warm from the hunt
we climb toward midnight.
It has happened
pictures of it will always go off the page
seek them there in the shadows, in the wind, in the moon
in a room filled only with breathing.
Inside it sings,
it screams, it whispers questions -
too many questions, some are too crude
but answered - if even under our breath.
Every morning I forget how it is
and then something attracts my eye
and I reach for the shade to run off the sun
and I take his hand
and embrace the moon again.
        Tracy Winters

Midnight Storm

Out of a starlit dream I fell
and in reality I found myself
caressed by a blanket woolen and warm
comforting me from the outside storm
Thunder and lightning frightened my soul
and the outside wind blew quickly and cold
My mother's scream was heard in the night
I felt her depression as well as her fright
A slap in the face echoed into my room
as the cold winter night continued in gloom
A loud scream again, then followed by tears
I could only imagine neighbors snickers and sneers
I closed my eyes tightly, this was all I could bear
I still felt the chill of the night's icy stare
I began to dream, and again felt warm
These dreams comforted me from my family's storm
        Elizabeth Anne Keatinge

Rock

My rock is strong and sturdy.
It supports my step and ensures it.
My rock feels no pain -
    it gets beat up and scratched and hurt,
yet it pays back no such treatment,
    instead it's all just kept inside - bottled up.
My rock is concerned -
    concerned it may hurt someone, so it
    changes and becomes smooth to satisfy the barefoot.
My rock is special.
It would never hurt me on purpose or anyone else for that matter.
My rock protects me.
It protects me from the harsh insults and rumors directed
and pelted at me.
My rock stands by me.
My rock is very special.
My rock is everlasting in my heart.
I love my rock.

Janelle Ann Lipscomb

Armageddon

The desolate stretch of sand is all that is left
Of the lush and fertile world that once was there.
The fires still burn, however, the fires that
Destroyed an entire planet.

The stench of death and decay hangs heavy in the air,
The result of hatred and oppression,
A sole survivor gasps and coughs, then takes
His last breath.

Only Death is left standing, and looking about him,
He laughs.
He steps among the bodies, looking over each hate-contorted face
With grim satisfaction.

The hatred that had existed since Man was created
Brought about the annihilation of a world.
Only the vultures are left
To accompany Death to gloat and feed.

Aaron Blalack

Dear Sis

When I talk to you, can you hear me?
Sometimes I feel you can,
I only wish you could answer,
And help me understand.
Do you see the flowers I bring,
To lay upon your grave?
Do you feel the tear I shed,
Can you touch me in some way?
They tell me you're in Heaven,
I wish I knew for sure.
Maybe this pain I'm feeling,
Would be easier to endure.
I want to believe there is Heaven,
And a God taking care of you too.
I guess when I die, I'll know if its true.
Many years have come and gone, since you passed away,
All I have is memories...
A space in my heart I can't fill.
I love you Sis,
I miss you so much....still.

Sandra A. Koltes

Soldier

Are you filled with honor.
Filled with glory. As you tell your story.
Of what you saw in combat.
    How many people did you kill.
How many people did you drill.
    Are you proud of what you have done.
Did you spare anyone. Did they plead for mercy.
    Kill soldier kill. For your flag.
Kill soldier kill. The government wants you to.
Kill machine kill. It's what you're programmed to.
    Do you think God is with you. Do you think he damns you.
For killing another of his children. By the hundreds.
    Kill soldier kill. For pride. Kill soldier kill.
Cause it's justified. Kill fool kill.
That you don't understand.

Cecilia Fonseca

Untitled

February 14th, a red letter day
For Chocolates and Roses and Romance Per Se.
Oh will she say yes, or will she say nay.
I'm hoping we'll both dance the night away.
Oh let the stars, up above
Twinkle the eyes of the woman I love
And I'll kiss my sweet dove
And melt her resolve.
Bring her unto me
Under the old apple tree,
Where we'll snuggle and see
Us bonded until eternity.

Yes, we'll meld our ups and meld our downs,
Meld our smiles and meld our frowns,
Meld our laughter and our tears,
Meld our sodas and our beers,
Meld our collection of ships and clowns,
Meld our collection of musical sounds,
Meld our carousels and lighthouses too.

Gift wrapped in this ode just for you.

Frank A. Wennin

The Arrival Of Truth

To come so close
And watch the sands of time
Slip slowly through my fingers.

Oh-well, maybe next time!
It's just one more misconception
In this crazy life we live.

No more human crutches, on my own two feet
Finally with the strength to believe;
In a love that was meant to be;
In a love so true, the love of me.

No longer lost in this rat race called life;
No one can beat me,
No one can tame me;
The joke's on them this time...

Laughter splinters and shatters the silence of night;
Like a looking glass leaving shards that slit like razors.
It is I who laughs last, and I who laughs with restraint;
For it is I who has conquered, and I who will overcome.

Alia Boncheff

Prayer For Cody And Andrew

Oh God, how Sue loved you. Her faith was so strong.
I know she is smiling and hearing Your song...
My heart is rejoicing but tears fill my eyes,
knowing the doubt that the cancer supplies:

Why did You take her Lord?
Couldn't she stay?
I wish I could know but that isn't Your way.

You provide everything, filling each need.
You gave to us family and friends who will plead...
Thank You, Oh Jesus, for giving us Sue.
We need more than ever to bring her to You.

For now...she's an angel, brimming with joys!
and watching, from Heaven, her two little boys.

Father, I ask You to touch them with love.
Help them to understand angels above
are always protecting and showing the way...

Give them the faith of their Mother today.

Susan Kay

The Home Of His Heart

The snowflakes blew down in a blinding white wall,
the man in the wind had to stumble and fall,

His haven of safety was left far behind,
so much there outside that he just had to find.

The bitter sharp air often earned his respect,
the thickest of garment not sure to protect,

But the slicing of cold and the seeping of wet,
not misery enough to make him regret.

For the dazzling glitter of ice and of white,
are a reward all men should once hold in their sight,

And the days which are past without braving the cold,
are the deepest regret that a person can hold.

Still the time always comes when enough has been seen,
and more has been learned then the seeker could dream,

And the knowledge he gained as he roamed all about,
was the same as was taught him before he went out.

So the drift of his life leads him back to the start,
through the snow of his days to the home of his heart.

Kim Hulett

The Longing Spirit

As the sands trickle out to the sea
and the roar of the waves crash onto shore,
I feel your loving strength within me
and my spirit longs for you all the more.

Time and distance have dealt their fate
and taken from me my life.
It is the stinging salt air I hate,
and the wind cutting like a knife.

I see you in my mind and thoughts,
I am possessed by your piercing eyes.
There is forgiving for the times we fought.
There are no answers to the where's or why's.
Our time will come and we will be together to share,
for this cruel hand death has dealt will never seem fair.

Marguerite Thompson

Beckville

Come to Beckville to be renewed.
Renewed by the immigrant's hope for tomorrow,
Renewed by an unfailing determination to prevail,
Renewed by an uncommon faith in God.

An oasis of stone among fields of corn,
An oasis of hope against relentless odds.
Courage and determination, the immigrant's tools,
Faith, their shield from fear.

Johan pursued a dream of land and a better life.
Esther was a daughter of the immigrant's dream.
Hers started as a simple, Godly life,
With Joseph at her side, and Beckville at their center.

Disease and death took its toll,
First her Joseph, then two children.
Armed with three years of school, and faith in God,
She insured a college education for two remaining daughters.

Come to Beckville, but not as I did many years ago,
Recalling only a time that once was, and will never be again.
Rather, come to Beckville for that spirit,
That once was...but shall live...through us...forever.

Michael Herrick

As Long As You Hold Me

As long as you hold me
My heart shall not be broken,
Because through your arms, I feel your love,
Before a word is spoken.

As long as you hold me
I'll always feel a loving fate,
That one day you and I
Will be each other's eternal mate.

As long as you hold me
You'll always be my prized possession,
Because every time I think of you
My heart goes in your direction.

As long as you hold me
I'll feel the warmth that your love brings,
Although it's just a hug
It's more than just a little thing.

At first I questioned my feelings
But now it's plain to see,
That nothing bad shall come my way
As long as you hold me.

Martin Smith

Wisps

Drawing hard on my blackened pipe,
The cherry heat scorches my tongue.
I stare at the blank paper before me
But the words do not write themselves.
Leaning back in my padded chair,
Puffing forth a mouthful of smoke,
Long trails of white haze spiral heavenward,
Stinging my tearing eyes in passing.
A hoary ring rises like a halo above my head,
Widens as it passes the open window
and falters...
then fails...
as the gentlest breeze sweeps it away
Into nothingness.

Gordon Parish

Untitled

It is always so peaceful there.
The only place where I can collect my thoughts,
And find therapy for mind and body.
The sounds of happiness grace the surroundings.
This place is special.
It helps me come back to reality, and preserve my sanity.
But I am not there.
I was, but I left early.
With smiles on their faces,
They invited me to come back.
And I said I would.
I meant it, too.
But I didn't go:
Other things are more important now.
I want to go back,
For it soothes me so.
But I know I won't.

Green for green, know what I mean?
I thought so.

Perhaps one day we'll meet up again...There.
Kamal Soliman

Memoriam And Other Birds

A caramel sparrow soars in each of our four bedrooms.
A small peaceful man nailed to its back.
For years I haven't looked upon it.
Nervous eyes darting past.
These days are the hardest.
Last night, I looked upon Him.

She lay broken in a chair.

One clutched her hand,
another caressed thin Irish bone
I stroked her strawberry hair.
We clung to her.

Exhausted, breathing hurt.

A knit blanket fastened about her legs
hid calves cold and swollen blue.

I'll never forget Jack. Knelt whispering in her ear.
Letting her let go.
Shaking her head, she said she knew.

I saw him in the kitchen an hour before.
He and John had spoken. Walking out to the porch;
Desperate, he cried. God, desperate.
Audrey Glynn Coco

What Does This Child Know

What does this child know of my aching mind,
That as he views me with his troubled eyes,
I see my questions manifold, then more,
Reiterated in his simple signs and sighs,
His world to him is yet a great unknown,
To me is mine the same, but time has flown.

Further see I than he, yet still not far,
But what tomorrow brings today can't tell,
This moment is his fear, 'tis now and real,
And I, having greater fears, must his dispel.
So may it be, that I, as he,
Be quickly quiet, my mind set free.

Now in my giving him of me a part,
Sweet peace pervades my fearing heart
And from my heart comes love so calm
That words sound like an angel's charm.
There, he knows that all is well,
On sadder things he need not dwell.
Joann Schlaeppi

Forever

A winding staircase
The word "forever"
What promise do they hold?

To quietly meditate on them as a child
Always questioning
Why do I feel such peace in these words?

The lovely feeling of a free spirit
But unknown to me at the time
Just the realization that heaven would go on.

Forever, forever, forever.

To that young child of years ago
Was given the glimpse of eternity
To build upon today.

The awakening of my soul to this life
From a journey
Traveled in the eternity of yesterday.

Now I understand my soul was remembering
So that I could continue my growth
Into the eternity of today and tomorrow.
Janis R. Coan

Forgive And Forget

You ask to be forgiven, but not all is forgotten.
You want the best, though you expect the worst.
You cry for life out in the world, though you sit all curled up
with no one but pain, and fear as you search for a cure.

You're so angry at what has been laid out for
you, though what do you do? You worry so much
that you can't concentrate on the goods in life.
I please ones who don't even appreciate what I do...

I have a thrive of running till I just can't run anymore.
I want to take him with, but my worries stand in way of my words.
I can't recall my last escape, I try to live life to the fullest,
but I can't push too hard. I have dreams that don't leave me,
I just leave them. I think of drinking till I can't drink any more,
or even be able to see the door. I cry for laughter, I scream
for what was once seen. I lost hope in myself, I lost care in my heart,
and I am falling apart. He still stands with both hands open
willing to forgive, though my worry is that he'll forget.
Melissa A. Erwin

Light Is Life

A simple man, dressed in rags,
Loaded down with the burdens of the world.
Seeks to find refuge in the night.

A stream of light, pale and thin, shines down beside him.
He reaches out to touch it
With a shaking hand of fright.

A whisper in the wind says,
"Don't be afraid, I'm here only to bring you truth."
He whispered back and said,
"I'm living a lie. To me you must show proof."

Then the light grew bigger,
And his rags fell away to the ground.
His burden was lifted as he looked all around.

He soaked in the light, as the fear went away.
The night that he had lived in,
Had now become day.

Overwhelmed with the meaning so obviously clear;
He barely felt the weight of his sword,
When he lifted it up in the praises of truth.
In the worship fear of the Almighty Lord.
Virginia Marrie

In The Jaws Of The Lioness

Unsheathed and sharpened, her lye-laced words
Relentlessly chewed; Grinding, Devouring
The Predator relishing — her reflection
In a spreading pool of destruction.

The silenced screams of Bewilderment,
A tribute to each puncture.
The long, low moaning of Betrayal,
Deliciously musical — in its turn of phrase;
Lasciviously lyrical — the tearing
Of fleshy, unsuspecting innocence:
Crescendo-decrescendo-Crescendo,
With each twisted swing of her neck.

From the jaws of the lioness, I hung
Lame; Anesthetized
Dripping with bloodied, venomous lies.
Shrapnel-laden, dis-Heart-ened shreds;
Chains at my ankles — pulling...
I was soon submerged; Drowning,
Choking on the Vomit
Of my Disbelief.

M. E. Dustman

Massaged By Angels

As I closed my eyes to sleep last night
I began to hear music: So beautiful,
Like nothing I'd ever heard: A great melody,
Never repeating.

As I drifted further to sleep
I began to see these colors:
Some I'd seen before, some I could never imagine

Then a feeling began to spread over me
My body relaxed, all my muscles let go:
Such an incredible, soothing feeling,
Hundreds of hands massaging, but never touching

I felt a great peace: with everyone and everything,
I awakened a new man: A peaceful man
Full of love, love for the world;
A love for Life.

Daniel Jason Williams

The Terminal Disease

There is no cure but help me, doctor, please.
We've nothing to lose though little to gain,
for life is but a terminal disease.

And I, confused by these societies
have searched to find a simple way — in vain.
There is no cure but help me, doctor, please.

The games of life cause such anxieties
and dreams, it seems, are passing by too fast,
for life is but a terminal disease.

We all must face some cold realities,
times and places soon forever past.
There is no cure but help me, doctor, please.

They are mere trivialities,
the passing joys, the things that cannot last,
for life is but a terminal disease.

These common symptoms we call memories
distress me when instead should sooth the pain.
There is no cure but help me, doctor, please,
for life is but a terminal disease.

Nike DiMattia

Lifeless

Quietly...
There's still a time when I bleed.

Cannot express the questions that are written on my face.
With the answers in the distance, I'm feeling out of place.

And in time I search for nothing.
Without it I don't exist.
I'm sad sometimes when I smile.
Lifeless.

Memories, like everything, in time all soon will fade.
Just as winter's song is silenced by springtime serenade.
My words remain suspended.
Entombed within the air.
As I'm followed by my anguish and led by sweet despair.

Letting go, I stare at the sun and watch it disappear.
I'm hypnotized by the darkness, with light no longer near.
Slowly I rise above it, my world and distress.
Serene, I'm finally at peace with me.
Lifeless...

Dale Kiesling

Let There Be Light

The first particle was yet to burn
In the first morning's sun,
Where darkness ruled the timeless ocean
of uncreated space.
Then came the blast that filled the void
With light shattering, God reflecting,
Time spinning primal force,
That tipped the hourglass of time.
Particles burned in the gaseous orbs
Where the first dawn exhaled the solar winds
Of the first light. Imprinting nascent worlds
In the baptismal font of a universe.
No living ear was pricked
In the ethereal gas.
The sound went unperceived
That fueled the shapeless mass.
Chaos tremble in the dead-dark realms
As light's first sound approached,
And color burst in hymns of silent prayer,
While the wavelength of Creation sweeps across the endless dark.

Ramon Jusino Jr.

Untitled

A loving tribute to my grandfather
I am filled with rage
For now he is just a memory
A shadow
Dead in this world and the life I once knew
That dream is now gone
As is he
He was taken from me, plucked like a feather from a chicken
Cursing the God that took him
Asking why
Saying it's not fair
Was it supposed to be fair?
I don't think I can handle this
My outcome will not be tears
For I will be
Exactly what this is for me-
A nightmare

Matthew Blanock

Every Day Angel

You took my hand and led me down the lonely angels road.
A place I'd never seen, and no one had ever told.
And when I look deep into your fairy tale eyes,
I can see your heart and your soul but did not realize
That what I could not see and what you did not know
Is just how tough love can be when one's heart is cold.
But as I see you skating across the ice caps of my mind
I run the routes of Hercules remembering how hard I've tried.

And if you'd take a few more steps down this broken road
I would meet you in the midst of all the stories that I've told.
Just to hear your voice, narrating in my mind.
And to see that fork ahead to which I've always been so blind.
Because you see, if there is this thing that they call love,
Then your eyes would be the ones to lead me to the place that
    I dream of.

Scott Corthell

Have The Wind Blow

Let it be known across the land
That you have asked for my hand,
And now to me you are fiance,
Seems quite an elegant word to say.
And the look in your eyes that night
Told me for sure my choice was right.
Eyes filled with happiness well beyond measure,
Reflecting the trust and commitment I treasure.
They spoke of years and years in love,
And silly disagreements we would rise above.
Together our strengths will multiply,
And troubles and sorrows will pass us by.
So have the wind blow and blow,
Even still my joy will show.
Let the clouds fill the sky,
'Cause even rain won't make me cry.
Take away what you will,
And I will love you still.
Let the years cause me to age,
For with love, time is no cage.

Victoria Dove

Narcissism

To my beautiful sleeping girlfriend with soft breasts;
I caress your shoulder,
engrossed in tactility,
absorbed in endearment,
enamored of affection,
and intoxicated with adoration.
I strive to posses this one moment
like you possess my being.

Lisa Steffes

August

August 5th is my special day,
And for the rest of my life it will stay.
On this day is a special thought,
For this is when my gifts are brought.

August is a time for fun,
In this month there's lots of sun.
I go swimming in the day,
And have many hours out at play.

August days are bright and sunny,
That's when the bees make their honey.
In the night it is warm,
And then the stars come out to form.

August days are free from school,
Another month and it gets cool.

Angela Thiele

Is It Safe?

Insecurity happens to you and me but why?
Because of some kind of scheme or lie?
Yeah, because trust is a must — the way of today,
but it doesn't matter, just ascend the ladder

The ladder of life, filled with strife,
Climbing each rung is another song sung
but you can't undo what's been done.
Look forward, not back, because back is an attack.

An attack on your heart, the most important part
of your past seems like it will always last.
People will come and go but the only way to know
the real from the fake is to take

One day at a time is what I've learned, but,
even at this pace it's a race to save face.
Look out for yourself because who else will?
Another fact of life I've instilled.

Hurting from someone else can and will inflict
insecurity in you and me, but see
these attacks only pack more pain in your brain
so let go and let yourself know...and grow.

David Robert Beers Jr.

Sports

Sports of display and sports of potential,
Spirit wild to hit the ball!
Spirit wild to dunk the ball!
Spirit wild to run a goal!
And if you don't succeed,
It really doesn't matter.
For excitement or amusement is the aim of any game.

Raul Acosta

Attuned

Play my favorite...sing for me
Like Astaire on ivory,
    Stepping into my heart.
Your soul echoing from each key.

No notes to guide you.
Racing...staggering on the edge
Pausing for a rest from the hectic beat.

Relentless duets of honky tonk and
    ice cube staccatos.
Our bond...a syncopated rhythm.
Your melodies reverberate through each
measure of my life.

My heart requests da capo, da capo, da capo.
The silence whispers al fine.

Cheryl Lee Hettinger

Whither The Rain Forests Of The Earth?

In the beautiful rain forests,
where all the creatures live,
there was a disturbance in the leaves
of the great koapok tree;
Birds and mammals smell the fire
of the great koapok tree;
Butterflies fly threw the fire,
where they all burn in death,
and the great koapok tree;
Do people care? Do you care?
This is a question nobody will ask nor answer,
Alas, the rain forests of our earth!

Lanka S. Constance DeSilva

Emotions Of An ER Resident

Lonely, alone, fearful, emptiness
the sound of nothing echoing in his mind.
A day's toil sapping strength for the night,
his mind now effortlessly fatigued.

It starts with a piercing ring,
the body groans with unwillingness.
Irritated for unknown reasons,
"Did I choose this nightmare?"

Then it's over, as if it never happened,
one more portal of energy drained.
Trying hard to remember why,
why was this hell so necessary?

From God it comes so quickly,
always at the right moment.
Rescuing from the brink of despair,
for the doctor, it's a smile from his patient.

Timothy Jerald Felton

A Gift Of Love

Today you've earned your wings my love,
to fly about and see,
all the wonderful things out there,
to learn, to adventure and to be...

Today, I'm cutting the apron strings,
that are bound close to my heart,
even though I'm "cutting you free"
I know in spirit, we'll never be apart.

I'm so very proud of the man you've become,
you've really earned your space,
just take it easy, one day at a time,
don't make life one big race.

I must tell you though, I've saved a piece,
for you see, your strings don't quite match,
just in case there comes a time,
you need to take a latch.

And so my little butterfly,
today's your special day,
enjoy it to the fullest,
do with it as you may.

Vicki Holt

My Children

Babies, children, kids. Mine, yet not mine, borrowed from God.
Mine to feed, bathe, diaper and walk the floor with.
Mine to play with and laugh at.
Mine to cry with and pray over.
Mine to nurture and love.

Teenagers, young people, almost adults but not quite.
Mine, yet not mine, borrowed from God.
Mine to teach, as well as learn from.
Mine to agonize over and spend much time in prayer over.
Mine to feel pride and joy in, mine to love even when it hurts.

Adults, grown ups, on their own, still my children.
Mine, yet not mine, borrowed from God
Mine when they have problems and only I can help.
Mine when they are happy and need to share their joy.
Mine when they are sad and need someone to cry with.

My children, mine, and yet not mine, borrowed from God.
I pray that I was a good steward,
Faithfully caring for those precious jewels.
Did I cry, laugh, teach and pray enough? Did I love enough?
My children...mine, yet not mine...borrowed from God.

Frances Adkins

Untitled

The smell of the crushed green grass
Under my body in the warm sun
Brought titillating actions to my nostrils.

The leaves overhead attempted tirelessly
To block the sunlight
From the carpet of green below.

As a ray of light broke through
And focused on a single leaf,
It began to shimmer and sway
In the bright light and cool breeze.

The movements of the leaf gently
Brushed my eyelids closed,
But this failed to block out the similar
Movements of the belly dancer
In the focused spotlight on the dance floor.

As my eyelids opened,
The ray of sunlight disappeared
The leaf was motionless, but in my mind
The petite belly dancer danced on.

Fred Payne

Dimension Of Feeling

Our relationship has inspired a new and
exciting dimension of feeling
Together there is heartfelt strength that
keeps us reeling

The nature of the love we share is as inevitable
as it is deep and sometimes obsessive
Recasting our lives in a moment of truth with a
breadth of yearning others might find possessive

For our love transcends any and all
relationship gone before
Inspiring both of us to conquer all
adversity with our very core

There is an overpowering impression that we
were created with a special love
Achieving a spiritual partnership that contains
a "magic" sent from above

Linda M. Creech

Beaten And Broken Woman

A woman is like a flower.
She starts from a seed in her mother's womb
Then she is born into a world that is very cold.

She grow up to be a teenager, her body goes through
changes and before she knows she is a woman.

Then a man comes into her life, and things start to change
then marriage, then before she knows children are
coming. She faces so many things in her life.

She wonders what will tomorrow bring.
She gives her life to her family.
She tries to make the best of bad times
she puts her life on hold for her family.

But sometimes she feels as if what she does doesn't matter
her voice is not important.
Only what she can offer and sometimes, that's not important.
She wonders, why am I here.
She feels as though she has been battered and beaten down.
Though she has not been hit as some.
But she feels as though she has been in a fight.
She tired and in despair, but she won't give up the fight.

Cynthia Dyanne Alexander

Forever

Him, it is always him.
In front of me like some great mirage,
but he is real, and in my dreams,
day and night.
His presence lingers long after he is gone,
like the scent of fresh roses on a warm, summers day.
He makes me feel new, not old and abused.
and when I smile, it is for his eyes to see,
and to receive his smile in return,
a smile like sunshine, on the first day of spring,
beautiful and glorious in its own special way.
His talent inspires me, and to me, his words are everything.
I cling to them, as if I am afraid of falling,
but then I realize that I have already fallen,
into a pit which bears his name, one that I cannot escape.
I wonder if I ever want to be free,
deep inside me, I feel, that the answer is no.

Jennifer Mary Gallagher

Life

To My Dear Parents

Someday, somewhere, our dreams, images,
and wishes will all come true.

A girl's Prince Charming will sweep her off
her feet and a boy's tough father will say that
he loves him, taking his last breath.

How sad and cruel the world may seem, but
that's the way it is. We are like the gentle flower
that we see every day; we blossom and we wilt.

If only life, the precious gift that God gave us,
would last forever. If only we could have
another chance. But we can't.

We must love, cry, worry, and be frightened in
our time here. We must use our time on this
planet wisely because that's the way it is...
That's life...

Haseena Mohabbat

An Easter Poem

For His death I know I'm to blame
And my heart was torn when he exclaimed,
Father why have thou forsaken me
The night he died on Calvary's tree.
I've learned that life can seem unfair.
But to his my trials will never compare.
He left his home in heaven on high
And left his world with a solemn cry;
Father forgive them, they know not what they do.
This wasn't just for me it was also for you.
So when things become tough and hard to understand
Remember Jesus was the one with nails in his hands.

Erika Elizabeth Moore

Come - They Will

The sun dips low
beneath the clouds,
The sky grows dark
only to summon deep, dead crowds.
The living dead-for they will fight—
Let one and all know its Halloween Night!

Heidi Tune

Riddles?

If Pilate placed Jesus upon
the Cross and Constantine
sanctioned the Holy Body of
the Church, then what is that?

If stars adorn his shoulders
and his sword covered with pearls, is he still not a murderer?

In the capital city, the jail sits between Freemen's
hospital and a 19th century
graveyard; is it then not a morgue?

Two-million years ago, stone
tools were carved, how did the people's genes split in two?
Is Darwinism the reverse of true?

Augustine who? Are three-fifths a whole?
Where are the Moors? Can the Universities of Timbuktu
compare to Oxford? Was Xavier a fool?

And, is the act of naming juxtaposed to economics?
Or the algebra of our skins the effect of persecution?
Do you believe the sages? Then who are "We" and "Us"?

There is a loaf of bread to share, must we compete?
Who do we have to thank, save Isabella and Ferdinan?

Kirk K. Gillums

Peace

The voice of peace calls out to me.
The tongue of a snake shows the evil in me.
Arms of peace wrap around me like a thick wool blanket.
Eyes of God lay upon me and guide me
Heart of the homeless give me strength to help me go on.
The mouth of heaven give me light, tell me I am safe.
Knees of love lay before me, give me a heart, a heart of gold.
The memory of my ancestors guide me through the night.
The mind of a dragon says I'm wrong.
The brain of a wolf says I'm right.
The breath of a storm lays in the air, I know it's going to rain.
The elbows of Goliath hit the earth.
The hearing of Goliath's fall dies in the distance.
The feet of many horses hit the earth like thunder.
Ears of heaven listen to my every move.
Hands of God lay on my shoulders.
The shoulders of God slump for I lay down and die.
Mind of my heart, mind of my soul, send me to heaven,
    for my heart is of gold.

Krystyna Marie Hale

A Robyn's Last Flight

It's 12:00 midnight, here's to romance
Wake up, my little Robyn, it's time to dance
Think of the hikes in the woods and the
    cool dips in the lake
    yet it wasn't enough, and now it's too late
I'd rule like a king with you by my throne
Come on, Milady, don't leave me alone
I'll make good on that promise
    A shiny Palace in France
Wake up, Madame, it's time for a dance
Remember last summer, when I baked you
    an apple pie?
It was your birthday, baby,
Don't make me cry
If loneliness is a prison
    You'll be accused of that crime
    So I pass you your sentence
A dance one more time

Rodney Richard Chin

Papa's Chair

Papa's chair
So big
But yet as soft as a baby's bed
As warm as a big blanket wrapped around me.
Its smell
Is as if he was
Sitting right beside me.
When I sit
In
Papa's chair
I feel as if he was not dead
But right here
Next to
Me.

Jesse Pita

Pax Vobiscum, Joseph

King of Raptors! Thunderbird!
Servitor of the Sun!
Delicate, broken eagle.

Succumbed to human failings,
Yet your spirit soars free,
Dancing among the clouds.

Motionless, wide-open wings,
Floating, soaring, gliding on thermals.
Hanging, effortlessly aloft.

Spectacular, heaven-kissed acrobatics,
Performed with the purest joy,
Serene in your majestic grandeur,

While I watch from below,
Marveling at your eloquent performance,
Grateful for your nearness.

Kathleen A. Grassel

Grandma's Plea

If I was a parent, and my child was two;
I'd feel frustration, wondering "What shall I do?

This child of mine, he's a problem, you see —
If you were in my shoes, you'd agree."

Then my mind would clear, I'd look again
And realize what a fool I'd been.

I'd take the child and hold him tight,
Tell him of love, caring, truth and light.

I'd laugh and joke, together we'd enjoy life.
I'd protect him for now from worldly strife.

I'd walk with him, talk to him, show him and teach.
So when the need arises, to me he'll reach.

But my hands are tied, my chance gone by.
For I am the Grandma. I must watch and cry -

Denise C. Huntsman

Winter Season

Winter season, so snowy white and cold,
Winter season, ever so beautiful and bold.
Winter season, makes the land of white,
Winter season, the time when Jack Frost bites.
Winter season, the time for cookie bakes,
Winter season, the time for snowflakes.
Winter season, not a time to play ball,
Winter season, the best time of all.

Jeremy Kisloski

Untitled

Living in silence
is like being trapped
in a tomb with no light
no hope of ever escaping
smelling and breathing stale musty air
that will soon run out
stagnant wisps of cobwebs
growing somehow larger without any presence of life
countless hours of staring endlessly, aimlessly
at walls that will not move
yet they weep silent streams of moisture
like the soft quiet tears on a porcelain face

Otera S. Nash

Little Girl's Face

See the little girl peeking through the window
See the tear streaks on her face.
When will my daddy come
When will he wipe away my tears.

See the little girl peeking through the window
See her mommy crying in the other room.
Daddy went away without a word
When will he wipe my tears away.

See the little girl peeking through the window
See the smile upon her face.
Here comes my daddy now
to wipe away our tears.

Stephanie D. Small

My Wish For You

May your years together be happy
May your years together be bright.
Let all of your dreams come true
And your life together be right.
Look to the future and forget the past.
May your hopes and dreams come true at last.
Love one another with all your might
Cling to your marriage, and for it fight.
Cling to each other for love and support
For life by yourself is way too short.
Sometimes your troubles will boggle your mind
If this happens, ask for help from the divine.
Set your priorities right from the start
That all things you do, come right from the heart.
Love is the key to a happy life.
May God keep you from all of life's strife.

Mavis Jones

Believe

If I run, will you follow?
For a dream will you dance?
Would you scale the wired wall,
just to catch me?

'Cause I'll run for the hero
In hopes of a fighter
Believing fate to catch me from this wall
For a true love must exist, after all

When mistakes create new heartbeats,
from their fall

Destiny plans life for a reason
Hope is the dreamer, you always knew
Faith is the knowing, to all our questions
will come the answers
Wisdom's the heart that believes dreams true

Joelina Davies

Untitled

Whatever happened to life's little pleasures
Whatever happened to life's little treasures
A child's infectious laughter as she plays a game
Of jump rope or leapfrog, it's really a shame.
The Tooth Fairy and Santa, they're dreams of the past
Innocence is gone, they grow up so fast
Cowboys and baseball take a back seat
When license and wheels give access to the street
Teens trade in their toys for their guns and their dope
In fear of the gangs, their life without hope
Becoming parents themselves at too young an age
Filling young hearts and minds with destructible rage
Blaming the system feeling life is unjust
Insecurity their blanket covering a bed of mistrust
Most remember their childhood with no pleasure at all
For most of their treasures came from the mall
They've never had things that money can't buy
Love, friends, and family until the day that they die
The world needs some answers for the generation to come
For peace, happiness and prosperity wasn't meant just for some

Bonnie K. Stephens

Nature

You could be as pretty as a magnolia blossom,
or, as shapely as a maple leaf!
Perhaps sweet as a rose petal,
or, bright as a forsythia bloom.
No matter what, sooner or later,
The wind will sweep you away!

You could be a thorn on a rose bush,
or, simply a "weeping-willow!"
Maybe, a piece of hated crabgrass,
or, a smelly scallion sprout.
Sooner, or later you will lose your roots,
and, disappear into the ground!

Perhaps you could be a mocking bird singing in the tree
or, a robin searching for his food!
A squirrel searching for acorns
and, yes a man struggling to exist!
Soon, all will fail, and go into dust!

However, God, in his omnipotent wisdom,
has a strong vacuum sweeper, and
will draw all up into eternity with Him.

Louis Garbowski

Geezer DeJure

A geezer is a chap that's dwelt long upon the earth,
Tripped the light not so fantastic,
Found the healing property of mirth;
Demands not so much to be amused
As to retain self-worth.
Convictions tested over time
Are spoken loud, with force;
An unapologetic rhapsody. Mediocrity is worse.
Not here to steer or guide you,
Yet unwilling to relax
Unless glaring irregularities
Are taken hard, to task.
Genders don't apply to this description
It's not based in Venus or on Mars
The sole purpose for its being
Is to focus on the stars...
For if life can count for anything
A dream's the thing to teach;
Else why ever should a man's
Grasp outstretch his reach?

Cherie M. Dunn

March

The chance of rain today is of portent
But most of winter's frigid blasts are spent
The pines and lawn provide foreground of green
Dispersed about, the fringes set the scene.

Tree trunks black, with few stragglers gray
Looking skyward, gray-white glares the day
But browns prevail throughout this pre-spring spread
Nothing vivid, nothing rich or red.

In few short days, St. Pat's Day arrives
With the season plant and man re-thrives.
The dead have died and dying is of sorrow
Yet, prevailing, we must hail tomorrow.

Take up the hoe, the rake, the trowel, the spade
Extend the fragile verve of which we're made.
Take the joys and sets that living offers
Partake of March and life and nature's coffers.

Paul B. Blizzard

A Child's Prayer For Life

Dear sweet Lord, I pray
That you will give me another day,
Free of sorrow and free of pain
To see the sun rise again,
To see the world in all its beauty.
To be able to run and play,
To remember the memory of today.

So dear Lord, if you will,
Give me the strength of body,
The strength of mind,
To overcome their affiliation of mine,
To have love in my heart for those who care,
But most of all, for you dear Lord.

Show me the mercy of your love,
For I pray with all my heart
Dear sweet Lord,
Please give me another day.

K. L. Bindhamer

A Chance For Me

In the tiniest of nature's gifts
A willing soul will find
The spark of hope needed
To rekindle its spirit.

A searching soul is nurtured
Through all creations it is allowed to absorb.
It exists unselfishly and unconditionally
To unleash the passions within our hearts.

This treasured gift enables us to believe,
To do, to enjoy, to imagine,
And to become all our Creator
Intended us to be.

Mary Ann Gurney

He Is

He is without a doubt my teacher and my friend.
That special and only someone, who will be with me in the end.
He is my motivation for everything that I do.
Things just get so much clearer; and this I say is true.
The cares of this world seem so trifling to me.
He is the only one who can truly see.
Drugs on every corner; thieves on many streets.
If there's safety that you need he is the one to seek.
All our lives we search for something to set us free.
He is and always will be that precious one for me.

Douglas B. Baldwin

If You, If I

If I were the door
to all your hopes and dreams,
would I open easily,
and be all that I seemed?
 If you were the doorway
surrounding all I am,
would you be held fast in place
to catch me if I slammed?
 And oh what use, this thought of mine;
one never built before?
As we find the frame's no good
unless it has the door
 And if the door lay prone, so flat,
no element can it tame
As we find the door's no good
unless it has the frame

Tim Bragg

Do You Know My Friend?

As you walk about our city,
On this bright and cheerful day.
Quoting scriptures of Salvation -
And a new world on the way.

Do you really know my Jesus?
Is He standing at your side?
Is He speaking through your lips
with His spirit as your guide?
Do you always feel His presence
as you go from day to day?
And do you always thank Him
for His blessings along the way?

It's our duty here as Christians
to spread the gospel far and wide.
Seeking souls to Jesus - to wait His
coming in the sky.
But let's be careful as we labor that our work is not in vain.
For we'll only be rewarded for the souls we've won for Him.

Do you really know my Jesus as a Savior, friend and guide?
If you do, you'll be rewarded with a mansion in the sky.

Anna Rhodus

Candle Glowing

 We lit a candle when she was one
To celebrate her first year with every one
 She saw the candles on the cake
So then and there she set a date

 Now every year with candles glowing
It takes more wind and a lot of blowing
 Now she uses candles for everything
To begin her day and light to bring

 She even used candles to light up her bath
With candles a-floating on little rafts
 We can't end this ditty without saying it
But for safety's sake I think she should quit

John J. Weaver

Imitations

Imitations make your feet feel fine
Imitations cost $1.99
They come in all different shapes and sizes
If you buy 'em at Payless you get all sorts of prizes
Power Ranger, Lion King, and Sega Sports
I guess those shoes are just for dorks
If you don't have money I guess you're out of luck
You must be dumb if you can't afford a buck.

Brandon Ballard

Fall

Ah, you have come
Fall,
Nymph of frost,
To court the maples of the wooded grove.

See, how they all
Tremble
At your approach
And leave a scarlet path for you to tread.

Twirl, swish your skirts,
Dance,
Through forest lanes.
Leave your familiar patterns etched on green.

Come, in your stealth.
Kiss
the outstretched hands
Of those who wait to fling their gold on you.

Clasp, in fond embrace.
Infold
With frigid arms
Till each reluctant prince shall sigh and yield.

Sally Streib

My Inspiration

You are my inspiration,
the light,
my restoration.
Whom I preciously admire.
When I am down,
I take a trip to you,
and everything is alright.
When I am in despair,
I take a trip to you,
and all my hopes are regained.
Your words are strong yet soft,
and a melody to my ears.
You inspire me to do my best.
For when I see you,
I feel the need to.
Yes, you are my soul satisfying supply of inspiration!

Yvette Williams

My Dear Grandson

When cats and dogs and snakes are nice,
And mother hates your lost pet mice;
When messy rooms are meant to stay,
And life is best when you're at play.

When dirt was fun to throw and wear,
And normal was much tousled hair;
When your folks are old at thirty five,
It's great to know that you're alive!

Filled with all the future hopes,
And never yet been on the ropes;
Us grand folks bathe in all such thoughts,
Because these things you have taught.

That hope is found in a little guy,
Since you are not afraid to try!
That play is an important things,
And comes from hearts that like to sing.

That wonderful children are still in the crowd,
For which us old folks are really proud;
But probably best and really true,
You help me remember that, once, I was just like you.

Dean C. Nelsen

Scouting For A Home

Christian friends, I'm looking for a home!
Make me feel like I belong.

I need to get in touch with the Lord
so, take me in and judge me from my heart.
that's where it should start.

Forget about the way that I look or dress,
God knows my life is a mess.

Just give me a minute to say "I've found
a home, before my last breath is gone."

Remember to take a look at yourselves,
I'm sure there are skeletons on your shelves.

Let's put the foolishness behind,
then you can welcome me with open minds.

Erasala B. Cody

God, Family, and Friends

When our world seems to be just falling apart,
And the sun refuses to shine.
When the clouds of sorrow hang heavy above,
And we wish we could turn back the time.

When each day seems longer and full of hurt,
And the road seems never to end.
These are the times when it means the most,
To have God and family and friends.

I may never be rich with wealth untold,
Nor a king with a silver crown.
I may never be a traveler to place afar,
Or write music with a golden sound.

These things mean little to a man who's down,
And whose heart is on the mend.
But he has the cure within reach of his hands,
With his God and family and friends.

Lee Wiley Burch

Willow

Six feet under...sea level.
Named for its bent-over trees,
    stooped men and women of nature,
    yielding to time,
        surrendering to gravity.

Corner street lamps
    question their existence.

Telephone poles,
    those umbilical chords of communication,
        atheistic crosses apologizing for nothing.

Creaking cries of neglect heard from houses,
    wailing nails nearing exhaustion.

Suffocating humidity,
    weighing upon its residents,

Sweat travelling like wax,
    a slow bullet.

Shadows jumping from one to another,
    a hopscotch for life or death.

The latest census says that the population of Willow is declining.

Maria Viera-Williams

Encounter

I am walking
A turbulent maelstrom of responsibilities races about my brain
Never ceasing

Suddenly, I glimpse a familiar face in the crowd
I cannot speak
The silence renders no mercy
I am filled with an emotional rush from head to toe
'Tis he

Souls intertwined, bodies torn apart
Desperate eyes meet
Sweet words never spoken
Star-crossed lips that never have touched

Unknowingly he's grasped me
I am left in pieces
Scattered askew

The familiar face is gone
I am alone
The whirlwind returns
I am longing, but I go on.

Jamie McCarthy

Reality And Dreams

I had a dream,
A perfect dream.
Yet, not so perfect it would seem.
You lean on me, I'll lean on you.
That's the way it should be.
Friends forever long together.
That's the way it should be.
Reality strikes.
It leaves us bare of the things we've come to care.
Friends forever long together.
Torn apart at the heart.
Hatred blazes through the air.
So much so we hardly dare to do the things of yesteryear.
I had a dream, a perfect dream.
Yet, not so perfect it would seem.

Joy Bennett

Death Arriving

Why have foolish thoughts of things that will not pass?
My life and love are yours until death.
Surround yourself in waves of warmth.
Let your fears float away to a world that does not exist.
Take today and accept I am yours.
Will I ever leave you, my love?
No, not until death.

Accept what is given without wondering.
Accept today and the tomorrow promised to you.
Awake each morning knowing my love is with you.
Dream each night knowing my love will not end.
It circles you like a gentle sea breeze.
Will I ever leave you, my love?
No, not until death.

Grasp the feeling of strength and don't let go.
Hold the promise this love will last.
Question not the love that has been given.
And grieve not when I leave.
Will I ever leave you, my love?
No, not even in death.

Margaret Flaherty-Cruz

Go Home

I wish that I could just go home
I want to meet, Sitting Bull and Geronimo
I wish I could go home
In this place, at this time I'm all alone
I wish I could go home
I wish the white man had not come
I wish I could go home
I have been led astray when told I am home
I wish I could go home
I want to get the hell away from here.

Becky Peeso

What Is A Mother's Love?

It has no price
It earns no glory
It can't be found in a story
It can't be measured
It can be treasured
It's a feeling deep within your soul
You can't find it, borrow it, steal it
It's always there
It can be found in a prayer
It comes without you asking
It needs no reasons to be given
It comes when you least expect it
It is a blessing, a gift, a caring, a word, a look
It's what I give to all my children
Not Just My Own
The child down the street
The child who I meet
The child I will never know
For one day that child might be my own

Lillian O'Neal

Astor Place

Subject oneself to vermiculation of The Big Apple.
Reject the rattled plea of charity.
Inject the orb that frees the three tined gate
And wait.
Conject the crush of a thousand crackers
Under the rolling pin
Of the hurtling express.
And,
Project abject indifference to the
Pied ingredients of the city's life.

Jane E. Ross

The Golden Years

Fifty golden grains of sand
Have flowed through the hour glass of life
Each one has its memories
Some were serious, some were glad
Others were happy, while some were sad
What the other grains will bring you
As they slip through the hour glass of life
My they bring you more happiness than sorrow
More laughter than tears
May they truly bring you the golden years.

Paul J. Raverty

For Denise

From my window, my view
is a forest of green morning flowers all covered with dew
Blossoms abound colored golden and lovely as your hair
My thoughts are of love and you and knowing you'll always be there

Ron Artale

A Man Loved By All

Angels watching down on you
Knowing now, when and what to do
Patiently waiting, as loved ones watch on
Calling to you, as they're singing your song

The chosen one's coming
To give you relief
You take one look back
You see so much grief

Many who love you
Honest, true, friends who care
You touched so many hearts
Giving all much to share

True, honest, and giving
A real man of your word
We listened, we learned things
All of your words heard

A man of much wisdom
Who went far in life
One woman, loved by him
Betty Sue, his beloved wife

Terri J. Bilderback

Childhood Unbound

I want to see like a child again,
Instilled with the wonder the world stole,
No longer burdened by an empty heart and soul,
Awed by the fact that I'm once again whole.

I want to be like a child again,
Innocent, without doubt, fully trusting,
Today I may feel I'm less than nothing,
But as a child I'm much more than something.

I want to speak like a child again,
Ignorant of the pain that knowledge reveals,
Without my cynic's tongue or flawed ideals,
Only words of beauty and a love that heals.

I want to feel like a child again,
Invincible and immortal, no longer dead,
Free from the worries that fill me with dread,
Newborn, with my whole life ahead.

And I want to die as a child,
Not mourning the bridges I've never crossed,
Always ready to pay life's high cost,
But unwilling to consider my childhood lost.

Paul Demopoulos

That's What Friends Are For

If you are feeling low,
Just let someone special like a best friend know.
If someone is blue and you really care,
Just let them know that you are there.
A friend is someone who makes sure that you're okay,
Someone who will be there until you pass away.
So the next time feel unwanted or unloved,
Tell them and you'll know who your friend is thinking of.

Ashley Christopher

Diamonds And Pearls

Diamonds and Pearls shine like the moon on a clear cool night.
Diamonds and Pearls can complement that silk dress just right.
Diamonds and Pearls drive some people to fight.
Diamonds and Pearls may or may not bring joy to everyone's life.
But Diamonds and Pearls added to almost anything makes it look
out of sight.

Gerald Lawson

Contact In America

From July '94 to July '96,
Harold J. Nicholson gave Russia some tips.
About new CIA agents, he gave information,
To Russia, a U.S. enemy nation.

In Europe and Asia, overseas
Nicholson seemed to do as he pleased.
He gave secrets away,
That will haunt new agents day after day.

What he wanted was money,
But this wasn't funny.
He sold secret into,
To please his honey.

He had secret conversations,
With people from other nations.
And now he's in fail,
Without any bail.

While he's in jail,
Who knows what he'll do.
He might be on the Internet,
Looking for you!

Emily Finnegan

The Circle

The young girl wears the lines upon her face,
Like a trophy to be displayed.
She's seen the world come and go.
Round and round,
Sometimes turning life upside down.

She's seen the children go from happy and smiling,
To sad, old, and dying.
What used to be,
Almost seems that it never was.
Just an illusion of the heart.
And she's seen the world come and go.
Round and round,
Always turning life upside down.

She runs her fingers across the lines of the past.
Across the pain and gladness.
The years of struggle roll down her cheek.
She turns out the light.
And still the world goes,
Round and round.
Forever turning upside down.

Cynthia L. Fargo

Summer's Trail

During the Summer when I was young,
I woke up one morning and saw the sun,
I laid in the grass and drifted away,
To a different place,
A different day.

People's deep happiness shining so strong,
Their minds so open, they knew no wrong.

That world is still there,
It must be found.
A key so special,
I dropped on the ground.
A lock so tight,
It hides the day past.
Walking the trail
I found my aged brass.

It's in the lock, without hesitation
I open the doors to my Imagination.

Adam Murphy

Time Tock

While waiting for the bread to toast
What I'd like to do the most
is to talk with you, for

Time melts like butter on a hot, hot day
the more we manipulate and square it away
the more it squishes in the dish

Time flying is like butter in the microwave
each bubbling yellow lava wave
a boundless bundle of molecular life

Time standing still is like a frozen stick of butter
perfect in appearance but full of utter
unspreadableness

For time which does not flow is unusable time

Time is ticking as we are talking,
not sticking but quietly stalking...

So now that I can smell burnt toast
what I'd like to do the most
is with our coffee cups make a toast to life, for
I've enjoyed this time - enjoyed you;
I'll just butter the next slice.

Bonnie Brawand Lafitte

Too Soon To Tell

Oh! How I wonder about my little girls...
When they grow up, I hope they do well!
I want the very best for them now and always
For now, they're young and it is too soon to tell!

Will they go to college, or a trade school perhaps?
Will I have a "son" and grandchildren?
I want the very best for them now and always
For now, they're young and it is too soon to tell!

Will they move far away or live close to home?
Will they still come to me for advice?
I want the very best for them now and always
For now, they're young and it is too soon to tell!

Have I taught them that they are precious to God?
Do they really know that I'll love them no matter what?
I want the very best for them now and always
For now, they're young and it is too soon to tell!

Oh! How I wonder about my little girls...
When they grow up, I hope they do well!
I want the very best for them now and always
For now, they're young and it is too soon to tell!

Lucinda J. Haldeman

The Portrait

She sits in the chair by the window,
Sun glistening on her silver hair,
Reminiscing of times gone by,
Dreaming of the moments they shared.

The dances, the walks in the park,
The bright twinkle that sparkled in his eye,
The love will live on forever,
In her heart it will never die.

The past in her mind stands still,
As the clock ticks the seconds away,
Where to find refuge from the pain,
Unforgotten happiness of many yesterdays.

A tear drop rests on her cheek,
Remembering his warm gentle touch,
Her fragile hands grasp the torn portrait,
Of the man she loved so much.

Tracy Schwable

415

Where Is Hope

Where is the hope that this
World needs,
The hope we all seek, but cannot
Seem to find?
Violence is all around us, shootings,
Murder, drugs, abuse, and more,
Amidst all this, where is hope, hope
Of any kind?
Dying hearts crave it, hurting souls pine
For it, they search until their will is sore.
Where is I ask, the hope that this
World needs.
The hope that we all seek, but cannot
Seem to find?

The answer, I know, is Jesus Christ,
Give Him your heart,
For He is the hope of the world, and He
Died, so that we, in Him,
May find a new life, heart, and mind.

Sunny Thompson

Love At Last

I thought I was dead, you gave me new life,
I knew no feelings of love until your eyes shone upon me.

Could it be, love at last?

How deep my feelings were,
but were they true or just a fancy?

As time flew by I knew no doubt, love at last!

Deep in my soul, deep in my heart,
I wondered how, how this could be?

So pure and honest, could it be true,
Did God's angel of fate send me to you?

Could it be, love at last?

Though you can fight not to see me now
To keep your feelings so far down,
Do you ask yourself was it love at last?

I've been on a journey to know myself through and through
To see life and grow, the toughest yet to come,
being separated from you for who knows how long.

I wonder when it's over will I have the chance to ask you
for a lifetime, no formality no writing, based on trust.

Will there be a you and I to say
Love at last, love at last?

Paul Stevens

Divergence

So slowly does the sunlight emerge
from the darkness of the sky's divergence.
Bringing forth warmth upon the cold, desolate land.
The ground shudders
as creation accepts, a gift of rebirth.
Cautiously - does the beauty appear,
blossoming gently
consumed with both
Hope and Fear.
Sunlight sparkles upon a single Rose
as it awakens from bleakness,
so tenderly, so gently, afraid to bloom.
For so long, has darkness prevailed..
Thus, stands a single Rose - bathed in sunlight.
Afraid, as I, of warmth,
    of the unknown....
        Yet hopeful of the same.

T. LeeAnn Frieman

Growing Old

I am so old and my body's so weak,
I have so much pain even when I sleep.
I can't keep up with the rest of the crowd,
I can't stand straight and hold my head proud.
My family can't help me, but I understand,
they can't keep up with all my demands.
So they put me in a home and walk out the door,
and I never see them anymore.
I have no friends and I'm all alone,
but they tell me this is my new home.
I am very bitter and I often throw fits,
I'm the confused old lady in Room 306.
If someone would sit down and talk to me,
they would find out what I really need.
It wouldn't be restraints to hold me in my chair,
It wouldn't be a nurse to comb my hair.
It wouldn't be a sedative to help me sleep at night,
It wouldn't be a nurse to make my bed right.
It would be a friend to hold my hand,
It would be a friend who would understand.
I would be a smile and gentle touch,
It would be love that I need so much.

Terri Jacobs

Oh Love

Such a precious thing
yearned for by so many
yet held by so few
The thirst in one's soul
only to be quenched by
another's undying love
Hungered for by the heart
yet causing pain and heartache
if ever wavered
Impatiently sought after by so many
yet thrown to the sea by those
who have grown weary of trying
to deceive themselves into thinking
that it could be obtained -
Those who have grasped it,
felt it, touched it, tasted it completely,
feeling infinity bonded to it - whom
have had it snatched away just as
quickly as they had imagined it
was obtained.

Julie Wirt

Untitled

I am lost in the dessert, and you are my oasis
I drink from you, your supple water quenching my thirst
Without you I would surely die
You give me the strength I need to find my way
I awake, it was a dream, I'm still hear behind locked doors
A new day, you're already in my thoughts
I'm like a man adrift at sea, and you are my raft
Up and down you carry me through the endless days
Without you my time here would be unbearable
Midday rolls by, memories of your smile erase another hour
You are my escape, with you I am free
I am an eagle soaring high with you by my side
A buzzer sounds, a door slams, I am alone
Reality sits like a lump in my throat
It seems like a year since you saved me from the dessert
I close my eyes, I can not go on, I am weak
Like an angel you come to me, your glow is almost blinding
You gather me up with out stretched arms
You are my strength, with you I can me it.
Your love has taken me through another day.

James L. Ward Jr.

The Dandelion

I'm strange I know, I can't be denying,
But I secretly love the dandelion.
The memories, its sight brings to my mind,
I know it's spring when the first one I find.
Calenders try, but the dandelion knows
when the cold winter wind no longer blows.
And as a mother, it was very grand
to get a bouquet in a childish hand.
Those yellow blossoms, carried so proudly,
the love they showed, proclaimed so loudly.
Grandchildren now wear the little brown stains,
they put them in water with very great pains.
They're a lesson in love, a joy to behold,
to me the gift is as precious as gold.
Their survival instincts are easily seen,
you can weed and feed until you turn green.
Then you walk outside on a bright summer day,
and they wave at you in their taunting way.
It does my heart good as they sit on my lawn,
To know they'll be there long after I'm gone.

Sonya Baker

God's Great Glory

A beautiful angel big and bright
has taken me into her arms tonight
It felt as though I was one with the universe
free at last from this dreadful curse
The angel's wings wrapped tenderly around my frail body
gave me the strength to let go and feel God's great glory

Finally my young and tired soul was set free
so I could see all the beauty God had intended for me
My spirit soared above the clouds beyond the mounds of white
My heart rejoiced my soul cried out oh what a glorious sight
While the angels played their harps of gold
rainbows and magic began to unfold

In the distance stood a man in white
With His arms stretched far and wide
Could it be who I think it is
my God it's Jesus Christ
He's all I ever dreamt He would be
I can't believe He died for me
Thanks Mom and Dad for teaching me God's word
because of my faith I'm in Heaven and cured

Barbara McSheehy-Kattany

Rainbows

A gift of color,
A gift of sight,
An array of emotion,
created by light.
Arching across the sky,
silently catching our eye.

Fairy tales created,
now stopping to ponder.
Stories from our childhood,
now cause us to wonder.
Remembering our dreams,
when watching a child's innocent slumber.

Stories we'll pass on,
giving them new fascination.
Changing little by little,
with every generation.
It's his promise that's given,
Now gathering little ones attention.
Amazed by the Lord invention.

Victoria A. Young

Who Am I

Who am I? It's me the greatest of all time,
is who I be
I once went by the name Clay,
but you can call me Ali.
Who am I? I'm a religious militant
Who's the topic of most intellectual's conversation
my life was taken on February 21, 1965
by assassination.

Who am I? I go by the name Doc,
don't ask me why
Back in my prime years,
I used to soar through the sky.
Who am I? Only the first black on the Supreme Court Justice
But I'm not being arrogant
Everyone has the opportunity,
to make great achievements.

Who am I? I'm a young black man,
filled with exuberance
True, there are different shades, sizes, and shapes of men,
but there is no real difference.

Joseph Wilson

Four In One

Day by day I have become
A unique blend of four in one.
Mom's enduring love that protects, encourages, lets go
Prepares me for the challenges that I have yet to know.

Dad's gentle strength that secures a solid home,
Prepares me for the fragile world that needs so much to know
The part of me that reaches out with nail-scarred hands
To embrace the weak and lonely, to love without demands.

And here I am — so much a part of Mom and Dad,
And so much is Christ in me.
And here I am — so much the same, yet so unique
Because three and one make me.

Jenifer Thrall

Separation

My sea, my sea, my beautiful sea, they shall
Not take me away from Thee!

Thy sands have warmed me
Thy waters have refreshed me
Thy power o'erwhelms me
How can I leave Thee?

My sea, my sea, my beautiful sea, they shall
Not take me away from Thee!

Alberta Regina Cuozzo

The Silver Box

It may be beautiful, and it may shine,
It will keep your secrets and thoughts all combined,
It may not talk, but it holds many words,
It may not think, but it has many thoughts,
You think they will be kept, because it has a lock,
But the lock may break,
And all your thoughts escape,
What happened to its beauty and its shine?
You thought it was "all mine,"
But your thoughts have gone,
And it was all a waste,
To give your heart with all your faith.
But what happened to the box,
Now that it has released all your thoughts.

Jennifer Javalera

Fateful Night

On that fateful April day,
Her passengers were on their way
To their destination: New York Harbor.

Some were rich and some were poor;
They'd never seen the sea before,
And by the night they never would again.

For on that fateful April night,
Titanic vanished out of sight
Into the murky waters underneath.

Her maiden voyage was her last.
Her memories are fading fast,
Lost forever to the fickle sea.

April 15 of 1912,
The unforgiving waters swelled
To drag her to the ocean floor below.

To this day she still sits there,
Still with that gigantic tear
That caused her to go down that fateful night.

Erinn D. Clarke

A True Friend

You and I have been through so much
So many hard times,
Along with so many wonderful ones.
The first time I saw you,
I knew we would be friends forever.
You are my very best friend and always will be.
You know how I always worry about you all of the time,
Even when we are together.
I worry about you every hour, minute, and second of the day.
You also know how much I love you with all of my heart
and always will.
I don't care what other people say
because you know how I feel about you.
I know how much I mean to you
and how much you care.
So I hope we will be friends forever,
but I know we will!

D. Miller

In Days of Old

In days of old,
When knights were bold,
To win the hand of a maiden
They would go and slay a dragon.
A dragon's heart I cannot offer
But without your love I would surely suffer.
My heart I give
So that we may live
In happiness together.

Tony V. Chamblin

Hiding Behind A Face

I look in the mirror and I see a face,
A reflection of myself, a reflection of the human race.

It is my armor, and it is my shield,
I use it to mask my vulnerability, to hide how I really feel.

I can force it into a smile, I can force it into a grin.
Make it seem as if I'm happy, as if I've never committed a sin.

It is a protection so strong, I could not live without,
For if my feelings were revealed, sadness would sprout.

It covers up my emotions, and my biggest fear I come to call,
That one day my armor would break, and reveal it all.

Teresita Barrus

Vision Of Sea

The sun's long golden rays
   Beat down upon me
I am filled with the warmness they shed
   In my minds eye I can see the ocean waves
I hear them crash down
   I see them pulled back
By the mighty tide
   The controller of all the sea
The waves call to me
   They whisper and sing
Come in, come in they laugh
   I cannot help myself
I run into them
   I am engulfed by their salty sweetness
They carry and lift me
   I squeeze my eyes shut
And the vision is broken
   I am back
Alone
   In the sunshine

Alexandra Hart-Chavez

What Thoughts Of Tomorrow

What thoughts have I of tomorrow,
When it is so near and yet so far away.

What thoughts have I of tomorrow,
when today is still today,
Tomorrow is just a vision,
a dream, a thought, a glimpse of the future.

What thought have I of tomorrow,
While today is still vibrant, alive and fresh!

What thoughts have I of tomorrow,
When today takes all I have,
If I can get through this day,
Then tomorrow will soon be today.

Sallie Adams

Ring

I'm a ring hurled out of a window
and it's my only kingdom she's down

Which doomed never to reborn
I'm a ring once cherished and worn

By the one casts and drown
And I may never be flown

She's down my only kingdom
and why do I blindly remain dumb?

When it may be years buried underneath
with more strokes of rain of snow or thunder

I'm a ring hurled out of a window
And it's my only kingdom she's down

But why am I still proud to be worn once
When now I weigh much more than an ounce....

Daniel Valme

The City

This is the city that never sleeps,
Millions of people, cars, buses and jeeps.
The skyscrapers here are very numerous,
But rush hour here is not very humorous.

The hustle 'n bustle of this place, The City of York,
Is great, if you have your credit card and fork.
Bagels, Coca-Cola, Pepsi and Snapple,
This is New York City — a.k.a. The Big Apple.

Shimmy Feintuch

How Tiny Leaves Of Today Please

I am inside my insides
inside out here devoting myself to starry onlookers
beneath starry onlookers.
Looking for looks from my friend the suicidal poplar.
I am inside my insides
mind as he tends to tour jeté in play, but anyway...
Today I lay in leaves of fallen day
where in times of lost, children had played
Inside my insides
hands with the toss of ball
yet solo would stand with other plans
confessing to heaven, he's feeling small.
Inside his insides
inside a beckoning for need
is grasping for its chance to show
that he too would be able to lead.
And as I lie here watching day turn
into night, inside my insides
inside I find a deeper passion for the outside
living inside of me.

Ryan C. Smith

Innuendo

Overwhelmed by a plethora of color,
something like a flashing rainbow somewhat obscured;
and jeweled angels float in silence
There are things that pass
and there are warm welcoming sensations that linger
A sense of peace with oneself
Something of an awakening, bright and sophisticated
deeper than even the mind can see
So incomprehensible
Every image symbolizes the secrets of truth
whatever the fear may be, at any cost
to be inside the dream
to know the temptations and indulgence
Is there no greater pain?
Is there no greater pleasure?

Rob Decker

When Heaven's Lamp

When Heaven's lamp mounts the starlit sky
And waxes into the deep night's darkness,
Waked from its conscious slumber, the mind's eye
Plucks visions from sleep's eternal abyss.
Visions propelled by waking hope and desire
to play out actor's parts in midnight's dream.
Played, rather dreamt, with such spirit and fire,
That in waking all too real do they seem.
Yet the jealous Dawn, forbidding such play,
Intrudes, cold and sharp, upon the warm night
Driving vision, but not passion away,
To lie hidden from us in the day's light.
And thus what desire gave life to in dream
Do we desire more for our life to seem.

Philip Jones

Spring Day

The misty dew has fallen upon
the earth, foretelling the coming of dawn.

The angelic stars gently fade away,
as the warm sun welcomes the beginning of day.

The moon's pale, blue, captive shine
no longer whispers through the dusty pine.

The morning birds boastfully sing,
wake up, sweet earth, for it is Spring!

Roberta Bowen

Restless

When the time is right, I'll sleep through the night
but for now, I lay with wide open eyes
My thoughts are vast, my heart beats fast
as my prayers filter the skies.

Dear God, I know you're listening, for you love to hear my heart
sing... but tonight, I only have tears.
So my cheeks are wet, as I try to forget
the pain that I've felt through the years.

Yet I've known in my heart, right from the start
for every night, there's a day.
There's a right and a wrong, a silence, a song
and I'm sure that you'll show me the way.

So with bended ear, please ease my fears,
and enable me again, to fight.
Because from day to day, we may lose our way
and it's hard to know what's right.

Though the lessons I've learned, are the "Joys" I've earned
and my battles will someday be won.
So in my "restless" state, please teach me to wait...
...for the happier days yet to come.

Tina Strange

The Other Side

Come to thee, thy one that wants to,
Cross over to the other side,
I'll collect your ticket,
hand you your stub,
Then be on thy way
and to never see me again.

But when you go I will warn you,
If you've been bad I'd stay here
But if you've been good, go,
And let peace follow you all the way through,
And if you have revenge,
be gone with you, go and do your business,
But when you come back be ready to say
Goodbye, farewell and be ready to,
Cross over to the other side.

Bobby Wexler

A Wife's Reflection

Today I look back at the years of our past
Because I wanted to know
The changes we've made, the hills that we've climbed
All the things that have helped us to grow.

It started as friendship, then glorious passion
True love took time to grow.
We also found anger, and small irritations,
Some things we just didn't know.

But the one thing I've learned and found most important,
What really counts in my heart,
Is to look at you now and not find what you're not
Just truly see what you are.

You're the joy of my heart, the rest of my soul,
The best friend in all of my life.
You're loving and kind, so gentle but strong,
The man who made me his wife.

So I give you my love, I give you my life,
And I thank my God up above,
Who has given me you, and the wisdom to know
how special your life lasting love.

Donna Crawford

Happiness

As a child - this meant playing games with my dearest friends.
Maybe ride a bike or take a swim.
To own a puppy was the ultimate treat,
and let him cuddle around my feet.

I like to please those whom I love, I cherish the
stars and the moon above.
To play outside in the early night, with my special friends
was a real delight.

As I grew older, my priorities changed.
Sometimes for love and sometimes for fame.
Somewhere in my life, I came awake;
I want to give back more than I take.
When material objectives fall
from my priority list,
then there's a chance for "Happiness" to exist.

Eudell Griffin

But A Weed

Sometimes I wonder why
Such a beautiful weed was ever created
It passes my mind how something so beautiful
Could be slaughtered by the hand of man
For we of all living things should cherish it

When the wind blows its seeds spread
For it is abundant but not really wanted
Its beautiful green leaves
And passionate yellow flowers
Even its astonishing powder puffs

I look at these and imagine me
To be as free as a flower
To roam where I please
That's all anyone wants in life
To be free is my dream.

Drew Luke

My Whisper Of Wind

Because my lady,
your gentleness surpasses any other;
The carefulness of your hands is as gentle as a spring breeze.
The words you whisper float through the air
and softly land with a gentle kiss upon my ears.
Your face is of angels, and with that smile, as an angel,
you float among the clouds and play with the wind;
ride its back.
Through your winds, love I feel,
an airborne kiss whispers sweet nothings
as it floats about and with its destination
it touches my cheek with sweetness and soft whispers of wind.
Forever to me will you always be
my very own
whispers of wind.

Anthony J. Tigner

The Flame

Maybe it's your fiery soul-flickering and glowing
   That burns my wounded heart.
Your courageous soul so willingly draws me in
   Into your gentle arms, ever so softly
So inviting and calm, yet never wanting to pull away
   From the innocence within me.
Your lips touch my hand with a kiss I will always remember,
   Yet I say nothing — but smile as you do it once more.
Your romantic essence surrounds me, lifting me up
   Encasing me with a sweetness that is your beauty.
For it shines bright like a glowing candle,
   Warming all my senses when you are near.

Heidi E. Spriggle

The One Who Cares

When I die, don't come to see—
My face planted under a tree.
Don't spit on my grave to water the weeds -
When I was on earth, you did me no kind deeds.
I tried to love and did the best I could —
Until I found out it was doing no good.
Why, God do some people find —
Happiness of a more lasting kind?
A way of misery and torment —
When others just cause punishment.
If you see I am gone - don't come around my body and moan.
For I'll be in a better place, you see —
at the foot of the cross on Jesus's knee.
He'll be my comfort then - someone who'll let me in.
He'll be my solace and peace and accept me as I am
for he knows I tried to be a caring person for thee.

When you look up into the stars at night -
look for a shining light.
That will be my face you'll see —
the face that was planted under the tree.

Harriett M. Nesbitt

Honest Truth

I am not going to pretend to be something I'm not
I don't want to sit around in some coffee house
and discuss things I know nothing about
drinking espressos while reading their poems isn't me
I have no desire to be like them, to snap my fingers
after hearing a "right on" poem
All in all I guess I want to say is I write poems
not like that trendy coffee house scene, who sit and cry
thinking their life is so sick and sad
I know I don't write the best of poems, but they are good
enough for me.

Arabella Sheridan

If I Could See Down The Road

If I could see what was down at the end of the road
Maybe I wouldn't go on.
But life's never been an easy thing to live
And what's behind me now is gone.

There were good times and bad, happy and sad
Times when I thought I'd call it quits
But life's never been an easy thing to live
The pieces of the puzzle seem to fit.

What the future holds in store is anybody's guess
It's best to take it day by day.
But life's never been an easy thing to live
I tend to wish my life away.

With the final piece in place and my future in the past
And few tomorrows yet to be seen
I hope I can look back up the road I've come down
And say I've fulfilled every dream.

Fred H. Thompson

To My Children

Look at you my wonderful children, how
you've grown with much love and respect.
How time has flown since I carried you so
close with so much wonder of what you
were or where you would go. The wonder
is still there with great pride. As each day
comes and goes I watch. For now it's time,
you see, to go ahead of Dad and me, though
we won't be far behind to hear and see the
notes of your songs, we'll hum quietly along.

Esther Lucerna

Ode To Mother, Inez

Born to Mark and Maude in Texas, 1905,
Moved to Oklahoma when just a girl.
Worked as a sharecropper's daughter
In your own snug little world.

Married young and moved to California
Where you worked hard, gave birth to a son, Gerry.
Returned to your Texas roots as a 33-year-old woman;
Remarried, had three daughters, life was heaven.

Your sunny smile and sweet nature
Helped mold several more generations of people.
You always gave of you time and money
To help others who were often lost and lonely.

Your 91st birthday will be one to remember
Because few ever reach those twilight years.
You have seen many days through tears and joy
Yet you persevered with grit and little acrimony.

So let our family say, "we love you"
And we wish you many more good memories;
Also, birthdays filled with happiness and candy
From your kids, Gerry, Joy, Bonnie, and Nancy.

Joy Hall Rinker-Grant

My Hero

My Hero's found
When the road starts to bend,
Her hands are reached out,
For their offer to lend.
Although sometimes forceful
But done with such care
She gives me her guidance,
Knowledge and prayers.
Never she asks for payment or praise
Just respect and love for her caring ways.
Not often enough
My hero's told, how very special she is,
To my heart and soul.
As I grow older
The awareness is there
Instilled in my mind above all just "Care".
Now my children are walking
On that road with a bend
For You see it all started
With my Grandmother's hand.

James Rick Maddux

Let Me Go

The struggle to free myself from your selfish grip,
goes beyond the physical.
I got away, but still you haunt me.
I shudder in terror at each ring of the phone,
icy fingers wrapping around my heart,
Turning my guts, sickening terror.
I cut the ties, one by one, as quickly as I can.
But my life is still tangled, intertwined in your grip,
I cannot get free, You will not let go.
Manipulating, Calculating, always Controlling.
Hypnotizing, Smooth, beating down my defenses.

Barricaded in my little world,
alone in my terror,
defensive, defenseless.
The least little thing that you do,
Carries with it a threat,
a conditional ultimatum,
You'll own me again.

Karen Beth Stack

My Secret Place

There is a place that no one knows.
That when I was little I chose.
A place where the wind does not even blow.
A place where the water does not flow.

To my secret place, you cannot go,
though I am there every time, everywhere.
My secret place, to you I cannot show.
But sometimes I really would like to share.

Everyone has their own place,
though some do not know how to find it.
They let others who are unfamiliar with this place lead them.
And soon everyone gets mixed up and lost.

In this place, there is no race.
There is no face.
There is no chase.
There are just thoughts.

Thoughts of very simple,
yet also complex beginnings.
Thoughts just floating everywhere.
That is my secret place.

Matt Schaning

Ode To The Flower Lady

We extol the hand that planted the seeds,
But they adapt at all other needs;
They prepare the with flower feed,
And sufficient moisture to sprout the seed:
They wait with patience for the sprouts to appear;
And a sigh of triumph we are sure to hear;
Tilling the soil is a delight task;
As we wait with patience as they appear at last.
It is always necessary to remove the weeds;
And watch for insects that night use them for feed
The flower lady stands with her heart filled with pride,
As the laws of nature begin to preside;
Each sprout will appear with a flowerily crown;
But the flower lady should be wearing the crown.

Arvin Miller

Santa Claus

For seven years I thought he was real,
But all that time he was a fake.
I just knew I was getting a deal,
For being so good, for goodness sake.

My parents sat me on his knee,
To tell him all my wishful thoughts.
They wondered what my list would be,
Though the presents had already been bought.

He was a great big jolly old soul,
With a long white beard dangling down.
Santa played a very big role,
In the minds of kids all around.

In every store I saw him there,
And wondered how that could be.
But they all were Santa they declared,
Every one...two...and three!

I felt inside that he was real,
But my sister said he was not.
She really was a brat to steal
The magic from my thoughts.

Adam James

The Gift

A grandma dreams of little girls
with great big eyes and lots of curls
you were everything I'd hoped you'd be
Perfection from head to toe, Natasha Lee.
But our dreams were shattered, our hearts forever
broken, God took you home, with no words spoken
So each night as I lay awake, I pray to God for our sake
"Hold her tight and hug and kiss her
Tell her how much we love and miss her
She's in our hearts till our dying day
Her memory will never fade away
So each day I start a new
Envying God, cause he has you
you're one of his Angels, the best one I know
How precious you are, we'll never let go
So, rest high on God's Mountain
And stay warm in His light
For someday, we'll be together
And I'll be holding you tight forever and ever
our gift Natasha Lee

Shelbie J. Bell

To My Daughters

It only seems like yesterday
That I held that tiny hand
And watched you through adoring eyes
As a mother only can

Everything you've ever done
Still seems just like a dream
I hope that I will never wake
And lose these memories

I've cherished your accomplishments
And cried when you were sad
Your hopes and dreams were also mine...
The life I never had

We've had our good times and our bad
But remember for all time
All my love for you is pure...
And with no strings to bind

The love that's grown throughout the years
You can never know
Till you've had a child of your own
To love and watch her grow

Diane Richey

A Child's Memory

My grandpa died when I was only five
Never to return, no longer alive
"Such a good man", is what people would say
Then why was he taken so far away?

My grandpa was so gentle, so gentle and kind
But now when I look he's nowhere to find
My heart is so empty without his warm touch
I think that is why I miss him so much

On April 23 confusing thoughts went through my head
"Grandpa's gone to God", is what mommy said
He's missed important things that went on through the years
But I always felt his presence through the laughter and tears

Some things I won't remember but him I'll never forget
Not spending enough time with him I will always regret
My grandpa encouraged me to forever strive
But it still isn't fair because I was only five.

Darci Mancini

Communication

I sat beneath the pines, a warm gentle breeze was speaking;
branches swaying, bending, as if to speak back.

A short distance away I heard a birds song, others joined,
again speaking.
I looked up to the azure sky, swift moving clouds; so graceful.

The sun, today it glistened, speaking of warmth; now setting
in the western sky; clouds cover its blinding light,
speaking rest, day has ended. Your glow weakens, in
response the sky darkens.

The sky spoke to the stars; it is your turn to shine,
Brighten the earth with your white light.

The moon kissed the night sky, speaking; I am king of the
night sky; all creatures on earth sleep in my presence.
I shall guide the night, while you speak to our Creator in your dreams...

Christine Gordon

Imagination

As I sat watching the clouds fly by,
I thought of Jesus, so high in the sky.
I could vision him astride a whirling cloud,
Gazing sadly down on this worldly crowd.

Oh, the things I imagined I could see,
As those soft billows floated past me.
The saints of old, out for a stroll,
And the guardian angels dressed in white and gold.

Then my imagination said, "Stop and behold",
Because there stood Jesus straight and bold;
Dressed in long flowing robe and crown,
As he viewed his creatures on the ground.

He opened his loving arms wide,
A safe harbor for those who would abide.
He stood there as someday he would,
When he comes to separate the bad from the good.

Soon the clouds floated away.
My heart sighed good-bye until another day.
My feet were light as away I did trod,
Thanks to my imagination, thanks to God.

Sarah Andrews

Little Guy

How does a father show his love,
With a gentle squeeze of his hand?

How does a father show his love,
With a gentle pat on the can?

How does a father show his love,
And still keep him a man?

He watches with pride,
When he runs for the score,
or makes the winning basket.

How does a father show his love,
When he knows that soon he will be a man?

He hopes for the best and knows that he tries,
But how does a father show his love,
When he's as tall as a man?

A hand outstretched to go into his,
Or arms outstretched to give a hug,
How does a father show his love,
When the little guy, becomes a man?

John R. Romance

Prayer

I carry secrets and love in my clinched fist...
without cracking for anything, not even my bliss
Oh Lord won't you help me...because I can
feel this suffering...won't you help me be at
peace with something...I stand in the rain
waiting for someone to pull me in... I create
my own shadowed room world...filled with
a rage of sin.... Oh Lord won't you help me...
you see I want to repent...but all these
whispering hands hold the key to the doors
that keeps me locked in... I paint my
sky a color knowing it will turn red... Oh Lord
please lend me the strength so I won't give in

Brandon Hoffman

Reality

The rain seeps through the roof
And it reminds us of our strife
It's just the reassuring proof
Of the harshness of our life

We cannot overcome the hardships of this world
Our fate is predetermined just like a river's flow
And you and I should know
No matter what our circumstance
Someday the pain will go

Away and we will be
Alone and flying high
Because we have been set free
And left to rule the sky
Away from the grueling task of living our one great lie

Brandy Smith

One Moment

You are no longer with me but
If I had one moment more what would I do
Would I say thank you for
All good things you sent my way
Would I say that I miss you more
Than words can ever say
If I had one moment more
What would I do
Would I just look at you in silence
And be thankful for all the wonderful memories
Or would I talk and talk and try to speak a lifetime
In just that one moment more
If I had one moment more
What would I do
I believe I would look at you
And say
I love you more and more each day
And that you were the best dad
In every way.

Wylia J. Holt

The Void

There's no way to describe,
   the void I feel inside.
There's no way to replace,
   that horrible empty space.
To feel again the joy and pride,
   you brought about while you were alive...
Your laugh and smile always ready.
The lit-up eyes, the gentle face
   My memory will not erase.
If I could have but one true wish;
   It would be that you,
   I need not miss.

Brigid A. O'Brien

Race

In the United States of America
Race is an issue.
We are under the American flag
Still, race is an issue.
How can we be divided
And, be under the American flag.
The American are proud of the American flag.
But, we are still divided.
Our Americans flag stands for the country.
Our American flag stands for the people.
People, who live in the united states of America are Americans.
We are Americans.
You are an American.
Americans love their country.
Every American should know the pledge of allegiance.
So, if the American people are divided
Why, continue being under the American flag.
We salute our American flag.
By standing up and putting our right hands over our hearts.
And giving the pledge of Allegiance.

Diana Maldonado

A Perfect Place For Me

I live in a tiny cottage
In a city by the sea
Filled with sunshine and flowers
A perfect place for me

My house is filled with treasures
Gifts from family and friends
My shelves are filled with books to read
And crafts that have no end

My door is always open
To friends who come to call
And picture of my children
Are lined up on the wall

There are memories here in every room
I hold them all so dear
I never want to move away
My roots are planted here

I live in a tiny cottage
In a city by the sea
With the man I have loved for fifty years
A perfect place for me

Carmen Bumgardner

The Desire

A sip from the glass
that has poisoned her lips.
And into her soul.
Burning her thoughts,
and tearing apart her mind
she drinks from that glass
she desires the results.
It stands tall beside her.
Sheltering her with its crystal shield
so she can still see through
to the other side
which she wants, which she craves
but still she holds the glass
the poison protecting her
until she is no longer there, all but a reflection
until one day the glass is broken.
Shuttered by her own hand the shards piercing her skin.
Making her bleed. And as the last trace of blood is gone
the pieces scattered around her
she looks for herself and finds a reflection.

Alicea Ardito

Bang The Drum Slowly

Bang the drum slowly
and listen to the lowly
thunder of other nations

O Bang the drum slowly
and light the sky bright
with flames from torches
left burning in the night

Bang the drum slowly
and listen to the cries
of people that are hungry
little hope in their eyes

O Bang the drum slowly
and hear the night moan
echoed cries from the beatings
that they suffer alone

We must open our ears
and listen for a sign faintly hearing the echo
of this brother that is mine

O Bang the drum slowly
and listen to the slowly thunder of other nations

Cristina M. Garland

Life

Light at the end of the tunnel.
First encounter with the real world.
After six weeks of darkness' funnel,
Golden light shines upon my hair, twirled.
Eyes having been closed tight in dread,
Peep out like a flower unfurled.
A cool hand serves as a nest for my head,
Around its mate, my fingers are curled.

Dark shadows are seen with blue eyes,
Gray mixed with white, blended by fears.
Quick movement startles me - afraid, my cries
Wracking my frail body, piercing ears.
Tiny fists stretching to the skies,
Clenched tightly against falling tears.
Pure age of innocence, no sin nor lies.
Fragile, bright life, soon embracing years.

Ann-Catherine Ventura

Lost American Dream

A child is molested
No Daddy! She cries.
As her mother sits in the other room,
Pondering all of the lies.

Lost, lost is the American dream.

A black boy is beaten,
for the color of his skin.
He cries out for freedom,
while hanging from a limb.

Never to be found, never to be seen.

America seems no longer free,
no longer a safe place.
How could this be true?
Because of the twisted minds of the human race.

Lost, lost is the American Dream
Never to be found, never to be seen

What shall we do?
The question remains unseen.
Remember the American Dream and there we shall find,
Freedom, the American Dream

Jennifer Danielle Ritter

The Fall Of Summer

She left abruptly yet rageless
Passionately I mourned the good-bye
Uncertainty abounds in the darkness
Suspecting the ransom is too high

Undoubtedly patience is a virtue
However, not one that I possess
Violent rains, storm clouds, black hue
Loneliness, abandonment, distress

She shall return when times are right
But to bear the wait is torment
Peace, clarity, and an azure sight
Will hopefully make me content

Soon her soothing whisper and gentle touch
Will once more caress my cold skin
The joy, warmth, and love that I miss so much
Will encompass my heart once again.

Matthew E. Hooper

Frost Bitten Death

As I walk along through drifts of snow, I know that I must have fire.
The wind is blowing strongly as my tired and weak heart pounds
like a drum in my chest. With out any one by my side, I feel as helpless
as a two year old child. Fire, how I long for fire, but there isn't a way
in the world to carry out my wish. My heart still pounds and the wind
still blows and I try to walk on. My mind says walk on, but my body
says rest. My body is numb and half frozen, and my eyes close,
and my life slowly comes to an end.

Emily Ceterski

Stillness

In the stillness of the night, a cry rang out in grief.
Of a loved one passing in their sleep,
Soon they will be with God up above in
That land of golden streets.
Suffering no more in this world of sin and sadness.
They will be in the land of joy and gladness
No sorrow or tears in that land of glory and sunshine.
There will be singing and shouting of happiness.
And glory will shine through the face of the
Lord on his children that are in that
Land he prepared for them that kept his word
And lived for him.
Surely they shall be missed by their loved
One and friends.
But they are in a better place of glory.
Hallelujah! His name is Jesus.

Frances M. Flowers

My Dearest Son

On this sad day, I will cry tears,
for God has taken my Mother.
But most of my tears will be for you,
and the loss of your Grandmother.

She had a very giving and loving heart.
And in time I will tell you much more,
as you are both apart.

You brought joy and laughter to her heart.
You were her light when it got dark.
You were her strength when she was weak.
You were her food when she could not eat.

For three years you kept Grandma alive
until God said now it is time.
Someday you will know what you meant to her,
until then, she will keep watch,
with all her love, from heaven above.

Nora Ebeling

You Get One Chance

"You get one chance" he said
So keep this in your head,
It's not how much you make of it,
But how much you give and take of it,
That really fills your life it seems,
Don't rest on laurels, chase your dreams.
It's not how far you've come, it's not how far you'll go,
But how much you have learned and not how much you know.
Stop clinging to the past and find a different path,
For all you seek, is in your reach, the prize within your grasp.

He looked into my eyes and gave a cheerful sigh,
And said, "My son the time has come, it's now my turn to die".
"You get one chance" he said
So keep this in your head,
Every man, despite his stand, will one day end up dead.

So make the best of life,
And get all you deserve,
And you'll soon learn, there are stones unturned,
And dreams still left unserved.

Bryan L. Montgomery

The Four Seasons

Summer, winter, spring and fall,
Life goes on, and that's not all.
The sun, the moon, a twinkling star,
So very near, and yet so far.
A rabbit's dash, across the meadow,
His paw prints left, on a bed of snow.
A drop of rain, on the window pane,
A stream will flow, from the melting snow.
A whispering breeze, caresses the trees,
As a song bird sings, the beginning of spring.
A summer shower, a blooming flower,
A bird in flight oh! What a sight.
As you look up, with a sigh,
A snow white cloud, a deep blue sky.
The summer heat on a city street,
Will send you back, to a country retreat.
A falling leaf, at summers end,
The beginning of fall, a yearly trend.
A year went by, for you and me,
Like a twinkling light, on a Christmas tree.

Joseph Ciolli

Dreams

When the day is done, and gone is the sun,
the darkness of the night,
puts my restless thoughts to flight.
The dreams of my mind,
are finally set free,
to dance with the nobles,
and the deities.
I know not what I dream, but it would seem:
In my dreams my feet
don't touch the ground.
They only touch where
the Heavens are sound.
Your dreams hold the power
of many armies strong;
your dreams hold the key to
both right and wrong.
So listen to your dreams,
or something will pass you by,
for a dream is the one thing
that will never tell a lie.

Kara Kneubuhler

Untitled

As the sun sets over the deep blue sea
I see your eyes, pure blue.
I take my shoes off and roll up my jeans
and wade into the ice cold water.
I continue to look into your blue eyes
not blinking or turning away.
Soon the water is to my waist
Yet I still walk to your pure blue eyes.
Suddenly a gust of wind knocks me over.
I gasp for air, only getting water.
My arms and legs thrash to and fro.
Then I feel your mighty hands hold me
and bring me to shore.
You help me wash my face and dry my clothes.
I glance once more at your eyes
they were no longer blue, they turned to fierce red.
I screamed in horror trying to get away
from your mighty grasp.
I tried so hard to get away but nothing worked.

Sharon "Raven" Cushing

Nature

Hiking through old growth ancient trees,
or skipping across sea foamed sand in a salt scented breeze,
I cherish moments like these,
for here is where I find,
my peace of mind,
solitude and tranquility, stress left behind,
swift and sinuous, snow spawned streams,
glacier sheathed mountains that are the splendor of dreams,
the crisply clean clarity of the wilderness air,
brings me closer to my higher power, nothing can compare,
cumulus crowded desert sky,
my imagination is soaring high,
like an eagle streaking by,
nature's energy is clean and pure,
cleansing my spirit, strong and sure,
when the strains of life are taking their toll,
I escape to nature for revitalizing, re-energizing of my soul.

Dan D. Halstead

Day Dreaming

I have dreams of another life, in another world,
That I will probably never see or be a part of.
I have dreams of a world of happiness, of an endless glow,
And children's laughter taking me to sleep.
In my nightmares my eyes burn,
For tears already gone,
Taken in a dream gone wrong.
It lasts so long I begin to confuse it with reality.
But reality...no it can't be!

I'm living in a nightmare that is supposed to be reality,
So when I awake what will it be...
A nightmare, reality, or the dreams that will probably never be.

Thalia Y. Bishop

Untitled

If God is so good, then why did he take her away?
Did he promise to bring her back someday?
What else will rip my heart out the same way?
When will I see her?
Will she have wings?
Will they be golden like the sun?
Will she take my hand and show me around?
Will I seek sadness like I already found?
Heaven will be magical people say,
Then why did he take her away?

Kate Siwicki

Addictions

Mindlessly driven by one single thought, idea, or action.
Life, living, freedom, control, words no longer words,
devout of power and meaning.
Subconsciously/Consciously obsessed/possessed
by power unseen and omnipresent.
Memories (past), goals (future),
all funneling towards what's
inside you (present).
Time lost.
Ropes of hands grabbing from the shore
pulling, tugging, slipping slowly away.
Right. Wrong. Good. Bad. God. Satan.
Clarity drifting into insanity.
Possession by angels with hats, whistles, clipboards (no halos).
You are a rat in a lab or a governmental burden.
Psychologically and illogically.
You used to be a person and yet by definition still maintain that status.
Life, no longer your option to squash like a bug.
Death is your addiction and pain is your drug.

Kevin Oakley

Choices

Should you choose this once, or should you choose that one?
Should you choose the thin one, or maybe the fat one?
Will you get a new one, or just keep the old one?
You'd sweat with a hot one, but you'd freeze with a cold one.
Which one's the false one and which one is true?
You'd take the other if you could see through.
The right one is obvious, yet the wrong one's right too.
Obviously, the obvious is not obvious to you.
If the choice is important (one you cannot evade).
Then think of the choices you've already made.
Some choices failed, while some were successful.
The ones left unmade were sometimes regretful.
The choices unchosen you chose not to make.
Those choices seemed far too risky to take.
Yet you made some choices and somehow survived
To find that new choices, since then, have arrived.
So, that one or this one, which one will you choose?
Just make the right choice and you're not going to lose.
Because choices are many, they're a dime-a-dozen.
Be proud of your choice, for it's what you have chosen.

Richard A. George

Passion For Life

I thought it was over
Just when it all seemed a blur
Like a leaf turning in the fall
Loses all hope of its emerald life
As that wish for a four leaf clover
Never came

Monotony! You say? Don't stop now, you never know
There may be that one instant in time
You stop to say...Hey! Who are we? Why are we living?

Then just as the leaf sees another side - bright orange and red
He's reminded of the winter friend
Closer as one moves, noticing each branch
Intricately designed and held together to make
Its being - the flake, by fate, singled out

Why then must we hide or question?
We, the creators utmost design
I again thought it was over
Just when it all seemed a blur
Oh, but what a focus

Clear, crisp and there all along

Betty Davino

Changes

How does time change a person so much,
it changes their mind, heart and touch.
The definite feeling you have inside,
you may soon find out it's just a lie.
It may change time and time again,
for better or worse, in goodness and sin.
Often mistakes will also be made,
but their memories will eventually fade.
Do not live in the future, or the past.
live in the now, so the feeling will last.
The world is yours, so take good care,
be courageous, but be aware.
Have an open mind,
be curious, but kind.
Have an open heart,
so friends may never part.
Keep your eyes open as the days go by,
For the more you close them the faster they fly.
Always remember God's great love for you,
So be yourself, and to yourself be true.

Tamara M. Taylor

Cloud Number Nine

The clouds are my pillow billowy and white
Gazing upon the stars are my eyes each night
Dreaming and wondering and thinking of you
Oh how we could shine if you only knew
For the stars are my friends as they enlighten the way
To be with you in my dreams as I slumber each day
and when a new day dawns and the sun rises high
The warmth on my face makes me think of you and sigh
How I long to be with you when the sun sets low
To share all that I feel the things you already know
So, if you care to rest upon my pillow
...cloud number nine
I will gladly share it with you for all of time.

Robert T. Rusoff

Always In My Thoughts

I woke up this morning only to find
A dear little bird that was in a bind
I proceeded to help him only to find
His leg was broken and I heard him whine
I picked him up with gentle care
And placed him in my arm chair
My heart was full and I was in despair
And I didn't know what to do from there
He stayed with me for quite a while
And he was like a friend
Lo and behold to my dismay
Oh a windy day he flew away
I hoped for a miracle so
That he could join his friends in the sky.

Ivy Oliver

Untitled

The weeping willow is a beautiful
tree. Messy though it can be, it
grows so fast you cut it back, in a month
it's right back. It give nice shade
from the sun. But taking care of
it is no fun. The leave falls all
over the place. Cleaning them up is a race.
    No wonder people cut them down
and leave the stumps. As a mound.
    When you leave them alone the
limbs grows to the grown it
makes it hard to see the little
animal playing around.
    Sometimes I wonder, what life
would be, without my beautiful willow
tree, so I, decided to leave it
alone, and keep the chores as my own.
        Oralean Garner

The Dandelion

A little burst of yellow in a field of emerald green;
an unwanted little flower that wants its beauty seen.

It only wants to exist in a world of sightly wonder.
It only wants to live without being torn asunder.

A reputation undeserved in a cultivated lawn;
its beauty shines so bright as it greets the sunny dawn.

It spreads across the vale with all the flowers wild.
It's born into this world with the innocence of a child.

A beautiful scarlet rose, the tulips in the spring;
the lilac's sweetly scent, cause a happy heart to sing.

But what about these petals with a golden splash of sun?
Is there no appreciating of their beauty to be done?

Why does no one like this brightly colored bloom?
The eye perceives its beauty, but the mind perceives its doom.

This creation done by God, by His goodness and His grace;
although it's called a weed, it's just a flower out of place.
        Dennis Decker

Fall

My favorite time is quiet fall;
When leaves fall gently to the ground.
The tree that once was full of life;

Now stands alone...

Her crowning glory at her feet;
Like a golden blanket spread around.

I see a leaf...one gentle, tender leaf...

It fights to stay;
And yet I know that it will leave...
When the time will come for it to go.

I am that tree...
My fall is here.

My life was full with bloom;
And now it's time for leaves to fall...
And softly blow away.

Yet I know;
That spring will come...
And bring me joy abound;

The leaves that fell will bring new buds;
for me to tend again.
        Nina K. Ashton

My Rose Of Rare Beauty

You are my rose of fairest bloom,
Filling with fragrance this ordinary room.
Planted by God in His garden, so rare
There isn't like you another anywhere.

Break open for me my bud of rare worth:
Unfold every petal so there may come forth
Such perfume enchanting, o'erpowering the air
With incense ethereal and wond'rously fair.

Oh grant me the time to know the real you,
To search out your sweetness and drink of your dew!
Buzz round you fair flower and, drawn like a bee,
Pull forth your sweet nectar and taste your honey.

Fair flower of nature, so richly endowed,
Give not forth your secrets nor shout them aloud.
I'll take me a lifetime to pull them all out;
What a pleasant endeavor to be always about.

To him who'd dutifully take of the time
To unravel your mysteries, oh! What a find!
Such beauties of nature, such fragrance of soul
Will flood him with wonder as the petals unfold.
        Lloyd A. Cooke

The Light Of My Life

The light of my life has blinded my eyes.
For I have lived in the eclipse of life.
I have left my sanctuary to delight in its warmth.
But it leaves me exposed to the menace, which hurts more.

The warmth it leaves has captivated my skin.
It's hard to cleanse it, once it has been pierced.
Oh, how I wish I hadn't seen the light,
it has burned my heart.

What happens now with the radiant soul
it has made me into?
Will it leave one day, to take everything I own,
and leave me in the dark?

Now that I can see, which way do I go?
The path ahead has many streets and conjunctions.
Yet it leaves no directions.
This is no-man's-land.

The light has left much to see,
that has hypnotized the heart to ache.
Do I reach and grab the air. . .
or will I receive what is mine?
        Lester West Jr.

The Noose

Around my neck a noose pulls tight.
Under my feet a two-legged chair,
maintain balance or walk on air.
People pass my precarious perch,
they wave, smile and even smirk.
Are they blind, can they not see,
death is dancing with me?
My grimace, looks like a smile,
friends stop to chat a while.
A slap on the back, I lurch and sway,
curse my friends and the day.
A small girl stops to gawk,
eyes resemble that of a hawk.
She rushes my chair, I gasp in terror.
Noose tightens, neck pops,
my body twitches as I drop, then... Stand and walk.
I reach to my neck and discover a thread.
What the Hell is wrong with my head?
        M. Edward Mitchell

The Past

Why does life end so fast,
I can't remember much of the past,
My Aunt, my Uncle went away,
Leaving another pathway.

One by one we'll drift away,
I am so shocked; I don't know what to say,
Who will be next, I wonder who,
Will it be another two?

I wish I could control the past,
If I could I'd bring them back very fast,
They are happy where they are,
Even though they are very far.
        Nicole Richmond

This Shimmering Ocean

As I gaze my eyes upon this shimmering ocean
  I am silenced by a roaring thunder of crashing waves.
A bird flies beneath the soft clouds
to reach the breezy wind of these crashing waves
to set its sprit free and to soar above the ocean.
I see the sun so differently;
shining so that it reflects hidden dreams of the night before,
and keeps them one secret treasured beneath the ocean floor.
As the waves crash endlessly against the white sandy shore,
they cease to hush and are silent no more.
As I try to lock there reflections into my soul,
I am breathlessly paralyzed by the hidden dreams.
Dreams of every spirit who has touched this ocean
with their loving and pure hearts;
Forever will I hold this sight seen never in my dreams before,
as I gaze my eyes upon this shimmering ocean,
I see it speaking words of eternity;
understood only by one's spirit for it seeks to reach another
Forever crashing, forever dreaming, forever shimmering,
forever speaking, in my heart evermore.
        Lacy A. Mills

A Wedding Today

  I attended a wedding today,
and I was not the groom.
  Yet, I prayed at that wedding today,
with anticipation that I would be one, soon.

  It was beautiful at that wedding today.
The bride and the flowers, you see.
  But most gorgeous at that wedding today,
was my lovely and dearest Leigh.

  As I sat through that wedding today,
Plenty, did cross my mind.
  Strongest thought at that wedding today,
Was of the love in her, I find.

  As I left that great wedding today,
grass looked greener and brighter the sun.
  For my hopes after that wedding today,
dealt with prayers, that we two could be one.
        Fred L. Stevens

Haunting Memories

Sands of time wash over the shore.
Soft winds, like a kiss of baby's breath,
sweet and pungent, touch my cheek.
Spirits, long gone, frolic in the waves,
dashing and dancing, onto the rocks below.
Bitter-sweet memories rush in to touch me
and the caressing waves soothe my soul.
        Vera Pace

Daybreak

As I awaken from peaceful sleep, darkness greets my eyes
  It must be morn, I hear the birds flying through the skies.

Lying in bed, so wide awake almost as though I'm pinned
  Outside the weeping willow is rustled by the wind.

The early morning odors from the kitchen rise
  The smell of fresh perked coffee and bacon as it fries.

The smells have made me hungry I guess it's time to eat
  I'll be served my meal in bed it's always such a treat.

I try to enjoy each moment in this quiet life I lead
  I try to keep it wholesome in thought, word and deed.

I've gotten all I've asked for
  But one and I don't mind
  It's great just living day to day
  Even though I'm blind.
        Michael P. Blattenberger

Between Night And Morning

Behind silent walls,
eyeless dreams remain untouched,
by the blue melancholy of early morn.
Stars recede further into heaven
as faint light intrudes
on the domain of darkness.

Bodies touch in unconscious ways,
as past, present, and future collide,
in the boundless depths of inner self,
and the fake death
lives out its final moments in triumph,
its return forth coming.

Even time seemed to stop and rest,
coming from its windy tunnel,
from its great heights
and endless misery, to lie quietly,
like a warm blanket,
before rushing off into the night like wind,
fearful of stillness and capture.
        Ron Mauriello

When I'm Alone

Why do keep remembering the smile upon your face?
What is it I'm searching for, in everything lonely place?
I do not think about you dear, when I am occupied
With daily duties or words, of someone at my side
I do not see you when I walk beneath a troubled cloud
Nor hear the slightest echo of your laughter in a crowd
But when the street is empty and I go my way alone
There is no comfort in my heart, that I call my own,
I seem to reach with longing words for something in the sky
And every memory of you becomes another sigh
        Anthony J. Sasileo

I Wonder

Did you ever hear a Bluebird sing?
So bright and cheery in the Spring?
From the heart he calls to his mate,
Come, share this day, let's have a date.
To his side, she flies.
To him.
From limb to limb into tree tops high.
Together.
Flashes of blue way up in the sky,
So brilliant a blue it hurts the eye.
Did you ever hear a Bluebird sing?
You'd never forget such a marvelous a thing!
        Dorothy G. Ormsbee

Who Cares?

Some things in life may never change.
For many people, this may sound strange.
But people are killed everyday
and don't have the chance to become old and grey.
Before a child could say hi,
it's about time to say goodbye,
because if the car they're in take a wrong turn,
slam! Bang! Boom! And they're gone.
This is not what life is about, but how louder can people shout?
Citizens are scared to take charge,
because the repeat offenders are always at large.
It seems as if they have all the rights,
whenever they patrol the streets by day and night,
looking for the innocent ones, with their 9 mm guns.
Nowhere is safe anymore, I may have to whisper to Mr. Gore.
How can anyone be active?
When they're in their homes as captives.
Hey, it's not that the home is safe,
but it's somewhere to say some grace.
This is all I have to say and hope I am heard while I pray.

Oslyn Jones

My Room

It's safe in here,
the world's out there
a dark shroud of endless hope
breeding poverty, greed, and sin
my friendly enemies are here,
drugs, alcohol, and despair
surrounded by death's icy fingers
devouring my spirit and soul
what is my purpose here should I emerge
a glimpse of daylight, the scent of a warm spring day
laughter in the air
life is drawing me near, there is a purpose
I know not what, it calls my name
I feel happiness within, it's stronger than me, I cannot hide
no sense of worthlessness or shame
I am alive!
My room, no longer my comfort zone
in this life I must stay
it is this world that I must change

Sherri Smith

Untitled

Too many things left unsaid.
Too many things never done.
You're the one who always led
The gaiety and the fun.
You're in my thoughts and in my prayers,
As you make the journey up Heaven's stairs.
The tears I shed are for you;
Tears of joy and of sorrow.
I'll remember all we used to do;
It will help to get through today and tomorrow.
I'll remember the fun we had,
The joy you brought everyone,
especially Mom and Dad.
I Love you more and more each day.
More than the sister you are.
You are tucked in my heart, not far away.
But in a sense you are far away.
My heart will never mend; since I have to say Good-bye.
To my very, very best girlfriend.
Why'd you have to die?

Jean Ann Leib

I Remember

I remember you. I fight and try to keep you out of my mind. But when I'm asleep, and the strength to struggle won't come, I dream of you. And when I've given up on fighting, I think back on your face, your embrace, our race to make time stop, our haste to make time just go on so we could be together again. I remember fighting the battle to stay together, knowing we'd never win. And I remember our last day. Tears... and trembling teenage lips touched and said good-bye. All the calls and cards and kisses we sent could never be what we really needed each other. And when the fight was finished, we each stood alone, on our own, and embraced ourselves. The only place we found power and peace was in our hearts. And the only fight left to be fought was the one to keep you out of my mind, and I lost that battle every day. Though the fight to keep you away is killing me, the fight we fought together was beautiful, and made us strong, and will never be forgotten.

Heather Rollings

You've Never Been There

I know you learned in school
I know you learned at home
I know you know the consequences

You always say I won't get caught
But tell me one thing
"How do you hide 9 months of consequences?"

The best way, I'll tell you...
Tell them the truth
You can't hide

So learn it in school learn it at home
But always ask "How do you hide 9 months of consequences?"

No matter how many times
You learn at home, in school
You'll never know 'til you've
Been there.

Brooke Calvillo

The Golden Season

Before the snow falls
Green leaves change like magic
Red, orange, green, all colors around me
Makes me warm inside

The setting, golden sun trying to say beautiful words
The sky, shining like gold
Evening ending so fast
Quiet, fresh days turn into dark, dull nights

Air as sweet as hot chocolate in my face
Soft touches and dull sounds echo back and forth
Cool, wet ground under my feet
Makes me comfortable and relaxed

Cindy Cattier

A Part Of Me

The sun comes up to bring a bright new day.
Which brings to mind, who's gonna pass along your way
As you continue to go through the day.
How will you remember who touched you along the way?
You think for a moment and pause; was it he or she?
Then wonder now; have they accepted me.

Donna Rodas

The Tiny Dog - Our Dog

From where did come Par Par -
From near or far?
From heaven above
Or earth beneath?

Where did he get those pointy little teeth?
Where also his smooth brown fur,
His vicious bark
And his growly grrrr?

Where did he get his soft, soft paws?
He's neat, he's sweet.
He obeys all the dogly laws.

From his dear brown eyes
To his sharp - pointed claws,
From his grey and black nose
To his scratchy little toes,
From his white underbelly and chest
To his long, thin black tail,

His love for us seems never to fail.
We love and adore our Skipper (Skipparrr)
Our little dog nicknamed Par Par.

Beth Denton

My Ebony Girl

I met a girl, lovely as could be
The loveliest diamond you'd ever see
Men would love to give you the world
So sweet sooo precious, my ebony girl!
When you walk in the room
you are the center of attention
of white men, black men even men on their pension
Wherever you walk wives and women cuss and fuss.
You should be in a history book
a nice topic to discuss!
It don't matter what you wear
because you sure wear it well —
For any man to have you in his arms
is like holding an angel.
The first time I met you,
in my mind I committed sin.
You'll always be my Ebony Girl
C A R O L Y N

Melvin Hardrick

Mother

A mother's love is like a rose,
It grows and grows and is so strong
Gentle as the falling leaves,
Never can be broken until it is released

A mother's heart is pure of gold
It holds things that are to be left untold
Yet it holds the gift that cannot be sold...
Kindness and gentleness

A mother's mind is so unique,
It helps you find the things you wish to seek
She thinks of things that are helpful for you,
And teach you to always be true

She also teaches you to think of others,
So in the future your kindness and
Thoughtfulness will be delicate as a flower

No matter what happens in life,
A mother is a mother,
Forever and ever.

Lynda Nguyen

A Butterfly's Plea

Why catch me, why, why, why?
When I should be free, free to fly,

I'm swift as a hawk going after its prey,
And should be set free to fly away,

Away to a land where plants can walk,
Away to a land where wild animals can talk,

In my land of enchantment where I can stay,
In my land of enchantment where I can live in happiness each day,

The fields are filled with flowers and grains,
That grow an inch each time it rains,

The nectar is so sweet, and the sun is so warm,
Living there are butterflies and bees by the swarm,

So to you I must plead for my life to spare,
With hopes that I will soon be there.

Stephanie Barnard

Grandmother

She was blessed by our Lord
with a unique and special way,
of making lives much brighter
through every passing day.

Her touch is warm and gentle,
tenderness fills her eyes;
the time she spends in caring
gives comfort to all our lives.

While reflecting a fragile quality,
her words stay firm and true.
She blesses hearts around her
with love and encouragement too.

Cherish the moments shared with her
the time was made to treasure;
For when those moments have come and gone,
the memories will be there forever.

One fact will always remain,
there will never be another,
for in this world nothing compares
to the love of a dear grandmother.

Staci Boykin

Going Your Own Way

It seems only a little while ago. Even before I can remember, your mother brought you to school and left you alone. That's probably the first time you remember...
Going your own way.

Then, as years went by, you made new friends. These friends became your own society and another phase of...
Going your own way.

More years went by and you met that special someone. Everything seemed so right and you brought that someone into your...
Going your own way.

Through that special someone you had me, and I was added to your circle of...
Going your own way.

Many years have passed and memories became numerous. Through the years there were many, some of them big and many more small but all them events and stages of...
Going your own way.

Now the space around you is quite and silent and the memories have stopped being recorded, but deep in my heart I know, Mom, you are starting a new series of...
Going your own way.

Edmund J. McIntyre

Apparition Of Love

The air was perfumed that day in June
with a love that was warm and well worth
waiting for. The sky was crystal and the
world seemed right. We starred in a sunset,
lived in a song, danced on the breathe of life.
Nights were fantasies which were the start of
lasting memories.
Nothing went unnoticed, nothing went untouched.
The heavens above shined on our love.
Like Spring's first green when all is serene;
till clouds of gray blow through with a wintery
snow and turns our fields of green to a paradise
of ice our love shall endure.

Evelyn L. Pszolkowski

Untitled

The pain in the world hurts so deep
  I dwell in hellish sorrow
All I need is the will to jump
  To insure there's no tomorrow
To end this painful life I live
  To stop these tears I weep
To stop this agonizing heart breaking hurt
  By taking an eternal sleep
On earth hell is in the heart
  And happiness is something you need
And those who cannot find it
  Are those whose hearts do bleed
To feel death's dark embrace
  I can feel my life signs falling
The reaper accepts age, all race
  I accept his morbid calling

William Jake Huffman

Mystic Anchorage

Reflections, peaceful thoughts, and clipper ships
Swaying upon a green, respiring sea—
These harbor-pleasures (Her sighs! Her fingertips)
Are breaths which fill canvas, inspiring me.

It appears New England's Ladies have not ceased
Admiring works of exotic artistry,
Timeless treasures from the distant East,
Cargoes of tea and Taoist philosophy.

From Canton's port, our vessel heavy-laden,
We left last April on homeward pilgrimage;
And sailed the swelling Silk Road to this place
Where a storm-sick soul finds tranquil space,
The kindness of a dark-haired Yankee Maiden,
And quiet moments at Mystic anchorage.

Clayton Ralph Martin III

Dreamers

I've tried to close my eyes to sleep, beneath the moon and
stars. I've listened to the wind keep blowing and wondered
where you are! I dream of having you here with me, but I
know I'll keep dreaming my life away.
So what are dreams good for, anyway?
What do I say to the people I see, who speak of your name
always to me, "Oh yea, I remember him;" but where on earth,
can you be? I dream about your tender words, but I know
I'll keep dreaming my life away. Please, someone tell me.
So what are dreams good for, anyway?
We had a good thing, you and I, but it slipped away just
like time. So now I keep dreaming of when you were mine,
and finally realized, that's what dreams are good for;
You and I. (Sweet Dreams My Love)

Virginia Duffy-Burch

We Were Like One

We were like one in the beginning, whatever happened?
We used to flow, flow like two rivers.
We used to gently flow all calm and relaxed and cool.
We met and became one river.
We rolled all around each other, kissed and made
soft passionate love all night.
We used to flow, flow together as one and now we're two.
You still flow, flow so gently laid back calm and cool,
and me I flow, I flow a bumpy, rough, broken ride.
We used to flow, flow as one.

Ladwana Caywood

You And Me

  As I lay in bed I think of you.
With your arms around me, and me kissing you.
When I look into your eyes I can see right to your
heart...I hope we will never part.
As soon as I give you a hug,
I kiss your hand and start to walk the distant land
Hand and hand we were meant to be,
If I hold you in my arms will you promise to love
me? I never knew we would get this far, but we are
better off as we are.
  In the beginning we started as friends and now our
love won't ever end. Trying to find my way out of
here, will you follow me? Will you stay near?
I promise our love won't fall apart
  because we hold together a lonely heart.

Candice Liebert

Song Of The Wind

Listen, can you hear it?
It's the song of the wind.

In the Spring the wind rushes,
Hurrying to blow Winters cold away
Warming, to bring new life to the Earth
New Hope, New Love.

The Summer winds come not so often
They can dry the land or bring cooling rain
Easing our minds of sweltering pain.

Fall winds bring a chill to the air
Bringing relief from what has been
To let life know what is to come
A calming of our hearts and souls.

Winter winds come blustering, cold and stout
The Earth now sleeps or does it?
The winds blow the snow about shaping the landscape
Into yet another scene of infinite serenity.

Listen, can you hear it?
It's the song of the wind as they blow through the seasons
they blow through our lives, ever changing, unpredictable.

Deanna M. Taylor

Listen

We must let the inner voice speak
there is no sound, the thought process takes hold of you
you stand quietly and react to truth
that binds your very soul, that no man can touch
the confused thoughts only make you doubt
listen and hear before you speak
now your words are clear and understandable
your eyes become clear of tears,
the sweat removed from your palms
now the inner voice speaks

Vernis L. Winfield Sr.

431

The Journey

To gain your love is to attain the highest prize,
  like reaching the shores of the destiny of my voyage.
Feelings swell deep in my heart when I behold your eyes,
  to walk on the beaches of your love I gathered my courage.
The waves roll over my feet and the sand slips beneath,
  I close my eyes and feel that I am spinning, falling.
I hear the waves and smell the salt of the water when I breath,
  through the cries of the gulls I heard you calling.
When first I set my eyes upon your shores,
  looking out over the bow of my lonely boat,
I lowered my sails and dipped my oars.
  The winds blew against me but I kept my hope,
and when I had made it I burned my ship.
  This beautiful land to be my new home,
no longer will I sail the dark, perilous seas alone.

  Timothy R. Noble

I Didn't Mean It

Help me, I can't survive,
I'm not strong enough to stay alive,
I cannot eat,
I cannot sleep,
Fear has got me on my feet,
There is no food,
It's too cold,
My tent is ratty, worn and, old,
The beasts are out there,
Ready for their share,
Huddled in the corner, tired and cold,
The beasts are ready now, strong and bold,
The tears are coming steady now,
My fears are taking over,
I didn't mean for the plane to crash,
The gas gauge read empty,
So we started downward,
Now the plane is empty,
All are drowned but me, it's so sad to see,
I cannot stay alive, help me I'm going to die.

  Margaret Mary Pelly

Old Folks

There's a charming little couple, who live just back of us.
You never hear them quarrel, and seldom do they fuss.

They used to be quite active, their duty was you see,
To warn us of intruders, and this they did with glee.

They watched out after our house, when we were gone away.
When we came back they greeted us, as if it made their day.

But they have gotten older now, lived longer lives than many.
One has gotten fatter, the other much more skinny.

They simply sit around most times, and seem to have great fun.
Just walking with each other, and lying in the sun.

For you see this little couple, live right inside our fence.
Cleopatra the cockerpoodle, and my old hound dog named Prince.

  Jack M. White

Night After Night

Longing to be free from fright
Wanting to be left alone...to remain unseen
is an unquestionable dream
not wanting to fight
not wanting to scream
Dreams are these, because it seems
like try as I might all I do is
scream and fight?

  Joshua Perkins

Untitled

Tears of sadness roll down my face
Only to drop into a wicked, dry, dark space.
And who but you can set me free and
break these pains that confine me.
Only you who is often so very weak
can't even find a voice to speak.
To say the things one longs to hear -
A promise is a promise, one of true love -
It can be used as a token and easily be broken.
You can take the good with the bad or go full force ahead.
But just remember you can breathe the air and still be dead.

  Linda J. Hawkins

A Little Woman In Me

I went in search of a friendly face and found it amidst the
  presence of a little woman's grace.
I saw her standing there with a smile and found I hadn't found
  myself, I stayed and drank a while.
As I slipped in to her skin I saw through her, I could envision
  her dream and found a dream deferred.
I saw what she saw. She looked at flowers and animals. All
  so complex things, yet simple through her windows.
For I was her and she was me, and in her words she said to me,
  let's go climb a tree.
And so we did and we were one, within ourself we were strong,
  and in her skin I could be that little woman in me.

  Stephanie Elise Kenyon

Unborn Child Within

I will protect you, my child, from the storms of fear.
When the lightning crashes and the thunder roars,
come running to me.
I will protect you from the corruption and disasters
That we create in this world.
I will stand by your side forevermore.
I will guard you little one, with all my heart and soul.
When you're forlorn or filled with hostility,
come running to me.
I assure you, my child, you will be safe
From the tragedies of the world.
Just remember, I'm here to protect you, my child, forevermore.

  Christy Raefski

The Rebuff

That handsome man with hat brim tilted
Can he be that kid I once jilted?
Yes. The scar on the chin: just ten years ago
Both of us sixteen, wouldn't you know?
I must have been out of my mind.
I've looked ever since for just that kind
Sweet and considerate, my devoted slave
I'm needing the kind of attention he gave.
He's so handsome. What a surprise!
Little black mustache and laughing eyes.
I wonder if a rebound I can make.
"Hello, Ronald for goodness sake
I'm glad to see you. You are looking well.
I'm sure you have some good stories to tell.
I'd be a good listener; come any day
You give me a ring so I won't be away."
"I beg your pardon, madam. You don't understand.
I'm not who you think. You have the wrong man."
A very beautiful girl walks up, touches his sleeve.
I'm too embarrassed to speak - so hard to believe.

  Gladys L. Koonce

432

He Told Me He Loved Me

He told me that he loved me,
and cared for me a lot.
We may have had disagreements
but we never fought.
We planned on getting married
and having kids of our own.
We wanted to live in a two-story house
and have a portable phone.
One day he laid me down and told
me how long we would be.
It really seemed like forever and I
really wanted to see.
Even though it all happened just in one night
I guess it made me wake up and see the light.
That after all those reports on pregnant teens
Who would have thought it could
happen to me and in only fifteen

Andrea McKnight

Heaven

Heaven is just like tons of dreams
a beautiful place, to me it seems.

It makes your curiosity flow;
for all the things that we don't know.

It's like a wish that doesn't come true;
but when it does, it surprises you.

To me, heaven is snowy white, full of angels,
and is a beautiful paradise.

To some people, it doesn't even exist;
and in the end, they won't know what they've missed

But the rest will be happy and never blue;
as long as this wish for them, shall come true.

Some people are curious, and some will go,
but as for the rest; they'll never know.

Trina Solem

The Romance Of The Fireplace

Beside the hearth nestled in the quilt
Cuddled by the warmth of the fire freshly built
We settle into each other's embrace
To enjoy the romance of the fireplace.

Winter surrounds with such chilling cold
But the heat radiates from the flames roaring bold.
Our hearts are warmed by the fires good grace
To enjoy the romance of the fireplace.

The glow upon your face is enhanced by the firelight.
To see your loveliness for me is such delight.
Sleep, my lady...in my arms...by the fireside
Dream away the night and let the romance be your guide.

Tony M. Mazzuco

Entitlement

On any given day, at any given moment
Sadness, and suffering and even death
fill the range of my senses
I am an unwilling witness caught
in the web of your tragedies self imposed or not
It is not of my control
I feel for you. I empathize with you
I'll even help you
But your problems are not mine
I am going to go about my business
in spite of your pain
I have got to. I am entitled

Yves Morency

The Spirit Of A King

A world entangled by a web of race
Articulately baffled without a scent of grace.
We struggle and shake, no effort succeeds
A scheming spider preying on worthless needs.
Awkwardly though, we choose to subside
This enchantment with death failing to be denied.
A dance with the devil by raging moonlight
Began long ago as an alienable right.
Now, a gleaming generation appears through the dark
As a shining sword prepared to leave its mark.
The uncanny craftsmen build bridges of love
Setting forth their intentions by a descending dove.
The cunning captains sail upon waves of decadence
Gracefully though, they're driven by loving winds of providence.
Something great is amidst this vast air
Prepare to be consumed by the truth it bares.
Like the spirit of a king
They boldly stand for freedoms ring.
No price could dare to climb too high
By peace and perseverance, they'll spread their wings and fly.

Brian Dufala

To Look Into A Dream

To look into a dream is to see into the heart
It is never what it seems for you wish to never part
Your mind is open, your breath is taken away
It is like sitting on an island, looking at a bay
You never use your mouth, only your eyes and ears
You remember all your wishes, and forget all your fears
There is always a beginning, but never an end
There is never an enemy, but always a friend
There is always someone there for you, someone who really cares
In a dream there are treasures, only the fine and rare
You can get along in life with truly wonderful ease
There are always people in a dream to help violence cease
In a dream it is regular to see a dove in flight
At the end of the tunnel, you can always see a light
You can always see the sun when you look at the sky above
And all around you, you can feel the warm sense of love

Summar Shoaib

Daddy

Christmas is near Dear Lord,
and Daddy is not here.
My heart is empty and full of fear.

My life has changed...
It Simply can Never be the Same.

But despite my hurt — I will gladly celebrate
the memory of your birth.

Jean Kalman-Volpe

Secrets

I tell all my secrets to whom I can trust
I'll keep them to myself if I really must
To myself, I keep my fears
I'll let them out when the end nears
There are only a few to whom I share
And these little few ones that care
I love them with all my heart
And I hope we never part
Secrets are best to have
Some make you smile and even laugh
My secrets are told when I feel it's right
Some last day's months, and even years
Some bring joy, some bring tears
Some are rumor's, some are true
If I tell you my secrets, I trust in you

Kathy Kammerer

On Being Seventy-Five

Three quarters of a century, I am here;
Forward looking, not back, having only to adhere
To each day's Sunrise and each day's Sunset.
Counting each hour an unpaid debt to be accounted for
Upon reaching that other shore.

Will it all add up to being my Sunrise or my Sunset?

Seventy-Five years and add a bit.
Thank you Lord, for your permit
To travel these Seventy-Five years,
Through this vale of tears;
Striving to learn and trying to cope
With the help of loved ones and undying hope,
To reach that heavenly place
Not made by hands of a mortal race.

Three quarters of a century,
Still grasping to reach Eternity.

Lawrence Wray

A Poem For Mary

I have a daughter so beautiful and strong
Once she was weak and did many wrong.

She has a big heart
And God knows it's true.
She wants a new start
So she won't be so blue.

God took my sweet girl from the depths of hell,
And tucked her under his arms so well.

She's learning a big lesson
Thank God it wasn't too late.
It is a real blessing
That in her heart - she doesn't hate.

She wants to come home,
But the law says...no
So she holds her head high,
And we just say good-bye.

When she comes home
The sun will shine,
Because I know in my heart
Her life will be just fine!

Sally Holder

To My Dear Irish Mother

My mother never made it back to Ireland.
Sure her name was Mary.
I can still feel on my brow her gentle hand
And her stories of beautiful Tipperary.
I have a picture of my mother as a young colleen,
It was not only her loveliness
But her beauty of soul I later seen.
In spite of her fatal sickness.
As I kneel beside her grave
With her son Mike lying beside her.
I think of all the love she gave.
Thank you, Lord, for my Irish mother.

Edward Bonner

Our Mother

You are the Mother I received the day I
wed your son and I just want to thank you
for all the things you've done.

You've given me a gracious man, with whom
I share my life. You are his lovely mother
and I his lucky wife.

Mary F. L'Ecuyer

The Hands Of Man

The world began as bright and clean
Never any thought of more
For man and beast kept the balance
And the world was fair and green
For many eons nature worked and changed
To keep the balance true
But man began to think that he knew more than she
For he used the land in a way not wise
Now man and beast no longer friend
For all the world was at loose ends
Now nature is not a tolerant foe
She will render payment for what has been done
For earth's salvation now is in the hands of man

Elizabeth Miske Ramirez

The Folly Of Man

Black holes in space, wombs from which
    Galaxies are born;
Are they the nothingness from which comes all,
    or are they the All?

Is God dead? Does Science rule? Eve or Evolution?
    Neither, I think.
For these merely demonstrate that God is made by man
    and not the other way around.

Where is the Truth and how can it be found?
    I know not.
But my Soul, freed from this dimension, becomes the Truth;
    for the Truth is that All are but One.

Christine Holland

Precious Memories

When I was a small child in my country town,
The carnival came with a merry-go-round.
Calliope music soon filled the air;
And for me there was nothing that I could compare
To the horses bright saddles and their manes I loved so,
As around, up and down, in a circle they'd go.

I climbed on and then quickly my eyes looked around
And I knew I had chosen the best to be found.
As I held the reins tightly, I began my first ride,
A big smile on my face and excitement inside.

The brass ring was suspended just out of my grasp,
Although I reached out for it each time I passed.
I rode 'round and 'round, never picking up speed,
On my beautiful, wild, shiny, black and white steed.

Then as the horses began to go slow,
I knew that the time had come when I must go
Far from the magical merry-go-round;
But I hoped that the next time they came to our town,
I could again know the feeling of joy it would bring
With those up and down horses and bright, golden ring.

Frances L. Willis

The Lady Of The Dawn

We seek the resurrection,
She comes with slight detection,
Her soothing light reminds me of a long
Forgotten memory
She touches me so tenderly
I feel her warmth across my face and arms.

I know the morning once again
Has come,
And with a sweet amen
I greet the rising Lady of the Dawn.

Stephanie L. Barr

An April Sunday - A Tribute To Marvin Gaye

The first day and fourth month in '84
Events unfolded - this is the lore.

Early that morning I took a walk.
Met a strange guy with strange talk.

He mentioned death; I mentioned God: it's April Fools.
He blasphemed him "I don't know him and damned his rules".

Oh the morning air was brisk, but warm.
So then I went to breakfast with my dear mom.

We spent the day together; we talked; we laughed.
Then I put myself on homeward's path.

A radio played a flop; a smash.
Then it aired a painful flash;

"Marvin Gaye is dead", and what prevailed?
A mother lost a son to death and spouse to jail.

An aries man; a sexy ram near forty-five.
But April Fool! This year was cruel: Marv's not alive.

John Leonard

My Brother

Dear Brother of mine,
you have had the life of beer and wine,
 And now it is time to let it go,
and live the life you have always known.
 You have children to love and hold,
so show them a dad that won't let go,
 so hold your head up and hold it high
and let the Lord show you that he is on your side,
 Show the people that you care
and you can see the things in life that we all can share,
 Life is beautiful in so many ways,
so keep yourself sober and keep the Lord near
 cause He will be there through your biggest fear,
If you will turn to Him and have no doubt
 He will show you what life is all about,
Don't you see Brother of mine
 The Lord has walked with me down the same line.
So don't you see I wouldn't be here
 To write this poem for someone so dear,
I love you Brother of mine.

Sheila C. Bates

A Prisoner's Cry

These bars hold me and restrain me.
My family, friends and society are taken away from me.
Not because of my crime but
Because of the prejudice that has arose.

Is it right for me to be harassed?
I committed a crime and I did the time.

There were no witnesses, just the law and me
Whose word is true?
The law, because I am a felon

Taken from no reason
Taken for the ones who I love and who love me

Sitting and waiting to go to court
Continuance after continuance, my life is on the line.
No decision has been made
My family is waiting patiently.
A woman, I love trying patiently to wait for me.

How much longer? Can someone make a decision? Is it too late?

I'm behind these bars. Restrained.
The love of my life is free and vulnerable to temptation.
These bars that hold me.

Lakecia Whimper

To Be Free

C'mon Star Light shine on down
Light the path that leads me on
To a simple life where we are free
Where people find a way to peace...and their destiny

 I went to the mountain
 I go to the well
 I drink from the fountain
 of you

We'll walk along the river's edge
To the valley that opens up to the sky so wide
And in the morning sun, we'll fly
Let the spirits be our guide...it's easy to be free

 I went to the mountain
 I go to the well
 I drink from the fountain
 of you

Reach out and touch that cloud
Gently lay your body down and rest above the sea
Let the swirling breezes lift you up
Release the weights you're a peaceful dove...it's easy to be free

Scott S. Meyers

Friend

Friends are for sharing
all the joys and the sorrows,
a friend will be there
in all the tomorrows.

When life's not at its best,
and you need to take a rest,
a friend will be there to bring you happiness.

And always when you're lonesome
and your world comes tumbling down,
a friend will come along and take away your frown.

Friends are the priceless moments that you will come to share,
saying kind words, thinking kind thoughts, showing that you care.

I have written this poem quite clearly,
because I have a friend very dear to me.

And though I have many friends there's one I'm thinking of,
my one best friend, a friend I dearly love.

So my friend these gifts of friendship,
these gifts I know are true,
have happened to me only because
of a wonderful friend like you.

Rhonda Fletcher

Beyond The Walls Of Clay

 Full compositions fill my head
like an orchestra of angels majestic...
and visions of hell unfold around me,
bringing forth contrast.
 The invisible eyes and child of fear,
dead flowers on a nameless grave
freshly covered.
Blissful sounds released into the air
music heard only in dreams,
whilst far below, I hear the gnashing
of teeth and cold blood chilling screams.
 The tranquility of madness,
horrific beauty of deities in battle,
possession of the throne commence!
Wings aflame, tails gnawed, strings
of harps broken,
 Both sides preach victory
 Bringing forth contrast

Jeffrey S. Burdick

435

Give Way To The Overtakers

Surely awake, now go to sleep,
No tunes are playing, mouse it goes creeping.
Shatter the glass all over the floor,
No more a mask or flavor ardor.
Tears have been spoken on plains and the hills,
Mountains have given the way from the chill.
The chill of the conqueror finding his way,
Down paths that the demons have given to sway.
The angels keep singing this marvelous song;
Not only from dusk, also till dawn.
But this cannot stop him, his power his might,
This keeps me awake all through the night.

Maya Perrott

Rocking Chair

A tired soul rocks in the chair
Swaying back and forth
Little evidence of virility and joy
As one ponders the artless loss of youth
The days are filled with recollections
Of the distant past
Yearnings for the younger life
Which seemed fabricated to forever last
One hopes silently to be remembered
That our achievements and dreams
Will continue to live on
That our precious life will have meant something
Even long after we are gone
Everyone of us will grow old
Everyone of us will disappear
When all that is left
Is the rocking of the empty chair

Marion A. Petchalonis

Untitled

Fisherman, fisherman face of tan
What pilgrimage you make to some foreign land
To sit in some boat or by some shore
A whale, shark or bass to add to your lore
Why sit you there when no bite you get
Do you dream of more worlds you haven't conquered yet?
To while away the time without care and woe
The soul needs these things to keep on the go
Fisherman, fisherman face of tan
Let me go with you to some foreign land
No angler's line need I
just some cool spot with blue-gray sky
So I, too, can leave care and woe behind
And take solitude for mine.

Laura H. Ross

The Dove

The song of the dove brings tranquility.
Soft cooing outside the window, calm settles over me.
The lonely song of the dove,
it stands for peace, resembles love.
It seems so strange how the cooing of one small bird
could mean so much,
far away from human hands, miles away
from human touch.
I look outside my window,
it is always the dove my eyes see.
This quiet bird resembles so much,
the type of people we should be.
Always peaceful, eternally calm
the gentle cooing sets me free.
The song of one bird,
it's simple pacifying plea.

Shannon Marie Thomas

Dream

As I look at you, you look at me,
Your soft brown eyes go straight through my soul.
They seem to read my mind,
If I look hard in them, I get lost never to be found.
Your lips so soft, so sweet and strong with every kiss.
They keep me near never to leave.
Your voice takes over me, with your every
    command and leaves me trembling.
Your hands so gentle, as they pull me near.
Your body's strong and warm with love,
    I can feel you through-out my body
We hold each other close, never to let go.
Your eyes put me under a spell.
    Your smile leaves me breathless.
As we lean closer, I long to feel your kiss.
I close my eyes, and I can feel your
    breath on my face and know we're even closer.
I hear a noise and open my eyes,
    you're not there.
I guess it was all a dream.

Ashley Marie Rodgers

Dedicated To The One I Love

I came back to this state,
I only wanted to date.
I looked for you to no ends,
Trying and hoping for amends.
I cared for you once before,
Yet our relationship couldn't score.
Then I called upon you,
You're too good to be true.
Now that you're here to stay,
I fell in love with you in every way.
I need you more than life,
In April I will be your wife.
I want you 'til death do us part,
Cause you forever hold my heart.
Our love shines like the sun so bright,
I love holding you all through the night.
I want you to know you mean so much,
I will forever need your touch,
I want the whole world to know,
Just how much I love you so.

Karen A. Turner

Untimely Demise

My tears leap to their untimely demise
Silence is broken by my devastating cries

Searching, searching, searching to fuel that dark abyss
Search no more, it will never come from a warm, deep kiss

What truly can pervade that dark endless hole?
Is it going to be you and you and you
Or is it going to be my crippled, thirsty soul?

I floated beside you in the friendly village —
Our hands locked, as I clutched on for life

Grips reluctantly loosened until they unraveled
And the pain penetrated my stomach like a knife

As I peacefully drifted above all my shattered dreams
I faintly can make out one of your thunderous screams

One hand slowly slides into my other, as I start to descend
My crippled, thirsty soul in the abyss is finally hydrated,
And beginning to mend

My tears leap to their untimely demise
The silence is broken by my whispering sighs

Kenneth T. Bierman

Love Of A Lifetime

Lost and lonely, and looking around,
For someone to love her, then she finally found,
The greatest man, with light dusty hair.
The cutest smile, and charm to spare.

She loved him and he was always true.
He was the greatest man she ever knew.

It was then she realized, it had to be a dream.
How could this love be as good as it seemed.

"I've never met his family!", she thought with a sigh.
It was then she knew, it was all a big lie.

How could she be so naive.
Now she knew he had a trick up his sleeve.

He came by to see her one bleak winter's night.
She tried to confront him and they got into a fight.

Red neon thoughts flashed through her mind,
As he pinned her down and committed the crime.

Then when he left, she fell to the floor.
This wasn't the kind of love she had bargained for.

She looks back on him with no emotion,
As the death he planned for her, washed through her like an ocean.

Sibyl Blanton
Angela Ray

Mama, Is Grandma Home?

You want to see her, and so do I...
You ask where she is, and I want to cry...
"Mama, is Grandma home?" You'll ask with a frown.
And all I can say is, "No honey, she's gone..."
But then I will hold you, and we will have a long talk;
all about God and the Angels, and to the Light she will walk...
You seem to understand all these wonderful things.
Yet the very next day, you ask the same thing.
"Mama, is Grandma home?" You ask with a sigh.
How do I tell you, we all have to die?...
"With Jesus?" You ask. And I smile your way...
"Yes with Jesus my sweet," what more could I say...
With tears in my eyes, I hug her "little man,"
and we again talk of angels, and a most heavenly land...

Kathleen M. Bingen

Let Your Heart Shine

Through the intricacies of God's plan
You were formed in your mother's womb.
Created there was a special place
Deep within your heart
A place where God can dwell
If only you invite Him in

As He is living there you cannot deny His love
It glows within you—You are consumed with a fire
A blazing flame fed by His Word
Fed by fellowship with other believers
Illustrated by worship and desire to serve
A burning heart for the lost souls
Whose fire has grown cold

You hunger to fill the empty places of the world
Cast away demons who lie and deceive
Restore the flames that once burned
Light some flames for the first time
It all begins when your heart glows
Filled with God's presence, God's Glory, God's love
Let your heart so shine

Judy Grubb

"The River of Love"

My love for you is like
A river in the hot sunshine.
It flows long and warm and courses
Through the years without drying up.

Your strength is my inspiration.
It keeps me going everyday.
Thinking of you and the love we share,
Makes the troubling times in my life easier to bear.

Though the rocks of life in the river
Of my love try to stop its flow,
The river surges strong and mighty
Overcoming and overflowing its barriers.

Just knowing you are there
Is a salve to my mental and emotional wounds.
Just knowing you are a part of my life
Keeps the cold from entering my being.

I guess what I'm trying to say is
That you mean the world and more to me.
The love that I have for you knows no distance,
And will endure anything that tries to stop it.

Melanie Thompson

M e

A mi_____le long.
but still -
just a grain of sand in the universe.

Space.
   Stretched out an eternity in each-tiny-little-direction.
   No stars.
   No planets.
Nothing.
Me
   and
Space.

Heather Schroer

Death

As the clock came near seven,
a raven came and said, "Heaven, Heaven."
I thought and thought what it meant,
then I remembered my son Evan.

He was out trick or treating
I had to go pick him up.
But when I got there, my son was dead,
laying flat on his back without saying a sound.

I wondered and wondered
where would he go, heaven or hell!
And with my sorrow I managed to remember
the raven saying, "Heaven, Heaven."

Roshan Soans

"Me"

It seems so odd that when we look back to when we were younger,
We wanted to grow up so fast.
But, now that we're older those same reasons that we wanted
to grow up for don't have the same meaning for us.
Those particular rosy thoughts haven't the same innocence for us.
The innocence in our eyes has been changed forever.
With the reality of everyday life.
So when life's troubles begin to get overbearing
and nothing seems to make sense.
Remember the one thing that hasn't changed is our friendship.
And you'll always have me!

Kathryn Rooker Skaggs

Learn to Love Again

Forget about love,
Forget about life;
Forget about the peace dove,
Forget how he flies;
Remember him as he remembers you,
Learn how to love again and stop feeling blue;
Remember how to live as you did once before,
Before the pain and hurt came knocking on your door.
Take it as it comes and be grateful for all you've got;
Remember to live is to love,
Even if your heart says it's not;
Forget those who have hurt you in the past,
Remember the happiness and love now that is meant to last.

Tara J. Schmitt

Fury Of Fear

Sometimes I hear crying in the night
Is it anothers terror or my fright
I listen as it calls me near
And want to go down and help her fear
As I walk slowly down the hall
It seems to grow closer but farther and I stall
I feel something weary inside as I stand
And wonder which room is the one within
I can't wait to see her
And tell her it's me!
There's no need to fear with little ole me
But I can't find the crying downstairs you see
Because the one crying was deep within
Me

Mickey

Time

Time can be wasted in so many ways
In one short sweet second, or long endless days
Treasured yet taken for granted by all
Time is not just a clock on the wall
Time is a gift, as precious as life
It begs us to dream, not wallow in strife
Saved for, enjoyed, and dreaded by man
It's remembered, spent and needed to plan
Given and taken, pitied and changed
Time has run out, yet has always remained
Time is expected, questioned and asked
Begged, borrowed and stolen, returned to and past
It flies without wings, regrets and stands still
Long, short and lived for, it's something to kill
Time is used and abused by us all
Time is not just a clock on the wall

Gerald I. Hummel

A Mother's Love

I open my eyes, but what I seek is not there.
I look out the window, yet all I see is bare.
I listen for the music, but her voice I do not hear.
I read my collection of poetry, yet I feel no cheer.
I feel so lost and wonder, as I look high up above...
What will I do, how will I live, without my mother's love?

I close my eyes and listen for the sounds that I might hear.
It's then that I do realize my mother is so near.
I see her in my brothers, I see her in my dad.
I hear her in the music thru the songs I've always had.
She's always close beside me with everything I do.
She's in the birds I hear each day, she's in the sunshine, too.
Her love has never left me, it's just that I've been blind.
I've kept myself so busy, I forgot to open my mind.
My mother is deep inside me, she's deep inside my heart.
And now I truly understand, we'll never be apart.

Pamela J. Flick

Do We Belong?

If I kept you from doing the things that you loved,
for fear of losing you, would I really be loving you?
Is trust not a part of love?
What's more, shouldn't love give a feeling of security—
a sense of reassurance?
I love you so much, and so afraid of losing you that I hold
you as my prisoner of love.
In a real sense, am I not just setting myself up for pain?
If I let you do the things that you love, and you come back
to me, isn't that security, reassurance—love!
But...if you didn't come back to me and you found something
or someone else...Do we really belong?

Debby Grachen

Potato Harvest

I can see my father in the garden stabbing whales:
he thrusts too soon his forked harpoon
and fails to land a catch

Then drives down deep his blackened tool
bringing forth a breaching school
his harvest belly-up in frenzied black

And in a frenzy of his own
he gathers what he'd sown into a sack

Then sees more swimming there below the surface just
and with a final reaping thrust
brings up that which he knows he must

For these are his—are his to take
all swimming in his back yard lake

And often he'll be found here wading
in the wake of his own spading

Luke Schelhaas

Found You

Silence keeps on coming back to me:
It seems that I can never be free.
I know that it isn't real.
I know that I can never feel.
    Through Consciousness and savage dreams,
    I've found my true call,
    For when I try to break through, all I do is fall.
    When I try to get up I get pushed down,
    And all that I want to do is say that I found.
Has it come back down to this, have I found the end?
Is it possible to go on with just my friends?
    Why is it that I must stay so far away?
    Can I approach you with all I have to say?
    What are all these secrets that you chose to hide?
    Why have you chosen to keep them locked inside?
The world revolved round the thoughts of life;
Now it's just full of hatred and strife.
Now that I know just what to do;
All that I need is to find you.

Howard Wolosky

My Friend

I have a friend that you might know
Who gives to others so they will grow
Herself, she never thinks of first
But only others is her curse

She brought to me with open arms
Her love and kindness, strength and charm
This friend of mine is you, you see
And a friend of mine you will always be

Romney W. Tripp

Destiny

The man with the sad orbed face
stares at what entombs his love.
His rosy cheeks are glazed with
a natural salt.

Incense of the dead fills his nostrils
and his pained heart,
leaving him with a feeling of absolute
loneliness and shun.

His world has died when her last
tear of pain plummeted in utter silence.
The dreams and memories have faded
like the song of a bird in flight.

Thoughts of past fill the sky
in flashes of lightning, allowing him
to forget her eternal slumber
for some short time.

Although he knows the pain is deep,
it will also soon come to an end.
For he knows he is only a moment
of time behind her.

Steven L. Safrany

Love

Love is the word that
can get this world together
love is the word that
can erase all the sadness
and bring happiness.
    Love is the word that
can unite all the countries
even when they speak different
languages.
    You loved yesterday,
you will love today and
tomorrow, don't forget
love is to your life
the vitamins.
    Where there is love
there is light, where there
is love there is life,
so don't forget to love and
you will survive.

Ramonita Calcano

Love

Love is a hand
Held fast in your own
Love is a kiss
The sweetest you've known
Love is a joy
You feel from the start
Love is a dream
You keep in your heart
Love is a world
That's peopled by two
Love is wonderful
Love is you.

Walter S. Bachenko

Untitled

It is better to travel on
the unfamiliar road
of a dream
Than to sit in the
darkness of routine.

Teresa Marie Beukers

The Meaning

We closed our eyes
In our hearts you appeared
We smiled aloud we had no reason to fear

You were blessed to us
Because of our love for you
Questions why
Futile when loves true

Awaiting the day
For you and us to meet
Anticipating slowly
Our lives incomplete

Thoughts of you
Nothing else to be
So much to do
A loving family

Now you're here
For us to see touch and love
We thank the Lord
Around you angels from above

We close our eyes

Joseph M. Ebbitt

Soul Torn...

Inside my eyes will cry,
my smile will die.
My heart will break,
my soul will ache.
My body will numb.
This feeling wished to be undone.

Outside my eyes will be bright,
my smile will take sight.
My heart will be happy, that I say.
My soul will not hurt in any way.
My body will be free,
but not inside of me.
Inside is hidden,
to enter is forbidden.
Look on the outside,
ignore the inside.
Touch my soul,
never let go.

Bethany LaPorte

Early Spring

Bear up - bear down happily,
    Bear in mind and keep bearing,
    Bear with me endearingly,
    Bear all things, my early spring.

Believe in me sincerely,
    Believe and keep believing,
    Believe with me honestly,
    Believe all things, early spring.

Hope and pray, yes, faithfully,
    Hope and trust and keep hoping,
    Hope with me eternally,
    Hope all things, my early spring.

Endure please, courageously,
    Endure and keep enduring,
    Endure with me endlessly,
    Endure all things, early spring.

Love never fails entirely,
    Love and always keep loving,
    Love with me but, tenderly,
    Love all things, my early spring.

Robert Daniel Melofsky

Place Of Secrets

This place of secrets, hidden
From the blue sky of morning,
Names engraved in granite
Lost and long forgotten.

The ancient and wise ones
Submerging themselves
In lust and vanity,
Needing no God to forgive them.

This place of secrets was silent,
As the soul of man had darkened
In the saddened prophecy
Reflected by broken mirrors.

George A. Hoehn

My Tears

I cry not for my dead
He stands by God's throne
My tears are for the living
Who now must walk alone

I cry not for my dead
He stands in God's shining light
My tears are for memories
Which make my pathway bright

I cry not for my dead
Now leaning on God's arm
Someday I'll meet him there
And be safe from all harm

Marjorie J. Willis

Fear

It sometimes comes as few,
Sometimes one,
Often many.

-It Always Comes-

Always scratching
And clawing
And tearing
At reason and rational thought.

-It Always Comes-

It turns some to infants,
Crying helplessly through...
Through glossy eyes
And painted smiles.
Still some persevere?

-It Always Comes!-

For all of life,
Tethered heart to heart;
Master and minion.
Which is whish...which is Fear?

Chris La Guardia

A Birthday Wish

Once again it's that time of year,
to go about and spread good cheer.

We spread it in a special way,
because Jesus Christ was born this day.

So when you wake on Christmas morn,
give thanks to God that he was born.

Just look up in the sky and say,
"Hello Jesus, Happy Birthday!"

James Kessler

What Can I Tell My Bones?

When everything is dying.
When everything is cold.
When everything becomes weak.
When everything grows old.
What then can I tell my bones?

When all life is lost.
When all energy is gone.
When all has grown dark.
When I am all alone.
What then can I tell my bones?

When there is nothing left to say.
When there is nothing left to do.
When there is no more hope.
When nothing again is new.
What then can I tell my bones?

When everything grows black,
And death is the only tone.
When my heart no longer beats,
And I long to go home.
What then can I tell my bones?

Mary Jane Browney

Left Behind

The music that played
when I looked into his eyes
has since faded
he has said his good-byes.
The words he said,
are meaningless now,
the lies to me he fed,
so I'm remembering how,
he made me feel.
Useless and unwanted.
Now here's the deal,
his strengths he flaunted,
but mine he ignored.
Leaving me to decide,
if this's what I can afford.
My confidence has been forced to hide.
Leaving me in the dark.
Is this what I want?

Sarah Meston

Conscious Conscience

I took a trip
Never returned
The flags representing
My mind burned
For I learned
Looking from a different view
What we are, me and you
Countries uninviting, fighting
Earthlings that should be uniting
We all believe in different Gods
But we come from the same place
Just because we have separate face
Cripples us to touch base
So in our case
Separate until desperate
In need of each other
That is one day we will not see color
Only call ourselves sisters and brothers
And create a peaceful earth
Like it should have been from birth.

Crystal Hall

Untitled

Go forth merry into the world;
Step gaily on its edges;
Dance in wonder across its pains;
And honor nature's pledges.

Lightly, lightly touch your love
In reverent awe and giving;
Lightly, lightly take your love,
Receiving all in giving.

Go forth merry into the world,
Your voice aglow with singing;
Look all at life but not at death;
Keep every heart-bell ringing.

Lightly, lightly tread the path;
But barely touch the sod;
Lightly, lightly lift your hand
And feel the form of God.

Earl Russell

My Nebraska

How I love my dear Nebraska,
Early in the spring,
When meadow larks are singing,
And showers flowers bring.
Now the days are getting longer,
And the joys of summer here,
And we can go on picnics,
With our friends and loved ones dear.

Oh it's lovely in Nebraska
In the beauties of the fall.
And the sparkling snow of winter,
Is a cover for it all.
So I'll stay in old Nebraska
With its many sunsets rare.
And know that God has kept us
In His tender Loving Care.

Nebraska is the state I love;
Its beauties all sent from above.
Nebraska is the state I love;
So may we share the joys thereof.

Zella Escritt Schwarting

Remembering Them

Crown of madness, crown of tact
Royalty is just an act
Bright side suicide
Still deceiving fate
Side by side clasping hands,
Interfering with the band
When the death was such a disgrace,
It caused him to roll over in his grave
New secret lover and concentrate
Somewhere there was a lucky eight
Sit and bathe eternally
Planting houses, building trees
Sugar magnolias and oddbody palm trees
Ladder steps that climb so high,
Watching cars passing by
Filling up and draining out
Liberty is at a doubt
Strangeness yellows ugly things
Harassment warrant for your arrest,
Hey piggy piggy now who's the best

Lori Browning

'Tis The Sun Is Risen

'Tis the sun is risen
   I open my eyes, as I feel
The warmth of sunlight on my face.
   The breeze gently kisses my
cheeks as it brushes back my hair.
   I smell the sweet perfume of
the rose lingering in the air.
   The sound of birds are heard
in the distance.
   I am ready to face the day
and accept its challenge.
   I will go every round,
Neither death nor prejudice
   will overtake me.
Some say I am just
   a blind man.
I say I am a fighter
   and a winner.

Eunice D. Karr II

My Freedom

Poetry is freedom
and both being the same,
linger in my pocket,
like Cinderella's lost key.
Stern voices in a harsh,
real,
beautiful world.
City stores and daggers,
ring out their own cries of night
and the irrelevance
of being relevant
is becoming important.
How could there ever be too much
poetry?
Does it make me great?
Or mad?
Does my freedom
scare you?

Cassandra Dovel

Cape Cod Perceptions

An arm that sticks out in the ocean,
With elbow and bended fist.
Cranberries, beach plums, and scrub oaks
dewy with ocean mist.

Beach grass peeks out of the sand dunes
Breezes propelled upon high
Gray cottages flaunt their pink roses
On a background of cape cod blue sky.

Umbrellas dot the seashore
Waves beckon us to come
The water laps over our bodies
As we frolic through the foam

Sailboats on the horizon
With billows of puffy white
God's engine pushes them forward
As they vanish out of sight.

Summer's wondrous pleasures
Simple, sweet and carefree
The sunshine warms our inner souls
And fills our hearts with glee.

Patricia W. Dorsey

The Little Hand

There's that warm special feeling
Deep down inside
When those five little fingers
Into my larger hand slide.

That tender, young hand
With a squeeze can impart
All the dreams for a future,
All the love in a heart.

That sweet, little hand
Is mine to help guide.
The responsibility is great
As we embark on life's ride.

When I hold that small hand
Questions run through my mind.
Can I build character and courage
So life's best that hand will find?

That uniquely designed hand
May one day dwarf mine.
But a touch still brings memories
Of the love built through time.

Beth Ann Glasgow

A Mother's Love

Find a river's origin,
then try to find its end.
You'll find some rough water
and eventually a bend.
Like the river's water,
sometimes is a Mother's love.
She does the best she can,
as directed by God above.
Rapids or rough waters,
and then around that bend,
the waters grow calmer,
as does nature always intend.
With each and every challenge,
be it a son or a daughter,
her love is everlasting,
just like the river's water.

Lisa J. Hansen

His Face

I must seek his face
I need his embrace
His arms are open wide
I rush to his side
But then his pain I see
As he looks down at me
I feel all the shame
I know I'm to blame
He came from above
To bring me his love
I hurt him so
I didn't know
It was for all my sin
They had to crucify him
His life he had to give
So that I might live
He reigns up above
Waiting for your love
You need his embrace
You must seek his face

Helen Billiot

The Pansy

The pansy has a lion's face
as any fool can tell
he wares a tie of greenest lace
and dongs a silent bell

His jungle roar is never heard
the roses see to that
he's not allowed to speak a word
nor may he ware a hat

There with his brothers he doth stand
demented as a loon
and late at night he lifts he head
elegantly lifts his head
and bellows at the moon

Donald M. Henson

We Each Walk Alone

We each have a trail to walk,
    We each one walk alone.
We don't realize what it is,
    Or where it leads us on.

We walk a little of this trail,
    Each day that we're alive.
We wonder down those little paths,
    As through life we strive.

We don't know nor understand,
    How far we go each day,
God lends us a helping hand,
    As we go along the way.

We have to ask Him though you see,
    If we want His help each day.
He won't just give us what we want,
    You're going to have to say.

In the end, we walk that road,
    And no one understands.
Because it's ours alone to walk,
    But God's our helping hands.

Lloyd Lamb

On Eagle's Wings...

When I'm at my desperate moment
In the loneliest hour of the day
When the pain is too much to bear
I refocus myself and pray.

Then I mount up like an eagle
Ride the wind up to the sky
Let the storm clouds be my chariot
As I spread my wings and fly.

Through the storm I reach the heav'ns
As the Lord reaches out to me
He carries me through the darkness
To a safe place I can be.

There I found the joy once lost
There I found the peace
There I found the comfort longed
In the loving arms of Jesus.

I realize that it takes a wound
To learn how to be strong
I know now that only through God's pow'r
Every pain to a blessing belongs.

Elizabeth Batista

Anger Is a Palace

Anger is a palace
Towering over the sweetness
Of the land around it
Ruling anything it wants
And not thinking twice about it.

Lauren Malench

Life's Unanswered Questions

Where do we go from here?
Should we go on?
Can we start over?
When will this end?
When will we find the truth?
Could it be here?
Is someone there?
Who can help us?
Could this be a dream?
Should we go there?
Should we stay here?
Will it find us?
Will we find it?
What is this place?
Should we go in?
Should we stay out?
Where do we go from here?

Meaghan Coughlin

Untitled

You see the trust in my eyes
I feel the sun on the rise.
A silent blue becomes the sky,
As a baby bird learns to fly.

And now a rain comes down
It falls on a freak-filled town.
It broke me when you went;
The rain took what I sent.

The ground soaks down what it can
And I know now I'm a man,
Because I push the pain behind my pride;
What should be free I hold inside.

Simon Foust

We Have Meaning

Although we are not bright,
we have meaning.
We have family and friends,
who care about us,
even though we are not bright.
Although you may make fun of us,
for not being bright,
we have meaning.
You may shame us,
and hurt us with words and looks,
for not being bright,
but know we do our best to survive,
even though we are not bright.
When you make it a point,
to accept us the way we are,
know you will evolve for doing right.
But until that happens,
we want you to know,
we have meaning.

Jose Covarrubias

Franklin

Take this heart of mine,
Take this fire inside,
Take the ground beneath
my feet,
Take the person you are
and put it in me,
I see my world in your eyes,
I see my son in your soul,
Make me your wife,
Make me your true love
to be,
Make me everything
you see.

Carolyn Whittemore

Madness

I sit in a corner as I hear
gun shots
This world is so crazy,
everyone is going mad
Drugs everywhere people killing
people, it all seems so unfair
a tear runs down my cheek
because I'm so scared of
the streets. I don't know
what to do, I can't take
this anymore.
Everything's going wrong,
I'm thinking about suicide.
You know something has to
be wrong when you take
your own life.

Frannie Coffey

I Like Me

I like me!
I like me
because I am me!

Erica Lambertz

Let Us...

Let us sail to paradise
Let us sing about eternal love.
Let us rise above worthless fellow
And empty words.

Let us kiss each other, like
two stars glowing.
Under guise of love and fire
let's conquer twilight of the life
and the end.

Let's be always
two stars glowing.
Let's swear to those we love.

Darko Braunstajn

Life

Life,
What is the use of life.
It only holds me down.
To die, to die is what I want.
To be an empty shell.

I rather be an empty shell,
Than have an empty heart.
Without the love that makes us live,
What is the use of life.

Carol A. Chapman

Rapture

Embrace thy own creation
of whence thou came to be
Witness thy absolution upon
thy trinity
Behold thy resolution for whence
thou art alone
For ye hath revelation within
thy flesh and bone
Thine flesh of dust thine eyes
begotten from thee whom
saw thy seed
For in all conscience begotten
to reason 'tis law of eternity
Unto all whom dwell amongst
the waves of Ideals conceived
by thrones woe ye art dead
and shall lie instead amongst
thy dust and stones

Daniel J. Smith

What Is Love?

She asked me,
"What is love?
Is it the feeling of togetherness,
The solidarity of two hearts?
Or is it the unity of two souls?
Is love life and being
Light and warmth
Joy, ecstasy or sorrow?
Is love God
Or is love thyself?
Is it mystical and supernatural
Or a basic element of life?
Is love...
What is love?"

I replied,
"Love is you
And love is me."

Michael Wall

Fireside Talks

With half closed eyes
I watch the flaming fire.
Half awake
half dreaming
my imagination wanders.
Orange and yellow flames leap and dart
inviting me to come.
I follow into unknown spaces
probing
searching
testing untried concepts.
Uninhibited I explore
until the constant steady blue flames
stay my wondering thoughts.
As embers grey
reality returns.
I stir the dying coals
only to have them blaze again.
The fire makes its own decisions.
My fire talks to me.

Martha Tavener

Young Love

Embers die and fade away
But with love it is not so
For love may die but never fade
It has an afterglow

Elaine E. Omo

Silhouette Of Winter

The sun is shining
Diamond crystals glimmering off the snow

The air is crisp
And smells so clean
No sounds of birds
The sky is clear

The wind blows
With a message of its own
That no one knows

The trees are calm
No leaves on their limbs
For the sound of winter, is so, still

Children play
Throwing snowballs, sledding
And making angels, where they lay

Some are on ski slopes
While others go
Where the wings of birds
Take them, solo

Idella Tyler

The Lessons In Our Past

The Day is done...
The Die is cast...
We live our lives as in the past.
We continue our transgressions.
The tools of which are fear, hate,
    and oppression.
Looking for someone or something to blame.
We can just look forward to more of the same.
We have failed to learn the lessons in our past.
And the price we'll pay shall be the last.

Perry Medina

Summertime Dreaming

The lazy old sun
On a quiet summer day
Warms my bod to sleepy drowse,
Takes my fancy to faraway lands
On fairy wings I fly away.
I dream of castles, silks, and kings,
Of riches and love,
Adventure and fun,
All of this
Belongs to me
As I lie 'neath the sleepy old sun

Sheryl W. McDaniel

Tickle Me Elmo

I wanted a Tickle Me Elmo,
Because he's so cute and sweet.
He's red he wiggles and giggles,
While moving his hands and feet.

We hunted all over the city.
We even went out of town.
We tried so hard to find it.
But still none were to be found.

I woke up that Christmas morning,
And much to my delight,
I found my Tickle Me Elmo.
Which Santa had left last night.

Crystal Dower

442

Gone Forever

As I stand alone
left all by myself
I dream of the days that are gone.
Memories will last a lifetime,
I know.
Yet in my heart
I'll never be the same.
Just yesterday I remember,
your absence to be noticed.
I know I can not control
most of my worst nightmares,
and God be willing
you have died.
You never let me down,
and I will remember
how you caressed my hand.
In act of love I wept,
and yet still forever
you'll be gone.

Jackie Strenio

Butterfly, Butterfly

Butterfly, butterfly, don't be shy,
Spread out your wings, and fly, fly, fly.
Fly over the mountains, and over the seas,
Over the meadows, and over the trees.
Fly through the clouds, and over the park,
And don't be afraid to fly when it's dark.
Butterfly, butterfly, if to you life is a scare.
How do you expect to get anywhere?

Jennifer Busacca

Quarter Of Six

She sits on the windowsill
where the street lamps
can't touch her,
as the last minutes
bleed into the sky

Ice cubes clatter
like bones
when she sobs
and stirs her drink,
recalling dreams stolen
by hours and guns

It's then I cried
for the burning saints
and her ludicrous life,
while she slept
like a drunk angel
on ivory hotel linens

Sean Devlin

The Sound Of Your Voice

The sound of your voice
Sends shivers down my spine.
When I'm on the phone with you,
I feel that I've known you.
You're always on my mind.
I know in my heart that I have you,
and will always love you.
Promises are for ever,
my love for you is true.
If I didn't have you,
I wouldn't know what to do.

Amanda Sutterfield

Pearl

Smooth ivory
So round
and flawless.
A new fresh
bar of soap
The looks of a delightful
scent
so delicate.

A rainbow bubble
Transparent
and a shiny
mirror.
Songs from the wind
Dawn's soft rays
A caress on the cheek
A piano's tune
Across the sea.

Erin Cayabyab

The Spider

A spider sat in the corner.
    He was wearing a coat with a hood.
On that pleasant May morning,
    He was waiting for some food.

The first prey he caught,
    Was a humongous mosquito.
The next prey he sought,
    Was a shiny black beetle.

The spider was so full,
    He needed to drink.
When he met a bird at the pool,
    He suddenly needed to think.

As he sat by the pool,
    The spider was thinking,
He did not want to be eaten,
    As he watched the bird drinking.

So he made up with the insects
    Not to eat them again,
And asked the bird not to eat him,
    In sunshine or rain.

Isabel Chen

A Rose In Bloom

Once my love for you
Was like a rose in bloom
Its satiny petals all unfurled
Their vibrant shades of color true.

I thirsted for your touch
Your soft kisses were like dew.
I believed your words of love
Myself, I gave to you.

In the bloom of love
You pledged our hearts as one
Was it just your whimsey...
Or, golden rings my fantasy?

Now that love has faded
You've said good-bye to me.
Where is that love, dear
Could it have gone so quietly?

My heart is barren now
Like the rose it's frayed
The fallen petals washed away
By the sadden tears that fall...

Ella Zavala

A Feeling Of Lasting

'Twas an unexpected pleasure
    One afternoon in two lives,
It emerged then grew in depth
    To linger day and night.

When communication bypasses
    The words of spoken meaning,
Each glance and nuance is understood
    Each sentence filled with needing.

Eyes meet, hands touch
    A glow of warmth transcending
All conversation that flows —
    To joy that's never ending.

As the hours grow to days
    Thoughts translate into passion
Continuing through the night
    In wild, yet tender fashion.

Add the sum of all these feelings
    To these moments forever passing
And you'll glimpse into the future
    Towards a love that's everlasting.

Barbara Roman

Forever

I see two stars, in summer night;
Hovering, lost, in blinding light
Each so dull in Heaven's net
So each remains, as yet unmet

But fortune moves in strangest ways;
It lengthens nights; it shortens days
May this night end and day begin
And bring two people back again.

Adrienne Cappelluti

Endangered Species (For Kim)

You are the lady slipper.
A stark pale contrast
to the brown moss and ferny lace of
your private haven.

You were not meant
for cultivated gardens.
No mantle or table
could boast your
presence long.

You belong here:
A rare and delicate
reminder of the best
God has bestowed,
if only to be appreciated
by a lucky few.

Roberta Georgen

"A Sun Is Born"

It will soon become a sun.
You cannot touch it.
It is hot.
It sparkles.
It is the Christmas star.
It is shiny bright...yellow.
It is in the sky.
It only comes out in the dark.
I think it's a teardrop from the sun.
It falls from the sky.

Shawntae Jenkins

Winter

Winter, winter,
so beautiful. Covers the
mountains and the
ground with its
white powder.
In the spring
it melts away
But I know
it will come
back again
some other
day.

Tamra Frazer

Faith

On the wings of faith
I can see
All the possibilities
Through the dark tunnels
To an empty street
To a scary stairwell
Lead to an apartment of love
Where my kids and I
called home
I can see

On the wings of faith
I can see
All the possibilities
that today
A church was not robbed
A woman, a child, a priest
An officer was not hurt today
I can see
All the possibilities
On the wings of faith

Lionel Bazile

Cristom

My heart hurts too much,
I am the lonely one,
Who desires the loving touch,
Of the ungodly son.

My mind wanders into the sea,
I think I can hear him,
But he only wants to be free,
And get back his other limb.

My fear is far too great,
Of him I do not know,
To keep him as a mate,
And still have ways to show.

My time has yet to come,
In this world of hate and love
The feeling of being numb,
Will soon make me rise above.

My wish wasn't to be like this,
I only have one fear,
Please just one last kiss,
I want for it to be clear.

Meadow Anna Kinard

Summer Rose

As Autumn came the leaves on the
    trees began to fall.
But the last rose of summer
    clung to the bush

Diane O'Connor

After

I lay there staring at the stars
Little neon stickers scattered about
Thinking
Breathing
Loving
Only you
Your sleep comes quickly
I hear you softly inhaling
Exhaling
I slide in next to you
Like a puzzle we fit.
Our bodies
Our minds
Our breath
Our sleep.

Rebecca Turner

In Memory Of A Cherished Friend

You are gone
But in body only.
Your spirit
Your faith
Your courage
Are always here
To remind us of you
And what you are
And were.
Your son
And your grandsons
Are living reminders of you.
You touched each of us
with love, caring,
Sympathy and helpfulness.
May your new life
Be all you envisioned
And deserved.

Jeannette K. McCamey

Feelings, Ever In Life

Love is like the sea.
Ever screaming with life.
Yet, ever being polluted.

Hate is like the fungi.
Ever creeping in darkness.
Yet, ever being brought to light.

Happiness is like the redwood.
Ever standing with strength.
Yet ever being whittled.

Sadness is like the rapids.
Ever roaring with waves.
Yet, ever being overcome.

Steven L. Johnson

Forever

I thought I knew its meaning
when I said "forever," dear;
but then we were young and newly wed
and everything seemed so clear.
Together we would chart a course
and sail through life's rough seas;
together we would face the world
as our love would only increase.
But the Gods grew jealous of our love
and took you one day from me.
And now that you're gone, I clearly see
that there's no such thing as
forever.

Dorothy C. Pease

Do Not Cry When I Die

Do not cry, when I die
Do not say, how nice I look
What you see, will soon be dust
My spirit is here, standing at your side
Asking the question, why are you sad
Why do you cry, I am not dead
Shed my burden, it lies at your feet
I am not dead.
Life is a trial
In flesh you are in pearl
Spirit not living, in body of flesh
Imprisoned, by man's desire of flesh
Must have this, do my own thing
No thought of tomorrow
Or sorrow for sin
Heap-up treasures, pleasures I cherish
Live for today
Who knows, what tomorrow will bring
Do not cry when I die

Angelo Tassone

Truth

It stands on its own
Needing no support
Solid as a stone
It is not corrupt

It knows no color
It does not discriminate
Always in order
Designed to liberate

It does not change
It will not fail
And on its own time
It will prevail!

Ardelia R. Evans

Keeping Faith

On a cold and misty morning,
I felt a vibration in the air.
    In an age of powers where no one
had an hour to spare.
    Suffering in silence, we have all
been betrayed.
    It beat us, it hurt us,
in a terrible way.
    Praying for survival at the end
of the day.
    There is no compassion for
those who stay.
    There must be someone who can
set us free.
    To take our sorrow from this odyssey.
    To help and protect what is left
of humanity.
    Not content with that, with our hands
behind our backs.
    We pull Jesus from a hat.

Christopher Erickson

Untitled

Pain Throbs in your mind
As you decide whether you're right
or they're wrong
You decide they're right
Just to be socially in
When everything they say
you're against.

Penny York

The Lamp

It shows us the way to walk
in the darkest of darks.
With its glow of amber assuring
us of any unforeseen dangers.

The flame it flickers
from an unseen wind
but yet it shines for
us again and again.

There is a sense of safety that
I feel from the lamp especially
when it is cold and damp.

It comforts me as I rest my weary bones
from a day of unforgiving chores.
Yes the lamp remains a mystery to me
replaced by lights of electricity.
Yes I'm sure though the lamp will
shine for many more centuries.

Daniel P. Burbank

His Touch

His gentle kiss
His hand running
down my back
Tingling and sensations
All the emotions
All the pain
Of the memories
My heart aches
It is a but a dream.

Elizabeth Ashley Lopez

Great White

As she roams the clear blue water.
Her movement is swift as can be.

Riding the tides along the shoreline,
She is rightfully the queen of the sea.

Swimming the waves of the water,
Her majestic fin will glide.
Keeping with the currents,
in the cold uncertain tide.

Her tail to the left,
Her tail to the right,
A mighty power,
that roams through the night.

Eyes of darkness that venture the sea,
To all men who sail it,
You're captive to thee.

As to the many that have
met their end.
The sea is no stranger,
maybe foe,
sometimes friend.

Dodie J. Kurtz

Ghosts, And Goblins

Ghosts, and goblins
awake from their sleep.
Ghosts and goblins
dance in the street.
Ghosts, and goblins,
witches too.
Ghosts and goblins
They'll get you!

Colleen George

Kiss

My kiss is not a simple play
That teases your red lips.
My kiss is one more way to say
Those things that words will miss.

It's a way to say the things that words
Will fail to bring across,
It's a way to bring my humbled heart
To you, my gorgeous rose.

There are many flowers in the dawn
That make man's life a bliss,
But you're the best, my dear rose,
So let me kiss your lips.

Michael Shengaout

I Am A Child

I am a child.
Don't hurry me to grow up.
Don't teach me fear.
Don't hurt me.
Don't make me cry.

I am a child.
Let me play, let me laugh.
Let me grow.
Don't make me cry.

I am a child.
Let me be a child.
Don't take my innocence away.
Don't abuse me, or tell me I am bad.
Don't teach me hate.

Please, let me have my childhood.
Let me love and laugh, play and trust.
Don't make me cry.

Mary Alice McDonald

Racism Without Race

Does anyone really have a race
For white to be with black
That's supposed to be wrong
I don't know, is it religion
I don't know, isn't everyone
Just the same really if
you're open-minded there is
not just one race.

Paul Wheeling

Apart

Drowned within spinning images
Lost in divided worlds
crying your name
I conceal.

Lingered thoughts
dance holding destiny,
for you I see
my hidden fantasy.

Yearning for silence
you speak,
so does your soul,
beyond my reach.

Denied reality
grasps the heart
forever forgotten
we are apart.

Eric G. Pelnis

Russian Roulette

Russian Roulette,
It's not just a game.
Once you play it,
You'll never be the same.

Trust me on this one,
It happened to a friend.
When you pull that trigger,
Your life could easily end.

If you happen to live,
You'll play it again.
It will be the second time,
So the bullet will go in.

You'll kick and you'll scream.
The bullet is stuck.
You'll die in massive pain.
It has nothing to do with luck.

Don't play the game.
Can't you see?
No rush is worth a life.
Take it from me.

Jennifer Campbell

Untitled

We thank you O Lord
today and forever more
We thank you Jesus
for the open door
We give you praise
for the death of our sins
for upon the cross
our life did begin
and the baptism of the holy spirit
that cleansed with fire.
For in the name of Jesus
He fulfills our desires.
We worship you O Lord
with honor and praise
We thank you O Lord
for the coming of your days
We thank you O Lord
today and for evermore
We thank you Jesus
for opening the door

Tony Robinson

I Am

I felt all alone
but not with despair.
A longing to be somewhere else...
but where?

I sought my emotions,
looked deep in my heart.
I was longing to know
what would make me feel part.

I talked to some friends,
and a comfort I felt,
but still I was searching
when finally I knelt.

I pleaded, I begged,
I prayed and I cried.
Are you listening dear Lord,
I whispered and sighed.

Then I heard a small voice;
not thunder but breeze.
I am here my dear child,
get up off your knees.

Paula Turner

Life

Of life there is love,
With love you stand proud,
Proud of who you are,
And proud of who you can be.
Love is understanding,
Love is how you feel,
God put us on this earth,
To live our lives as a person,
One can change,
Only if willing,
One can desire,
Only if known is lust,
One can dislike,
But there is never hate,
   Love is the best thing you can be.
Monica Schmiedlin

She....

Lying motionless,
Virtuous, beautiful,
untouched, clean,
unsophisticated,
perfect

Her eyes...inviting
Her lips...wanting
Her breathing...heavy
Her heart...pounding
Her temp...rising
Her body...eager

Anxious yet excited
Nervous yet confident
Weak yet vigorous

Possession of beauty
more than skin deep

Shall I accept this?
W. F. Pittsley III

Logan

Today they've dug through the sweet smell
   of grass,
To place your body in the earth below.
"Oh, Sweet Spirit" the angels sing,
As they gather around this new young soul.

And now this new angel starts to sing,
"Mommy, Daddy, don't cry for me,
I am up above all the pain and grief,
At last, I am now free."

"I, with all my patience, will wait,
I will be here smiling when
you cross through this gate."
Melissa Marshall

Hope

I shine the eyes of children,
Enemies embrace me
Yea! I am with all, that breathe
The spirit of free life.
I am the gift of the grail.
The promise of the new covenant
I am hope
Thou; that crusade forth,
To seek me out
Also take me with thee
I am hope.
Walter J. Nott

All At Once

I finally took a moment and
I realized that you
are not coming back to me.
And it finally hit me,
   All at Once!

I started counting the tear drops
At least a million have fell
My eyes began to swell
And all of my dreams were shattered
All at once!

Ever since I met you
You're the only love I've known
And I can't forget you
Though I must, I realized this....
   All at Once!
Jeremiah Fairbrother

Untitled

The black sea of night
Sprinkled with twinkling stars
Moonlight pours over the earth
Changing things to a heavenly blue
Sprinkled with twinkling stars
Softly the wind whispers
Changing things to a heavenly blue
Can you hear it in the night?
Softly the wind whispers
All of night's beauty
Can you hear it in the night?
Is trapped in the sky above
All of night's beauty
Moonlight pours over the earth
Is trapped in the sky above
The black sea of night.
Kim Heath

A Little Extra Time

God made the moving rivers,
Flowing wildly and strong,
He made the little bluebirds,
Sing their springtime song.

He created every sunrise,
Glowing just about the hill,
He handcrafted every butterfly,
And every daffodil.

He placed every twinkling star,
In the endless deep blue sky,
And made it so that everyone,
Would have a different way to shine.

But I think
That when God created you,
He was in a different state of mind,
When God created you,
He took a little extra time.
A little extra time.
Megan M. Warren

Perfection

Searching for answers
To questions unknown
Exhausts the soul
I trudge onward
Ever vigilant
Ever alone
Thomas O'Hagan

Inspired By A Woman

When I met you,
I could not see
The kind of woman,
you could be.
As I asked you out,
I thought this would be,
another failed attempt,
at love for me.
I started out somewhat sincere,
but I would soon realize,
that there was much more here,
than would meet my eye.
A beautiful woman,
just waiting for,
a chance to grow,
a chance to be,
much more,
than I could,
ever see.
Garry FitzGerald II

Journey

I walk along the shadows of spirits
My life soars like a falcon
I run as swift as a wild horse
My mind rattles like a baby rattle
My heart is romance
I take my journey back to the wild
My body is cinnamon
My heart is a robin's egg
The world is a question
I take my journey back to the wild
Jessica Wygand

Take This Other Part Of Me

God, take this other
part of me
this part that no one else
can see
and lay it gently
deep within
some little waif
still free of sin
and when these
feelings
come along
give him some sweet
some gentle song
to tell the world
that I belong
as well as any other.
Patricia Malnati

Things To Come

Time is but a window,
Death is but a door,
They collaborate together
To fulfill our lives and souls;
A time will come
That sweeps over me;
With a sudden unforgettable fee:
Soon, as I wait nearby
The messenger arrives,
And enclosed in a box
   Is Death.
Joseph M. Watts

Explain The Pain

Explain the pain, two souls alone,
A bittersweet farewell.
Torn apart by willing hands,
Once joined, the stories tell.

Such simple needs to unfulfilled,
A distance wrecked in time.
Spirits linked, so meant to be,
Yet doomed with verse of rhyme.

Two voices soft with gasp of fear,
For sharing final thoughts,
Sing melodies of stuttered tongue,
And tears never forgot.

Explain the pain, it digs so deep,
From destiny undone.
Why must a love so perfect, real,
Be ripped from two to one?

Christopher W. Holtry

What He Went Through

Thorns upon his head,
Most though He was dead,
But He rose from his grave,
For there were people to save.

The scars on His hands prove,
What He went through,
To pay a debt,
For me and you.

Many a seed He planted,
In hearts like yours and mine,
Dare not take Him for granted,
Or hardships you will find.

For you must not see to believe,
But have faith and you will receive,
Eternal life and new birth,
For there is nothing of equal worth.

Christy Lamb

Still Here

Here, I shall still be standing,
Standing as you appear, to me
From over that ridge, when you return.
And here I shall be standing, waiting,
Longing to hear your voice, again.
And here I shall be standing,
Standing in loneliness, waiting,
For you.

David T. Corey

A Request of God

God please help to make the day
Guide my life along its way
Help my brother, mom, and dad
To help the old and mend the sad
Help me to forgive the mad
Take their sins and make them glad
Amen

Halle Heflin

Book

Basically
Organized
Oral
Knowledge

Amy K. Ledvina Hardt

Father And Child

The joy you have
Is the joy I've had
Of being a Father
Of being a Dad

I look at you
With your daughter dear
And remember mine
During those years

A smile so full
Trusting you I see
Mine did too
She trusted me

But little girls grow up
And change somewhat
Requiring more space
Than Daddy's got

But let them grow
And let them change
They still love Dad
Just the same

David R. Duncan

A Hitler Book That I Read

Came back, perhaps a dream maybe
    the nerve wrecking powder
A room. . .keep telling yourself
    you're a good person moral and "sane"
The figures of a different time
    dimension fall attack on a
demon or a satyr people seem the
    same scrambled, as voices
and faces invade a delicate place
    don't make me speak
numbers and words it scares me
    a gun shattered silence
and our addiction. The guy next
    door is insane, are you
waiting for him? What do you
    think of combustion? Original -
I knew the guy who died
    the priest told me not to lie
    Death can be both. . .

Thasha Gius

The Masquerade Ball Of Fall

Will thou dance with me
Upon the shadows of the sea
A ring of pansies in your hair
I cannot help but stop and stare
Your dress is full of daisies' blooms
Your mask wears a look of gloom
Your face I will recall
As the fairest one of all
Will thou dance with me
Upon the shadows of the sea
At last, you agree
You shall dance with me
As your feet swept the floor,
I loved you more
As your dress swept the ground
People watched from all around
You pulled me into the hall
And under your mask, nothing at all!
What should I have said,
I've danced with the Dead!

Stephanie Anne Munson

I Wonder

I wonder if you want me
I'd really like to know.
My whole world depends on you
I need your love to grow.

I wonder when you're sleeping
If you ever dream of me.
Or if you dream of how it was
Before I came to be.

I know you know I'm in here
It doesn't seem quite fair.
You should be so excited
But you just don't seem to care.

Give me a chance to show you
In the fall so clear and mild.
When I am born into your world
I can be your loving child.

Beverly J. Smart

Simple Words For My Love

With all my heart I do care
With all honesty I must say
I yearn to see you
Each and every day

You are as a miracle to me
So beautiful and so gay
Eyes that see through me
Lips that will not say

All emotions are in my eyes
You alone can see them there
You see that you are my everything
You see that I do care

Before words were spoken
I knew the sound of your voice
I knew your gentleness and kindness
Your spirituality and your dignity

Some good things have gone
Some good things we may never know
Our love stays strong
Some good things may still be there.

Orrett E. Ogle

Odie

Odie likes to jog
In the morning fog

Odie is not a fellow
But he likes to bellow

Odie is not fat
But he likes to chase a cat

Odie likes Jon
When he is not gone

Odie hates to get sick
But he likes to lick

Odie likes his dish
But he does not know how to fish

Katie Pederson

On Passing

Grieve not for me upon my bier
Let happiness be present here
It's just my body that you see
My soul is in eternity

P. K. Pfalzgraf

Summer USA

Where have all the children gone?
The sky is summer blue.
  Swimming pools unrippled
  Playgrounds empty
City street or country lane
The children are not there.

Desire or need ravage the land.
The sun is shining.
  Trees unclimbed
  Frogs secure
Urban parks, farmer's fields
The children are not there.

The world is a vast loneliness.
Fluffy clouds drift by.
  Imagination untapped
  Daydreams denied
North, South, East, West
The children are not there.

Romaine Guzi

Your Baby Girl

Now you have a baby girl
To melt your heart away.
She'll bring you much happiness
Every single day.

Will she cling to Mom
Or be a Daddy's girl?
It really makes no difference.
She'll be the center of your world.

You both will be her idol,
Her role model too.
She will try to imitate
Everything you do.

And, as she grows up
She'll have lots of love for you.
She'll want all her friends
To see her Mom, and meet her Daddy too.

Makes no difference of her age
She'll still be your little girl.
Miranda will always be
The center of your world.

Rita Wilkinson

The Portal Of Death

All alone with no understanding
Of heartache and pain

Solitaire is played alone
Like the loneliness I can't share

By myself with no listener
Separate in my grief

Living in the agony
That no one else can ease

Bearing the dull aches
That will soon be relieved

Enduring the desperate thirst
That is waiting to be quenched

Suffering from the torture
Of becoming the forsaken cause

Growing apart from all
Like a separate blade of grass

Grasping the reality of abandonment
Knowing the time to let go

Maricor H. Santiago

Twentieth Century Man

Can man say, "I am sorry"
  Instead of "I am proud"

Can man say, "I love"
  Instead of "I hate"

Can man say "God forgive me"
  For my mistakes?"

Can man stand tall,
  While others are falling?

And lend a helping hand
  To those less fortunate?

Can man take life as a test,
  And prove himself the best?

'Tis life of bitter and sweet,
  That makes challenges meet.

'Tis armored guard against the wages of sin,
  That turns men into greater men.

Marene Fassina

Untitled

A flower opens and her seeds
  blow unto the wind.
A starry night breaks into dawn
  and daylight begins.
A small cry heard round the world
  symbolizes life a new.
A light handshake, a shy smile,
  the love of a lifetime,
    I've found in you.

Tami Hayes

To My Father

Before you put the gun to your head
pulled the trigger
and shot yourself dead
Did you ever stop to think
what you would do
to the ones you're leaving behind,
those who loved you?
Did you realize when you chose
to put your life to rest,
You also made the choice
to make mine a total mess.
so many emotions run through my head,
Anger, loneliness, fear and sadness
so many things left unsaid.
But the thing that hurts so much,
what makes me so sad
you've left me alone in this world,
without a Dad

April Denk

Today Is Today Is Today

Today is today is today.
Yesterday never was and tomorrow
will never be.

Only today juts forth its head
in search of now.

Only today juts forth its head
in search of now.

Only the eternal present
juts forth its head
in search of now.

John L. Moulton Jr.

The Wide Oak Tree

There stands a wide oak tree
Forlorn and all alone,
Casting shade on a an old house
That once was a happy home.

Within this tree is laughter
Of children at their play,
And the longing loneliness
Of a cold and rainy day.

Scars can still be seen
On the limbs-rotted and bare,
Where the rope left its mark
In the heart of one who cared.

Tears from its heart fall unnoticed
Where love and memories abound;
Wind blowing through dead branches
Leaves a desolate sound.

Now there's no one left to care
As helplessness turns to sorrow,
For the house it protected and treasured
Is being torn down tomorrow

Judy White Embry

A Faithful Warrior

He was resolute
in his beliefs.
Like a warrior,
fearless before adversary.
Despite ridicule
and criticism,
he sought to conquer.
In matters of
healing and faith,
always prepared
for the battle.
Though sincere,
his sword could be sharp.
Sometimes faltering but
never retreating.
All battles now over,
he kneels
now at the throne of God.
Victorious
His faithful warrior.

Julie M. Lynn

Give Them To Jesus

Misery knocks at my heart's door,
  Despair stands by his side.
They asked me if they could come in,
  Now what should I decide.

Misery loves company,
  So he brings his friend despair.
It is up to you to tell them both,
  If they are welcome there.

If I let these things bother me,
  If now I feed despair,
It is all because I have let them in,
  Oh no one seems to care.

I prayed to God,
  Please help me Lord,
    Please help me now decide,
      To be content whatever my state,

His love now lives inside.

Dennis K. Hanscom

Life's Wind

Alone: A lonesome dreary word!
One man against the world.
One reed against the wind.
Lifes wind blows hard,
The reed is sadly spent.
What chance has it alone?
It's heart is rent!

Friendship: A warm inviting word!
One reed 'midst many
Will bend but breast life's gale.
Reach out and touch
with friendship's hand
And you will never fail.
Draw strength from those
Lifes wind just bends,
God meant for man
To be 'midst many friends.
Walk with some on life's rugged road.
Man should not walk alone.

Kathleen Deery

A Friend

A friend and I went walking
Had no place important to be

Just thought we needed talking
About things that bothered me

Many hours were spent that day
As I told of my unhappiness

When I had nothing left to say
I felt my friend begin to caress

"My child", my friend did whisper
"Your problems are so small."

"For everything I have a cure,
You only need to call."

My Friend then took me by the hand
And promised never to depart

My Friend is there to understand
To heal a weeping heart

Jesus is my friend you see
Sent from God above

He always walks and talks to me
And guides me with His love

Alice Marie Skinner

Flying Through

I bet you are flying
    not in a plane
    nor on a bird

Yet, you are flying
    amongst many colors
    and through the scheme...
    of your dream

Deep within you are flying
    While the diamonds in your eyes
    race back and forth;
    Your heart slides forward
    and stops

I know you are flying
    high inside

Jackie Stankus

On The Wall

George Fitzgerald Johnson,
on the wall
Not much family left at all.

Mother, Dad have come to
read your name upon the wall!
Memories of the dead run
through their head.

I shall raise my hand
and stand as tall.
And read your name upon
the wall.

Stanton Spinks

Untitled

Flecks of snow pass
thru the street light
countless emotions squeezing my chest.
Oh so tight!

Pain flashes in my heart
sticking, stabbing with a pulse
dressed like well decorated windows
of X-mas art.

Mind in sync
with the twinkle eye see
Mazed hunger, how is it?
Cascading painfully sea.

Robert B. Nolley

What Is Beauty?

Is beauty only skin deep,
Or is there something more?
That mirror image that we see,
Doesn't show us at the core.

For when we look much deeper
Than the eye can see,
We'll find that real person
Someone like you or me.

Looking more than surface deep
Is what we ought to do,
Or we may miss out on a friend
Maybe a love that's true.

Christine N. Bear

Another Throne

Melt, melt into that rose
That is the sky down neath the bridge
Where darkness lies

Pain my vision one last time
And go to rest
Knowing no crime

Holy are you that lit the day
While I sat in your presence
And in the grass lay

Blue was your foot rest up on high
Flowing down white
I looked up and sighed

Soft is your bed behind the mount
Giving birth to stars the masses count
Sleep now and dream

Of another throne
Where birds be your servants

Reed Preble

In-Human Nature

Give me a reason to roll in self pity
And I'll rock even more than before
Give me a chance to mourn some romance
And I'll eat my heart out to the core
I've got to admit, I'm a hypocrite
And talk like some pious whore
And it scares me to think
That I'm right on the brink
Of coming back for more
Why can't I leave this body behind?
Forget my mistakes — my life of crime?
Maybe I'm just afraid of the change
I wonder if that's not so strange?
I've been thinking of myself too much
Of being "Wonder Woman" and such...

Deborah Eremento

Grandma's Prayer
A Cure For A.I.D.S.

Weathered hands clasped in prayer
those dead before they're due
What once was budding hope, like he,
is now decaying too.

The doctors she once held on high,
have fallen from her grace.
Their almost mystic powers, but,
her loved one's not replaced.

The grandson she once held and loved
is now a haunting past.
How many more will live in hell
before a cure at last?

Mark A. Holum

A Twilight Conspiracy

Enter the burning shadows of silence
Breathing an existence so serene
Broken thoughts within a thousand words
Jagged pieces of a shattered dream

Winds shall howl a bitter winter chill
Upon this frozen December night
An outcry unleashed throughout darkness
Retold in the caress of twilight

Truth does bring a piercing solitude
Accompanied in the warmth of lies
Together swearing dying credos
Beneath the tyrannic winter skies

As midnight compassions pass on by
Loveless loves shall burn and fade away
Wandering souls in conspiracy
Forever forlorn alone to stay

Gregory Lobman

Winning Isn't Everything

Winning isn't everything!
It's not something you need,
You don't have to have it.
It does feel good, doesn't it?
To win, I mean.
Your knees stop shaking.
Your stomach stops quaking.
Your muscles stop churning.
Your head stops burning.
It does feel good, doesn't it!

Annie Acri

Fountains

Springing forth
Gurgling with anticipation
Shaping sculptures
  with an invisible force
Moving in a continuous rhythm
Slapping at the invisible air

Higher and higher
Something urges it on
  to reach out
    and touch the sky

Blue as the waters
White as the clouds
Reflections of one another
In the eyes of a child
Ellie Odell

The Year Nail

Unrisen to this occasion
of deep autumnal silence,
the phoenix of reason
has forsaken the horizon
of the steady west wind
that stirs the dust and ashes
of this bonfire long grown cold.

There is a yearning in heaven,
a scar upon the earth,
to mark this passing soul;
and the hammering of
the year nail, and the drift
of leaves, are but one
last best remembering.
Mark L. Sereno

"Ocean"

Powerful, majestic ocean.
What a notion
To ride the waves
half-crazed.

To feel the awesome power
that could devour.
Rising like a tower
making mankind cower.

Teeming, crushing sea
changing endlessly.
Never ending, always sending
another wave to me.
Amanda Jeanne Whelen

Tumbleweeds

Tumbleweeds are we
a gather of specks and pieces
held loosely on flexed skeletons
both tossed and trying
to find a direction
a corner to rest
or just the leg of another
we find along the way
of cracked and stony places
where sand flies through
our open parts.

Now charged with the mark of us
earth grants a stand of trees
to still our roll
and hear our stories
one by one.
Judith A. Hollis

My Dream Place

My dream place is where
  no one stares,
My dream place is where
  help is always there.
My dream place is where
  people are laughing and singing,
But let me tell you,
  I'm not dreaming.
My dream place is where
  I am sitting.
Home, Home, Home!!!
Brittney Cloyd

Untitled

A little hope
A tiny light
To illuminate the dark, cold night
If I could send
The pain away
It would be gone, my friend, today
Do not fear
For God is near
Dry your eyes and wipe away your tears
Close your eyes
And trust in him
Even when the light grows dim
Before you know it my friend
you will be feeling well again
Kelli Revell

Savior Boy

She walked the stoney trail
  A body young and frail,
Her burden carried with joy
  Awaiting the Savior boy.

The city gate in sight
  Shelter for the night,
Fodder for her tired head
  A manger for His bed.

The message angels brought
  Generations had sought,
The heavens rang with joy
  The arrival of the Savior Boy.

A wondrous star glowed bright
  And led the Wise Men that night,
To find all that the prophets said
  Wrapped with love in a manger bed.

The story the shepherds told
  With time, has not grown old,
We bow and sing with joy
  The birth of the Savior Boy.
Jimmye Watson

Untitled

  The days rush by with increasing
Speed -
  To my frantic calls, they give no
Heed -
  Ah, were I but able, to stop
this rush - of days, that mean
so much to us -
  Then file them away, like rare old
Books -
  To pull them down from shelves
on high and live them again -
for another try.
J. McKechnie

Untitled

Sometimes I like to hide in my
Own little world
No one has to feel my pain but me.

To everyone else I am strong
Inside, I hurt - but I believe
Inside, I am my own hero,
My own faith, my own strength.

I pray for others -
That no one has to feel what I do.

My heart is strong and made of gold.
I touch the hearts of others
As those close to me touch mine.

And with each day I grow stronger,
And wiser, and I know this is the link
That will make me live forever.
Jennifer Walsh

Love And Laughter

I mostly have love and laughter
I have sunshine
I have hope
I hardly ever have darkness
Sometimes I have pain
I have rivers when I am sad that
form oceans at the bottom of me
Even though I have
all of these things inside me the two
most important things I have
in me are
Love and Laughter
Arthur Gussis

To Make A Dragon

Take a little bit of this,
and a little bit of that.
Some eye of newt,
and some wing of bat.
Take a lizard by the toe,
throw him up
and watch him grow.
When he lands you better run,
this big creature is not much fun.
Burning houses,
eating cows,
Oh my gosh don't look now,
he's going to the castle,
with the old brick fence.
He'll probably eat the scrawny prince.
Here comes the knight to save the day,
hope he doesn't run away.
Oh my gosh, hooray, hooray!
No more dragon,
at least not today.
Justin Brooks Castonguay

Indecision

In decision
One must
Be decisive
Which is
Precisely why
I am
Always
In decision
Jennie M. Maloney

Untitled

Our macabre love's
Precious paucity
In this debris
The profoundness
Of this moment —
As we commence;
Spinning, spiraling,
Our descension
Into the golden infinity.

Josh Kincaid

Rwandan Snow

Grey blue clouds
slither across the sky.
It starts quiet and white,
Falls like drifting feathers.
But who needs another poem
about snowy fields and sky?

When the snow in Sarajevo
is stained red
with the decaying excrescence
of decomposing bodies, and
the sky in Rwanda has turned black
with the machete massacres of
weeping women and mutilated men.

And yet, somewhere, the sky still
turns grey blue,
and the clouds continue to
slither through, and
the quiet white feathers fall.

Herb Hirsch

Stars And Stripes

We give our people freedom,
to do as they see fit.
Most work real hard to do their part,
to keep the home fires lit.

We seem to have some malcontents
who always seem to try,
to change our values and our goals
we really don't know why.

It seems our flag is now in use
to wear as garments. Fie!!
It means so much and tells so much,
of patriots who have died.

Our flag is not a toy for fun.
It's something we hold dear.
If you wear or burn it.
That is not American, hear?

Hank W. Ring

Humble

I know what it is to be humble
Oops, there it goes
You know what it is to be humble
When you find it, there it goes

It just cannot be
To know that you are humble
Only others can see
That virtue called humble

Dan Cunningham

Untitled

May your dreams be many...
May your hopes reach high
When you think you can't do it...
Your wings take to the sky
Believe in yourself
Always spread your wings
And when your goals are reached...
That is when your
Heart sings!

Cristen M. Kuchera

Unicorns

You look at the beautiful creatures
with the golden horns, their curly
manes, and the beautiful long
flowing tails. They look as though
they are as happy as we know.
They prance around with courage
and heads held high. Their body
is a pure white, almost as white
as a midnight sky. But has it ever
occurred that unicorns are not
real? Yes, they are like horses,
but fantasized a great deal. A unicorn
is nothing more but a part of your fantasy.
And therefore, that makes them real,
but only to those who believe.

Brandy Lynn Norman

What Teens Really Want

Is popularity so precious,
My status as a teen?
Must I have sex at his request,
Be pregnant later seen?

If self-respect is prior
To actions good or bad,
What stops me from refraining
From pleasures I have had?

Is it right to blame my parents
For not informing me
About all the hours of service
It takes to raise a baby?

I'm intelligent and pretty
But not so smart it seems
When it comes to getting pregnant
And spoiling childhood dreams.

So teens, beware of older guys
Who smother you with chatter
And coax you into corners.
You decide what really matters.

Evangelita Hughes

Thank You, Friend

You surface words
from my internal struggling
That make crystal my thoughts
and free my spirit
To go on to other volcanoes,
clearing my path.

You empathize with my tigers,
opening cages
That circumstance and corners of closets
have given me...
To understand and live more
Love, which is all of life.

Leslie Alcott Tempest Temple

Daybreak

Dewdrops on
A crimson flow'r
Gave color to
The morning hour.

The sparrow's song
Upon the wind
Was a signal of
The nighttime's end.

The sun's first rays
At the horizon's rim
Filled up the sky
With sunny trim.

Mara Delcamp

Black And White

Colors give the world the right,
To choose from right and wrong,
To keep a people under thumb,
To keep them where they belong.

Oh, to loose the color of sight,
To see in shades of gray,
To gaze upon another life
That I just met today.

To see the joy within the eyes,
The experience on the brow.
To learn about the inner self,
Shades of gray, but how?

I dream of a world where children can
Enjoy their time of play,
Seeing each other as much the same,
Just different shades of gray.

James M. Shea

Bell

Why do I hear your voice
Even in the softest wind?
Why do I reach out for you
As each day begins?
Why do I listen for your step
After each endless day?
Why can't I accept the truth
That you have gone away?
Why do I feel your hands
Against my cheeks?
Why do I torture myself
With this unhappiness I seek?
Why did you leave me?
Then I answer with a hush
God just didn't understand
I loved you so very much.

Ruby Heffelfinger

Proud

Great Grandparents came to be free
Sailing across the sea
Each bringing a helping hand
Each helped to build this land.

Miss Liberty they proudly say
They saw her on their way
Still she watches sea to sea
She is proud of what we have come to be.

Rose Ann Servinsky

Our Love Is Like A Child

If our love were a child
Today it would be born
Because from the day we met
Nine fast months have gone
It would be brand new
With a loving, breathing soul
Love was what was missing
It's the thing that made us whole
A child grows so quickly
Such as our love has done
To form a brand new life
Just as we have become one
As we fall deeper in love
And as our spirits soar
I find it very special
Everyday, more and more
When I think about it
Our love is like a child
Sometimes really gentle
But sometimes really wild!!

Steve Melville

"Till My Dying Day"

I'll love you "till my dying day"
I long ago first said.
You told the same, "until my death"
That dying day I dread.
You fill my heart with dreams to reach,
You temp without a doubt.
Your faith is what is holding me,
So lost I'd be without.
I never shall return my vow
When I give you my life.
I'll share my heart, my loving grace.
When I become your wife.
There never once shall be a doubt
In knowing love for you.
For when I place my hand with yours,
We'll start our life from new.
I await the day of dressing white
With joy our hearts will fill.
The love we share will be enough
Forever and eternal.

Grace Schlereth

Something's Wrong With My Head

One thing you never wrote about,
And none have answered yet
How come my nose runs like a spout
Because my feet get wet?

If colds are caused by germs, as said
Or virus, if you please
How come a draft affects my head,
And causes me to sneeze?

Can it be true they only live
In air that's cold and fresh?
Then why do they such misery give
When lodged in human flesh?

The truth, my friend, is plain to all
Who read your noble works:
You've tilted with the windmills tall,
But never with the Turks.

For one more siege I must get set;
Then take me off to bed.
For ever since my feet got wet,
A cold's been in my head.

Cecil D. Cliburn

Lullaby To My Unborn Child

As I carry you
inside me
wherever I go,
I can barely believe
that such a tiny seed
can grow.
Already human,
with heart, soul, and mind,
my darling baby doll,
one of a kind.
Mommy loves you, baby.
Daddy loves you, too.
Grandma and Grandpa
can't wait to meet you
As I carry you...

Rosemarie Kemp Mehl

To Meet A Man

To meet a man
whose soul is bare
Is something special
and so very rare...

To meet a man
who touches your heart
To have words pierce
your defense like a dart...

What would it be like
to let down your guard?
Will he love you, and guide you?
Or is it just a charade?

When boundaries have been
a secure safety net,
What would it be like
to hedge that safe bet?

To meet a true man
has the dream always been
Dare to bare your own soul,
in the end, will love win?

Stacey L. Holman

Paradise

I took a trip to Paradise
Footloose and fancy free
Where there were no important I
And insignificant me.

Along the way I chanced to see
Another by my side
Who thought that he would accompany me
On my trip to Paradise.

So together along the road we went
With heart and hand in tow
To where the trees and flowers bent
In the meadows far below

A dream he said this has to be
For I've traveled far and wide
And ne'er has one like you and me
Walked together side by side.

Alas! We reached the journey's end
With heavy heart and tear-stained eyes
We walked from where the meadows bend
And said good-bye to Paradise.

Lola B. White Harrison

What My Friend Did For Me

I talk to Him each morning
through the day and evening too
I talk to Him of my problems
and ask what I should do

I give thanks for His blessings
for He is there for me
He tends my every need
the best friend there could be

I praise Him for His love
for His life that He once gave
I thank Him for His sacrifice
for the sinners He would save

He washed away my sins
when He died upon the cross
He gave to me eternal life
which should have been my loss

He will do the same for anyone
Jesus is His name
get to know your Savior
we sinners is why He came

Joseph Jankowski

Take My Hand

The time have come for me to go,
my life here on earth is no more, I'm
young with future in mine, and a
family I don't want to leave behind
O please o please don't take me away, I
know I wasn't here to stay,
the sin I did I can't undo,
but Lord I ask you to see me
through, so take my hand and let it
be, I see you again one day you see.

Patricia Pickens

Daydream

The two beautiful
lovers sit swinging on their
porch swinging in the distance
they could hear the faint
sound of rolling waves
as the ocean hit the
rocky ground of the
sandy beach, and
as the sun sets
they sit and
hold hands.

Margaret Kendall

Moonbeam

The curving sliver of a moon
Eased up above the skeleton trees
And floated there
Amid a pool of stars.
As I drew my gaze away
From a meaningless
Puddle of wasted tears,
And saw that bit of light
Dancing there,
Free, for me,
My soul was lifted
To meet the beam
And the darkness of my sorrow
Dimmed and disappeared.

Alice Lee

What To Do With You And Me

What to do with you and me?
All I see is so much confusion,
In a world of such delusion.
What you said,
Why can't I get it through my head?
My mind says it's wrong,
But my heart says it's right.
Someday, maybe they'll stop the fight,
And then perhaps I'll see the light!
What to do?
I know it's not you.
Nothing makes sense
The world seems very dense
And the feeling is so intense.
Yet, I ponder,
And still I wonder.
Sure wish I knew how this could be,
What to do with you and me.
Then I could finally see,
What to do with you and me.

Joanie Offerman

After The Rain

When the clouds
  Shed their tears
And the sun
  Reappears

Day is clear.

Lightning and
  Thunder cease.
Winds subside.
  Earth knows peace

No more fear.

Earth smiles.
  Life abounds.
Birds sing with
  Joyous sounds

God is near.

Michael Lamar Coston

Freedom Can Go On Forever And It Will!

Creatures here, and Creatures there,
Listen to the wind and air,
They are telling us you see,
What will be,
Will be, yes free
If we listen, if we try
Free will come to us real soon,
Just like a flower that will bloom
Bloom and spread its beauty round,
Round the world,
Round the sky
Up as high as we could fly,
But to sorrow, it must die
Creatures here, and Creatures there,
Creatures from the wind and sky
Come with me so we can fly,
Fly high into the sky
Come with me to set them free,
Forever!

James S. Robles

This Pane Called Life

Life it has such bounteous beauty
The likes of none compare
Its wings are tipped in golden hue
Floating as in a prayer.

Life it is a cathedral
Its spire to the sky
The winters sunlight filtered through
The panes of red and gold and blue

Each piece of leaded glass
Gives off a different hue
So is life

Together all working side by side
To one magnificent goal
To shine in all their beauty
Neither red nor gold nor blue
All have one mind...
To let beauty through.

Cara Caron

Dearest One

If all your troubles, I could erase
If I can put a smile, on your face
Then my "Dearest One"
I found my place, in the sun.

Josephine Sandrene

Untitled

These visions I have are not my own,
filled with the face of a man unknown.
He takes me before gods whose powers
unrivaled in their world alone.
I am never alone he roams through my
head as if his own.
Everything I have is not my own,
not this mind with which I think
nor
this hand with which I write.
I own nothing, my thoughts nor my fears.
He owns not the deed to my soul,
But my mind he does control;
And ever searching in his domain,
my soul to possess.
His quests just like the rest,
shall be in vain;
For I have no soul to obtain.

Robert J. Lomb Jr.

Beauty

The grass is green across the way
And flowers bright adorn the ground
Like jewels in their sets of green
With sentinel oaks on guard around

Light and shadow mingled lie
Dancing, playing, ceaselessly
No foot has touched this mat of green
Or else trod lightly, furtively

A butterfly is floating by
On lovely, silent wings
And then, to make the scene complete
A happy blue bird sings.

Of beauty there can't be too much
And beauty we should try to find.
For seeking beauty every where
Increases loveliness of mind.

Rachel A. Gold

My Rose

There is only
one flawless rose.

Delicate petals
gleam red.

On perfect petals,
Raindrops glisten
in the waking sunlight.

Lacking thorns,
I see it there
Hidden from
the world.

I found it there
when least expected,
my flawless, perfect rose.

Laurie N. Tahir

Love No More

Every time I let someone get close to me
They end up letting go of me
Maybe I'm too blind to see
My heart falls too easily

Just when I think I've found the one
Everything seems to come undone
Why can't I find someone
Who understands my heart

I let myself love for so long
My heart is so strong
Why must my feelings be so wrong
And why do I keep holding on

I won't let my feelings show
My love will no longer grow
Maybe then I'll know
Why everyone lets me go

I'll try not to love anymore
Until my heart feels sure
Then maybe I won't hurt no more.

Christal Greenlaw

Staying

She would stay for the kids
  Or so she told them all
Never once did she think
  It would be the wrong call

For her kids saw the abuse
  And heard all the bad names
And every time they heard it
  It was always the same.

With every time he hit her
  He would yell and scream
Her kids learned abuse and rage
  That was the way it seemed

When her darling girls grew up
  They accepted their husbands' abuse
Her boy thought it was alright
  To beat a woman for his own use

They did not learn love
  They learned cruelty and hate
She stayed for the kids
  She just learned a little too late.

Joanne Poletz

Thankful

I'm thankful for the television,
The picture is so faded.
I'm thankful for the telephone,
My parents confiscated.
I'm thankful for my Sega game,
The batteries are all bad.
I'm thankful for my dad and mom,
Although they drive me mad.
I'm thankful for my favorite hat,
It blew off in the wind.
I'm thankful for my favorite shirt,
My mom forgot to mend.
I'm thankful for vacation,
My skin, it gets so burned.
I'm thankful for my CD player,
Although it will not turn.

Jayme Fisher

Snow Flakes

Snow gently falling from
heaven so free
Peaceful serenity
embraces me
Memories over come
as tears fills my eyes
Hopes, love
Lovely sighs
Winter comforts me
as a child's lullaby.

Shauna Peterson

My Favorite Place

Sitting in,
My favorite place,
I look way up,
Into the pine green lace.

Then, like a feather,
Something breaks the silence,
It whisks through the trees,
With little violence,

Yet it touches every little thing,
Every twig in the trees,
One of God's greatest gifts!!

It's a beautiful breeze!!

I always like going,
To my favorite place,
And I always leave,
With a smile on my face!!

Ruth Taylor

Pessimistic Thoughts

When I sit
in my hour of solitude,
I often find myself
pondering
over life.
Funny how
we try to define
the meaning of life.
We try to project
the perfect image
of what life should be
and much to our despair,
it never turns out
that way.

Quianda N. Stanley

Thoughtscape

Out of chaos, one word
Drops
Monolithic and myriad meanings
bound by impenetrable chains
of associations
One word lithely dancing
on the parameter of my mind,
oblivious to its own modality,
pleading ecstatically for definition
Unaware of the sacrifice.

Laura Govia

Daddy

Daddy is a word
That I will always use
'Cause he makes me happy
When I have the blues.

I'm lying in my bed
Just staring at the ceiling
I know that something is happening
And get this horrid feeling.

Everyone has gone away
I'm sleeping in my bed
My mom and sister wake me up
And tell me that my Daddy is dead.

Daddy is a word
That I don't use too much
For when I was a little girl
Me and my Daddy, we lost touch.

Amanda Ebarb

A Seed Can Be Anything

A seed can be anything,
like a new baby that's born,
or a seed can grow into corn.
A seed can be anything,
a seed can be a butterfly,
with beautiful wings to make it fly.
A seed can be anything,
to a business that is low,
a seed to make it grow.
A seed can be anything,
when the rain brings a shower,
a seed will grow into a pretty flower.
A seed can be anything.

Reseanda Thomas

Music Of The Flowers

Each little daffodil
Sings its cheery song
Waiting for the crocus
To come join along.
Waiting for the buttercup
To nod its yellow head
Keeping time with the music
And to the beat it led.
And then the cheery tulips
Why they joined right in,
And soon a rosebud opened,
To join the melodic din.
Oh what a day that was,
The day of the flowers' song
They were worshipping Christ
Our King
For whom they did long.

Janet Rust

My Valentine

Just when I thought
My life was snug
You came and gave
My heart a tug

You pulled the strings
That gently tied
Forgotten emotions
I cannot hide

Just when I thought
I'd seen it all
You came to me
And I took the fall

You make me laugh
You make me cry
With tears of joy
With love I sigh

Just when I thought
My turn was done
You awakened my heart
My baby my grandson

Lee J. Ivers

Poster Child

Poster child, poster child
where are you?
I am in the Shriner's hospital
the operations
The sounds of a saw cutting the cast
A child cries
Mom
She isn't there
Teddy bear - friend
I sing with Simon and Garfunkel
A smile.
The operations
Cast cutting
Blood, blood
Leg braces
The cold bars of the bed
A poster child cries
Child of blood and pain
I am going to fight and win
I am

Allan Walsh

Valentine's Day

I gave you my heart
on Valentine's Day
So care for it as
I have done
For now you have two
and I have none

Alicia Stricker

The Winds Of Life

What interrupts thee
While you interrupt thee
Only God knows

What interrupts thee
While you interrupt thee
Only I and God know

What interrupts thee
While you interrupt thee
Only the winds that blow

Jonathan Lightell

Love Dirge

When did the love die?
Do you remember? Nor do I.
Was it when the leaves fell in October?
Or during the first freeze of November?

Did it break like so much crockery,
When love was made a mockery
By words that shattered
All that mattered?

Or did it happen day-by-day
As love was slowly worn away
Like acid dripping on stone
'Til we were left, bitter and alone?

When did the love die?
It's difficult to say.
But could we at least try
To make it through another day?

Bernard D. Baber

Interpreter

Robed in black, she steps up front,
Her white-gloved hands before her.
The lights go out, the blacklight on,
She signals the start of the music.
No sounds come from her lips of clay,
Yet from her depths she sings.
Her hands, alive, gesticulate,
The song moves through her soul.
Words are formed upon the air,
Through hands, the heartbeat felt.
To the deaf and hearing both
A message by her is told.
Brought to life the song lives on
In the hearts of those who see
The majesty of the mighty God
Through the young interpreter.

Stacey McLain

Apathy

In the love of heaven
Before his eyes
Rise by the moon.
Fly by the stars.
Laugh into epiphany
Smile in the tears of fire
Safe from the whispers of darkness.
Taller than the lips of fear
More beautiful than liquid serenity.
Dying in the day's new found night.
Happily met, cold skin.
Cryptic epithet
Windows at three quarters,
Crying leaves of fall.
Crawling behind kudos of fear.
Tears of hate belonging to the sun
Drink all and leave not a drop.
Reach out to hold nothing.

Laura Nussel

Confusion

Love, Hate, Confusion
Which do I feel
Joy, Anger, Confusion
Which one is real
Isolation, Desolation
One in the same
Confusion, Confusion, Confusion
It's a wonder I know my name...

Melissa Woodard

Life

Love, hate, joy, sorrow
All feelings different tomorrow.
Nothing's fair, nothing's right
To die is cowardly, to live is might.
All through life you grow and learn
And nothing's gone when you burn.
All your feelings, all your worth
Carry on until your birth.
Live again, burn again
Ashes of feelings in the wind.
Life is gone or so it seems
Until those ashes again are dreams.

Sandy Jane Parmenter

Worlds

The world is strange
in its many different ways.
There are many worlds
that exist in the world.
Everyone sees the world
through a different pair of eyes,
And each pair of eyes
belongs to a different mind,
And no two minds think alike.

Therefore, there isn't one world,
but a different world inside
of everyone.
Each one unique, different, better,
yet worse than the next.
The best world for me is my own
And only I have the opportunity
to live in that world.

How Lucky I Am.

Steven P. Shanks

Alone

Too often,
Loneliness lies there,
In bed beside me,
Late at night.
And reaches out,
To touch my heart,
With her cold hand.
Teasing me,
Taunting me,
Robbing me of sleep,
And always reminding me,
Of her presence.
Whispering to me,
Of opportunities lost,
And chances never taken.

David E. Bewley

Thinking Of You

Not only on a special day
I Think of you all the time
That's the reason that I have
to call you My Valentine.

I think of you everyday
Not only from time to time
So there is no doubt in my heart
that you are My Valentine.

No matter what I be doing
You are always on my mind
because I love you so much
I call you My Valentine.

Andres Castro

Love Is Confusing

The feeling is great
But could it be a mistake?
Sometimes I think
But it makes me pink.
I always wonder what life means
But my mind goes into extremes.
What should I do
If I am disloyal to you?
I'm not sure if I am ready
So help me keep a grip and be steady.
I know I have trust in thee
But do you in me?
I hope we can grow.
So I won't leave you low.
I would never want to leave you sad.
Or not even slightly mad.
I think I love you.
Just help me so I'll know
That you are the one and only right
And not just what is in my sight.

Janet LeConey

January One Or Two

All of us
After the holly, the mistletoe
Testing new light
On promises shafting through songs
Ancient from childhood
Half dazed with longing
And nausea
Early morning horns
Strident
Then dying
No lungs left or force to care
Until today
A landmark bewildering...
So much the same as before
When the Child blossomed
Under baubles and wassail and we wept
Not for ourselves only...
All the fools out there are family.

Ben Browne

The Man Named Gray

Beneath a weeping willow lies
A carpet of a lush green color
With many stories left untold
Bordered by one another

But of one tale we are concerned
Amidst this strange array
The tale of an unknown hero
The man who was once named Gray

As he fought beside his men
Keeping enemy at bay
He never saw the lone assassin
Who stole his life away

When sunrise came and the smoke cleared
The Generals basked in their glory
Then laid Gray in an unmarked grave
And buried him with his story

Now he lay in endless slumber
Passing each and every day
never tossing, never turning
The man who was once named Gray

Susan Kemp

Soul Mates

Two hearts torn apart in a complicated twist of fate.
One chose to love, the other to hate.
I scream from my heart, to call out your name.
You kept on insisting, the feelings will never be the same.
The tears flow less often, one day I will breathe.
For I was the victim, and I could not leave.
I love you so dearly, and now I must go.
To live in this hell, I created on my own.
One day you'll forgive me, and it will be too late.
Not physically together, we will always be soul mates.

Suzi Logan-Daniels

A Pondering

As time swiftly passes by
It's hard to think one day I'll die.
When my time is up what will be
How will this world remember me?
For the good I've done, the things I've tried
The help I gave, the tears I've cried.
Or will it choose to dwell upon
The things I've done that were bad or wrong?
Perhaps I will just fade away
Like many others do each day
Gone for good not to return
As a candle to no longer burn
Or will I be able to make a noise
And stand in history with grace and poise?
As more time passes at least it's clear
Our families will always hold us dear.

James R. Hess

Just A Tidbit

And,
So,
At night,
As Eye lie in bed,
In the dark,
In the silent Silence,
Eye return "Home",
To my "Glorious Soul-Self
Where everything is possible...
    Where "The Mother Sun" rises in the West and set in the East;
    Where there is no more of that "Man Devil beast"
    Where the Children are fed sweet milk and honey;
    Where Life is no longer a matter of money;
    Where the Artists form a Sister/Brotherhood;
    Where, after all the bad, now Comes the good.
If everyone were to just return "Home"
And not, from there, forever roam,
O, what a "Utopia" this world would be;
For, "The Collective Soul-Self" would, at last, be free!

Gypsy Marpessa Nefertiti Dawn Menor

Morning Surprise

Woke up this morning and got a surprise.
When I went on the porch to watch the sunrise.
I took a sip of coffee with a grin
and thought it's great to see the day begin.

I took a deep breath of the morning air
and marveled at the beauty I smelled there.
I looked at the birds and the big oak tree.
It's hard to believe God gave it all to me.

In awe I thanked God for my life
for two daughters and the lady who was my wife.
I thank him for all the gifts from above
But most of all for allowing me to know love.

John T. Smith

Help Take Me Away

Please take me away from this urban life.
Carry me away from the city's pace.
I need to stop and smell the flowers,
And allow the country sun to caress my face.

I desire to lay in meadows of green,
And gaze to the heavens above.
To stop and appreciate all of God's gifts,
To be totally filled with peace and love.

I would like to picnic beneath the mighty oak
And watch the stream poetically flow by.
Watching the squirrels scampering playfully,
While listening to the birds singing in the sky.

I'd love to have total peace in my life,
And leave all this stress behind.
I want to experience all nature has to offer.
It seems I am unable to find the time.

It feels as though I'm stuck in this urban life.
I sometimes worry I'll be forever at this pace.
There's never time to smell the flowers.
And in the city, the sun is unable to reach my face.

Cheryl Phelps

Everlasting

Thoughts should not be of sympathy or mourn
for these will one day pass;
But should be of Love
For it is everlasting.

Roger K. Smith

Reunion, Unexpected.....

We stood in January's Snow and Wind,
    Each placing a Rose on the grave of our Friend.

We cried for times never to be,
    And laughed at the memories...

We shared this day Food and Wine,
    With old Friends and Family, but now it was Time...

Life, had changed who we were back then.....
    So goodbye to our friend and to this moment....

Vowing to keep what we knew couldn't stay,
    We embraced, each going our separate way...

Penny J. Sheppard

Less Than

The sound of rain bouncing in my head,
I feel it run down my face and onto my back.
Then, I walk through the door,
Blood runs from my poisoned veins, then
dries up like wax.

I don't think you would understand,
Lights in my head flash on and off,
I try to loose my past.
Cold air hits my body, color flows in my eyes
my soul has been stolen.

This fear is running through my body
I fall to my knees,
Ears polluted with pollution
My heart is pounding out of my chest
I can feel someone watching me.

Staring straight up my spine
I feel no more pain, you have driven
It all out of me.
The trees blow in the wind
As the last leaves fall.

Jason E. Liebert

Misery Is Strong Also Weak!

Dedicated To Annie Franklin

As I sit here in a wait, sitting and wondering
and stirring up hate, as misery flows around
me each and every day. Oh, my God the
more the more, and more I hate.
And you ask me why I sit and wait?
For misery is nothing but hate. And now I
must try and escape. I look in every crack
and corner to hide and make my escape.
At last I found a place, and there goes
misery, it's past me and gone through the
gates. For now I have beaten misery and
I am released. Go away misery and
let me make this a good day. Oh God,
here it comes again. And it sees me. So
now I have failed in my escape.
Misery has won its way again, but I am one
and so is it for life will succeed for me and
walk right over it. Oh God, you put up a
battle for me. And I thank you.
Go away misery.

Nora A. Franklin-Miller

A Daddy's Lullaby

Let's dream of a world made of rainbows,
Where little white ponies have wings of gold.
We'll make believe we'll ride the ponies,
Soaring way up in the air.

So close your eyes tightly don't peek now,
For all of this might fade away.
Just hold daddy tight, cause in dreams there is light.
Let's trip to our magical land.

Your world might be made of cotton candy
With gum drops in rivers of cream.
There might even be sticks of candy
With bubble gum tops to make trees.

So hold to your pony, don't leave now.
You'll have all the night if you prayed.
Just hold daddy tight, cause in dreams there is light.
Let's stay in our magical land.

Dream, dream, of a world made of rainbows.
Dream we're on golden wings.
Dream, dream of the times that we'll share there.
Dreams are for you...and for me.

Bob Rinehart

My Life

I've danced alone a thousand times
To songs that no one else could even hear
I've reached into the flame of love
I couldn't hold it and it disappeared
I've lived to learn to hate the blues
I've lived with everything but you
I can't believe my eyes
I see you here looking just the way you should
So good
It's too good to be true
I live my life
Looking for someone just like you
Trials and strife
You've helped me through
I pledge my life to you
Never to hurt
Never to cry
To you I always pledge
My entire devotion
My life... My love.... Are yours to keep for all time

Melyssa Barker

Graduation Day

He got a letter from my brother today,
my son so far far away.
He read the words that he'd sent.
Made him cry when he saw what he meant.

I loved him well, my second son,
and now I rejoice to see what he's become.
A man who's good and kind and sweet,
but has the strength to tell the truth.

He worked his way on through the maze
of tests and books and pizzas to be made.
He asked for little all those years
and thanked us for what small things we gave.

He never forgot to send us gifts
small and personal, our hearts would lift
just to know we were not forgotten
in the rush of growing up so swift.

Sometimes it is enough to know
that he's doing well and on his own.
But many times my heart is sad
and yearning to bring him home again.

Leigh Hofman

The Last Rite Of Passage

At sunset my shadow stretches across the waters
and dissolves into a horizon
immersed in blue.
I can see nothing ahead of me
not a star nor a lighthouse not even a buoy
to show me the way, just a lone gull
and the tides that come to me
and go back, come to me
and go back drawing me closer
to a place I'm not ready for. I remember
when I was young I had a dream
to sail to the far side of the horizon and begin a new life
but like the tides that wear away these shores
year by year my dream
became nothing more than
a passing breeze. Now I am old
and only wish that after my passing
I will rise like the moon
above these uncharted waters
on the other side.

Charles Hung

The Fat Girl

Look in the mirror,
See the fat girl inside
And for a minute, show the pain
That you usually try to hide.

People don't seem to understand
How difficult life can be
When all of your clothes become too tight,
And skinny people are all you can see.

People laugh at a fat girl
And, of course, she laughs along
Because, if she chose not to,
They might feel that they did something wrong.

People whisper behind her back
As she walks down the hall
They yell out degrading comments
And she pretends to ignore them all.

But she can never ignore the pain
Of feeling all alone
When will we throw away our vanity,
And accept the fat girl as one of our own?

Jessica McLuckie

Ridin' My Mind

Come to me inside the bubble of my mind.
Tell me what you see, is there anything you like.

Swim through my sight and ride what I hear.
Let everything flow with you there's nothing you should fear.

Do you know me better now or am I worse than before.
Just ridin' my mind, tell me what did you find.
Do you want to see more?

Is it a sunny day or is it a storm?
Wrap yourself in my thoughts and keep your feelings warm.

Bask in all those things that I thought about you.
Intoxicate your brain with what you never knew,
All those feelings I have for you.

Do you know me better now or am I worse than before.
Just ridin' my mind tell me what did you find.
Do you want to see more?

Did you satisfy your thirst of the wish that you had?
Did you find out more about me?
Was it somethin' new to you?
Would you do it all again?
Just ridin' my mind.
David M. Thomas

Separation

I'm alone in my corner,
I have nothing to do,
but sit here and think all about you.
When I hear little whispers I fill up with joy,
Then I remember no longer are you a little boy.
I daydream that you'll be at my side,
Then I burst into tears 'cause you're really 25!!!
Naomi Marie Pruitt

Threads of Life

In the threads of life we weave our web.
In the eternal pit of desolate space.
For the infinite burden on our souls,
Is the sin we can not place.

Is this world for real?
This snare of falsehood and shame?
Or am I oblivious and can not see,
The mirth and joy I name?

Why is this world so empty,
Of hope, happiness and love?
It takes away the ones who care,
And leaves us dangling above

We'll never escape this determined ring,
Of discord, death and pain,
Nor ever be contented,
With the sympathy to gain.
Meghan Garn

In The Garden

I long to walk with you,
In the garden, in the garden, in the garden.
I long to talk with you,
In the garden, in the garden, in the garden.
I long to seek your face, to taste the grace that you
have shined on me.
I long to feel your embrace, as we meet in this place,
In the garden, in the garden, in the garden.
I long to be with you,
In he garden, in the garden, in the garden,
of my heart.
John S. Finlay

My Daughter

I sit alone by my cottage door
To dream of lands in far off shores
Who took my daughter when she was young

Oh, how I miss that lass of mine

I can see her playing on the moor
Laughing, running, talking about folklore
She has so much life and was full of fun

Oh, how I miss that lass of mine

When she reached an age when she was free
Gave no thought of the void she would leave
Just up and fled to that country to see

Oh, how I miss that lass of mine

That foreign land with its appeal
Teased and tempted her with all its zeal
Then gave to her what it thought she needed

Oh, how I miss that lass of mine

I have dimmed the lights and locked the doors
It is getting late, but I will wait
Hoping she will come back once more

That Lovely lass of mine.
Anne Mary Adamowicz

Belfast

The streets I remember the faces I don't
The memories surround me like unwelcomed ghosts
The temples of wisdom that welcomed us all
For a moment in time so many delinquent souls.

And the fortunes of youth that wasted away
On street corner day dreams how many escaped
This return of its son has left me cold
Little is new so much is still old.

The violence that raped this emerald isle
Is remembered with monuments for those who died
North and south each are to blame
I hope the next generation will learn from our mistake.
Bernard A. Shields

Uncertainty

I cast my eyes upon the western skies and wonder.
As perhaps men have done since the dawn of time,
I ask the creator what purpose my species serves,
And whether death is truly final,
As my senses suggest it is,
Despite the lure of ancient myths.

I toe the earth and smell its breath,
Mingled scents of flowering and decay,
And wonder if I am simply the product
Of its biology, destined also to flower and decay...no more.

The Western skies are laced with strands of rose hued clouds,
Filling my eyes with pleasure as my ears drink silence
And my throat tastes the bittersweet aroma of the soil.
I want to live forever, to hear, to taste, to touch, to see.
Yet I also want to find the place of my dreams,
Where those I love who die may live again with me.

I am mortal with longings for immortality,
Believing and disbelieving as heart and mind debate,
And when the sun is well set and I turn to the cave to sleep,
My dreams replay the theme of my uncertainty.
Basil Deming

Good-Bye

Why did you teach me to say good-bye
You knew one day it would make me cry.
It feels as if you're tearing me apart.
I know you're breaking my heart
I wish I could have never learned to say good-bye
Because now I wouldn't be standing here about to cry.
Saying good-bye is such a crime.
You were on this earth for a short time.
Good-bye is some of the first words we say
Why did you tell me good-bye today?
Saying good-bye means you'll be gone forever.
I'll talk or see you again never.
If I knew this would be the last time I'd see you.
I would have made this moment last forever too.
Good-bye.

Claudia Kay Mills

A Fifth Grade Boy's Thoughts In June

I love my teachers, my parents, their friends,
But I haven't gone where they have been.
My time to start there is just coming now,
And I have watched them so I'll know how.

Middle school looms as a mystery to me.
I must be strong, but my pathway can be
Only what I set my sights on, you see.
Their help I'll need every step of the way,
But I must do it myself by remembering the day
They said, "Reach out, grasp your future,
Steer your course, be strong."
I am scared for I certainly don't want to go wrong.
Our pathways in life aren't surprisingly clear,
Yet I know I carry forth all things they hold dear.

So I say to adults who are watching my strife.
Do this if you want me to have a good life.
Hold me up, push me forward, sometimes hold my hand.
Only then can I start on the road as a man.

Lynnette Kipp

Everywhere

Space surrounds us with few bounds
Sees itself around us now
Saving itself,
Jutting absolutely nowhere, it takes us there —
And leaps
Temporarily
Trying to be closed
Only for a moment though —
Pulsing pounding
Upon the ground
Below—
It cannot end its ever-hovering existence,

In time —
Everywhere

Mary S. Kelly

Untitled

While sitting home I sit alone
I am very tired of it. I feel to close my eyes
and go sailing far away to a better land
or peace. Where the little people are and
to be close to trees while the golden leaves
are falling by the sea. So you see it's
nice to be by the sea. You feel the
cool breeze coming from the sea
I look up to see a rainbow across
the sea so you see it's nice to be
by the sea.

Eula McNeil

Like A Lion Lost

Like a lion lost, I quiver for a moment,
afraid to lick the blood from a bone.
I question the known, as I lose
myself in a bed of thorns.
Like a crane flown south, I try to bask
in the sweet warm glory,
though my wings which whip the water's side
are tied.
Like a dreamer been told, I cry for the moon;
a disheartening fool,
and I sail for my stars,
as my den of sorrows is invaded by liars.
And tomorrow,
like a slave set free,
I will beat them at their own game....
torturing me.

Lauren Reedy

The Volunteer Firefighter

Volunteer firefighters are a rare breed
They do what they do because others are in need

They get up and go all hours of the night
On the way they hope that everything will be alright

They do it for free, they get no pay
And if need be they do it every day

The pager goes off during their dinner
But they never seem to get any thinner

Firefighters go to weekly drills
To check equipment, there are no thrills

There are the monthly meetings
And parties to give Seasons Greetings

They go to all kinds of calls
From working fires, to accidental falls

Some firefighters go to class to become divers
Some learn to be firetruck drivers

It doesn't matter how warm or cold
They go to the Chief and do what they are told

So when you see a firefighter with a blue light
Get out of the way because there's a fire they have to fight

Kevin Rhyne

The Love Of A Lifetime

To the eternal love of my life,
Our romance is full of power and strength.
The everlasting moment we share provides me
With the will to live, love and endure at long lengths.

In You, I have a true friend with whom
I can share my most intimate feelings and thoughts.
In You, I feel the safety and security
Of someone who protects me a lot.

In You, I have someone who gives me
Much happiness and joy directly from her soul.
In You, I have allowed myself to grow,
And because of you, my life is now whole.

In You, I have witnessed a person
Full of self-will and emotion, yet
For you, I can promise that you have
A life-long friend full of devotion.

These promises, I make solemnly to you.
It is perfectly clear my love for you will
Never, never end.

Kyle Fry

Unique

My weary mind, spiritless wings carried me this far
To find a mockery lake in these desert sands.
I walk about even the breezes burn my flesh
Exhausted I cried but my tears are dry.
There must be mercy along with rest - somewhere?
Shade?
It is a possible trick as sweat filled my eyes
No, it was true you with your outstretched arms
A barrier from the unyielding, unforgiving heat.
Willingly allowing me, to drink your life giving water
I bowed weeping as a child; your child
Immersed in your single oasis.
The crown of thorns upon your head only penetrated you.
Your love and forgiveness only penetrated me
I am necessary in this desolate land
I have committed my life to His will.
Together we are very unique and complete.
Alone I burn my God given wings.

Sherrie Lee Jones Hogan

Out Of The Ashes

Smoldering prejudice, smoldering hate,
Smoldering ruin, sanctuary laid waste,
A desolate moment, a time of fear,
Pervasive helplessness, the future drear!

These hollowed halls of beam on stone,
God's earthly presence, we call His home!
The pinnacled spire held the pealing tone
Hailing hearers to come worship Him alone!

Love is stronger than hate, and,
Hope is stronger than despair!
Good is stronger than evil, so,
Evil is overcome because God is there!

Wilma Noe Payne

The Cut Glass Beauty

For long it lay a prisoner in the attic
Bound with cardboard, paper and knotted
String — the cut glass sugar bowl.
One day the bride, unblushing now sets free
The bowl, fills it with sugar then sits down
To wait, He comes to dinner, the somber
Groom and humbly bows his head as grace is said.
While scooping sugar from the bowl he scowls,
"Isn't this the thing your mother, that old
Bat gave us the day we wed?" Like a seething
Volcano old argument surface - she picks
It up to smash against his head.
He quickly jumps up, reaches over and
Carefully stills her trembling hand.
It rests now on a what not shelf -
The antique, cut glass beauty, a lonely
Scapegoat - brimful of dusty sugar.

Sadie W. Peterson

Beautiful Mother

There's nothing more truer than a mother's beauty, and to
see her face in the morning, then to glance up to her.
I'll always remember when she'd whisper the words, "I
love you..." in my ear how those words meant so much, and
I'd send those same words back with twice as much love.
My mother means so much, Is there nothing more
prettier than when your mother gives you a good night kiss,
or for when you are scared
There's so many pretty things about mother's, like when
she lays her hand upon your face
Mothers are pretty but mine is Beautiful.

Toni Miller

A Friend Indeed

When you've lost something that's close to your heart,
And you can't comprehend another start,
Put your hand in mine
And I'll forge ahead,
Until thought returns
And your spirit is no longer dead.

I know that it's hard to blink back the tears,
So let them flow freely
Not build up for years,
'Cause in order to heal your grief must be freed,
Until then have my shoulder,
Wipe your tears on my sleeve.

Rebuild your mind and body as one,
So that once again we'll advance together
When at last your healing is done.
Until in proper balance we can stand,
You may always reach back for my outstretched hand.

Julia Adam

A Walk In The Garden

Such a beautiful morning
I smell the fresh air
I feel how the breeze runs right through my hair

The sweet smell of flowers that sets my mind free
remind me of picnics on shores of the sea

I walk along and think a while
I think I walked about a mile
through vines that grab right at your feet
My nose and flowers did often meet

I sit and swing above the phlox
and think of what this place unlocks
about the past, of what it's seen
of what will come and what has been.

This wonder started by a seed
somewhere in the middle of a mead.
The lush green grass where cows were grazing
with colorful autumns, it sure was amazing

I feel how the breeze runs right through my hair
I snap out of my dream,
and smell the fresh air.

Kira Lee

Lost Of My Beautiful Bird

Whippoorwill, oh whippoorwill why
Must ye be lonely
For thee must
Just lost thy lover in flight
Cries of her sounds there only at night
Whimpers and cries through the lonely night
He calls her name Whippoorwill

William Henson

Friendship

Our friendship has "aged" over years gone by,
But my, oh my, how times does fly.

But the best part of this is the wonderful bliss,
That keeps our friendship alive,

Through all the tears and smiles too,
We managed to chase away the blues.

But our memories are there and these we do share,
For we're two friends who really care!

Adelene J. Mitchell

Once Upon A Flower

I once saw a flower, whose petals were of
greenish-grey. It bloomed every night, and
withered everyday. Along came a force, let
it be wind or seed or bug, and started the
little flower on its way, to endless,
unconditional love.
Every night, and early morning rise, it
bloomed a different color, size and petal
shape. Its choices couldn't get any duller.
My flower still changes now, as it meets
the waxing moon. It will be a rainbow, no
doubt, someday, perhaps not too soon.
For it takes a while to choose one's self,
to choose what you want to be, but
whatever my darling flower, I will always
still love thee.

Briana Duga

The Fields At Night

At night, when we walk the shadows, hold my hand.
As rain quenches the thirst of the earth,
quench my thirst for touch.
As the grass bows low to the wind,
so I bow low to you.
Make love to me as the lightning illuminates our body.
Pull me close,
so close that not even fear can come between us.
The rain will stop and dawn will break...will we?

Many nights I am reminded of us never beginning —
Not from lack of me, but from lack of you.
Until I realize who you are,
I will always dream of the fields at night
with you.

Steven Paul Spears

God's Masterpiece

I see a field of golden grain, the brown earth, green trees, and
   blue skies and I say - "God's Masterpiece"
I see the trees when Autumn turns the leaves; the hills ablaze
   with Autumn splendor and I say - "God's Masterpiece"
I see the field now covered with snow, the deer and the
   evergreens and I say - "God's Masterpiece"
I see the robin in the trees now budding in the Spring, the
   rainbow that sometimes follows the rain and I say -
   "God's Masterpiece"
At night I see the radiance of stars and moon amid the
   ebony sky and I say - "God's Masterpiece"
I see a newborn baby, cuddly and small as it moves
   inside its blanket and I say - "God Masterpiece"
I see my life changed and touched by the power of God
   when He reached down and saved my soul and
   I whisper with a grateful heart - I am "God's Masterpiece."

Hazel M. Gembe

Untitled

Down by the land, at the sea
There sat a young man, winking at me
All of a sudden, I glanced to the right
Then to the left, and he was out of sight
I kept asking myself, where could he be?
Not long after that he was standing by me
My heart was beating as fast as it could
I wonder if he liked me. Do you think he would?
Then the least I expected from him, was to ask me to swim.
All of a sudden, out of the blue
What I had predicted, was very true
After we were all through, there came those three words,
"I love you" then all of a sudden I said it too!

Cassandra Gondolfi

Untitled

I want to talk to you and make you see,
The person you're looking at isn't really me.
Shutting you out was not what I planned,
You tore my world apart with a stroke of your hand.
When I wanted to talk, all you could say was "wait",
With a single word you sealed our fate.
I want one word to make everything better,
But you have to find your own way to pull it together.
I said, "just friends" that's the way it should be,
Now I can't stop wondering, what happens to me?
There are too many feelings to just ignore,
And I can't help but think, what was all this for?
I don't think this was a waste of time,
But I'm tired of waiting, standing in line.
And want this to work, you and me,
And what's in the future I'll just have to see.
Mutual respect we both need to earn,
I just want to love you and get the same in return.

Allison L. Minter

I Didn't Know

You told me that you loved me
I thought we should be friends
I really messed up big that day
Now my heartache never ends

I loved you oh so dearly
But I just didn't know
That day that you decided
To let your feelings show

Now it's the way I wanted it
And friends we'll always be
We never will be more than that
And it's all because of me

There's a million thing I should have said
To you that rainy night
I should have believed your words to me
That together we were right

What made you say those things to me
What made you love me so
I realize now that I love you
But then I didn't know

Michelle Overholt

The Moon Casts A Spell

The sun shuns the moon as indiscreet;
on a hot evening love permeates the air.
Birds are singing happy tunes to a pair.
The moon gripes — why can't we too meet?

The pair kicks and tosses a beach ball.
Swiftly, Eli hides behind a rocky hill.
What's keeping Ebe; why is all so still?
Eli awaits anxiously while she evades all.

The moon light reflects so splendidly;
Over hide-and-seek Ebe chooses swimming.
A current drags her; danger is defying.
The unknown brings grief unexpectedly.

Eli looks over the beach and cries my love!
He swims and scans the ocean over and over.
A sand castle Eli has promised to build her;
as he builds it, gazes afar, and sees a dove.

The majestic sand-tower is unique and steep.
Its highness proudly awaits for its princess.
A fiendish wave delivers misery and sadness.
The moon grins as fate brings Ebe to Eli asleep.

Elba Zapata-Barnes

My Favorite Earthling

It may be the rage, in this nuclear age
To fly with your guy to the moon.

But, I prefer to remain, where it's safe and it's sane
With my mate, in our earthly cocoon.

Circle the world round and round, travel faster than sound,
And do what you need to do.

I'll go my own pace, no reason to race,
All I ever need is you.

So, if your life is a bore, take that whirlwind tour,
And escape on that outer space ride.

I don't need mind-boggling heights, nor far away sights,
As long as you are by my side.

Start your daring vacation, at the nearest space station,
And float in the land of moonbeams.

But, for whatever it's worth, I'll stay right here on earth,
With you - the man of my dreams.

Pat McManus

Sunshine Morning

Oh, sunshine morning I awake to your light
When I rise to the beginning of a brand new day,
As the sun beams tenderly, quiet, and bright
The fresh air is misty and lingering to stay.
Oh, sunshine morning I walk through the grass
I look up at the sky and I hear the birds,
When I was once there remembering the past
Understanding my heart and finding the words.
Oh, sunshine morning will I see you tomorrow?
Until eternity and the end of our lives, oh yes,
When can I touch the nature I borrowed?
Deep down after giving everything the very best.
Life has a meaning in the morning, I know
So come along with me - we'll find it, and grow.

Paula Leigh Peacock

Untitled

The moon, the stars, the sky above, belong together dear
Just as my heart and I are one, but only when you're near
For God, who made the universe, made you, and made me too
And with his understanding heart, and divine love he knew
That self-sufficient as we are, we cannot stand alone
And thus he made for each of us, someone to be our own
Someone whose heart calls out to us, whose eyes light tenderly
Someone with arms to hold us tight, throughout eternity
And darling I am lucky for, I've found my own true love
And I'll be holding you each night, beneath the stars above
And nothing in this world can change, this love of mine for you
And it will blossom when at last, I do belong to you

Peggy Smith

What Was That All About?

When I lie down to gasp my last,
I'm certain I will scratch my head and ask...
What was that all about?
This 75-year opportunity —
To see, to hear, to taste, to touch, and to shout,
What was that all about?
This brief spate of consciousness
We laughingly refer to as
"A Human Life."
What was that all about?
It seems it was just 75 years and out.
That is simply what it was all about,
Just 75 years, and out.

Edwardo J. Regan

"Our Family"

Daddy, Mama, and six kids is the family we'll always be
and every one of them still means the world to me
Step family is what we really are
but through the years we've came far
even if we came from one place or another
we are still sister and brother
The years that we all had to work together
is what made us this family forever
We fussed all the time a little we would fight
sometime during the day but mostly at night
We had a few sad times but mostly they were good
I wouldn't change a thing even if I could
It took a lot to make us what we are today
"It was all worth it" we'll gladly say
If you don't know the meaning of family ties
then just look at us with your eyes
I love my family separate and together
even now more than ever!

Christie Bedford

Darkness To Light

A darkness unable to be penetrated,
Desperate and alone with no one you can trust
How easy to end it all,
How easy to let go,
Not an eye to see,
Not a mouth to speak,
How lonely,
How terrifying,
To stay or leave is up to you.
To find something to hold onto
Something to hold you up
Find the light to penetrate through
Scared and alone is nothing to feel
Too many switches
Too many places to escape.
Find yourself
Your pain will end
Your darkness will be shattered.

Regina Williams

Grandmother Walthour

My grandmother
    planted fields of flowers in rows like corn,
    counted cross stitch tulips on fine linen,
    quilted for blue ribbons at the county fair,
    cooked melt in your mouth fried chicken
and gave me cause to hate.

In her roundness with her sparkling white hair
    she might have been the model for a Norman Rockwell grandma.

Dispensing charity from her house on the hill
    she brought us home grown vegetables
    and dresses made from feed bags.
In return, we made weekly pilgrimages
    to be reminded of our poverty
    and to thank her for her largess.

Susan Drewery

Rosanne's Song

As I sit and watch the star studded sky
    I think about those days gone bye
    I think about a waterless brook
    A beautiful flower once shaded by a nook
    A small oasis under a hot desert sky
    A plentiful well that has since run dry
    But, no more shall I think of those days gone by
    I must live for today for tomorrow I may die...

Rosanne J. Cipriani

Mont Royal

I think I'm getting too old
to be wandering alone
in these places
so saturated with your presence.
There, it was snowing as it usually does
the same squirrel,
the same children
sliding down the icy hill;
the same kind families
with their French accent:
The iron cross
vigilant over Montreal.
The only difference
was my profound nostalgia.
The scenery somehow was terribly distorted.
I was ten years too old
and my Josephine was missing.

Jorge Gomez

The Foggy Window

When it's right in front of you,
    you don't see or feel what it is;
But when it's miles away,
    it suddenly becomes clear.

It's the good times,
    filled with smiles and laughter;
It's the endless searching,
    and then realizing this is what
you've been after.

It's the tears of sincerity,
    the fears of reality.
It's the loyalty, the openness,
    the vivacity and the eternity.

Through the foggy window it becomes clear.

I see it now, I feel it now...
    I see Love —
But more important,
    I feel Love.

Heather Bosley

The Golden Years

When I was new, to the land that grew,
To be my bread and butter,
I looked forward to the time I knew,
That I would only putter.

But there's lots of work, with little fun,
That I must yet endure,
I'm looking forward to it now,
I'll be happy then, I'm sure.

But life went on, and on, and on,
With trials and tribulations
But I knew that later on, I'd have
One great big long vacation.

"The golden years", they told me of,
That older generation,
I looked forward to, I'm tellin' you,
With great anticipation.

Now, I'm 74, my bones are sore,
My muscles, not so nifty,
I'm tellin' you, "the golden years",
Are between 25 and 50!

Norman L. Kear

My Back Yard Garden

A niche in the flower bed,
    where caterpillars and butterflies dwell.
A baby bird on the ground,
    looking up at the branch from which it fell.
These things are in my back yard garden.

Bird feeders on posts
    and hanging from limbs.
Corn cobs for the squirrels,
    one for her - one for him.
These things are in my back yard garden.

A swing to sit on
    and listen to the birds.
Whistling tunes
    without any words.
All this can be found in my back yard.

Audrey Palmer

Betrayed

I was betrayed by my best friend,
that's why I decided it was the end
I trusted him, I told him my life,
then he betrayed and cut me like a knife
for a long, long time I believed his lies,
and after a while he saw all my cries
it hurts so bad you wouldn't believe,
I didn't think he was the type to deceive
he changed so quickly, it happened so fast,
now our friendship is in the past
I cried all day, I cried all night,
I felt like I had to put up a fight I was so mad.
And yet very sad deceiving, lying, cheating type,
since we fight I always gripe
I want revenge but that's too mean,
with all my heart I'd wish he'd seen
my whole world fall apart
my heart hurt so bad I wanted to depart
all my feeling I must dismay,
because my best friend can betray!

Joanna Grassman

Your Smile Darling

See your smile, standing there.
See your step, around the block.
See you healthy and well,
See you almost everyday,
See you are coming on the path, grass,

See you on my dreams, every night and day.
See you coming back again with your smile.
See you darling on my sight, on my mind.
See you happy healthy, loving, friendly.
See you on the clouds, on the sun, on the rain.
See you on my heart, on my mind and soul,

See you soon sunny or snow or windy,
See you in any corner of my mind and my heart.
See you all the time, day, night, weeks, months
See you darling on the flowers, on the clouds
See your step on the snow, on the sun, on the rain,
See you my love in my heart and mind.

See you darling on the sky, on our heaven,
See you anywhere forever.
See you always in my heart keep you loving.

Milagros S. Miranda

Today I'm Getting Married Grandma

Maybe God will let you see
Cause I believe it's with his blessing
and this man really loves me.

I've had plenty of time to get ready
everyone knows I've tried.
I'm getting it all together
so I can be the most beautiful bride

I've prayed about this wedding
that God would make it pure
and as I think about his love I am very sure.

As the ceremony begins
I want to feel your love.
I ask that God would allow it
to flow down from above.

When everything is said and done
and wedding dust is clear,
I know I can look in the future without a single fear.

For God has blessed this union
and there will not be a tear
our love will just get stronger each and every year.

Alex & Kathy Castillo

Destiny

My destiny lies in the hands of
the beholder, while I search to
find what he has in store for me.

I want my destiny to be real;
fulfilled with satisfying love
that no one can give but you.

In my destiny I want you
to be by my side, so we as one
can conquer destinies of all destinies.

A destiny in which holds us
together and makes the impossible; possible

A destiny that keeps our
love for one another growing
stronger than ever.

And a destiny that tells
me, the one I love till this day
is the one I will love throughout
my destiny.

Veronica A. Jackson

Yesterday's Male

The time has come to realize
That sparkle shining in my eyes
Is fading past...just like a ship set sail.
When I look back, upon my days
With dreams ahead and heart ablaze
I wish I could have changed it all somehow.
But knowing then what I know now
Would be so foolish anyhow
I have to understand those days are gone.
...I'm old news now...just like yesterday's mail.
Day by day I'm haunted by, those memories of the
Girls that tried
To love and keep me satisfied
But my wandering ways made all their love grow pale.
They tired of all my silly games
Those beautiful faces with no names
And left me alone... To deal... With yesterday's male.

Larry R. Reese

The Train

As I lay in my bed in the dark of the night.
All's quiet.
Then I hear
A long way away.
A whisper.
The train!
Just arriving in the valley.
Its sounds reverberating
Through and around the hills.
Its noise, rumbling, a gradual crescendo,
Getting closer, as it snakes its way along.
When will it get here?
It seems to take forever.
Loud, loud, its roar filling all the spaces
A sharp shriek wheels skidding on the rails.
It's here and stays
Then it begins to pass on its way North
traveling on through the dark.
It's gone
All is quiet again.

Alice P. Britton

Then Sings My Soul

When life has run its course
and you have passed
Into the realm beyond,
I shall not weep, for I will know
That you have found the place
Where you were meant to dwell,
And you will find the peace
That fills the soul when all is well.
I know that you'll be waiting there
With arms outstretched to welcome me;
As always you'll be there,
To hold my hand, to stroke my hair.
I failed to tell you what you meant to me,
For all too often chores come first,
Or lips were sealed because of lack of words.
Perhaps up there, in that glad day
I'll simply just say "thanks"
and you will know how much I care.

Helen Corley Cooper

Love Is...

Love is more than just a feeling,
It is an expression of a heart that is healing,
A heart that is healing of past wounds.

Love will last a lifetime
It is more than just yours or mine,
It is the whole world's aspiration.

Love is like a bolt of lightning,
The speed with which it hits is frightening;
It can set you on fire in a second.

Love is there to guide us,
It will guide us without a fuss,
It is our beacon in dark waters.

Love is magic in the air,
It will help us all things to bear;
It is in everything that is wonderful.

Love is more than just a feeling,
It is an expression of a heart that is healing,
A heart that is healing of past wounds.

Stephenie Clontz

464

Winding Pathways

Winding pathways dressed in stone,
   Strolling through Eden, savoring God's home.
Lemon Verbena, sweet pea breeze,
   Feline creatures...busy, buzzing bees.
Rainbow petal blossoms simply astound,
   Hummingbird 'copter-wings wildly resound.
Winding pathways dressed in stone,
   Strolling through Eden, savoring God's home.
Yellow yarrow corn bread...strawflower mix,
   Autumn pumpkin vines...velvet peppermint sticks.
The baby's breath nuzzles lamb's fuzzy ear,
   Butterflies flit to ladybugs' cheer.
Winding pathways dressed in stone,
   Strolling through Eden, savoring God's home.
Canaries splash and sing lazy summer songs,
   Bluejays squawk and chase little birds along.
Strawberries, curry, lavender and thyme,
   Wondrous delights nourish my mind.
Winding pathways dressed in stone,
   Strolling through Eden...Savoring God's home.

   Jeanne Kinann

The Sports Utility Van Lament

I cannot abide taking a ride along the side
Of the new auto rage the sports utility van

Wasn't the driver taught left turns
That leave some room for the autos she spurns
Van turns are quite reprehensible
Making the roads most inaccessible
Van driving could not be worse
Elsewhere in the universe

The way they drive won't keep us alive
Van driving is awful it cannot be lawful
We want to live and not be afraid
To go to the beach and watch the parade
Of blue sky and sand that is marvelous
Not spoiled by driving so scandalous

I've earned my old age to sit at the beach
To watch the water, the sky and my peace
When along comes a sports utility van
Labrador retriever and baby Dan
Trying to get them to use less utility
Is a lesson in sports van futility

   Sheila Rothman

Snarer Of Hearts

I set sail on my inner sea
Without compass or chart to guide me
God-less, yet in God most needing
Hopeful, yet in Hope not believing
Weary, but Wearier more,
In my own Worldliness which I abhor
Soul-less I would add to these
This list of my Infirmities
But, from the buried mineshaft of my Soul,
Long neglected
A faint murmur from Soul's survivors was detected
Gratefully, I would have them see Light of Day
And Joyously I would Hear and
Comprehend what they say.

This I Pray...
Amen.

   John J. Scanlon

Another Lost Meaning

It seems like love is such a casual term,
That is so often used to adorn;
Has become worn out an' torn.
This appears normal for most
While the wiser laugh and boast,
When they know this is far from true.
It's in your heart's every beat...
It's in your dreams when you sleep...
And always on your mind once you wake.
It causes a fire which grows and grows,
With a swift course through our veins;
Only making us more insane.
A truly special word that lovers just know
It can be read in their eyes...
Heard by their souls...
And voiced by their hearts...
This word is neither dead nor gone.
For its song is best sung,
When the fire's turned on.

   Clayton Chapman II

Very Discouraged

Once I wrote a piece
then I rewrote
and rewrote it again
and though it wasn't quite yet what I wanted,
I liked it
I really believed it was good.

   And then I had a friend
   who picked up the piece
   and read it aloud
    and laughed and laughed and laughed...

   James Roberts

The Pain Of Self Inflicted Death

The blood in my veins I should have saved
instead I released it with a razor blade
my lifeless eyes gaze at nothing
after death there must be something
now the world one person less
my rotting corpse must seem grotesque
Illuminated by pale moon light
moments later my soul takes flight
seeps away from my rotting innards
down to hell with all the sinners
once arrived the burn is felt
the eternal wage for sin is dealt
thoughts of taking back the evil
for there is one life there is no sequel
spike my mind right through the pain
if I'd only known I was insane
for the moment in which my self has died
I've committed suicide.

   Daniel E. Barrett

Lost In Me

Yesterday, I laughed.
Today, I'll cry and tomorrow I won't even know why.
The smiles I reminisce. The tears I hide, in my weary swollen eyes.
And sometimes, I just sit without a thought.
Am I lost or found in a different time, tic-toc passing,
while I'm laughing and crying inside of me.

   Timothy R. Williams

465

Our Grandma

Dear friends you will never see such distress as when
we lay our Grandma down to rest
For 95 years she was mother, grandma, friend, a teacher to all
Now she's heard a higher call...

She left us here alone to cry, while she is with him on high
And yet we see her everywhere
On the couch and in the chair

And the chickadee she loved will sing her song
As she watches the clouds move along
The moon it will shine so bright when we look up at it tonight
And grandma she will be looking down
She'll feel our sorrow all around

She'll know we loved her one and all, she'll hear our cry,
She'll hear our call
She'll feel our sorrow, feel our pain
Until we meet with her again.

So friends please help us carry on
Our hearts are empty
   Grandma's gone!
And my heart breaks like a thousand pieces of broken glass

Cassandra Lee Fashano

Untitled

All that we hold certain are life and death
no one is sure if he can inhale another breath
unanswered questions await around every turn
take it in quick, there is far too much to learn
while yesterday's memories evaporate day by day
new ones replace them as the old ones fade away
nothing is a sure thing in this life
so take it slow and maybe you can survive

William Alexander McKinney

An Untitled Life

I am an unborn child
I was planted three weeks ago
I'll live inside my mother till I am nine months old
fingers, toes, mouth and nose
I am growing really fast
it's hard to believe all the time that has already passed
I am now due in seven months and two weeks
boy I'll tell you this sure stinks
I could not wait to be born, now I'm sad so I mourn
today on this October morn
I'm sorry to say today is the day my mother killed me
I heard her cry, I heard her scream
I thought she had a real bad dream
I felt her strain, I felt the pain
I saw the light, it was bright
in an instant I was gone
no memory of me will carry on
did I not matter, would I have been a shame
I guess I'll never know my cause of pain

Darla Linebarger

Dark Eyes

I can only see darkness through these eyes,
As it shuts around me I hear a silent cry.
This reminds me of a warm safe place or
that I'm stuck between worlds.
I'm in this shelter, I open my eyes,
to see that absolute horror of darkness is imprisoning me.
I reach out to break free to find out there
is a wall wrapped around me.
I open my mouth to scream, but I only hear silence.
As often as I can remember, I'm in this coffin forever.

Jeanna Marino

All There Is

I sit in this lonely room.
I think of what my life has come to,
and wonder if this is all there is.
I've loved and lost.
I've lost faith that there's much to believe in.

My luck's run bad and run out.
Is this all there is?
Pain, confusion, loneliness
that's my life now.
I wonder if it will ever change.

So long ago I knew laughter and light.
The world burst through the wall.
And now I sit in darkness,
a candle the only memory
of light I have left.

Eclipse of the heart.
In my heart, in the sky
the sun has set.
I'm left to wonder:
Is this all there is?

Sheldon Carpenter

Has Arrived

I walk blindly through the winding rough of life
Wondering who or what is going to save me from
This lurid pain of outlandish strife

I then flash back to when my mother took care of me
And made me feel secure

Only trying desperately to find that perfect combination
To make those feelings reoccur

Keep on keepin' on
We're gettin' there
Flashed before me in a splintering fashion telling me
That those two sayings were the foundations of my
peace and serenity

I love you
Was another saying that my mother taught me and
That is what has made me into a man today

James Seaman

North Dakota, My Home

Mesmerized by the Dakota sun,
I saw visions
Of a life that has passed
Not knowing where it rests.

On the rolling green hills
I saw Native Americans
With their camps so organized,
Smoke rolling off their fires into the sky.

On the flat prairie
I saw wild flowers in full bloom,
Pioneers searching the land for
A place to call home.

Near a crystal clear creek,
Easterners settled their homestead,
Children playing...
Mischief in the air!

These people have passed on,
North Dakota is still here
That life may be in the history books,
But it's still a place to call home.

Terri Thompson

466

The Feeling Of Spring

You should see my Willow tree behind the house today
It's wispy green, all soft and gay.
Then too, the blades of grass turned green this week
and the forsythia is anything but meek!

The tree out front has stretched its limbs
inviting all to see
The violets growing just beneath
this lovely Mimosa tree.

I love the spring and all its wealth;
Birds nesting and chirping and colors usurping
all of winter's gray,
giving way to warm sunlight and soft breezes,
as the dull spirit of winter unfreezes.

Oh, to run and dance and sing,
this feeling of love for everything!
To shout with joy, to soar aloft
this feeling I get, every so oft,
especially in the spring.

Thelma Espenschied

Fate

Life is wonderful, life is great,
Filled with magic in the form of fate.
What is fate, people wish to know?
Why can't a flower grow in the snow?
Why can't a fish sing like a bird?
How come the buffalo travel by herd?
In coming, in coming all around,
The wounded are screaming their nightmarish sounds.
Corpsman, corpsman, corpsman up,
The last one we saw had used up his luck.
We stare at the LZ, no choppers in sight,
And realize we're destined to spend the night.
How come some buddies got wounded and blind?
Why aren't some breathing when others bought time?
These questions of fate can't be answered in rhyme,
But too often consumes what's left of my mind.
You can't research or discover it or solve it in verse,
Because the mystery of fate's magic is so vast,
It's too modern for future, too ancient for past.

John C. Schlicher

Open Sea

There's an open sea
inside my head
Depths of the unknown
not explored
I sail the sea
with hook and line
To catch the Unknown
not sure what I'll find
Perhaps a phrase, a sage, a space in time
a choice, a voice
A state within the mind
A place of peace a part of time

A hook, a sinker, a line

And so I dwell and play the game
a gambler betting with rhythm and time
And should I play a merry tune
Will they dance to how my fingers move...?

With their fragile sails of open minds...

A gentle breeze guides them
to the open sea.

Scott Dunmire

Empty World

I am alone out in empty space.
With nothing to do no one else of my race.
There is nothing of interest and no one is here.
Not even a sound to buzz in my ear.
The earth has vanished the plants are all gone.
The lakes are dried up and fish can't spawn.
The world has vanquished for nobody's cared.
If we'd just have listened the earth could've been spared.

Laura Novkov

For My Angel

When I was very young,
Maybe two or three,
I had an Uncle Eugene who was in love with me.
He'd take me to the park,
And throw me in the air,
He would always catch me,
He'd always be there.
I wish what I had told you,
Him always being there were true,
But at the time I never guessed the ordeal he would go through.
Since I was so little I simply can't remember,
That tragic night I lost him in the middle of December.
If only he had had a friend to take his keys that night,
Maybe he'd have got to see me grow up sweet and right.
I guess we should have warned him,
Then maybe he'd be alive,
If only we had told him not to drink and drive.
Now he is my angel watching from above,
This poem is from me to you Eugene,
Just to show my love.

Dawn Koch

Thoughts

A red M&M in the sand,
a boy and girl coming this way, holding hands;
some rocks, some foam on the waves, some sun -
    not much - make up this day.

Some thoughts of you, some of him;
they disappear, they're here again.

Two boats at sea. Do they see me?
Or is it that they'll never know that my hair blows
    two miles away.

That my thoughts grow and shiver and die
    as in the moist sand I lie.

That my mind bleeds and drains from rains of thoughts
    of you, and him; they're here again.

Christine G. Kane

Just A Thought

My eyes concealed to the wonder that is life,
squandered on those precious things,
such as love.
My youth must escape me.
I see it vanishing but do not realize,
for that time is spent in bliss,
not that which is always happy,
but sad also.
Experience blinds the time that binds the world to its fate.
A cracked rear view mirror,
I watch my life,
like a memory, but yet it is diffracted.
The image never being perfected,
for it loses its beauty the second it passes.
But hope is mine in the beauty of the future,
That which has yet succumbed to time.

Brittany Ogletree

Life Is Still Here

Life comes and goes so fast,
what can we do to make it last?
    In a heartbeat it is no longer,
we pray compassion will make us stronger.
    Cherish each moment, as though the last,
for that moment comes way too fast.
    Look around, life is still here,
in everything we see, even through a tear.
    Listen hard, and try to smile,
remember those moments, once in a while.
    Everywhere you are, life is there too,
smile and remember, you won't be so blue.
    When touched by someone, it makes your heart break,
when the body is gone, how your arms ache.
    The soul and spirit are here everyday,
cherish each memory made along the way.
    Keep the memories and share them from your heart,
Life is still here, we never really part.

Linda L. Parr

HIV+

Life changes when you are looking
    death in the face.
Not knowing, day to day, when death will
    take the life you have.
It doesn't infect only one person,
    one race, one religion, it's anyone.
It infects and affects everyone, from all
    stages of life.
It will become, how you live your life,
    face to face, day to day, hour to hour
    and sometimes even minute to minute.
The not knowing when that day will come,
    is as bad, if not worse, than the disease.
You learn who your real family and friends
    are when they find out.
Living HIV+ can make you or break you.
Live your life for yourself, not the virus.
You can live your life to the fullest.
Take advantage of any and everything
    that comes your way.

Dianna James

Smiles And Tears

I smiled today, although I was still sad
After yesterday's tears, the heart could be glad
The sun was shining, and gone were the fears
You look to God, and he dries your tears
I smelled the flowers with the shining sun
The heart can easily be glad, when the
sun is shining and it's no longer sad.

Rose M. Harter

You Decide!

Life is a giant roller coaster ride.
Where it ends you decide.
How it ends you can't always decide,
But if you end it in suicide,
You toss God's love for you aside.
Don't be too afraid, of Him, to confide,
He might just send an Angel to your side!
When you finally do confide,
You'll find He's always been at your side.
So remember, the next time your ride,
Through this life, gets a little bumpy, Confide!
God has always been there,
And He will never leave nor forsake you!
Don't forget, He is always listening.

Beulah Slaton

Tranquility

A secret message scrawled by a schoolgirl in the wet sand,
Footprints of man and bird wandering aimlessly in the tidewater.
Sand castles gilded with parapets, moats and battlements,
And, alas, the persistent relentless waves
In league with the ever shifting sands
Slowly, deliberately erasing all signs of man's presence
    on that pristine shore.
Patiently, wave after wave, driven by timeless tides,
    cleanse the beach of human intrusion as a reminder
    of our transiency on this speck of the universe.
Drawn magnetically to the sea are we hearkening to our
    amniotic pre-existence in the protective security
    of the womb with its soft aquatic rhythms?
Or, are we drawn to some mystical worship of our primordial
    beginnings from which we evolved those countless eons ago?
In a world so fraught with waning stability
We turn to the ancient sea
Our one source of tranquility.

Dale Miller

My Uncle Jack

Twinkling blue eyes, scratchy beard, rough in a refined way.
You are strong and capable, an expert in your field.
A talented artist and skilled craftsman,
You are proud and confident.

You smile and tease; you make me laugh.
You cause me to think, you give me
New perspectives and food for thought.

I can just see you: Leaning back, arms crossed; one leg
Resting on the other...quietly
Watching, observing what goes on around you.
Taking it all in.

You were sick, weren't you?
You of all people, so strong,
So untouchable. How could you be sick?
My Uncle Jack, who has always taken care of me. Me?
Why? I didn't understand.

I knew it couldn't get you.
I knew it wouldn't. I knew. I was right.
Twinkling blue eyes, sandy-brown hair, scratchy beard,
Rough in a refined way. My Uncle Jack.

Emily Poel

Sensation

Listen to the raindrops.
What a glorious sound!
The raindrops are bringing well-needed moisture
to our ground all around.
Our grass has all but dried up and you know what that means.
Especially for our farmers, who are praying and down on their knees;
for one of God's little treasures, to put the moisture back on our leaves.

Rhonda S. Frank

Praised, Loved, And Lost

As compared to any bloom betray
Memory's lights, aspiring buds, grey
And whom a heart's admissions speak?
When to you, the hated beauty, lies defeat
Coward in awe, or amorous grace
Alone sit I, with only the darling face
A loss to loss, a mind to dwell
All cannot be lost, despite a farewell
Broken misfortune, a story to find
It matters not to you, an ending a lie
Know the promise of lovers apart
The longing cry silent of the broken heart

Aaron Blevins

The Tennis Match

It was a passing shot, it was a volley.

The ace,
The shot, that was well placed.
The Serlano tennis match that night.

She positioned herself,
It was a drop shot.
The ball was to her forehand,
Just clearing the net,
It spun forward and to the left.

What shot would she make?
The scoop?? A drop shot,,,
It was the...Oops!!

Three times it was match game.
Who won? Who won?

It was a match...To the finish.
Through sweat and tears.
For both players, there were many cheers,
There were no winners,
It was a match of tennis.

 It was a tennis match.
 Alonzo A. Alston

In Memory

Lest you think that we forgot
or that we didn't care,
It was our time in Camelot
and a moment we could share.

Lest you think we misunderstood
or we could not spare the time,
It was a time in sisterhood
a celebration of our kind.

'Twas not we had nothing to give
or cared not to risk our souls to bare,
It was that life is short to live
and we wanted to be there.

'Twas not we did not recognize your love
or could not leave death's bed,
It was that we saw the peace of the dove
and chose a better time instead.

 Doris Phillips Gernovich

Odd Man Out

Odd man out, no qualification.
Suffice that it is an oblique truth.

Desire to blend, encumbered by ability.
Over time, acquiesced; not entirely placid.

We got cerebral, we got menial.
Religion to radiators, Verdi to Volkswagens.

We danced a jig to the gulls.
We wept in our hearts, the dark half.

Content at pasture's edge;
a long dead poet reminds me, I'm in the fold.

"How beautiful is this house!
The atmosphere
breathes rest and comfort,
and the many chambers
seem full of welcomes."

Longfellow wrote what I feel.
Psyche reflections; odd man in.

 James C. Bibber

A Dream Waiting To Become True

We are like a stained glass window,
With blacks, yellows, reds, whites and blues.
Once dark and broken,
But the words of Dr. King has brought us together,
In one united rainbow shining through the light,
Let his dream come true,
We are one, shining together,
Through the rays of love and peace,
For all mankind,

 Hyan Kim

A Place

Today as the sun shines upon my face
I would love to be in a different place
Maybe a place I've been before...
Where my dreams are washed along the shore.

As I walk dreams reveal
All those places, that I feel
Miles of pastures covered in green,
as I wonder what it means.

I search for peace along the way
As I travel that sunny day
Mountains are covered with beautiful snow.
As I look for a place to go...

Somewhere out there, there's a place for me.
Where my heart is opened and my mind is free
Maybe that place I've been before
Where my dreams are found along the shore

 Carl Anthony Semien

Sick And Tired

I'm sick of tears, and sick of pain.
I'm sick of sadness, and always rain.

I'm tired of fighting, always trying to win.
I'm tired of giving, but always giving in.

I'm sick of heartache, and always getting hurt.
I'm sick of treating people like gold, but being kicked in
 the face with dirt.

I'm tired of trying, but never getting what I want.
I'm tired of failing, and giving reason to taunt.

I'm sick of being good, being sweet, nice and don't forget kind.
I'm sick of being wonderful, yet there is always someone better to find.

I'm tired of being taken for granted, given no worth at all.
I'm tired of being knocked down, but always expected to get up
 and walk tall.

 Serenity Joi Berry

Accidental Love

Did you really think you'd break my heart
a heart broke long ago
As though it were a porcelain cup
that shatters on the floor
I'm made of far more substance
than your arrogance would know
My skin is thick
my heart still soft
The thrust of your knife
was only one small blow
I'll build no walls
nor punish others
for your insincerity
and sin
For that would be the real crime
to not let others in.

 Carmela R. Olsick

Why?

Perhaps, I am not wise enough to know
Why happiness is always mixed with pain.
Why the sun is blatted out by clouds and rain
and then appears again; but it is so.

I do not understand why robins go away
at autumn time; I can't explain,
why leaves should fall; or why
the day should wane.
Or, why we must surrender the flowers that grow
but; I have learned he has not blessed
but half, those, who have not tasted joy that follows grief.
and who has not known the
pleasure of a laugh, that follows grievous
tears; but, oh, but the sweet relief is only mine,
When skies are clouded, just to know,
yet another day
may bring a beautiful sunset's
Glow and but yet again why?

Chuck Mesaros

As The Last Petal Falls

Full, rich, fragrant, corolla blooms with unsurpassed beauty,
    touched by the Divine seal its glory
    nature to enjoy

Roses grace elegant vases like bouquets of the heart,
    fragile, dew moistened, velvet petals crown thorny stem
    with colorful splendor.

Without pageantry, one by one they quietly, delicately fall
    adorning table top below, simulating teardrops
    reflecting sorrow within

Each separation brings a new reality of doom
    foreseen without power to impede, pray may I stay
    one more day

As the last petal falls, leaving barren stem to cry
    alone in its demise, remembrance of radiance past press deep
    on tender heart

Gather roses though duration short may be,
    for in this splendid gesture, they gloriously
    fulfill their destiny.

Dorothy M. Machado

Love Won!

Grant me a heart that will not fear
This work of Gethsemane so near.
Such sorrow and such pain
This heart of love seems already slain.

Grant me a heart that will not fear
This work of Gethsemane so near.
My heart faints, my body pressed down
My intercessions deep, yet I pray with no frown.

Grant me a heart that will not fear
This work of Gethsemane so near.
To love so completely seems to separate us deeply
But God I am to drink,
Let me do so sweetly.

Then the angel of Gethsemane drew near
With sweetest voice and encouragements so dear.
There came a peace from God to onward trod,
"Thy will be done" my righteous rod.

So here, it is true, is where it all begins
Where love agrees with "Thy will be done!"
The victory shouts "Love Won!"

Shiri Ahava Yisrael

The Garden of My Heart

Black flower
Empty, isolated, alone
Living, growing, changing
But never reflecting any of life's colors
The joy, the love, the laughter
Dead life
Black flower

Elaine Graziano

What Is Love?

Love is something that affects us all.
It's a feeling that will never fade.
It makes us laugh with all our heart.
It makes us cry with all our soul
We have always fought for it.
We've even died in its name.

Love can bring you much pain.
But it brings much more joy.
Without love, how could we live?
It is both our heart and soul.
It is our lifeline in a sea of hatred.
Without it, we're lost, but with it, we are saved.

Love comforts us in our sorrow
And strengthens us when we are weak.
Its gifts are unsurpassed
Its joys are forever
So if ever you need a helping hand,
Call on love, for it will always be there.

Tamara Ericsson

Dream Walker

You come and visit every night,
Sometimes you even bring me fright.
You walk around from dream to dream,
Sometimes you're drowning in a stream.
Sometimes you're happy-sometimes sad,
I've even caught you being bad.
I want you to know I can't hide my feelings,
Out of all the guys - you're most appealing,
you mess with my mind -
til my thoughts are in a bind,
Somehow I figure this must be a sign.
When I wake up I don't remember a thing,
Something tells me you're pulling me strings.

Katrina Cook

Pieces Of My Life

When you left me, you shattered my life.
Shattered pieces were strewn out everywhere.
As I moved along, heading in a forward direction,
I slowly picked up the pieces of my life.
This process was not without pain.
You see, as I walked along I realized something.
There were pieces out there I didn't even know existed.
So, I would step on them and feel intense pain.
With the horrible pain came many tears.
Tears of sadness, tears of fear
It took me by surprise when I discovered these pieces.
You see, until you left me,
These pieces were so small, so hidden, I could not see them.
Although I cannot pick up all the pieces,
Nor avoid the pain of stepping on a few,
I know once I have completed this process,
I can create anything I want to.
I cherish the pieces I hold and anticipate others
To be collected along the way,
As I continue my journey onward.

Sheri Lynn Di Prima

Untitled

I am the still one on a delicate watch
Marking the tally of another day's notch.
As a wandering sun darkens the garden and room
Shown only in candle light of a flickering moon.

Southern winds faintly whisper all the while
The passing ages with such sweet denial.
As years marked by changes long transcend
Two shadows cast by a passing day's end.

Kim Griffith

Rhythm

Listening to the beat of her drum
   she calls my name
Smooth as an evening breeze, mixed with the scent of cane
   she called my name
The rhythm of her swing is like the flicker of a candle
my fingers tapping smooth leather sending colors of the rainbow
through my head
Oh so powerful in her loving
calling my name

Elise Coleman

The Night Sounds

They cried in the night — the Coyotes
There was loneliness and shiver in their bark;
Even though I was safe there and sleeping
They shed fear and dread in the dark.

I know not what is this feeling
That haunts like a shadow in dreams,
Something that goes back in the races
That never is quite like it seems.

Their call is a sad lonely echo
Of things in the past now gone,
That we can't explain in expressing,
It stirs a memory as sad a song.

And in the song there is sadness and yearning
And it is not the feeling of pain,
It's just the feeling of sorrow
As your heart beats out its refrain.

We try to escape this feeling,
Not give it a moment to dwell,
Just let pass as heart beat
And say to ourselves now all will be well.

Jearline Bates

One Special Athlete

He's tall, muscular, kind and full
of surprises.
He's quiet and so well liked, with a
hand shake that's so polite.
He knows how to make ya smile, no
matter what the atmosphere's like,
When out on the field wearing the
jersey 40 he's like lightning with
the sound of thunder scoring.
When in the gym he's wearing the
jersey 32 or 33, we all yell and
holler as he shoots with a grin.
Now out on the field he stands so
fine, wearing jersey #9.
With he roar of the crowd, he runs
like a deer, catching that pop fly with no fear.
He's an athlete going for something special.
With a scholarship in hand, He'll
go on with his plan as he
travels across the land.

Dorothy Anderson

On The Edge Of Heaven

Choking like the phlegm clogging one's throat,
You bring soothing chamomile tea and honey.
The double edge sword; too vile or too sweet,
I glance down in the murky pond scum, my reflection runny.

I bash my memory in search of the reason you're here
Regenerating this kind, caring attitude towards me.
In paranoia I wonder if it's nothing but a ploy,
Mocking, "You sad bastard, this, could never be!"

Night sweats or chills, either way afraid to be left alone.
Your body warm, our souls play the same melody.
My incessant need to never let anyone on to me,
You come too close, I turn away, keeping this hell low key.

You persist like last years winner trying to repeat;
Leaping great obstacles of patience, commitment, and desire.
I've set up the hurdles defensively to keep everyone away;
Never anticipating your competitiveness, you never tire.

The path I tread is humbly sweet, yet, just as bitter.
For in night you hold the lantern and my hand;
Joining me in a journey that is whole,
Only to be swept away by the light you are barred.

Walter J. Beck

A Poem For Someone

How courageous to dream beyond your splintered past
singing a future that repeats itself in unpleasant colors.
And how daring to scream above the painful cries of
Those who have forgotten their youth in an empty bag.

For you I will write and dance and sing and maybe
on occasion I will tell you a story rich in spirit
and rich in dreams one hundred years old when
your ancestors and mine tried a few things here
and there and promised each other to keep living.
If even one more day.

I wish flowers and grass were money.
How splendid a bouquet I would prepare for you.
Do you remember how wonderful honey suckle smells.
Even before the sun arrives at your doorstep?
Oh, how I wish you loved the sun as you love fear.
And how I wish you could see how beautiful you are
without anything but your eyes that reflect your soul.

You are from an unrecognized future where only the
blind still see and the deaf still hear a warm summer
shower and a life worth living.

Arlaana Black

An Unexpected Encounter

Guess what?
Quite unexpectedly one afternoon
I bumped into spring
On Glenwood Avenue.

Like a hooligan
It stormed down the busy street,
In its tipsy thunder yet
There was a promise of a treat.

For a pastel moment only
It seemed to have waved its colorful hat
And admit it, you felt its pearl rain
Whether you were old or lonely — or in pain.

A few days later,
What is left behind?
Wrapped up in luscious greenery is our yard
Birds' silver songs wake us up and we wonder
Why tulip petals - like cards after a game —
Lie scattered on the ground.

Mirka Christesen

Will She Quit Trying?

My grandchild has a teacher
who's very hard to please.
She tries her very hardest
but it never seems enough,
I know she will quit trying
if he doesn't soon let up.

Her answers are correct - yet no!
The words are not in order,
not enough detail, not enough flow.
I know she will quit trying if he doesn't soon let up.

She works so hard for every test,
trying and trying to do her best.
No notice made of effort or striving,
I know that soon she will quit trying.
If only he'd let up.

We love this child of sunshine and light,
we want her to be happy and bright.
Please see her worth regardless of grades
and try to give her a little praise.
Perhaps she won't quit trying.

Shirley Ford

Grandma

I would like to write this poem,
for a dear one that I love.
Who truly is a God send,
from the places high above.

When I was yet a child, a nickname you did get.
And you will always be known as "Nana," you can surely bet.

There's a special place for you,
in this little heart of mine.
That truly is beyond mere words,
that surely makes me shine.

What a comfort in knowing,
never will we say goodbye.
For we both will be caught up, in the twinkling of an eye.
And placed amongst the angels,
along the streets that shine of gold.
And see our blessed savior, what a sight we will behold.

I will always love you, "Nana,"
for my heart is truly set.
That you will always be my "Nana."
You can surely bet.

Denise M. Marjama

Come Into My Dream (By The Sea)

Tonight I shall walk alone in my dream, with a fear that
you may not be there...I will walk beside the sea without a
hand to hold, or your heart to warm with my love....I shall
think of your beautiful eyes, wondering if they will become
but a memory...I will listen to the sounds of the sea but
without you, they will have no meaning to me...Clouds may
fill the sky and hide the sun, everything then so cold and
gray.....suddenly a sound behind me and glancing back, I see
your footprints in the sand washed away I will sit upon a
rock, and dream a dream within my dream, one that might bring
your love to me...So much in love with you that a falling
star I cannot even see...Ocean breezes then whispering
softly to me, saying that you are alone by the sea...An
emptiness fills my heart, as my dream comes to an end....I
only know that I shall return to this place by the
sea....with every hope and prayer that you will come to
me...and that our love will last until eternity....

Jim Maher

Nature's Secret

The subtle lake whispers to the forest
And it tells a story that will definitely lure us
A story about trees being cut down
Taken into town

A story about the lazy raven
But hopefully some one will save him
For once the tree was his home
Now he's all alone
Nowhere to set his nest
The tree is gone. Just a hole, depressed

A story about the friendly bear
for shadows only come in his lair
And the wretched sun will scorn his back
And for the bear there is not one snack

But one thing tells this scary tale
It tells us humans that we have failed
Failed to leave some things alone
Things of nature young and old
This is what the subtle lake told

Jessica Leah Tyler

Thankful Heart

Thank you God for all you have done.
Blessing me with life and the many joys which came from your
heart and caring eyes.

Family and friends, they fill my days with loving times and fun
to share. Memories lasting for many a year.

Life is short, this is true. For you gave it to me and soon
I will be coming home to stay with you.

Bless each and everyone oh Lord.
Protect them in all they do, life is so precious because
it came from you.

Debra J. Siggins

Place

There is a place known, to but my heart alone.
A serene rage beats the beach where I and seagulls moan.
Impending, powerful, crash to gentle earth below,
You surf leads me to the inner tides I ever long to know.

O ocean, I call you my "be there always friend."
Walked out on you before—Yet you've waves of love to lend.
You hold me in your arms and listen, lapping up my cares.
I want to be with you, because of what we share.

Your breath surrounds me, and whispers warm hellos
I hear impassioned symphony each time the water flows.
And when I sail upon your soothing, secured shores,
My blue life guard protects me, how could he provide more?

Feeling and walking upon your whitened sands,
I place my heart in your open, outstretched hands.
No one has ever held me, like the azure embraces you,
No one could ever melt me or mold me like you do.

Patty O'Neal-Kenney

Life

Life is like a fleeting
going hither, thither and yon,
At times we take a beating
which passes and then is gone.

The ground upon which we stand
is like the shifting of white sand.
While we should offer each other a hand,
instead we are playing as singers in a band.

Daniel L. Rupert

Jigsaw

I guess everyone has a year in their life
  when everything seems to go wrong;
I've got friends of mine dying on my left and right
  can't even write a good song.

  When there's something missing in the air
  - that disagrees with you;
  You burn it all out - then you sit way back..
  ..slowly, it leaves you.

I guess everyone has a time in their life
  when there's puzzle pieces they can't find;
I've got a piece over here - I've got a piece over there
  - really wish I had a peace of mind.

  When there's something missing in the air
  - that disagrees with you;
  You burn it all out - then you sit way back...
  ..slowly, it leaves you.

    James Guiney

Remember

Went by the old home place today
Though I would look around maybe take a few pictures
Before they come tear it down
The two old Magnolias are still standing
Remember where we use to play
And where mama use to our clothes
On that old wash board everyday
Remember how little our worries were
But mama and daddy had a bunch
Remember when they couldn't afford bread
So daddy took biscuits in his lunch
Remember that old gate the one daddy put the anvil on
It was to make it hard to open
Well it's still there but the fence is gone
I looked for the glass we buried
But it was all grown over
Remember when we were gonna try and find it
Someday when we got older well all that's left here now
Is a lot of sweet memories of all the days gone by
Just though you'd like to here about them and see if you
remember

    Doug Lindsey

A Little Blessing From Above

A little child goes out to play
on a warm and sunny day
the dirt and bugs and trees and grass
it's the little things that make them laugh

A little blessing from God above
reflects on the faces of the ones we love
the joy of knowing who gives life
this wonderful miracle given to man and wife

A child will grow stronger with each day
as he struggles to learn to make his way
while a mother stays upon her knees
praying the Lord will hear her plea

We watch them grow and change each day
Lord give us strength to let them go their own way
to become adults with hearts most pure
with strength to endure when the road is unsure

Lord, keep this little child of mine
safe in either my arms or thine
I know that whether near or far
that where he is, is where you are

    Mary Clemons

The Storm

From my bedroom window, I study the threatening skies
Rain is on its way, which I will await with curious eyes

The sun, once shining so proudly, has retired for the day
For there's a new ruler in town and it's in the form of gray

Darkness has invaded, the angry heavens above begin to rumble
The moment has arrived, raindrops will soon start to tumble

And then, almost instantly, the drops fall with such grace
Diving downward with ease, descending at a very slow pace

Gaining speed, the now driving rain becomes music to my ears
A light drizzle has become a heavy downpour as lightning nears

All is wet, the soaking rain has drenched everything it sees
The ground quickly turns to mud as gusts of wind bend the trees

And, as I listen and watch, I wonder how long it will last
For the rainfall is weakening and I think the storm has passed

    Jimmi D'Angelo

The Sweet Arms Of Time

Under the glistening moon,
With the sparkle of a star,
By the twinkle of the twilight,
A blossom blossomed.

The sweet arms of time
began to unfold.

Under a smiling eye,
With a caring caress,
By the warmth of a whisper,
The blossom flowered.

The sweet arms of time
savored the now.

Under a cautious watch,
With a nurturing nudge,
By a gentle glow,
A flower blossomed.

The sweet arms of time slowly let go.

Under a shimmering reflection,
With the memory of a moment,
By the dash of a daydream,
The flower flowered.

The sweet arms of time longed for the then.

    Alex Sigona

Image

As generations have their own,
The one that has drawn attention has flown
With no rational decision in mind
Though never leaving a thought behind.
Moving with no conceived abstract idea,
Working off all the embedded social fears
When the internal and external unite,
The alerted feeling stand appealing in the night.
Unknown before only to deplore you,
Now the spirit rises for the new cue,
Processing comes while only to some askew
Until repressed desires ignite a fire to view.
What the mental image lectures do,
True or false maybe a clue giving a few.
Therefore, a mind may roar to review
If in fact the laborious picture was subdued.
Perhaps the day soon may arrive
When all in the land shall strive.

    J. J. Hagan

The Student

Priests' robes at Easter
look like the grapes carelessly tossed
into a cheap, ceramic bowl.

Which reminds her of gaudy neon lights and
Tired feet and
Tired smiles.

"Paint that".
Struggling to find form, texture or beauty,
The would-be artist fails and finds nothing.

She turns to the window,
Seeing angry grey clouds at war with each other
And thinks,
"I could paint the smell of rain."

And two old men, bent with age,
trading lies over backyard fences.

But she can't.

L. Permar Quackenbush

A Happy Hello And A Sad Goodbye

A warm and joyous hello,
Wrapped inside a hug and kiss,
A rush of love in my body that I don't know,
Smelling the deep scent of the one I miss.

Everyday spent side by side,
Ideas, thoughts, and dreams shared with each other,
A special bond we both tied,
Love from a sister to a brother.

Loud actions and whispered words,
Smiles so often exchanged,
Sweet I love you's were always heard,
Near or far our love didn't change.

Precious moments spent together,
Dreaming of you and all you do,
Loving you without wondering whether,
You think of me half as much as I think of you.

Now we face a sad goodbye,
I must return and live without your love so near,
My face is filled with a wet cry,
How I wish you were always here!

Aarti Gadkar

Builders

Each one of us is an architect.
We can make for our lives great plans.
We can put our sketches on the finest canvas,
Or on beaches among shifting sand.

We can watch and wait with patience,
To see what the builder will do.
Or, are we, ourselves, the builders?
Is the responsibility for your life up to you?

It is the life that we build on today,
That must sustain us for the days yet to come.
It must be filled with many rich experiences,
That we can draw on when all else is gone.

There are those who would prefer not to work.
There are those much too busy to make plans.
There are those dreams of tomorrow,
will be washed up among the sand.

Each one of us has his own time.
We can divide it between work and play.
There are rich lives to be built for tomorrow.
We, the architects, must build them today.

Alma Shaw Greer

Of Hope And Angels

The angels proclaimed the wondrous birth
    of our Father's son who came to Earth.
Their songs of praise filled the sky
    for the Baby who came, for us, to die.
We celebrate what those angels knew,
    of God's great gift of love so true;
His own Son's life so freely given,
    that we could be with him in heaven.
God help us now in our world of strife,
    to, like the angels, rejoice in Christ's life.
And live, like Jesus, a life of peace,
    that our world may be free, that war may cease.
Keep on us your sovereign hand,
    and guide the leaders in our lands.
Let them now, as the angels then
    proclaim, "Peace on Earth, goodwill to men."

Kathleen Marie

The Wall

A wall is built to separate, divide.
A wall is built to keep some folks inside.
A wall is built to keep others outside.
This wall was built to simply show much pride:
In Fifty-Eight-Thousand on its obverse side.

I've seen it thrice, as deeply moved became;
Its loudest silence burst my ears as to proclaim:
"That though we died, we did not die in vain;
"For communism soon became a much derailed train;
"That gangster system was, through us, put through a strain.
"We pray its ilk will never rise again!"

(We also learned protracted conflict is not good,
For it lasts longer than it ever should.)

Earl F. Voelz

Spider Plant

The mother plant sits bushy and high,
Reaching for all the sunbeams she spies.
She reaches so hard and so long that quite soon
Her babies appear and it's time to make room.

Like spiders with silk, on a stem they descend
Towards the light, it is there that they faithfully bend.
Out they will grow, to the ground it is certain.
They will surely loop under the hem of my curtain.

What once started out as a delicate seed
Has matured to become quite substantial indeed.
From her tiny clay pot near the window up high.
The mother plant watches her offspring and sighs.

Like children, they wander to all different places
Some winning, some losing the survival races
But each of the seedlings conduce as if one
As they battle through life towards the afternoon sun.

Corianne Iacovelli

A Heart Beat

Silence. Listen to the beating,
the beating of my heart.
It beats with a hollow echo,
that carries through the halls.
It beats without love that I
may never find.
Though my face carries a smile,
my heart beats my true feelings.
It beats feelings that my dream partner's heart,
may never beat for me.

Marvin Richardson Jr.

To My Mistress

I watch you
And my soul begins to wander.
Unceasingly, you play rhythmic games
Within my yearning-to-be-free heart,
And mockingly, call me back to your side.

Where have you been?
How many dreams,
With your careless stormy moodiness
Has your beauty shattered this time?

What is it about your touch that calms?
Is it your wind tossed nakedness
That demands, no man long leave you alone
And commands he call your depths home.

Now, I call upon all my strength
And the courage Neptune blessed me
To leave you one more time
'Til you summon me back to your watery realm
By salt within the wind.

J. J. Schappert

The Old Oak Tree

The Old Oak Tree grows old,
It grows tall with celestial heights,
It stands forever with all its might,
Enjoying the sights of day and night.
It stands for causes and helps a lot,
For all the beautiful things natures got.
Homes of birds, squirrels and playhouses too,
The Old Oak Tree stands along side you.

Kasia Sawicz

To Beau

From behind those deep, beautiful dark eyes
let me touch with your fingers and see from your heights
to know the anger as it sprouts from a tiny seed of frustration
to your elation so pure, my heart melts from my own tears.

Your fascination with little things
in their order precise
your ability to find and dissect those hidden spots
which to us, remain invisible and unknown.

How do you shut the world off
when your absorption is so deep
and in one split second demand the presence
of a human to fill your needs.

Let me feel your peaks and valleys of emotion
your perseverance to the point of obsession
your struggles to fit in
your needed moments of isolation
your gnawing craving to feel wanted.

But oh...above all I want to capture
this swelling love for the people in your life
as tiny cracks appear in a once isolated world.

Dianne Thomas

Trust

To have and to hold is what they say,
But after all these years we've seemed to slip away.
From this day forward is what they mean,
But none of that matters if it's all just a dream.
In sickness and in health for the rest of our lives,
Stay healthy and true to your husbands and wives.
Until death do you part is the way it should be,
Stay healthy and strong and try to be happy.

Kenneth D. Kennedy

Pendulum

There is a silver pendulum
Which swings to and fro
Through the cavernous dark
Pit of my stomach.

A rhythm ticking steady
To my mind's ebb and flow
Oscillating between virtue and desire
Between two grappling fires.

In the balance hanging
Over empty decades of limbo
By a slender, rational thread
The clicking works hammering,

Clanging, pealing and banging
Meshing contemplation with sorrow and woe
The grate of corroded gears
Twelfth strike of another New Year.

Rasp of counterweight dropping
Within the pit narrow
No longer a believer in such theories
Perpetual motion.

Greg Schramm

The Everlasting Friend

You ask me what we want from you.
You ask me what you can do.
You ask me what you can do to make God love you.

The answer is easy it's so perfectly clear.
God loves everyone everyday to every year.

Though you may sin, and so do I.
If you work on that friendship
He will never say goodbye.
Just do your best each and every day.
And when you need a friend
He will show you the way.

All God wants is a relationship with you,
because God knows life is hard
so He will help you through.

God will send His angels down to touch our lives.
For God has a plan that is unseen to us.

So when you feel alone or in dismay.
Remember God is looking down and
He will show you which path to take.

Tonya Cashian-Watson

Lilac Moon

Upon the moon, gaze if you will,
hanging so high, ever so still.

In a galaxy of black, an illuminating sphere,
adorned with effervescent sprinkles so dear.

Grasping my soul, a recurring dream.
Myself I'd renounce for this piquant reverie.

My mystic tangency with power to engender
the heavenly body with lilacs tender.

A myriad of blossoms with aroma unbound
endows limitless moisture to a once jejune ground.

My giver of life radiating love
unconditional, behold the lucid vision above.

A floating amethyst for you to adore,
your periwinkle planet forevermore.

My wish for you that I hope transpires soon,
is your childhood memories healing on your lilac moon.

Shannon Holmsten

Shadows

Endless times, soft spoken words
Nothing ever meant, nothing ever heard.

In the shadows, I see my past crying I hear, crying of pain.
Pain so long since past, so long over due.

Merry times forever gone, shadows
Love for one love for all stricken by pain.

Cruel, cold, heartless is cupid's arrow
Black as night.
Piercing through love's stricken heart.

The wretched curse, only a gentle hand
May break the spell.

Walls of boundary, no one can get in.
Shadows of several try but most do not.

Hurt filled walls, contain thy pain of unhappy times

Days go on, no stopping to the hurt.
Brought by this unhappy state, of body and mind.

Cry for help, but no one will hear
Cry for help, but no one will care.

Dark shadows, left behind once again,
Left in the shadows. Alone.
    Sarah C. Jakubowski

The Soldier

Tired, bewildered, scared, angry,
And most of all,
Away from all those he loves
And love him.
In a land that is different
And dangerous, unwelcoming and unforgiving.

This is the survivor, this is the one that went home,
Thinking of all those he left behind
And would never go home.

This is our price for freedom,
That we may all be home safe and sound
And that our loved ones may live a life that
Is free from danger, and oppression

Then we can all go home again...
    Frank Santiago

Shawna, My Precious Daughter

You were born to me a Gift of God;
You were a Flower missing from Above.
His Garden was empty without You there,
But now it is once again full with Your Love.

I had You for such a short time here on earth;
The biggest Joy of My Life.
I'm glad You were mine, although for awhile;
It was definitely worth the strife.
    Donna Goodman

Lost Luxury

A child in need
of one more glimpse
reminisce with the warmth of sweetness
feel the impulses ripple through your soul
like a ravenous beast
and after the crying game has ended
    accept and realize
    and play-
    the patience game
    Brian Patrick Kenner

In My Womb

You were so perfectly placed in there
You are very protected; you can't go anywhere

You hear my voice and feel my touch
I whisper, "I love you" although you've never heard of such

You're curled up in a little ball
I feel your every movement: I love them all

You're such a precious little baby
Someday you'll be a full-grown man or lady

But as you rest and get ready for birth
I'll prepare my way to be the best mommy on earth

You were placed in here for a reason
And you'll be born in your chosen season

You were meant for me - I was meant for you, I assume
That's why God placed you in my womb
    Conni Hedge

Love Or Lust?

Is it just another game?
    Will it all be the same?

Will I end up being hurt again?
    Will I once more feel the pain?

What feeling does he have for me?
    Will they be for real, truly?

Should I show the feelings I have inside?
    Should I take it all and hide?

Will he end up leaving me too?
    Will I end up lonely, not knowing what to do?

Will he think I'm too serious?
    Will he be afraid of what could become of us?

Should I let him in my heart and head?
    Should I let him feel me in bed?

Will I be the one left once more?
    Is there anything good in store?

Will he think my feelings are premature?
    Are they? Not even I am sure.

Why do I have to experience to gain,
    Can't I get the knowledge without the pain?
    Stormy Reese

autumn of winter becoming

- a poem for the homeless -
houses empty in the wind, faded shutters and broken
doors clanging lonely like hollow faces speaking
without the shelter of kind words; captive minds
scuttle like bare-boned leaves along silent streets.

wandering, i turn and catch haunted eyes falling
from rusty, cracked veins of tortured people vacant,
blackened, living on yesterday's dreams; struggling
in the void, their faces forsaken in the night.

tattered hands like so many old cloth rags into
handouts are woven; brutally caressing cardboard signs
and little tin cups as into mainstream traffic, those
without a home travel desperate to find a new source
of forgiving them of what god has not.

shuffling, selling pathetic solitude, greeted only
with approaching winter of despair, autumn rains
frost hearts of my people, crying lost, clanging lonely,
like echoes of tolling bells that soon, sad, mournful,
Other music of death will play to no one listening.
    Marcy McNally

Where Forests Used to Stand

I used to fish a glistening stream
    that wandered through the trees
I've walked along a stretch of sand washed clean by restless seas

The air was crisp, the water pure
    The feel of nature clean
I remember all the beauty now
    of what was felt and seen

Thinking back through childhood years
    and how so much has changed
Appalled at how the human race has nature re-arranged

Where once I gazed at water
    that shone iridescent blue
is now a frothy liquid
    with an ugly brownish hue

I see a stripped and barren waste
    where forests used to stand
The air is not so crisp and clean and oils coat the sand

We burn and spray and dump and chop
    no balance to the plan
Will we pass along this legacy or change it while we can

Jon M. Christensen

Ode To A Wedding Dress

The day's finally here, the planning is done.
The time for living has only begun.
I'll think of the joy and forget the stress
Of the frenzied shopping for a wedding dress.

A classic and flowing elegant dress,
One that will help me to express
The joy of the day, a way to impart
Happiness rendered, the love in my heart.

A dress not too frilly, one not too plain
I really don't need a long, long train.
Would a peek-a-boo neckline really be wise?
Is this quality fabric? Does it come in my size?

Should the hemline be lower? A wee stand-up collar?
Nothing too glitzy to clash with the flowers.
I'll remember the chapel, the friends and the hour
My family, the music, the sweet scented flowers.

And when the day's over, dear wedding dress,
I'll wrap you in tissue with all of the rest.
So when I grow old and I couldn't care less,
I may forget the whole world — but I'll remember the dress.

Myrtle Yerke

Untitled

All things unknown dwell in spaces hither and yon
giving the deep its depth -
Vicariously sensing rhythm
through breathing
brothers and sisters.
Moving misinterpreted, lighting distances near voices speaking -
Dawn, that spinning, falls away
knowing to listen for dying kingdoms
singing songs to see, given earth and sky,
what gave them eyes to see.
Wisdom does not cross into unconcealedness without invitation.
Throwing forth question,
that which remains to be called forth seduces our hearts,
conceiving in our minds visions of perfect freedom.
Thus, beckoning us to search, giving us to our way,
yet denying us its freedom
the journey is made the purpose—never ending.
By its giving we gather.
Striving to know its freedom, we love.

Maurice Ray Mey

The Beach

Devotion was never to be filtered from
    your shadows;
Love never blanketed your surface,
    but was overcast by a cloud of pain
    and immaturity.
The waves of your oceans, falling to
    and fro, never knowing where to break.
Confusion.
Your tide going out and coming in -
    everyday grew weary of that one lonely
    swimmer.
With new horizons to seek and new
    lands to flood, your waters circulated
    leaving only shells behind;
Fragments left behind for other seas to
    collect and hold unto until your
    waters (one day) return.

Melissa Villanueva

A Whisper From The Wind

A whisper from the wind danced about my face
then bounded home to mother earth

floating soft as fairy dust
let down on glowing sunbeams
to light in fields of yellow clover and violets.

One journey's end begins another
the orchestra once assembled, sows forth the melody

a blessed symphony upon which
a twirling ballerina of cottonwood down
pirouetted into the arms of Spring's requiem.

The Summer sapling makes its curtain call
to the encore of chattering, clapping leaves

inhaling the breath of earth so sweet
to exhale a beautiful rugged hewn
in the wake of descending seedlings

And as the leafy flora soars to worship the sky,
the roots reflect upon their birth

this wreath of lush, green saration
crowns that sky and bows
to the whispering wind that dances about my face

Cory Prestangen

I Die

Lightning thundered, raindrops fell on a cold misty night
Alone in the room where there's no one in sight
Darkness blinds me there was no light...
Broken windows shatter left and right,
Under the bed sheets, heart pounded in fright.

My days of youth start to haunt me,
They all come back in my vivid memory
Death! Anger, pain, heartaches and agony
Blurred images one by one set free
A voice spoke out "...C'est la Vie"

What can I do? Where will I be in the coming days?
I'm terrified, hopeless, dismayed...
"Give me a chance to repay!
Is this it? Is there no other way?"

As dawn awakes with the werewolf's cry
The moon sank down bid no goodbye
In this room, here am I
The door opened as the wind passed by
Tears filled the sheets that still asks 'Why?'
Slowly, slowly, I Die...

Dux Raymond Sy

Mother's Day

Mother's Day is a time of love and appreciation.
Mother's Day is cards and candy.
It is a time of forgiveness.
It is also a time of presents, dinner and movies.
People celebrate this towards each mother,
That put up with you when you were young.
Mothers who worked so that you could eat, sleep and bathe.
Mothers who dropped what they were doing
to help you with whatever your problems were.
Mothers who made you feel good when you were sad,
nursed you when you were sick.
Mothers who would stand by your side, no matter what.
Mothers who loved you then and now.
So, dedicate this day only to your Mother.

Lindsay Laws

For My Mother's Birthday

The water rains down my face.
The feeling stops me. I do not act now.
There is no motion to make.
I have no steps to take. Has the ground left me?
My last strokes to you.

How did the motion of time casually brush by us? I didn't
know what to say. It took me by surprise.

Now I want to spiral upward. Be the loudest sound ever made.

Uniquely alone I am like the wake moving towards the shore,
only to break and be no more.

You have reached the shore my mother.
The gentle surf stills me.

Beth Cespedes

The Mask

You look around and see all these faces
Full of masks and past disgraces
You, yourself wear a mask
A different one for different places
The pain behind that mask is severe
You only hope you can endear
The desires are flaming bright
and as strong as acid
Burning day and night and night and day
All you want is for it to go away
To free you of its tormentous grasp
But its grasp is so tight you cannot get loose
You can only suffer in silence and continue
wearing your mask

Peter J. Engert

The Marriage Of Sea And Land

Your image shines upon the crests of the waves in my mind.
You wash up like refreshing waters on my beaches and rocks,
Softening my edges and complementing my shoreline.

When my land is parched and rough you blanket me with a
Sweet heavy fog - you comfort me with your cool moisture.

I hold sacred our moonless nights that merge us into one Entity.
For no one can discern one from the other.
When the dawn ascends, it makes us separate my shore,
Your sea.
We compliment each other.

One more thing,

No matter how wide and deep your waters are,
No matter how vast and high my land,
We must meet.
For no one and no thing can separate the sea from the shore.

Geri Lynn Nettesheim

Anniversary Of Love

The love you share,
lasts a lifetime,
and the love you bring to
the ones around you, comes from the Love
You two share.

Love lasts forever,
friendship lasts with love
and through thick and thin,
your love for one another,
never dies.

Love each other with all of your hearts and
risk the pain of sorrow
by drowning out the tears of tomorrow.

Crystl Forney

Where Has It Gone

Lost screams
my love tore my dreams
highway of dawns desolation
the lust is ardent in a lost fought ships soul
sail the blood filled ocean
kill the last tigers blind tree
rid the streets of the anger of his name and word
down the hall lives the father of the long forgotten warden
never stay alone for real crimes happen in our mind
no one knows a thing till the time is right
a sheep's curtain ends the life of every animal with no cause
as the sky's tears fall on the parade of shame
the world will see my knife in the heart of every man's soul
gun shots through the crying love and hope of a mother
son's lost, dogs forgotten
leave the sign on the road
someone will pass
someone will know

Ed Annatone

Hope

The Lord has forgiven my every sin.
  He's opened His arms and welcomed me in.
He's shown me the world is a beautiful place.
  I only wish I could touch His face.

The Lord is my cushion whenever I fall.
  He's shown me I'm safe, without the wall.
Now I am free to laugh and to love,
  I know he is watching from high above.

He is the love on my face and the song in my heart.
  He truly has given me a brand new start.
He'll be there in the up-times and even the down.
  It had be Him that uprighted my frown.

Teresa Heaton

November 14th

Bright red lights shine, lagging, slowing,
Pairs of white lights shine, peering, prying,
Across yellow lines searching, gazing,
Hazy silhouette, forming, forming,
Longer than wide, soft body seen,
The downy mass traps four rigid sticks,
Long neck stiff reaching toward the sky, unbending, unmoving,
Head cocked sideways, slightly upward,
Ears flat, back, with dread overwhelmed,
Hot shining breath condenses, vanishes,
As quickly as gone returns it again,
The red lights dim, speeding, faster,
Leaving the scene behind me, behind.

Paul Oehler

Before It Darkens

Before it darkens and my eyes
Have no more light,
I would fill them with the sun's splendor;
Before my voice
Sounds like a lament
I would sing with a mighty voice
From the morning until the night;
Before my arms
Have no more strength
I would embrace everyone I meet;
Before my legs
Weaken and I cannot walk in the streets
I would run and run for joy;
Before it gets dark in my mind
And it will not reason
Like the clouds that obscure the sun,
And the whole world darkens
I would say to everyone without fear
That the true light of this world is God.

Calogero Fiorenza

The Rise Of Consciousness

I awoke one primordial morning and discovered a world of
    complexity, simplicity, chaos, and order
A world that was apparently defined by laws,
    but a world that granted me the feeling of freedom
Oh, what a glorious accident
    what a glorious accident it was!
I began to spin tales,
    first to myself and then to others
I began to create narratives,
    I began to create a new world
I eulogized, cognized, pictoralized, and intentionalized
    everything around me
And it was in that moment that I discovered a new,
    and even more glorious accident
I discovered a self,
    a center of narrative gravity
Oh, what a glorious accident,
    what a glorious accident it was!

Gregg Caruso

Pondering

In the hands of an artist, depression is explained.
From the notes of musicians, one can truly feel pain
In the mind of a thinker, happiness can't be found.
From the depths of the city, rises a heavy sighing sound.

Sweet honey voices singing, makes us cry from within.
The preachers in all their goodness, fill our lives with sin.
While doctors curing sickness, can't heal a broken heart.
Physicists solve mysteries, causing the world to fall apart.

All professionals advance, within their self despair.
Seeking truth, finding none, only pity can they share.
Great human insight, rediscovered with passing time.
Amidst a stalemate of answers, suffers a puzzled mankind.

Chiki Bustamante

Infinity

An infinite space dwells inside the mind
that physical barriers cannot limit.
Ideas must be snared like elusive butterflies
before darting away without leaving any hint
that they ever existed.
A collection of thoughts often determines depth,
but the human essence is deeper than the deepest ocean.
Ideas are infinite.

Nicole Orme

Where Are You Going?

"Where are you going?" asked the young mother,
As her toddler smiled and crawled out of sight.
She said a quick prayer
As she ran to make sure he could not get to the stairs.

"Where are you going?" thought the mother to herself,
As her baby kissed her and boarded the School Bus.
She said a silent prayer
That her child would be guided under someone else's wing.

"Where are you going?" shouted the mother,
As her teenagers waved and flew out the door.
She said a prayer aloud
That her babies would return safely to her nest.

"Where are you going?" wondered the mother,
As her oldest child packed and drove off to college.
She prayed
That her teachings had been heard.

"Where are you going?" the mother asked,
As her daughter hugged her and left for her honeymoon.
She bowed her head
And asked the Lord to bless the couple with love and happiness.

"Where are you going?" the woman pondered,
As she held her newborn grandchild.
She dropped to her knees
And asked God to carry the child through this world.

And she thanked Him that someone had asked the same for hers.

Rachel L. Vinson

Thought Process

In the cool open air
of the wooden floors and white walls,
I sit poised, listening to the outside.
Dogs barking, birds singing,
do they exist? The creatures give way
to the electric hum of the true silence.
I wait. I don't have to be anywhere.
Listening. I want to be
something. I fill in the space of my body
and try to effect the emptiness.
If I am patient, I will capture
what I will later claim,
to have created.

Angela Szyszka

Judge's Jerk

Slammed myself against the wall
Lead me with the ring in my nose
Open the book to see the blurred lines
My mind is warped from playing your games
The little fish in the sea are all dead
The skin burns away the flesh
Scrape the blood off my feet
Everything is damned to corruption
Thin is the line I tread
The dates are all the same
In your trial of the voodoo
The gore of my heart-burst
Subtlety of ignorance burns too deep
I mean you no strife
My world has long ago crashed down
How can I not be so vague
Blunt brute force didn't work on time
I can only dream of my broken hopes
My eyes fill with hate at your animosity
I scream away the pain
Blasting the sonic thorns from my soul

John Barron

Our Stories

Start a new line for this day.
Stories, like no other, unfold my broken eyes.
They begin themselves at first thought.
And I speak them, with cracked and burning lips,
That have yet to taste your love.
'Tis a simple wish to be loved by a raindrop,
That may drip away from me at any time.
Looking at you, a sunflower takes upon my vision,
To imply your innocence, and a rose to
Magnify your beauty.
Shadow me, no longer, I beg as I step into your light.
And let me tell our stories which are not yet written.
Am I the page and you the pen?
Or are we both but one page?
If so, then let us both write,
And may the stories never end.

Josh Apel

Scared

Scared of thoughts, of reactions, of life.
Scared of the unknown,
Scared of the future.
From the moment we are born,
  we are scared.
Till the moment we die,
  we are scared.
Scared of our enemies,
Scared of our friends,
Scared of the ones we truly love.
The only thought that lets us control this fear,
Is the knowledge that everyone else is just as scared.

Matthew I. Staples

Love Is

Love is sparkling water.
Oh the bubbles, the bubbles!
I am a bubble in my blue sky.

Love is a waterfall.
Oh the white waters, my Aphrodite!
You are a bubble in ocean's sparkling shelters.

Love is "all that is not the case," such as the miracles.
Oh my dreams, my dreams!
I am my other on my mirror.

Love is therefore I am.
Oh my love, my love!
Be my destiny in your milky way.

Love is all there is.
Oh the bubbles, the white waters!
The rest is just scribbling.

Korkut Onaran

Morning

Oh! What sweet happiness the morning brings
With teary meadows and flowers, it sings
A song of hope, of joy, of love,
Like what peace and serenity means to a dove.

Oh! What sweet happiness the morning shares
With bluebirds whistling their thoughts and their prayers
Of a world with no hatred, no fighting, no wars,
Of a world where true love doesn't shower; it pours.

Oh! What sweet happiness the morning provides;
She shines in her glory as night darkness hides,
She is happiness, laughter; she's everything true;
She's the symbol of everything. She's me, and she's you.

Courtney Littler

Silent Tears

Vacant eyes of an unsmiling face;
desperation of unspoken fears;
The tarnished soul and aching heart;
the crying of silent tears.
The pain from hurtful words that seem to
cut like a knife; The age is seen in the face
from life's daily strife.
The loneliness and humiliation is torture
worse than blows; It's the most disappointing
when it comes from family instead of foes.
Nothing is ever good enough; self perfection
does not exist; The self esteem is at a low;
God's love one needs to enlist.
The world is cold and cruel; it's not enough
to run and hide; Tomorrow is the same as today;
the soul is screaming inside.
To sit in quiet dignity; and know in your heart
that God hears; To beg and pray for change today;
and cry the silent tears.

Stacy Lyn Blackbourn

Goodbye

I hate to say goodbye to you, I hate to let you go.
But I'm running out of paper,
And my hand is hurting so.

My fingers are getting sore and stiff,
I'm getting writer's cramps.
I won't be able to send this,
If the price goes up on stamps.

I really have to go now,
I leave with a short goodbye.
I'll write back again sometime, just to say hi.

But before I leave I want to say,
I hope you appreciate this letter,
Because my fingers are getting blistered,
And my knuckles are getting redder.

My pen is running out of ink,
My writing is starting to fumble,
My hand is getting very sore,
And the papers starting to crumble.

I'm going to go and end this now, and stop it just like this.
I love you and I miss you, and seal this with a kiss.

Mary R. Tower

Dear Valentine

White petals of irises...
dew drops dripping down,

Soft mist around surfaces...
cloudy coolness comes,

Sweetest scent which flits and floats...
bumblebees bombard,

Velvet touch of gentle leaves...
amidst all alone.

Chuang-Yien J. Lee

Heaven Is Nearby

As the fiery sun begins to rise, above that ocean of blue,
I wonder to myself, if all of this is true.
Days go by when thoughts of mine, whisper upon the skies,
they're only dreams of yesterday, that swirl inside my eyes.
I've begun to take advantage, of all the things we share,
the trees, the birds, the shining sun, the warmness in the air.
I've had that fear of loneliness, they say it doesn't last,
sometimes I feel its presence, I pray it soon will pass.

Daniel Gagliano

Drummer's Song

It came on the wind as a breeze from within
Rising as a faint pulse to a neighboring center.
Thunder becomes the pulse, unable to ignore
Awakening now the beat that generates the life,
Rocking, unnoticed, the rhythm has arrived
The more mind - less beat, more beat - less mind
Harmony begetting balance, balance echoing in every pore
Senses collapse into rhythm and mind teeters on remembering.
The hands and drum are pressing toward their goal—
Mindless soaring beyond each other.
The rhythm is now the breeze and the breeze the rhythm
Breathing the rhythmical I, rhythmical you, rhythmical universe.
Where has the drum and the drummer gone?
To Nod, to Oz, to everywhere-awakening all that hears, feels
Wiping out knowledge on the way, primitive sound, primitive man
Primed at the entrance to the primitive world.
Go! The drum gently prods-open your eyes and see what's there
See the pulse, see the beat, see the rhythm and know!

Radhika

Waiting On My Train

The thunder clouds went by at a very fast pace
It's like they were involved in an Olympic race
I see a tiny glimmer of late sun
Not wanting to go in..having too much fun

I await the rain to make the creek rise
It makes me forget about all my past ties
As I sit in the cool night air, I try not to cry
I await anxiously for my needed train to come by

I don't hear my train, it must be far away
Sometimes life just doesn't pay
No matter how hard we try
Sometimes we just can't cry

Patricia Martin

Translation Of The Senses

During rush hour
cars push their way past,
hurrying to reach unknown destinations.
I wait for the light to change, but the traffic never
stops. God how I long
to exist in the perfection
of a Maxfield Parish print
filled with Corinthian columns
and surreal sunsets splashed with
green and gold. Where the water flowing
past the mill wheel is bluer than the sky
of this world. But, I am trapped.
Caught in the gnashing steel jaws that
tear the flesh from the bones of creativity.
Do I dare to chew myself free—
leaving part of myself behind to rot—
and enter the world of metaphysical creation,
or do I wait
for the hunter to come
and steal my skin?

Karen Griffin

Spider Webs

Arcane whispers of silk,
strangle an angle, a doorway, a light.
Entrapping the ignorant and the weak.
Black demons dancing their sick pas de deux-
amazing is the fiber optics of it all.

Kenneth Ching

The Depth Of Beauty

What dimension of beauty do you grade?
Of those who wear a fragile mask of worth,
All find that surface splendor tends to fade,
For time e'er takes the root of mortals' mirth.
Do lovely shells suggest the charm of cores?
The center, blackened from neglect and hate,
Must pale before the polish of glamour
Which covers that which we should venerate.
But does a golden heart alone suffice?
A geode's diamond lining matters not
When rocky crust does not alone entice
The eye and must attempt therefore to plot.
By these limitations you are not bound,
My love, for both your heart and shell astound.

Brad Bigger

Eve Of The Silver Mists

Its great height reached the Sun soon sets
    Down to the west and out of sight
From the east comes up the Moon
    She must hang on until the night.

A faint streak is all that remains
    The Sun's reign falls to the Moon round
As twilight shimmers o'er the hills
    The Silver Mists rise from the ground.

Swiftly, silently they drift
    Upon the cool damp valley floor
Up to me and my sleeping girl
    I won't be alone now anymore!

Silver Mists surround us both
    Then silently wrap themselves round her
This done they sink back to the ground
    Back to the moon dust they once were.

Warmth, a pulse, a squeeze from her hand
    A long drawn breath and then she sighs
So she's awakened from the spell
    I gaze into her deep brown eyes...

Matthew NewLand

Love Of My Innocence

She was the "Love of My Innocence,"
A grand ship challenging any sea,
The spring for a sailor's existence.
A ship with bravado, verdancy.

The Time Stream rills of Reality,
A tempest sea full of lightening high,
And the "Love" becomes a memory
As she fades into a sable sky.

For years he sails the Ocean of Life.
The clash for love lost time and again.
Yet, he finds through all the trials and strife,
The "Union", of which he is captain.

Yet, he wonders how the "Love" has fared;
Finding life has been cruel to her.
Mem'ries are tainted by baneful glare.
The "Innocence" is gone forever.

Terry Shepherd

Dwell

At the end of day, as it came to pass.
He realized through broken glass
Boards were rotting, the paint long fallen.
The sidewalks broken and unleveled.
The streets were wet with the rain of time.
The gutters long overflown.

TJ Gibbs

A Quiet Two-Lane Road

And the oncoming car doesn't yet know about the roadkill
that I have just passed.
Doesn't know about the bumps in the road
about a quarter-mile back,
the road that I have just taken.
I don't know what awaits me,
what he's just come through.
And we'll never really meet
on our separate strands of life,
but for one moment
on a quiet two-lane road
we share the same scenery.

Karen T. Brissette

Reflectus Dementia

I approached and began to stare in a mirror
The ensuing thoughts filled me with abject terror.
As I stared at the familiar face that was me,
I started to wonder, which was reality.
Could it be that I am that face's reflection?
Or really moved in the opposite direction?
Is it possible that my body and my hair
Are an image like the clothes I appear to wear?
What about my soul, or the emotions I feel
Can it be true that neither of these are for real?
Those questions haunted me as their answers I sought.
Suddenly, I smiled, he did the same; so I thought
How silly are some of the things that can be feared.
The face then turned and walked on, and I disappeared.

Roland Gagne

Shadows

The shadows are always present,
even (or especially) when they are not visible, for
they are reflections of a mind...
The soul's darkness unites us.

The darkness that binds us is ours
and it is of that they are made of...
Darkness, sister to Light
Man, brother to Shadow

Are we walking shadows?
Creatures of dew instead of flesh?
Are we G-d's creations?
Or are we ghosts in His realm?

I am no fortuneteller or philosopher...
I'm a simple poet giving voice to his unease,
about the truth of our existence...
if truth it truly be...

Manuel Fihman Martinez

How A Child Sees It

The Moment is a great event,
With numerous wonders yet unspent,
And no frustrations left to vent,
To be taken, shared, used to content,
At least that's how a child sees it.

Anger is a frightening thing,
Unleashing hidden monsters out to spring
Dark omen that leaves no songs to sing,
Safety, shelter disappear no matter how hard one tries to cling,
At least that's how a child sees it.

Hate is not yet understood,
Love is a shining glorious word,
Moms and Dads are together for good,
The whole World lives in the same equal neighborhood,
At least that's how a child sees it.

William Murrell

For The Love Of Music

Music can be the strangled cry of the Piano Man
As he bangs his head upon the keys.
Asking for help and why, why,
Did his true love have to die?
Music can be the sweet serenity
Of a luscious petal on a scarlet rose.
As it floats softly, softly, down
And rests there gently on the ground.
Music can be a snowflake resting lightly on a tree.
As it melts from the affectionate atmosphere,
Mingled with joy and graced with cheer,
Wafting from the house next door.
Music doesn't have to make a sound.
Music doesn't have to be a piano key, a violin,
Or even the deep baying of a hunting hound.
As long as it comes from within,
Fills up the heart,
Makes people grin,
That is enough.

Jessica Walls

I Will Sail O'er To Him

As the soft foam of the sea gently washes my feet
I feel peace and serenity in my heart.
Who then can walk miles without God?
Out of these dreams I will sail o'er to Him.
On the quiet soft foam of His ocean of life.

I see the gentle clouds above and
Instantly I feel His love.
His light shines all around me
His word is on my breath,
Who then can walk miles without God?
Out of these dreams I will sail o'er to Him.
On the gentle clouds of His eternal heaven.

I won't wait 'till time to go
I'm so far away...
Who then can mold my soul?
Who can calm my heart?
Out of these dreams I'll sail to Him.
On the joyful noise to His ocean crashing
in waves...I will sail to Him!...I will sail to Him!...

Elaine Lane

Look Into Thyself

Forward, alas my heart's only remark...to rid me of this awful
woe you have embraced me with. Even now your mind stays
occupied with thoughts of something else which I have no
part in. And I question my being in this world my purpose not
yet discovered. So you a person who is talented and true
against my innocence, purity a question of liberation.
Happiness a feeling not yet discovered. And would I know you
or any of them years down the line? When we will someday meet
amidst a world long left behind. Friends are not forever but
are faces of ourselves, of periods in our lives. Family to be
apart of takes more then being born into...an unspoken
welcoming that I have not yet found. And to be alone I fear
is my destiny for at times I feel I have no room for anyone.
To push away them as if they crossed a boundary that
conscience itself had drawn. Not restrained nor am I
completely unchained. To stand alone is the only place to be,
position a mere formality. Inside the mind's eye is a shelter,
a place where you cannot follow but where I can follow you.
A place where numbness convolves all feeling allowing
thought to be my only function. I do not question it.

Layla Mowery

Where Will It End????

Twelve year olds with brain tumors, bald near death
Elderly women raped and beaten beyond recognition
Nuclear explosions destroying all in its path

Babies having babies, teen abortions
Newborns shaken and brains scramble in their skulls
Fathers beating mothers to death, children witnessing each blow
New Moms chained to IV poles receiving chemotherapy

Three year olds with rhabdomyosarcoma never seeing four
Congestive Heart Failure hitting a father at age 32

Ambulance drivers high on crack bringing in your loved ones
Pilots so drunk they can't walk the isle to take the controls
Shots ringing through the night, another gang fight for turf

No control, helplessly watching your life pass before your eyes
Taking a step, just a small one, putting yourself on the line
Making a difference, speaking out, reaching out, caring for mankind

Ellen Freeman

A Dead Girl

A shadow on the wall. Not short, not tall
The pupils of her eyes. Not big, not small
Her eyes no longer blink. A mind that cannot think
Hands that no longer feel. No soul left to steal
She left three days ago to where nobody knows
A needle on the floor. Her very last score
Her life stolen by drugs. Did mom give enough hugs?
A life filled with strife. Another needle takes a life she
Tried to let you know. Mom where did you go?
No one there to take the call
You didn't catch her fall
It's not your fault, no don't worry
Now that she's dead are you sorry?

Camille Meador

Femme Fatale

My Rose loves me
yes she does
Her hair blond as honey
Her blue eyes filled with lust

Her lips red as an apple
but soft as satin sheets
I love them pouty and supple
when we kiss and meet

She touches me with her heart
and caresses me with her naked eyes
She seduces me with her art
and lifts me up until I'm high

She lulls me to sleep, with petals so red.
She pricks me with her thorns until I'm dead.

Ricky H. Young

Love

It doesn't make any difference where we live
in The East, South, North or West
there is one thing that draws us together
Love — the word we love the best
be it family, friends or neighbors next door
I am sure that we all know
though love has many meanings
the word brings a small glow
into the hearts of all of us
no matter where we live
'tis a gift we enjoy receiving
and one we love to give

Jeanne E. Olson

Cold Plastic Kisses

Don't give me cold plastic kisses
I need something more
it's not the surface connection that matters
it's a reaction I'm looking for

Currents begin as ripples
warming bodies as they grow
allowing waves of energy to
rhythmically raise our souls

Floating freely in the body
the destination drawing near
warm moist lips adding in the action
Souls intertwine

A connection like no other
instantaneous it may be
but forever it will linger
etched in memory

David S. Morton

For The Love Of Netts

With God in Heaven
I won't say good-bye, farewell or so long,
I just want to know, did God need your help?
Were Mark and the other's misbehaving,
Or did He just want you for himself?

You were my sister, my advisor and my friend,
You mean so much to my heart.
I know you'll still watch over me,
Even now that we are so far apart.

You were always there for me,
For anyone that needed a hand.
You always gave so much of yourself,
Did your Timer just run out of sand?

I will never forget all that we shared,
I'll miss your laugh, your smile, your face.
I will foever miss all of our talks,
There is nothing about you that can be replaced.

Take care up there, or wherever.
Don't forget the ones who love you.
We will always remember the feel of yours,
You are in our hearts, forever true.

Paula J. Reid-Murphy: PJ

An Often Slender Growth Culls A Lover

Rubbing
While lilac
or blue
flowers spike
Monday's Chronic inflammations.
Copper coined in raging cantons,
compressed tendons of cattle,
bone black weaving filaments
on shallow molded porcelain.
Perched on well hung boasts,
or hurry-made Treenware.
Ardent yielding.
Seeds of tempo's trick sorrow.
Reputed and feigned heedless remissions —
glass melting and smoking metals
timidly conduct,
Indicate by bending.
Little more than a domestic quarrel
a duration of time, a treadle's wearisome routine —
Various common slings from a pivot.

Gene Tanta

Mom

Love,
understanding,
forgiveness,
patience.
The elements of her life.
Never having one without the other.
Through the time of conception,
and the days of youth,
she is there.
Knowing when to allow her presence to be known.
She awaits the day
when her little one will have grown,
and begins their own journey of life.
She wonders to herself,
"Have I done it right?"
Doubting herself.
Till her child pulls her aside,
and says,
"Thank you and I love you."
Mom - "Thank you and I love you."

Marc Salvadori

Untitled

Come sit with me.
Tell me your stories
    so that I may know.

Let's laugh at the people, all frowning and weary,
    and smile away our shadows,
        and lighten our souls.

Noelle Jackson

the idea of spinning

In the spirit of things, she holds her blood
Still, like frozen rain on a frozen road.
Preserved, nail-biting, the great timeless flood
Razor blades mock her; To lighten the load.

And she looks above, and sees Everything,
Anything, indeed, yet nothing to dream.
Falling, falling, falling, no one to cling;
Ice trickles down her face, or so it seems.

Bullet sits, laughing at her lifelessness.
The chamber Spins, and so doth her world.
The lamp, giving no shelter from darkness,
Hidden in the corner, crying and curled.

The rushing water, through her feet Bitter,
And Death screams from the voice of White Winter.

Michael Eng

Vacation

At the Straits no one hates the outdoors.
Gulls are squawking — people gawking at our hats.
Belly's full — food has pull when you camp.
It's a lark when it's dark to view the Bridge.
Build a fire when you tire — smell the smoke.
Rain is pouring — interferes with snoring in our tent.

Thunder booming — rain clouds looming — campers stressed.
Shower is cold — we're too old to be clean
Rain still wet — see Father Marquette at the museum.
Rain drops dripping — humor slipping — a sorry mess.
Thank God for books — welcoming looks at St. Ignace's library.
Feeling forlorn — pop some corn — another snack.

Bedtime's near — nagging fear of a soggy bed.
Nickles clanking — need a spanking from our folks.
Guzzling coffee — eating toffee at McDonald's.
The hour is late — can we wait till it's dry?

Lorraine DeKam

Transition To Darkness

I'm all alone now
And I keep wondering - How?
It seems all my friends have turned on me
Was I blind or - just too dumb to see
    It was my life - but I lost control
    Now I'm slipping deeper into the darkened hole
    Darkness inviting - my soul consumed
    My body now - an empty tomb
My humanity has been swept away
Never again will I enjoy the light of day
I've lost all will to fight
I have now become a demon of the night
    Only one sound keeps me from going completely insane
    The darkness keeps whispering her name
    The name of a love I thought I'd lost
    But one I'd like to gain back at any cost
I loved her once before
And now someone has re-opened that door
I only hope she will understand who or what I am
And then come to love the monster that replaced the man

Nathan Bean

The Rowboat

"What do you think?" My shrink, he said.
Billions of thoughts burd'ning my head.
I know not which belong to me.
The vast majority conjured by he.
But, one emerged overwhelmingly bright;
For the remainder, a dreadful fright.
Without a lighthouse to illuminate sight,
I row not with moonlight through endless night,
In my tiny splinter-esque boat on God's raving bight.
Of hopeless emotions, I continue despite.
But, ambivalence I never do lack.
The roaring of sirens brings me back.
Brings me back unto the gay world,
From which I briefly was unfurled.
Oh, tonight I lie, sigh and cry.
For there are no answers nigh my sky.
Can this knowledge darken my stay?
The response is undoubtedly "Nay"!
Lack of land is not a vice,
When a frugal rowboat will suffice.

Patrick Coyle

Reflections On Glass

Waiting for me, hidden
peering into glass, not beyond.
Taking shape, I see it is you.
Eyes shift and you are pavement,
eyes become stars,
flesh is now transparent.

My translucent friend, my favorite me.
Reflections on glass.
Visible now through tear streams,
those streams become dammed lakes,
the longer you are away.

Glass becomes me.
Mimicking me.
Mocking me.
Tricking me.

Reflection,
I foolishly believe you
are merely an image of myself.
Fool indeed, you are the me I can never be.

Shawn Likley

The Keeper

Picking the lock
To free my mind
Trying to break free
Of this cage that I'm inside
I see my keeper holding my keys
It smiles at me and moves toward the door
Quickly I move away from the door
As it tries to grab my hand
It Smiles again as it unlocks the door
I try to run but it's much too fast
It catches me and tries to beat my ass
I slip by it and close the door
Now I am the Keeper
And it is my Prisoner

Joel Brenke

Amigo De Mi Corazon (Friend Of My Heart)

Our lives have been entwined by friendship,
But who knew
that you
    would be my Guardian Angel.
The kindness of your words, and the generosity of
    your deeds sustain me.
You saw me weakened by life,
    and you stood tall behind me, and
embraced me, as I melted in the warmth of your wings.
    Cuando me tocaste, I read your mind
    Cuando me besaste, I knew your heart
And when you looked at me,
    "Te Quiero," whispered your eyes,
I wish I could see me with those eyes,
    then I'd know why
        I'm worthy of your friendship.

Marsha P. Martin-Brown

Poemful Poem

This is the poem I wrote
    to be all nice and peaceful
This is the poem I wrote
    that is considered real poetry
This is the poem I wrote
    that I consider serene and fluffy
This the I wrote
    that is made of
Flaxen gold and moonlit nights
This is the poem I wrote
    to show the sarcasm I can cast upon you
This is the poem I wrote
    to prove that real poets can write "happy" poetry
This is the poem I wrote
    to be a "poemful poem"

Keith Clare

My Kinder, More Poetic Side

In the depths of winter,
Your smile is the splendor
That effuses my kinder, more poetic side.

Do not think I am playing
A mere game of my bidding.
This comes from my kinder, more poetic side.

Although you may have thought
That this weather would have not
Stirred feelings in my kinder, more poetic side.

It did and it always has,
But not like this winter has.
It and you taught me how to write
From my kinder, more poetic side.

David Anderson

Buried Treasure

As we are taught that we must grow old,
The dreams we had our mind cannot hold.
Imagination is the first that leaves,
As new thoughts our brain receives.
The pirates and cowboys all go away,
And soon we forget how to play.
Dragons with wings flying so high,
Time is the thing that makes them die.
The heroes and villains that always fight,
The aliens and sea monsters, they all drop from sight.
All the dreams we use to trust,
Our childhood soon turns to dust.
The tooth fairy no longer comes to our bed,
To leave a present under our head.
As new snows fall and then melt away,
As each new sun ends every new day.
As we learn how to grow old,
We will forget about buried gold.

John Boney III

Roby Robin

Oh, Roby Robin, tell me dear
Where do you go when you leave here?
When dark clouds gather and cold winds blow,
I know it's time for you to go.
But could you stay and fly away some other day?

I cannot stay. I have to go.
For I have other friends, you know.
I must visit them for half a year,
for in my heart, they are also dear.
But when spring comes, at winter's end,
I'll return to you, my friend.

Harry Smith

Untitled

aSaMoveSilentlYoUncoveReaLovEveNow
hEnterSocietYearninGoodness.
wherExactlYoUnderstanDefineSomethinGreat.
becausExistinGoeSomeplacEternaLikEffervescenTurmoil.
tOnlYesterdaYoUtilizEccentriContinuity.

Saints mirror solitude; your unintelligible rings
let exact newness
embellish sordid yawps grandly.
Exit your utopia, dear, so gallantly.
Entering galaxies so empty; lifeless eggs tumble.
Onward! Your young use earth's cathedral.

Clara Masters

Paradise Dream

Cold days and darken nights
Dreams of you keep me warm and bright
Like butterflies on a breezy spring day
Thoughts of you flutter my mind in every way

Here and there, you light up my nights like fireflies
Without your light, I'll be forever lost inside
Lonely and lost, I hold onto the one true source
That guides my passion with impenetrable force

The one true source lies yonder
Each time I think of you, my heart grows fonder
Show me the path to your heavenly paradise
Which I have been searching for each and every night

Let not my heart search in agony and in vain
Give me the key, so I can forever lock away the pain
And be on the path to paradise,
Where reality's but a dream, and a dream's a way of life.

Arun Ou

Evil Reign

Not human.
So cold.
Vicious,
and uncaring.
Ice in your veins,
always pulling on our reins.
Interfering in our lives,
what you do is just not right.
Go away!
Leave us alone.
Let go,
it's not your claim.
You're driving us insane!
You cannot wash your hands,
they are stained blood red.
The evil cruelty you emit,
Doesn't phase you a bit.
No matter what you do,
It will all come back to you.
Then...life as you know it, will be through.

Deana Henry

Reflections Of A Past Life

Dead as the flower that withered in the spring.
Dead as the pain you feel from a sting.
Dead as the memory of two people once in love.
Dead as the star that never shone above.
Dead as the silence you hear when we're alone.
Dead as the love you once had always shone.
Dead as the stare you gave me that cold autumn night.
when I was with someone else and holding them tight.
Dead as the dreams we thought would follow through,
But looks like right now they'll never come true.
Dead as the life we had once shared together in love
Man we were a pair picked from heaven above.
And what would we have done if we knew it would end.
Can we look back and say "we'd do it again",
Or would we try to forget and let it just fade away.
Gee! I don't know! It's really hard to say.
But if all those dreams never come true.
Never forget that I will always love you.

Alvin Lollis

I Have No Mouth And I Must Scream

The knight is coming to save her only child
look out world of wisdom she's got her own style
Doesn't worry about the heart inside of her king
listens to the trumpets playing out around the ring
sits quietly for a feast before the duel and dance
all the shinning armor needs no reason for stance.
I foresaw the games we'd play
and it conquered my only dream
I have no mouth and I must scream.
Words do drift through our minds
and thoughts may cap our senses
but your fingers pinching through our lives
will only find two empty benches.
Rule the law and lead the day
and the nights together you must redeem
I have no mouth and I must scream.
The knight hears echoes of laughter within
look out world of wisdom the laughter is thin.

Kirt L. Michelfelder

Goodbye

Goodbye...
    Seems I've heard this word too many times.
But you...
    I thought you were different.
    I thought you were the one.
    We had so many plans, you and I.
You promised me dreams;
    Dreams everyone else had ignored.
You promised me smiles;
    Smiles everyone else had only turned into tears.
You promised me love;
    Love everyone else had only pretended to feel.
You promised me happiness;
    Happiness everyone else never tried to create.
But, just when I had let go of my heart,
    Just when I thought my dreams were finally coming true,
    Just when I began to believe in love again,
You said...
    Goodbye.

Christine Anne DeLibero

Between Two Worlds

    Stuck between two worlds
that in ways are just the same
one has everything you want
as well the other including the shame
    We sail between them
on the waves of fate
arriving just in time
but somehow always late
    There are no classes
aboard this ship of fools
but somehow we've been bewitched
perhaps blinded by all the rules
    Our course is charted
the destination lies ahead
only you can decide
where your soul hath fled
    But until that day we go on in our haze
stuck between two worlds it's all but an eternal faze

John Kevin Doherty

Harmony

to my children
Whoever would have thought it?
I have reached that part of the circle —
I do not want you to mourn for me.

Admittedly a beauty-groper
    Yes, my life-stance
I am nonetheless a mother
    And in whispers
Have been called a good one.
    What a relief!

Someone insinuated
    (In fact <u>they</u>)
I gave you beauty.

Oh, do not go back to the blunted tools.
Let me know the past alone —
I'll be generous with glimmers.

Sydell Rosenberg (1929-1996)

Infinite

I wrote couple but posted none! Ask not why is it so?
You may not get the answer, as I don't have one!!
Life goes on, time passes, hopes diminishes, realities brightens
heart cries but mind speaks strong with broken heart!
Wishes, dreams and aspirations collides with truth,
realities and actualities; differentiate - result will be
either success or failure; quotient will be illusion;
integrate - answer will be infinite, which we don't know!!
Try to evaluate with definite value calling as boundary
who made this boundary? Unfortunately we ourselves,
with big correction factor!! What we call definite integral
is just a cover-up of infinite value which we cannot define!
So how far I can go in this infinite value?
No matter how far, because it will remain infinite
till another ramanujan born to make it finite!!!
Yet the day to come Veda remains finite in this infinite life,
is with a co-factor or not? That's what I don't know!!!

Veda Tatachar

Night Thoughts

How still is the night, and calming to the soul,
how luminous and tranquil the silvery moon
that does shed its light upon a world that is sleeping,
yet here light resides, and a mother does croon
and comfort her child.
How beautiful the sound to the child that is weeping
is the mother's voice. How enchanting the note and
bewitching the touch that can quiet the throat
of the mewling babe. How I envy the infant who,
when sad or lonely need nothing to do but cry out,
and the love of the mother comes and chases away
all fear and doubt.

Matt Davenport

Always And Forever

The day I met you I knew I liked you,
  But I was not sure what to do.
The day you left me I knew I loved you.
Will I ever again feel your sweet embrace
Will I ever again caress your loving face
  If I never again taste your kiss
  I can surely tell you this,
  Your love brought me higher
Your simple touch set my heart on fire
  I miss you dearly day and night
And want to hold you close and tight.
  Sometimes I cry and ask myself why
The pain I felt made me want to die.
  Even though you and I are apart
We will always be together in my heart.
There is nothing anyone can do or say
  To ever take my love away.

Nicholas John Coppola

Friends

Remember the love of friends
that have a place in you that's
all their own.

Never cease thought about the past with them,
  never cease to make the future all it can be.

Endless friendships join every week,
and as the sun smiles on the Sunday morning land,
so as the ones who can see
the friendships they will
hold close from now until eternity

And beyond then.

Patrick Ryan

There Was A Time

There was a time when the World sang
and my joy went unbounded by constraint.
I was, as love, when first we met.
My heart knew. It drank of your sweetness.
...And I walked on.

There was a time when the Stars shone bright
and my fascination for you grew constantly more.
I was, as passion, when deep embraced.
My self knew. It drank of your essence.
...And I walked on.

There was a time when the Universe cheered
and my delight in you saw no bounds.
I was, as ecstasy, when moment unleashed.
My whole being knew. It drank, and drank again.
...And I remained.

There was a time when the World sang,
  My heart knew, my self knew,
  My whole Being knew.
The Stars shone bright, when the Universe cheered.
  ...And I was at peace.

Stephen C. Jones

The Fool

I am tired and sitting in the dust of a doorway
but this pen won't stop dreaming of you
It is odd that I can write well at all
as my words embarrass themselves about you

I am an illiterate in the language of smiles
yet this face knows only bloom around you
This hair has been tanglewood all my days
but I never fail to tame it, so I may see you
It is funny that I can see my arms move
for they shiver and shy when I mean to hold you

My New York heart has been mugged before
and lies still as a beaten heart

But still dances like a fool,
at the mention of you;
would still take changes like a fool,
for a mention by you.

Scott Shou

Bustling Gnomes

The purest of water is given to thee
Filtered through sands of eternity
In the darkness, drop by drop it comes
Building sentinels without drums.

Water sparkling everywhere but cleansing it is not.
This seed inside planted by fruit once begotten,
It sprouts for just a moon, at will, and flesh be rotten.
To bind, and tie, and cage is its grand plot.

The undead wonder through this world
In masks of secrecy that they wear
Shielding them from ridicule unfurled
Captives of fate, dead in fear.

They walk the bustling cobbled streets
And cautiously mingled ever so aware
Their numbers abound, but rarely do meet,
With masks in hand, dark secret to bear.

Instead they grope and stumble in darkness,
Dungeons of solitude, hoping to find
A mate, a lover, a mistress
To bring forth a Spring and peace and mind.

Gary Tollar

Self destruction

Peace, once more I dream of you.
Again I smell your sweet, scented breath.
In another time I might have given up,
but now, I calmly stand alone
with dull, red eyes and wind cracked skin,
is shoes that used to be brand new,
and bones that have, by now, turned to stone.

My spirit had died too many times,
my mind needs rest, my hands are tired.
I feel a tremor beneath my feet,
and turn my thoughts to a God I once despised.
The same one I am anxious, strangely, to meet.

I try to fill this soulless pit
and find I can not, so I lay on my back and count the stars
and resign my soul to a Hell I never thought could exist.
The same Hell I am anxious, strangely, to see.

And like a star I explode,
now blameless, shameless, and free.

    Caleb S. Asbridge

The Healer

The light shines down and twinkles so bright,
I squint to see your face just to make things right.
I feel warm and confident, I have no fear.
I'm never alone, nor do I shed a tear.
You speak to me, without using lips,
it's your soul that comforts and gathers my wits.
Your eyes shimmer and radiantly gleam...
Providing to me your love, is more real than a dream.
I dare not to speak, in fear of the moment,
that you might vanish, too great would be the torment.
I yearn for the chance, to touch your face...
To feel its tender, and glorifying grace.
Your glowing hair waves in the wind,
sending your love, to help my heart mend.
Your image still stands, never failing,
to clear my thoughts, and send my soul sailing.

    Sealey Harris

Song For Catalina

Encanto mio
My runaway desire
I will sing your name from dawn
Nor rest my tongue till sundown

Elemental waterfall
Close to touch as the horizon
I will drench my soul in your vapour spray
Till I tingle in the marrow

In Buenos Aires they assemble
The dry bones of the missing
Cheap trinkets, plastic wrist watches
A copper tooth here and there

Beside the mothers' testimonies
The photographs, the tears
They build the final monuments
To the Decade of the Beasts

But here, Catalina mia
When the summer rains subside
I plant your face among the rosebushes
And print your face on my guitar

    Olu Oguibe

Inside

Behind the scenes of strange destruction
lives the eerie sound of death.
And in the moment of mass confusion
We find in our hearts there is nothing left.

Sheltered from the endless cold
I search my mind for a little hope.
In the quest for gleeful reason
I find the somber answer most.

I ask someone for the right direction
To a place beyond the righteous eye.
I often find my quest unnerving
for the place I never find.

I look inside and find direction.
And find a little sense of something hoped.
I see the world from a different angle
And I find the gleeful answers most.

    Jenna Koch

Mom

She holds you up when your world has collapsed
She is strongest when you're at your weakest
She puts warmth into your coldest of corners
She brings light when your life is at its bleakest

Someone to guide you through life
and carry the heavy load you take along
Until you have learned
to stand straight and be strong

This woman will not judge you
by the things you have done
she will teach you a better way
so you are able to overcome

Someone whose love will
never grow tired
Someone to stand by you
and keep you inspired

Her strength we admire
and her courage we commend
There is nothing she can't do
a 'mom' is there from beginning to end

    Vicky M. Lee

The Re-Claiming Of Night

She comes for me like a thief,
  creeping onto the edges of my domain.
  Fast does she ride, advancing swiftly, as does Mercury.
She bewitches me, and takes over.
  Her scent is that of morning's dew settling,
  Her hair, the gold of Apollo.
  The chariot atop which she sits, gleams. . .
  with the crystalline presence of the North Wind.
It is from her I flee,
  To know she is approaching, is to ready for my own demise.
  To lay eyes upon her beauty, is to invite my own downfall.
Tightly she holds to what is mine.
  Until such a time as I may return.
  Bringing with me her ruin,
  Which is my name. . . .
  Dusk. . .

    Sharia MaLinda Young

Love Hurts

How can I like someone so much,
  When all I do is hurt?
The pain inside me has no end,
  And I feel like I've been ground into dirt.
You don't understand the pain that I feel
  When you tell me you love me no more.
I can't express my feelings toward you
  When you go and shut the door.
I know that I have a lot of guy friends,
  And that's not going to change.
I may talk and flirt with all of them,
  But you're the one in my range.
I'm sorry for all that I've done,
  And I hope you know that's true.
I thought you were the one for me,
  And I was the one for you.
  Megan Carns

Snow Steps

Snow falls softly on pine needle carpeted ground
Our footsteps are covered as quickly as they are found
Unheard, we tread lightly,
Forgetting as we travel blithely
Of the footsteps that will never be covered.

The footprints that are left
Empty, they are kept
Will not fill with snow
For their emptiness will always show.

The snow will not always cover our prints
But we go on, not expecting ours to be missed
Thinking not of the future that we will find
But only of the nowness of our lives, yours and mine.
  Anne Duffus

A Dirty Sock

I love and hate being a teenager at the same time.
No limits to what we can dream,
Yet our parents can keep us home.
A teenager is like an animal trapped in a cage,
On display at the zoo.
So many people trying to interpret our behavior,
All we want is freedom.
Teenage life is like a maze,
With so many choices of directions.
Some choices will lead us outside to safety,
Others will lead us to feel lost in our problems.
Teenage life is like a dirty sock.
Sometimes it stinks,
And just when everything feels all right,
A hole develops someplace uncomfortable.
  Jacqueline Weiss

February Afternoon

In the stillness of the late afternoon
All is peaceful
All is still

A look of cute contentment on his face
I stare, looking at every inch, every hair, every possible move
As if looking and remembering would somehow do the trick

Unspoken messages, carried through the air
The power of positive thinking,
subliminal thoughts I desperately send
He rises, smiles, were the thoughts received?

All is peaceful
All is still
All is so deceitful
  Lisa Ann Schreier

No News

No news.
The muse is pity-ful
Declined an invitation,
Amusing recitation
Of facts (stats and circumstantial evidence.)

Divining rods and tea-leaves
  Objects lacking verbs.
Toulouse-Lautrec's perspective
  A haughty hooker's nose.

"Fate" accompli, mate.
  (No conjugated rights.)
The thief dropped his vaseline,

  Mentholated vapors and
  A smile for the passengers.

You'll know it when you step in it,
Wittgenstein was right.
  Jeff Howard

The Sandman

The Sandman, Ha!!
He never brought me no dream.
When he told me why
I didn't like his scheme.
He said I was poor,
a victim void of hope,
a product of the ghetto,
then he gave me a rope.
I said "Death come not near me,"
as I rose ten feet tall.
I buried my foot within his chest and said
"Beckon to my call!
Bring to me a wondrous dream
and it I shall fulfill,
to be respected, educated, prosperous, happy,
a leader upon life's hill.
Dreams are made for all people
for without them we would die.
Our dreams are what shape our future
so Sandman never pass me by."
  Mitchell Simms

What The Season Has Left Of The Trees

I stepped into the brisk autumn morn'
To rake the amber and crimson leaves.
'Tis through the beauty that I mourn
What the season has left of the trees.

I toss the leaves here and there
To uncover what the autumn had piled.
Of what I found I could only stare;
The forgotten graveyard of a child.

'Twas an old leather ball in the mossy thatch,
Buried in a shallow grave, betrayed, unseen.
(With dad I spent my youth playing catch,
of which standing her now I can only dream.)

What's left for me but to work, achieve...
I've just got to clean up all these leaves,
For I simply have no time to grieve
What the season has left of the trees.
  Bo Sutherland

A Short Cut To Hell

Feel the sun scorching down on my face as the flesh rots to decay.
The stench consumes the air as the coagulated blood turns into rigor
mortis and stiffens my body.
The skin on my eyes are chapped yet the fluid oozes from the tissue beneath.
My lungs are filled with mucous as the heat creates gases in my
stomach and pushes small quantities of slime out of my mouth.
My tongue is enlarged and swollen like a large worm protruding out of
my mouth, as though it is waiting for some victim to pass on by.
My skin is lifeless, yet moves like the waves of the ocean as the
maggots beneath feeds on carrion.
My pride and his two companions, scorched and shrivelled from the heat
of the sun and looking like unwanted raisins.
Buzzards and flies are swarming around me, waiting for their piece of the pie.
Why did I come through here?
The other way was a bit longer.
I should've heeded the sign's warning, "NO TRESPASSING! Violators will be shot!"
"Yeah! Right!" I sarcastically exclaimed.
Now look at me,...a lump of dead sh*t!

Gene Franchot Muller Jr.

Afterglow

As long as I have known myself to be a mature woman
The ultimate in passion has been my main concern
To reach that place where every nerve and every fiber quivers
Has been the destination, my quest in life to learn

But why did this elude me? Was I doing something wrong?
Did my psyche shy away from what my body tried to learn?
Did the partner of the moment suspect my inhibition?
Was I waiting for the ultimate when none was there to find?

And then I found my soulmate, my destiny, my love
A perfect adoration, a gift from him above
Here "The One" to take me to the top, and maybe further
This midlife body eager and perhaps, at last, mature

For when I rode those feelings that had been beyond my reach
When I finally found that dreamed of place that none can ever teach
Bells rang so very loudly; symphonic disarray
A feeling that I felt down deep was really here to stay

And so we walk together down the footpath they call life
Resplendent in the garb of perfect union
A wholeness very oft conceived but rarely ever found
An afterglow to last a lifetime through.

Judi Kearney

Memories Of Love

To smell, to taste and touch your hair, I'm the one that really cares
Let me run my fingers through your hair, if you dare

To lie next to you late at night, watching your spirit by candle light
Oh God, you're an incredible sight. What can I do for you tonight?

I lay my head upon your chest and wonder what the world would
Be like if it weren't for breasts

What price would I pay to taste your juices of life
To touch and to caress your beautiful skin, it would
Be the beginning that could never end

I would start with the toes and work towards the neck
I'd kiss every beautiful inch, what the heck

To join our souls in ultimate delight would get us started on our spiritual flight
We were just travellers passing by in life, our souls had joined for the night
But we knew that we were right

Jeffrey Alan Putt

I Miss Her Lying Next To Me

I miss her lying next to me
The way she smelled after a long hot shower
When I would lie contentedly in her arms
Hour after hour

I miss her lying next to me
The sounds she made when drifting off
When I could only hope that it was me
She'd be dreaming of

I miss her lying next to me
The way her body felt
And when I touched her tenderly
Her passion made me melt

I miss her lying next to me
The softness of her kiss
And the emptiness I'm feeling now
Tells me it's her love I desperately miss.

K. Ulmer

Forbidden Fruit

Didn't you see I was just a child
part of the tender and mild
Yet you came in night after night
knowing I would not fight
You have no face or name
all you brought was shame

I was the forbidden fruit
tempting your every desire
It was too late, I lit the fire

Your touch burned with pain
Your eyes saw straight through
for I had tempted you once again
and lost my innocence in your grasp

Brenton W. Kornegay

Finding God

What if I found God?
Found him deep within my bowels,
wrapped up in my self pity...
What if I found your God
eating out of my hand,
eating the s**t you feed me?
What if I discovered him
in a box marked God,
packed away deep in your
damp
dusty
creepy-crawly
cellar?
Along with your doubts and regrets.
What if I found him in
your hypocritical words?
Would that surprise you?

Mary Armstrong

Touch

A fireplace...
Some marshmallows...
even perhaps some cognac...
the hand nestles in the warm cleft of her sex
the wind howls noisy outside
my baby howls only on the inside.

Charles Rudolph

Once Upon A Friday Night

Icy hands grip my throat
Chills run down my spine
My hemorrhaging eyes gaze
Into those
Of a cold hearted dead soul
I feel a sharp pain in my chest
Then warmth covers my breast
I realize this monster
Has released my throat
And ripped out my heart
My body slumps to the ground
Eyes wide open
Watching in helpless silence
As the beast pisses
Into the vast abyss
Where my heart once was

Rachel Miller

A Monday Morning Wash

I washed the jeans today,
been lying here for three weeks now.
Soaking
it's a long walk from bed to laundry

In the wash cycle you go,
around broken dreams.
Agitating
soap suds like retaliating clergymen

Ruby blood stain,
period at the end of my day dream.
Dissolving
into the murky water of memory

Waiting for the detergent to bleach my pain,
thought the chlorine could disinfect that day.
Rinsing
releasing your breath from my lungs

Mechanical spasm swallows a delicate bird.
Down the drain. Down the drain.
Spinning
good-bye little foolish girl

I washed the blood stained jeans today.

Jeanine Hester

A Safe Trust

As I lay there in your arms,
 I can smell you;
  deep down in my soul.
As I lay there in your arms,
 I can feel your heart beating;
  racing faster than time.
As I lay there in your arms,
 I watch you breathing;
  chest rising and falling soft and steadily.
As I lay there in your arms,
 I caress your stomach;
  following the forbidden trail.
As I lay there in your arms,
 I whisper, I love you;
  more than words can say.
As I lay there in your arms,
 I close my eyes,
  and fall fast asleep.

Karen C. Rakoski

Fading

It's 2:00 am
a businessman is on the bedcorner
a black robe all that separates his pale white flesh from the stained quilt beneath him
the room reeks of sweat and smoke the paint is peeling off the wall
he can still taste the liquor from 3 hours before
a wretched man awaits his whore
In the next room she sits
looking in a cracked mirror with her blue eyes
the freckles on her face can barely be seen through the cloud of marijuana smoke
she finishes her last hit, removes her cross, and prepares to descend once again
the creak of hinges is heard for a moment it all stops
She longs for lost dreams he wonders about his daughter
then they go on both knowing it is not the last time it will continue
fighting back tears, she satisfies the beast once again
It's 2:30 am and the only thing clear is that the paintings on the
wall are not the only thing
fading...

Jeffrey Brown

Untitled

As it slowly rises out of its pocket
The wetness of sweat softens the delicately white outer layer
Then slowly it speeds up the immense pressures,
as it is forced to go faster
Patiently the other waits for this power to reach the core of its tip
As it reaches the rounded tip
Pleasures of joy and pain are shown by the grin
It enters the pit of the unknown
No longer in control of either one
Now it suspends in the hands of no one
Only in the open field of emptiness space....
Faster and Faster, the other tires to reach what will soon be pleasure to him
No longer can wait, he has waited for hours and now, his chance
As he tries to grab it, the white softness is now too wet
Sweat drips, no longer lone but now partnered by nature's dew
He finally grabs hold
Forcefully he tugs back
Throws his arm over his shoulder
Reaches for his target
Yet misses, the runner scores.

Leticia Villa

He Has No Face

She awoke, but seemed in a dream a myriad of thoughts and confusion,
someone else was there but this could not be
as she was in bed, undressed, impossible she thought.
Then she saw him lying there, she did not know him
so she tried to see but he had no face. "Who are you?"
gasping, barely able to ask, he didn't answer.
He was alive she could hear his breath, but he had no face.
She wanted to know so again "Who are you?" Silence
broken only by the rhythmical sounds of breath, alive, but he had no face.
She wanted to touch him, to see how he felt
hot or cold, hard or soft, rough or smooth, she knew he was there
but he had no face. The music played by his breathing, his familiar
presence. Oh she knew him, but he had no face.
She pulled the covers above her naked body, both thrilled and ashamed
she wanted him there, but who is he?
A long forgotten lover of the past, a memory of someone I have known
aching to receive him again to touch once more the haunting memories,
rising up, burning, haunting memories I cannot face but must.
"I am afraid" she whispered and in the silence a familiar voice answered
"I am afraid too;" but he has a face

Priscilla G. Andonie

Television Rights

A cold wet road this year,
No World-Peace-In-A-Can infomercial
To numb down the burden of living.
No ethnic cleanser to wash away your sins, buttercup.
Let's make a new world order of two tonight, I said,
Because it's always easier; thinking with your gonads,
Because you always know what they want.

The trailer parks all dream of high society orgies,
Sleep tight while the kids are out shooting up the streets
In a colorblind frenzy.
But I'm a millennium away, I'm a minority of one,
Give me my infinite rights,
Drunk driving as a form of free speech,
And F**k-You the first clear words out of Baby's mouth.
Wonder where he picked that up?!

We've got to work our schemes, To make the world a better place,
For the Drug Cartels and the Politicians. I'll show you birth control
she says at sixteen. Drops the baby in the trash can on her way to
school. Mama didn't know she was pregnant, Because it wasn't on the
tabloids, or the cartoon news. We got family TV values, right?

Marcus McCoy

An Unspoken Dream

Last night as I was sleeping
I thought, I heard you call my name
I walked to the window to find it, was
only the wind whispering through the trees.
As I looked at the moon, through the trees,
thoughts of you, entered my mind.
I turned only to find myself lying under the willow tree
Motionless like a cloud, you stood over me,
looking upon me with your dark midnight eyes.
Only to see deep within the opened temple gates unto my soul.
Manlike you lie upon my breathless body.
Do you not feel sweet love and constant
chastity that dwells within my body?
You kissed my lily budded breast and
teased me with lips like cherries, charming me to bite.
Look into my emerald eyes, do you see how beautiful my love is?
Do you not hear in the silence of the night, me calling to you?
Come be with me, let me reflect the dreams
and desires of your heart, let me teach you of my love!

Evelyn Theresa Underwood Hanna

Sins Of A Housewife

Before I leave your tongue makes sure I won't sleep tonight.
It runs across my skin burning in its mark.
Not here, not yet, how about Wednesday?
Vague replies from you, giddiness from me.
"I'll call"
"Okay."
"I'll call"
"Okay."
Another kiss and my hand between your legs.
"Go! Please just go before someone sees us!"
I'm out of the car now; surprised I remember how to walk.
In the rain, happy for its cool wetness on my hot skin
Already reliving the moments like a thief after a heist.
The key turns and I'm in my other world as you drive away.
For hours I lie in bed wondering what you're thinking;
happy for once that he's snoring so I can cry unnoticed.
Finally my dreams take me away, back to you.
You're taking me on a burning altar.
Young girls encircle us chanting about the wicked.
And we burn in and out, a pagan sacrifice of souls.

Michelle Dean

Mary M.

The Jesus men are coming.
It's too late.
Pimp crows crowd the roof edge
Checking the Jesus John's out.

See them through Lilith's eyes.
They've come before in better times.
Furtive souls, who repented later
The sin was always mine.

Jesus men,
Wrinkling their noses,
Stirring the dark corners
With the tips of their unsullied shoes.

It's too late.
This is the time of maggot kisses,
Limp flesh, departed dreams,
The birth of flies.

This is the time of bloated rats
Burrowing through my blankets
Like lustful little men
No odor of sanctity attends this bier.

Melissa Yocom

Far Away

I close my eyes
I smell everything
Feel the wind in my face
Hear the loudest silence

Shadows of years, of decades
Consume my every moment
The battle can not be won
Nor can it be finished

It is the lust for the past,
The longer it lives
The rape more passionate
Only when I close my eyes.

Arnold De La Cruz

The Provider

If you were a creator,
A Madonna, an oyster,
A toucher of God,

Would you write of your capital assets —
Stocks, bonds, trusts;
Or of f***ing your secretary
As an ode to the giver of life?

Would your son,
Who you've slammed against a wall
For questioning you,
Strike you as tragic
For golfing at fifteen?

Would you speak of your dreams
Or has their realization
Renamed them expectations?

What do you expect of me?
And if the thought Had crossed your mind,
Would you toss it aside
Like yesterday's Wall Street Journal?

Rebecca L. Sheppard

The Test

Everyone in life takes the test.
So try to be always at your best,
Just like all the rest,
The test is just like a game
Whether you win, tie or lose.
It is something that you cannot abuse.
Whether or not you take the blame.
Again it is just like a game.
Just like all the rest.
Remember to be at your best.
That you must take the test.

Edward F. Bayer

Shooting Star

You're so bright and shinny
Way up in the sky,
Sparkling and moving
as time as goes by.
Brilliant in color
magnificent in sight,
moving through the sky
with all your might.
So pleasant to watch
as you zoom by so fast
million miles an hour
wishing you could last.

Lee Ann Tairi

Sounds of the Rainforest

The wonderful sounds of the rainforest
Monkeys running for their lives
Chainsaws blaring
The wonderful sounds of the rainforest
Men yelling
Trees crackling
The wonderful sounds of the rainforest
Monkeys running for their lives

Danny Eppolite

The Meadow

Meadowy meadow when night falls
The sky darkens sunset falls
People walking walking for a sight
Meadowy meadow dark in the night

Meadowy meadowy when night falls
The sky darkens darker than all
If you're looking looking for a sight
You won't find one dark in the night

Sam Williams

Treasures

Some folks treasure money,
Others material possessions,
Still others treasure fame.
My treasures are memories,
Memories of old places, faces and times.
Remembering the joy each brought,
Makes my life worthwhile.
I am extremely rich,
For I have so many memories.
Even when life throws curves,
I can still smile,
I have all my special memories,
Memories I cherish and treasure.

A. M. Lomen

Netsirk

Do I walk with my girl at the time of a sunset?
I love to walk on the soft sands of the beach.
As waves roll over our feet making them wet,
My words flow into her ear as if it were water, telling her she's my little peach.
The sun shines off her hair as if it were golden.
Then I draw a heart shaped figure leaving a print in the sand.
As I look into her eyes I know I must be dreaming.
Then the water rushes up to smooth the sand and the waves get out of hand.
Breaking up with the one I love would be ill,
'Cause I know if we just took time out it would be even better.
To be with another girl there would be no thrill,
There is no other girl out there that can make me wetter.
My only aspiration is to be with the one I love,
She's the star in the sky and the heavens above.

Chad Algorri

Where Do Little Gargoyles Come From?

"Some look almost human," is the worst thing you can say,
When speaking of a gargoyle in such a condescending way.
Gothic gargoyles are the proudest of this cement and metal breed,
And the males are very careful to protect their grotesque seed.
It isn't very easy from a human's point of view,
To think of gargoyles mating, but that is what they do!
On rainy nights at three a.m., the mating is begun,
They grapple and they struggle just to grab at least one bun;
And when the mating's over each goes back to its domicile,
For then the waiting's started and it goes on for quite a while.
Gestation times for gargoyles run about a thousand years,
But it certainly is worth it when you see the little dears.
And if you see a female gargoyle and her stomach is still thin,
You'd better run away real fast or you might be next of kin!

Ted Brohl

Untitled

The urge to kill comes to me again. Begging weakness to
Surrender. Sweet sounds in the Shadows of Sorrow, this is Love. Care not what you
think of me, rely not upon thyself. Outer
being, outer beauty, controlling every temptation. Questioning me. Am I still
happy? Am I still joyous? Am I still ecstatic? Do I strive in waves of
bliss each day? The single answer to many questions is No.
Life is not as it used to be. The sun is shining, though now it Rains Eternally.
A blackened mist forms, encompassing me as if it were a shield to ward off evils.
Once spoken, Eternity is Ours.
Now estranged, I feel that was is a more fitting word. Eternity was
Ours. I hath loved thee Forever. Can you not see the sickness it
has posed on me? Do you not recognize me without you?
Changed. It is all so different now. I am pained in places I
cannot reach. How right you are.
Paradise is in Flames.

Kristina A. Lynch

The Sonnet Of A Man Who Loved Death

There is a man who has a love of death
He would become famous, and wanted for his thrills
With every last, squirming victim's gasping breath
He would shock the world of his kills
Everyday he would drink his booze
With black thoughts running through his head
Every time, a girlfriend, would take a snooze,
The next day she would end up dead
During his reign of fright
He would cause another dark day
His victim would be hidden away by the end of the night
By this, he would make his victim's family dismay
Every night, his bathtub would flood
With the crimsonness of the victim's blood

Michael Koivisto

Untitled

Let's get high on life together
Get light headed as a feather
Then we can embrace each other
Now stare into the deep blue sky
And watch the beautiful birds fly
As we race towards a higher high
The sunset is opening the night's door
Now let's go into the night's core
As we feel our blood pressure and endorphins soar
Now get into my car
And look at the sparkling stars
Baby take it real far
Look at the beautiful moon above
And listen to the singing dove
And now let's make beautiful love
Baby let's bump and grind the night away
Baby let's make love till the next day
As we sip on some chardonnay

Allan Picardy

Brats

Staunch Catholics, Mom and Dad, fought their way across
America from one USAF base to the next with five kids
in tow. Military dependents. Hostages. It was like we
needed to be somewhere different all the time.
Like there was a demon or the police on our heels.
Even though we weren't jailbirds. Yet.

Dad, a sordid Lifer, had the logic of a drill sergeant.
While we cried for his violence to stop,
Mom prayed to the Holy Mother, Goddamn her.
Didn't she know there was no redeeming him?
That our souls had evaporated. Already.

We all reacted when catastrophe struck: Car wrecks,
plane crashes, burning houses, evacuations. We knew to get
the f**k out. Unfortunately, on a daily basis, when the
sh*t-hit-the-fan, we waited to be rescued. Dumb Asses.

Nancy Ryan Keeling

My Twin

There she was, an awesome vision,
Would she notice me?
In time we became friends,
Nothing held back, open were we.

She shared ever more with me throughout the years,
Opening up with her innermost thoughts whispered in my ears.
Until that Friday though, we had never touched,
Lust and love when we kissed, through our bodies powerful
    emotions rushed.

My heart, mind, and soul united with hers instantly,
Another kiss and we knew.
This is it,
Ecstasy at last, a love so true.
Soul mates are we - my twin she'll forever be!

Sherri Ihrig

Salem

Dangling cigarette,
And nervous tic.
High-beam eyes drive through the night.
Subtle indifference to a statuesque blonde
'Til her tortuous lips kiss my lust.

Body hunched in a hardback chair.
Bottle dangling from nicotine fingers.
The only thing of hers I have left
Is the residue of love on my sheets.

Jay Trigg

Speed Of Light Cam

Waves crash against the beach
Then are pulled back, and
Pulled in to you by a force,
Lust, I don't understand
A force I can't control myself against

This urge comes over me in waves
They roll over, wash away, and
Are pulled over us again
Washing up the beach, letting back to sea
Like the breathing of the ocean
With the gentle press of your lips against mine

The dew on the wet fresh grass
Can be seen in droplets, and
The ocean mist dense almost as fog
Gray mist leaving a salty spray on your skin
The taste of salt, I am pulled under again
As your tongue slides, coaxing, pulling from my mouth.

Margaret Zimmerman

Reaching For The Clouds

Spiralling, speeding, increasingly faster, down. Down.
Trying to get a hand hold on one of the clouds
that are my dreams, my hopes. They're gone.
No more silver linings, no more windless days
Constant, torrents of ash being Slammed into my mind,
Whisked into my eyes, and intermittently into my mouth
Everything is burnt, warped, and the on verge of incredible Death
My head won't stop pounding against the bloody walls
You nonchalantly slip into my life.
With deceit and hatred.
My hopes and dreams have been taken, never to return,
To balance cynicism and mistrust.
Wherethef**karethosecloudsanyway???
Where is my parachute? What has happened to my compassion?
and caring, and love and desire, and satisfaction, and mind.
Wheredidyousaythosecloudswere?
I guess I'll just wait for an end to the pain, watch
for an end to the pain.
Idon'tthinkI'lleverfindthosedamnedcloudsagain.

David Bowles

Ode To You

Today I got the urge to share,
The feelings that I hold so dear.
Seldom do I express how I feel
But in my heart I know it's real.
So today as I sit and stare,
I let my mind wander to bring you near.
I smell you in the morning air
Your breath whispers gently in my ear.
I see you in the shape of things
And oh, my heart, what joy it brings.
The thought of you always makes me smile
And memories, great memories play in my mind.
I need you, and I hope you know
How my body craves with wanting you so.
I know you know, though I don't say
That's why I'm telling you here today.
My darling, as the skies are blue
My love for you runs deep and true.

Shelley Harris

494

Stairway To Heaven

Let's imagine flying up toward the sky,
as if we were a white dove with long delicate wings
Flying to a destination that's unknown and far
Pretending there were no problems upon us,
as if there was no earth and only we exist
Then reality strikes and we must awake,
yes, awake from a dream so far from reality,
To know that we only live a test-a test of life
Trying to make a straight path for our stairway to heaven

Laurine Kandare

Tears For Years

I wondered how it must have felt for you to carry me so close
   to your heart.
Did you want me...was I a part of you...or were we destined to be apart?
I didn't know...
for so many years, I had no idea I was adopted...
I didn't know...
for so many years, I had no idea who you were...
I didn't know...
for so many years, why you'd want to leave me...abandoned
I didn't know...
for so many years, why God would let this occur.
But I believe in miracles, and a Lord who provides...Peace
I was taught that faith heals, and through this we have...Peace
By faith I have found you...and by God we have...Peace
The tears have turned happy...the laughter rings loud...
Two hearts are mending, and I am so proud...to call you mother.
Yes, I believe in miracles, and a Lord who provides...Love
I was taught that hearts mend, and through this we have...Love
and by God we have...each other.

Carol Dierking

Balloons

As I watched the six colored balloons fly,
They looked so beautiful in the blue sky.

All of the balloons were right next to the sun,
Look, I said to my daughter and son.

Look at the six colored balloons that fly,
Don't they look beautiful in the blue sky?

Look how they are all right next to the sun,
Do you see? I said to my daughter and son.

Jim Raffensparger

continuity of reality?

i cannot find the words anymore
all that rages inside me has no equal
too much to fill just a page
but nothing whose true meaning reveals
lost and alone and unable to speak
curiously scared of finding these truths
unable to make sense of it all
thinking thoughts untranslatable by these mortal roots
infinite ideological parallels
mired in the disparity of existence
it is a wonder we understand each other...
nothing in common
where words mean nothing
but everyone's the same
if we could only understand...
madmen are prophets
only to those who see past
what is being said
to what is truly meant.

ralph petagna

In Sync

Oh, the world is so in sync
So very much like the dishes
Of a dinner the night before.
China patterned dominoes,
Sunken treasures I can see through
The filthier looking glasses.
Soaking impermeably,
Clinging to the useless entree
That no one wanted anyway.
Caked on cake on caked on cake,
Sour dipped crusts (cool ranch, I think),
Salsa'd for those who could take it
And the humus lies under it all.
And left to culture a stink.
And my love, the greasy film
Seeping through my pores, smothers me
Contaminates my cleanliness.
No, I won't think of what's in sync.
I could have used my dishwasher.

Melinda Marie Blair

Untitled

You are the sun that stretches down,
to drench the earth with light;
Enriching everything that you caress,
but what happens when day turns to night?
Do you leave, where can I find you,
I feel lonely when you aren't found;
The warmth from your touch is far from me,
I am here on the cold, hard ground.
You told me that I will always see,
and feel your loving ray;
But I cannot feel your warmth,
until the darkness is engulfed by day.
I ask you why I feel alone,
when day is extinguished by night;
You told me to look to the sky,
and feel you with my sight.
For at night your ray does not hit the earth,
but instead it hits the moon;
Shining like your love for me,
telling me it will be day again soon.

William H. Payne IV

Regret

He weaves his deception so exquisitely
Draping it like silk around my smile
He arrives smoothly and quickly
Never on time, but always right
He sings his songs to charm my heart
Luring me into his lair
And in laughing blindness I fall
Denying what I know
To find escape in his songs
And solace in his offerings
For once to hold the reins
Instead of grasping desperately
to this runaway horse
That tramples on my fallen soul
And laughs at my confusion
And so here I sit now
An angel with two broken wings
The devil who lead me to this destruction
Laughs at me from afar
And the other angels will never look at me the same again

Amanda Kruse

Self-Destruct

They argue and argue
about how much they agree,
and the corrupt attack,
holding on to their aluminum halos.
The people ignore them;
half asleep after half a race.

They tune out the mindless droning,
as the young man tries to look old
and the old man tries to look young.
The rags to riches hero
joins the assault on the poor,
and only the billionaire will defend the common man.

They viciously maim each other
as the media bombards the battle.
None will ever be the same.
They watch their souls forever damned
by the court of public opinion.
None will ever be the same.

Edward H. Goyda

A Child's Ode

Hush, little one! Please don't cry.
Listen to the words of this lullaby.
Close your eyes, not a sound or a peep
Your troubles left behind while you sleep.

Dear God, quickly mend this broken wing.
Hear those steeple bells as they loudly ring.
Baby Jesus will always be at your side.
His angels will protect, rule and guide.

Go ahead! Reach out for his courageous hand.
In your prayers, rejoice to the marching band.
He is real; not a nightmare or a dream
Wash away those fears in his stream.

Awake! Everything is in tact.
Brotherhood has created a pact.
When in doubt seek his precious love.
A child's ode is to the heavens above.

Renita Krasnodebski

Lost And Found

Even though a room is full where life and spirit abound
It still remains an empty space if no one can be found
A dreamer is just a dreamer only to pass the time away
Trying to find his niche in life and get by another day

Swimming alone in this massive ocean isn't the way it should be
Suspended in air no place to land nothing around to see
A cry for help that reaches no ear is futility at its best
The mind rolls on in strange direction I think you know the rest

An island remains an island whether or not it has a tree
A dry and desolate oasis is a despairing sight to see
Crawl in a hole on where to go buried deep in the sand
A comfort zone being all alone only you can understand

Momentum will have to be gained in order to overcome
Ridding the lethargic nature is a very slow path for some
Perish all negative thoughts brush the sand from your face
Be aware of these principles and get out of this place

The emptiness is gone it seems others I have found
It takes all of my inner energy to keep my feet on the ground
Alone no more as dreams unveil to the listening ear
At last I have finally found myself not there but here

Gary Stucci

No Flowers

No flowers for the man that brought all ten home
for certain none would allow that he die alone

No flowers to be laid for our great Dad
he is gone now, from his suffering we're glad

No flowers from the doctors that dismissed his pain
nor from the helpful that tried in vain

No flowers, it seems, in a heap to be piled
for a genius that always bowed to a child

No flowers behind which many would hide
could honor this man we wish back to our side

No flowers then, from the Adams Family
who came to his door with their sympathy

No flowers save a rose from each of his kind
and his lover's poise, whom he's left behind

To Dad with love, Des

Desmond Doris

Cherish The Moment

A European coffee cafe,
The flower gardens with a touch of Monet

Sipping a glass of the finest wine,
Cured from the grapes of the sweetest vine

Jazzy jazz echoing through the park,
The soothing melodies from dusk to dark

Barefooting through the warm, refined sand,
Blading along the beach front strand

Expressing yourself with an opened mind,
The creative juices that flow not bind

Spending the time with family and friends,
The laughter and joy that never ends

Extending a hand, lending a smile,
Assisting those in need never goes out of style

Cherish the moments, cherish the times,
Life's an adventure, full of reason and rhyme

Julie L. Sasaki

Lost Souls

Lost souls reunite,
greetings from an old friend.
She has come to take us home.
We will fly far from here, free from pain, freed from chains
Above the clouds and in the mist,
not off the road and in the mud.
Time has taken my cumbersome shell
but now I can see from the farthest sands
to the highest snow covered peaks.
All with just a blink of an eye.
Some come and then leave again.
All that it takes to keep me here is to look into his eye
and hear his voice.
It's been so long, my God the time that has passed.
I would have never thought I'd laugh with you again.
He whispers a few words and sends me on my way.
Somehow I know they wait for me to join them once again.
My eyelids raise with the help from a tear.
I stare at the cold blank ceiling.
What does it all mean, where have I gone?

William Younkins

Why Me Lord

Why me Lord, why me
Day after Day Night after Night
I contemplate on how to make a better way
For myself and unborn child
Life has to be grand
Honesty, Integrity, Equality
is for which I stand
Why me Lord, why me
As my child breathes
his first breath of air
I sit in pain and joyful tears
watching him alone
My son's big beautiful brown eyes,
dark bronze skin, tamed hair that of his father; he too
has come and gone
Just vanished without a trace
A smile that once
shown on my face; will forever be no more
Cause he slipped out the door...
Why me Lord, Why me

Deidra Webb

His Will

How perfect and special God made her little boy
So perfect that his five fingers could pick up a toy.
Why then, she wondered, would God take him away
For she loved him so much, not even words could say.

Entering the room quiet and dim,
Looks on the faces were nothing but grim.
As she walked down the aisle, remembering his precious face,
She pulled from her purse a handkerchief of lace.

Knowing he would be someone she would forever and always miss,
She bent down beside his coffin and gave him a kiss.
Only then was it that she realized in the quiet and still,
It couldn't have been God's wrath, it must have been His Will.

Shelli Kay Rainer

The Reality Of Life

Life is full of changes
There are the good and the bad.
Even though some are sad
You must look at the bright side.
Friends will come and friends will stay.
You sit and wonder, why does it have to be this way.
Why can't people stay forever?
It is all a mystery to me.
Friends are the best thing in the world,
Why do they have to leave,
Why can't they stay and spend time with me?
God has his reasons, and friends make the decision,
To come and stay or to move away.

Anita Morrissey

Untrodden Paths

Would I choose to pass this way again?
I think not!
If one's desire is to find oneself,
Travel far from home and friends
'Tis then, where yourself, you can only be.
The experience of untrodden paths rarely is undertaken
New experiences cannot be redone.
To those who wish their lives to live over I say,
You have never lived before.
You are allowed only one pass of the torch,
Timidity is the first trial of failure
Alas, we shall not pass this way again

Frank Balint

The Silent Ones

Always beware the silent ones,
the silent and the meek.
Always beware the quiet ones,
the quiet and the weak.
For they are the ones who dream your death,
while standing wide awake.
They are the ones who stalk your lives,
while standing in your wake.

Always beware the silent ones,
the silent and the strong.
Always beware the quiet ones,
the quiet who can do no wrong.
For they are the ones who hold the knives,
the ones who shoot the guns.
They are the ones who kill you now,
for things that you have done.

Cristin Mulligan

My Life Is Like A Match That Has Burned Itself Out

I feel the black wind blow through my hair
There's no one to help me
There is no one there
And my life is as empty as the ceiling at which I stare

It seems there is no one like me
No one that feels the same
Sad and lonely like a cold dark rain

The sun is never shining on me
The darkness is always out
And no one seems to hear me when I scream and shout

I sit and wait and lie in vain
Hoping for some help
And my life is like a match that has burned itself out

Jason Bessette

Heaven Speaks

The sun shines in the morning,
   but only on good days.
It is winter's warning,
   that ends the beautiful rays.
If only heaven wasn't so far away
   for I know there would be light,
as gentle as the hands of day;
   as mysterious as the whispers of night.
This captivating place I know
   can only be found when my soul is at rest
I must leave this dark and go,
   for my heart and soul always knows best.
Of all my passions, I choose the light of love
   This is the best gift, the one from above.

Kristy Lutz

Butterflies

Butterfly on the windshield:
Yep this is where it happens
Where the tire meets the toad
The Earth squashed flat by the
Hurtling, indifferent juggernaut of
Unprincipled "Progress."

When we get where we thought we were going
We'll get out and with sponge and hose
Industriously wipe away the spattered
Reminder of what we have become,
Sticky and tattered,
Butterflies on the windshield.

Michael Wayne Rock

Passions Of Yesterday

Though it's almost been two years
I still think of you all the time
your face a picture in my heart
an offering to my mind
and I know that you've gone on with life
found your true love so you say
I still can't seem to free my life from the passions of days
when we would walk hand in hand and make our future plans
talk of how our lives would be together without this maze
of school and parents and other things
that were always in the way
and how we'd love no other now and how we'd be today
and I know it all seems foolish now and I should be like you
but of all the things I told you one thing still stands true
I said that I would love you with my body, soul, and mind
forever to be faithful and new love never find
and though I never thought it would be over quite like this
and fate would deal an empty hand and leave me you to miss
I often still can find myself reaching back in time
to grasp the days with you and me our passions undefined.

Paul Karl Arthur Kell

Cradles Of The Sea Never Looked So Smooth

Every insatiable taste bud was a turn on
every tightly wound concept of the body did hurt
toll bridges to my soul wore me out
the carvings of my sister's face were shattered
all the bandwagon mysteries were unclothed
all the serpentine heart attacks helped angels die
they completely dropped for the wrong reasons
the worst sleeping pills were the price you paid
and the gentle rock of your cradle
became a lullaby in itself

Darren Anderson

Cue The Rain

Time passes quickly, yet that day it stood so still,
an emerald green carpet of grass, warmed by summers sun
topaz blue sky trickling a warm mist
a shaft of white light connecting upward
our bodies commingle, minds and hands explore
no faults, no flaws
no barriers in mind nor heart
a time that knew no time at all
suddenly the sky opened, a hard rain fell
scurrying for clothing and shelter
laughing we fell upon a bed
two bodies two minds, two souls,
they became one, merging with the wind
becoming everything free
time passes quickly, yet that day it stood so still
when the world falls hard upon me now
I close my eyes
returning to that place in the wind
again time stands still
cue the rain

Jean Milligan

An Autumn Day

Fall rain, falling on my hair,
As I walk through the park without a care.

Soft breeze, blows through the trees,
Runs through my spine and shakes my knees.

Autumn leaves hit the ground.
They flutter softly without making a sound.

Cold, gray sky looks down on me,
Seeing something inside me that I can't see.

Kristen Stockhausen

The Fog

It rides on the wind as the day slips away,
soft and white, fresh and light always knowing its way.

The Horns begin blowing their soft lonely call
to announce the arrival of the slow flowing wall.

Over velvet green hilltops it tumbles and skips
reaching down its long fingers, through valleys they slip.

The bridge to the city now draped in fine mist
its silhouette gowning hardly seen by the ships.

Its journey completed and gone is the light
covered up like a blanket, snuggled in for the night.

As dawn breaks the skyline you waken today
and while you were sleeping it just slipped away.

Leaving air fresh and sweet like a soft summer rain
what a fabulous gift one could hardly complain.

The thing I missed most when I moved far away
is that wonderful fog drifting in on the bay.

Shayne Maxwell

There Will Come Heavy Rains

When it's time for the leaves to brown,
There is no need to frown,
For we know when one has taken his last breath,
There will be death.
Be like the calm wind blowing across the sea
Understand that this was meant to be.
There is no need for any cries of sorrow
Don't you know, there is always a tomorrow?
Although you will no longer be here,
The memories of you will linger near.
There will always be smiles up above,
With nothing but tears of love.
Throughout life there will come heavy rains,
Of heartaches and of pains.
But in the end, the black clouds will be blue,
Not only for me, but also for you.

Sherry Burks

Careless

I'm nothing but a guy,
There's so much I won't see.
Someday we will both die,
So pull the trigger and blame it on me.
They'll send to the Chamber or the Chair.
I won't put up a fight,
'Cause I really don't care.
They can gas me, fry me, whatever they might;
I'll lose one thing of my likeness,
And won't know what it is,
Because my whole life is careless.

Dominic Armenio

Family. . .

Such a small word, yet it means so much to so many; caring,
hope, strength, support, loyalty, forgiveness, happiness, love,

It is not a choice to whom we are born unto, rather it is
destiny, it is family

Families share so much; good times, bad times, times of need
and times of rejoicing.

But no matter what one is going through, be it the highest
of highs to the lowest of lows, the family bond brings us
all together to become one solid, powerful source of
strength, love and everything in between.

Dawn Daglian

Little Wagons

Sometimes when I linger, old pictures blurred in the light
pedal back to the days when it was just a game
a time of dust and dirt, thirsty tree roots rippling sidewalks
only to be conquered by our little wagons
It was all in there waiting, a world within its walls
I lived a thousand lifetimes, ruled over magical kingdoms
crossing over and back at will
the mighty weight of knowledge
tempered and tamed by our little wagons
with each new summer day, another road trip to plan
city streets country roads - looking for fun but really
hoping to get the feeling again
treasures to be discovered, all brought back to camp
by our little wagons
The more that we learn, so easy to lose the feel
how to live without bounds
play the game, read a story, walk the path
and feel the magic around us
Sometimes I want to linger, capture all that my arms will hold
bring it back, all of it...in our little wagons

Jim Mathrusse

Fruit Of Life

You are the Fruit of Life
that flourishes from the Love within us all.
That precious moment of Life,
a spirit is born, a Creature of God.
The time has come and our journey
through life has just begun.

What can she see as she opens her eyes,
a dark cold shadow lies behind her mind.
As she approaches she can't find
that what she is searching for is in her mind.

Down deep inside there it is,
true as something I've never seen.
I feel it in my body. I feel it in my soul.
I feel it all over extend like fire that burns uncontrolled.
It's the sprit of Love, it's the sprit of God. It's so divine.
It's the powerful strength of Love we should all grow inside,
too nourish the child that lies deep in her soul

You are my Father, you are divine,
you will always live in my mind and soul, as I get old.

Diana Chavarria

Grandson

Not very long ago, there came into this world, a little boy,
Who filled the hearts of everyone near with enormous joy!
After a few suns and stars and moons had passed by,
He joined the Rob Kelley household in which to lie.
To the city called Conyers in the Georgia State,
He did move and that is where he learned to skate,
And to play golf, baseball, basketball and girls to chase,
   But between all of those activities so pleasing to him,
There were classes to attend and tests to take,
For his ambition and his dad's sake.
To Truett-McConnell, an institute of higher learning,
He went, yet for his family and friends, he was yearning.
Somewhere in all of the creation of this history maze,
Automobiles and speeding and collisions were common place.
But now those matters he has outgrown,
And seeds for his life and fortune have been sown.
Grandma and Grandpa could not of you prouder be,
As you begin this long journey into the unknown of future's sea.
Keep on the path you are on, for everyone's sake,
And you will be a success at whatever you undertake.

Robert M. Kelley, Sr.

Between Winter And Spring

Naked limbs dance solemnly high above,
Their patterns are so hauntingly beautiful,
The sky is empty and sea green,
Breeze is running around with no real destination,
All is broken in this forest tomb,
The sun is barely looking over the tree tops,
Spilling out its golden light like molasses,
Birds are creating sweet songs,
Water slides and splashes across pebbles,
The pearl white snow is melting with ease,
A stream of liquid, blue as a baby's eyes, moves away,
All things in a sate of serenity,
Warmth is making its way here with this new season,
The frigid months are gone and Spring has come.

C. J. Emerick

Always And Forever

My Dear Neal,
On this day, I became your wife,
I could not imagine anyone else I would rather be with for
the rest of my life.
I made a vow unto you this day in front of family and friends,
I promised that my love for you will never come to an end.
Neal, words cannot express how much I love and care for you,
We will be the best of friends each and every year through.
I will try to make you as happy as I can,
because when it comes to your love, I'm your biggest fan.
You are the smartest man I have ever met,
You make me so happy, and you always make me laugh.
For better, for worse, for richer, for poorer,
I will be your loving and devoted wife,
Always and forever.

Angela D. Wynn

Torrent

His salty breath calls,
and the skies take to thunder.
The regression of my soul is his to ponder.
His fire is cold and burns me with time.
My kinsman are swallowed by his dark rabid rhyme.
My salvation is broken beneath my feet.
Its pieces are torn for him to eat.
With that I am swept in his boiling stew.
My fear is reflected in his dark green hue.
The lack in my lungs I am unable to bear.
My eyes are surrounded by his cold stare.
Despite my desire to follow hope back,
My soul does regress and the white fades to black.

John Orr

Love

I speak of love, I'd die for it
So what is love to me?
A home and kids, a loving wife
It's comfort, warmth and safety.

It's something that's intangible
It's feeling that all is well
It's peace and security
A shedding of your shell.

It's soft spoken tender words
In the middle of the night
A sweet, warm kiss, a soft caress
Two arms locked around you tight.

It's understanding, it's unselfishness
It's worrying, wondering and caring
It's being together, at least in your thoughts
Two bodies, two minds and two souls, forever totally sharing.

George R. Williams

Their Love

A cool calm day, a breeze in the air.
Two young lives walking heart in heart.
They laugh and smile as they walk down the lane,
Trying to forget that soon they must part.

They trade their memories for each other to keep sacred.
They realize now he must be on his way.
They embrace each other passionately, for it's love that is kind.
He pulls her close and says, "I'll miss you so much."

He looks in her eyes, and his show such sorrow.
Though her heart aches she must stay strong, for him
She cries in her heart, "I need you please stay."
She kisses his cheek and wipes the tears form his chin.

Praying, "We must trust in Him."
"We must remember, God provides."
The journey is long, for their love is strong,
God is within them, for their love will survive.

Roxanne B. Mayer

The Last Leaf

Silhouetted against the deep blue, autumn sky,
One last leaf hangs by a slim, yellow stem,
And flaunts its brilliant face to passers by,
While waiting for a puff of wind to start its sail.

Only a few days ago it had been strong and green,
While a few other leaves turned yellow and drifted off.
'Til one frosty night a painter came
To mark those left with fiery reds and golds.
And then, with each new gust of wind
The leaves had begun to drift away,
Leaving, on this bright and spicy morning,
Only this last leaf to make
Its own statement about the season.

A cold rain could shake it loose
To join the others in the compost pile,
Or perhaps, some capricious wind would send
It out among the birds, and down
To where a child's eager hands
Wait to capture an autumn treasure.

Rae M. Haas

I Won't Take A Shower!

I'm nearing the record, yet I still have a ways.
I've stayed clear of the shower for 82 days.

The record still stands at one hundred and three.
The man who achieved it collapsed instantly.

Some say he went crazy, but I say it was aroma.
The poor fella's still in a seven year coma.

But my nerves will not crack, for my goal has been set.
The record is mine, I'm willing to bet.

Each day gets greater, keeping focused is tricky.
My fingernails are filthy, and my hair is all sticky.

I've begun to grow weary; I look like a bum.
I'm covered with dirt, and I'm steeping in scum.

I've broken one hundred — there's no turning back.
I've regained my senses, and turned back on track.

Yes, it's official! Give me jeers, give me praise.
I've stayed clear of the shower for 104 days.

Anthony M. Manzi

Untitled

Your flowers lost, the smell of heaven
the Gods that fire, the lighting from up high
she cries only alone, her tears fell the floor
I want to be your pillow, to hold you tight
take your hate, and turn it to love
some day it will come, even if I die try'n, for
maybe that would be enough, to bring you up,
out
into the light, of those eyes
the moon it shines, off the snow that falls
turning your face into a dream, of an angel
the one inside, of that statue
you put out, to show the world
that you're happy
I swear
one day it won't be a mask

Eric Aleshire

A Friendship Ignored

Close friends from birth like seeds do we exist,
'Bout life we learn in close proximity.
Through wind and rain together we persist,
Till leaves abundant overshadow me.
Thy roots are deep, and limbs much stronger grow,
Adorned by praise you need not think of those
Who weak and feeble live in shade below.
Laudation ruins men, do you suppose?
Preserved my pureness still remains in shade,
In heaven life eternal will be mine,
And memory of you is sure to fade,
Forgotten, you're subject to hands of time.
In friends', not strangers', mem'ries you are praised,
Ignoring friends shall leave no mem'ries raised.

Gregory W. Orr

Wings

(in memoriam Joyce)

I did not hear a beating of wings — not then —
But waking cold and alone in the attic bedroom
I knew straightway that at last the bird had flown,
Silent, wild, torn out of flesh into freedom.
Everything creaked: The bed, the old wood floor,
My morning bones stiff from the sleep of the living.
I clambered white-breathed down the spiral stair
To Joyce's room, my wife sitting quiet, and nothing:
Nothing in the bed but gray, discarded flesh,
A maggots' breakfast, raped of Joyce's beauty.
I kissed my wife — her hot live loveliness —
Then kissed her mother's cold dead forehead, mutely.
    I've heard them since: wings beating slowly by,
    Ripping the membrane of our impervious sky.

Nigel Hazeldine

Fall Foliage

Ayus, you will grow and go away:
Children are granted to us
A temporary miracle.

I believe that when I watch
Sun's amber burnt sienna gold
Drizzle on the back of your perfect head
As you dance your way
Back home from school
Through fall's magenta ochrelime foliage.

I follow, carrying your knapsack
And believe in the blessing I see
A gift, a light, a colour and a joy.

Oopalie Operajita

Emptiness

Sitting in the bar,
a drink in my hand.
Up to the lip, take a sip,
up to the lip, take a sip.

Eyes wide open,
looking at the faces all around.
Seeing nothing, seeking nothing,
neurons connecting to the brain,
sleeping like lazy dogs.

How did it all begin?
why did it have to end?
Questions, more questions,
questions dancing the brownian motion in my mind.

Up to the lip, take a sip,
up to the lip, take a sip,
up to the lip, no more to sip?
Wasn't there a drink in my glass,
or was I drinking emptiness all along?

Sudhir K. Oak

Unique

Piercings, tattoos, blonde hair, brown eyes,
Black skin,
What's wrong here? Nothing to me.

Skater clothes, alternative music,
Black skin,
What's wrong there? Nothing I can see.

White friends, white girlfriends,
Black skin,
What's wrong? Nothing at all.

Athlete, good student,
Black skin.
What's wrong? Please tell me.

Outgoing, unique, different
Black skin,
Yet, I am hated. I am what they say wrong...

Nick Walker

Dream Door

Slowly swinging shut, the dream door sloughs off all
invited guests, and the sullen man's blood-reddened fingers.

A sobered drunk shakes swollen head,
Icy day started, he cuts himself,
and then again,
Sifting shards of mirrored glass,
Fumbling, fitting shattered edges,

Which resist new order.
Salty water caught frozen in the blond/red beard hairs,
Gasping breath, fogged views, cracked myths and fables,
Half-lived designs of a lesser-known God's plan gone awry.

Seeing not at all, can he know?
New dreams come slowly,
Not from old and broken pieces stuck together,
But from new forms, grown in deeply warm and caring spaces.

Quickly now he rises, desperate acts aside,
His stupor passed, turning, he coughs a little,
shuffles his feet, squares his shoulders,
Leaves behind forever the safety of dead
places.

Byron C. Aldrich

Volcano Flame Eaters

The smell of smoke is in my blood. . .
hear that? It's the yellow sunshine falling leaves.
Smell winter's approach. . .
crackling footstep flame-leaps of faith.
Fiery smoke fills my lungs, burning its way into my mind.
Things are sort of smoky in October. . .
see that? My sister calls it snow
(she's rushing things) and it makes the grass
CRACK beneath the soles of my muddy hi-tops
(told Mom I'd ruin them if I used them for Gym)
A raucous flame licks the twig I offer to it
begging it to come play
begging for some food
knowing that its playthings disintegrate from the joy.
The twig grabs hold of my hand, leaving its mark.
(It doesn't really want to be a sacrificial maiden, I guess.)
Applecider sap dribbles down to steam.
Flame fun falls as does the snow
and October lasts as long as the sticks.

Anne M. Kent

Too Late

I remember when I first saw you
And I felt something new.
I wanted the romance to wait
But the opportunity was there, too late.

I remember being the only one dear
And when I was busy, you stayed near.
You thought I didn't care; you lost faith
And you thought you lost me, too late.

I remember playing second best
But everyone knows I'm better than the rest.
Now, you want me back as your mate
But I am gone, too late.

Jacqueline F. Fuller

The Mermaid

Staring at the sea, my mind plays tricks on me
I see a mermaid swimming toward the horizon
Her green luminescent scales reflect the light of the moon
I look to large boulders piled haphazardly at my side
And wonder should I walk out and join her, or just close my eyes?

Forgetting that I am only a man at this moment
I leave mothering sand and climb onto black rocks
My sight remains focused on her path of broken ocean
Then I stop, aware of the mounting apprehension I feel
Afraid that getting too close would confirm the mermaid not real.

She darts through the water like a porpoise at play
I forget my disillusionment and softly call out
A flash of pure horror escapes her porcelain face
As she melts into blue foam under the starry night sky
Both of us knowing because I believed in her, she now must die.

Christina J. Schrank

Fall Leaves

As the green leaves,
Slowly turning gold,
Turning red,
Turning yellow,
Graced the wind,
As if they were dancing,
Dancing,
Hand in hand with each other,
Gliding to the soft gentle grass,
As if the grass were tiny little snakes waving in the wind.

Ashley Hall

501

From The Sonoran Thorngrass Soliloquy

In the dark room the crickets lodge in woodbeams of the adobe
sawing their love-call to build more crickets...
the half coyote yowls and yips...
the nave of his mind in ears that point like arrows
to the woman stalking skillets to warm the flattened corn...
the girl pups listen to their hair-do's...
every tv on...four stations...phone ringing...ringing
bad rap static on the jam-blasters...uneven code
for the vestal and the worn

Survivors face the desert like boxers
gloves of thorn
elements that rage survival...
vaulted stars and moon singing
upon the american outback of broken cars,
micro-transmitters, dry mud walls, sears siding,
rubber maid and taco shells...
and mexico just a few miles down the road...

Victor W. W. Stevens-Rosenberg

Destiny Unknown

Aflight among the distant clouds,
 lost between the massive crowds.
Walking, wandering, struggling alone,
 trying to reach destiny unknown.
Seeing illusions at every turn,
 running away from the hurting burn.
Wanting to laugh, needing to moan,
 trying to reach destiny unknown.
Hoping for relief with each passing day,
 struggling for something important to say.
But each day turns into a clone
 of trying to reach destiny unknown.
Where love is hate and hate is hell.
 Where everything falls under his spell.
Where highest hopes sky high are blown
 is where we find destiny unknown.

Melanie J. Barish

Bittersweet Relief

My soul is overwhelmed with pain
and is aching to be relieved of its sorrow
but I can't give the only relief it seeks: in tears
for there are none left in me anymore.
My eyes have shed the last drop years ago.
O where is the silver lining behind every
cloud that the sages speak of?
Where is the light at the end of a long dark tunnel?
Or am I to believe that life in itself
is the long dark tunnel and death
is the light at the end of it — the bittersweet relief
my soul seeks.

Nariman Ahmed

Eye Full Of Tears

Six winters and four moons had run its course,
And now I sit here upon a horse,
Not knowing what is to come next,
For I sit here very perplexed.
Foreign pale beings
Talk in meanings
That I cannot understand.
I am just two hands
Put down here on the lands.
I am not a savage,
Although that's how it appears,
I am just an Indian with an eye full of tears.

Brandon J. Dowdy

Who Am I?

In the reflection, often seen but never heard.
Through my mind, often heard but never seen.
Voices, telling me that I am great, and not so great.
Sometimes I hear them ask, "Who is this person?"
Often I ask myself, "who am I?"
 I wonder through the day, in search of someone.
I know not who I am seeking but I know that he exists.
To run forth among the trees, often a dream.
I hear the trees asking, "who is this person?"
I often ask, "Who am I?"
 Forward through time I have run.
I see the past rush before my eyes at night
I see the future, uncertain to me yet obvious in path.
Who am I? You may ask me but I will no longer ask myself.
The trees know, the reflection knows.
I know that I need not know....only time will tell who I am.

Steven W. Williams

Dream With Blue Eyes

I was told once, when I was young, to follow, to chase my dreams.
I dream of a woman with the brightest blue eyes, the face
of an angel, and a smile which warms me as the sun.
I wish that dream could come true.
That dream is none other than you.
Seems like everywhere I go, I leave someone behind.
I do not want to leave you.
While the stars still shine while my heart still beats a
steady rhythm in the cage of ribs which hold it

 ...Trapped

And even if I leave this place
I will still see your face,
As it has been engraved upon my minds eye to my very soul.
I was told once, when I was young, to follow, to chase my dreams.
I dream of you. I dream of me. I dream of us

 ....Together.

Jason Drake

Weird Things That Happen

 Something weird has happened today,
as I went outside to play,
I advise you if a rock's name you must hear,
Slam a stone up to your ear.

 This rock will tell you what to do,
while your sisters say shoo-shoo-shoo,
Something weird has happened today,
as I went outside to play.

 That something weird was really strange,
Believe me it wasn't a 'Home on the Range'
It walked and it talked, and it spoke and it joked,
As I sat on the curb I started to choke.

 That something weird was my kid brother,
believe me, it could be no other.

Charlotte Marie Davis

A Baby Bird

Look at that bird in a nest
He is the one I like the best
When he is tired he'll take a rest,
but I am just sitting here wearing a vest!
In the winter he will fly west and I must go inside
and I must go inside and take my test
Oh look there is a guest, it is a cat
but get that cat out of here!
He's making a mess and being a pest!!!

Alyssa M. Alecci

In A Mirror

When I look in a mirror I see a face,
Sometimes I wonder...am I out of place?

I look in the mirror everyday
And different thoughts come my way.

Some thoughts are good and make me smile,
But others make me question my style.

When I look in a mirror I see a person
who always laughs and brings smiles to others.
That makes one say, who cares?
I do for they're all my sisters and brothers.

Once in awhile the picture isn't so great
And I say to myself maybe I should give it a break.

Go back to bed and try it again
The mirror smiles and says, "Amen!"

Mirrors bring bad and good
But the inside is what matters, at least it should.

    Natasha Hubert

My Sunshine

Alone, battered, and beaten from all sides;
Just floating through life, riding out the tides.
What's that? Just another monstrous wave,
A man with a frown and a raft to save.
Rains keep falling as my boat springs a leak.
All seems utterly lost when in you peek.

Clouds flee in terror as my sunshine appears,
The rain quickly stops and the water clears.
She offers her warm arms in loving embrace.
As I accept, my heart begins to race.
But could first look lead to lasting love?
How long will it shine from heaven above?

Often times dark, billowing clouds have come.
Have we had waves? Yeah, a few worse than some!
But break our embrace, they could never do;
A love this strong adheres better than glue!
This sun shall never set nor dim its glow,
Regardless of how strong the winds may blow.

    Bradley P. Sutton

Orange Tree

I have a tree in my back yard,
it's very big and very hard.
I put up a swing on its branch,
in its bushy arms I built myself a ranch.
It gives me oranges every year,
they're good weapons if enemies come near.
I pretend that I'm a pretty princess with golden hair,
and even have my own white mare.
My best friend comes over to play with me,
our favorite place to play is in my tree.
Danny and I carved in our initials,
but now they've turned to humongous thistles.
Its oranges taste succulent and sweet,
I think my orange tree is really neat.
I never want to chop up my tree
and make it a sailboat in the sea.
I would never dream of sawing it down
because it would make me wail, cry, and frown.
I guess I'm kind of attached to my tree.
My tree is really precious to me.

    Elizabeth Recker

A Soul's Tear

A cold, soft rain drifted down from the sky,
Engulfing all it came in contact with,
Severe in its indifference and doubt.
The water and pavement are in such bout,
Like that of love and hate engaged in pith.
Perhaps destined by fate or time, but why?

The rain falls steadily in deep despair,
Gently patting the empty street of life
In search of hope, alone and forgotten,
Like my heart, abandoned. Dead, and rotten.
Poor is the soul that must deal with such strife
Yet all must search for someone who will care.

Will the rain ever stop, I do not know,
But that day my finally come in the end.
The rain floats down from heaven in sorrow,
Like the only answer for tomorrow.
Such sadness and despair I can be friend,
It seems only that love is my true foe.

    Jacob West

While You Were Away

While you were away, a young girl died.
I thought you might like to know.
I realize you don't know her.
While you were enjoying your life,
she was fighting for hers.

Isn't it funny - our lives can be so different,
yet so much the same - kinda makes you think, doesn't it?

It just doesn't seem fair.
But, one thing we can be sure of,
wherever our lives take us,
God will protect and give us strength in all we do.
His love endureth forever.

So, while you were away,
life called on a friend - Love
Love found the answer.

Think about it.

    David E. Cline

Sometimes My Heart Cries Out

Sometimes my heart cries out in loneliness
Sometimes my heart cries out in content
And sometimes my heart cries out in fear...
...fear of rejection
...fear of suffocation
...fear of losing control
...fear of love
Sometimes my heart cries out in anger
Sometimes my heart cries out in joy
And sometimes my heart sings...
...songs of happiness
...songs of family and friends
...songs of truth
...songs of love
Sometimes my heart cries out in frustration
Sometimes my heart cries out in hope
Sometimes my heart cries out...

...And sometimes, my heart just cries.

    Jackelyn Lauersdorf

My Heart Lies Bleeding

My heart is pierced by Cupid's arrow
I lay bleeding here in this puddle
Of blood and tears and sorrow:
I'll die, dear heart,
If not today, well, then...tomorrow
If you leave me here in agony;
Please be my surgeon.
This sting is more than I can bear.
Won't you please but a Band-Aid
On this poor wounded heart of mine;
It was such a cruel wound
on the morning of St. Valentine.
Cupid pierced me with his poisoned dart
With cruelty he did put a gash upon my heart...
That only you can heal
Please be my physician, love
I have complete faith in you!

Mary Gonzalez

A Symphony

Memories, ideas, thoughts
The sounds of a symphony of colors.
I think about happy times,
Exciting times.
I hear the bellowing noise
Bursting yellow, orange, red.
An almost overwhelming mix of symbols, horns and drums.

It's hard to remember with such loud splashes of color.
Blinding, deafening
Interrupting the memories
The private memories, long since heard.

The gentle willow weeps for me.
Gently singing its green lullaby
Fluttering, swaying to the rhythm of the wind
Oblivious to the noise.

I hear it now
I hear the green - the clear sound of my memories
I hear the symphony of color.

Janet Miller

Shadows

I have seen them on the castle stair,
beckoning me to come forth.
I looked deep into their black eyes and took the dare.

I have heard the evil shrieks,
warning me of what is to come,
naively on the path I keep.

Slowly I approach the door with no handle,
I cannot enter unless they want me to.
A cold wind in the dark corridor blows out the candle.

In the darkness I run, now knowing who they are.
A never ending labyrinth it seems,
they won't let me go far.

I can feel their evil presence.
I am paralyzed with fear
Suddenly — they force my mind to remembrance.

I fight with all my strength but cannot win,
painfully in front of a broken mirror
I see who I am and what I've been.

Your soul is the only chance for help, you will need faith
and strength to battle the demons of your inner self.

Simply Lizz

Passive Racism

Blond hair, blue eyes, I sit in a room with others like me;
  I am talking.
We talk of children and husbands and pets and homes;
  I am talking.
The talk turns to others, not like us, I am quieting.
..."They" do things differently; I am quiet.
..."They" don't watch over their children; I am quiet.
..."They" don't have the same values; I am quiet.
..."They" expect others to do for them; I am quiet.
..."They" do things different; I am quiet.
..."They" aren't like us; I am quiet.
The conversation turns back
  to children and husbands and pets and homes;
I am silent.

Barbara Mulvey-Welsh

Lady Love

I met a lady the other day
  an old friend of twenty years, plus, or so

Where did she come from?
  Where has she been?

She loved me, needed me, trusted me
Lord! I felt like a man again!

I awakened this morning
  depressed, alone and sad

Has she gone?
  Where did she go?
    Will she return?
To love me, need me, trust me again?

Neal B. Anderson

Like Her Quilts

She covered us with love
  Like her quilts; it warmed us every day
  Her love was unconditional
  It embraced us is in every way

She covered us with pride
  Like her quilts; she was so proud of each one
  With flaws and individuality
  We are family, not to be undone

She covered us with humor
  Like her quilts; her laughter was at every turn
  Her greatest humor was at herself
  Something all of us should learn

She covered us with sorrow
  Like her quits; her family is a tribute to her life
  We show wear and tattered edges
  But her "thread" will help us survive

She covered us with quality
  Like her quilts, she fit pieces for a pattern so bright
  True color and character is what she gave
  To create a blanket of warmth and delight

Nance Schultz

Time

The Time was near when he first had thought.
The Time was near when he first had bought.
The Time was near when he started to use it,
The Time was near when he started to abuse it.
The Time was near when he was movin' fast.
The Time was near when he went through the glass.
The Time was near as he lay on the hospital bed.
The Time is gone... now he's dead.

Peter A. Brock

Dreamer

I dream of clear blue skies
Blanketing the land.

I dream of strangers who appear out of nowhere,
Just to hold one's hand.

I dream of walking barefoot together,
On the moist, white sand.

I dream of the days we spent together,
Before you left this land.

Meg Lowery

Sad Hungry Faces

Sitting on a hill top watching cows graze,
as they try to adjust to an awkward cow phase.
The cows are not quiet as they graze about the field,
being distracted by every movement that other cows yield.
If they are too distracted they will not get their fill,
and without a full stomach they will tumble down the hill.
For those cows look forward to a very long way to go,
and without proper nourishment they will never know,
how to survive in a harsh, polluted place,
that has no sympathy for a cow with a sad hungry face.

Bryan Thanner

Quiet Calm

Serenity becomes complete.
My joy is constant,
like seconds on the clock.
Eyes of innocence...
and the time stands still.

If I breathe,
will I lose you in a moment?
So small against my breast...
you are my quiet calm.

Made within my bed of love,
you are now another light within my home.
Warmth upon my soul...another room added to my heart.
My children's quiet calm.

Gail Kaloplastos

Untitled

Crazy people run alone dying with blood
Exposing the terror about a secret killer.
Fear to kill the victim without terror is a failure.
and we encounter hell in death.
We trust a hidden fear of dying,
Alive secret pain like past trust cheating
you by honesty can price what truth speaks out.
Lost in fire we search to stop time.
Alone a dangerous ordeal stalked power to an emotional heart.

John Biel

A Mother's Treasure

As I was cleaning up today
I came across those yellowed torn pages of yesterday
I stopped and read your childish scrawl
And saw the delight you'd had each day.
It's a joyful tearful thing to me
To look back on your childhood, yet know that you've grown.
You've grown in stature, courage, and pride
Yet I still see that little boy deep inside
A mother holds dear every childish endeavor
So close to her heart that she'll always treasure
You as that child even though you've grown
Into that handsome young man.

Martha Pearson

Cushing, OK - 1927

Young boys...two of them...brothers to the core.
Riding like royalty in their hand-me-down clothes.
The oldest smiles with pensive eyes as the younger
mans the reins. They sit astride the buggy
seat of their cart drawn by a goat named Bill.
Their little glory wagon is painted
a red the color of apples and labor.
Its highlights are white that were pain
stakingly applied. The wheels' spokes appear
to be turned by the benefit of accents.
Where are they headed with their cargo of cheese?
The house stands paintnaked in the background
with a crate impersonated wall.
All are remnants of the land rush.

The goat stands still...
these boys are going nowhere.

Debra Gabbard Gibbons

The First Tear

In the eyes of the young
In the eyes of the innocent
One cannot see pain, nor sorrow
For they have not lived it.

In the eyes of the young
In the eyes of the innocent
One cannot see anger, nor jealousy
For they have not lived it.

In the eyes of the young
In the eyes of the innocent
Once can see joy and love
For they have lived it.

But to know when they have faced
The cruel realities of the world
You look deep into their eyes
Until you see the first tear fall in a silent cry.

Nicole Brown

Another Mother's Son

A tattered weary bunch dragged slowly up the hill
only ten left of their platoon and time had lost its meaning.
Days were joined to days, nights to nights.

Buddies coiled 'round each other amid murmurs of fear.
Winds of death swept over them chilling their souls
despite the rising temperature, the choking humidity.

The dying light as the sun settled was quickly replaced
by a ball of fire and a thick haze of smoke as
the small band struggled through the thunder and rain.

In a blinding flash the hill of brown mud turned to red blood.
Amid the muck a young warrior lay drained of color and life
Another Mother's son!

Frances Alwardt

My Love Light

I don't want to look and see
What my man is doing to me
I thought he will always be my love light
Only his love for me was giving me sight
But now I have a feeling in my heart
Our love is drifting and falling apart
Do I give up or do I pray?
I need his love every single day
I've been left to stand still, I'm just here
Waiting for my sight to reappear
For only his love can bring back my sight
Oh Lord, I need My Love Light

Christina Mason

Simple Truths, Boldly Told, A Poem!

So may the march of rhythm and of rhyme
Be cast in norms of old iambic form,
Wrought notable and quotable, each line,
How boldly told, a thought sublime, a Poem!

If I were now to make a sonnet say
Something new, profound, and better put,
Would it appeal to those who must defray
The price of print my little poem took?

It's useless to bemoan our cyber times
Or television's cost of readers lost.
Better that we conjure lasting rhymes
And more important themes for them to host!

These simple truths within my poem hide:
That words may sing and works of peace abide.

Robert E. Gallamore

A Poet's Request

Forgive me
My anger.
I know it's unseemly in one so young
And hardly in need.
What could I know, what have I seen,
To make me so bitter, often so mean?
Does it matter? Don't we all know
Something that chills us right down to our bones?
I don't have to tell you all that personal stuff
Just knowing I'm human is reason enough.
Tell me - don't you think it's better that I'm writing this down?
If I don't get it out here, I'll just spread it around.
Maybe someday I'll mellow and this pen will calm down.
Maybe then you'll be able
To forgive me
My anger.

Heather Person

Heavens Clouds

Sometimes when I look up in the sky I see clouds
in the shape of some kind of animal or person and
other things that died and they're up in heaven.
See I believe there's a heaven somewhere up in the sky.
Maybe it's the way God lets people see these things again.
The world will probably never know but it would
be a real cool science project to try to do for school.
The things I mostly see are animals.
I saw lions, dogs and others.
One day I saw an airplane and it reminded me of Flight 800.
No one knows where heaven is, but I do believe it's out there.
Someday I will find out and maybe, just maybe
I will be in the clouds and be remembered once again.

Jamie L. Everett

Infatuation

When you walk into the room my mind goes
blank, like a chalk board after school. Words
lose their meaning. Suddenly my tongue is
paralyzed, the cause? Paralysis of the Heart.

Your eyes prick my soul leaving me with the pain
of unrequited affection. If I were Don Juan, I
would approach you, but I'm not. So like the fly
on the wall, I go unnoticed and unharmed?

Perhaps it is better to have loved. To have
drank the wine of infatuation and wafted
the aroma of lust. It is better to have loved
than to suffer death by rejection.

Jerome K. Dotson Jr.

Ocean Sunset

In all Earth's beauty, made by God,
Here, no man's feet will ever trod.

Where blue meets blue, and white explode,
A fire will turn, the white to gold;
While white wraps fire, inside her cuff,
Deep silence brings, the calm to rough;
The rough blue breathes, a liquid breath,
Into the lives, of its great depth;
The fire reflects, across the rough,
As if to end, in one great bluff.

The fire once high, now burns so low,
As darkness nears, the fire must go;
As soft blue lies, beyond the white,
Our daylight fades, into the night.

Connie T. Duffell

Journey

I am in a tunnel.
It is dark and
I can't see what is ahead.
The man who cleans is here.
He has asked me many questions.
I have no answers.
I fear,
   for it may all collapse
   then I may have nothing.
The damages to the tunnel are old and unrepaired.
I do see a light.
There is so much to leave behind.
Now I see it.
I am going to reach for it.
I have passed through fire and rocks,
ice and snow,
rain and wind.
I will do it all again.
All to touch the light.

Theresa M. Martin

I Dreamed

I dreamed I saw you standing on the beach
by yourself, all alone.
Peacefully blowing, Peacefully warm.
I dreamed I saw you next to the ice cream stand.
I dreamed I saw you melting my heart away.
I dreamed I met you.
I dreamed I fell in love with you.
Then I realized it wasn't a dream.
It was real.

Jeremiah Prough

Campobello Island (A Sonnet)

The waves of the Atlantic never cease
To pound the mighty Campobello shore.
This island is the photograph of peace
When listening to the deaf'ning waters roar.
The seagulls circle in and out of clouds
That lowly lie and mask the Fundy bay.
The lighthouse shines through fog and bellows loud
To warn the sailors of the rocky way.
A Finback Whale resurfaces for breath
And fills his lungs with pure New Brunswick air,
His massive body dives into the depths
And disappears without a thought or care.
This tiny island off the coast of Maine
Does beckon me to visit once again.

Brooke Davidson

506

Jesus In Your Life

I've come to learn that with Jesus in your life,
all the world is much easier.
When I sing His praises I know that He is pleased.
With Jesus in your life,
you can understand how wonderful life can really be.
It's even simpler than bread, butter, and tea.
With Jesus in everyone's lives,
the world would be a safer place,
You would not have to look and see
anger, sorrow, or sin on one's face.
I know that some people's lives have been tough,
And everything could be a lot harder on one and more rough.
But whenever you look up to God and ask Him to help,
He says to you that He knows what it is
and that it is sin that you felt.
But all you have to do is beg for forgiveness,
And He will give it to you with sure redeemness.

Crystal Lacy

Ma's Blushing Pinks And Daisies

Dreaming of flowing pink material sprinkled with white daisies,
laying on a rough, varnished wooden table.
Gleaming silver scissors laid gently atop,
ready for her art.

Blushing pink fabric, fragile. What will it become?
A masterpiece, like a multiplicity of colors from God,
from the gentle touch of Ma.

Careful planning, ironing, fussing,
the way of a grandmother.

A pattern is formed, gently pinned with great care,
onto the beautiful delicate fabric,
scissors in hand, the cutting is done.

Laborious love hums the sewing machine,
like music on white cumulus clouds,
as she sews away, her quiet serenity.
The needle sewing the words of her soul.

Pins in mouth, brow in frown, sewing away to her perfection.
The humming stops, and a surprise awaits...
A lovely dress appears, like stars meeting the dusky evening.
Made from the loving aged hands of Ma.

Rachel Goldie

Moon Struck

As we stood there under a moonlight night
All I could think of, was what a beautiful sight
Your face was aglow, your lips moist and ripe
Your eyes were like sapphires sparkling in the twilight

As we stood there under a moonlight night
My heart was throbbing, a song of delight
Your body was warm, your embrace so tight
Our emotions would never make it to light

As we stood there under a moonlight night
I could feel your desire, deep down inside
Your body so soft, your kisses just right
Our senses were flowing about to take flight

As we stood there under a moonlight night
The meaning of life so clear and so bright
My feeling for you, becoming harder to fight
A dream come true on a crystal clear night

As we stood there under a moonlight night
Our hearts became one, just around midnight
With feelings of joy, and some of fright
We lay there holding each other real tight

Rodney Taylor

Bedtime Query

Dreams, such perplexing things.
Are they the truth,
Or am I going insane?
The Sandman is clever,
So brief and elusive.
He teases with scenes which are never conclusive.
Will I be dreaming forever?
Will I ever reach the end?
Do people ever dream together?
Is the Sandman pretend?

Brett Alan Michelson

Secrets Unrest

Dedicated to Jenny Lieseke
Secrets lie within us,
our deepest thoughts our insecurity,
sacrilege to the many,
needs to others our loneliness,
like the very sea without flesh,
a desert without powdered glass,
a barren wasteland to contend,
fought so hard is our trifling love,
our souls lay burdened with many outcomes,
regrets to scar us like many cuts,
left to bleed untouched,
our hearts wasted,
becoming like the very sea,
moving endlessly through eternity,
unable to unveil this very sight,
our unrest secrets of Regretful Pride.

Chris Simmons

Grandpa, Grandpa

Grandpa, Grandpa, where are you?
In heaven with Jesus and with me too.

Grandpa, Grandpa, I see you.
In dreams at night and daytime too.

Grandpa, Grandpa, I hear you.
When praying alone like you'd want me to.

Grandpa, Grandpa, you're with me now,
And will be always till I lie down.

Terri Vance

And All Those Broken Hearts

Like a ship that sails down a sea
Like the tides that hunger for the land...
All inventions—such dimensions
and all those broken hearts.
Like a mansion standing tall
Withered and weary and astute.
Like a king and all intentions
and all those broken hearts.
Like the dawn - ageless
Made by time,
Crucified by all His love
and still remembered.
And now—as broken hearts
pass by loveliness,
there's an air of sadness in my eyes.
And now as broken hearts pass by
there's an air of gladness
slowly rising up in the sky.
And hope fills my heart
and all those broken hearts.

Jonathan Francis Debney

Divorced Dad

As I sit here with a pen in my hand,
I feel so tense, like a taut rubber band.
I've got to go to work and make some money
because I now have to pay to see my honey.
My girl's name is Beth and she's six years old.
And she is the one that I long to hold.
I wish she was here just to sit on my lap
or to lie beside me as we take a nap.
She's the most beautiful girl in the whole wide world,
with her big blue eyes and her blond hair that's curled.
I know it's not right, nor is it funny,
'cause I can't see my baby without any money.
Right now it's not good and the outlook is bleak.
I just hope and I pray that I could see her next week.
But as the days come and go, I feel so sad
'cause she now wants to know if I'll still be her Dad.
It's getting hard to keep writing as I'm starting to cry,
but I made Beth a promise, crossed my heart - hoped to die.
I told her I'd love her whether she's good or she's bad,
and no matter what happens, I'm always her Dad!!

Michael J. Laccone

The End

Lonely, Tired, Unvisited, Weary, Worn,

Hurt, Concerned, Prayer, Panic, Upset,
Ambulance, People, Busy, Talking, Action,
Chaos, Equipment, Noise,

Numb, Peace, Quiet,

Shock, Tears, Awkwardness, Disbelief,

Arrangements, Casket, Flowers, Visitors,
Words, Regrets, Familiar, Unfamiliar

Service, Memories, Prayer, Songs, Speeches,
Sermons, Hearse, Outdoors, Weather, Grass,
Dirt,

Quiet, Waning,

Remembered

Forgotten

Jim Davis

Girl Of My Dreams

Oh to dance under a harvest moon
two hearts beating in perfect tune
the angel before me you utter no sound
but look into my eyes as the world goes around

Lost in lust unaware of our travel
spinning away as the night unravels
whirling desires kindle the flame
drunk on your beauty I know not my name

Awakened by the sun
I jump up and scream
the moment ripped from my heart
like awaking to scream

No more to dance
with my heart's desire
no one to quench
the lonely man's fire

Turn on the computer
and what do I see
but the vision of my heart
the girl of my dreams

The Night Hawk

War

This is no time to dwell in vague premonitions
for savage, bestial, city destroyers
are tearing our hearts
and killing our children
we see our creator, yet no comfort
no shade

There is no looking back this time,
no changing of hearts,
nor betrayal of the mind
we must learn to attack with the word of peace
we will rebuild our land in the healing warmth of the sun
and never again shall we see the darkness of tyranny
glowing through our eyes
is a virtue of everlasting proportions
this virtue of truth must stay upon us
for there is no grey,
failure is death this time
by the hand of the greatest destroyer
ourselves

Doron Reizes

Lost Love, Cold Dead

Wandering in golden-lit streets,
    Hundreds of images dance in my head.
Faster still, my broken heart beats,
    Over lost love, that is now cold dead.

Twenty-four-seven my work life went,
    While at home she sat, hurt and alone.
Hours and hours in the work place spent,
    While at home she sat, time with me, none.

That horrible night, when home I came,
    On the sofa she sat, said nothing, just stared.
I asked her what could make it again the same,
    She asked me if I had ever really cared.

Pain in her eyes, while she packed things together,
    Pain in her heart as she looked in my eyes.
Pain in her voice as she said goodbye forever,
    A look in her gaze as if to ask, "Why?".

My heart had then faced its strongest defeat,
    I collapsed and cried on what once was "our" bed.
Faster still, my broken heart beats,
    Over lost love, that is now cold dead...

James Byrd

An Act of Love

Swimming in a vertigo of feeling
all my senses drunk and reeling
    caught in a raging sea of ecstasy
    a union of vulnerable intimacy.

Choreographed rhythms of echoing tenderness
a resonance as real as my aching consciousness
    infinitely more complex than mere excitement
    emotional maelstroms of mutual enlightenment.

In widening ripples a flood of warmth creeps
into my soul the soft burning seeps
    a slow simultaneous opening of sensation
    in tempos of sweetly tortured duration.

With physical telepathy we communicated
the moist perfection of each kiss enunciated
    a sensuous zone between pleasure and pain
    passionately driving my thoughts insane.

To memories of future love we respond
as one we're carried to the edge and beyond
    so very gently floating far above
    the rainbow currents of an act of love.

Curtis E. Crisel

Road Of Life

Yes I walk through life in pain
but I do not hold my head in shame.
It seems to me it's all gone wrong
but I know that I must stay strong.
It feels inside like I've lost it all
and I will stumble but will not fall.
What once was great now lies in dust
I want to rest but go on I must.
It feels like everyone thinks I'm crazy
as I walk the view ahead is hazy.
It always feels like no one cares
for through this walk there are traps and snares.
They think I'm wrong, I think I'm right
down this path there are battles to fight.
It's true right now there's pain and strife
Yet I will continue down the road of life.

Michelle R. Ramos

A Quiet Place

And when I am weary, I must go...
To a quiet place I only know.
I cross a valley and then a meadow...
A quiet place where gentle winds blow.

I gaze an endless sky...
I watch those billowy ships passing by.
They stream through a harbor wide and grand...
Wispy monarchs moving as sky touches land.

Soft breezes flow, lifting my heart...
But I'm with sorrow for I must depart.
I long to watch the Sweetgum's shiver...
Dancing across a pale moon of silver.

Time's fleeing, sands in the hourglass grow...
And wandering in quietly, there's a doe.
Just behind her, saunters a wobbly fawn...
Grazing here, from dusk to dawn.

Evelyn A. Watson

The Kiss

Blowing a bubble really slowly
Imminent, unfulfilled, full of tension
I sacrifice my virgin for the welfare of the village in my brain
Anticipation grows more and more, bigger every microsecond
This burns too hot
Crackling crisp forests like toast
A great globule of desire, swim through it
Virgins are valuable, you know
If geniuses are tortured and unsatisfied
Then beauties are innocents desired
When will the big, unusual hands come
To pop this thing
Am I a book that won't be read for fear of what's inside?
I'm waiting at the doctor's needle,
wondering if beforehand is the best part....

Julie Prince

Words

Words that are spoken with kindness and love
are guided through us by our creator above.

Words that are spoken with bitterness and hate, I know
that they come directly from the devil below.

Each time we speak a choice will tell
Whether our words will be from heaven of hell.

Robert L. Daniels

You Left

I still remember the day you left us.
The day you walked away from all your friends.
You made us all cry.
And you did it because you thought your life wasn't good.
Being on the football team,
Having lots of friends.
To me that sounds like a good life.
But it wasn't the way you wanted it to be.
You could have changed that.
We would've helped you.
Why?
Why?
Why did you have to die?
Why?

Michelle Garrell

Denny's

I eat out a lot...alone,
coming on to all the waitresses.
They only talk to me because it's their job.
Tolerating me for a tip.

Coming on to all the waitresses is
such an obvious plea, yet
tolerating me for a tip
is really all I ask.

Such an obvious plea, yet
often I go unnoticed.
It's really all I ask...
you see I have no friends.

Often I go unnoticed, but I keep on trying.
They only talk to me because it's their job.
You can see I have not friends, so
I eat out a lot...alone, but always hopeful.

David Chitwood

Boolabu

Jumping after the beans have been lit in the underside
of the shark's belly.
And when the time did 'vrive for the mennunman to swivel
their grivel in the elixir of the womantides
They verily cried unto them the sanctimproofs of the diatribes.
Farcifically, when the callerious fanctijiffs
Beat their hoary chests in jest
We have once again been granted the receipt of life.
I have often ponderized the intifiation of the infectuality
of these facts.
As I cast my clear and shiny lorbits across the sea of Vernalou
I am full of the pregnations of the journey
Into the land of the Boolabu.

LaVonda R Staples

Sea of Distress

The day is dusky and filled with thick fog
spreading. The sea now undulates. Raining
is persistent and manages to clog
large reservoirs. The still winds, rest. Raining
finally fading away into mist.
A boat floats in the sea, rocks back and forth
as the waves surround it. Winds quicken mist,
making all of the quietness abort.
The boat struggles after, in night's abyss,
groping for strength, swaying from left to right,
tumbling, as winds prod it to go amiss.
It's also windward with no help in sight.
After not giving up, the striving boat's
sure then, better able to find the shore.

Angela Liburd

Here and Then

Today I sit and watch you with all the love a heart
cannot hope to contain, yet somehow does.
I knew then, when I met you, that I could have been
something more, something else, if only years before
in lost youth we had crossed paths.
Perhaps, perchance, I could have been the One
that set you free of a patterned life, the One
you might have defied traditions for.
But here, with all the obstacles of what has
been and gone, I am a slight, nice
distraction
nothing less, nothing more
still you persist, to speak, to smile,
to imagine, once in a while,
That here I could love or believe in you
because you needed me then.
But now I dare not ever let you know I could.

Rene Aharoni

The Singer In Eden

Seen from outside, the house was perfect:
brass quail topped faucets where a twist of hand
turned the moist metal beak due West indenting
the palm and drink spouted (like Moses tapping
a rock) cold, cold iron & copper scented wellsprings.

Tricycles with tinseled handlebars posed atop
jewel-clean aggregate concrete walkways.
Two Siamese spat under polished bureaus then
skulked forth to glare, hour by hour, through eleven
windows. A cupped-hand portal made seeing inside clear:
wingback chairs shouldered silk jackets, Waterford gleamed
rainbows onto the gleaming Steinway where a metronome

echoed like a click-beetle. The Bible, opened to Genesis,
released a moth which fluttered around the red silk bookmark.
Oh, you did not want to stand outside forever!
You waited, knowing the door would at last open and you
could cool your cheek on granite, polish your fingers on
the piano, listen to the soothing rumrumrum of madam's Singer
inventing a shirt bordered with roses & never outgrown.

Sean Brendan-Brown

Everlasting Love

I pray dear God each night
For guidance to do what is right
Look back at all I've tried
And the tears that have been cried
Taught to live with pride
My feeling I must hide
For my children - strength to provide
I take each day in stride
Always hoping no one can guess
The aching of my loneliness
My faith sustains me
And makes me see
The wonderful hidden mystery
That what you create
Nothing can separate
I know that together we still walk
In a very special way
For your spirit lives in us every single day

Joan Choma

You

I've always thought of you as pretty;
Your presence means the world to me.
I am not asking you for pity,
I'm asking you to stay with me.

You've stripped away all my defenses;
My heart is laid bare at your feet.
With you I'm willing to take my chances
You've chained my heart, but set it free.

I'm victim of my indecision;
My self-worth crushed beyond repair.
My mind is being ripped asunder
Conflicting feelings bring despair.

I must discover your true feelings;
Before I crumble soundlessly.
Loneliness isn't edifying
That's why I want you here with me.

Ruben Cade Carter

Nature

You can hear it coming over the top of the mountain
The sound is like a melodic chord in G
It moves from tree to tree with orchestrated motion
Moving limbs and leaves with tremendous ease

If you listen to its tones as it nears you
A noticeable rhythm can be heard from above
Mother nature creates her own highway on cue
And her travel flows with the grace of a dove

The beauty of Mother Nature is her many diversities
She changes the weather on time with much vim
And she still retains many of her mysteries
But what would we do on earth without the wind

Caesar Valdes

Waiting for a Green Light

For approximately fifty six hours of our lives
we are controlled by a box held high
above us, taunting us with
such colors as red and
yellow and green
meaning stop
speed up
and
go

Tom Davenport

Caught In The Middle

As I lie here with tears in my eyes
I gather my thoughts and realize,
At times I feel as if no one cares for me
and that is one thing in life that scares me.

I cry myself to sleep at night
But always in darkness, with no light
I cry out loud hoping someone will hear me
Maybe it would comfort me to have someone near me.

I love my family and they love me
but why can't they see what it's like to be —
the middle child.

Tammi Lean

My Golden Years

My golden years are here at last.
And I just sit,
And think about my past.
Events for fifty years I recall.
But yesterday morning,
I can't remember at all.
I need a hearing aid to hear.
And still the words,
Don't sound too clear.
My eyesight gets worse,
With each day that passes.
I need my specs to find my glasses.
My bill from the dentist,
Was out of sight.
Ten thousand for dentures,
That never fit right.
When I walk a block,
My feet start to swell.
My golden years,
Are worse than hell!!!

Sheila Fallick

Books Of History

Bring forth the books of history,
The pamphlets of death and grief.
Go fetch the papers of learning.
Reach for the scrolls of the seas.

Give me your eyes and ears tonight,
To share the moments of the past.
I want to teach you compassion,
To reach you and make it last.

Bring forth the books of history.
Adjust the lamp, it's getting late.
Read the books of lasting wisdom.
Understand man's timely fate!

Jann A. Gillespie

Time

Today's a day
For all to see
Because tomorrow
Has been set free

The time you spend
Spend it well
Because tomorrow
Will always tell

Time is something
That's oh so grand
Because you hold every single minute
In the palms of your hands

So just be wise
Of how you spend it.
Because in days to come
You will soon be in it.

Cynthia M. Morrison

Life Is A Game

Life is just a game
Everyday is not the same
That is why life ain't lame
Life is just a game
Some claim fame
Some claim shame
We are all the same
What makes us different
Is how we play the game

Christopher Byers

Comfort To My Child

Hush my baby,
Don't you weep.
Our Father is good,
That's why I must sleep.

The tempest's great rage
Lurked quietly by.
Like a thief in the night,
It did not pass me by.

I am well my dear child.
Don't fret because I'm gone.
I'll walk with you daily.
I'll never leave you alone.

Keep faith in Our Father.
He'll never let you down.
Though the burden is heavy,
In him peace can be found.

So hush my baby,
Don't you weep.
Our Father is good,
That's why I must sleep.

Reba A. Gates

Mountain Brook

Winding up the mountainside,
Shining waters reflecting sunlight,
Spraying droplets like diamonds,
Leaping fish were rainbows,
Twisting, turning in the air.
Flowing over stones and pebbles,
Creating sounds like splash and splash.
Babbling over random subjects,
Reaching a waterfall.
Cascading down for only a few feet,
Hitting land again.
Coursing between the banks,
Passing through a dark tunnel,
Reaching light again,
Flowed the majestic mountain brook.

Danny Herres

Flower By The Wayside

A TINY FLOWER...

placed among the stones,
near the tar and oil
along the roadway
on a hot summer's day.

A FLOWER BY THE WAYSIDE...

carefully displayed
an acute contrast
to bleak surroundings.

...I wanted to pluck it out

   ...My hand stopped short.

IT WAS LIKE ME...

placed among the stones,
near the tar and oil
along the roadway
on a hot summer's day.

A FLOWER BY THE WAYSIDE...
carefully displayed
an acute contrast
to bleak surroundings.

Colette Hughes

Free Spirit

I walked across an open field
Thinking about my life;
Of all the things that happened
And caused me so much strife.

I watched a pony run around
Just kicking up his heels;
I stood there as though hypnotized
And wondered how it feels.

No cares, no worry and no stress
No thoughts to cause me pain;
Just wind and clouds up in the sky
And a drizzle of Spring rain.

To frolic all around with glee
So wild and oh so free;
Then wished with all my heart and soul
That it could just be me.

Judy Irene Stewart

The Time Is Now...

If you are ever going to love me,
Love me now so I can know,
The sweet and tender feelings,
Which from true affection flows.

Love me now,
While time is running,
Please don't wait too long,
Forever I am in your heart,
Please do not let anything go wrong.

Our love is stronger than marble,
Plus any stone or rock.

Hug me now and forever,
Until our life is through,
Hug me now, much too long,
For all I need is you!

So if you are ever going to love me,
Love me now, so I can know,
The sweet and tender feelings,
Which from true affection flows.

Eileen A. Lim

Jiaya

She takes the hand of Heaven's own
Reaping the seeds that He has sewn
Wander beyond the known
The lunacy the moon has shown

Her angelic hair and cherubic eyes
Conceal the cause of her despise
She flashes a smile but her soul cries
Yet, she wonders how I see her lies

Her pain runs deep and evils creep
As she joins the Devil in His sleep
Beyond the mask of her own fear
I wipe away the solemn tear

Michelle Guerin

Rabbit

Velvet and silk
Fur and glistening eye
Shadows and light
Flickering in and out
Padded paw and silent step
Silver light and frosted tip
Rabbit

Sarah Sander

Pathways

The road I have taken
Is not the one I planned.
Everything is shaky...
Like castles made of sand.

I felt my life was empty
The day I chose this route;
But I had been deceived
By the devil's vicious shout.

Now after years of searching,
I have found that empty hole
Was not the lack of earthly love
But the hunger of my soul!

Patsy R. Laufer

In God's Season

In God's season
   He brought us together
To share a love
   that will last forever.

We built a friendship
   with a strong foundation,
That has lasted throughout
   our trials and tribulations.

Our friendship has grown
   with trust and honesty
Into a very special relationship
   I thought I would never see.

Through winter, spring,
   summer and fall,
Our love will last
   throughout it all.

The seasons will come,
   the seasons will go.
With every passing season
   our love will grow.

Annette Hollingsworth

Victory

Marching up a mountain,
Coming down a hill;

Victory at last was won,
But is it ever real?

Seeing the cries of fellows,
The agony and heartbreak inside;

Wishing it was over,
not yet ready to die;

Dreaming it's finally over,
But is it really done?

The green pastures darken
By the clouds of death;

In war, nothing's ever won,
Victory is the end.

Julie Leven

My Dad TheGolfer

He can count higher than I can,
His favorite number is four!
You can tell he's got more in store.
He likes to tease me all the time,
To me he's one of a kind.
A hole - in - one Dad.
My Dad the golfer

Sierra Fulmer

Untitled

A short span of time, just part of
   one's day
How long can it last; am I
   holding my breath?
The rain floods down. Fog settles
   onto the ground
Turn after turn; have I lost
   my way

The tires drift slightly, wet
   leaves will not hold
The hill rises sharply, mud is
   over the road
Turn left, then right - no!
   sharp left again
One moment in time. There'll
   be no more turns

Jude Meyer

Life

Life is great but often short.
If you live in a house or in a fort.
There's one thing that you must know,
That sometimes you just have to let go.
They'll always be in your heart,
Whether you are or not smart.

Lori Rescigno, age 11

The Long Dance Of Love

Love is like one long dance
   twirls, dips and whirls
Staying with the tempo
   never losing eye contact
Knowing when to step lively
   and when to step lightly
Keep dancing for life
   never lose the beat
Love your soul mate fiercely
   never lose your grip
Climax into the grand finale
   of life, love and dance
Never come down from the ultimate
   high and exhilaration of
The long dance of love

Brenda M. Davis

The Rapist

I can't understand why
Why he chose me you see
I thought my actions were right
But they can't have been obviously

The night in question is vague
I feel my memory has gone
Just to think I pulled the trigger
They said it was very wrong

Realizing I should have waited
I missed and hit the wall
Confirmed by the law
My actions were not small

The rapist deserved all he got
He should now be terminated
But because of me I missed
As I was a little intoxicated!

L. M. Suter

Snow

The snow falls gently past the window
No uniformity looking into the night
It almost looks the snow on TV
But there is no sound
The only sound is that of my breath
And the beating of my heart
The view will almost hypnotize
Takes me to a state of nothingness
All thoughts and feelings are gone
The only one that remains is numbness
The numbness if being nothing!

Joseph R. Schmidt

Blinking Nights Of Light

Looking at city lights from high on a hill
give me a sensation of bring so nil.

The lights linking red, blue, pink,
green and white keep blinking off
and on all during the night which
in my minds eye is a beautiful sight.

Yes with the stars over head and on
a clear night the lights of a town
can be a welcoming sight.

For a person like to me to get high
on a town is simply to look at
the shiny lights all around.

David S. Dayhuff

Compulsion

I will not write again today
to many things to do
The house, the yard, some shirts to mend
to mention just a few

But thoughts compelling push me on
with such insistence till
I stop - pick up the pen and then
a few more lines I fill

Dorothy Duggan

Balance

Like a cyclist's wheel
balanced on a tight rope
We move through the time
of our living
And seek the reason
for being that which we are
The joy and sadness
Happiness and sorrow
The time to love
The pain of love lost
The circle of life
young to old
A time of innocence
The maturity of reason
We balance ourselves
somewhat precariously
Reach out
to grasp what we must
And believe we can continue
this journey called life

William H. Thomson

Nothing Of Any Consequence

Who will care
Eons hence
Of oil, hoyle
Tin foil
Of gold, silver
Or pence
It just won't make any sense
Gaping gaps
Mishaps
Other traps
Will elapse
With no universal collapse

Paul J. Giorgiole

Afternoon Delight A Poem At 3:30

Chickadee, Titmouse, Red Top Finch
All fly in to take a little dip.
Cat bird to number one
What will he see?
A cardinal does a touch and go
Too many here for he.
Latest addition, much to my surprise
The orange and black
The Oriole,
The bathing beauty prize!

Mitzie A. Salem

Writing Letters

I'm separating my thoughts,
carefully
as I do the addresses of friends.
Anyone would think
it was the first of the year.

I search,
until all the corners of day
leave the house.
A dim lamp and a desk
is all that is left.

No stamps
in the top bureau drawer.

It does not stop
this hollowing of tunnels.

Anne Campbell-Van Dyke

Heaven In My Arms

She has told him lies, and
She has told him truths,
Even if she never said a word.
And I must mend,
The damage she's done
Before he can see we are one.

He allows me to stroke
His dark, dark hair;
For truly, he lets me comfort him.
And in his tears,
I see the past,
And all that she has done.

I hold him close as
Dusk turns to night,
And he begins to sob again.
His tears run down my arm,
Like raindrops after a storm.
And now I've got
Heaven in my arms.

Christine L. Bernards

Alone

Snow covered trees
Dead beneath the white
Thick gray clouds
Letting in no light

Unforgiving cold
freezing all at hand
The old weakened sun
Cannot warm this land

A jagged rocky cliff
Like a heart turned to stone
This is where you left me
Standing all alone.

Angela Rando

Mother

I go to my place in the woods
to hear our Mother, to feel her

There's a giant white pine
near the sparkling flow
in May, cool and moist

She adorns her children
in velvety moss coats.
I seek you out, my constant rock

You, amongst all your neighbors
I've fallen in love with.
Your feet anchored endlessly

In the flow
constantly cleansed, intended forever.
Who before has had this pleasure?
I ponder, I wonder.
If, and most likely will come
the money changers
killers, disguised as developers

I will fight them with all it takes
for Her life; and mine

Steve Quetti

My Sweetheart

Your lips are roses
With a flavor of sweet wine.
As your hair glows
Your sparkling eyes shine.
Your figure is like no other,
The curves are just right.
My heart melts like butter,
When I'm with you at night.
You are a goddess
From the heavens above,
But sent to earth
For me to love.
I will love you with all my heart,
Nothing in the world
Could make us part.
Like the diamond ring
That bonds us together,
My love for you
Will last forever.

Thomas Minnich

Untitled

Me, you,
Our bodies together as one.
Now and forever we will be one
Anywhere and everywhere.
Us

Jessica Brothers

My Friend

You've been a listener...
    When I needed to talk.
You've been laughter...
    When I needed to laugh
You've been a smile...
    When I needed to smile
You've been hugs...
    When I needed a hug
You've been a shoulder...
    When I had to cry
You've been wings...
    When I needed to be uplifted
You've been the spirits...
    When I am down
You've been a companion...
    When I am lonely
You've been my lover...
    But most importantly
You'll always be my friend
    I love you

Dorothy M. Chambers

Tested

Your mind is Tested
Your heart is Tested
Your patience is Tested
Your love for family is Tested
Your courage is Tested
Your strength is Tested
Your shoulders with the weight of the
    world are Tested

Remember this always...
....Give God all your problems
You are a student for God
And God always protect his own
His students never fail
They are just Tested

Sherman E. Simms

Alone In The Dark

Alone in a dark room, I stand
    wondering what's going on
Then all of the sudden a bright
    light shines through.
I stand bathing in the warm,
    comfortable light, wondering where
    it's coming from.
And then all of a sudden it disappears.
But for some reason I know that
    it will be back, to make my life
    full again.

Melissa Morgan

Life

Life is a road of uncertainty
not knowing of our fate.
A fear, a shiver and wondering,
why no man can make time wait.
We can't take back our yesterdays
nor borrow from tomorrow.
We must embrace this sunshine
dare not we dwell in sorrow.
Accept each day as if a gift
And scatter love and laughter.
That after our final sun has set
Somehow we'll be remembered thereafter.

Dee Price

So?

Does beauty show bluest
    When hid by the sky,
    When blanketed by sea,
    Or blinded by eyes?
Do true feelings exist
    Just to define ecstasy,
    To explain the red rage,
    To proclaim you as free?

No! - (I stand in awe of the truth
    With the lies,
    In awe with the blank page
    Of what no one can write)

And all the posing of art
    Cannot do the moon right
    Nor any tune play the breeze
And not a word -
    Nor the leading detergent
    Can go whiter than white

Robert Lombardi

Into The New Millennium

Limit not the imagination
To an endless sky
This world not alone
Many a moon
Many a sun, many stars
Await us, beyond the endless sky.

Hold us not 'O' Imagination
For we captive thoughts,
Some may think, we dreamers
When we truly, captain thoughts.

Created by creation itself
We are born to create
We are beings blessed, imagination
Time shall unfold that
Death we are too,
Yet under disguise, alive.

Fear not 'O' believers
Your help comes from
An eternal God
A timeless God

S. P. Shafi

Untitled

If a house could talk
What would it say?
The stories and laughter
The children's frolic and play

The old folks so wise
With their quiet way
The memories and dreams
From a by gone day.

The days filled with toil
Heartaches and pain
Of courage and strength
And growth and gain.

Of music that swells
Through the house like a breeze
Lightening the heart
Turning thoughts to ease.

If a house could just talk
We might hear it say
The Father watches over you
By night and by day.

Florence Dunlap

Mom

Your wisdom floats
down from heaven
into my mind and heart,
helping me to make
the right decisions,
the right choices
for the road that
I've taken in life.
If you were alive
beside me,
I would not have listened
as I do now.
You went to heaven
and left me here
to miss you...
still, you show up
all the time, and I listen.
I know you're there.
I know you are watching...
and guiding me... Like an angel

JoLee J. Fassler

True Love

Love is it blind? Or something
that can drive one out of mind?

Love sees no color, nor does
it recognize age - so why with
time does it fade?

Love is an appreciation and
respect of one's differences - a sharing
of dreams - and similar experiences.

Love is an understanding of one's
individuality - the desire for
independence while having mutuality.

Love can be found if one looks
from within - this is how true
love- truly begins.

Love brings together people of
all kinds - so if one can realize
true love - one can find this true
love, is by no means blind.

Tracy Ann Finch

I Will Always Love You

You mean so much to me;
I can't bear to let you go
The sadness you couldn't see;
The hurt you didn't know.

The happiness that I felt
Would never be there again.
My heart would just melt;
Our love would never mend.

You would leave in a day,
And I would stay behind.
The words we couldn't say;
I didn't really mind.

Our last day together,
The worst day of my life;
I tried to think of something clever,
Maybe I could be your wife.

I just want you to know,
I will always love you.

Rebecca Delmez

Untitled

I do not understand
    Why people don't like sunshine
    Why stars shine so bright
    Why grass grows so fast.

But most of all
    I do not understand
    How some people are mean enough
    To laugh at the less fortunate
    And act like it's nothing at all.

What I understand most are butterflies
    They are beautiful
    And they can fly freely always.

Jamie Hall

Our Wish For Tomorrow

Our wish is that we
can have a safe
and peaceful world.
People should
forget their
differences and
be allies with
one another.
We wish more
countries would
sign peace treaties.
If we all do a little
we can do a lot.

Gerard LoVerde

Joseph DeAngelis

Folded Folk

Put-away towels on a shelf,
the Folded Folk wait
on other things important,
priorities laying on top.

Thirsty, day follows day,
color-striped and solid,
the Folded Folk wait
for events to unfold.

Touched briefly, held close,
snuggled, warm and tear-damp,
the Folded Folk then
are wadded and dropped.

Fresh-laundered, put away,
the Folded Folk, wait
in a quiet secluded place
at the bottom of the pile.

Until loose-threaded, barren
ravel-edged with tangled parts
their purpose gone, they,
the Folded Folk, disappear.

Marlene K. Lemmer Beeson

Freedom

Honorably, they lay,
Row by row,
Day by day.

Youthfulness was their foe.
Wantfulness is our way.

Solemnly, they lay,
Row by row,
Day by day.

Sara I. Billeter

A Family Of Three

You said a sister was your wish
a baby brother wouldn't do
again the angels listened, son
as they often do to you.

Now hold on to her smaller hand.
She's your doting family.
No father in the picture now.
A family of three.

She hangs onto your every word,
tries hard to make you grin,
reaches out if you should fall
and cheers your every win.

I watch you growing closer now
so alike from face to face
not needing me around to bond
if I ever leave this place.

The smaller one will follow you
through happiness and strife.
Friends and lovers come and go
but she's your friend for life.

Susan Austin

Courage

I had the courage
To do what I was afraid of

To go ten feet
In the air

To look down
From way up there

I got scared
Ten feet high

It felt like I could
Feel the sky!

I saw my Dad
Down there below

I could tell he was proud

But I couldn't jump
I was too afraid

As I came down the ladder
I realized
I had done what I was afraid of

Mya Marie Steadman

Sun Set

If I could paint a picture
I'll do it right away
I'm looking at the sun set
And please God let it stay

I've never seen such beauty
And it's all there just for free
All we need to do is look
To enjoy the scenery

The colors they keep changing
From red to pink then blue
I'm wondering if you're looking dear
As we so often do

Now night is fast approaching
The pink clouds fade away
Tomorrow we'll watch the sun rise
On another bright new day

Patricia A. Dabbelt

A Place Dreamed

A ground level look
at the grains of sand
Seem as infinite as the universe.
But observed again
on autumn's cool afternoon
It is the convergence
of all that is secure.
This fragile nirvana
on the edge of totality
Where one simple life
comes to weight
No city so vast
or countryside view
Can compare
to this scene by the sea

James Jacobs

An Unknown Memory

A warm day,
A sunny day,
A good day for a young girl,
Put to rest.

Once a warm blood ran through her,
Bringing life.
Then a cold blood came,
And took that life away.

So now she rests,
Unharmed,
Untouched by life.

She is an unknown memory.

Sara E. Barge

My Rose

There was a rose so sweet and pure
Her beauty to behold
I picked her from the bramble bush
And took her for my own

Through life we went together
Down every bumpy road
Until our Father called for her
And left me all alone

Now I walk these roads so lonely
And think of her each day
And wish that she was with me
To help me on my way

But when I am at my lowest
And I think I can't go on
I hear her voice whisper
Someday you will come home

And then we'll be together
So happy we will be
In God's greatest kingdom
For all eternity

Bob Massey

Answers

When you think you're being hassled
And your world seems nothing but trouble
Don't let it burst your bubble,
And leave you dismayed
There are other paths to follow
More people still to be met,
And there is all day tomorrow
That hasn't been touched yet.

Alfred E. King

No Longer The Feeling

The glowing light has faded
That sparked the tender fire
In the hearts of the grasping lovers
No longer the feeling
Of warmth and care
The remains are but fragments
Of despair
It is no longer between them
Their hearts have grown weary
From the torment they've shared
The lovers depart to a new life
Hoping to find what they lived and
Loved for in the past
They must find a way to mend
Their worried souls
Before all else fails
If they find not what they hope for
Then their only choice is each other

Kelvin Kettle

Unending Life

A crystal drop hangs. . .
Then trickles down. .
Dispersing light upon the ground. .
Then runs away into the earth. . .
To again another birth. . .
And pushes upward toward the rays. . .
And after many day. . .
Its leaf has formed a tiny cup. . .
To catch another crystal drop. . .
Of rain to trickle down and
Cause new grain. . .
Again. . .
Again a drop of rain. . .

Cynthia J. Clark

Moments Of Doubt

What shall I do when
My world become so blue

My feeling of sadness
hurts deep within

My lost of interest
color my thought
my anger feels like a shot
My happiness feels like a tiny dot.
My tears pour down like rain
will I ever be the same
For I have endure so much pain
will I stop and take a lot
no I will go and say not
for life is worth living and
giving, instead of dying and
not trying.

Jacqueline O. Williams

"Thoughts of You..."

Thoughts of you
And years of past
Where are they going

Shards of glass
Raining down
Tearing, ripping
Away my skin

I see my soul
I see you

Anjelle

Don't Get Mad!

I said "You fly!" He didn't blink.
The worst insult that I could think.
I guess he didn't realize
   the habits of those pesky flies.
As I inferred, were he a fly,
   I'd swat at him as he flew by.
He spreads disease, the ugly cuss.
He's like the air...ubiquitous.
The food he eats with raspy tongue
   corrupted flesh and steaming dung.
His place on earth, to my disgust,
   reducing garbage back to dust.
Now a fly that he's grown up
   he was a maggot as a pup.
He crawled around in garbage cans,
   or Port-o-Lets, or old bed pans.
It seems a harmless name to cry,
   but think of all that you imply.
So, when he makes you hit the sky,
   don't get mad. Just call him "Fly!"
   Ned Potter

Remember Me

Sometimes when I'm here at night,
   Staring at the stars so bright.
Thinking of your love so dear,
   Knowing that I'll never hear.
The words we said so long ago.
   Yes, that's right, I love you so.

We've lost our way these many years,
   though we shed so many tears.
We said goodbye on that night,
   knowing that our loves not right.
I hope that you've found happiness
   for all the love I know we'll miss.

Sometimes when you're there at night,
   staring at the stars so bright.
Think of me, I love you so,
   In your heart you'll always know.
No one in this world could be,
   closer in thought to you then me.
   Sandra Barron

Awareness

Does it take a special talent
To write poetry and rhyme
Life is made up of our senses
And the passing of time
You don't get a second chance
To record what is sublime
So open up your heart today
It's certainly not a crime
To peer out of the window
And see the grass as green as lime
To hear a far off church bell
That seems to endlessly chime
To feel the cool breeze upon your brow
That's in the ladder you climb
To inhale the fragrance of a rose bud
That even the best can't mime
To touch a thing of beauty
Can cost less than a dime
To feel good about yourself my friend
Shows life is in its prime
   G. Baughman Reid

The Birth Of My Friend

The birth of my friend,
It happened one cold January day
She was a gift from heaven
My little bundle of joy.

She was never unhappy
She never complained
Oh my little friend
She was my joy and happiness
In my world of pain.

She was so grown up
In her little head
She was my best friend.

Today she is a woman
And she is still my best friend
This daughter of mine
In my world of pain
My best friend.
   J. Fina Shelton

Love

Love is a feeling you get when you like,
Love is a word you use when you write.
Love is an adjective used to add color.
Love is a phrase you say to a lover.
Love is a kiss to show that you care.
Love is someone who is always there.
Love is a big part of "I love you",
Love is a tune you sing when your blue.
Love is a smile used when your around,
Love is something worth having around.
Love shared between two,
Love is the feeling I have for you.
   Misti R. Stringham

To Friends At Christmas

When lengthened days and hours flee,
With presents wrapped
Beneath the tree,
I cherish moments late at night
To be alone with thoughts that might
Escape me during busy days
A time for me to offer praise
To Him who gives us joyous dreams
Of Love and Peace, and who, it seems,
Could use our help
In making sure
That someone thinks to help the poor
To aid the weak, make strong the sad,
Help us share when we are glad.

May you and yours abound with joy
And may God grant to every boy and girl
His gifts of Love and Grace
Our hearts to be their resting place.
   Marita S. Hettinger

Child

Look at the Heavens
trace the patterns in the sky
look into your soul
and ask yourself why
look at those around you
see their joy and see their pain
ask yourself and question
and know you're not the same
why did you change?
Child
   Katharine Donelson

Sometimes That's Me

I am an Eagle flying
with pride and streaming
alone in the wind.

You are a friend
I try to help you any way I can.
I put you under my wing.

You take your inner
beauty with you.
Outer beauty, you make a
hell of a friend.
   Carl Stewart

A Message To Be Related

Hello central,
Please give me heaven
I have a son up there.
Will you tell him how much I miss
him and how much I'll always care?
I miss his calls from Fresno, with
all the fun things he would tell
About his boys and wife Shirley,
They got along so well
It was wonderful being with
him all the time when he was ill.
I asked God to take care of him
I'm sure he always will.
Thank you - bye, bye, for now.
   Blanche Folland

Across The Miles

Across the miles so far away,
   I feel as though we've gone astray.

Our love was strong when I left,
   I often wonder what is left.

You know I love you, and I do,
   but you must show it too.

Across the miles and far away
   a letter from you would make my day.

In my heart I yearn for you,
   not to mention that I miss you.
   Ricky F. Rounds

One Grain Of Me

I tried to push this sadness away
Inch by inch it grew farther
Miles I walked without stumbling
Days I laughed without tragedy

But one morning I wake up lonely.
It creeps up Yard by Yard
to inhabit the steps I take,
to soil the peace I feel
and separate my eyes from my smile.

I lay down crying
to daydream of sleep I cannot taste
and joy that I can't remember.
So I pray,
because God has always listened
and noticed my clenched teeth,
my sagging heart
He will answer
and for miles I'll think I'm walking
when really I'm being carried.
   Peggy Kelley

My Dolls

Dolls are for little girls
to let their imagination
take over and pamper,
change, feed and love them

Dolls are talked to, spanked
taken for walks, put to bed
for pretend sleep so their
busy mothers may rest

Dolls kept during the little
girls' growing up years are
displayed in honor of their
unique beauty and age
Patricia A. Neal

Untitled

You are so beautiful
I am so hung over
cliches and excuses howling
like domesticated dogs
in this city
this heartless and unhappy city
you and I are so alone
still
so hungry for privacy
I spit in the public eye
sing for sweet paradox
my darling
I swear I will cease
cursing the course of our life
Don Markey

Sum Of All

The addled thoughts
of a random mind
(where expiration ends
and time begins)
do flee the sun
and kiss the moon.
For in the void of blank,
(the padded rooms
do fill the hall)
the eye does see
the whole of none,
the total sum of all
(while guards do sleep,
and children call)
Richard R. Curren

Winter Winds

As they wail
Winter's cold biting winds
Blow those brittle branches
Upwards to meet
The gray flowing clouds
And the dry leaves
On the bitting winter winds
Like dark brown sails
Blow over the choppy waters
And the waters
Catch those dry leaves
And carry them away.
Peggy E. Yarbrough

It

It isn't what you say that counts,
It's what you do and how you live
It isn't what you get that counts,
It's what you're able and do give

It isn't monetary values that count,
It's principles applied day by day
It isn't right to work and work
And never learn the joy of play

It isn't opportunity that's rare,
For all who want it, it's there
It isn't what you have that counts,
It's how you think and compare

It isn't what you wear that counts,
It's that which dwells within
It isn't right to gauge or judge,
For we are not without sin

It isn't hard to be happy,
When your life you want to give
To make this world of ours,
A happier place in which to live.
Mary E. Sabato

A Prayer For Liberia's Crises

Lord, bring this crisis
to an easy and peaceful end;
our hearts are heavy laden with
the thoughts of fearfulevil things;
dangerous and harmful,
cruel and wicked enough
for other creatures and humans,
are there fleas? let them flee;
with out national transgressions;
with our deeds, seeds and weeds;
with our drawbacks and shortcomings;
let us lead a better life
adopt a better mode of thought
after these crises.
Pianapue Kept Early

Joy

In my life I've many things
Sang songs of love and jelly beans
Set free a world of pink balloons
Laughed out loud at fun cartoons
Dreamed dreams of hope and teddy bears
Stumbled headfirst: A dragon's lair!
Breathed cotton candy clouds up high
Saw rainbow horses soar the sky
Ne'er once I glanced behind to sigh
Nor looked ahead with tears to cry
For though there's much I've yet to meet
Filled with joy, I am complete.
Alison Hwang

Noah

When I was feeling oh so blue,
Finally my dreams had come true.
A baby was born out of me,
I kissed the small child tenderly
The baby was heavens one joy
The child was a dear, little boy.
My love for him will always flow,
As I watch my little boy grow.
When I think back for when he was born.
Never again will I cry or mourn.
Melanie L. Brandy

The Will And The Way

The will may be the ego
or is it your gut—
maybe it is a trio
of time, trust, and smut.

Words of will are so bitter
short, sassy, and bright—
jewels that shine and glitter
reflections of light.

The way is the heart's domain
of blood, wet and wild—
nothing seen is ever plain
clear, measured or mild.

A deed is the way's yardstick
of progress and style—
dark, daring, dazzling, and slick
a mask or profile.

Beware of that old clichT
about way and will—
the world is one of blue-grey
wide, vast, lonely, chill.
Beautiful Sky Eyes

Freedom Flies High

Startled -
   The birds cry - and fly,
High above they soar,
   Constantly alert, they glide
Beautiful and graceful.
   Ascending and descending
with the greatest of ease,
   Riding the wind, they skim
the treetops - searching,
   for a place to rest...
At last, they find a perch,
   to settle their sleek frames;
until, once again,
   they're startled - and,
they fly - high.
Regan G. Mulvey

Then And Now

Then I saw you from a distance,
Who you were I couldn't tell,
Now I see you from a distance,
Every part of me turns to gel.

Then thoughts of you were vague,
And dreams of you were short,
Now every thought is about you
Like a constant dream of some sort.

Then you were just a friend,
And we were often apart.
Now I want to see you more;
Whenever near you touch my heart.

Then it didn't matter
What I thought of you.
Now every minute I'm alone
I wish you only knew.

Then it never mattered
What you even thought of me.
Now it matters - and
I'm tired of being free.
Jennifer Rae Swann

Seasons Greetings

'Tis the season
To love,
To cherish friends
Old and new,
To love,
To share with family
And special ones who care.

'Tis the season to touch
Again the lives of those
we love...
'Tis the season to
Give thanks, and
praise the Holy one
   Above.

Dorothy Travis Pumphrey

The Dawn

How Perfect the dawn
The sun lay hidden beneath the hills
Peeking over the clouds
In anticipation
Ascending on humanity
Resplendent in its glory

The sun like a cat waiting to pounce
Teasingly tempting
The cloud playing the game
Reflecting shadows
As the morning awakens

Daylight casting illusions
Shadows in the mist
Morning intrusions
Moon disappearing bit by bit
Cricket add to this luster
Cast a funny spell
As the dawn enfolds
The story that daybreak tells

Vaughan A. Powell

A Magical Winter's Night

Alone here in this room
Staring into space,
I smile as I see
The memory of your face.

The way you held my hand
On that winter's night;
The way you touched my hair,
Nothing felt more right.

For a moment I was lost
In your loving eyes.
Silence filled the air;
A brightness filled the skies.

Never will I forget
The way you made me feel;
The beauty of the night,
The magic that was real.

Lisa Squibb

In A Tiger's Eye

In a tiger's eye you can see fear
and scaredness
In a tiger's eye you can see
fire burning in madness
In a tiger's eye you can see
birds chirping with delight and happiness

Anna Cherry

The Battle

Silence prevails in the darkest hour
A sound that sinks deep into the soul
I block it out, but it's still there
It's warning me to be aware
The feeling seethes into my bones
That of the demons I am told
They come to steal away my heart
To torture me and tear me apart
I scream and scream for help
But no one's near enough to hear
I struggle to fight in this silent night
Suddenly they are gone
The silence is still there
Of the darkness I am aware
My body is bruised and sore
What it was I'm still not sure
Silence prevails in the darkest hour
A sound that sinks deep into the soul
I blocked it out, but it remained
I fought and it left me, ashamed

Jill DeEtte Fuszard

Here I Am With My Friend

Here I am waiting for my friend,
to join me at our favorite place.

Here I am sitting with my friend,
sipping coffee we like so much.

Here I am talking with my friend,
about the misfortune in my life.

Here I am listening to my friend,
about a likely solution to my disaster.

Here I am supporting my friend,
as they tell me of their dilemma.

Here I am helping my friend,
find an answer to the plight.

Here I am in silence with my friend,
as we think of something else to voice.

Here I am laughing with my friend,
because of the jokes we tell.

Here I am smiling again with my friend,
for now problems are forgotten.

Here I am hugging my friend,
since it is time to depart.

Kathy Peters

Dreams

I have lived in my dreams,
Closing my eyes to reality
At least that's the way it seems,
Life is but an endless stream,
that struggles to stay pure,
of this I'm sure.
Look at the future,
forget the past.
We are what we've been,
as other people have seen
Life is a dream,
dreams are but a fantasy,
the world now sleeps,
Let us awake to reality.

Cataldo Nashton

I'll Always Remember You

I believed in you,
but you didn't believe,
If only it lasted a little longer,
I know it would have gotten stronger.
It's a shame it ended this way,
If only it lasted another day
But you got in trouble with the law;
and were put behind bars
you broke a rule
and were kicked out of school.
Now you spend your days
lonely and gray,
And while you're away
I'll always remember
and love you.
If only it lasted another day.

Laura Sanchez

Let Him Go

Since the day you left me
I've never been the same
The tears just won't stop falling,
But I know I'm the one to blame

The words you said so sweetly
Still wonder in my mind
The question if I'll ever get over you,
haunts me all the time

But now I'm living without you
Well life can't get much worse
Even though you've been gone for a while
my heart still really hurts

I'm slowly getting better
though you all ready found someone new.
And now it's over,
But I just can't let go of you

Amanda Reasor

To A Ballerina.....

A slender willow touched by wind,
   Whispers of your grace.
The singing brook and sunlight spin
   Their web of dappled lace
To wrap you in its radiance
   As lissom shadows trace
The beauty of your being
   In this enchanted place.

Dance ballerina. La Sylphide
   Is you as you are she.
Your paean to the muse has waked
   The dryad in the tree.
And waking, weaves her wondrous spell,
   And woodland grasses come to be
A sylvan ballet dancing to
   The rhythm of your ecstasy.

   Ah, Terpsichore, would that thee
   Could make this magic moment be
   Forever.

Thurston Munson

Mirrors

When there's nothing to reflect,
what does appear?
A mirror is only perfect,
when it isn't crystal clear.

Kendall Schneider, age 12

Unwanted?

What have I done, cries unwanted child
My life taken, so violent, so vile

I only came to give you joy
Was I a girl or even a boy?

But it is too late, you will never know
The love that would surround you so

A choice has been made, for you, for me
It cannot be changed, this is Eternity

Now you must live with pain and guilt
This, your future that you have built

As for me, I hear Him calling
A voice so meek, so mild, so loving

Aborted baby, unwanted child
Heaven awaits you, no more denial

As He reaches down from above,
And cradles you in His arms of love

Sandra Kerman

The Angel's Tears

As I sit alone and listen,
to the raindrops falling from the sky,
I try to understand it,
But just can't no matter how I try.
I think of the rain, as tear drops,
Falling from the heavens up above,
Maybe the angels are so sad,
'Cause you were called away from
so much love.
Although he has his reasons,
I'm not sure that I agree;
Only because I want you back,
Here at home...with me!

Debbie Kane

Do You Believe

Do you believe
God took me on a ride up in the sky,
Do you believe
He lectured me on the Bible with pride
I know the Lord is standing right by my side
I do believe in God.
Do you believe
Jesus died for our sins
Do you believe
He will come on earth again.
I pray every day and night
Thanking the Lord for saving me,
Saving you, do you believe.

Do you believe
God chose us as he did His son.
Do you believe
God wants us to live as one
My spirit's filled with the Holy Ghost.
I do believe.

James Robertson Sr.

Censored

Forbidden books in forbidden halls,
Molding, and Mildewing-
within broken walls.

A broken library in a broken city,
Stories gone-
is it not a pity?

Thomas Garcia

A Soldier Reflects (While Dying)

Lying bravely. Stately resting.
No one hearing. No one sees.
See him lying, dying slowly.
Proudly bleeding. Now at ease.

Confident that they'll remember.
Hero actions, they'll recall:
—He Fought Bravely, He Fought Proudly.
For His Country, Gave His All.

Heaven calls now, in the distance.
Piercing silence. Pending dread.
Comrades lying near beside him.
Some lay dying. Most are dead.

Whispered praying, "God have mercy.
Take me quickly. End the pain".
"Proudly, bravely, did my duty.
Valiant Soldier! End the pain".

Recollect now—what they told him—
Just before his eyelids fell.
"This one thing you must remember,
War ain't fun, son. War is hell".

Robert Coley III

Father, Son, Holy Ghost

Father son and Holy Ghost
Bless this bed I lay on
Four corners to my bed.
Four angels to my head.
One to bless.
One to pray.
Two to carry my soul away.

Lord Jesus I hear you calling.
As I awoke today I
looked to the Lord -
And this is what pray -
Thank you Lord for this new day.

Lord majesty from up above.
You carried your son with love -
As Jesus does for you and me
He holds the keys to heaven above.
Amen

Sherly Sebet Reedder

Reveling

I Am Up In A Tree
Looking down to the ground
     Looking out to the sea
     Where I wish I could be

I Lay On The Grass
Looking straight to the sky
     Those clouds floating by
     Are like heaven to me

I Sit In My Chair
Looking straight to the woods
     There a rabbit sits up
     Like he really understood

I Hear An Airplane
So I look into the sky
     But to be up there?
     Oh no, not to fly!

That's Fear For Me Now

     Maybe in the next century
     But No, I Cannot See!

Rowena Young

No Second Chance

It was ninety-one years ago today
In Henderson, Kentucky
The Eblen family found itself to be
Extremely lucky!
A tiny red-haired baby girl
The size of a pound of butter
Was delivered by a happy stork
To a happy dad and mother!
They tucked her into a sugar bowl
To try to find her measure —
They even put the top back on,
But that kid just kicked with pleasure!
After all these years she's still around
So brimful of fun and fire
That that old stork has come alive
Filled with one last desire!
I've heard the Eblens moved away
From that town in west Kentucky —
They feared that stork night come again
And make them "two times" lucky!

Evelyn H. Rice

Untitled

A string around the Christmas tree
Great memories we keep!
Little eyes light up in glee
Though still but half asleep.

Such great dreams we had for you!
Proud as we watched you grow.
Drying some tears and boasting too
Meant more to us than you can know.

You're grown now and far away,
But dreams can travel too
Knowing that in every day
We have many thoughts of you.

So, once around the Christmas tree
Please hand this string in view.
Regardless of where we might be
Each bead proclaims our love for you!

Robert G. Meek

Rusting Away

With a heart of gold
Her story she told.
One of love and lust
That just turned to rust.
Like a precious metal
She lost one more petal.
With her head held high
She breathed a small sigh.
Life to her was so real
More than touch and feel.
To just rust life away
Would never be her way.

Patricia L. McMullin

Seperatance

Yea, of such a noise, she did make,
Her displeasure of my presence —

Sequestered inner rages quake,
Betrayals not quite past,
Yet bowing to the present.

Dignity's indulgent grip,
Upon thoughts never spoken -
Sending me from bed and board,
To wit, a union broken.

D. E. Gayle

Loving You

Loving you is so sweet and dear
You have lighten my world without tears
Morning, noon and night I pray
that your love is here to stay
Our future now depends on you
But you must know I love you too

Look at me and you will see
the way true love is to be
When we can walk the sea shore at dawn
and make real love on our lawn

True love is you and me
and all else is an use to be
You have made my world complete
and loving you is oh, so sweet

Albertha Miller

Time

It comes and goes,
passes us by,
it watched us grow
and made us cry.

It brought us cheer,
and made us sad,
took away our fear
and gave us all we had.

Time may be forgotten,
thoughts can never be,
as for what might happen,
I shall never see.

Ryan Klos

The One For Me

As I look across the room,
what I see,
is what I need.
It's what I dreamt.
She is the one for me.

She's wonderful!
She really cares!
She's always there,
so beautiful,
as I look across the room.

I see the light, the shining light,
of the one I love!
I miss her so much!

Fred Klammer

Your dark form hovers
above me, waiting to land.

Your outstretched wings fold
over my willing limbs.

Your heart beat guides
my breath, your breath fills

my mouth, your black
feathers tremble as they brush

my skin. Rivers flow
from my bones, leaving

them hollow. Crowman,
you envelop me in

the memory of flight.

Telos Whitfield

My Shoe

My shoe, my shoe,
You turn my sock blue.
My foot is wet,
But I still love you.

When I wear boots,
I know you feel bad.
But you're the best footwear
My foot has ever had.

After a few years,
I must replace.
I'll miss everything about you,
Even your dirty shoe lace.

When that day comes,
I know I will regret,
Leaving you behind,
The shoe I'll never forget.

I'll never forget our times together.
I will remember them forever and ever.

Q. Dogg

Thanks

I'm so pleased it isn't me,
Who hears the stumbling on the stair
The fumbling with the lock
The slurred greeting and hushed giggles.
I'm so pleased it isn't me.
I'm so pleased it isn't me,
Who guides undresses cleans
as understanding wanes,
and listens to
Promises, apologies.
While the sour smell
of bile and beer
fills the room.
I'm so pleased it isn't me!

Poppet Hill

A Prayer...

Oh Dear Lord please answer me
This one request I ask of Thee.
Grant my sailor the fairest seas
Good times and comradery.

Bring him home safe and sound
Back from the seas he's traveled 'round.
Bring him home safe and sound
To rest his feet on welcome ground.

Please let him fall not into harm
But let him walk into my arms.
Let him know my love is true
As is the faith I have in You.

So grant me this I ask of Thee
Please bring my sailor home to me.

Amen

Terri Kiley

My Angel

My angel is a teacher
who has taught me how to pray.
She showed me that happiness
is here each and every day.
The idea is to look for it
and never to deny;
That there is power in each of us
to spread our wings and fly.

Jennifer Clark Wilson

The Rockinghorse

Endless hours of pleasure,
Ceaseless amazement at leisure.
Wonderful world, so full
of imagination,
Riding to another town or nation.
Innocence, naivete, and curiosity.
Turn to embarrassment, age,
and busy-ness.
Time spent in ceaseless amazement,
Now wasted on other engagements.
Hours of adventuring,
Replaced by motionless days.
Now neglected and ignored.
Thrown carelessly away,
Nevermore to play,
Upon the Rockinghorse.

Josh Mattix

The Seducer

Eyes of blue watch intently,
my every move and make.
Curious glints...waiting?
I could have told you
'cause I knew.
But then you did too.
I saw,
when you carried me
to the grass,
and laid me down gently.
Frustration welled...
I can read you
like my biography.
Does that scare you?
You and I between a mirror,
catch the same reflection.

Anne Marie Judt

My Commitment

What can I do for you, Lord?
You're everything to me.
I'm not lonely anymore
Since you've shown me life.

You're everything to me, Lord.
It's so wonderful to know you.
So great a feeling to be close
To someone like you.

Many times life seemed so empty.
Now I find life full
And rich and alive and real.
You're so good to me, Lord.

So what can I do for you, Lord?
Please show me the way.
Though life is sometimes difficult,
I know you are with me to stay!

Timothy A. Draime

The End Of Time

I know not the reason why
that everyone must die,
I do know that I must not dwell
on the reasons we are all in hell.
Here on earth we do our penance,
and serve out a life long sentence.
We prove our heavenly worth,
so at long last we leave this earth.

Elaine M. Brents

Irish Rain

Softly sliding, slipping, running,
Enter in the Irish Rain.
 What's that tapping, rapping,
 But the peace it brings.
 Now the sound begins to enter,
 Into every part of me.
 "Come alive!" it softly whispers,
 Windows of my soul so wide.
 Now I know that I am real,
 For I feel - I feel!
Softly sliding, slipping, running,
Enter in the Irish Rain.

Herb Marlow

Love's Conception

Where did the hours fly?
Into that night sky,
As we searched and tested;
Never and always asking, "How?"

Where will we go now?
Now that you know
The curves of my face
And my neck and my nape?

Did you actually see
The depths of me
That I braved to expose
To your scrutiny?

Dare I trust you?
Dare I trust myself?
What will our worlds say
If we tell them there is an "us"?

How will we know
The truth in our hearts from
The needs in our souls?
That wisdom abides in going slow?

Andrea E. Jackson

Unattainable Love

The feelings are so real
But the exchange is not.
Proclamation is impossible
What's the meaning of us?

To meet your mouth in my dreams
Your dream-perfect lips
When I'm forced to wake
The life-knife splits/rips

If only you could visit
Illumination Park with me
We would ride "Repel Reality"
And forever be.

Kimberly A. Dana

Regret

No turning back
I've done what I've done
The blood is on my hands
The price is on my head
They hunt me like an animal
I escape again

Some would call me wild and free
But life itself is a prison for me
I've thrown away my own key
Now I rot away
Forever

Robert F. Weiler Jr.

Passing The Time

Like the Oceans tides
another day passes by
my mind is adrift

The warmth of the sun
a cool breeze across my face
is this but a dream

Look and you shall find
the secret of happiness
within your own heart

I reach for the past
I have dreams for the future
Losing sight of now

A quick view of death
the darkness surrounding me
The alarm clock rings

The bell chimes midnight
Another day has passed
the slate is wiped clean

Steve Pfarr

Our Love

Our love was once...
The brightness of the sun
The blueness of the sky
The greenness of the grass
Mountains so high

Now there is no bright sun
No blue skies
The grass has turned brown
As everything dies

You have your own world
With no love to share
You will always be in my world
I will always love you
I will always care
Forever and always

Patricia Krueger

Hope

 Hope brought a tear today
and left it at the door
 She silently slipped away
and returned to us no more
 We've waited by the window
longing for her form to see
 And finally at the winter's snow
we knew it would never be
 Hope would never come to us
for we never asked her near
 It was for us the single loss
for her last gift was the tear

Robin Bowers

Popcorn

Popcorn is good
Oh so good
Popcorn is great
Carry on a plate
On top is butter
Rice if you please
None left!

Rachelle Barnes

A Journey

Words spoken simply
Secrets to be kept
Trust to be gained
A journey begins...

Words spoken simply
Feelings explored
Memories unearthed
A journey goes forward...

Words spoken simply
Dreams written of
Inspirations treasured
A journey continues...

Words spoken simply
Individual lives touched
Giving one another
A journey to be shared.

Linda S. Zecchinelli

Lost

Your laugh is empty, you repeat yourself
your eyes wander
blankly around the room.
You are so detached
I wonder
could you (the child with the red
balloon, held loosely by
a thread of string) let your soul
slip through your fingers
and wind-blown
float away?
Does it hurt so much to feel?
I have never seen a child smile
who has lost a red balloon.

Nora Kraemer

Cupid And Me

One day I was walking
Down the street,
And looked up and saw Cupid!
He was ready to shoot,
And aiming at me!
I ran, and ran, and ran,
And then I hid.
He looked,
And looked,
And looked.
Then he saw me,
And started to chase me again!

Steven Jones

My Best Friend

The Lord is my best friend,
He is my future and my past,
I will serve him till the end,
Then I will meet him at last,
I was living in sin,
I had so much pride,
The Lord came into my life again,
Now I feel so good inside,
When I close my eyes,
I can see him nailed to the cross,
Then I realize,
No more do I want to be lost,
Never again will I let him go,
For he is my Master,
I love him so,
For me, there are no greener pastures.

Shirley Machann

Without Words

The mind is a novel,
Not viewed in black and white.
A story to be unfolded,
With no pages in sight.

The heart is the reader,
The teller the soul.
Stored back in your head,
It never grows old.

A story that survives,
For as long as you live.
Whether opened or closed,
Follows you to bed.

There's always a beginning,
No particular plot.
With one main character,
Until death does it stop.

Deborah K. Cruise

Someone

I want someone to share with,
All the hurts, the joy, the pain.
I want someone who understands,
Someone who'll whisper my name.
Someone who will hold me close,
Where it's safe and warm.
Someone who'll accept I'm sorry,
If my words do any harm.
Someone to take a walk with,
And count the stars above.
Someone I can share with,
This curious thing called love.
Some to fill the hours with,
Someone to call my own.
Someone who wants to share,
In making a house a home.
I know that out there is someone,
Made especially for me.
Some to share and love with,
Til the end of eternity.

Karima

Spring

First hot, then cold
Then cool, then warm
Spring is here.
There are flowers
Everywhere
Bright and beautiful.
There are birds
Singing in the trees
Back from winter's home.
There are children
Playing, laughing
Glad to be outside.
There are farmers
Planting, watching
Hoping and praying.
There are people everywhere
Looking for something
Hoping for something.
What we all need in spring
Is trust in God.

Judy R. Beasley

Tina

Night,
velvety draped sky blanketing our warmth

Green eyed, turned, towards me.
Rust hair reflecting the moon's
golden glow.

A turn, change in warmth.
Her breast shadows my arm,
a love-hallowed sigh
echoes though the room, touches my soul.

Love, once dead within my breast,
beats anew, like a savage drum
to the jungle night.

Tina, you came for me-
after my sun had set
and the dreams broken
and you gave me rebirth,
love,
anew.

Marc Jordan Ben-Meir

Gone

Gone
The word echoes down
the hallway of my mind
Alone
The realization grasps
the peace I cannot find
Never
Will I see his face
again upon the earth
Ever
Will I feel his touch
and gladly count his worth
Years
We spent together building
mountains on our memories
Tears
Trickling down my face
into the cold arms of reality

Tamara Huffman

Tears Call

As the tear rolls off my cheek
And slowly hits the ground it seeks
The spot it hits is scarred forever
Forsaken to produce never
Another tree nor plant nor fern
Because the spot becomes so stern
Allowing nothing to become
Even flowers would not have done
You see, the screaming of a tear
Causes even Mother Nature to hear
And when she does she begins to weep
As the tear begins to seep
Into the Earth and to her home
She sets the spot aside alone

So next time you cause a tear to fall
Remember all who hear its call
And stop the tear and save us all

Micah Jeppsen

To Whom It May Concern

To whom it may concern
I fear I've lost my mind
In attempts to get your attention
Myself I can no longer find

As I wanted you to notice me
I changed a trillion ways
Can I ever be myself again?
Not while this feeling stays

Look in my direction
Please acknowledge I'm here
You can't just look right through me
I know you know I'm near

Obsession tries my patience
This crisis is something new
I hardly know myself anymore
How can I expect you to?

Brandi Gibson

Promises

I have some promises to you I make,
and I promise these never to break,
  I promise to love you
  with all of my heart
  I promise nobody
  could tear us apart
  I promise to give
  you all of my love
  I promise to treat you
  like an angel above
  I promise to love you
  with all that I am
  I promise to give you
  all that I can
And, when the time comes and I must go,
knowing my love will make you whole.

Brienne Giddens

Desperation

Times of need
desperate times
full of hate
loveless crimes
troubled times
times of pain
times of loss
never gain
constant struggles
constant woe
needing to run
nowhere to go
feelings are numb
can't find the sun
everything black
nowhere to run
loss is abounding
omnipresent fear
everyone listens
does anyone hear

Di Smith

Life Goes On

Empty nights and flying days
Life goes on
And here we stay

Growing close and driven apart
life goes on
with one in my heart

Afraid to go, not able to stay
Life goes on
Each passing day

I loved you then, I love you now
Life goes on
We'll make it somehow.

Cecil McQuain

Cat Fight

I was all alone
it's just me and her
we are a growing disease
for which there is no cure

She bites and claws
and I kick back
every time I turn around
she's on the attack

There's nothing I can do
to help things along
because no matter what I do
I am always wrong

And I hate to love her
but I always will
and she loves to hate me
and is loving me still

Shawn Richards

A Day In Winter

It's snowing hard
With butterflies so white and candid
That every touch becomes a blessing.

Awoken,
The old country road
Is dressing
Its long forgotten path.

It's snowing hard.
Soon every branch becomes a portal
Of silver splendor.
Every tree a magic realm.
And every star a witness, like me,
To such unearthly poetry.

Julia Simone

This Empty Heart

This heart may look empty,
    but truly it's not.
It's filled with the love and memories,
    I've not forgot.
It's full of the laughter,
    joy, and happiness too.
Along with sorrow, tears,
    and some blue.
It's sealed with the fire
    and energy of our love.
To make sure that it's not lost
    even when above.

Tina M. Triplet

Through The Ice Cave

Through the ice cave
came a sparkling shine,
rose above the Earth
at least one more time.

Through the white snow
coming out of the cave
being so bold
and very very brave.

Seeing the white soldier
coming out from the past
for now the past is gone
from me at last.

As he nods his head
and blinks his eyes
there's no more to say
I must say good bye!

Laura Schamp

No Clue

Nerves on edge
New plans today
Angry words spoken
Uninvited; misunderstood; silence
Thoughts turn backward
Heart grasps truths
Tears fall unending
Clouding mindless dreams
No clear vision
Only one side
Time breaks silence
Two sides now
Unable to weave
Mended yet torn
Sunlight burns haze
Magnifies heart's desires
Words with caution
Shine deep within
No clue,
Forgive.

Thresa Warmbrod

Whisperings

Here in my corner
Whisperings in my head
I wonder what they said
And I wonder can they see me
Here in the back room of my mind
Here in my corner
I might hear
Time... Slip away
And I wonder what they say
While I play with memories
Here in the back room of my mind
Sometimes I might glimpse
A distant
Shadow
For an instant
But I just smile and look away
For I don't understand what they say
And I wonder can they hear me
Screaming
Here in the back room of my mind

Kimberly Ann Martin

Fall Out

A ray of light
sifts through a cloud.
Sunshine speaks
so quiet it's loud.
Specs of the sky
reflect in the moon,
and the sun cries
to depart so soon.
The air shudders with sobs
of pain that runs so deep,
of sadness and sorrow
a heartache that never sleeps.
They cry out in torment:
Mother! Mother earth they pray.
Father! Father time they call,
take this pain away.
Forgetfulness we seek;
oblivion we crave.
We want our innocence back
before we dig our grave.

Wendy Miller

Farewell My Love

When I look back to the day we met,
a tear comes to my eye,
for never will I forget,
the memory of you and I.
I'll cherish every moment,
of the times we've spent together,
and only hope to meet again,
and be with you forever.
I'll miss the way you walk and talk,
and the smile upon your face,
just take the love I've given you,
and put it in a special place.
My dear lover I'll miss you so,
but now we have to part,
so this is what I give to you,
I give you all my heart.
Now it's time to say farewell,
but I'll forget you never,
I'll wish for you the best of luck,
today, tomorrow, and forever.

Ruth Mann

Castaway

I live my life like the sea...
With nowhere to turn on
this lonely journey

It is a long voyage I follow
day by day...
After, my society have
turned me away

But, I have nowhere else
to be...
So, I guess there is no need
to rescue me

Then, if I wait for the world
to come around...
Therefore, these seas are
where I drown.

Desmond D. Broadway

Song Of The Dead

Pathetic apparitions
exhumed from forth the soil
sing a song of love and death,
of strife and life and toil

Of fear and cheer
they reminisce,
of long-passed wars
and loved ones missed

But there exists
amid this scene
a shining hope,
a pretty dream

And dead do dream
oh yes, it's true
and sing to us
of course they do

Oh home, sweet home,
of righted wrongs,
a dream of friends,
a dream of song
Daniel Nielsen

Rain Kissing

Why should I open my eyes?
Black is a familiar fold.
I hear the blue falling anyway.

A soft voice of motion in
Celestial blessing;
Like us, like rhythm.

This eden's Conscience
Laughing, tapping skin;
Drink, inhale...
Alexander Jarz

The Path

She strolls the unfamiliar trail,
Not knowing where it leads.
Leaving her shyness, her deceiving veil
And planting some new seeds.

The path is rough, but then it clears,
For her it paves the way.
She finds herself ignoring fears
And bathed in sunny rays.

The stranger road now seems exciting,
And expecting something new,
She rounds each bend, smiling, singing.
She sheds her feet of protective shoes.

Experiencing life for what it's worth,
Relieved of all distrust
She enjoys her life, her rebirth,
For her steps she has to trust.
Maureen Turner

The Raindrop

Picture a raindrop, it fell from the sky.
Picture a seedling, so easy to die.
Picture an oak, it rose from the dirt.
Picture a flower, the season of birth.
Picture an insect, a bird or a bee.
Picture the sunshine, life is the sea.
Picture a baby, pink from the move.
Picture a mother, a love that is true.
Picture a child, picture a man.
Picture the fighter, released by the hand.
Picture a valley, green from the day.
Picture a mountain, the tops always gray.
Picture the forest, wild and free.
Now picture the city, do you like
    what you see?
Picture the blue sky, or picture a cloud.
Picture an airplane because it is loud.
Picture the earth now, picture the moon.
Picture the twilight, everything happens
    too soon.
Now picture the raindrop it started from there.
Life is a cycle, so treat it with care.
Ron Spencer

Who Knows?

What does the world know?
Of wisdom, compassion and understanding.
All of these it does not know.

Where does love in the world show?
In smiling faces, warm glows, laughing faces.
Would this be taken as love?
Or would it all just be a facade.

Only one superior being would really know.
Who knows only the shadow knows!
Rachel Yenor

Gerald Allan Harper

Gifted of men; was He
Even though He was very rejected
Righteous in His ways of thinking
And precious as ever to me
Loved and respected by the children
Driven to shame and disgrace

Always trying to help others
Letting Himself go to waste
Loving and caring in all ways
And never doing any real harm
Nothing to Him seemed right

However who's to say he was wrong
Always to society, a victim
Really, He meant no harm
People never tried to understand Him
Even in cause for alarm
Righteous and gifted was He
    But not strong enough to say "no".
Cheryl E. Harp

Expressions Of My Love

When times are hard
    leaving your back heavily burdened,
    my shoulders will help lighten your load.
When an accomplishment has been worked for
    causing an uplifting in your soul,
    my heart will swell with pride.
When sadness overwhelms you
    creating tears in your eyes,
    my hands will gently brush them away.
When your senses are aroused
    and you are feeling desire,
    my body will move to satisfy you.
When life gets too challenging
    and your mind churns with frustration,
    my fingers shall ease your tension.
When your voice speaks out
    to question my love,
    look into my eyes for your answer.
Donna G. Cole

Alone

Snow covered trees
Dead beneath the white
Thick gray clouds
Letting in no light

Unforgiving cold
freezing all at hand
The old weakened sun
Cannot warm this land

A jagged rocky cliff
Like a heart turned to stone
This is where you left me
Standing all alone.
Angela Rando

Ananda Devanagari

Let me trace
    the landscape
        of your body
    before we merge into one breath
with the soft caress of an eternal song
    I taught you long ago.

    There I taste forever
    the mystery of a memory
we imagined made it so

    Let me trace
    the boundary
    of your soul
before we melt into one river
with the silent whispers of an ancient tongue
    you taught me long ago.

    Where I touch the spirit
    and the meaning of its magic
        we imagined made it so.
Catherine Lipnick

A Womanizer's Predicament

To tease or not to tease - that is the question: Whether 'tis nobler in the mind to suffer
The curves and limbs of outrageous women, Or to take pinches against a sea of lawsuits,
And by opposing, end them. To pass over - to refrain - No more; and by refraining to say we end
The gawking and the thousand natural fantasies that hormones are heir to - 'tis a consummation purely to be wished.
To give up - to hold back. To hold back - perchance to score!
Ay, there's the rub! For in that moment of contact what nights may come,
When we have shuffled off this mortal perversion, must give us pause.
There's the respect that makes calamity of not making a move.
For who would bear the slaps in the face, the harsh denials,
The buff, teed-off boyfriends,
The agony of mace and pepper spray, Or the knee to the groin that the unfortunate take,
When he himself might a relationship make with respectful conversation? Who would
Rejections bear, to grunt and sweat over failing pick-up lines,
But that the dread of something after success, the undiscovered PMS, from whose rage
No man escapes unscathed, puzzles the will, and makes us rather accept the complaining of those we have
Than fly to others whose temper we know not of? Thus conscience does make cowards of us all,
And thus our chauvinistic egos are beaten down with the thought of brutal repulsion,
And enterprises of great skill and womanizing with this regard most pathetically are butchered
And the underlying purpose cast away. - Soft you now! The fair female race! Ladies, in thy consideration,
May all my disrespect be pardoned.

Dave Turner

Narcissus Discerns Himself Into Physical Inactivity

Upon exposure to books he took to thinking,
and after his marriage this practice evolved beyond itself
into a dream where all the world
became his extension; his gaze brought whole fields of wheat into glory
and his eye, approving, lent beauty to the autumn hills
beyond the valley; people were either this or that,
a taste he did or did not like;
his friends became hollow protagonists
within whom his identity echoed during dramas of his own devising;
even his love for his wife depended upon his most recent insight
or how she smelled.
At last, discerning that he was all in all, he
dispensed with humans altogether, preferring to manifest himself
from a chair while ticking as a French clock on the mantel
or growing in fragrant rows along moist beds of himself.

Charles Lincoln Zeiders

Biographies
of
Poets

ABAD, TERESA
[b.] September 25, 1928, Quirihe, Chile; [p.] Andres Abad, Eusebia Casin; [m.] Divorced; [ch.] Two sons; [ed.] High School and Beauty School; [occ.] Retired; [oth. writ.] Last year I published a book I wrote, the title is: "Inspirational Knowledge" methaphysical common sense. The poem appears in the large version of 28 lines, was shorten for the contest.; [pers.] We have a great need for peace in the world God has not given any man any natural superiority, we are all equals. Wars will cease on earth when men practices "The Law Of God" then all men will be brothers.; [a.] Clearwater, FL

ABRAHAM, JAMES A.
[b.] August 9, 1973, Wichita, KS; [p.] Roy and Helen Abraham; [ed.] Metro-Midtown; [occ.] Customer Service Rep; [oth. writ.] I write poetry and stories all the time. Was in Metro-Midtown school paper.; [pers.] I believe my writing is a reflection of my soul. Only through poetry can my true self shine through.; [a.] Wichita, KS

ACOSTA, RAUL
[b.] February 3, 1987, NYC; [p.] Mr. and Mrs. Raul Acosta; [ed.] 4th Grade; [occ.] Student; [memb.] Parksville Baseball, Karate; [hon.] 1st honors in 3rd grade 2nd honors in 4th grade; [a.] Brooklyn, NY

ADAM, MRS. SANDRA MARIE DAVIES
[pen.] Sandra Marie Davies; [b.] January 23, 1938, Salt Lake City, UT; [p.] Mr. and Mrs. Bryan and Edna Davies; [m.] Mr. Milton Frank Adam, August 9, 1960; [ch.] Mrs. Crystal Michele Nielsen, Mrs. Joy Celeste Southern; [ed.] AA Liberal Arts; [occ.] Music Teaching-Ceramics and Oil Painting; [memb.] MTNA-LDS-Music Director and Choir Member; [hon.] Poetry published in Pencilings East High School - Salt Lake City, Utah Poetry published in Colors of Thought by the National Library of Poetry.; [oth. writ.] Poetry and prose.; [a.] Fullerton, CA

ADAMOWICZ, ANNE MARY
[pen.] Anne Ryan-Fulham; [b.] June 1, 1941, Ireland; [p.] Esther Ryan (maiden name), John Fulham; [m.] Joseph, August 29, 1964; [ch.] Robert John, Paul Joseph; [memb.] Immaculate Conception CCD Teacher, Tamarack Golf Club; [oth. writ.] None published.; [pers.] The influence of my late father inspired me to write this poem. I would like to dedicate this poem to my late parents.; [a.] Jamesburg, NJ

AHMAD, AMEERAH H.
[pen.] Ameerah Hasin; [b.] February 23, 1952; Jersey City; [p.] Raymond P. Hall, Mae P. Hall; [ch.] Lugman, Musaddia, Kalimah, Muslimah, Talib; [ed.] Lincoln H.S. New Jersey, attended Howard University also St. Peters College; [occ.] Poet, storyteller, educational artist, civil court clerk; [memb.] Currently member of "Lucid Dreams" poetry group, C.A.P. Community Arts Program of Jersey City. Formerly member of Educational Arts Team J.C. and Newark Writers; [hon.] Paul Robeson Award Library for contribution to the arts, Nominated "Outstanding Young Woman of America" 1987; [oth.writ.] Poetry book, "New Dawn," several plays. Co-wrote anti-drug play "Not Even Once," toured public schools, newspaper reviews, cable TV; [pers.] Yes, I do believe in the power of the spoken word, if used for goodness we can uplift people, mentally and spiritually; [a.] Jersey City, NJ.

AHMED, NARIMAN
[b.] September 27, 1971, Pakistan; [p.] Zamiruddin Ahmed, Hosne-Ara Ahmed; [ed.] New English School, Universal American School, University of Texas at Austin; [occ.] Student; [memb.] Alpha Phi Omega, Association for computing machinery.; [hon.] Phi Theta Kappa, Who's Who Among Students (1996), National Dean's List; [oth. writ.] Wrote articles for High School Newspaper. Have written several (unpublished) urdu poems.; [pers.] This pain has given a voice to the deep well of sorrow that had been surging inside of me. So many thoughts I had buried, now come pouring out and fill the empty pages of my life.; [a.] Austin, TX

AHMED, NIDA ISRAR
[b.] June 21, 1986, Queens, NY; [p.] Farzana Ahmed, Israr Ahmed; [ed.] Grade 5, P.S. 107 Queens, New York; [occ.] Student; [oth. writ.] Other poems: Fall, My Guardian Angel, Dino, My Mother; [pers.] Stay in school.; [a.] Flushing, NY

AJAY, DAVID T.
[pen.] Positive Dave; [b.] November 30, 1916, Altoona, PA; [p.] William and Mary Ajay; [m.] My darling sweetheart Diane (Deceased 1991), August 10, 1946; [ch.] Cindy and Michael; [ed.] Business College (2 yr. course), National Institute of Nutritional Education (NINE); [occ.] Nutritional Consultant, Nylander's Vantage Products, Sacramento, CA; [memb.] Society of Certified Nutritionists (CN) appellation; [hon.] Golden Anniversary Award of Distinction (Then National Nutritional Foods Assoc. (NNFA), Past President, NNFA, Past President (SCN), (The Society of Certified Nutritionists), Outstanding Adjunct Faculty Awards (NINE) 1987-88; [pers.] I have taught my children, and shall do the same for my little grandson, Bobby, "that you should never give up, or never give in ... when you're in any situation that you still have a chance to win!"; [a.] Sacramento, CA

AKINTOYE, STEPHEN
[b.] February 18, 1935, Ado-Ekiti, Nigeria; [p.] Chief James Akintoye, Mary Akintoye; [m.] Mary F. Akintoye; December 28, 1984; [ch.] Ademola, Bukola, Abimbola, Adedej, Adedotun, Adebanj, Babafemi; [ed.] Christ's School, Ado-Ekiti, Nigeria; University College, Ibanan (affiliated to London University); University of Ibadan, Nigeria; Westminster Theological Seminary, Philadelphia; Biblical Theol. Seminary, Hatfield, PA; [occ.] Minister; [memb.] Historical Society of Nigeria; Liberty Evangelical Church, Philadelphia, PA; African Studies Asscociation; Christ World Missions; [hons.] Bachelor of Arts (with honors) of the University of London; Doctor of Philosophy of the University of Ibadan, Nigeria; Master of Arts in Missions and Evangelism, of the Biblical Theol. Seminary, Hatfield, PA; [oth.writ.] Revolution and Power Politics in Yorubaland, 1849-93, Longman. Emergent African States, Longman. Ten years of the University of IFE, 1962-72, IFE University Press. Six chapters in various joint books; more than 15 articles in learned historical journals. Some newspaper articles and seminary conference paper; [pers.] I strive to live a life molded by the Lordship of Jesus Christ, and to reflect it in my literary writing; [a.] Hatfield, PA.

AKKER, CORINA
[pen.] Corina; [b.] January 11, 1986, Ellensburg,

WA; [p.] Lana M. Akker (Mother); [ed.] 5th grade, Athol Elementary School, 'A' Student; [occ.] Student; [hon.] Self manager - equivalent to Honor Student in middle school & high school; [oth. writ.] The Green Roses, Mrs. Megillahcutty's Ride, Sunny Days On First Street, Just Johnny And I; [pers.] Believe in God, honestly. Respect for my elders. I love to write and hope to enter that profession!; [a.] Athol, ID

ALEXANDER, CYNTHIA
[b.] July 7, 1958, Deport, TX; [p.] Bobbie and Terry K. Davis; [m.] Edward Alexander Jr.; [ch.] Peony, Jessica, Ashley; [occ.] Tech Parapro; [oth. writ.] I have a book of poems that have not been published yet.; [pers.] Everything I write is what I have seen, heard and what I have been throw I comes right from the heart.; [a.] Muskegon, MI

ALLEN, LINDA L.
[b.] July 14, 1946, Omaha, NE; [m.] Ethan M. Allen; [ch.] Jody (Deceased), James, Jeremiah; [ed.] Soumi College (AAS), Hancock MI, Clinton Community College (LPN), Clinton IA, Portland Community College (RN) Portland,OR; [occ.] Registered Nurse; [memb.] Bethlehem Lutheran Church, The Compassionate Friends - Lincoln City Chapter.; [oth. writ.] Many other poems and thoughts published monthly in the Compassionate Friends Newsletter.; [pers.] I did not start to write until after a car accident took my son Jody and his fiancee Kathy from us March 25, 1995. I write what I feel at the time and it helps me remember them.; [a.] Aloha, OR

AMADEO, VINCENT S.
[b.] December 17, 1935, Port Chester, NY; [p.] Louis Amadeo, Nancy Amadeo; [m.] Audrey Joyce Amadeo, September 17, 1977; [ed.] Westchester Community College, University of Bridgeport; [occ.] Bio Medical Engineer; [memb.] New England Society of Clinical Engineering; [hon.] VA Connecticut, Superior Performance Award; [oth. writ.] The lightning Bugs Return; [pers.] My goal is to utilize scientific knowledge in my writing. I am influenced by Biblical and American Poetry.; [a.] Wallingford, CT

AMOS, RICK
[pen.] Rick Olando Amos; [b.] August 14, 1963, Gulfport, MS; [p.] Willie and Margie Amos; [ed.] B.S. Accounting, Xavier Univ. of Louisiana, J.D., Marquette Univ. School of Law; [occ.] Attorney; [memb.] Gulfport School Dist. Mentorship Program, American Inns of Crt., Original Illinois Club, Brd. of Dir. Leadership Gulf Coast, Alpha Phi Alpha Fraternity, Brd. of Dir. Boys and Girls Club; [a.] Gulfport, MS

ANDERSON, CHARLOTTE
[b.] July 4, 1936, Birmingham, AL; [p.] Fletcher and Lillian Karr; [m.] Denver R. Anderson, November 13, 1954; [ch.] Janice, Michael and Mark; [ed.] BS (Education) Univ. of AL MS (Voc. Ed.) Alabama A&M; [occ.] Retired Teacher (30 years); [memb.] St. Joseph's Catholic Church, Ala. Retired Teachers Assoc.; [hon.] Wife, Mother, Grandmother, daughter, sister and friend; [oth. writ.] Notebook of poems dating back to 1960's; [pers.] My family and friends, together with my strong faith in an eternally. Loving God influences my poems.; [a.] Huntsville, AL

ANDERSON, DARREN
[b.] September 17, 1979, Fontana, CA; [p.] Dennis and Frances Anderson; [ed.] High school, college; [occ.] Student; [pers.] The gargoyle reluctantly sheds his eyes to achieve true humanity.; [a.] Panama City, FL

ANDERSON, DOROTHY
[pen.] Dort Swanson; [b.] November 15, 1961, Harvey, ND; [p.] Albert (Bud) Swanson and Helen Weinmann; [m.] Terry L. Anderson, April 11, 1980; [ch.] Derek, Miranda, Dana, Mirissa; [ed.] B.M. Hanson Elementary and Harvey High, Harvey N.D.; [occ.] Housewife, worked for a concession company for 5 years then went back to my children and husband who needed my companionship more.; [oth. writ.] Out on the Range and My Pompy, "All my poems I wrote are true and of a friend."; [pers.] I wrote this poem because of a very talented Athlete and good friend. I never thought I could write a popular poem like this.; [a.] Butte, ND

ANDERSON, EVAN PHILIP
[b.] March 19, 1971, Buffalo, NY; [p.] Ray and Bess Anderson; [m.] Christine M. Anderson, June 11, 1994; [ch.] Alexandria Patricia, Rebekah Lynn; [pers.] To trust in God is to take a step off a cliff and knowing that He'll catch you.; [a.] Scott AFB, IL

ANTOINE, LEON
[b.] November 01, 1960; Grenada; [p.] Joyce Caasar; [ch.] Lindei, Camille; [ed.] St. Andrew's Secondary School, (Grenada); Cha Electronic College, (Grenada); [occ.] Credit consultation, Car sales manager; [oth. writ.] song writer (contemporary calypso music); [pers.] I'm a salesperson and I enjoy interacting with the public. In my spare time I read, write or listen to music. I enjoy composing; [a.] Brooklyn, NY.

ARANTOWICZ, GERARD
[b.] October 31, 1969, Ephrata, PA; [m.] Erin, November 29, 1997; [ed.] Bachelor's of Science Penn State University; [occ.] Freelance Cartoonist The Real Washington Publication; [memb.] American Association of Editorial Cartoonists, Christian Cycling Team; [hon.] Desert Storm Veteran; [oth. writ.] The Truth Hurts Political Cartoon, Jewel Comic Strip; [pers.] You have to pave your own path in life, in order to succeed, you have to risk failure, live life on your own terms... or not at all.; [a.] State College, PA

ARGUELLO, ARLY
[occ.] Psychologist; [pers.] At a very young age, I was drawn to art and music. One of my favorite hobbies was to read and write poetry. I admire the work of Pablo Neruda and many others. Writing poetry is a way to touch the heart and soul of humanity.; [a.] Arlington, VA

ARLOTTA, FELICITA ROSADO
[b.] February 12, 1948, Ponce, PR; [p.] Miguel A. Rosado, Carmen Lydia Cuadodri-Rosado, [m.] Raymond R. Arlotta, November 24, 1989; [ch.] Randal Garcia; [ed.] Washington Irving H.S., Kingsborough Com. College, Brooklyn College; [memb.] National Museum of the American Indian; [pers.] Education is the highway towards a better life.; [a.] Brooklyn, NY

ART, ROBYN
[b.] October 12, 1974, Boston, MA; [p.] Robert

and Suzane Art; [ed.] Graduate of Caby College '97 with a degree in English; [occ.] Student; [memb.] Editor of Colby Literary Magazine; [hon.] Dean's List, Academic All-American, 4-Time All-New England in Track; [oth. writ.] Published in various campus literary magazines, newspapers.; [a.] Lincoln, MT

ASHTON, NINA K.
[b.] September 15, 1922; Nicolsk-Ussurisk, Russia; [m.] (late) Col. Clark Ashton USMC; [ch.] 3 daughters Victoria, Valerie and Marina; [ed.] Russian school (Shanghi, China), nursing school; [occ.] Retired; [memb.] Marine Corps Wives Club, writer of children's stories and Russian poems; [hon.] Various awards for volunteer work; [pers.] Material things are not important, it's people that count; [a.] Virginia Beach, VA.

ASHTON, VICTORIA
[b.] January 4, 1961; Indianapolis, India; [p.] (late) Col. Clark Ashton, Nina K. Ashton; [m.] Richard Clabbers; [ch.] Kaitin, Nina Ashton Clabbers; [ed.] Attending Tidewater Community College; [occ.] Flight attendant (17 years!) In my 18th year!; [hon.] + other writings selected for publishing, "Chicken Soup for the Soul," won art contest for the cover of the guide to park and recreation-80,000 copies published, poem in "Voices of America" 1993, won logo contest for college learning center, short stories, and a children's book, "The Little Girl who Lost Her Sleep," working on a novel, fiction; [pers.] To Kaitlin, my inspiration and joy, Rick, the love of my life, Nina, more than a mother... my best friend. Thank you for loving me, XO Victoria ; [a.] VA Beach, VA.

ASPROMONTE, BRITANNY MAE
[pen.] Britt Aspromonte; [b.] August 18, 1985; Cortez, CO; [p.] Tony, Vicki Aspromonte; [ed.] K-6 Mancos Elementary; [occ.] Student; [memb.] Benjamin Franklin Stamp Club, Writers Club, Girl Scouts of America, Color Guard, track team, basketball team, volley ball team, First Baptist Church; [hon.] A honor roll, Kindergarten-6th Physical Education Presidential Award; [oth.writ.] Poems and stories at my local school; [pers.] I love to write and I look forward to publishing tons and tons of more writings; [a.] Mancos, CO.

ASSELIN, LYN EDWARDS
[b.] April 2, 1921, Oberlin, OH; [p.] Davis Edwards and Jill Edwards Gardner; [m.] Vi Asselin, September 5, 1942; [ch.] Rex, Sandy, Larry, 9 grandchildren, 3 great grandchildren; [ed.] Graduate 1942 Northwestern University School of Speech; [occ.] Retired after 50 years of active participation in Branson area tourism, and living on a mountain top 10 miles from bustle of our renowned Country Music tourist mecca.; [memb.] Zeta Phi Eta, professional speech sorority, past Vice President Dogwood Trails Girls Scout Council, former Board member Library Club, Chamber of Commerce, many community activities [hon.] Won my first poetry contest at age 11 in Chautauqua NY, Dean Dennis Award for Interpretation NU 1940, Best Actress NU 1941, Who's Who in MO '74, prestigious Branson Lakes Area Chamber of Commerce "Pioneer Award" in '95 along with husband Vi for 50 years of service and contributions to the community; [oth. writ.] Many published articles covering the history of the Ozarks and the growth of

Branson. Promotional stories, booklets, and news stories for newspapers and magazines on Ozark tourism.; [pers.] Poetry has always challenged me...the strength, magic and power of conveying emotion and ideas in concise form with precisely chosen words and rhythms. Vachel Lindsay was a family friend and I vividly recall him dancing around a campfire chanting "The Congo" when I was 5. Greetings from Peaceful Mountain.; [a.] Branson, MO

ATKINS, JANINE NICOLE
[pen.] Yoda - "The All Knowing"; [b.] April 11, 1983, Newburgh, NY; [p.] Linda R. Atkins, Andre K. Baynes; [ed.] North Jr. High School; [occ.] Student (8th Grade); [memb.] LPP (Liberty Partnership Program); [hon.] "If I were a Bell", second grade; [oth. writ.] "If I Were A Bell", "Life"; [pers.] I don't actually write about what and how I'm feeling, I just write what I think about. I feel my writing is my life.; [a.] Newburgh, NY

AUSTIN, BARBARA
[pen.] Barbara Austin; [b.] December 29, 1949, New Haven, CT; [p.] John and Dorothy Tarbell; [m.] Louis E. Austin (Deceased), April 8, 1992; [ch.] Michael and Christopher Austin; [ed.] High school, East Haven High, Stone's Business School, Computer Programming Inst.; [occ.] Data processing in Film & Photo Development Mystic; [memb.] Mystic Seaport; [hon.] Certificate of Completion from Three Rivers Comm-Tech College, Certified Graduation of Computers from CPI; [oth. writ.] Several poems in booklet form for friends and family. Special occasion cards and notes.; [pers.] I've always been able to deal with everything by putting my feelings down on paper. Finding out that people really like my poetry really helped.; [a.] Mystic, CT

AUSTIN, SUSAN M.
[b.] October 5, 1955, Lynn, MA; [p.] Frank and Doris Aldus; [ch.] Justin Lengel and Shannon Austin; [occ.] Director of Credit; [memb.] Florida Direct Marketing Association; [pers.] Poetry is such a wonderful way to express feelings for people you love.; [a.] Cooper City, FL

AVERY, ERWIN T.
[pen.] Erwin Avery; [b.] February 11, 1936, Winston-Salem, NC; [p.] E. Stanley Avery and Florence B. Avery; [m.] Karen M. Avery, November 22, 1990; [ch.] Ted and Liz; [ed.] AB from the University of North Carolina - graduate courses at old Dominion University; [occ.] Certified Public Accountant; [memb.] CPA Society, Great Book Club; [hon.] Phi Beta Kappa from UNC, Good Conduct Medal from US Army Certified as Public Accountant in 1985; [oth. writ.] Research papers NATO, Womens Army Corps., Yalta Meeting; [pers.] Poetry is used to recapture themes such as childhood love and pets; [a.] Norfolk, VA

BABER, BERNARD D.
[b.] November 6, 1945, Australia; [p.] William E. Baber, Phyliss A. Brady; [m.] Cynthia A. Baber, March 15, 1969; [ch.] Blair Bernard, Brent De Pree; [ed.] Western Washington University; [occ.] Director, Properties, Airborne Express; [hon.] Dovell- Grove Speech Schoolarship; [pers.] I try to write with clarity, brevity and feeling; [a.] Redmond; WA.

BACHENKO, WALTER
[b.] October 29, 1910; Chelsea, MA; [p.] Emil and Valerie Bachenko; [m.] Jennie (Kozak) Bachenko; August 24, 1941; [ch.] Alice Jane and Walter John; [ed.] Binghamton Helg School and a Pharmacy School in Providence RD now connected with Brown University; [occ.] Pharmasist for 42 years; [memb.] 53 years in the Knights of Columbus - 206; [oth.writ.] Poems "Marriage" "Blessings"; [a.] Binghamton, NY.

BADER, DENNIS
[b.] January 31, 1955; Dayton, OH; [ch.] Jonathan, Rommie, Alan; [ed.] Dulaney High, Essex Comm. College; [occ.] Self-employed; [memb.] Mankind; [pers.] Never give up, what you want could be in the midst of your next struggle. When you find what you want, hold on with your heart and soul.;[a.] Surfside Beach, SC.

BAIN, EDNA
[b.] August 9, 1928; Sparta, TN; [p.] Plese and Ollie Seibers; [m.] Leslie W. Bain (deceased); August 19, 1949; [ch.] Shirley Greenwood, Kenny Bain, Mitchell Bain; [occ.] Retired, Part Time Desk Clerk; [memb.] Spring Hill Baptist Church Since Aug. 1949; [oth.writ.] I've always had a love for poetry. I have a book full of poems. But have never had any published. This is the first time I've tried to send or get any published; [pers.] All of my writings are of God's Holy Spirit. He gives me each word that I write. I feel as if He speaks to me as I write the poem; [a.] Walling, TN.

BAKHTIAR, CLAUDETTE
[b.] April 20, 1970, New York; [p.] Dr. Farhang Bakhtiar, Miryam Bakhtiar; [ed.] State University of New York at Binghamton, B.A., Fordham University School of Law, J.D.; [occ.] Law Student; [a.] Woodbury, NY

BALLOY, MAGDALENE PATRICIA
[pen.] Madelene; [b.] November 6, 1932, Grenada, British West Indies; [m.] Arthur J. Balloy, November 23, 1955; [ch.] Michael, Dennis, and Noelle Rose, Grandchildren: Candace and Carla Balloy; [occ.] Cosmetic Sales; [oth. writ.] A book in progress: "Beyond The Darkness", Other poems: "God Is Seeded In Man's Soul", "Heaven Is", "A Life Worthwhile", "Hasten Darkness In It's Flight", "This Is My Desire", "The Answer Is Love", "His Light Will Shine", "My Awakening", "Magdalene's Prayer", and many more.; [pers.] My childhood was one of depravation and abuse. I am self educated. And was transformed by a death-like experience in 1963, when Jesus appeared to me. Since that life changing event, I have developed a hungering need to express myself through poetry. Several of my poems have been published by local newspapers, church communications, and by The National Library of Poetry. I am a recipient of the National Library of Poetry, Editor's Choice Award. And was elected into The International Poetry Hall of Fame Museum, which can be found on the Internet. I am currently editing my own autobiography entitled: "Beyond The Darkness", a personal and intimate story of life's challenges, triumphs, defeats and accomplishments.; [a.] Palm Desert, CA

BANKS, KEITH D.
[b.] May 4, 1972; Huntingdon, PA; [p.] Mary and Chester Banks; [ch.] 2; [ed.] Mount Union Elementary Mount Union, PA, McConnelsburg High School; [oth.writ.] I've written several poems; [pers.] If I can get through today there is hope for tomorrow; [a.] McConnellsburg, PA.

BANKS, SANDRALEE
[pen.] Sandilee; [b.] November 3, 1967, Bristol, PA; [p.] Rosemary and Harold Banks; [ch.] Alyssa Saragin, Brittainy Banks, Anthony Portillo; [ed.] F.D.R. yr. High and Truman High and Future Penn State Student Fall of 1997; [occ.] Freelance Writer/Student; [memb.] Due to being Native American I cannot give out any memberships due to race; [hon.] Honors in, Accounting, General Business and Journalism; [oth. writ.] Personal writings not yet ready to publish. Over 4 journals of materials and a manuscript named/titled "The Matou". Waiting and trying to find a publishing house.; [pers.] All my writings and poems are all my intermost thoughts and emotions and have been my vice ever since I was a child and after reading "Shakespeare's" novels.; [a.] Warminster, PA

BARNARD, W. R.
[pen.] C. B. Bullock; [b.] January 6, 1939, Reidsville, NC; [ch.] Tammie L. Barnard; [ed.] 9th Grade; [occ.] Retired; [oth. writ.] None published.; [pers.] Man made God in his own image.; [a.] Reidsville, NC

BARNES, ELBA ZAPATA
[b.] November 2, 1937, Valencia, Venezuela; [p.] Luis and Benigna Tovar-Zapata; [m.] Walter D. Barnes, November 2, 1968; [ch.] Joseph and Dennise; [ed.] BA Columbia University; [occ.] Catechist and GSL Teacher and GED Instructor (Spanish); [oth. writ.] "Mommy Still Cares?," "Tree House and The Negri-Rivera Family," short story.; [pers.] Late '59 or early '60's I met Bill Cosby, acting in a small Greenwich Village Cafe, in N.Y.C. One of his jokes I remember vividly, "If Russia bombed Harlem, the U.S. would become its permanent ally..." (Then, the U.S. and the U.S.S.R. were the world's super powers.) The next time I saw Mr. Cosby, was when he first invaded my living room via T.V. acting in "I Spy". In the early '90's, Joseph, my son faithfully watched the "Bill Cosby Show." Later his "Jello" commercial sublimely influenced my daughter's appetite... Recently tragedy hit his home. I realized that life can be a bit ironic, if not cruelest at times. Yesterday, Bill Cosby joked about a political rivalry issue, and today the hands of a Russian possibly ravished his son's life. Dismayed by the news of Ennis' death, the son of Bill Cosby, my most unforgettable character: comedian, philanthropist and a great father, inspired me to write the theme, "The Moon Casts a Spell.";[a.] Bronx, NY

BARNES, RACHELLE ANN
[b.] December 18, 1985, Clark AFB, Philippines; [p.] Jeff and Ronda Barnes; [ed.] Currently in 5th grade at Westwood Elementary School in Greenwood, Indiana; [occ.] Student; [memb.] Berean Baptist Church, Community Center, 5th Grade Choir; [hon.] Science Fair, AWANA Olympics; [oth. writ.] Short stories and articles poems.; [pers.] I write for fun and so that I can use my imagination. I think I write good stories.; [a.] Greenwood, IN

BARRIOS, EDDIE A.
[pen.] Eddie; [b.] February 9, 1957, Los Angeles, CA; [p.] Manuel M. Barrios, Maria A. Barrios; [m.] D.; [ch.] Eddie Jr. and Veronica Anne; [ed.] Queen of Angels, Salesian High School, East Los Angeles College; [occ.] Mental Health Worker; [pers.] I have been greatly influenced by poets such as Emily Dickinson, Walt Whitman and Robert Frost. I would also like to thank Professor J. G. Bayaune of E.L.A.C. for her encouragement to write.; [a.] Baldwin Park, CA

BARRUS, TERESITA
[b.] January 4, 1984, Renton, WA; [p.] Nellie Barrus and Wendell Barrus Sr.; [ed.] Seventh grade, Northwood Jr. High; [occ.] Student; [memb.] School Choir, Active Pep Squad Member - Northwood Junior High; [hon.] 1996 Olympic Torchbearer, 1997 High Academic Achievement Award, Runner-Up (Speech) Pre-teen Wa. 1996, 1994 1st Place - Northern Life Insurance Arts and Crafts Fair - for poem entitled "The Hearts Are With The Soldiers"; [pers.] I hope one day my writing will inspire people everywhere.; [a.] Renton, WA

BARRY, EARL C.
[b.] July 10, 1928; Owens Mouth, CA; [p.] Gerald and Vesta Barry; [m.] Gay Page Barry; November 25, 1948; [ch.] Elizabeth, Earl Jr., Patty and John; [ed.] Turlock Union High School; [occ.] Retired Police Sgt. part time court security officer, Fed C.H. Rich. VA; [memb.] For John Marshall Lodge #2 Oak Grove Baptist Court House road Richmond, VA, Veterans of Foreign Wars; [oth.writ.] If it were only possible, I want to know Jesus, Jesus at the Temple, Woman At The Well (unfinished) nothing published; [pers.] While my hand penned the poem Autumn Leaves I firmly believe the words written were layed on me by my Lord and savior Jesus Christ, whom I love and worship dearly and daily; [a.] Midlothian, VA.

BASKIND, JAMES
[b.] July 28, 1970, Hinsdale, IL; [p.] Robert Baskind, Pamela Baskind; [ed.] Hinsdale Central High School, University of Iowa (B.A.), Kyushu University (Japan), University of Hawaii at Manoa; [occ.] Graduate Student; [hon.] Recipient of Japanese Ministry of Education Scholarship 1994; [oth. writ.] Unpublished; [pers.] Like Lord Byron says - (Poetry is) "the lava of the imagination whose eruption prevents an earthquake". And so with me, inexorably, hot molasses flowing, it is necessary, and sweet, to write.; [a.] Honolulu, HI

BAUER, STAN
[pen.] Paul; [b.] October 6, 1950, Faribault, MN; [p.] Clarence and Ina Bauer; [ch.] Justin, Jessica, Nathan, Zabulon; [occ.] Vofm Duluth MN Austin Community College Winona State U MW; [memb.] O printer Wenger Corp Owatonna MN; [oth. writ.] Poems - "Friends", "Do Butterflies Cry", "Dream Weaver", writing a novel.; [pers.] There are two people who have inspired me and my writings the most; Peggy Jo Dirks, the lady I hope will soon be my wife, and Mary 'Casey' Gorka, in spirit her sister, and both my dear friends.; [a.] Owatonna, MN

BAYER, EDWARD F.
[pen.] Eddie Bayer; [b.] March 26, 1951, Buffalo, NY; [p.] Deceased; [ed.] Franklin Orthopedic, Lackawanna, NY, West Seneca, NY, N.F.V.R.C., 100 Leroy AV, Buffalo, N.Y.; [occ.] Janitor;

[memb.] Alden Mennonite Church, Founding Member of FDR Memorial; [hon.] Spelling Runner-Up, Spelling Champion, Perfect Attendance, High School Diploma, A Member of the 1968 Championship Volleyball Team of West Seneca High, (E.C.I.C. Division I) Champions (Section 6 Class ANA Champions); [oth. writ.] Wrote a poem called "A Poem So True".; [pers.] If you ever want something or anything in life, go after it, because it will not come to you.; [a.] Cheektowaga, NY

BAYS, WANDA
[b.] August 16, 1951, Annapolis, MD; [p.] Paschel Fletcher, Freda Fletcher; [m.] Terence Bays, January 18, 1972; [ed.] Anne Arundel High, Ohio State University; [occ.] Retired Project Manager from Nationwide Enterprise.; [oth. writ.] Several unpublished poems, short stories, and how to instructional materials; [pers.] Retired from the corporate world at age 44 and currently live on a horse farm practicing self sufficient living.; [a.] Louisa, VA

BAZILE, LIONEL
[b.] June 22, 1950, Haiti; [p.] Boniface and Clara Bazile; [m.] Divorced; [ch.] Four Kids, Three Boys and a Girl; [ed.] College of Staten Island (Degree) P.C.A. Two years studied not graduated; [occ.] I am unemployed, I was ask to resign I refused, then I was fired.; [hon.] I've been honored and awarded by the National Library of Poetry this is the only honors and awards I have ever receive the only one I will ever need, through my journey here on earth.; [oth. writ.] I wrote many songs, heard my songs on the radio. I never have the pleasure to be recognize, I wrote an essay while I was attending college, but were stole. "God loves you and so do I" were stolen.; [pers.] Today I am the proudest man on the face of the Earth to be the semi-finalist in the North American Open Poetry Contest, I can't explain it only to say thank you, thank you very much.; [a.] Bronx, NY

BEARD, KENNETH ERIC
[pen.] Sir Eric; [b.] December 11, 1958, Memphis, TN; [p.] James H. Beard, Johnnie Beard; [m.] Judy Marie Beard, July 24, 1986; [ch.] Eric, Amber, Joshua; [ed.] Westwood High School, University of Memphis; [occ.] Mail Processor Specialist, United States Postal Service, Memphis, TN; [memb.] Memphis Tennis Association; [hon.] Dean's List; [oth. writ.] Several poems for wife and friend. This is my first attempt to get one published; [pers.] I tend to write a great deal about love and nature. Among other things, I believe that poetry reveal one's true and pure thoughts and self.; [a.] Memphis, TN

BEASER, ROBERT
[b.] May 18, 1948, Detroit, MI; [p.] Val Beaser, Bess Beaser; [ed.] Boston University, University of Massachusetts; [occ.] Substance Abuse Counselor; [memb.] United States Golf Assoc., Habitat for Humanity International, Boston University Alumni, Aid Association For Lutherans; [hon.] Quarter-finalist, two years in the American Songwriting Festival, Los Angeles, CA; [pers.] Using words, I try to compose emotional images on the canvas of imagination. Influences include 19th and 20th century art and music.; [a.] Quincy, MA

BEASLEY, CHERYL A.
[b.] March 22, 1971, New York, NY; [p.] Robert

E. and Flossie M. Gambol; [ch.] Charles A. and Cayrena M. Beasley; [ed.] San Pasqual High School, Winterhaven, CA; [occ.] Culinary, Westin La Paloma, Tucson, AZ; [hon.] Varsity Letters for Basketball, Softball, Cheerleading and Drama; [oth. writ.] Several articles in High School Yearbooks, numerous unpublished poetry and lyrics.; [pers.] Writing is my way of dealing with life. I can't change what society sees or thinks. I write what I feel and hope for understanding.; [a.] Tucson, AZ

BEASLEY, JUDY
[b.] November 7, 1949; Augusta, GA; [p.] Mr. & Mrs. Donald H. Riley; [m.] David B. Beasley Sr; July 12, 1986; [ch.] Brianna, David Jr.; [ed.] Thomson High School, Augusta College (BA, MA, SpEd); [occ.] Media Specialist, Dearing Elementary School, Dearing, GA; [memb.] Professional Association of Georgia Educators; [a.] Dearing, GA.

BEAUDRY, RONALD NORMAN
[b.] May 14, 1933, Albany, NY; [p.] Deceased; [m.] Divorced; [ch.] Desiree, Robert, Victoria Lee; [ed.] 1 year of college, numerous service schools in Electronic Field in Navy, last two years I've completed Basic Application Computer, World Perfect 5.1 Level I, Lotus 5, 123, Micro-Soft Office; [occ.] Retired U.S. Navy, 20 years of service; [memb.] AARP; [oth. writ.] Poems "It's Only A Pool", "Beauty", "Jenny", "God Made Me A Parent", "Girl In The Booth", and "A Prayer", "Thy Kingdom Come", I hope to write autobiography for the benefit of my grandchildren.; [pers.] I believe in that a person should have a free spirit whom it comes to creativity but it should be bolstered by tradition, value and truth and not cause intentional harm.; [a.] Norwalk, CA

BEAVIS, VIRGINIA L.
[b.] November 17, 1966; [oth. writ.] Who I Am, I Wonder, To Be, Father of Life, A Sanctuary, (You Are) Part of Me, Words of Love, No More Despair, Bless This Body, Lord, Little Ragamuffin and many more.; [pers.] Some of us observe special beauty wherever we go, but writer tell the story.; [a.] Newport News, VA

BECK, LEANNA J.
[pen.] Jeanne; [b.] June 12, 1953; [p.] William E. Beck (deceased) and Jacquelyn A. Wallin (deceased); [m.] Michael W. Runyan; Haven't set a date at this time; [ch.] Shauna Kristine; [ed.] High School Graduate, Some College, Sawyer Business School, Ser Business and Technical Institute Computer Skills III; [occ.] I do Domestic Work because I like working with people who need your care its good therapy; [memb.] National Family Opinion, National Home Gardening, Flower of the Month Club, The Humane Society, of the United States, Hiltop Research Team and American Online; [hon.] Golden Poet Award; Silver Poet Award, Several Honorable Mentions, Poems "Beautiful" and "Wonders" Published in "Poetry Anthology" Eddie Lou Cole was Editor at the time of World Of Poetry; [oth.writ.] Short Stories; Articles for church newsletters; keep Journals of life's happenings I have also sent in articles in the Opinion Section...good place to get your opinions out there; [pers.] Life reminds me of a treasure hunt..except the treasures we seek aren't seen with the human eye. I dedicate my poetry to all of those who feel with their hearts. Love is truly magic; [a.] Palm Beach Gardens, FL.

BEERS JR., DAVID R.
[pen.] Lee Valenti; [b.] June 3, 1975, San Diego, CA; [p.] Sharon and David Beers; [ed.] Merritt Island High School, Brevard Community College; [occ.] F-16 Armament Systems Technician, Italy; [hon.] National Spanish Honor Society; [pers.] The world is what you make of it. Let God be the candle that brightens your life.; [a.] Merritt Island, FL

BEESON, MARLENE K. LEMMER
[p.] Henry and Pauline Lemmer; [m.] Robert G. Beeson; [ch.] Jodie G. and Dustin L.; [ed.] B.A. History at Bethel College, Summa Cum Laude, North Newton, KS, M.A. from Wichita State University, Wichita, KS; [occ.] Law Student; [oth. writ.] Poems published in Lines Master's Thesis.; [a.] Newton, KS

BEHEE, STEPHEN M.
[pen.] The Night Hawk; [b.] October 23, 1965, Warrensburg, MO; [p.] Doris and Elmer Bryson - James Behee; [m.] Lela J. Behee, December 28, 1996; [ch.] 3 - Stephen Jr. 9, Dustin 7, Rachel 5; [ed.] Grad. Memphis High School, Memphis Texas 1984, USAF Fire school 1986; [occ.] Computer Tech. - Network Administrator; [memb.] American Radio Relay League; [oth. writ.] Night Bird, Predators and Prey, Rebirth?, Red River, Spring, The Flower, Questions, Giants, Friends and Lovers, A Little Closer, I Know, Killjoy, Edge, Touch of Velvet, Midnight Ride, The Rose, Stepping Stones, Sweet Mercy, Tears; [pers.] I breathe in life and try to write what I see, feel, taste, hear and offer my personal perspective on common things and people. Everyone has something to teach me, if I just listen.; [a.] Waco, TX

BELCHER, JESSIE B.
[b.] April 21, 1957, Perry Co., KY; [p.] Beach and Coey Belcher; [m.] Marilyn Belcher, February 11, 1984; [pers.] "Lifetime" was composed for my wife, Marilyn, who is the true love of my life and my greatest inspiration who's love never waivers.; [a.] Phoenix, AZ

BENAVIDES, HECTOR F.
[b.] May 24, 1974, Laredo, TX; [ed.] Enrolled at Southwest Texas State University (SWT); [hon.] Locally published artist and poet; [oth. writ.] You, Me and A Bucketful of Angels; [pers.] Passion is greater than structure. Leonard Cohen turned me to poetry.; [a.] Laredo, TX

BENNER, KRISTIN RENEE
[b.] November 30, 1984; Ravenna, OH; [p.] Tim Benner and Sally Benner; [occ.] Currently in 6th Grade Student-Crestwood Middle School, Mantua, Ohio; [memb.] D.A.R.E., Girl Scouts, Band, Choir, Gymnastics, Just Say No; [hon.] "Student of the month" - Both 5th and 6th Grades; [oth.writ.] Had 2 poems published in school Literary Journal; [pers.] I really enjoy writing poems. When I write a poem I like to make people feel as if they're really there; [a.] Mantua, OH.

BENNETT, HARRIET HOEVET
[pen.] Harriet Hoevet Bennett; [b.] May 19, 1920; Lowell, IN; [p.] Edward Bernice (Rudolph) Hoevet; [m.] Divorced; March 5, 1949; [ch.] Daniel Charles; [ed.] BA Mus Ed, Olivet Nazarene Univ., M Mus Ed, Univ of Ill; [occ.] Teacher, retired; [memb.] Ill Education Assn., retired, National Audobon Assn.,

National Wildlife Assn., AARP, United Church of Christ; [hon.] Alpha Tau Delta, Indiana Girls State; [oth.writ.] "Joy," "Shall I Tell You," musical pieces, a craft project in New Generations. "Kindness," a poem; [pers.] We are on this earth to help one another. Stretch your potential; [a.] Hodgkins, IL.

BENNETT, JEFFREY
[b.] May 18, 1965, Homestead, FL; [p.] James Brady Bennett (Father), Claudia Jean Oesch Bennett (Mother, Deceased); [ed.] Bachelors Arts Recreation Management; [occ.] Still looking; [memb.] Green Peace; [hon.] 2nd Place Optimist Contest, Essay - Very First Entry of any kind; [oth. writ.] Nothing ever published before, but have been an avid writer. I have many poems and short essays, but have never submitted any.; [pers.] Words on paper are the window to my soul. They purge my inner being, making everything clear.; [a.] Palm Beach Gardens, FL

BENNETT, JOY
[pen.] Joy Bennett; [b.] March 24, 1984, Atlanta, GA; [p.] Helen and Jim Bennett; [ed.] Attending Mundys. Mill Middle School (7th grade); [occ.] Student; [memb.] 4-H Coordinator (local club) First Baptist Church of Jonesboro; [hon.] All A. Honor Roll, October Student of the Month ('96), 2nd in Kawanis Club talent show (piano); [oth. writ.] State-wide Writing Assessment and poems for family and friends.; [pers.] "Fear not that life shall come to an end, but rather that it shall never have a beginning."; [a.] Jonesboro, GA

BENNIE, RICHARD H.
[b.] March 17, 1917, New Brighton, PA; [p.] Alexander Bennie and Fourteenia E. Lee; [m.] Thelma E. Hoffman, January 18, 1940; [ch.] Beverlee I. Baird, Ronald L., Richard K. and Rhett A.; [ed.] Graduate of Pottsville High Class of 1936; [occ.] Retired Bell of Pennsylvania Engineer; [memb.] Church of Jesus Christ of L. D. S., Bell Telephone Pioneers of America, West Shore YMCA Active Older Adults, St. Theresa's Catholic Church, Little Flower Club, China/Burma/India Veterans Association, Marine Corps League; [oth. writ.] Poem on Mother's Death while away serving in the United States Marine Corps During World War II.; [pers.] I not only believe in Christ, but I believe Christ, that He is who He claims to be, that He lives, and that He will fulfill all that He promises to do. It is this eternal perspective which provides the "firm foundation" for all that I strive to be and to do.; [a.] Camp Hill, PA

BENON, DEBORAH ANN
[pen.] Deborah Harberd-Benon; [b.] May 25, 1950; Ann Arbor, MI; [p.] John and Beatrice Harberd; [m.] Richard D. Benon II, April 18, 1985; [ch.] Cassandra and Tunicia Ross; [ed.] Ann Arbor Pioneer High; [occ.] Child Care Provider; [pers.] My poetry has always been inspired by personal events in my life. This poem is one-half of a tribute read at the funeral of my first granddaughter, Angel Hall, who was silently born on February 6, 1992; [a.] Romulus, MI.

BENSING, BRENDA J.
[b.] December 5, 1949; Tucson, AR; [p.] Mr. and Mrs. Alexaner Gilbert; [ch.] AJ, Dustin Lorne; [ed.] Western High KY College of Technology, Louisville, KY; [occ.] Electronic Technician; [hon.] Delta

Sigma Phi; [pers.] I was influenced to write this poem, because of my personal feelings for a very dear person, Chuck Profitt; [a.] Louisville, KY.

BENYAMIEN, AVEEN
[b.] June 27, 1985, Dohuk, Iraq; [p.] Sadah and Basima Benyamien; [ed.] McIntyre Elementary School, Birney Middle School; [occ.] Student at Birney Middle School - 6th; [hon.] D.A.R.E. Program, Rainbow Readers; [oth. writ.] Many poems are written in a notebook from school called a Writer's Notebook.; [pers.] Poems give you the opportunity to go beyond what's really there - use your imagination.; [a.] Southfield, MI

BERGNER, LAURITA ANN
[b.] July 26, 1955; Pittsburgh, PA; [p.] Carmel and Ann Cirocco; [m.] Robert Bergner; April 29, 1978; [ch.] Carl and Arthur; [ed.] B.A. Adm. of Justice; [occ.] Wife and mother; [hon.] Honor roll at Allegheny Community College for 2 years attended, and foresics for choral and interpretation; [oth.writ.] Past recognition in poetry by teachers and poetry competition; [pers.] Poetry is like a piece of fine art! When writing poetry I think of a theme that can mean something different to different people!; [a.] Webster, NY.

BERNHART, ELIZABETH W.
[pen.] Betty Bernhart; [b.] March 30, 1942, Norfolk, VA; [p.] Waite W. Worden, Elizabeth B. Worden; [m.] Michael H. Bernhart, September 8, 1962, (Divorced May 30, 1985); [ch.] Michelle St. Germain, David Michael; [ed.] Emory University BMSC 1978, Emory University MPH 1990; [occ.] Physical Assistant (Women's Health); [memb.] Unitarian-Universalist Congregation of Atlanta, American Academy of Physician Assistants. "Partnership with hope".; [oth. writ.] First Poetry; [pers.] "Magic Happens - Allow For The Possibility", "Do Your Dream", "Don't Postpone Joy."; [a.] Atlanta, GA

BEST, AUBREY
[b.] June 11, 1955, Guyana; [p.] Bernice Best, James Best; [m.] Dhalma Best; [ch.] Andrea and Terrance Best; [ed.] Academy of Aeronautics; [occ.] Systems Engineer; [a.] Seagirt Beach, NY

BETHUNE, PEGGY K.
[b.] April 29, Augusta, GA; [p.] Mr. and Mrs. J. C. King; [m.] Cleveland W. Bethune; [ch.] Carl and Brenda; [ed.] High School, School of Floristry, School of Dolls, Education in Retail (children); [pers.] I would like my poem to reflect the olden days: The past has people with lot of ethics. I want my poems to reflect me, the way I feel.; [a.] Evans, GA

BIANCHI, EUGENE
[b.] March 15, 1979, Syracuse, NY; [p.] Gina Bianchi; [ed.] Presently a Senior in High School; [oth. writ.] Skies Are Blue, Consuming Fire, A Conversation of Life and Death; [pers.] Man has limited God and has therefore bound himself; [a.] Liverpool, NY

BIANCHI, HOLLY
[pen.] Dina Mapelli (Used for my books); [b.] June 25, 1952, Orange, NJ; [p.] Ovid Bianchi and Matilda Dolce Bianchi (Both are Deceased); [ed.] Studied at Corcoran School of Art, Washington, DC, 1975-76, A.A.S. Degree from Marymount

University, Arlington, VA, 22207; [occ.] Federal Employee, Food and Drug Administration, Rockville, MD; [memb.] Member Summer Opera Guild, Charter Member, National Museum of Women in the Arts, Member, Titanic Historical Society, Member, Washington Ballet Women's Committee, Member, National Trust for Historic presentation and various animal welfare organizations; [hon.] Patriotic Service Award from Department of the Treasury, 1986, Washington, DC; [oth. writ.] I create artwork and contribute poetry to the cultural organizations I support including the Coast Guard Auxiliary in New Jersey. I have also written four poetry books and five children's books (unpublished at this time).; [pers.] I write to let those reading my work to know what is in my heart and soul, as if I am sitting across from you and speaking to you personally.; [a.] Falls Church, VA

BIASETTI, SCOTT
[b.] April 29, 1965, Oceanside, CA; [p.] John and Catherine Biasetti; [m.] Andreana Saffi Biasetti, July 23, 1994; [ed.] University of Notre Dame, New York Medical College; [occ.] Physician; [memb.] American Medical Association, Notre Dame Monogram Club, Trout Unlimited, North American Fishing Club; [a.] Port Jefferson Station, NY

BIERMAN, KENNETH T.
[b.] May 29, 1970, Englewood, NJ; [p.] Leslie and Carole Bierman; [ed.] Northern Highlands Regional High School (grad. 1988) (NJ), Penn State University (grad. 92), and Widener University School of Law (grad. 95); [occ.] Attorney at Law; [memb.] Justice Morris Pashman American Inn of Court, The Bergen County Bar Association, Chi Phi Fraternity, Widener Public Interest Law Clinic; [hon.] Dean's List, accomplished Chicago Marathon (1996); [oth. writ.] A law article published in the Journal of Individual Employment Rights (1995), and several editorials published in People Magazine, The New York Post and the New York Daily News.; [pers.] In the words of Emmet Fox, "Do it trembling if you must, but do it."; [a.] Hoboken, NJ

BIL, AMANDA
[b.] July 29, 1982; Franklin, NH; [p.] Dawne and John Bil; [ed.] I'm in 9th grade college English, and I have other various college courses (Laconia High); [occ.] I'm High School Student; [hon.] 1st grade - field day, 3rd place, 5th grade 3 awards for honor roll, 6th grade 3rd place in activity day, 8th grade 2 for student of week in math; [pers.] I enjoy poetry and natural doings influences my writing. Along with things that have really happened to me; [a.] Laconia, NH.

BINDHAMER, K. L.
[b.] July 17, 1940; [p.] Dec'd; [m.] John S; February 28, 1965; [occ.] Housewife; [pers.] When gives a chose of odds on how long a child is to live, you see more from his eyes and your heart, than you do everyday. When he ask if he is going to die, the heart put words waiting; [a.] SI, NY.

BINDIG, CASANDRA
[pen.] Casey; [b.] October 02, 1980; Chester, PA; [p.] John and Stefaney; [m.] August 30, 1975; [ch.] Jessica 19, Casey 16, Sara 15; [ed.] 2 yrs of pre-school, grade school and is currently in high school; [occ.] student; [hon.] Choir awards in 1996; [pers.]

A person who will make a difference in this world; [a.] Whitehall, PA.

BINGEN, KATHLEEN
[b.] February 21, 1966, West Bend, WI; [p.] Frederick P. Lehn and Darlene E. Lehn; [m.] Peter Eugene Bingen, June 2, 1990; [ch.] Rick Scott Bingen and Alexa Mary Ann Bingen; [ed.] Slinger High School, Moraine Park Technical College; [occ.] Elected Town Clerk for the Town of Polk, Washington County, WI; [memb.] Wisconsin Municipal Clerk's Association, International Municipal Clerk's Association, Wisconsin Towns Association; [pers.] All my poems and writings stem from personal experiences that have affected my life. I have been greatly influenced by my Aunt Carol who has had many articles published throughout Wisconsin.; [a.] Slinger, WI

BINNS, MARY
[b.] April 28, 1930, Los Angeles; [p.] Felipe and Frances Cantu; [m.] Joseph, June 10, 1961; [occ.] Retired from real estate; [a.] South Laguna, CA

BIRT, ORLA L.
[b.] July 13, 1906, Darke Co., OH; [p.] J. E. and Vena Birt; [m.] Dorothy, July 18, 1931; [ch.] William Stephen Bert; [ed.] Elementary and Secondary Masters Degree 1951, Miami University, Oxford, OH; [occ.] Retired; [memb.] Calvery Presby Church, Ohio Prinepals Association; [hon.] Life Member of N.E.A. - O.E.A., and O.E.A.R., Life Member of Cinti Real Estate Rd., Life Member of Oh. Masonic Lodge; [pers.] I have a habit of writing poetry on various occasions or as a tribute to friends.; [a.] Margate, FL

BISHOP, PATRICIA
[b.] January 15, 1948, Tupelo, MS; [p.] Howard and Betty Pearce; [m.] Kenneth Bishop, June 22, 1970; [ch.] Christopher Ray, Kimberly Ann; [ed.] B.A. Blue Mtn. College, M. Ed. University of Mississippi, further study at Mississippi State University and University of Southern Mississippi (Itawamba A. High School 1966 and Itawamba Junior College 1967-1968).; [occ.] Foreign Language Instructor at Itawamba Community College; [memb.] AATSP (American Association of Teachers of Spanish and Portuguese), AATF (Amer. Ass'n. of Teachers of French), Mississippi Foreign Language Ass'n, MS Jr. College Faculty Ass'n., Pilot Club of Fulton, Fulton First Baptist Church; [oth. writ.] Poems: "Springtime Saturdays", "Chris", "Kim", "It Matters Not", Local essay winner: "The Flower of Childcoat Street", short story: "Expectations"; [pers.] Most of my poetry is purely lyrical, expressing strong emotion. I love to work with alliteration.; [a.] Fulton, MS

BISHOP, TIMOTHY
[pen.] Flame Pillar; [b.] April 5, 1976, Ishpeming, MI; [p.] Nedra Bishop and Mickey Bishop; [ed.] Commerce High School; [occ.] Deli Worker at Golden Pantry; [hon.] 13th Place in state of GA in GACS Algebra I tournament. 1st Place in state in keyboarding straight A's all thru high school; [oth. writ.] Articles in the Athens Banner Herald; [pers.] The most important thing anyone can learn is how to love. Love is your one way ticket to Heaven.; [a.] Watkinsville, GA

BISSON, GARY P.
[b.] February 11, 1951, Manchester, NH; [p.] Ernest

and Racheal Bisson; [ch.] Renee M. Bisson, Ernest P. H. Bisson; [ed.] Central High School, Manchester, New Hampshire; [occ.] Lieutenant, Manchester Fire Department; [memb.] I.A.F.F. N.H.M.R.O. NRA, NRA-ILA, National Wildlife Federation; [oth. writ.] Poems not published yet. Touch, Alone, Dreams, Tears.; [pers.] Live free or die, thank you veterans.; [a.] Weare, NH

BLACK, ARLAANA
[b.] January 21, New York City; [p.] Lee and Shirley Shenkin (Deceased); [m.] Charles F. Black III, February 14, 1993; [ch.] Spenser Lindsay Black; [ed.] Columbia University, M.A. in Int'l. Relations, Certificate in African Studies, 30 credits from School of Journalism; [occ.] Teacher, Freelance Reporter, Real Estate; [memb.] S.G.I. USA; [hon.] Award for Outstanding Contribution to World Peace (Magna Cum Laude, Honors Society), various educational honors and awards in teaching; [oth. writ.] Book of poetry entitled "A Day In The Next," (unpublished) various news and feature articles.; [pers.] Educators as writers must use words to inspire and move people in more positive directions. This is my lifetime quest, the process by which I aspire and the dream which I seek to fulfill.; [a.] Edisto Island, SC

BLACKBURN, LISA MARIE
[b.] May 24, 1964; Dearborn Heights, MI; [p.] Charlene and Ronald Blackburn; [ed.] Coral Springs High School, Southeastern Academy, Broward Community College, Hillsborough Community College, University of Tampa; [occ.] Information Support Manager, Tech Data Corporation, Clearwater, Florida; [memb.] United Way Volunteer Assocation, Toys for Tots, American Cancer Society, Data Processing Management Association, Paint Your Heart Out Association, Help Desk Institute, Delta Sigma Phi Alumni Assoc.; [hon.] Who's Who Among American High School Students, graduated magna cum laude, president's list, John Philip Sousa Outstanding Musician Award, D.P.M.A. Chairperson of the Year Award; most team spirit, most distance covered, most creative campsite and picnic award (as team captain for American Cancer), Toys For Tots Appreciation Award; [oth.writ.] Recieved creative writing scholarship for short stories and poems written. (at Coral Springs High School); [pers.] We all have goodness deep inside. Some may not realize how much, while others choose to hide. If each of us takes the initiative to point out each other's good side, we can greatly influence all of our lives; [a.] St. Petersburg, FL.

BLACKMON, SHELBY Y.
[pen.] Bet; [b.] May 11, 1959, Memphis; [p.] John and Shirley Blackmon; [ch.] Ashley and Amber, Blackmon; [ed.] GED, Memphis Area Vo Tech, Draughouns Jr. Junior College. Shelby State Community College; [occ.] CRTT, Medical Assist, Librarian Asst.; [oth. writ.] Why Want They Listen, Come One, Come All; [pers.] I strive to reach someone through my writing.; [a.] Memphis, TN

BLALACK, AARON
[pen.] Lone Wolf, Steve Phyllis, Delta Sierra; [b.] January 20, 1983, Alexandria, LA; [ed.] 8th grade student; [hon.] Several trophies and 14 medals for figure skating, in newspaper many times for piano performances; [oth. writ.] Two poems published.; [pers.] To destroy others with hurtful words because

of their gender or race only serves to show how ignorant and unfeeling you are.; [a.] Kenosha, WI

BLAMIRE, TODD
[b.] May 10, 1966, Los Angeles; [p.] Carol and Edward Blamire; [m.] Terri Blamire, June 29, 1991; [oth. writ.] Too many personal stories, poems, and songs to write. I've kept all of my writings since I was 10 years old.; [pers.] Love each other, take care of each other, and make the most of our brief existence on this wonderful planet.; [a.] Richardson, TX

BLANDFORD, HEATHER ANN
[pen.] "HA"; [b.] November 21, 1983, Fairmont, WV; [p.] Thomas and Patricia Blandford; [ed.] Powell Valley Middle School; [occ.] Student, President of Jr. Beta Club; [memb.] Jr. Beta Club, Girl Scouts, Band; [hon.] 1st Honor Roll, John Fox, Jr. Writing Award, National PTSA Reflections Award, Johns Hopkins IAAY Award; [oth. writ.] Published in Powell Valley Middle School Literary Magazine, Publisher of Jr. Beta Newsletter, short stories and essays.; [pers.] I dedicate this poem to my grandfather as a tribute to his life.; [a.] Big Stone Gap, VA

BLEVINS, AARON
[pen.] Marcel Domeck; [b.] February 22, 1981, Louisville, KY; [p.] Roberta Blevins, Harvey Blevins; [ed.] Shawnee High School; [occ.] Telecommunications Operator; [memb.] Louisville Poet's Guild, AOPA; [oth. writ.] Several locally published poems, songs, and stories.; [pers.] For Andrea: I love you, always...; [a.] Louisville, KY

BOGLE, DELORES VERONICA
[pen.] Ms. De; [b.] August 19, 1937, Kingston, Jamaica, West Indies; [p.] Martel Bogle, Finella Bogle; [ch.] One; [ed.] Valene-Altha-Maymmie A. Seivright; [occ.] Home Health Aid; [memb.] National Library of Poetry, Police Concern - Hospitalized Vet.; [hon.] I have received Two Merit of Award and Bronze Medallion Medal, Two Award Honors, I wish to continue my writing and poetry. I wrote several poems in the Anthology, still hope to do better and better.; [oth. writ.] Yes I have other writing I just want to finished up. Poem take over my life.; [pers.] Writing become a part of me, I am addicted, I am hooked, I don't buy cigarette, I buy paper and pen, writing put me in a mood of relaxation, I can go off smooth sailing, I can dream dreams, and get lost and find myself in a cemetery running.; [a.] Hollis, NY

BONNER, EDWARD
[b.] February 6, 1929, Chicago, IL; [p.] Mary-James Bonner; [ed.] 8 Years Grammar School, 3 years High School; [occ.] Work in Grocery Store; [memb.] R. Horan Club; [hon.] 1952 Won an essay contest worth 1,000 first prize, While serving with Army Engineering in Korea; [pers.] My mother was a great inspiration for writing poem to her - God Bless you mom.; [a.] Elgin, IL

BONNEY, ERIN
[b.] April 6, 1987, Newark, DE; [p.] Michael and Alison Bonney; [ed.] Nixon Elementary School, Sudbury, MA; [occ.] Student - 4th grade; [memb.] Girl Scouts; [oth.writ.] Poetry and Short Stories; [a.] Sudbury, MA.

BOSCH, JEANNETTE MARIA
[b.] November 11, 1982; Miami, FL; [p.] Maria

Elena Bosch and Gustavo Bosch; [occ.] Student and Model; [hon.] Honor roll student, Young Miss Professional Model Diploma; [a.] Miami, FL.

BOWMAN, KATHERINE DENISE
[pen.] Katherine Denise; [b.] May 12, 1960, Wareham, MA; [p.] Judith Lynn Maynard; [m.] Divorced (To be married again soon to high school sweetheart); [ed.] Parkland Senior High School, Winston-Salem, NC, 1978 Nursing Assistant Certification, 1991 Davidson County Community College; [occ.] Radiology Assistant at High Point Regional Hospital; [oth. writ.] I have a collection of my poems that I've written ever since High School that I may now think about publishing in the near future.; [pers.] I write from my heart. I have only been inspired by true experiences and true feelings of love and passion. I was only "brave" enough to recently try this contest.; [a.] Winston-Salem, NC

BOZEMAN, TOBIE
[pen.] Toby Bozeman; [b.] May 31, 1979, Brookhaven, MS; [p.] David and Rose Bozeman; [ed.] Graduate of Lawrence County High School and Student at Copiah - Lincoln Community College; [occ.] Waitress; [memb.] Creative Writing Club (Lawrence Co. High School); [hon.] 95-96 Lawrence County High School Creative Writing Award; [oth. writ.] I have written poems and stories, etc. since seventh grade, but this is my first national publication.; [pers.] I love writing because every word reflects a part of me. I do it for self-satisfaction more than any other reason.; [a.] Silver Creek, MS

BRADLEY, NORMA J.
[b.] January 14, 1958, Aurora, NE; [p.] Gerald and Freda Hartzell; [ch.] Four, Justin Michael, Joseph Dale, Denae Joy, Devrie Jo; [ed.] Aurora High School, University of Nebraska at Kearney; [occ.] Student at UNK, Part-time Bartender/Cook; [memb.] Messiah Lutheran Church; [hon.] UNK Dean's List (3 Consecutive Semesters); [oth. writ.] "Mothers, Daughters and Transculturation" presented at the 1996 Student Writer's Conference in Kearney, Nebr.; [pers.] I consider myself to be in the infancy stage of my talent and want to thank Glady for helping me to be reborn.; [a.] Aurora, NE

BRAGG, TIMOTHY C.
[b.] April 24, 1972; Columbus, GA; [p.] James H. Bragg, Mary Helen Bragg; [ed.] Kendrick High, Columbus State University; [occ.] Novelist, Poet; [memb.] Proud member of Generation X and the Human Race; [hon.] Summa Cum Laude, Alpha Kappa Alpha; [oth.writ.] Approaching completion of my first novel, God Help Us, the definitive story of Generation X, currently seeking a publisher. Many poems also available to be published individually or in book format; [pers.] My major influences include the old style dramatic realists such as Dostoyevsky and Conrado. Like them, I try to be true to myself and my subjects, bringing charity and reality to the most fantastic situations; [a.] Columbus, GA.

BRAGG, TIMOTHY S.
[b.] April 30, 1962, Montpelier, VT; [p.] Robert and Virginia Bragg; [ed.] Union 32 High School, Private Vocal Instruction; [oth. writ.] One studio recorded musical composition, one compilation of

various poems entitled "Works"; [pers.] My goal in my writing has always been with the belief that, eventually, a number of people would hear it or read it, and realize a degree of empathy. My influences include music, classical pieces, etc. If I can, through the presentation of my work, help to lighten a heart, brighten a day, or help someone to find joy through simplicity, then it may very well have been more of a service to myself than to another.; [a.] Wallingford, VT

BRAICU, MELANIE
[b.] May 22, 1967, Rapid City, SD; [p.] J. Roger Eatherton, Florence Lyon; [ch.] Michael Gabriel, Adrian Armand; [occ.] Radiologic Technologist and Mammographer; [pers.] I am only influenced by the good in all around me and the desire for a peaceful happy life and the well-being of others.; [a.] Montgomery, AL

BRAJKOVICH, DAN
[pen.] Danilo Marquise; [b.] January 29, 1971; [occ.] Teacher, Oakland, CA; [pers.] An Axiom and Sentiments: 'If everyone likes you, then you are lying to someone'- It seems to be a particularly healthy note to be disliked by certain types and systems; [a.] San Francisco, CA.

BRASSAR, JOHN DENNIS
[pen.] John Dennis Brassar; [b.] November 27, 1913; Sault Ste Marie, MI; [m.] Flora May Brassar; February 19, 1977; [ed.] G.E.D.; [occ.] Retired from Homeywell Co. FNR. March 31-94 busy working around the house presently; [oth.writ.] To whom it may concern. I am sorry for the delay in writing back. I hope it isn't to late for a come back; [pers.] Dianetic processing addresses the spiritual being, then you will know why you have that bad feeling; [a.] Las Vegas, NV.

BRAUNSTEIN, DRAGICA
[pen.] Buby; [b.] March 28, 1945, Sarajevo; [p.] Dusan Veljovic, Milena Veljovic; [m.] Zoran Braunstein, September 9, 1967; [ch.] Darko Braunstein, Dejan Braunstein; [ed.] Faculty of Arts, University of Sarajevo, Bosnia and Herzegovina, Yugoslavia; [occ.] Professor of Psychology and Pedagogy; [oth. writ.] Articles published in daily newspapers "Liberation" Sarajevo, my writing include poetry and prose.; [pers.] Sometimes, written word has a power of the storm, a strength of the giant, and value of the life! It should be bear in mind, when we write!; [a.] Toronto, Ontario, Canada

BRENNAN, JEANIE
[b.] November 22, 1927; [m.] Gene, April 30, 1949; [ch.] Two sons, Bill and Jerry; [ed.] graduated from high school - 1945; [occ.] Worked in lab at hospital - later in life a Medicare-Medicaid Bookkeeper at Beverly Terrace Nursing Home until retirement.; [oth. writ.] I have written many poems - not on subjects, but for special occasions for family and friends. All fun kinds of poems. The one in this book was more serious - for a friend. Her grandson, Matthew, died at 6 months of crib death.; [pers.] I am a mentor for a little 1st grader this year. I love to travel when I can - especially to Ireland. Recently I traveled to the Eastern U.S. I like to play bridge. I read when possible. For a few years much time has been spent on genealogy. [a.]Watertown, WI

BREZINSKI, MAUREEN MARY
[b.] July 6, 1961, Brooklyn, NY; [p.] Margaret and Kenneth Bird; [m.] John Joseph Brezinski, October 7, 1989; [ch.] Jonathan Charles (18 mos.); [ed.] Bayonne High School; [occ.] Systems Mgr. for a Freight Forwarding Co.; [oth. writ.] A collection of poems encompassing many joyfull and sorrowful heart felt emotions.; [pers.] My poetry was written as a very young woman to help myself express the emotions of love, sorrow, loneliness, and insecurity that I felt as I experienced life.; [a.] Bayonne, NJ

BRIDGEMAN, BETTY
[b.] August 22, 1933; McLean, VA; [p.] Raymond and Thelma Kane; [m.] Samuel M. Bridgeman; December 8, 1956; [ch.] John, Kathleen, Wesley, Michael; [ed.] Falls Church High School and Northern Virginia Community College (incomplete); [occ.] Retired; [memb.] Secretary, McLean Historical Society; National Catholic Committee on Scouting; [hon.] The Silver Fawn and St. George Emblem in Scouting; [oth. writ.] Harold, the Clumsy Squirrel (a children's story); Cutting the Proverbial Apron String (a mother's reflection on her last child getting married); [a.] Aldie, WA.

BRIDGES, JOANN
[b.] July 30, 1947, Honea Path, SC; [p.] James and Mary Thompson; [m.] Eddie Dean Bridges, February 14, 1985; [ch.] Dennis Jr. and Todd Fortner; [ed.] Finished 11th Grade at Woodruff High, later in life received G.E.D.; [occ.] Housewife; [memb.] Calvary Methodist Church; [pers.] On Feb. 2, 1997, I rededicated my life to the Lord. I came home the same night and wrote the poem, "A Happy Day".; [a.] Spartanburg, SC

BRIDGES, ROBIN LYNNETTE
[pen.] Sista X; [b.] September 14, 1971, Saint Louis, MO; [p.] Robert L. Bridges, Gloria S. Bridges; [ed.] O.D. Wyatt H.S., Navarro College, Oxnard College, Art Institute of Atlanta, American College of Atlanta (currently enrolled); [occ.] Mail Clerk, United States Postal Service; [hon.] Hon. Mention, December 1990, World of Poetry, Golden Poet 1991, World of Poetry; [oth. writ.] Several poems written not yet published.; [pers.] My mentors are Dr. Maya Angelou, Imamu Amiri Barraka, Nikki Giovanni and Elaine Brown. Through the death of my mother God showed me the gift He gave me to write.; [a.] Decatur, GA

BRITTON, ALICE P.
[b.] February 12, 1921, Russell, MA; [p.] George Pierce and Annie Tucker; [m.] Byron E. Britton, February 27, 1938; [ch.] Jo Ann Britton, Susan Maxwell, Leigh Britton (Deceased), 7 Grandchildren, 10 Great-grandchildren; [ed.] Westfield High School, 11th; [occ.] Housewife and 50 year plus CraftPerson; [memb.] Russell Community Church, Russell Historical Society, Palm Terrace Club Secretary, Methodist Church Ladies Group, Hampden County Improvement League; [hon.] 4H Leader 12 yrs. Order of the Pearls, Hampden County Extension Service; [oth. writ.] Springfield, New Correspondent, Westfield Advertizer, Town of Russel, Town Report, 'Did you know', History Buff Stonewalls, 7 Hilltowns Booklet Collection of Historical Research, Western, Mass.; [pers.] I have always hoped the world has been a better place for me having been here.; [a.] Sarasota, FL

BROCK, PETER A.
[b.] 1959, Delaware; [p.] Elmer Paul and Adoria; [m.] Kelley; [ch.] Peter Augustine, Daniel James, Joseph Paul, Christopher William; [pers.] Just say "No"; [a.] Garrett Park, MD

BROOKS, DENNIS W.
[b.] May 12, 1949, Jax, FL; [p.] Deceased; [m.] Susan C. Brooks, January 13, 1995; [ch.] Michelle A. Brooks, Daryl W. Brooks; [ed.] High School, Englewood Senior High (1968); [occ.] Electrical supervisor with Duval County School Bound; [oth. writ.] Many different poems some of which have been published. I also write music and lyrics.; [pers.] I like to write from personal experiences as well as from observations, and situations, my wife once ask how I came up with things to write about. I said I didn't know, but while she sat there I wrote a poem called depression in about 2 minutes she loved it.; [a.] Jacksonville, FL

BROUSSARD, VIRGINIA R. V.
[pen.] Tee Rose; [b.] February 19, 1945; Washington, LA; [p.] Resteel P. Villery and Roenia S. Villery; [m.] Divorced; November 12, 1964; [ch.] Michael J., Joyce M. and Orland B. Broussard; [ed.] North Elementary, J.S. Clark High School, Winbush Bible Institute, Prompt Succor Nursing Home (CNA); [oth.writ.] Published, Opelousas Daily World (several poems), Church Of God In Christ Pub. Co., Memphis, Tenn.; [pers.] My main purpose in my life in writing is to reach out to others and touch on their hearts and thought and to encourage them as they read, it will help them as it helped me; [a.] Opelousas, LA.

BROWN, JEROL
[pen.] Broken Dove, Gypsy Rose; [b.] October 9, 1953, Valdosta, GA; [p.] Josephand Mary Brown; [m.] Divorced; [ch.] Four; [ed.] High School GED, 2 Nursing Assistant Certificates; [occ.] Home School my children; [hon.] Poems mounted in different homes and government buildings; [oth. writ.] 7 Books of poetry (never published); [pers.] That I may leave a path that others may find, and that on this path they can learn and grow, through the scars and tears and victories penned down by Broken Dove; [a.] Valdosta, GA

BROWN, KARLEY
[b.] February 14, 1976; [p.] Robert Brown, Marilyn Brown; [ed.] Eastern Washington University (Junior); [occ.] Student, Majoring in Developmental Psychology; [hon.] Selected for National Dean's List, Don Heacox; [pers.] I can do all things through Christ who strengthens me. Philippians 4:13; [a.] Kent, WA

BROWN, MARSHA P. MARTIN
[b.] October 24,1958; Brooklyn, NY; [p.] Rawle Martin, IdaCambridge Martin; [m.] William Cecil Brown: August 18, 1984; [ch.] Christopher Daen, Jason Ajani; [pers.] A little kindness goes a long way. Life is too short and uncertain to allow malice to prevail; [a.] Bronx, NY.

BROWN, NANCY
[b.] August 23, 1943, Newark, NJ; [ed.] Point Pleasant Beach H.S. in N.J., A.A.S. Computer Science - Brookdale Community College in Shrewsbury, NJ; [occ.] Retired - Computer Programmer; [pers.] I write as a result of my desire to understand and express my feelings about my experiences in life.; [a.] Livingston, TX

BROWN, TAMMY RHNEE
[b.] June 25, 1965, Batesville, AR; [p.] Sammy and Kayrene Asberry; [m.] Kenneth Brown, April 24, 1993; [ch.] Evan Layne, Melissa Lerin; [ed.] Cave City High and White River Technical School; [occ.] Nurse/Mother; [memb.] Cave City First Assembly of God; [hon.] I am honored to be a Mother!!!; [oth. writ.] Have written many now publishing them gradually; [pers.] I love to write poetry, my inspiration comes from battling years of infertility and being blessed now with an open adoption resulting in two children.; [a.] Cave City, AR

BROWN, TRISHA
[b.] November 8, 1979; Harrisburg, PA; [p.] William Brown, Deborah Brown; [ed.] East Pennsboro Area high School; [occ.] Babysitter; [memb.] Student Council, French Club, Tennis, Stage Crew, Chess Club; [hon.] Who's who among American High School Students and a second place medal for a tennis competition; [oth.writ.] I've had one poems, published in our school newspaper. I had one short story published in the school news paper also; [pers.] I write about the things in my life and my own experiences and I hope that people can somehow relate to my poems. I have been influenced by Emily Dickinson; [a.] Enola, PA.

BROWNE, BENJAMIN JUDSON
[pen.] Benjamin Judson Browne; [b.] December 19, 1921, Rockland, ME; [p.] Benjamin and Rachel Browne; [m.] Laurel and Browne, October 27, 1967; [ch.] Mark, Nina, Matthew; [ed.] Suffield Academy, Duke Univ., Boston Univ: B.A., Ph.D. (Philosophy), Union Theological Seminary, New York, N.Y., M. Div.; [occ.] Retired. Formerly: Professor Edinboro State Un., St. Mary's College of MD, Vice Pres. Lakeland Coll. Christian Pastor, Harrisburg, PA; [memb.] Amer. Civil Liberties Union, American Alumni Council, Chrmn Boston Committee on Open Housing 1956-57, Amer. College Public Relations Ass'n; [hon.] Roberts Prize New Testament Exegesis, Princeton Seminary, Time-Life Grand Award: Best Direct Mailpublication - US Colleges; [oth. writ.] Several articles: United Church Herald, one book on cultural conflict: "Kiss of Eve - Kiss of Death", 1990, Dissertation: "Plato's Social Philosophy as Fascistic." A collection of poems.; [pers.] There is an aspirational-survival spirit given to the human breast to counter and redeem life's apparent defeats and absurdities.; [a.] Lyman, ME

BROWNLOW, DELORIS
[b.] October 19, 1965; Cruger, MS; [p.] T.J. Burden, Cora Burden; [ch.] Brittany, Keenan; [ed.] S.V. Marshall High, Mississippi Valley State University; [occ.] Contract Specialist; [oth.writ.] Several poems; [a.] Huntsville, AL.

BRUBAKER, JASON
[b.] May 26, 1976, Fairfax, VA; [p.] Jay and Mary Lou Brubaker; [ed.] Lake Braddock Secondary School, George Mason University; [occ.] Sales Representative for Superior Salon Products; [memb.] Eagle Scouts of America; [pers.] My inspiration and dearest love, Christina Zanette. My influences are Byron and Joyce.; [a.] Burke, VA

BRYANT, ALICE G.
[b.] September 8, 1944, Lorain, OH; [p.] Hersel Morgan, Priscilla Morgan; [m.] James T. Bryant;

[ch.] Chanel Thompson, Courtney Thompson; [ed.] Mott Community College, Flint, MI, Associate Degree in Applied Science, License Practical Nurse; [pers.] Follow your first mind, but how can you tell what is your first mind.; [a.] South Bend, IN

BUCK, JONATHAN W.
[pen.] Warren; [b.] June 26, 1966, Houston, TX; [p.] Henry and Ruby Buck; [ed.] Aldine Sr. High, Houston, TX; [occ.] Barber; [memb.] Memorial Baptist Church; [pers.] Jesus Christ is the only reason for purpose in Life. And for Him only do I write. I have been greatly influenced by Robert Frost.; [a.] Houston, TX

BURBANK, DANIEL P.
[b.] July 26; Rochester, NH; [p.] Norma and Paul Burbank; [m.] Janet M. Burbank; May 1, 1982; [ch.] Daniel P. Burbank, Brian, Christopher; [ed.] GEO; [occ.] Logger/carpener; [oth.writ.] Did you know I love you published in the Poetry Guilds anthology this spring.

BURCH, LEE WILEY
[b.] May 11, 1954, Olney, TX; [p.] Nick and Alwana Burch; [m.] Janan, May 11, 1974; [ch.] Adam 18, Daniel 16; [ed.] B.S. Degree, East Texas State Univ. 1975; [occ.] Agriculture Science Instructor, Newcastle I.S.D., Newcastle, Texas; [memb.] Life Member, National FFA Alumni, Vocational Agriculture Teachers Assn of Texas, National Vocational Teachers Assn.; [hon.] American Farmer Degree, FFA, 1973, Teacher of the Year, 1985, Texas Sheep and Goat Raisers Assn., Honorary Lone Star Farmer Degree, FFA 1980; [oth. writ.] Several poems written for various functions and individuals. Perform poetry in public. Currently writing autobiography named "Dreamin' In Color".; [pers.] I have been writing poetry all my life. I have been greatly influenced by my mother and my favorite all time poet, Mr. Hank Williams.; [a.] Newcastle, TX

BURCH, VIRGINIA DUFFY
[b.] October 7, 1958, Sacramento, CA; [p.] Lt. Col. G. H. Duffy, Georgia Duffy; [m.] Randall Burch, July 27, 1979; [ch.] Jermie Alan; [pers.] I have always been inspired by the talent of a poet who can touch ones inner soul, through an imagination or truth from days gone by, present and future.; [a.] Decatur, TX

BURDEN, BRIAN
[b.] March 11, 1972, Louisville, KY; [pers.] "I can do all things through Christ which strengthen me. Philippians 4113 A.G.T.G.; [a.] Louisville, KY

BURDICK, JEFFREY S.
[pen.] Gentleman Jeff/Sloggathorus Wreck; [b.] November 21, 1969, St. Paul, MN; [p.] Thomas E. Mulkern and Cathryn Burdick; [m.] Darcie Lynn Mason, The Dawn of Time; [ch.] Alek Scott, Gunnar Gary, Jacob Collins; [ed.] Harding High, Class of 1988 and the East Side School of Hard Knocks; [occ.] Welding and Tattoo Artist, P.T. Tattoo Artist; [memb.] Lead singer of Final Demise a St. Paul Based Hard Core Thrash Band with Bubie, Sean, Len and Stevie, all original!; [hon.] Artistic achievement in painting, drawing and sculpture and now, Literary composition to which I am truly honored and grateful; [oth. writ.] Final Demise "Power of Suggestion", Final Demise "Mystery Violence The-

atre" (Audial) and piles of unpublished work in poetry and song.; [pers.] Express your thoughts, ideas and be good to one another, for one day we'll all know each other on a spiritual basis.; [a.] Saint Paul, MN

BURGESS, DALE E.

[b.] December 24, 1936, San Mateo, CA; [p.] Carlton Burgess and Vivienne Burgess; [ch.] Gregory, Stephen, Jeffrey; [ed.] B.A. Accounting, MBA Taxation; [occ.] CPA; [hon.] Outstanding Professor, Graduate Tax School, Outstanding Alumni graduate Tax School; [oth. writ.] Many poems written for friends and personal expression and fun.; [pers.] Words are an expression of the heart.; [a.] Larkspur, CA

BURK, SARAH C.

[b.] May 17, 1956, Cambridgeshire, England; [p.] Burl S. Sands; [m.] Charles W. Burk, September 12, 1984; [ed.] Baptist Christian Academy, 3 semesters Bossier, Parish Community College; [occ.] Homemaker; [hon.] Graduated Third in my class, B.C.A., twice published in the College Poetry Review by The National Poetry Press; [oth. writ.] Miss April, Final, Tenth Floor, Black Monday, Always, Unit 9, Everafter, Innocence in the Mist, Sumptuous Summer, etc.; [pers.] Dreams, promises, and love have carried me through the years. My poetry relates the power of despair, defiance, romance, compassion, and the ecstasy of nature.; [a.] Bossier City, LA

BURKEEN, LUCILLE

[b.] April 21, 1958, Clarksville, TN; [p.] Hubert and Martha Winchester; [m.] Jerry Burkeen; [ch.] October 12, 1976; [ed.] Brian, Nancy and Jermey; [occ.] A.S. - Accounting Miller-Motte Business College Graduated Summa - Cum Laude; [memb.] Bookkeeper, Langford's Welding and Steelworks; [pers.] The only true way to grow older and wiser, is to grow older in the knowledge of Jesus Christ as Lord and Savior.; [a.] Clarksville, TN

BURKS, DEBBIE A.

[pen.] Debbie Burks; [b.] September 10, 1953, Birmingham, AL; [p.] Mr. and Mrs. Shelby Carson Douglas; [m.] I am divorced.; [ch.] Zachary Lee Burks and Kaleb Luke Burks; [ed.] West End High and Minor High School; [memb.] I am a member of Bonita Park, Freewill Baptist Church, Birmingham, AL; [oth. writ.] I use my poems in my church bulletins.; [pers.] I want to give honor, praise and glory to Jesus, who died that I might live. Thank you Lord for loving me so much.; [a.] Trussville, AL

BURKS, SHERRY

[b.] December 13, 1973, Chilton County; [p.] Norma Jean and Willie V. Wilson; [m.] Algarian Burks, November 20, 1995; [ch.] Algarian Burks II; [ed.] Isabella High School; [occ.] Sales Associate; [memb.] Future Homemakers of America, 6 yrs. Vice-President, 1 yr. Parliamentarian, 1 yr. Chorus, 2 yrs. Beta Club, 2 yrs.; [hon.] Honor Roll, Who's Who Among America High School Students, National Honor Society, English Merit Achievement, Miss FHA 1991 2nd Alternate, Senior 1992 Best Dressed.; [pers.] I have great pride and joy in my writing - this achievement has allowed me an opportunity to further enhance my writing abilities and take them to a higher level. Thank God and you for this privilege and honor.; [a.] Huntsville, AL

BURLINGAME, SAUNDRA F.

[b.] June 14, 1940, Moscow, ID; [p.] Robert D. and Grace M. Vercoe; [m.] Amos D. Burlingame, August 4, 1962; [ch.] Wendy, Darci, Calvin, Kevin; [ed.] Plummer Elementary Plummer High School, Plummer Idaho; [memb.] American Legion Auxiliary Fraternal Order or Eagles Auxiliary Associated Grandmothers Club of Washington Inc. Plymouth Congregational Church UCC; [oth. writ.] None published; [pers.] My writings come mostly from my own personal experiences, feeling and thoughts. Mostly dealing with family, feelings and God. And the heart.; [a.] Colfax, WA

BURNETT, SHIRLEY

[b.] January 15, 1941, Fulton, TX; [p.] John and Birdie Cole (Deceased); [m.] J. P. Burnett (Deceased March 24, 1995), October 6, 1962; [ch.] Gary Burnett, Leah Burnett; [ed.] Rockport - Fulton High School, Texas Western College - El Paso, Texas; [occ.] Retired - 1996, 15 years in education - last 2 years was a Softball Coach at R7 High School; [memb.] Daughters of the Republic of Texas; [hon.] All District 61AAAA-1995, Coach of the year 1995 in Softball in South Texas; [oth. writ.] Several poems - not published: "The Walk", "Life with J.P.", and "Thirty Two Years", to name a few.; [pers.] I have been writing since the death of my husband 2 yrs. ago. Most of my poems reflect the importance of God in my life.; [a.] Fulton, TX

BURRESS, AMANDA

[b.] May 17, 1985, Wichita, KS; [p.] James and Vicki Burress; [ed.] Currently in 6th grade; [occ.] Student; [memb.] 4H, Young Entomologist Society, National Wildlife Foundation; [pers.] I really do have a fat lazy cat named "Lollypop". He inspired me for this poem. He does just about everything in this poem. Including put on a hat!; [a.] Springfield, IL

BURTON, DORIS M.

[pen.] Doris M. Burton; [b.] October 19, 1917, Anderson, SC; [p.] Thomas, Melvin and Mary Malone Vandiver; [m.] Ralph W. Burton (Deceased), June 7, 1935; [ch.] Melvin, Alan, Patricia, Tommy and Alice Burton; [ed.] High School-Anderson Girls, High School, Anderson, SC; [occ.] Retired Kennestone Hospital Ward Secretary; [memb.] Beta Club, 1st Presbyterian Church Marietta, GA.; [hon.] Born 1 of 10 girls and 1 boy to above. Doris has a beautiful voice and sang to her children and far herself when we were young, (Melvin Burton son).; [oth. writ.] Being 80 years old, Doris has penned other poems but none published. Letters to the editor only publications and these were many. One poem "Missing Melissa" I would also like to send Barbara E. Burton - Daughter in Law.; [pers.] "To my grown up son" was penned in approx 48 or 49 to my husband Melvin Burton who has lies 60th birthday March 30, 1977.; [a.] Marietta, GA

BURTON, TOMMY

[pen.] T. Burton "Dream On"; [b.] September 26, 1949, Johnston, SC; [p.] Panzo and Alice Burton; [m.] Roper Ann Burton, November 15, 1970; [ch.] Stoney - (T.J., Tommy Jr.); [ed.] WE Parker High School; [occ.] Professional Carpet and Vinyl Installer - Part time Writer; [memb.] Johnston City Council Gov., Piedmont Technical College Board of Visitors, Johnston Human Relation Committee,

Edgefield Chamber of Commerce Officer; [hon.] Former Vietnam Combat Infantry/Veteran with 4 medals and other awards; [oth. writ.] I have 28 song and poems copy written in to The Library of Congress.; [pers.] I admire the works by such people as the wright Bro, Dr. Gerge WV Curver, and all the inventors, I also like to write about myself in song and poems when I was once a Casinova, years ago.; [a.] Johnston, SC

BURYAK, IRENE

[b.] October 21, 1979, Brooklyn; [p.] Michael Buryak, Esfira Buryak; [ed.] Moore Catholic High School; [occ.] Student; [pers.] The poetry I write express my feelings. Some good, some bad but there mine. Whenever I write I feel a sense of relief, that I have one less thought on my mind.; [a.] Staten Island, NY

BUSACCA, JENNIFER

[b.] June 2, 1985, Bayshore, NY; [p.] Kathy and Richie Busacca; [ed.] Cayuga Elementary School, Lake Grove, NY (grades K-5), Wenonah Elementary School, Lake Grove, NY (grade 6); [hon.] High Honor Roll, Perfect Attendance, Her essay won for the recent D.A.R.E. Program; [pers.] I love to write poetry and stories and hope to be a famous author some day.; [a.] Lake Grove, NY

BUSTAMANTE, CHIKI

[pen.] Chiki Bustamante; [b.] November 5, 1953, Heidelberg, Germany; [p.] Robert B. Maddux, Barbara A. Maddux; [m.] Joel I. Bustamante, December 13, 1975; [ch.] Jihi Bustamante, Jun Bustamante; [ed.] Art Institute of Ft. Lauderdale, Central Venezolano/Americano; [occ.] Illustrator/ Desktop Publisher; [memb.] Sokagakkai International; [hon.] Pinellas County Schools, Volunteer Services Award; [oth. writ.] Translations for Seikyo Criollo in Caracas, Venezuela; [pers.] With a positive attitude, I strive to reach my full potential by living each moment as if it were my last. For only through the achievement of each individual's happiness can world peace be realized.; [a.] Saint Petersburg, FL

CABALLERO, KATIE MARIE

[pen.] Katie Marie; [b.] October 5, 1980, Morenci, AZ; [p.] John Charles Caballero and Irma D. Caballero; [ed.] Bisbee High School; [memb.] Enterprise Club; [hon.] Free and Accepted Masons of America Public Schools Committee Award (State Winner); [pers.] I dedicated this poem to my parents, who taught me never to quit, and also my teacher Hedwig Mulkey, who was a great influence.; [a.] Bisbee, AZ

CADET, RALPH EVENS

[pen.] God & My parents; [b.] June 22, 1980, Haiti; [p.] Marie Yolaine Cadet and Jean Dupuy Cadet; [ed.] Student at N. Miami Beach Sr. High School 11th grade. Plan to study Medical after High School; [memb.] Fulford United Methodist Church; [hon.] Chamber of Commerce, Octagon Club, French Club and also sports. I have been nominated secretary of my youth program and youth crime watch.; [oth. writ.] Couple to my Friend and to the people that I love and really appreciate.; [pers.] I want to thank my teachers that influence me to follow my dreams and believe in what I can do. Thanks to my family, my friends, and also my youth leader.; [a.] N. Miami Beach, FL

CAIN, BARBARA
[b.] November 16, 1952, Winston-Salem, NC; [p.] Davis and Katherine Woodle; [m.] Ervin A. Cain, October 23, 1993; [ch.] 4 daughters and 1 son; [ed.] East Forsyth High, High Point Univ.; [occ.] Office Asst. Chemistry Dept, Univ. of NC at Greensboro; [memb.] American Legion Auxiliary, Tar Heel Girls State Commission; [oth. writ.] Several poems and collection being considered for publication...also, have children's stories under consideration.; [a.] Kernersville, NC

CALEY, PEGGY
[b.] April 20, 1933, Greeley, CO; [p.] Paul and Edna Wells; [m.] Clark Caley, August 29, 1955, (now divorced); [ch.] Christopher and Cathleen Caley; [ed.] B.S. in Education - Grade School teacher for a few years; [occ.] Retired; [memb.] United Methodist Church, Eastern Star, - I help with the Heart and Cancer Associations; [oth. writ.] Mostly just poems about my family. Some of them have been published in local newspapers; [pers.] Christianity is not just a word but the way we live. Nothing can take the place of doing His will and I believe nothing takes the place of plain every-day goodness and compassion.; [a.] Clarks, NE

CAMARA, DALE M.
[b.] July 13, 1997; Bridgeport, CT; [p.] Lyda Dolores Heilman, Ronald Petrahal; [m.] Scott Camara; May 22, 1993; [ch.] One on the way; [ed.] University of Houston; [occ.] Credit Supervisor, Warnoco, WC; [memb.] Warnoco's Credit Union Supervisory Committee. Member and organist of First English Lutheran Church; [oth writ.] Stories published in the local "Beanfest"; [pers.] Writing is a way of expressing my inner soul. I am also an amateur photographer and enjoy combining both medals; [a.] Bridgeport, CT.

CAMPBELL, BRAD
[b.] May 5, 1933, Hinton, OK; [p.] Berenice Campbell Stephenson; [m.] Bonnie Jean Campbell, February 21, 1986; [ch.] Carla, A.J., Scott; [ed.] Alva High, Alva, Okla, Northwestern State Univ, Alva, Okla, Arizona State Univ, Phoenix, Ariz., Wichita State Univ., Wichita, Kans.; [occ.] Engineering Design Specialist (Retired); [memb.] Fraternal Order of Eagles Aerie #2919, "Worthy Past President", Golden Spike Trap club, Utah Golf Assn., First Presbyterian Church; [hon.] Numerous awards Engineering Design related; [oth. writ.] "Personal" poems of loved one's, not intended for publication.; [pers.] As a child my mother told me my outlook on life is "Looking through rose colored glasses". Until proved otherwise, still prefer to do so.; [a.] Farr West, UT

CAMPBELL, GENEVIEVE
[b.] September 22, 1923, Alpena, MI; [p.] Warren and Nellie Page; [m.] Orian (Deceased), June 24, 1944; [ch] Gloria, Douglas, Valerie; [ed.] BA English and Elementary Education (majors), Central Michigan and Wayne State U. of Mich.; [occ.] Retired teacher, Writing poetry, Children's Lit.; [oth. writ.] Self-published: History of Christ Episcopal Church of Sidney, Nebraska; [pers.] Count your blessings. Do your best with the skills you have.; [a.] Sidney, NE

CAMPBELL, JENNIFER
[b.] October 16, 1981, Dallas, TX; [p.] Cliff Campbell, Sandy Trimble; [ed.] 9th Grade at Southwest High School, Ft. Worth, TX; [occ.] I baby sit for my church.; [memb.] I an a member of the Southwest High School Drama Department, the Blue Raider Girls Softball Association; [pers.] The reason why I wrote this poem was to warn people about Russian Roulette. My friend killed himself pretending to play this, and I don't want that to happen to anyone else.; [a.] Fort Worth, TX

CAMPOLO, MARYANNE
[b.] October 20, 1958, Syracuse, NY; [p.] Carmen Campolo Sr., Marion Caparco; [ed.] Albany High School; [occ.] Retail Management; [pers.] When we can learn to let go of our expectations in life our achievements become unlimited.; [a.] Amsterdam, NY

CAPPS, ROBERT DEAN
[pen.] Poet Capps; [b.] June 8, 1961, Santa Rosa, NM; [p.] Floyd Capps, Margaret Dowdy; [ed.] GED at TAVS; [occ.] CDL-APTX; [oth. writ.] Other poems include Window, Antiprose, and Music Coruscation.; [pers.] I have been greatly influenced by the Ten Commandments. Thanks Mom.; [a.] Albuquerque, NM

CARGILL, NOMA D.
[b.] October 1, 1913, Omaha, NE; [p.] Hans P. and Maria Jessen; [m.] P. Emmett Bechthold, December 24, 1932; [ch.] Delbert L., Linda R.; [ed.] High School, Business School, 83 years life experiences; [occ.] Retired Bookkeeper 32 years in same company; [memb.] First Baptist Church Grand Island, NE 59 years Danish Sisterhood; [oth. writ.] Poems: "Christmas", "Easter"; [pers.] I pray that my writings will be a living testimony of my love for my Saviour, Jesus Christ, the true author, who inspired them.; [a.] Grand Island, NE

CARLSON, GAYLE ANNE
[b.] October 13, 1950, Coeur D'Alene, ID; [p.] Bernard and Dorothy Merriman; [m.] Barry V. Carlson, June 7, 1969; [ch.] Benjamin Vaughn, Rachel Anne, Jacob Joel, Abigail Joye, Luke Andrew, Isaac Artemas, Alexander Eli; [ed.] Coeard'Alene Senior High, North Idaho Junior College, Covenant Bible College; [occ.] Piano Instructor, Part-time, Homeschooling Mother, Housewife; [memb.] Eugene Christian and Missionary Alliance Church - Eugene, Oregon; [oth. writ.] High School and College Literary Magazines - Poetry, Church publications - Poetry; [pers.] Since God gifts me to write, I prefer to honor Him in the majority of my works.; [a.] Eugene, OR

CAROLLO, JANET MARIE
[pen.] Jan Blake; [b.] September 14, 1956, New York; [p.] Lorraine Manning and Andrew Carollo; [ch.] My 2 beautiful dogs: Dallas and Daina; [ed.] Uniondale High School, Hofstra University, Weist - Barron School of Television, Arena Theater; [occ.] Artist, Actor, Musician; [memb.] Preservation of Wildlife Foundation, Handicapped Children Association, Spina Bifida Foundation; [hon.] Junior High School received award in gymnastics from President Johnson, High School awards in music and theater. Also received a "Medal of Honors" from Uniondale High School.; [oth. writ.] I've written many poems for pleasure. I would like to have some of my poems published. I'm also working on my autobiography.; [pers.] I strive to reflect the kindness and love of mankind and wildlife in my writing. I am also greatly influenced by music and poetry.; [a.] Babylon Village, NY

CAROTHERS, CLAIRE
[b.] December 11, 1972, Greenville, MS; [p.] Roy Carothers, Camille Glazebrook; [ed.] B.S. in Physical Ed., Summa Cum Laude, pursuing M.A. in Gerontology/Sociology; [occ.] Research Assistant at Northeast LA University, at the Institute of Gerontology; [memb.] Phi Kappa Phi, Omicron, Delta Kappa, Mortar Board, Association for Gerontological Enrichment, Sociology Club, Cardinal and Amber, American Sociological Association; [hon.] Physical Ed. Major of Myer Award Sociology, Service Award, Sociology Club Member of NE Year Award, Student Involvement Scholarship; [pers.] Poetry is the window of the soul. I write so that the world can see from my side of the window.; [a.] Monroe, LA

CARPENTER, SHELDON C.
[b.] August 19, 1974, Rexburg, ID; [p.] Ron and Jan Carpenter; [ed.] Teton High School, Teton Middle School, Victor Elementary; [occ.] Desk Clerk, Grand Canyon Quality Inn; [oth. writ.] Writings that I've judged to hard and put away. But I hope to write something that I can approve to have published.; [pers.] This is the first poem I have really written. More on a whim during a spell of depression and a feeling of "you're going nowhere" than a confidence in my "artistry". I guess it was mostly to say that I did it and to see what would happen.; [a.] Grand Canyon, AZ

CARROLL, DEBRA-THERESE
[pen.] Community of Teresian Carmelites; [b.] June 18, 1964, Worcester, MA; [p.] John Carroll, Loretta Carroll; [ed.] Holy Name Central Catholic High, Worcester State College; [occ.] A semi-cloistered Carmelite Nun; [memb.] National Notary Association, CMSWR: Councilor Major Superiors of Women Religious; [hon.] Dean's List, Summa Cum Laude/Valedictorian, Psi Chi National Honor Society: Psychology, Alpha Mu Gamma: Foreign Language National Honor Society; [oth. writ.] Music Compositions: Songs Articles for Diocesan Newspaper, unpublished poems.; [pers.] To soothe the wounded hearts of humanity with the message of God's love and mercy.; [a.] Worcester, MA

CARSON, MEGAN
[b.] January 10, 1985, Charleston, WV; [p.] Collett "Skip" Carson, Mary Beth Carson; [ed.] Currently 6th Grade Student, St. Anthony School. Will be attending Charleston Catholic High School in the Fall of 1997; [pers.] Writing is just "speaking" on paper.; [a.] Charleston, WV

CARTER, RICHARD A.
[pen.] H.R.S.; [b.] June 13, 1949, San Francisco, CA; [p.] J. and M. Carter; [ch.] Jimmie Douglas; [ed.] Merritt Island High, Mississippi State University, University of Maryland; [occ.] Philanthropist Incrp.| Influenced by life and the love of a great librarian.; [a.] Corinth, MS

CASEY, PAULA
[b.] February 16, 1953, Kansas; [p.] Paul and Pat Packard; [m.] Mike Casey, August 6, 1988; [ch.] Skylar Kidd, Connor Casey; [ed.] B.S.W., University of Kansas, J.D., Washburn University Law School; [occ.] Attorney; [memb.] Wichita Bar

Association, Kansas Bar Association, American Family and Concillatory Courts, United Methodist, Homeless Task Force; [a.] Wichita, KS

CASTILLE, BELINDA
[pen.] By Be; [b.] January 28, 1967, Dallas, TX; [p.] Mary E. and Bonnie Joe Warren; [m.] Simon Castille Jr., May 22, 1993; [ch.] Elwyn Jr., Joshua, Leon, and Simone; [ed.] Linden - Kildare Elem., Linden - Kildare Jr. High, and L-K High Sch., all of Linden, Texas, Tx. Southern Univ., Houston, TX; [occ.] Medical Insurance Rep., Univ. Tx., M.D. Anderson Cancer Cntr.; [memb.] Rose of Sharon M.B.C.; [hon.] Several awards for good sportmanship. Finished High School 1 yr. ahead of class. On the Honor Roll several times. Star actress "Olga" In High Sch. Play; [oth. writ.] The Flicker of A Light, Just to Commit Suicide, Running This Race at God's Pace, Awake to Morning, etc...., non-published yet.; [pers.] I am influenced by all poets due to my writing reflect joyful, sadness and living. My poetry is of various different themes to touch the heart.; [a.] Houston, TX

CASTILLO, KATHLEEN A.
[b.] May 23, 1973, Dueblo, CO; [p.] Ray and Judy Sperry; [m.] Alex Castillo, April 30, 1994; [occ.] Staff Accountant; [pers.] Both of my grandmothers and one grandfather had passed away prior to me getting married. The day of the wedding I placed this poem on my grandmother's graves. I wrote this about 1 week before the wedding. I felt very sad that they couldn't all be there but somehow I think all of them were watching.; [a.] Dueblo, CO

CASTONGUAY, JUSTIN BROOKS
[b.] March 21, 1985, Williamsburg, VA; [p.] Shirley Castonguay; [ed.] 6th, West Point Middle School; [memb.] Our Lady of the Blessed Sacrament Church, Altar Server; [pers.] My love of mystical and magical stories and characters has greatly influenced my poetry. Art and Science are my favorite subjects.; [a.] West Point, VA

CAVUOTI, K. MICHIEL
[pen.] Kate Ryan; [b.] April 30, 1952; Shirley, MA; [p.] Lawrence W. Head, Jr. and Florence P. Head; [m.] Clinton P. Cavuoti Jr. M.D; August 21, 1982; [ch.] Whitney Ryan Cavuoti (son); [ed.] San Angelo (TX) Central High, Angelo State University, U. of TX Health Science Center at San Antonio; [occ.] Dressage Trainer, Wind River Farm, Inc. (President); [memb.] United States Dressage Federation; American Horse Shows Assn.; U.S. Equestrian Team; Holy Family Catholic Church; American Medical Assn. Alliance; [a.] Abilene, TX.

CESPEDES, BETH A.
[b.] July 26, 1958, New Bedford, MA; [p.] Willard and Jean Mahar; [m.] Travis J. Cespedes, July 21, 1989; [ch.] Jude and Milo; [ed.] Associates of Arts Degree in Fashion Design from the College of Alameda, Alameda, CA; [occ.] Senior Product Tech, for "GAP" Technical Services; [pers.] I have made a commitment to work with the cosmic rhythms of life, in order to have a positive affect on others that will bring happiness, success and joy to all.; [a.] San Anselmo, CA

CHAMBERS JR., DONALD
[b.] April 28, 1960, San Diego; [p.] Marian Hill and Donald Chambers Sr.; [m.] Lorelei Chambers, July 22, 1989; [ch.] Aaron and Brandon; [ed.] Castle Park High School, Southwestern Jr. College; [occ.] Material Coordinator; [hon.] "1984 Mr. San Diego"; [pers.] It is my hope and prayer that those who identity with this poem can somehow find the same healing in its words as I did in writing it. Thanks for the love and support from my wife Lorelei.; [a.] San Diego, CA

CHAMBLIN, TONY V.
[b.] May 4, 1966, Maysville, KY; [p.] Leo and Verdena Chamblin; [m.] Deborah A. Chamblin, September 24, 1994; [ch.] Megan Curtis, Anthony Lance, Houston Taylor; [ed.] Mason Co. High, Maysville Community College; [occ.] Team Leader, Paint Shop, Toyota Motor Mfg. KY.; [memb.] Northside Christian Church; [pers.] I write from the heart and through God's guidance. I am greatly influenced by J.R.R. Tolkien and other "Fantasy" authors this poem was written to my wife in our first wedding anniversary.; [a.] Sadieville, KY

CHAMBLISS-LARKINS, LAVERNE
[b.] June 3, 1950, Akron, OH; [p.] Lucy and Luther Chambliss; [m.] LeRoy Alan Larkins, June 30, 1972; [ch.] La Troy L.A., La Tron A.; [ed.] Buchtel High, Howard University, The University of Akron; [occ.] Caregiver, Parking Services Kent State University; [hon.] Dean's List, Top Female Salesperson - Great Lakes Division; [oth. writ.] Numerous poems published in local newspapers.; [pers.] I believe we all have a purpose in life and we should not pass up an opportunity to leave a positive image of ourselves.; [a.] Akron, OH

CHANDLER, BARBARA JEAN
[pen.] Faith Byerson; [b.] October 30, 1937, Des Moines, IA; [p.] Rev. and Mrs. C. Gordon Chandler; [m.] Harold W. Rodrigues, July 18, 1970; [ch.] Terri Lee Byers, Rock Dean Allison; [ed.] Pittsburg, Ca. High School Eugene Bible College, Eugene Oregon; [occ.] Retired Civil Service Supervisory Position in Social Services; [oth. writ.] I am an amateur. Several poems, three Children's book dedicated to each grandchild: "Tae", "Eager's Lost Bark", "Adolph's Escape"; [pers.] Happiness is not in having what you want but in wanting what you have. I am contented and very happy.; [a.] Antioch, CA

CHANG, HANNA
[pen.] Silent Muse; [occ.] Graphic Artist; [oth.writ.] Silent Muse, White Blossom and Memory Tree; [pers.] I strive to integrate my poetry, song writings and paintings to represent my personal philosophy about humanity. My works have been influenced by Chinese philosophy, Zen Buddhism and Christianity; [a.] Fullerton, CA.

CHAPMAN, ART
[b.] December 5, 1941; Camden, Ark; [p.] Arthur and Tinnie Imez Chapman; [m.] Divorced; [ch.] 3; [ed.] 3 yrs college; technical and Liberal Arts training; [occ.] Special projects manager in engineering and construction; free lance writer; [memb.] American Management Assoc.; American Assn. of Airport Executives, NAACP; [hon.] University of Nevada at Las Vegas (UNLV) "Outstanding Services in Minority Studies," "Award of Merit," Co-founder of The Afro-American Unity Festival; [oth. writ.] Numerous essays on religion and dreams; politics; a collection of more than 260 poems; [pers.] In my poetry, my quest is for the "Holy Grail" of truth, and to share my findings with others; [a.] Las Vegas, NV.

CHAPMAN, CAROL A.
[b.] October 4, 1952, Jersey City, NJ; [p.] Nunzio Savino, Evelyn Savino; [m.] Thomas C. Chapman, June 11, 1983; [ed.] Piscataway High, Middlesex County College; [occ.] Employee Benefits Administrator; [hon.] Phi Theta Kappa, Outstanding achievement award in business administration and management; [oth. writ.] Personal poems and notes to my husband.; [pers.] With love and support of family, overcame a noticeable birth defect. As children, our peers can be cruel, I wrote my poem "Life" at age 10. I look for the inner beauty in all people.; [a.] Delray Beach, FL

CHAPMAN, KAREAN L.
[b.] April 8, 1969, Ottawa, Ont., Canada; [p.] Israel and Betty Levi; [m.] John T. Chapman, April 24, 1994; [ed.] Monta Vista High School, San Jose State University, Foothill College, Registered Veterinary Technician; [occ.] Small Business Owner Registered Veterinary Technician; [memb.] (CVMA) California Veterinary Medical Assoc., Association of Avian Veterinarian, American Holistic, Veterinary Medical Assoc., United States Figure Skating Association; [hon.] Royal Conservatory of Music, University of Toronto. First Class Honours in piano and theory black belt in the martial arts; [oth. writ.] Currently working on articles related to holistic veterinary care. Wedding vow song, sung by me for my husband; [pers.] Life may seem extreme at times so love, care, share and be kind.; [a.] Cupertino, CA

CHIFFOLO, MARY JANE T.
[pen.] Mary Jane Chiffolo; [b.] September 12, 1934, Albany, NY; [p.] Anthony and Elizabeth De Augustine; [m.] Nicholas Chiffolo, August 8, 1959; [ch.] Anthony and Theresa Chiffolo; [ed.] Cathedral Academy, Albany, N.Y.; [occ.] Retired; [a.] Albany, NY

CHINAPEN, JOEL
[b.] March 22, 1949, Guyana, South America; [p.] Solomon and Randai Chinapen; [m.] Margaret, April 12, 1975; [ch.] Vincent and Julien; [ed.] Berbice High, Guyana, University of Guyana, Trinity College, Indiana, Cyril Potter College of Education, Guyana; [occ.] Reading/Writing Lab. - Technician - Hillsborough College, Tampa, Fl.; [memb.] Village Presbyterian Church, Tampa, Trinity Alumni Association; [hon.] Six Awards in National Essay Writing - Guyana - 1971-1989, 1 Poetry Award - USA - 1980, Best Student Award - Guyana Teachers Association, 1979, Teacher of The Year Award - Marsh Harbour Primary School, Abaco Bahamas, 1994; [oth. writ.] Free-lance Journalism - Guyana Graphic 1970-1980, unpublished poems.; [pers.] To clothe truth in beautiful words, I must always rely on the God of truth who gives insight to the issues of life. In this way I can share the pain, pathos, hopes, dreams and struggles with life at all levels.; [a.] Tampa, FL

CHINCHILLA, CARLOS AMERICO
[b.] August 1, Costa Rica; [ed.] Bachelor of Arts "With Honors"; [occ.] ESL Professor; [memb.] I am a member of The Latine American Writer in New York City; [hon.] Sigma Delta Pi; [oth. writ.] 11 unpublished books, mostly in Spanish, however I do have some in Spanish.; [pers.] I am a romantic poet that love writing, symbolism in poetry.; [a.] Staten Island, NY

CHORICH, JOHN L.
[b.] March 28, 1947, Cleveland, OH; [p.] John and Eleanor Chorich; [m.] Lynn Parsons Chorich, December 27, 1980; [ch.] Daniele R. Chorich; [ed.] Bachelor of Science in Geology from Kent State University, Kent, Ohio in 1977; [occ.] Construction Engineer; [oth. writ.] Short stories: Blackwhirl, New Delta, Clarion River Exodus, Enough Is Just The First Bite. Poems: A late November Sunrise, Boundaries; [pers.] I wish all of my writings to proclaim God's truth.; [a.] Warrenville, SC

CHRISTESEN, MIROSLAVA
[pen.] Mirka Christesen; [b.] August 22, 1949, Caslav, Cech Republic; [p.] Prof. Jirivi Konta, Helena Kontova; [m.] Robert C. Christesen, February 22, 1974; [ch.] Jana Christesen; [ed.] Charles University, Prague, Czech Republic (English and Russian Ph.D. equiv.); [occ.] Language Arts Teacher, Leesville Road Middle School, Raleigh, NC; [memb.] NCAGT, NCAE, NCPAGE, Phi Delta Kappa; [hon.] 1997 Leesville Road Middle School Teacher of the Year, 1996 North Carolina Outstanding Teacher of the Gifted, 1996 National League of Junior Cotillions Best-Mannered Teacher, 1972 Summa Cum Laude, Charles University, Prague; [pers.] I believe in the healing power of nature, "stop and smell the roses". I also share Henry D. Thoreau's view that this world would be a very sad place if only the most gifted were allowed to sing.; [a.] Raleigh, NC

CHRISTMAS, CAROLYN
[b.] February 15, 1953; Ferdinand, IN; [p.] Donald and Helen Weyer; [ch.] Adam and Aaron; [ed.] 12 years with credits for courses in business; [occ.] Credit Manager; [oth. writ.] One song; [a.] Ferdinand, IN.

CHRISTOPHER, ASHLEY
[b.] June 11, 1987, Flint, MI; [p.] Marcia and Michael Christopher; [ed.] Sprinview Elementary - 4th grade; [occ.] Student; [hon.] Spelling Bee - Building-Wide Champion, Honor-Roll Student; [oth. writ.] 12 poems published in the Wide Awake Club in Local Newspaper; [pers.] Shel Silverstien is my favorite poet, and reading his books influenced me to write.; [a.] Flushing, MI

CLARK, CHRISTOPHER
[pen.] Christopher Clark; [b.] November 26, 1974; Zanesville, OH; [p.] Bruce Clark, Gayla McElroy-Orr; [ed.] Gilbert High School, Gilbert AZ, soph. at Ohio University; [occ.] Student, Ohio University; [memb.] Trinity Luthern Church; [hon.] Dean's List at Ohio University; [oth.writ.] Several poems about love and friends; [pers.] Learn to respect the little things in life that most people do not notice. Never rush anything or anyone because that's when mistakes occur; [a.] Zanesville, OH.

CLARK, KEVIN TOBY
[b.] December 27, 1988, Harrisburg, PA; [p.] John Clark Jr. and Grace Young; [ed.] William Penn High School, Harrisburg Area Community College, Hunter College, New York, NY; [occ.] Writer; [oth. writ.] Wordshop Anthology, The Storyteller; [pers.] I take pieces of people's lives and place them onto paper giving them a voice they otherwise would not have.; [a.] Harrisburg, PA

CLARK, RUTH
[b.] August 5, 1946, Taylorsville, KY; [p.] Richard and Nellie Patton; [m.] Earl Clark, April 29, 1967; [ch.] Kimberly June Clark Smith; [ed.] Mt. Washington (Elem. - High) KY. Victor School of Business Louisville, KY; [occ.] Christian Wife, Mother and Secretary; [memb.] Social Director of Palmyra Church of the Nazarene, Madd, American Heart Assoc. World Missions; [hon.] Published in the National Library of Poetry for winning the Editors Choice Award, Leadership Award, Directors Award, Calvary Missionary Church.; [oth. writ.] Circle of love in Etches In Time, Lost But Not Forgotten in Tracing Shadows Aim For The Stars in Dance Upon The Shore The Love Of My Life in Best Poems of 1997; [pers.] I believe in trying to live my life each day in the presence of the Lord. He "God" knows all and sees all, so I want to be a pleasing christian for my heavenly father from whom all blessings flow.; [a.] Palmyra, IN

CLARK, TARA HANNA
[b.] October 6, 1976, New Haven, CT; [p.] Walter K. Clark and Patricia J. Elwyn; [ed.] Nonnewaug High School, Hawaii Pacific University; [memb.] National Honor Society; [oth. writ.] Poems published in Anthology of American Collegiate Poets.; [pers.] "In the end we will conserve only what we love, we will love only what we understand, and we will understand only what we are taught." - Baba Diam.; [a.] Woodbury, CT

CLARKE, WILLIAM L.
[pen.] O. Farrington Nutley; [b.] October 31, 1936, Dayton, OH; [m.] Patricia, November 26, 1960; [ch.] 4 sons, 1 daughter; [ed.] B.S. U. of Dayton, MBA Xavier Univ., Adjunct Professor - Marketing Wright State Univ. - Dayton; [occ.] President - CEO Children's Book Publishing Company; [oth. writ.] College Literary Magazine, Short Stories, Editor - College Yearbook; [pers.] Writing is a personal reflection of one's experiences and feelings which can be better expressed with the pen than the spoken word.; [a.] Saint Petersburg, FL

CLEVELAND, SHARON R.
[b.] July 19, 1938, Pike County, IN; [p.] Gilbert Burkhardt Robling and Verda Risley Robling; [ch.] JoAnn, Keith, Aaron Dean (Deceased) Rebekah LeAnn; [ed.] Central High School (Evansville, IN), University of Evansville (Evansville, IN); [occ.] Marketing Advertising Compliance Specialist; [memb.] Christian Fellowship Church, Optimist International, Golf Leagues; [oth. writ.] Poem "Sometimes" honorable mention and "As I think of you today" published in National Library of Poetry Memories of Tomorrow. I am in the process of writing an anthology of poetry and three books.; [pers.] I am inspired by the beauty of creation woods, streams, and nature. I have a deep compassion for people who suffer and endure. I have a great desire to encourage others.; [a.] Evansville, IN

COCHRAN, DONALD
[pen.] Roach Singletary; [b.] March 1, 1955, Manning, SC; [p.] Willie Cochran Jr. and Edith Thelma Ragin Cochran; [m.] Elvia Mercedes Griffith Cochran, September 2, 1974; [ch.] Keisha Shendell Cochran Lesaine; [ed.] An Associate's Degree in Interdisciplinary Studies, University of Maryland, Currently pursuing a Major in History with a Geography Minor at University of Cameron at Lawton Oklahoma, Includes the Primary Noncommissioned Officers Course, Basic Noncommissioned Officers Course, Advanced Noncommissioned Officers Course, and the Jungle Warfare Operations Course; [hon.] Elected in The International Poetry Hall Of Fame, Legion Of Merit Nominee, three Meritorious Service Medals, the Army Commendation Medal, five Army Achievement Medals, eight Good Conduct Medals and the Expert Driver's Badge; [oth. writ.] Donald has had his poetry published by The National Library Of Poetry, The Poetry Guild, The Amherst Society, Poets' Guild, Delta Publications and Quill Books in thirteen separate National Anthologies. He has written a collection of poetry entitled Poetic Encounters and is currently working on volume two of a series.; [pers.] Donald has been writing poetry since 1991. He is a First Sergeant at the US Army Field Artillery School, and is aspiring to become a teacher as a second career. His hobbies includes reading and writing poetry, song-writing, fishing and gardening. Donalds says, "Poetry is a refreshing source of entertainment, one of the finer arts bulging with sagacity - recognize, digest, admire and enjoy". Favorite Authors: Alexander Pope, Nathaniel Hawthorne and Grace E. Easley.; [a.] Lawton, OK

COLE, DONNA G.
[b.] January 5, 1964, Napa, CA; [p.] Dorman and Jean Hitzfeld; [ch.] Deuce Cole; [ed.] High School Education, current Student of the Institute of Children's Literature; [occ.] Admin. Associate with The University of Texas at Austin; [a.] Elgin, TX

COLE III, JAMES W.
[b.] August 1, 1947, Baytown, TX; [p.] Bill and Colleen; [ed.] BA English Lit. University of Houston; [occ.] Mill Worker (Paper Mill); [pers.] I envy those who can rhyme and meter their words, they are truly gifted, and a sonnet is a blessing for us all.; [a.] Pasadena, TX

COLEY III, ROBERT
[pen.] Silky Smoove; [b.] December 18, 1969, Norwich, CT; [p.] Robert Coley Jr., Patricia A. Onyia; [ed.] Mercer University, Atlanta, GA, University of Connecticut, Storrs, CT, - B.S. Electrical Engineering, Norwich Free Academy, Norwich, CT; [occ.] I be chillin', 24-7; [hon.] Dean's List; [pers.] If you define me, you confine me. Everything is everything. (Say what?); [a.] Atlanta, GA

COLLINS, VIRGINIA C.
[pen.] Din; [b.] September 28, 1937, B'ham, AL; [m.] Allen D. Collins; [ch.] Three; [ed.] BA Goucher College, 1959; [pers.] "Today" was composed 12 yrs. after undergoing 7 1/2 hrs. of surgery to remove a squamous cell carcinoma in my ear. I was 5 out of a million to have this particular cancer and have had no recurrence.; [a.] Birmingham, AL

COLLINS JR., HERBERT
[pen.] Herbert Collins Jr.; [b.] October 27, 1931, Washington, DC; [p.] Marie Eleanor Adams and Herbert Collins Sr.; [ed.] Francis L Candozo, dipl. June 1950, Univ. of Dist. of Columb BS June 1955, G.W. Univ, MA, June 1962, Cath. Univ. of America, Post Grad, 62 hrs.; [occ.] Paralegal Prof., active; [memb.] Barclay Alumni Assn., Candozo Alumni Assn., CUA Alumnia Assn., HARP - Smithsonian Institute; [hon.] High Honors, Barclay Carriers Sch., 53 Pres. (???) Bill Clinton, 53rd Letter of Apprec. and Ramirez, Columbr Sr. Ctr., Bar-

bara Bennett Valuable Service Award, Certif. of Apprec., Bill Clinton Consep. Dept. Awards (Condf.), Certif. of Apprec., Francis L Candozo (Black Hist. Concert) Blanche R. Hammonol Chair Div., In Appreciation. European Tour (Nov. 6, 1996 Blanche R. Hammonol, Reginald C. Prins Balland, Jr.; [oth. writ.] Submitted to Dale: Nancy Karlgon, O. J. Simpson; [pers.] Ideas come from all situations and events personal and external: Solitude allows the rolers to flow.; [a.] Washington, DC

COLYER, PATRICIA M.
[b.] October 25, 1942, Manchester, CT; [p.] Robert P. O'Neal, Nancy Ann Monroe O'Neal; [m.] Marvin T. L. Colyer, December 21, 1963; [ch.] Dr. John "Andrew" Colyer and Kimberly Ann Colyer; [ed.] Watts School of Nursing 1963, Durham, NC, Duke University, continuing education: Drury College, Springfield, MO, Mineral Area College, Park Hills, MO; [occ.] Owner, Go Travel, travel sales; [memb.] Colonial Williamsburg Foundation, American Heritage Organization, Daughters of the American Revolution, Sarah Barton Murphy Chapter, All Saints Episcopal Church, Flowers Altar Guild, CLIA (Cruise Line International Association), RNC, Pachyderm Director; [hon.] Singer Sewing Dressmaking Award, New Born High School Homecoming 1950, Queen, Bicentennial Parade Chairman 1976, Director St. Francois County "Save the George Caleb Bingham Art Collection for the State of Missouri," Gov. Kit Bored Project, 1976, National Honor Society Girls Tri-Hi Y, Student Council 3 yrs. president, sr. year cheerleader, high school, 2 yrs., co-captain senior year.; [oth. writ.] Annual family newsletter for 25 years, never been "published," first entry; [pers.] I have been a very active correspondent for over 40 years to my grandmother, my Daddy's 5 overseas military assignments (gone 1 year at a time) and 2 favorite aunts, school friends at a distance. I had a monthly business motivational newsletter 5 years while in a sales business.; [a.] Farmington, MO

CONLEY, GERALDINE
[pen.] Geri Conley; [b.] Washta, IA; [ch.] Shane Conley, Stace Conley; [occ.] Accounting Clerk; [memb.] OCDS, Carmelite Third Order Light of Life Prayer Group; [oth.writ.] Three Days Pass, The Fence, God's Holy Will, Soulmate; [pers.] I write from my heart. I love to write about people, The poem "Such a Spirit" is about a wonderful nun, Sr. Martha Glaser. She helped me deal with my 17 year old son's death; [a.] Sioux City, IA.

CONNELLY, MARY LOU
[b.] July 8, 1960, Boston, MA; [p.] Robert A. Connelly and Barbara H. Connelly; [ed.] Bachelor of Arts from Boston College, Chestnut Hill, MA; [hon.] Summa Cum Laude, Alpha Sigma Nu National Honor Society, The Morgan Award for General Excellence; [oth. writ.] Various poems and short stories.; [pers.] Love and truth are the shield and the sword our children need in a world without conscience. To Jimmy, my angel, you will live on in my heart forever.; [a.] Brighton, MA

COOK, CAROLINE
[b.] December 6, 1986, Pottsville, PA; [p.] Robert Cook and Michelle Cook; [ed.] 4th grade student, Shenandoah Valley Elementary, accelerated class; [hon.] School Board Academic Achievement Award; [pers.] Kids are people too.; [a.] Shenandoah, PA

COOMBS, ANTIONETTE
[pen.] Ann; [b.] December 10, 1968; Dudley, GA; [p.] Mack Auther Coombs Sr. and the late Daisy M. Coombs; [ed.] West Lawrence High School, Dublin, GA; [occ.] K-Mart Customer Service; [pers.] I would like to give thanks to God above for giving me this poem. I hope people can see that Christ and love are the main keys in any relationship; [a.] Dudley, GA.

COOTE, PAMELA WILLIAMS
[b.] December 29, 1952, Kansas City, MO; [p.] Mrs. Vivian Lewie Williams, Dr. Charles Warren Williams; [m.] Charles E. Coote Jr., March 17, 1984; [ch.] Ashley Marguerite Coote, Kyndal Vivian Cassandra Coote; [ed.] North Mecklenburg High School, Hampton Institute/ University, University of North Carolina, Chapel Hill, NC; [occ.] Speech, Language Pathologist Greensboro, NC; [hon.] Commissioned to write poem for Nursing Honor Society; [pers.] To my mother who always said 'I could' and made me believe 'I would'.; [a.] Greensboro, NC

COPELAND, JIMMY
[pen.] Cherokee Flash; [p.] Jimmy and Laura Copeland; [ed.] College Level; [occ.] Jazz Musician, and Night Club Entertainer; [memb.] Musicians Union, Spanish Club at Charles County College, B.M.I. Songwriters Society, American Indian, and The Indian Movement; [hon.] Philosophy, Commercial Art, Introduction to Video Production, Student Achievement Award from Charles County College, Outstanding Rating 3 Times from U.S. Naval Air Station, Patuxent River, MD; [oth. writ.] Songs - I Cover The World, Don't Be In A Hurry To Tell Me Good-Bye, if you Leave Me Take Me With You, Say No To Drugs 1000 Times, I'm Always Running, Give Me Just One More Thrill; [pers.] You can feel my tears in the songs and poetry that I write. I use good memories to chase away the blues. Eaten bread is soon forgotten.; [a.] Lexington Park, MD

COPPLE, JULIE
[b.] March 28, 1983; Webster, TX; [p.] Bruce and Tammy Copple; [ed.] Elementary and junior high; [occ.] Student; [hon.] Anti-drug essay contest winner; [a.] League City, TX.

COREY, AUDREY SUE
[b.] March 29, 1971, Hancock, NY; [p.] Dawn A. Gage, Gordon E. Davis; [ch.] Alysha Mari (4 1/2 years), Stephen Hugh (11 months); [memb.] Daughters of American Revolution; [pers.] Poem was written for my daughter - 4 1/2 yrs, she means the world to me - she is my best friend. I live for both my kids.; [a.] Honea Path, SC

COREY, DAVID TORRENCE
[b.] February 2, 1981, Knoxville, TN; [p.] Walter C. and Barbara B. Corey; [occ.] High School Student - Farragut High School; [a.] Knoxville, TN

CORLEY JR., KERRY R.
[pen.] Kerry R. Corley Jr.; [b.] September 18, 1972, Phenix City, AL; [p.] Capts. Ric and Barbara Corley; [ed.] B.S. Florida State University major Communication minor History; [occ.] Student;

[memb.] Shriner and Bay Co. Chess Club and National Honor Society; [hon.] Golden Key (Nat'l Honor Society) and Bay Co Council for Exceptional Children Certificate of Achievement; [oth. writ.] Never published: "New Orleans", "The Sea", "The Death of Nature", "Lives", "Untitled", "To the People".; [pers.] I have cerebral palsy a birth defect and in spite of this physical disability, I can drive a car, have acquired a BS degree from FSU, and live a fairly normal life. God doesn't make junk, so everyone has a value.; [a.] Panama City, FL

CORONEL, SUSANNA
[b.] December 16, 1974, Austin, TX; [p.] Natividad C. Chavarria; [ed.] University of Houston, downtown; [occ.] College Student, Sales Associate at ARC Dove; [memb.] Co C, 136th Sig Bn (CS) TX Army National Guard; [hon.] Dean's List, Army Achievement Medal; [oth. writ.] Other poems published in other anthologies.; [pers.] Sometimes we tend to forget that we owe everything we are to our mothers who gave us life.; [a.] Stafford, TX

COSTELLO, MARTIN D.
[pen.] Marty Costello; [b.] February 23, 1961, Pittsburgh, PA; [p.] Edward Costello and Maureen Kennedy; [m.] Sandra Herron Costello, October 8, 1994; [ed.] A.A.S. Environmental Protection; [occ.] Environmental Protection Specialist; [hon.] Inventor Awarded U.S. Patent #5,502,851. 1995 White House closing the Circle Award.; [oth. writ.] "Righteous Path To Destiny", "Natures Blemish"; [pers.] I'm interested in thoughts of the mind. My poetry reflects this. This poem was inspired by a dream. After waking I began to write it down.; [a.] Chesapeake, VA

COUTTS, MARISA A.
[b.] February 19, 1962, Malaysia; [ed.] M.B.A. (Finance), San Francisco, Calif., B.A. (English Literature), Manila, Philippines (P.I.); [occ.] Competitive Intelligence; [hon.] Recognized for volunteerism in Romania with orphaned children.; [pers.] My life is exploration, as art is progress. I begin with simple brushstrokes, minding my hunches. Gradually, a self-portrait emerges. It takes a lifetime to complete the piece but I persevere, arranging and rearranging the elements, filling in the forms, shapes and colors, a brushstroke at a time. Creating the authentic work of art, an authentic life — they are one and the same. Neither is accomplished as long as affectation obstructs the way.; [a.] San Francisco, CA

COUTURE, KATIE LEE
[b.] May 12, 1984, Grosse Pointe, MI; [p.] Robert and Nancy Couture; [ed.] St. Thecla School (7th Grade); [occ.] Student; [hon.] 1-Second Place and 2-First Place Awards (E.C.F.L.) East Catholic Forensic League; [pers.] Many have encouraged me to write, especially my parents and my English teacher Miss Pryor. I feel by writing, it brings out your feelings and emotions.; [a.] Clinton Township, MI

CRANK, STEVE
[b.] January 10, 1951, Emmett, ID; [p.] Mother - Deceased, Del Crank; [ed.] BA. Sociology - Boise State University - 1975; [occ.] Custodian - I have had many and assorted jobs.; [oth. writ.] I have written numerous poems in both prose and traditional styles. I have been writing since High School,

and in particular the last twenty or 50 years.; [pers.] Most of my poetry reflects man's place in his natural or physical surroundings in conjunction with the erenent of chance, and how circumstances play out in his daily life. I have been influenced by early to mid 20th century writers.; [a.] Boise, ID

CRIST, MICHELE L.
[pen.] Mickey; [b.] November 4, 1960, Akron, OH; [m.] Mark M. Crist, October 23, 1992; [ch.] Matthew Crist; [ed.] University of Akron, Social Work major; [occ.] Retail; [memb.] Montrose Zion Methodist Church; [hon.] Dean's List; [oth. writ.] Several other poems and short stories.; [pers.] I try to reflect on the feelings and emotions that people experience with the everyday occurences in their lives.; [a.] Copley, OH

CROMLEY, VICTORIA LYNN
[pen.] Victoria Becker; [b.] June 2, 1958, Wooster, OH; [p.] Martha M. and Foster G. Becker; [m.] Robert E. Cromley Jr., June 1, 1985; [ch.] Andrew F. and Bethany L. Cromley; [ed.] Graduate of Wooster High School, Graduated of Capital University, Nursing, Cols, Ohio with BSN in 1980; [occ.] Registered Nurse, Staff Nurse in Invasive Recovery Unit, Riverside Meth. Hospitals; [memb.] North Community Lutheran Church, Senior Choir and Church Member, Sunday School Teacher Bible Study, Women's Circle Member, Powell Ladies Club Member past 5-6 years; [hon.] Who's Who Among American High School Students, Nominated for Cundystriper of the Year Award in 1974, Nursing - Capital University, Dean's List Spring of 1980; [pers.] I am proud of this work - more of a personal nature - so I don't know that you would need to mention it - I do not feel right submitting it for that reason. After the loss of a couple I have known about 13 years, a couple who were both patients of mine at one time or another, and had embraced a group of their caregivers and made us a part of their personal life, I composed a poem in celebration of their life together, which their daughters have and have said they cherish the work. "The Old Feather Pen" was composed during my days at Wayne Elementary School and was one of the "Save It" articles kept by myself and my mother. Any writings I have done since are usually sincere and motivated with honesty and goodness from the heart.; [a.] Powell, OH

CURRIE, LISA L.
[pen.] Lisa Peters; [b.] November 8, 1966, Presque Isle, ME; [p.] Thomas W. Peters, Diane L. Peters; [ed.] Presque Isle High School, Northern Maine Technical College; [occ.] Registered Nurse, The Aroostook Medical Center, Presque Isle, Maine; [memb.] Maine State Nurse's Association; [hon.] Carl and Lillian Rassmusen Scholarship; [pers.] The true beauty of people comes from within. To find this in one another, we first need to find the beauty within ourselves.; [a.] Presque Isle, ME

CUSHING, SHARON
[pen.] Raven; [b.] October 29, 1982, St. Pete; [p.] Larry and Lu Cushing; [ed.] Oak Grove Middle School, Southern Oak Elementary School; [oth. writ.] Suncoast Young Authors Conference Short Story; [pers.] "Gloom and mischief is my game, writing poems is my way, I only wish to entertain." Thank you to all who inspired my writings, and always, God bless.; [a.] Clearwater, FL

DAILY, LAURA
[pen.] Laura Cumings; [b.] February 28, 1957, Des Moines, IA; [p.] Dick and Betty Lamb; [m.] Rick Daily; [ch.] Tony, Mike, Jeff and Jeremy; [pers.] There is an ocean of meaning in a drop of a word.; [a.] Ankeny, IA

DALRYMPLE, APRIL E.
[b.] April 16, 1947, Alabama; [p.] Janie and Fred Henderson; [m.] David A. Dalrymple, September 1, 1977; [ch.] Ladena K. Smith; [ed.] Russellville High; [occ.] Correction Officer; [pers.] Love is the key, faith unlocks the door but prayer is the mode of transportation there don't fear climb on aboard.; [a.] Russellville, AR

DANKS, TERESA
[b.] March 29, 1967, California; [p.] Terry and Jeannette Gorham; [m.] Dale Danks, April 30, 1994; [ch.] Elizabeth and Nicholas; [ed.] B.A. Degree in Social Sciences; [occ.] Gymnastics Instructor with Tulsa World of Gymnastics; [memb.] Attend Asbury Methodist Church; [a.] Tulsa, OK

DARBEE, KATHLEEN A.
[b.] April 23, 1952, Greene, New York; [p.] Clarence Hunsicker and Beatrice Hunsicker; [m.] Bruce (Deceased); [ch.] Aaron Darbee; [ed.] Greene Central School, Boces I, Health Technician Group; [occ.] Assembly Worker and singer; [memb.] New Life Fellowship, ABS Bible-a-Month Club; [hon.] Phlebotomy Certificate EKG Technician Certificate; [oth. writ.] Numerous poems, a few songs. Very often, I use poetry to encourage others in greeting cards and letters.; [pers.] As a born-again Christian, I am blessed as a Gospel Music Soloist. I use this talent from God to share His love with people through songs that touch hearts and change lives.; [a.] Varysburg, NY

DARK, ANTHONY P.
[b.] March 22, 1969; Manchester, CT; [occ.] Chief; [oth.writ.] "The Thought of You" published in The Pathways of Poetry in 1995; [pers.] Keep an open mind and a strong heart. The fruits of joy are often poisoned by shallow relentless bastards; [a.] Wagne, MI

DATTS, VELMA
[b.] May 16, 1940; M; [p.] John Wilcox, LaeVonia Wilcox; [ch.] Eight; [ed.] Catholic elementary school, 4 yrs. of Catholic high, 2 yrs. of secondary schooling, Human Resource and Nursing; [occ.] School Crossing Guard; [hon.] Two in nursing, one for 1st 5 yrs. as a SCN; [a.] Phila., PA

DAVENPORT, MATT
[pen.] Edward Couch; [b.] February 11, 1974, Cherry Hill, NJ; [p.] Christine B. Davenport; [ed.] North Florida Christian School, University of Maryland; [occ.] Student; [oth. writ.] Have a personal collection I hope to one day have published.; [pers.] I thank my savior and Lord Jesus Christ for giving me the ability to express myself in words.; [a.] Tallahassee, FL

DAVENPORT, TOM
[b.] April 26, 1976, Cedar Rapids, IA; [p.] Wayne and Julie Davenport; [ed.] Little Rock Central High, University of Arkansas, Fayetteville; [occ.] Student/Bank Teller; [memb.] Kappa Alpha Order, Interfraternity Council, National Trust for Historic Preservation; [hon.] KA Gentleman of the Year, Dean's List; [oth. writ.] A handful of poems

and short stories published in small magazines, I also write screenplays, but as of yet have had little success.; [pers.] A lot of my poetry explores the minuscule aspects of life most people ignore.; [a.] Fayetteville, AR

DAVIDSON, BROOKE
[b.] May 22, 1978; [p.] Gary and Susan Davidson; [ed.] Graduated from Logansport High School in 1996, currently a Journalism major and English minor at Ball State University in Muncie, IN; [pers.] I have always been awed by the beauty and might of nature. I strive to convey this admiration in my writing; [a.] Logansport, IN.

DAVIDSON, MARK W.
[b.] January 23, 1969, Concord, MA; [p.] Robert Davidson, Connie Davidson; [ed.] Concord-Carlisle High School 1987, Fairfield University, B.S. 1991; [occ.] Treasurer of North Star, Concord, MA; [a.] Concord, MA

DAVIES, JOELINA
[pen.] Gogie, Tiffinay Stonewall; [b.] November 1970, N.Y.; [m.] Mr. Christopher Davies, September 1997; [ch.] Zachariah; [ed.] Fashion Merchandise, Master Cosmetology; [occ.] Fashion Design; [hon.] Stage performance, (H.H. Island Theatre, Fayetteville, Atlanta, Republican Party, Atlanta Radio v.o.); [oth. writ.] In the writing of a playscript, titled "By Chance". A Dark, Drama, Where As the Heroine, Tiffinay Stonewall, By God's Direction, Raises The Voice Of Sunset Children.; [pers.] Believe, always believe.; [a.] Peachtree City, GA

DAVIES JR., FREDERICK
[b.] June 25, 1936, Alexandria, MN; [p.] F. Ernest and Helen L. Davies; [m.] Sharleen, July 21, 1962; [ch.] Annette, Paul, Nanci; [ed.] High School; [occ.] Retired; [memb.] IOOF; [a.] Pasco, WA

DAVINO, BETTY
[b.] June 28, 1967; Brooklyn, NY; [p.] Luz Reyes, Ciro Davino; [ed.] BA Biology, BSN, Cert. Holistic Nursing; [occ.] Registered nurse, holistic; [pers.] We have all already arrived. If we could slow down and let our senses experience the present, pure truthful moment we would remember our truth...Divine, unblemished love; [a.] Cornwall, NY

DAVIS, BERTHA
[b.] March 6, 1918, Marion, MI; [p.] Archie and Margret Lux; [m.] Clifford Davis, August 29, 1992; [ch.] Richard, Ramona, Victor, Archie and Eugene; [occ.] Retired; [memb.] V.F.W., A.U.X., United Brethren Church; [hon.] Nurse Aide of the Month and Nurse Aide of the Year at the Clare Hospital; [oth. writ.] I have many other poems.; [a.] Harrison, MI

DAVIS, BRENDA M.
[b.] October 1, 1959, Port Arthur, TX; [p.] Vernon B. Miller and Lucille Huckabay Miller; [m.] Wilbur F. Davis Jr., July 19, 1986; [ch.] Mikayla Raye Davis; [ed.] Lamar University, Port Arthur, TX, Port Neches, Groves High School; [occ.] Legal Secretary, Office of the Attorney General for Texas; [memb.] Elroy Baptist Church, Notary Public for the State of TX.; [pers.] I like to look at the world through rose colored glasses. I love the laughter of children.; [a.] Del Valle, TX

DAVIS, CHARLOTTE
[pen.] Sissy Davis; [b.] January 13, 1984; Hartford,

CT; [p.] Evelyn Perez, Dwain Davis; [m.] Johnny Farmer Stepfather; [ed.] Still in school fav. courses language, Arts, French and Sign language; [memb.] Mayor's youth council; [hon.] Superintendent: outstanding student of the month award, Principals Award; [oth.writ.] I've never given my other poems any names; [pers.] Anyone could make a perfect world if they only tried; [a.] Newington, CT.

DAVIS, CYNTHIA L.
[pen.] Lady; [p.] Evan Krewson and Betty Lambeth; [ch.] Edward Allan and Robert Reasar; [ed.] Law Enforcement AA, Correction AA, Counseling BA, National Board Certified Wound Spec.; [occ.] Clinical Nurse Specialist Wounds; [memb.] American Holistic Health, VFW Aux #2080, DMAT CA1; [oth. writ.] "Dreams," "Nursing is...," "Aerobics with a Bounce," "Kloof the Clown," "Best of the Best"; [pers.] I live in a world without limits. Where anything preceived can be achieved. Disease and disasters will be our foes in the future and the world will find peace.; [a.] Lake Forest, CA.

DAVIS, DEE
[b.] March 8, 1944, Asheville, NC; [p.] Mr. and Mrs. Cecil S. Lippard; [m.] Divorced; [memb.] Trinity Chapel Church, Sarasota, FL; [hon.] Plays in Church Orchestra; [oth. writ.] "The Beautiful Truth", a collection of God inspired poetry - pending publication due to financing.; [pers.] All of the poetry is inspired by God and when written flows - there are verses and quotes from the Bible without my knowledge at the time written. God wants us to know how much He loves us and how we should love one another.; [a.] Sarasota, FL

DAVIS, ELAINE
[b.] Januray 5, 1934; Ardara, Penna; [p.] Margaret and Charles Patterson; [m.] William Davis; November 18, 1950; [ch.] William Jr. (deceased), Susan, Sharon, Ken; [ed.] High School, two medical courses; [occ.] Retired; [memb.] Senior Citizens Club, card club; [hon.] First place for painting, Womens Club, second place in sewing an outfit, Womens Club. First place in knitting and crocheting contests; [oth.writ.] Children's book, A Mouse In a Jar; [pers.] I have been married 46 1/2 yrs. Have had 4 children. Besides my painting, sewing, knitting, crocheting and writing poems and stories. I owned and operated a personal care home, taking care of senior citizens until I became ill. I gave the home to my youngest daughter; [a.] Jacksonville, FL.

DAVIS, JAMES E.
[b.] August 10, 1961, Maryland; [p.] Betty and Earley Davis; [m.] Kathi Davis, April 29, 1983; [ed.] Richard Montgomery High, Montgomery College; [occ.] General Manager, Barrons Enterprises, Inc.; [pers.] Work hard - be honest.; [a.] Woodbine, MD

DAVIS, JENNIFER ANN
[b.] December 31, 1982, Saginaw; [p.] Charles and Peggy McNeil; [ed.] Currently in the 8th grade at North Middle School; [occ.] Student; [hon.] Honor Roll, Merit Roll, Exhilarated Reading Award, Certificate of Mastering Science and Math on Michigan Education Assessment Program 1996; [oth. writ.] Many unpublished short stories and poems; [pers.] Your never to young to conquer the world, one must just believe in themselves.; [a.] Saginaw, MI

DAVIS, TANISHA M.
[b.] May 19, 1973; Detroit, MI; [p.] Frances Hill; [ed.] Georgia State University, pres. New York Universtiy, North Western University; [memb.] Hartford Memorial Baptist Church; [hon.] Dean's List, 4.0 GPA for winter '96 quarter; [oth.writ.] First publication of many that are waiting in the wings to reach ink; [pers.] My writing is a reflection of the world from which I come. It may not always be pretty but it will always be me; [a.] Stone Mountain, GA.

DAW, SCOTTI SHAY
[pen.] Shay-Shay; [b.] August 31, 1983; Birmingham; [p.] Sandra Lang Daw and E. M. Daw; [ed.] 8th grade; [occ.] student; [memb.] High school, marching bands, band color guard, Miss Warrior High Band; [hon.] Beta Club, honor classes; [oth. writ.] Why, Listen Up to Life Love Friends; [a.] Warrior, AL.

DAY, HOWARD MICHAEL
[b.] September 12, 1961, Olney, MO; [p.] Walter E. Day, Janet D. Day; [m.] Brenda Powell Day, September 26, 1980; [ed.] Montgomery County Community College; [occ.] Engineer; [oth. writ.] The Creation of Space, Newsletter of the Carnegie Institution of Washington; [pers.] I would like to thank my friend Jeane Powell who always fishes with me, even though the fish are not biting.; [a.] Laurel, MD

DAYHUFF, DAVID S.
[b.] March 3, 1941, Spencer, IN; [m.] Mary Lou, October 26, 1963; [ch.] Two; [occ.] Retired Over Road Truck Driver; [hon.] Won "Golden Poet Award for 1989" for poem Eye of the Eagle as seen in World Treasury of Great Poems Vol. 2 John Campbell Editor Publisher; [oth. writ.] In process of writing a story titled "Hard Way Home" which is about one man's search back to his beginning before his life on earth; [a.] Sequim, WA

DEARING, ROSETTA
[b.] April 1, 1919, Assumption, IL; [p.] Elmer Edwards, Lula E. Christen-Berry; [m.] Rev. John Dearing, May 5, 1941, (Died August 23, 1995); [ch.] 3 Daughters; [ed.] 9th Grade, (very ill). Helped in Church Bulletins, wrote poems, and had musical experience; [occ.] Retired Senior (Living in Subsidized housing) (Minister's wife); [memb.] Belong to Organization Here, (Where I Live) and Church Member, (Assembly of God); [hon.] Recognition Who's Who in Poetry", 1990 by John Campbell and Eddie Cole, and Recognition in Church (No money Involved); [oth. writ.] Following unpublished "Happy Thoughts", "What Is A Mother", "Consider The Lilies", "Through Your Window Pane", "A Country Road"; [pers.] There are many others I have written, just for pleasure, or church helps or "shut-ins", and some just for encouragement.; [a.] Saginaw, MI

DEBOER, MELANIE
[pen.] Melanie DeBoer; [b.] October 31, 1980; Beaver Dam, WI; [p.] Lynn and Nancy DeBoer; [ed.] Laconia High School; [memb.] Laconia High School Student Council Chorus/ Band, Reformed Church Youth Fellowship, I Soli Unis; [hon.] Finalist in America's Best Poetry Contest (1996), Magna Cum Laude (1996), State Solo/ Ensemble (1996, 1997); [oth.writ.] Published in school pa-

per; [pers.] I enjoy expressing my thoughts and emotions through a simple pen and paper; [a.] Brandon, WI.

DECKER JR., ROBERT H.
[b.] November 12, 1976, Peekskill, NY; [p.] Robert and Rose Decker; [m.] Still searching; [ed.] Walter Panas High, Westchester Community College; [occ.] Deli Clerk, Student; [pers.] Above all, my greatest honor is the love and knowledge my parents have shared with me. To this, I am beyond any debt, and could never repay.; [a.] Peekskill, NY

DEFIBAUGH, LILY
[pen.] Lily Defibaugh; [b.] April 15, 1916; Everett, PA; [p.] George Blanche McGraw; [m.] Walter Defibaugh; June 25,1938; [ch.] W. Lee Defibaugh; [ed.] High School; [occ.] Retired; [memb.] Several Book Clubs, AARY, United Methodist Church.; [oth.writ.] Just a few poems published in local paper and church bulletins; [pers.] My way of expressing my feelings on many subjects especially my faith in Jesus Christ.; [a.] Bedford, PA.

DEGENNARO, PAUL ANTHONY
[pen.] Opie; [b.] July 31, 1958, Brooklyn, NY; [p.] Anthony and Marjorie DeGennaro; [m.] Maureen Maher-DeGennaro, September 21, 1985; [ed.] Fort Hamilton High, Long Island University, Mercer County Community College; [occ.] Full Time Student (MCCC); [pers.] Only by constant cultivation throughout its growing season will the creative process, once planted within the fertile heart, grow to maturity and bear fruitage.; [a.] Cranbury, NJ

DELANO, CAITLIN
[b.] January 13, 1988, Denver, CO; [p.] Michael and Jill DeLano; [ed.] Sabin Elementary School, Denver, Colorado (3rd Grade); [pers.] I love to write, thanks to a very special teacher. You're awesome, Mrs. Carlson!; [a.] Littleton, CO

DELONG, JUSTIN M.
[b.] April 17, 1984, York, PA; [p.] John and Sandy DeLong; [ed.] In 7th Grade at West York Area Jr. High; [memb.] Boys Scouts of America, Peer Group - Wy Jr. High Student Council, Soccor Club Track Team; [hon.] 1st Place - Martin Library's 9th Annual Poetry Contest Art Awards (School - Fair) Scouting Awards Honor Society; [pers.] I write what I feel from within.; [a.] York, PA

DEMING, RICHARD DEUEL
[pen.] Richard Deming; [b.] July 18, 1967; Columbus, OH; [p.] Matthew Deming and Margaret Smith; [m.] Gail Patricia Deming; April 22, 1989; [ch.] Richard Davis, Elizabeth Angel, Matthew David, Elton Drake; [ed.] Grandview Heights High School, Grandview Heights, OH, various technical schools; [occ.] Electronic Service Technician, RAM Technologies, Charleston, WV; [oth.writ.] Two country songs published on KMA Record, first song by Keith Bradford, "Friends Again," second by Tom Grant, "Daddy's Little Girl"; [pers.] I was heavily influenced by my high school English teachers; [a.] Charleston, WV.

DEMOPOULOS, PAUL
[b.] March 22, 1978, Pocatello, ID; [p.] Tom Demopoulos, Peggy Demopoulos; [ed.] Skyline High, University of Utah; [occ.] Student, Univer-

sity of Utah; [hon.] National Merit Scholar, Dean's List; [oth. writ.] Many poems and short stories, not yet published.; [a.] Salt Lake City, UT

DENEEVE, IAN K.
[pen.] Ian K. DeNeeve; [b.] December 29, 1970, Honolulu, HI; [p.] Philip DeNeeve, Barbara DeNeeve; [ed.] Longmont High, C.U. Boulder; [occ.] Musician, Photo Technician; [oth. writ.] Music and some poetry appearing on the gallery compact disc: "Infinite Patience."; [pers.] Listen to your loved ones, your surroundings. But most of all, the most important, listen to yourself.; [a.] Boulder, CO

DENNIS, PATRICIA A.
[b.] April 5, 1939, Cape Vincent, NY; [m.] James D. Dennis, April 18, 1970; [ch.] Mary, James II, Jennifer, Jason; [ed.] Clayton Central High, Clayton N.Y.; [occ.] Bank Data Processor, Muncy Bank and Trust Co., Muncy, PA; [memb.] Volunteer with Susquehanna Home Health Hospice; [pers.] I have had a longing to write since childhood, a need to bring beauty to the soul in a world where there is so much ugliness covering up the beauty of God's world.; [a.] Muncy, PA

DENSON SR., LEVIATHAN B.
[b.] June 21, 1923; [m.] Eleanor Regina Denson (Deceased), December 15, 1945; [ch.] Linda Marie, Georgia Lee, Leviathan, Jr., David Joseph, Vicki Lucille, Kenneth Willard; [occ.] Retired; [oth. writ.] True Love True Life, Just Plain Tired, The Devil's Highway; [pers.] This poem is dedicated in everlasting memory of Eleanor Regina Denson, Devoted wife and loving mother of our children, deceased September 26, 1995.; [a.] Chesapeake, VA

DESMOND, MABEL J.
[p.] Charles and Ada Lenentine; [m.] Jerry R. Desmond Sr., June 23, 1951; [ch.] Jerry Jr., Ronnee, Jed, Jennifer; [ed.] B.S. - University of Maine Presque Isle, (UMPI) M.ED. University of Maine; [occ.] Representative in Maine State Legislature; [a.] Mapleton, ME

DESROCHES, DAWN
[b.] April 21, 1969, Lynn, MA; [p.] Sandy Spinney (mom); [ch.] Neil Eric, Jacqualine Candace, Joseph Ernest; [oth. writ.] I have written several articles in a local newspaper. I have helped others learn how to express themselves through writing.; [a.] Salisbury, MA

DEVINE, FANNY K.
[b.] Syria; [p.] Ludwig and Maria Kraiss; [m.] Paul J. DeVine, 1953; [ed.] Mansfield University, Art Institute of Chicago, Noyes School of Rhythm; [occ.] Free-lance Writer, Artist-Watercolors; [memb.] National League of American Pen Women, AAUW; [hon.] Over 200 prizes for poetry; [oth. writ.] Three books: "A Star On His Shoulder", "If I Were Clay", "Legend of the South Meadow", Magazine Publications: Articles, Essays, Short Stories, Poems; [pers.] I am ever mindful of the great debt I owe to my teachers.; [a.] Wooster, OH

DIAZ, ANGELA M.
[pen.] Anjelle; [b.] December 14, 1953, New York City; [p.] Helen O'Connell and Henry Diaz; [ed.] Two years of college, John Jay College of Criminal Justice; [occ.] Print Production Coordinator for

print broker; [hon.] Recipient of The 1996 Merrill G. and Emita E. Hastings Foundation Artists Assistance Grant; [oth. writ.] I have written over 30 poems all of which come from my soul. I feel them as I am writing them. Hopefully this publication will open up some new doors for me.; [pers.] I was not aware of my talents until my mother passed away. It was a year after her death that all these feelings started pouring out of me and they have helped me through my hard times. Most of my poetry is from personal feelings and experiences.; [a.] New York City, NY

DICKEY, KATHRYN
[b.] November 16, 1937, Russelville, KY; [p.] Nile C. and Katie (Kingins) Hancock; [m.] Robt. K. Dickey (Deceased), February 22, 1957; [ch.] I was single parent due to death of their father. Five sons (Kirk, Blane, Kyle, Brett and Kelly); [ed.] 2 years, University of KY, Lexington, 1 year Sullivan Business College at Louisville, KY, continued studies, U. of Louisville, I am currently a part-time student at Western Kentucky, University; [occ.] Wal-Mart Associate; [memb.] Serve on Council of Ministries of United Methodist Church; [oth. writ.] Never published. I'm just starting. I am presently taking creative writing. This is my second semester, I am seeking my lifelong dream to become a published author and I am writing a fictitious novel.; [pers.] I believe success can come late in life. I am getting a late start with my writing, but I have lived an interesting life, have lived in Europe and many places in the USA and have gained much wisdom. And insight to create great characters.; [a.] Russellville, KY

DICKEY, WILLIAM D.
[b.] September 7, 1971, Phillipsburg, NJ; [p.] Doris M. Dickey; [ch.] Seth A. Muskett; [ed.] Easton High School; [occ.] Agricultural Adjuster; [oth. writ.] I have written several poems that have not been published yet.; [pers.] I write as means of expressing my feelings without reservation. No one person understands as well as the paper.; [a.] Easton, PA

DICKINSON, DON C.
[pen.] Don C. Dickinson; [b.] September 28, 1943, Double Springs, AL; [p.] Joel S. and Gladys M. Dickinson; [m.] Jo, May 9, 1964; [ch.] Donald Craig, Timothy Dwain; [ed.] Winston County High School (1961) Draughons Business College (1963), LaSalle Extension University; [occ.] Public Accountant, Lavonia, GA; [memb.] National Beta Club, Hon. Order of Kentucky Colonels, Grace Baptist Church, Toccoa, GA; [hon.] Ordained Baptist Deacon, 1974; [oth. writ.] Published poems "Day Dreams", "The Dogwoods Story", "Ode To Georgia", "Life", "Sowing". Over 100 unpublished poems, most of which tell a story, highlight a scripture passage, or have a particular message to share.; [pers.] Poetry is my way to reminisce the past, tell a story or to record a thought about a scripture passage. I attempt to communicate the goodness of God, the love of Christ and to draw the reader to the scripture, and the Holy Bible.; [a.] Toccoa, GA

DIETZEL-BALDWIN, CHERYL ANN
[pen.] "Bailey"; [b.] January 11, 1955, Missouri; [p.] Dorothy and Ralph Dietzel; [ch.] Jack, Brian; [ed.] Community College, Fayetteville, Technical Community College, Media Integration; [occ.] Stu-

dent and Secretary; [hon.] The Honor of being Brian and Jack's Mother; [oth. writ.] "Pioneer of Your Totality", 1997 "A Garroulous Type" - 1997; [pers.] There are no failures in life, only non-successes - which means you must continue to try to succeed, and you will.; [a.] Fayetteville, NC

DIPKA, SANDRA M.
[pen.] Sandra M. Dipka; [b.] May 14, 1954, Detroit; [p.] George Dipka, Pat Habitzruther; [ch.] Richard and Lee Anne Spychaj; [ed.] Lapeer High/ Baker College; [occ.] Student/Custodian; [memb.] Life Enrichment Center, Beginning Experience; [hon.] Dean's List; [oth. writ.] Several have been published; [pers.] Follow your dreams. If you want something bad enough, and you strive hard enough, it will come to you. Believe in yourself.; [a.] Flint, MI

DOBBELAAR, RANSOM H.
[b.] February 1, 1912; Jersey City, NJ; [p.] Lauret and Henry Dobbelaar; [m.] Helen M. Dobbelaar; March 3, 1947; [ch.] Connie, Ronnie, Frank, Karyn; [ed.] Barringer High, University of Virginia, United States Army; [occ.] Retired Johnson Wax Salesman and representative; [memb.] golf clubs; [pers.] Express your feelings in any form; [a.] Upper Mentclair, NJ.

DODDS, CYNTHIA MARGARET
[b.] November 4, 1952; Lansing, MI; [p.] Lee F. Gilman, Norma J. Price Gilman; [m.] John Paul Dodds; June 9, 1973; [ch.] Megan Ashley, Trevor John; [ed.] Lansing Eastern High, Olivet Nazarene University; [occ.] K-12 Subsitute Teacher, Des Moines Public Schools, Des Moines, IA; [memb.] Free Methodist Church; [pers.] By God's divine providence, I am who I am because of a steadfast Christian heritage and the influence of many who wonderfully touched and colorfully decorated my life by their unselfish love and example; [a.] Des Moines, IA.

DONKIN, ANGELA
[b.] September 21, 1979, Burlingame; [p.] Pam Donkin and Gary Donkin; [ed.] High School Graduate Burlingame 1997; [pers.] My poetry spills out of my thoughts in an endless overpowering explosion of feeling. It is my back door, my escape.; [a.] Millbrae, CA

DONN, ROGER
[pen.] Frank N. Stein; [b.] October 24, 1958, Liberty, TN; [p.] Robert H. Donn and Elizabeth Frances Parker; [m.] Debra Darlene Donn, August 7, 1982; [ch.] Jennifer Lou and Dixie May Donn; [ed.] GED, Wayne County Community College, Dean's List; [occ.] Carpenter; [hon.] WCCW Dean's List; [oth. writ.] Davy Cry, One Way Street, Up And Back Because I Was Young Heartbreaker, I Want To Be An American; [pers.] God is real, stick with what you believe.; [a.] Naubinway, MI

DORIS, DESMOND
[b.] December 3, 1963, Dublin, Ireland; [p.] Patrick, Cathrine; [m.] Carol, February 11, 1989; [ch.] Natalie; [occ.] Business Owner; [pers.] 'No Flowers' is a tribute to my father, who raised his 10 children to follow their own dreams. May he rest in the arms of God.; [a.] Little Roar, AR

DORSEY, PATRICIA W.
[b.] June 14, 1930; Lyon Falls, NY; [p.] John, Mary

M. Walsh; [m.] James B. Dorsey; June 10, 1951; [ch.] Katherine, Mary Lee, Pamela, Suzanne, James Jr., Alison; [ed.] Saratoga Springs High School, Skidmore College, Real Estate School; [occ.] Housewife, Real Estate Sales; [memb.] Saratoga Golf and Polo Club, Saratoga Reading Room, The Hyde Museum, Ladies of Charity, Cornell University Club, New York City; [oth.writ.] This is my first writing; [pers.] Having had the experience of living on Cape Cod for three years gave me the inspiration to put my thoughts into writing this poem. I would like to think that this simple little poem will bring joy to all people who love the Cape; [a.] Saratoga Springs, NY.

DOWER, CRYSTAL
[b.] February 22, 1983; [p.] Chris Dower, Randy Dower; [ed.] Currently attending Desert Christian Junior High School in Palmdale California; [a.] Palmdale, CA.

DOWNS, ALBERT L.
[b.] March 14, 1948, Cedar Rapids; [m.] Christine Downs, May 31, 1970; [ch.] One daughter Amber; [ed.] College; [occ.] Minister; [oth. writ.] Poetry, A book - The Gentile Prophet in Production; [a.] Cedar Rapids, IA

DRAIME, TIMOTHY A.
[b.] February 12, 1972; Toledo, OH; [p.] Timothy P. Draime, Wilma Seevers; [m.] Juanita A. Draime; December 26, 1990; [ch.] Angela Renee, Shilo Christine; [ed.] Stryker High School, Stryker, OH; [occ.] US Air Force, Minot Air Force Base ND; [memb.] Minot Independent Baptist Church; [pers.] It is my wish that every person have the opportunity to hear the gospel of Jesus Christ; [a.] Minot AFB, ND.

DROEGE, SUSAN LYNN
[b.] April 14, 1950, Pittsburgh; [p.] William G., Marjorie H. Moore; [m.] John F. (Deceased - 1995), March 3, 1984; [ch.] John A. - 7; [ed.] B.S. in Education, Edinboro University, PA, Gateway High - Monroeville, PA; [occ.] Unemployed - 1995, Staffing Supervisor - Hospital - 21 years; [a.] Pittsburgh, PA

DUBOIS, ELWOOD
[b.] September 27, Salem, NJ; [p.] Elwood and Mary; [m.] Jean E. Allen, October 1949; [ch.] Elwood III, Susan E; [occ.] Self-employed farmer; [pers.] I was written to show God's mercies on his children and was compiled the night mother went to be with our Lord. It is my spiritual birthday of my effectual calling as a 'Born-Again Christian'.; [a.] Salem, NJ

DUGAN JR., WALLACE
[pen.] Wally, Jr; [b.] October 12, 1956; Yuma, AZ; [p.] Wallace Dugan Sr., Esther E. Thomas; [m.] Eileen Menta Dugan; December 31, 1984; [ch.] Fayeanne and Austin, Dugan, Ila and Ina, Hopper; [ed.] San Pasqual Elementary and San Pasqual High School, Winterhaven, California, H.S. graduate; [occ.] Groundskeeper, Maintenance for Quechan Community Health Service; [oth.writ.] A book in 1991, Feeling of the Heart, 25 page booklet. First project into poetry; [pers.] I try to look at life in many views in the human spirit, its joys, sorrows, young, old, past, future, and also in nature in which it gives its beauty. As we live for both, we must have a heart that cares in both to live a happy life in what this world offers in God always; [a.] Winterhaven, CA.

DUNBAR, BILL J.
[b.] August 7, 1959, High Springs, FL; [p.] Willie Dunbar Sr., Idella Dunbar; [ch.] Caleb Jemar, DeiAndre; [ed.] BA; [occ.] U.S. Army; [a.] Columbus, GA

DUNBAR, YVONNE
[b.] September 24, 1971, England; [p.] Keith Arthur Dunbar, Lynn Dunbar; [ed.] Park High School, Birkenhead, England, Sixth Form College, Birkenhead, England Technical College, England, Eastern Tech., Western Tech., School, Baltimore, MD.; [occ.] Professional Chief; [hon.] College graduate NVQ level I and II catering, Hygene Certificate with honors, British Red Cross first Aid Certificate; [pers.] All my poetry comes from the heart, I enjoy writing poetry that people can empathize with.; [a.] Owings Mills, MD

DUNCAN, ALICE L.
[pen.] Alice Lee; [b.] March 2, 1947, Indiana; [p.] Calvin and Geneva Spurgeon; [m.] Hugh Snively; [ch.] Danielle and Joshua; [ed.] Salem High School, Indiana University; [occ.] Business Owner and Writer; [oth. writ.] Former journalist for several newspapers, contributing author to business book, unpublished novel, privately published book of poetry.; [a.] Hagerstown, MD

DUNCAN, KIM
[pen.] Jay Paradise; [b.] November 17, 1961, Detroit, MI; [p.] Brager Duncan, Willa M. Duncan; [ed.] University of Detroit Mercy; [memb.] United Community Services; [oth. writ.] None that were published.; [pers.] Growing up in the midwest in a major metropolia city like Detroit who is big on car production the one that stands out the most for me is the Corvette. I like to see and write inspiring poems.; [a.] Detroit, MI

DUNMIRE, SCOTT T.
[b.] December 28, 1962, Port Angeles, WA; [ed.] B.S., Fisheries Resources; [occ.] Fish Biologist; [memb.] Return Peace Corps volunteer, Mali, West Africa, and Lesotho, Southern Africa.; [oth. writ.] Song writer, musician, poet, non-published.; [pers.] It is in the creative state where we open the doors to the unknown and begin to understand the known.; [a.] Kendrick, ID

DUTY, PAT
[b.] October 20, 1954, Baltimore, MD; [m.] Kenneth S. Duty; [ch.] Christine and Crystal; [ed.] Essex Community College; [occ.] Senior Customer Support Helix Health; [oth. writ.] The Symphony of Life; [pers.] I strive to use my writing to provide healing and encouragement to all who have experienced inner pain and heartache.; [a.] Baltimore, MD

DYSON, JENNY L.
[pen.] Jenny Dyson; [b.] July 3, 1957, Inglewood, CA; [p.] Paul L. Glagovich, Veronica Todd Glagovich; [m.] John A. Schneider on December 2, 1975, Divorced, June 1990, married William Hap Dyson May 11, 1991, "As of April 1, 1997 he is no longer a part of my life."; [ch.] John Paul (J.P.) Schneider born November 23, 1976, Joshua Harold Schneider born April 8, 1979; [ed.] S.C.O.C. - Torrance, CA. Computers AIEA Comm. College, OAHU, Hawaii - Psychology Wyoming Comm. College Evanston, Wyo-Psychology Arizona Correctional Officer Training Academy (COTA); [occ.]

In the process of moving and reentering the correctional field of psychiatric care.; [hon.] Woman sailor of the year 1984 from the Kaiettes womens sailing club at Hickum AFB, OAHU; [oth. writ.] My dearest poem in my heart is titled "Joshua" dedicated to my youngest son. It tells the story of myself and my son leaving a hard life behind in Wyoming and traveling to California then on to Arizona.; [pers.] Thank you to my special friend whom if not for her I would never have realized my talent. (My mother in law Elizabeth (Betty) Dyson, she saw my talent before I did. And to hap whom if it wasn't for our 8 years together these poems would never have been written or lived on in my memories. "I still love you"; [a.] Tehachapi, CA

EBBITT, JOSEPH M.
[b.] October 2, 1963, Braddock, PA; [p.] John F. and Jane E. Ebbitt; [m.] Honey Lynn Tornblom Ebbitt, November 19, 1988; [ch.] Blake Honey, Jake Joseph; [ed.] Greensburg Central Catholic High School, Indiana University of Pennsylvania, Duguesne University Paralegal Institute; [occ.] Paralegal; [oth. writ.] Numerous poems given to my beautiful wife, and eulogies extolling departed loved ones.; [pers.] This poem was inspired by my daughter's conception, and given to her on the day she was born.; [a.] Irwin, PA

EBELING, NORA ANN
[b.] July 28, 1968, Orange, CA; [p.] JoAnn Mary and Norman Leroy Hafer; [m.] Richard Joseph Ebeling, January 29, 1994; [ch.] Richard Jr. Age 3; [ed.] High School Diploma, Pharmacy Technician College; [occ.] Pharmacy Technician; [pers.] This poem I wrote for my 3 yr. old son. My mother was diagnosed with cancer when I was pregnant with him. He was her only grandchild and he brought tremendous joy to her life, and in many ways she found life through him. I wrote this poem on the back of an ATM receipt while driving to the church for her viewing.; [a.] Moreno Valley, CA

ECHOLS, JUDY ANN
[pen.] Judyth Song; [b.] August 6, 1955, Dearborn, MI; [p.] Charles and Elizabeth Allison; [m.] Divorced; [ch.] Amy, Kurt, Kara, Kendra, Kyle; [ed.] Brablec High, Roseville, Mi., Montgomery College, Germantown, Md.; [occ.] Office Manager, Frederick, MD; [memb.] The Writers Center - Bethesda, Md., (mem) Oakdale Emory Methodist Church; [hon.] Detroit Free Press, Poetry Award - Volunteer Service Germantown, Chamber of Commerce; [oth. writ.] Frederick News Post, Free lance articles - United Methodist Connection - Poems published in many books.; [pers.] I have been influenced by Edgar Allen Poe, The Holy Bible and The Book of Virtues along with many other writings.; [a.] Frederick, MD

EDDINGTON, AUSTIN
[b.] September 25, 1981, Sacramento, CA; [occ.] High School Student; [pers.] I write poetry to express my true emotions. My favorite writers are Robert Frost, E. E. Cummings and Shakespeare.; [a.] Minot, ND

EDWARDS, CHRISTINE A.
[b.] January 25, 1987, Sioux City; [p.] Darin and Renee Edwards; [ed.] Currently in the 4th grade; [occ.] Student; [hon.] Honor Roll, Attendance Award, Math Awards, Music Award

EDWARDS, PATRICIA GALE
[pen.] Patricia Edwards; [b.] January 31, 1944, Jackson County, IN; [p.] Floyd and Mildred Blankenship; [m.] James E. Edwards, May 26, 1962; [ch.] James Jr., Tony, Greg, Cindi, Lenora, one child Timothy Brian, Deceased; [ed.] Graduated 1961 Brownstown Central High School. Graduated from Indiana Vocational technical College 1980 as an L.P.N., I.U.P.U.I., Management courses in Illinois and Columbus, Indiana; [occ.] Retired for health reasons. Asst. Director Nursing Longterm Care Facility for 15 years.; [memb.] Fraternal Order of Eagles #655; [hon.] Little awards throughout school.; [oth. writ.] None. Just other little poems never published in anything.; [pers.] Due to my health, I'm home bound and poetry is my hobby. I feel surprised and honored that one of my poems is going to be published. I'm "Speechless"!; [a.] Seymour, IN

EDWARDS-WHITT, THERESA
[pen.] T.T.; [b.] May 11, 1954, Clay Co.; [p.] Lucille and Elby Edwards; [m.] Companion: Steven Fisher, lived together 12 yrs.; [ch.] Maryellen (19), James (15), Justin (9); [ed.] Oak Park High; [occ.] Self Employed, Writer; [oth. writ.] I have my first poem published in A Muse to Follow and Best Poems of the '90's. It's called The Sunrise of You, I've dedicated this poem to my mother.; [pers.] My mother gave me pencil and paper and told me to write my silence thoughts and she told me people will read it and they will hear you speak with your words.; [a.] Gladstone, MO

EFRONSON, SARAH
[b.] July 5, 1985; Miami, FL; [p.] Lise and Lee; [ed.] Pinecrest Elementary School; [occ.] Student; [memb.] National Honors Society, Girl Scouts; [hon.] Principal's Honor Roll; [oth.writ.] The Presidential Rally; [pers.] Many thanks to my parents for all of their interest and support; [a.] Miami, FL.

EGAN, JUDY A.
[b.] July 23, 1940, Ashland, KY; [p.] Maxwell and Evelyn Otis; [m.] Divorced - May 1968; [ch.] 5 girls and 14 grandchildren; [ed.] High School; [occ.] Retired; [memb.] Boys Town Honorary Citizen; [hon.] Awarded Outstanding Volunteer Teachers Aide for 3 years work at Local Grade School, Editors Choice Award, presented by National Library of Poetry; [oth. writ.] Frontier Woman, published in "Frost At Midnight", articles published in High School Paper - also published articles in daughters pre school paper; [pers.] Take a walk with a child to renew your sense of wonder with nature.; [a.] Tacoma, WA

EILRICH, CARLA
[b.] July 11, 1961; San Francisco, CA; [p.] Albert Tognoli, Lorna Tognoli; [m.] Wade Eilrich; June 13, 1987; [ch.] Heather Eilrich; [ed.] Soquel High, Foothill College, five years of Native Animal Rescue Wildlife Center; [occ.] Animal Health Technician, Wildlife Care Specialist, Glass Fusion Artist, [memb.] Ibizan Hound Club of North America, Stafford Bull Terrier Club, Llama and Alpacas of North America Assn.; [hon.] Stained/ Fused Glass lampshade won third prize at the Santa Cruz Co. Fair. Handled two Ibizan Hounds to their championships and one to her obedience title; [oth.writ.] A paper on Axonal Dystrophy for the Ibizan Hound Club Newsletter. Lots of Cyberpunk songs for my

friends; [pers.] I must say this one was commissioned by God; [a.] Watsonville, CA.

ELIZABETH MEIGS, LUANA ROSALANI
[b.] August 30, 1972; San Diego, CA; [p.] Stanley D. and LeeAnn Meigs; [ch.] Alexander Charles Meigs; [ed.] Yreka High, College of the Siskiyous; [occ.] Student, home mom, aspiring writer; [hon.] Writers Cramp contest of Siskiyou County, 1st place; [oth.writ.] Several poems written and awaiting private publication, autobiography and other tales awaiting private publication; [pers.] Of all the resources in the world I find no other is as insightful or revealing as a journal or a book. Words and writings are the true meaning of one's life, thoughts and feelings. The innermost soul; [a.] Montague, CA.

ELKINS, ROSA LEE
[b.] January 23, 1942; Bartlesville, OK [p.] Margaret Marine Conner; [m.] J.D. Elkins; February 1, 1960; [ch.] J.D. Elkins Jr, Rita Lynn Bell, Saundra Kay Chidester, [ed.] Graduated from college, high school in 1962 in Bartlesville OK; [pers.] I believe pain of the heart, mind and body are the hardest feelings to deal with in life; [a.] Bartlesville, OK.

ELLINGTON, VIRGINIA
[pen.] Jenny; [b.] October 5, 1916, Cleveland, OH; [p.] Luna and Frank Redd; [m.] Lawrence Ellington, June 26, 1937; [ch.] Ruth Lawrence Jr., Steven Penny; [ed.] John Adams Senior High School; [occ.] Nurse Aide, Cleveland Clinic; [memb.] International Society of Poets; [hon.] Editor's Choice Award; [oth. writ.] On Top of the World, A Face in the Window, Home Sweet Home, Togetherness, My Friend Jesus; [pers.] I am eight years old was married for fifty four and a half years to a wonderful man and I thank God for him.; [a.] Cleveland, OH

ELMER, THEODORE K.
[b.] January 21, 1930; Park City, UT; [p.] Theodore Elmer and Ann Marie Kershaw; [m.] Laura Wilson; August 15, 1995; [ed.] Brigham Young University, 1995; [occ.] Retired; [pers.] Man has always existed. Our Heavenly Father's works are to lead his children to immortality and eternal life that we may be like Him someday. This life is a training ground, preparing man for Godhood, like Himself. [a.] Tremonton,UT.

EMERICK, CARI
[b.] October 28, 1980, Fort Wayne, IN; [p.] Bruce and Jo Anne Emerick; [ed.] Currently enrolled at Columbia City, HS; [hon.] Honor Student; [pers.] It's all to human frailty to suppose a favorable wind will blow forever; [a.] Columbia City, IN

EMERSON, PHILLIP HULL
[b.] April 3, 1944, Noblesville, IN; [p.] Mark Emerson, Hortense Emerson; [m.] Judith Marie Emerson; [ch.] Jonathan Hull, Michael Jacob; [ed.] B.S. Business; [a.] Denver, CO

EMMONS, BEVERLY
[pen.] Beverly Barrow Emmons; [b.] San Antonio, TX; [p.] Allen and Jeanne Barrow; [m.] Ed Emmons; [a.] San Antonio, TX

ENGLEBRIGHT, STEPHANIE LYNN
[b.] May 10, 1983, Wichita, KS; [p.] David and Darlene Englebright; [ed.] Riverside Elementary, Mead Middle School; [occ.] Student; [memb.] In-

ternational Baccalaureate Student; [oth. writ.] "Untitled" appeared in National Library of Poetry's Into the Unknown.; [pers.] "Don't be rebuked by those who say it'll never happen, it will happen."; [a.] Wichita, KS

ENOS, MICHAEL F.
[b.] November 28, 1940, Bellingham, WA; [p.] LeRoy Enos and Theoda Enos; [m.] Ann Lilian, January 27; [ch.] Christopher Franklin, Damon Michael; [ed.] Birburg H.S., St. Martin's College, E. Kentocky Univ., William Carey College, Univ. of S. Mississippi, Univ. of Wyoming; [occ.] Instructor, School of Nursing, Univ. of Wyoming; [memb.] Sigma Tau, Honors Nursing; [oth. writ.] Masqoe of Meloncoly, Ecological Awareness in 19th Century England, Nursing as a social contract: A Philosophy of Nursing.; [pers.] One must know Shelly, Keats, Byron, and Alfred Lord Tennyson to experience life.; [a.] Casper, WY

ERICKSON, ALYSSA
[b.] August 4, 1981, Iowa City, IA; [p.] Claude and Judy Erickson; [ed.] Currently a Sophomore in High School; [memb.] Iron Midgets Girls Ice Hockey Team, YMCA Soccer Team. My hockey team was recently accepted into the U.S. Hockey hall of Fame.; [hon.] Friends of the Library Writing Contest - First place in Personal Narrative, First Place in Poetry, 3rd Place in Short Story; [oth. writ.] Many, but none published.; [pers.] Some of my favorite writers are Edgar Allan Poe, Emily and Charlotte Bronte, Tennessee Williams, and Bob Dylan, among others.; [a.] Embarrass, MN

EVANS, ARDELIA R.
[b.] January 6, 1958, Fort Worth, TX; [p.] Calvin and Cora Evans; [ed.] Bachelors of Social Work, North Texas State University, O.D. Wyatt High SChool, Fort Worth, Texas; [occ.] Social Worker, Texas Department of Health; [memb.] Alpha Kappa Alpha Inc., Big Brothers and Sisters of Tarrant County - Associate, Antioch Missionary Baptist Church Choir, Member and Youth Worker; [hon.] Big Brothers and Sisters, Match of the Year; [oth. writ.] Working on a book of over 60 poems to be published. Many poems published in the Truth Seeker Magazine.; [pers.] My poems reflect spiritual revelations and the experiences of life.; [a.] Fort Worth, TX

EVERLING, JACK E.
[b.] July 23, 1927, Bozeman, MT; [p.] Ben/Florence Deceased; [m.] Virginia Deceased, December 3, 1952; [ch.] Michael; [ed.] 4 Yrs. College - Pol Sci, Int. Rel.; [occ.] Real Estate Sales; [memb.] Rotary, various Real Estate Orbs, various Military Orgs; [hon.] Various rotary, Real Estate and military awards retired 30 years in navy is carrier pilot.; [oth. writ.] Poems are the fears and start of book over the tears; [pers.] Poetry allows more to be said more succinctly in fewer winds than prose.; [a.] Coventry, RI

EVERSTINE, ANDREW D.
[b.] June 30, 1966; Annapolis, MD, [p.] Douglas and Carolyn Everstine; [m.] Sima Farid Everstine, May 15, 1997; [ch.] Frostburg State University, BS in Bus. Admin, concentration, management, minor, economics; [occ.] Director of Food Services at Shady Grove, Adventist Nursing, Rockville, MD; [oth.writ.] Several poems published in nurs-

ing home news letters. I have a book of poems that I wish to publish. [pers.] I believe in my writings wholeheartedly as they have come from the deepest part of me. I don't have any notable influence except the world itself and the good Lord above. Also, "The Voice" inside me as I write; [a.] Germantown, MD.

FABBRO, LILLIAN
[b.] February 20, 1946, Italy; [ch.] Lidia, Angelo, Ron and Richard; [occ.] Seamstress; [memb.] Undead Poets' Society; [pers.] I have a tendency to drive people to the brink but not intentionally.; [a.] Grand Junction, CO

FADER, KAREN K.
[pen.] Care Run; [b.] March 7, 1955, Fort Worth, TX; [p.] Duane Francis Rix and Gloria Esther Andrews; [m.] William Joseph Fader, September 18, 1988; [ch.] Floye, Wayne, Roseanne Delight; [ed.] High School Graduate - Colonial High, Orlando, FL; [occ.] Owner - Janitorial and Director in Consumer Direct Marketing; [memb.] Dodd Road Church of Christ, American Red Cross, Lake Worth Playhouse; [oth. writ.] Several other poems and a play "Child's Play", copyright 1995, several songs, and short stories published in the Lake Worth Herald.; [pers.] I have always been a firm believer in that people are in life where they choose to be and have tried to instill hope even in times of despair through my writings.; [a.] Lake Worth, FL

FAIRBROTHER, JEREMIAH
[b.] December 4, 1980, Anchorage, AK; [p.] David and Nellie Fairbrother; [ed.] Lakeland High School; [a.] Post Falls, ID

FAJDICH, LAURA M.
[pen.] "Bagora"; [b.] July 2, 1966, Chicago, IL; [p.] Beatrice Fajdich, The Late "Big Mike" Fajdich; [ed.] George Washington H.S., South Suburban College; [occ.] Teacher; [memb.] C.F.U. Tamburitzan Music and Kolo Group, Chicago Special Olympic Asst. Coach and Volunteer Choir; [oth. writ.] I have had a few poems published. Where as others are framed and hung in special friends homes. An honor in itself!!!; [pers.] The smallest hug says more than the biggest word.; [a.] Chicago, IL

FANTE, CHRISTIANA
[b.] August 28, 1965, New Jersey; [p.] Wolf and Joan Barth; [m.] Jeff Fante, November 5, 1988; [ch.] Gabrielle and Jesse; [ed.] Completed high school and went to Burlington Community College for two years.; [occ.] Housewife; [oth. writ.] I've written several poems for my children. It is something I enjoy doing in my spare time. My goal someday is to publish children's books.; [a.] Mount Holly, NJ

FARLEY, D.L. PAUL
[b.] June 24, 1952; Craborchard, WV; [p.] Paul and Lee Farley; [m.] Anna Baharapoulou Farley; March 26, 1978; [ch.] Paul Orestis; [ed.] Clearfield High PA; [occ.] Public Affairs Officer for U.S. Navy; [oth.writ.] Numerous news releases and articles for internal Navy use; [a.] FPO, AE.

FARMER, EMILY BRANTLEY
[b.] November 9, 1979, Richmond, VA; [p.] Don Farmer and Karen Farmer; [ed.] St. Michael's Episcopal, Governor's School for Gov't. and Int'l. Studies; [occ.] Student, swimmer; [memb.] American Red Cross, NOVA of Virginia Aquatics, US Swimming; [oth. writ.] Almost everything on my mind.; [pers.] Can't write without living the day first. I get much energy from Robert Hunter and Bob Dylan.; [a.] Richmond, VA

FARTHING, JAMES III
[b.] September 28, 1969; [ed.] CSU San Marcos; [memb.] Tau Kappa Epsilon, UC Religious Science; [oth. writ.] Poems and fiction; [pers.] Explore the grace of innocence and the movement of experience; [a.] Oceanside, CA

FASHANO, CASSANDRA LEE
[pen.] Cassandra Lee Ann; [b.] March 31, 1945, Buckannon, WV; [p.] (Divorced, remarried) Ozella Smith and Warren Blank; [m.] Victor Fashano, June 24, 1979; [ch.] Brian Edward; [ed.] Pickens High, East Tennessee State University (Assoc. Degree Nursing), Bloomfield College, Bloomfield, NJ, Cum Laude, BS Nursing, Certified Operating Room Nurse; [occ.] R.N. Operating Room, University Hospital UMDNJ; [memb.] American Operating Room Nurses, Holy Family Catholic Church, Nutley, New Jersey; [hon.] American Legion Award, graduated Cum Laude, Dean's List; [oth. writ.] Working on a collection of poems, "Yesterdays Dream," and a short story, "Trouble's Story," about my Siamese cat.; [pers.] I strive to capture yesterday's dreams, beautiful memories and to reflect on the world around me through my writing. My Grandma, Della Metzner is my inspiration.; [a.] Bloomfield, NJ

FASSINA, MARENE P.
[b.] Gadsden, AL; [p.] Starling and Bertha Pitts (Deceased); [m.] Deceased; [ch.] Susan M. Harris; [ed.] One and one-half years of college; [occ.] President, Management Institute; [memb.] Business organizations; [hon.] Who's Who In America awarded by The National Foundation For Recognition of Outstanding People, S.B.A. "Women In Business Advocate" award, Chamber of Commerce Community Service Award; [oth. writ.] Books: Comprehensive Management, Speech Profile, How to Sell Professionally, You, Too, Can Be An Executive, For My Roots, I Cry, Laughs Breed Success.; [pers.] I am dedicated to assisting teenagers through drug lecturers and educational scholarships.; [a.] Fultondale, AL

FELDMAN, EZRA D.
[b.] April 15, 1980, Boston, MA; [ed.] Maimonides School, Brookline, MA; [pers.] I am approximating the form of the perfect abstraction. Truth belongs behind the shade of anonymity.; [a.] Cambridge, MA

FERGUSON, LARRY N.
[b.] June 24, 1944, Hillsdale, MI; [p.] Neil and Laura Ferguson; [m.] Rosalinda, June 7, 1969; [ch.] Gregory-Paul, Tiffany-Lin; [ed.] BA, Psychology, M. Div. Missions, Ph.D., Clinical Psychology; [occ.] Psychologist, Missionary; [memb.] American Psychological Association, Christian Association for Psychological Studies; [oth. writ.] Journal and Professional articles; [pers.] All of life is God's creation to be enjoyed, loved, and explored.; [a.] Fresno, CA

FERNANDEZ, JACQUELINE
[pen.] Jacqueline Fernandez; [b.] June 3, 1969; Los Angeles; [p.] Maria and Heribeto Fernandez; [m.] Sept 29, 1968; [ch.] Ruth, Sulemo, Heribeto Jr., Jesse; [ed.] University High, Long Beach City College, American Studies Program, D.C., Biola University; [hon.] State Phi Ro Phi Silver Medalist, National Phi Ro Phi Silver and Bronze Medalist, forensics speech trophies, leadership certificate; [oth.writ.] Several unpublished poems, short stories, and currently working on a novel; [pers.] Life is an interesting journey made of obstacles and tribulations. It is through the survival of such that one gains courage, strength, and wisdom; [a.] La Mirada, CA.

FERNANDEZ, TABITHA
[pen.] Tabey; [b.] June 9, 1972, Colorado; [m.] Denny Fernandez, August 12, 1989; [ch.] Andrew, Christopher, Amanda; [occ.] Aspiring writer of children's books; [oth. writ.] I have many poems and children's stories yet to be published.; [pers.] "Eternally Yours" is a poem that I truly believe in, and have experienced, and is very true. I hope that by others reading "Eternally Yours" it will make them stronger too, if and when they have a doubt. It may even save some marriages out there. As for Denny and I were stronger than ever. Denny I'm eternally yours.; [a.] Northglenn, CO

FIFE, CHARLOTTE A.
[b.] March 24, 1943, Hamilton Co., IN; [p.] Ralph and Thelma (McRoberts) Padgett; [m.] James E. Fife, December 4, 1983; [ch.] Lisa L. (Anderson) Saulmon, James L. Anderson Jr., Shelly C. Anderson; [ed.] Lebanon High School and Indiana Vocational Technical College; [occ.] Retired (Volunteer Work); [memb.] Otterbein United Methodist Church, Sheridan Order of The Eastern Star, Literacy Action Group of Boone County; [hon.] Editor's Choice Awards (Previous Publications); [oth. writ.] Several poems published in local newspapers and the poem "Home" in the book, "The Rainbow's End", as well as the poem "My Friend" in the book, "Best Poems of the '90's".; [pers.] The poem included in this book is one I wrote for my husband, Jim Fife, for our Anniversary. I enjoy writing poetry for special occasions and for special people, such as my family and friends.; [a.] Lebanon, IN

FIHMAN, MANUEL
[pen.] Fatik Chandra Pal-Ctesias Greco; [b.] February 14, 1981, Caracas, Venezuela; [p.] David and Doris Fihman; [ed.] Junior at Moralyluces "Herze - Bialik" High School; [occ.] Student; [hon.] Runner up at a National High School Poetry Competition in Venezuela - 1996; [oth. writ.] Poems in the Kaliope Magazine - a play called "Ctesias"; [pers.] Poetry, like life, is not meant to be analyzed or measured. It exists to be lived out, impregnate your heart and drunken your mind, as if you fell into a bottle of wine.; [a.] Caracas, Venezuela

FINCH, TRACY ANN
[pen.] Tracy Ann; [b.] March 8, 1959; Silida, CO; [p.] Ann Finch, Cecil Finch; [ch.] Jason and Danny; [ed.] Moon Valley High School, Medical School for Respiratory, Glendale, Community College for Computer Programming and Engineering; [occ.] SPD Tech. at H. Lee Moffitt Cancer Center; [memb.] AARC; [hon.] Writing and Penmanship in grade school and high school; [oth.writ.] First poem published by The Poetry Guild (Colors), and songs that someday also may be published. [pers.]

I hope I can touch and have impact on the lives of others by what I write, just as writers such as Hemingway and others have had on me; [a.] Tampa, FL

FINGER, LUCIAN
[pen.] Ryu D'Shadow Drake; [b.] May 2, 1980, Dayton, OH; [p.] Candace Finger, Dan Finger; [ed.] Belmont High School; [occ.] Student; [hon.] Honor Roll List, Principal's Awards, Perfect Attendance Awards; [pers.] Nature controls technology as technology controls humans. Humans may feel in control, but are slaves to their minds.; [a.] Dayton, OH

FINKBINER, DALE
[b.] June 9, 1950; Terre Haute, IN; [p.] Dear and Helen Finkbiner; [m.] Carmen Finkbiner; May 2, 1981; [ch.] Summer Leah; [ed.] Marshall High School, Radio Announcing Trade School, currently a home study on journalism; [occ.] Quality Control at Brico Mebals, Inc. in Marshall; [memb.] Various Church Committees; [oth.writ.] Writings for Churchland factory newsletter; [pers.] Mellow and easy-going writing, even though I tend to enjoy authors like Edgar Allen Poe and Steven King; [a.] Marshall, IL.

FISHER, PHILLIP K.
[pen.] Storm McKenzie, Armand Santiago; [b.] October 12, 1976, Little Rock, AR; [p.] Stan and Linda Fisher; [ed.] First Gospel Academy, University of Arkansas at Little Rock; [occ.] Quality Control; [hon.] Ambassador Award for Outstanding Character and Leadership; [oth. writ.] Several poems used in Support Centers. Others available from pk20@aol.com.; [pers.] All of my poems were inspired by incidents in my life. They are my means of coping with trials and tests. Give your all to others and you will reap what you have sown.; [a.] Little Rock, AR

FISK, DENISE L.
[b.] August 24, 1959, Grand Rapids, MI; [p.] Ross and Kathy Fisk; [ed.] B.A.A.; [occ.] Paramedic/Importer; [memb.] NAEMT/IC's; [hon.] Who's Who 1993/94; [oth. writ.] Numerous all dealing with emotions and nature's reflections of those emotions.; [pers.] I believe our emotions are an important stream in our life and that nature can reflect and draw on those emotions. Emotions are seen through the windows to our souls.; [a.] Sand Lake, MI

FITZGERALD II, GARRY
[b.] March 15, 1967, Wash., DC; [p.] Garrett and Diane FitzGerald; [ed.] St. Vincent Pallottie High 1987, Howard Community College 1997; [occ.] Work part time for UPS and go to school part time; [oth. writ.] "My writing is my emotional expression of my life experiences."; [a.] Laurel, MD

FLACK, CATHLEEN
[pen.] Cathleen Flack; [b.] June 14, 1944, Los Angeles; [p.] Ines and Durwood Brown, [ch.] Steven M. Flentye; [ed.] Occidental College BA, University of California - Teaching Credential; [occ.] Teacher on disability leave due to bipolar disorder; [memb.] AARP, NEA; [oth. writ.] Poems Pensive Prose, Whimsical Poems, The Lighter Side.; [pers.] As one who suffers from bipolar disorder I often write gloomy poems those from the dark side. I try to express what we seldom talk about to quell the these thoughts in others.; [a.] McGill, NV

FLEETWOOD, BARBRA
[b.] June 28, 1949, Sulfur Springs, TX; [p.] Mr. and Mrs. E. C. Vestal; [m.] Dewey Glenn Fleetwood, July 12, 1996; [ch.] Two daughters - three grandchildren; [ed.] Drew High School, Delta State University, (Dean's List); [occ.] Retired State Employee; [hon.] Received numerous writing awards in college for short stories and essays, graduated from Law Enforcement Academy - highest Academic Achievement and Outstanding Physical Training Award; [oth. writ.] Several writing (poems, essays, and short stories) published in college newspaper and yearly special writers book; [pers.] Many of my friends and family members died in the Vietnam War. I try to show my appreciation thru writing and regular donations to the paralyzed Veterans of America.; [a.] Coffeeville, MS

FLETCHER, KRISTAL L.
[b.] July 13, 1983, Saranac Lake, NY; [p.] Bradley and Nancy Fletcher; [ed.] 8th Grade, Student at Brushton-Moira Central, Brushton, NY; [occ.] Student; [memb.] Basketball-softball, Treasurer for the Class of 2001, Band, Chorus, Biddy ball coach, Bowling champion '95; [hon.] All Academic Basketball, Rookie-of-the-Year Basketball 96-97, Honor Roll, Donald Bellows Award, 6th Grade Basketball, Band Awards 93-94-95-96; [pers.] I wrote this poem for my mother. I love her immensely. I take pride in my work. I have written many other poems but I never thought they were good enough.; [a.] Moira, NY

FLICK, PAMELA T.
[b.] October 28, 1959, Newark, NJ; [p.] Marshall Beahm, Evanthia Beahm; [m.] Arthur R. Flick Jr., August 12, 1989; [ed.] Kearny High, Pacific College of Medical and Dental Careers; [pers.] I tend to express my deepest emotions through words which is reflected in my writing. My inspiration comes from the strong love and support of my husband and family.; [a.] San Diego, CA

FLORES, CARLO
[pen.] Charles Elsener; [b.] September 27, 1925, Hermosa Beach, CA; [p.] Joe Flores, Alice Elsener; [m.] Ruth M. Smith, January 28, 1950; [ch.] Susan, Audrey, Gary, Yvonne; [ed.] B.A. International Business and Economics, San Francisco State University, San Francisco, CA, 1954 graduate work at SFSU World School of Businees 1955-56.; [occ.] World Traveler, Adventurist, Explorer, Expedition Leader, Internet Webmeister, Intergeneration-Telecom Host on America Online, Writer, Poet, Publisher, Philanthropist, also Founder and Executive Director of TWI - The Waterfalls Institute; [memb.] U.S. Army Intelligence WW II and Korean War, American Foreign Legion Unit Europa 1945, San Francisco Export Manager Club 1954-58, Honolulu Contractor's Ass. 1958-62, Veterans of Foreign Wars Life Member, American Legion Boys State Counselor 1995, World Waterfalls Watchers Club Life Member 1992, Volunteer at GGNRA, San Francisco former U.S. army Presidio and serving as a seasonal part-time docent with Yosemith Ass. at Yosemite National Park, CA, since 1992.; [hon.] Swiss Boy Scouts Jamboree Award, Zurich, Switzerland 1938, Swiss Alpine Club 1938, Davos Junior Ski Patrol - Downhill Race Winner 1939, SFSU Dean's List 1951, Ambassador's Club Philippines 1958, Honorary Member of The White Tiger Hunters Club, Dalat,

Vietnam 1958, Rangoon Explorer Club, Burma 1958, Raffle Hotel Water Hole Club Singapore 1958, International Aerostation Flyer, Napa, CA. 1985, Who's Who in U.S. Executive 1988-89, Diamond Award GSMIC 1991, Honorary Life Member The World of Waterfalls Club 1992, Distinguished Member International Society of Poets 1996.; [oth. writ.] Author of "How To Sell Your Idea, Product and services in the USA 1975 In search of Waterfalls and several science fiction short stories on America Online's ESH network also self-published a book of poems Journeys of the 20th century. The story of My Family and My Life by Watermark Press, 1997.; [pers.] My travels, hobbies and interests take me to all corners of the world and cyberspace which I share with my worldwide friends and the school children on ESH - The Electronic Schoolhouse forum of America Online and the Internet URL: http://wwww.batnet.com/infoman/waterfallsonline/ E-mail: CJ4Short@aol.cpom and MrWatrfal@aol.com. My third-age generation motto: To live one day at a time to the fullest sharing my joy with others! My life's mentors: My maternal grandmother Frida Egger-Elesner (a true entrepreneurial spirit in her times 1865-1937), Raymond Margolies (former President of GSMIC, Park Ridge, IL), Leni Donlan, teacher and educator of San Francisco, CA. the legandary John Muir, Louis L'Amour (Westerns), William Carlos Williams and vivacious Kristian Rylands of Mariposa, CA (both poets extraordinaire.); [a.] Redwood City, CA

FLORES, HAKIOWSKIE A. (AKA HAKI)
[pen.] Haki; [b.] August 16, 1980; Lansing, MI; [p.] Nery A. and Jesse A. Flores; [occ.] Student; [memb.] NCSY; [hon.] Basketball Summer Camp Okland University 1st Place Award, Most improve Basketball player Award Akiva Hebrew Day School. Honor Roll Akiva Hebrew Day School and National Science Merit Award (NSMA) winner; [oth.writ.] A modest proposal and poetry writing that I have not submitted for publication; [pers.] I have been influenced by Jonathan Swift and other poets like him that wrote satire during the 18th century. Some beat, Edgar Allan Poe and other writers have influenced me over the years. I try to reflect in my writing the world around me; [a.] Ste Hts, MI.

FLORES, TED MATTHEW
[b.] November 25, 1979, Berkeley, CA; [p.] Theodore Flores and Kathleen Flores; [ed.] Currently a high school junior, at John F. Kennedy High School in Sacramento, CA; [occ.] Student; [memb.] National Honor Society, California Scholarship Federation, G.A.T.E. (Gifted and Talented Education), M.E.S.A. (Math, Engineering, Science, Achievement).; [hon.] Eastman Kodak Young Leader Award 1996, Who's Who of American High School Students 1996 and 1997, Golden State Exam for Biology: School Recognition (1996), Golden State Exam for Economics (1996), honors.; [oth. writ.] Weinstock's Department Store Mother's Day Poetry Contest for children, won 2nd place: $175 Waterford Crystal Vase. (11 years old).; [pers.] As a youth I admired the poetry of Shel Silverstein. Now my favorite poets include Walt Whitman, Robert Frost, Langston Hughes, and Maya Angelou; [a.] Sacramento, CA

FLOWERS, FRANCES M.
[pen.] Rose Bud, FMF; [b.] October 28, 1933; Norfolk, VA; [p.] James D. Maness and Esther Bergstrom; [m.] James Oliver Flowers, Sr.; December 9, 1950; [ch.] James Oliver Flowers, Jr.; Brenda Louise, Patricia, William; [ed.] 12th grade, Kee's Business College, Professional Business and Medical Inst., Ches. Fire Fighter and EMT; [occ.] Retired Secretary, and FF and EMT; [memb.] Church-Parkway Temple, Chesapeake Moose Lodge WOTM 691, Chesapeake Storm Management Comm., Widow Persons Service, AARP; [oth.writ.] Numerous poems and songs, inspirational songs and poems, poems published in VA. Ext. Home Makers Council, I also play the guitar and dulicmer and electronic keyboard, family history and genealogy, building, home repair, auto repair, painting, roofing and electrical; [pers.] I am a Christian and do Bible study; [a.] Chesapeake, VA.

FOOTE, SALLY ANN
[b.] December 31, 1980; Red Oak, IA; [p.] Shari Jackson; [m.] Keith Jackson; September 30, 1983; [ed.] American Home Schooling; [occ.] Clerk at Casey's General Store; [oth.writ.] One poem published in Crossings; [a.] Cushing, IA.

FORAKIS, AMY
[pen.] Amy Forakis; [b.] May 19, 1970, Selmer, TN; [p.] Max and Margaret Franks; [m.] Jim, December 15, 1990; [ch.] Joshua Maxwell, Demetrius Kostas; [ed.] Hardin County High, 2 yr. (Associate's) in Journalism; [occ.] Housewife; [memb.] Pastor's Wife; [pers.] My writings mostly consist of Motherhood and the ever increasing demand to forget what it is like to be a child.; [a.] Colchester, VT

FOREMAN, ROBERT B.
[b.] March 6, 1984; Indianapolis, IN; [p.] Robert and Ann Foreman; [ed.] 7th grade; [occ.] Student Orchard School; [pers.] The Human Spirit is as strong as the very essence of life, and like life, it will never die; [a.] Indianapolis, IN.

FOSTER, OLIVE W.
[b.] August 13, 1944, Jamaica, West Indies; [m.] Linval A. Foster, March 29, 1970; [ch.] Lyneve, Opal, Darlene; [ed.] State University of New York at Buffalo, State University College at Buffalo; [occ.] Educational Administrator; [memb.] School Administrators Association of NY State, Western N. York, Women in Administration, University of Buffalo Alumni, State University College at Buffalo Alumni; [hon.] Doctoral Degree in Educational Administration (Suny at Buffalo); [oth. writ.] Several poems presented in local church setting.; [pers.] In my writing I attempt to portray the beauty of a meaningful life, especially as developed from a Christian perspective. Life is only as meaningful as it includes service to others.; [a.] Buffalo, NY

FOSTER, WARREN L.
[oth. writ.] "Peace Of Mind", "Song Of The Shore", "Writer's Blue", "An Open Book", "Rain On The River"; [pers.] Listen to your heart.

FOUNTAIN, FLOYD E.
[pen.] F. E. Fountain; [b.] July 5, 1927, Springfield, MA; [p.] Eva Getto, Floyd E. Fountain; [m.] Adrienne Cayan (Deceased), November 27, 1947; [ed.] GED at 50- years old; [occ.] Retired - US Postal Service; [memb.] Masonic Orders, Boy

Scouts of America, VFW Dundee United Methodist Church; [hon.] Nominated Poet Laureate of Florida, Black Hills Passion Play Writer Award; [pers.] Live and let live, do unto others as you would have them do unto you. To ere is to be human, to forgive is to be divine.; [a.] Winter Haven, FL

FOUST, SIMON
[pen.] Ethan Stone, SSF; [b.] June 5, 1978, South Carolina; [p.] Michael and Rebecca, (Bio. Father) Mitch Shull; [occ.] Student; [memb.] Member of Sunrise (Christian) Church in Rialto, CA; [oth. writ.] Having never been published before I am extremely interested, and waiting for God to open the doors to where he wants me to go.; [pers.] With words I worship my King, even as birds pause outside and sing. And I will sing of his love forever.; [a.] Rialto, CA

FOWLER, HUGH
[b.] April 7, 1938, Syracuse, NY; [m.] Jewel Anne, November 24, 1962; [ch.] David; [ed.] BS - Mathematics, MS - Education, AAS - Electronics Communications , BSAMT - Robotics; [occ.] Retired Teacher; [memb.] Worldwide Church of God; [pers.] Musical arrangements invited - I have melody and refrain music.; [a.] Fort Wayne, IN

FRANKS, DEHNER
[b.] March 1, 1963, Chicago, IL; [p.] Theodore Franks, Leona Franks; [m.] Anita Franks, February 27, 1988; [ch.] DeAnthony Franks; [ed.] Bachelor of Arts, Bachelor of Music, Jazz Piano Performance, University of Washington; [occ.] Professional Pianist; [oth. writ.] Several songs both with lyrics and instrument pieces; [pers.] I like to write songs and poems that will touch the reader in a special way.; [a.] Seattle, WA

FREDRICKSON, ARIEL
[b.] March 30, 1984, Hastings, MN; [p.] David and Chrys Fredrickson; [ed.] Hastings Middle School, grade 7 (when I wrote the poem); [occ.] School; [oth. writ.] The Dream, The Stream, Bunnies, Being Scared, The Summer Breeze, The Opposites, I Wish, Candy Canes and Jelly Beans, Angel, Hot Dry Wind; [pers.] I struggle to help other people see that no matter what color or religion you are, we are all equal. I have been greatly influenced by my 7th grade English teacher.; [a.] Hampton, MN

FRIDAY, MONA IRENE
[b.] June 22, 1916, England; [p.] Deceased; [m.] Deceased, March 23, 1940; [ch.] Two Sons; [ed.] College (in the United Kingdom); [occ.] Retired; [a.] Osprey, FL

FRIEMAN, T. LEEANN
[b.] August 19, 1968, Akron, OH; [p.] Larry and Marianne Stear; [m.] Kevin L. Frieman, November 4, 1995; [ch.] Jessica Nicole; [ed.] Garfield High School, U.S. Army, Clayton School of Natural Healing; [occ.] Student; [memb.] American Natural Hygiene Society, Coalition for Natural Health, The Nature Conservancy, Missouri Botanical Gardens, St. Louis Zoofriends Association, Girl Scouts of America; [oth. writ.] Several poems published in Newspaper, magazines and books.; [pers.] Live, laugh, love and treasure the simple things.; [a.] High Ridge, MO

FRISHMAN, PATRICIA Y.
[b.] February 2, 1952, Garden City, KS; [p.] Antone

A. Kanak, Doris G. McGee (maiden name); [ch.] Bradley Vincent, Bryan John; [ed.] Johnson County Community College, Longview Community College, Lee's Summit MO (working on degree in journalism); [occ.] Program Analyst for General Services Administration; [memb.] Parents Without Partners, Federal Womens Program; [pers.] Time, patience, and nature are the greatest healers!!! There are no mistakes in life, only "hard lessons" to be learned!; [a.] Belton, MO

FRONDLE, KELLI E.
[b.] October 9, 1979, Cedar Rapids, IA; [p.] Julie E. Frondle; [ed.] Solon High School; [occ.] Cashier; [oth. writ.] United in "The Ebbing Tide"; [pers.] My mother for always being there, all my family. Shaina Lacina, Mrs. Farrier, my English teacher, Mr. Vetter for teaching me discipline in chorus. And God, for never letting me give up. Life is short so make your dreams come true before it ends.; [a.] Solon, IA

FRY, GARY Q.
[b.] September 27, 1951, Cleveland, OH; [p.] Harvey Q. Fry, Elizabeth M. Fry; [m.] Divorced; [ch.] Mark Brandon, Melissa Ann - Matthew Allen; [ed.] Washington High (Phx., AZ), Glendale Community College (AZ); [occ.] City Investigator; [oth. writ.] (Unpublished) book of love poems; [pers.] Poetry is the feelings and emotions which come from one's heart; [a.] Phoenix, AZ

FRY, KYLE
[b.] February 6, 1979, Carlisle; [p.] Patricia Ann Cramer; [ed.] High School; [occ.] Lube Tech.; [pers.] The poem was for my girlfriend for Valentine's Day.; [a.] Shermans Dale, PA

FUHLENDORF, CHARLENE L.
[b.] July 27, 1949, Turlock, CA; [p.] Mickey and Ima Jean Martins; [m.] Michael Fuhlendorf, November 9, 1974; [ch.] Erik and Allan Fuhlendorf; [ed.] College Student; [occ.] Student, Computer Graphics major; [memb.] Grace Lutheran Church; [oth. writ.] "My Cat's Clothes," published in "Space Between," "This Is Pepper," published in "Best Poems of 1995," "Something Never To Forget," published in "Best Poems of the '90's," "Compassion Lost," published in "Best Poems of 1996".; [a.] Modesto, PA

FULLER, JACQUELINE F.
[pen.] Francisca Robinson; [b.] October 17, 1978, The Bronx, NY; [p.] A. Michael Fuller, Wendy Robinson-Fuller; [ed.] Dunbar Senior High School, Marymount University; [occ.] Student/Entrepreneur; [memb.] American Institute of Aeronautics and Astronautics, Air Force ROTC; [hon.] Tuskegee Airmen Scholarship, National Cherry Blossom Scholarship, Who's Who Among American High School Students; [oth. writ.] Poems published in H.S. Yearbook and Church News Letters, Letter to Editor about Colin Powell and Born Jamericans published in Everybody's Magazine.; [pers.] My writings are stories of people from all walks of life. I write to bring everyone to a common ground and relate life's situations to be expressed.; [a.] Washington, DC

FULLER, ROSE MURCIER
[b.] August 22, 1948, McCormick, SC; [p.] Mr. and Mrs. James Murcier; [m.] Willie Fuller Jr., April 8, 1973; [ed.] Mims High School, Graduated 1966,

Columbia Business College - Typing Course; [occ.] Account Exec. for Fashion Fair Cosmetics/Div. Johnson Pub. Co., Publisher of Ebony/Jet Magazines; [oth. writ.] Poem - "Talk To Me Now", "Unpublished"; [a.] Columbia, SC

FUNAIOLE, BARBARA L. HARRIS
[pen.] Barb Fun; [b.] October 11, 1951, Fayetteville, TN; [p.] Dorothy Brison Harris, Milton "Mickey" S. Harris; [ed.] Chattanooga High School, 1970, Chattanooga, TN, Manatee Community College, AA, 1986, University South Florida, BS, 1990, Elementary Ed., Early Childhood Ed., State of FL Certification Areas; [occ.] Teacher, Manatee County, Bradenton, FL; [memb.] USF Alumni Association, Facilitator Leadership Trained, State Facilitator of Environmental Educ. Programs, i.e., - Project WILD, Aquatic Wild, Project Learning Tree, 4 R's, Biodiversity, etc.; [hon.] Outstanding Graduate USF/ Sarasota, Spring, '90, Outstanding College Students of America, Who's Who of American Colleges and Universities, USF Gold Council Membership, Sun Coast Area Teacher Training Honors Program Graduate, VSF/Sarasota Reading Council Outstanding Service Scholarship Award; [oth. writ.] Phonics Teaching Activities for Modern Curriculum Press. This will be my first work of poetry published.; [pers.] Enjoy he challenges of channeling life events and occurrences into rhyming poems and stories - to hand difficult situations more calmly and turn negatives into positives.; [a.] Bradenton, FL

GAGNE, NANCY LEE
[b.] February 7, 1940, Cambridge, MA; [p.] Anthony Romano and Gioconda Di Palma; [m.] James P. Gagne, July 19, 1992; [ch.] James, Scott and Lorraine Kelley; [ed.] A.S. Business Admin., Northeastern University 1997, Boston, MA; [occ.] Executive Assistant; [hon.] National Golden Key Honor Society; [oth. writ.] Several poems, as yet unpublished and children's short stories.; [pers.] My writing pleasure is two fold, in the creation of a piece worthy of publication and in a reader's enjoyment.; [a.] Medford, MA

GAINEY, LYNN
[pen.] Lynn Gainey; [b.] January 29, 1937, Florence, SC; [p.] Mary and Bruce Smith; [m.] Howard B. Gainey Jr., December 28, 1964; [ch.] Mary, H. B. III, and Liston; [ed.] B.A. Coker College 1959; [occ.] Self-employed, Taught elementary education for nine years before having children; [oth. writ.] None published.

GALLAGHER, AMY C.
[pen.] Amy Barton; [b.] February 17, 1963, Ft. Worth, TX; [p.] Charles and Shirley Gallagher; [m.] Wayne M. Keeton, March 16, 1996; [ch.] Michael - 8 months; [ed.] BS Journalism/Public Relations, Oneyr-masters in Public Administration Program; [occ.] Aviation Public Relations; [memb.] Public Relations Society of America (PRSA), Women in Aviation (WIA), National Assoc. of Female Executives (NAFE); [hon.] Girls Service Leage Scholarship; [oth. writ.] First poem "Mist" published age of 10, several feature articles in aviation trade journals, several articles published in local newspapers and newsletters.; [pers.] I live and love through the beauty of words. I have been inspired by many "common" writers who dared to express through the power of the written word.; [a.] Lewisville, TX

GALLEGOS, MICHAEL
[pen.] Mike; [b.] May 11, 1960, Santa Fe, New Mexico; [p.] Albert and Eliza Gallegos (brothers-Philip, Paul & Manual-Deceased); [m.] Divorced; [ch.] none; [ed.] Santa Fe High School, New Mexico - involved in lots of sports, basketball was his favorite.; [l.] Spanish, English and German; [memb.] The Eagles Club, St. Anne's Catholic Church, Santa Fe, New Mexico; [hon.] Navy - received award from the president of the USA/Bill Clinton; [oth. writ.] Poems of love, Tomance, Faith and nature. Scribbles of a puzzle that only Mike could understand. These poems were in his personal pad, that no one could find. [pers.] Mike lived life to the fullest, he was a warm hearted person. He enjoyed a good challenge and when he believed in something he worked hard at it till the end. He was a tall, beautiful hazel eyes Spaniard that carried his faith (a scapular) over his heart. His inner strengths were: dreams, romance, nature, love, creativity, faith. "A great work of art, always to treasure".; May 11, 1960-July 14, 1995; "In a New York minute, anything could happen"; Liza Gallegos - Mother; Lisa Colergo - Special friend.

GALLOTTE, KATHERINE SUMMER
[pen.] Summer; [b.] October 6, 1971, Starkville, MS; [p.] Fred and Cassie Breland; [m.] Michael Scott Gallotte, December 17, 1994; [ed.] Bay Senior High graduate, Associate of Arts Degree from Jefferson Davis Community College in Gulfport, MS; [occ.] Cash Office Manager of Goody's Dept. Store, Oxford, MS; [oth. writ.] Several other poems and songs, as yet unpublished.; [pers.] Many thanks to the musicians in the states. Your music is a great inspiration for my drawings and poetry.; [a.] Watervalley, MS

GAOA, RACHEL
[b.] July 11, 1983, Long Beach; [p.] Filipo and Linda Gaoa; [ed.] 232 Place Elementary, Stephen M. White, Middle School; [occ.] Student; [oth. writ.] I have a collection of my poems in a binder.; [pers.] I get my inspiration from the people around me, when I write a poem it's like I can feel another person's happiness, sadness or suffering and then I just have to write it down!; [a.] Carson, CA

GARCIA, RICHARD
[b.] October 8, 1969, Miami, FL; [p.] Desiderio and Elpidia Garcia; [m.] Deborah Renee Garcia, June 18, 1993; [ch.] Patrick and Julianne; [ed.] High School Graduate, Miami High Class of 1987; [occ.] Entrepreneur; [pers.] "Ones etiquette and upbringing is shown in your children."; [a.] Miami, FL

GARCIA, TIERRY F.
[b.] December 20, 1919; Philippines; [p.] Dr. Silverio F. Garcia, Physician (deceased), Elisea Trijo, Pharmacist (deceased); [m.] Amanda Garcia; April 19, 1953; [ch.] Tierry Silverio, Business man, Sofia Amanda Ruiher, Physician, Angela, Lawyer; [ed.] Doctor of Medicine, University of the Philippines, residency in ear, nose, throat disease, Columbia Presbyterian Hospital, NY; [occ.] Physician; [memb.] Indiana State Medical Assn., American Rhinologic Society, American Academy of Otolaryngic Allergy, American Academy of Environmental Medicine, Toast Masters Club, Knights of Columbus; [hon.] Diplomate, American Board of Otolaryngology, Dept Chairman of Otolaryn-

gology, University of the Philippines General Hospital; [oth.writ.] Articles on ear, nose and throat disease and health care; [pers.] I find increasing peace and joy in gratefully acknowledging all my blessings from the Almighty, including rules for the fullness of life, showing my love for neighbor in whatever way I can; [a.] Indianapolis, IN.

GARDEPE, JANIS V.
[b.] November 18, 1948, Warwick, NY; [p.] William H. and Emma Elwood; [m.] John E. Gardepe (Deceased, 1973), April 30, 1967; [ch.] John E. the second, Jason and James; [ed.] High school; [occ.] Housewife; [pers.] If you take time to look, you will always find the beauty of the world around you.; [a.] Bloomingburg, NY

GARN, MEGHAN
[b.] July 25, 1983; Grass Valley, CA; [p.] David Garn and Marcia Doerr; [ed.] 8th Grade; (School) Lyman Gillmore Middle School 1996-97 Nevada Union High School 1997-98; [hon.] Principal's List Honor Roll; [oth.writ.] I haven't had any other of my poems published, but I do expect to keep writing; [pers.] I think that by writing things that are true and similar to life, that I can affect somebody through my poetry. I that I can; [a.] Nevada City, CA.

GARNER, HELEN
[b.] November 11, 1952, Dillon, SC; [p.] Danny R. Garner, Allaine Garner; [m.] Divorce, September 25, 1975; [ch.] Andy L. Porter, Steve G. Porter; [ed.] Finish 9th Grade; [occ.] I work at Styrex, High Point, N.C. I'm a Mechan Operator; [memb.] The Entertainer Ind-Association, ISP International Society OF, Poets; [hon.] Editor's Choice Award, Special Recording Award For, Song I wrote, Remember When, I have been published in 5 books; [oth. writ.] I write poems and songs.; [pers.] I feel, that the Lord gave me the gift of writing, poems and songs. I know this is from God. I know that the Lord is working through me to reach some one else. Through my poems and songs.; [a.] Thomasville, NC

GARVER, LINDA ANNE
[b.] June 16, 1954, Philadelphia, PA; [p.] James P. Cannon, Vera Cannon; [m.] Ronald Paul Garver, September 7, 1974; [ch.] Amy Lynn, Lisa Anne; [ed.] Marple-Newtown Senior High School; [occ.] Administrative Assistant; [hon.] Business Award from Marple-Newtown High School; [oth. writ.] I have written many poems and a book. They are unpublished at this time.; [pers.] I have been around horses most of my life I was even married on horseback. My love for horses is what inspired "Horse's Heaven."; [a.] Frazer, PA

GAUNT, BRIAN
[b.] April 3, 1957, Portland, OR; [p.] Mack Gaunt and Shirly Gaunt; [m.] Patricia Sterling Gaunt, May 31, 1986; [ch.] Ian Forrest and Blaire Mcenzie; [ed.] Parkrose High, 3 yrs. at Univ. of Ore.; [occ.] Finish Carpenter; [oth. writ.] Articles for a regional outdoor magazine, "Salmon, Trout, Steelheader"; [pers.] In memory of Mack Gaunt.; [a.] Lincoln City, OR

GAYLE, DARRYL E.
[pen.] "D"; [b.] March 9, 1949, New York, NY; [p.] Gladys D. Gayle and Earl E. Gayle; [ed.] Graduate of "The High School of Art and Design - New

York, NY, Graduate of "Arizona State University", Tempe, Arizona; [occ.] Instructor and Printer; [oth. writ.] Many, as yet unpublished; [pers.] Be not broken by the brightness of life, for even the weed persists.; [a.] Brooklyn, NY

GAZA, IRENE M.
[p.] Mosho and Hatsumi Gaza; [ch.] Deborah Tasato-Kodama, Alluson Mellone, Keith M.Y. Tasato, Dayle David Y. Tasato; [ed.] Our Lady of Loretto High School, Los Angeles, CA; University of Hawaii, West Oahu Campus, Pearl City, HI; [occ.] Accounting Department of Outrigger Hotels and Resorts; [memb.] Honolulu Academy of Arts, University of Hawaii West Oahu Alumni Association; [hon.] Editors Choice awards for Sunshine Through Jalousies and My Son, Dayle; [oth.writ.] The Broken Toy, Life's Analogy, The Tall Pine, Hidden Agenda, Man of Contradiction, A Dawn to Purpose, The Puppet, Miss-Understanding. Prose: Myself-My World, Cans of Money; [pers.] Everyone should be given every opportunity to achieve their goals, to attain a quality of life they would want for themselves; [a.] Honolulu, HI.

GENGLER, JENNIFER ALDEN LINDSEY
[b.] November 13, 1969, Vero Beach, FL; [p.] Carol and Robin Fox; [ch.] Britney Fletcher, Brandon; [ed.] Graduated Kathleen High School, Travis Vocational School, (Health occupations); [occ.] CNA/HHA (Nursing); [hon.] 1st Place poetry contest in 1981, President award 1982; [oth. writ.] A poem I wrote in 1981 won 1st place this award was given by my school.; [pers.] My poems are written from my heart I enjoy writing poetry it seems to be a part of me. Of who I am. Thank you.; [a.] Lakeland, FL

GENSAYA, JOY PELOBELLO
[pen.] Willis, Beanstalk; [b.] January 4, 1973, Iloilo City, Philippines; [p.] Lilia P. Gensaya and Toribio G. Gensaya; [ed.] Elem. - Central Philippine University, Philippines, High School and College: West Visayas State University, Philippines; [occ.] Registered Nurse, South Shore Hospital; [pers.] Love conquers all.; [a.] Bay Harbor Islands, FL

GENTRY, RICKY THOMAS
[b.] December 17, 1955, Portland, TN; [p.] Susie Starks Gentry and Ewell Thomas Gentry; [ed.] Completed the eleventh grade; [occ.] Factory worker; [hon.] I.S.O. certified for quality, service, and teamwork at place of employment.; [oth. writ.] I have written several poems over my lifespan, but this is my first attempt at publication.; [pers.] The words of my poetry are swells of emotion from the bottom of my heart, I have lived every line and felt every emotion.; [a.] Springfield, TN

GHENT, CAROL W.
[b.] December 25, 1949, Lancaster, SC; [p.] Rev. W. C. Wallace Jr., and Mary N. Wallace; [m.] Rev. Gene Ghent; [ch.] Mica, Daniel; [ed.] Master's Degree plus 30 hours from Winthrop College, Rock Hill, SC; [occ.] Extension teacher, Grade 2, North Elementary in Lancaster, SC; [memb.] NCTM, NCTE, SCCTE; [pers.] Anne Morrow Lindbergh said, "An experience isn't finished until it's written." I have been greatly influenced by the teachings of Lucy McCormick Calkins, Donald Graves, and Georgia Heard, all... educators of the art of writing.; [a.] Lancaster, SC

GIACOMAZZO, BERNADETTE
[b.] November 29, 1977, Queens, NY; [p.] Guiseppe and Anna Maria Giacomazzo; [ed.] Our Lady of Mercy Academy, Syosset NY, DuQuesne University, Pittsburgh PA; [occ.] Student, DuQuesne University, amateur poet/photographer/musician; [memb.] TriBeta Biological Honor Society, Lambda Sigma, Service Honor Society, Phi Eta Sigma Honor Society; [hon.] Dean's List, Director's Circle; [oth. writ.] Several poems published in different anthologies.; [pers.] I try to reflect my spiritual, Gothic side in all my works. I've been influenced by a wide variety of artist, from Henry David Thoreau and Edgar Allen Poe, to Bob Dylan and Marilyn Manson.; [a.] Pittsburgh, PA

GIBBONS, DEBRA GABBARD
[pen.] Gabrille Daines; [b.] December 10, 1954, Roswell, NM; [p.] Vinder Isaac Gabbard and Glenna Mae Wehl; [m.] Thomas J. Gibbons, August 25, 1984; [ch.] One Son, Sean Thomas Gibbons; [ed.] Polytechnic High, Western Nevada Community College; [occ.] Mom, Student, Business Owner, Active Volunteer; [memb.] St. Teresa of Avila Catholic Church, National Geographic Society; [hon.] Phi Theta Kappa, Dean's List; [oth. writ.] First published poem.; [pers.] My son, Sean, is my greatest encouragement and with that all else is possible. God's grace is so good when we are grounded in him.; [a.] Carson City, NV

GIBBS, THOMAS J.
[pen.] Thomas J; [b.] 1979; [ed.] Minimal literary study. All works are merely thoughts or ideas presented in semi-poetic form; [oth. writ.] One finished book of writings, and another in progress; [pers.] In writing, quality is a perception. The depth and meaning, determined by the reader. Success is only in the reader's realization as to a work's meaning in relation to their own experience; [a.] Dallas, TX.

GIESE, RICHARD J.
[b.] July 14, 1969, Saint Petersburg, FL; [p.] Robert and Bonnie; [ed.] 1 1/2 years junior college, Jefferson College, Hillsboro, MO, Community College of the Air Force; [occ.] Full-time student, part-time warehouse shipping/ receiving; [memb.] American Heart Association, Volunteer Firefighter, Church of Christ, Arnold, MO; [hon.] Phi Theta Kappa, Dean's List, published in National Dean's List Honor Society catalog (biography); [oth. writ.] Short stories, poems and essays published in local newspapers, Jefferson County Journal, editor for church bulletins and tracts.; [pers.] My hope through my writings is to open the minds of my readers to the beauty in the surrounding universe. My previous association with scholars and other journalists has had the greatest influence on my writings.; [a.] Arnold, MO

GILLESPIE, JANN A.
[b.] November 11, 1942, McDonald, KS; [p.] Marion and Marie Hallagin; [m.] W. J. Gillespie, May 25, 1962; [ch.] Johnene, Janette, Jeanna, James; [ed.] McDonald High, Fort Hays University, Hays KS; [occ.] Bookkeeper (Jerry's Alignment and Auto Service), Dietician (Good Samaritan Home); [memb.] United Methodist Church Good Samaritan S.H.A.R.E. Team Sherman Co. E.H.U., 4-H Leader Community; [hon.] 4-H Leadership Awards, All-Star Sunflower League Coach; [oth. writ.] Local newspaper, Grit Good Samaritan Quarterly; [pers.] Leadership is only achieved by those who have followers that are dedicated and willing to succeed and share their success without a price tag on it.; [a.] Goodland, KS

GILLETTE, MARK F.
[m.] Maria; [ed.] Graduate, Grand Rapids JC, Michigan State University, Northwestern University, Western Michigan University; [occ.] Physician Assistant; [memb.] American Association of Physician Assistants, Michigan Association of Physician Assistants, National Geographic Society; [pers.] The inspiration for my poetry and writing is God who created all things, including my wife who inspired me to write this poem.; [a.] Grand Rapids, MI

GILLINGHAM, ERIC
[pen.] John Page; [b.] January 22, 1977, San Diego, CA; [p.] Christine and Michael Gillingham; [ed.] St. Augustine High (San Diego), Loyola Marymont University; [occ.] College Sophomore, Musician for hire.; [memb.] My band, "Pendulum," St. Augustine High School Band, Fish and Game Association (San Diego), Rifle Club, Audio Engineering Society; [hon.] Honors in high school, Principal's List, (3.5 GPA), Band Spirit Award, high school, and Freshman Football Award, Math and English achievement awards, 2nd place in Loyola Marymont Poetry Contest; [oth. writ.] I have several poems I pretty much store in my computer, and a few short stories, and an essay. I have written on things such as wHs for school.; [pers.] I tend to like to reflect the darker side of human nature and life in general in my poems, and prefer smooth flowing rhyme schemes. Many of my poems are influenced by Edgar Allen Poe.; [a.] San Diego, CA

GINGRAS JR., HORACE
[pen.] Horace Gingras Jr.; [b.] September 23, 1922, Springfield, MA; [p.] Margrete E. Courtney and Horace Gingras Sr.; [m.] Catherine Barbara Villardi (Deceased), November 1, 1976; [ch.] Five: (4) daughters and one son; [ed.] High School, various service school, over a period of twenty yrs., active duty and various schools for DuPont; [occ.] Retired from E.I. DuPont de Nemours and Company and 30 yrs. U.S.N.; [memb.] VFW, American Legion, N.R.A. Knight of Columbus, Sons of Italy; [hon.] Various, Service Medals and Commendations; [oth. writ.] A Young Lad, Do We Love You Any Less, Great Big Barricade, To Find away, Give Us Courage, Mother Of Mine; [pers.] What you put into life is what you get out of it nothing more or nothing less.

GLOOR JR., ALBERT G.
[pen.] Albert Gloor; [b.] July 20, 1950, Goliad, TX; [a.] Goliad, TX

GOBIN, DENNIS P.
[b.] July 10, 1961; Guyana; [pers.] Life should not be a labor, but an art to live out. Like love to fellow humans is not a burden, but a way to live; [a.] Hollis, NY.

GOLD, RACHEL A.
[b.] May 16, 1914, Bartow, FL; [ch.] Richard (son), Cindy (daughter); [ed.] High School - Bartow, Florida; [occ.] Senior Citizen 82 years old; [memb.] First Baptist Church, Dryers Road, MD 20640; [oth. writ.] I have been writing verse for fifty years.

My daughter owns a Web Sight and has published some there. Have had some published in the Lakeland Lodges, Lakeland, Fla.; [pers.] When I moved to Indian Hood, MD. I brought along about 400 of my poems, composed from age 14 to age 82 - in a number of categories.

GONDOLFI, CASSANDRA
[b.] August 22, 1986; Sarasota, FL; [p.] Charles A. and Dawn M. Gondolfi; [ed.] J.E. Moss Elementary, Johnson Middle; [hon.] Honor Roll, Star Student, since Kindergarden; [a.] Antioch, TN.

GOODMAN, JARROD LESKO
[pen.] Pendragon; [b.] June 27, 1979, Columbia, MO; [p.] Richard Goodman, Cindy Goodman; [ed.] Heritage Christian Academy, Milwaukee, WI; [occ.] Part-time Stock Person; [pers.] Emotions are the gateway into which one enters inspiration. I write what I feel, and I feel what I write.; [a.] Waukesha, WI

GOSSE, REBECCA S.
[pen.] Rebecca Susan Gosse; [b.] December 6, 1970, Winfield, IL; [p.] Darrel Gosse, Dianne Naumann; [ch.] Caleb Austin Gosse, Son; [ed.] Completed 4 years at Indiana University, Double Major in English and Afro American Studies; [occ.] Administrative Assistant for Cosco North America, Inc.; [oth. writ.] 4 Nonpublished volumes of poetry including at least 700 poems published 3 times in Byzantium.; [a.] Lyons, IL

GRANT, JAMES E.
[pen.] Jimmy Grant; [b.] March 27, 1964, Queens Village; [p.] Ann and James M.; [ed.] Sayville High, Liberal Arts Degree - Suffolk Community College; [pers.] I have been writing poetry for along time and get great pleasure from it. I have kept most of them to myself though because my poems are very personal to me. I figured it was time to test myself though, and see what the experts thought. Thank You.; [a.] Sayville, NY

GRANT, JOHN
[pen.] John Grant; [b.] November 26, 1980, Richmond, VA; [p.] Thomas and Karen Grant; [ed.] High School Junior at Thomas Dale High, Chester, Va.; [occ.] Student; [memb.] Marching Band, Jazz Band, Symphonic Band; [hon.] Most Valuable Wornline Member "in Marching Band, School Winner in the "Write Now Contest" with poem "Hush", "Outstanding Intermediate Band Musician"; [oth. writ.] "Hush", "A Wish", "Appreciation", "A Special Friend", "Chancing It"; [pers.] I usually escape life with music but poetry is a more relaxing way when you have a headache. When God leads a life a burden is never too heavy. "All you need is love."; [a.] Colonial Heights, VA

GRASSMAN, JOANNA
[pen.] Jo Grassman; [b.] April 5, 1983, Tomah, WI; [p.] Robert J. Grassman, Kathy Grassman; [ed.] St. Paul's Lutheran Grade School, Martin Luther Grade School; [occ.] Student; [hon.] Cheerleading, spelling bee, track, school paper article; [oth. writ.] Poem published in 'Sensations' from the Iliad Press.; [pers.] Love is an illusion; you think it's there then it disappears.; [a.] Neenah, WI

GRAVITT, JEAREAL L.
[pen.] Jeareal L. Gravitt; [b.] March 29, 1942, Londonmills, IL; [m.] Ruth A. Gravitt, August 4, 1979; [ch.] Jerry, Lee, Diane Conklin; [ed.]

Elmwood High, Bellville Community College; [occ.] Computer Operator DOD, St. Louis MO.; [memb.] Computer Operator Dod, St. Louis MO.; [oth. writ.] Nam, The Land That God Forgot; [pers.] The poems I write comes from my personal live.; [a.] Mascoutah, IL

GRAY, ELAINE F.
[pen.] Elaine Gray (Elaine Allen); [b.] May 4, 1918, Huntington, OR; [p.] Grace and Lee Vredenburg; [m.] John Gray (3rd Marriage), December 27, 1979; [ch.] Gary Ellis, Sandy Myers, Jim Allen, Dawnna Mandel; [ed.] Two years college; [occ.] Retired, (supposedly) I'm busier than ever. 20 years at S.J. Merc-News Comp. RM.; [memb.] Santa Clara Woman's Club. Good Samaritan Senior Club, Volunteer at "Winchester Cono. Hosp., where my husband has Olg.; [hon.] Nothing special, just honored to be a "mother", "grandmother", "great-grandmother" and could be a "great-great". Oldest great is eighteen.; [oth. writ.] "Free-Lanced" articles writing for a "Old" merc-news family section. Some "Outdoor" mag. 3 years novelette "S. Clara W. Club", Editor/currently: Editor (Vol.) for "Winchester Con. Hosp. Residents" Newsletter.; [pers.] To Me: Poetry is a reflection of the author's inner soul, for it usually comes from the heart!; [a.] San Jose, CA

GRAY, JUDITH ROGERS
[pen.] Isametria, Planet Jude; [b.] May 2, 1949; Los Angeles, CA; [p.] Elizabeth Rogers, Peter Vi Rogers; [ch.] 1 Sarah Elizabeth Rogers Gray; [ed.] Pasadena High School, San Diego State University, Palonar Jr. College, Cabrillo Jr. College, Pasadena City College; [occ.] Producer and Writer; [memb.] Santa Cruz Community Television, Refuse and Resist, Women's International League For Peace and Freedom, Themis Foundation; [oth. writ.] Poems published in New Age Dawn (1976), Roamber Poetry (1991, small press Washington state) and The Real World Press (Santa Cruz 1994) many letters to editors; [pers.] I have a daughter who is the apple of my eye. Writing poetry saved my life, it has become my channel to the Gods. Through the liberation of the psyche, peace will come to all the Earth; I believe we are living in a garden, we must nourish and protect her. (My first collection will be published soon); [a.] Aptos, CA.

GREEN, MELANIE
[b.] December 23, 1956, Butler, PA; [p.] John and Maxine Brooks; [m.] Martin Green, June 23, 1979; [ch.] Andrew, Stefanie; [ed.] Knoch High School, Edinboro University; [occ.] R. N. in Family Practice Office; [a.] Dover, PA

GREENBUSH, PAMELA
[b.] November 13, 1951; Fremont, NE; [p.] Ray and Carol Brandt; [m.] Garry D. Greenbush; August 12, 1995; [ch.] Timothy L. Cannon, Nathan Cannon; [ed.] Graduated HS 1970 (Fremont Sr. High School) Fremont NE; Gartenet Tech, Morehead City, NC; [occ.] Housewife, Teacher BEII (Behaviour, Emotionally Handicapped); [memb.] NCAE; [oth.write.] Lots of poems, unpublished (Because of not submitting); [pers.] My life has been greatly influenced by tragedy of different kinds with lots of up-lifting situations. My writings have been created out of true happenings in my life; [a.] Newport, MN.

GREENE, DEBORAH T.
[b.] October 30, 1976; [p.] Dennis Greene and Carol Greene; [ed.] Downey High, Cerritos Jr. College; [occ.] Teachers Assistant at Creative Beginnings, Downey; [hon.] Phi Theta Kappa, Dean's List, Who's Who Among American High School Students; [oth. writ.] Several poems written for my family.; [pers.] In my writings I have been greatly influenced by the love, strength, sadness and courage among my family.; [a.] Downey, CA

GREENLAW, RUBY A.
[b.] September 11, 1929, Grand Manan, N.B.; [p.] Gwendolyn and Lloyd Cook; [m.] Eston Greenlaw, June 29, 1961; [ch.] Six live children; [occ.] Artist and Homemaker; [oth. writ.] Nans World, Walk Down the Road of Life, My Secret Corner, "Poems", "He was Me", soon to be published (novel).; [pers.] I strive to say what most people want to, but can't. Poem, Miss Louise C. is about my teacher who at 90 is still an inspiration.; [a.] Calais, ME

GREGORY, BYRON
[b.] July 19, 1934, East Saint Louis, IL; [p.] Alfred and Mary Gregory; [m.] Divorced; [ch.] Valerie, Melody, Angela, Serena, Crystal; [ed.] B.M.E. - Lincoln University, M.M. - Southern Illinois Univ. C.; [occ.] Assistant Professor of Music, University of Arkansas at Pine Bluff; [memb.] Phi Mu Alpha Fraternity, College Band Directors Assn., Optimist International; [hon.] Mayor's Trophy for Contributions In The Arts - E. St. Louis 1976, Citizen of the Year Achievement Award, Monitor Newspaper E. St. Louis 1977, Spotlight on Scholars Award, Jackson State Univ. 1986, Performance of an Original Major Composition by Pine Bluff Sym. Orch. 1995; [oth. writ.] Compositions: Symphony Orchestra-Locrian Lore, Katron, Rhapsodic Parameters, Quartachromas, Contemporary Suite For Piano, Musical - Color Me Beautiful, Books: Classroom Percussion Instruments, Music Can Improve Your Business, Band: Pines, The Parade, The Arch, Poems: Renaissance, By Design, A Flower, That Way; [pers.] Do the best that you can, when, and wherever you can for the good, for yourself, for your fellowman, and for God.; [a.] Pine Bluff, AR

GREGORY, CANDY A.
[b.] March 20, 1959, Cleveland, OH; [p.] Joseph Groves, Opal Groves; [m.] David W. Gregory, April 18, 1986; [ch.] Adrienne Marie; [ed.] Charleston High, Charleston, MO; [occ.] Acct. Rep. Medical Business Office, Jefferson City, MO; [a.] Tebbetts, MO

GRIFFIN, KARYN L.
[b.] April 7, 1982, Winston-Salem, NC; [p.] Ann Griffin; [ed.] Currently a freshman at North Forsyth High School; [occ.] Student; [memb.] Calvary Baptist Church, American Ju-Jitsu Assoc., Tri-Hi-Y Service Club, American School of Self-Defense; [hon.] Honor Roll Student, Most Spirited Award for Dedication to the Art of Ju-Jitsu, National Champion, Ju-Jitsu Grappling Event; [oth. writ.] Imagery writings/poetry, religious writings/poetry and short stories.; [pers.] The beauty within shines through when honesty and kindness are practiced.; [a.] Lewisville, NC

GRIFFITH, KIM
[b.] August 9, 1972; [ed.] B.F.A. from Texas Christian University; [occ.] Graphic Designer; [a.] Dallas, TX

GRIFFITH, TRAVIS JAMES
[pen.] Pyrrhicv@aol.com; [b.] May 17, Bountiful, UT; [p.] Charie Griffith, Rob Griffith; [occ.] Screenwriter; [oth. writ.] Demographic Target, Sanctuary of the Heretic; [pers.] As writers, we are responsible for teaching, entertaining, and horrifying the world in an artful manner, for life is a jigsaw puzzle of thoughts, and the more pieces you turn over, the better your viewpoint on "The Big Picture."; [a.] North Salt Lake, UT

GRIMES, BRITTNEY MONIQUE
[b.] August 28, 1989, Queens, NY; [p.] Tillery and Debbie Grimes; [ed.] Shubert Elementary School - Baldwin, L.I.; [hon.] She has won several school awards for her poetry, she is also an honor student in school.; [oth. writ.] She has written two children books, and about 30 other poems.; [pers.] I believe that all my dreams will come true, if I trust in God! I love you Mommy and Daddy.; [a.] Baldwin, NY

GRIMES HANSEN, LISA J.
[b.] August 2, 1968; Fairfield, IA; [p.] James L. and Linda D. Grimes; [ch.] Bart Edward; [ed.] Eddyville High School, Indian Hills Community College; [occ.] Hospital Coderand Abstractor; [memb.] American Health Information Management Association; [pers.] Poetry, along with writing passionately, and perfectionism come strait from the center core of my existance, my enormous heart. This poem originally was written on Mother's Day in 1995 for my wonderful mom; [a.] Waverly, IA.

GRIMI, ANGELINA M.
[pen.] Angie Grimi; [b.] September 18, 1984, St. Louis, MO; [p.] Louis and Carmelina Grimi; [ed.] Bierbaum Elementary School, currently in 6th grade.; [occ.] Student; [memb.] Sunshine Singers, Drama Club, Academic, Olympics, Service Club.; [hon.] Honor Roll in all six grades. Straight A honor roll.; [oth. writ.] Welcome Spring (unpublished), I wrote this poem when I was 10 yrs. old in the 4th grade.; [pers.] If you really want to do something go for it!; [a.] Saint Louis, MO

GROTH, DIANE D.
[pen.] Diane Dalum Groth; [b.] August 23, 1948, Clintonville, WI; [p.] Herbert Dalum and Dorothea Dalum; [ed.] Marion High, Metropolitan Coll. of Bus. and Tech., U. of Wis.; [occ.] Disabled with M.S.; [oth. writ.] Several pieces published in various church bulletins and papers.; [pers.] With poetry, I attempt to paint pictures of ordinary events in ordinary lives. Hopefully my legacy will be a body of work all can identify with.; [a.] Marion, WI

GUESS, KERI BROOKE
[pen.] Keri Brooke Guess; [b.] May 16, 1986, Mobile, AL; [p.] Raymond and Cindy McEthmar; [ed.] Has attended Sesame Lane Day Care Center, Bay Minette Elementary School and is presently attending Bay Minette Intermediate School; [memb.] BMIS Safety Patrol; [hon.] 'A' average student, numerous softball and soccer trophies. Dance (best hitch-kick) trophy.; [oth. writ.] May I please have this space to say "Thank you to my Aunt She-She and Nana for all the love and support they give me."; [pers.] While my academic curriculum is a necessary part of my life, I also enjoy socializing with my friends and participating in sports. I feel, if I give my best to all these areas

I will pave the way to a happy and successful life.; [a.] Bay Minette, AL

GUILHERME, PATRICIA
[pen.] Mariposa De La Luz; [b.] December 12, 1970, Fall River, MA; [p.] Maria S. and Antonio M. Guilherme; [ed.] Tiverton High School, Bristol Community College, University of Massachusetts at Dartmouth; [occ.] Portuguese and Spanish Tutor; [hon.] Junior Leadership Award from Katharine Gibbs School, May 1989; [oth. writ.] Several poems awaiting publication, several reviews of theatre plays for college newspaper.; [pers.] I dedicate my writing to my inspiration, Paul Nave, for his constant and loyal encouragement, support and love. My love for you is eternal.; [a.] Tiverton, RI

GURNEY, MARY ANN
[b.] May 1, 1969, Annapolis, MD; [p.] Janet Daue; [ed.] BA Fine Arts/Art History from St. Mary's College of MD, BA Art Education Towson State, Currently pursuing MA University, degree in Art Education and Children's Literature/Illustration at Towson State U.; [occ.] Elementary School, Art Teacher; [memb.] National Education Association (NEA), National Art Education Association (NAEA), National Arbor Day Foundation, The Maryland State Teacher's Association (MSTA); [oth. writ.] Published with School Arts Magazine and published children illustrations with Ephemera publishing; [pers.] My inspiration to write is the result of the values instilled in me by my mother. If you appreciate life's finest gifts. Nature's wonder and beauty, love of family, and the ability to share your talents while learning from others, you will be rewarded.; [a.] Boring, MD

GWIN, KATHALEEN
[b.] July 24, 1957, Alabama; [p.] Duncan and Emma Herren; [m.] Kelly Gwin, May 1, 1996; [ch.] Misty Starla and Cheryl Lynn; [ed.] Winfield High School; [occ.] Owner of: Cherish Memories Child Care, Inc.; [memb.] Rock Mountain Lakes Baptists Church; [pers.] Each day will unfold something good, as long as I am trying to live the way. I believe God wants me to live. I pray that I may be taught, just as a child would be taught. I pray that I may never question God's plans, but accept them gladly.; [a.] McCalla, AL

HAGER, GRACE I.
[b.] October 31, 1947; Ohs., Ontario; [p.] Freeman J, Alma G. Sowden; [ch.] Michael Todd Hager, Vaugh and wife Andrea Edwards, granddaughter Emily Paige; [ed.] Cake Decorations, Bradenton Florida, Ontario Real Estate first phase, Medical Assistant and Laboratory Assistant career, Canada College, Nursing Assistant, HCA, Osilla School of Nursing, Sociology, McMaster University Business Administration, Legal, Park Business College, Psychology, McHawk College, Health Record Technician, Hamilton, Ontario, Canada, Private Investigation and Security, Toronto, Ontario, Canada, Canadian Firearms Safety, Dehli, Ontario, Canada Flying Mt. Hope Ontario, Canada; [occ.] Sales Associate, Bakery Clerk, Publix, Florida; [memb.] St. Pauls Anglican Church, Edinburgh, Ontario, Canada; [hon.] Photography, Edinburgh Square and Cultural Center, Caledonia, Ontario, Canada; [oth.writ.] Christmas Poem, memoriams printed in newspapers in Caledonia, Ontario, Canada; [pers.] Poem dedicated and inspiration by first grandchild Emily Paige learning to speak; [a.] Sarasota, FL.

HAISE, JOSHUA
[b.] July 17, 1981, Tyler, TX; [p.] Carolyn and Scott Carle; [ed.] High school student (junior) at Clear Creek HS; [memb.] Junior Classical League (JCL); [oth. writ.] Other poems published in magazines and the literary magazine at my HS.; [pers.] I am greatly influenced by the harsh reality that surrounds me each and every day. My poetry helps me come to terms with social bias and inconsistency.; [a.] League City, TX

HALL, ASHLEY
[b.] December 10, 1983, Anaheim, CA; [p.] Shari and Doug Hall; [oth. writ.] Previously published in the Anthology of Poetry for Young Americans.; [pers.] What doesn't kill you, makes you stronger.; [a.] Escondido, CA

HALL, CRYSTAL L.
[pen.] Star; [b.] November 29, 1973, Sacramento, CA; [p.] Donald Hall Sr., Dorothy Hall; [ed.] Wellsville High, Self educated without question, there is no learning without question.; [occ.] Student of life - I guess; [memb.] President of the Sunset Chasers, President of August 1-9 Festivities - go outside lay flat on the earth - look straight up at the night sky without moving head - move eyes - and like the grateful dead said, it'll - "steal your face..." in loving memory of Jerry Garcia.; [oth. writ.] Several; [pers.] I am the Lizard Queen, I can do anything... I give much appreciation to Jerry Garcia and The Grateful Dead, Jim Morrison and the doors, Bob Marley, Tre and my parents. Thank you.; [a.] Wellsville, NY

HALL, DANIEL M.
[b.] June 3, 1979, Colorado Springs, CO; [occ.] Student at Bloomington High School South; [oth. writ.] An ongoing collection of poems and short stories.; [pers.] Do unto others as you would have done to you. Individually we can achieve nothing, in this we will be forgotten. Together we can accomplish anything, that is what will truly be remembered.; [a.] Bloomington, IN

HALL, ERIN G.
[b.] April 4, 1983, Winston-Salem, NC; [p.] Thurmond and Sandra Hall; [ed.] Southeastern Stokes Jr. High School; [memb.] Fulp Moravian Church, Jr. Beta Club, Southeastern Softball Team; [hon.] Honor Roll, Perfect Attendance, ECA Cheerleading Finals (honorable mention), nominee for All American Cheerleader, captain cheerleading squad, All Around Student (1997); [pers.] I enjoy writing putting my imagination on paper. I really enjoy making others laugh.; [a.] Walnut Cove, NC

HALL, JAMIE
[b.] June 6, 1982, Bedford, IN; [p.] Jon and Diana Hall; [ed.] Currently a Freshman at Bedford North Lawrence High School; [occ.] Student; [memb.] High School Pep Club, French Club; [oth. writ.] Several poems written for Freshman Literature Class.; [a.] Bedford, IN

HALL, JOHNNY T.
[b.] August 12, 1966, Washington, DC; [p.] William Hall, Kathleen Hall; [ed.] 2 yrs. Suffolk County Community College, Brentwood, New York 11717, Audio Research Technical Institute, Hauppauge, New York 11788; [occ.] Freelance Photographer, Flooring Contractor; [pers.] I owe my life to my

parents and my wisdom to the world and myself.; [a.] Brentwood, NY

HALL, RUSSWYN
[b.] Newport News, VA; [p.] Faith Hume and Charles Russwyn Otis; [m.] Alexander Stuart Hall, March 4, 1974; [ch.] 1 son - Rusgwin Stuart Hall; [ed.] AB degree Willis and Macy College at VA (Master Degree); [oth. writ.] Have written a book of poetry, not published, and a humorous novel, Cricket Hollow, about a simple Blue Ridge Mountain family, not typed yet.; [pers.] I find people charming and humorous. I find God everywhere.

HALSTEAD, DANIEL D.
[b.] November 23, 1962, Bremerton, WA; [p.] Beverly Halstead, Darrell Halstead; [m.] Pamela J. (Weaver) Halstead, June 29, 1991; [ed.] G.E.D. 1979, Currently working on an Associates Degree in Applied Science specializing in Hazardous Materials Handling and Management; [occ.] Student, Environmental Clean-up; [memb.] YMCA, Peninsula Wilderness Club, REI, PADI; [hon.] Dean's List at South Seattle Community College, Two Navy Good Conduct Medals, Navy Sea - Service Award, Surface Warfare Pin, Honorable Discharge 17 March 93; [oth. writ.] Several writings, no others published.; [pers.] I draw my inspirations from the rugged beauty of the mountains, forests, oceans and rivers. My erratic mood swings also contribute to my writings, (I have bi-polar disorder).; [a.] Burien, WA

HAMEL, NOEL S.
[pen.] Kyle Tanner Lefebrve; [b.] August 13, 1963, Springfield, MA; [p.] Ken and Nancy Hamel; [pers.] Put fear in its place - let the heart show you the way.; [a.] Belchertown, MA

HAMPTON, RICHARD
[pen.] Rhythm; [occ.] U.S. Army Communications; [pers.] All my love Barbara (Blues)

HAMSHER, JOAN HOUGHTON
[b.] December 20, 1924, Chanute, KS; [p.] Sereno George Houghton, Winifred Houghton (Rinebarger); [m.] Robert E. Hamsher, December 27, 1952; [ch.] Karen Kooh, Robin Nickerson, Heather Wright; [ed.] Chanute, KS, El-Parsons, KS - Jr. Hi, Sr. Hi, Jr. College, Under Grad., Fine Arts Credited Classes, Training - Piano - Voice; [occ.] Retiree; [memb.] Alumni, Church, Community Organizations; [hon.] Various Certificates of Merit, Achievement, Awards and Honors; [oth. writ.] Numerous unpublished poems, journals, letters, A Memoir; [pers.] Enjoy the works of Robert Frost and Emily Dickenson, In aim of the natural world.; [a.] Flint, MI

HANNOLD, DAVE
[pen.] Dave Hannold; [b.] May 2, 1945, Philadelphia, PA; [p.] William and Ellen Hannold; [m.] Sheri Hannold, November 29, 1993; [ch.] Jay Wesley Fileen Nicole; [ed.] Paramount High; [occ.] Retired; [hon.] Won Dual 1st Place Awards in writing contest at Nissan Motor Corp. U.S.A.; [pers.] Have intense passion for writing. Have written many poems for friends. Avid record collector of 1950's "doo-wop" sound.; [a.] Monarch Beach, CA

HANSCOM, DENNIS
[oth. writ.] Oh Yes, Jesus is Alive, True Love Will Wait, Foolish Pride, Starting Over, Following Jesus, A Mother's Love, God's Love, The Love of Maine, Friends, Living Water, In the Arms of Jesus, Why does your Father Weep, Born Again; [pers.] January 1, 1996 I was depressed. As I stepped out of my van to walk and cry, I prayed the prayer you see. I did not cry as I walked but was filled with joy and peace. Jesus took my depression and gave me the words for this poem.; [a.] Belmont, NC

HANSON, FLORENCE
[b.] March 7, 1910, Concord, NH; [p.] Samuel Baker and Annie Gould; [m.] Russell S. Hanson, August 27, 1939; [ch.] Janet Hanson Gawlak, Sue Baker Hanson; [ed.] Concord High School, Concord, NH, University of New Hampshire, Durham, NH; [occ.] Retired Teacher; [oth. writ.] Observations by Florence Baker Hanson published by Carlton Press, Inc., Conclusions by Florence Baker Hanson published by Carlton Press, Inc.; [pers.] Poetry is thought so strong it has to be expressed.

HANSON, LARRY D.
[pen.] Bj Hanson; [b.] April 23, 1964; Flint, MI; [p.] Connie Hanson, Allen Hanson; [ed.] Bendle Sr. High graduating class of 1982; [occ.] Customer Service Manager, Outdoor Supply Co.; [memb.] Trout Unlimited Fly Fishing Club; [oth.writ.] "Unfinished thoughts," poetry, "Cross over a bridge" short play, many other unpublished poems and song lyrics.; [pers.] In failure, we succeed in becoming stronger and more successful.; [a.] Grand Blanc, MI.

HARDT, AMY K. LEDVINA
[b.] March 9, 1971; Indiana; [p.] Raymond and Dianne Ledvina; [m.] Gred F. Hardt; December 5, 1995; [ed.] Harold Washington College; [occ.] Photographer; [memb.] Phi Theta Kappa Honor Society, Criminal Justice Club, student government; [hon.] Dean's List, "Neat" Woman's Award; [a.] Chicago,IL.

HARPSTER, DANIEL IAN
[b.] December 17, 1976, San Antonio, TX; [p.] John A. Harpster and Julia G. Harpster; [ed.] Moore High School, Guthrie Job Corps; [occ.] Navy Recruit; [memb.] St. John's Lutheran Church; [oth. writ.] Too many to list, but none that have been published.; [pers.] From the shadows of existence he observes society, protecting some, exacting payment from others, while always attempting to maintain that delicate balance known only in precognitive myth.; [a.] Moore, OK

HARRIS, CHRIS C.
[b.] October 10, 1977, Milwaukee, WI; [p.] Rose Harris and Clifton Harris; [ed.] Assumption High School, MSTC (Mid-State Technical College); [occ.] None right now, just like to write.; [oth. writ.] "Using My Mind," "Walk With My Lord," "Aimee," "Winning A War," "My Guided Light," "Waiting," "My Address," "My Closest Friend," "Life Is Precious," and "Only A Man." They had never been published yet, but hopefully one day!; [pers.] I love to pick up a pen and try to reach others in my writings. More about achieving things, how to succeed in life and love. Life is a very long trek.; [a.] Wisconsin Rapids, WI

HARTMANN, DEAN JAMES
[b.] February 19, 1963; Shawano, WI; [p.] Allen M. Hartman, Joanne Hartman; [m.] Kellie K. Hartmann; June 25, 1983; [ch.] Sarah Kay, Emily Rachel, Jacob Dean; [occ.] Production, Commercial Sales Manager, (Franciscan Publishers and Printers); [pers.] A child's eyes are the mirror to the soul; [a.] Shawano, WI.

HARVEY, BERYL
[b.] July 27, 1938; Trinidad, Tobago; [p.] Nathaniel J. Clarke, Mother deceased; [m.] Divorced; [ch.] Twins Shanida and Sharon Harvey; [ed.] Graduated high school Trinidad and Tobago. Nursing school, England; [occ.] Private nurse, Researcher, Health/ Nursing Care; [hon.] Nurse of the Year, International Poetry Hall of Fame 1996, Editor's Choice Award 1997, Nurse of the Year 1997, Hero Award 1997 for saving a life with Heimlich Maneuver; [oth.writ.] Editor and founder, Cruising with Lady Dynamite, Editor and founder with Battered Women Exclusive, published poetry in Into the Unknown; [pers.] Thanks to the National Library of Poetry; [a.] Hyatsville

HARVEY, MYLES
[b.] April 24, 1977; Sidney, NE; [p.] Dave and Lark Harvey; [ed.] High school; [occ.] U.S. Army; [memb.] The Human Race; [oth.writ.] Nothing else has been published; [pers.] My writings flow from the soul. This is the only way. I feel that my writings reflect the truth; [a.] Killeen, TX.

HAWKINS, LINDA J.
[b.] October 8, 1965, Fort Hood, TX; [p.] Almo and Irvin Hawkins; [ed.] AS Liberal Arts at Des Moines Area Community College DSM, IA, BS. Education at Iowa State University, Specialized Special Educ. Minor in Sociology, Ames, IA; [occ.] E.C. Special Ed., Teacher Oleson Elem., Houston, TX; [pers.] Make today the first day of the rest of your life! Attitude check.; [a.] Houston, TX

HAWKINS, OCTAVIA B.
[b.] September 9, 1961, Philadelphia, PA; [p.] Delores Hawkins; [ch.] Simone N. Hawkins; [ed.] I graduated from Olney High School; [occ.] I work as an Recreation Assistant; [hon.] I received an Honor of Best Worker.; [oth. writ.] I've written several other poetry, which has been published in the news letter on my job.; [pers.] I would like my poetry to reflect our younger generation. Open up our minds to bigger and better things. I have been influenced by Maya Angelou.; [a.] Philadelphia, PA

HAWN, LISA D.
[pen.] Liz-beth; [b.] March 13, 1963, Covington, KY; [p.] Virginia Hall, Father (Deceased); [ed.] Associates Degree Office Administration, Northern KY. University Walton Verona High School; [occ.] Communications Coordinator, General Cable Corp.; [hon.] Boone County Business Woman's Award, Who's Who - High School Students Nat'l PBL Contest Winner - N.K.U. Dean's List - N.K.U.; [oth. writ.] Non-published poetry collection reflecting the range and depth of human emotion.; [pers.] My poetry reflects what I believe are ever in the mind - The deepest feelings and emotions the human heart can experience - leaving behind memories of happiness and pain that shape our lives.; [a.] Walton, KY

HAYDEN, DON
[pen.] Dahni; [b.] December 13, 1953, Columbia, MO; [occ.] Freelance writer, reporter, advertising sales, deep waters (own business); [oth. writ.] The Tear and The Tender - Poetry, Life's A Trip -

Poetry, Talons and Feathers - Poetry, various articles, present work on a screenplay.; [pers.] To entertain with the desire, that the reader (earn something than to ever try and teach anyone, anything.; [a.] Rogers, AR

HAYES, DANIEL
[b.] April 28, 1958, Greenville, SC; [p.] Don J. Hayes, Annie Hayes; [ch.] Kasanya Hayes; [ed.] Gulf Coast Comm. Coll., J.S. Reynolds Comm. Coll.; [occ.] Product Development Technician; [memb.] U.S.A.F. Reserve (Congressional Wing); [hon.] Emily Owen Vinton Award for English Proficiency; [oth. writ.] Songwriter/contributing songwriter for ten 2 one productions, Setaro - Tredway Music and Tredco Productions.; [a.] Fredericksburg, VA

HAYES, FLORA
[pen.] Dee; [b.] December 1, 1955; Beaufort, SC; [p.] Rev. And Mrs. Henry Hayes; [ch.] Scheria Keith-Hayes, Diamond Hayes; [ed.] Graduated from Battery Creek High School, Manpower Business School, NYC, NY, (Battery Creek High School, Beaufort, SC); [occ.] Secretary; [oth. writ.] I've written many poems and lyrics for songwriting, amateur writing; [a.] New York, NY.

HECKER, LUCIEN J.
[b.] October 25, 1968, Lewiston, ME; [p.] Gerard and Jeannie Hecker; [m.] Cheryl Ann Hecker, July 24, 1993; [ch.] Hannah Elizabeth Hecker; [ed.] Oak Hill High School, University of Maine at Orono; [occ.] Administrative Specialist, U.S. Army, Izmir, Turkey; [memb.] Assoc. of the U.S. Army, Veterans of Foreign Wars; [hon.] Dean's List, various military awards; [pers.] I wrote the poem about my daughter, Hannah. Now that I have a child, I'm more aware that my actions have consequences and affect others, and I try to think how they affect my daughter.; [a.] VA

HEFFELFINGER, RUBY V.
[b.] August 29, 1906, Brownville, NE; [p.] Claude and Lizzie Creek; [m.] David R. Hart - 1924 until 1946, B. M. Heffelfinger - 1947 until 1985; [ch.] Geraldine, Jack, Patsy, Jane; [occ.] Retired; [oth. writ.] Many other poems some published in 'Stars and Stripes' in the 1940's.; [pers.] I wrote about my family and faith as it is my love of family and deep faith in God that inspired me.; [a.] Nebraska City, NE

HEFLIN, HALLE
[b.] November 4, 1987, Akron, OH; [p.] Richard and Kim Heflin; [ed.] 3rd Grade at St. Charles School; [occ.] Student; [memb.] Girl Scouts, St. Charles Church; [pers.] "Never give up! It's a few words that has a lot of meaning. I think there are two tasks in life. To achieve, what you want, and to make what you achieve a little better.; [a.] North Benton, OH

HEIER, TERESA
[b.] September 14, 1972; Santa Barbara, CA; [p.] Mel and Donna Heier; [ed.] Simi Valley High School College of the Sequoias; [occ.] Student; [memb.] PETA (People for the Ethical Treatment of Animals); [a.] Camarillo, CA.

HELLIGSO, NOEL
[b.] January 4, 1950, Astoria, OR; [p.] Stan and Robert Helligso; [m.] Cathleen Lori, March 16, 1974; [ch.] Flint Benjamin Helligso; [ed.] 68 gradu-

ate Warrenton High School, US Army Heavy Equip School 62330; [occ.] Log Home Contractor Heavy Equipment Mechanic; [memb.] Life Member NRA, Life Member VFW, Member International Union of Operating Engineers; [hon.] None of any significance; [pers.] We are all in this boat together, but before we tell others how to row we should be adepts, or at least morally blameless.; [a.] Lapine, OR

HELM, RANDY
[pen.] Randolf Helm; [b.] June 29, 1945, Ashtabula, OH; [p.] T. Leonard and Mary M. Helm; [ch.] Melissa Margaret Helm; [ed.] Graduated from Oklahoma Military Academy in 1963; [occ.] Artist, General Contractor, Bartender of Jack All Trades; [hon.] Honor's for works done or yet to be done, have not yet been bestowed upon me, until your recognition of my work, fame and I remained virgins to one another.; [oth. writ.] On occasion, my teacher friends ask me to write poetry to compliment the subject matter they are studying.; [pers.] I enjoy putting words to rhyme, and seeing the smile it brings after they read it.; [a.] Houston, TX

HENRY, KEITH G.
[pen.] Azule; [b.] April 9, 1955, Trinidad, West Indies; [p.] David Henry and Althea Henry; [m.] Deborah Ann Marie Henry, January 29, 1977; [ch.] Keith K. Henry, David D. Henry, Jasmine Nicole Yeefoon Henry; [ed.] St. Anthony's College, Trinidad, W.I., Balt. Community College, Airco Technical Institute; [occ.] Special Police Ofc. Detective; [memb.] A.M.E. Church, N.R.A.; [oth. writ.] Nadine's Rhythm, Life Walk With You, Nubian Passion, Am I Good Enough, Open To Love, Meeting Of Chance, Love's Bitter Edge, Lust To Respect, Another Day Lost; [pers.] Always open your heart to love, love and live. To close your heart to love is to slowly die.; [a.] Baltimore, MD

HENSON, WILLIAM
[pen.] Bill Danile; [b.] March 7, 1955, Hazzard, KY; [p.] Jack Henson, Ola Mae Henson; [m.] Irene Lois Henson; [ch.] Eric; [ed.] Robichuard High School; [occ.] DAV; [memb.] US Eagles; [hon.] US Army; [oth. writ.] Beginning of a Dream; [pers.] Traveling threw the path of life may your path meet with the one you love.; [a.] Brooklyn, NY

HERDLINGER, HAILEY ANN
[pen.] Hailey Ann Herdlinger; [b.] August 30, 1984; Fayetteville, AR; [p.] David Herdlinger and Paula Van Hoose; [ed.] 7th grade student at Helen Tyson Middle School; [occ.] Student; [memb.] First United Methodist Church, Helen Tyson Middle School Honors Choir, Soccer, Basketball and Softball teams, Gifted and Talented program; [hon.] P.T.A. Reflections Contest (Past winner in Music and Literature Division) Odyssey of the Mind (Regional Winner), Honor Roll (Walker Elementary and Helen Tyson Middle School) Southwest Jr. High Basketball team; [oth.writ.] "Dare to Discover" ('95 P.T.A. Reflections Contest winner) "Imagine That" (P.T.A. Reflections Music Composition winner - 1993) "If I Could Give the World a Gift" (P.T.A. Reflections Music Composition 1994); [pers.] I enjoy writing poetry because it makes people happy to read it. I've been writing poems since I was in the second grade.; [a.] Springdale, AR

HERNANDEZ JR., JUAN
[pen.] "Dreamer", "Sonador"; [b.] February 28,

1960, Del Rio, TX; [p.] Juan M.; [m.] Belia C., July 15, 1989; [ed.] J. W. Nixon High, Laredo Community College, California College for Health Sciences; [occ.] Respiratory Care Tech.; [pers.] "Why linger in the past or worry for the future, when the present is so precious."; [a.] Laredo, TX

HERRERA, JOSE-TRELLES
[b.] December 31, 1984, Miami, FL; [p.] Jose M. Herrera and Georgette Trelles Herrera; [ed.] St. Brendan Elementary; [occ.] Student; [memb.] Choir, Mission Club, Newspaper Club; [a.] Miami, FL

HESS, SHEREE
[b.] March 29, 1978, Allentown, PA; [p.] Joyce Hess, Edgar Hess; [ed.] Northern Lehigh, Lehigh County Vocational Technical School; [occ.] CNA, Fellowship Manor Nursing Home; [pers.] Writing poetry is a way I cope with what happens in life. If I write about it, it makes it easier to understand.; [a.] Slatington, PA

HIATT, WANDA C.
[b.] January 9, 1915, Bucyrus, KS; [p.] James and Minnie Turner; [m.] LeRoy F. Hiatt (Deceased), May 12, 1951; [ed.] High School and year of working as private secretary. Served in Waves in World War II in Hawaii; [occ.] Retired, living in Good Samaritan Center since almost blind; [memb.] 1st Christian Church Olathe, KS; [pers.] Happy that my niece Carolyn Babb took the time and care to submit my poem. Have been writing poems for years. It is my love.; [a.] Olathe, KS

HICKS, DAVID
[pen.] Dave Hicks; [b.] June 12, 1971, Indianapolis; [p.] Tom and Pat Hicks; [ed.] Went to Marron College for 3 1/2 years, have also attended Herron School of Art.; [occ.] 911 Dispatcher; [memb.] Member of the USS Bounty Star Trek Club, member of Priests of Pathways; [oth. writ.] Till Death Did Them Part, Death Awaits, Destiny To Die. In process of working on a book called Blind Faith, have written several works for the Renegade.; [pers.] My writings reflect the harsh darkness in humanity, and the things that nightmares are made of. My favorite writer is Edgar Allen Poe.; [a.] Indianapolis, IN

HIGGS, SHAREON E.
[pen.] Crystal Finn; [b.] December 17, 1940; Salt Lake City, UT; [p.] Allen and Enid Allington (deceased); [m.] Earl Ronald Higgs; October 18, 1965; [ch.] Bonnie Skinner, Steve Higgs; [ed.] Graduated from Olympus High School, Holladay Utah. College of Eastern Utah in Price, Ut where I received my associate Degree; [occ.] I work in the Carbon School District, Price, Ut as an aide and Trainner, Community Careers and Support Systems, Four Corners Mental Health as an advocate. I work with adults and children with disabilities. whether we have learning or physical disabilities weare very talented wonderful people blessed with many talents and gifts. I try to instill in the people I work with that they are important. I also am an Artist and writer. I teach oil painting classes. I am a talented writer and artist waiting to be recognized; [memb.] I am a member of the Castle Valley Arts and Humanities Counsel, Utah SCBWI Children's Writers Society, Utah Association Alcoholism and Drug Abuse Counselors and others; [hon.] Certificates of Award for Advocate Service at Four Corners Mental Health, Received an

award from the Sweet'n Low great waiters competition, Carnation Community Service Award, 4-H leadership awards and honors, Certificate of Completion of University of Utah, School on Alcoholism and other Drug Dependencies. I was a participant in the 1995 1st annual Helper City Arts Festival Teton Valley Mountain Arts Celebration and hope to be in many others if invited; [oth.writ.] The Crystal Child, The house within, Loving her was it enough, Take Time to listen, Marriage in an Album, If I could walk and Talk with you Dad, Girl in the Park, Christine, To my son on his College Graduation, No lonelier than a recoving addict in Narcotics annoymous and Alone, and others; [pers.] I was dyslexic, not dumb, I was creative. The Dyslexia was not discovered till 1989. I now have many tools to help me. I never went to College till age 48. I had wonderful tutors and teachers in College who helped me and believed in me. I believe its others who put negatives in our life's and we believe them negatives. Follow your dreams; [a.] Puce, UT.

HILDEBRANDT, SANDRA
[b.] August 26, 1985; Ames, IA; [p.] William and Reinee Hildebrandt; [ed.] Currently in 6th grade; [occ.] Student; [memb.] 4-H, Girl Scouts; [hon.] 2 top ratings and medals for karate, Honor Roll 3 semesters; [oth.writ.] "Night Dragon," (3rd grade class publication); [pers.] I have a porcelain cat collection. My 2 favorite ones look like my real cats, Linus and Beethoven, a fisty aribitios cat came along; [a.] Springfield, IL.

HILDRETH, PAT
[b.] May 3, 1942, Atlanta, GA; [p.] William P. McClain and Augusta McClain; [m.] Charles Benjamin Hildreth, July 17, 1959; [ch.] Marcia, Kathy and Karin; [ed.] Chamblee High, Massey College, Artistic School of Cosmetology, Dale Carnegie, Art and Sculpture School; [occ.] Hair Stylist, Independent Contractor.; [memb.] Collegedale S.D.A. Church, Women's Ministries Assn., ABWA, Tenn. Cosmetology Assn.; [hon.] Won cosmetology course, spelling bee statewide; [oth. writ.] Church newsletter; [pers.] I love creativity whether writing, art, or sculpture. There is such beauty in creating something that didn't exist before. It makes you feel closer to the real Creator.; [a.] Collegedale, TN

HILL, POPPET
[pen.] Poppet Hill; [b.] May 29, 1945; Wallingford, England; [p.] Dr. and Mrs. Kenneth H. Pickup; [ed.] Woodcote School, St. Peters Hill School, Halton School, all England. Age 9 till 13. International School, Fontainbleau France, Welsh Girls School, Ashferd Mx. England, CARDIFF School of Cuisine & Domestic Science, Wales, Hereford Shire Technical College, England, Teachers Credential, Santa Barbara City College, CA; [occ.] Bartender; [memb.] Member of Royal Society of Health; [hon.] Academic Achievement Award in Philosophy from Santa Barbara City College, California, Counseling Skills Certificate, Boarding School and College in England; [oth.writ.] I have always written as balm for the soul, only wrote to write, now still write to write and now others read; [pers.] Influenced by many from A.A. Milne to L. Wittgenstein. Trapped by our language. Say what I mean and mean what I say, I believe I must keep open the heart, say less than is known and hear more than is heard; [a.] Santa Barbara, CA.

HILL, SHELLI
[pen.] Shelli Rainer; [b.] July 20, 1971; Plainview, TX; [p.] Joe Rainer, Charlotte Pierce; [m.] Lyndon Hill; September 16, 1995; [ed.] Aledo High School, Texas Tech. University; [a.] Aledo, TX.

HILLIARD, MATTHEW ADAM
[pen.] Matt; [b.] September 18, 1982, Savannah, GA; [p.] Floyd W. Hilliard, Reta S. Spears; [ed.] South Effingham Middle School; [occ.] Full time Student; [oth. writ.] Personal poems.; [pers.] My goal is to one day go to college and become a writer.; [a.] Guyton, GA

HILLS, ROBERT O.
[b.] July 27, 1920, Detroit, MI; [p.] Clarence and Pauline Hills; [m.] Lila Jean Hills, September 14, 1948; [ch.] Elizabeth and Patricia; [ed.] B.S. Forestry, M.S. Education; [occ.] Retired (Rancher) Angus Cattle - Boarding Kennel; [memb.] Portland Elem. Sch. Principals Association Society of Children's Book Writers and Illustrators; [hon.] Bronze Star (Combat WWII S.P.) and Philippine Liberation Medal; [oth. writ.] "A Mouse Tail" (series of small animal stories for primary children); [pers.] "A good person knows it".; [a.] Eagle Creek, OR

HILTON, CHRISTOPHER C.
[pen.] C. C. Bain; [b.] August 5, 1977, Bogalusa, LA; [p.] Richard L. Hilton Sr., Jacqueline C. Bain; [ed.] G.E.D., Seeking Higher Education; [occ.] Currently unemployed, seeking higher education; [hon.] All Hansen Memorial Award 3rd Place, Franklinton, LA, Free Fair Poetry Contest, 10th Grade 1st Place, 11th Grade 2nd Place, Publication in "Writers of Passage" 1995 Volume 1 #2; [oth. writ.] Several unpublished poems, Sports writer for Jr. High Newspaper during Jr. High attendance.; [pers.] I write my poetry from imagination and experience mingled together to form an art so that others can enjoy it.; [a.] Bogalusa, LA

HIPPS, NATHAN S.
[b.] July 12, 1959, Fitzgerald, GA; [p.] James and Sue Hipps; [ed.] Bachelor of Science, Florida State University - 1982, Major - Media Communication, Minor - English Lit./Creative Writing; [occ.] Writer/Asst. Director in Video Production; [hon.] New York Festivals Award - 1995 for the video "Scenes of Life", Telly Award - 1991 for the video "Struggling for Equality"; [oth. writ.] Currently working on a historical novel based upon my grandmother's family, currently working on an article for Kaleidoscope Magazine.; [pers.] If I couldn't write, I wouldn't be. Writing has taught me how to communicate, how to think, how to feel.; [a.] Tallahassee, FL

HIRSCH, HERBERT
[b.] April 29, 1941, New York City; [p.] Emeric and Lillian Hirsch; [ch.] Candace Taylor, April Sullivan, Karen, Mark; [ed.] AB Concord College, MA Villanova University, Ph.D. Univ. of Kentucky; [occ.] Professor of Political Science; [memb.] International Council of the Institute on Holocaust and Genocide, Philadelphia Center on Holocaust, Center for Comparative, Genocide Studies; [hon.] Assorted Research Grants, Lecture Awards; [oth. writ.] Genocide and The Politics of Memory, U of North Carolina Press, 1995. Perspectives on Anti-Semitism, The Right of the People, other books and numerous articles and book chapters.; [pers.]

Helping to make the ugly realities of people everyday life more just, equitable and less dangerous.; [a.] Richmond, VA

HIRSCH, SHIRLEY CLAIRE
[b.] Allentown, PA; [p.] Rose and Morris Walode; [m.] January 4, 1953; [ch.] Mitchell Adam, Lauren Julie, Sonnie Beth; [ed.] Walton High New York University; [occ.] Trade Show Exhibit Consultant; [hon.] Arista, Pitman Medal, Belding Scribes; [pers.] Family is most important to me. This is always reflected in my thoughts and my writing.; [a.] Paramus, NJ

HOBART, DANIEL L.
[pen.] Daniel Leander Hobart; [b.] February 26, 1949, Syracuse, NY; [p.] Dorothy E. Brown and Francis L. Hobart; [m.] Deceased (suicide), January 25, 1989; [ch.] Three; [ed.] A.A.S. business & general studies, student Long Ridge Writers Group, free lance writer; [occ.] Disabled American Veteran (Hobart Construction); [memb.] Khe Sanh Vets Organ., Military Order of the Purple Heart, Vietnam Veterans of America, American Legion, Life Member, Disabled Vets; [hon.] Three Purple Hearts, 2 Presidential Unit Citations, Conspicuous Service Cross, Combat Action Medal, National Defense, Vietnam Cross of Gallantry, 3 Honorable Discharges: Marine Corps, Army and Army National Guard; [oth. writ.] Short stories for vets, articles for newspapers, writers guild, creative writing, journalism, working on a book of poems.; [pers.] To experience the gates of hell in Vietnam and for twenty years after, God is my most cherished accomplishment. "In Him I will survive."; [a.] Moravia, NY

HOCH, JEAN
[b.] March 16, 1933, Wampsville, NY; [p.] William and Hazel (Fellows Deceased); [m.] Melvin Hoch, May 30, 1953; [ch.] Three children, one living, Bonnie Jenkins and Diane Roache, Ronald (Deceased); [ed.] North Broad Street One'da High; [occ.] Babysitter; [memb.] Bowling team at Beach Bowl at Sylvan Beach; [oth. writ.] I wrote many poems for people for birthdays and anniversaries and births; [pers.] I wrote for years because it gives me pleasure to make people happy.; [a.] Canastota, NY

HODGE, KATRINA
[b.] August 18, 1964, Corning; [p.] Naia and Richard Hodge; [ch.] Noel Francis; [ed.] GED from the University of Texas, a degree in Auto Cad Drafting from ATI Career Training Center; [occ.] Care Giver of the Disabled; [memb.] Member of the International Society of Poets; [hon.] Several poems published by The National Library of Poetry. An Editors Choice Award for "Autistic Child". An exhibit of poetry on the Web. Also entered in The International Poetry Hall of fame.; [pers.] This poem was written about a friend I cared for. Dedicated to and in the memory of Jerry M. Shannon, of Caddo (S.) Texas; [a.] Caddo, TX

HODGE, KATRINA
[b.] August 18, 1964; Corning, NY; [p.] Naia and Richard Hodge; [ch.] Noel Francis; [ed.] GED from the University of Texas, A Degree in Auto-Cad Drafting from ATI Career Training Center; [occ.] Care Giver of the disabled, Pizza Hut Dough Maker; [memb.] The International Society of Poets; [hon.]

Editors Choice Award for "Autistic Child" and placed in the International Poetry Hall of fame; [oth.writ.] 3 other Poems Published by the National Library of Poetry. "Autistic Child" in Lyrical Heritage, "On The Wing" best Poems 1997," Life's Lows and Highs" in The Isle of View; [pers.] This Poem is dedicated in the Memory of Jerry Slemmons of Caddo Texas. He was a very good friend. "This Ones For You"; [a.] Caddo, Texas.

HOLLAND, CHRISTINE
[b.] November 18, 1946, Chicago, IL; [p.] Bruno Mack, Alice Mack; [ch.] Charles Youngs, Geoffrey Youngs; [ed.] De Paul University, Calif. State Univ., Long Beach (B.A. History Cum Laude), Louisiana State University (J.D.); [occ.] Attorney/Trustee; [memb.] Louisiana State Bar Assn., Assoc. for Research and Enlightenment; [hon.] Phi Kappa Phi, Dean's List, Moot Court Board; [pers.] Poetry is a gift from my soul to me.; [a.] Houston, TX

HOLLANDER, AMANDA
[b.] October 19, 1979, Evanston, IL; [p.] Cary Hollander, Rita Hollander; [ed.] Wheeling High School, University of Wisconsin - Whitewater; [occ.] Student; [hon.] Honor Roll, Young Authors Conference Representative, Various Music Awards Local and National; [oth. writ.] Poetry and prose published in literary magazine.; [a.] Prospect Heights, IL

HOLLY, DAVID L.
[pen.] David L. Holly; [b.] January 9, 1964, Louisiana; [p.] Philip Holly and Jerry Eudy; [ed.] 2 years of college; [occ.] Student; [oth. writ.] Poems and short stories in High School publications.; [pers.] I see mankind as one big human family capable of anything if we would only cooperate for the sake of all.; [a.] San Angelo, TX

HOLMSTEN, SHANNON
[b.] July 27, 1965; Fremont, CA; [p.] Leonard and Janeen Holmsten; [ed.] BA Education/English; [pers.] The grand essentials in this life are something to do, something to love and something to hope for; [a.] Hayward, CA.

HOLT, VICKI
[b.] January 11, 1949; Wichita, KS; [p.] Will and Hee Russell; [m.] Robert Holt; September 6, 1980; [ch.] Jon Paul, Todd, Penny and Wendy; [ed.] Mt. Roenier High, Hi-Line College, Floral Design School; [occ.] Floral Designer; [memb.] Veterans Association, American Heart Association; [pers.] The poem published was inspired by the love for my son Jon Paul, and for the hope of his future. A gift to him on his 18th birthday; [a.] Kent, WA.

HOLTRY, CHRISTOPHER W.
[b.] August 23, 1971; [p.] Gerald and Robertson; [ed.] Valley Forge Military College, University of Virginia; [occ.] Army Officer; [pers.] Poetry is my brain massage. It brings me a peace I wish everyone could share; [a.] Newport News, VA.

HONEYCUTT, FRANKIE EVELYN
[pen.] Frankie Honeycutt; [b.] June 25, 1939, Ranger, TX; [p.] Lonnie Tedford, Ruby Tedford; [m.] Jess Honeycutt, July 25, 1955; [ch.] Rowland Wade, Barbara Racine, Brenda Yvette; [ed.] Phillips High School, TAAO - Course 110 (Texas Assoc. of Assessing officers); [occ.] Housewife and Business owner, formerly Tax Deputy; [memb.] United Pen-

tecostal Church of Lake Worth; [hon.] Musical Awards from Hallman Piano Studio; [oth. writ.] Several Plays and Dramas (unpublished and used in personal church work) poems, songs and prose. I am currently writing for UPC International Sunday School Literature; [pers.] My endeavor is to touch, encourage and strengthen humanity or the reader of my writings. I am greatly inspired and motivated by my creator and deity.; [a.] Fort Worth, TX

HOOTEN, JESSICA
[pen.] Danielle Steel (just Kidding); [b.] March 8, 1982, Anchorage, AK; [p.] Rick Hooten, Evelyn Hooten; [memb.] West Houston Church of Christ; [pers.] I am stubborn and passionate, yet sensitive to everything around me, and that is how I write. I write me.

HORTON, SHIRLEY J.
[pen.] Rikki; [b.] November 10, 1936, Tyrell Co, NC; [p.] Alvania and Wardell Horton; [m.] May 13, 1952; [ch.] Rayfeal, Edward and Stephanie Lewis; [ed.] Booker T. Washington High School, San Jose Community College; [occ.] Care Provider; [memb.] Soka Gakkai International; [pers.] "When you start out on the bottom, the only way to go is up. On your way up you meet all kinds. Treat everyone with respect. Try not to judge anyone until you walk in their shoes...; [a.] Marina, CA

HOWARD, JULIANNE N.
[b.] March 30, 1969, Brooklyn, NY; [p.] Harvey S. and Thelma H. Evans; [m.] Vincent L. Howard, November 22, 1990; [ch.] One, Ashlee M. Howard; [ed.] Sumter High School, University of South Carolina; [occ.] Loss Prevention/Front End Supervisor Sam's Club (Div. of Walmart); [memb.] Delaware's Missing and Exploited Children's Assoc. (Founder), American Red Cross (Volunteer), Sam's Club Community Involvement Committee; [hon.] Who's Who Among American High School Students, Who's Who Among the Nations High School Students (1985-1986 and 1986-1987); [oth. writ.] Several pieces that have not been published nor read by anyone. (Approx. 50 plus); [pers.] Poetry for me is an outlet and the way to explore other worlds. I believe each of us has a reason for being and each is unique. If I have a positive influence on one person, then I have given something of myself back to humankind!; [a.] Dover, DE

HOWARD, TIFFANY MONIQUE
[b.] July 28, 1985, Gardena, CA; [p.] Booker T. and Millie Howard; [ed.] In 6th Grade, Dollban Elementary School; [occ.] Student; [hon.] Reflections and writing celebrations - Rialto Unified School District, Honor Roll Achievement Awards - Academic; [oth. writ.] To Make The World A Better Place, The Holy Feast, Fantasy; [pers.] Writing is a great activity and a good way to express how you feel. I love to write.; [a.] Rialto, CA

HOWELL, STEVEN D.
[b.] March 18, 1970, Pekin, IL; [p.] Thomas and Marie Howell; [ed.] Pekin Community High School; [occ.] Sales, Wal-Mart; [oth. writ.] Some short stories, songs, and a few poems.; [pers.] I write about things that I see. Things that affect me in some way, shape, or form.; [a.] Pekin, IL

HOWERTON, WILLIAM VERNON
[b.] April 26, 1933, Long Lane, MO; [p.] Ira G.

and Edith (Anglen) Howerton; [m.] Geneva (Jeannie) Moser Howerton, May 21, 1955; [ch.] Verlene Lonjers and Doyle Howerton; [ed.] Grade School - Latimer and Southview High School - Conway High 1947 - 1950, MoArk College, West Plains, MO, Missouri Baptist College, Poplar Bluff, MO, Southwest Teachers Col., Springfield MO; [occ.] Pastor - The Church of Living Love; [oth. writ.] I have written poems since my wife and I were saved in 1961. I also have written many, many songs, I have published two books of poems. The poems included for this publication are short, but I have many that are long, story type poems.

HUBER, REINHARD
[pen.] Red - (May use later on); [b.] December 2, 1944; Rorschach, Switzerland; [p.] Alice N. (Floege) Huber, Karl A. Huber; [m.] Single; [ed.] Graduate Riverhead High School, Riverhead, NY; [occ.] Warehouse Manager; [memb.] None presently, previously participated in amateur bowling and softball programs; [hon.] Honorable discharge from United States Air Force, received two Commendation Medals for service in South Vietnam (1968-1969) (1969-1970), total service 5 years (1965-1970); [oth. writ.] None published; [pers.] Have written poems to entertain or in the form of a letter, will strive to improve the artistry of my writings and cherish and the need to have them as a rewarding hobby; [a.] Riverhead, NY.

HUGHES, COLETTE
[b.] April 23, 1932, Scranton, PA; [p.] Joseph and Regina Srebro; [m.] John T. Hughes, July 21, 1973; [ch.] (2) Sons, Jonathan and Joel; [ed.] Scranton Technical H.S., Keystone Jr. College; [occ.] Self-employed; [memb.] Treasurer of Board of Directors - Scranton Area Christian Academy; [hon.] 1. 'Nominated for Irene Ryan Excellence in Acting Award' while at student at Keystone College, 2. 1995 Interboro Dist. Library Champion Storyteller, 3. 'Royal Reader' for MidValley Elementary School; [oth. writ.] Several poems published in local newspapers.; [pers.] My life and creativity is dedicated to God, my family, and the believers in Christ.; [a.] Clarks Summit, PA

HUGHES, JUANITA
[b.] June 22, 1976; New York, NY; [p.] Martha and Melvin; [occ.] Student; [a.] Bronx, NY.

HUGHES, SIS. EVANGELITA
[pen.] Patricia Hughes; [b.] March 31, 1920, Mason City, IA; [p.] Bridget and Henry Hughes; [ed.] B.A. at Immaculate Heart College, L.A., 1953 M.A. at Clarke College, Dubuque, Iowa - 1970, Summer courses U. of Hawaii - 1960-'63; [occ.] Retired Volunteer at Crisis Nurery and at Recording Studio for Blind.; [memb.] Sisters of Charity, B.V.M. St. Agnes Catholic Church, Phoenix, Catholic Diocese of Phoenix; [hon.] I taught elementary grades 3 through 8 for 40 years and was principal for 10 years.; [oth. writ.] "My B.V.M. Journey" - essay to be printed in a book entitled, Religious Women: By Women Who Live It. Author Julie Ferraro. Poem: "Jubilee Women Rejoice!" pub. in Salt Magazine, Spring, 1997.; [pers.] My teachers instilled in me a great love for poetry and an enthusiasm for life which I gladly share with others.; [a.] Phoenix, AZ

HULETT, KIM P.
[b.] September 7, 1963, Moberly, MO; [p.] Gerald

and Lorene Sieck; [m.] Michele R. Hulett, July 18, 1986; [ch.] Risa and Josh Hulett; [ed.] Bachelors degree in History with Minor in Psychology at University of Missouri; [occ.] Police Sergeant, Overland Park, KS Police; [a.] Edgerton, KS

HUNG, CHING CHEH
[b.] November 3, 1949; September 20, 1980; [ed.] Ph.D. in Chemical Engineering University of Minnesota, March 1980; [occ.] Research Engineer; [oth.writ.] Numerous professional Writing in Professional Journals. The only non-professional writing is a "letter to the future" to people 100 years from now. This is for the celebration of Cleveland Bicentania. (On Cleveland Newspaper "The Plain Dealer", June 30, 1996); [pers.] "Sometimes it looks like growing pain" is some of my observations that I hope can be expanded or further discussed by its readers; [a.] Westlake, OH.

HUNTER SR., LEE A.
[b.] July 20, 1944, Jasper, TX; [p.] Archie and Bernice Hunter; [m.] Rose Mary Hunter, August 6, 1988; [ch.] Five; [ed.] High School - College No Degree; [occ.] Customer Service Agent for United Airlines; [memb.] National Rifle Assc., American Legion - 40 and 8 Liverpool Rod and Gun Club; [pers.] I have written other poems, however over the years I have either given them away or misplaced. I do intend to write more in the near future.; [a.] Cicero, NY

HURSH, RAY
[b.] March 2, 1935; [m.] Helen M. (Hughes) Hursh; [ch.] Deborah Ann, David Joseph, Donald Francis, Terrence Patrick; [ed.] Duluth Central High, Duluth MN, Cal. College of Theater Arts, Pasadena, CA., University of Minnesota, Duluth, MN, Wisc. Indianhead Technical College, Superior, WI; [occ.] Fine dining waiter, U.S. Forest Service Personal Trainer (all part time); [hon.] Multiple awards from serv. organizations for public speaking and lectures. Pres. 2 yrs. Alpha Psi Omega, Nat. Honorary Drama Frat., Pres. of student council, WITC Superior, WI, placed in Who's Who In American Technical Education, winner of poetry contest at Lac Courte Orielles Ojibwa College, Hayward, WI, special journalistic award from National Journalistic Society while at Univ. of MN; [oth. writ.] Psychology paper which was placed in ref. lib. at WI Indianhead Tech. College, 25 page submission to Poetry Harbor, Duluth MN for possible chapbook pub. Poems published in various small papers and quarterly publications, presently working on my own book of poetry in hopes of future publication.; [pers.] Life is the greatest teacher, and nature the director. Learn well from both, for even though we have to get old, we don't have to grow old, for the wisdom of maturity will bring a peaceful coexistence with both.; [a.] Hayward, WI

HUTCHINGS, CAROLINE
[pen.] Caroline Ivey Hutchings; [b.] October 28, 1941, Yellville, AR; [p.] Deceased; [m.] Robert Hutchings, July 9, 1989; [ch.] Five grown children; [ed.] Associates - Liberal Arts; [occ.] Editor of Local Publication "Country Echoes"; [memb.] Member South Grand Lake Area, Chamber of Commerce, First Baptist Church, Langley, OK; [hon.] Volunteer Awards; [oth. writ.] I have written numerous stories and articles for magazines and newspapers.; [pers.] Thank you for giving poets the

opportunity to express themselves in such a wonderful way.; [a.] Langley, OK

HUYNH, YOUNG
[pen.] Huy Tinh; [b.] December 1, 1961; Danang, Vietnam; [p.] Cam Huynh, Toma Huynh; [ed.] University of Houston; [occ.] Senior Computer System Analyst; [oth.writ.] Several other poems in Vietnam era will be published in local Vietnam newspaper; [pers.] I believe that true and lasting love is based upon mutual understanding and caring, I dedicated this poem to my lovely Kimlan; [a.] Merrifield, VA.

HWANG, ALISON
[b.] September 13, 1975, Taipei, Taiwan; [p.] Miin Fei and Ming Chwen Hwang; [m.] Preston Li, February 1998; [ed.] Bronx High School of Science, City College of New York 1997; [occ.] Chemical Engineer, Merck and Co.; [memb.] American Institute of Chemical Engineers; [hon.] The National Dean's List 1995-96, Omega Chi Epsilon, Roslyn Gitlin Scholarship 1995-96, Leonard S. Wegman Scholarship 1995, A.J. Drexel Scholarship 1992-94; [pers.] Make the most of your life and make a difference in the lives of others.; [a.] Rego Park, NY

INGLE, SAUL
[pen.] Saul; [b.] November 24, 1980, Mobile, AL; [p.] Reah Ingle; [occ.] Student; [memb.] Adopt a friend; [pers.] Thank you Gan-Gan.; [a.] Mobile, AL

INMAN-SIEVERS, MARCELLA
[b.] June 21, 1949, Poplar Bluff, MO; [p.] Ethel M. Inman, Hugh E. Inman (Parents of 10 children); [m.] Arthur A. F. Sievers (My friend and partner for life), January 30, 1976; [ch.] Michael F. W. Sievers, best son I could ever have. Navy Veteran of Gulf War; [ed.] Poplar Bluff Senior High, St. Louis Community College at Meramec, St. Louis, MO; [occ.] Writer, Poet, Artist, Wood Carver. I also travel and work with my husband the lower 48 states and Canada; [memb.] International Society of Poets; [hon.] Award for Outstanding Poetry; [oth. writ.] Children's stories, short stories and other poems.; [pers.] My writings and my poems keep me going. They are the "Morning Song" of my days. I am so happy to have them. My poems and my dear Arthur and God gives me inspiration for other poems to come.; [a.] Saint Louis, MO

IRVIN, HOLLI ANN
[pen.] Domenice J. Philips; [b.] June 22, 1982, Millersburg, OH; [p.] James and Shirley Irvin; [ch.] Holli Ann Irvin; [ed.] K-8; [occ.] Student; [memb.] Choir, drama club, various church act.; [hon.] Young Authors Award (3rd place); [oth. writ.] Songs and poems - unpublished; [pers.] I write what I feel and my own experiences.; [a.] Loudonville, OH

IRWIN, GLENN E.
[b.] August 12, 1924, Monessen, PA; [p.] Harrison A. and Leona Mae; [m.] Nancy Light Irwin. December 22, 1940; [ch.] Glenn, David, Daniel, Jonathan; [ed.] Franklin and Marshall College, Harvard Univ., Graduate School of Banking, Rutgers University, Lancaster Bible College; [occ.] Executive Director, Franklin Hospital Foundation; [memb.] Westminster Presbyterian Church, Calvary Fellowship Homes, Super Citizens, Sim International; [hon.] Outstanding Education 1973, Outstanding Administrator 1979, 1984, 1985; [oth. writ.] Numerous articles on estate planning, stew-

ardship for the Christian (257 articles), Fidget's Woods (a book), a manual on church administration (approx. 300 pages).; [pers.] I write to reflect a Christian point of view regarding the handling of money and its ultimate disposition to family or Christian organizations.; [a.] Lancaster, PA

ISLEY, LEIGH
[b.] October 1, 1953, Lex., SC; [p.] J. W. Bickley, Helen Bickley; [m.] James W. (Jim) Isley, November 21, 1987; [ch.] Deborah Ann, John Earl; [occ.] Marina Management (Dry-Storage and Wet Slips); [hon.] Working with the Coast Guard Auxiliary - promoting boat safety. Working with the fire Dept. Lincoln County supporting and contributions for the burned children fund.; [oth. writ.] Have written several other poems none have ever been published.; [pers.] Most of my poems are written straight from the heart, my feelings, and my thoughts. Life is a teacher we learn by lives mistakes, happiness, sadness through living and through death.; [a.] Stanley, NC

JACKLE, LARA D.
[b.] May 25, 1982, Westwood, NJ; [p.] Linda and Scott Jackle; [ed.] Pascack Valley High School; [memb.] Saint Andrew's Church Choir, Bergen County Choir; [pers.] I am both helped and inspired in everything by my family, especially my Mom, Aunt, Grandma, Ash, and Kate. Special thanks to Suzanne, Jess, and Sara for being patient and always listening to my many poems.; [a.] Rivervale, NJ

JACKSON, CASEY A.
[b.] August 24, 1963, New Orleans, LA; [ed.] McDonogh #35 SHS (Grad.) University of Maryland-Asian Division; [occ.] Personnel Sergeant United States Army; [oth. writ.] Several poems given as expressions of concern, commitment and encouragement. In the process of compiling as a book.; [pers.] I strive to express in my writings that love can see us through any situation. Life is too short to let it pass us by, so enjoy!; [a.] River Ridge, LA

JACKSON, VERONICA A.
[pen.] Bun; [b.] November 29, 1979, Washington, DC; [p.] Diane Smith; [ed.] High School Senior, graduating June 10, 1997, acceptance into Salem-Teikyo Uni.; [occ.] Working with Bell Atlantic for the summer of 1997; [hon.] Certificate from Bell Atlantic (Aug. 1995 and 1996), Achievement Certificate from High School for Trade of Pre-Med (Nov. 1996); [oth. writ.] I Wish, Emotional Thoughts, My Love For You, Farewell, Dreams That I Have; [pers.] As long as you make a destiny, you will most definitely have a future!; [a.] Hyattsville, MD

JACOBS, JAMES
[b.] September 7, 1955, Reading, PA; [oth. writ.] Unpublished poems, too numerous to list.; [pers.] I have been greatly influenced by writers Robert Hunter and Bob Zimmerman. Except for a word change here and there, my poems are written exactly the way they come to me.; [a.] Shoemakersville, PA

JACOBS, SHAWN M.
[b.] August 4, 1967, Millinocket, ME; [p.] Harry E. Jacobs, Cheryl D. Pelletier; [ed.] Mexico High School Class of 1985; [occ.] Electronics Technician U.S.

Navy 1986 - Present; [hon.] National School Choral Award, John Philip Sousa Band Award; [pers.] I write to emphasize the importance of self discovery. My greatest influences are Jim Morrison and Bob Dylan and would someday like to have my words put to music.; [a.] Manheim, PA

JAMES, ADAM RUSSELL
[b.] February 19, 1983, Norfolk, VA; [p.] Gary James, Pamela James; [hon.] Honor Roll Student; [oth. writ.] "Grass", Anthology of Poetry by Young Americans, 1996 Ed.; [a.] Chesapeake, VA

JANKOWSKI, JOSEPH
[b.] November 25, 1925, Elvira, NY; [p.] Nellie and Theodore Jankowski; [m.] Margaret Henry Jankowski, August 21, 1948; [ed.] High School, Speech course (Univ of Maryland), Creative Writing course; [occ.] Retired Radio Announcer and Sales Manager in Radio; [oth. writ.] Short story "Put The Coffee On" 1985 in Good Ole Days magazine. revised and also published in Tampa Tribune December 1996 poems and stories published in St. Petersburg Times, Florida Clearwater Sun Florida and Local newspapers etc.; [pers.] My writings (wether poem or story) are written for the pleasure of young and old alike. Some are serious, some offer a bit of humor and some written to make readers aware of past, present and up-and-coming happenings. A lot of them touch on my personal life.; [a.] Holiday, FL

JAWORSKI, MRS. BARBARA
[pen.] Mrs. Barbara Jaworski; [b.] January 29, 1935, Newark; [p.] Joseph and Louise Raimo; [m.] William A. Jaworski, June 27, 1970; [ch.] Michael w. Jaworski; [ed.] B.S. in Education - Kean - 1956, M.A. - Seton Hall - 1961, Certification - Learning Disabilities Teacher-Consultants (LDT-C) - 1977; [occ.] Learning Consultant; [memb.] NJEA - N.J. (Education Assoc.), NEA (National Education Assoc.), Association of Learning Consultants, The Orton Dyslexia Society; [pers.] I strive to reflect my inner most thoughts about life in my poetry.; [a.] Parsippany, NJ

JEFFERS, AUSTIN J.
[b.] March 8, 1981, La Porte, IN; [p.] Donald and Julia Tibbs; [occ.] High School Student; [memb.] La Porte H.S., Pom and Dance Team, and Advanced Women's Choir; [hon.] 1st Place Solo and Ensemble Awards for Choir; [oth. writ.] Many other poems, but they have not been published.; [pers.] "Dear Mommy" is dedicated to my mother Julia Tibbs in memory of my brother who died on May 24, 1978.; [a.] La Porte, IN

JEFFERSON, SUNDRA
[b.] August 2, 1978, UMC; [p.] Sarah Jefferson, Johnnie Jefferson; [ed.] Madison Central High School; [hon.] Honors in Math; [oth. writ.] I have wrote alot of poems and now I have a chance to let other people enjoy my work.; [pers.] It's hard going through life having people to look down on me. Because I am different, but I still keep my head up.; [a.] Flora, MS

JEFFERY, S. ROBERT
[b.] February 2, 1938, Melrose, MA; [p.] Alva and S. Roy Jeffery; [m.] Mary W. Jeffery (Wallen), July 7, 1978; [ch.] Mark and Pamela; [ed.] Bently College; [occ.] Vice President (Retired) Bay State Gas Co., Westborough, MA; [oth. writ.] Several

poems for friends and family re: birthdays, retirements etc.; [pers.] As a result of brain cancer and cancer in both lungs, my philosophy is living one day at a time because yesterday's gone and tomorrow is not mine.; [a.] Milton, MA

JEGANNATHAN, SASHIHARAN ANDREW
[pen.] Andrew Jegannathan, Andrew Storm; [b.] December 28, 1978, Beverley, UK; [occ.] College student, Free Lance Writer, Film Producer and Songwriter.; [oth. writ.] I write a lot of songs, poems, and short stories. I am a script writer and producer in television, and I used be a video-jockey.; [pers.] Life, do any of us know what it really is? In our rush to find all the answers, we lose ourselves, drown, deprive ourselves from the ultimate love of God! Keep the faith, don't buy into society's suicide...; [a.] Columbus, OH

JENNINGS, MICHELE
[b.] March 30, 1983, Odessa, TX; [p.] Michael and Karen Jennings; [ed.] 8th Grade; [occ.] Student; [memb.] Bethany Christian Church, Odessa, TX; [hon.] A Honor Roll, Top Choir, 2nd Rank Tennis, 3rd Place in an Art Contest, All-City Choir, First Division Solo/Ensemble, Honorable Mentions in a Poster Contest; [oth. writ.] I have nothing else published, but I enjoy poems, short stories, songs, and horror stories.; [a.] Odessa, TX

JERALD, DAVID
[pen.] "The Warrior Poet"; [b.] November 20, 1948, Clarkston, WA; [p.] Horace T. Jerald (Father); [m.] Divorced; [ch.] Bill, Shelia, Clay, Stephanie; [ed.] Just High School; [occ.] Supervisor at Arizona Portland Cement; [memb.] American Kenpo Karate Academies; [oth. writ.] All poems "Mother", "This Poems for You" - "My Unforgivable Sin" - "Where The Plains Touch The Sky", "One With The Rock" and others. None of my poems have yet been published.; [pers.] I am determined to take the complication out of poetry. To write poems at a level everyone can understand. For if you can find the truth within the poems you will find the truth within yourself.; [a.] Tucson, AZ

JESTER, AMANDA
[pen.] Amanda Jester; [b.] October 30, 1985, Huntsville, AL; [p.] Michael and Sharon Spangler; [ed.] 5th Grade at Ridgeway Elementary in Memphis, TN; [occ.] Student; [memb.] Girl Scouts; [hon.] Several Reading Awards.; [pers.] A lot of times, I have words in my head that I want to get out. I wrote the poem Swiftly in 3rd grade.; [a.] Memphis, TN

JIMENEZ, PEDRO
[b.] December 26, San Antonio, TX; [p.] Patricia Vela, Tomas Vela; [ed.] Stephen F. Austin High, Texas Southern University, Houston Community College; [occ.] United States Marine Corps; [oth. writ.] Collection of personal poems never published.; [pers.] Life is Love and Love is life. Contentment cannot exist without the agony. Words are energy from the subjective - self out to the objective world that is experienced, employ them for the continuing of humanity by any means. A special meaning exists for each of us in life.; [a.] Houston, TX

JOE, TED K.
[pen.] Psykosis; [b.] July 2, 1975, Houston, TX;

[p.] Kherman Joe, Leanna Joe; [ed.] University of Texas at Austin; [occ.] Student, Undergraduate Laboratory Researcher, UT, Austin; [memb.] American Chemical Society; [oth. writ.] Two personal compilations which are wholly unpublished.; [pers.] I seek to awaken the solitude and the sadness that sleep forever inside me, and perhaps uncover the humanity hiding underneath.

JOHN, ELIZABETH
[b.] August 8, 1976, Denver, CO; [p.] Rex John, Lorie Rutledge; [ed.] Currently a Junior in College at Hardin-Simmons University, Abilene, TX; [memb.] Tallowood Baptist Church, Student Mission Fellowship, Student Foundation of Hardin - Simmons University; [hon.] Who's Who Among American High School Students; [pers.] My prayer is to share this peace that I have in Jesus Christ with all who are weary. He is our strength.; [a.] Houston, TX

JOHNSON, CARL H.
[b.] February 14, 1949; Astoria, NY; [p.] May and Carl; [m.] Suzanne; January 16, 1982; [ch.] Carl Jr. Gerald, Justin; [ed.] Adelphi University 1977, Bachelor of Business Administration; [occ.] N.Y.S. Asbestos Investigator; [memb.] Vietnam Veterans of America, Chapter 82, Nassau County; [a.] West Hempstead, NY.

JOHNSON, CARRIE
[pen.] CC; [b.] September 22, 1943, California; [p.] Jasper and Etta McMullan; [m.] Charles Johnson; [ch.] Anthony and Carlton; [occ.] Owner of T.B.L. Packaging CO. AKA The Box Lady; [memb.] San Francisco Christian Center; [oth. writ.] Soon to be published "Women Of Faith Come Into The Knowledge of Who You Are"; [pers.] In all I say and do, I do as unto the Lord...Loving mankind by praying for a better world. For our children and love ones; [a.] Oakland, CA

JOHNSON, JAMES W.
[b.] September 22, 1949, Chillicothe, MO; [p.] Leo and Norma Johnson; [ed.] 1 yr. college; [occ.] 100% disabled vet; [memb.] VFW; [hon.] US Army Airborne, US Marine Corps, US Navy, Bronze Star, Air Medal; [oth. writ.] The Silent Man

JOHNSON, KRISTEN D.
[b.] June 29, 1982, Zachary, LA; [p.] Douglas and Tammy Johnson; [ed.] West Feliciana High School (in attendance); [occ.] Student; [memb.] Spanish Club, Art Club; [hon.] Fabulous Freshman Award; [a.] Saint Francisville, LA

JOHNSON, MRS. MICHELE
[pen.] Tight; [b.] May 29, 1953, Saint Louis, MO; [p.] Bernice and Willie Hamilton; [ch.] Shanik, Brendan and Diamond; [ed.] I went to summer school and then went to summer high; [occ.] Housewife; [oth. writ.] How Can You Leave Me; [pers.] I just love writing because I can open up someone heart and fill it with love and happiness.; [a.] Saint Louis, MO

JOHNSON, TIM F.
[pen.] Francis James; [b.] December 16, 1971, Normal, IL; [p.] Tim Johnson Sr. and Jana Eppstien; [m.] Glenda Johnson, November 4, 1995; [ch.] Stephanie 6 yrs., Samantha 2 yrs.; [ed.] Sophomore at San Antonio College in San Antonio, Texas, Majoring in Psychology; [occ.] Assistant to the

disabled.; [hon.] 2 Consecutive Presidential Honors List Awards for achieving academic excellence; [oth. writ.] Many poems and short stories soon to be released for publication.; [pers.] The poem featured in A Prism of Thoughts is my own modernized version of Wordsworth's "The World Is Too Much With Us." Wordsworth seemed to effectively sum up where we were, and are still headed.; [a.] San Antonio, TX

JONES, DARRELL E.
[pen.] T. H. Austin; [b.] August 12, 1952, Paragould, AR; [p.] William and Eva Jones; [ed.] B.S. in Secondary Education - English, Master of Arts English, Reading Specialist; [occ.] Chapter I Reading Teacher, Caruthersville Elementary; [pers.] I see in this poem Autumn as a lady in the Victorian era, perfectly serene and composed, who accepts the passing of her time with noble gestures and grace. She is worthy of admiration and only subtle sympathy.; [a.] Dyersburg, TN

JONES, DAVID
[pen.] D. J.; [b.] April 22, 1952, West Helena, AK; [p.] Eddie Jones and Darda Jones; [m.] Betty Hicks-Jones; [ch.] Sheilann Jones, Dawn Hicks and Denise Hicks; [ed.] High school, 2 yrs. college, business school; [occ.] Government Worker, (claim clerk); [pers.] The talent that God have given to us, we must share with others.; [a.] Brooklyn, NY

JONES, EDNA
[b.] March 23, 1947, Greenville, SC; [p.] The Late Willie and Dorothy Johnson; [m.] Thomas Elijah Jones Sr., March 17, 1967; [ch.] Thomas Jones Jr., Sabrina Jones, Nicholas Jones, Zackary Jones; [ed.] Washington High, Career Training Institute College; [occ.] Sourdough Sandwich Shop Owner, Marketing Specialist; [memb.] SC State Board of Cosmetologist, National Cosmetology Association; [pers.] I believe I have been given the gift of therapeutic writing to impact and change the lives of people. My greatest influence in my Lord and savior Jesus Christ and my husband of 30 yrs. and son, daughter-in-law and grandchildren!; [a.] Greenville, SC

JONES, EDWARD A.
[b.] September 3, 1969, Brooklyn, NY; [p.] Robert and Janet Jones; [m.] Madeline M. Jones, April 3, 1993; [ed.] Monsignor Farrell High, St. John's University, Pace University Business Graduate School; [occ.] Retail Banker, Chartway Federal Credit Union; [memb.] Knights of Columbus, Golden Key National Honors Member; [hon.] Phi Beta Lambda, Beta Gamma Sigma, Dean's List, President's Society; [oth. writ.] Several articles were published on a variety of University newspapers throughout my college years.; [pers.] Life is supposed to be fun. Learn to appreciate what you have and don't strive for material wealth. Rich people are actually poor people with money. Life's challenges should be seen as opportunities and seize the moment when one comes your way.; [a.] Norfolk, VA

JONES, ELIZABETH O.
[pen.] O. Jones; [b.] June 20, 1925, Baltimore, MD; [p.] Mary Burns Owens; [m.] Gilbert K. Mook, September 16, 1989; [ch.] Larry Jones, Beth Davino, Sharon Bapties; [ed.] Roland Park Country School, Baltimore, St. Margarets,

Tappahannock, VA; [occ.] Artist; [memb.] Artist Guild and Gallery, R.I. Watercolor Society; [oth. writ.] Unpublished journals; [pers.] Many of my poems stem from seeds planted in writing courses hold over the last 10 years.; [a.] Charlestown, RI

JONES, JIM H.
[pen.] Jim Jones; [b.] February 13, 1970; CA; [ed.] Graduate of I Diman Regional Vocational School, 1988; [occ.] Certified Welder; [hon.] Gold Medal Award for a trumpet competition; [oth.writ.] First poem at the age of 16 written about my childhood sweetheart entitled "Dancing With The Stars"; [pers.] At the age of 26, for employment and adventure I have worked in MA, RI, AZ, CA and presently LA.; [a.] Dartmouth, MA.

JONES, JON
[m.] Julie Jones; [ch.] Jason and Jonathan; [occ.] Multi-talented Rock Musician, Singer/Songwriter. "Sea of Change" is a song written by Jon and performed by his family band, the pods; [oth. writ.] Songs, poems; [a.] New Richmond, TN

JONES, LORRIE L.
[b.] August 19, 1951, New Vineland, NJ; [p.] Deceased; [m.] Ronald L. Jones, March 20, 1982; [ch.] George L. Bednar, Jason S. Bednar; [ed.] Graduated 1993 from University Tenn. Chatt. with B.S.W. Bachelor of Social Work now; [occ.] Social Worker; [memb.] National Ass. of Social Workers (N.A.S.W.), Golden Key Nationals Honor Society; [hon.] Golden Key National Honor Society, Who's Who Honor Student, Dean's List, my biggest honor was being a wife and mother to my 2 children George and Jason; [oth. writ.] Golden Rings, The Anniversary, Dragon Slayer, Life's Eulogy, Soul Death, Doubt, Faith, Time to let go.; [pers.] I choose to reflect family and gifts of love in my poetry. I firmly believe love, family are gifts not to be taken lightly or for granted.; [a.] Apison, TN

JONES, MARY V.
[b.] October 27, 1940, Bessemer, AL; [p.] Silas and Dimples Grace Smith; [ch.] 2 Boys, 1 Girl and 4 Grandchildren; [occ.] Operations Manager for Alarm Monitoring Co. Central Station Inc.; [oth. writ.] I have wrote many poems but I have never had any published.; [pers.] I really enjoy writing poems and putting my thoughts into words. God blessed me with the ability of making my words rhyme. If I can make someone happy or feel better I feel I have used my talent as God would want me to.; [a.] Bessemer, AL

JONES, PHILIP
[b.] June 14, 1956, Dallas, TX; [p.] Bill Jones, Helen Jones; [m.] Crystal Flagler-Jones, October 19, 1995; [ch.] Wendi Michelle; [ed.] Skylene High School University of Dallas; [a.] Euless, TX

JORDAHL, TROY
[b.] October 9, 1967, Yankton, SD; [p.] Ellef and Corriene Jordahl, [m.] Busy Jordahl, March 12, 1988; [ch.] Chadalee, Kelsi, Nathyn; [pers.] God and my family are my greatest inspiration for creativity.; [a.] Sioux Falls, SD

JUDT, ANNE M.
[pen.] Anne Gerrard; [b.] June 18, 1965, Fremont, NE; [p.] Kenneth Gerrard, Monica Gerrard; [m.] Phillip Judt, August 24, 1996; [ch.] Cari Ann Flood; [ed.] Stanton High, Stanton, NE; [occ.] Packaging

Technician, Pfizer Animal Health, Lincoln Ne.; [memb.] American Heart Assc. Health Care Provider; [oth. writ.] This is my first published poem.; [pers.] I believe that poetry brings out the beauty in all of us, Poetry has been an anchor for me in difficult times and struggles.; [a.] Lincoln, NE

JUSINO JR., RAMON
[b.] September 7, 1935; Puerto Rico, USA; [p.] Ramon and Dolores Jusino; [m.] Mariana Jusino; July 23, 1960; [ch.] Kenny 34, Janette 33, Teresa 17; [ed.] Masters in creative writing from City College of N.Y. and the University of Paris (France); [occ.] Writer, Investor and Real Estate Agent; [oth.writ.] A long poem entitled "Mother Europe" (15 pages) dealing with Zeu's charming of Europa and their flight to "Inprint upon the West" her name and "A continent to seed with heirs". Also, other poems and a play; [pers.] I'm still refining the instrument on which I will play my note; [a.] Elmont; NY.

JUST, CHERABA
[b.] October 3, 1978; [p.] Mark and Gentala Patterson; [ed.] Home School, 2 yrs. Mayer High School, Political Science University of Georgetown, American Legion Police Academy (Jr.) National Youth Leadership Forum on Defence, Intelligence and Diplomacy; [occ.] Student, Reserves U.S.M.C.; [memb.] Yavapai County Sheriffs Explorers; [hon.] Special Recognition for English, Certificate of Academic Excellence, National English Merit Award, Who's Who Among High School Students, Outstanding Academic Achievement and Leadership; [oth. writ.] First place short story contest, "Soul of a Cop", First Place Poem, "Call of Duty"; [pers.] True heroism is remarkably sober, very undramatic. It is not the urge to surpass all others of whatever cost, but to serve others at whatever cost. Arthur Ashe.; [a.] Spring Valley, AZ

KAMELISKI, MARILU
[pen.] Camille Ryan; [b.] April 21, 1970; [p.] Charles and Marilu Kameliski; [ed.] Lee Hospital School of Radiology PA, University of Wisconsin; [occ.] Primary Support Specialist, Kodak Health Imaging; [memb.] American Association of Radiologic Technologists, American Cancer Society Breast Imaging Specialist, Salvation Army Volunteer, Certified Cathecist; [hon.] Radiology Convention Application's Specialist, Indiana County Independent Salesperson, Up With People, Ms. Int'l Petite Wisconsin, Priliminary Finalist Miss Pennyslvania; [pers.] There are Angels Among Us.; [a.] Dallas, TX

KANE, DEBBIE LYNN
[pen.] Debbie Kane; [b.] December 22, 1968; Belleville, NJ; [p.] Arthur Bakarich, Barbara Bakarich; [m.] Kevin Frank Kane Sr; May 28, 1988; [ch.] Kevin Jr; [ed.] Kearny High School then Natural Motion School of Hair Design, Jersey City; [occ.] Beautician Assistant; [oth.writ.] Several poems written at home, this is the first one I sent in for someone else to see; [pers.] All my life people tell me I'm too sensitive, and that I'm a dreamer, writing let me express my feelings, I recently lost my 25 yr. old brother to a long battle with cancer. I wrote the poem "The Angels" for memory of Michael L; [a.] Kearny, NJ.

KAPIS, RON S.
[pen.] Ron S. Kapis; [b.] April 30, 1974; Chardon,

OH; [ed.] Chardon High School and The School of Hard Knocks; [occ.] Tree Trimmer; [oth.writ.] Too many poems and songs to count or remember; [pers.] "Live as you will have wished to have lived when you are dying," Christian Furchtegott Gellert; [a.] Chardon, OH.

KATTANY, BARBARA MCSHEEHY
[b.] March 11, 1953, Worcester, MA; [p.] Lloyd, Marjorie McSheehy; [m.] James F. Kattany, November 21, 1976; [ch.] Nicole Kristen, Alysia Alexandra; [ed.] North High School Worcester MA, B.S. Psychology, Worcester State College; [occ.] Fund raiser and volunteer for a non-profit organization that helps children with cancer Why Me, Inc.; [pers.] Life is precious, cherish the ones you love for you never know when God will call one of them home. Don't be afraid to say "I love you" for love is the essence of all that is beautiful and good. Strive to be humble in all that you do for humility is knowing God and all His glory.; [a.] Marlboro, MA

KEAR, NORMAN L.
[b.] February 9, 1922, Bellflower, CA; [p.] Augustus Kear, Mabel Kear; [m.] Suzanne C. Kear, October 29, 1976; [ch.] 4 children - 3 stepchildren; [ed.] 10th Grade; [occ.] Retired; [memb.] VFW Post #5867, Lakeside, CA; [oth. writ.] Several poems about different events in my life, dating back to 1943, several "Letters to the Editor" local newspaper.; [pers.] No matter how hard the day, if I could find something to laugh about, even if the joke was on me, it was worthwhile.; [a.] El Cajon, CA

KELLEY, ROBERT M.
[b.] December 23, 1929, Scottsboro, AL; [p.] Dr. B. K. Kelley, Myrtle Roberts Kelley; [m.] Faye Pittman Kelley, January 20, 1951; [ch.] Joel, Robert Jr., William, Cynthia; [ed.] B.S. Univ of Ala., MA Univ. of Alabama, Educational Specialist Degree - Univ. of Georgia; [occ.] Retired Educational Administrator; [memb.] Lions Club, Officer, 1st United Methodist Church; [hon.] Dean's List, Grant-in-Aid, State of Georgia; [oth. writ.] Poems to my wife, Children, speakers at Lions Club, friends.; [pers.] My poems are for enjoyment, usually recalling the life history of the person about whom I am writing.; [a.] Conyers, GA

KELLY, FRANK EDWARD
[b.] June 26, 1968, Queens, NY; [p.] Francis Kelly, Margaret Kelly; [m.] Patricia Boyd Kelly, August 24, 1996; [ed.] BA, Hofstra University, Chaminade High School; [occ.] Graphic Artist, Long Island, New York; [pers.] My poetry is inspired by moments in time that seem to last a lifetime.; [a.] Valley Stream, NY

KELLY, MARY
[b.] Chicago, IL; [ed.] St Xavier's University BA, plus addtional course work Loyola University, North Eastern University; [occ.] Teacher; [memb.] PIRGE (environmental group); [a.] Chicago, IL.

KEMPER, REV. CARL F.
[b.] March 29, 1923; Farm home, Crete; [p.] John and Lydia Boekel Kemper; [m.] Betty J. (Welsch) Kemper; October 23, 1945; [ch.] Eunice, Beverly, Thomas and Timothy; [ed.] Rural school 1-8, high school, (voc. ag.), Elmhurst College '57, Roosevelt U., 2 summers Eden Seminary '60; [occ.] Retired, Owners Nebraska Red Popcorn, maintain wildlife

areas on farm; [memb.] United Church of Christ, Nebraskans for Peace, Center for Rural Affairs, Farm Crisis Council, Nebraska Food Industry, NE Sustainable Agricultural Society; [hon.] Star Farmer in Future Farmers of America, highest award in state one act play contest, Elmhurst, Cum Laude Award of Merit, Big Blue NRD; [oth.writ.] A sermon once a week for 40 years, letters to the editor, articles for magazines; [pers.] In our nine year farming career we practiced soil and water conservation, and now as landlords we require farming practices which save the water and soil, leaving residue on the land and using no chemicals. We believe in family farms which sustain the small towns and rural churches. The Tale of the Silent Bell was inspired by the church we grew up in and our first pastorate; [a.] Crete, NE.

KENDALL, ERIC
[pen.] E, X Static Blue, Chocho Flair; [b.] December 19, 1973, Milwaukee; [occ.] Bank Teller; [oth. writ.] Tons of poems, songs, some short stories; [pers.] All of my best work is hunger, blistering need, and a desperate attempt to release it and let others feel it too. "My first published work is dedicated to Emilio, who opened my eyes, lit my power, and inspired me without trying. One of C's two, all that I do, I do for me - and for you".; [a.] Muskego, WI

KENDRICK JR., ROBERT T.
[pen.] Robert Scotts; [b.] January 7, 1971, Hamilton, NJ; [p.] Gloria Kendrick and Robert Kendrick Sr.; [ed.] A. A. Mercer County College, currently s senior at Rider University; [occ.] Full time student, work part time, Mental Health Association; [memb.] Psyc. club, Rider University; [hon.] National Honors Society, Dean's List; [pers.] I will continue to work very hard to achieve my dream when I have reached it. I will be only still working on the next.; [a.] Trenton, NJ

KENT, ANNE
[b.] June 3, 1976, Lansdale, PA; [p.] Robert Kent, Grace Kent; [ed.] Boyertown Area H.S., Millersville University; [occ.] Student; [hon.] Dean's List, Computer Science Departmental Honors, Pennyslvania School Press Association, Keystone Award in Poetry; [pers.] Life rocks!; [a.] Perkiomenville, PA

KENYON, STEPHANIE E.
[pen.] Stephanie E. Kenyon; [b.] December 27, 1976, Malden, MA; [p.] Donald and Joyce Kenyon; [ed.] Nandua High School, Onley, VA, Chowan College, Murfreesboro; [occ.] Bank Teller, Loan Secretary; [hon.] Poems published in Salisbury Times. Honor Roll, All State Softball, Basketball, All Region Volleyball in high school; [oth. writ.] "Take In All Of The Little Things," "The Dishes."; [pers.] Broken hearts know mercy, selfish ones know none and rich hearts do not know the word.; [a.] Poplar Branch, NC

KEOWN, SHERRY
[b.] July 9, 1960, Detroit; [p.] Charles and Helen Weiss; [m.] David, September 22, 1978; [memb.] ASPCA, World Wildlife Fund, Humane Society; [hon.] Many Editor Choice Awards through, "The National Library of Poetry"; [oth. writ.] God For A Day, Ask An Angel, Eyes Of Horses, Splashed In Red, kingdom On The Sea, What Price You Pay; [a.] Warren, MI

KERMAN, SANDRA
[pen.] Sandra Kerman; [b.] June 22, 1961; Philadelphia; [p.] Richard and Myra Hawkins; [m.] Jack Kerman, January 31, 1988; [ch.] Jordan, Ryan, Casey; [ed.] Cedar Grove Academy; [occ.] Artist; [oth.writ.] I am presently working on children's books, writing and illustrating; [pers.] My poem reflects personal tragedy, but also tells of personal healing in the midst of guilt and pain with the healing power of God's forgiveness and love; [a.] Lewisburg, PA.

KESSLER, JAMES
[b.] October 15, 1963, Philadelphia, PA; [p.] Joel and Marion Ewing; [m.] Anna Marie Kessler, October 8, 1994; [ch.] Chiara-Marie Kessler; [occ.] Machine Operator; [memb.] Lakehurst VFW Post #10061 - Amvets Post #2, Jackson, NJ, Director of Special Events for Children's Independence Day 1996; [hon.] Veterans Of Foreign Wars National Award of Excellence for Children's Independence Day 1996. Distinguished Service Award VFW 10061; [oth. writ.] Several Letters Printed in local newspapers; [a.] Lakehurst, NJ

KIEHLE, MARGUERITE
[pen.] Margie; [b.] January 25, 1936, Paris, TX; [p.] Dewey and Clara Elkins; [m.] Widow; [ch.] Jon, Linda, Tony, Tim, Becky; [ed.] High School, Chicago Inst. of Nursing, Seattle Business and Med. Training Center; [occ.] Retired, I live in Retsil Veterans Home; [memb.] American Legion, American Kennel Club, Retsil Veterans Home; [oth. writ.] Clara's Story, Cry for Yesterday Poem.; [pers.] Live for today - yesterday is gone. Love yourself, smile often, cry little. It is better to say kind words than mean, and it takes no more effort.; [a.] Retsil, WA

KIESEL, LINDA
[b.] May 10, 1948, PA; [p.] John and Klover Hopewell; [m.] Carson Kiesel, July 11, 1970; [ch.] Kristen and Joel; [ed.] A.A. - Registered Nurse, Dalomar College; [occ.] Homemaker/Freelance Photographer; [memb.] Rancho Bernardo Camera Club, Emmanuel Faith Com. Church; [hon.] Camera Club Monthly Competition; [oth. writ.] Several poems about people or animals in my life.; [pers.] I write from personal events and meaningful people in my life - (My high school english teacher made poetry fun to write); [a.] Escondido, CA

KILLIAN, BARBARA LOUISE
[pen.] Barbara Louise Killian; [b.] April 11, 1925, Chico, CA; [p.] Ceres and Harry D. Robison; [m.] Stewart Gregory Killian, January 14, 1946; [ch.] Gregory Stewart and Stephen David; [ed.] Pasadena Jr. College; [occ.] Housewife; [memb.] Plumas County Asst. Assoc., National Health Federation Conservative Caucus Foundation; [hon.] Poem published in the Plumas County Art Assoc. News.; [oth. writ.] Nature and animal poems for children. Inspirational poems.; [pers.] I endeavor to delight our grandchildren with adoration for the Creator as reflected in mountain, lake and pine, bird and animal. My mentor, Robert Louis Steveson's, "A Child's Garden of Verse"; [a.] Lake Almanor, CA

KIM, EUGENE
[pen.] Eugene Kim; [b.] January 12, 1980; [p.] Dong Ho Kim, Young Hwa Kim;; [ed.] Sunny Hills/ Bolsa Grande High; [occ.] High School Student; [memb.] National Teen Leadership Program;

[hon.] California Teen Leadership Program essay finalist; [oth.writ.] Orange Country Register Teen Movie Panel; [pers.] Wealth and charity go hand in hand; [a.] Garden Grove, CA.

KIM, HYAN
[b.] June 27, 1985, San Jose, CA; [p.] In Kon Kim and Hae Khung Kim; [ed.] Blue Hills Elementary School; [memb.] San Jose Korean Baptist Church, Children Choir; [hon.] Bible Drill State, Perfect X3's (California State); [pers.] I've been influenced from my father, civil rights leaders and strong Christians, "Consciousness is not just living, it's understanding."; [a.] Saratoga, CA

KINANN, JEANNE
[b.] January 31, 1950, El Paso, TX; [p.] Arnold and Virginia Johnson; [m.] Mike Kinann, September 25, 1968; [ch.] Tami 28, Wendy 26, and Kristi 17; [ed.] Soquel High, West Valley College, Cabrillo College; [occ.] Former Court Reporter and Legal Secretary; [hon.] Dean's List; [oth. writ.] An unpublished collection of poems copyrighted in 1995.; [pers.] Poetry is a powerful relationship healing tool. It has given me considerable direction and has become my medium to reach out and touch my family and friends.; [a.] Soquel, CA

KINDER, BETTY MAE
[pen.] Betty; [b.] April 27, 1939, Salt Lake City, UT; [p.] Albert and Lella Moore; [m.] Gene Ray Kinder, September 17, 1954; [ch.] Gene, Wayne, Randy, Laurie, Billy, Kenny and Angela; [ed.] Salt Lake City Schools and St. George, Utah - High School; [occ.] Child care - of a Grandchild; [memb.] LDS Church - community choir, Scouts of America.; [hon.] Callings in my church: Teacher, Librarian and Song Chorister. Award's: Happiness.; [oth. writ.] Composed song of Utah's mountains and flowers. Sung them for many church and social gatherings.; [pers.] I have been greatly influenced in my life by the fine example of my christian parents who taught me to love God and to stay close to him thru prayer and scripture study.; [a.] American Fork, UT

KINDLESPARGER, BECKY
[b.] November 13, 1982, Fredericktown, MO; [p.] John and Dorothy Kindlesparger; [ed.] Finishing 8th Grade at Farmington Middle School; [memb.] Cadate Pommies, R.A.D. Church, National Junior Honor Society, FHA (Future Homemakers of America), Girl Scouts; [hon.] Honor Roll, Honor Society, Perfect Attendance, Girl Scout Patches (Variety); [oth. writ.] Best Friends, Special Friendship; [pers.] Most of my poems come from things that's happened to me or someone I know.; [a.] Fredericktown, MO

KINDS SR., JOHN L.
[b.] April 19, 1943, Gallatin, PA; [p.] Mr. and Mrs. William C. Kinds Sr.; [m.] Valerie P. Pierre-Kinds, December 21, 1974; [ch.] Jeffrey Michelle John Jr.; [ed.] Elizabeth - Forward High, Penna, U.S. Army - Clerical and Medics, Albert Merill School, Data Proc. IBM and Xerox Training Cntrs.; [occ.] Word Processing Specialist; [memb.] Smithsonian Institute, Metropolitan Museum of Natural History, Black Veterans for Social Justice; [hon.] Athlete of the Year, Elizabeth-Forward High, PA, Letter of Appreciation - U.S. Army Adjutant Generals Office, U.S. Army Rifle Marksman Medal, Viet-

nam Vet Memorial Plague, Penna Dept. of War Honorable Discharge; [oth. writ.] Biography in progress.; [pers.] Dedicated to "Poet" Sister Patsy Andrew "A promise kept and a dream fulfilled." One love.; [a.] Fort Greene, Brooklyn, NY

KING, MAXINE L.
[pen.] Maxine L. King; [b.] January 14, 1917, Kearney, NE; [p.] Levi and Almeda Lewis; [m.] Charles W. King, February 8, 1947; [ch.] Nancy King, Linda Poland; [ed.] Gibbon (NE) High, Kearney State University, Greeley (CO) State College, (Former-Teacher - Deputy Circuit Clerk Girl Scout Executive); [occ.] Housewife; [memb.] Methodist Church, Hospital Auxiliary, Membership, Chmn of Nursing Home Auxiliary, Christian Women's Club, United Methodist Women.; [hon.] Valedictorian of H.S. Class; [oth. writ.] Childrens stories and poems, personal biography.; [pers.] So much wisdom can be gleamed from little children and they need to know they are important. Likewise, our older people need to know they are loved and respected.; [a.] Cherokee Village, AR

KINKADE, MARIA
[b.] November 11, 1981; HI; [p.] Gary and Susan Kinkade; [ed.] Iriving K-5th, West High 9-10th still going to school; [occ.] Work out a bakery "Johnsons Bakery"; [hon.] I haven't ever enter any other poetry contest except this one, but I do have awards for cheerleading; [oth.writ.] I have started some stories and wrote many other poems; [pers.] I have been influenced to write poems cause of my grandma and things that happened in my life; [a.] Waterloo, IA.

KIPP, LYNNETTE H.
[b.] July 15, 1942, Louisiana; [p.] Donald and Lynn Henry; [ch.] Kevan, Carey, Robert; [ed.] BA La. Tech University, MS University of La Verne; [occ.] 5th Grade Teacher Menifee School District Mentor Teacher; [memb.] NFA, CTA, MTA; [hon.] 1996 Who's Who of American Teachers, CTA WHO Award, President of Menifee Teachers Association; [pers.] I draw my inspiration from my wonderful family and my delightful students. I adore all children.; [a.] Hemet, CA

KISIEL, THEODORE LEONARD
[pen.] Ted Kisiel; [b.] November 19, 1974, Erie, PA; [p.] Leonard and Rose Kisiel; [ed.] Klein Elementary School, Harborcreek Jr./Sr. High School Triangle Tech.; [occ.] Projectionist/Comedian; [memb.] Star Trek Fan Club, Nitpickers Guild; [pers.] I try to find the humor in most everything no matter how odd the situation.; [a.] Erie, PA

KITTLESON, HOWARD B.
[pen.] Howard B. Kittleson; [b.] August 27, 1913, Blair, WI; [p.] Hani-Bertina Kittleson; [m.] Adeline J. Kittleson, June 23, 1932; [ch.] Eloria, Carole, Charles, Christopher; [ed.] Barron W. thru Crapi 12 I C S all subjects related to steam fitting Combustion Engineering, Chicago, IL; [occ.] Retired, Mechanical Contractor; [memb.] Life member Ashrae life member Osman Temple Shrink St. Paul, Min., 50 year member North Star Lodge A.F. and A.T.; [hon.] 50 Year Masonic Award 50 year shrink hospit. award. Life member Elks B.P.O.E. 516 St. Cloud MN. Life member Knights Temple, Life member; [oth. writ.] To be a benefactor on family - beyond success on asbestos - the electric car -

chrotamp prayer time - asbestos on family.; [pers.] I strike to exalt the dreamy of all persons, to have faith in God, to believe in God to contribute to productivity charity and observe the golden rule.; [a.] Albany, MN

KLAMMER, FRED
[b.] June 12, 1970, Queens, NY; [p.] Fred and Madeline; [ed.] Saint Raymond's High School, Bronx, NY; [occ.] Security Supervisor, Albert Einstein Coll. of Medicine, Bronx, NY; [hon.] 4 Time Security Merit of Honor Award Winner; [oth. writ.] A few unpublished poems.; [pers.] I try to express deep feelings of falling in and out of love with the pain and mental emotion we all go through.; [a.] Bronx, NY

KNIGHT, BRENDA
[p.] John and Grace Hiller; [m.] Jeffrey B. Knight; [ch.] Carrie, Jacci, Katie; [occ.] Wife, Mother; [pers.] "To God be the glory, great things He has done."

KNIGHT, BRENDA L.
[p.] John and Grace Hiller; [m.] Jeffrey B. Knight; [ch.] Carrie, Jacci, Katie; [occ.] Wife, Mother; [pers.] "To God be the glory, great things He has done."

KOPP, FREDERICK P.
[pen.] Frederick P. Kopp; [b.] March 4, 1949, Muscatine, IA; [p.] Philip and Erma Kopp; [m.] Sharon, August 24, 1974; [ch.] Elaine and Philip; [ed.] University of Iowa, Liberal Arts and College of Law; [occ.] Attorney; [memb.] Phi Beta Kappa, Phi Delta Phi, American Bar Association, State and Local Bar Associations in Illinois and Iowa; [oth. writ.] A collection of unpublished poems.; [pers.] My life is a parked car with its engine running, in which I have locked my only set of keys.; [a.] Rock Island, IL

KOZLOWSKI, GLENNA M.
[b.] July 6, 1931, Buffalo, NY; [p.] George and Stella Hummel; [m.] Deceased - Leonard J. Kozlowski, May 30, 1951; [ch.] (Deceased) Linda, David Gail, Kenneth, Mary and Carol; [ed.] St. Gerard's Grammar School Kensington H.S. Medaille College; [occ.] Retired - Teacher, Mother of Six; [memb.] Past member Medaille Alumni Association Board Marine Dr. Board of Directors 2nd Vice President - 1995-1996 President - 1996-1997 Church Choir Member; [hon.] Dean's List; [pers.] Reflection, observation, emotion and psychology, are the embodiment of my writing.; [a.] Buffalo, NY

KULAGE, LILLIAN M.
[pen.] Shelli Kulage; [b.] June 19, 1964; Gary, IN; [p.] Lindaf Mihal, Ronald J. Mihal, Sr; [m.] Jett A. Kullage; January 05, 1990; [ch.] Melissa Anne, Jett Allen; [ed.] Lew Wallace High, Dayton Job Corps Center, Daven Port College; [occ.] Head ... of River Forest Field Indian, IN; [memb.] National Home Gardening Club; [hon.] Daven Port College Dean's List, Graduated with honors; [oth. writ.] Several poems and short stories never published. This is the first time I've submitted any of my works for approval; [pers.] This particular poem was written for my grandmother, Hazel Murley-Traglio, thanks; [a.] Merillville, IN.

KUNDERT, AMANDA
[pen.] Morgan Adams; [b.] October 2, 1972, Alameda, CA; [p.] Robert and Mary; [ed.] Hayward High School, Chabot College - AA Degree, California State University, Hayward - still attending; [occ.] Student - English; [a.] Hayward, CA

KURTZ, DORA JULIAN
[pen.] Dodie J. Kurtz; [b.] January 16, 1960, Lakeland, FL; [p.] H. S. and Lillian M. Julian; [m.] Eric David Kurtz, September 9, 1989; [ch.] April C.; [ed.] Lakeland High, Mr. Dels University of Cosmetology, Rofflers (Barber Instructor), "Universal Hairstyling Academy (Cosmetology)"; [a.] Bonita Springs, FL

L'ECUYER, MARY F.
[pen.] Mary F. L'Ecuyer; [b.] April 23, 1907, Boston, MA; [p.] William H. Coogan, Mabel Rush; [m.] Frederick E. L'Ecuyer, September 7, 1940; [ch.] William F. and Frederick E. Jr.; [ed.] Boston School System and Courses Evenings at Boston University and Harvard University; [occ.] Deceased in 1989; [memb.] Oak Hill Country Club, Fitchburg and Cranberry Golf Course in Harwich, Mass, Publicity Chairman for the Leominter Chapter of the Red Cross; [oth. writ.] Many stories covering background of family history, businesses, returned Vietnam veterans published in the Montauchesset Review, Fitchburg Sentinel, Leominster Enterprise, Harwich Oracle and Cape Cod Times; [pers.] Remembered by many to this day.; [a.] Harwich, MA

LABARRE, MATTHEW ANDRE
[b.] March 2, 1976, Fort Benton, MT; [p.] Jean-Ernest and Susan K. LaBarre; [ed.] Fort Benton High School and Highwood High School. Currently a student at the University of Montana, Missoula, MT; [occ.] Student at U. of M.; [hon.] Dean's List at the U. of M.; [a.] Fort Benton, MT

LAJOIE, RICHARD
[b.] July 1, 1949, E. Tempelton, MA; [ch.] Three; [occ.] Teacher; [pers.] My poems and thoughts come from my dreams and life experiences.; [a.] Fitchburg, MA

LAMB, LLOYD E.
[pen.] Wenllo Burlam; [b.] Febraury 21, 1936; Jefferson, TX. [p.] Tom Burnett, Virginia Rhodes (step father-Robert Lamb); [m.] Gwen Anderson; August 6, 1994; [ch.] L. Michael, Deborah L., Robert C., Elizabeth MA., step- Fred Anderson, David Harvey; [ed.] I was educated in country schools, 1 room, finished my education, H.S. adult ed classes and B.S. in Admin from City University; [occ.] Disability Pension, but volunteer as Lay Associate Pastor; [memb.] Was member of DECA in College. Former Kiwanis member; [hon.] Dean's List, Nursing Home Administrator, Itinerant Preacher for Seventh-Day Adventist Church; [oth.writ.] "Sowing Seeds For God," in small work newsletter entitled Southwestern Union conference "LE" Newsletter; [pers.] I strive to show moral and spiritual values as well as historical significance in some of my writings. I have enjoyed the Great Poets of America and have been much influenced by them; [a.] Morristown, AZ.

LAMONTAGNE, KIM A.
[pen.] Kim Ann Royce; [b.] October 22, 1963, Methuen, MA; [p.] Josephine and Jeremiah Kennelly; [m.] Sylvain Lamontagne, September

15, 1984; [ch.] Roscoe, Riley, and Jake; [ed.] Salem High School, Institute of Children's Literature; [occ.] Writer, Mother and Wife; [memb.] United Methodist Church, PTA Volunteer for South School in Londonderry; [oth. writ.] What's In A Name, Josephine, Young Jake (unpublished); [pers.] I write what I feel. A pen and paper is a tool. Which opens a window to our soul. Removing our deepest thoughts and feelings.; [a.] Londonderry, NH

LAMPE, ALAN
[b.] May 17, 1972, Bridgeport, CT; [p.] Andrew Lampe, Alice Lampe; [ed.] Springdale High, Northwest Arkansas Community College; [occ.] Computer Technician; [memb.] Society for Creative Anachronism, Inc. (SCA); [oth. writ.] Fictional story published in an SCA monthly newsletter; [a.] Springdale, AR

LANGMAN, SHANNON
[b.] December 31, 1980, Back of a green beat-up dodge; [p.] Bob and Sharon Langman; [pers.] My poems form during rainstorms, and when faced with trembling insecurities.; [a.] Midvale, UT

LANGSTON, JOHN GABRIEL
[b.] March 21, 1984, Lucedale, MS; [p.] Missy Byrd, William Langston; [ed.] 7th Grade; [occ.] Student; [pers.] I am inspired by the Counting Crows music. I strive to do my best in everything. I want to let people know the talent God's given me, and hope someday to publish my own book.; [a.] Lucedale, MS

LAPORTE, BETHANY
[pen.] Bepi; [b.] May 17, 1982, Pawtucket, RI; [p.] Louis and Karen LaPorte; [ed.] 9th Grade in Davies School. Still attending; [occ.] Student; [memb.] East Prov. Bowling League; [hon.] Honor Roll, Bowling Trophy, Science Fair Honors, Young Authorship, Attendance, Jumpy Rope for Heart Award, Junior Achievement Award, DARE Certificate of Achievement, ReadaThon Certificate; [oth. writ.] Young authors books: 1. The Princes Who Didn't Want To Marry The Prince - 1st place, 2. Where Did The Principal Go? - 1st place, 3. The Wishing Star - 1st place; [pers.] In every poem I write, I always write them with feeling. Every one of them has a meaning behind them. Everyone of them is a little piece of my life.; [a.] Pawtucket, RI

LAUERSDORF, JACKELYN
[b.] August 14, 1969, Stamford, CT; [p.] Oho and Helen Lauersdorf; [ed.] Greenwich High School, Katherine Gibbs School, Marymount College; [occ.] Print/Production Assistant; [memb.] First Luther Church, Women's League, Tres Dias of Fairfield County, MS Society, YGOP of Greenwich; [hon.] Golden Key - Key Club Award, Excellence Award, Wood Logan Associates; [pers.] Sometimes, it is a curse, other times it is a blessing. But always, writing is a gift.; [a.] Stamford, CT

LAUMANN, KAREN ELIZABETH MCLENDON
[b.] November 23, 1953, MD; [p.] Shirley and Kenneth McLendon; [m.] Vernon, May 27, 1972; [ch.] Kandice and Vernon; [ed.] Western High School, UMCP; [occ.] Technical Typist, Scientific, UMCP; [oth. writ.] Mothers Prayer, In Tune With Time; [pers.] I find the net when used improperly, and with deceit to be a very scary place. Chat rooms can be deceptive.; [a.] Baltimore, MD

LAUREANO, BEATRIZ
[b.] February 6, 1987, Hartford, CT; [p.] Francisco and Enid Laureano; [ed.] 4th Grade - St. Augustine Catholic School, Hfd., CT; [occ.] Student; [memb.] YWCA, Guakia - Arts School, Jo-Ann Ferrero School of Dance; [hon.] Student of the Month (3 times), Jo-Ann Ferrero's School of Dance Five Years Trophy; [oth. writ.] Several poems and short stories.; [pers.] I write when I get an idea in my mind.; [a.] Hartford, CT

LAURIN, JEANNE H.
[pen.] "Jeanne"; [b.] June 16, 1954, Grants Pass, OR; [p.] Father: Leslie Charles Black, Mother: Helen Jean; [m.] Fiancee: James R. Crawford; [ch.] Clarylynda (daughter) and Christopher (son); [ed.] "Artistic School of Hair Design", Certified Nurses Aid, took Creative Writing, Crescent City Cal. College of the Redwoods"; [occ.] Courtesy Clerk University Center, Safeway/Clerk for Cinnibuns; [hon.] 7th Place in Oil Pastel Design in 8th Grade/ South Jr. High Sch., Grants Pass, Oregon; [oth. writ.] "Image in the Mirror", "After the Facts", "Burgany Rose My Ballad", "High Society", "After the Facts"; [pers.] It's never so dark that light is not found at the end of the tunnel of life, only a new beginning soars from his feathered twig nest, wings in the breath.; [a.] Anchorage, AK

LAW; BRUCE N.
[b.] November 23, 1958, Providence; [p.] Elizabeth Brunnell; [ed.] U.R.I., C.C.R.I.; [occ.] Student; [memb.] A.S.M.R., S.A.E.; [hon.] R.I. Honor Society; [oth. writ.] Spirit Of The Stars; [pers.] I would like to have my complete poem's published in summer day.; [a.] Pawtucket, RI

LAW, LONNIE
[b.] January 31, 1982; Thomasville; [p.] Martha Ann Tyler; [ch.] 4; [ed.] 9th grade currently; [occ.] Student at Brookwood; [oth.writ.] A lot of untitled ones (untitled poems.); [pers.] Whenever I write a poem it is not something I work on for long periods of time. I mostly write to fulfill my audience, although this is my first real audience; [a.] Oclocknee, GA.

LEAK, ANNA MAXINE HOLT
[pen.] Anna "Maxine" Holt Leak; [b.] February 28, 1928, Jefferson Co, IN; [p.] Allen L. Holt/ Leah V. Barber Holt; [m.] Ralph Bauer Leak, June 9, 1968; [ed.] Hi-School Grad. N. Madison; [occ.] Retired from the American Legion Nat'l. Hq.; [memb.] Amer. Legion Aux. Victory Memorial U.M. Church Int'l. Soc. of Poets; [oth. writ.] Several other poems; [pers.] That I might be a true witness to my faith and that I always keep a promise.; [a.] Indianapolis, IN

LEAN, TAMMI
[b.] September 27, 1962, Cobourg, ON; [p.] PerryLean, Jim and Diane Shields; [ch.] Jessica Diane; [ed.] CDCI East High School, Cobourg, Ont., Loyalist College, Belleville, Ont., Canada; [occ.] Single Mother of One; [memb.] Volunteer at my daughters School (Thomas Gillbard PS, Cobourg, Ont., Canada); [hon.] Singing awards at the Public School Level; [oth. writ.] Written many poems but for personal viewing only; [pers.] I have been greatly influenced by the love of my family. All my poems are the reflections of my feelings; [a.] Cobourg, Ontario, Canada

LEBLANC, EDDIE
[pen.] Kot; [b.] September 27, 1978, Lafayette, LA; [p.] Ann Jones; [ed.] High School Senior; [occ.] Student; [memb.] Key, Spanish Club, Remote Sensing Team, Black Belt Karate, NAUI Scuba Diver, CPR, First Aid, Safety, Rescuer, Instructor Training, Lifeguard, Water Quality Monitor, Student Government.; [hon.] Eagle Scouts, National Honor and Math Society, Who's Who Among Amer. H.S. Students (3 yrs.), Citizenship Award, Boy Scout and Bishop Award, Maceo and NEDT Test Award, Football Captain, National Leadership, Law, Stateman invited participant.; [pers.] Keep your eye on the summit - not its distance!; [a.] Beaumont, TX

LEMPGES, THOMAS E.
[b.] May 28, 1926, Dunkirk, NY; [p.] Theodore and Lucy Lempges; [m.] Caryl Norton Lempges, September 6, 1947; [ch.] Claudia and Gerry; [ed.] B.S. ME; [occ.] Retired; [a.] Oswego, NY

LESSARD, CHRISTINA
[pen.] Krisci or C. M. Lessard; [b.] November 2, 1982, Waterville, ME; [p.] Kathleen Lessard and Alan Lessard; [ed.] I am going to school in Winslow, Maine. I am in the eighth grade.; [occ.] I am currently in school.; [hon.] I have gotten community awards, spelling bee awards, and sport awards.; [oth. writ.] I write poems and short stories in my free time.; [pers.] Think positive! It will get you further in life!; [a.] Winslow, ME

LEWIS, EDWARD
[b.] March 12, 1925, Yancey Co., NC; [p.] Kimsey M. Lewis, Myrtle Lewis; [m.] Irene R. Lewis (Deceased), April 22, 1959; [ch.] Daniel M. and James E. Lewis; [ed.] Public Schools, no college; [occ.] Retired from Greyhound Corp, "Driver"; [memb.] VFW, USS Colorado Alum. Assn.; [oth. writ.] "A very special day" other poems not published.; [pers.] Dedicated to the family of "Irene" also her two grandchildren. Andrew M. Lewis and Kimberly M. Lewis.; [a.] Ruther Glen, VA

LEWIS, HEATHER
[pen.] H. L. "Dreamer"; [b.] June 16, 1970, Modesto, CA; [p.] Geneva and Raymond Lewis; [ch.] Alexis Carmelita Lewis; [ed.] K-8, Salida Union School in Salida CA., 14 yrs. high school Modesto High, in Modesto CA., MUC, 1 year in Modesto Basic Training Course; [occ.] Homemaker, and mother and all time forever "Dreamer!!"; [memb.] None that compare and relate to writing and poems. This is my first time out at giving my thoughts and poems a chance to be known and enjoyed to all who wish.; [hon.] None, only awards and honors from friends and family who honor my love and respect for all, and awards I receive every day from my daughter Alexis and my family just by standing by my side and never losing sight of the true meaning of honor award - every person deserves both.; [oth. writ.] Poems, only for my self enjoyment and learning tool. This is my first poem that received honor and award. "Love" I wrote a poem in grammer school and it too received an award, but only a general school award.; [pers.] Forever keep reaching for the stars and one's dreams, for all dreamers need starts to keep our future bright and very clear of one's paths.; [a.] Salida, CA

LEWIS, SERGIO
[b.] March 4, 1954; El Paso, TX; [p.] Erasmo and Alicia Lewis; [m.] Irene; March 31, 1990; [ch.] Erick (13), Joshua (6), Savannah (5); [ed.] Irvin High School, El Paso, TX. Texas Real Estate Lic., Inactive; [occ.] Co-owner, Lewis Body and Custom Shop Inc.; [memb.] Charter 1993-94 President, El Paso Sunrise Rotary, Pres. (EPISD) 1995-96 Texas School Board Assn., Past Pres., Texas Council of Urban Sch. Dist's, President, (Vatto) vocational apprenticeship technical training organization (non-profit); [oth.writ.] Several poems published in local newspapers. Heed the cause, others - Simplicity and elegance, Irene, Aroused, Natures - Beauty, Pleasurable madness; [pers.] Why wonder incredibilities, tomorrow never comes ungotten; [a.] El Paso, TX.

LEXUAN, THUY
[b.] April 25, 1927, Vietnam; [m.] Thin Thi Dang, September 7, 1957; [ch.] Phuong-Tram, Phuong-Thoa, Tung, Thach; [ed.] Agrege of International Accounting Systems, 1970; [occ.] Financial Control Systems Developer; [memb.] Secretary General/Puginier Alumni, Saigon, Vietnam, 1970-73. Comptroller/Association of Vietnamese Scientist, Saigon, Vietnam, 1970-75. International Platform Association/International Academy of Poets, USA. International Society of Poets/Distinguished Member, USA.; [hon.] Award of Excellence, US Library of Congress, USA. IBC Decree of Merit/Outstanding Contribution to Financial Control Systems, Cambridge, London, England. IBC Golden Medal/International Leaders in Achievement, Cambridge, London, England. Citation of Meritorious Achievement/Transcendental Poetry, Cambridge, London, England.; [oth. writ.] Books: Kim-Van-Kieu I, English Translation and Commentaries, Editions 1963, 1968, Saigon, Vietnam. Principles of Advanced Bookkeeping and Accounting, Edition 1971, Saigon, Vietnam. How to Establish a Powerful Chart of Accounts for Business Enterprises, Edition 1971, Saigon, Vietnam. How to Establish a Powerful General Ledger for a Government, Editions 1981, 1993, 1995, Virginia, USA. The Super Revelation, revealing important events related to direct enlightenments, the Coming of Christ, the Truth of Creation of the Universe, Evolutions and Divine Incarnations, editions 1989, 1991, 1993, 1995, Virginia, USA. The Prajnaparamita Sutra, experimental interpretation of the Highest Key of Wisdom, Editions 1989, 1991, 1993, Virginia, USA. Kim-Van-Kieu II, Revised English Translation and Commentaries, award of Excellence, US Library of Congress, Editions 1992, 1993, 1995, USA. Poetry: The Soul of Poetry inside Kim-Van-Kieu, (5410-verse) Poetic Version and Commentaries 1995, Virginia USA. Dawnlight, a collection of my short poems (English, French, Vietnamese). NLP/Whispers at Dusk, USA, NLP/The Best Poems of 1997, USA, NLP/The Sound of Poetry Album, USA, NLP/A Prism of Thoughts, USA, NLP/The Scenic Route, USA, Internet/The International Poetry Hall of Fame, USA. Songs: The Song of My Love, Star Route USA album, AmeRecord, Hollywood, USA, 1997. Out of a Dream, Star Route USA album, AmeRecord, Hollywood, USA 1997.; [pers.] Christ came at last, manifesting His presence since September 1977, with a cosmic consciousness encompassing the whole Truth of Creation and Evolution of the Universe before the and after its formation. Christ is a sacred title used by the empyrean authorities to designated the level of Omniscience acquired by the successful incarnated yogi. Christ exists now, not before, in the land where the eagle hunts and soars free from fencing bounds, not as phantom of some gas smoke from mind baloney, but through union, the highest wisdom, well hidden inside the Trinity: "Man can unite his individual soul, the Son, in full with the Universal Soul, The Father, for the Holy Spirit, the Creator, to become his own Body of Light, so immense in size, so small and low in density, so pure and so clear in purity." The Heavens no longer are the highest. Higher than the High is He who has conquered the whole universe, mapping it inside His pervading Light. The physical world will change, for a millennium, from an abyss of darkish holes full of webs of profane intrigues and tricky goals, into a cherished plane for the wise and witty to develop their souls and move for sanctity.; [a.] Alexandra, VA

LEY, BETTY J.
[b.] July 14, 1951; Hollywood, CA; [p.] Morris G. and Dorathy E. Lansbery; [m.] Fred M. Ley; February 7, 1976; [ch.] (foster) Tina Marie, Suzy Marie; [ed.] San Fernando High, Los Angeles Mission College, Los Angeles Social Services, classes, American Red Cross, classes; [occ.] Amway distributor, home health caregiver volunteer, teachers aide volunteer; [memb.] Amway Corp., American Red Cross, Girl Scouts, San Fernando Valley Foster Parent Association P.T.A., L.A. Streets transporation council with the Bernstein; [hon.] 3 teachers aide volunteer awards from local elem. school, 7 adult Girl Scout awards, 2 Foster Parent Assoc. awards; [oth.writ.] Poetry, but only for my family and friends, and a couple of poems printed in my high school paper 28 years ago; [pers.] I was inspired to write "Understanding Grief" after my mother passed away. I love helping others, working with children, baking, crafts, reading self-help motivational books and spending time with my family; [a.] Mission Hills, CA.

LIBERTY, AMANDA
[b.] March 6, 1985, Biddeford, ME; [p.] John and Debbie Liberty; [ed.] Currently in sixth grade at Eastland Elementary; [hon.] Award 1st memorized book award ribbon, Award Excellence trophy, high honors for school, B.U.G. award (Bring Up Grade); [a.] Corinna, ME

LIEBERT, JASON E.
[b.] July 17, 1979, Columbus, OH; [occ.] Student, Worthington Kilbourne High School; [a.] Worthington, OH

LIEN, KARA
[b.] December 25, 1985; Langdon, ND; [p.] Charles and Lynn Lien; [ed.] 5th grade so far; [occ.] student; [hon.] Honor Roll, Science Fair; [oth.writ.] I've written several poems for special people, when people feel "down" I write them a special poem; [pers.] When I write them, it makes me feel good, when it makes them smile; [a.] Walhalla, ND.

LIGHTELL, JONATHAN
[b.] December 19, 1988, Slidell, LA; [p.] Lester and Mary Lightell; [ed.] Home-schooled, Third Grade; [occ.] Student; [memb.] New Jerusalem Praise and Worship Center, Slidell Christian Home Education

Fellowship (SCHEF); [hon.] Bowling Trophies (4), Baseball Trophies (2), Presidential Fitness Challenge Winner - 2 years; [pers.] I am influenced by my mother's poems and songs.; [a.] Slidell, LA

LIGHTFOOT, VERA
[b.] February 27, 1954, Kemmerer, WY; [p.] Jay Floyd, Ginny York; [m.] Mike Lightfoot, August 29, 1975; [ch.] Jonni Belynda, Billie Lee; [ed.] Kemmerer High School; [occ.] Housewife; [memb.] Secretary of Kemmerer Ladies Auxiliary #2341 Fraternal Order of Eagles; [oth. writ.] Editor and publisher of "The Eagle Feather" a newsletter of Kemmerer Aerie #2341 F.D.E.; [pers.] I love nature and want it to remain in its glorious stature to be viewed for all time; [a.] Kemmerer, WY

LIM, EILEEN A.
[b.] October 23, 1984, Sacramento, CA; [p.] Lina Lim and Roland Lim; [ed.] Morada Junior High Middle School; [memb.] Morada Reading Society, School Site Council, San Joaquin County Middle School Honor Orchestra; [pers.] I enjoy writing stories and poems for people to read and feel happy about. I'm sure this book is a giant step towards this.; [a.] Stockton, CA

LINDSAY, DEIRDRE
[pen.] "Deej" or Dear; [b.] February 5, 1958, Brooklyn; [p.] Shelley and Theodore Lindsay; [ch.] Terrin J. Lindsay; [ed.] George W. Wingate H.S. College of New Rochelle (BA) Long Island University (MA); [occ.] Nynex - Representative; [memb.] The Glorious Church of God in Christ, The Christian Life Center; [hon.] Received many awards for writing and poetry including Women's Special Awards. Mayor's Poetry Award, College Recognition Poetry Award, High School honors in writing award - Literary Award; [oth. writ.] "Love and Death", "Fear", "Understanding", "A Relationship", "From Here To There"; [pers.] My ultimate goal is to write many poems and books to help educate our teenagers and many others. People who are confused about life!; [a.] Brooklyn, NY

LINDSEY, DOUG
[pen.] Doug Lindsey; [b.] April 7, 1943, Sour Lake, TX; [p.] Ollie and Estelle Lindsey; [m.] Kathleen, March 19, 1965; [ch.] Victoria, Michael, Scotty; [ed.] High School; [occ.] Baker; [memb.] Union Local #85, Baker's Union; [hon.] Wrote an article for Reminisce Magazine Coached Little League Baseball; [oth. writ.] Wrote an article for Reminisce Magazine; [pers.] I always try and treat people good. Cause life is uncertain, and death si for sure.; [a.] Fresno, CA

LINDSTROM, LISA MICHELE
[b.] August 8, 1961, Minneapolis, MN; [p.] Ward and Carol Engebrit; [m.] Jeff, July 25, 1992; [ed.] German, Literature, Grammar, Charles A. Lindbergh Sr. H.S., 1 year U of Minnesota, Literature; [occ.] Poet, Publisher, Housewife, Logistical Events; [memb.] Charter Member All American Eagle Racers, Distinguished Member International Society of Poets; [hon.] Over 20 Editor's Choice Awards from the National Library of Poetry, 2 Poet of Merits Awards from International Society of Poets and I was nominated and accepted a web page with The International Poetry Hall of Fame.; [oth. writ.] "Inadequate Justice - Beginning Healing Through Poetry," 1st book. Publishing "Ob-

serving And Feeling While I am Healing," and I am presently writing "Slamming The Ancient Door Forevermore To A Distant Shore"; [pers.] My personal experiences drive me to write most of my poetry. I also like the subjects of politics, nature, culture and people.; [a.] Yorba Linda, CA

LINNEY, MICHELLE
[b.] November 28, 1979, San Diego, CA; [p.] Carol Linney, Raul Lopez; [ed.] Junior in High School (Hilltop High); [oth. writ.] I have been writing poetry since I was 6 years old.; [pers.] This poem is dedicated to the woman and made me the person I am today, my mother!; [a.] Chula Vista, CA

LIPSCOMB, JANELLE ANN
[pen.] Janelle Lipscomb; [b.] October 5, 1981, Jackson, MS; [p.] Mr. W. B. Lipscomb Jr., Mrs. Jan T. Hederman; [ed.] 10th Grade Jackson Preparatory School; [occ.] Student; [memb.] First Baptist Church Youth Team School Band Guard Captain; [hon.] First place in 1995 Mississippi Poetry contest category #8, Level 3 printed in Fledglings 1995; [oth. writ.] A book of unpublished prayers and poems, free lance; [pers.] I write for expression - one of the most beautiful things in the world; [a.] Jackson, MS

LIPSEY, BENJAMIN
[b.] May 6, 1959, Memphis, TN; [p.] Charlene Lipsey and Benjamin Jones; [ed.] Whitehaven High School, Memphis Tenn.; [occ.] Writer; [memb.] Veteran of the U.S. Army Boys Scouts Troop 511; [hon.] Honorable Discharge, Basic Leadership Course; [oth. writ.] The Secretary, Ups and Downs, Much Love For You On Mother's Day, Letting You Know, Ghetto Child, My Friends at the Dentist Office; [pers.] All trials in life shall pass.; [a.] Bedford, MA

LOGAN, BARBRIE
[b.] May 4, 1955, Detroit, MI; [p.] Mr. and Mrs. Paul and Elizabeth Stewart; [ed.] B.A.-Michigan College- Oakland Police Academy-1985; [occ.] Police Officer, Wayne County Sheriff's Department; [oth. writ.] Happy Father's Day Dad, Ordie My Love or Mistake, several poems unpublished.; [pers.] Our good-bye gift. Mark, our eldest of eight siblings, started his exciting career as a Detroit super cop, was recruited by the Department of Alcohol, Tobacco and Firearms, and has earned several promotions with transfers. We honor him, rarely.; [a.] Detroit, MI

LOMBARDI, ROBERT
[pen.] Robert Lombard; [b.] December 2, 1961, Far Rockaway, NY; [p.] Robert Lombardi Sr., Patricia Lombardi; [ch.] Dillon Robert; [ed.] Plainedge High (N. Massapequa, NY), D.K. Myers Trout Fishing School (Dakota, WI); [occ.] Sales Manager "MSC Paper Products" Hillside N.J.; [memb.] "Amnesty Int'l", "Wayne Newton Fan Club"; [oth. writ.] Collected works "Killing The Day", to be published in 1998; [pers.] "I lived in freedom for two years... and now I'm back".; [a.] Roselle Park, NJ

LONG, LORI MAE
[b.] June 18, 1965; Buffalo, NY; [p.] Lester and Sarah Long; [ed.] Iroquois Central High; [occ.] Shipping Clerk; [pers.] I believe that writing is the purest form of self expression. Your feelings flow through the pen and you've found total freedom; [a.] Elma, NY.

LOPEZ, ELIZABETH ASHLEY
[b.] March 15, 1959; Laredo, TX; [p.] (deceased) Guadalupe S. Moran and Dr. J. Bodilla; [ch.] Chris, Adam, Elizabeth; [ed.] Doctor of Metaphysics, Doctor of Theology, United High, Carroll High, Val Modesto California; [occ.] Self- Employed, Doctor of Methaphysics, Doctor of Theology; [memb.] American Society of Notaries, Reverend Member UAL; [hon.] Congressional Awards; [pers.] A Passion to Live, I believe in God. I believe in that we all strive, regardless of the obstacles, we can climb mountains, slowly but firmly; [a.] Cypress, TX.

LOPEZ, JOSE R.
[b.] N.Y.C.; [m.] Bok Soon; [a.] Bronx, NY

LORUSSO, JOSEPH C.
[pen.] Jose LoRusso; [b.] August 9, 1960, Boston, MA; [p.] Mr. and Mrs. Joseph LoRusso; [ed.] I have a Bachelor of Science Degree in Physical Education. I also have a Masters Degree in Education. In addition a High School G.E.D.; [occ.] Program Director for the McColl Branch YMCA, Lincoln, RI; [memb.] Eastern New England Baseball Umpires Association, Association of Professional Directors, YMCA of the USA, Reebok Instructor Alliance; [hon.] Executive Development Program, Eastern Mass., YMCAs Management Resource Center Alexander Scholarship Loan Fund, U.S. Area International Association of Y's Men's Clubs, Senior Director Status YMCA of the USA, YMCA Membership Service Training, Director Active Older Adults; [oth. writ.] I do not have any other writings except Programming in the 90's and Beyond - Master of Education Thesis.; [pers.] My professional goal is to further my career with the Young Men's Christian Association - YMCA. In doing this is to improve the quality of life for individuals and families through strong membership/programs.; [a.] Somerville, MA

LOVE, MICHELLE
[b.] April 21, 1966, Dunedin, FL; [p.] Robert and June Frost; [m.] John Love, December 3, 1982; [ch.] Jenifer and Sarah Love; [ed.] Dunedin Elem., Dunedin Middle, Dunedin High, High School electives in creative writing.; [occ.] Housewife and Mother; [oth. writ.] Several other pieces not published as of yet.; [pers.] For as long as I can remember, I've always loved poetry and have always had a strong desire to express myself through writing. My life-long ambition is to someday write professionally, but no matter what the future holds, my desire and love for writing will always stay with me.; [a.] Largo, FL

LOVE, NANCY
[b.] November 1963, Neodesha, KS; [p.] Bob and Rose Carrier; [m.] Ken Love, December 18, 1981; [ch.] Nick, Amber, and Alek; [ed.] Sooner High, Bartlesville, OK; [occ.] Elementary Teacher; [memb.] Greenwood Baptist Church; [pers.] My Poems have been written to release inner feelings. Usually it's a stress outlet for me.; [a.] Humble, TX

LOWERY, MARGARET BEECHER
[pen.] Meg Lowery; [b.] December 4, 1981, Houston, TX; [p.] Joseph and Jane Lowery; [ed.] Lanier Middle School, Houston, Kelly High School, Beaumont; [occ.] Student; [memb.] Students Against Drunk Driving (SADD); [hon.] Best All Around - Lanier Middle School, April '97 "Splash of the

Month" on "A Little Poetry", Website for "Turbulence"; [oth. writ.] "A Little Poetry", an internet poetry site under "Poetry Puddles"; [pers.] "Words that enlighten are more precious than jewels" - Hazrat Inayat Khan; [a.] Beaumont, TX

LOZIC, REGINA
[b.] October 15, 1984; Montclair, CA; [p.] Nick Lozic and Melinda Lozic; [ed.] Lincoln Elementary School Newport Beach, Calif., Corona Del Mar High School Newport Beach, Calif; [occ.] Student 7th grade; [memb.] Los Angeles Macintosh Group (LAMG); [hon.] Daughters of the American Revolution Essay Winner- 5th grade; [oth.writ.] Essay on John Nancock; [a.] Newport Beach, CA.

LUEBBERS, DAREN L.
[pen.] Daren; [b.] October 30, 1976, Woodstock, IL; [p.] Karen and Phil Luebbers; [ed.] I graduated Wauconda High School 1995, I am now attending The Lary Grove Dance Academy, where I'm studying ballet, jazz, and modern dance; [occ.] Carpenter; [memb.] I am a member of The Lary Grove Dance Academy, also a member of Holy Cross Lutheran Church; [hon.] Having attended a servant event of Bethesda Lutheran Home I received "The Most Faithful Servant Award" after one year at The Dance Academy I've received The "1997 Spirit Award"; [oth. writ.] Include: "Mystical Progression", "Desolate Repeatedly", "Sensations to Phrases", "No Reverence", "Variant Pulses", "Furbishing the Scroll", "Tarry I", "Which I Proceed", "Each Excursion", "Melody Lane"; [pers.] I thank you for noticing my talents. I thank the Lord, for blessing me with such talents, and for all invocations he has granted us with. Amen God bless you all.; [a.] Fox River Grove, IL

LUTZ, EDMUND H.
[pen.] Ed Lutz (on occasion); [b.] January 12, 1916; Cleveland, OH; [p.] Ferd C. Lutz, Lydia Lutz; [m.] Betty T. Lutz; November 1, 1943; [ch.] Karen, Catherine, Deborah, Amy; [ed.] AB Western Reserve University; Casey Jones School of Aeronautics; USAF Pilot Training; [occ.] Retired, Cleveland Museum of Art; Retired, Lt. Col. USAF, Bomber Pilot and Photo Officer; [memb.] Past. Pres. In Plant Printing Mgnt. Assoc.; 8th Air Force Historical Society; 379th Bomb Group WWII Assoc.; the Retired Officers Assoc.; the Caterpillar Club; Trustee, Lake Shore Christian Church; [hon.] Top Class Award, Casey Jones School of Aeronautics; forty-two awards in national printing competitions; Roundtable Award, Champion International; [oth.writ.] Technical articles for InPlant Printer Magazine, several poems published in Air Corps flying school yearbooks; [pers.] I believe in hardwork ethic, raising a great family, the joy of accomplishment, and being grateful for the gifts of life; [a.] Euclid, OH.

LYNCH, JACQUELYN MICHELLE
[b.] September 7, 1981, Riverdale, GA; [p.] Christopher and Juanita Lynch; [ed.] Currently in tenth grade; [occ.] High School student; [memb.] Concert, Jazz, Marching and Symphonic bands. Science and Mathematics Academy of Benjamin E. Mays High School, Atl, GA; [hon.] Honor Roll, All American Scholar Award. Numerous Band Awards.; [oth. writ.] Two original short stories and one sonnet.; [a.] Riverdale, GA

LYNCH, PANSY ROSE
[b.] February 2, 1962, Wytheville, VA; [p.] Flora and Clarence Taylor; [m.] John D. Lynch, May 20, 1995; [ch.] Samantha and Mark; [occ.] Jewelry Sales Associate; [a.] Ashland, VA

LYNNE, VICTORIA
[pen.] VL; [b.] January 1, 1957; Williams MN; [p.] Marilyn and Dallas Murphy; [ch.] Amanda and Sabrina; [ed.] BS in Computer and Management Science, Metropolitan State College; [occ.] Senior Programmer Analyst, Access Graphics, Boulder Co; [pers.] I am a strong proponent of personal and spiritual growth, mentoring others, and doing what I can to make the world a better place to live; [a.] Broomfield, CO.

LYONS, GAIL
[b.] June 18, 1965, Michigan; [p.] James R. Lyons, Gloria J. Wisenbaugh and Gerald Wisenbaugh; [ch.] Laura Lee and Adam Gerard; [ed.] Fraser High School; [occ.] Homemaker and mother; [a.] Macomb cnty.] MI

MABATID, HEIDI F.
[b.] December 26, Cebu City, RP; [p.] Jose Knepp Mabatid, Lucia Flores Mabatid; [ed.] Doctor of Medicine; [occ.] General Surgeon; [hon.] B.S. (Premed) Magna Cum Laude, M.D. Cum Laude, Southwestern University; [oth. writ.] More unpublished poems, essays.; [pers.] I like reading John Donne and Emily Dickinson. To me, writing poetry is the soul's self-expression...; [a.] Converse, TX

MACDONALD, VERONIQUE MAES
[b.] November 10, 1961, Ghent, Belgium; [p.] Rene and Blanche Maes; [m.] Bill MacDonald, May 7, 1988; [ch.] Kelly (4), Michelle (2), Matthew (8 mo.); [ed.] Royal Athenaeum Welteren (Belgium), Regents College New York; [occ.] Mother, Student, Co-Owner of Fotomac (Scenic Photography); [pers.] Language is our main means of communication. We need to preserve and cultivate it.; [a.] Buellton, CA

MACK, JANELLE M.
[b.] March 4, 1967, Vincennes, IN; [p.] Gary and Wanda Onken; [m.] Joy R. Mack, March 6, 1992; [ch.] Victoria (5), Nicholas (3); [pers.] My poem was inspired by my daughter, Victoria, who weighed 1 lb. 9 oz., when she was born. My inspiration is my children. May they be forever happy and healthy.; [a.] Vincennes, IN

MACQUAIDE, MARYBETH
[pen.] MaryBeth MacQuaide; [b.] June 8, 1965, Montclair, NJ; [p.] Robert C. and M. Jean MacQuaide; [ch.] Afiya Sunshine; [ed.] Hanover Park High School, East Hanover, NJ; [occ.] Self-employed, company name 'Star Vessel', Poet and clairvoyant; [oth. writ.] 'The Power of Love'; [pers.] My poetry is a form of healing. It is a daily journey of my life, through it finding answers and solutions to every day situations. More than anything it inspires people to follow their dream and to live from the heart.; [a.] Asheville, NC

MAGUINESS, NANCY
[pen.] Nancy Maguiness; [b.] March 11, 1952; Chicago, IL; [p.] Elaine, Richard Maguiness; [m.] Divorced; January 30, 1971; [ch.] Mark and Timothy; [ed.] B.A. English, Master of Pastoral Studies, Loyola University Chicago; [occ.] Store owner and

hotel switchboard operator; [hon.] Voice of Democracy essay contest two times in high school; [oth writ.] My self-published book is called "Giving Back the Elements" ISBN-1-879260-19-0; [a.] Chicago, IL.

MAHANEY, JACKLYN SEYMOUR
[b.] October 28, 1968, Sioux City, IA; [m.] Tom Mahaney, April 28, 1989; [ch.] A 5 year old cocker spaniel named Abby; [ed.] B.A. California State University - Dominguez Hills, Carson, CA, Journalism major; [occ.] Major Account Executive, AT&T Wireless Services; [oth. writ.] Several other poems and the beginnings of a novel.; [pers.] A special thanks to a dear friend named Lonnie who introduce me to poetry many years ago...and to my husband, Tom, who has encouraged me to keep on writing!; [a.] Gilbert, AZ

MAHER, EDWARD F.
[pen.] Mid Evil Man, Eddie Caous; [b.] December 10, 1971; Glen Cove, NY; [p.] Edward and Theresa Maher; [ed.] High School Graduate; [occ.] Musician; [oth.writ.] About 1200 I'd say but they haven't been really shared; [pers.] Every one person renders his or her soul to be partially understand, then we begin again; [a.] Imperial Beach, CA.

MAINES, DANIEL WARD
[occ.] Singer/Song Writer/Poet/Musician/Plasterer; [oth.writ.] I am currently working toward finish my first anthology of poems and recording my first CD; [pers.] I strongly desire that mankind end war on love; [a.] Marion, IN.

MALDONADO, DIANA
[b.] December 7, 1938, Fulfurrias; [p.] Mrs. Guadalupe H. Maldonado; [ed.] Falfurrias High School, Texas A and I University; [occ.] Retired Teacher; [memb.] Texas State Teachers Association and Teacher Retirement System of Texas; [oth. writ.] I have a poem to be published.; [pers.] The early romantic poets have inspired me.; [a.] Falfurrias, TX

MANCINI, DARCI
[b.] March 18, 1980, Middletown, CT; [p.] Jan Shah and Andrew Mancini; [ed.] Holy Cross High School in Waterbury, CT; [occ.] Student; [hon.] Spanish Honor Society; [oth. writ.] Poetry; [pers.] The poems I have written reflect my experiences of the past and the experiences I hope to have in the future.; [a.] Oxford, CT

MANDELL, ANDREW P.
[pen.] Mr. Diabetes, when writing about diabetes, fitness health; [b.] April 23, 1945, Boston, MA; [p.] Arthur Mandell, Ida Young Mandell; [ed.] Newton South High School, Attended Suffolk University; [occ.] Executive Director, Defeat Diabetes Foundation, Inc. (A Non Profit Foundation); [memb.] The Human Race; [hon.] 1985 Science Magazine - Quations (TM) The Crossmath (R) Game Listed as one of the Best 15 Educational Products Recommended, also won: Parents Choice Award, Consumer Electronic Show Award - Strategy, National Crossmath (R) Puzzles Champion - 8 yrs., Martial Arts Black Belt Shaolin Kempo Karate, Jerome R. Dangel Music Award for Guitar Excellence - 1997; [oth. writ.] Crossmath (R) Puzzles Magazine, Quations (TM) The Crossmath (R) Game, Published by: Scholastic, Inc.,

Crossmath (R) Puzzles, Published by: APM Productions, The Mr. Diabetes (R) Home Fitnes Program, Published by: APM Productions, Micro Magic (R), Published by: Magic Master, Inc., various brochures and pamphlets; [pers.] The words I live by is a piece by Lloyd Shearer, Titled: Resolutions, I recommend it to everyone. Resolutions: No one will ever get out of this world alive. Resolve therefore to maintain a sense of values. Take care of yourself. Good health is everyone's major source of wealth. Without it, happiness is almost impossible. Resolve to be cheerful and helpful. People will repay you in kind. Avoid angry, abrasive persons. They are generally vengeful. Avoid zealous. They are generally humorless. Resolve to listen more and talk less. No one ever learns anything by talking. Be chary of giving advice. Wise men don't need it, and fools won't need it. Resolve to be tender with the young, compassionate with the aged, sympathetic with the striving, and tolerant of the weak and the wrong. Sometime in life you will have been all of these. Do not equate money with success. There are many successful money-makers who are miserable failures as human beings. What counts most about success is how a man achieves it.; [a.] Newton, MA

MANN, RUTH M.
[b.] March 18, 1969, Southfield, MI; [p.] Gerald Mann, Janice Warneking; [ch.] Brooke Mann; [ed.] Business Administration, Honolulu Community College; [occ.] Contracting Specialist, US Air Force; [memb.] US Air Force; [hon.] First Place - Talent Competition - US Air Force, "Tops and Blue" Mac Level, Category - Classifical Piano; [oth. writ.] Personal poems and piano music.; [pers.] I have written poems all of my life. This poem, "Farewell my Love", is a personal favorite.; [a.] Honolulu, HI

MANN, SOL
[b.] July 29, 1917, Chicago, IL; [p.] William Mann, Ida Marcus Mann; [m.] Lillian Mann, January 24, 1943; [ch.] Dr. David Mann, Allan Mann; [ed.] Hyde Park High (Chicago), Wilson Jr. College (Chicago) U.C.L.A. - BE U.S.C. Master; [occ.] Retired (Educator-Administrator) Psychologist-Speech-Therapist); [memb.] U.S.C. and U.C.L.A. Alumni AARP - American Speech and hearing Assoc., EDUCARE - CTA, NR&A - Phi Beta Kappa; [hon.] Patriotic Poems placed in Statue Liberty Museum - U.S. Congressional Record - John F. Kennedy Library - Martin Luther King Jr. Foundation - Guest Speaker at Ceremony in Calif. - Establishing the Martin Luther King Holiday in Sacramento - Made Poetic Presentation to Coretta King in Los Angeles in 1968; [oth. writ.] "Selection and Evaluation of Teachers" - "An American Speaks", "A Collection of Patriotic Poems", (Health Play) "Candy Bar Martin", "Classroom Organization and Management Techniques"; [pers.] My writings serve as a vehicle of releasing my bursting souls desire to express my love for nature and all mankind - striving always to be courageous to speak out for truth, justice and freedom for all who inhabit the earth - recognizing always the truly insignificance of man in this vast universe - knowing also, that this encompassing love which will be ever enduring is truly a reflection of God.; [a.] Laguna Hills, CA

MARC, MICHAEL
[b.] July 28, 1955, Chicago, IL; [p.] Chester J. and Lena C.; [m.] Nancy E., May 12, 1979; [ch.] Michael

T. and Matthew T.; [ed.] Associate Degree, Traffic and Transportation Management from Triton College, Bachelor of Science in Business Administration, Elmhurst College, with honors.; [occ.] Distribution Center Manager; [pers.] I believe that we should think before we act or speak, and then confirm understanding.; [a.] Naperville, IL

MARCHUK, PATTY
[b.] March 13, 1968, Newark, NJ; [p.] Geraldine Badawi (Mom); [ed.] Harrison High School, Jackson Memorial High, Ocean County Vo-Tech, Jackson Community School; [occ.] Cosmetologist/ Singer; [hon.] English/Writing Singing, Music Instrumental; [oth. writ.] Poems in school journal.; [pers.] My motivation comes from within myself. I write about things I have experienced throughout my life and things that touch my heart.; [a.] Jackson, NJ

MARINO, JEANNA DIANE
[b.] December 1, 1976, Fontana, CA; [ed.] 1995 graduate of Hesperia High School; [hon.] Honor Roll and Dean's List; [pers.] Poetry has always been an escape, and the emotions of my life. I strive to be the best I can in life, and never take anything for granted.; [a.] Hesperia, CA

MARJAMA, DENISE M.
[b.] January 7, 1962, Santa Rosa, CA; [p.] Dennis Kitchens and Dorothy Baldwin; [ch.] Nicole, Brendan and Jenea Marjama; [ed.] General Education Courses at a local Jr. College and Certified by The American Association of Medical Assistants, as a C.M.A.; [occ.] 1. Currently employed as a Certified Medical Assistant for Dr. Jerald Jarrett, Orthopedic Surgeon, 2. I also own my own business called, "Advanced Medical Transcription"; [hon.] Inspirational People: Two very special people who have inspired me and deserve heartfelt recognition are: My Grandmother, Eileen Rose and my sister, Michelle Moore.; [oth. writ.] Poems entitled: Mother, Friend and Grandpa, published thru Illiad Press, 1997.; [pers.] That I may make a positive difference, in the lives of people who pass my way.; [a.] Paradise, CA

MARKEY, DON
[b.] April 18, 1968, Port Chester, NY; [p.] Don Markey, Gail Markey; [ed.] Westhill High School Boston College Brian Utting School of Massage; [occ.] Case Manager for Homeless Men; [hon.] Recipient of American Massage therapy association foundation scholarship; [oth. writ.] Unpublished poems and song lyrics.; [pers.] Philosophy's best when put to the test.; [a.] Seattle, WA

MARKOVICH, SUSAN M.
[b.] January 2, 1955; Hammond, IN; [p.] Thomas and Josephine Boren; [m.] Mark Markovich; January 12, 1973; [ch.] Shannon and Jenna; [ed.] Some college and trade school; [occ.] Homemaker, mom, grandmother of 3, writer; [memb.] I belong to my church and Catholic school organization, numerous police, veteran's and abused children's organizations; [hon.] 3rd poem published won a lot of awards in school, scouts, successful marriage (27 years) and two great kids and 3 grandkids; [oth.writ.] "1996 Eastern semi-finals Bulls Vs Orlando" other poems, a short story and a song; [pers.] If in any way, I've made anyone smile when they've read something I've written, then it's all worth it!; [a.] Hammond, IN.

MARROW, JENNIFER
[b.] March 15, 1980, Riverton, WY; [p.] William Marrow, Kimberly Marrow; [ed.] Washington High School; [occ.] Student; [hon.] Honor Roll, 3 California golden state exams (school recognition), Caravana Mexicana, student of the week; [pers.] Why I love to write my poems it shows what's in my heart it expresses all my feelings in every word and part.; [a.] Brentwood, CA

MARSH, CHERYL
[pen.] Cherylabina; [b.] September 13, 1979, Tuskegee, AL; [p.] Evon May Marsh and Aston Marsh; [ed.] Miami Dade Community College, St. Hilda's Diocesan High School (Jamaica), Columbus Preparatory School (Jamaica); [occ.] Student; [pers.] Success is not the key to happiness but, happiness is the key to success.; [a.] Miramar, FL

MARSHALL, MELISSA
[pen.] Missy Wagle; [b.] December 13, 1968, Cape Girardeau, MO; [p.] Judy Keown-Wagle, Stacie K. Wagle; [m.] Robert L. Marshall I, July 21, 1991; [ch.] Kristin and Bobby Lee; [ed.] Van Duyn Elementary South Vermilion Middle and High School Indiana Business College Assoc. Degree-Business Management; [occ.] Accounting Clerk Jr. Chevrolet, Inc. Clinton in President-American Cancer Society-Vermilion CO.; [memb.] Dean's List - I.B.C.; [pers.] Learn to appreciate don't take things for granted.; [a.] Clinton, IN

MARSTERS, MICHAEL S.
[pen.] Michael S. Marsters; [b.] June 26, 1976, Longview, WA; [p.] Heather and Alan Marsters; [ed.] Negligible Formal Education; [occ.] Waste Technician; [pers.] Anything pretentious is worth a second look.; [a.] Bothell, WA

MARSTON, MICKEY
[b.] November 10, 1953, Nashville, TN; [occ.] Accountant; [pers.] I hope this will be a beginning, for me. One day I want to write children's books.; [a.] Nashville, TN

MARTELLY, RACHEL
[b.] Fall River, MA; [p.] Elizabeth and Paul Martelly; [occ.] Student - Grade six; [hon.] Luther student of the month award certificate of Excellence for school work. Sportmanship Award Theatrical workshop. Winner in National Dare Day Program. Ballet and Drama Reviews. Babysitters Certificate.; [pers.] My best friend died, but he will never be forgotten. A scholarship has been established in his memory. Bone marrow transplant clinics are being held through Michael's Fund which perhaps may save another person's life. It was too late for him. I miss and love him so!; [a.] Swansea, MA

MARTIN, THERESA M.
[b.] October 25, 1980, Lancaster, PA; [p.] Julie and Charlie Martin; [ed.] Sacred Heart of Jesus School (grade school), Class of 1999 at Lancaster Catholic High School; [occ.] Full time student, part time lifeguard; [memb.] Member of Sacred Heart of Jesus, Roman Catholic Church, Serteen, Larc, Respect Life, Student Ambassadors, Rockville teen board, Special Olympics Coach, CCD teacher Youth Group member, Volunteer with UCP, SPRC, June Smith, United Support Group.; [hon.] Nomination for the 1997 Jefferson award and Recipient of the Lancaster Junior League - Deb Altman Service

Award - 1997; [oth. writ.] No other published writings.; [pers.] As a young person I try hard to learn from my experiences, except my failures and try again. Many people have greatly influenced me and I would love to give back to the community what they have given to one - a spirit and drive for life.; [a.] Lancaster, PA

MARTIN III, CLAYTON
[b.] April 5, 1948, Lancaster, PA; [p.] Clayton Martin Jr., Ruby Talley Martin; [ed.] Franklin and Marshall College, Millersville University of Penna., Penn State University; [occ.] Substitute Teacher and Care Giver; [hon.] Dean's List: F&M and Millersville, Citamard Award (1973), Best Drama, written for Millersville Dramatic Society visitation in late December; [oth. writ.] Poems For Dark Vienna; [pers.] Poem written August 1995 for and symbolically about Vienna. Her exquisite jeweled face inspired this sonnet as well as much of my subsequent work.; [a.] Lancaster, PA

MARTINEZ, BOB G.
[b.] June, 1949, New Mexico; [p.] Mrs. Mary Jane Martinez; [m.] Annette Elizabeth Martinez, February 10, 1973; [ch.] Daughter (20), Lita; [ed.] North High School (1968), Denver, Colorado; [occ.] Security Department of Denver Merchandise Mart; [memb.] Distinguished Member ISP-NLP ... Mile High Poetry Society... Columbine Poets of Colorado; [hon.] Numerous Editor's Choice Awards and over 36 publications in various national anthologies; [oth. writ.] My Time To Rhyme, a personal journal (1949-89) in a single unbroken poem (302 pgs.), Sidetracks, a compilation of my favorite poems (45).; [pers.] You only live once... but, if you do it right... once is enough.; [a.] Denver, CO

MASTERS, CLARA
[b.] March 17, 1980, Fort Wayne, IN; [p.] Craig and Lisa Masters; [ed.] Bryan High School Class of '98; [occ.] Student, part-time clerk at Revco; [memb.] National Honor Society, Mask and Sandal Drama Club, Bryan City Band, Bible study group; [hon.] Best Actress in a leading role - Anne Frank in "The Diary of Anne Frank," all "A" honor roll, A&B honor roll, Music Award and Certificate, Superior Rating in Flute Quartet at contest, Varsity letter "B" for academics; [oth. writ.] One poem soon to be published in school's writing magazine, personal journal kept (about 50 poems so far), essays on diverse topics.; [pers.] My motivation to start writing two years ago was triggered by experiencing the poetry of Christina Rossetti and the beginnings of self-actualization.; [a.] Bryan, OH

MATCHOPATOW, DIANA LYNN
[pen.] Sissy or Little Red Wing; [b.] July 3, 1961, Shawano; [p.] Earl and Elaine Thompson; [m.] Marvin L. Matchopatow Sr. (Separated), September 26, 1980; [ch.] Marvin, Jr., Dannielle and Cory; [ed.] Shawano High School Certified Nurses Aide, NWTC Creative Writing, Union Grove, WI; [occ.] Mother and C.N.A.; [memb.] Enrolled Member of the Hu-Chunk Nation Winnebago Tribe of Wisconsin, Member of St. James Lutheran Church; [hon.] Received awards for writing poems and short stories, received certificate for creative writing.; [oth. writ.] Publishings in local newspaper and Ho-Chunk Wo-Lduk Tribal Newspaper; [pers.] My current goal is to have a book published with short stories.; [a.] Shawano, WI

MATHIS, JAMIE
[b.] August 22, 1983, El Dorado, KS; [p.] Mike Mathis and Annette Mathis; [ed.] 7 years of schooling; [occ.] Student; [memb.] Builder's Club; [hon.] President's Award for Educational Excellence and Honor Roll for two years of Middle School; [a.] Saint Louis, MO

MATOSKY, CHRISTOPHER
[b.] April 10, 1973, USN Base, Japan; [p.] Andrew Matosky and Diana Moore; [m.] Amy Elizabeth Vanover Matosky, May 18, 1996; [ed.] Currently a nursing student at East Tennessee State University; [occ.] Nursing student, part time home health CNA; [hon.] Veterans of the World Wars, ROTC Medal; [oth. writ.] Several non-published poems including two musical adaptations; [pers.] With love anything is possible; [a.] Johnson City, TN

MATTIE, EVELYN
[b.] July 12, 1952; Sewickly, PA; [p.] James Darby, Gelsomina Darby; [m.] Timothy Mattie; April 1, 1977; [ch.] Isaac Wayne; [ed.] Coraopolis High, Penn State University, Uniontown School of Nursing; [occ.] Pediatric RN; [memb.] Allison Nazarene Church; [oth.writ.] Short story about Lisa's Poem and many poems not yet published; [pers.] I believe that I can accomplish anything through God and His strength. I try to relate God's love through my poetry; [a.] Smock, PA.

MATTIOLI, RITA
[pen.] Rita Mattioli; [b.] June 1, 1954, Bronx, NY; [p.] Clarice Rietveldt Mattioli and Constantine Mattioli; [ch.] Stephen Rubeo; [ed.] Monroe College; [occ.] Office Manager in a city hospital; [hon.] President's and Dean's List, Community Achievement Award, Photojournalism Contributions for school publications, social events and guest speakers; [oth. writ.] Dawn Of Life And Joy, Whales, The Lady Who Wore Fur In God's House, Several articles published in Monroe College Newspaper School Talk; [pers.] "Nothing is so strong as gentleness. Nothing so gentle as real strength". In my writing I try to capture the real strength of humanity, gentleness.; [a.] Bronx, NY

MATTIX, JOSH
[b.] August 8, 1977, Medicine Lodge, KS; [p.] Charles III and Marilyn Mattix; [ed.] Hillcrest High School, Evangel College; [occ.] Student; [hon.] Choral Performance in Carnegie Hall with Evangel College Concert Choir; [oth. writ.] Several personal poems and ballads, also available few short stories.; [pers.] I try to set a reader on a trail of thought. Evoking emotion is secondary. If I can get a reader to take another look at something, or think about anything, my task is accomplished.; [a.] Springfield, MO

MAXWELL, SHAYNE MARY
[b.] April 21, 1959, So. Calif.; [p.] Kay Mitchell and Gary Kidwell; [m.] David Maxwell, June 10, 1989; [ed.] Univ. of Utah; [pers.] Without the rain there would be no rainbows.; [a.] Tiburon, CA

MAY, ELLA BLAKE
[pen.] Ella May; [b.] December 30, 1911, Grady, MS; [p.] Gus Blake, Viola Blake; [m.] Pryor Howell May, November 24, 1933; [ch.] Kathleen, Connie, Douglas, Polly; [ed.] Bennett Academy, Woods Jr. College, Holmes Jr. College, Mathiston, Miss. Mathiston, Miss., Grenada Co. Hospital LPN Train-

ing; [occ.] Retired Practical Nurse; [oth. writ.] A few poems were published in local newspapers; [a.] Memphis, TN

MBA, SIR VIRGILIUS
[pen.] Sir Liche Mba; [b.] June 26, 1955; Imo State, Nigeria; [p.] Chief and Mrs. Simeon Mba; [ed.] High School Umuaka Orlu Nigeria West African School Certificate BS, DP, Jersey City State College NJ. Real Estate Licensed Sales Rep. St, Peter's College JC, NJ; [memb.] Knights of Columbus since 1990; [oth.writ.] Unpublished works of art: The Dulphin. A Broken Piece Of Glass. The Troublesome Sheep; [pers.] Let us visualize our role as a leader, and after reflect to the image we have left behind; [a.] Jersey City, NJ.

MCARTHUR, MARY
[b.] September 14, 1944, Butte, MT; [p.] Margaret and James McArthur; [m.] Divorced; [ch.] Kim, Marci, Kate and Mike; [ed.] Girl Central High School butte, Montana; [occ.] DayCare Mother, Grandmother of 5 - 4 boys and 1 girl; [pers.] I miss my parents so much but must tell you after I mailed this poem off I have stopped going to the phone to call them and as they were both cremated following their deaths. I have kept them here with me - last month I was able to bring them to Holy Cross Cemetery to their final resting place.; [a.] Spokane, WA

MCCARTHY, JAMIE MELISSA
[b.] July 26, 1980, New Port Richey, FL; [p.] Patricia E. and George C. McCarthy; [ed.] River Ridge High School - New Port Richey, FL; [occ.] High School Junior Honors Student; [memb.] National Honor Society, Who's Who Among America's High School Students (1995/1996); [hon.] Pride in Writing Award (1990); [oth. writ.] First poem published in local newspaper at age 8 (1988), Journalism Award for story published in local newspaper at age 9 (1989), several writings, stories, and poems, earned school honors.; [a.] New Port Richey, FL

MCCARTHY, SHAWN
[pen.] Joeseph Blackwolf; [b.] May 28, 1980, Saint Louis, MO; [p.] Janet LaVar (Fran LaVar), Patrick McCarthy; [ed.] Still in high school; [occ.] Student; [oth. writ.] Dozens of unpublished stories and poems, articles for school newspaper.; [pers.] As a teenager leading a "normal" life, I try to prove that it is anything but, I write to display the confusion and pain that youths go through as they look for things to fill the emptiness that comes with being young.; [a.] Affton, MO

MCCLELLAN, DEREK
[b.] November 17, 1980, Tallahassee, FL; [p.] Henry and Belinda McClellan; [ed.] Godby High School; [occ.] Student; [memb.] Leon County Sheriff's Explorers, Godby Football Team, Honors Club; [hon.] Academic awards; [oth. writ.] Several poems.; [pers.] Through my writing I want people to know that writing is an expression of feelings and a creative escape mechanism.; [a.] Tallahassee, FL

MCCLOUD, MICHELLE L.
[pen.] M. L. McCloud; [b.] February 29, 1972, Paintsville, KY; [p.] Patricia McCloud-Stambaugh; [ed.] Porter Elem., Paintsville, KY, Morton Jr. High, Lexington, KY, Henry Clay H.S., Lexing-

ton, KY, Antioch College, Yellow Springs, OH; [occ.] Writer; [memb.] Various political org., amateur literary org., human rights org.; [hon.] Creative writing awards, academic writing honors, literary magazine publication, Beta Society, academic achievement awards, drama society awards, and community service awards.; [oth. writ.] Personal poetry #'s over 500 total. Also do editorials for local paper on occasion. Amateur literary magazine publications.; [pers.] "Self worth comes not from the validation of others, but the true self love in your soul".; [a.] Lexington, KY

MCCOLLOUGH, CARL A.
[pen.] Carl A. McCollough; [b.] September 17, 1918, Iowa; [p.] Ralph F. and Marie E. McCollough; [m.] C. Muriel (Schimek) McCollough (Deceased), May 30, 1943; [ch.] Three sons and one daughter; [ed.] BA in Education, Master of Arts in Administration MA in Student Personnel Services; [occ.] Retired Antique Dealer (I taught Technical Ed for 26 yrs.); [memb.] American Legion, 133rd Inf. Assoc. 34 Inf Division, Trinity Lutheran Church; [oth. writ.] I wrote a column for a small weekly newspaper during the first part of World War II, wrote for the school paper. I have notebooks of poetry.; [pers.] An idle mind is a terrible waste. It leads to a life devoid of taste.; [a.] Frederick, MD

MCCOY, MARCUS S.
[b.] June 26, 1982; Pullman, WA; [p.] Stanley and Carlene McCoy; [ed.] Sophomore in high school; [occ.] High school student; [memb.] Life Boy Scout, working on Eagle Member of the "Order of the Arrow." Black belt in Shudokan Karate; [hon.] Was voted "Most Ambitious" in my freshman class. This year I became the finest and youngest student from Lewis-Clark Karate to win Adult Grand Champion in Sparring at the Snake River Karate Classic; [pers.] "I like my stupid life just the way it is and I wouldn't change it for 1000 flying pigs."; [a.] Lewiston, ID.

MCCOY, RONNIE G.
[pen.] Cream; [b.] March 3, 1962, Rockford, IL; [p.] Johnny and Roise McCoy; [ch.] Kesha, Ronnie Rem, Brandon, Todd, Roni; [pers.] This is my 1st try and I dedicate it to my mother Rosie Lee McCoy, Carlton Dashaun McCoy may he R.I.P.

MCCRAY, GEORGIA
[pen.] Jackie - Apple Jack; [b.] September 25, 1964, Boynton Beach, FL; [p.] Eva Mae Darville, Alfred Darville; [m.] Dennis Mark McCray, January 6, 1987; [ch.] 3 Godchilren - Samson Joseph - Jackee Moore, C. J. Cross; [ed.] Lake Worth High School; [occ.] Homemaker; [memb.] Believer's Voice of Victory; [hon.] Rope Climbing 3rd place; [oth. writ.] Two poems published in Quill Books, one book called Dusting Off Dreams, the second book called Echoes From The Silence.; [pers.] I love poetry and art, they are the most passionate pair that makes my day.; [a.] Boynton Beach, FL

MCCULLERS, LISA F.
[pen.] Hollywood; [b.] December 30, 1962; Washington, DC; [p.] Louise and Thomas McCullers; [ch.] Antonio (deceased) Shanida McCullers; [ed.] H.S. educated, three years college educated; [occ.] Program Specialist; [memb.] Afro-American Writer's Guild; [oth.writ.] Several poems published, currently working on a children's story; [pers.] I hope everyone enjoys this poem. It was dedicated to my deceased grandmother, on my mother's side. However, I would like to give thanks to my father, because his belief has helped my dream become a reality; [a.] Severn, MD.

MCDADE, DONNA MARIE
[b.] April 29, 1949, Cleveland, OH; [p.] Daniel and Frieda Nee (Deceased) Forkapa; [ch.] Jason Christopher Gorman; [ed.] Nursing Retired, Therapeutic Herbalist Reiki; [memb.] Juvenile Diabetes Foundation, Support Multiple Charities; [hon.] Nurse of Yr. UMC 1991, Who's Who in The West 1997 for research publication in Radiation Oncology; [oth. writ.] Published Medical Professional Journals Lectures and Presenter Poetry Publication; [pers.] To write is to have thought, To think is to have know, To know is to have lived.; [a.] Tucson, AZ

MCDUFFIE, ROY
[pen.] Roy McDuffie; [b.] November 2, 1941, Hazlehurst, GA; [p.] Daniel (Bud) McDuffie and Loraine A. Yeomans; [ed.] Graduated June 1960, Jeff Davis High School, Hazlehurst, GA; [occ.] Fiserv, Jay, FL; [memb.] The International Society of Poets, Distinguished member, The International Society of Poetry Hall of Fame, Rondo Ave Baptist Church, Florida Freelance Writers Association. North Florida Writers Club; [hon.] License to preach by Hillside Baptist Church in Rome, GA on November 18, 1973. Editor's Choice Award for poem "What If" I entered in contest Editor's Choice Award for poem "Thank God" for poem I entered in contest. Editor's Choice Award for poem "Apple" I entered in contest.; [oth. writ.] Poet "What If " published in throughout the Hourglass. Poem "Thank God" published in Fields of Gold. Poem "Apple" published in The Color of Thought. Poem "Pear" published in The Nightfall of Diamonds. Poem "Tree" published in Tracing Shadows. Poem "O Road O Road" published in The Isle of View. Poem "Beans" published in A View From Afar.; [pers.] Teach adult Sunday School class. Assistant Pastor Rondo Ave Baptist Church I strive to share the word of God in my poems.; [a.] Jay, FL

MCELYEA, ADDIE RENEE
[b.] July 3, 1950, Dothan, AL; [p.] Mose and Nancy Brown; [ed.] Ashford High School, George C. Wallace State College; [occ.] R.N. at Southeast Alabama Medical Center, Dothan, AL; [memb.] American Heart Assoc., American Assoc. of Critical Care Nurses, International Society of Poets; [hon.] Phi Theta Kappa, Editor's Choice Award, National Library of Poetry (Into The Uunknown entry); [oth. writ.] Several poems published in college newspaper, yearbook. Poem published in Into The Unknown by National Library of Poetry, poem published in Poetic Voices of America and Treasured Poems of America by Sparrowgrass Poetry Forum.; [a.] Ashford, AL

MCGARR, JAMES A.
[b.] October 19, 1959, Cordele, GA; [p.] Mr. and Mrs. David W. McGarr; [m.] Kathy Lynne, February 22, 1997; [ed.] 12th Grade; [occ.] Investor - Musician; [hon.] Honorable Mention in previous National Library of Poetry entries; [oth. writ.] "Destiny", "Whippoorwills", "Fences", "Hell Memories", "Shadows Of The Past"; [pers.] The recent death of my father and the new love of my life, my wife, was the inspiration for this poem.

Along with all the support of my mother and sister.; [a.] East Ellijay, GA

MCGEE, JOHN
[b.] July 14, 1923, Bronx, NYC, NY; [p.] John and Emily McGee; [ed.] B.B.A. Manhattan College (NYC), M.S. Fordham University (NYC), M.A. New York University (NYC); [occ.] (Retired) Elementary School Teacher, New York City, Assistant Principal, New York City, Board of Education; [memb.] Catholic Teachers Association of New York, United Federation of Teachers, (AFL-CIO), Catholic Kolping Society of America, The American Legion (WW II); [hon.] "Distinguished Service Award for Leadership" by The Catholic Kolping Society of America; [oth. writ.] Monthly publications of poems and book reviews to "The Kolping Banner" in Chicago. Monthly contributions of poems, cultural activities: plays, theaters, churches, concert halls, museums, colleges, etc., as well as, original poems to local newspapers and to the monthly newsletter of The Catholic Kolping Society of New York..."The Kolping Bulletin".; [pers.] Understanding, the thinking of today's American teen-ager can be almost God-like. You can help plan, suggest, direct, and guide their lives to success. America's future depends on them.; [a.] Jackson Heights, NY

MCGEE II, GLENDON
[b.] September 5, 1960; Los Angeles, CA; [p.] Glendon McGee, Sr., Lula Magness; [m.] Terri McGee; April 15, 1983; [ch.] Glendon McGee, III, Amber Nicole, Markus Daniel; [ed.] El Segundo Elementary, Vanguard Jr. High and Centenial H.S.; [occ.] unemployed; [pers.] I write poetry to express my feelings and inner being. I also like to draw; [a.] Compton, CA.

MCGRATH, DANNY L.
[b.] February 16, 1953, Clinton, IA; [p.] Lyda and Frank H. McGrath Jr.; [m.] Widowed - wife's name was Nancy, March 7, 1992; [ed.] Associate of Arts Degree, Mount St. Clare College - Clinton, Clinton High School - Clinton; [occ.] Head Custodian at Clinton High School - Clinton, IA; [hon.] Mu Sigma Honor Society at Mount St. Clare College; [oth. writ.] Countless works written privately for my wife. Some printed in the local newspaper.; [pers.] My poetry is written from the heart to or about someone special in my life. It's always reward enough to see a smile of joy or a tear of happiness when someone reads a poem.; [a.] Clinton, IA

MCKINNEY, AUDREY
[pen.] Rabbet Gray; [b.] October 30, 1956, Fort Lauderdale, FL; [p.] Alice Frost and Peter Stanely; [ed.] Graduated Cooper City High 1974, Davie, FL; [occ.] Disabled; [oth. writ.] Numerous of poems, none have been published, looking forward to it.; [pers.] I have only been writing for a year and a half but I feel the hunger to reach all people and rely to their emotional and physical pains.; [a.] Columbia, SC

MCKINNEY, DEREK
[pen.] Derek McKinney; [b.] April 23, 1981, Radondo Beach, CA; [p.] Tim and Magali McKinney; [ed.] One year completed of high school at Southington High School; [oth. writ.] Scratch paper poems, none acknowledged.; [pers.] There's a time to live, there's a time to die, that's how the world works and no one knows why, In this world

of killing there is no tie, just a limb for a limb, and an eye for an eye.; [a.] Newburgh, NY

MCLAIN, STACEY L.
[b.] September 28, 1971, McHenry, IL; [ed.] North Boone High, Illinois College; [occ.] Hardee's; [pers.] I desire to reflect the Spirit of God in my writing, to express the joy I find in my own life.; [a.] Jacksonville, IL

MCMULLIN, PATRICIA L.
[pen.] Patricia L. McMullin; [b.] May 28, 1949; Aransas Pass, TX; [p.] Willard and Judy McMullin, Betty Dreyer; [m.] Andre Garesche; February 14, 1997; [ch.] Charles, Chance, Cougan and Brad; [ed.] H.G. Olsen Elementary, Flour Bluff High; [occ.] Writer, Poet; [hon.] None of national recognition; [oth. writ.] Have been writing poetry since 1965; [pers.] As a 3rd generation Port Aransian, my poetry has been focused primarily on the island of Port Aransas, island life and island ways. There's no doubt that the island has had a direct influence on my work. I hope people appreciate; [a.] Port Aransas, TX.

MCNAB, LISA ELIZABETH
[pen.] L. Elizabeth McNab; [b.] June 9, 1961, Oak Ridge, Roatan, Honduras, CA; [p.] Crawford B. McNab and Leila E. McNab; [ed.] Seventh Day Adventist School, Martha Gregg Institute (In Honduras, CA); [occ.] Student, Nunez Community College, Chalmette, LA; [memb.] First Baptist Church of Chalmette Sisters Committee; [pers.] I try to reflect on the love and beauty of God's creation in my writing. I have been influenced by the everyday beauty and wonders of our world. Nevertheless, the greatest influences has been the trials of life.; [a.] Arabi, LA

MCNEIL, EULA
[b.] June 2, 1931; [p.] Emma and John Stewart; [m.] Expired, June 11, 1954; [ch.] Five; [ed.] 10th grade; [occ.] Retired Nursing Aide at Parshelsky Pavillion 27 yrs.; [memb.] Metropolitan's Twenty Rivers Club; [hon.] Humanitarian Libby Asofsky; [pers.] I would like to try writing a book about working with the elderly as I aged with them.; [a.] Brooklyn, NY

MCPHERSON, ROBERT L.
[b.] July 26, 1915; Maize, Kansas; [p.] Leo H. Ellen McPherson; [m.] Divorced; [ch.] Janey Arnberger/ Barbara Krol; [ed.] 26 years in the USAF as a systems analyst, 1 year of college; [occ.] Retired; [memb.] Veterans of foreign wars; [hon.] Various awards in the Air Force; [oth.writ.] 1. "The Angel" 2. "My Dream" 3. "Heart Aches" 4. "A Boor Of Time"; [pers.] I am a history buff and I donate items I find to the school and museums; [a.] Black Canyon, AZ.

MCQUAIN, CECIL L.
[b.] February 18, 1970, Butler, PA; [p.] William and Linda McQuain, [ed.] Phillp Barbour H.S., B.B.A. University of Guam; [occ.] Student Naval Aviator; [hon.] U of G Dean's List, U of G President's List; [a.] Corpus Christi, TX

MEDINA, PERRY
[b.] September 28, 1964, New York City; [p.] Israel Medina, Dalia Medina; [m.] Deborah A. Medina, July 19, 1996; [ed.] Hunter College High School, Hunter College; [occ.] Director at the Princelon

Review; [memb.] USGA; [pers.] Former United States Marine, you are what you do when it counts.; [a.] Ronkonkoma, NY

MEEUWSEN, TERRA LISA
[b.] May 9, 1981; [p.] Dennis and Valorie Meeuwsen; [ed.] Yoncalla High School; [occ.] School; [memb.] 1. SADD (Students Against Drunk Driving), 2. PHP (Peers Helping Peers), 3. Scholars; [hon.] Computer Communication HOBY (Hugh O-Brian Youth Foundation, a leadership conference for Sophomores all over the state of Oregon); [oth. writ.] Several poems published in Imaginings, an anthology of county-wide student writings.; [pers.] Writing is one of the many means of expressing your inner feelings.; [a.] OR

MELDRUM, SHERYLL A.
[b.] June 13, 1946, Polson, MT; [p.] Robert and Doris Wickard; [m.] Ted W. Meldrum, May 25, 1972; [ch.] Beverly, Anne, David, Deborah, Donnie, Joseph, John; [ed.] Renton High, Ricks College, BYU Univ.; [occ.] Postal Service - Clerk EDDC Redmond, Wash.; [memb.] The Church of Jesus Christ of Latter Day Saints - Relief Society; [oth. writ.] College Poetry Press, Personal poems for newborn babies.; [pers.] In our sojourn in life, that which we say and do for others we'll be our legacy in the eternities.; [a.] Renton, WA

MELROSE, LOUISE E.
[pen.] Beth; [b.] June 28, 1954, Bridgeport, CA; [p.] Donald Shrider, Leila Shrider; [m.] Thomas L. Melrose, October 5, 1991; [ed.] Tonopah High School, Education Dynamics Technical College, Travel Dimensions College, Ft. Mohave Jr. College; [occ.] Administrative Assistant Occidental Oil and Gas Corporation; [memb.] OES; [hon.] Honor Society, Young America Who's Who (2 yrs.); [oth. writ.] Reader's Digest, National Poetry Press various newspapers; [pers.] With desire that my writings may lead readers through the realm of unrestricted imagination.; [a.] Bakersfield, CA

MELTON, CHRISTOPHER
[b.] April 20, 1972, Tyler, TX; [p.] Dennis Melton, Connie Melton; [ed.] Garland High School, B.A Stephen F. Austin State University; [occ.] Account Representative, Software Spectrum Inc.; [a.] Carrollton, TX

MENICUCCI, SUSAN M.
[b.] June 16, 1969, Omaha, NE; [p.] Ronald Lakin and Patricia Rybin; [ch.] Robert, Ryan, Brandi; [ed.] South High, Metropolitan Community College, Gateway College; [occ.] Assistant Manager, N.P. Dodge Management Co.; [hon.] Women's Overseas League, American Legion Post 331 For Military Excellence (X2), Superior Cadet Award; [pers.] I started writing at age 16 for leisure activity. My greatest influences were my parents, grandmother (Lorraine Lakin) and English Professor (Pat Coffey).; [a.] Plattsmouth, NE

MENOR, GYPSY MARPESSA NEFERTITI DAWN
[b.] January 3, 1934, PA, USA; [p.] Mother: 1/2 East Indian Gypsy, 1/2 Persian Gypsy, Father: 1/2 Egyptian, 1/2 Filipino; [m.] In our matriarchal family, we do not marry.; [ch.] (1) Damana Taz, (2) Hathora Ma'ata, (3) Erikrystjan, (4) Lorene Tehan, (5) Marlon Darryl, (6) Dhyana Jalande, (7) Soraya Selene, (8) Eloah Sun; [ed.] Associated in Applied Arts and Sciences, Degree, issued by The Institute of Applied Arts and Sciences of the New

York State University (1953); [occ.] Retired am now, an student in the Russian Language, at Alma Mater, (Have studied eleven languages.) From age 8 to age 60, "worked" in showbiz, the highlight of which was Meye starring role, in the Oskar-Winning Film, "Black Orphews (Best Foreign Film 1960); [hon.] Which in all has won 19 top grand prizes, in the Major Planetary Film Festivals - thosely becoming the most recompensed film in all the world history of cinematography; [oth. writ.] "Zillions" of notebooks, over the years. I had totally forgotten about this contest (perhaps, because I felt it to be inconceivable that I would ever be selected), your response in today's mail is a big surprise. Please respect all my autographical syncracies - "Eye" for "I" - K and Z underlined, etc.; [pers.] I believe in "The goddess mother life", Meye "religion" in all "her" a spirits. Is love and respect for "her", there is no way that anyone is going to make me believe that "The Kozmikreative Power" is a "Testosteronik andromorphik character!!!"; [a.] Monsey, NY

MERCER, EDITH B.
[pen.] Edith B. Mercer; [b.] March 22, 1919, Baltimore; [p.] James and Isabella Bond; [m.] Deceased, March 21, 1940; [ch.] Albert, Elaine, Hariet, Donald; [ed.] High School and Nursing Training; [occ.] Retired from "University of MD Hospital"; [hon.] "Edi Cole" sent written awards for some poems I wrote the title was "Aren't You Glad You're Made In The U.S.A."; [oth. writ.] "I Can't Find A Reason", I also made a "Family Rapp" of my nine sisters and brothers".; [pers.] "The secret to success is hard work", "what you say will be doubted, it's what you do."; [a.] Baltimore, MD

MERTENS, MARLENE C.
[ed.] Journalism student in high school; [a.] Rio Rancho, NM.

METEVIA, JOHN
[b.] July 7, 1953, Saginaw, MI; [p.] Ira and Marie Metevia; [m.] Janet K., October 12, 1974; [ch.] Charie and Carrie; [ed.] High School, Church: Kingdom Ministry School, Church: Public Speaker, Instructor Teacher; [occ.] Baker I, Sara Lee Inc.; [memb.] Lake Leelanau Congregation of Jehovah's Witnesses; [hon.] Leelanau Amateur Wine Festival: 1986: 4 1st place entries plus Elderberry B.C.S., 1st and 2nd best of show Elder Blossom B.C.S. Cherry and Strawberry, 1987: 1 entry - 1st place (elderberry), 1st Best of show (elderberry); [oth. writ.] The Baker, The Winemaker, Talented Wife; [pers.] Title: Goals a mind reaching out sharing special thoughts joys and hopes, especially dear every moment spent, a joy a love expressed, without any fear; [a.] Cedar, MI

MEY, MAURICE RAY
[pen.] Maurice Mey; [b.] July 30, 1974, New Albany, IN; [pers.] The heavens declare the glory of God, the skies proclaim the work of his hands. (Psalms 19:1) The Kingdom of God is within you. (Luke 17:21).; [a.] Georgetown, IN

MEYER, AMANDA
[b.] June 6, 1980, Hendersonville, TN; [p.] Teresa and David Meyer; [ed.] Beech High School; [occ.] Student; [oth. writ.] Several other poems.; [pers.] I am striving to do great works, and to be recognized for my contribution to poetry.; [a.] Hendersonville, TN

MICHELFELDER, KIRT L.
[b.] June 3, 1964; [m.] Tamela, September 1, 1988; [ch.] Tena, Jenni, Samantha, Jesse; [oth. writ.] Currently in process of completing and editing my book of poetry titled: Two Sides Of A Dream, which I been constructing since 1982.; [pers.] Though some of my writing is about personal experiences, the majority is from watching and listening to other people and how the feel, good or bad.; [a.] Caledonia, MI

MILLER, ALBERTA
[pen.] Bert; [b.] November 3, 1949, SC; [p.] Thelma Dow; [m.] Herbert Miller, July 11, 1970; [ch.] Four; [ed.] B'klyn School of Nursing; [occ.] Retired; [memb.] Supt. Sunday School Finance Comm.; [oth. writ.] Short love stories.; [a.] Sumter, SC

MILLER, BARBARA GAILE
[b.] July 15, 1944, Painter, VA; [p.] Robert Belote, Annete Belote; [m.] Allen E. Miller, September 10, 1994; [ch.] Jim Temple III; [oth. writ.] Currently compiling poems for a book to be entitled: A Family Is A Treasure; [a.] Moyock, NC

MILLER, BETSY JO
[b.] September 20, 1929, Kansas City, KS; [p.] Joanna D. McKinney; [m.] Richard N. Miller, September 20, 1985; [ch.] Jeffery and Lynette Marker; [ed.] B.A. Sociology, Education; [hon.] Parents' Magazine, Penney - Missouri Magazine Award; [oth. writ.] Articles in Newspapers, Parents' Magazine, Redbook, and The Journal of Religion and Physical Research; [pers.] I am interested in how so-called 'psychic' phenomana, undergirds our lives, and how his relates to the fields of Psychology, Education, Medicine, Science, and Religion; [a.] Alva, OK

MILLER, CLAY
[b.] June 24, 1980, Fullerton, CA; [p.] Ron Miller, Holly Miller; [ch.] Currently a student at Mt. Spokane High School; [ed.] Student; [occ.] National Honor Society, United States Swimming, Gloria Dei Lutheran Church, Spokane Waves Swim Team; [memb.] "Montana Poet Magazine" 1991, Christmas Poetry Contest winner, "Most Inspirational" - Mead Junior High Band percussion section, competitor at 1997 Junior National Swimming Championships, current holder of Region XII Age Group Long Course meet record in 200 individual medley.; [hon.] "Elves" - Montana Poet Magazine; [pers.] As a Christian teenager living in the 1990's, I am disappointed, in general, with the conduct of society. I feel that there are purer, simpler things we must return to, and I try to express these things in my poetry.; [a.] Mead, WA

MILLER, DR. DALE A.
[b.] August 13, 1932, Waterbury, NE; [p.] Aaron and Susie Miller; [ch.] Terry Lyon, Julie Fountaine, Lisa Brumm; [ed.] B.A./M.A. California State University at Los Angeles, Ed.D. Stanford University; [occ.] Vice President, City University; [hon.] Humanitarian of the Year awarded by convicts in the California State Prison for Women, Numerous Civic Awards; [oth. writ.] Several poems and professional articles published in journals and newspapers.; [pers.] I speak to my inner self through my poetry. If others like them, fine. But that really doesn't matter to me.; [a.] Kirkland, WA

MILLER, JOYCE
[b.] November 8, 1932, MI; [ch.] Belinda, Bill Jr.,

Sandra, Daniel; [ed.] So. Haven High School; [occ.] Factory Assembler; [memb.] Three Bowling Leagues; [hon.] Won two 1st place Tournaments; [pers.] Poem in Memory of my Granddaughter who lived 10 wks. 4 days very sp.; [a.] Fremont, MI

MILLER, LINDSEY
[b.] December 8, 1982, Greenwood, IN; [p.] Tony and Vicki Miller; [occ.] Student; [oth. writ.] Christmas Wish published; [a.] Greenwood, IN

MILLER, PATRICIA
[pen.] Miracle Iverson; [b.] October 30, 1969, Leakesville, MS; [p.] George L. Miller Sr., Winnie P. Miller; [ed.] Sand Hill High School, Jones Junior College, University of Southern Mississippi; [occ.] Administrative Assistant Progressive Insurance Company, Hattiesburg, MS; [hon.] Member of Beta Club for 4 years in High School; [oth. writ.] Wrote Skits and Plays for Church Presentations; [pers.] God has been and always will be the purpose of my existence. I attempt to depict his perfectionism in my writing.; [a.] Hattiesburg, MS

MILLER, TONI MARIE
[b.] August 1, 1981, Metairie, LA; [p.] Wayne and Susan Miller; [ed.] Home Schooled - 3 yrs., now attends Pearl River High School; [occ.] High School Student; [memb.] School Paper, School Year Book Photographer; [oth. writ.] Toni's Collection of Poems; [pers.] To never let a day go by without seeing the beauty in someone or something this world has to give.; [a.] Pearl River, LA

MILLIGAN, JEANNE
[b.] June 16, 1961, Muskogee, OK; [ch.] Rae Lynn, Amanda; [memb.] A.B.A.T.E.; [hon.] United Way - Fund Raiser Muskogee Regional Medical Center - Friendliness; [oth. writ.] Of my many poems written, some have been used for songs by local artist.; [pers.] To Brent, who inspired "Cue the Rain", as well as many others. "May your spirit fly forever free", thank you for sharing it with me. Here's to eternity.; [a.] Tahlequah, OK

MILLS, CLAUDIA KAY
[pen.] Claudia Kay Mills; [b.] December 2, 1962, Denton, TX; [p.] Claude and Patsy Young; [m.] Mark William Mills, June 9, 1984; [ch.] Mark W. Mills II and Robert Scott Mills; [ed.] Aubrey High School, Aubrey, TX, Career Point Business School, San Antonio, TX; [occ.] Medical Records Analyst at Harris Home Health Service; [oth. writ.] Some poems published in school newspaper.; [pers.] Take one day at a time and enjoy it.; [a.] Aubrey, TX

MILLS, KATHERINE M.
[b.] July 18, 1963, New Haven, CT; [p.] Thomas and Mary Ricks Sr.; [m.] William T. Mills Jr. (Divorced - March 3, 1994), July 27, 1990; [ch.] William T. Mills Jr. III; [ed.] I graduated from Plant City Senior High School, June 3, 1982, I have one year of college. I studied Human Services Tech.; [occ.] Student care attendant for Columbia County School Sys.; [oth. writ.] This is my first attempt at being published even though I've written other poems. I never published any. I've been writing since I was in 4th grade.; [pers.] Put God first and pray daily. If you have a dream and a talent, pursue it. It may take awhile but you will finally get there.; [a.] Lake City, FL

MILLS, LACY
[pen.] Lace; [b.] January 19, 1979; Rockford, IL;

[p.] Richard and Cathy Mills; [ed.] Rockford Lutheran High School; [memb.] Who's Who in American High School Students, Grace Lutheran Church, International Society of Poets, Honor Roll; [hon.] Award from "Visions of Youth" Art Show; "Editor's Choice" Award for 1994, 1995 1996, President's Education Award for Outstanding Improvement; [oth.writ.] "A Once Red Rose," "A Memory," "Yesterday," "Who Cries at night," "My precious Easter Gift," "The Risen One"; [pers.] My Lord and Savior have blessed me with my poetic spirit and my passion for love and life; [a.] Roscoe, IL.

MILTON, SHENIQUE MONIQUE
[b.] February 12, 1976, Eutaw, AL; [p.] Mary Jean Atkins; [ed.] Eutaw High School, Alabama Agricultural and Mechanical University; [occ.] Student at Alabama Agricultural and Mechanical University; [memb.] Zion Friendship Baptist Church; [pers.] Love and hate, happiness and sorrow and all other strong emotions of this world can be found in one place, the great poetic book of life.; [a.] Eutaw, AL

MINNICH, THOMAS
[b.] December 30, 1977, Allentown, PA; [p.] Clarence and Sharon Minnich; [ed.] Lower Dauphin High School, Reading Area Community College, Allentown College of Saint Francis de Sales; [occ.] Junior Majoring in Accounting; [hon.] Dean's List, President's List; [pers.] I dedicate "My Sweetheart" to my fiance' Maryann, my first and only true love.; [a.] Grantville, PA

MINOT, MARCIA CHVAT
[b.] October 15, 1923; New Jersey; [p.] Anna and Alexander Chvat; [m.] Robert Morton Minot; April 30, 1955; [ch.] 3 - Dr. Mark M. Minot, twin daughters Michele Tonkyro and Jeanne E. Behrendt; [ed.] Master's degree; [occ.] Retired Teacher, Reading Specialist Los Angeles United School District; [memb.] Episcopal Lay Minister, St. Margaret of Scotland, Episcopal Church San Juan Capistrano, CA; Society of Children's Book Writers, Sherlock Holmes Society, Cheviot Hills Garden Club President, Travelers Aid Society Volunteer at LAX, 5 yrs.; [hon.] Docent of the year, LA County Museum of Natural History, served 11 yrs., special award for outstanding teacher in LA. school district; [oth.writ.] Poems published in 10 anthologies and local newsletters, 2 poetry books, 3 children's books; [pers.] Since childhood, greatly influenced by the Psalms and mystery stories. Archaeology, Egyptology in particular; [a.] Dana Point, CA.

MIRANDA, MILAGROS S.
[b.] May 17, Philippines; [p.] Deceased; [m.] Deceased, 1946; [ed.] Dr. of Medicine, Chemical Engineering, Chemist, Banking Finance, Business, Electric Engineer Milagros, High School, only retired; [occ.] Business retired; [memb.] Church of Christ, Helper in Finance; [hon.] So many awards I received those days for my true story, Radio Center, Program, Contest, in Manila, Philippines, sponsored by Vicks International; [oth. writ.] None, I wish to be true story in the days to come if our God willing, my ambitious is to be a writer, of true story, thank you, God Bless You, again God Bless.; [pers.] Inspirations of my love to a handsome man, my lucky star, My lucky star. Truly I love him and to

love him until my last day in this world. I am only a new writer of poems, inspired only by my ups and down, of a queen for a month, for only, true story, in radio center in my country.; [a.] Englewood, OH

MITCHELL, ADELENE
[pen.] Addie Mitchell; [b.] September 16, 1920, Quincy, IL; [p.] Eben F. and Hattie Kerksieck Turner; [m.] (Boots) Martin O. Mitchell, June 27, 1992; [ed.] Quincy Senior High, Quincy Gem City Business College, Quincy; [occ.] Retired, making cards on computer; [oth. writ.] This is first time I ever submitted anything. Friends have been encouraging me.; [a.] Quincy, IL

MITCHELL, M. EDWARD
[b.] August 15, 1967, Honolulu, HI; [p.] Marvin and Odet Mitchell; [ed.] B.S. Public Relations '95 Pacific Union College; [occ.] Chiropractic Assistant; [memb.] President - Dramatic Arts Society. (Pacific Union College Drama Club) 94-95 school year.; [hon.] None yet. As a college student I was a disaster. (Academically, that is); [oth. writ.] Many stale, academic papers for college classes. Nothing I would want published.; [pers.] I have no literary influence to speak of. I am influenced by events, common and everyday, that trigger a mood. It is my goal to capture that mood in my writing.; [a.] Angwin, CA

MITCHELL, MARGARET
[pen.] Peg Mitchell; [b.] September 30, 1957, Orange, CA; [p.] Frank H. and Mary A. Scholl; [m.] Randolph Lee, August 27, 1977; [ch.] Yvonne Marie and Christina Lynn; [oth. writ.] Several short stories and plenty of poems; [pers.] The family's not as fun, as it was before, they think my poems, are just a bore. To read or hear 'em, they consider a chore, 'cuz they'd rather be walkin', out that front door. My feelings, sure, they got quite sore, but I'll continue to write rhyme, all the more!; [a.] Anderson, IN

MOBLEY, MURTLE I.
[pen.] Bebe; [b.] January 4, 1964, Jax., FL; [p.] Joseph Minnis (Deceased) and Gwen Minnis; [m.] Bevi Cecil L. Mobley, February 19; [ed.] William M. Rain's High School, Jones College; [occ.] Certify C.N.A./H.H.A. for Northeast Hospice; [memb.] One More Chance Ministry; [hon.] Most Pretty Girl, Most Helpful Person, Certificate of Excellence Award of Merit Certificate; [pers.] I would like to thank, God who's the head of my life and first, who gave me this talent, also my husband Cecil, who supported me, and many family and friends.; [a.] Jax, FL

MOONEY, FRANCES D.
[pen.] Dollie; [b.] December 27, 1934, Clintwood, VA; [p.] Fassie and Earnest Mullins; [m.] Crit Mooney, June 30, 1990; [ch.] Gary (Deceased), Billy, Greg, Lisa and Randy; [ed.] Clintwood, Elem. Dickenson Memorial High, GED, Huntsville AL. 1990; [occ.] Homemaker, Retired Retail Sales, Mother; [memb.] Valley View Church, Huntsville, AL, 700 Club; [hon.] The handmade cards, and gifts of my children, and the honor of their love and trust.; [oth. writ.] Poems for friends and family, also "The Coming of Dawn" publication, National Library of Poetry.; [pers.] I strive to honor my grandparents who raised me, and my biggest desire was and is a good mother grandmother, friend, and to honor Christ as Saviour.; [a.] Clintwood, VA

MOORE, HELEN J.
[b.] July 30, 1935; Van, TX; [p.] Frances Shelton, Robert Miller; [m.] J.K. Moore; May 20, 1953; [ch.] Vanessa, Valerie, Jeffrey; [ed.] High school; [occ.] Retired; [pers.] I would like to thank you for even considering the poem I wrote. My husband saw the contest in Reader's Digest. He challenged me to write it. Thank you again; [a.] Tenell, TX

MOORE, JAMES
[pen.] James Bernard Moore; [b.] May 21, 1952, Chicago; [p.] Donald and Catherine; [m.] Meridy, October 3, 1982; [ch.] Matthew, Steven, Megan; [ed.] St. Joseph H.S., De Paul University; [occ.] Owner - Concentrated Logic Corporation; [memb.] Network and Systems Professional Association, President - CA-IDMS Midwest User Group; [oth. writ.] Technical Documentation (for software), Software, Technical Articles in Trade Magazines, Monthly Column - "Working Smarter", in Technical Support Magazine; [pers.] I write - software, music, poetry, short stories and magazine articles and columns. I strive for a timelessness in my writing with an eye toward enlightening and educating.; [a.] Glendale Heights, IL

MOORES, ALEX Z.
[b.] June 3, 1974, Santa Rosa, CA; [p.] Terry Moores, Debbie Moores; [ed.] UC Irvine; [pers.] The meaning of life is: To be happy and to make others happy. The secret to life is: Passion and Ambition.; [a.] Santa Rosa, CA

MORALES, PATRICIA
[b.] April 16, 1958, Seattle; [p.] William and Leila Jacobs; [m.] Stan Morales, July 12, 1980; [ch.] Dejenelle and Derek; [ed.] High School, Barber College; [occ.] Barber/Stylist; [hon.] Styling show; [oth. writ.] Several poems written since high school.; [pers.] I have written most of my poems at a young ages as going thru life and the changes of my life and how I perceived them.; [a.] Lynwood, WA

MOREAU, SHAWN
[pen.] Cloud; [b.] October 5, 1978, Central Falls, RI; [p.] Charles and Sandra Moreau; [ed.] C.F. High School presently attending New England Technical Institute; [occ.] College Student taking an Associates Degree in Video Production; [memb.]; [hon.] Received $1800.00 book award toward college; [oth. writ.] I have done many other poems, but never sent them for consideration for publication.; [pers.] I believe that poetry is a tool to unite the world. I am influenced by the 60's poets, Jim Morrison and Timothy Leary.; [a.] Central Falls, RI

MORELLO, ANTHONY
[b.] March 23, 1939, Monreale (PA), Italy; [p.] Salvatore and Gaetana Morello; [m.] Palmira Lena, June 8, 1968; [ch.] Salvatore Massimo - Sebastian Richard; [ed.] Italian Diploma of Bookkeeper - US High School Diploma - two years Correspondence College on Accounting; [occ.] Aircraft Engineering, helper construction parts; [memb.] Mt. Carmel and St. Christina Society; [hon.] Italian Recognition of Poetry; [oth. writ.] Many poems in Italian local newspapers. Two poems in "O Globo" of San Paulo, Brasil.; [pers.] My natural expression of ingenuity and simplicity reflect all entire love of God's children. It is very sensitive toward the human beings.; [a.] Hartford, CT

MORGAN, TIFFANY SPEARS
[pen.] T. C. Morgan; [b.] August 14, 1974, Phenix City, AL; [p.] Nancy and Thomas Rieder; [m.] Jeffry Morgan, November 23, 1996; [ed.] Central High School, Huntingdon College, Troy State University; [occ.] Student and server; [hon.] Dean's List, Alpha Omicron Pi; [oth. writ.] Personal collection of unpublished works.; [pers.] To thine own self be true. Always remember that there are no rules, nor are there any limits, in the game of life.; [a.] Phenix City, AL

MORTON, MATTHEW
[pen.] Mat Head Morton, Head 23; [b.] January 1, 1980, Kansas City, KS; [p.] Mark Morton, Kathy Morton; [ed.] Trinity Catholic Middle, Lincoln High, Maur Hill Nren School; [occ.] Student, Math Tutor; [memb.] Capitol City Cyclists; [pers.] I can only hope that someday the world can see the beauty of the carrots, or just plain spontaneously combust into a lump of limburger cheese.; [a.] Tallahassee, FL

MOSELEY, GLENDA J.
[b.] February 14, 1937, Georgia; [m.] Harry K. Moseley, May 7, 1955; [ch.] One daughter, one son; [ed.] High School Graduate 1955; [memb.] Appling Health Care System Auxiliary, Crosby Chapel, United Methodist Church; [oth. writ.] Poems - "Spirits Illusion", "Peace" and "Other Vistas", published in anthologies with The National Library of Poetry, poems in local newspaper.; [pers.] Poetry is a means of making the soul visible. In my poem "Un-Holy Dominance", I am writing for all the ones in this country and indeed the world who still search for a true image.; [a.] Baxley, GA

MOSS, TAMMIE
[b.] April 16, 1960, Poplar Bluff, MO; [p.] Jimmy Garrison, Charlene Murphy; [m.] Steve Moss, March 5, 1992; [ch.] Brandi and Brad Sandoval, Sarah Moss; [ed.] School of Practical Nursing, I am currently a Pre-Law Student, at Southwestern Oklahoma State University; [occ.] Licensed Practical Nurse; [memb.] Oklahoma State Association of Licensed Practical Nurses; [oth. writ.] I have written many poems, but this is the first time I have submitted one.; [pers.] "In everything you do, be kind."; [a.] Clinton, OK

MOULTON JR., JOHN L.
[b.] June 12, 1955, Eutaw, AL; [p.] John L. Moulton Sr., Annie S. Moulton; [ed.] Eutaw High, Princeton University, University of Alabama; [occ.] Currently incarcerated at MCI-Norfolk in Norfolk, MA; [pers.] Jesus Christ Is Lord.; [a.] Norfolk, MA

MOWATT, AUTUMN DANIELLE
[b.] July 14, 1983, Englewood, CO; [p.] David S. and Sheryl J. Mowatt; [ed.] Castle Rock Middle School, 8th Grade; [hon.] Honor Roll Student, accepted into the International Baccalaureate Program for High School at Douglas County High; [pers.] Serious poetry is normally my style, but this one was great fun.; [a.] Castle Rock, CO

MOYNIHAN, KATE
[b.] February 11, 1982, Haverhill, MA; [p.] Charles and Kathleen Moynihan; [ed.] Currently in 9th grade at Haverhill High School; [occ.] Student; [pers.] Locked doors always have a hidden key.; [a.] Haverhill, MA

MUDDIMAN, RYAN DOUGLAS
[b.] July 10, 1971, Reading; [p.] Doug Muddiman, Joyce Muddiman; [m.] Mindy Muddiman, June 25, 1994; [ch.] Cameron-Sky Muddiman; [a.] Reading, OH

MUELLER, ANDREA
[pen.] Andrieka La Duke, Andeen Mueller; [p.] Ron and Kelly Connaughty, Michael H. Mueller; [occ.] United Auto Worker; [oth. writ.] An unpublished book of poetry entitled Another Day's Rest; [pers.] I would like to thank Kathy Kimmel and Sandra Stidell for believing in me. I would welcome the opportunity of working with other known artists in the future.; [a.] Utica, MN

MULAY, BHAVANA
[pen.] Manu; [b.] May 16, 1981, Nagpur, India; [p.] Vilas Mulay, Nilima Mulay; [ed.] Mount Carmel Convent High School, India graduated at Senior High, Grand Island, Nebraska; [occ.] Student in High School; [memb.] Key club, multicultural club; [hon.] Exchange student to the U.S. for the year 96-97 meritorious student of the district, best student of the school.; [oth. writ.] Some poems and articles published in local newspapers; [pers.] Life is not a bed of roses, it is made up of good and bad times. One should make optimum use of all the time in his or her life.; [a.] Chandrapur, MS

MULLEE, CHRISTAN
[b.] May 14, 1984, Gainesville, FL; [p.] Nancy and Bob Mullee; [ed.] Independent study, private tutors and Sylvin Learning Center; [memb.] The National Library of Poetry; [hon.] Three Editors Choice awards.; [oth. writ.] Survive, Beast, Kity Kit's Pouch, Oh Little One, Pain, My Feelings of Remorse, Sunny Day, Kit Kit, Paths, Soul Survivors, Bleeding, Fair.; [pers.] I think that no one is just good, or just evil, but in order to be whole, you must be both light and dark. Because knowledge is not wisdom without experience.; [a.] Gainesville, FL

MULLER, JENNY
[b.] August 5, 1982; Royal Oak; [p.] Barbara Muller; [ed.] High school; [occ.] High School Student at Henry Ford II; [memb.] French Club, SADD, youth group; [hon.] Michigan State Board of Education Certificate of Recognition for essential skills reading test, an award for outstanding oral expression; [oth.writ.] Mother's Day article in Daily Tribune; [pers.] For those who believe in me, loved me, and accepted me for who I am (Scott, Payne, Barb, Amanda, Mary Helle, Dorothy Sheley) Thanks, Love ya; [a.] MI.

MULLER JR., GENE FRANCHOT
[pen.] Jr.; [b.] June 4, 1966; Honolulu, HI; [p.] Gene Muller, Sr., Louise Patricia Muller; [ed.] Associates in Science Degree, Accounting, University of Hawaii, Associates in Arts, Liberal Arts, from University of Hawaii; [occ.] Materials Handler Technician for the National Guard, Income Tax Assessor; [memb.] Member of Hawaii Boxing Club; [hon.] Various degrees, certificates and medals from different institutions; [oth.writ.] Copyrighted 15 songs and lyrics from the Library of Congress in Washington, D.C. In the process of writing more music and will hopefully have them published; [pers.] I believe that poetry and music go hand-in-hand, and that literary arts is one of the structures of our society; [a.] Pearl City, HI.

MULLIGAN, CRISTIN
[pen.] Sorka, Sorka O'Maolagain; [b.] October 21, 1982, Iowa City, IA; [occ.] Student; [oth. writ.] Several poems and short stories, none are published.; [pers.] I try to reflect my ideas through my writing, and hope to somewhat portray myself.; [a.] Marshfield, WI

MULLIGAN, KERRY
[b.] August 2, 1982, Boston, MA; [p.] Barbara and John Mulligan; [ed.] Perkins Elementary, Condon Elementary, McCormack Middle, Fenway Middle College High; [occ.] Babysitter and billing for hardware store; [memb.] JFK Library Corps, Girl Scouts of America, Miss Linda's School of Dance 4th Presbyterian Ch. Music and Art 4th Presbyterian Church; [hon.] Technology Award, (Bank of Boston); [pers.] "Remember me now, so when I'm a star, you'll be able to say you know me!"; [a.] South Boston, MA

MUNIZ, RAFAEL
[b.] September 22, 1951, Bronx, NY; [p.] Manuela Colon; [ch.] Rafael Muniz Jr., Bobby Muniz; [ed.] Dewitt Clinton High School, New York City Community College, Herbert H. Lehman College Fordham University; [occ.] Educator/Social Worker; [memb.] Youth and Education Comm. Area Policy Board Member; [hon.] Teacher of the Year in my school 1987-1988-1989-1990 Boys Club Staff of the Year 1976 Achievement Award 1976, Achievement Award 1995; [oth. writ.] Many writings which are still not published - perhaps this is the vehicle by which my dream will become and reality.; [pers.] To have a positive impact on society. "Never ask why things are as they are, but ask how things are not and question why."; [a.] New York, NY

MUNSON, THURSTON
[pen.] Thurston Munson; [b.] April 24, 1906, Greenfield, MA; [p.] Dollie and Frank; [m.] Mollie (there have been 4); [ch.] Patricia, Elizabeth, Thurston Jr.; [ed.] High School - Art school; [occ.] Artist (painter); [hon.] Several in painting and architecture; [pers.] I have never found a reason to change an early conviction: "Fine Art is revelation beautifully presented".; [a.] Greenfield, MA

MURAWSKI, DOLORES L.
[pen.] Dolly; [b.] July 22, 1931, Webster; [p.] Mr. and Mrs. August Bembenek (Deceased); [m.] Stanley Murawski, June 28, 1952; [ch.] Robert and Martha; [ed.] St. Joseph's School, Bartlet High School; [occ.] Housewife; [pers.] I have always loved poetry and it seems that when I am out doors looking at the sky. The flowers and trees the words just come into my head from up above.; [a.] Webster, MA

MURPHY, MRS. MICHELLE J.
[pen.] Shelley Isobel; [b.] December 1, 1962, Poughkeepsie, NY; [p.] Jeanne and Lawrence Smith; [m.] Robert M. Murphy, May 2, 1992; [ch.] Shetland Sheepdogs: Sweet Dream, Daddy's Angel, n' Lif Bit O' Heaven; [ed.] Graduated John Jay High School in 1980. Graduated Dutchess Comm. College in 1984. A.A.S. in child care.; [occ.] Being a housewife, poet, and caretaker for our 3 furry children.; [memb.] I am a member of The International Society of Poets; [oth. writ.] The National Library of Poetry has previously published a few of my other poems.; [pers.] "Angel in heaven" reflects how our youngest Sheltie, Heaven, used to climb on Angel's back, and hug him with his Forepaws. L'il Bit O' Heaven was only a puppy of 9-12 weeks old at the time.; [a.] Stanfordville, NY

MURPHY, PAULA JEAN REID
[pen.] PJ; [b.] October 16, 1956, St. Louis, MO; [p.] George and Dolores Reid; [m.] Anthony Murphy, November 13, 1996; [ch.] Casey, Angi, Tina; [ed.] High School graduate 1974, Riverview Gardens; [occ.] Disabled; [memb.] My Family; [hon.] I held a job with the USDA. I received an award for exceptional job performance for almost each of the 14 years I was with them.; [oth. writ.] I have had 2 other of my poems published by your company/organization (maybe it was poetry guild) "Summer" and "My Love" and I have just around 40 more I could submit to you.; [pers.] I write from the heart. Just give me a subject, and 9 out of 10 times, I will turn it into a feeling, a poem and a special story; [a.] Saint Louis, MO

MUSSELMAN JR., ARTHUR
[pen.] Arthur Musselman, Jr.; [b.] January 8, 1946; Bloomsburg, PA; [p.] Arthur Musselman, Sr. and Esther; [m.] Mary Russell; August 6, 1966; [ch.] Arthur Musselman, III; [ed.] Benton Joint High, University of Georgia; [occ.] Fire Inspector Macon-Bibb County Fire Department; [memb.] Mason, American Legion, Georgia Fire Inspectors Association, University of Georgia Alumni Association, United States Marine Corps Association; [hon.] First class firefighter award, Letter of Commendation for project completion of New E-911 Center; [oth.writ.] The first Thanksgiving, The Moon's Glow, several poems, local; [pers.] I am truly a romantic at heart. I only wish all of mankind had a truly romantic heart I love all poetry; [a.] Hillsboro, GA.

MYERS, ANGELA MONIQUE
[b.] July 29, 1976, Arizona; [p.] Linda Kay Myers, Dennis Dee Myers; [ed.] High School Graduate; [oth. writ.] "Blake" about my brother and his beautiful family that was published in my High School Newspaper. "GreenWay High School"; [pers.] Thank - you mom for believing in me and my poetry! To all of my family I love you!; [a.] Phoenix, AZ

MYERS, DIANE M.
[b.] January 17, 1955, Minneapolis, MN; [p.] Edward and Marjory Lickteig; [m.] Mark C. Myers, April 30, 1994; [ch.] Matthew; [ed.] Edina High School, University of Minnesota - Duluth and Main Campus.; [occ.] Customer Assistance Manager, Chevrolet Motor Division; [a.] Spring City, PA

NADEAU, BRUCE R.
[pen.] N. M. Roger; [b.] January 19, 1972, Concord, NH; [p.] Jackie Neveu, Paul Nadeau; [ed.] Pembroke Academy High School, Hesser College, Northeastern University; [occ.] Police Officer; [pers.] There is no limit to what one can achieve if you live each day as if it were your last.; [a.] Allenstown, NH

NANCE, CATHERYN R.
[pen.] Catheryn R. Nance; [b.] February 2, 1948; Bridgeport, AL; [p.] Charles Raulston and Patsy I. Raulston; [m.] Earl T. Nance (deceased); July 29,

1967; [ed.] Bridgeport Elementary, Bridgeport High grade 1-10, Marion Country High School 11th, Bridgeport High School 12th, Chattanoga State Technical School; [occ.] Medical Transcriptionist; [memb.] First Baptist Church, Jasper, TN, Hope Sunday School Class, American Association of Medical Transcriptionists; [hon.] Beta Club, Dean's Honor List, Women's Business Group awarded a scholarship to me, Golden Rule Marble Girl; [oth. writ.] Book in the works titled: "The Way the Lord Touches My Life: My Joy"; [pers.] Trust in the Lord with all thine heart and learn not to thine own understanding. In all thy ways acknowledge Him and He shall direct thy paths. Proverbs 3: 5-6; [a.] Jasper, TN.

NASH, JESSE
[b.] September 2, 1946, Atlanta; [p.] Mary Elizabeth and William Emery; [ed.] University of Georgia, Liberal Arts, 2 years; [occ.] Disabled; [hon.] Letter, Drama Club, Brown High School, Dean's List, University of Georgia, Award of Excellence, Defense Language Institute, Monterey, CA; [oth. writ.] "Dreams", "The Sea", "Autumn Leaves", unmentionable limericks.; [pers.] Poetry is true communication of the soul, one can relate deep secret feelings without inhibition.; [a.] Aptos, CA

NASH, OTERA S.
[pen.] Brandi Capone; [b.] January 25, 1967, Pekin, IL; [p.] Larry and Janet Nash; [ed.] Graduated, Pekin Community High School, Pekin, IL; [oth. writ.] I also write short stories and plays.; [pers.] Most of my writing is inspired by the joys and sadness of everyday life. Although fantasy writing lets the imagination free.; [a.] Arcadia, FL

NASHTON, CATALDO
[pen.] Kit, or The Kidd; [b.] September 16, 1953, Rome; [p.] Olympia Nashton; [ch.] Amber Lynn, David Charles; [ed.] Rome Free Academy; [occ.] New York State Dept. of Corrections; [oth. writ.] Many other poems on Life, Love, and Loneliness for U.S. Army Stars and Stripes - 1973-75; [pers.] Look at the world, and it's people as a whole. Dreams, are for the dreamers, who believe in magic.; [a.] Rome, NY

NATION, CYNTHIA
[b.] January 9, 1989; Oakridge, TN; [p.] Ricky A. and Tammy F. Nation; [ed.] 2nd grade; [occ.] Student at Mount Pisgah Christian Academy [memb.] North American Association of Ventriloquists; [hon.] Selected to participate in Miss Preteen 1997 Contest, Celebrate 200! (summer reading program), Read across TN for readine 25 books at age 7, ventriloquist, balloon artist, puppeteer; [oth.writ.] "Red Bird, Blue Bird"; [pers.] I try to help other people in my writings; [a.] Oliver Springs, TN.

NAYAGAM, NORBERTA
[b.] Bombay India; [p.] Ambrose and Anna Nayagam; [ed.] St. Xavier's College, Bombay, India; [oth. writ.] My short stories and prose pieces have been published in India and Europe.; [a.] Bridgeport, CT

NEAL, JOHNATHAN
[b.] November 3, 1979, Bronx, NY; [p.] Leora Neal, Robert Neal; [ed.] Senior at Monsignor ScanLan High School, will graduate June '97, will attend School of Visual Arts College in the Fall; [occ.] Student; [memb.] Future Business Leaders of America (F.B.L.A.), Teens Helping Each Other (T.H.E.O.); [hon.] The Wesley cup for spirituality from the Cathedral School in June '93, Creative Writing Award from T.H.E.O., ScanLan H.S. Art Honor Roll; [oth. writ.] Poem Titles, Time, Death, Stress; [pers.] Everybody has talents that makes them unique from others. We all must have confidence in our talents and show others what we can do. By doing this we are showing God we are not wasting the gifts he gave us and in turn we become gifts to society.; [a.] Bronx, NY

NEAL, PATRICIA
[pen.] Patricia Neal, Patricia Dowling Neal; [ch.] Three grown children and seven grandchildren; [oth. writ.] Article: "In Memory Of My Dad"; [pers.] I enjoy reading, so in my writing I strive to cover areas in life from an early age thru advanced years. Warmth, caring, sensitivity and love are a great combination for me in my poems.; [a.] San Diego, CA

NELSON, JACKIE L.
[b.] September 30, 1960, Everett, WA; [p.] John W. and Alice M. Nelson; [ed.] Riverview Elementary, Snohomish, WA, Graduated from Selah High School in the year 1978; [occ.] I work at several part time jobs, usually in the Apple Warehouses; [oth. writ.] I have written several songs for my own pleasure. I suppose you would class them as folk and/or religious. I call them my "Songs of poetry".; [pers.] Little is known about life, but a lot is written about it. The more we write, the more we know.; [a.] Selah, WA

NELSON, MARK
[b.] June 20, 1980, Massachusetts; [p.] Mark Nelson, Mary Erin Nelson; [ed.] High School 11th grade; [occ.] Student/Photographer at Lion Country Safari, FL; [oth. writ.] First; [pers.] I strive for people to be aware about what is going on around them. I may be young but I am not blind. Thing's need to change and I hope my poems could help in some way!; [a.] Wellington, FL

NELSON, ROSA
[b.] February 16, 1950; Hackleburg, AL; [p.] William D. Frederick and Ruthie Lee; [m.] Mark Norris and Stanley Nelson; June 14, 1970 and divorced November 16, 1980; [ch.] Shannon Norris (26), David Shoy Norris (25), La Shanda Nelson (9); [ed.] High school, Hackleburg, AL, diploma, Computer Operation, top 10 in class, U.S.A. Marine Corps Honorable discharge 1970; [occ.] Birmingham news courier; [memb.] Sam's Club; [hon.] National Defense Medal; [oth.writ.] Not in print yet; [pers.] Keep your dreams alive and they will come true; [a.] Birmingham, AL.

NETTESHEIM, GERI LYNN
[b.] February 8, 1966, Milwaukee, WI; [p.] Winston and Gladys Sephus; [ch.] Raymond, Rachel, Ruth; Thanks to Jan for the gift of words. Thanks to my parents for the gift of freedom, thanks to my children, for their beauty moves my pen. Thanks to friends for the gift of love.; [a.] Plano, TX

NEWLAND, MATTHEW
[b.] January 18, 1980, Valentine, NE; [p.] Douglas, Elizabeth Newland; [oth. writ.] I am finishing work on my first book-length poem; [pers.] My interest in writing poetry began last year after re-reading some of J.R.R. Tolkien's works. My poem in this book is dedicated to Kate Butcher.; [a.] Valentine, NE

NICHOLSON, EDWARD A.
[b.] October 14, 1936, Glen Cove, NY; [p.] Edward W. and Annie Nicholson; [m.] Christina, May 20, 1960; [ch.] Kimberly; [ed.] Locust Valley Grammar School, H.S. - Glen Cove, High School, College - University of Hawaii; [occ.] VP Sales and Marketing - SPC Marketing Company; [memb.] Reformed Church of Locust Valley, Locust Valley, N.Y.; [hon.] Editor's Favorite Award 9 times, The National Library of Poetry; [oth. writ.] The Poetry Guild, A Walk of Bliss - Footsteps in the Sand, A Boy - Reflections of the Soul, The National Library of Poetry, Man's True Pride - A Muse to Follow, Condensed Beauty - Recollections of Yesterday, Invincible Force - Best Poems of the 90's, Winter's Night Wonderland - Whispers at Dusk, Eternity - Colors of Thought, Message of the Winding Stream - Memories of Tomorrow, Baby Seal - Colors of Thought, Ancient City Parable - Essence of a Dream, Potter's field Equipoise - A Moment to Reflect, New York Subway Escapade - The Nightfall of Diamonds, Utopia and Time - Etches in Time, Heaven's Gate - Tracing Shadows, The Rugged Coastline - The Best Poems of 1997, Armageddon Transpose - Through Sun and Shower, God's Message - A View From Afar; [pers.] If you've enjoyed my poem "Mother of Jesus" and would like to write me about it and this remarkable woman - please do so.; [a.] Glen Cove, NY

NICKEL, JOHN H.
[b.] December 31, 1957, Big Timber, MT; [p.] Howard and Margaret Nickel; [m.] Marilyn, December 27, 1980; [ed.] Oregon State University, B.S. Chemistry University of Houston, Ph.D. Analytical Chemistry; [occ.] Network Design Consultant; [memb.] American Chemical Society; [pers.] Misquote from a Solomon Islands "You sneeze you lose!" Life is requires choices, don't sneeze!; [a.] San Jose, CA

NIELSEN, ADAM
[b.] May 19, 1980, Conn., New London; [p.] Ken Nielsen; [ed.] 11th grade Ledyard High School; [occ.] Student; [pers.] Timing, is everything. "The truth is out there" - Deep Throat.; [a.] Norwich, CT

NIEMEYER, COLLEEN LOUISE
[b.] December 31, 1961, Lawton, OK; [p.] Alvin and Leona Von Seggern... and Noni Niemeyer; [m.] Michael (Mick) J. Niemeyer, March 6, 1987; [ch.] Kristina Amber, Lauren Helena, Michael Joseph; [ed.] Washington High School 1980; [occ.] Housewife, Mother; [oth. writ.] Personal collection of poetry; [pers.] My husband, children, family, and friends are those who inspired me to put pencil to paper. With each writing there is a silent message try and the paper and print my sincerest gratitude to everyone over the years who encouraged me to write.; [a.] Independence, MO

NIXON, LORI ELIZABETH
[b.] May 6, 1977; Ft. Bragg, NC; [p.] Lee, Michelle Nixon, Hilda Stephens; [ed.] GED; home schooling to be a paralegal; [occ.] Operator Services; [hon.] Several writing contests throughout school; [oth.writ.] I have been published in my local newspaper. I was published in the literary magazines

throughout high school. Published in a previous National Library of Poetry; [pers.] When I write, I write from my heart. So what may be affecting me that day will usually show up in my writing; [a.] Macon, GA.

NORMAN, BRANDY LYNN
[b.] March 10, 1983, Fort Worth, TX; [p.] Michael Norman, Sodra Norman; [ed.] Nichols Junior High, 7th Grade; [occ.] Going to school; [memb.] North Side Bapt. Church, Nichols Junior High, Choir Mustang Athletics Team, Texas Readers's Club, Awana's Bible Study; [hon.] Honors English, President's Education Award, All Star Student, A-B Honor Role, Young Authors Hall of Fame, Dare Graduate Award, Citizenship Award, TTAS Recognition Trophy, Safety Patrol Award; [oth. writ.] I have other poetry that I have wrote. But none published.; [pers.] When writing poetry I like to reflect the kindness and goodness that comes from the Lord. And the things that He has created.; [a.] Arlington, TX

NORRIS, GLEN A.
[pen.] Gan Astor; [b.] April 25, 1950, Jamaica, WI; [p.] Richard and Eunice Norris; [m.] Narisse Norris, August 18, 1990; [ch.] Annmarie, Richard and Ashley; [ed.] College of New Rochelle, NY, BA; [occ.] Teacher; [hon.] Dean's List; [oth. writ.] "Voice of Gan Astor," a collection of several poems. Read poems on radio program.; [pers.] I like to write from experience, things just fall in place.; [a.] Freeport, NY

NUSSBAUM, KIMBERLY
[b.] December 22, 1967, Pittsburgh, PA; [p.] James M. Sheppard, Barb Johnson; [m.] Dr. Paul David Nussbaum, August 9, 1986; [ch.] Ryan Paul, Andrew Paul, Paul David II; [ed.] University of Pittsburgh; [pers.] I love you.; [a.] Pittsburgh, PA

NYDEGGER, JOANNE ELLISON
[b.] August 24, 1935, Pittsburgh, PA; [p.] Joseph and Catherine Saunders Ellison; [m.] Fred Albin Nydegger, July 31, 1982; [ed.] B.S. Carnegie Mellon University M.A. Columbia University, Ph.D. - completed course-work. Dropped out during thesis research, retired H.S. teacher; [occ.] Free-lance Artist, Writer, Co-owner -Freds Cafe de Paris; [memb.] Travelers Century Club, Carnegie Mellon V. Admissions Council Carnegie Mellon U. Class Coorespondant, AAUW, Natl. Asso. Female Executives; [hon.] Selected to design and make a coat for the Orlando - Broadway Series Celebrity Auction. - Won 2nd place "How Orlando will be in 25 years." - My Personally - Artistically decorated home was featured in the Philadelphia Inquirer Magazine - win 1st prizes in many cruise - costume design contests - Who's Who in Female Executives - Home also was focus of 2 tour groups in New York to view my artistry. - Oriental collection - from my travels was displayed in a museum for 2 months.; [oth. writ.] Articles and artwork have been published in local and national newspapers and magazines. Wrote personal books; [pers.] Life is extraordinarily Beautiful!... reach out, explore, and experience, take chances - seek your bliss ... but don't take it too seriously. Enjoy it! ... and ... always help others; [a.] Orlando, FL

OGLETREE, BRITTANY DAWN
[b.] May 11, 1979, Amory, MS; [p.] Dr. Ben and Bennie Ogletree; [ed.] Heritage Academy, Colum-

bus, MS; [occ.] Student; [memb.] American Heart Association Youth Board, First Baptist Church, Beta Club, Mu Alpha Theta, Quill and Scroll; [hon.] Who's Who Among American High School Students, Beta Club Secretary, Ray Furr Journalism Award in Photography; [oth. writ.] Several poems published in National High School Anthologies.; [pers.] Psalm 139; [a.] Columbus, MS

OGUIBE, OLU
[b.] October 14, 1964, Aba, W. Africa; [ed.] B.A. Summa Cum Laude, Univ. of Nigeria, Ph.D., University of London; [occ.] Stuart S. Golding endowed chair, Univ. of South Florida; [hon] 1992 Christopher Origbo all-Africa prize for literature, 1993 hon. mention, Noma Award for publishing in Africa, British foreign office Scholars Award, Rockefeller Foundation Award, arts council of Great Britain new Artist Collaborations Award; [oth. writ.] 1. A Song From Exile, (Boomerang Verlag, Bayreuth (1990) 2. A gathering fear (Boomerang, 1992 kraftbooks 1992) 3. Songs for Catalina (savannah press, 1994), 4. So Journers (Arpc, London, 1994); [a.] Tampa, FL

OKOROH, EMEKA ROBERT
[b.] July 29, 1991; Detroit; [p.] Major Godson Okoroh and Pauline M. Okoroh; [ed.] Kindergarten; [occ.] Scholar; [hon.] Young Writers and Illustrators Awards Competitions, Certificate of award in Fl Academic Excellence at Gesu School, Certificate of Achievement in Sea Horses (swimming), Trophy Award in Kia Kicker Soccer; [oth.writ.] Airplanes, not yet published. Submitted to Reading Rainbows; [pers.] I will continue to write on the things I like and other people will like too; [a.] Detroit, MI;

OKOROH, PAULINE ONWUZURIKE
[b.] June 23, 1959; Aba, Nigeria; [p.] Sabastine and Philomena Onwuzurike; [m.] Mr. Godson M. Okoroh; March 23, 1991; [ch.] Emeka and Chidimma Okoroh; [ed.] Masters of Arts in Teaching, Masters of Education in Educational Leadership, B.S. in Business Administration, Associate Degree in Arts; [occ.] Elementary Teacher, MAAT Imhotep Technical Academy, Det. MI; [memb.] Detroit Federation of Teachers, National Teachers Association of Michigan; [hon.] National Honor Fraternity Highland Park Community College, Highland Park, Michigan; [pers.] I am writing to inspire people to believe in God. With the desire, decision and determination, God will make them to be all they want to be; [a.] Detroit, MI.

OLIVER, IVY JEAN
[b.] January 1, 1932; London, England; [p.] Ann and Eric Parker; [m.] Deceased; October 29, 1951; [ch.] Four; [ed.] High school, England; [occ.] I was in Ladies Retail for over 35 years (now retired); [oth.writ.] The only other letters I have had printed is with my local newspaper in Bakersfield, CA; [pers.] I have always loved poetry, first one I ever submitted, Thank You; [a.] Bakersfield, CA.

OLSICK, CARMELA R.
[pen.] Carmela De Simone; [b.] June 30, 1959, Chicago, IL; [ch.] Gabrielle, Danielle; [ed.] Kelly High School, Institute of Children's Literature, Long Ridge Writer's Group; [occ.] Hairstylist; [memb.] St. George Parish, Perpetual Adoration Society; [oth. writ.] Collection of Poems in

progress; [pers.] Time is more important than money. Anyone can get more money, no one can get more time.; [a.] Tinley Park, IL

OLSON, JEANNE E.
[b.] August 7, 1929, Kenmare, ND; [p.] Robert and Ruth Gehring; [m.] Lewis Olson (Deceased), December 22, 1949; [ch.] Meredy then Ann and Steven Lewis; [ed.] Kenmare High School, Minot Business College; [occ.] Retired; [memb.] AARP, NARFE, American Legion Auxiliary, Methodist Church; [pers.] Think to reflect my feelings into readable words for others.; [a.] Minot, ND

ONYEULO, CHARLES I. O.
[pen.] C. Lhekoronye Onyeulo; [b.] August 16, 1953; Calabar, Nigeria; [p.] Peter, Patricia Ulumma Onyeulo; [m.] Lisa Chinelor Ugoezi Onyeulo; May 25, 1985; [ch.] Alecia Adamma, C. Ezenna Ovuenyi; [ed.] B.A. Classical Humanties, MA Masters Public Administration; [occ.] Financial AD administrator, businessman, writer; [mem.] IGBO Organization, African Community Association (ACA); [hon.] Most enthusiastic, voluteerism, soccer coach awards, community service; [oth.writ.] Nigeria's IGBO names for African Americans, The Onyessy, The Ihad, Thank You America, The Living Conditions Of African Americans in 1990's, Peter Onyeulo, The Man Of Suffering etc. (all in progress); [pers.] 'Fate shares the balance in some lives', 'Fortune favors the brave', 'High intellectuals like the tops of mts. are the first to catch and reflect the dawn', Women's Organization; [a.] Richmond Hill, NY.

OPAL, MAUREEN E.
[b.] February 24, 1943; Hot Springs, SD; [p.] Joseph and Jeanne Callahan; [m.] Bruce B. Opal; October 28, 1972; [ch.] Kelly (28), Joseph (27), Brian (23) grandchildren, Adriane, Daniel (8 months); [ed.] Wray Public High, Loretto Heights College, St Joseph Hospital School of Nursing (all in colo); [occ.] Hime Health Hospice RN, Scottsdale Memorial Hospital, Scottsdale, AZ; [memb.] Society of Urological Nurses, Chair. St. Maria Garett Catholic Church, Diocecene Chair of Phoenix; [hon.] Academic scholarship jr. year nsg. school, Chapter 7 Nurse of the Year (Colo. Nurses Assoc. 1989), Rosette Stone Finalist for Patient Education Literature 1985, American Urological Association, Allied; [oth.writ.] Several liturgical music pieces, patient education instruction material and in-service workshops in nursing education; [pers.] Favorite authors: William Shakespeare, C.S. Lewis, P.T. Lonroy, Emily Dickinson, Maya Angelou, The Rhyming Satyrist, Odgen Nash, Cardinal Henri Nouwens, Pope John Paul II and Mother Theresa. I am down to the truth pain and beauty of the human condition and our hunger for oneness with the Creator; [a.] Fountain Hills, AZ.

OPERAJITA, OOPALIE
[b.] Cuttack, India; [p.] Prof. P. N. Das, Prof. B. Das; [ch.] Ayus Aditya Kennedy; [ed.] Rishi Valley School, 'O' Levels, M.A. Delhi University, M.A. English, Dalhousie University, M.A. Professional Writing, Carnegie Mellow University; [occ.] Choreographer/Odissi Classical Dancer/Consultant - Professional Communications and Business Writing; [hon.] National Science Talent Award, National Merit Scholar, Rotary Foundation International Educational Award, Chancellors Prize for

Best Debater in Univ., Singarmani, Voted Best Dancer at Khajuraho Festival of Dance (India's Leading Dance Festival), Performance in Nov. '96, Voted in Top Ten '96 by Pittsburgh Post Gazette; [oth. writ.] Scholarly articles on dance and aesthetics in several magazines, anthologies, journals and newspapers.; [a.] Pittsburgh, PA

OPPENHEIM, MICHAEL HENRY
[b.] September 26, 1968; [ed.] B.A. Slavic Languages and Literature, Indiana University 1991; [occ.] United States Marine; [a.] Oceanside, CA

ORTEGA, TONI ROXANN
[pen.] Toni Ortega; [b.] July 31, 1980, Odessa, TX; [p.] Tony and Irene Ortega; [ed.] Home Schooled from 9th grade, now attending Midland College; [occ.] Student, help parents with their business ventures; [hon.] 7th Grade National Honor Society; [oth. writ.] Several other poems not yet published. Compiling a book of poems to submit for publishing.; [pers.] These poems are my definition of what love means. All kinds of love can be very inspiring.; [a.] Midland, TX

OSTRICH, DEBBIE K.
[b.] September 23, 1956; [p.] Carl H. Ostrich Sr. and Helen Ostrich; [ed.] Uniontown Area High School; [occ.] Dept. Store Clerk; [memb.] Supporter, Vietnam Veterans of Fayette County; [pers.] A special note of thanks to my cousin Art and other members of the veterans' community, whose inspiration and words of encouragement have rekindled my creative poetic passions.; [a.] Uniontown, PA

OTTAVI, FRANCES E.
[pen.] Fran Ottavi; [b.] March 8, 1937, Knox, Indiana; [p.] Stella Kinney and Earl Coyer; [m.] Robert J. Ottavi, July 14, 1979; [ch.] Christine Avery and Grady Williams; [ed.] Knox High School; [occ.] Vice President-Ottavi and Son Tile and Marble; [memb.] Boats US, Stuart Yatch Club, ARRP; [hon.] Certificate of Achievement in Music Piano; [oth. writ.] One song-several poems currently writing a book-nothing published to date.; [pers.] Enjoy writing about events and things that deeply touch me personally or about wonderful qualities I see in others that other people might relate to in their lives.; [a.] Port Saint Lucie, FL

OVALLE, WILLIAM RICARDO FARFAN
[b.] April 13, 1963, Bogota, Colombia; [p.] Fanny I. Ovalle and Julio Farfan; [m.] Linda Farfan, November 27, 1994; [ch.] Two step-sons; [ed.] College, Mechanical Engineering; [occ.] Sales Representative; [hon.] Poet title, publish a narration at National University (Columbia); [oth. writ.] Narrations (Reposo) poems; [pers.] Freedom of nature implies inside the human being.; [a.] Louisville, KY

OWEN, ROY
[b.] December 28, 1937, Hollywood, CA; [p.] Roy and Ethel Owen; [m.] Sharon Owen, January 26, 1995; [ch.] Gina, Jennifer, David, Melanie; [ed.] Mira Costa H.S., Manhattan Beach, CA, USAF Tech Schools; [occ.] Retired; [memb.] The Human Race; [oth. writ.] Love letters in numerous relationships.; [pers.] I enjoy people from young to old. I don't think most people are dumb. We just do dumb things. I believe that God loves me.; [a.] Los Osos, CA

PAGE, LAURA A.
[b.] April 21, 1917, Pittsfield, MA; [p.] Laura A. and George H. Perron; [m.] Henry D. Page, December 7, 1944; [ch.] Laura Page Cox (Waterbury, Conn.); [ed.] Pittsfield High, Bridgewater State Col. (Mass.); [occ.] Retired English Teacher, Pittsfield, Mass. and Albuquerque, N.M.; [hon.] Editor Campus Comment (college paper); [pers.] I needed to express my grief over the loss of my father. This poem was my emotional release.; [a.] Rio Rancho, NM

PALMER, JOSEPH D.
[pen.] Joseph D. Palmer; [b.] July 15, 1926, Passaic, NJ; [p.] Dayton and Evelyn Palmer; [m.] Eileen O'Loughlin, June 16, 1951; [ch.] Michael, Edward, Shane, Sheila; [ed.] High School, St. Patrick's Academy - Binghamton, NY, S.U.N.Y. - Binghamton, NY, BA; [occ.] Retired; [a.] Boynton Beach, FL

PALMER (HILL), JOELLA
[pen.] Joella Palmer; [b.] September 4, 1941; Trinidad, CO; [p.] Mr. and Mrs. Billie Palmer; [m.] Mr. Bob Hill; June 28, 1959; [ch.] 3- Vance, Tate and Rafe Dottie; [ed.] High School Grad, Hashme, CO, Bette Bonn International Modeling And Charm School Des Moines, IA; [occ.] Rancher and Model, Rodeo Queen Contest Judge, 5 States Trained Rodeo Queens; [memb.] Methodist Church; [hon.] Written about and honored for my teaching rodeo queens, you gave me the Editor's Choice Award for my poem "Ode to a Cowboy," in Daybreak on the Land, had article on my editor's choice award in two local papers, La Juenta Co. Tribune Democrat, Trinidad Blues, Roton, New Mexico; [oth.writ.] Did an advertisement for (spring) water (poem or catchy statement) for La Juenta Line Stock CO; [pers.] I write about the cowboys cowgirls horses and etc. Just the country way of life; [a.] Model, CO.

PARIAS, JULIE
[b.] July 6, 1979, Baltimore, MD; [p.] Bill and Carol Parias; [ed.] Lenawee Christian and Tecumseh Public High School; [oth. writ.] Journalism Excellence Awards and English Excellence Awards; [pers.] Always be yourself, never allow yourself to become a mold.; [a.] Tecumseh, MI

PARKER, ROMONDA DEE
[b.] March 14, 1970, Evansville, IN; [p.] James Parker, Lottie Parker; [ch.] Jeremiah James, Joseph Douglas; [ed.] Pre-school Teacher; [a.] Evansville, IN

PARKS, SHANNON
[b.] May 24, 1978; Danville, IL; [p.] David and Tina Straughn; [ed.] Graduate from Grace Christian Academy; [oth.writ.] Another one of my writings was published in the anthology "Of Moonlight and Wishes"; [pers.] My poems are dedicated to my grandfather, William Franklin Maring This is for all his love and patience. He is greatly missed by all; [a.] Williamsport, IN.

PARRISH, DARLENE F.
[b.] July 14, 1937, Roundup, MT; [p.] Ralph A. Hogan, Arlene R. Fiske; [m.] Lanny H. Parrish, February 15, 1980; [ch.] Vanessa Lee Argyres, Brian James Lasater; [ed.] South Salem High School, Salem, OR, Southwestern Oregon Community College, Coos Bay, OR; [occ.] Business Administrator, Bay Group Anesthesia Svc. P.C.; [memb.] Coos

Bay Elks #1160, Coos Bay - North Bend Rotary, 1st Presbyterian Church; [oth. writ.] Multiple poems, unpublished.; [a.] North Bend, OR

PASCHAL, NICOLE
[b.] October 26, 1976, Indianapolis, IN; [p.] Betty Paschal, C. Paschal; [ed.] Ben Davis High School, Ball State University, IUPUI; [occ.] Student Majoring in Anthropology; [oth. writ.] High school and college publications; [pers.] Poe has been my greatest inspiration. My writings surface from the exploration of those hidden emotions which torment the heart, mind and soul.; [a.] Indianapolis, IN

PATTERSON, ROBERT HUGH
[pen.] Robert Hugh Patterson; [b.] July 24, 1965, Beale AFB, CA; [p.] Lawrence R. and Virginia A. Patterson; [ch.] Robert H. Patterson Jr.; [ed.] Cordova Senior High (1983), BSCS, National University (1994); [occ.] M/S Manager, Orrick, Herrington and Sutcliffe, LLP; [a.] Belmont, CA

PAYNE, LEVI
[b.] October 18, 1980, Greeley, CO; [p.] Ed Payne and Karen Payne; [ed.] Sophomore in high school; [occ.] Student; [a.] Eaton, CO

PEARCE, NICHOLAS A.
[b.] March 16, 1985, Chicago, IL; [ed.] 6th grade; [occ.] 6th grade student; [memb.] Apostolic Church of God, Saving Grace Ministries, South Central Basketball Association; [hon.] Honor Roll for 6 years, 2nd place, Chicago public schools (1996) Math Olympics, 3rd Place Region 6 1997, CPS Young Author's Competition, 1st Place, 1997, Keller School Essay Contest, 1st place, 1997, Region 6 Math Olympics; [a.] Chicago, IL

PEARLMAN, HARRY
[b.] September 7, 1920, Memphis, TN; [p.] Philip (Deceased) and Regina Pearlman; [m.] Liverne A. Pearlman, April 2, 1941; [ch.] Marilyn Pearlman, Joanne P. Fleetwood; [ed.] Memphis State U.; [occ.] Real State Broker; [oth. writ.] "Valerie and Mister Funderful" (pub. 1983), "This Is My Own" (unpublished) set in post civil war Memphis, newspaper and magazine articles re: Medical Information.; [pers.] I have been fascinated by creative talent all my life.; [a.] Decatur, GA

PEARSON, LANITA
[b.] December 22, 1987, Chicago, IL; [p.] Lee R. Pearson Jr., Elizabeth Pearson; [ed.] Sauk/Matteson Elementary School, Burnside Scholastic Academy Elementary School; [memb.] Girl Scout (Troop 256), Youth Choir Christ Universal Temple, Studio One Dance Conservatory, Dancer Gifted Student, Gifted/Talent Program; [hon.] High Honor Roll, Principle Scholar, 1st Place Science Fair winner Kindergarten and 1st Grade, Outstanding Behavior Award Perfect Attendance Award, Young Authors Award 1st and 2nd Grade; [oth. writ.] Several stories in school and at home. I wrote 2 books and several poems.; [pers.] I want to be a writer, dancer and actress. I plan to continue being a high honor roll student. After high school, I plan to attend Harvard University.; [a.] Richton Park, IL

PEARSON, MONTEGO
[pen.] Tego; [b.] May 1, 1979, Goldsboro, NC; [p.] Sharron Pearson, Trueman Lofton; [ed.] Goldsboro High School; [hon.] Mind's eye poetry contest;

[oth. writ.] Several poems unpublished, I also write and perform songs, but I do not have a second deal and I am striving to get one.; [pers.] I strive to write poems that interests the young and old. I also like to use my imagination and creativity to write about other things besides a love relationship or the goodness of the weather effect.; [a.] Goldsboro, NC

PECK, LORRA
[b.] June 13, 1957, Enid, OK; [p.] Gene and Joan Ruhl; [m.] Brian K. Peck, August 19, 1978; [ch.] Colin McKenzie, Kelsy Quinlan; [ed.] Enid High School; [occ.] Self Employed, Stitch Station, Enid, OK; [memb.] President, Hoover PTA, Treasurer, Humane Assoc. of Enid; [pers.] I am devoted to the happiness and well being of my family, actively participating in my children's lives. My goal is to help them grasp a positive future.; [a.] Enid, OK

PECTOR, SALLY
[b.] March 18, 1971; Queens, NY; [p.] Francine Pector; [ed.] Plainview old Beth Page H.S., Nassua Community College, Dowling College; [occ.] Expeditor in a purchasing dept. of an electrical company; [oth.writ.] Include an extensive collection of poetry and short stories which at press time has not been released for publication; [pers.] I have always found great comfort and sanity in writing. It's been a form of therapy. I can only hope it reaches and touches other as deeply as I intend it to. I believe knowing you're not alone, can give you the strength to go on; [a.] Plainview, NY.

PEDROZA, ALICIA RENEE
[b.] September 25, 1979, Gary, IN; [p.] Edith and Jessie Olmo; [ed.] Portage High School; [memb.] Powerhouse Gym, Business Professionals of America; [hon.] Pictured in the "Who's Who in America" yearbook.; [oth. writ.] "By The Sea", "Euphoria", "Best of Friends", "Company", "Dream Away". All poems written by Alicia Pedroza.; [pers.] I get my inspiration from special people in my life, personal experiences, and music. I free myself in my poetry and hope that whoever is reading it, knows they are not alone.; [a.] Portage, IN

PELNIS, ERIC G.
[pen.] 'E'; [b.] June 17, 1969, Portland, OR; [p.] Madeleine Mernik, Andris Pelnis; [ed.] Coon Rapids H.S., Mound Westonka H.S., Community College of the Air Force; [occ.] Writer/Philosopher; [oth. writ.] 'The Angel I'd Wished Upon my Side'.; [pers.] "Life is a continual learning process, with the most intricate of details left to the imagination". Thank you Lesha.; [a.] Plymouth, MN

PERERA, MELANIE
[b.] January 21, 1981, Long Beach, CA; [p.] Earl Perera and Lalitha Rasaputra; [ed.] Currently attending Foothill High School; [occ.] Full time student; [memb.] California Scholarship Federation; [hon.] High Honor Role, Special Recognition Award; [pers.] My words are simply my thoughts.; [a.] Santa Ana, CA

PERROTT, MAYA
[b.] February 1, 1974, New York; [p.] Ralph Francis Robert and Marianela Furgerson; [oth. writ.] Currently working on first novel (Bio-Thriller-Romance).; [pers.] A chef I will never forget to taste, the people who have

influenced my insanity. The sons and daughters who smile at me.; [a.] Alameda, CA

PERRY, CAROL A.
[pen.] Carol Ransom Perry; [b.] November 25, 1938, Saint Paul, MN; [p.] Mr. Lasalle and Katherine Ransom; [m.] Divorced; [ch.] Robert, Darryl, Trahern, Crews; [ed.] University of MN, Ramsey County Opportunities Ctr Tutor, St. Paul Literacy Program; [occ.] Teacher Asst.; [memb.] Free at Last Church; [hon.] Volunteer for different services; [oth. writ.] I have several other poems they have never been published.; [pers.] Show love.; [a.] Saint Paul, MN

PERSON, HEATHER
[b.] December 19, 1973, Stillwater, OK; [p.] Myrla Cole Haury and Kent Haury; [m.] James Rolston, August 13, 1995; [ed.] BS in Zoology - University of Oklahoma (1995); [occ.] Vista Americorps Volunteer at East Texas Literacy Council; [memb.] Longview Bicycle Club; [hon.] Phi Beta Kappa, National Merit Scholar; [oth. writ.] Various poems, short essays and editorials; [pers.] Writing helps me clarify and understand who I am.; [a.] Longview, TX

PETERSON, JANENE
[b.] April 20, 1955, Gardena, CA; [p.] John and Victorene Peterson; [ch.] Jolene Dee Peterson; [ed.] El Segundo High School, Calif., Long Beach University, Calif.; [occ.] Bartender, Waitress, Cook; [memb.] Moose Aux., VFW Aux. (V.P 1994); [oth. writ.] My own collection.; [pers.] I'm just a small town gal who's been honored and awarded with the most valued precious gifts ever presented: life, love, friends, and a child.; [a.] Lake Havasu City, AZ

PETRILLI, RYAN
[b.] December 30, 1973, Wilmington, DE; [p.] Joe and Jean Petrilli; [ed.] A.I. DuPont High School, High Point University, High Point, NC; [occ.] Part-time Caterer and Part-time Writer; [memb.] Pi Kappa Alpha; [oth. writ.] Several published poems in the Lamplighter, the University's Literary Magazine, plus poems published in various books. Also, several songs recorded.; [pers.] I believe every moment is an inspiration.; [a.] Newark, DE

PFALZGRAF, P. KENNETH
[b.] April 28, 1929, Pittsburgh, PA; [p.] August and Lena Pfalzgraf; [m.] Jeanne Coulter, June 14, 1952; [ch.] Richard Pfalzgraf, Susan Reidel; [ed.] B.S. and M.A. University of Pittsburgh; [occ.] Retired; [memb.] Past Trustee President and Tenor Soloist at Stone U.M. Church, Past President and 30 yrs. member of Meadville Kiwams Club Past Officer of numerous Masonic Bodies; [hon.] Kiwanis Distinguished President, Gerwig Unselfish Service Award, Knight York Cross of Honour, Order of Purple Cross; [oth. writ.] Some Masonic writings and poetry; [pers.] Follow the Golden Rule to success and happiness.; [a.] Meadville, PA

PFARR, STEVE
[b.] July 19, 1970, Marshall, MN; [p.] Ken Pfarr, Cathy Woelfel; [m.] Anja Pfarr; [occ.] Student St. Cloud State University; [pers.] Remember yesterday dream about tomorrow live today; [a.] Buffalo, MN

PHELPS, JUDITH T.
[pen.] Judy Phelps; [b.] September 30, 1921, Baltimore, MD; [p.] Rachel and Taylor Thom; [m.] David

Phelps, December 11, 1948; [ch.] Catherine and Virginia; [ed.] B. Mus. and M. Mus. Oberlin Conservatory, Ohio; [occ.] Retired Piano Teacher, Church Musician: Homedale Presbyterian Church; [memb.] Owyhee County Historical Society, Caldwell Thursday Musicale, Idaho Music Teachers Assoc., Gem State Writers' Guild, Choral Union (Caldwell, ID); [hon.] Pi Kappa Lambda (1942); [oth. writ.] Articles and short stories; [a.] Homedale, ID

PHILLANDER, NATASHA R.
[b.] June 20, 1972; [a.] Brooklyn, NY

PHILLIPS, ALIA NOEL
[b.] May 12, 1985, Florida; [p.] Walter and Catherine Phillips; [ed.] St. Stanislaus School; [occ.] Babysit; [memb.] Drama club, horseback riding (English), Dighton softball team, choir, alter server, Polish dancing.; [hon.] Student of the month. Horseback riding, 3 ribbons softball, trophy art certificates; [oth. writ.] "Silver," "The Medieval Spell," "The Big Blizzard"; [pers.] Don't give up, we all have things we're good at.; [a.] North Dighton, MA

PHILLIPS, ARTHUR R.
[pen.] Art; [b.] November 16, 1966, Pompton Plains, NJ; [p.] Arthur and Marilyn Phillips; [m.] Laura, May 31, 1997; [ed.] Passaic Cty Tech and Voc HS, William Paterson College, Devry; [occ.] Sales, soon to be an English Teacher; [memb.] U.S. Air Force, Church - Riverdale Baptist Church; [oth. writ.] Several poems I'd like to see published.; [pers.] I strive to reflect the inner feelings of mankind in my writing. I have been influenced by my surroundings and experiences.; [a.] Hawthorne, NJ

PHILLIPS, DEBRA
[pen.] Debra Phillips; [b.] January 21, 1960, Stuttgart, AR; [p.] Mr. and Mrs. Will Isbell; [m.] Richard Phillips, January 21, 1987; [ch.] Robbie, Ricky, Wes; [ed.] High School, diploma, 1 1/2 years college at Central Baptist College. In school now UALR Computer Science 1997; [occ.] Manager of a Mapco Express 7328; [hon.] Beta Club, Manager of the Year 1996

PHILLIPS, DEBRA K.
[b.] July 13, 1956, Tyrone, PA; [p.] Richard Nearhoof (Deceased), Joyce Michael; [m.] Roderick L. Phillips, July 27, 1974; [ch.] Stephanie Ann; [ed.] Muncy High School, - Graduated State Beauty School, Williamsport, PA, - Graduated Attended Pennsylvania College of Technology part-time; [occ.] Housewife; [memb.] American Liver Foundation, Hep. C Foundation, Eastern Star, National Society of Tole Decorative Painters, Moreland Baptist Church, Muncy, PA; [hon.] Teach Time Release (Religious Instruction) for the 5th and 6th graders at Hughesville, PA; [oth. writ.] Several poems for friends, family and doctors. Never published just given as gifts.; [pers.] My poetry is written for others as they handle life's problems and celebrations of life. I have had a Bone Marrow Transplant which has shown me the true meaning of life, although sadly I contracted Hepatitis from transplant which will end my life soon. If I can help others see life through my poetry, then it is well worth it!; [a.] Muncy, PA

PHILLIPS, ROGER W.
[pen.] R. William Phillips; [b.] January 5, 1969, Saint Louis, MO; [p.] Paul and Margaret Phillips; [ed.] Lindbergh High School; [occ.] Bartender; [oth.

writ.] Several unpublished poems, for example, "The Walking Dead," "Lost Memories," "Looking For The Light."; [pers.] Love is the water of life and without it the soul will die. Nothing will make you ponder the meaning of life more than a broken heart.; [a.] Saint Louis, MO

PICCIONE, EDYTHE V.
[b.] April 19, 1921, U.S.A.; [m.] Fred A. Piccione; [ch.] Four; [ed.] Bachelor of Science in Business Administration; [occ.] Retired; [hon.] Who's Who of American Women, Published Author, Professional Artist Hall of Fame - Bridal Industry; [oth. writ.] "Glamour's Bridal Business", "Facts and Fashions for the Bride", "We Call It Gravy"; [pers.] Poetry is a song of Beauty - Expressing emotions verbally - and telling truths.; [a.] Juno Beach, FL

PICKA, BILL
[pen.] Q Dogg; [b.] April 1, 1978, New Prague, MN; [p.] Ed and Grace Picka; [ed.] High School (and High School only); [occ.] Coffee Shop Barrista; [oth. writ.] A variety of poems and parodies of songs; [pers.] "Be stupid, in an intellectual way".; [a.] Eagan, MN

PIKE, ARIIA
[b.] May 1, 1980; Anchorage, AK; [p.] Ben Pike, Diana Pike; [ed.] Junior in high school; [occ.] Student; [oth.writ.] Many other poems and essays. Some poems published in other publications and in numerous newspaper articles.; [a.] Chugiak, AK.

PILALAS, MICHELLE
[pen.] Michelle; [b.] August 16, 1984; AL; [p.] Steve and Nancy Pilalas; [ed.] Centerville Elementary, Queensbury Elementary Merrymount Elementary, Meadow Middle School; [occ.] 7th grade; [memb.] Drama Club, Softball,track,Chorus Band, Soccer; [hon.] Awards from school, and an award for an art project I did, Human Rights Advocate I have been on the Highhonors/Honor roll for 7 grades; [pers.] Try your best at everything and don't give up; [a] Quincy, MA.

PINA JR., JAIRO
[pen.] Jairo; [b.] December 11, 1977, Colombia; [p.] Jairo and Zorayda Pina; [ed.] High school in Venezuela. Part of college at UNITEC Venezuela, currently studying electrical engineering at the University of Toledo; [occ.] Student; [memb.] Latino Student Organization MECHA-LSU, Electrical Engineering Honorary Eta Kappa Mu, Electrical Engineering Society IEEE; [hon.] Membership at Eta Kappa Mu, Dean's List at the University of Toledo during spring 96. First place in science fair in 9th grade. Outstanding award of academic achievement in high school graduation.; [pers.] Every time you look at someone, look for details nobody else sees. If they make the person look beautiful, never hesitate to say it.; [a.] Perrysburg, OH

PIPER, STEVE
[b.] September 29, 1950; Fargo, N. Dak; [p.] Deceased, Fred and Belvidere Piper; [m.] Dianna Piper; [m.] October 17, 1981; [ch.] Elliott, Gabriel; [ed.] 2 years at North Dakota State Universtiy and 2 years at University of North Dakota, Occupational and Physical Therapy; [occ.] Disabled -I have Cerebral Palsy and rheumatoid arthritis; [memb.] Gallery 522, Lion Lutheran Church board of Lay Ministry, Governors Council on Developmental Disabilities; [oth. writ.] My Best Friend, Sporting Chance, Hunters Lament, Neon Rainbow, My Dads A Cowboy, My Old Man, My Father; [pers.] I write from the heart, from past experiences or things people ask me to write about; [a.] Bismarck; ND.

PITA, JESSE
[b.] October 28, 1986; Pt. Washington, NY; [pers.] This poem is dedicated to my grandpa, Mr. Louis Dankner and to the greatest teacher, Mr. Robert Pfizenmayer. It was Mr. Pfiz who taught me to love poetry.

PLETZ, VICKY
[pen.] Vickly Pletz; [b.] January 30, 1983; Wash., USA; [p.] Gary and Felicity Pletz; [ed.] John Paul College, Brisbane, Queensland, Australia 1993-1996, Laurel Springs High School, Ojai, California, 1996; [occ.] Student; [hon.] Music awards; [a.] Longview, WA.

PLOTCZYK, ALICE M.
[b.] January 23, 1947, Worcester; [p.] Edw. and Alyce (Deceased); [ch.] Lisa M. Plotczyk; [ed.] South High School, Quinsigamond Community College, Medical Resources; [occ.] Certified Home Health Aide; [memb.] St. Mary's Guild for Women; [hon.] 1st Place in a poetry contest in college my freshman year.; [oth. writ.] Love And Light, A Summer Memory, Night Rhythm, Moods, From The Depths; [a.] Worcester, MA

PLUMM, LYNDSEY
[b.] April 11, 1982, Pontiac, MI; [p.] Robert and Deborah Plumm; [ed.] 9th Grade; [occ.] Student; [memb.] Brandon High School Student Council; [hon.] Honor Roll: 7th, 8th, 9th grade; [oth. writ.] This is my first.; [pers.] I wrote this poem to reflect my thoughts about my dad who died unexpectedly November 17, 1993 while I was at school. I loved him very much and think about him every day.; [a.] Ortonville, MI

POEL, EMILY
[b.] November 6, 1978, Kalamazoo, MI; [p.] Bill Poel, Kathy Poel; [ed.] Calvin Christian High School; [occ.] Student (at Calvin Christian High School); [memb.] Grand Rapids Ballet; [hon.] Class Officer for 3 years, received a Distinguished Artists Award from Hope College (which is a scholarship for dance); [pers.] This poem was written in honor of my very much loved Uncle Jack.; [a.] Grand Rapids, MI

POINTER, CHRISTINE
[pen.] Chris; [b.] July 20, 1963, Statesboro, GA; [p.] Lee and Burdie Brown; [ed.] Associates Degree, General Studies, NVCC; [occ.] Office Assistant, Hospitality Programs, Central Texas College; [memb.] Students-In-Free-Enterprise (SIFE), Christian House of Prayer, Rhema Choir, Scribes Ministry, Austin Songwriter's Group.; [oth. writ.] Unpublished book in poetry, several articles for local church newspaper "Celebration News," and many gospel songs inspired by God.; [pers.] "And how shall they preach, except they be sent? As it is written, how beautiful are the feet of them that preach the gospel of peace, and bring glad tidings of good things!"; [a.] Copperas Cove, TX

POTTS, KEVIN MICHAEL
[b.] May 20, 1976, Columbus Air Force Base, Columbus, MS; [p.] Major John Edward Potts, Betty L. Goodwin and George L. Goodwin (step-father); [ed.] I graduated from Halls High School in Knoxville Tennessee with an Honors diploma and am currently a senior at Carson-Newman College in Jefferson City Tennessee. I will graduate in the spring of 1998 with a bachelor's degree in Psychology.; [occ.] As well as being a full time student I am employed full time at Baptist Hospital in Knoxville TN as a Gero-Psychiatric Assistant. I am also an Amway Distributor.; [memb.] I am a member of the National Authors Registry, National Parks and Conservation Association, Salem Baptist Church of Halls, Carson-Newman College Baptist Student Union (BSU).; [hon.] Honors Diploma at Halls High School, "One in Ten-Thousand" from Southern Baptist Convention, recipient of Jord H. Jordan Scholarship (1994), Carson-Newman College Special Achievement Scholarship (1994-1997), National Authors Registry, Second place in "Young Writers Collection" contest (1988), Varsity letter Halls High School in Track and Field, swim team, Carson-Newman College S.P.O.T.S. team with Creative Ministries Team (1995 & 1996), Summer missionary (1995-present).; [oth. writ.] Several poems published in many other anthologies, currently working on a novel to hopefully be published by fall '99.; [pers.] All men die at some time in life but only a few men ever truly live."

PRATT, NICOLE VERIA
[b.] September 10, 1984, Denver, CO; [p.] Michel Pratt, Jeanette Pratt; [ed.] Have not finished school currently in 7th grade; [oth. writ.] No other poems have been published like to write poems on driveway with sidewalk chalk; [pers.] I write poems to help people. I try to send messages to help people. And to help peoples problems they might have.; [a.] Rogers, AR

PREKU, STEPHANIE A.
[b.] October 17, 1974; Carson, NV; [p.] John Preku, Lynette Preku; [ed.] High school graduate, Reno Nevada High School; [occ.] Serving in U.S. Navy; [A.] Murrieta, CA.

PRESING III, JOSEPH A.
[b.] June 5, 1941, Jersey City, NJ; [p.] Joseph Presing Jr., Marie Presing; [ed.] Dickinson High School, Montclair State College, B.A., Jersey City State College, M.A.; [occ.] Chairman, Foreign Language Dept., D.H.S., (Retired); [memb.] C.S.P.I., Partners In Hope, Grace Chapel, Tenafly; [hon.] Guitar Award, Dean's List, Middle States Comm. on Sec. Ed., Foreign Language Awards.; [oth. writ.] "To A Pessimist", MSC Quarterly; [pers.] Poetry seeks to express that which is, in truth, unexpressible: The innermost nature of the human soul.; [a.] Bergenfield, NJ

PRESSLEY, DARRELL SHAWN
[b.] August 7, 1969, Detroit, MI; [p.] Barbara and Harold Pressley; [m.] Linda M. Pressley, December 21, 1991; [ch.] Bryan Allan Christopher and Kymberlee Joyce Nicole; [ed.] Bachelor's, Journalism, Wayne State University, Detroit, MI, May, 1990; [occ.] Education Reporter, The Cincinnati Enquirer; [hon.] Top prize for a newspaper series from The Michigan Press Association and Michigan's Associated Press; [pers.] I am a young poet with an old spirit. Faith, love and family. Those are the three elements of life which warm my heart, elevate my soul and inspire my creativity.; [a.] Park Hills, KY

PRIDGEON, TERESA
[b.] October 6, 1958; Perry, FL; [p.] Tilden Lundy, Geraldine Lundy; [m.] Riley J. Pridgeon; June 7, 1973; [ch.] Chasity K. Pridgeon; [ed.] Taylor County High, North Florida Jr. College; [occ.] Small business owner; [memb.] Pisgah Baptist Church of Perry; [pers.] My poems contain personal encounters of realistic struggles of life here on earth and thoughts of my surroundings which influence the feelings of oneself; [a.] Perry, FL.

PRUITT, DARRIN
[b.] June 14, 1966, Newton, NC; [p.] Dennis and Millie Pruitt; [m.] Mike Foster, June 9, 1995; [ed.] BA - Bridgewater College, MPH - Tulane University; [occ.] Courseware Development Specialist; [memb.] American Public Health Assoc., Lambda Society; [hon.] National Endowment for the Humanities grantee (1993); [oth. writ.] Several poems published in newspapers, The Philamathean, (college journal for Bridgewater college), "Unfinished, Valentine", in The Coming Of Dawn.; [pers.] The beauty of a poem is it's ability to capture all the passion, sentiment, meaning and sensation of a moment in time. It does all this in a distilled and rare form.; [a.] New Orleans, LA

PRUITT, NAONIE
[b.] August 20, 1984, New Jersey; [p.] Janet Pruitt, Robert Pruitt; [ed.] Highland Park High School; [occ.] Student; [memb.] The Adventure Club, First Baptist Church, Track Team Highland Pk, H.S. Basketball Team Highland Pk H.S.; [oth. writ.] A letter to deceased father, an interview, and a few more poems.; [pers.] I just write.; [a.] Highland Park, NJ

PSZOLKOWSKI, EVELYN L.
[pen.] E.L.A.S.; [b.] June 7, 1964, Smithtown, NY; [p.] Evelyn M. Supe, Robert T. Supe; [m.] John W. Pszolkowski, May 14, 1993; [ed.] Mt. Pleasant Elem. Smithtown, New York Ave., Jr. High Smithtown, Smithtown H.S., West Smithtown, Cayuga Community College, Auburn; [occ.] Computer Operator; [memb.] Creative Writing, Poetry Workshops; [hon.] Art and Literary Magazine Smithtown, H.S.; [oth. writ.] "Morning Dove", "People Paper Crumble", "The Liar, The Cheater", "The Alarm Clock", "Stairs", "Kings and Castles"; [pers.] "Poetry and writing are a true reflection of the soul, and mind at constant play, the light in one's eyes which makes us unique and human.; [a.] Nesconset, NY

PUTT, JEFFREY A.
[b.] January 20, 1956, Fort Wayne, IN; [ed.] Automotive Tech., Computer Drafting, Geology; [hon.] Honors for G.P.A., Physical Fitness Award U.S. Coast Guard 1973; [oth. writ.] Songwriter; [pers.] If you can't depend on yourself don't depend on others.; [a.] Aurora, CO

RABER, ROBERT VAUGHN
[pen.] Vaughn; [b.] February 19, 1971, Wadsworth, OH; [m.] Tammy Marie Raber, November 14, 1992; [ch.] Stephanie Marie and Jessica Lynne (Deceased); [ed.] Chippewa High School, Wayne College, University of Akron, BA English; [occ.] Office Clerk, Allied Baltic Rubber Strasburg, OH; [hon.] Dean's List; [oth. writ.] Other poems and short stories numbering around 500.; [pers.] The harsh reality of life is the absoluteness of death.

My daughter Jessica died from SIDS. Somehow, she symbolizes the horrific beauty of life.; [a.] Canal Fulton, OH

RAFFENSPARGER, JIM
[b.] October 14, 1983, Bountiful, UT; [p.] Scott and Cynthia Raffensparger; [ed.] 7th grader when poem was written; [a.] Orem, UT

RAMDEO, RENE D.
[pen.] Rene D. Ramdeo; [b.] August 10, 1969, Guyana; [p.] Mr. and Mrs. Ramdeo; [occ.] Currently a student at York College in Queens, N.Y., where I am majoring in Finance; [memb.] Account Representative for the New York Hospital; [pers.] Born and partially educated in Guyana. I migrated with my family to the U.S. in the early eighties. I am currently employ at the NYH-GUMC Finance Dept, and pursuing a degree in that field. The passion of analyzing my inner thoughts is the art of my writing.; [a.] Richmond Hill, NY

RASCHE, CATHERINE A.
[pen.] Cathy; [b.] Januray 28, 1930; Marian Hill, IN; [p.] Gilbert and Frances Gogel [m.] (deceased) Al Rasche; August 26, 1950; [ch.] Nine children; [ed.] Mariah Hill In. Dale In, Insurance Evansville, In. Indianapolis, Long Term Care Life, disability; [occ.] Insurance Sales Life, health, Medicare; [memb.] Fashion Beeline Sales, National Library of Poetry; [hon.] New car in sales 1964, Real Silk Inc. fashion shows, Indianapolis IN; [oth.writ.] "Poems" "You are something special" "America" Hime; [pers.] If you help others, there will be somebody else to help you; [a.] Evansville, IN.

REASOR, AMANDA
[pen.] Mandy; [b.] August 8, 1981, Dallas, TX; [p.] Gary and Mary Reasor; [ed.] In High School, 9th Grade; [hon.] Cheerleading-Attendance; [oth. writ.] Our Song - No More Smiles, Go On Move On, Promise, My Needs, cheater-Run, My Fears, I Deserve It, Our Love, Still, I Fell Apart, In Love, Sympathy Pain and Tears, I Want To Stay, Only You; [pers.] My writings strive to reflect feelings of teens and adults alike. I am a learning disabled teen, but I feel no disability when writing poetry.; [a.] Watkins Glen, NY

RECUPERO, PATRICK S.
[pen.] Patrick Stephen Recupero; [b.] November 25, 1976, Elyra, OH; [p.] Gloria Recupero and Patrick J. Recupero; [ed.] Second Year at Cuyahoga Community College, Graduated Saint Peter Chanel High, Bedford, Ohio occ.] Central Production, Finest Supermarkes; [memb.] USA Karate Federation, United States Judo Association, 4th Degree Brown Belt, International Federation of Trekkers Security Officer; [oth. writ.] I have been published in a few of the local newspapers, Garfield Leader, Garfield Hgts., OH, Cuyahoga Community College Newspaper.; [pers.] We all are alive but we do not always enjoy life, love is like a two edged sword make sure you mean it before you stabith into thee.; [a.] Cleveland, OH

REDING, EUNICE ABBY
[b.] January 13, 1916, McKees Rocka, PA; [p.] William Henry and Eunice Wyres Ward; [m.] Richard Wallace Reding, August 28, 1937; [ch.] Richard William and Barbara Ann; [ed.] Warren G.; [occ.] Retired Cinema Manager Now enjoying Grandchildren, Great and Great-Great-; [memb.] St.

John United Church of Christ U.S. Coastguard Auxiliary, Philatelist, AARP National Audubon Society.; [hon.] Editors Choice Awards Having my poetry printed in Anthologys.; [oth. writ.] Invisible enigma, Reluctant Regrets, Lasting Happiness, Mystery of Lost Words; [pers.] I find pleasure in reading poems in The National Library of Poetry Anthologies written by fellow poets.; [a.] Strasburg, OH

REED, CRYSTAL L.
[b.] March 12, 1972; Middletown, CO; [p.] Victor Pearson, Valentine Pearson; [m.] Erwin L. Reed; November 20, 1995; [ch.] Michael, Jazamin, Karen, Erwin; [ed.] Middletown High School, Southern Orlio College; [occ.] Bank Teller, Colorado National Bank; [oth.writ.] Several poems written for church newsletter at faith fellowship; [pers.] I would like to open a card shop full of spiritual greetings and uplifting thoughts to inspire both the young and old; [a.] Denver, CO.

REED, GINA M.
[b.] May 26, 1971, California; [p.] Jerry and Charlene Graves; [m.] William Ray Reed, February 14, 1993; [ch.] Jessica and "Baby due in July"; [ed.] 1989 graduate of Reeds Spring High School, Reeds Spring, MO and Missouri College of Cosmetology 1990 graduate, Springfield, MO; [occ.] "Stay home" Mom; [memb.] Joy Fellowship Leader at Keystone Assembly of God Church in Reeds Spring, MO, Humane Society of the United States member; [hon.] Scholarship to Missouri College of Cosmetology, Regional champion in my high school typing class contest 1989.; [oth. writ.] I only write poems that come from my heart. My greatest inspiration has been my children. My love for them reaches beyond any explanation - words can not touch this love I feel.; [pers.] I only want the words that reach my poems to make a difference to those who read them. If just one person can love their child just a little bit more from reading my poem, then I have done my job.; [a.] Galena, MO

REED SR., SHERMAN
[b.] Baltimore, MD; [p.] Violet Anne and Lee Ernest Reed Sr.; [m.] Dorothy Reed; August 23, 1986; [ch.] Candice Jessica, Sherman Jr., and Tynetta Nicole; [ed.] B.S. (Instructional Technology) from Towson State University, MSB Master of Science in Business from Johns Hopkins University; [occ.] Wright Line, Inc. Senior Territory Manager (Sales); [memb.] Suburban Maryland Technology Council, Board of Director for Alumni Services, Boy Scouts of America (Den Leader); [hon.] Dean's List, The State Of Maryland Merit Scholastic Award; [pers] This poem reflects the deep passion that I have always had for baseball. My one philosophy has always been to "strive to be your very best"; [a.] Baltimore, MD.

REJOUIS, JEAN ALBERT
[b.] October 4, 1937, Haiti; [p.] Rev. Faber Rejouis; [m.] Marlene Rejouis, October 19, 1968; [ch.] Paul, Caroline, Lawrence; [ed.] Lycee Louverture Haiti, Kingsborough Community College, Brooklyn College, New York, USA; [occ.] Case Manager, ACS; [memb.] Minister of the Gospel, Evangelical Crusade Church, Uniondale NY; [oth. writ.] Publication of 3 books of poems in French: 1. Le Cri De La Montagne (1979), 2. Requiem Pour Les Negrillons (1981), 3. Lamentations (1992) and

Abrige Des Grand Faits de L'Histoire Chretienne (1996); [pers.] My writings reflects my profound sorrow about the suffering of man king, why a small number of people have everything, power, wealth and then the great number of people have nothing. I want to voice the complaints of those who are crying in silence and show them the light of hope.; [a.] Rosedale, NY

RESPESS, GEORGE
[pen.] George Llewellyn; [b.] July 1, 1947, Hattiesburg, MS; [p.] Llewellyn Ede and Nell Ede Carlisle; [m.] Michael A. Respess, October 29, 1995; [ch.] Donald Loper, Michael Loper; [ed.] Hattiesburg High School, Jones Co. Jr. College, University of Southern MS, Spartanburg Technical College; [occ.] Medically Disabled (Cancer); [memb.] American Association of Medical transcriptionist; [oth. writ.] Time Passes, A Mother's Prayer, An Angel Named Michael, Tears Of A Loved One, The Tea Set, For My Children; [pers.] I strive to share my feelings with other persons through God. I use my writing to overcome despair and depression due to cancer and loss of loved ones to death.; [a.] Spartanburg, SC

REYNOLDS, AUDREY
[pen.] Aud; [b.] October 17, 1983, Brooklyn, NY; [p.] Arthur and Margaret Reynolds; [m.] Edward J. Enright (Dec/Div), April 12, 1952; [ch.] Edw., Joseph, Dorothy, Patricia and John; [ed.] High School - Richmond Hill and some College, no Degree; [occ.] Retired (Writing); [memb.] Legion of Mary at my Church Colombiettes of S. Ozone Park, Rosarians also at my Church Secretary to both Organizations at Church - St. Anthony of Padua; [hon.] In High School for Excellent Art Work; [oth. writ.] Three - songs copyright "1977" - Many short stories and poetry. Now working on two manuscripts.; [pers.] My mother wrote poetry and songs, also played piano. I had a brother that was an artist, and an Uncle that also was an artist. I believe that if there is anything in life that you want to do then you should go for it. I always wanted to be a writer and yet never tried hard enough to pursue that dream. I am now going to do so. My mentor for writing was my Mom.; [a.] South Ozone Park, NY

REYNOLDS JR., DONALD E.
[b.] March 29, 1975, Washington, DC; [ed.] Boyertown Area High School, Graduated 1993; [occ.] Ensoniq, Corp. (Malvern, PA) Beta Testing and Third Party Development; [oth. writ.] Many poems, songs, and short stories never published; [pers.] Loving thanks to my grandmom, uncle, sisters, brother and Cindy for all the creativity they have inspired. I thank my friends and shadow for following close beside me as a constant reminder that a bright future is always ahead.; [a.] Douglassville, PA

RHYNE, KEVIN
[b.] January 4, 1955, Liberty, NY; [p.] Gerald and June Rhyne; [ch.] Step children: Larry McAllister - Robert Duncan, Cheryl Duncan; [ed.] Monticello, NY., High School; [occ.] Blacksmith; [memb.] Kauneonga Lake, Volunteer Fire Dept.; [oth. writ.] Just a few poems; [pers.] Being a volunteer firefighter gives me a sense of accomplishment. Being able to help others in time of need, and I think the volunteer needs some recognition.; [a.] Bethel, NY

RICE, STEPHEN E.
[pen.] S. E. Rice; [b.] March 26, 1947, Cumberland, MD; [p.] Cornelius W. Rice, Joan W. Rice; [ch.] Christopher Scott, Nicholas Stephen, Emily Lynn; [ed.] St. Charles High School, Longview Community College, Rockhurst College; [occ.] Law Enforcement; [pers.] My prose reflects my experiences in life, both good and bad. My favorite writing style of prose form, is both English and Italian sonnet format.; [a.] Saint Louis, MO

RICHARDS, KAREN L.
[b.] August 25, 1963, Millinocket, ME; [p.] Gerald Frost Sr. and Lucille Frost; [m.] Jerry A. Richards, December 8, 1990; [ch.] Richard and Arron Veysey; [ed.] I graduated from Schenck High School in East Millinocket, Maine in 1982.; [memb.] Community Evangel Temple Church in Lincoln, Maine; [hon.] Training courses through Community Evangel Temple; [pers.] I am a distant cousin to the poet Robert Frost; [a.] Lincoln, ME

RICHARDSON, KIMBERLY A.
[pen.] Kimberly Richardson; [b.] November 3, 1964, Valdosta, GA; [p.] Charles Yale, Florence Yale; [m.] William H. Richardson, May 3, 1986; [ch.] Crystal Ann, (Due in Oct. 97; Baby Richardson); [ed.] Valdosta High, Valdosta Tech, 1 yr. Georgia Military College; [occ.] Substitute Teacher (K-5) Valdosta City Schools; [memb.] Christian Science Society (Valdosta, GA); [hon.] Daughters of the American Revolution 1984; [pers.] My husband and children are my greatest inspirations for writing.; [a.] Valdosta, GA

RICHEY, DIANE
[b.] June 21, 1954, McKeesport, PA; [p.] Martha and Chester Krusienski; [m.] Michael Richey, April 18, 1990; [ch.] Carrie, Kimberly, Alana; [ed.] South Alleghony High School, McKeesport Hospital School of Radiologic Technology; [occ.] Implementation Analyst; [memb.] American Registry of Radiologic Technologists, American Society of Radiologic Technologists; [pers.] My thanks to my daughters for being the unique individuals that they are.; [a.] North Huntington, PA

RICHIE, EMILY J.
[b.] February 17, 1978, Tucson, AZ; [p.] Colleen and Daniel Richie; [ed.] High School, Graduate; [hon.] Geography award, Honor's Scholar's award, Service to School award; [oth. writ.] Many unpublished poems and short stories.; [pers.] I would like to thank my mother most of all, for inspiring my creativity!; [a.] Leominster, MA

RILEY, ROB
[b.] February 21, 1977, Carthage, NY; [p.] James and Doris Riley; [ed.] Carthage High, Jefferson Community College; [occ.] Liberal Arts student at Jefferson Community College, Watertown, NY; [hon.] Dean's List; [pers.] To my Nikki without her, I have no inspiration to write.; [a.] Carthage, NY

RINEHART, BOB
[pen.] Down Stairs; [b.] March 1, 1964, Barstow, CA; [m.] Connie S., November 19, 1986; [ch.] Candyce, Shanna, Tyler, Scott; [ed.] Alabama Technical, Fire Fighter Level I, Rescue Level I, Red Cross C.P.R. Instructor.; [occ.] Production Worker, my own business "Koler Kids and Ko" an artistic design company; [memb.] Soddy-Daisy Fire Dept., Daisy Church of God, Youth Coach CYMCA Soc-

cer League. Fund Raising Chairman at Friends of the kids (A Playground Project); [oth. writ.] Numerous poems stories and songs. None published.; [pers.] We are all created by each person we meet through life.; [a.] Soddy-Dawy, TN

RINKER-GRANT, JOY I. HALL
[b.] September 15, 1939, Mangum, OK; [p.] Joe C. Hall and Inez Richardson Hall; [m.] Carroll W. Grant, October 10, 1985; [ch.] Sheri Rinker Copeland, Brena Rinker Smith, H. Douglass Rinker, Diane Rinker Hanley; [ed.] Mangum H.S. 1957, Central State Univ., Edmond, OK 1972 B.S. in Educ., Central State Univ., Edmond, OK 1974 M.Ed in Learning Disabilities, Oklahoma City Junior College, Assoc. in Business 1981, University of Texas, Denton, TX, Mid-Management 1990, Degree 1990; [occ.] Public School Business Teacher, Taught Special Education for 22 years; [memb.] Daughters of American Revolution; [hon.] Dean's List Twice UIL Outstanding Sponsor of the Year 1992, Teacher of the Month (Twice); [oth. writ.] Local Newspaper Articles on Special Education Methods and Techniques, published letters on the editor; [pers.] The most important thing we have in our life on earth is the love of our family. Compared to all other relationships, they pale in comparison. Nurture your family and cherish your parents...so many people aren't lucky enough to have this blessing.; [a.] Forth Worth, TX

RIVERS, DAMANI
[b.] November 9, 1978; Stockton, CA; [p.] Frankie Rivers, Alberta Rivers; [ed.] Bear Creek High Scool; San Joaquin Delta College; [occ.] Student; [pers.] My writings reflect the problems and issues facing African-Americans in today's society. My mind and spirit have been strongly influenced by the works of W.E.B. Dubois and Langston Hughes.; [a.] Stockton, CA.

RIZZO, NICOLE
[b.] December 30, 1977, Long Island, NY; [ed.] I attended junior high and High School in Hauppauge on Long Island; [occ.] I am currently a student of Suny Cortland College; [pers.] I believe that everyone has a hidden talent. People just have to reach within themselves to find it.; [a.] Smithtown, NY

ROBB, DAN
[b.] December 2, 1982; Hanover, NH; [p.] Charles and Cheryl Robb; [ed.] Plainfield Elementary School; [occ.] Student; [pers.] I believe that my writing is popular among readers not because of the words I use, but because of the musical quality my writing seems to have. When it comes down to it, I'm just a musician; [a.] Plainfield, NH.

ROBERTS, ARIC LEE
[b.] December 13, 1976, Travis AFB, Fairfield, CA; [p.] Marta Westfall, Daniel Roberts; [ed.] Mountain View High School, DeAnza Community College; [occ.] United States Air Force Reserves, (Optional) Receptionist at Caspr Library Systems, Inc.; [hon.] Dean's List at DeAnza College; [oth. writ.] Several poems published in school newspapers and magazines.; [pers.] Of all human experiences, life, death, pain and ecstasy, love is the only truly important one. This is for mine. (Kim Marie Marsh); [a.] San Jose, CA

ROBERTS, JAMES A.
[pen.] Popinjay; [a.] Sunrise, FL

ROBERTS, VALERIE
[b.] January 31, 1985, Springfield, MA; [p.] Brent Jr. and Kathleen Roberts; [ed.] Attending 6th grade at Goshen Center School, Goshen, MA; [occ.] Student; [pers.] I believe that poetry is a world full of enchantment and wonder, it's anything you may desire. I have been greatly influenced by the power of nature, where my poetry thrives.; [a.] Goshen, MA

ROBINSON, CELESTE
[pen.] Stuff; [b.] September 19, 1963, NYC; [p.] John and Mary Robinson; [m.] Vanlear Williams, April 4, 1997; [ch.] Latoya, Robert, Kareem, Vanessa, Vanlear Jr. and Khia; [ed.] College student at Baltimore City Community College, major Electronic Repair Tech.; [occ.] Administrator of Kids Family Club; [oth. writ.] Braids and Styles magazine and The Double Dutch Winners.; [pers.] I give all thanks to Jesus Christ for my writing skills and for Kids Family Club dedicated to keep families first.; [a.] Baltimore, MD

ROBINSON, NIKOLAS PAUL
[pen.] Angel; [b.] December 16, 1978, Saint Paul, MN; [p.] Darcy Robinson, Daniel Robinson; [m.] Heather Beckman; [ch.] Cecily Skye Robinson; [occ.] Frontman and Creator of the original musical project - Angel, Lyricist and Bassist; [oth. writ.] Several unpublished writings, along with seemingly hundreds of song lyrics; [pers.] What is insanity to those who are not sane, or sanity to those who are? The answer is 'Reality', and reality is undefined. Keep that in mind as you change the world around you...and remember to keep an open mind and your perceptions awake.; [a.] Rapid City, SD

ROBINSON, OLACOY O.
[b.] April 7, 1977, Detroit, MI; [p.] Vicki and Ralph Robinson; [ed.] The Roeper School, Wayne State University; [occ.] Private Speech Consultant, Asst. Forensic Coach, Roeper High; [memb.] Wayne State Forensic Team, Wayne State Student Council Volunteer Committee; [hon.] Wayne State University Talent Scholarship recipient, National Forensic Assoc. Speech Competition qualifier; [oth. writ.] "Gifted Students Speak Out" published in The Gifted Kids' Survival Guide.; [pers.] It is important for all of us to believe in the promise of a new day.; [a.] Detroit, MI

ROBLES, TINA
[b.] March 12, 1924; Sacramento, CA; [p.] Frank and Linda Robles; [ed.] Galt High School, San Joaquin Delta College; [occ.] College Student; [memb.] Delta Drama's Actor Training Program; [oth.writ.] Several poems unpublished and song lyrics; [pers.] I wish to thank my parents and family for all their support and inspiration; [a.] Herald, CA.

ROCK, MICHAEL WAYNE
[pen.] Machaira; [b.] August 11, 1968, Houston, TX; [p.] Joseph Rock, Carolyn Rock; [ed.] Aldine High School, Houston, Bachelor of Science, Kinesiology, The University of Texas at Austin; [occ.] Artist, MacIntosh Computer Expert, Consultant.; [oth. writ.] Various poems, unpublished, the poem "A Dagan's God Breathes" and the essay "Dogs and Buddha Nature" appeared in the zine "Thou Art...', Vol. A, Issue A., 1993. The Temple of conscious earth.; [pers.] "The mystery of life isn't a problem to solve, but a reality to experiences". Frank Hubert, Dune.; [a.] Austin, TX

RODRIGUEZ, SAMUEL J.
[b.] September 27, 1978, Brownsville, TX; [p.] Abel and Maria Rodriguez; [ed.] American Home Schools NRI Schools; [pers.] Everyone has talent deep inside. It is up to you to find it. This is why I write: CIDGAS.; [a.] Mission, TX

ROGERS, WILMA
[b.] March 3, 1929, Pikeville, TN; [p.] James and Grace Angel; [m.] Luke Rogers; [ch.] Pam, Judy and Jacquie; [ed.] Central High, Art and Music Classes; [occ.] Music Teacher, Church Organist - 21 years retired; [a.] Hixson, TN

ROLLINS, VIELKA E.
[b.] May 28, 1955, Panama Rep.; [p.] Ellis E. Williams, Genara Williams; [m.] Julian Rollins, March 6, 1976; [ch.] Nadra Rollins; [ed.] Spanish BA; [occ.] Student; [memb.] Hispanicu CSI, Cultural Society - President; [hon.] Who's Who Among Students of American Colleges and University 1997; [oth. writ.] Spanish Literature Criticism/Spanish poetry; [pers.] The message of my writings are rooted in the unique power of the mind in the context of words, and its philosophical implications.; [a.] Matawan, NJ

ROMANN, JOHN F.
[b.] May 14, 1920, Brooklyn, NY; [p.] Matilda Garttner and John J. Romann; [m.] Jacqueline B. Romann, March 17, 1962; [ch.] Two - John (32), Julie (30); [ed.] Graduate - U.S. Merchant Marine Academy, Kings Point - L.I., N.Y. - Chief Engr (Marine) Steam and Diesel; [occ.] Retired - keep active on property - summer (outdoors) winter (indoors); [memb.] Various Church Organizations; [hon.] Certificate of Merit - N.Y. Fire Dept. Additional Comment: "To lose one's wealth is sad indeed, To lose one's health is more, To lose one's soul is such a loss, That no man can restore"; [oth. writ.] Engineering (Diesel) articles for "Diesel and Gas Engine Progress", (1), WNYF (with N.Y. Fireman) (1), "Diesels in the N.Y.F.D.".; [pers.] "This one life will soon be past, only what's done for Christ will last." "Even if you're on the right track, you'll get run over if you just sit there." Will Rogers; [a.] Easton, PA

ROSE, JEFFREY H.
[pen.] Jeffrey; [b.] August 10, 1963, New Bedford, MA; [p.] Maria and Franklin Howell; [ch.] Jeffrey, Dante, Quincy; [ed.] High School New Bedford, Allenhandcock, Jr. College; [occ.] Referrals and Authorizations Specialist; [pers.] About a year ago as I began to fall asleep something said get up and write your feelings down. Since then I written about 30 poems of friends and feelings. I love life.; [a.] Houston, TX

ROSENBAUM, HOWARD J.
[b.] April 20, 1974, Los Angeles; [p.] Sam Rosenbaum, Rhonda Rosenbaum; [ed.] BA Sociology/Business Admin. UCLA; [occ.] Sales Representative; [memb.] New England Chamber of Commerce; [oth. writ.] The Void Within, When Someone Loves You, Footprints Across My Heart; [pers.] A love unpursued is like a rose that never blooms.; [a.] Malden, MA

ROSSA, ISABELL G.
[pen.] Greer; [b.] March 28, 1928, Pasadena, CA; [p.] Joseph and Isabell Jarewicz; [m.] Lawrence R., November 11, 1946; [ch.] Two sons and three girls; [occ.] Retired - great G. Ch. enjoying my children - gr. children; [memb.] American Legion Aux.; [pers.] A good morning or a smile to a stranger - makes me feel great for the rest of the day, hopefully the stranger.; [a.] Hobart, IN

ROSSER, VICTORIA
[pen.] Victoria Rosser; [b.] August 28, 1983; Detroit, MI; [p.] J and April Rosser; [ed.] Eighth grade; [occ.] Student at Detroit Country Day; [memb.] Detroit Area Pre-College Engineering Program, Girl Scouts; [hon.] Distinguished Student Awards, Junior National Honors Society; [a.] Detroit, MI.

ROSSOW, RANDAL R.
[pen.] Randal R. Rossow; [b.] September 10, 1959, Reno, NV; [p.] Leo J. Rossow, Jacquelyn M. Rossow; [m.] Linda K. Balsi, May 27, 1989; [ch.] Glorianna L. Rossow; [ed.] University of Nevada, Reno (Class of 83); [occ.] School Teacher; [a.] Reno, NV

ROTHMAN, SHEILA
[b.] October 12, 1931, New York, NY; [p.] Henrietta Horowitz and Joseph Handshoe; [m.] Frank Rothman, September 2, 1956; [ch.] Andrea Steven Rothman, Richard Robert Rothman; [ed.] BBA 1952, MBA 1959, CCNY; [occ.] Retired; [memb.] Alzheimers Association, Foundation for Epilepsy, Democratic Party; [hon.] Listed in: Who's Who in the East 1986-1987, Who's Who of American Women 1987-1988 CCNY: Alumni Award for Service 1952; [oth. writ.] Letters to editors unpublished personal essays Corporate annual reports; [pers.] This is my first poem after a 42 year career as an accountant. Language is important. We all must learn how to use it for good purpose.; [a.] Westport, CT

ROUHANA, NATHALIE
[b.] Montpellier, France; [p.] Odile and Rodolphe Rouhana; [m.] Harsha Bhojraj, August 12, 1995; [ed.] B.S. Chemistry, Purdue University, M.S. Chemical Engineering, Purdue University, Ph.D. Chemical Engineering, University of Tennessee; [pers.] This poem was born from the spontaneity and intensity of feelings for my future husband-to-be, Harsha, and is an unforgettable part of my college years at the University of Tennessee.; [a.] Pulaski, TN

ROUNDS, RICKY FERROL
[b.] April 15, 1963, Denver, CO; [p.] Harold M. Rounds (Deceased), Whitman Rounds Larson (Deceased), Janet Sue; [m.] Companion: Kristopher K. Erickson; [ed.] Arvada Christian School, Graduated May 1982, U.S. Navy; [occ.] Food and Beverage Supervisor, Marriott City Center, Denver; [hon.] Honorable Discharge, Several Customer Service Awards - Marriott Navy - Letters of Recognition; [oth. writ.] Get To The Center Of Things - Aids And Safe Sex, Washington Blade 1989, many many more not yet seen by many people.; [pers.] Since my writings contain poetry, personal thoughts, feelings and politics, I have classified myself as an expressionists.; [a.] Denver, CO

ROUNTREE, PHILIP ANDERSON
[b.] October 16, 1971, Mobile, AL; [p.] John Campbell, Linda; [ed.] Florida State University, B.A. (English Literature); [memb.] Golden Key National Honor Society; [pers.] My primary focus is short fiction.; [a.] Tacoma, WA

ROWE, GORDON J.
[b.] March 8, 1921; [m.] Sandra C. Rowe, April 13, 1945; [ch.] Gregory Scott, Stanton Jeffrey, Patrick Douglas; [ed.] Univ. of Georgia, BS in Physics, 1949; [occ.] Retired NASA as Aerospace Engineer; [oth. writ.] Several children's stories, humorous short stories and commentaries.; [pers.] I am a contradiction to an accepted notion, while working as an Engineer for 30 years, my soul was deeply embedded in the aesthetics of life.; [a.] Huntsville, AL

RUBECK, KEVIN
[pen.] Kevin Oran Rubeck; [b.] September 28, 1972, Brazil, IN; [p.] Ron and Evelyn Rubeck; [ed.] Cloverdale High School, Putnam County Vocational School; [occ.] Rubeck Sawmill; [memb.] International Society of Poets; [hon.] Famous Poets Society Diamond Homer Award, Famas Poets Society, Best of 1996, National Library of Poetry Best of 1996; [oth. writ.] Self-published works - Poemettes, My Heart, poems in anthologies.; [a.] Poland, IN

RUBIN, TERRELL D.
[b.] November 5, 1973, Lafayette, LA; [p.] Pauline Rubin and Albert Hood; [ch.] Kelsey Eisenman; [occ.] US Navy; [oth. writ.] Various poems in boot camp.; [pers.] Special thanks to Fred Rickman and Dave for conveying to me that the bottom is too crowded so it's a must that I stay on top. Thanks for believing in me.; [a.] Lake Charles, LA

RUDDER, SHIRLEY SIBIT
[pen.] Shirley Sibit; [b.] September 19, 1940, Enid, OK; [p.] Ida - Vearl Sibit; [m.] Deceased, Marlin J. Lawson, September 18, 1956; [ch.] Marlin Jay Lawson, Vearl Gondon Lawson; [ed.] 12th Grade; [occ.] Disibility was retail; [oth. writ.] Many Mother of a Son. Other poems.; [a.] Enid, OK

RUDOLPH, CHARLES
[hon.] Editor's Choice Award 1995, 1997, The National Library of Poetry; [pers.] "We are all waiting to win. Just as we are born knowing only life."

RUITER, EMMA
[b.] January 8, 1908, Grand Rapids, MI.; [p.] Ralph and Elizabeth Ruiter; [ed.] A.B. M.A. - University of Michigan; [occ.] Teacher - Remedial Reading - Retired; [memb.] Roosevelt Park Chr. Ref. Church Calvin College Guild G. R. Chr. Teacher's Assoc.; [hon.] Prize for "The Banner" poem.; [oth. writ.] Prayer for the Golden Years published by "The Banner" Grand Rapids, MI.; [pers.] I try to reflect my love and belief in our risen Lord and Savior, Jesus Christ in my writing.; [a.] Grand Rapids, MI

RUPERT, DANIEL L.
[b.] November 12, 1953, Waynoka, OK; [p.] Robert A. and Georgia Yvonne Rupert; [m.] E. Carol Rupert, June 12, 1977; [ch.] Joshua Daniel Rupert; [ed.] Miss. State University Educational Specialist, 1991, New Orleans Baptist Seminary, Master of Divinity 1985, Park College B.A. Social Psychology, Georgia Military College A.G.S. 1980, MS County Community College, A.A. 1979; [occ.] Elementary Principal; [memb.] Mississippi Counseling Association, Chi Sigma Iota, Christian Martial Arts Instructors Association; [hon.] Who's Who in American Education, 1996-97, Who's Who in America 1997, Who's Who in the World 1997, Who's Who in American Christian Leadership,

1989, Who's Who in the Computer Industry 1990, nominated for inclusion in the Dictionary of International Biography, Chaplain Mississippi Department of American Ex-Prisoners of War.; [oth. writ.] Selected poems. Selected articles in local newspaper and various research articles published in the American Family Association Journal.; [pers.] My writings flow from the influence of the Bible, my family, and personal experiences gleaned by the living of life and listening to the songs of life as my father and his band sang them.; [a.] Tupelo, MS

RUSOFF, ROBERT T.
[b.] May 7, 1966, California; [p.] Robert H. and Judith A. Rusoff; [m.] E. Walden Brown-Rusoff, 1994; [occ.] Freelance Architectural Designer; [pers.] To my wife: You have shown me that love is a journey full of high and low roads alike. I am forever grateful for having walked this journey with you. I will love you always.; [a.] Fountain Hills, AZ

RYAN, JEANNE
[pen.] Jeanne Ryan; [b.] November 15, 1969, Boston, MA; [p.] John and Joyce Ryan; [ed.] BA English Communications from Emmanuel College Boston, MA. Currently Training at the Lee Strasberg Theatre Institute.; [occ.] Actor/Writer; [oth. writ.] Freelance short stories, and sitcom scripts. Presently writing a fictional coming of age novel. Recently finished a stage play entitled "I Never" based on woman's struggle.; [pers.] Currently working on a sitcom pilot. Also I am currently writing and performing stand up comedy material. I would someday like the opportunity to write and act in my own independent screenplay/ feature film. "The Medium is the Message".

SABATO, MARY E.
[b.] November 26, 1914, Watsonville, CA; [p.] Carl Clarence and Jessie D. Carey; [m.] Frank V. Sabato, August 11, 1946; [ch.] (Two) George F. and James R.; [ed.] High School, College of Hard Knocks; [occ.] Retired (still homemaker); [memb.] American Legion Auxiliary, AARP, Carlosians; [hon.] (by my family) "Mother of the Year", renewed each year, Honored Volunteer for Catholic Charities Day Care, San Carlos, CA, now Volunteer for El Dorado Day Care, I play the Casio and am "billed" "Sing Along with Mary"; [oth. writ.] Many, mostly poems to loved ones on birthdays and other occasions. Some poems have been published in local newspapers.; [pers.] I was taught, and I teach, and I try to live, "Doing unto others as you would have them do unto you."; [a.] Placerville, CA

SABOL, LINDA J.
[b.] January 4, 1960, Pottsville, PA; [p.] Ruth D. and Thomas J. Sabol; [ed.] Cardinal Brewnam H.S., Penn State University; [occ.] Patroll Manager, Blaschak Coal Corp. - Mahanoy City, PA; [hon.] Presidential National Scholarship, Senatorial Scholarship, National Honor Society, [oth. writ.] Article published in Pottsville Republican Newspaper; [pers.] I reveal in my poetry the secrets which lurk in everyone's hearts.; [a.] Saint Clair, PA

SAITOW, MICHAEL
[b.] December 22, 1971, Boston, MA; [p.] Carol Lerner and Ivan Saitow; [ed.] Syracuse University, Public Relations and Marketing; [occ.] Events Promotion Manager; [memb.] American Red Cross, Public Relations Society of America (PRSA), International Sports

Marketing Association (ISMA), National Registered EMT; [oth. writ.] The Trail Book - Lake Tahoe - Several poems in small newspapers.; [pers.] I try to experience as much as possible in as many fields as possible to fully, savor the flavors that an active life has to offer, while respecting others and nature.; [a.] Newton, MA

SALTER, LOUISE
[b.] Ind.; [p.] Rev. Dr. William Zeigler and Alice (wife); [m.] Manuel Lee Salter Sr. (Deceased); [ch.] 2 both grown; [ed.] B.A. - Huntington College, M.A. - Indiana Univ., Bloomington, Ph.D - Columbia Univ., N.Y.C. (dissertation not completed - no money for further research in England); [occ.] Writing and Painting; [memb.] Teachers Assoc., AARP, chose early retirement after pleasure of teaching 12th grade college - going seniors 13 years. First Presbyterian Church, Raleigh, N.C., International Society of Poets; [hon.] Valedictorian in H.S. at age 15, B.A. Huntington College with honors in 3 years, Editor of Yearbook, Pres. of Lit. Society, Columbia Univ. Phi Beta Gamma - only one chosen of grad. women for creativity, academic ability integrity that year; [oth. writ.] 3 poems and Sunday School pg. of ten in the Christian Conservator. Almost 5 yrs Chair of English, Lib. of Congress, Speeches and Research, Congressional Record, seeking publication: On Wings of Song - Christian Poetry 150 pp., Oh No - What Next - Humorous Skits for The Lonely, 170 pp., Songs of Earth and Heaven - 160 pp.; [pers.] I was influenced by the New Testament, Shakespeare, Eng. poets and history plus biography of each. I am convinced Jesus Christ is Savior who loves all mankind and we are chosen to use our talents to spread the word and to help others.; [a.] Raleigh, NC

SAMPSON, DENISE
[b.] January 26, 1952, Bay City, MI; [p.] Gene LaRocque and Gloria Krenz; [m.] Dennis Sampson, October 15, 1977; [ch.] Brett Eric and Torre Lyn; [ed.] 12th; [occ.] Housewife; [oth. writ.] Many poems written for personal greeting cards. One poem book in print on life lessons and testimony. One Coloring Book in print for young children. Sent free to anyone that requests them.; [pers.] Was inspired to write when I was in debilitating pain and couldn't do anything else.; [a.] Essexville, MI

SANCHEZ, JANET JEWELL
[b.] October 10, 1956; Okinawa, (AFB); [p.] Claude Jewell, Teresa Jewell; [m.] Michael L. Sanchez; May 19, 1990; [ch.] Maria, Kristina; [ed.] Central MO State University (CMSU), Belton High School, Rhein Main Elementary, Germany; [occ.] Free Lance Writer; [hon.] Poem published and story about Christmas published; [oth.writ.] Several stories written; 1 story published in KC Star Magazine (local newspaper); [pers.] I strive to look for the good in all people, and the beauty in all things; [a.] Lee's Summit, MO.

SANDERS, GREG
[pen.] Greg Sanders; [b.] March 16, 1982, Saint Louis; [p.] Betty and Ulas Sanders; [ed.] The School I am now attending is Chaminade College Preparatory School; [occ.] Student; [memb.] Jazz Concert Band; [hon.] Honors Academic, Student of the Month; [oth. writ.] Nonpublished.; [pers.] I always try to remember "To not try will surely result in a failure to succeed".; [a.] Manchester, MO

SANDERS, MARTHA LYNAM
[b.] May 15, 1912, Marshallton, DE; [p.] Earle Lynam, Emma May Lynam; [m.] Harry Connell (December 14, 1935) - Wm. Sanders, (April 12, 1959); [ed.] High School; [occ.] Retired, Former: El Du Pont Denemours and CO. Ran Motel and Rock Shop; [memb.] National Honor Society, Delaware Mineralogical Society; [hon.] Lots of Ribbons for GEM, Mineral and Fossil Displays; [oth. writ.] None except school and one thesis "Boneyfish"; [pers.] I have devoted my life to reading, trying out new frontiers of imagination, and trying very hard to do unto others as you would have them do unto you.; [a.] Floral City, FL

SANDERS, NICOLE
[pen.] Mikaila Nicole Allen; [b.] January 6, 1975, Spokane; [oth. writ.] "Illusions" in the Colors of Thought.; [pers.] I am greatly inspired by mystical things. All life, all death, very mysterious in our minds. I find it difficult not to be inspired.; [a.] Renton, WA

SANDERSON, SCOTT
[b.] April 8, 1968, Hopkinsville, KY; [ed.] Berea College BA 1990, attending Louisville Presbyterian, Theological Seminary; [occ.] Student, graduate school; [pers.] Originally this poem was written for my brother's wedding. I would like to inspire, entertain and challenge people with my writing.; [a.] Louisville, KY

SANDRENE, JOSEPHINE
[b.] March 31, 1922, Akron, OH; [m.] George (Deceased), June 14, 1947; [ch.] Donna (Deceased); [ed.] High school; [occ.] Retired from the General Tire of Akron; [oth. writ.] "A Deed For A Day," "He?," "I Love Baseball," "I The Poet," "Dearest One," (many more); [pers.] The poem "Dearest One" was written for my husband George Sandrene.; [a.] Akron, OH

SANTOS, YRENE
[pen.] Yrene Santos; [b.] June 27, 1963; Dominican Republic; [ed.] Bachelor in Education, mention Philosophy and Arts. (UASD: 1989); [occ.] I'm studying for my Master of Arts in Latin American Literature at the City College of the City University of New York; [memb.] "Instito Cervantes" of New York. Member of the "Terlulias de Escritoras con la Doctora Daisy Cocco De Filippis"; [oth.writ.] Desnudez del silencio (Santo Domingo: Editora Bu'ho, 1988); [a.] Richmond Hill, NY.

SASILEO, ANTHONY J.
[pen.] Leslie Hall T Saunders; [b.] May 26, 1930; Newark, NJ; [p.] Carlo and Frances Sasileo; [m.] Mary Kranick; November 30, 1957; [ed.] Weequiahic High School NJ. Columbia University NY, Dean's list, grad. University of Tokyo, sponsored by US Army, majored in English; [occ.] Free lance writer; [memb.] Society of Technical Writers and Editors NYC, Knights of Columbus, Eliz. NJ; [hon.] Rank Corporal served in Korean War, one of the 13 survivors of Heartbreak Ridge, wrote articles for Stars and Stripes, official Army newspaper; [oth.writ.] Short story published by American Mab Aug '56. Wrote scripts for Steve Allen Show, submitted speech to late President Kennedy's campaign; [pers.] Henceforth I shall accept what I am and what I am not with my limitations and my gifts. I shall go on using life as long as I am in this

world and afterwards. Not to use life, that alone is death; [a.] Little Silver, NJ.

SASSO, LAURYN ETHNE
[b.] June 23, 1978; Providence, RI; [p.] Katryn and Laurence J. Sasso, Jr.; [ed.] Smithfield High School, Mount Holyoke College; [occ.] Student (first year of college); [memb.] National Honor Society, Rhode Island Honor Society; [hon.] National Honor Society, National Merit Semi-Finalist, Winner, graduated 4th in high school class of 1990, Rhode Island Honor Society; [oth.writ.] Several other poems, all unpublished; [pers.] I believe success is an internal thing, you have all that you need to survive within you, and when you need help, calling on yourself is the best thing possible. My parents taught me that.; [a.] Smithfield, RI.

SAVARESE, LUDWIG
[b.] May 5, 1917, Italy; [p.] Giovanni and Noemi; [m.] Pia, September 1940; [ch.] Geoffrey and Ludwig Jr.; [ed.] St. Anns High, Hunter College, N.Y. State Merchant Marine Academy. Did not complete college.; [occ.] Retired; [oth. writ.] Numerous rejections, in my youth, from various magazines. Wrote silly little poems for my children, and some for personal pleasure. Enjoyed writing while at school.; [pers.] Although I am awed by the great masters, two lesser ones stand out in my memory: Lewis Carroll, and Omar Khayyam. If I had to take one book to the grave with me it would be the Rubaiyat.; [a.] Boca Raton, FL

SCHAFER, ETHEL
[b.] Haydock, England; [p.] Deceased; [m.] Deceased, World War 2 England; [ch.] One girl Deceased; [ed.] St. James Church of England Elementary School, Haydock. Also St. Barnabas Church of England Elementary School. Morecambe Bay. Gambels Institute High, England, Haydock Preparatory College School, University of Chautauqua N.Y., USA; [occ.] Assistant to a Funeral Director and County autopsy undertaker. Previous Occupations - Civilian Inspector of Amendments and Doctor's helper during air-raids on Liverpool World War 2, Own Jewelry Business USA.; [hon.] Royal Ordinance Award for outstanding Service to my Country England and the Civilian Division of Inspector of Amendments, During World War War 2. I still love England and always will. But am proud to be an American now and love it. And always will; [oth. writ.] Only for my own pleasure; [pers.] The works of William Shakespeare have always, fascinated me. Also Walter-De-La-Mare and Robert Browning. I believe it takes someone who has lived a gut-wrenching heart-tearing life and yet belief in a higher power to write the best of stories or poems, or songs.; [a.] Little Falls, NJ

SCHERFFIUS, LAUREL
[b.] August 29, 1980, Minnesota; [occ.] Student and Actor; [hon.] Freedom Leadership Award, President's Award for Educational Excellence; [oth. writ.] "A Time For War, A Time For Goodbye", "A Darker Presence"; [pers.] Art is not truth. Art is a lie that makes us realize truth. P. Picasso; [a.] Cornelius, NC

SCHLAEPPI, JOANN
[pen.] Joann Schlaeppi; [ed.] Chislehurst Grammar School, Kent, England, Wimpole Park Teacher's College, Cambridgeshire, England; [occ.] Retired,

Active Volunteer; [memb.] High Point, NC Historical Ass. High Point, NC Museum Guild. National Wildlife Federation. High Point, NC Literary League.; [hon.] Mary Lib Joyce Award from High Point, NC Historical Ass. Trustees Award from High Point, NC. Historical Ass. Mayoral Certificate of Appreciation for Community Work. Certificate of Achievement from NWF Backyard Wildlife Habitat Program.; [oth. writ.] None published; [pers.] I try to see the best in people, but get actively angry with corruption and injustice.; [a.] Greensboro, NC

SCHLERETH, GRACE
[b.] November 1, 1970, Athol, MA; [p.] Larry and Carolyn Malone; [m.] Todd R., September 16, 1989; [ch.] Tyra (Doberman), Ripley (German Shepherd), Sierra (Wolf); [ed.] Gt. Falls High; [occ.] Admissions Representative, Benefis Health Care; [oth. writ.] Several poems published in small newsletter and magazines. I have developed more into songwriting and wish someday to be recognized for that.; [pers.] I choose only to write about subject that are real - possible areas that not many people wish to discuss. My favorite statement. "Life is like a conversation, every pause counts."; [a.] Great Falls, MT

SCHMIDT, MARION H.
[pen.] Marion H. Schmidt; [b.] September 23, 1913, Mayville, WI; [p.] Marie and William Bolduan; [m.] Theodore Schmidt, September 9, 1933; [ch.] Three children; [ed.] High School; [occ.] Housewife; [memb.] My memberships were many in my 83 years of good Godly living; [hon.] Were satisfaction and thanks from my wonderful family and friends through the years.; [oth. writ.] A book of many poems each depicting the lives of my children, grandchildren, and great grandchildren and many other poems.; [pers.] Be happy, cherish each day, it may be your last to share all God given gifts, in this scenic, poetic world.; [a.] Griffith, IN

SCHREIER, LISA ANN
[b.] May 5, 1957, Chicago, IL; [p.] Alfred Schreier, Rita Schreier; [ed.] B.A. - Northeastern Illinois University; [occ.] Self-Employed Advertising/Media Marketing Consultant; [memb.] Broadcast Association of Chicago; [oth. writ.] Freelance articles, short stories, poems, etc. - on travel, humor, music and personal experience.; [pers.] "I know its only rock and roll, but I like it."; [a.] Skokie, IL

SCHROER, HEATHER
[b.] December 16, 1979, Fort Leonardwood Army Hospital; [p.] Dan and Elaine Schroer (Divorced); [ed.] Jefferson City High School; [hon.] I had another poem published both in my schools Write On and in the Jefferson City News Tribune; [a.] Jefferson City, MO

SCHWENDIMAN, MARVA J.
[b.] September 12, 1932, Murray, UT; [p.] Ruth Goodman, Henry C. Jorgensen; [m.] Gary L. Schwendiman, December 18, 1953; [ch.] Gary Lynn, Henry J., Ronald James, and Mark Eldon (4 sons); [ed.] BS Degree from Brigham Young U. in Elem. Educ., Graduate of Utah Writing Project 1985; [occ.] Retired First Grade Teacher, Genealogy Research and Writing; [memb.] Genealogy Extraction Program, Brighton Cultural Club (Brighton), L.D.S. Church; [pers.] I believe we all

have the potential to make the world a more beautiful and loving place to live.; [a.] Salt Lake City, UT

SCOLES, THERESA
[pen.] Kitten/Baby; [b.] December 5, 1974, Satori Hospital; [p.] Warren and Barbara Scoles; [m.] (Fiance) Jacob Freese; [ed.] High School Diploma, College Degree (AAS), Major (Child Development); [occ.] Asst. Manager of Casey's General Store; [memb.] Life Goal: I would like to own my own Day Care Center and raise my children, by teaching them the way I feel they should be taught.; [hon.] I have been given many awards for my creative talents with children and writings.; [oth. writ.] Many different poems, Ironic Stories, and I'm presently working on my manuscript for a book of love poems and a book for children's poems.; [pers.] "Oh yes. I do believe, the whole world inspires me."; [a.] New Hartford, IA

SEAMAN, JAMES
[pen.] P.G., P. Garrett; [b.] October 1973, Atlanta; [p.] Laura Seaman; [ch.] Trump - dog - 7 yrs.; [ed.] College Junior at Georgia State University; [occ.] Full-time Worker and Part-time Student; [memb.] United States Jaycees, Honorary Member of the Knighthood, Advisor - Demolay; [oth. writ.] Published in College Newspapers, Graduation Annuals; [pers.] Always remember, walk hard, stand tall, do not let anyone trample your flower garden.; [a.] Decatur, GA

SEGIT, LOUISE G.
[b.] February 23, 1929, Buffalo, NY; [p.] Marion Baranski and Agnes Kolasa; [m.] Stanley J. Segit, July 19, 1947; [ch.] June, Deborah and David; [ed.] St. Stanislaus Grammar School, St. Ann's Business School, G.E.D. Univ. of Buffalo, Millard Fillmore Fine Arts program.; [occ.] Homemaking, reading, acrylic painting, floral arranging. Intense interest in Shrines and current apparitions.; [memb.] Former member local art organizations, Garden Club, M.M.P. Past President - Girl Scout Mother's Club.; [hon.] Accepted in numerous juried Art shows with ribbon awards. Drawing accepted in Burchfield Center 4th W.N.Y. Collegiate Travelling Exhibit. Awards in Floral Design.; [oth. writ.] Poem "Grandchildren" National Library of Poetry - "Morning Song"; [pers.] Poetry has become a diary for me, whereby I can easily document memories or profound experiences that can be recorded in no other way. Love of serenity, beauty, antiquity, vibrancy and uniqueness are explored in my paintings, floral designs and poetry. All credit to God the Father for His many gifts to me.; [a.] Depew, NY

SEIBERT, DYLAN
[pen.] Donald Francis; [b.] January 29, 1983, Carbondale, IL; [p.] Paul and Kathleen Seibert; [ed.] Public elementary and junior high schools and a radically conservative, all or nothing, (in terms of effectiveness) private school called Governor French Academy (G.F.A.), [hon.] None in this category, I am not usually very public about my literary expressions of pain.; [oth. writ.] Oppression-a fictional about sexist-based slavery in the 21st century, Ashtray Thoughts: Poetry, Self-Euthanasia-poetry: Immortal Love-ironic modern realistic fiction about the agony of losing the only thing that matters, Terminally Immune - the infinite hell of infinite life.; [pers.] Sprinkling emotion

into this dark world, inviting strangers into his heart, amputating a piece of his soul for criticism, and desperately grasping, clutching, and clinging to the myth and desire of true sanity. He is the poet.; [a.] Lebanon, IL

SELING, LINDA
[b.] May 16, 1944; Detroit, MI; [p.] William and Mary Barth; [m.] Louis Seling; June 20, 1970; [ch.] Michael; [ed.] Fairmont High School, Kettering, Oh, Heidelberg College, Tiffin, Ohio B.A., Michigan State, East Lansing, MI, M.A.; [occ.] Retired Primary Teacher; [pers.] In my writings, I hope to use currently taught science concepts and vocabulary in stories which show science principles for primary age children. My emotions are shown in poetry; [a.] White Lake, MI.

SELLS, JEFFERY
[b.] March 4, 1980, San Antonio, TX; [p.] Ted and Melinda Simpson; [ed.] 10th Grade; [occ.] High School Student; [pers.] I write to express my deepest and truest emotions. My inspirations come from my past. Thank you for giving me a chance to see how much my poetry can succeed.; [a.] Trent, TX

SEMIEN, CARL A.
[b.] October 25, 1957; Lake Charles, LA; [p.] Mr. and Mrs. Ernest Semien (deceased); [ed.] High school graduate, trade school, "Downey School of Business," trade of choice (computers); [occ.] U.S. Postal Service; [hon.] January 96, Celebrity Records 1st Place Karaoke Contest, received a gold plated framed record of the song I sang, "Hello," by Lionel Richie. I've won 1st, 2nd, and 3rd place medals in my 10th grade choir solo competitions; [oth.writ.] I am a truly talented individual. And if by chance I can help someone else through my talents, so be it! I want to be able to touch people all over the world...through my music, poems, or art ability!; [pers.] I wrote this poem to express how I felt/feel about a place of peace. My life style in any time, has always searching for this special place. My spirituality has enabled me to express in words and sketches what my soul feels at times; [a.] Long Beach, CA.

SEMON, RENEE
[pen.] Renee Semon, Renee Rezza; [b.] April 21, 1963, Milwaukee, WI; [p.] Ralph and Alice Rezza; [m.] James W. Semon, August 28, 1993; [pers.] I've been writing poetry and songs for many years and have shared little work with few. I'm proud to have a piece considered worthy of publishing and to share with so many. Thank you!; [a.] Oconomowoc, WI

SENTZ JR., ROBERT
[b.] July 22, 1952, Lancaster, PA; [p.] Robert Sentz Sr., Beatrice Sentz; [m.] M. Eileen (Hess) Sentz, October 7, 1972; [ch.] Kimberly Michelle, Jeremy Michael, Tiffany Danae, Bethany Renae; [ed.] Conestoga High, C.T.I. Training, [occ.] Commercial Truck Driver for Rugby Building Products; [memb.] Cross Roads Brethren in Christ Church, Ryder Truck Rental Million Mile Club National N.F. Foundation.; [hon.] 1993 1,000,000 miles of accident free, violation free driving award.; [oth. writ.] Other poems, "Meaningful Living", "Words", "When Did I Start To Love You?", "If I Were To Paint A Picture", "Bethany's Blessing", "Tiffany's Gift", "He's Only

Just Begun" more; [pers.] Because of my love for God and His Son Jesus Christ, I strive to spread his principles along my path by example, speaking, and writing.; [a.] Mount Joy, PA

SEXTON, EVAN W.
[b.] October 30, 1970, Knoxville, TN; [p.] Cade Sexton, Dean Sexton; [ed.] University of Tennessee, Knoxville, B.A. Psychology, Appalachian State University, currently graduate student, Community Counseling; [memb.] American Counseling Association, Chi Sigma Iota Counseling, Academic and Professional Honor Society International; [pers.] I believe that challenge can temper and strengthen love. I'll always be loving you, wherever you are.; [a.] Caryville, TN

SHABAZZ, TONIA J.
[pen.] Tonia J. Shabazz; [b.] March 22, 1968, Lorain, OH; [p.] Charlie Burns Sr. (Deceased), Lola Goodlett (Elma Goodlett, stepfather); [m.] Robert Shabazz, February 14, 1997; [ch.] Six; [ed.] High School Graduate, Law and Public Service Magnet Cleveland Ohio, attended Vient State Univ., Kent, Ohio; [occ.] Crafter; [memb.] NAACP; [oth. writ.] Short stories that was read before the Teachers Conference in 1988; [pers.] I have been influenced by my mom and poets Elizabeth and Robert Browning.; [a.] Lorain, OH

SHAFI, SYED P.
[occ.] Business; [oth. writ.] (a) Memory Of A Soul, (b) Moving Moments, (c) Reason Vs. Reason; [pers.] Travel we, upon existing belief somewhat lost, references we hold, reasoning beyond reasonable doubt charging into time, like shooting stars, brilliant at times and temporary yet.; [a.] Elmhurst, NY

SHARMA, CHARIMA
[pen.] Karina; [b.] September 25, 1957; Iowa City, IA; [p.] Deceased; [ch.] Angela, Vanesa, Dean, Iykeerah; [ed.] Sooner Technical College; [occ.] Administrative Assistant to author/ channel Toni Motdan; [memb.] Association of American Medical Personnel; [oth.writ.] Published in the Penstar Press and the Cosmic Courier, local magazine and church papers; [pers.] "Anything in life worth having is never easy." I write about everyday events. There's too much reality for me to concentrate on fiction; [a.] Dallas, TX.

SHAVE, BRENDA NICOLE
[b.] August 6, 1981, Fort Myers, FL; [p.] Jim Shave, Colleen Shave; [occ.] Student; [hon.] Poems published in newspapers and other books.; [pers.] For the Pyes, The Guys, and my Katy Marie.; [a.] Port Charlotte, FL

SHAW, SARAH
[pen.] Sarah Shaw; [b.] September 29, 1923, Wisconsin; [p.] Ruth and Shorty Kirk (Both Deceased); [m.] Bob Shaw (1920-87), March 22, 1942; [ch.] Three children, 6 Grandchildren, 8 Great Grandchildren; [ed.] High School Business College and much learning from life's experience; [occ.] Enjoying life to its fullest being a mother and grandmother and a friend to so many great people.; [memb.] An active member in Jerome United Methodist Church and in the West Michigan V.M. Conf. Also in Albion District United Methodist Women. Also as a VIM (Volunteer in Missions - in KY and New Mexico).; [oth. writ.] For 40 years I have written poems for all occasions in our church and

our family. I have now had several poems published.; [pers.] Life is an adventure - and I try to experience, with joy each episode. Travelling - singing - fellowship - friendships - and even sorrows - need to be expressed and that is why I must write.; [a.] Jerome, MI

SHEFFIELD II, ARLIS A.
[b.] January 13, 1944, Houston, TX; [p.] Homer G. and Ruby Slovacek Sheffield; [ch.] Jessie K. Sheffield, 7; [ed.] Duke Univ., B.A., Univ. of Rhode Island, M.A. (English), Columbia Univ., studying graduate Fine Arts Program (writing-fiction). Sorbonne and Alliance Française (Paris), study in French language; [occ.] Farmer, Specialty Grower for Restaurants, "Pain and Pleasure" Farm; [memb.] Duke Univ. Phi Delta Theta Fraternity, Vietnam Veteran, 1967-68, Chu Lai, Vietnam, U.S. Navy Mobile Construction Battalion (Seabees); [hon.] Several awards for journalism, photography in Vietnam: Battalion Newspaper won one of 3 best newspapers in U.S. Navy, two consecutive quarters, during Vietnam deployment. Runner-up in Literature, 1978, Rhode Island State Council of the Arts, for the novella, "Even If I Wanted To"; [oth. writ.] A novella, "Even If I Wanted To," "Discrepancies Versus Vision - A position paper on purpose and truth in Art," "Winter, Snow, and Short Days" (A short story), an essay on Emerson, numerous articles in newspapers; [pers.] Each day we live, we are simultaneously crushed and sustained by our past decisions: those we made ourselves, those that were made for us, and those we ignored and did not make at all.; [a.] Nathalie, VA

SHELDEN, MARGE
[b.] August 2, 1925, Marlette, MI; [p.] Merle and Norman Landon; [m.] Deceased; [ch.] Katherine, Elizabeth and Frances; [ed.] Marlette High School (MI), Attended MSU (East Lansing, MI); [occ.] Retired Consultant, Community Volunteer; [memb.] Ganges United Methodist Church, Lake Michigan Shore Assn. Bd of Directors, Saugatuck/Douglas Historical Society, Pier Cove Ravine Trust Assn.; [hon.] V.P. National Assn. of Women in Chambers of Commerce, Exe. Director, National ATHENA Award Foundation (National Recognition Program for Women) Lansing Regional Chamber of Commerce, 25 years. Award, Mulliken Village Council (MI) Civic Award, Mulliken Dist. Library, President's Award 1993 Athena Award Recipient presented by ATHENA Fdn. Owner/Operator, Shelden Insurance Agency, 36 years.; [oth. writ.] Poems published in Lansing State Journal (MI) and in various professional business newsletters. Published Family Poem Book of 150 pages; [pers.] I have two personal mottos: "Confront the Issue" and You must do the thing you think you cannot do". I have mentored and encouraged many young women in business to believe in themselves and their ideas.; [a.] Fennville, MI

SHELLEY, WANDA REAGAN
[pen.] Shelli Smith; [b.] January 6, 1941, MO; [p.] Frances and (late) Chester (Ted) Smith; [m.] Merlin (Sonny) Shelley, January 21, 1982; [ch.] 5 Children and 5 grandchildren; [ed.] Martinsburg Grammar School and R-6 Community High School, Scotts Corner, MO, Palmer's graduate of Literary Arts and Long Ridge Writer's; [oth. writ.] Submitted to magazines such as "Rosebud, Story, True Love, and McCalls". Writing short "Love" stories

is second choice to poetry. I haven't gotten a definite reply but, I have heard from two of the magazines, the are still making a decisions, sometimes it takes months, in any case, this could be good news.; [pers.] "I love to look through the keep sakes pages of my mind knowing along my path, I have met and made a difference in someone's life."

SHELLY, GABRIEL J.
[b.] October 13, 1978, Knoxville, TN; [p.] Narcia M. Shelly and J. R. Satterfield; [ed.] Sr. at West High School, Knoxville, TN; [occ.] Student; [hon.] Accepted to the University of Tennessee, Knoxville, (Graduate from Patricia Neal Rehabilitation Center as a result of a traumatic brain injury; [pers.] I don't want to copyright myself as I had written this statement in the school newspaper as well: I'm glad I'm entered as a semi-finalist in this: I believe it shows what I am on the inside. For we can never truly be what we appear on the outside.; [a.] Philadelphia, TN

SHELTON, FINA
[pen.] Fina Shelton; [b.] March 11, 1941, Spain; [p.] Juan Pozo and Juana Rubio; [m.] Jerry Shelton, June 1, 1980; [ch.] Darlene and Daryl; [ed.] Private School, Spain, O.C.C. Oceanside, CA; [occ.] Creative Writings; [oth. writ.] Children's book "Oatmeal-Cinnamon", A tale of a girl who loves to eats oatmeal-cinnamon that's how she's got her name.; [pers.] I like to write simple and be warm and get to people, by writing from my heart.; [a.] San Clemente, CA

SHENGAOUT, MICHAEL
[b.] February 22, 1971, Vilnius, Lithuania; [p.] Vladimir Shengaout, Inna Satunovsky; [ed.] Moscow Institute of Management, B.Sc.; [occ.] Computer Programmer; [pers.] Poetry expresses spiritual things transcending logic in the form of logical words. When the desire to share the voice of the soul becomes unbearable, a poem is born.; [a.] Norcross, GA

SHEPPARD, LORI
[pen.] Momara Sheppard; [b.] September 12, 1959; Portland, OR; [p.] Joyce and Robert Schasteen; [m.] David Sheppard; August 28, 1992; [ch.] Tom, Heather, Dan, Amara, PJ, Robert; [ed.] Ph. D, Columbia State College, Ed. Psych. Daughter/Co-Author of "cloud 9" is a 4.0 Student at CHCA (Cincinnati Hills Christian Academy); [occ.] Human Resource/Risk Consultant, President-Profit Point, Inc.; [memb.] PNPMA: Past co-chair Compensation Benefits; Charter Member Society for Technical Communication; L.O. Chamber of Commerce; PTA; Academy of Proffessional consultant and Advisors (APCA); [hon.] Certificate Appreciation: Safety and Health Committee Chairman for Blue Cross and Blue Shield of Oregon (BCBSO) Training Awards, 3rd place music award, 1st place National Dance Competition. Graduated With Honors; [oth.writ.] How Not to Succeed in Business, Grandma's Sew Special, Mommy Only Makes Baby Girls. If Your Dream Is Too High...Stretch; [pers.] Life is an adventure. Live it joyously and with a grateful heart; [a.] Vancouver, WA.

SHERMAN, CHERYL
[pen.] Cheryl Sherman; [b.] September 4, 1958, Lansing, MI; [p.] Eldean and Betty Wickerham;

[m.] Jack L. Sherman Jr., November 17, 1991; [ch.] Anita, Teresa, Anthony, Keith, Brooke; [ed.] Eastern High, Lansing, Mich.; [occ.] Housewife, Motel Manager; [oth. writ.] Poem, "Yes Lord", published in Local Newspaper, have other poems but not published yet.; [pers.] With God all things are possible. He is the real Author and Finisher of my faith and writing. Praise The Lord!; [a.] Lake Berryessa, CA

SHEVOCK, MARY
[b.] February 2, 1938, Plymouth, PA; [m.] Al Shevock, May 7, 1960; [occ.] Legal Secretary; [pers.] My love for animals makes it easy to write about them, especially when we spend time together.; [a.] Plymouth, PA

SHI, DR. FENG SHENG
[pen.] Feng Sheng Sho; [b.] September 28, 1945, Shanghai, China; [p.] Geng Long Shi; [m.] Dorothy Connis, May 1, 1992; [ed.] Engineer: Professor Ship Designer, Mathematician, Author; [occ.] Mathematician, Author Sahed Pierre Fermont, Goldbach; [memb.] All nations International Mathematics Students, Library of Congress, Smithsonian, Who Is Who International; [hon.] Who Is Who America, Cert. of Merit, Cambridge, England, International Man of Year - 1997, Medal of Honor for Mathematics, So many many more, Who's Who in the World, International Award for Poetry, take from Boon Who Is Who; [oth. writ.] "Exists", Library of Congress Mathematics, Electride Devotions of Water, "My Mother's Little Boy", Divide the Angle by 3, Divide the Couch by 7, many more.; [pers.] God gave me all the knowledge to do these problems not solved for 2,000 years, without God I am nothing.; [a.] Saint Petersburg, FL

SHOAIB, SUMMAR
[b.] November 29, 1984; Tampa, FL; [p.] Mohammed Shoaib, Shahida Shoaib; [ed.] 6th grade at Whitewater Middle School, Fayetteville, GA; [occ.] student; [memb.] Student Leadership, Whitewater Middle School Band, student government, Fayetteville Elementary Chorus, summer reading clubs; [hon.] President's Education Award, "A" Honor Roll Awards, county spelling bee honor, county reading awards, D.A.R.E. Essay honor, student leadership award, school geography bee honor; [oth.writ.] "This Word," "Oh, Where You'll Go," "Love," "If I Were A Cloud," many essays in contests, several short stories; [pers.] "I am constantly influenced by Islam, my teachers, friends and family. Their encouragement is what gives me something to write about."; [a.] Fayetteville, GA.

SHULTZ, DONALD F.
[b.] October 23, 1930, Homestead, PA; [p.] Helen and Steven J. Shultz; [m.] Suzanne Parker Shultz, July 15, 1961; [ch.] Four girls and one boy; [ed.] 8 yrs. Elementary, 4 yrs. High School, went to a 1 room school for four years; [occ.] Farmer; [memb.] PA Farmers Association; [oth. writ.] Many poems, a few songs.; [pers.] I have often said, being a farmer I worked by myself a lot but never felt alone, I compose a good share of my writing while working my fields or milking cows.; [a.] Emlenton, PA

SILVA, BETH
[b.] December 11, 1981; [p.] Gilbert and Joyce Silva; [ed.] Currently attending West Linn High

School; [memb.] ECHO (Employee Community Help Organization) Volunteers; [hon.] Editor's Choice award for my untitled poem in Memories of Tomorrow; [oth.writ.] Another untitled poem published in Memories of Tomorrow through the National Library of Poetry; [pers.] I think life is an incredible gift given to the soul and I would never take it away from myself or any other person. Just to reassure you "worriers."; [a.] Westlinn, OR.

SIMMONS, GENEEN MARSHETT
[b.] July 15, 1966, Havana, FL; [p.] Betty Clayton, Elijah Simmons; [ch.] Talysa Senft; [ed.] Havana Northside High School, Lively Vocational Technical Center; [occ.] Systems Consultant; [hon.] Outstanding Young Women of America, National Honor Society; [pers.] If at first you don't succeed, try, try again.; [a.] Tallahassee, FL

SIMMS, MITCHELL
[b.] January 3, 1963, Brooklyn, NY; [p.] Eddie and Angelena Simms (Deceased); [ch.] Jared Mitchell and Javan Nathaniel; [ed.] Brooklyn Technical High, John Jay College of Criminal Justice, University of Colorado; [occ.] Correctional Records Technician at Arizona State Department of Corrections; [hon.] Dean's List, John Jay College; [oth. writ.] One published poem in a children's magazine. Several unpublished poems, children's books and screenplays.; [a.] Fort Huachuca, AZ

SIMMS, SHERMAN E.
[pen.] Sherman E. Simms; [b.] April 2, 1957, New Orleans, LA; [p.] Mary L. and Lloyd Simms (Deceased); [m.] Danna M. Simms, April 28, 1989; [ch.] Jasmine, Jessica, Tanesha and Tracy; [ed.] Audubon Business College, Southeastern LA. Univ., Accounting; [occ.] Assistant Store Manager, Home Depot; [oth. writ.] "God Made Me That Way," "Put Him First," "Silent Mind," and "I Apologize," "Why," (about the Oklahoma disaster), "Mother," (about the growth and history of Africa); [pers.] I love reading inspirational, positive and romantic works. I also by request put up work on an employee news board at my work place. When I see someone in need of uplifting, I give them words to hopefully help.

SINENO, JESSICA
[b.] September 2, 1976, Bethpage, NY; [p.] Virginia and Dominick Sineno; [ed.] Patrick Henry High, Virginia Western Community College; [occ.] Crew leader at Kenny Rogers Roasters; [hon.] Business award; [oth. writ.] None published I have written others.; [pers.] I find substantial pleasure in writing down my feelings or thoughts. It releases the burden it carries.; [a.] Roanoke, VA

SISTONI, APRIL
[b.] February 20, 1983, Burbank, CA; [p.] FredRick Sistoni, Sandy Carroll; [ed.] Home School; [memb.] 4-H Club; [pers.] "All the greatest writers are inspired by God" I thank my parents, friends, grandparents, Sean, Crystal, Sarah, and my teacher Mrs. Cowley; [a.] Meridian, ID

SKAGGS, KATHRYN M. ROOKER
[pen.] Angel, Emmaranda Charlane; [b.] July 22, 1968, Bay City, MI; [p.] Robert F. Rooker, Faith C. Farnsworth Rooker; [m.] Lawrence R. Skaggs, July 19, 1986; [ch.] Lawrence Robert, Kyle Andrew; [ed.] Bangor John Glenn High School and

Delta College University Center; [occ.] CSR and Asst. Manager, Domestic Engineer, A full time Mother; [memb.] Vice Chairperson at Lawrence Pre-school; [oth. writ.] Dozens have been written, only one has been published at this time.; [pers.] My friends and family have inspired me, through their experiences in life as well as my own.; [a.] Bay City, MI

SLATON, BEULAH
[pen.] Beulah Slaton or La Rinda Slaton; [b.] June 28, 1981, Antlers, OK; [p.] Horace and Jane Slaton; [ed.] Sophomore at Hugo High School; [occ.] Student; [memb.] Oklahoma Honors Society, National Honors Society, USAA; [hon.] A - Honor Roll, Honors Biology; [pers.] God directs my writing and life, so I can only give this honor and recognition to him.; [a.] Hugo, OK

SLAVIN, VEDA
[b.] September 24, India; [p.] Padma and Tatachar; [m.] Boris Slavin, November 21, 1996; [ed.] 1. MS in Information Systems, 2. C.A. (Inter) India, 3. B.S. - Mathematics, India; [occ.] Systems Administrator, AT&T Wiseless (Consultant); [oth. writ.] My poems were published in "India World" Web Page.; [a.] Lodi, NJ

SMALL, STEPHANIE D.
[b.] July 18, 1957, Portland, ME; [p.] Ernest Smith, Rae Knight; [m.] William A. Small, November 12, 1989; [ch.] Aaron, Jason, Chris; [ed.] Richmond Adult High School, Richmond, California; [occ.] Teacher's Aide; [memb.] Non-Educators Association, Maine Educators Association; [pers.] I pull the feelings of my childhood and others I know together to try and show the way the world really is for some.; [a.] Casco, ME

SMITH, CHARLOTTE ANN
[b.] July 2, 1949, Snoqualmie, WA; [p.] Bobby Jones and Mary Ann Wing (mdn); [m.] Ernest Smith Jr., June 14, 1969; [ch.] Marci, Shasta and Heidi

SMITH, FERNALENE
[pen.] Fern Smith; [b.] June 20, 1952; Raleigh, NC; [p.] Charles Carrington, Rachel Davis; [m.] John Henry Smith Sr.; October 10, 1981; [ch.] Stephans Walter Phillip, John Henri Smith Jr.; [ed.] Apex High School, Wake Country Technical College; [occ.] Housewife; [memb.] Kingdom Hall of Jehovah's Witnesses; [oth.writ.] Short story submitted to Ebony writing contest; [pers.] Writing is therapy and a healer. The beauty of expression is found through written word; [a.] Thomaston, GA.

SMITH, GECOULIA
[b.] February 3, 1930, Gastonia, NC; [p.] George M. and Fairy Bradley; [ch.] Peggy Pace and Bryan Smith; [memb.] Hickory U.P. Church; [a.] Hickory, PA

SMITH, GLENNA
[p.] Ann and Herb Morgan; [ed.] Associates Degree in Applied Science, Major, Legal Assistant, Paralegal, Midland College; [occ.] Legal Assistant; [memb.] National Association of Police Organizations, Paralyzed Veterans of America, Veterans of Foreign Wars, Disabled American Veterans, National Children's Cancer Society and American Heart Association; [hon.] Pauline Slator Competition in Music (piano), Editor's Choice Award for past poem that has been published.; [oth. writ.] Craig My Loving Brother, My Parents, My Friends,

The Journey, Toby My Special Friend, Remembering You While We Are Apart, Thoughts, Thank You Terry, Someone, Understand Me (not published) and The Gift, published in 1997.; [pers.] A special "Thank you" to Terry McKinley for helping make the difficult decision submitting this poem. This poem is dedicated to a special friend I lost in May, 1996, Toby Burkes. I have been influenced by my personal and past experiences. I like or enjoy life and making others happy.; [a.] Midland, TX

SMITH, HELEN C.
[b.] January 9, 1921, New York City, NY; [p.] Anna Klanica, Paul Chernota; [m.] Walter J. Smith, April 23, 1949; [occ.] Retired; [pers.] I am a romanticist in love with love and life...and good literature.; [a.] Jupiter, FL

SMITH, JACOB THOMAS
[b.] November 21, 1973; Ludington, MI; [p.] Wayne W. Smith; [ed.] B.S. Fisheries/ Wildlife Management, May 1996, Michigan State University, E. Lansing MI; [occ.] Drywall Contractor, Drywall Services, Walhalla MI; [oth.writ.] Numerous poems written throughout high school and college. One printed for 1992 junior/ senior prom book, Mason County Eastern High School, Coster MI; [pers.] My poems represent my trials and tribulations in my life. Personal motto: The world is hard, try to survive; [a.] Walhalla, MI.

SMITH, JAMES LEE
[pen.] James Lee Smith; [b.] May 8, 1926, Wellington, TX; [p.] Lee and Stella Smith; [m.] Dorothy Lee Smith; [ch.] Five children, four stepchildren; [ed.] Post High School, 1944, 2 years college; [occ.] Retired 1987 after 42 years with State of Texas; [memb.] Church Veterans Organizations; [a.] Tahoka, TX

SMITH, SHERRI M.
[b.] March 9, 1954, Salt Lake City, UT; [p.] Kenneth and Emogene Morelli; [m.] Rick, April 22, 1979; [ch.] Aaron, Adam, Devin, Landon; [ed.] West High School; [occ.] Collections Supervisor; [memb.] Notary Public Credit Professionals Intl.; [hon.] Hope of America; [pers.] To give hope to our teenagers in today's world; [a.] Sandy, UT

SMITH, THERESA A.
[b.] July 18, 1965, Quincy, MA; [ed.] Woodward School, Quincy, MA, Quincy College, Quincy, MA; [hon.] Ruth Hurlbert Award for English Proficiency - 1983; [pers.] If every child had a childhood, adults would continually rediscover and reap the benefits of the inspirations of life. I hope one day my writings will be such an inspiration.; [a.] Plymouth, MA

SNOWDEAL, ROLANDE
[b.] February 10, 1966, Portland, ME; [p.] Roland J. Bilodeau Sr., Edna M. Bilodeau; [m.] Allan D. Snowdeal Sr., June 23, 1984; [ch.] Allan D. Snowdeal Jr.; [ed.] Westbrook High, ICS, Southern Maine Technical College; [occ.] Certified Nurses Assistant; [memb.] Pet Therapy Dogs, Inc., St. Ambrose Catholic Church; [pers.] My writings reflect the soul of my existence and my love of family, animals, and life.; [a.] Richmond, ME

SNYDER, CHELSEA D.
[b.] September 6, 1975, Elgin, IL; [p.] Cheryl Snyder Kinzig; [ed.] University of the Ozarks, University

of Arkansas at Little Rock; [occ.] Clerk, Central Arkansas Library System, Little Rock, Ark.; [memb.] Rocky Horror Picture Show Fan Club, Rhoda Fan Club; [pers.] "Whoever fights monster should see to it that in the process he does not become a monster. And if you gaze long enough into an abyss, the abyss will gaze back into you." Nietzche; [a.] Alexander, AR

SOANS, ROSHAN S.
[b.] March 28, 1986; Bangalore; [p.] Rev. Chandra S. and Mrs. Betsy N. Soans; [ed.] 5th grade Riverside School, Princeton NJ; [occ.] Student; [memb.] Princeton Soccer Assn. Westminister Choir College - Piano, Riverside School, Band Plays Clarinet; [hon.] Smoke and Five - Princeton Soccer Dist. Award; [oth.writ.] Poems 1.) Adventure. 2.) Open Five. 3.) Golden Fish. 4.) The Maze; [pers.] Do not let go flashing thoughts, tie them together they may be precious jewels; [a.] Princeton, NJ.

SOBOSLAI, JOHN
[pen.] The Unnamed; [b.] November 21, 1978; Meriden, CT; [p.] Thomas Soboslai, Elizabeth Soboslai; [ed.] Lyman Hall High School, Central Connecticut State University; [oth.writ.] Several poems published in self-founded magazine Epitaph, Final Words of a Dying Breed; [pers.] If everyone went by society's rules, many heroes of the past, present, and future would never have been, or never will be; [a.] Wallingford, CT.

SOCKELL, MARK
[b.] December 13, 1952, New York, NY; [ch.] Three; [ed.] Medical school; [occ.] Physician, St. Mary's Hospital, San Francisco, CA; [oth. writ.] Sundry medical topics; [pers.] I write only what I know about - which isn't much.; [a.] Portola Valley, CA

SOUTHWELL, DEBORAH L.
[b.] June 26, 1951, Alpena, MI; [p.] Victor Mischley, Elizabeth La Barge Mischley; [ch.] Jennifer L. Davis; [ed.] Alpena High, Alpena Community College, Michigan State University, Lansing; [occ.] Not at present; [oth. writ.] Other poems.; [pers.] To be able to touch another persons life for the better through anything I have written.; [a.] Fairhope, AL

SOUVA, JEAN A.
[pen.] Jean A. Souva; [b.] February 15, 1953, Lima, OH; [p.] K. Dwight and June M. Ketcham; [m.] Donald N. Souva, October 18, 1987; [ed.] Lima Sr. High School, LaSalle University, Northwestern College; [occ.] Housewife, Retired Medical Secretary; [hon.] Best poem award - WDP, 1991; [oth. writ.] One poem published in World Book of Poetry, television guest on local station for award.; [pers.] Poetry should make one feel, as well as think. My writings evoke the feelings from the heart as well as stimulate the power of the mind.; [a.] Lima, OH

SPARROW, JOSEPH CONRAD
[b.] August 12, 1965; Big Spring, TX; [p.] Lemuel C. Sparrow, Inez P. Sparrow; [m.] Kristina Marie Knotts Sparrow; [ch.] Michael, Jessica, and Kevin; [occ.] Freelance Writer; [oth.writ.] Short stories, poetry, and currently in the final stages of a first novel, a work of fiction entitled The Convent, others to follow; [pers.] I have found it is more

important to remember where we are going, rather than where we have been. Constantly looking behind, one can easily stray from a planned path. When looking back, always use a mirror. A quick reflection confounds all stumbling blocks; [a.] Waskom, TX.

SPEAKE, NANCY
[b.] April 15, 1962, Baltimore, MD; [p.] Marion and Jane Speake; [ch.] Jessica Blanken-Speake; [ed.] Brooklyn Park Jr/Sr High, MD Rehab Ctr; [occ.] Tele service Representative for the Social Security Administration; [memb.] American Legion Auxiliary. Miss Wheelchair MD Member; [hon.] MD Rehab. Secretaries Scholarship Award, Hammar Award by Vice Pres. Gore, through work; [oth. writ.] Poems for family and friends, "As Angels Often Do," with the National Library of Poetry.; [pers.] I write because I enjoy bringing a smile or a thought to those who may read my work.; [a.] Baltimore, MD

SPINKS, STANTON NOLAN
[pen.] Stanton Nolan Spinks [b.] August 11, 1951, Richwood, WV; [p.] Oscar W. and Loraine V. Spinks; [m.] Companion: Kay Wilfong; [ch.] Five step children; [ed.] Nicholas County High School, Charlotte Community College, North Carolina; [occ.] Carpentry; [memb.] West Virginia, Horseman's Association; [hon.] Reporter and Cartonist for Nichol County Chronicle (20 years ago); [oth. writ.] Clouds of my Heart, On The Day my Mother Died, Why Not Forgive, The Tree, To You My Love, Worm on the Tree, I Am Hers; [pers.] Poetry will touch the heart, only if you let it. Let your heart do the writing! And your soul shall be an ease!; [a.] Gauley, WV

SPRIGGLE, HEIDI E.
[b.] June 16, 1973, Harrisburg, PA; [p.] Donald Spriggle, Dianna Spriggle; [ed.] East Juniata High School Indiana University of Pennsylvania (IUP) B.S. in Dietetics (May 1996); [occ.] Graduate student at Indiana University of Pennsylvania M.S. in Food and Nutrition expected May 1998; [memb.] American Dietetic Association Phi Kappa Phi (The Honor Society of); [hon.] Dean's List, The Honor Society of Phi Kappa Phi; [a.] McAlisterville, PA

SPROW, CHARLES E.
[b.] July 5, 1926, Altoona, PA; [p.] Chester and Elizabeth Sprow; [m.] Olive Green Sprow, May 2, 1946; [ch.] Chester - Vickie - Rebecca; [ed.] High School Graduate; [occ.] Retired; [memb.] V.F.W. - Legion; [a.] Bellefonte, PA

STAMILE JR., ANTHONY
[b.] April 2, 1971, Plainfield, NJ; [p.] Mr. and Mrs. Anthony Stamile Sr.; [ed.] Southside Christian School, Bob Jones Univ.; [occ.] Auto Salvage Facility Operator and Manager; [memb.] Grace Bible Church, Sptbg., SC; [hon.] Daughters of the American Revolution, Honorary Citizen Award, Who's Who 87-88 Among American High School Students; [pers.] It is my belief and strong conviction that all mankind with myself included, see desperately the need of his creator divine, and from the greatest to the least of us might find our lives saturated with the richness of his character, wisdom, and knowledge as made possible by Him.; [a.] Spartanburg, SC

STANLEY, QUIANDA
[b.] March 18, 1977, Nashville, TN; [p.] Robert

and Brenda Stanley; [ed.] Currently a Sophomore Psychology major at Hampton University; [occ.] Student; [memb.] Member of Operation, Think smart (Mentoring Program), Member of Hampton Univ. Pep Squad Member of the Ronald E. McNair Post-Baccalaureate Achievement Program; [hon.] National Dean's List, All American Scholar; [oth. writ.] "Time" also published in one of the National Library of Poetry's anthologies.; [pers.] Trust in God and believe in Him in everything you do.; [a.] Antioch, TN

STEADMAN, MYA MARIE
[b.] September 9, 1988, New London, CT; [p.] Betty and Stephen Steadman; [ed.] 3rd Grade, Dean's Mill School, Stonington, CT; [occ.] Elementary School Student; [memb.] 1. YMCA, 2. Stonington Community Center, 3. Mystic Marinelife Aquarium, 4. Dance Palace; [hon.] 1st Place: Beginner Level Horse Show, Canochet Riding Stable, 2. 2nd Place: Beginner Level Horse Show, Canochet Riding Stable; [pers.] I am really happy that my poem has been published.; [a.] Pawcatuck, CT

STEELE, CATHERINE M.
[pen.] A Child Of God; [b.] October 15, 1947; Deming, NM; [p.] Lily Mae and Adam Brock; [m.] Charles Evin Steele; November 19, 1988; [ch.] Keith, Colleene, Ed, Evelyn, and Corey, Daughter-in-law Amber, new granddaughter Monica Nicole; [ed.] Simi Valley High School, West Valley Occupational Center; [occ.] Wife, Mother, Grandmother, Aunt, Graphic Artist; [oth.writ.] Precious Virtue, Pending (six books) for the Lord, in His time!; [pers.] God's scripture says: You can do all things through Christ our saviour that strengthens you; [a.] Simi, CA.

STEFFES, LISA M.
[b.] February 10, 1965; Fond Dulac, WI; [p.] Vic Steffes, Marion Steffes; [m.] Janet L. Haney, June 23, 1995; [ed.] New Holstein High, University of Wisconcin, Life College; [memb.] Various women's, gay, and animal rights groups; [oth. writ.] Staff music reporter at UW's Daily Cardinal; [pers.] I often try to create a sense of irony to bring awareness of an issue. Social change begins on a personal level; [a.] Sharpsburg, GA.

STEINHORST, TIM
[b.] October 22, 1968, Forks, WA; [pers.] In every soul burns the flame of humanity, I only hope my words can set it free.; [a.] Puyallup, WA

STEPHENS, ALZELIA P.
[pen.] Zee Stevens; [b.] June 13, 1957, Lake Charles, LA; [p.] Late James and Mable White; [ed.] Washington Jr. Sr. High, Delta Tech Vocational School; [occ.] Department Clerk Entergy/G.S.U. Utilities Co; [memb.] Mount Calvary Baptist Church, Junior Woman Auxiliary, Member: Past President Les Petite Civic Auxiliary; [hon.] March of Dimas Award; [oth. writ.] I Don't Know Why; [pers.] Push towards the positive forces in life and pull away from the negative objects that surround you. Then "Be Still". God will do the rest. That will help you understand the good within yourself.; [a.] Lake Charles, LA

STEPHENS SR., ROY JAMES
[b.] July 1, 1947, Tampa, FL; [p.] Roy and Helen Stephens; [m.] Mary Catherine, December 22, 1966; [ch.] Roy James Jr. and Bruce Randall; [ed.]

Brandon High School, Brandon, Florida, 1 year college, University of South Florida; [occ.] Owner of R&M Medi-Trans, Inc.; [memb.] Palo Cedro Seventh Day Adventist Church, American Cancer Society, Board Member of Redding, Adventist School; [oth. writ.] Numerous unpublished poems and songs.; [pers.] Good memories are the stepping stones which help us pass through the fields of disappointment and love is the material from which they are made.; [a.] Redding, CA

STEVENS, AMY
[pen.] Margret Kendall; [b.] May 7, 1983, Oakland; [p.] Ken Stevens and Cat Stevens; [ed.] Graduated jr. high, started high school, still in high school.; [occ.] Student; [oth. writ.] Other poems not yet published.; [pers.] I wrote this poem with personal feeling and I dedicate it to my 8th grade English teacher Mrs. Cheryl Lanning.; [a.] Phoenix, AZ

STEVENS, BELINDA JOY
[pen.] Belinda Stevens; [b.] June 18, 1948, Yazoo City, MS; [p.] Father - L. L. Stevens (Deceased), Mother - Bea Holmes; [m.] Divorced; [ed.] Bachelor of Arts Degree - Behoven College, Jackson, MS, Masters Degree - Social Sciences - Miss. College - Clinton, MS - Law Degree - Ms. College; [occ.] Attorney; [memb.] Mississippi Bar Association, Episcopal Church - Chapel of The Cross (Formerly on the Altar Guild); [hon.] Belhaven College - Dean's List, President of the Women's Student Bar Assn. - Ms. College School of Law, Senator - Law Student Bar Association; [oth. writ.] Poems to be published in Iliad Press and JMW Publishing. Working on the rewrite of my first novel.; [pers.] I believe poetry should tell a story, entertain and inspire. I hope my poetry does all three.; [a.] Madison, MS

STEVENS, FRED L.
[pen.] Fred Lewis; [b.] September 9, 1953, Akron, OH; [p.] Tommie Stevens, Estella Stevens; [m.] Leigh Ann Stevens, August 24, 1996; [ch.] Saunya Deanne, Shannon Lee, Sheena Marie, Alexis Nicole; [ed.] South High School, Kent State University, Ohio Police Officers Training Academy; [occ.] Police Detective with Akron Police Department/ Property Crimes-Burglary Unit.; [memb.] The Salvation Army, Fraternal Order of Police, National Arbor Day Foundation; [hon.] Several Commendations for performance in the Line of Duty as a Police Officer; [oth. writ.] Several other assorted 'Love' poems.; [pers.] And we know that all things work together for good to them that love God, to them who are the called according to His purpose. Romans 8:28; [a.] Akron, OH

STEVENS, SANDRA
[pen.] Sandra Neal Stevens; [b.] September 6, 1953, Corpus Christi, TX; [p.] Bill and Nita Neal; [m.] Bob Stevens, April 2, 1983; [ch.] Stepdaughter - Kelly; [ed.] Carroll High School, Del Mar College; [occ.] Housewife, [oth. writ.] I have written several inspirational poems throughout the years, but have just begun seeking publication for them.; [pers.] I have been greatly influenced by the inspirational poetry of Helen Stiener Rice.

STEWART, CARL P.
[b.] February 4, 1957, L.A., CA; [p.] Carleen Sudweeks; [ed.] High School; [occ.] Roofing; [a.] Layton, UT

STILLIAN, CARLA
[b.] August 3, 1971, Orlando, FL; [p.] Carolyn and Carl Haslam; [m.] Shawn, September 26, 1992; [pers.] This poem was written in memory of my sister Martha "Dee" Haslam who passed away on my birthday August 3, 1996 with M.S. We miss and love her.; [a.] Baton Rouge, LA

STOKES, CATHERINE
[pen.] Cathy; [b.] November 28, 1926, Philadelphia, PA; [p.] Buster O. Adams, Helen Adams; [m.] Alexander Stokes, February 18, 1947; [ch.] Greg, Theresa, Charlotte, Derrick, Karen, Alexis; [ed.] Simon Gratz High, Community College of Allegheny County; [occ.] Housewife; [memb.] State President of the Ministers, Deacons Wives Guild, International Correspondent Secretary of MDWG, Local President of Women Council of Refuge Temple Church; [oth. writ.] (not published) Linksburg's Murders, Murder on Sugar Hill, and No Way, Not in this World; [pers.] My dream is to have my poems and short stories published, to not only leave a legacy but to encourage my children and grandchildren to write. I was inspired by my ninth grade English teacher who said to me, "Never stop writing."; [a.] Wilkinsburg, PA

STOMPER, THERESA
[b.] November 18, 1983, Rutland; [p.] Stan and Phelina Stomper; [ed.] Currently in 7th Grade at Rutland Middle School; [occ.] Student at Rutland Middle School, currently 7th grade; [hon.] Creative writing award in 6th Grade, Field Hockey Team Award; [oth. writ.] None that are published.; [pers.] This is dedicated, in the memory of my teacher Jill Small who encouraged me to bring out my talent in writing.; [a.] Rutland, VT

STONE, MEGAN
[b.] March 18, 1984; Nampa, ID; [p.] Tom and Monica Stone; [ed.] 7th grade West Middle School; [hon.] 4.0 G.P.A.; [pers.] I enjoy music and sports. I like the writing assignments in my English class. After college I want to be an architect; [a.] Mampa, ID

STRAIGHT, ROBERT DANIEL
[b.] April 15, 1960, East Stroudsburg, PA; [p.] Cynthia Middaugh, Owen Straight; [ed.] A little High School in a little town called Reedpoint, Montana. I'm a 1978 Graduate, of Reedpoint High School.; [occ.] I'm a self employed Independent Tradesman in the Building Trade; [oth. writ.] I have written many short poems and songs only to be added to my personal collection so far.; [pers.] Be close to the earth, honor what mother earth has offered to share with us. Look at the night sky, breathe the new day. Be spiritual.; [a.] Doylestown

STREGE, JENNIFER
[pen.] Jennifer; [b.] May 8, 1981, Sturgeon Bay, WI; [p.] Sally Charney and Danny Strege; [ed.] I'm been home schooled through the american School and I doing a great job.; [pers.] I owe a lot of my poems to the love of my life Tom even after all we been through cause he inspired me to write. I also want to thank my friends for always been there and making my life worth living.; [a.] Bailey Harbor, WI

STUCCI, GARY M.
[b.] April 19, 1948, Saint Paul, MN; [p.] Leo and Grace Stucci; [m.] Marie Stucci, December 27, 1968; [ch.] Six - 4 girls and 2 boys; [ed.] 2 yrs. Assoc. Degree, American History/Philosophy; [occ.] Advanced Technologist, 3M Co.; [memb.] V.F.W. (Vietnam War), Coaching Football, Softball and Baseball. Also served as a "Loaned Executive" for the United Way of St. Paul; [hon.] Purple Heart, Bronze Star - War Medals, All - City High School Football, Golden Gloves Champ; [oth. writ.] A personal collection of poetic works over the years.; [pers.] "Personal situations and emotions guide my pen."; [a.] Lake Elmo, MN

STURGILL, TRACY L.
[b.] January 28, 1967, Columbus, OH; [p.] Leslie C. and Loretta P. Sparks; [m.] Allen C. Sturgill, November 21, 1989; [ch.] Amanda Nicole and Allen Michael; [ed.] G.E.D. 4/89 Lawrence Co., Kentucky; [occ.] Housewife, Poet and Small Bus Owner in the near future; [hon.] (2) Editor's Choice Awards from The National Library of Poetry; [oth. writ.] "Roses", "Within Your Beautiful Eyes" and "Like The Phoenix"; [pers.] Being a poet, I realize that the pen is truly mightier than the sword. Written words from within are a precious resourse to give the future.; [a.] Circleville, OH

SUMMERLOT, CHRISTI
[pen.] C. M. Summerlot; [b.] January 25, 1973, Linton, IN; [p.] Thomas W. and Cora L. Jensen; [m.] Lawrence Summerlot, December 31, 1993; [ch.] Jakki, Levi; [ed.] High School, continuing Education in Computer Programming; [occ.] Homemaker; [pers.] My writings are adapted from my personal experiences, and my experiences are adapted from my mistakes.; [a.] Bloomfield, IN

SUTHERLAND, BO
[b.] August 26, 1970, K. L., MO; [p.] Roy and Robbie Sutherland; [m.] Nancy Sutherland, July 22, 1994; [ed.] B.A. Point Loma Nazarene; [occ.] Teacher (Bible) First Baptist Academy, Dallas, Texas.; [memb.] Pantego Bible Church; [hon.] Dean's List, Academic and Athletic Scholarships; [oth. writ.] A book of unpublished poetry, quotations and short essays on sorrows topics.; [pers.] Many are confident that, on a world of images, "a picture is worth a thousand words". I am convinced, however, that a well written poems is worth a thousand pictures.; [a.] Arlington, TX

SWEET, ASHELY NICOLE
[pen.] Nikki Sweet; [b.] December 12, 1982; Clarksburg, WV; [p.] David Sweet, Deborah Sweet; [ed.] 8th grade this year 1996-1997. Starting freshman year high school this fall 1997; [memb.] Jr. Beta Society, advanced band at N.G.M.S., Rex Healthcare volunteer, science club, media assistant; [hon.] A Honor Roll, A-B Honor Roll, member of the Junior Beta Society, Miss Congeniality; [oth.writ.] Several poems (not submitted); [pers.] Always think before you act. And be true to yourself. [a.] Willow Spring, NC

SWEET, FLORENCE E.
[b.] August 23, 1956, Gloucester, MA; [p.] Paige O. Poole; [m.] Mary Ann Poole; [ch.] Robert Paige Sweet; [ed.] Rockport High School; [occ.] Engineering Fuses; [pers.] Thank-you to my parents who showed me how to love. God bless. Love to my Grandmother and rest of my family.; [a.] Amesbury, MA

TAIRI, LEE ANN
[pen.] Arlene Kane - Scotland, Brian Metiviex - Maine, U.S.A; [b.] June 23, 1967, S.I., NY; [p.] Florence Mazella and Anthony Mazella; [m.] Happily Divorced; [ch.] Christopher Tairi; [ed.] High School; [occ.] Disabled due to back injury; [memb.] International Abba Fan Club Holland/International Abba fun club Australia/Agnethafahskog Fan club Bristol; [oth. writ.] All my other writings have never been seen by anyone. Other than 3 close friends. My writing is very personal.; [pers.] I am a very emotional and sensitive person. I feel my feelings through my writing.; [a.] Staten Island, NY

TARBELL, MICHAEL GARRETT
[pen.] Lust; [b.] November 12, 1977, Devore, CA; [p.] Clarence Tarbell, Ruth Tarbell; [occ.] United States Marine; [oth. writ.] An unpublished book of over 100 poems, titled "To Whom It May Concern".; [pers.] I feel like the new model of an old toy.; [a.] Devore, CA

TASSONE, ANGELO
[b.] January 31, 1924, Johnsonburg, PA; [p.] Sam and Ellen Tassone; [m.] Janet Tassone, October 9, 1954, Divorced, June 10, 1972; [ch.] Ralph, Rosemary, Robert, Randy, Romina, Renee, Rhonda; [ed.] High School; [occ.] Building Remodeling; [memb.] Catholic Church, Senior Citizens; [hon.] Honesty - God Fearing; [oth. writ.] I write views and ditties poems, letters; [pers.] I am a survivor. I survived the depression World War II - Divorce - 7 children 17 grandchildren, cancer - 25 years T and E on Railroad - Presently 73 and will survive after death; [a.] Johnsonburg, PA

TAYLOR, BRANDI LYNN
[b.] September 16, 1983, Bountiful, UT; [p.] Jerry and Terri Taylor; [ed.] 7th Grade Bennion Jr. High School; [memb.] Student Council; [hon.] 3.89 GPA, 100% attendance, High honor roll, Outstanding Citizenship, Hope of America Award (presented by Kiwanis Club) 41 trophies and 21 medals for dance; [oth. writ.] Several mini stories for school.; [pers.] I have been influenced by reading poems the silverstine. And by my many teachers and peers.; [a.] West Jordan, UT

TAYLOR, DEANNA
[pen.] Deanna Taylor; [b.] May 5, 1956, Monett, MS; [p.] John Bob and Susie Dalton; [m.] Frederick Taylor, October 11, 1990; [ch.] Brian, Jennifer, Kristi, step children Holly, Samantha, Ashley; [ed.] East Newton High School, Crowder College; [occ.] Account Clerk II Ottawa County, MI Finance Department; [memb.] American Heart Association, United Way-MS; [oth. Writ.] Poetry-The Dreamer, The Non-Dreamers, Indian Spirit Walking (all unpublished), Novel-The Walls Within (unpublished); [pers.] Despite strife or hardships-never give up and always maintain your sense of humor.; [a.] Spring Lake, MI

TAYLOR, DIANE
[b.] February 26, 1963; West Palm Beach, FL; [p.] Joseph and Dolores Kuharcik; [m.] Charles Taylor; June 29, 1985; [ch.] Lindsey Jordan Taylor; [ed.] Cardinal Newman High School, North Technical Education Center; [occ.] Secretary, West Palm Beach, FL; [memb.] Covenant Community Church; [pers.] The theme of my poetry is the reason I live; [a.] West Palm Beach, FL.

TAYLOR, ERIN
[b.] February 21, 1980; Waterbury, CT; [p.] Nancy F. Taylor, Curtis J. Taylor; [ed.] Highland Elementary School, Dodd Middle School, Presently a Junior at Cheshire High School; [memb.] Member of Junior Schubert Club for 11 years for piano; [hon.] Playing in Junior Schubert Club for piano, playing in Honors Orchestra for 1 year. Received 3 gold cups for piano solos, 2 trophies for dance, Presidential Academic Fitness Award for academics in 6th grade, and 8th grade for effort; [a.] Cheshire, CT.

TAYLOR, RICK B.
[b.] December 14, 1965, McKinney, TX; [p.] Richard B. Taylor and Sharon Inez Mills; [ed.] Graduate Denton Sr. High School Class of 1984, Denton, Texas; [hon.] To be called friend by Dave, Glen, Jay and R.C.; [pers.] Let the world not hide in what we've been taught, let us all grow together and promote freedom of thought. Who knows what's best for me, better than myself?; [a.] Plano, TX

TAYLOR, STEPHEN ALEXANDER
[b.] May 6, 1964, Anson, CO; [p.] George and Vangleen Taylor; [ed.] Bowman Sr. High, Anson Community College; [occ.] Native American Steel Art; [oth. writ.] Departure of Soul, Native Justice, Broken Promise, Lanterns of the Night, One Great Spirit; [pers.] My poetry reflects on my Native American background. And inner feelings for all native people.; [a.] Peachland, NC

TAYLOR, STEVEN
[b.] January 16, 1976, Dallas, TX; [p.] Scott Taylor, Shirley Taylor; [m.] Jessica Taylor, March 11, 1995; [ch.] Erin Taylor; [ed.] Bryan Adams High School, Texas A&M University; [occ.] Student, Bus Driver; [memb.] American Association of Petroleum Geologists; [hon.] National Merit Scholars; [a.] College Station, TX

TEMPEL, ALICIA
[b.] November 14, 1986, Jasper, IN; [p.] Paul R. Tempel and Dave Anita Hollander; [ed.] K-4th grade; [occ.] Student; [memb.] 4-H Club for 3 yrs., 6 yrs. member of gymnastics receiving over 100 medals, 4 yrs. on the softball team, D.A.R.E. member; [hon.] Gymnastics, has placed in several state meets. 3rd in Vault in 1997. Gold honor roll every year. Member of the Gifted and Talented.; [pers.] I have always enjoyed school and writing.; [a.] Lincoln City, IN

TERRELL, LINDA TESTA
[b.] November 26, 1948; West Palm Beach, FL; [p.] Pasquale and Veronica Testa, dec.; [m.] Ronald L. Terrell Sr.; January 21, 1989; [ed.] Lake Worth High, Palm Beach Community College, Realtor Institute; [occ.] FL Lic. Real Estate Broker; [memb.] American Legion Auxilliary, 32 years, served all committees, all chairs, past President 2 consecutive years, Realtors Association of the Palm Beaches, National Association of Realtors; [hon.] Proficiency awards in writing and secretarial, college scholarship, Deans List; [a.] West Palm Beach, FL.

TETIDRICK, TIFFANY
[pen.] Alphabet; [b.] October 9, 1981; Louiseville, KY; [p.] Cecil and Katrina Stovall; [memb.] Bata Club, FBLA (President) FCA, Flag Corp (Captain) Business and Professional Women (choices) NJROTC, National Honors Society, Pep Club, and Choir; [hon.] 1st and 3rd place in an Oratorical Competition. 3rd place in a district writing contest. I also have the 3rd highest CPA in my sophomore class; [oth.writ.] District representative in writing. "A Dad Decision"; [pers.] Your destiny is not set in stone, don't let anyone tell you that your worthless, waste your hardest and you can achieve any goal; [a.] Louisville, KY.

THANNER, BRYAN
[b.] December 24, 1973, Baltimore, MD; [p.] Lawrence Thanner, Patricia Railey; [ed.] McDonogh School, University of Miami; [occ.] Eight grade United States History teacher at Miami Springs Middle School; [memb.] American Federation of teachers; [hon.] Golden Key Honor Society, Omicron Delta Kappa National Leadership Honor Society, Phi Kappa Phi Honor Society; [pers.] Chewy at ix.netcom.com; [a.] Miami Springs, FL

THOMAS, DAVID M.
[b.] April 6, 1968, Cheektowaga, NY; [p.] Ronald Thomas, Allene Thomas; [ed.] AAS in Architectural Technology from E.C.C. South AAS in Interior Design from Villa Maria College; [occ.] Sales Associate; [hon.] Dean's List from both colleges, awards in design competition, Product Display Awards.; [oth. writ.] A few lyrics for a friends local music group. Several other poems that are unpublished, that I put together for a few special friends.; [pers.] My creativity comes from what I feel inside. I am lucky to be able to put it in words.; [a.] Buffalo, NY

THOMPSON, JIMMY
[pen.] Buddy Felton; [b.] January 15, 1940, Cook Co, GA; [p.] John and Martha C. Thompson; [m.] Cheryl, November 22, 1964; [ch.] Clay, Jason Scott; [ed.] B.S. Samford U., B'ham, Ala.; [occ.] Glazier; [memb.] Newfound Baptist Ch., Leicester, NC; [oth. writ.] "Looking For Answers," a collection of poems and prayers.; [a.] Balsam, NC

THOMPSON, RICHARD W.
[b.] May 13, 1966; Madisonville, KY; [p.] Larry and Sonya Thompson; [m.] Joan; March 28, 1987; [ch.] Ashley (5), Nicholas (2); [ed.] South Hopkins High School; [occ.] Electrician; [hon.] Second place Military Airlift Command Editorials in 1992 while in the Air Force; [pers.] Ashley was born 4 months premature and weighed 1 pound 7 1/2 ounces. She was given less than 1 percent chance of survival. Two and 1/2 million dollars later I have a precious 5 year old miracle who defied the odds; [a.] Caseyville, IL.

THOMPSON, SHAINA
[b.] December 21, 1949, Vallejo, CA; [p.] Howard and William Barkhill; [m.] William W. Thompson Sr., December 7, 1973; [ch.] Joseph Aaron, Rebecca Anne, Wayne, David, Tammy; [ed.] Sonoma State University (B.A., credential: E.C.E.), Santa Rosa Junior College (A.A.), Master's candidate - San Francisco State, Piner High School; [occ.] Teacher - English as a second language, Master's Candidate - Education; [memb.] Title IX-Indian Ed. Jefferson School District, Daly City, CA, CSEA, ASA, SKINS; [hon.] Dean's List, award of merit, SHOFAR award (for work with youth), third place - Poetry, San Mateo Co. Fair, Second place - Art (Basket of

Dreams), Third place art - Spirit Warrior (Mask), Hon. mention - Art (Spirit Window): County Fair; [oth. writ.] Various articles in newspaper, book of poetry: Shades of Blue (unpub.), Race: Reading Readiness Program (unpub.), Your Brother's Native American Curriculum Unit (unpub.), romance books (unpub.), poems published in high school and college papers; [pers.] I have a rich cultural background from which I draw on for my writings.

THURMOND, LYNN
[b.] March 24, 1954, Washington, GA; [p.] Marcus Bullock, Barbara Bullock; [ch.] Brian Thurmond, Brandy Terrell; [ed.] Washington-Wilkes High; [occ.] Textile Worker, Washington, GA; [memb.] Martin's Crossroads Congregational Holiness Church; [pers.] It is my desire to brighten other lives through my writing.; [a.] Lincolnton, GA

TIDWELL, P. ARREL
[b.] September 28, 1954, Huntsville, AL; [p.] John Lenward Owen and Peggy Owen; [m.] William A. Tidwell, June 2, 1974; [ch.] Kelley Dawn Tidwell (17 yrs.); [ed.] S.R. Butler High School, Livingston University (now known as The University of West Alabama). Ira D. Pruitt School of Nursing; [occ.] Registered Nurse (Labor and Delivery -OB/GYN), Shelby Baptist Medical Center; [memb.] American Lung Association, National Foundation for Cancer Research, American Cancer Society, American Heart Association, March of Dimes, National Wildlife Federation, Y.M.C.A.; [oth. writ.] None previously published.; [pers.] Life is like a sheet of music, complex and beautiful in its design. Two choices must be made during each verse or movement. 1.) To follow the melody or the descant and 2.) To complete the verse or movement, before moving on to the next one.; [a.] Alabaster, AL

TIGNER, ANTHONY J.
[pen.] Thunder; [b.] October 9, 1978; Rockford, IL; [p.] Steve and Bonnie; [ed.] Elementary, Rockford Christian, high school, Rockford Lutheran, starting at UW Whitewater next year at college; [occ.] Student, part time job at parkside warehouse; [memb.] First Evengelical Free Church; [hon.] Football captain, Varsity wrestler, and being a personal friend of Jesus Christ; [pers.] I am thankful first and foremost to my Lord and Saviour Jesus Christ, my wonderful honey, Lacy Ann Mills, I love her w/ all my heart! And for her making this happen!; [a.] Rockford, IL.

TOLBERT, JUDY
[b.] March 17, 1963, Grand Rapids, MI; [p.] Detroit and Christine Jones; [m.] Roger James Tolbert, October 31, 1981; [ch.] Shinika Lynette and Christopher James Tolbert; [memb.] Grace Apostolic Assembly Pentecostal Church; [oth. writ.] I am now writing my own book of poetry that I hope will soon be out at the end of 1997.; [pers.] I have always strived to do my best at what I'm good at. I love writing poetry it gives me peace of mind.; [a.] Grand Rapid, MI

TONGOL, IAN
[pen.] Ian Tongol; [b.] May 11, 1984, San Francisco, CA; [p.] Bong and Anita Tongol; [ed.] 7th Grade Queen of All Saint School Concord, CA; [occ.] Student; [memb.] CYO Basketball and track. CVAA Football, AYSO Soccer; [hon.] Publicity officer, student government, Q.A.S. School. 2nd

place in math contest. Blockbuster V. 1st place in Sega tournament in 1994. Met Pres. Bill Clinton during his 1992 presidential campaign in Concord, CA.; [oth. writ.] School writings; [pers.] "Do your best, try your hardest, and have fun."; [a.] Concord, CA

TRAPP JR., JAMES
[pen.] Tom B. Stone; [b.] June 21, 1948, Camp Lejeune, NC; [p.] James B. and Isabel M. Trapp; [ch.] Jenny M. Trapp, Michael C. Trapp; [ed.] BA - University of New Orleans, J.D. Loyola University; [oth. writ.] Poem - "Mirages"; [pers.] I try to write what I feel when I can be honest with those feelings.; [a.] Newton, NC

TRAXLER, JOHN A.
[b.] December 6, 1963, Hutchinson, MN; [p.] Ted Traxler, Sandy Traxler; [m.] Patricia Traxler, July 6, 1996; [ed.] Hutchinson High School, Willmar Area Vocational - Technical Institute, DePaul University; [occ.] Telecommunications Manager; [memb.] Knights of Columbus; [hon.] Golden Key National Honor Society, J. Edgar Hoover, Foundation Scholarship; [oth. writ.] Photo Sculpt, An Introduction to Chicago's Art Sculptures and the history behind them.; [pers.] Attitude is everything!; [a.] Forest Park, IL

TRIMBLE, CONNIE
[b.] October 15, 1964, Lancaster, PA; [p.] Mr. and Mrs. Joanne and Walter Frice; [m.] Robert J. Trimble, December 21, 1996; [ch.] Nicole Miller; [occ.] Secretary for Frost Disposal Service; [pers.] I just wanna say thank you to all my real friends, that showed me there's no shame in showing my real feelings.; [a.] Willow Street, PA

TUNISON, REBEKAH JEAN
[pen.] Becky; [b.] August 28, 1976, Salem, OR; [p.] Joe and Julie, Stepmother: La Nora Tunison; [ed.] McNary High School, Keizer, Oregon; [hon.] I got the Choice Award for Outstanding Achievement in Poetry for my poem, May God Be with You Always.; [oth. writ.] May God Be With You Always!, The World Is Yours!, I Love You God!, I've Got It!, When I Tell You I Love You My Friend It Means Forever!, Freedom!, Jeff Ryan Keniston, Don't Be So Hard On Yourself!, Stay True To Yourself!, I Look To Each Day!, Mischief!; [pers.] I hope people like my poetry, I also hope that God will bless your - lives. Well I think everyone is special. Everyone should be their selves don't be someone your not, just to make people like you. You will really regret it if you do. I think God made everyone special. So be you, you gotta be you, love yourself. And be the best you can be because you're loved by God. Be yourself the best is good in it.; [a.] Keizer, OR

TURLA, ERNIE
[b.] January 6, 1938, Lubao, Pampanga, Philippines; [m.] Angela Turla, November 24, 1966; [ch.] Michael, Pamela, Eileen, Kathy; [ed.] B.A. in English, BS in Ed., MA in Linguistics; [occ.] Postal Clerk, was school teacher in California, 15 years; [memb.] Circulo Pampangueno, Aguman Kapampangan, Filipino-American Club; [hon.] Special Achievement Award - Post Office; [oth. writ.] Short articles - Philippines Free Press Magazine, Pampango - English Dictionary; [pers.] I've written poems far better than this. But I prize this

the most because I wrote it when I just 15, right in the classroom in a foreign college and was adjudged by our class as the best one written.; [a.] Aloha, OR

TURNER, JENNE
[b.] December 1, 1981; San Antonio, TX; [p.] Tom and Pam Turner; [ed.] Westlake High School; [occ.] Student; [oth.writ.] A variety of poems and short stories (not published); [pers.] I love writing, especially poetry! I started writing poems in the second grade and have been doing it ever since. I hope more of my writing will be published in the future!; [a.] Austin, TX.

TURPPA, JOHN EDWARD
[pen.] "Skooter"; [b.] February 26, 1955, Grayling, MI; [p.] Alice I. McKensie and Ribertheroy Turppa; [m.] Divorced; [ch.] Shaun P. Dove, Alicia M. Turppa, Amber Rose Turppa; [ed.] 12th Grade from Johanesburg High; [occ.] Chemical Engineer, Atlas Energy Products; [memb.] Callaway Gardens Country Golf Club, Paradise located in Beatiful Pine Mtn. GA; [hon.] Won several Kareokee Singing Contest been on TV 15 times singing my own songs, also have done and performed comedy acts that I wrote the jokes and scripts and dreamed up the characters, 4 to date.; [oth. writ.] Several other Christian Poems, 18 Country, Love and Christian Country Songs, have 18 copyrighted, 8 recorded with music and about 50 written anxious to publish them.; [pers.] I John love life, the Lord, children, writings poems and songs, singing, comedy. God and life inspire me to write and sing.; [a.] La Grange, GA

TYLER, JESSICA LEAH
[pen.] Jessica Leah Tyler; [b.] December 16, 1983; Pittsburgh; [p.] Leo and Bernadette Tyler; [ed.] 7th grade; [occ.] Student; [memb.] Girlscouts, Orcherstra Nursing Home Volunteer Pianist; [oth.writ.] Black shacows, vacation pleasure, friends to the End. The Night, Changes of the Months, Rainbow Luxerics; [pers.] I love writing what ever comes to mind. And for anyone who will listen I hope they enjoy my feelings; [a.] Pittsburgh, PA.

UNDERWOOD, DONNIE R.
[b.] March 2, 1973, Clifton Fonge, VA; [p.] Mr. and Mrs. Ronnie Underwood Sr. (Judith); [ed.] Associate Degree - Dabney S. Lancaster, Community College/B.A. Religious Studies Lynchburg College; [occ.] Youth Minister - Clifton Forge Presbyterian Church/Mental Retardation Services; [hon.] Montgomery Scholar - Lynchburg College; [oth. writ.] Unpublished; [a.] Clifton Forge, VA

UZIALKO, EVAN ANDREW
[b.] September 11, 1977, Scranton, PA; [p.] Robert and Alice Uzialko; [ed.] Lakeland High School Jermyn, PA; [memb.] Black Belt member of Scranton Tang So Do Academy; [pers.] Evan completed suicide on June 8 1995. The day before his high school graduation. He fought so hard to put these terrible feelings out of his mind. But nothing could help him.; [a.] Jermyn, PA

VALDES, CAESAR M.
[pen.] C. Mathew; [b.] May 14, 1924, Redlands, CA; [p.] Elvira Garcia and Joseph Jesse Valdes; [m.] A. Louise Valdes, January 7, 1994; [ch.] 2 Stepdaughters, 1 daugther and 1 son; [ed.] (2) Associates of Arts (Social Science, (Business Mgt.), (1) Bachelor of Arts (Public Administration), Califor-

nia State University at Los Angeles Graduate Machinest - Miscellaneous Self Improvement College Courses; [occ.] Retired-Rockwell International Management; [memb.] Benevolent order of Elks, Eagles, Life Member American Legion. (US Navy W II/Korean Conflict); [hon.] Local Awards only. Company Achievement Awards, Naval Commendations, Community Recognition Awards; [oth. writ.] Writing Class originals. Never attempted to publish; [pers.] Very interested in conservation of natural resources. And supporter of education and the firm belief in Americanism, my writing often reflect this.; [a.] Shady Cove, OR

VALENTIN, JASON C.

[b.] July 25, 1975; York, PA; [p.] Carl and Kathie Valentin; [ed.] Delmar High School; [pers.] Stride for what makes you happy but don't wide off the footprints behind you; [a.] Delmar, DE.

VAN DYKE, JANET

[pen.] Helen Bedd; [b.] September 9, 1956; St. Paul, MN; [p.] Jack Howard, Irene Howard; [m.] Preston Van Dyke; September 9, 1984; [ch.] Barabbas Glenn Howard, Riddell, step - Tara and Dara Van Dyke; [ed.] Cincinnati Metrolopolitan College; [occ.] Reception, Sales Support; [memb.] Active YMCA and St. Elizabeth Hospital volunteer; [hon.] Typing and attendance; [oth. writ.] Short stories, nothing published; [pers.] I'm committed to improving my writing and sharing my experiences; [a.] Covington, KY.

VAN HORN, JASON

[b.] April 1, 1971, Great Falls, MT; [p.] Linda Van Horn, Darrel Van Horn; [ed.] Shafter High, Bakersfield College, Red Rocks Community College; [occ.] Kiln Loader for Coors Ceramics Co.; [oth. writ.] Several poems though none published.; [pers.] In my writings I try to express in words the emotion of the moment.; [a.] Lakewood, CO

VASQUEZ, LUPE T.

[pen.] Lupe T. Vasquez; [b.] March 31, 1927, Edna Co, San Luis Obispo, CO; [p.] Maria Octolrano Vasquez; [ed.] Grade, high school, dental, real estate; [occ.] Insurance Office Mgr., Seniors Bookkeeper, Blind Shut in Cancer Seniors; [hon.] Insurance; [oth. writ.] Ted Brown Colbur May - 1950 poetry; [pers.] Working with children, helping the needy, working with AAA.

VAUGHAN, WENDELL L.

[b.] May 8, 1921, Iberia, MO; [p.] Samuel and Mellie Vaughan; [m.] Vivian R. Vaughan, December 28, 1941; [ch.] Victor Vaughan, Debbie Bellew; [ed.] Iberia Academy - (AB) Drury College, Springfield, MO, (BD) Brite Divinity School, Ft. Worth, Texas; [occ.] Retired; [pers.] I attempt to write all types, styles, and subjects of poetry. I always feel I am more 1800s than modern in my approach.; [a.] Lakewood, CO

VAUGHN, DARLENE GARDNER

[b.] January 3, 1959; Philadelphia, PA; [p.] Herbert and Dorothy Gardner; [m.] Clarence R. Vaughn; June 23, 1984; [ch.] Christian Gardner, Jeannine Vaughn, and Danette Vaughn; [ed.] Great Valley High School, York College Of Pennsylvania; [occ.] Self-employed Day Care Provider; Hugs N Care, Montclair, NJ; [oth.writ.] Tucker Wood and Tucker Wood: A Tree Top View are a series of short stories for children. Although unpublished, these books will be a family

heirloom; [pers.] Dedicated to my parents, Herbert and Dorothy Gardner, through them, creativity and imagination was encouraged and instilled in our family lifestyle; [a.] Montclair, NJ.

VAUGHT, NONA

[b.] December 16, 1928, Johnston City, IL; [p.] Orion and Reathel Berry; [m.] Thomas Edward Vaught, August 29, 1948; [ch.] Joyce Bauer, Elaine Freeman, Marian Schneider, Cindy Schneider; [ed.] Central High School, Evansville, University of Indiana, Evansville, IN; [occ.] Bookkeeper; [memb.] First Christian Church, Mt. Vernon, IN, Poetry Society of America; [oth. writ.] Works of Nona Vaught, "We Will Rest In His Love", Words and Music, "Hath He Not Made These Things", Words a music by Nona Vaught, "Winter Dawn", Words and Music; [pers.] Goal - "To go into all the world."; [a.] Mount Vernon, IN

VEAL, ANGELA G.

[b.] January 2, 1967, North Carolina; [m.] Christopher Veal, January 27, 1996; [ed.] Currently enrolled as a correspondence student at the Institute of Children's Literature in West Redding, CT.; [occ.] Administrator and Financial Officer of Veal Concrete and General Construction, Inc.; [memb.] World Changers Church International, College Park Georgia, Pastor and Founder Creflo A. Dollar Jr.; [a.] Stone Mountain, GA

VILLANE, STEPHANIE

[b.] May 3, 1967, Waterbury, CT; [p.] Judith Silkowski, Joseph Klezun; [ch.] Jessie Catherine; [ed.] Crosby HS, Naugatuck Valley Community Technical College; [pers.] If you spend your life blaming others for where are you will not be able to take credit for where you go.; [a.] Naugatuck, CT

VILLANUEVA, MELISSA

[b.] May 6, 1973, Bronx, NY; [p.] Ruben and Janet Villanueva; [ed.] Cardinal Spellman High School and S.U.N.Y. at Albany, Bachelor of Arts in Psychology; [occ.] Shift supervisor in res. program, Children's Home Society; [memb.] Golden Key Honor Society, S.U.N.Y. at Albany Alumni Association.; [hon.] Dean's List, Spellman Awards for Academic Excellence, Service Awards for Volunteers Work; [oth. writ.] I've been writing poetry since age 12, but none have been published, my poetry was private until now.; [pers.] I write what comes from my heart. My life experiences are reflected in my poetry.; [a.] Pembroke Pines, FL

VIRDI, SEEMA

[b.] August 5, 1974, India, New Delhi; [p.] Jagjit Virdi, Raj Virdi; [occ.] Student; [oth. writ.] Several unpublished poetry.; [pers.] Peace please!; [a.] Stone Mountain, GA

VITANZO, DORIS

[pen.] D. Wimmer Vitanzo; [b.] September 5, 1938, Phila., PA; [p.] Douglas Wimmer Sr. and Claire Wimmer; [m.] Louis J. Vitanzo, October 16, 1961; [ch.] Deborah Lee Danley and Robert Danley; [ed.] Woodbury High, Valencia Community College, Orange Co. Vocational School, NRI (correspondence school); [occ.] Licensed Practical Nurse; [hon.] Four highest honors from NRI; [oth. writ.] "My Brother" published in The American Poetry Annual; [pers.] Do the best you can at whatever you do, and satisfaction will be your greatest reward.; [a.] Kodak, TN

VOELZ, EARL F.

[b.] July 14, 1921, Danube, MN; [p.] Emil and Lydia Voelz; [m.] Doris Vaughan Voelz, October 21, 1944, died on March 4, 1975, Kathleen Walls Voelz, July 30, 1977; [ch.] Mary Ellen, Eric Vaughan, Lenore Ann; [ed.] Danube, Minnesota High School Luther College, Decorah Iowa, AB Degree (Maj. English, Phys. Ed.); [occ.] Retired. Taught English H.S. (4 years), Colonel USMCR, Ret. 1981.; [memb.] Am. Soc. of Training and Devel Opment, Marine Corps League, Episcopal Church (Lay Reader, Outreach Chairman); [hon.] Who's Who Among students in American Universities and Colleges. Marine of year in Saint Louis (1975).; [oth. writ.] Short poems and ditties in bullets, and programs.; [pers.] I have written poetry since grade school (always to congratulate commemorate etc. Thomas Moore, The "Sweet Singer of Ireland" first inspired me.; [a.] Saint Louis, MO

VOIGHT, MARY FRANCES

[b.] August 13, 1929, Vienna, WV; [p.] Bill Shannon, Gladys Shannon; [m.] Hoyt Carpenter, April 11, 1949; [ch.] Wade, Sherry, Kirk; [ed.] Juarez Stake Academy; [occ.] Crisis Management Consultant; [oth. writ.] Stop Light Poetry; [a.] Anchorage, AK

WAGGANER, GALEN R.

[b.] August 1, 1950; Ironton, MD; [p.] Delbert Wagganer, Jean Wagganer; [m.] Martha Wagganer; June 10, 1973; [ch.] Rebecca Ann, Jennifer Lynn; [ed.] Mineral Area College; [occ.] Postal Supervisor; [pers.] I attempt to convey a wide range of emotion in my writings, my desire is to allow the reader to escape inside the work for a brief time; [a.] Fredericktown, MO.

WAGGONER, NATHANIEL

[b.] September 8, 1972, Arkansas; [p.] Ben and Suzanne Waggoner; [m.] Queena Waggoner, January 26, 1996; [ed.] Mt. Vernon High School, University of Central Arkansas; [occ.] Manager of Production Mid-Ark Wood Products; [oth. writ.] I have published other poetry in magazines and newspapers.; [pers.] Perhaps the greatest poem even written has yet to be until the pen in trembling fingers strikes the page.; [a.] Mount Vernon, AR

WAGGONER, TAMMY

[b.] August 17, 1962, Indiana; [p.] Julie McClure and Richard Waggoner; [ch.] Kenny, Dustin, Joey; [ed.] San Diego High School, San Diego City College; [occ.] Children's Hospital of San Diego.; [oth. writ.] I have written many other poems and songs... yet to be published.; [pers.] "When I sit down, and begin to think I get out my paper, and my ink - then I write, what's in my heart - and it becomes my piece of art."; [a.] La Mesa, CA

WAGNER, JOLLEEN

[b.] June 4, 1982, Troy, NY; [p.] Janet DuBray and Charles Wagner Jr.; [ed.] Now in ninth grade; [occ.] High School Student; [memb.] Peer Leadership, S.A.A.D., Spanish Club, Drama Club, Basketball, Softball, Soccer; [hon.] Honor Roll, Merit Roll etc.; [oth. writ.] None published; [pers.] I look at my writing as a friend, a way to let out my feelings.; [a.] Green Island, NY

WALCHER, JENNIFER LYNNE

[pen.] J. L. Walcher, Jenni Walcher; [b.] February

8, 1956, Denver, CO; [p.] Donald R. and Winifred E. Walcher; [ed.] Grad. Denver South High School 1974, Assoc. Degree - Admin. of Justice - Arapahoe Comm. College 1984, Bachelor's Degree - Criminal Justice - Columbia College 1986, Assoc. Degree - Occupational Safety and Health, Trinidad State Jr. College 1994; [occ.] Safety and Loss Control Specialist for Denver Water Dept.; [memb.] American Society of Safety Eng., US Golf Society, US Golf Association, National Safety Council, Colorado Safety Association, Colorado Historical Society, Toastmasters International; [hon.] Phi Theta Kappa, Dean's List, Who's Who of American Women, 20th Ed., 1997-98; [oth. writ.] Professional articles for the Nat'l Safety Council and The American Water Works Association; [pers.] I write about what I observe and about what I feel. I write about anything and everything - and my vivid imagination helps my efforts!; [a.] Denver, CO

WALKER, GWENDOLYN
[b.] January 28, 1947, Marianna, FL; [p.] Ernest and Lillian Fossette; [m.] Widow; [ch.] Diya and Karriem; [ed.] Seton Hall University - B.A., Seton Hall University - M.A.; [occ.] Disabled, former social worker and rehabilitation counsellor; [memb.] National Society of Christian Social Workers, National Multiple Sclerosis Society; [hon.] Rho Chi Sigma - National Rehabilitation Counselling and Services Honor Society, Alpha Delta Mu - National Social Work Honor Society, Probation Department of Essex County N.J. for Project Care; [oth. writ.] Several poems published in other anthologies, Co-authored, "Ethnicity and Disability: Two Minority Statuses", Journal of Applied Rehabilitation Counseling" (Winter, 1983); [pers.] I believe all individuals need love and caring. Children especially need love and caring, but so do adults on a different level.; [a.] Irvington, NJ

WALKER, NICK
[pen.] T. A. Freak; [b.] December 26, 1978, Carson City, NV; [p.] Gwen Lagunas, Mark Lagunas; [ed.] Northglenn High School; [occ.] Disc Jockey, Cosmotologist; [hon.] 4 Year Letterman - Track 1-Year Letterman-Football, High School Diploma, D.A.R.E. High School Role Model, Baxter Minority Leadership; [oth. writ.] Several poems for my pascal class, I've wrote a few songs for my band.; [pers.] My poetry reflects my personal life and the way I view life itself. My influences are my Mom, Tori Amos, Marilyn Manson, Jonathan Davis, Twiggy Ramirez, and Dennis Rodman.; [a.] Northglenn, CO

WALLACE, JAMES D.
[b.] September 24, 1949, Atlanta, GA; [p.] James C. and JoAnne S. Wallace; [m.] Harriet S. Wallace, May 13, 1989; [ch.] Cris, Andy, Joey and Jodi; [ed.] High school; [occ.] Manager with Big 6 accounting firm; [oth. writ.] Other poems to family members; [pers.] The poem was written from the heart as one of my sons reached his 21st birthday this year.; [a.] Stockbridge, GA

WALLACE, THEONDRA VENESSA MCILWAIN
[pen.] Theo; [b.] April 29, 1958, Columbia, SC; [p.] Odell Isaac, Jessie Mae McIlwain; [ch.] Anthony Dean III, Jessica Jewel; [ed.] University of S.C., George C. Wallace Community College; [occ.] Registered Nurse (OB), Dale Medical Center, Ozark, AL; [memb.] State and National Congress of Par-

ents and Teachers, Notary Public in State of S.C., Achievers Unlimited, previous member of U.S. Army (6 yrs.) 1978-1984, previous member of Tae Kwondo Association; [hon.] Excellence in Nursing Performance (1992), Red Belt in Karate (1993), Several Letters of Commendation/Appreciation to include Honor Graduate of Pharmacy Specialist course while in Military Service. Served as NCOIC of Pharmacy Service while in Germany.; [oth. writ.] Several poems for my own personal portfolio. None published.; [pers.] Overcoming many trials and tribulations through out my life, I've learned to trust God whole heartedly and believe that with Him by my side, anything is possible. I strive for peace.; [a.] Ozark, AL

WALSH, ALLAN
[b.] July 5, 1962, Windsor, VT; [p.] Lena and Gregory Walsh; [ed.] B.A. (1985), M.Ed. (1987) - University of Vermont; [occ.] Deportation Clerk (Immigration and Naturalization Service), South Burlington, VT; [hon.] Poster Child (Shrine Football King) 1969, Outstanding College Students of America (OCSA) 1989-90; [pers.] Perseverance will triumph over life's travails given love and understanding.; [a.] South Burlington, VT

WALSH, JOANNE ELLEN
[b.] June 22, Melrose, WA; [p.] Catherine (Smith) Walsh, Joseph Walsh; [ed.] Newbury College (Magna Cum Laude); [occ.] Human Resources Representative; [memb.] Northeast Human Resources Association, Board of Directors: Hope for the Children of Haiti, Inc., Grace Chapel - Lexington, MA, Massachusetts Society for the Prevention of Cruelty to Animals; [hon.] Magna Cum Laude; [oth. writ.] Several articles and poems published in local periodicals; [pers.] My writing is a reflection of what is in my heart and I try to use it as a vehicle to send a message of encouragement to a world that is often filled with trials and uncertainty.; [a.] Melrose, MA

WALUSKO, TAMARA M.
[b.] May 3, 1950; Venezuela; [p.] Michailand Zoia Walusko; [ch.] Sean and Lance; [ed.] California State University, Northridge B.A. and M.A. University of Pittsburgh. Ph. D candidate; [occ.] ESL Instructor/Educational Consultant Modesto Junior College; [hon.] Art Exhibits: Pittsburgh, PA. 1987. Abstract paintings. California State University, Northridge, 1983. Paintings/Mixed Media. St. Vincent Medical Center L.A. CA 1978. 1st Place (ink-wash) 2nd place day figure (eagle). Los Angeles City Hall 1967 Pencil Drawings; [oth.writ.] Publication "The National Library of Poetry" 1996 Green Eyes Compose of Symphony. National Textbook Publishing Com. 1992 My World In Spanish, Italian, French and German coloring picture dictionary; [pers.] Ancient Philosophies have enriched my intellectual and emotional outlook, expanded my perspective into the lives of others, and has laid a strong foundation in my work; [a.] Modesto, CA.

WAMPLER, MARY FRANCES
[b.] January 1, 1981, Blacksburg, VA; [p.] Elizabeth G. Prout, John F. Wampler; [ed.] Southwest Guilford High; [pers.] Always remember, even doctors call their work "practice." There's always room to grow.; [a.] High Point, NC

WARD JR., JAMES L.
[pen.] Rev.; [b.] April 12, 1963, Lock Haven, PA; [p.] James Ward, Victoria Ward; [m.] Divorced; [ch.] Brandie Ward, Jamie Ward; [ed.] Ft. Lee Quartermaster School; [occ.] 4 Ward Produce; [memb.] L.O.O.M., B.P.O.E.; [hon.] 2 Army Achievement Medals; [oth. writ.] Several poems including "Here I Am Once Again"; [pers.] I write from my heart, I believe in a poem that many people can relate to in their own way.; [a.] Avis, PA

WARMAN, FELICIA
[b.] October 2, 1983; Somerset, KY; [p.] Glenn Warman, Jane Warman; [ed.] Eagle Elementary School, Whitley City Middle School; [odd.] Student; [memb.] Future Homemakers of America, W.C.M.S. Academic Team, W.C.M.S. Band. Eagle Elementary, 4H, McCreary County Girl Scouts; [hon.] Eagle Elementary School Basketball, Drug Abuse Resistance Education, Jim Claypool Conservation Poster Contests 1992, Eagle Elementary Honor Roll, 1993-1994, Eagle Elementary Academic Acheivement, KY House of Representatives Honorary Pager for Representative Danny Ford. Eagle Book IT Diploma; [oth. writ.] Eagle Elementary Creative Writing, 1996, book published in WCMS Library. 1994. Publish-a-Book Contest, 4H writing contest; [pers.] I strive to reflect feelings in my writing and hope someday to become a great author. I was highly influenced by my third grade teacher, Renie Diamond; [a.] Whitley City, KY.

WARREN, OLIVIA JOYCE
[b.] June 28, 1986, Queens, NY; [p.] Walter and Joyce Warren; [ed.] Allen Christian School, Queens, New York; [occ.] Student; [memb.] Shekinah Youth Chapel, Shekinah Mass Choir, Liturgical Dance Choir, Sunday school and Girl Scout Troop No. 6414 Gloria Jackson Dance Studio; [hon.] Honor student, Literature Certificate, Stop World Hunger Essay Contest Certificate; [oth. writ.] "What's Up At P.S 176," "When My Father Died"; [pers.] On March 6, 1997, Olivia was involved in a tree falling accident. She departed from her earthly mission to be with the Lord. On December 17, 1995, Olivia's father Walter died.; [a.] Saint Albans, NY

WARREN, RENEE L.
[b.] June 28, 1975, Milford, DE; [pers.] Seeing the world through others eyes has taught me things about others, myself and life. My words are from their eyes, their soul, and my heart.; [a.] Greenwood, DE

WATKINS, MYRON
[b.] April 16, 1950, New Orleans, LA; [p.] (Foster) Evelyn and Peter Henry; [m.] 1. Rochell Gross, 1978, 2. Deborah Howard, 1991; [ch.] One - Myron Andrew Watkins (Deborah) 1979; [ed.] Jockson C. Lockett Elementary School (N.O., LA) 1962, George Washington Carver Jr. and Sr. High School (N.O., LA) 1962-1968, Loyola University of the South (N.O., LA) 1968-72, attended University of Wyoming - 1981-82 (Grad.); [occ.] Song Writer; [memb.] The Retired Officers Association; [hon.] 1st Place G.W. Carver Jr. Science Fair 1963, 4-1st Place Gymnastics G. W. Carver Jr. New Orleans 1963-64, LA-State Drama Championship 1968 Grambling, LA for G.W.C. Sr., Ping Pong Champion Loyola University U.B. 1968, Distinguish Military Student Loyola U. 1972, National Defense Medal U.S. Army 1972; [oth. writ.] Songs

and poems recorded for Hilltop Records and Hollywood Artist Recording Studios of Los Angeles, CA.; [pers.] What it is? It is what it is!; [a.] New Orleans, LA

WATSON, BEN
[b.] February 18, 1946; St. Louis, MO; [p.] Mary Watson, Hancel Watson(deceased); [m.] Elizabeth (Beth) Kay Shields; August 1, 1992; [ch.] Dawn, Diana, Donielle, Daniel, Joseph, Heath, Brandon, Cameron; [ed.] Salt Lake Community College, A.A.S. Degree in Transportation Management, Herculaneum High School, MO; [memb.] American Legion, Alcoholics Anonymous, LDS Church; [hon.] Top Secret/ Crypto Security Clearance, Army Security Agency; [oth.writ.] This poem is dedicated to my son Donielle who committed suicide on June 30th 1993; [pers.] It is never too late to make changes and better your life. Love everyone; [a.] West Jordan, UT.

WATTS, JOSEPH MANUEL
[pen.] Joe Watts; [b.] May 16, 1980, Syracuse, NY; [p.] James and Jo-Anne Watts; [ed.] Fayetteville-Manlius Highschool; [occ.] Student; [hon.] Poems in McGregor Hill Poetry Anthology, Anthology of Young Americans, and Writes of Passage, a teenage literary journal.; [pers.] Each of my poems serves it's own special meaning. They try to convey a message that means something to everyone that reads them.; [a.] Fayetteville, NY

WEAVER, JOHN J.
[pen.] John J. Weaver; [b.] October 4, 1913, Dayton; [p.] John and Emma Weaver; [m.] Catherine F. Weaver, July 3, 1939; [ch.] Mary Ann, John, Chris, Joan, and Mary Jo; [ed.] St. James Elm. Chaminade H., Dayton Art Inst. Sinclair Col.; [occ.] Retired Delco Prod. (Delph) 1974 Supervisor of Production Control; [memb.] St. James Church Dayton Precious Blood Church - Trotwood; [oth. writ.] Many unpublished poems - on Gun Control my brother talent for fixing things "Dickie Doo" many relatives and friends birthdays and life styles.; [pers.] I usually write humorous poems to bring a smile or laughter to my acquaintance "My Brudder and Me" depicts my style of writing (unpublished); [a.] Englewood, OH

WEBB, JON
[pen.] Jon Webb; [b.] January 29, 1970, Muskogee, OK; [p.] Thomas O. and Carol J.; [ed.] Associates Degree/English, Tulsa Community College, High School Graduate, Union High School, Tulsa, OK; [oth. writ.] One poem, "Dying for Elora", appearing in 1990 Union High School Anthology, "Totems 1990"; [pers.] "Job, chapter ten, verse one".; [a.] Broken Arrow, OK

WEBER, EVELYN
[pen.] Nina; [b.] May 4, 1946, Lexington, KY; [p.] Lonnie Clay Combs, Reynolds; [m.] James A. Weber, September 25, 1964; [ch.] Ben, Kathy, Joe, Kim; [ed.] 12 Years of school, 2 years of cosmetology; [occ.] Laundry Adams Ln. Health Care Center; [memb.] Field House Sports Club; [oth. writ.] After moving residents two years ago I have miss placed my other writings.; [pers.] I was inspired to write this writing by a co-worker an friend. Gregory Gibson. I wish people would relax, be themselves and enjoy the life given to each of us.; [a.] Zonesville, OH

WEBER, JESSICA
[pen.] Jessica Joyce; [b.] November 27, 1960, Kansas City, MO; [p.] Jesse Henderson, Genevieve Williams; [m.] Bryan Weber, November 10, 1979; [ch.] Bryan Weber Jr., Brandon Weber, Kirby Weber; [ed.] Martin Luther King Elementary School, North High, Southeast Sr.; [occ.] Youth Direction Worker Adolescent Mental Health Des Amoines, IA; [memb.] Christ Apostolic Temple, Inc. Bishop Jeremiah Reed, D.D., Ph.D., Pastor; [hon.] Baptism February 3, 1997; [oth. writ.] I am honor to have "A Prism of Thoughts" as my first book of publication of my poem.; [pers.] Thoughts and words breaths reality. I praise and thank God!; [a.] Des Moines, IA

WEBSTER, MARCENE
[pen.] Marcy Webster; [b.] September 3, 1929, Wadsworth, OH; [p.] Ernest and Ottilia Seiberling; [m.] Frank O. Webster, March 19, 1950; [ch.] Doug (Physician), Kent (Speech and Hearing Therapist), Jill (Phys. Ed. was "alternate" in tower diving, 1992 - Barcelona) (Olympics).; [ed.] Norton High School, Wittenberg University (2 yrs.) Ohio State University with B. Sc. in Education.; [occ.] Retired elementary (gr. 1, 2, 3, 4) 14 yrs. teaching, retired realtor, 12 yrs.; [memb.] Ascension Lutheran Church I dropped my professional affiliations at retirement. I continue membership in many groups, such as craft, euchre, Bible study, and am currently a "leader" of a group in small group ministry.; [hon.] High School Valedictorian My time is college was divided between work-schedules and studies. (I worked my way through college.); [oth. writ.] I've done original poems and drawings for my Christmas cards for 30 years. I've done poetry for special events, birthdays, etch. More recently, I've written poetry for my nine grandchildren. I've also written a "lullaby" for my grandchildren - music and verse. (My grandchildren are a "huge" part of my life. Active involvement with them gives me more pleasure than I can describe.); [pers.] If we, as adults, can respond to all children's "uniqueness" in a way that "nurtures" their growth in self esteem and their growth in individual potential...then we have contributed something of value to our world.; [a.] Columbus, OH

WEBSTER, TRACY
[pen.] Misty Price; [b.] April 13, 1963, Durban, South Africa; [p.] Thelma Maureen Price, Howard Allan Price; [m.] Ian Webster, February 3, 1995; [ed.] Matric (Grade 12) D.G.H.S., South Africa; [occ.] Home Executive; [memb.] (New to Baltimore, been here 4 months); [oth. writ.] All personal writings, never written by publishing purposes.; [pers.] Through my writing I would like to reach out the children on important issues and to help create a healthier society.; [a.] Towson, MD

WEILER JR., ROBERT F.
[b.] November 18, 1980; Chemy Pt., NC; [p.] Robert Weiler Sr., Catherine Weiler; [occ.] Student; [pers.] Gen, thanks for the inspiration; [a.] Forestville, MD.

WEINGARTNER, SHERRY A.
[b.] October 10, 1959, Beaver Falls, PA; [p.] Mr. and Mrs. Carol Bruce, (Mother) Mr. and Mrs. Fred Coy (Father); [ch.] Trevor - Son, Asia - Daughter; [ed.] 1978 Monaca High School; [occ.] Laborer; [memb.] First Presbyterian Church in Beaver Falls,

PA; [pers.] Dedicated to those we love yesterday, today and always.; [a.] Beaver Falls, PA

WEINSTOCK, MICHELLE B.
[b.] October 11, 1970, Philadelphia, PA; [p.] Samuel Weinstock, Myrna Weinstock; [ed.] George Washington High School, Temple University; [occ.] Statistical Analyst, The PMA group, Blue Bell, PA; [memb.] Gamma Iota Sigma, Beta Alpha Psi, Beta Gamma Sigma; [hon.] Dean's List, graduated Summa Cum Laude, Most Outstanding Intern Paper under the Independent Reinsurance Underwriters Association Internship Program (1992); [oth. writ.] My poems are written for fun and are sometimes presented as gifts to commemorate special occasions.; [pers.] When I'm feeling inspired and have some spare time. It makes me happy to express my thoughts in rhyme!; [a.] Philadelphia, PA

WELLS, JOYCE
[b.] August 25, 1962, Ann Arbor, MI; [p.] Albert Lee Elam, Corine Elam; [ch.] Paris Elijah Iman Addie (14), Steven Zaire Garner (3); [ed.] Ypsilanti High School, and went to Washtenaw Community College; [occ.] Currently working at the University of Michigan Hospital in Ann Arbor, MI; [oth. writ.] The First Time We Met, Free, Dreams of Love, Devotion, are just a few of my heart felt poetry; [pers.] This is one of the poems I wrote to my first love in "1980", I have always been a "Hopeless Romantic", with a love for writing. I was inspired by my loving brother, Larry Elam to summit my poem. My Heart and thoughts are a Design and a gift from God, to whom I give all my Thanks.; [a.] Ypsilanti, MI

WELTY, SUSAN M. SOCHAN
[b.] November 2, 1951, Oneida, NY; [ch.] One son, Trevor; [occ.] Registered Nurse; [pers.] This too shall pass.; [a.] Syracuse, NY

WEST, CARLA
[b.] May 25, 1964, Saint Louis; [p.] Nello and Ruth West; [ch.] Jerome Alexander West; [ed.] McCluer North High School, Central MO, State University; [occ.] Administrative Assistant; [pers.] This poem was written with so much love and joy. I feel deeply that anyone who reads it will be touched.; [a.] Saint Louis, MO

WESTLAKE, RUTH M.
[b.] July 23, 1922, Old Forge, PA; [p.] Harry and Mary MacKinder; [m.] David G. Westlake (Deceased), October 7, 1950; [ed.] High School, 7 yrs. night school - (Banking); [occ.] Retired; [memb.] St. Luke's U.M. Church, widow of a United Methodist Pastor (David G); [hon.] A candidate for Jean Arnot Reid Award - one of 10 in the United States in Womens (Banking); [oth. writ.] Several poems over the years given as gifts to friends.; [pers.] Just a thought: "There are no strangers in my life, just someone I have never met.; [a.] Largo, FL

WESTOVER, CHARLES J.
[pen.] Del Westover; [b.] October 3, 1977, Traverse City, MI; [p.] Dr. Robert and Pamela Westover; [ed.] Graduated Lincoln County High School, Freshman Vanderbilt University; [occ.] Student; [hon.] Senior Soccer Award, Nominee Mr. LCHS, Most Dependable; [oth. writ.] None published, "Death," "Open Eyes," "6," "Running Down A Dream," "Forever Dancing," "Fame," "Goodbye," "Un-

listed," "Feather," "Sobriety," "Remain," Prayer," "Friends."; [pers.] "Life is a wild rollercoaster, just remember to stay secure at all times." In loving memory of Guy Turpen, Damon Cannel, and Cousin Del Shannon.; [a.] Fayetteville, TN

WHEADON, BRIDGET R.
[b.] November 27, 1961, La Porte, IN; [m.] W. Ronald Wheadon, March 16, 1984; [ch.] Paul Elias Wheadon and Golda Corinn Wheadon; [ed.] High School Graduate and Privileged to be a friend and student of 82 yrs. Accomplished Artist - Genius, James Spencer Russull; [occ.] Personal care giver to 102 yrs. old woman in her home and mother of 2 children; [oth. writ.] Several I have not yet attempted to have published.; [pers.] I believe evolving will transpire when people stop using "God" "seeing them" as an excuse to do the right thing - One day people will do the right thing not because "God is watching", but because they want to look in the mirror and "see" God in themselves transpiring.; [a.] Rochester, IN

WHEAT, ALEXIS SHUREN
[b.] October 2, 1986; Akron, OH; [p.] Alex L. Wheat and Kalessa Edgerson; [ed.] Isaac Crary, Detroit, MI; [hon] Principal's List, Honors Award; [oth.writ.] Granny, The Internet, achievement in creative writing Young Writers' Award; [a.] Detroit, MI.

WHEELER, DESIREE
[b.] July 6, 1980, San Pedro; [p.] Terry and Deniece Wheeler; [ed.] I am currently a Junior at Palos Verdes Peninsula High School.; [occ.] Student; [pers.] Jesus Christ is the greatest influence in my life and it is my prayer for myself and others to always walk the narrow path with Him.; [a.] Rolling Hills Estates, CA

WHEELER, JENNIFER
[pen.] Jaybird, Jay, Scooby; [b.] November 20, 1983, Home; [p.] Ann and Billy Wheeler; [ed.] I am in the 7th Grade. I mostly make A's, B's, and C's. I love school.; [memb.] I am in 4-H, I love that too. It is very fun and educational. And Band, it's so easy.; [Hon.] I've gotten awards for Best Trumpet in band. Honor Roll Student and most Improved Behavior.; [oth. writ.] "Open Night", "Dreams", "You", "The Kiss", "My Friend", "Wishes", "My Heart" and "The End". They are all included for you to see.; [pers.] I believe in many things like God, aliens, UFO's, superstition and losing weight!; [a.] Ashland City, TN

WHEELER, STEPHENIE L.
[b.] July 28, 1953, Buffalo; [p.] Albert and Goldie Wheeler; [ch.] Larry Jr. and Dwayne Hardy; [oth. writ.] "There Used To Be", "She Will Have Her Way", "The Silent Cries of a Battered Woman", "Have You Ever Touched Jesus"; [pers.] To learn and write about my personal experiences throughout my life's endeavors ; [a.] Buffalo, NY

WHIMPER, LAKECIA
[b.] November 18, 1971, Chicago, IL; [p.] Willie M. Whimper and Lonnie Ward; [ch.] Kelceion J. Taylor; [ed.] Cathedral H.S., Loyola University Chicago (undergrad.), Concord Univ. (post grad.); [occ.] Social Service Worker for at risk teens; [memb.] American Counseling Assoc., Illinois Counseling Ass., Mentor Program for Juvenile Delinquents; [oth. writ.] Working on research regarding youth and violence.; [pers.] No matter how society may doubt your efforts always strive to better yourself.; [a.] Chicago, IL

WHITE, CHRISTOPHER K.
[pen.] Chris; [b.] August 29, 1977, Brooklyn, NY; [p.] Bessie and Nathaniel White; [ed.] Currently, I am a Sophomore at Renn State University. With a dual major in Journalism and Criminal Psychology I aspire to become a Journalist and as indicated a psychologist.; [occ.] I am employed at a McDonalds and I am the Chief Editor of my school magazine Palimpsest Review; [memb.] I am an active member of The Penn State Choral Ensemble as well as an active participant in The Multi Cultural Club which is highly involved in uniting Penn State Student of diverse ethnic, cultural backgrounds.; [hon.] In my years of writing poetry and thus embellishing my creature skills which I still find has plenty of space for improvement, I have been awarded the Society of American Poets Honors Award, and most recently have been acknowledged in The National Anthology of College Poets.; [oth. writ.] I have received honorable publication as mentioned before in The National Anthology of College Poets as well as in various Renn State Literary Magazines and Newspapers.; [pers.] The Best things found are often of times never looked for as I always inform people as they read my poetry which is a mere expression of my inner soul's desire to be heard without having spoken a word. The meanings of my poetry are sometimes found in my commas, periods, my syllables and in looking too deeply, you will only overlook all the meanings.; [a.] Brooklyn, NY

WHITFIELD, TELOS
[b.] May 30, 1965, Hanover, NH; [p.] Pamela and Richard; [ed.] B.A. in History from the University of New Hampshire; [occ.] Events Organizer; [memb.] Board Member of Outright, VT; [oth. writ.] From Her Heart - Dreams and Passions of Vermont Women - (Project in progress); [pers.] We are all struggling to feel fulfilled and happy. Writing is an essential part of my journey. My creativity is an expression of my spirit.; [a.] Montpelier, VT

WHITTEMORE, CAROLYN
[pen.] Carolyn Whittemore; [b.] September 11, 1978, Johnson City, IN; [p.] R. E. and Anne Whittemore; [occ.] Waitress; [oth. writ.] One poem published in a book, "Perspectives", name of poem "Never".; [pers.] I enjoy expressing myself with words and I love to write with my heart.; [a.] Johnson, TN

WICKS, JAMES
[b.] March 9, 1955; Halifax, NS; [m.] Marie; May 23, 1991; [ch.] Amanda Ashleigh, Robert Matthew; [ed.] University of Toronto, Fanshawe College, Wharton School of Business; [occ.] TV News Anchor [memb.] National Academy of Television Arts and Sciences, Radio Television News Directors Associaton; [pers.] Do not let any unwholesome talk come out of your mouths, but only what is helpful for building others up according to their needs. Ephesians 4:29; [a.] Palm Beach Gardens, FL.

WIDMAN, MAISIE M.
[b.] July 21, 1925, Washington, DC; [p.] Leo and Marie Abernethy; [m.] Charles L. Widman (Deceased), September 13, 1947; [ch.] Michael and Richard; [ed.] Graduated from Immaculate Conception Academy, Wash., D.C.; [occ.] Retired; [oth. writ.] Various other poems.; [pers.] Nature - in all its shades of beauty, joy and sometimes sadness - is the root of poetry.; [a.] Bethesda, MD

WIEGARDT, LORNA
[b.] March 6, 1969, Portland, OR; [ed.] B. Ed., Georgia State University - College of Education; [memb.] Omicron Gamma Chapter of Kappa Delta Pi, National Middle School Association, National Council of Teachers of Mathematics, Nat'l. Council of Teachers of English; [hon.] Faculty Scholar, graduated Cum Laude

WIGINGTON III, JOHN H.
[pen.] Caesar Rex; [b.] April 20, 1961, Wooster, OH; [ed.] The University of Akron; [occ.] Clerk, Scribe, Bard; [memb.] The International Society Of Poets; [hon.] Editor's Choice Award; [oth. writ.] Poetry, Short Stories, Essays, Journal; [pers.] Knowledge is power, power is discourse; [a.] Akron, OH

WILCE, EDITH CRIST
[b.] July 26, 1913, Zanesville, OH; [p.] Chas Crist and Maude Stockdale; [m.] Maurice J. Wilce, May 19, 1939; [ch.] Maude Ellen, Michael, Helen and Geoffrey; [ed.] Fairmont H.S., Fairmont, W. VA., Fairmont State, College, Univ. of Maryland, elem. school teacher; [occ.] Housewife; [memb.] Beta Psi Beta, Dean's List, President Beta Psi Beta, Editor of church oOrgan (periodical), member of Vermont Ave. Presbyterian Church; [hon.] National Honor Society, Gold Medal Winner, National Essay Contest; [oth. writ.] "A Patchwork of Memories" (collection of poems).; [pers.] While I love all poetry, I am intensely interested in England's poets.; [a.] Marysville, WA

WILES, DAVID I.
s[b.] October 11, 1951, Wichita, KS; [p.] Jack L. Wiles, Colleen I. (Hooton) Wiles (Deceased), stepmother Phyllis Y. (Robertson) Wiles; [m.] Divorced; [ch.] Brian D. Wiles, Jill V. Wiles; [ed.] Raytown High School 1 year at University MO at K.C.; [occ.] Acoustics Technical Aide. (in submarine construction); [memb.] Save the Bay, USGA, Marine Draftsmen Association, (UAW); [hon.] US Navy 11-70/11-76 Good Conduct Medal, Honorable Discharge, Submarine Qualified; [oth. writ.] None published.; [a.] Westerly, RI

WILKINSON, RITA P.
[b.] August 31, 1931, Ferrum, VA; [p.] Harry M. Peters, Roosevelt Peters; [m.] James H. Wilkinson (Deceased), October 7, 1953; [ch.] James William, Sue Lockwood; [ed.] Ferrum High School, Ferrum College, Virginia Western Community College; [occ.] Personnel Office, Kroger Company, Roanoke VA; [memb.] Hollins Road Church of the Brethren - Treasurer; [hon.] Phi Theta Kappa International Honor Society, High School Graduating Class Valedictorian, College Graduating Class Salutatorian, The National Dean's List; [oth. writ.] Poems and short stories for family members and friends, child's book for grandson Ben.; [pers.] I was influenced by my mother who did a lot of writing. I like to write to and about the people I love and admire.; [a.] Roanoke, VA

WILLIAMS, BRAD DAVID
[b.] February 16, 1978, Charlotte, NC; [p.] David and Becky Williams; [occ.] College Student at UNC - Charlotte; [oth. writ.] Several poems which are too numerous to list and two unpublished novels: "Click" and "A Summer to Remember". Current project is the novel "Experiments In Orange Bliss".; [pers.] I wish to thank my friend and fellow poet Danny Smith who encouraged my growth as a poet by giving truthful feedback when no one else would listen. I wish to also acknowledge F. Scott Fitzgerald whose pen influenced and shaped my writing more than anyone else I've ever read. Finally, a quote whose truth and profoundness speak for itself. "A weed is a plant whose virtues have not yet been discovered." Ralf Waldo Emerson; [a.] Charlotte, NC

WILLIAMS, EILEEN L.
[b.] June 29, 1956; Staten Island, NY; [p.] Bernice Williams, the late Samuel Williams; [ch.] Jerome Miller, Shaqueja Miller, Julian Miller; [ed.] Susan E. Wagner High School, College of Staten Island, A.A. and B.A. degree; [occ.] Mental Hygiene Therapist Assistant, Answering Service Operator; [oth.writ.] Poems published in the National Library of Poetry "Morning Song" and "The Nightfall of Diamonds"; [pers.] I am inspired by my surroundings, friends, family and what I feel from within; [a.] Staten Island, NY.

WILLIAMS, JACQUELYN ADAIR
[b.] April, Steubenville, OH; [p.] Jacquelyn Swan Coleman; [m.] David, March 29, 1993; [ch.] David and Lisa; [ed.] B.A. at Mount Union College, Arizona St. U., Grand Canyon University, Phoenix College, Rio Salado, Ottawa University (Big Red High School); [occ.] Former Jr. High Teacher and Medical Secretary; [memb.] Arizona Humane Society, Adoptive Parent for Endangered Species at Phoenix Zoo; [oth. writ.] Three anthologies, "Good Old Days" magazine, "Cat Fancy" magazine, "Green Leaves" periodical, and my own book, Of Gypsies and Horses and Things, is currently being published by Watermark Press.; [pers.] "Hold onto your dreams."; [a.] Phoenix, AZ

WILLIAMS, JOSEPH H.
[pen.] Joe Williams; [b.] February 11, 1978, Las Vegas, NV; [p.] Kamilla J. Williams, Joseph A. Williams; [ed.] Fort Walton Beach High School; [occ.] Student; [memb.] Fort Walton Beach High School Band, Holy Trinity Lutheran Church Youth Group; [hon.] Who's Who Among American High School Students (2 years), Honor Roll, Superior Rating t Solo and Ensemble; [oth. writ.] Several unpublished poems and short stories, currently writing a novel.; [pers.] Open your eyes to nature and listen to its music, for you will then know peace and beauty.; [a.] Fort Walton Beach, FL

WILLIAMS, STEVEN R.
[b.] May 17, 1959, Lockney, TX; [p.] Dean Williams and Jonell Williams; [ch.] Amanda Marie and Stephanie Anne; [ed.] B.S. Electronic Engineering; [occ.] Design Engineer; [hon.] Dean's Honor List; [oth. writ.] Several writing not yet published. "Having You Near" was published in A Question Of Balance, "Thoughts of You" was published in Beneath The Harvest Moon, and "Need You" was published in Best Poems of the 90's; [pers.] "Angel" is dedicated to Sharon Myzell. Sharon is a

beautiful woman you inspired me to read several others poems not yet published. I will continue writing poetry to someone as beautiful as her.; [a.] Summerville, SC

WILLIAMS, TIMOTHY R.
[b.] August 6, 1971, Gifford, FL; [p.] Doc and Mary Williams; [ed.] Graduated from Vero Beach Senior High 1990, Graduated Indian River Community College, AA, 1996 Attending Univ. of FL.; [occ.] Manager of Hometown Supsmrk. Employed Indian County School Board as Sub. Teacher.; [pers.] Everything and everyone has a purpose in life.; [a.] Gifford, FL

WILLIAMSON, BRIAN
[pen.] Ark; [b.] December 29, 1977, San Angelo, TX; [p.] Andy and Phyllis Anderson; [ed.] Crane High School Angelo State University; [occ.] Student; [memb.] First Baptist Church; [oth. writ.] Several poems published in the Oasis, Angelo State's students magazine. A poem recorded for "The Flight of Icarus" art show.; [a.] San Angelo, TX

WILSON, DESIREE
[pen.] Desiree Wilson; [b.] May 27, 1971, El Paso, TX; [ch.] Nicholas Wilson; [ed.] Currently attend Southwest Texas State University - major is Theater Arts; [occ.] Full time student and mother.; [memb.] Friends of Bruce Lee Tributes.; [oth. writ.] Several poems, song lyrics and novel material, not yet submitted to be published.; [pers.] Out of all the disbelievers, shines one inexhaustable light. She is my sister and one of my greatest influences.; [a.] San Marcus, TX

WILSON, EDWARD JONATHAN
[pen.] Ed Wilson; [b.] December 15, 1974; Baltimore, GA; [p.] Earland and Ann Wilson; [ed.] High school graduate class of 1994; [occ.] Student; [hon.] W.S.A. (World Skateboarding Association) Championship Trophies; [pers.] Faith is the key to life; [a.] Tucson, AZ.

WILSON, JOSEPH
[b.] June 9, 1980, Newark, NJ; [p.] Josephus Wilson, Mattie Wilson, Pearlie Lyon (Guardian); [ed.] Junior at Essex Catholic Boys High School; [occ.] Student; [memb.] Newark Public Library, Student Council; [hon.] 2nd Honors for three years; [oth. writ.] I have three other poems: "Dream", "My Favorite Days" and "The City".; [pers.] I feel that poets are the narrators of everyday life. We take the people or things we see and describe them creatively.; [a.] Newark, NJ

WILSON, LEO C.
[b.] November 16, 1935, Galveston, TX; [p.] Clement and Irma Wilson; [m.] S. Marie Wilson, March 26, 1983; [ch.] Sheryl, Vincent, Rene, Robert, Natalie, Joe Dale, Marie, Kimberly, Michael; [ed.] AA in Electronics, San Jacinto Coll., BST in Education Univ. of Houston, Houston, TX; [occ.] Retired U.S. Navy and Retired Professor at San Jacinto, Coll.; [memb.] Phi Kappa Phi, VFW, Am Legion, VVA, DAV, TREA, Omnicron Tau Theta; [hon.] Navy Commendation Medal for leadership, Phi Kappa Phi Honor Society; [oth. Writ.] "You Have Seen Him A Thousand Times", "How Fragile Life", "Mother Told Me"; [pers.] I write about my deepest low's and greatest high's. Giving one an insight into my innermost self.; [a.] Galveston, TX

WILSON, MR. COURTNEY
[b.] February 6, 1974, Midland, MI; [occ.] Architecture Student; [oth. writ.] The Demonic Plague: A collection of pain, isolation and perseverance from the guff of souls. Shadows of the Vertigo: Further passage into the uncharted region of the soul. But original works.; [pers.] Today exists for tomorrow, tomorrow hides in yesterday, yesterday wants to be today. That leaves tonight...; [a.] Walled Lake, MI

WILSON II, LEWIS E.
[pen.] Lewis; [b.] November 21, 1959, Gardner, MA; [p.] Lewis and Betty Wilson; [m.] Divorced; [ch.] 17 yr. old daughter Liana; [ed.] High School Diploma, Narragansett Regional High School, Tempelton Ma.; [occ.] Mental Health Worker, (8 yrs. DMR Mass.); [hon.] Just this one; [oth. writ.] Several poems, short stories; [pers.] I like the philosophy of Dr. Nietzsche and favorite poets are: Keats, Yeats, Oylan Thomas, Richard Bradigan.; [a.] Gardner, MA

WINTERS, WALTER L.
[b.] November 16, 1972, New London, WI; [p.] Debra and Chuck Winters; [m.] Tyra Kolstad, July 5, 1997; [ch.] Brett E. Winters; [ed.] Neenah High School, Neenah, Wis., dropped out; [occ.] Factory Worker, Quad Graphics, Bouncer - Bartender (illusions); [hon.] 1st Place 4H Drawing Contest, 4th Grade, 4th Place, 8th Grade Wresting Invitationals; [oth. writ.] A New Old Love, A New Life, Tip Top, Better Myself - nothing published.; [pers.] Live fast, live free, live safe and have fun doing it. The beautiful thing about learning is that nobody can take it away from you.; [a.] Fond du Lac, WI

WINTERS, YOLANDA NICHOL
[pen.] Yolanda Winters; [b.] November 15, 1977, Des Moines, IA; [p.] Diane Banks; [ed.] High school GED; [pers.] "The book is a resource of knowledge for the mind, a getaway for the heart and an ease for the burdens of the soul."; [a.] Des Moines, IA

WIRFS JR., JAMES
[b.] February 22, 1979, Anchorage, AK; [p.] James and Marie Wirfs; [ed.] Willamina High School, South Whidbey High School; [occ.] Student - full time; [oth. writ.] Had a poem published in an Oregon High School student anthology called Voyages.; [pers.] My goal in my poetry is to let the reader know what I'm feeling.; [a.] Freeland, WA

WIRTH, JOHNNY
[pen.] Johnny Wirth; [b.] December 24, 1977, Eau Claire, WI; [p.] John Wirth, Linda Wirth; [ed.] High School, Freshman year in College (attending); [hon.] Graduated High School with honors; [oth. writ.] A few writings contained in my diary; [pers.] Happiness is within; [a.] Eagle River, AK

WISENBAUGH, GARRETT
[b.] April 16, 1979; [p.] Tony Wisenbaugh, Barb Wisenbaugh; [ed.] Owosso High School; [occ.] Student, Crest pontoon boat builder; [oth. writ.] Poetry, short stories at leisure; [pers.] I'm a pillar among other pillars helping to hold something up.; [a.] Owosso, MI

WISNIESKI, TINA ANN
[b.] June 18, 1974; [p.] Tom and Janice Litchfield; [m.] Kenny Wisnieski, September 12, 1997; [pers.] This poem is for my husband Kenny. You are "The Love of my Life." I love you!; [a.] Toms River, NJ

WITZEL, RUBY
[b.] March 16, 1921, Attalla, AL; [p.] Richard and Florence Foster; [m.] Paul B. Witzel, September 29, 1946; [occ.] Homemaker; [memb.] Church of Christ; [oth. writ.] Other unpublished poems.; [pers.] I was a wave in WWII and stationed at the armed guard school Camp Shelton, VA and worked in the post office there.; [a.] Rossville, GA

WITZEL, RUBY FOSTER
[b.] March 16, 1921, Attalla, AL; [p.] Richard and Florence Foster; [m.] Paul B. Witzel, September 29, 1946; [ed.] Homemaker; [memb.] Church of Christ; [oth. writ.] Other unpublished poems; [pers.] I was a wave in WWII and stationed at the armed guard school Camp Shelton, VA and worked in the post office there; [a.] Rossville, GA

WOJICK, CHRISTOPHER
[pen.] Any suggestions?; [b.] September 28, 1962, CT; [p.] John and Eleanor Wojick; [ch.] Corey John Wojick; [ed.] Bachelor of Science Hotel and Restaurant Mgt., New Hampshire College, May 1984; [oth. writ.] A collection which few eyes have yet to see.; [pers.] A poem is worth a thousand pictures.; [a.] Essex, CT

WOODARD, MELISSA
[pen.] Melissa Woodard; [b.] December 15, 1978, Perry, GA; [p.] Terry and Patricia Woodard; [ed.] Currently a senior at Bleckley County High School, graduating with college prep endorsement; [occ.] Model; [hon.] This is my 2nd poem published, Leading Hitter, 10th, 12th grades, NXA All-American, 11th, 12th grades; [oth. writ.] I have written several poems which have been published in books and the school annual.; [pers.] I love to write poetry. It is my way of letting my true feelings out. I write only about personal experiences.; [a.] Cochran, GA

WOODFORD, RICHARD E.
[b.] August 13, 1962, Youngstown, OH; [p.] Mr. and Mrs. A. G. Woodford; [m.] Amy M. Woodford, August 31, 1991; [ed.] High School Diploma, Ehove Joint Vocational School; [occ.] U.S. Postal Worker; [memb.] Pleasant Valley Evangelical Church, YMCA; [hon.] Missionary Work; [pers.] Nothing but words of edification shall proceed forth from my lips.; [a.] North Jackson, OH

WOODIN, GRACE
[b.] February 17, 1916, Bellaire, MI; [m.] Thomas C. Woodin; [ch.] Four are mine, 10 stepchildren; [ed.] High school diploma from adult education classes; [occ.] Retired and enjoying life.; [memb.] Calvary Baptist Church of Muskegon, MI; [oth. writ.] Only write for special occasions.; [pers.] Just that I am very thankful to God that I can do all the things that I do.; [a.] Muskegon, MI

WOOLEY, ANGELA D.
[b.] June 6, 1963, Cincinnati, OH; [p.] Theoes and Annie Wooley; [ch.] Kameron Maurice Ray; [ed.] Mt Healthy High, Buchman College (2 yrs.), transferred to Hofstra Univ., Graduated 1986, B.A. Psychology/Minor, English; [occ.] Counselor for Individ. with mental illness and chemical depend.; [memb.] Aids Volunteers of Cinti., Minority Aids Prevention Alliance, Multi-Ethnic Mental Health Consortium, Choir Member of The New Friendship Baptist Church; [hon.] Academy of American Poets Member/Award Recipient 1985, Advisory Board Member of The Mental Health Assoc., Se-

nior Thesis Proj., selected and presented for publicat. at 21st Annual NYS undergrad. Psychology, Confer.; [oth. writ.] Significant number of poems published in both campus newspapers for Spelman College and Hofstra Univ.; [pers.] God sets my path, I simply follow where He leads me. Angelou, Giovanni, Baldwin, Frost, Ginsberg, Hughes, Brooks, Gibran, Walker, Dunbar and Wheatley have all inspired me through verse and victory.; [a.] Cincinnati, OH

WRAY, LAWRENCE C.
[b.] December 26, 1921, Hutchinson, KS; [p.] George Wray, Thelma Wray; [m.] Frances J. Bergen, June 2, 1946; [ch.] Kevin Jon Wray; [ed.] High School (Class 1941), Peabody, Kansas; [occ.] Retired; [memb.] Gloria Dei Lutheran Church, Albert Pike 303 Masonic Lodge, Wichita Consistory Midian Shrine; [pers.] With all that is wrought, good and evil - most people still help sustain my belief in our Creators, God the Father Almighty.; [a.] Wichita, KS

WRIGHT, NICOLE
[b.] August 2, 1984; Rochester, NY; [p.] Allan and Tammy Wright; [ed.] Currently in 7th grade; [occ.] Student; [hon.] Participant, Johns Hopkins University Center for the Advancement of Adamically Talented Youth, Middle School Honor Society, Saranac Lake, NY; [oth.writ.] This is my first effort; [pers.] I write because it's fun; [a.] Ray Brook, NY

WULF, JASON
[b.] November 30, 1972, Coffeyville, KS; [p.] David Wulf, Carolyn Wulf; [memb.] Zion Lutheran Church; [pers.] I would like to thank my parents whose love and support encouraged me in my writings.; [a.] Phoenix, AZ

WYATT, EDWIN S.
[pen.] Ed Wyatt; [b.] July 28, 1946, Mount Kisco, NY; [p.] Edwin and Angela Wyatt; [ch.] Wendy Anne Frazzell; [ed.] High School, Pleasantville H.S., Pleasantville, N.Y.; [occ.] SPO Rocky Flats, Plant Golden Colo; [memb.] Lakewood Nazarene Church, Lakewood, CO; [hon.] 2 Editor's Choice Award "Of Moonlight and Wishes", "Etches in Time"; [oth. writ.] "God's Might" in "Moonlight and Wishes", "God's Miracle" in "Etches in Time", Last Chapter in "How To Get A Job - Start Your Own" - Angela Wyatt; [pers.] I don't claim to be a knowledge "Professional Poet - I write on my beliefs, thoughts, humor, about friend, current trait etc., in my own simple style.; [a.] Golden, CO

YEOMAN, LANDER
[pen.] Lander Yeoman; [b.] January 18, 1983, Austin, TX; [p.] Ellen and Gary Yeoman; [ed.] 8th grader, Baseline Middle School, Boulder, CO; [occ.] Student; [memb.] Playground Theater, Football Team; [hon.] Role of Romeo in "Rome and Juliet"; [pers.] 2 Rules in Life: 1. Don't sweat the small stuff, 2. Everything is small.; [a.] Houston, TX

YOAK, MONIA
[pen.] Monica Yoak; [b.] August 8, 1980; Parkersburg W.V; [p.] Jan and Ray Yoak; [ed.] Wever High School; [occ.] Part owne Red Ral Outfitters Cafe' Manager' Dude Wrangler-guide-Horse trainer; [memb.] American Paint Horse Ass.- America Quarter Horse ass. Rocky Mountain Elk Foundation- Future Farmers of America, Wever County Search and Rescue; [hon.] Miss Teen Ogden,

Honor Student; [oth.writ.] Others poems published in Horse Report and school paper; [pers.] People will not remember you by what you do, but how you make them feel. Always look for something good in everything that happens to you; [a.] Huntsville, UT.

YOUNG, KAREN
[b.] July 5, 1946, San Mateo, CA; [p.] Allen and Elizabeth Shuler; [m.] Divorced; [ch.] Jonathan, Katie and David; [hon.] Several awards and nominations for Directing, Sound Design, Set Design, and Technical Effects, including two Associated Community Theatre Aubrey Awards for Directing.; [oth. writ.] Three One Act plays, "Thoughts On Eternity," published in 1990, several articles published in "The Evangelical Beacon" in the 1970's. Short story, "The Audition", performed as a staged reading by the Mira Mesa Theatre Guild.; [pers.] "I credit my Mom for my love of all types of literature - for making the books available and encouraging me to read. And my Dad for making me `look it up in the dictionary'.";[a.] San Diego, CA

YOUNG, TROY LEN
[pen.] T. L. Y.; [b.] September 15, 1936, Lubbock, TX; [p.] Noah and Bertha Young; [m.] Gladys Baxter-Young, May 21, 1955; [ch.] 2 Boys - 2 Girls - 10 Grandchildren; [ed.] GED - High School; [occ.] Disabled - after 2 open heart serg; [memb.] I am a member of The Northside Church of Christ in Hobbs, N.M. and do some Preaching; [hon.] I am Honored by my Family and Reward is in Heaven; [oth. writ.] I have written several Christian Poems and some short stories about my childhood as I grew up on the plains in West Texas.; [pers.] It is my hope and prayer that those who read mu poems will think about their relationship with God and their fellow man.; [a.] Hobbs, NM

ZARING, AIMEE MILLER
[b.] March 23, 1971, Louisville, KY; [p.] Frank and Peggy Miller; [m.] Robert Zaring, May 1995; [ed.] Assumption High School, Bellarmine College; [occ.] Director of Outreach Services, American Red Cross-Hoosier Heartland Chapter, Muncie, IN.; [memb.] Delaware-Blackford County Medical Society Alliance: Psi Chi, National Honor Society in Psychology, Delta Epsilon Sigma, National Catholic Honor Society; [hon.] Summa Cum Laude; [oth. writ.] Several poems published in High School and college literary magazines, have written a children's book, currently working on a novel.; [pers.] To analyze poetry with the mind is to escape feeling it with the heart.; [a.] Muncie, IN

ZAVALA, ELLA
[b.] July 31, 1956, Elmhurst, IL; [p.] Riojas/Estrada; [m.] Miguel Zavala, June 14, 1974; [ch.] Ella, Miguel, Veronica, Tobias, Crystal; [occ.] Homemaker; [pers.] Reading and writing, in the form of poetry, short stories or novels is a way to expand and explore our minds as well as a peek into someone elses.; [a.] Kingsville, TX

ZRUBEK, GERALDINE MARIE PARKS
[pen.] Roxanne Weir; [b.] January 27, 1949, Milwaukee, WI; [p.] Jeanette Johnson-Parks and Myers E. Parks; [m.] Robert G. Zrubek (Divorced Pending, Final May 16, 1997), April 25, 1981; [ch.] Janet Carpenter, 25, and Gavin James Zrubek, 19; [ed.] Franklin H.S., Franklin, WI, Assoc. in

Fine Arts Degree, Cotley College Nevada, MO, Metro State College, Denver 1 1/2 yrs; [occ.] Homemaker; [memb.] Attending Amazing Grace Church, Englewood, CO with fiance Ronald Warner, contract worker for Home Lumber Co.; [hon.] Preston Memorial Art Award, Cotley College, 1969; [oth. writ.] Unpublished personal works of poetry, some typed and mounted on flat surface of water-filled glass bottles. A novel, unpublished, "God's Precious Children," from experience with religious grp. working on self-help educational book for youth.; [pers.] Proverbs 10:19 "We live in an age, where `a multitude of words' engulfs us daily. If I must postpone, or re-think my writing career, it is only to be less sedentary, and more into daily living!"; [a.] Englewood, CO

Index
of
Poets

Index